THE ROUTLEDGE HANDBOOK OF ENVIRONMENTAL ECONOMICS IN ASIA

Problems of climate change, biodiversity and air pollution are clearly growing globally, but more particularly in Asia because of its economic importance and richness in nature. The increasing interest in environmental and resource economics applied in regions of Asia will make this book an outstanding resource to the existing literature, particularly in the fields of environmental and resource economics and the integration of applied content in traditional and agricultural development.

At present there is no single handbook or text on the state of current knowledge in environmental economics in Asia or one which offers a comprehensive guide to students and academics on the subjects of environmental economics research. This book will help to fill the gap in the existing literature.

Shunsuke Managi is Professor of Technology and Policy in the School of Engineering at Kyushu University, Japan, while also holding positions as IGES fellow at the Institute for Global Environmental Strategies and as an Adjunct Professor at the University of Tokyo. He is an editor of *Environmental Economic and Policy Studies*, a lead author for the *Intergovernmental Panel on Climate Change*, and is the author of *Technology, Natural Resources and Economic Growth: Improving the Environment for a Greener Future* and editor of *The Economics of Green Growth*.

THE ROUTLEDGE HANDBOOK OF ENVIRONMENTAL ECONOMICS IN ASIA

Edited by Shunsuke Managi

LONDON AND NEW YORK

First published 2015
by Routledge

2 Park Square, Milton Park, Abingdon, Oxfordshire OX14 4RN
52 Vanderbilt Avenue, New York, NY 10017

Routledge is an imprint of the Taylor & Francis Group, an informa business

First issued in paperback 2018

British Library Cataloguing in Publication Data
A catalogue record for this book is available from the British Library

Library of Congress Cataloging in Publication Data
The Routledge handbook of environmental economics in Asia / edited
by Shunsuke Managi.
    pages cm – (Routledge international handbooks)
Includes bibliographical references and index.
    1. Economic development—Environmental aspects—Asia.   2. Environmental
policy—Asia.   3. Environmental protection—Asia.   4. Sustainable development—
Asia.   I. Managi, Shunsuke, editor of compilation.
    HC415.E5R68 2015
    333.7095—dc23
    2014021091

ISBN: 978-0-415-65645-0 (hbk)
ISBN: 978-0-367-17297-8 (pbk)

Typeset in Bembo
by Apex CoVantage LLC

CONTENTS

TABLES

Tables

FIGURES

Figures

CONTRIBUTORS

Akira Maeda is a Professor at Graduate School of Arts and Sciences, The University of Tokyo, Japan.

Ashok Chapagain is a Science Director at Water Footprint Network (WFN), Netherlands.

Beng Wah Ang is Professor at the Department of Industrial & Systems Engineering, National University of Singapore.

Clem Tisdell is an emeritus Professor at School of Economics, University of Queensland, Australia.

Clevo Wilson a Professor at the School of Economics and Finance, QUT Business School, Australia.

Dabo Guan is an Associate Professor at Sustainability Research Institute, University of Leeds, UK.

Diptiranjan Mahapatra is an Associate Professor at Adani Institute of Infrastructure Management, Ahmedabad, India.

Eriko Miyama is a post-doctoral researcher at the Graduate School of Environmental Studies, Tohoku University, Japan.

Hainan Shi is a graduate student at the faculty of Economics, Kyushu University, Fukuoka, Japan.

Hajime Sugeta is a Professor at the Department of Economics, Kansai University, Japan.

Henrik Lindhjema is a researcher at the Norwegian Institute for Nature Research (NINA) and senior partner at Vista Analysis, Oslo, Norway.

Jan Minx is the Head of Technical Support Unit of IPCC Working Group III, Potsdam Institute for Climate Impact Research, Potsdam, Brandenburg, Germany.

Jing Cao is an Associate Professor at the Department of Economics, Tsinghua University, China.

Kazushi Hatase is a research associate at the department of Economics, Kobe University, Japan.

Kei Kuramashi is a PhD student at the Graduate School of Environmental Studies, Tohoku University, Japan.

Keisaku Higashida is a Professor at the School of Economics, Kwansei Gakuin University, Japan.

Keisuke Nansai is a senior researcher at the Center for Material Cycles and Waste Management Research at the National Institute for Environmental Studies (NIES), Japan.

Ken-Ichi Akao is a Professor at the School of Social Sciences and Graduate School of Social Sciences, Waseda University, Japan.

Klaus Hubacek is a Professor at the Department of Geography, University of Maryland, USA.

Koichi Kuriyama is a Professor at Division of Natural Resource Economics, Graduate School of Agriculture, Kyoto University.

Makiko Nakano is an Associate Professor at the Graduate School of Environmental Studies, Nagoya University, Japan.

Martin Bruckner is a researcher at the Sustainable Europe Research Institute (SERI), Vienna.

Masako Ikefuji is Assistant Professor at the Department of Environmental and Business Economics, University of Southern Denmark.

Masayuki Sato is an Associate Professor at Graduate School of Human Development and Environment, Kobe University, Japan.

Paramjit is Associate Professor at Department of Economics, Delhi School of Economics, University of Delhi, India.

Peng Zhou is Professor at College of Economics and Management, Nanjing University of Aeroneautics and Astronautics, China.

Priyadarshi Shukla is a Professor at the Public Systems Group, Indian Institute of Management Ahmedabad, India.

Regina Betz is a senior lecturer at the School of Management and Law, Zurich University of Applied Sciences (ZHAW) and Research Coordinator at the Centre for Energy and Environmental Markets (CEEM), UNSW Business School, University of New South Wales (UNSW), Australia.

Ryo Horii is a Professor at Institute of Social and Economic Research (ISER), Osaka University, Japan.

Shigemi Kagawa is a senior researcher at the Research Center for Material Cycles and Waste Management, National Institute for Environmental Studies, Japan.

Shunsuke Managi is an Associate Professor of Resource and Environmental Economics at the Tohoku University, Japan, while also holding position as an Adjunct Associate Professor at the University of Tokyo. He will be Professor of Technology and Policy, School of Engineering at Kyushu University, Japan.

Shunsuke Okamoto is an Associate Professor at the faculty of Economics, Kyushu University, Fukuoka, Japan.

Sören Lindner is a researcher at European Commission, Spain.

Suduk Kim is a Professor at the department of Energy Systems Research, Ajou University, Korea.

Surender Kumar is a Professor at the Department of Business Economics, University of Delhi, India.

Suresh Jain is a KTP Visiting Fellow, University of Technology, Sydney, Australia and a Professor of Department of Natural Resources, TERI University, India.

Takahiro Kubo is a Visiting Researcher at the Department of Resource Economics and Environmental Sociology University of Alberta, Canada.

Takayoshi Shinkuma is a Professor at the Department of Economics, Kansai University, Japan.

Takayuki Takeshita is an Associate Professor, Nagasaki University, Japan.

Takeshi Ogawa is an Assistant Professor at Hiroshima Shudo University, Japan.

Tania Bhattacharya is the Founder & CEO of The Celestial Earth consultants, India.

Tetsuya Tsurumi is an Assistant Professor at the Faculty of Policy Studies, Nanzan University, Japan.

Toshi H. Arimura is a Professor at the School of Political Science and Economics, Waseda University.

Tran Huu Tuanb is the Dean of Faculty of Development Economics, College of Economics, Hue University, Vietnam.

Vincent Hoang is a Senior Lecturer in the School of Economics and Finance, QUT Business School, Australia.

Wasantha Athukorala is a senior lecturer in the Department of Economics, Faculty of Arts, University of Peradeniya, Sri Lanka.

Weijia Dong is an Assistant Professor at the School of Economics of Nagoya University, Japan.

Yanfei Li is an Energy Economist at the Economic Research Institute for ASEAN and East Asia (ERIA), Jakarta, Indonesia.

Yasuhiro Takarada is an Associate Professor at Nanzan University, Japan.

Yohei Mitani is an Associate Professor at the Division of Natural Resource Economics, Graduate School of Agriculture, Kyoto University, Japan.

Youngho Chang is an Assistant Professor at the Division of Economics, School of Humanities and Social Sciences, Nanyang Technological University, Singapore.

Yungsan Kim is a Professor at the College of Economics and Finance, Hanyang University, Korea.

Yutaka Ito is an Assistant Professor at the Graduate School for International Development and Cooperation, Hiroshima University, Japan.

ZhongXiang Zhang is a Distinguished University Professor and Chairman at the School of Economics, Fudan University, China.

INTRODUCTION

Shunsuke Managi

There is increasing interest in the environmental and resource economics applied in regions of Asia-Pacific among economists and engineers, policy analysts, and other social scientists. Problems of climate change, biodiversity, and air pollution clearly are growing globally but, more particularly, in Asia-Pacific because of its economic importance and richness in nature. There is also a discernible increase in (under)graduate courses on environmental and resource economics and in the integration of applied content in traditional agricultural and development economics courses. At present there is no single handbook or textbook on the state of current knowledge in environmental economics in Asia-Pacific or which offers a comprehensive guide to students and academics on the subjects of environmental economics research. More in general, there are three handbooks of environmental economics in the literature. None of these comprehensively surveys the subject area in the way intended by the proposed companion as a focus on Asia-Pacific.

This handbook is designed to provide a prestige reference work which offers students and researchers an introduction to current scholarship in the expanding discipline of environmental economics applied in Asia-Pacific. The expected readership is students and researchers in economics and environmental schools; academics and students seeking convenient access to an unfamiliar area; and established researchers seeking a single repository on the current state of knowledge, current debates and relevant literature.

As shown in the Table of Contents, this volume of 31 chapters is organised in the order of more traditional topics of economic growth and environment, tax, emissions trading, and energy, to more growing topics, including biodiversity, coastal management, and representative country applications. Our handbook is *intradisciplinary* in character, seeking to explore the comprehensive aspects of economy and environment questions in Asia-Pacific. Next, we cover the discipline of economics theory, actual practice in policy, and conventional applied techniques used for Asia-Pacific. The remaining sections cover specific characteristics and areas of study where environmental and resource economists analyse applications in Asia. The structure is intended to reflect the increasing diversity of contemporary research on economics history.

The chapters are written by an international selection of authors drawn from Asia, the UK, the US, Australasia and continental Europe. The authors comprise leading experts in the relevant subjects. They are selected based on the criteria of being either senior recognized contributors or up-and-coming names in the field who have a proven track record of publication. Each chapter provides a balanced overview of current knowledge, identifying issues and discussing relevant debates.

Shunsuke Managi
Sendai, Japan
2014-12-2

1

ENVIRONMENT AND GROWTH[1]

Ryo Horii and Masako Ikefuji

Keywords: Environmental Kuznets Curve, Limits to Growth, Poverty-Environment Trap, Sustainability, Natural Disasters

1. Introduction

One of the most important and challenging questions for economists has been how to harmonize economic growth with the natural world. Since the Industrial Revolution, the growth rate of income per capita has been fairly stable in the United States. As shown in Figure 1.1, the measured per capita real GDP in the U.S. has been expanding exponentially, with its growth rate after the mid-19th century being around 2 percent. Figure 1.1 also shows that a number of Asian countries are in the process of catching up to the U.S. income level. Although they differ in the timing of when modern economic growth took off (e.g., Japan's modern growth started relatively earlier, while China's rapid growth is a much more recent phenomenon), their growth rates were typically higher than the U.S. after the second half of the 20th century. As long as this trend continues, the per capita income of successful countries will converge to the exponentially expanding U.S. per capita GDP level.

However, given that the world's economic growth means the exponential expansion of output, especially if it requires ever increasing inputs of natural resources, it is obvious that this process cannot be continued for a very long time. This was the theme investigated by Meadows et al. (1972) under the title of the "Limits to Growth," which subsequently led to a large body of literature that examined the possibility of economic growth under resource scarcity (seminal studies include Dasgupta and Heal, 1974; Smith, 1974; Stiglitz, 1974; see also a survey by Krautkraemer, 1998).

In addition to resource scarcity, the pollution that accompanies the production or use of particular kinds of inputs poses another constraint for economic growth. Although the literature on pollution and growth has been largely disjointed from that on resource scarcity,[2] the fundamental root of the problem is the same: the finiteness of the natural environment. Suppose that the aggregate production function has constant returns to scale and that all inputs are reproducible or non-exhaustible. In such a setting, long-term growth typically is achieved by a homothetic expansion of all inputs and outputs.[3] However, if the production or use of some types of inputs involves pollution, such an expansion will result in an increasingly deteriorating environment.

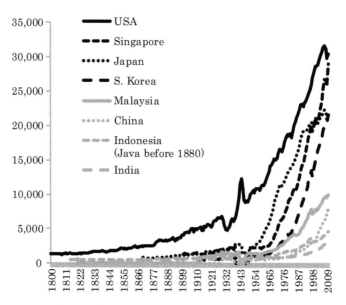

Figure 1.1   Long-term evolution of per capita GDP in the U.S. and Asian countries (in 1990 international dollars)

Data source: Bolt and van Zanden (2013).

Given that nature itself cannot be expanded along with other inputs, the intensity of pollution (i.e., the ratio of pollution to environmental capacity) will increase with the growing production. The deteriorated environment in turn makes sustained economic growth difficult for a number of reasons, such as health problems and frequent natural disasters caused by global warming. In the paper "Are there limits to growth?," Stokey (1998) considered this type of problem using an AK growth model with pollution and showed that it is not optimal to pursue sustained growth as long as the technology level is constant.

In this chapter, we explain the implications of the interrelation between the environment and economic growth. In particular, we focus on two issues. The first is the feasibility of economic development in stagnant poor countries that are suffering from both low income and environmental degradation. Second, at the global scale, we consider the sustainability of world economic growth in the future. While these two issues have so far been treated in two separate bodies of literature, we show that the key to understanding both issues is the same: the mutual causality between the environment and economic growth. After intuitively explaining how this interaction works in the next section, we introduce two formal models that focus on the two issues in Sections 3 and 4.

2. Mutual causality between the environment and economic growth

As we discussed in the introduction, we will inevitably face the "limits to growth" problem if the environment continues degrading as the economy develops. The consequences of "limits to growth" are illustrated in Figure 1.2, which depicts the mutual relationship between pollution and the income level in one phase diagram. In the figure, the $\dot{Y} = 0$ curve reflects the causality from pollution to long-term income: for a given intensity of pollution P, the output can grow up to the $\dot{Y} = 0$ curve in the long run.[4] The downward slope of this curve means that the

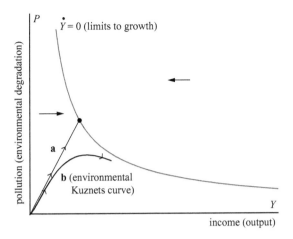

Figure 1.2　The relationship between income and pollution

potential for economic growth is adversely affected by environmental degradation. For example, when air pollution harms human health (WHO, 2006), it not only lowers the productivity of workers but also reduces life expectancy and, hence, the return on education, which in turn lowers the incentives for parents to provide their children with higher education. Without sufficient educated workers, (foreign) firms with advanced technologies will be reluctant to invest in such regions. These considerations imply that higher pollution (i.e., environmental degradation) will adversely affect long-term income.

What, then, determines environmental quality? We may think of economic growth as a determinant of pollution. At the initial stage of economic growth, the scale of production is small, and, thus, both income and pollution would be small. In the figure, this means that the economy starts from a point near the origin. Then, as the economy develops, the scale of production increases. As long as the economy operates under the same technology and the same relative factor prices, the pollution P would increase proportionally with output. In the figure, this means that the economy moves to the upper right direction and will eventually reach the $\dot{Y} = 0$ curve, beyond which the economy cannot grow (denoted by path **a**).

While this seems a pessimistic result, in reality the technology level is not constant but improves as income grows. If improved technologies cause less pollution for a given amount of production, economic growth could mitigate the environmental problem through technological change.[5] This consideration leads to the *environmental Kuznets curve (EKC)*, a hypothesis that there should be an inverted U-shaped relationship between per capita income and various pollutants or environmental indicators. If this hypothesis is correct, environmental degradation continues until the income per capita reaches a certain level, but beyond it environmental quality will improve as the economy grows. In Figure 1.2, the path denoted as **b** shows the movement of the economy following this hypothetical EKC. If pollution begins to decrease before the economy hits the $\dot{Y} = 0$ locus, it might be possible that the economy can grow beyond the "limits to growth." In fact, many studies, including seminal studies by Grossman and Krueger (1991, 1995) and Selden and Song (1995), confirm the existence of the EKC for local air pollutants, including sulfur dioxide (SO_2), suspended particulate matter (SPM), and oxides of nitrogen (NO_x).

Note, however, that the existence of the EKC does not always mean that every economy can overcome the "limits to growth." Because of the differences in the characteristics of countries, including technology, resource endowments, and institutions (particularly institutions for

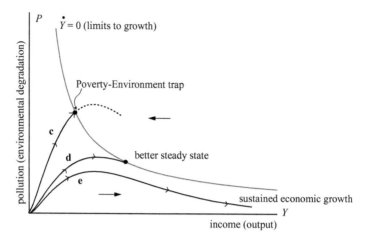

Figure 1.3 Poverty-environment trap

environmental protection), the shape and location of the EKC vary across countries. Three paths in Figure 1.3 illustrate the consequences of different EKC shapes. Path **c** illustrates the case in which the economy hits the $\dot{Y} = 0$ curve before reaching the top of the EKC. At this point, the economy is trapped by the mutual causality between environmental degradation and poverty. The environmental quality is low because the economy is poor. Such an economy cannot afford to employ better and cleaner technology because everyday consumption is their first priority, and they cannot finance the costs of required investments that would improve their life and environment in the future. Similarly, it would be difficult for people in such an economy to agree to set stricter environmental regulations because such regulations would seem to (at least temporarily) further reduce their low incomes. At the same time, the economy is poor because environmental degradation lowers the productivity of workers, reduces their life expectancy, gives less incentives for parents to provide good education for their children, and so forth. We call such a situation the "poverty-environment trap."

In Figure 1.3, path **d** shows that an economy that maintains low pollution intensity along the process of economic development can get over the top of the EKC and reaches a steady state in which both the environment and income are better than those of economies trapped by the poverty-environment trap. Path **e** shows that it is theoretically possible that an economy can grow indefinitely without facing limits to growth. These considerations suggest that in the long run we will observe large differences across countries in terms of the intensity of pollution and income level and also will find a negative relationship between these two variables. Figure 1.4 confirms this expectation, which shows that there is a negative relationship between air pollution (PM10 concentrations) and the per capita income level among Asian countries. In Section 3, we present a formal model with a microeconomic foundation that explains the existence of multiple steady states – the poverty-environment trap and a better steady state – and we discuss how the environment is related to international income differences.

Pollution is a serious problem not only at the level of individual countries but also at the global scale, particularly regarding the issue of global warming. In this case, we should view the whole global economy as one entity because the emission of global warming gases depends on the economic activities in all countries. Can we then observe an inverted-U relationship between the average income in the world and the emission of greenhouse gases? Thus far, the answer is negative. In many papers (e.g., Dinda, 2004; Kijima et al., 2010), the existence of the EKC has

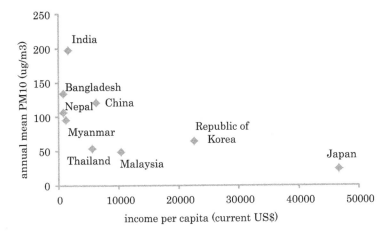

Figure 1.4   Income and Air Pollution in Asian countries. Vertical axis: Annual mean PM10 concentrations in the capital city, where PM10 means particulate matter with a diameter of 10 πm or less.

Source: Urban outdoor air pollution database, Department of Public Health and Environment, World Health Organization, September 2011. Per capita income is from World Development Indicators (WDI), Worldbank.

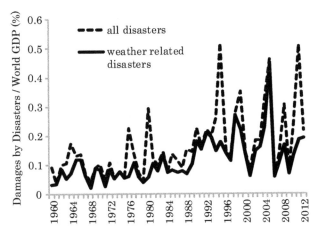

Figure 1.5   Ratio of Economic Damage from Natural Disasters Worldwide to World GDP. The solid line indicates the sum of damage from climatological, hydrological, and meteorological disasters.

Source: EM-DAT, the International Disaster Database, CRED, the Université Catholique de Louvain. World GDP is from WDI, Worldbank.

not been supported for the global warming gases such as carbon dioxide (CO_2). If global pollution continues to increase as the world economy grows, it will pose a threat to the sustainability of future growth.

In fact, NASA suggests that an increase in global temperatures results in an increased intensity of storms, including tropical cyclones with higher wind speeds, a wetter Asian monsoon, and, possibly, more intense mid-latitude storms.[6] Figure 1.5 shows that in the last 50 years, total economic damages in the world have increased more rapidly than the world's GDP, and most of the increase was due to weather-related disasters. For example, Hurricane Katrina in August 2005 caused total economic damages of $125 billion in the United States. More recently, typhoon Haiyan (or Yolanda) in the Philippines in November 2013 generated $12 billion in economic damages, an enormous sum for a small country. CRED (the Centre for Research on the Epidemiology of Disasters) reports that floods appeared to be most frequent during the last two decades, and the highest number of floods occurred in Asia.[7] The total damage and losses from the 2011 floods in Thailand amounted to $40 billion, more than one-tenth of the country's GDP. Given that the economic damages from natural disasters come primarily in the form of capital destruction, a higher risk of natural disasters inhibits the process of capital accumulation, not only by direct destruction of the stock but also by reducing the expected return from investing in new production facilities. If global warming continues with economic growth, and if these weather related disasters are intensified accordingly, it is clear that at some point further economic growth will become unsustainable.

We can again illustrate such a consequence in a phase diagram. Two panels in Figure 1.6 show the hypothetical evolution of the income of the world Y and the intensity of greenhouse gases P in a phase diagram. We again have a downward sloping $\dot{Y} = 0$ curve. A higher intensity of greenhouse gases will cause a higher risk of natural disasters. Given that the risk of natural disasters lowers new investments for production, it will lead to a smaller steady-state stock of capital and, hence, a lower steady-state level of world income. One difference from Figure 1.2 is that we now consider the possibility of endogenous growth. In the literature of endogenous growth, it is considered that physical and human capital can be accumulated without reaching a steady state and that the rate of accumulation is determined endogenously by underlying economic conditions such as technology and preference (we will present a formal model in Section 4). In the current setting, a key factor in the economic conditions is the risk of natural disasters, and it would be legitimate to suppose that the long-term rate of economic growth becomes positive only when the greenhouse gas intensity P is lower than some threshold value $\hat{P}$. This means that the $\dot{Y} = 0$ locus asymptotes to the $P = \hat{P}$ line as Y becomes larger.

Path **f** in Figure 1.6 (i) shows the evolution of the economy when there is no effort to reduce emissions per output. In this case, P/Y is constant. As the world's income grows, the pollution increases proportionally, as does the risk of natural disasters. The magnitude of the risk eventually reaches the point at which firms do not want to invest in additional stock of capital, and this is the

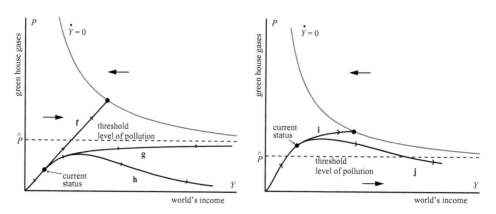

Figure 1.6   Global pollution and sustainability of growth

limit of growth for the economy in the case of a constant P/Y ratio. To sustain economic growth, the economy needs P to stay below the threshold value of $\hat{P}$, and this requires continued reductions in the P/Y ratio as Y increases. The P/Y ratio could be reduced by a number of factors, including the introduction of more advanced production technologies, the substitution of polluting inputs for cleaner ones, and abatement activities. However, because it often is costly for private firms to reduce pollution, it is necessary for the authorities to encourage them to do so by appropriate policies; for example, by raising the rate of environmental tax on the emissions of pollutants.

Path **g** in Figure 1.6 (i) shows one such possibility, where the amount of pollution is kept barely below threshold $\hat{P}$. On this path, the P/Y ratio is continually reduced, for example, by increasing the environmental tax rate, but the amount of pollution P itself increases gradually toward the threshold level of $\hat{P}$. In this case, economic growth can be sustained in the meaning that the amount of output increases without bound, but the long run rate of growth will become lower because the risk of natural disasters gradually rises, which gives disincentives for further investments. Path **h** illustrates a growth path under a stricter environmental policy, for example, where the tax rate is raised at a quicker rate than in path **g**. When such a policy induces the amount of pollution to become lower than the current level, we will eventually observe the EKC for global pollution. In this case, the adverse effects of global warming on growth (including the risk of natural disasters) will become milder in the long run. If the positive effect of the lower disaster risk exceeds the negative effect of higher taxation, such a policy will enable a higher long-term rate of economic growth than in path **g**.

The preceding discussion implicitly assumed that the current level of global pollution has not yet exceeded the threshold level, but this is actually far from obvious. Figure 1.6 (ii) depicts the possibility that the current level of pollution is already too high to maintain long-term growth. If this is the case, it is necessary to adopt a stricter environmental policy that reduces not only the P/Y ratio (e.g., path **i**) but also the global level of pollution P (e.g., path **j**). This means that economic growth is sustainable only when the amount of global pollution follows the EKC; in other words, the EKC for global pollution is a *requirement* for sustained growth. Although it might be considered that the EKC is a result of a successful process of economic growth, the above discussion suggests a possibility of reverse causality in that the sustained economic growth can be a result of appropriate environmental policies that achieve the EKC.

Note that even when a strict environmental policy is required for maintaining economic growth, it does not necessarily mean that this is always desirable in terms of welfare because in the short run consumers might need to reduce consumption because of increased production costs (and, hence, higher prices). Even in the long run, a stricter environmental policy does not always imply a higher long-term rate of growth because increased production costs mean lower profits, which might reduce the incentives to invest even under favorable natural environments. Therefore, we need to develop an economic model to explicitly investigate the mutual causality between the environment and growth and, by using it, examine the desirable policy. Also, in the case of local pollution, it is necessary to develop a formal model to see the precise cause of the poverty-environment trap, which will be indispensable in understanding the root of the international income inequalities and helping those trapped countries. The next two sections are devoted to these tasks.

3. The poverty-environment trap and international inequalities

In this section, we develop a model of local pollution and economic development and explain the mechanism of the poverty-environment trap. The following model is based on a simplified version of Ikefuji and Horii (2007).

3.1 A model of local pollution and technological choice

Consider an overlapping generations model where each individual lives for two periods. Individuals in their first and second periods are called young and adult agents, respectively. In youth, agents invest in human capital through education, which is necessary if they want to adopt both more productive and cleaner technology later in their life. In adulthood, each agent works and bears a single child (a young agent). The efficiency of both education and production depends on their health, which in turn depends on the amount of pollution in the environment.

Let us call an agent who is born in period t a generation-t agent. We normalize the number of agents of each generation to one. The lifetime utility of a generation-t agent is given by

$$U_t = \log c_t^y + (1-\beta)\log c_{t+1}^a + \beta \log x_{t+1}, \quad 0 < \beta < 1, \tag{1}$$

where, c_t^y c_{t+1}^a and x_{t+1} represent the amount of consumption in youth, in adulthood, and the amount of transfer that is given to their children, respectively.

Suppose that the health status of a generation-t agent is negatively affected by the amount of pollution in her youth. Specifically, we assume that the ability of an agent is given by $\ell_t = L - P_t$, where L is a constant representing the ability of an agent under the pristine environment, while P_t denotes the actual amount of pollution in period t.[8] Let x_t be the amount of transfer that each young generation-t agent receives from her parents. We consider a situation of a developing country where the credit market is imperfect, and we assume, therefore, that agents can neither borrow nor lend. For simplicity, we also assume that goods are not storable, so they must be used within a given period. A part of the transfer is used for consumption c_t^y. The remaining e_t is used as an input to human capital investment, which is combined with her ability to learn ℓ_t and yields $h_{t+1} = \phi e_t \ell_t$ units of human capital for her adulthood, where $\phi > 0$ is a parameter. The budget constraint in her youth can be written as:

$$c_t^y + e_t = x_t, \quad 0 \le e_t \le x_t. \tag{2}$$

In adulthood (period $t+1$), each agent produces goods by employing two types of technologies. One is sustainable technology, which produces goods from labor and human capital according to

$$y_{t+1}^s = A^s (h_{t+1})^\theta (s_{t+1}\ell_t)^{1-\theta}, \quad A^s > 0, 0 < \theta < 1, \tag{3}$$

where s_{t+1} denotes the fraction of generation-t agents' time devoted to sustainable technology. This production technology does not cause pollution and, in that sense, is clean. The other technology is called primitive technology, which uses only labor to produce goods, according to

$$y_{t+1}^p = A^p (1 - s_{t+1})\ell_t, \quad A^p > 0, \tag{4}$$

but it emits pollution. We assume that the emission is proportional to the amount of output from the primitive technology and that the amount of pollution in the environment evolves according to

$$P_{t+1} = (1-\delta)P_t + \hat{\eta} y_{t+1}^p, \quad 0 < \delta < 1, \hat{\eta} > 0. \tag{5}$$

An adult agent uses her total output $y_{t+1} \equiv y_{t+1}^s + y_{t+1}^p$ for consumption and transfer for her child:

$$c_{t+1}^a + x_{t+1} = y_{t+1} \equiv y_{t+1}^s + y_{t+1}^p. \tag{6}$$

3.2 Choice between dirty and clean technologies

The problem of a generation-t individual can be described as follows: given the amount of transfer from her parent x_t and the pollution P_t, she chooses education e_t, the fraction of time devoted to sustainable technology s_{t+1}, consumption c_t^y and, c_{t+1}^a and transfer to her child x_{t+1}. Her objective is to maximize lifetime utility (1), subject to budget constraints (2) and (6), and production technology (3) and (4). Because condition (2) includes inequality constraints due to credit market imperfection, this problem can be solved by the Kuhn-Tucker method. We find that the solution to the problem critically depends on the amount of transfer from her parent x_t. Note that under the utility function (1), $x_t = \beta y_t$ holds because adult agents always leave the fraction β of their income for their children as a transfer. Because it is easier to interpret the result in terms of income level (rather than amount of transfer), we describe the solution using y_t.

If the parent generation was poor and their income y_t was smaller than a threshold level of $\underline{y} \equiv (1-\theta)/2\sigma\theta$, where $\sigma \equiv (1/2)\beta\phi(A^s(1-\theta)/A^p)^{1/\theta}$, agents cannot receive education ($e_t = 0$) and have to rely completely on the primitive technology ($s_{t+1} = 0$), which worsens the quality of the environment.[9] Conversely, if the income of previous generation y_t was higher than $\overline{y} \equiv (1+\theta)/2\sigma\theta$, i.e., if their parents are sufficiently rich, agents can receive sufficient education ($e_t = \theta\beta y_t/(1+\theta)$) such that they rely only on the sustainable technology ($s_{t+1} = 1$), which improves the environmental quality. Finally, if y_t was between $\underline{y}$ and $\overline{y}$, agents receive some education ($e_t = \beta(y_t - \underline{y})/2$) but have to rely partly on the primitive technology ($s_{t+1} = \sigma(y_t - \underline{y}) < 1$). Still, it can be seen that the dependence on the primitive technology decreases (s_{t+1} increases) as the parents become richer. To summarize, we can write s_{t+1} in terms of y_t as:

$$s_{t+1} = s(y_t) \equiv \begin{cases} 0 & \text{if } y_t \leq \underline{y} \equiv (1-\theta)/2\sigma\theta, \\ \sigma(y_t - \underline{y}) & \text{if } y_t \in (\underline{y}, \overline{y}), \\ 1 & \text{if } y_t \geq \overline{y} \equiv (1+\theta)/2\sigma\theta, \end{cases} \tag{7}$$

which is consistent with the observation that richer countries tend to use cleaner technologies in a larger fraction of their production.

The amount of production $y_{t+1}^s + y_{t+1}^p$ is determined by the relative dependence on the two types of technologies $s_{t+1} = s(y_t)$ in (7) and the ability of agents $\ell_t = L - P_t$ as well as human capital $h_{t+1} = \varphi e_t \ell_t = \varphi e_t (L - P_t)$. We thus obtain the evolution of income y_t over the generations:

$$y_{t+1} = \tilde{y}(y_t)(L - P_t), \text{ where } \tilde{y}(y_t) \equiv \begin{cases} A^p & \text{if } y_t \leq \underline{y}, \\ A^p(\underline{y} + y_t)/2\underline{y} & \text{if } y_t \in (\underline{y}, \overline{y}), \\ A^s[\varphi\theta\beta y_t/(1+\theta)]^\theta & \text{if } y_t \geq \overline{y}. \end{cases} \tag{8}$$

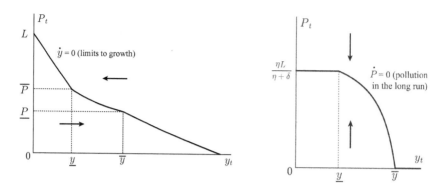

Figure 1.7 Evolution of income (left) and pollution (right) over generations

Let us examine the "limits to growth" of this economy. The $\dot{y}_t = 0$ locus can be derived by setting $y_t + 1 = y_t$ in equation (8).[10] The result is

$$
y^*(P_t) \equiv \begin{cases}
\left[A^s \left(\varphi \theta \beta / (1+\theta) \right)^\theta (L - P_t) \right]^{1/(1-\theta)} \geq \overline{y} & \text{if } P_t \leq \underline{P}, \\
A^p (2/(L - P_t) - 1/(L - \overline{P}))^{-1} \in (\underline{y}, \overline{y}) & \text{if } P_t \in (\underline{P}, \overline{P}), \\
A^p (L - P_t) \leq \underline{y} & \text{if } P_t \geq \overline{P},
\end{cases}
\tag{9}
$$

where $\overline{P} \equiv L - y / A^p$ and $\underline{P} \equiv (1+\theta)\overline{P} - \theta L$.

Figure 1.7 (left) depicts the $\dot{y} = 0$ locus (i.e., function $y = y^*(P_t)$ in equation 9) in (y, P) space. The level of income increases over generations if and only if the (y, P) pair is to the left of this locus. Similarly to Figure 1.2, the $\dot{y} = 0$ locus is downward sloping. This means that the economy can grow to a higher level of income when pollution is lower and, hence, the environment is better. In this economy, this occurs for two reasons. First, when the environment is better (P_t is lower), the agents have greater ability to work ($\ell_t = L - P_t$), such that they can produce more output. This is a direct effect of the environment on income. There is also an indirect effect that is manifested over the generations: when the environment is better, parents can leave a larger amount of income to their children, and children themselves also have higher ability to learn ($\ell_{t+1} = L - P_{t+1}$), both of which enable agents in the next generation to adopt a better technology. In Figure 1.7 (left), the effect of the environment on the technological shift appears when the amount of pollution is between $\underline{P}$ and $\overline{P}$. When P_t is within this range, a marginal change P_t has a larger effect on long-term income through inducing agents to employ the productive (and sustainable) technology in a larger portion of total production (i.e., the long-run level of s_{t+1} increases with P_t). This explains why the $\dot{y} = 0$ locus is flatter in this segment than in other segments.

3.3 Dynamic interaction between income and environment

We have shown that, given the amount of pollution P_t, the evolution of income is determined by equation (8). How, then, is P_t determined? Will it follow the environmental Kuznets curve? From (4), (5), (7) and $\ell_t = L - P_t$, the evolution of the amount of pollution in equilibrium can be written as

$$
P_{t+1} = (1 - \delta)P_t + \eta(1 - s(y_t))(L - P_t),
\tag{10}
$$

where $\eta \equiv \hat{\eta} A^p$. Equation (10) shows that the evolution of P_t is also determined by the (y, P) pair. By applying $P_{t+1} = P_t$ for (10), we obtain the stationary level of pollution for each given income level y_t:

$$P^{\ast}(y_t) = \begin{cases} \eta L/(\eta + \delta). & \text{if } y_t \leq \underline{y}, \\ \eta L/\left(\eta + \delta/\sigma(\overline{y} - y_t) \right) & \text{if } y_t \in (\underline{y}, \overline{y}), \\ 0 & \text{if } y_t \geq \overline{y}. \end{cases} \tag{11}$$

Let us call the curve given by (11) the $\dot{P} = 0$ locus, as depicted in Figure 1.7 (right). The amount of pollution in this economy increases toward the $\dot{P} = 0$ locus whenever the (y, P) pair is below this locus. Observe that the $\dot{P} = 0$ locus is (weakly) downward sloping because a richer economy can afford to invest more in human capital and, hence, can employ cleaner technologies (recall equation 7), which implies lower pollution in the long run. Note, however, that the amount of income y_t itself changes depending on P_t, and hence we need to examine the dynamic interaction between y_t and P_t over the process of economic development. This can be done by combining the $\dot{y} = 0$ locus and the $\dot{P} = 0$ locus in one figure.

Figure 1.8 depicts the phase diagram of the dynamic system in (y, P) space.[11] We can observe that there are two stable steady states, T and B, and one saddle point U. It depends on the initial conditions which steady-state the economy converges to in the long run. In this system, both y_t and P_t are state variables, and, therefore, the initial condition is given by a pair of the income of the initial adult generation y_0 (i.e., the parents of generation-0 agents) and the initial amount of pollution P_0.[12] Because we are interested in the process of economic growth, we suppose y_0 to be small so that we can examine the process from the initial stage of development. It also will make sense to assume the initial amount of pollution P_0 to be small if we consider that the economy starts from a pre-industrial society, but the precise values of P_0, as well as the parameters of the model, will vary across economies.

Figure 1.8 shows three representative equilibrium paths that start from slightly different initial combinations of (y_0, P_0). Path **k** illustrates an equilibrium path when the economy starts from a low P/Y ratio. On the first half of this path, pollution gradually accumulates while the output increases. However, once the income level sufficiently rises and the path moves past the $\dot{P} = 0$

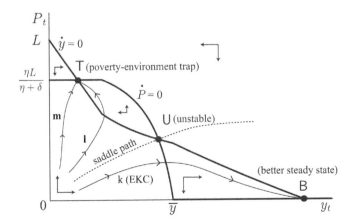

Figure 1.8 The poverty-environment trap and the environmental Kuznets curve in equilibrium

locus, the accumulated amount of pollution begins to decrease. This is because the economy now has enough income to invest in human capital and, therefore, no longer needs to rely as much on dirty primitive technologies. Thereafter, as the environment improves, the ability (or health status) of the workers also improves, which enables the income level to increase further toward the better steady state B. This path explains that the interaction between the income level and pollution can endogenously generate the EKC. However, this path is not the only possibility.

Path **1** in Figure 1.8 illustrates another equilibrium path when the economic development begins with a higher P/Y ratio. In this case, the economy hits the $\dot{y} = 0$ locus (the limits to growth) before encountering the $\dot{P} = 0$ locus. This means that the economic growth has come to its limit due to the environmental degradation before the income level reaches the top of the EKC. This is not the end of the story. From this point, environmental degradation further continues because the economy is still below the $\dot{P} = 0$ curve. After passing the $\dot{y} = 0$ locus, the income actually decreases due to the deteriorated ability of workers who are seriously affected by a poor environment. The economy eventually converges to steady state T, which we call the poverty-environment trap. In this trap, workers cannot escape from poverty because the deteriorated environment lowers their ability and productivity. At the same time, the economy cannot escape from the deteriorated environment because workers are too poor to obtain human capital and, hence, cannot employ cleaner technologies. This mutual causality creates a stagnating economy that suffers both from poverty and a deteriorated environment. Path **m** in Figure 1.8 shows the case where the initial P/Y ratio is even higher. In this case, the economy converges directly to the poverty-environment trap T, which is locally stable and can be approached from any direction in the phase diagram.

These two long-term possibilities, the better steady state and the poverty-environment trap, are grossly different both in terms of environmental quality and income. What, then, separates the successful economies that get past the peak of the EKC from the economies that stagnate in the mutual trap of poverty and environmental degradation? Observe from Figure 1.8 that there exists a saddle path that converges to the saddle point U. Because both y_0 and P_0 are predetermined state variables, there is virtually zero possibility that the economy happens to be on this path. However, the location of this saddle path is important because it separates the two long-term outcomes: the economy converges to the poverty-environment trap if and only if the initial (y_0, P_0) pair is above the saddle path. Therefore, even when all parameters are identical, a slight difference in the initial conditions (which depends on many factors, e.g., whether a country has been colonized or not and, if so, by what country) may explain persistent international inequality in income and environmental quality. In addition, if the parameters of economies are not identical (e.g., because of regional characteristics), the location of the saddle path as well as the locations of the steady states would differ across countries. This explains another possible reason why some economies have successfully developed along with a cleaner environment, while others are still suffering from low income and poor environmental conditions, as we have observed in Figure 1.4.

3.4 Environmental policies for trapped economies

Now let us discuss how environmental policies can or cannot save economies that are currently trapped in the poverty-environment trap and whether such policies can mitigate the international inequality both in terms of income and the environment. We have explained that, in a trapped economy, the environmental quality and, thus, the productivity was low because people rely on the primitive technologies that emit pollution. A direct approach to solve this problem is to limit the use of such technologies, i.e., to force them to reduce pollution even if it is costly for individuals. Alternatively, the authorities can tax the use of dirty technologies (or, equivalently, tax emissions) and use the tax revenue for pollution-abatement activities. In either case, the net income from using the primitive technology A^p will fall,[13] but the amount of pollution per unit output from the primitive technology, given by parameter η, also will fall. To examine the equilibrium outcome of such policies in a convenient way, we suppose that both A^p and η are functions of the strictness of the environmental policy, denoted by $\alpha \in [0,1]$, and that both are decreasing in α.[14]

Figure 1.9 illustrates how such environmental policies affect the trapped economy. Recall that in the poverty-environment trap, both the environmental quality and the income are low so that $P_t > \overline{P}$ and $y_t < \underline{y}$ hold. In this region, from (9) and (11), we can confirm that the locus $\dot{y} = 0$ shifts leftward, while the $\dot{P} = 0$ locus shifts downward. This implies that there are two opposing effects of environmental policies on the income of a trapped economy. First, the leftward shift of the $\dot{y} = 0$ locus means that, given the quality of the environment, the household income declines. This result comes directly from our assumption that environmental policies that aim to reduce emissions are costly for individuals. If it takes time for the environmental quality to change, as assumed in equation (10), then the short-term effect of environmental policy on income is necessarily negative.

In the long-run, however, the environment improves, as reflected in the downward shift in the $\dot{P} = 0$ locus. With a better environment, the productivity of workers will improve, increasing

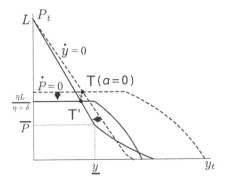

Figure 1.9   Effect of a small environmental tax or the enforcement of mild pollution reduction in a trapped economy (a magnified view around steady state T). The dashed loci show the phase diagram without the environmental tax. The solid loci show the case of $\alpha = 0.15$ (i.e., when both A^p and η are 85% of their original values).

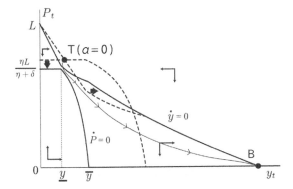

Figure 1.10   Effect of a large environmental tax or the enforcement of large pollution reduction in a trapped economy. The dashed loci show the phase diagram with $\alpha = 0$. The solid loci show the case of $\alpha = 0.27$ (i.e., when both A^p and η are 73% of their original values).

their incomes. The long-term net effect of environmental policy on income depends on the relative magnitude of these two effects. (In other words, it depends on the relative significance of the reductions in A^p and η, or more generally, it depends on the elasticity of the productivity loss to the reduction of emissions). As illustrated in Figure 1.9, the net effect can be negative even in the long run. The steady state level of income in steady state T' under an environmental policy of $\alpha = 0.15$ is lower than the income in steady state T with $\alpha = 0$.

The results suggest that it is not easy to form a consensus on the environmental policy to reduce emissions in a poverty-environmentally trapped economy because it will further undermine the already low income in the short run, and it is not certain whether it will raise income even in the long run. However, a sufficiently strong environmental policy can have quite different implications. As illustrated by Figure 1.10, the $\dot{P} = 0$ and $\dot{y} = 0$ loci become detached from each other when α is large enough. This means that the poverty-environment trap no longer exists in the new phase diagram, and because of this structural change the economy necessarily converges to the now unique steady state B. In this transition, the environment improves simultaneously with the rising income, as in the latter half of the EKC.

Why does a strong environmental policy give rise to such a drastic change? One possible reason is that a better environmental quality improves the productivity and, hence, the incomes of workers and enables their children to invest in human capital and cleaner technologies. However, as we have explained earlier, environmental policies to reduce emissions do not necessarily improve income as long as individuals are relying on dirty primitive technologies (i.e., when $P_t > \overline{P}$ and $y_t < \underline{y}$), and, therefore, this first cause does not always work. The second and more definite cause of the structural change is that because a strong environmental policy reduces the private returns from adopting primitive technologies, workers are induced to invest in human capital and adopt cleaner technologies even at lower income levels. This can be confirmed by the fact that the threshold levels of income for education, $\underline{y}$ and $\overline{y}$ in equation (7), become smaller when A^p falls.[15] Obviously, such a policy temporarily reduces the income of poor households (given that the environmental quality does not change instantly). As time passes, however, the environment improves gradually, which increases productivity and income. Once the income level passes a threshold level (specifically, when y_t and P_t pair falls below the saddle path in Figure 1.8), workers are now willing to invest in human capital and cleaner technologies even without further policy interventions, and the economy autonomously improves toward the better steady state.

To summarize, once an economy falls into the poverty-environment trap, it is difficult to build a consensus on environmental policies because such policies are likely to worsen income and welfare, at least temporarily. In addition, when the policy intervention is insufficient, poverty can be aggravated even in the long run. However, the situation can be solved permanently if a sufficiently strong environmental policy is continued for a certain period until the economy reaches the autonomous process of economic growth and environmental improvements. Given the short-term cost of such a drastic intervention, assistance from developed economies (e.g., by providing funds for the abatement cost, subsidies for education, or income assistance for households whose earnings are adversely affected by environmental policies) will certainly be a key in helping economies escape from the poverty-environment trap, thereby reducing the wide international inequality both in incomes and environmental quality.[16]

4. Sustainability of long-term growth under global warming

In the previous section, we examined the problems of large international differences in income and environmental quality. We showed the possibility that the interaction between the environment and growth within each country creates a poverty-environment trap and that this mechanism can explain the long-lasting international inequality in terms of both environmental quality and income. Now, let us turn to the growth of the world economy as a whole and examine how can it be harmonized with the global environment, particularly regarding the problem of global warming. As we have discussed in the latter half of Section 2, the growing world economy emits increasing amounts of global warming gases, which is suspected to intensify the risk of natural disasters. The aggregate economic damage from natural disasters, which mostly takes the form of the destruction of capital stocks, has been increasing at a speed faster than the growth of the world GDP (see Figure 1.5). If this trend continues, the risk of losing the capital stock will sooner or later exceed a threshold at which the economy does not want to invest further in capital stock. This is the "limits to growth" for the world economy (see path **f** in Figure 1.6). Can any environmental policy prevent such a situation from occurring and sustain long-term growth? Based on a simplified version of the endogenous growth model by Ikefuji and Horii (2012), this section presents a formal model of emissions, natural disasters, and the "limits to growth."

4.1 A model with global pollution and capital destruction

While the previous section considered only human capital, in this section we consider explicitly the accumulation of physical and human capital. Note that the damage from natural disasters occurs most strikingly in the form of capital destruction. In addition, natural disasters entail many human casualties and, therefore, destroy a substantial amount of skills and knowledge (i.e., human capital). A knowledge-based economy with a large stock of human capital can be vulnerable to natural disasters once its telecommunication network is damaged. Therefore, it is appropriate to develop a model where the economy accumulates both physical and human capital and where both are subject to the risk of natural disasters. This specification also allows us to examine the properties of long-term economic growth, rather than one-time transitional dynamics from a poor to a rich economy.[17]

However, considering two types of capital simultaneously makes the analysis substantially complex. Therefore, we make several innocuous simplifications. First, rather than explicitly considering different generations (youth and adults, as in the previous section), let us consider a representative household and assume that they divide their human capital (or their disposable time) between production (fraction u_t) and education ($1 - u_t$). In addition, rather than considering the choice between the two technologies, we suppose that production always uses fossil fuels P_t that cause the emission of greenhouse gases of the same amount P_t but that it is possible to adjust the amount of such an input in the production process. The output of the world economy is then given by a constant-returns-to-scale production function:

$$Y_t = AK_t^{\alpha}(u_t H_t)^{1-\alpha-\beta} P_t^{\beta}, \tag{12}$$

where K_t and H_t are the aggregate amounts of physical and human capital, respectively. It is possible to interpret that the primitive technology in the previous section corresponds to the situation where the economy uses a large amount of P_t while making little use of H_t. Sustainable technology corresponds to the opposite combination. Because this section's objective to examine how the economy's reliance on fossil fuels P_t limits the possibility of sustained growth through global warming and increased risk of natural disasters, we do not explicitly consider the finiteness of such resources.[18]

We also simplify the process of education. When the representative household uses amount $(1 - u_t)H_t$ of their human capital for education, it produces additional $B(1 - u_t)H_t$ units of new human capital, where B is a constant parameter for the efficiency of education (see equation 14).

In the model of the previous section, we assumed that local pollution reduces the productivity (ability) of agents. Instead, we now assume that global pollution (i.e., the emission of greenhouse gases) raises the risk of capital stock destruction. Suppose that when the world economy emits amount P_t of greenhouse gases, then, on average, a fraction ϕP_t of physical capital is destroyed by natural disasters within a year.[19] Natural disasters also will erode a fraction ψP_t of human capital, where we assume $0 < \psi < \phi$.[20] Then, the aggregate amounts of physical and human capital evolve according to

$$\dot{K}_t = Y_t - C_t - (\delta_K + \phi P_t)K_t, \tag{13}$$

$$\dot{H}_t = B(1 - u_t)H_t - (\delta_H + \psi P_t)H_t, \tag{14}$$

where δ_K and δ_H are depreciation rates of physical and human capital, respectively, excluding the effect of global warming. Because we are concerned about long-term growth rather than short-term fluctuations caused by individual events of natural disasters, we simply assume that the whole economy consists of many regions and, by the law of large numbers, there is no aggregate uncertainty on the aggregate damage in each year. In this setting, the use of fossil fuels P_t in effect accelerates the depreciation of capital through the larger damages caused by natural disasters.

The representative household has the standard CRRA utility function:

$$\int_0^\infty \frac{C^{1-\theta} - 1}{1 - \theta} e^{-\rho t} dt. \tag{15}$$

Let us consider a market economy where the authorities levy a per-unit tax of $\tau > 0$ on the use of fossil fuels P_t (or, equivalently, the amount of greenhouse gas emissions). Here, we abstract from the international politics and assume that the whole economy (i.e., the world's economy) can set a common rate of environmental tax.[21] Suppose the markets are perfectly competitive and there is a representative firm that produces output Y_t according to equation (12). Let the price of the output be normalized to one and assume that there are no other costs of using P_t other than the environmental tax τ.[22] Then, the first order condition for the profit maximization implies

$$P_t = \beta Y_t / \tau. \tag{16}$$

Equation (16) clearly shows that the emission of greenhouse gases P_t increases proportionally with the world's GDP, Y_t, if there is no strengthening of environmental policy τ. At the same time, this equation shows that emission P_t can be reduced if the environmental tax rate τ is raised, confirming the discussion in Section 2. However, this does not come without a cost. By substituting (16) into production function (12), we see that output can be expressed as

$$Y_t = \left(\tilde{A}\tau^{-\frac{\beta}{1-\beta}}\right) K_t^{\hat{\alpha}} (u_t H_t)^{1-\hat{\alpha}}, \tag{17}$$

where $\tilde{A} \equiv \beta^{\beta/(1-\beta)} A^{1/(1-\beta)}$ and $\tilde{\alpha} \equiv \alpha / (1 - \beta)$. Equation (17) can be interpreted as the aggregate production function given the level of environmental tax τ. It has the form of a standard Cobb-Douglas function with two inputs, K_t and $u_t H_t$, and its total factor productivity (TFP) is given by $\tilde{A}\tau^{-\beta/(1-\beta)}$. This expression clearly shows that, given the current amounts of physical and human capital, the environmental tax lowers the productivity.

4.2 *"Limits to growth" under constant tax rate*

We first show that if the environmental tax rate τ is kept constant, the interacting processes of economic growth and environmental degradation eventually lead to the "limits to growth."

In this economy, the only source of externality is P_t, which represents the use of fossil fuels and, hence, the accompanying emission of greenhouse gases. Other than this aspect, the conditions for the market equilibrium with the representative household and the representative firm coincide with the conditions for the welfare maximization problem.[23] The problem is to maximize the utility (15) subject to the production function (12) and the resource constraints (13) and (14), where we take the evolution of P_t in (16) as given. By setting up a Hamiltonian, we obtain the following first order conditions for this problem, which should also hold in the market equilibrium:

$$\frac{\dot{C}_t}{C_t} = \frac{1}{\theta}\left[\left(\alpha\frac{Y_t}{K_t} - \delta_K - \phi P_t\right) - \rho\right], \tag{18}$$

$$\frac{\dot{H}_t}{H_t} + \frac{\dot{u}_t}{u_t} - \frac{\dot{Y}_t}{Y_t} = \left(B - \delta_H - \psi P_t\right) - \left(\alpha\frac{Y_t}{K_t} - \delta_K - \phi P_t\right). \tag{19}$$

Equation (18) is the Euler equation for the intertemporal consumption. Note that the term $(\alpha Y_t/K_t - \delta_k - \phi P_t)$ in the right-hand side (RHS) represents the (expected) rate of return from physical capital investment, i.e., the marginal product of capital $\alpha Y_t/K_t$ minus the depreciation rate δ_K minus the expected loss from natural disasters ϕP_t. Recall from (16) that if the environmental tax rate τ is constant and the economic growth continues ($\dot{Y}_t > 0$), the representative firm uses an ever increasing amount of fossil fuels P_t. The resulting increase in the risk of natural disasters lowers the rate of return from physical capital investment $(\alpha Y_t/K_t - \delta_k - \phi P_t)$. Equation (18) shows that economic growth can be sustained ($\dot{C}_t/C_t > 0$) only when the rate of return from physical capital investment is kept above the rate of time preference, ρ. For this condition to hold along economic growth, the continual rise in the expected damage ϕP_t must be offset by an increase in the marginal product of physical capital $\alpha Y_t/K_t$.

Will such an increase in $\alpha Y_t/K_t$ actually occur? Note that under production function (17) the marginal product of physical capital $\alpha Y_t/K_t$ rises when the economy uses more human capital $u_t H_t$ relative to the amount of output Y_t. The rate of change in this ratio, $u_t H_t/Y_t$, is represented by the left-hand side (LHS) of equation (19). The first term in the RHS, $(B - \delta_H - \psi P_t)$, represents the rate of return from investing in human capital. The second term is the rate of return from physical capital investment, as previously explained. Therefore, equation (19) shows that the household uses more human capital in production if the rate of return from human capital investment is higher than that from physical capital investment.

As the amount of emission P_t increases in the RHS of (19), the rate of return for physical capital falls more rapidly than that for human capital (recall that $\phi > \psi$), and therefore, the economy increases its reliance on human capital. This is consistent with the empirical findings of Skidmore and Toya (2002), who suggested that a higher frequency of climatic disasters leads to a substitution from physical capital investment toward human capital. This substitution process actually increases the marginal product of physical capital $\alpha Y_t/K_t$, which encourages growth. However, this process cannot perpetually sustain economic growth under a constant tax rate. As we discussed, Euler equation (18) implies that nonnegative growth in consumption requires the rate of return from physical capital $(\alpha Y_t/K_t - \delta_K - \phi P_t)$ to be at least ρ. However, as $P_t = \beta Y_t/\tau$ rises with economic growth, the rate of return from human capital investment $(B - \delta_H - \psi P_t)$ will eventually fall to ρ. This means that the RHS of (19) becomes zero (or negative), and substitution from physical capital to human capital stops. This means that $\alpha Y_t/K_t$ cannot rise further, and, therefore, the rate of return from physical capital investment $(\alpha Y_t / K_t - \delta_K - \phi P_t)$ must eventually fall until it reaches the rate of time preference ρ. At this point, people are unwilling to invest further in physical capital to increase their consumption and economic growth comes to an end.

By setting time derivatives to zero in equations (18) and (19), we find that this steady state, or the "limits to growth," is reached when the amount of emissions increases up to

$$\hat{P} = \frac{B - \delta_H - \rho}{\psi}. \tag{20}$$

Figure 1.11 illustrates the processes of economic growth in (Y,P) space for three different environmental tax rates. These three paths start from the same level of capital accumulation. However, as we have shown in equation (17), the initial amount of production (income) Y_t varies negatively with the environmental tax rate because the higher tax rate reduces the effective TFP. When the tax rate is higher, the initial level of emission $P_t = \beta Y_t / \tau$ is also lower due to both higher τ and lower initial Y_t.

As the economy grows, the amount of emission P_t increases proportionally with output Y_t. Observe from the figure that the slope of the path, $P_t Y_t = \beta / \tau$, is less steep when the tax rate is higher. This means that the level of income at which the economy reaches the "limits to growth" (i.e., when P_t reaches $\hat{P}$) is proportionally related to the environmental tax rate:

$$\hat{Y} = \frac{\tau}{\beta \psi} (B - \delta_H - \rho). \tag{21}$$

Therefore, although a higher environmental tax initially corresponds to a lower output, it also implies there remains larger room for economic growth.

While Figure 1.11 illustrates the existence of the limits to growth of the world economy under a constant environmental tax rate; it also suggests that economic growth can be maintained if the environmental tax rate is continually raised. Whenever the world economy reaches the limit of growth, it is possible to bring the economy to a less steep path of growth that leads to a higher long-term level of output, although output temporarily falls (e.g., from point A to point B, or from point C to point D in Figure 1.11). It might be even better to raise the environmental tax before the emission P_t reaches $\hat{P}$ because doing so will allow the possibility of keeping the rates of return from physical and human capital investment higher, thereby encouraging faster

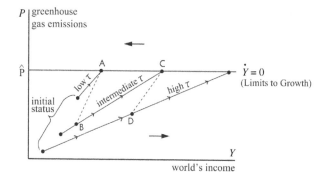

Figure 1.11 Evolution of the global environment and the world's income under different environmental tax rates

capital accumulation. However, it is not always better to raise the environmental tax faster because it lowers the effective productivity of production. In the next subsection, we examine the desirable environmental tax policy both in terms of the long-term economic growth rate and in terms of welfare.

Before leaving this subsection, let us explain the difference between Figure 1.6 and Figure 1.11. While we discussed in Section 2 that the $\dot{Y} = 0$ locus would appear to be downward sloping (see Figure 1.6), the $\dot{Y} = 0$ locus we derived so far (Figure 1.11) is actually horizontal because $\hat{P} = (B - \delta_H - \rho)/\psi$ does not depend on the income level Y_t. This result is due to several simplifications. In particular, we simply assumed that δ_H and ψ do not change with the income level or the level of human capital. At the initial stage of economic growth, however, when production relied more on basic labor than advanced human capital, we may interpret that δ_H and ψ must have been smaller. As the economy develops and the aggregate human capital accumulates (i.e., the development of complex systems of skill, knowledge and information in the world economy), the depreciation or the obsolescence of existing human capital will accelerate (i.e., δ_H increases). In addition, as the system of human capital becomes more complex, it might become more vulnerable to natural disasters (i.e., ψ rises). If we incorporate these changes into the model, the $\dot{Y} = 0$ locus ($\hat{P} = (B - \delta_H - \rho)/\psi$) will become downward sloping, as depicted in Figure 1.6.

Note, however, that if we do not expect δ_H and ψ to rise indefinitely, they will converge to certain constants in the very long run. Because this section examines the long-run consequences of the interaction between the environment and economic growth, we consider the situation where economic development has already sufficiently advanced so that δ_H and ψ can be seen as constants. In Figure 1.6, this corresponds to the region where Y_t is sufficiently large that the $\dot{Y} = 0$ comes close to the dashed horizontal line at $P_t = \hat{P}$.

4.3 Environmental policy and sustained growth

In the previous subsection, we confirmed that economic growth can be sustained only when the environmental tax rate is continually raised. Now let us define the rate of tax increase $g_\tau \equiv \dot{\tau}_t/\tau_t$ and examine how it determines the long-term rate of economic growth $g^* \equiv \dot{Y}_t/Y_t$.[24]

The long-term rate of economic growth g^* cannot be higher than the rate of tax increase, g_τ, because otherwise $P_t = \beta Y_t/\tau_t$ would continue to increase and eventually face the "limits to growth," $\hat{P}$. Therefore, sustained growth ($g^* > 0$) requires a positive rate of environmental tax increase. Under such a policy, there are two possible outcomes in the state of the environment. If the long-term economic growth occurs at the same rate as the tax increase (i.e., $g^* = g_\tau$), then the growth rate of $P_t = \beta Y_t/\tau_t$ will become zero, and, therefore, the amount of emissions will converge to a constant, which we denote by P^*. Another possibility is that output grows slower than the tax rate ($g^* < g_\tau$). In such a scenario, the amount of emission $P_t = \beta Y_t/\tau_t$ falls at the rate of $g_P = g^* - g_\tau < 0$ and will converge toward zero. That is, the emissions are asymptotically eliminated in the long run; $P^* = 0$.

In either case, the amount of emissions and, hence, the risk of natural disasters converge to a constant level. This by itself should be good for economic growth. However, when the tax rate τ is continually increased, is it possible to maintain output growth, given that a higher τ reduces the effective productivity? Calculating the rates of change on both sides of equation (17), we find that the growth rate of human capital $g_H \equiv \dot{H}_t/H_t$ should be higher than the output growth so that it offsets the effective productivity loss caused by $g_\tau > 0$.[25]

$$g_H = g^* + \frac{\beta}{1 - \alpha - \beta} g_\tau. \qquad (22)$$

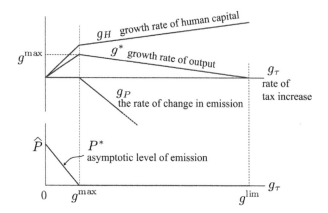

Figure 1.12   Rates of changes in output, human capital, and emissions (above) and the asymptotic value of emissions (below) as a function of the rate of environmental tax increase

Note that (22) means H_t/Y_t increases over time, whereas the constancy of P^* implies P_t/Y_t will fall. Equation (22) also can be understood in such a way that the environmental tax policy induces the substitution from fossil fuels to human capital in the production process. In other words, the policy encourages the shift toward a knowledge-oriented production process rather than heavily relying on natural resources. In a broader sense, this can be interpreted as a process of technological shift, as in the model of Section 3.[26]

Using the above properties in equations (13), (14), (16), (18) and (19), we obtain the asymptotic value of emission P^* and the long-term growth rate g^* as a function of environmental policy g_τ. The result is summarized in Figure 1.12, which also depicts g_H from (22) and $g_P = g^* - g_\tau$. Let us first explain the case in which the rate of tax increase g_τ does not exceed a threshold of

$$g^{\max} \equiv \left(\theta + \frac{\beta}{1-\alpha-\beta}\right)^{-1}(B-\delta_H-\rho). \tag{23}$$

When the tax policy is within the range of, $g_\tau \le g^{\max}$, we find that the output of the economy can grow at the same speed as the tax increase, i.e., $g^* = g_\tau$. In this case, $P_t = \beta Y_t / \tau t$ converges to a positive constant

$$P^* = \frac{1}{\psi}\left[B-\delta_H-\rho-\left(\theta+\frac{\beta}{1-\alpha-\beta}\right)g_\tau\right], \tag{24}$$

which is decreasing in g_τ. This means that by raising the tax rate faster, it is possible to reduce the long-term level of emissions and, hence, the risk of natural disasters. The lower risk of natural disasters encourages the economy to accumulate more capital, thereby enabling faster economic growth. Thus, g^* increases with g_τ.

Figure 1.13 depicts the growth paths of the economy in (P,Y) space under different tax policies. Suppose that thus far the tax rate on fossil fuels (or, more generally, the user cost of pollution-generating inputs) has been constant and that P_t and Y_t have increased proportionally to the current status of (P_0,Y_0). As we have seen in the previous subsection, the economy will face the "limits to growth" if the tax rate is kept constant (path **a**). However, if the tax rate is continually raised at an appropriate speed, the economy can overcome this limit. Path **b** depicts the evolution of the economy when the tax rate is raised gradually, but the rate of tax increase $\dot\tau_t / \tau_t$ is small. Under such an

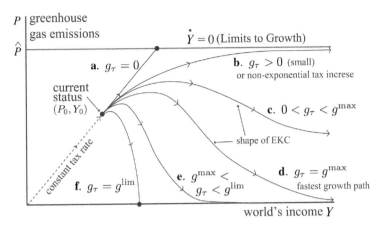

Figure 1.13 Environmental tax policy and the future evolutions of income and environmental quality

environmental tax policy, the amount of emission P_t can be kept below the threshold $\hat{P}$ but will come close to it. Then, the long-term rate of economic growth g^* is positive but not large (see Figure 1.12). Note that when the speed of increase in τ_t is positive but less than an exponential increase, $\dot{\tau}_t / \tau_t$ will fall to zero as the denominator τ_t increases. In such a case, the economy will grow similarly to path **b**, but in the limit the long-term rate of growth $g^* \equiv \dot{Y}_t / Y_t$ will fall to zero. This is a natural result because Y_t cannot grow more than proportionally with τ_t, and hence, if τ_t is not raised at an exponential rate, an exponential growth of Y_t (i.e., $g^* > 0$) is not possible either.

If the environmental tax rate is raised at a faster rate, the long-term level of emissions can be reduced to a lower level, as shown by path **c**. (See also equation 24 and Figure 1.12). The long-term rate of growth, then, is higher than that in path **a** because the environmental tax rate is raised at a faster rate and the output grows at the same rate. The fastest rate of long-term growth can be obtained when τ_t is raised at exactly the rate of $g^{\max}$ in (23). This environmental tax policy achieves asymptotically zero emissions in the long run. This does not mean P_t becomes 0 at some date t, which is not possible because the production function (12) always requires a positive input of P_t. However, it is possible to reduce P_t toward zero while using increasingly more human capital H_t over time. With the risk of natural disasters falling to the minimum level, the economy is encouraged to accumulate physical and human capital at the fastest speed. In this sense, such an environmental policy perfectly harmonizes the maximization of economic growth with environmental improvements in the long run.

Note also that under a policy such that the long-term level of emission P^* is lower than the current level of emission, P_0, we will observe the EKC in the future. Therefore, in the case of greenhouse gas emissions, the EKC does not emerge automatically but will only be realized when the world economy agrees on setting sufficiently strict environmental policies that enable faster long-term economic growth. In other words, following the EKC is a requirement for achieving a high rate of economic growth in the long run.

What will happen if the world economy decides to adopt a stricter environmental policy? If $g_\tau > g^{\max}$, the negative effect of tax on the productivity dominates, and the economy cannot grow at the same speed as the tax increase ($g^* < g_\tau$). Specifically, the long-term rate of growth becomes a decreasing function of g_τ,

$$g^* = \frac{1}{\theta}\left(B - \delta_H - \rho - \frac{\beta}{1 - \alpha - \beta} g_\tau\right). \tag{25}$$

The emission P_t falls to zero ($P^* = 0$) at the rate of $g_P = g^* - g_\tau$ (see Figure 1.12), which becomes more negative when g_τ is larger. Therefore, as depicted by path **e** in Figure 1.13, when the environmental tax rate is raised too quickly ($g_\tau > g^{\max}$), the emissions can be reduced at a faster rate but at the cost of a slower long-term rate of growth. Path **f** shows that the extremely strict environmental policy actually chokes economic growth, which occurs when the rate of tax increase is raised to $g^{\lim} \equiv (1 - \alpha - \beta)\beta^{-1}(B - \delta_H - \rho)$.

4.4 Welfare-maximizing environmental policy for global warming

We have seen that an appropriate environmental policy can both maximize the long-term rate of growth and reduce emissions toward zero. This particular policy ($g_\tau = g^{\max}$) can be characterized as the mildest environmental tax policy among those that asymptotically achieve zero emissions.[27] Note that this is still a strict environmental policy in the sense of reducing emissions toward zero, and such a policy incurs a substantial cost in terms of productivity loss in the short run, as we have seen in Subsection 4.2. While this policy can minimize the risk of natural disasters, is it desirable in terms of welfare?

Thus far, we have considered the equilibrium in the market economy. As we mentioned, in this economy the only difference between the welfare maximization problem and the market economy is the determination of the amount of emission (or, equivalently, the use of fossil fuels) P_t. In the market economy, the amount of emissions is determined as $P_t = \beta Y_t / \tau_t$ by (16). In the welfare maximization problem, the social cost of using P_t, including the negative externality from a higher risk of natural disasters, should be determined such that it is equalized to the social benefit of using fossil fuels, i.e., the marginal product of using fossil fuels. This condition can be written as

$$\phi K_t + \psi H_t \frac{(1 - \alpha - \beta)Y_t}{Bu_t H_t} = \frac{\beta Y_t}{P_t}, \tag{26}$$

Note that ϕK_t and ψH_t represent the marginal increases in the damages to physical and human capital due to a marginal increase in P_t, while $\beta Y_t / P_t$ is the marginal product of P_t. The fraction $(1 - \alpha - \beta)Y_t / Bu_t H_t$ represents the value (shadow price) of human capital relative to output. Condition (26) can be solved for the amount of emissions as:

$$P_t = \beta \left(\phi \frac{K_t}{Y_t} + \psi \frac{(1 - \alpha - \beta)}{Bu_t} \right)^{-1}. \tag{27}$$

Figure 1.14 illustrates the determination of the welfare-maximizing tax policy. Once g_τ is given, the capital output ratio K_t/Y_t and the fraction of human capital used for production u_t becomes constant in the long run. Therefore, equation (27) implies that it is optimal to keep emission P_t at a positive constant value in the long run. On the other hand, the actual amount of emissions under environmental tax policy g_τ is determined as in Figure 1.12, where its long-term value is positive only when the rate of tax increase g_τ is slower than $g^{\max}$. The welfare-maximizing rate of the tax increase, g_τ^{opt}, is determined so that the two coincide with each other. Observe that in our model framework it is neither necessary nor desirable to pursue zero emissions even in the long run. As a result, if welfare is the main concern, we should adopt a milder environmental policy than when long-term economic growth is the first priority. In other words, growth maximization is achieved when the world economy adopts a stricter policy to improve the environment than is actually desired by the general public.

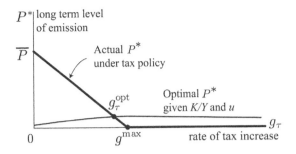

Figure 1.14 Welfare-maximizing environmental tax policy

This result might be contrary to the common perception that there is a trade-off between growth and environmental conservation. Because the welfare-maximizing environmental tax policy falls within the range of $g_\tau < g^{max}$, it is quite unlikely that international politicians will agree on a tax policy that is stricter than g^{max}, which is neither desirable in terms of growth or of welfare. Therefore, for the purpose of policy comparison, it will be sufficient to consider the tax policy within the range of $g_\tau < g^{max}$. Then, the presented model of the global environment clearly shows that although there is a short term trade-off between the environment and income, in the long run the environment and growth are positively linked. An acceleration in the rate of tax increase simultaneously improves the long-term level of emissions and economic growth. Of course, adopting too fast a tax increase ($g_\tau > g^{max}$) will be harmful both for growth and welfare and will not improve the long-term quality of the environment ($P^* = 0$). However, it will be safe to rule out such a possibility given that the global environmental policy must be agreed upon by the majority of countries.

5. Conclusion

In this chapter, we have discussed the implications of the mutual causality between environmental quality and growth. If the economy simply expands the scale of production, it will cause increasing amounts of pollution, which will deteriorate the environment. The environmental degradation in turn harms economic growth in various ways. Local pollution (such as air pollution), for example, adversely affects the health of workers and, hence, the productivity of the economy. Global pollution, particularly in the case of global warming, will destabilize the climate and raise the risk of natural disasters. When such negative effects become too large, the economy is no longer able to accumulate physical and human capital, which we call "limits to growth."

This mutual link creates serious problems, both at the level of individual countries and at the level of the global economy. We have shown the possibility that in the least developed countries (LDCs), poverty and environmental degradation reinforce each other, creating the "poverty-environment trap," in which people cannot afford to obtain adequate education and, therefore, have to rely on dirty technologies that cause further pollution. The existence of such a trap can be a cause of long-lasting international inequality both in terms of income level and environmental quality. The growth potential of the global economy also is limited by this mutual link if greenhouse gas emissions increase proportionally with the world's output.

The key to overcoming the "limits to growth" is technological change, or the transition from "dirty" to "cleaner" inputs, which enables the production of outputs with less pollution. In fact, the EKC is observed for some air pollutants, which means that while the intensity of pollution increases with income for some range, once the income level exceeds a threshold value the pollution declines with income. It seems that developed countries mostly have already exceeded the threshold level of income and, thus, have achieved better environmental quality along with higher income. However, this situation does not hold for every economy. It appears that the LDCs and some developing countries are trapped before they exceed the threshold income. In such a case, the authorities need to adopt appropriate policies to encourage technological change, such as taxing dirty technologies. Such policies will help them escape the poverty-environment trap and achieve better environmental quality in the long run.

In the case of global pollution, the emission of greenhouse gases is still increasing along with the world's increasing output, and thus far there is no sign that it follows the EKC. Our theory suggests that emissions will increase proportionally with output if the environmental policy is unchanged. Therefore, to make the world's economic growth sustainable, it is necessary to strengthen environmental policies over time so producers will rely less on pollution-generating output (e.g., fossil fuels) and more on new technologies, skills, and knowledge (i.e., human capital). If such a policy is successful at achieving a high rate of long-term growth, we will observe the EKC for greenhouse gases in the future.

For both local and global environmental issues, we have shown that the appropriate environmental policy improves both the environmental quality and income level by altering the mutual causality between the environment and growth that leads to the "limits to growth" if there is no such policy. Therefore, although it may appear counterintuitive, economic growth and the environment are not subject to trade-offs in the long run. However, there are short-term costs of environmental conservation that must be incurred by the economy. Banning dirty primitive technologies in LDCs will certainly lower their income, which is already quite low, in the short run. This creates a significant hurdle for such countries to adopt stronger environmental policies that are necessary to escape from the poverty-environment trap. The same can be said of the global economy. Raising the environmental tax rate will reduce the effective productivity of aggregate production, which will lower the growth rate for some time. However, such a cost is necessary to sustain economic growth in the long run. Still, this temporary adverse effect on the world economy makes it difficult for international authorities to agree on strengthening environmental policy at a sufficiently fast rate. Overcoming this political situation is not easy and is clearly beyond the scope of this chapter, but a correct understanding of the long-term positive relationship between environmental quality and growth, as examined in this chapter, will certainly facilitate international cooperation for environmental conservation.

Notes

1 The authors are grateful to Iain Fraser and Katsuyuki Shibayama for their helpful comments and suggestions. We also thank Stefan Jungblut, Nobuyuki Hanaki, and the staff at Paderborn University, GREQAM (Aix-Marseille University), and Kent University for the opportunity to write this chapter. This study was financially supported by the JSPS Grant-in-Aid for Scientific Research (23730182, 23530394), DAAD, the Daiwa Anglo-Japanese Foundation, the Nomura Foundation, and the Asahi Breweries Foundation. All remaining errors are our own.

2 Theoretical models of economic growth that examine the relationship between pollution and growth often assumed away the finiteness of pollution-generating inputs. Besides the analytical tractability, one substantial reason for this is that when the emission of pollutants binds the possibility of economic growth, the constraint of resource scarcity becomes slack and will not affect the equilibrium or optimal outcome. Similarly, those that focus on the resource scarcity typically assume away pollution, because if the resource constraint is stricter, pollution will only have secondary effects on the possibility of economic growth. Nonetheless, some recent studies numerically examine the intricate interaction of

pollution and the finiteness of resources and obtained quantitative implications of the interaction (for example, see Acemoglu et al. 2012).

3 In the endogenous growth literature, this type of model is called the "AK" growth model because, in the simplest form, the production function can be written as $Y = AK$, where A is a constant technology parameter and K is the reproducible input, which is usually called capital (e.g., Rebelo 1991).

4 The income (output) of the economy can grow only up to this downward sloping curve. For a given level of pollution, if Y is smaller than this long-term level, the growth rate of output is positive, while the growth rate is negative if Y is already larger the long-term level.

5 More precisely, there are both supply-side and demand-side factors behind the effect of economic growth on the environmental quality. Grossman and Krueger (1991) assessed three supply-side determinants for the EKC: *scale effects, composition effects, and technological effects*. The scale effect simply means that pollution increases with the level of economic activity, as discussed so far in the main text. Second, the composition effect reflects a general structural change from pollution-intensive production to less pollution-intensive production in the development process. Third, the technological effect refers to an improvement in environmental quality through the introduction of cleaner technology resulting from economic growth. The shape of the EKC will reflect the aggregate magnitudes of these three effects (see a review by Brock and Taylor, 2005). Our models in Sections 3 and 4 formally consider the composition and technological effects and show that EKC emerges endogenously. On the demand side, the people's demand for environmental quality tends to increase as their income grows because they can afford to devote more resources to abatement. This mechanism critically depends on the income elasticity of environmental quality (see John and Pecchenino, 1994; McConnell, 1997; Andreoni and Levinson, 2001; Lieb, 2002, 2004).

6 "The rising cost of natural hazard," by Holli Riebeek, March 28, 2005, NASA Earth Observatory.

7 CRED Crunch, Issue No.32, August 2013, Center for Research on the Epidemiology of Disasters.

8 Here, we simplify the model of Ikefuji and Horii (2007) and ignore the variations in the abilities among individuals in a generation, abstracting from the issue of income distribution within an economy.

9 As can be seen from equation (8), $\sigma \equiv (1/2)\beta\varphi(A^s(1-\theta)/A^p)^{1/\theta}$ represents the response of technology choice s_{t+1} to a change in the parent's income y_t when y_t is in the intermediate range.

10 Because the model in this section is formulated in discrete time, it is more precise to call it the $y_{t+1} = y_t$ locus. However, for comparison between the results of this model and the discussion in Section 2 (e.g., Figure 1.2), we intentionally do not make a clear distinction here between continuous time models and discrete time models.

11 Here, we assume that the parameters satisfy $\eta L/(\eta + \delta) > \overline{P}$ and, $\underline{P} > 0$ so that the two loci have intersections.

12 Strictly speaking, the predetermined variables in this system are x_t and P_t. However, because $x_t = \beta y_t$ always holds, specifying is y_t equivalent to specifying x_t.

13 Originally we assumed A^p to be a technology parameter. Here, we reinterpret A^p as the productivity after deducting the cost of abatement activity or after deducting the environmental tax.

14 Specifically, in Figure 1.9 we assume that a stricter α reduces the two parameters proportionally: $A^p(\alpha) = (1-\alpha)A_0^p$ and $\eta(\alpha) = (1-\alpha)\eta_0$. Equation (10) implies that for a given amount of labor input the increments of pollution are reduced by a factor of $(1-\alpha)^2$.

15 Recall that $\sigma \equiv (1/2)\beta\varphi(A^s(1-\theta)/A^p)^{1/\theta}$, $\underline{y} \equiv (1-\theta)/2\sigma\theta$ and $\overline{y} \equiv (1+\theta)/2\sigma\theta$.

16 Ikefuji and Horii (2007) also examined the effect of income-redistributive policies within the economy. It is found that at the initial stage of development, a smaller redistribution might help economies escape the poverty-environment trap, while in developed countries a larger redistribution will contribute toward a better environment.

17 While classical growth models require exogenous technological change to explain long-term growth, the literature on endogenous growth (with a seminal study by Lucas 1988) has shown that long-term growth can be explained within a model if we consider both physical and human capital accumulations simultaneously.

18 See note 2 for the relationship between the finiteness of resources and the problem of pollution.

19 For simplicity, we do not explicitly consider the accumulation of greenhouse gases in the atmosphere. Ikefuji and Horii (2012) show that the basic property of the result is the same when we explicitly consider the accumulation process.

20 While human and physical capital are vulnerable to natural disasters, it is reasonable to think that physical capital suffers more directly from natural disasters and, therefore, that the damage fraction of physical capital ϕP_t would be larger than that for human capital ψP_t.

21 Of course, this is a mere abstraction. Among countries that differ in many aspects, such as income levels and geography, it is not easy to agree on a common standard for greenhouse gas emissions, and it will be even more difficult to strengthen it over time. As we will see, such conflicts in international politics will create a threat to the sustainability of the world's economic growth.

22 In the present setting, we assume that the tax revenue is returned to the household in a lump sum fashion. With a minor modification of the model, it is possible to interpret that τ includes other costs of using fossil fuels, such as extraction costs. In this case, only the remaining fraction of τ will be returned to households.

23 Aside from the use of fossil fuels and the resulting global warming, our model framework is similar to Lucas (1988), where it is well known that the market equilibrium coincides with the welfare maximization problem because there is no externality. For details regarding deriving the market equilibrium and the welfare maximization solution, see the online appendix of Ikefuji and Horii (2012).

24 Strictly speaking, because we are interested in the long-term rate of economic growth, not the growth rate in the transition, the precise definition of g^* should be $\lim_{t\to\infty}\dot{Y}_t/Y_t$, and it should be called the asymptotic rate of economic growth. Similar remarks can be applied to growth rates of other variables, such as $g\tau$.

25 To derive (22), we use $\dot{K}_t/K_t = \dot{Y}_t/Y_t \equiv g^*$ and, $\dot{u}_t/u_t = 0$ which is justified as follows. Observe from Euler equation (18) that steady-state growth (constant growth of C_t) occurs only when K_t/Y_t is asymptotically constant. Therefore, the growth rate of K_t should be the same as that of the output, g^*. Note also that $\dot{u}_t/u_t > 0$ is not possible because it has an upper bound of 1, whereas $\dot{u}_t/u_t < 0$ violates the transversality condition.

26 While we simplify the process of the technological change by focusing only on the relative use of human capital and the polluting input, a number of studies explicitly examine the determinant of technological change and how it is affected by environmental policies: see, for example, Gradus and Smulders (1993), Bovenberg and Smulders (1995), Groth and Schou (2002), Grimaud and Rougé (2003), Smulders and de Nooij (2003), Hart (2004), and Ricci (2007). Recent studies, such as Di Maria and Valente (2008), Pittel and Bretschger (2010), and Acemoglu et al. (2012), also examine the direction of technological change.

27 We can confirm that when $g\tau = g^{\max}$ while P_t falls to $P^* = 0$, the asymptotic rate of reduction $\dot{P}_t/P_t$ is $g^* - g_\tau = 0$. This means that P_t converges to zero at a less than exponential speed. If $g_\tau < g^{\max}$, P_t converges to a positive constant $P^* > 0$, whereas if $g_\tau > g^{\max}$, P_t falls to 0 at an exponential rate of $g^* - g_\tau < 0$.

References

Acemoglu, D., Aghion, P., Bursztyn, L., and Hemous, D., 2012. The environment and directed technical change, *American Economic Review* 102, 131–166.

Andreoni, J., and Levinson, A., 2001. The simple analytics of the environmental Kuznets curve, *Journal of Public Economics* 80, 269–286.

Bolt, J., and van Zanden, J.L., 2013. The first update of the Maddison Project; re-estimating growth before 1820. Maddison Project Working Paper 4, The Netherlands.

Bovenberg, A.L., and Smulders, S., 1995. Environmental quality and pollution-augmenting technological change in a two-sector endogenous growth model, *Journal of Public Economics* 57, 369–391.

Brock, W.A., and Taylor, M.S., 2005. Economic growth and the environment: a review of theory and empirics, In: Aghion, P., Durlauf, S.N. (Eds.), *Handbook of Economic Growth*, vol. 1B. Amsterdam: North Holland, 1749–1821.

Dasgupta, P., and Heal, G., 1974. The optimal depletion of exhaustible resources, *Review of Economic Studies* 41, 3–28.

Di Maria, C., and Valente, S., 2008. Hicks meets Hotelling: the direction of technical change in capital-resource economies, *Environmental and Development Economics* 13, 691–717.

Dinda, S., 2004. Environmental Kuznets curve hypothesis: a survey, *Ecological Economics* 49, 431–455.

Gradus, A., and Smulders, S., 1993. The trade-off between environmental care and long-term growth-pollution in three prototype growth models, *Journal of Economics* 58, 25–51.

Grimaud, A., and Rougé, L., 2003. Non-renewable resources and growth with vertical innovations: optimum, equilibrium and economic policies, *Journal of Environmental Economics and Management* 45, 433–453.

Grossman, G.M., and Krueger, A.B., 1991. Environmental impacts of a North American Free Trade Agreement, National Bureau of Economic Research Working Paper 3914, NBER, Cambridge, MA.

Grossman, G.M., and Krueger, A.B., 1995. Economic growth and the environment, *Quarterly Journal of Economics* 110, 353–377.

Groth, C., and Schou, P., 2002. Growth and non-renewable resources: the different roles of capital and resource taxes, *Journal of Environmental Economics and Management* 53, 80–98.

Hart, R., 2004. Growth, environment and innovation – a model with production vintages and environmentally oriented research, *Journal of Environmental Economics and Management* 48, 1078–1098.

Ikefuji, M., and Horii, R., 2007. Wealth heterogeneity and escape from the poverty-environment trap, *Journal of Public Economic Theory* 9, 1041–1068.

Ikefuji, M., and Horii, R., 2012. Natural disasters in a two-sector model of endogenous growth, *Journal of Public Economics* 96, 784–796.

John, A., and Pecchenino, R., 1994. An overlapping generations model of growth and the environment, *Economic Journal* 104, 1393–1410.

Kijima, M., Nishide, K., and Ohyama, A., 2010. Economic models for the environmental Kuznets curve: a survey, *Journal of Economic Dynamics & Control* 34, 1187–1201.

Krautkraemer, J.A., 1998. Nonrenewable resource scarcity, *Journal of Economic Literature* 36, 2065–2107.

Lieb, C.M., 2002. The environmental Kuznets curve and satiation: a simple static model, *Environment and Development Economics* 7, 429–448.

Lieb, C.M., 2004. The environmental Kuznets curve and flow versus stock pollution: the neglect of future damages, *Environmental & Resource Economics* 29, 483–506.

Lucas, R.E. Jr., 1988. On the mechanics of economic development, *Journal of Monetary Economics* 22, 3–42.

McConnell, K.E., 1997. Income and the demand for environmental quality, *Environment and Development Economics* 2, 383–399.

Meadows, D.H., Meadows, D.L., Randers, J., and Behrens, W.W., III, 1972. *The Limits to Growth*. New York: Universe Books.

Pittel, K., and Bretschger, L., 2010. The implications of heterogeneous resource intensities on technical change and growth, *Canadian Journal of Economics* 43, 1173–1197.

Rebelo, S., 1991. Long-run policy analysis and long-run growth, *Journal of Political Economy* 99, 500–521.

Ricci, F., 2007. Environmental policy and growth when inputs are differentiated in pollution intensity, *Environmental and Resource Economics* 38, 285–310.

Selden, T.M., and Song, D., 1995. Neoclassical growth, the J curve for abatement, and the inverted U curve for pollution, *Journal of Environmental Economics and Management* 29, 162–168.

Skidmore, M., and Toya, H., 2002. Do natural disasters promote long-run growth? *Economic Inquiry* 40, 664–687.

Smith, V.L., 1974. General equilibrium with a replenishable natural resource, *Review of Economic Studies* 41, 105–115.

Smulders, S., and de Nooij, M., 2003. The impact of energy conservation on technology and economic growth, *Resource and Energy Economics* 25, 59–79.

Stiglitz, J., 1974. Growth with exhaustible natural resources: efficient and optimal growth paths, *Review of Economic Studies* 41, 123–137.

Stokey, N.L., 1998. Are there limits to growth? *International Economic Review* 39, 1–31.

World Health Organization (2006). *Air Quality Guidelines: Global Update 2005*. Copenhagen: WHO Regional Office for Europe.

2

ECONOMIC ANALYSIS OF ZERO-EMISSIONS STABILIZATION

Kazushi Hatase and Shunsuke Managi

1. Introduction

At the Group of Eight (G8) Summit of 2009, the powerful industrialized countries that attended the summit declared that the global mean temperature must not exceed 2 °C above pre-industrial levels, a decision made in recognition of the scientific findings of the Intergovernmental Panel on Climate Change (IPCC). However, maintaining temperature rises within 2 °C of pre-industrial levels is quite a stringent target, considering the prospect of future emissions increases from developing countries. Practical strategies to keep temperature change below this limit remain in the planning stage. However, the mere fact that a target has been agreed upon amounts to progress. During negotiations on greenhouse gas (GHG) emissions reductions, the international community failed to reach any such agreement. The Kyoto Protocol, which was initially adopted in 1997, obliged industrialized countries to reduce their total emissions of six GHGs by at least 5 percent for the 2008–2012 period relative to emissions levels in 1990. However, the Kyoto Protocol did not establish mandated targets for GHG emissions reductions for developing countries, despite the predictions that future emissions from developing countries would be larger than those from industrialized countries. This contradiction later led to a severe altercation between the industrialized countries and developing countries over their respective obligations with respect to GHG emissions reductions. For example, at the 15th Conference of Parties (COP-15) of the United Nations Framework Convention on Climate Change held in Copenhagen in 2009, industrialized countries demanded that legally binding targets for GHG emissions reductions be imposed on developing countries, resulting in a fierce confrontation between the two groups. Furthermore, although industrialized countries largely had agreed on the direction of the GHG emissions reduction policy since 1990, differences of opinion became apparent at COP-15. In short, practical policies on climate change mitigation have not been fully established, particularly because of tensions between industrialized and developing countries.

In this study, we note that the IPCC's climate change mitigation scenarios all presuppose the stabilization of GHG concentrations. Proposals for large emissions reductions in the near future are based on the IPCC's concentration stabilization scenarios. For example, one IPCC plan calls for maintaining CO_2 concentration levels below 450 ppm.

Other researchers, however, have sought approaches that avoid this potentially difficult-to-attain prerequisite. Matsuno et al. (2012) proposed a "Z650 scenario" that approaches climate change mitigation from a different perspective than the concentration stabilization scenarios. Matsuno et al. (2012) referred to the IPCC's concentration stabilization scenarios as "emissions-keeping stabilization (E-stabilization)," wherein GHG concentrations become stable at some future time. By contrast, in the Z650 scenario, GHG emissions are reduced to zero at some future time; thereafter, GHG concentrations decrease via natural removal processes, finally reaching an equilibrium state that Matsuno et al. (2012) termed "zero-emissions stabilization (Z-stabilization)." The "Z" in Z650 comes from the "Z" in zero-emissions stabilization, and the "650" comes from the assumption under the Z650 scenario that cumulative CO_2 emissions in the 21st century will be 650 GtC.

If zero emissions are required in the medium- to long-term future but a feasible emissions reduction rate is allowed, then greater quantities of emissions remain permissible in the near future. Thus, we can infer that Z-stabilization is more advantageous than E-stabilization for minimizing long-term risks while meeting short-term needs for high emissions levels. Given that post-Kyoto Protocol negotiations have reached a stalemate and that GHG emissions in developing countries continue to increase, the Z650 scenario is more realistic because its emissions path is close to that of the current "business-as-usual" scenario. However, as businesses have failed to adapt and countries have failed to enforce even the relatively modest changes required by past climate change reduction policies, it is clear that attempting to achieve even a slight change from "business as usual" can present significant problems, especially in an economic climate that prioritizes short-term profits over increased spending on environmental policies that yield only long-term benefits. Therefore, to be feasible for widespread adoption, climate change policies must also make economic sense. This chapter examines Z650's potential advantage in that respect.

Although meteorological and atmospheric studies of the Z650 scenario have been conducted, this study adopts a fresh approach in conducting an economic analysis to assess the economic efficiency of the Z650 scenario. In this study, we employ the DICE and RICE models, which are the most widely used models to simulate the economic effects of climate change. Assessing the adequacy of the Z650 scenario is more easily and accurately achieved by comparing its economic efficiency with that of other scenarios than by investigating the economic efficiency of the Z650 scenario alone. Thus, we compare the economic efficiency of the Z650 scenario with that of two traditional E-stabilization scenarios: 500-ppm stabilization and 450-ppm stabilization.

The structure of this chapter is as follows. Section 2 presents a brief overview of the simulation models that are used in this study. Section 3 presents the simulation results for climate change and the global economy obtained using the DICE model. Section 4 presents the simulation results for regional economies obtained using the RICE model and shows how the economic figures differ by region. Section 5 focuses on the Asian region, presenting an analysis of the effects of CO_2 emissions reductions on the economies of China, India, Japan, and other developing Asian countries. Section 6 presents an evaluation of the economic efficiency of CO_2 emissions reduction scenarios using two analytical methods. Section 7 summarizes the findings of this study and the main conclusions.

2. Model description

2.1 Overview of the models

The DICE and RICE models were used in this study, with a novel improvement. First proposed by William Nordhaus in 1991, DICE is an acronym for "Dynamic Integrated Model of Climate and the Economy," and it treats the world as a unified single region. By contrast, RICE, which is an acronym for "Regional Dynamic Integrated Model of Climate and the Economy," divides the world into multiple regions. In this study, the RICE model is used to analyze the world divided into 12 regions. The equations used in RICE and DICE are the same; thus, we can regard RICE as a regionally disaggregated companion model for DICE. We employ the DICE and RICE models in this study because these models are the most widely used models for simulating the economic effects of climate change (Hatase and Managi, forthcoming).

The DICE model, which is an improved version of the model that preceded it (Nordhaus, 1991), was given the name DICE in 1992 (Nordhaus, 1992). Nordhaus has continued to develop and improve DICE. The latest version at the time of conducting this research is DICE-2010 (Nordhaus, 2010a). The RICE model appeared as a reconstructed version of DICE in the mid-1990s (Nordhaus and Yang, 1996). The latest version at the time of this study is RICE-2010 (Nordhaus, 2010b). In this study, DICE is used for simulations covering the world as a whole, and RICE is used for simulations in which the world is divided into multiple regions. In short, we use the DICE and RICE models in a complementary manner.

The DICE and RICE models consist of an economic sub-model, a CO_2 accumulation sub-model, a temperature change sub-model, and a climate damage sub-model. The economic sub-model is a standard dynamic economic model of the Ramsey type that maximizes the total utility over the entire simulation period. We first present an overview of the equations for the DICE model. The objective function (which maximizes the total utility) of DICE is as follows:

$$\max \sum_{t=1}^{Tmax} U\big[c(t)\big]\big(1+\rho\big)^{-t} \tag{2.1}$$

where $U[.]$ is a utility function, ρ is the pure time preference rate, and c is consumption per capita. The production function of DICE follows the form of the Cobb-Douglas function:

$$Q(t) = \Omega(t)\big[1-\Lambda(t)\big]A(t)K(t)^{\gamma}L(t)^{1-\gamma} \tag{2.2}$$

where Q is the gross world product with net abatement and damage, Ω is a climate damage function, Λ is a function of CO_2 abatement costs, A is the total factor productivity, K is capital, L is the population and labor inputs, and γ is the capital's value share. DICE uses the following standard capital accumulation equation:

$$K(t) = \big(1-\delta_K\big)K(t-1) + I(t-1) \tag{2.3}$$

where I is investment and δ_k is a capital depreciation rate. The CO_2 abatement costs Λ in Equation (2.2) are calculated using the following function:

$$\Lambda(t) = \theta_1(t)\mu(t)^{\theta_2} \tag{2.4}$$

where θ_1 and θ_2 are the parameters of the CO_2 abatement cost function and μ is the reduction rate of CO_2 (relative to the business-as-usual scenario). The economic sub-model of DICE is closed by the following identity of the macro economy:

$$Q(t) = C(t) + I(t) \tag{2.5}$$

Next, DICE assumes that CO_2 emissions E consist of industrial emissions E_{IND} and emissions from land use change E_{LIND}:

$$E(t) = E_{IND}(t) + E_{LAND}(t) \tag{2.6}$$

The industrial CO_2 emissions in Equation (2.6) are calculated as follows:

$$E_{IND}(t) = \sigma(t)[1 - \mu(t)]A(t)K(t)^{\gamma}L(t)^{1-\gamma} \tag{2.7}$$

where σ is the CO_2 emissions intensity. The emissions from land use change E_{LAND} in Equation (2.6) are given exogenously. DICE's CO_2 accumulation sub-model is a box model consisting of a single atmospheric layer and two ocean layers (dividing the ocean into upper and lower oceans). In the CO_2 accumulation sub-model, CO_2 emissions $E(t)$ are added to the atmosphere as follows:

$$M_{AT}(t) = E(t) + \phi_{11}M_{AT}(t-1) + \phi_{21}M_{UP}(t-1) \tag{2.8}$$

where M_{AT} is the CO_2 concentration of the atmosphere, M_{UP} is the CO_2 concentration of the upper ocean, and ϕ_{11} and ϕ_{21} are the parameters of carbon circulation.

Finally, we calculate the climate damage in Equation (2.2) using the simplest damage function employed by Ackerman and Finlayson (2006):

$$\Omega(t) = \frac{1}{1 + \pi_2 T_{AT}(t)^2} \tag{2.9}$$

where T_{AT} is the temperature increase in the atmosphere and π_2 is a parameter. Because of space limitations, we do not show the CO_2 accumulation sub-model and temperature change sub-model of the DICE model, but readers may refer to Nordhaus (2008) for details on these sub-models.

The equations for the RICE and DICE models are essentially the same, but the models diverge at the point at which RICE calculates Equations (2.2)–(2.7) by region. However, DICE and RICE use the same CO_2 accumulation and temperature change sub-models. Readers interested in the equations of the RICE model may refer to the supporting information found in the work of Nordhaus (2010b).

2.2 Adaptation of the models

The latest versions of the DICE and RICE models mentioned previously are not entirely suitable for use in evaluating the Z650 scenario. Thus, we adapted DICE-2010 and RICE-2010 in the following ways.

First, the CO_2 accumulation and temperature change sub-models in DICE-2010 and RICE-2010 cannot recreate the CO_2 concentration and temperature increases in the Z650 scenario described by Matsuno et al. (2012), which uses a more detailed climate change model. Therefore, we used the CO_2 accumulation and temperature change sub-models in an older DICE model, DICE-2007 (Nordhaus, 2008). In fact, these sub-models of DICE-2007 can rather accurately recreate the CO_2 concentration and temperature increases of the Z650 scenario in Matsuno et al. (2012).

Second, DICE-2010 and RICE-2010 incorporate temperature increases and sea level rises as elements of the climate damage sub-model. However, the Z650 and 450-ppm stabilization climate mitigation scenarios do not reduce the estimated damage associated with sea level rise to the same degree, and as a result, the benefits of CO_2 emissions reductions are small if we use the default climate damage sub-model in DICE-2010 and RICE-2010. Therefore, we regard the climate damage sub-model of DICE-2010 and RICE-2010 as premature and instead use the simplest climate change model proposed by Ackerman and Finlayson (2006). Note that the actual damage function that we use is Equation (2.9) in the DICE model and Equation (2.10) in the RICE model.

2.3 Parameter settings and other calculation conditions

The simulations are conducted for ten-year increments beginning in 2005. The simulation period is 600 years (60 periods) in the DICE model and 300 years (30 periods) in the RICE model. We shortened the simulation period in the RICE model to 300 years because of the computation times required (note that RICE consumes more computational resources because it analyzes multiple regions rather than the world as a whole). We established three simulation scenarios: the Z650 scenario, which is the main focus of this study, and two E-stabilization scenarios, one for the E500 scenario and one for the E450 scenario. In the work of Matsuno et al. (2012), the Z650 scenario is compared with the E450 scenario because these two scenarios are similar from the perspective of atmospheric science; for example, the Z650 and E450 scenarios consider similar degrees of climate change mitigation in the next 150 years. Although this study primarily compares the Z650 scenario with the E450 scenario, we can also draw comparisons with the E500 scenario. Although it is difficult to view the E500 scenario as a practical climate mitigation policy from the perspective of atmospheric science (note that the E500 scenario may cause dangerous climate changes), the Z650 and E500 scenarios are anticipated to have similar economic effects in the first half of this century; thus, the E500 scenario is a convenient referential scenario for economic analysis. This study primarily focuses on comparing the Z650 and E450 scenarios, as in Matsuno et al. (2012). Table 2.1 explains the calculation conditions for the three scenarios.

The parameter settings differ among the economic, CO_2 accumulation, temperature change, and climate damage sub-models. First, in the economic sub-model, the DICE-2010 and RICE-2010 default parameter settings are applied in the DICE and RICE models, respectively. In the CO_2 accumulation and temperature change sub-models, the DICE-2007 default parameter settings are applied in both the DICE and RICE models. In the climate damage sub-model, the parameter settings differ slightly between DICE and RICE. In the DICE model, we apply the default parameter settings of the DICE-2007 climate damage sub-model. In the RICE model, however, we adjust the parameters of the climate damage function as described in the following equation.

The RICE model estimates climate damage by region, and we apply the following damage function, consistent with Equation (2.9) in the DICE model:

$$\Omega(t,n) = \frac{1}{1 + B\left[\pi_2(n) T_{AT}(t)^2\right]} \tag{2.10}$$

Table 2.1 Simulation scenarios

Scenario	Explanation
E500	Set the upper limit of CO_2 at 500 ppm
E450	Set the upper limit of CO_2 at 450 ppm
Z650	Fix CO_2 emissions at Z650 scenario of Matsuno et al. (2012)

where n is a region of the world, Ω is the rate of climate damage per gross domestic product in each region, T_{AT} is the temperature increase in the atmosphere, and $\pi_2(n)$ and B are parameters. In the parameter settings, we use the default parameter values of RICE-2010 for $\pi_2(n)$ which determines the regional allocation of climate damage, and we adjust the values of parameter B such that the climate damage estimated by DICE and RICE approximately correspond to the business-as-usual scenario.

3. Simulation of climate and global economy

This section presents the simulation results for both climate change and the global economy according to the DICE model. We first show the climate mitigation paths for the three mitigation scenarios considered, including Z650. We then present the results for the global economy. Note that all monetary values are shown in 2005 US dollars.

3.1 Simulation of climate change mitigation

The Z650 scenario assumes that zero emissions are achieved in the year 2160 (i.e., the middle of the next century). Under the E-stabilization scenarios proposed by the IPCC, large emission reductions from the early 21st century levels are imperative for avoiding dangerous climate change. In contrast, under the Z650 scenario, higher levels of emissions in the near future are permissible as a result of zero-emissions stabilization, which leads to sufficient climate change mitigation in the future. First, we show the simulation results for climate change mitigation under three mitigation scenarios according to the DICE model.

Figure 2.1 shows the CO_2 emissions for each scenario. Note that the legend "BaU" denotes the business-as-usual scenario. In the climate change mitigation path, we focus particular attention on the difference between the E450 and Z650 scenarios, following Matsuno et al. (2012). In the E450 scenario (450-ppm stabilization), substantial CO_2 emission reductions are achieved beginning in the early 21st century, whereas the Z650 scenario permits some increase in CO_2 emissions. By contrast, in the Z650 scenario, emissions are reduced more than in the E450 scenario by 2075, before becoming roughly zero in 2155. Incidentally, the emissions paths

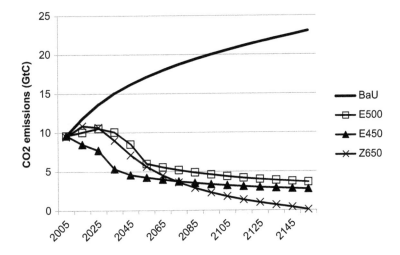

Figure 2.1   Global CO_2 emissions

of the Z650 and E500 (500-ppm stabilization) scenarios are similar in the first half of 21st century.

Figure 2.2 shows the atmospheric CO_2 concentration for each scenario. The concentration paths of the E-stabilization and Z-stabilization scenarios follow different trends: CO_2 concentrations become stable at some point in the E450 and E500 scenarios, whereas CO_2 concentration first peaks and then begins to decline in the Z650 scenario. In addition, in the Z650 scenario, CO_2 concentration reaches a peak at approximately 500 ppm in the middle of the 21st century and then begins to decline, becoming smaller than in the E450 scenario after 2135. Incidentally, the CO_2 concentration levels before 2045 are similar in the E500 and Z650 scenarios. The simulation results shown in Figure 2.2 reveal the outcome of the DICE model. Figure 2.3 compares the CO_2 concentration in the Z650 scenario according to DICE with that of Matsuno et al. (2012), which uses a more detailed climate model. Figure 2.3 demonstrates that the simplified climate module in DICE can reproduce the results of Matsuno et al. (2012) fairly well.

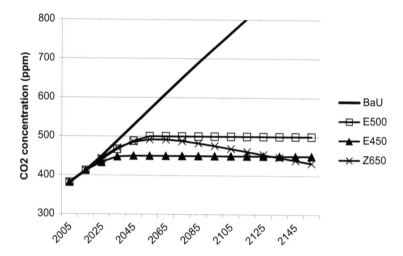

Figure 2.2 Atmospheric CO_2 concentrations

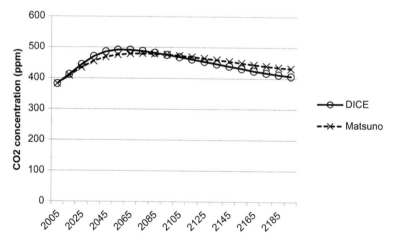

Figure 2.3 Comparison of CO_2 concentrations between DICE and Matsuno et al. (2012) for the Z650 scenario

Figure 2.4 shows projected atmospheric temperature changes since 1750 (during the pre-industrial era). The trends of the temperature change paths between the E-stabilization and Z-stabilization scenarios differ as follows: temperatures continue to increase after CO_2 concentration stabilization is achieved in the E450 and E500 scenarios, whereas temperatures initially peak and then begin to decline under the Z650 scenario. In the Z650 scenario, temperatures increase with respect to the pre-industrial level peaks at approximately 2.2 °C at the beginning of the 22nd century and then begin to decline until temperatures finally become lower in the Z560 scenario than in the E450 scenario after 2155. The results shown in Figure 2.4 clearly indicate that Z-stabilization is more effective than E-stabilization for long-term climate change mitigation. Figure 2.5 compares temperature changes in the Z650 scenario, as calculated by DICE and Matsuno et al. (2012). In the DICE scenario, temperature increases begin slightly sooner; the

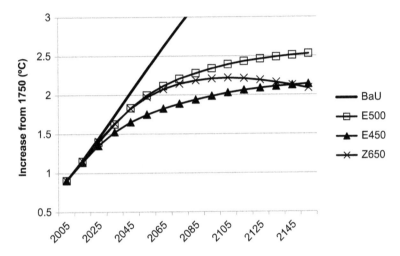

Figure 2.4   Temperature increase from pre-industrial levels

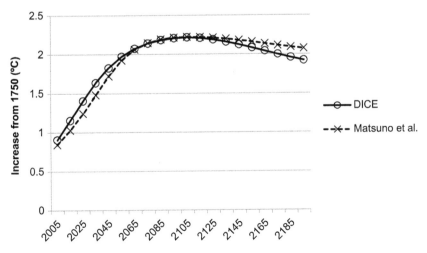

Figure 2.5   Comparison of temperature increases between DICE and Matsuno et al. (2012) for the Z650 scenario

temperature decreases in the 22nd century also begin slightly earlier compared with that found by Matsuno et al. (2012), but the peaks in the temperature increases match in the two models.

To summarize the climate change mitigation simulation results, we first confirmed that zero-emissions stabilization is more effective than "emissions-keeping" stabilization for long-term climate change mitigation. For instance, the E450 scenario is an ambitious climate mitigation scenario requiring drastic CO_2 emission reductions beginning in the early 21st century. However, from the perspective of long-term climate change mitigation, the Z650 scenario, which permits some CO_2 emission increases in the early 21st century, has a greater effect on climate mitigation than the E450 scenario. Second, we confirmed that a simplified DICE climate module can reproduce the results of Matsuno et al. (2012) fairly well, thus demonstrating that the adapted DICE and RICE models are fully applicable for use in simulations comparing the E500, E450, and Z650 mitigation scenarios.

3.2 Simulation of the global economy

We next focus on simulating the global economy under the same three mitigation scenarios. If zero emissions are achieved in the middle of the next century, then some increase in emissions is permissible in the near future, and economic losses associated with CO_2 emissions reductions are expected to decrease in the Z650 scenario. We also observe the shadow price of carbon (which reflects the amount of carbon tax) and the amount of climate damage in this section. Note that we evaluate the economic efficiency of all three mitigation scenarios in Section 6.

Figure 2.6 shows the GDP loss predicted for each scenario as a result of CO_2 emissions reductions, expressed as a percentage of GDP for the business-as-usual scenario. The GDP loss in the first half of the 21st century is roughly proportional to the level of CO_2 emissions reduction; thus, the GDP loss in the E450 scenario is substantial, whereas the GDP losses in the E500 and Z650 scenarios are relatively small. Conversely, the GDP losses in the 22nd century are fairly consistent among the three scenarios. For the DICE parameter settings used in this study, the GDP losses in the E500 and Z650 scenarios are roughly the same throughout the simulation period, but the outcome depends on the parameter settings and other calculation conditions. For example, the simulation results obtained with the RICE model in Section 5 show that the

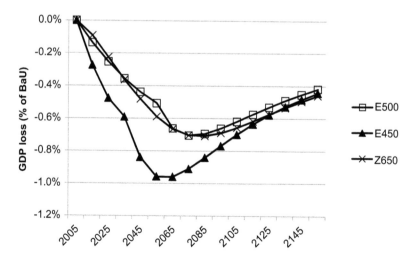

Figure 2.6 GDP loss caused by CO_2 reduction (% of BaU)

GDP loss in the Z650 scenario is significantly larger than that in E500 in the 22nd century (see Figures 2.17 (a)–(d)). In any case, as the GDP loss in the first half of the 21st century is roughly proportional to the level of CO_2 emissions reduction, the GDP loss in the Z650 scenario is much smaller than in the E450 scenario, although the Z650 scenario has a greater long-term climate mitigation effect than the E450 scenario.

Figure 2.7 shows the shadow price of carbon in each scenario. The shadow price of carbon is the marginal abatement cost of carbon (the cost of reducing one additional ton of carbon) and the amount of carbon tax in each scenario. The shadow price of carbon in the Z650 and E500 scenarios remains roughly the same until the middle of 21st century, but the shadow price of carbon in Z650 continues to increase, and the Z650 shadow price of carbon outpaces that in E450 in 2075. As noted previously, the GDP loss in each scenario is roughly proportional to the level of CO_2 emissions reduction only in the first half of 21st century, but the shadow price of carbon is roughly proportional to the level of CO_2 emissions reduction throughout the calculation periods. In the E500 and E450 scenarios, the increase in the shadow price of carbon slows in the middle of the 21st century when CO_2 concentrations are stabilized, whereas in the Z650 scenario, the shadow price of carbon continues to increase through the middle of 22nd century when zero emissions are achieved.

Figure 2.8 shows the amount of climate damage in each scenario. The estimated climate damage in the business-as-usual scenario in 2095 is $13 trillion, a value that is similar to that predicted by Nordhaus (2010b), who used a different damage function than that used in the current study. Because climate damage, according to the function used in this study, is proportional to the square of the temperature increase (see Equation (2.9)), climate damage reductions are proportional to the square of the temperature decrease with respect to the business-as-usual scenario, and the estimated climate damage in the Z650 scenario decreases to $5.2 trillion in 2095. The estimated climate damage in the Z650 scenario is close to that in the E500 scenario in the 21st century, but the estimated damage in the Z650 scenario becomes smaller than that in the E450 scenario after 2155. In the E500 and E450 scenarios, the climate damage amounts continue to increase exponentially, rising to $20 trillion by the end of the 22nd century in the E500 scenario; by contrast, in the Z650 scenario, climate damage increases become smaller with

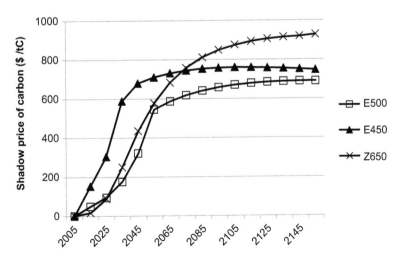

Figure 2.7 Shadow price of carbon for each scenario

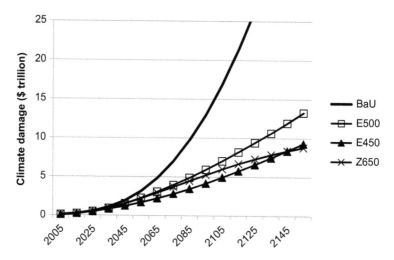

Figure 2.8 Amount of climate damage in US$ trillions

time, rising to merely $10 trillion by the end of the 22nd century. Thus, we can confirm that from an economic perspective, Z-stabilization is more effective than E-stabilization in climate damage mitigation.

We summarize the simulation results for the global economy as follows. First, GDP losses and the shadow price of carbon are roughly the same for the E500 and Z650 scenarios in the first half of this century. Thus, economic losses for Z650 in the near future will be much smaller than those for E450, the scenario often recommended by the IPCC. Second, the level of climate damage estimated for the Z650 scenario is similar to that for the E450 scenario in the middle of the 22nd century, but in the longer term, the level of climate damage estimated for Z650 is smaller than for E450. Thus, in comparison to the two E-stabilization scenarios, the Z650 scenario results in less long-term climate damage while also producing relatively small GDP losses.

4. Simulation of regional economies

RICE is a regionally disaggregated companion version of DICE, as explained in Section 2. Following Nordhaus (2012b), this study utilized 12 regions of the world. The RICE economic sub-model parameter settings used in this study are the same as those in the RICE-2010 model. For information regarding the regional partitions, readers should refer to the legends in the figures showing the simulation results (the following abbreviations are used: US: United States; EU: the European Union; MidEast: the Middle East; LatAm: Latin America; OHI: other high-income countries; and OthAsia: other developing Asian countries).

Figures 2.9 and 2.10 show the CO_2 emissions for each region in the E450 and Z650 scenarios, respectively. Because of space limitations, we do not show the regional CO_2 emissions for the E500 scenario, but the regional emissions paths for the E500 scenario are similar to those for the Z650 scenario for the first half of this century. As is evident in Figure 2.9, large reductions in CO_2 emissions beginning in the early 21st century are essential, and emissions reductions must be particularly substantial in China and the US. Thus, in reality, it will be difficult for the global community to agree to the CO_2 emissions reductions required based on the E450 scenario. Compared with the E450 scenario, however, the Z650 scenario permits some emissions increases

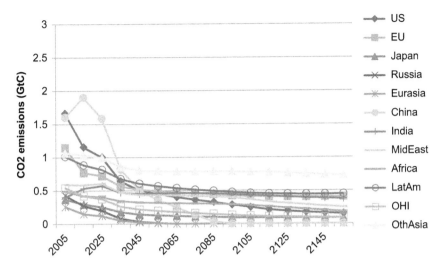

Figure 2.9 CO$_2$ emissions by region of the world (E450 scenario)

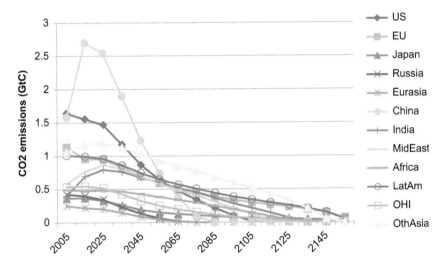

Figure 2.10 CO$_2$ emissions by region of the world (Z650 scenario)

in developing countries in the near future, as shown in Figure 2.10; thus, the Z650 scenario will be more agreeable for the global community. However, we must emphasize that increases in CO$_2$ emissions are permissible only until 2025, and substantial emissions reductions are required beginning in the middle of this century, even in the Z650 scenario. Thus, in any case, we must prepare for high levels of emissions reductions in the future.

Figure 2.11 shows the GDP loss from emissions reductions in each region in the E450 scenario, expressed as a percentage of the emissions associated with the business-as-usual scenario. Figure 2.12 shows the GDP loss in each region in the Z650 scenario. Because of space limitations, the GDP loss in the E500 scenario is not shown, but it is similar to that in the Z650 scenario in the first half of this century. Concerning Figure 2.11, GDP losses in the E450 scenario are large in developing countries, particularly in China, Russia, and Eurasia, up to 3 percent compared with

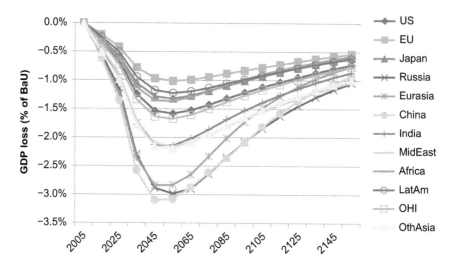

Figure 2.11 GDP loss caused by CO_2 reduction by region of the world (E450 scenario)

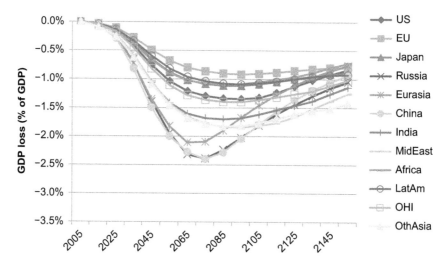

Figure 2.12 GDP loss caused by CO_2 reduction by region of the world (Z650 scenario)

BaU levels. By contrast, the EU suffers a maximum GDP loss of only 1 percent from BaU in the E450 scenario. Differences in GDP loss of this magnitude between industrialized and developing countries may hamper agreement on CO_2 emissions reduction levels. However, GDP losses in the Z650 scenario, as shown in Figure 2.13, are significantly smaller than those in the E450 scenario in the early 21st century, although the paths have similar shapes in both the E450 (Figure 2.11) and Z650 (Figure 2.12) scenarios. For example, in 2025, GDP losses of more than 1 percent from BaU levels occur in some regions in the E450 scenario, whereas GDP losses in the same period increase to 0.3 percent in the Z650 scenario. However, we must emphasize that GDP losses after the middle of the 21st century are considerably large even in the Z650 scenario; for instance, GDP losses in China and Russia increase by up to 2.4 percent from BaU levels. As noted previously,

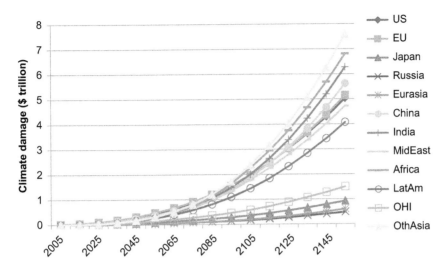

Figure 2.13   Climate damage by region of the world (business-as-usual scenario)

there are differences in the level of GDP losses between industrialized and developing countries even in the Z650 scenario, which may hamper international agreement on a CO_2 reduction policy. However, it should be noted that the advancement of new energy technologies and carbon capture and storage (CCS) may reduce GDP losses, thus facilitating international agreement.

Figure 2.13 shows the estimated climate damage in each region in the business-as-usual scenario. The estimated damage amounts are large in developing countries, especially in Asia and Africa. The estimated damage amounts also are large in the US and in EU countries, but these countries have large GDPs and the damage as a percentage of GDP is not as large. Climate damage amounts as a percentage of GDP are larger for Africa, India, and other developing Asian countries.

Figure 2.14 shows estimated climate damage amounts for each region in the E450 scenario, whereas Figure 2.15 shows estimated climate damage amounts in the Z650 scenario. In the business-as-usual scenario, the estimated climate damage amounts are 4.2 percent to 7.1 percent of GDP in 2155. In the E450 scenario, the estimated damage amounts are 0.9 percent to 1.5 percent of GDP in 2155. In the Z650 scenario, the estimated damage amounts are only 0.8 percent to 1.4 percent of GDP in 2155. In both the E450 and Z650 scenarios, the percentage of climate damage reduction is roughly the same for all regions, at approximately 80 percent of the business-as-usual level in 2155. In fact, the estimated climate damage amounts do not differ greatly between the E450 and Z650 scenarios in terms of long-term climate damage mitigation, despite the fact that the estimated damage amounts for Z650 are slightly larger than those for E450 during the 21st century. It should be noted that regions that suffer greater climate damage would experience larger reductions in climate damage with the E450 and Z650 scenarios; thus, developing countries with high levels of climate damage will have an incentive to reduce CO_2 emissions to mitigate climate damage.

We summarize the simulation results for regional economies as follows. First, the Z650 scenario permits developing countries to have some increases in CO_2 emissions until 2025. Thus, the global community is likely to attain agreement on Z650 easier than agreement on the E450 scenario. However, large reductions in emissions are necessary after 2025 even in the Z650 scenario. Second, the GDP losses from emissions reductions in some developing countries are relatively larger than those that industrialized countries would experience even in the Z650 scenario, and this difference may hamper international agreement on a CO_2 reduction policy. Third,

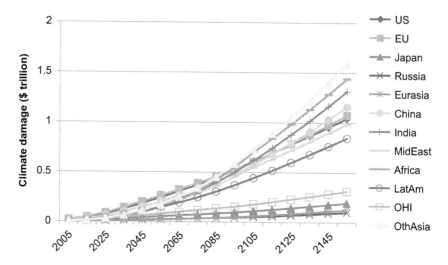

Figure 2.14 Climate damage by region of the world (E450 scenario)

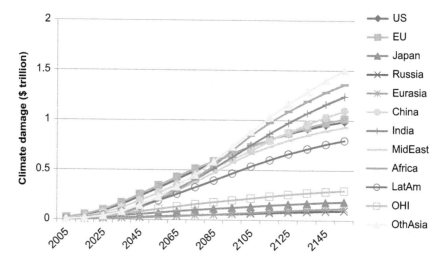

Figure 2.15 Climate damage by region of the world (Z650 scenario)

regions with greater climate damage have higher levels of damage reduction under the Z650 scenario, which will incentivize CO_2 emissions reductions in developing countries with greater climate damage. These findings indicate that the factor that hampers international agreement on a CO_2 reduction policy will be the differences in GDP losses across world regions. Thus, efforts will be needed to overcome such differences in GDP losses.

5. Simulation of the Asian economy

Following the analysis of regional economies in the previous section, this section focuses on the analysis of the Asian economy using the RICE model. The previous section showed the simulation results for 12 world regions, whereas this section focuses on four Asian regions: China, India,

Japan, and other developing Asian countries (this category, referred to as "other developing Asian countries," is the same as the "OthAsia" category mentioned in the previous section). The parameter settings used for RICE are the same as those described in the previous section. We show the simulation results for CO_2 emissions, GDP loss, and climate damage, which are the same categories of data discussed in the previous section. However, this section analyzes those results from different perspectives.

Figures 2.16 (a), (b), (c), and (d) show CO_2 emissions in China, India, Japan, and other developing Asian countries, respectively. First, Figure 2.16(a) shows that China's CO_2 emissions increase steeply in the early 21st century in the business-as-usual scenario. Such a steep increase in CO_2 emissions, which is permitted until 2025, influences the emissions reduction paths of the E500 and Z650 scenarios. However, in both the E500 and Z650 scenarios, China is required to reduce

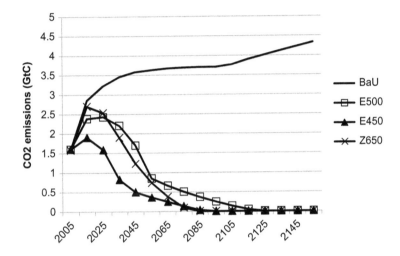

(a) China

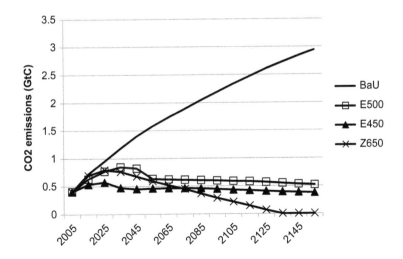

(b) (India)

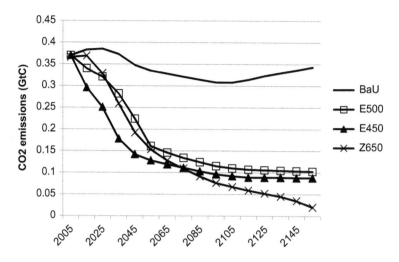

(c) Japan

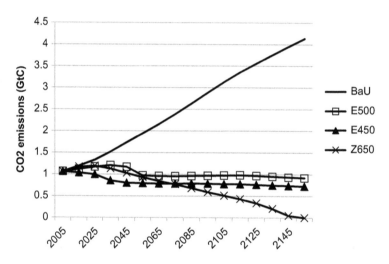

(d) Other developing Asian countries

Figure 2.16 (a)–(d) CO$_2$ emissions in four Asian regions

emissions drastically beginning in the middle of the 21st century. In the E450 scenario, China is required to reduce emissions beginning in the early 21st century, but such a requirement is not realistic. Second, Figure 2.16(b) shows that India's CO$_2$ emissions increase gradually throughout the simulation period in the business-as-usual scenario. In the E500 scenario, India is allowed to increase CO$_2$ emissions until 2035, as opposed to 2025 in the Z650 scenario, after which emissions must be gradually reduced. Third, Figure 2.16(c) shows that in the business-as-usual scenario, Japan's CO$_2$ emissions will increase only slightly until 2025 before beginning to decline. This decline in Japanese emissions will result from population shrinkage and technological advancements. In all three mitigation scenarios (E500, E450, and Z650), Japan is required to reduce emissions by approximately two-thirds by the middle of the 21st century. Incidentally, the difference in emissions reduction paths between E500 and E450 is smaller in Japan than in the other three regions. Finally, Figure 2.16(d) shows that CO_2 emissions in other developing Asian countries follow a trend that is similar to that observed in India: in the business-as-usual scenario, CO_2 emissions increase gradually throughout the simulation period, whereas in the Z650 scenario, gradual emissions reductions are required beginning in 2025. On the whole, the Z650 scenario requires drastic emissions reductions after 2025 for China and after 2010 for Japan and gradual emissions reductions after 2025 for India and other developing Asian countries. Compared with the E450 scenario, the Z650 scenario is considered more realistic for Asian nations, but drastic CO_2 emissions reductions are required from China and Japan, as noted previously.

Figures 2.17(a), (b), (c), and (d) show the GDP losses associated with CO_2 emissions reductions in China, India, Japan, and other developing Asian countries, respectively. First, Figure 2.17(a)

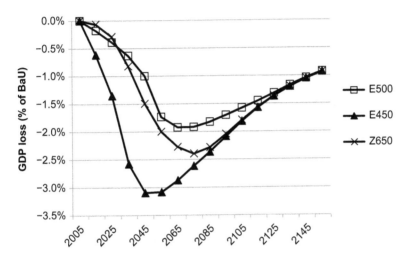

(a) China

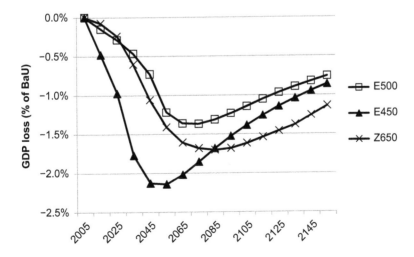

(b) India

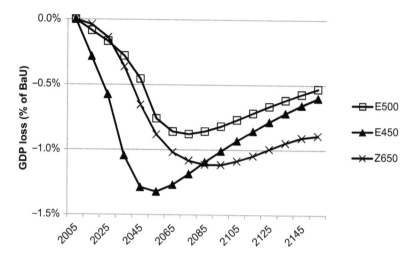

(c) Japan

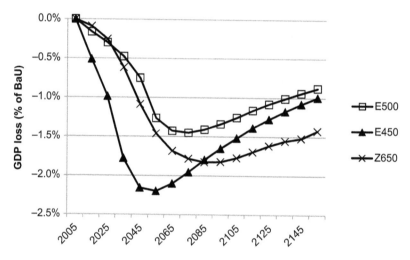

(d) Other developing Asian countries

Figure 2.17 (a)–(d) GDP loss caused by CO_2 reduction in four Asian regions

shows that China's GDP loss could reach up to 3.1 percent in the E450 scenario, up to 2.4 percent in the Z650 scenario, and up to 1.9 percent in the E500 scenario, compared with the business-as-usual scenario. China's GDP loss is among the largest in the world's regions, as noted in Section 4. Second, Figure 2.17(b) shows that India suffers only moderate GDP loss: up to 2.1 percent in the E450 scenario, up to 1.7 percent in the Z650 scenario, and up to 1.4 percent in the E500 scenario. Third, Figure 2.17(c) shows that despite Japan being required to reduce emissions drastically, its GDP loss is relatively small: up to 1.3 percent in the E450 scenario, up to 1.1 percent in the Z650 scenario, and up to 0.9 percent in the E500 scenario. Finally, Figure 2.17(d) shows that the GDP losses of other developing Asian countries could reach up to 2.2 percent in the E450 scenario, up to 1.8 percent in the Z650 scenario, and up to 1.5 percent in the E500 scenario. These values are similar to those for India; because India and other developing Asian countries have similar economic situations, they also have similar simulation results. Although the specific values for GDP loss are quite different, as shown previously, the trends in GDP loss are fairly similar among the four Asian regions. For example, the GDP losses in the E500 and Z650 scenarios are similar in the first half of the 21st century, and the GDP loss in the Z650 scenario becomes larger than that in E500 in the latter half of the 21st century. In any case, the difference in GDP loss among the four regions is likely to be problematic for policy decision-makers in Asia.

Figures 2.18 (a), (b), (c), and (d) show the climate damage estimates for China, India, Japan, and other developing Asian countries, respectively. The figures show that the climate damage estimates for the countries in the "other developing Asian countries" group are the largest of the four Asian regions, and those for India are the second largest. Although the climate damage

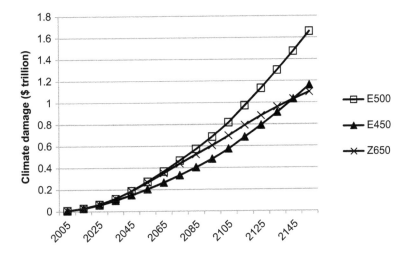

(a) China

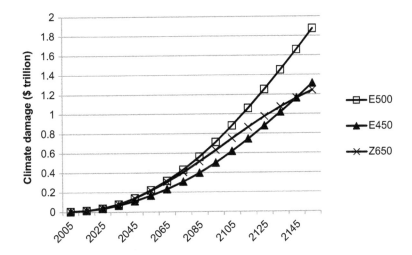

(b) India

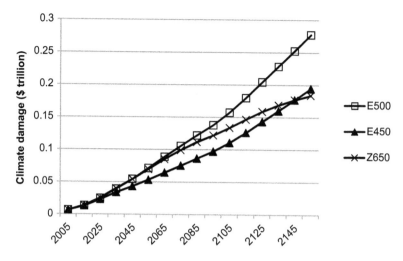

(c) Japan

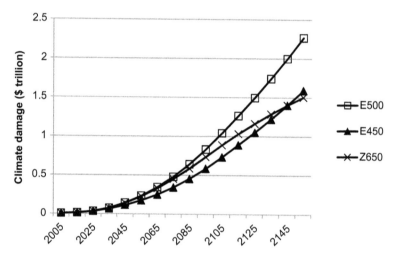

(d) Other developing Asian countries

Figure 2.18 (a)–(d) Climate damage in four Asian regions

estimate for China is similar to that for India, China's climate damage as a percentage of GDP is relatively small compared with that of other regions of the world because China has a large GDP. Thus, in terms of estimated climate damage, India and other developing Asian countries fare the worst of the four Asian regions considered. In fact, the climate damage estimates for other developing Asian countries are the largest of all 12 world regions considered in this study, as shown in Section 4. The trends in climate damage are similar for the four Asian regions, despite the differences in the values of climate damage among the regions. For example, in all four regions, the climate damage estimates for the E500 and Z650 scenarios are similar in the 21st century, but the estimates for the Z650 scenario are smaller than those for the E450 scenario in 2155. As already discussed in Section 4, regions with higher levels of climate damage have greater degrees of damage reduction in the Z650 scenario. Accordingly, both India and other developing Asian countries will have incentives to reduce CO_2 emissions.

Table 2.2 Rough summary of climate and economy in Asian regions

	China	India and other developing Asian countries	Japan
CO_2 emissions in the BaU scenario	Steep increase in the early 21st century	Gradual increase through-out the simulation period	Emissions begin to decline in 2025
CO_2 emissions reduction in the Z650 scenario	Drastic emissions reduction beginning in 2025	Gradual emissions reduction beginning in 2025	Drastic emissions reduction begin-ning in 2010
GDP loss from CO_2 emissions reduction	Large	Medium	Small
Estimated climate damage	Large in amount, small in % of GDP	Large in amount, large in % of GDP	Small in amount, large in % of GDP

We briefly summarize the findings of this section in Table 2.2. We summarize the simulation results for the Asian economy as follows. First, the CO_2 emissions paths in the business-as-usual scenario differ among the four Asian regions because of differences in their socioeconomic situations that significantly affect their CO_2 reduction paths. In the Z650 scenario, gradual emissions reductions after 2025 are required for India and other developing Asian countries, drastic emissions reductions after 2025 are required for China, and drastic emissions reductions after 2010 are required for Japan. The Z650 scenario permits CO_2 emissions to increase until 2025 for China, India, and other developing Asian countries but not for Japan. Second, GDP loss is not always proportional to the level of CO_2 emissions reductions. For example, the Z650 scenario requires Japan to undertake drastic emissions reductions, but Japan's GDP loss is small relative to that experienced by the other world regions. In the Z650 scenario, China's GDP loss is one of the largest of the world regions, India and other developing Asian countries experience moderate GDP loss, and Japan's GDP loss is small compared with that of other regions. Third, the climate damage estimates also are quite different for the four Asian regions. India and other developing Asian countries are predicted to experience more severe climate damage than other regions. Thus, India and other developing Asian countries will have incentives to reduce their CO_2 emissions. In general, the four Asian regions are quite heterogeneous in terms of CO_2 reduction paths, GDP loss, and climate damage.

6. Evaluating the economic efficiency of climate change-mitigation scenarios

This section evaluates the economic efficiency of the three climate-mitigation scenarios using two analytical methods. The first method is a cost-benefit analysis in which we evaluate the net present value of benefits minus costs. The second method is a damage-mitigation analysis in which we evaluate the net present value of mitigation costs plus climate damage. The analyses described in this section focus primarily on a comparison of the Z650 and E450 scenarios, as Matsuno et al. (2012) demonstrated that these two scenarios are competitive from the perspective of atmospheric science.

6.1 Cost-benefit analysis

We have already discussed the economic effects of CO_2 emissions reductions in the previous sections. This section presents an evaluation of the economic efficiency of the three climate-mitigation scenarios. First, we conduct a cost-benefit analysis in which we evaluate the net present value of benefits minus costs. In the cost-benefit analysis, a project is assessed as follows: if the net benefit (net present value of benefits minus costs) is positive, then the project is worth undertaking; by contrast, if the net benefit is negative, then the project is not worth undertaking. When we compare a number of projects, we use the guideline that the project with the largest net benefit is most worthy of undertaking. In this section, we assess three proposed projects for climate change mitigation (CO_2 emissions reduction): the E500, E450, and Z650 scenarios.

In the cost-benefit analyses that are presented in this section, we use the following formula:

$$\sum_{t=2005}^{Tmax} \frac{\left[Benefits\ of\ reduction(\ t)\right] - \left[Costs\ of\ reduction(\ t)\right]}{(1+r)^t} \tag{6.1}$$

where "r" is the discount rate for which we use the shadow price of GDP (which is the same as the interest rate of the global economy). Note that the "benefits of reduction" in Formula 6.1 is the climate damage avoided as a result of CO_2 emissions reduction.

Figure 2.19 shows the net present value of benefits minus costs for each scenario, as calculated by the DICE model. When *Tmax* in Equation (6.1) is within the 21st century, the net benefit remains a negative value for all three scenarios. By contrast, when *Tmax* is in the middle of the 22nd century, the net benefit is a positive value for all three scenarios, and the project (CO_2 emissions reduction in each scenario) is judged to be worth undertaking.

The Z650 scenario has the largest net present value of benefits minus costs under the calculation conditions of the DICE model used in this study. However, because the net benefit of the Z650 scenario is barely larger than that of the E500 scenario in the 21st century, the net benefit of the E500 scenario actually could be larger than that of the Z650 scenario, depending on the parameter settings and other calculation conditions. The E450 scenario has the smallest net present value of the three scenarios because of the high costs of CO_2 emissions reduction in the 21st century. To reiterate, the comparison of the Z650 and E450 scenarios is the main focus of the cost-benefit analysis in this study, and the results of this analysis confirm that the Z650 scenario is more advantageous than the E450 scenario.

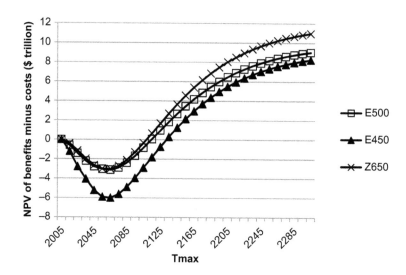

Figure 2.19 Net present value of benefits minus costs

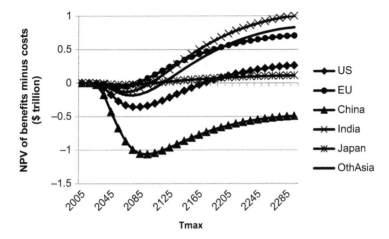

Figure 2.20 Net present value of benefits minus costs by region (Z650 scenario)

Figure 2.20 shows the net present value of benefits minus costs in the Z650 scenario for the four Asian regions (China, India, Japan, and other developing Asian countries) as well as for the US and EU. The calculation was performed using the RICE model, with the same calculation conditions as those used in the preceding calculations. The figure shows that India, other developing Asian countries, and the EU have relatively high net benefits, whereas China has a low net benefit. The time when the net benefit becomes positive varies among the regions. The net benefit becomes positive in the 21st century for some regions, but in China, the net benefit remains negative throughout the calculation period. These results indicate that undertaking the Z650 scenario will result in disagreement between the global and local levels. On the global level, the Z650 scenario is worth undertaking; however, at the regional level, the Z650 scenario is not worth undertaking for China. Thus, we must take measures to ensure a positive net benefit for China. Accordingly, persuading China to participate in a GHG reduction scheme will be crucial.

6.2 Damage-mitigation analysis

We now turn to evaluating the three scenarios according to the second method. In this method, we calculate the net present value of mitigation costs plus climate damage for each project using the following formula:

$$\sum_{t=2005}^{Tmax} \frac{\left[Costs\ of\ reduction\left(t\right)\right]+\left[climate\ damage\right]}{\left(1+r\right)^t} \tag{6.2}$$

where climate damage is calculated from the damage function in Equation (2.9). In this second method, we use the guideline that the project with the smallest net present value of costs plus damage is most worthy of undertaking. Using this method, we evaluate the three scenarios at the global and regional levels.

Figure 2.21 shows the net present value of mitigation costs plus climate damage for each scenario at the global level, as calculated by the DICE model. The Z650 scenario has the smallest net present value of mitigation costs plus climate damage for the calculation conditions of the

DICE model that is used in this study. As Figure 2.19 shows for the cost-benefit analysis, the net present value of costs plus damage for the Z650 scenario is only slightly more advantageous than that for the E500 scenario, especially in the 21st century. However, our main focus is the comparison of the Z650 and E450 scenarios, and we can confirm that the Z650 scenario is more advantageous than the E450 scenario in this analysis based on the DICE model.

Figure 2.22 shows the net present value of mitigation costs plus climate damage for the Z650 scenario for the four Asian regions, the US, and the EU. The figure shows that the US, the EU, Japan, and other developing Asian countries have relatively low net present values of costs plus damage, whereas China and India have relatively high net present values of costs plus damage. India has a relatively high net benefit and is in an advantageous position in the cost-benefit analysis, but in the damage-mitigation analysis, India is in a disadvantageous position. Japan ranks particularly low in the net present value of costs plus damage, but this result is largely a reflection

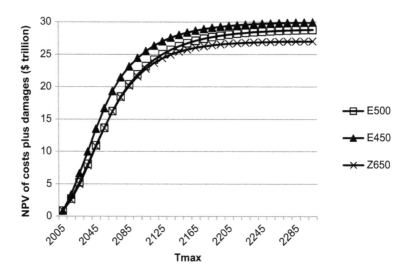

Figure 2.21   Net present value of mitigation costs plus damage

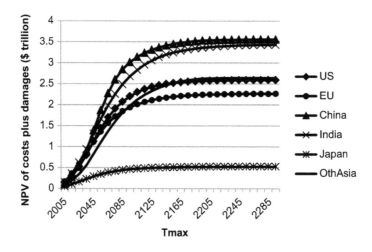

Figure 2.22   Net present value of mitigation costs plus damage by region (Z650 scenario)

of the country's size. As in the first cost-benefit analysis method, China is in a disadvantageous position in terms of its net present value of costs plus damage.

Figures 2.23 (a)–(f) compare the Z650 and E450 scenarios in terms of net present values of costs plus damage for the six regions. For China, the Z650 scenario drastically reduces the net present value of costs plus damage, compared with that for the E450 scenario. The US would experience a moderate degree of reduction in the net present value of costs plus damage with the Z650 scenario compared with the E450 scenario. For the other regions, the differences in the net present values of costs plus damage between the Z650 and E450 scenarios are small. Relative to the E450 scenario, the Z650 scenario drastically improves China's economic efficiency, although China is in a disadvantageous position compared with the other regions.

To summarize the results of this section, we found that the Z650 scenario is more advantageous than the E450 scenario in terms of two criteria: the net present value of benefits minus costs and the net present value of costs plus damage. In the cost-benefit analysis, the Z650 scenario is found to be worth undertaking at the global level, but the net benefit varies by region;

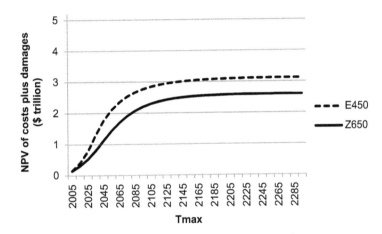

(a) US

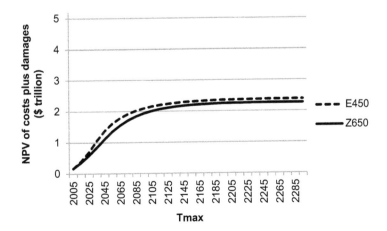

(b) EU

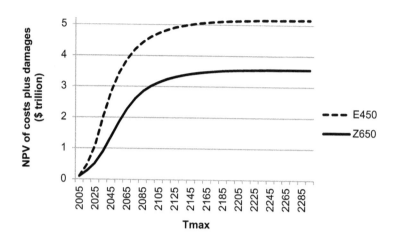

(c) China

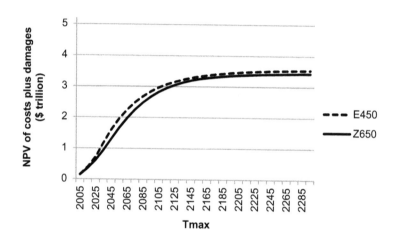

(d) India

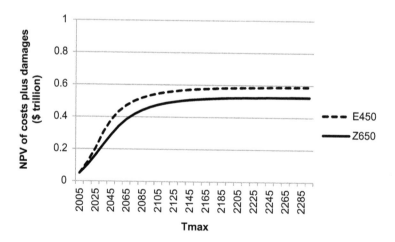

(e) Japan

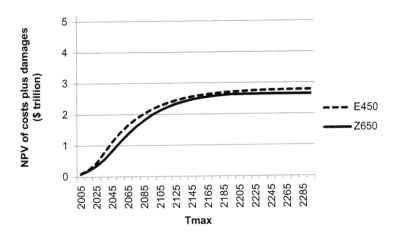

(f) Other developing Asian countries

Figure 2.23 (a)–(f) Comparison of E450 and Z650 scenarios in terms of net present value of mitigation costs plus damage

for China, we found that Z650 is not worth undertaking. Therefore, a conflict exists between the outcomes at the global and regional levels, and we must take measures to ensure a positive net benefit for China. Compared with the E450 scenario, the net present values of costs plus damage decrease drastically in China in the Z650 scenario; this result suggests that although the Z650 scenario drastically improves China's economic efficiency, China is in a disadvantageous position compared with the other five regions.

7. Summary

In conclusion, we summarize the main findings of this study. CO_2 emissions reductions in the Z650 scenario are small in the first half of the 21st century, but the long-term climate change mitigation of the Z650 scenario eventually exceeds that of the E450 scenario. This finding suggests that zero-emissions stabilization is more effective than "emission-keeping" stabilization in the long term. With regard to the economic effects of CO_2 emissions reductions, in the first half of the 21st century, GDP losses and the shadow price of carbon in the Z650 scenario are similar to those in the E500 scenario, in which emissions reductions are small. The economic effects of CO_2 emissions reductions on the world's regions in terms of GDP losses are significantly larger for some developing countries than for industrialized countries. Thus, agreement on CO_2 emissions reductions among the countries will be difficult to obtain even based on the Z650 scenario. Meanwhile, given the projections for the amount of climate damage, developing countries in which high damage levels are expected also tend to have expected benefits (in terms of reductions in climate damage) in the Z650 scenario, which may incentivize emissions reductions in developing countries. The evaluation of the economic efficiency of the three climate change mitigation scenarios using two analytical methods (cost-benefit analysis and damage-mitigation analysis) shows that the Z650 scenario is the most advantageous of the three scenarios.

The Z650 scenario has a large climate change mitigation effect, and its economic effect is relatively small, making it the most advantageous scenario. Given the current situation, in which post-Kyoto Protocol negotiations are at a stalemate, the Z650 scenario may break through the current deadlock of international negotiations. However, the differences in the economic effects among the world's regions (particularly the relatively large GDP losses for some developing countries and the negative net benefit for China) remain a problem, and efforts are needed to reduce regional differences in GDP losses.

The four Asian regions considered in this study differ in terms of the economic influence of CO_2 emissions reductions on their economies, and it is difficult to regard them as an economically unified region. One noteworthy finding is the contrast between China and Japan: China's GDP loss from emissions reductions is heavy, and climate damage as a percentage of GDP is relatively small, whereas Japan's GDP loss is small, and its climate damage as a percentage of GDP is relatively large. Thus, in theory, China is reluctant to undertake emissions reductions, while Japan has an incentive to undertake such reductions and wants China to reduce emissions. In such a situation, the transfer of new energy technologies and CCS from Japan to China may be the solution.

Acknowledgements

We would like to acknowledge the financial support of the Canon Institute for Global Studies. We would also like to thank Taro Matsuno (Japan Agency for Marine-Earth Science and Technology) and Junichi Tsutsui (Central Research Institute of Electric Power Industry) for providing data on the Z650 scenario.

References

Ackerman, F. and Finlayson, J. (2006) "The economics of inaction on climate change: a sensitivity analysis," *Climate Policy*, 6 (5): 509–526.

Hatase, K. and Managi, S. (forthcoming) "Increase in carbon prices: Analysis of energy economy modeling," *Environmental Economics and Policy Studies*.

Matsuno, T., Maruyama, K. and Tsutsui, J. (2012) "Stabilization of atmospheric carbon dioxide via zero emissions – An alternative way to a stable global environment," *Proceedings of the Japan Academy*, Series B, 88, 368–395.

Nordhaus, W.D. (1991) "To slow or not to slow: The economics of the greenhouse effect," *The Economic Journal*, 101 (407): 920–937.

Nordhaus, W.D. (1992) "An optimal transition path for controlling greenhouse gases," *Science*, 258 (5086): 1315–1319.

Nordhaus, W.D. (2008) *A Question of Balance: Weighing the Options on Global Warming Policies*, New Haven, CT: Yale University Press.

Nordhaus, W.D. (2010a) *DICE-2010 Model*, Online. Available HTTP: <http://www.econ.yale.edu/~nordhaus/homepage/RICEmodels.htm> (Accessed April 10, 2013).

Nordhaus, W.D. (2010b) "Economic aspects of global warming in a post-Copenhagen environment," *Proceedings of the National Academy of Sciences*, June 14, 2010.

Nordhaus, W.D. and Boyer, J. (2000) *Warming the World: Economic Modeling of Global Warming*, Cambridge, MA: MIT Press.

Nordhaus, W.D. and Yang, Z. (1996) "A regional dynamic general-equilibrium model of alternative climate-change strategies," *American Economic Review*, 86 (4): 741–765.

3

THE ENVIRONMENTAL KUZNETS CURVE IN ASIA

Eriko Miyama and Shunsuke Managi

1. Introduction

Kuznets (1955) argued that income inequality in a country first rises and then begins to fall at a certain point of economic development to form an inverted U-shaped curve, which is known as the "Kuznets curve." The environmental Kuznets curve (EKC) is a variation of the Kuznets curve that represents the relationship between economic development and environmental degradation instead of income inequality. The logic behind the EKC is that environmental quality may deteriorate as a result of economic development because of an increase in economically valuable activities that may have deleterious environmental effects, such as production and transportation. After a certain level of economic development has been reached, however, environmentally friendly innovations may be adopted that help improve environmental quality, but this is merely a hypothesis that has yet to be empirically tested. Knowing whether the level of environmental degradation will continue to increase or decrease after a certain level of economic development is critical to the pursuit of sustainable development.

Over a thousand empirical and theoretical studies have been undertaken to investigate the existence and shape of EKCs with respect to various pollutants and greenhouse gases (GHGs) since the 1990s. Grossman and Krueger (1991) produced an early and influential empirical study that showed that environmental degradation, as indicated by the ambient air concentration of SO_2, dark matter (fine smoke), and suspended particles (SPM), has an inverted U-shaped relationship with income per capita. EKCs are known to have different shapes depending on the characteristics of the relevant environmental degradation and the datasets employed. For example, other early studies on EKCs noted that levels of so-called "local emissions," such as SO_2, PM, and water quality, have inverted U-shaped curves and peak at lower levels of GDP per capita when compared to "global emissions," such as CO_2, which continue to increase. Panel data analyses of the EKC have shown that pollutant concentrations in major world cities have peaked at lower levels of economic development than country-level pollutant emissions because population and industrial developments tend to be centralized in urban areas in low-income countries (see Stern, 2004: 1423–1424).

Other characteristics, such as trade and type of energy source, have been suggested as factors that determine EKCs (Tsurumi and Managi, 2010b; Fujii and Managi, 2013). Managi et al. (2009) studied the relationship between the EKC and trade openness and found that open trade has beneficial effects for the environment in Organisation for Economic Co-operation and Development (OECD) countries but has detrimental effects on SO_2 and CO_2 emissions in non-OECD countries; nevertheless, trade openness does lower biochemical oxygen demand (BOD) emissions in non-OECD countries. Using data from 30 OECD countries, Tsurumi and Managi (2010a) investigated the EKC with respect to CO_2 emissions and showed that reducing the share of coal in energy production has a significant effect on CO_2 emissions, which implies that mere economic growth is insufficient to decrease GHG emissions.

Developed and developing countries may exhibit differently shaped EKCs because of differences in their technological levels, the international roles they play in the world economy, and their institutional development. Dasgupta et al. (2002) noted that environmental degradation would worsen in developing countries because firms in developed countries tend to relocate environmentally unfriendly production processes to developing countries as a consequence of stricter regulations in their home countries. This hypothesis has been investigated empirically; for example, Atici (2012) studied the relationship between CO_2 emissions and trade openness and found no evidence that foreign direct investment and Japan's imports from the region have a negative impact on environmental quality but did find that imports by China stimulate more pollution per capita.

Galeotti and Lanza (1999) estimated the EKC separately for developed countries (defined as Annex I countries in the Kyoto Protocol) and developing countries and found that the latter have higher CO_2 emissions growth rates. Similarly, P.K. Narayan and S. Narayan (2010) analyzed the EKC for developing countries and found that CO_2 emissions growth rates are higher in developing countries than in developed countries; these authors suggested that new policies should be designed for specific developing countries and regions with higher emissions growth rates. Coondoo and Dinda (2008) posited that income distributions among different countries affect their CO_2 emissions levels. Their empirical analysis indicated that an equalizing redistribution of income would cause the mean emissions levels in Europe and America to increase but not those in Asia and Africa. Marcotullio (2006) confirmed that emerging Asian economies have faster annual CO_2 emissions growth compared with the developed world.

Because there are better datasets for environmental quality in Malaysia than in other developing countries, a substantial number of analyses of Malaysia have thus been undertaken (Vincent, 1997; Saboori et al., 2012). Vincent (1997) investigated the relationship between GDP per capita and both air and water pollution solely in Malaysia. The results were inconsistent with global cross-country analyses. For example, the results indicated that ambient concentrations of pollutants would increase in Malaysia as the economy develops although these same pollutants were predicted to decline globally. Alternatively, other pollutants that were predicted to increase globally were shown to be declining in Malaysia. Vincent (1997) concluded that differences in the results were due to the country's natural resource endowments, shifting population patterns and, most importantly, because of various environmental policies (e.g., for BOD) and non-environmental policies (e.g., for energy independence and SOx emissions) (see Vincent, 1997: 429–430).

China is the most frequently studied country in Asia because of its population and the scale of its economic production (Coleman, 2009; Borhan et al., 2012; Jayanthakumaran and Liu, 2012; Shu et al., 2012; Song et al., 2013). Studies on economic development and the environment in China have forecasted further increases in emissions from China and recommend policies specifically tailored by province to mitigate environmental degradation. In addition, China frequently has been compared with other developed countries. For example, Yaguchi et al. (2007) compared SO_2 and CO_2 emissions between Japan and China and found that local communities in both countries are aiming to reduce the SO_2 emissions per energy use rate but are not aiming to reduce energy consumption or CO_2 emissions. Moreover, in both Japan and China, GDP per capita was not the determining factor of CO_2 emissions. These results demonstrate that neither government has the intention to reduce CO_2 emissions, in part because it is not a matter that is directly linked to their own communities.

As discussed previously, the range of analyses on EKCs are limited to certain countries because of data availability. The problem of missing data is widely recognized in the field of applied economics analysis, including EKC estimations, because necessary information about some countries and years is frequently missing in global datasets. Missing data also affect the projection of future emissions/concentrations. The literature has shown that model specification, econometric methods, and features of the dataset substantially affect the results of the analyses of EKC estimations (Millimet et al., 2003; Stern, 2004; Bertinelli and Strobl, 2005). In particular, deleting low-income countries from analyses because of data availability issues is common in the field and might bias estimation results.

In general, three types of methods are used to address missing data: deleting samples or variables with missing values, single imputation, and multiple imputation. Sample deletion may cause estimation bias if the missing pattern is not truly random. Single imputation is the most popular way of addressing the problem of missing values (e.g., as applied in World Bank databases) but tends to underestimate the error variance of missing data (see Junninen et al., 2004: 2906–2907).

Multiple imputation mitigates the problem; however, the method has not been widely used until recently because it requires substantial computational power to undertake the calculations required to generate a sufficient number of imputed datasets. Rapid development of computer technology since the turn of the century has shortened the computational time required for multiple imputation, which has made it one of the more common methods currently used to address missing data issues, particularly in medical science studies. Multiple imputation enables future levels of emissions for each country – even low-income countries – to be estimated and political goals to be set for such countries.

In recent studies on the EKC, analyses of individual countries and/or specific regional patterns have become increasingly important to decipher global trends and because developed and developing countries have different development paths. In particular, large emerging economies, such as China and India, are considered to be the world's largest potential sources of GHGs and other pollutant emissions. Thus, forecasting the levels of environmental degradation caused by the economic development of Asian countries is important, but data collection for those countries has been insufficient up to this point.

Thus, in this chapter, we apply the multiple imputation method to a global panel dataset to include as much information as possible about emerging economies in Asia. By imputing missing values in the dataset, we can include more Asian countries for longer time periods. We first estimate the EKC. Second, we compare the results of the estimation by multiple imputation with listwise deletion. Third, using the results of the EKC estimation, we calculate the future projections of these emissions in Asia by focusing on each country's share of the total emissions of the region.

We implement the analysis described previously on four environmental indices: CO_2, SO_2, PM10, and BOD. The missing rates vary for each of these four indices. CO_2 and SO_2 emissions are the most common environmental indices for EKC analyses and have low rates of missing data. PM10 also has a long and wide range of data collection and the lowest rate of missingness in our dataset. The BOD index is important to measure water pollution; however, only a small number of countries collect these data and this index thus has the highest rate of missing data.

In the next section, we first explain the missing mechanisms in the dataset that are the main reason for why we must use multiple imputation. Second, the data imputation and EKC estimation methods are described. Third, we check the missing mechanisms in the dataset and evaluate our imputation results before proceeding to EKC estimation. We use a global dataset for our imputation but estimate regional EKCs for Asian countries; in this way, we are able to derive a projection of future emissions. Finally, we summarize our findings and discuss the implications of this study.

2. Missing data mechanisms

Before choosing an imputation method, we must first identify the "missing mechanism" of the dataset, which is defined by Rubin (1976). The missing mechanism is classified into three separate patterns: missing completely at random (MCAR), missing at random (MAR), and missing not at random (MNAR) or nonignorable (NI).

Let D denote a matrix of $n \times k$, where n is the sample size and k is the number of variables. D embraces all dependent and independent variables – with some missing values – to be used in subsequent analyses. We denote D_{obs} as observed values and D_{miss} as missing values in D; thus, $D = [D_{obs}, D_{miss}]$.

2.1 MCAR

The missing mechanism is MCAR if the probability of missingness is identical for all the data units, i.e., $p(M|D) = p(M)$, which indicates that the missing pattern M is independent of D. For example, when the missing pattern is determined by coin flips, the missing mechanism of the dataset is MCAR. If the missing mechanism is MCAR, listwise/pairwise deletion and single/multiple imputation methods do not cause the estimators to be biased. Sample deletion in this context only affects efficiency.

2.2 MAR

The second missing mechanism is called MAR, such that the missing pattern M depends on D_{obs} but is independent of D_{miss}; more formally, $p(M|D) = p(M|D_{obs})$. In this case, missingness is determined by the observed values of variables without the missing values. For example, if the probability of the missingness of a variable is higher for older people, and the "Age" variable, which has no missing data, is included in the dataset, then the missing mechanism of the dataset is MAR. In the case of MAR, listwise/pairwise deletion causes estimation bias, whereas single/multiple imputation methods do not.

2.3 MNAR/NI

When the missing pattern is determined by the missing values D_{miss}, the missing mechanism is MNAR or NI. When the missing mechanism is MNAR, the probability of missingness is dependent on missing data; thus, the missing pattern cannot be predicted because we do not have information about the missing values. The methods discussed previously – listwise/pairwise deletion and single/multiple imputation methods – may cause the estimators to be biased when the missing mechanism is MNAR. However, we can convert the MNAR dataset to MAR by adding auxiliary variables (AV), by which we can predict the missing pattern M. The missing mechanism of a dataset cannot be determined with certainty because we do not have information about missing values. To avoid causing bias with MNAR datasets, we must use priors and expert information to make the dataset MAR when it is highly likely that the given dataset is MNAR.

3. Methods

3.1 Multiple imputation method with expectation maximization algorithm based on bootstrapping

There are two algorithms that are widely used for multiple imputation, the imputation-posterior (IP) approach and expectation maximization importance sampling (EMis) (King et al., 2001). IP is a method based on a Markov chain and Monte Carlo algorithm that requires both expertise and a lengthy computational time. EMis is based on the expectation maximization (EM) algorithm, the itera-tive estimation method, which requires less expertise and is faster than IP. These two methods have been used as major algorithms for multiple imputation. However, both IP and EMis have the disadvantage that they require considerable computational time and expertise. In addition, a large panel dataset, which includes cross-sectional and time series information, may not be properly treated by these methods.

The idea of multiple imputation was introduced by Rubin (1977). Different values are imputed for the missing elements in the multiple imputation process, such that m numbers of imputed datasets are generated based on observed values. In this chapter, we focus on a newly introduced method of multiple imputation, which is implemented by Amelia, a statistical package for R (Honaker and King, 2010) that addresses the missing data of a panel dataset. Amelia can handle both cross-sectional and time-series features of panel data.

The imputation method used in Amelia is based on an EM algorithm with bootstrapping (EMB), which can efficiently estimate missing values. The process of multiple imputation using EMB is shown in Figure 3.1. EMB is suitable for a large dataset because the drawing process of the mean vector and joint covariance matrix is simplified by bootstrapping. Bootstrapping has better lower order assumptions than the parametric approaches that both EMis and IP implement (see Honaker and King, 2010: 564–565).

The general concept behind the EM algorithm and its applications in statistics was introduced by Dempster et al. (1977). The EM algorithm is an iterative maximum likelihood method that is used to estimate parameters from incomplete datasets that consists of two steps – the (E) step and the (M) step. The (E) step calculates the expectation value of the unobserved data unit and estimates the parameter from the unobserved dataset. The (M) step estimates the parameter that maximizes the likelihood that distribution of the unobserved data is realized. The (E) and (M) steps are iterated until the estimated parameter is converged. Before beginning the analysis, the initial value for the missing data units must be set.

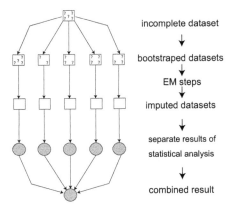

Figure 3.1   Imputation process by EMB algorithm

Source: Honaker (2011: 4).

After creating m datasets with imputed values by means of the EMB algorithm, we run m numbers of statistical analysis. For example, in the case of a parametric regression analysis, we calculate estimated parameters and standard errors for each imputed dataset. There are several methods that can be employed to combine these m results. In our study, we use the method developed by Rubin and Schenker (1986) because it can consider variance among m estimations. The combined estimation of the parameter $\bar{\theta}_m$ is simply an arithmetic mean of m estimations:

$$\bar{\theta}_m = \frac{1}{m} \sum_{i-1}^{m} \hat{\theta}_i \tag{1}$$

where $\hat{\theta}_i$ is an estimated parameter of the ith imputed dataset.

The standard error of $\bar{\theta}_m$ is calculated by "within–imputation variance" and "between–imputation variance." First, we calculate the mean variance of θ derived from m datasets $\bar{v}_m$:

$$\bar{v}_m = \frac{1}{m} \sum_{m=1}^{m} v_i \tag{2}$$

where v_i is variance of $\hat{\theta}_i$ in dataset i and $\bar{v}_m$ is the mean value of v_i, which is called "within–imputation variance."

Second, "between–imputation variance," which is the variance of estimated parameters among imputed datasets, is calculated by equation (3):

$$\bar{v}_b = \frac{1}{m-1} \sum_{m=1}^{m} \left(\hat{\theta}_i - \hat{\theta}_m \right)^2 \tag{3}$$

The combined standard error is calculated by equation (4):

$$\overline{se}_m = \sqrt{\bar{v}_m + \bar{v}_b + \left(1 + \frac{1}{m}\right)\bar{v}_b}. \tag{4}$$

The advantage of including "between–imputation variance" in equation (4) is that statistical significance is dependent on the missing rate of the original dataset, such that we can integrate the missing rate with the analysis result.

In addition, we assume that variables in a complete dataset follow multivariate normal distribution, indicating that each variable is explained by a linear function of all the others.

4. Estimation method of EKC

After the imputation, we estimate the regression model for the EKC. We recognize that there are arguments that using a parametric regression may not produce reliable results because the functional form and distribution are assumed in advance; therefore, semi-parametric methods have become commonly used to estimate the relationship between environmental degradation and income (Bertinelli and Strobl, 2005; Azomahou et al., 2006; Tsurumi and Managi, 2010a). However, the main purpose of this chapter is not to investigate the existence of the EKC but to compare the regression results from two methods: listwise deletion and multiple imputation. We, therefore, focus on a simple form of the EKC.[1]

We estimate the regression model described by equation (5). E_{it} is the emission/concentration level in country i at time t, X is GDP per capita, *Year* is a time trend variable, α is the intercept,

μ_i is a time-fixed effect of country i, and ε_{it} is an error term. To consider nonlinearity, we include the second and third power terms of GDP.

$$E_{it} = \alpha + \beta_1 X_{it} + \beta_2 X_{it}^2 + \beta_3 X_{it}^3 + \mu_i + Year + \varepsilon_{it} \qquad (5)$$

In addition, we focus on the EKC in different areas in Asia, South Asia, Central Asia, Southeast Asia, and East Asia. In the EKC literature, geographical information is treated either as larger categories, such as Asia, Europe, North America, and Africa, or as individual countries (Lee et al., 2010; Grossman and Krueger, 1991; Orubu and Omotor, 2011). CO_2 and SO_2 levels are analyzed both locally and globally, but PM10 is studied only for a limited number of countries and cities, i.e., US, Mexico, and Italy (Dasgupta et al., 2002; Mazzanti et al., 2007).

5. Data

We include industry- and environment-related variables in the imputation model, as shown in Table 3.1.[2] The data sources are the World Development Indicators (WDI) 2012, the Penn World Table (PWT) Ver. 7.1 (Nov. 2012), and the Environmental Performance Index (EPI) 2012. The data periods that are used in this study are 1970–2010 for CO_2 and SO_2, 1990–2010 for PM10, and 1990–2007 for BOD.

Countries are categorized by geographical region and income level, which are controlled by dummy variables. In all, 181 countries are included for CO_2, SO_2, and PM10, and 97 countries are included for BOD, based on data availability.[3] The 181 countries are categorized into 12 regional subcategories (Table 3.2): (1) South Asia, (2) Central Asia, (3) Middle East and North Africa,

Table 3.1 Variables used for multiple imputation

Variables	Label	Unit	Source	Period
GDP per capita	GDP	1,000 constant 2005 international dollars (I$) per person	PWT	1970–2010
Investment share of GDP per capita	INV	% of PPP Converted GDP per capita at 2005 constant prices	PWT	1970–2010
Openness of economy	OPN	% at 2005 constant prices	PWT	1970–2010
SO_2 emissions per capita	SO2CAP	SO_2 emissions kg per person	EPI	1970–2010
CO_2 emissions per capita	CO2CAP	CO_2 emissions kg per person	EPI	1970–2010
School enrollment, primary	SCH	%	WDI	1970–2010
Total population	POP	person	WDI	1970–2010
Manufacturing, value added	MNF	% of GDP	WDI	1970–2010
Organic water pollutant emissions★ (BOD)	BOD	kg per day per worker (country level)	WDI	1990–2007
PM10 concentration	PM10	micrograms per cubic meter	WDI	1990–2010
CO_2 per GDP	CO2GDP	CO_2 emissions kg per GDP	EPI	1970–2010
Renewable electricity	RNW	% of electricity production	EPI	1970–2010

★ Organic water pollutants are measured by biochemical oxygen demand (BOD), which refers to the amount of oxygen that bacteria in water will consume in breaking down waste.

Note: PWT indicates Penn World Table Version 7.1 (2012 November), WDI indicates World Development Indicators 2012, and EPI indicates the Environmental Performance Index 2012.

Table 3.2 List of countries categorized by region

Region	Country
South Asia	Afghanistan, Bangladesh, Bhutan, India, Maldives, Nepal, Pakistan, Sri Lanka
Middle East & North Africa	Algeria, Bahrain, Djibouti, Egypt–Arab Rep, Iran–Islamic Rep., Iraq, Israel, Jordan, Kuwait, Lebanon, Libya, Malta, Morocco, Oman, Qatar, Saudi Arabia, Syrian Arab Republic, Tunisia, United Arab Emirates
Sub-Saharan Africa	Angola, Benin, Botswana, Burkina Faso, Burundi, Cameroon, Cape Verde, Central African Republic, Chad, Comoros, Congo, Dem. Rep., Congo–Rep., Côte d'Ivoire, Equatorial Guinea, Eritrea, Ethiopia, Gabon, Gambia, Ghana, Guinea, Guinea–Bissau, Kenya, Lesotho, Liberia, Madagascar, Malawi, Mali, Mauritania, Mauritius, Mozambique, Namibia, Niger, Nigeria, Rwanda, São Tomé and Principe, Senegal, Seychelles, Sierra Leone, Somalia, South Africa, Sudan, Swaziland, Tanzania, Togo, Uganda, Zambia, Zimbabwe
Latin America & Caribbean	Antigua and Barbuda, Argentina, Bahamas, Barbados, Belize, Bolivia, Brazil, Chile, Colombia, Costa Rica, Cuba, Dominica, Dominican Republic, Ecuador, El Salvador, Grenada, Guatemala, Guyana, Haiti, Honduras, Jamaica, Mexico, Nicaragua, Panama, Paraguay, Peru, Puerto Rico, St. Kitts and Nevis, St. Lucia, St. Vincent and the Grenadines, Suriname, Trinidad and Tobago, Uruguay, Venezuela–RB
North America	Bermuda, Canada, United States
Western Europe	Albania, Austria, Belgium, Bulgaria, Cyprus, Czech Republic, Denmark, Estonia, Finland, France, Germany, Greece, Iceland, Ireland, Italy, Latvia, Lithuania, Luxembourg, Macedonia–FYR, Netherlands, Norway, Poland, Portugal, Romania, Russian Federation, Slovak Republic, Spain, Sweden, United Kingdom
Central Asia	Kazakhstan, Kyrgyz Republic, Tajikistan, Turkmenistan, Uzbekistan
Western Asia	Armenia, Azerbaijan, Turkey
Eastern Europe	Belarus, Georgia, Hungary, Moldova, Switzerland, Ukraine
Pacific Oceania	Australia, Fiji, Kiribati, Marshall Islands, Micronesia–Fed. Sts., New Zealand, Palau, Papua New Guinea, Samoa, Solomon Islands, Tonga, Vanuatu
Southeast Asia	Brunei Darussalam, Cambodia, Indonesia, Lao PDR, Malaysia, Philippines, Singapore, Thailand, Vietnam
East Asia	China, Hong Kong–SAR, China, Japan, Korea–Rep., Macao–SAR, China, Mongolia

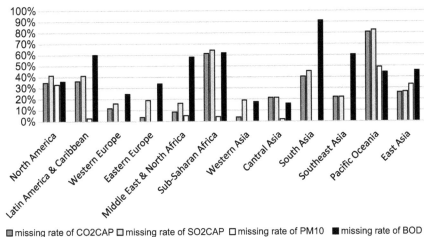

Figure 3.2   Data missing rate of each region

(4) Sub-Saharan Africa, (5) Latin America and the Caribbean, (6) North America, (7) Western Europe, (8) Central Asia, (9) Western Asia and Eastern Europe (10) Pacific Oceania, (11) Southeast Asia, and (12) East Asia. Thirty countries are categorized as high-income OECD countries, 19 countries are high-income non-OECD countries, 49 countries are middle-income countries, 49 countries are lower middle-income countries, and 34 countries are low-income countries.

The missing data rate is higher in Pacific Oceania and sub-Saharan Africa for SO_2, CO_2, and BOD. Data for PM10 are missing more often in the regions with developed economies compared with regions that have more emerging economies (Figure 3.2). The new database with estimated missing data is named as *World Resource Table* (WRT) (see also Yang, Managi and Sato, 2014; Miyama and Managi, 2014). WRT provides the most comprehensive data used in environmental and resource analysis.

6. Results of imputation

6.1 Checking the missing mechanism

Before moving to the imputation results, we check the missing mechanism of the dataset by using correlations of the indicator matrix and values of the dataset (see Kabacoff, 2011: 360–362). One way to check a missing mechanism is to examine the correlation of observed values and the matrix of a missing pattern.[4] We generate a dataset with indicator variables that are coded 1 for missing and 0 for observed. The resulting 0, 1 matrix is called the "shadow matrix." Tables 3.4–3.6 show the correlation matrix between the shadow matrix and the values of the dataset. The rows are observed variables, and the columns are indicator variables representing missingness. From the table, we can see that all the correlation between the shadow matrix and observed values is lower than 0.4, which indicates that the missing mechanism of the dataset can be assumed to be either MCAR or MAR.

Many articles in the literature have indicated that five to 20 imputations are sufficient for consistent analysis (see King et al., 2001: 53; Gelman and Hill, 2006: 542). However, most recent studies have found that estimation results with small numbers of imputed datasets can be biased and have recommended generating more than 100 imputations because of the reduced computational time of today's technology (Graham et al., 2007). Therefore, we execute 100 imputations for our analysis. Figures 3.7–3.9 show comparisons of relative densities between observed values

Table 3.3 The correlation matrix of variables used to impute CO_2 and SO_2 dataset

	CO2CAP	CO2GDP	INV	MNF	OPN	POP	RNW	GDP	SCH	SO2CAP
CO2CAP	/	/	0.20	0.19	0.20	0.06	-0.04	0.20	0.02	0.04
CO2GDP	/	/	0.09	0.14	0.09	0.03	-0.05	0.09	0.09	-0.03
Highincome: OECD dummy	-0.32	-0.32	-0.04	0.15	-0.04	-0.01	-0.21	-0.04	-0.11	-0.26
Highincome: non OECD dummy	0.02	0.02	0.11	0.04	0.11	0.06	0.03	0.11	0.11	0.03
Upper middle in come dummy	-0.09	-0.09	0.07	-0.11	0.07	-0.01	-0.09	0.07	0.03	-0.11
Lower middle in come dummy	0.07	0.07	-0.09	-0.01	-0.09	-0.01	0.06	-0.09	-0.04	0.07
INV	0.02	0.02	/	0.02	/	-0.01	0.06	/	0.01	0.03
MNF	-0.33	-0.33	0.03	/	0.03	-0.02	-0.28	0.03	-0.03	-0.32
OPN	0.10	0.10	/	-0.09	/	0.01	0.00	/	0.10	0.18
POP	-0.14	-0.14	-0.02	-0.07	-0.02	/	-0.13	-0.02	-0.03	-0.11
South Asia dummy	0.02	0.02	-0.04	-0.02	-0.04	0.00	0.02	-0.04	0.04	0.02
Western Asia (Eastern Europe) dummy	-0.07	-0.07	0.00	-0.07	0.00	0.00	-0.07	0.00	-0.02	-0.05
Eastern Europe dummy	-0.10	-0.10	0.00	0.06	0.00	0.00	-0.10	0.00	-0.04	-0.07
Pacific Oceania dummy	0.23	0.23	-0.04	0.03	-0.04	-0.01	0.19	-0.04	0.06	0.22
South east Asia dummy	-0.07	-0.07	-0.04	-0.05	-0.04	0.00	-0.07	-0.04	0.03	-0.09
Middle East & North Africa dummy	-0.20	-0.20	0.16	0.06	0.16	0.06	-0.14	0.16	-0.01	-0.17
Sub-Saharan Africa dummy	0.32	0.32	-0.10	-0.11	-0.10	-0.01	0.24	-0.10	-0.01	0.29
Latin America & Caribbean dummy	0.00	0.00	-0.08	-0.08	-0.08	-0.01	0.02	-0.08	0.00	0.01
North America dummy	0.00	0.00	-0.02	0.12	-0.02	0.00	0.01	-0.02	0.01	0.00
Europe dummy	-0.22	-0.22	0.12	0.14	0.12	-0.01	-0.18	0.12	-0.05	-0.22
Central Asia dummy	-0.04	-0.04	0.16	0.00	0.16	0.00	-0.09	0.16	0.07	-0.05
RNW	-0.12	-0.12	-0.12	-0.09	-0.12	-0.03	/	-0.12	-0.06	-0.04
GDP	-0.24	-0.24	/	0.07	/	0.06	-0.23	/	-0.03	-0.13
SCH	-0.20	-0.20	0.05	0.01	0.05	-0.02	-0.22	0.05	/	-0.15
SO2 CAP	-0.01	-0.01	0.20	0.19	0.20	-0.02	0.12	0.20	0.04	/
Year	0.00	0.00	-0.16	-0.33	-0.16	0.00	-0.36	-0.16	0.01	0.28

Table 3.4 The correlation matrix of variables used to impute BOD dataset

	BOD	CO2CAP	CO2GDP	INV	MNF	OPN	RNW	GDP	SCH	SO2CAP
BOD	/	0.13	0.13	-0.06	-0.06	-0.06	0.14	-0.06	-0.04	0.10
CO2CAP	-0.16	/	/	0.01	0.27	0.01	/	0.01	-0.05	0.03
CO2GDP	0.08	/	/	0.14	0.23	0.14	/	0.14	0.02	-0.06
High income: OECD dummy	-0.29	-0.25	-0.25	-0.05	0.12	-0.05	-0.25	-0.05	-0.17	-0.18
High income: non OECD dummy	0.00	-0.01	-0.01	-0.03	0.02	-0.03	-0.01	-0.03	0.14	-0.01
Upper middle income dummy	-0.05	-0.09	-0.09	0.07	-0.05	0.07	-0.09	0.07	-0.01	-0.06
Lower middle income dummy	0.24	0.07	0.07	-0.03	-0.09	-0.03	0.08	-0.03	-0.01	0.05
INV	-0.05	-0.08	-0.08	/	-0.06	/	-0.07	/	-0.05	0.00
MNF	-0.11	-0.23	-0.23	0.20	/	0.20	-0.23	0.20	0.01	-0.21
OPN	-0.16	-0.03	-0.03	/	-0.13	/	-0.02	/	0.09	0.07
POP	0.06	-0.10	-0.10	-0.02	-0.03	-0.02	-0.10	-0.02	0.03	-0.06
South Asia dummy	0.21	0.04	0.04	-0.02	0.01	-0.02	0.04	-0.02	0.19	0.03
Western Asia (Eastern Europe) dummy	-0.08	-0.06	-0.06	0.04	-0.05	0.04	-0.06	0.04	-0.04	-0.04
Eastern Europe dummy	-0.05	-0.07	-0.07	0.03	0.00	0.03	-0.07	0.03	-0.01	-0.05
Pacific Oceania dummy	-0.01	0.27	0.27	-0.02	-0.06	-0.02	0.28	-0.02	0.03	0.20
South east Asia dummy	0.08	0.02	0.02	-0.03	-0.09	-0.03	-0.01	-0.03	0.03	-0.01
Middle East & North Africa dummy	0.08	-0.15	-0.15	-0.03	0.19	-0.03	-0.15	-0.03	0.06	-0.11
Sub-Saharan Africa dummy	0.13	0.39	0.39	-0.04	-0.17	-0.04	0.40	-0.04	-0.01	0.29
Latin America & Caribbean dummy	0.09	-0.05	-0.05	-0.03	0.03	-0.03	-0.05	-0.03	0.08	-0.04
North America dummy	-0.03	-0.06	-0.06	-0.01	0.04	-0.01	-0.06	-0.01	0.00	-0.04
Europe dummy	-0.29	-0.19	-0.19	0.02	0.11	0.02	-0.18	0.02	-0.17	-0.13
Central Asia dummy	-0.11	-0.07	-0.07	0.19	-0.03	0.19	-0.07	0.19	-0.03	-0.05
RNW	0.03	-0.05	-0.05	0.04	-0.09	0.04	/	0.04	-0.03	-0.03
GDP	-0.28	-0.23	-0.23	/	0.12	/	-0.22	/	-0.07	-0.10
SCH	-0.03	0.01	0.01	0.01	-0.03	0.01	0.02	0.01	/	0.04
SO2CAP	-0.03	-0.05	-0.05	0.03	0.23	0.03	-0.01	0.03	0.03	/
Year	-0.26	-0.02	-0.02	-0.12	-0.17	-0.12	-0.01	-0.12	-0.06	0.35

Table 3.5 The correlation matrix of variables used to impute PM10 dataset

	PM10	CO2CAP	CO2GDP	INV	MNF	OPN	POP	RNW	GDP	SCH	SO2CAP
PM10	/	−0.10	−0.10	0.05	−0.02	0.05	−0.01	−0.10	0.05	0.06	−0.18
CO2CAP	0.01	/	/	0.01	0.21	0.01	−0.03	/	0.01	−0.03	0.04
CO2GDP	−0.04	/	/	0.15	0.17	0.15	−0.04	/	0.15	0.08	−0.07
High income: OECD dummy	−0.12	−0.28	−0.28	−0.03	0.08	−0.03	−0.04	−0.28	−0.03	−0.16	−0.22
High income: non OECD dummy	0.26	0.03	0.03	−0.02	0.08	−0.02		0.04	−0.02	0.10	0.03
Upper middle in come dummy	−0.08	−0.12	−0.12	0.05	−0.12	0.05	−0.05	−0.11	0.05	0.03	−0.09
Lower middle in come dummy	0.12	0.09	0.09	−0.01	0.03	−0.01	0.11	0.09	−0.01	−0.02	0.07
INV	0.23	0.09	0.09	/	0.16	−0.01	0.07	0.09	/	0.01	0.12
MNF	−0.16	−0.33	−0.33	0.16	/	−0.07	−0.02	−0.33	0.16	−0.04	−0.30
OPN	0.23	0.06	0.06	−0.01	−0.07	/	−0.03	0.07	−0.01	0.07	0.12
POP	−0.07	−0.14	−0.14	−0.01	−0.05	−0.01	/	−0.14	−0.01	−0.02	−0.10
South Asia dummy	−0.06	0.02	0.02	−0.01	−0.03	−0.01	−0.02	0.02	−0.01	0.08	0.02
Western Asia (Eastern Europe) dummy	−0.04	−0.08	−0.08	0.06	−0.05	0.06	−0.01	−0.08	0.06	−0.03	−0.06
Eastern Europe dummy	−0.05	−0.11	−0.11	0.08	0.05	0.08	−0.01	−0.11	0.08	−0.06	−0.08
Pacific Oceania dummy	0.43	0.27	0.27	−0.02	0.05	−0.02	−0.02	0.27	−0.02	0.09	0.21
Southeast Asia dummy	−0.06	−0.08	−0.08	−0.02	−0.09	−0.02	−0.02	−0.09	−0.02	−0.03	−0.07
Middle East & North Africa dummy	−0.03	−0.18	−0.18	−0.02	0.19	−0.02	0.23	−0.18	−0.02	−0.06	−0.14
Sub-Saharan Africa dummy	−0.07	0.31	0.31	−0.04	−0.07	−0.04	−0.05	0.31	−0.04	0.04	0.23
Latin America & Caribbean dummy	−0.08	0.03	0.03	−0.03	−0.10	−0.03	−0.04	0.03	−0.03	0.04	0.02
North America dummy	0.13	/	/	−0.01	0.12	−0.01	−0.01	0.03	−0.03	0.03	/
Europe dummy	−0.12	−0.25	−0.25	0.02	0.04	0.02	−0.03	−0.25	0.02	−0.15	−0.19
Central Asia dummy	−0.03	−0.10	−0.10	0.14	−0.01	0.14	−0.01	−0.10	0.14	0.03	−0.07
RNW	−0.11	−0.04	−0.04	0.01	−0.11	0.01	−0.07	/	0.01	−0.02	−0.04
GDP	0.11	−0.21	−0.21	/	0.11	/	−0.02	−0.21	/	−0.06	−0.10
SCH	0.09	−0.15	−0.15	/	−0.01	/	−0.06	−0.15	/	/	−0.07
SO2CAP	0.12	−0.04	−0.04	0.02	0.16	0.02	−0.05	−0.15	0.02	−0.01	/
Year	/	0.10	0.10	−0.09	−0.05	−0.09	−0.01	0.11	−0.09	−0.06	0.43

and the means of the imputed values. In most cases, the distributions are not substantially different between the imputed mean values and the observed values. Thus, the imputation models are considered suitable.

Figures 3.3–3.6 are scatter plots of imputed mean values and observed values. The open circles are imputed mean values, and the filled circles are observed values. For CO_2 and SO_2, the data for

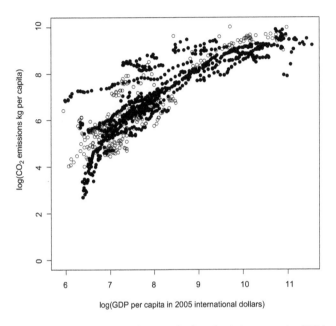

Figure 3.3 Scatter plot of observed values and imputed values for Asian countries (CO_2)

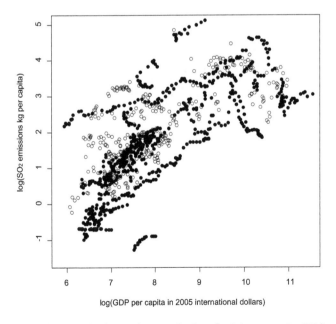

Figure 3.4 Scatter plot of observed values and imputed values for Asian countries (SO_2)

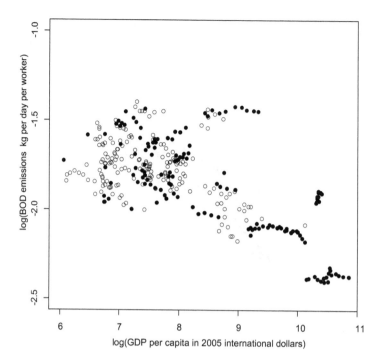

Figure 3.5   Scatter plot of observed values and imputed values for Asian countries (BOD)

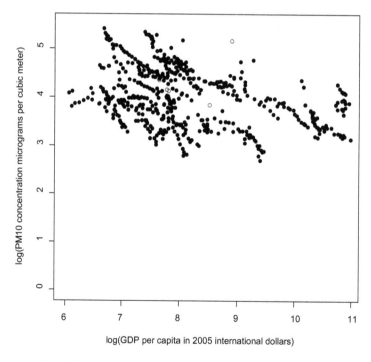

Figure 3.6   Scatter plot of observed values and imputed values for Asian countries (PM10)

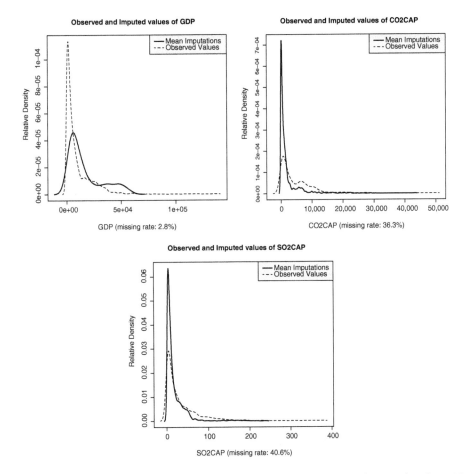

Figure 3.7 Comparison between relative densities of observed values and imputed mean values (CO_2, SO_2)

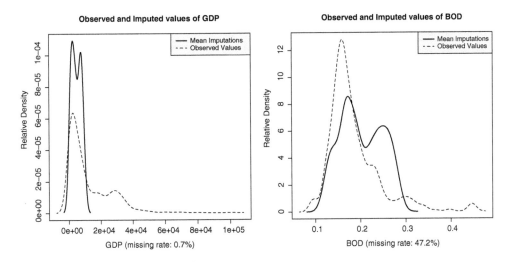

Figure 3.8 Comparison between relative densities of observed values and imputed mean values (BOD)

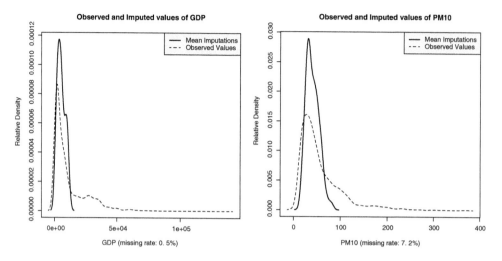

Figure 3.9 Comparison between relative densities of observed values and imputed mean values (PM10)

the countries with lower levels of GDP per capita are more likely to be imputed than the data from countries with higher levels of GDP per capita, whereas PM10 is more likely to be imputed at higher GDP levels. The data for BOD are more scattered compared with other indices, and the deviation of relative density of the imputed mean value from the relative density of observed values is larger than in other indices.

7. Results of EKC estimations[5]

Tables 3.6–3.9 show the results of the EKC estimations in Asia. The tables on the left show the results from listwise deletion and those on the right show the results from multiple imputation. CO_2 and SO_2 emissions per capita levels exhibit a significant relationship with GDP per capita

Table 3.6 Results of the EKC estimation (CO_2)

Dep. var: CO_2 emissions kg per capita	*Listwise deletion*		*Multiple imputation*	
	Coefficient	*Std. Error*	*Coefficient*	*Std. Error*
Intercept	−556***	177	−394*	220
GDP	667***	36.5	897***	132
GDP squared	−13.2***	0.961	−16.4***	3.65
GDP cubed	0.0735***	0.00681	0.0879***	0.0257
Year	7.59	4.85	−15.4	11.1
Country Fixed Effect	Yes		Yes	
Number of Obs.	750		1058	

*** Significantly different from zero at the 1% significance level
** Significantly different from zero at the 5% significance level
** Significantly different from zero at the 10% significance level

Table 3.7 Results of the EKC estimation (SO₂)

Dep. var: SO₂ emissions kg per capita	Listwise deletion		Multiple imputation	
	Coefficient	Std. Error	Coefficient	Std. Error
Intercept	−1.96***	1.62	5.42***	1.63
GDP	1.95***	0.353	4.23***	0.797
GDP squared	−0.0426***	0.00994	−0.113***	0.0216
GDP cubed	0.000269	0.0000714	0.000755***	0.000150
Year	0.0669	0.0440	−0.221***	0.0749
Country fixed effect	Yes		Yes	
Number of obs.	712		1058	

*** Significantly different from zero at the 1% significance level
** Significantly different from zero at the 5% significance level
* Significantly different from zero at the 10% significance level

Table 3.8 Results of the EKC estimation (PM10)

Dep. var: BOD g per day per worker	Listwise deletion		Multiple imputation	
	Coefficient	Std. Error	Coefficient	Std. Error
Intercept	0.132***	0.0101	0.180***	0.0252
GDP	−0.00509***	0.00182	−0.00495	0.00606
GDP squared	0.0000633	0.0000710	0.000170	0.000238
GDP cubed	−0.000000231	0.000000868	−0.00000181	0.00000297
Year	0.00200***	0.000273	−0.000318	0.000697
Country fixed effect	Yes		Yes	
Number of obs.	144		356	

*** Significantly different from zero at the 1% significance level
** Significantly different from zero at the 5% significance level
* Significantly different from zero at the 10% significance level

both before and after imputation. The signs for the terms of GDP per capita do not change after imputation, although their magnitudes are slightly different.

For PM10, depicting a significant relationship between its concentration and GDP per capita after imputation is difficult (Table 3.8). Such difficulty may arise from the fact that this analysis is a cross-country analysis. Many articles in the literature that have found an inverted U-shaped relationship between PM10 concentration and GDP per capita have used city-level data for air pollution (e.g., Grossman and Krueger, 1995), which may have a strong relationship with GDP per capita because population and industry concentration in urban areas is strongly related to GDP growth.

BOD has the highest missing rate among the four environmental indices in our analysis. As we discussed in the explanation of the methodology, the integration process of the standard error

Table 3.9 Results of the EKC estimation (BOD)

Dep. var: PM10 concentration micrograms per cubic meter	Listwise deletion		Multiple imputation	
	Coefficient	Std. Error	Coefficient	Std. Error
Intercept	121***	4.26	119***	4.73
GDP	1.72	1.18	−0.151	1.40
GDP squared	−0.0203	0.0450	0.0390	0.0669
GDP cubed	0.0000599	0.000527	−0.000522	0.000802
Year	−2.39	0.126	−2.30***	0.136
Country fixed effect	Yes		Yes	
Number of obs.	532		580	

*** Significantly different from zero at the 1% significance level

** Significantly different from zero at the 5% significance level

* Significantly different from zero at the 10% significance level

reflects the missing rate of the original data; thus, none of the estimated parameters of GDP is statistically significant for BOD (see Table 3.9).

Overall, the significance of the estimated parameters differs between listwise deletion and multiple imputation. For PM10 and BOD, GDP per capita is insignificant in the results for multiple imputation because the standard error has a tendency to become larger for the imputed dataset as the result of data missingness. In this way, we can better evaluate the uncertainty of the missing data by multiple imputation than by single imputation, which generally ignores the missing rate of the original data.

Figures 3.10 and 3.11 show the relationship between CO_2/SO_2 emissions per capita and GDP per capita after controlling for year trends and country-fixed effects. The broken line is the estimated line derived from listwise deletion, and the solid line is the result of multiple imputation.[6] The figures are presented only for CO_2 and SO_2 because their results in the multiple imputation show a significant relationship between emission/concentration per capita and GDP per capita, whereas the results for PM10 and BOD do not. In addition, each country's emission and GDP levels in 1970 and 2012 are plotted with circles overlapping the estimated lines to show which country's emissions level exceeds the estimated average line.

The curve for CO_2 emissions per capita has an inverted-U (N) shape in Asia (see Figure 3.10). The emissions peak is at 47,600 international dollars per capita. The results of the listwise deletion show that emissions peak at a lower level of GDP per capita compared with the results of the multiple imputation. Such a difference indicates the possibility of bias caused by listwise deletion.

Many empirical studies have found a monotonously increasing relationship between CO_2 emissions per capita and GDP per capita within the observed income levels (e.g., Shafik, 1994; Heil and Selden, 2001), but our study suggests that a regional inverted U-shape curve results from imputed complete data. Our results thus confirm the empirical results of Holtz-Eakin and Selden (Holtz-Eakin and Selden, 1995), who found an inverted U-shaped relationship between global CO_2 emissions per capita and GDP per capita. Their estimated emissions peaked at 35,428 US dollars of GDP per capita, whereas our estimation of EKC peaked at 40,600 international dollars, which is a reasonable level of GDP per capita compared with former research results.

In general, the emissions of lower middle-income countries tend to largely exceed the average level compared to 1970, whereas developed countries and low-income countries realized a lower emissions level than the average in 2012. Most countries continue to be on the left side of the

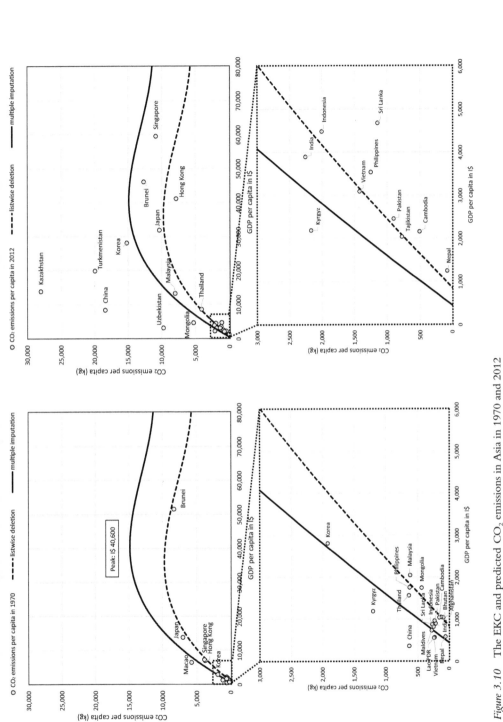

Figure 3.10 The EKC and predicted CO_2 emissions in Asia in 1970 and 2012

Note 1: The denominator of GDP per capita for Singapore includes only Singaporeans living in the country. Thus, GDP per capita is relatively higher for Singapore than in other countries.

Note 2: The estimated lines are identical for all three figures.

Note 3: The emissions levels are taken from the EPI. Missing values are imputed by multiple imputation, and the mean imputation is plotted.

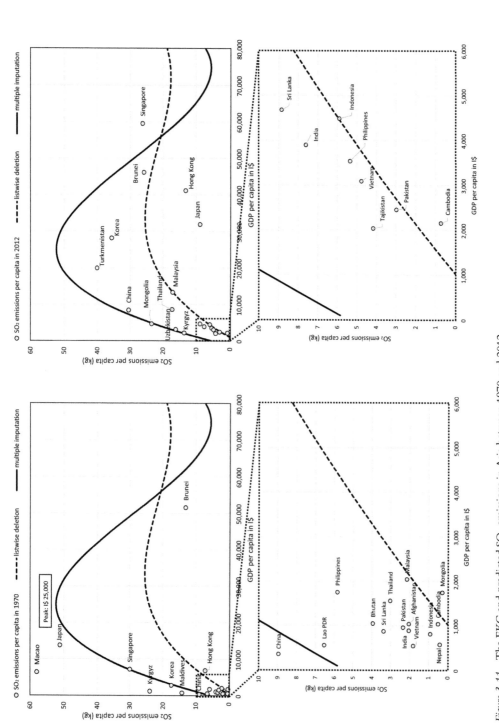

Figure 3.11 The EKC and predicted SO₂ emissions in Asia between 1970 and 2012

Note 1: The denominator of GDP per capita for Singapore includes only Singaporeans living in the country. Thus, GDP per capita is relatively higher for Singapore than for other countries.

Note 2: Estimated lines are identical for all three figures.

Note 3: The emissions levels are taken from the EPI. Missing values are imputed by multiple imputation, and the mean imputation is plotted.

U-shape in 2012, which indicates that they remain in the emission increasing phase (Figure 3.10). For CO_2, Singapore, Brunei, and Hong Kong are in the emissions decreasing phase. The CO_2 emissions level of most of the low-income countries has been lower than the estimated EKC line since 1970 (Figure 3.10), but these countries are still near the soaring stage of the EKC, which indicates that the trend of increasing emissions has not changed for more than 40 years, although GDP per capita in these countries has grown.

Hong Kong improved its CO_2 emissions level between 1970 and 2012, and Japan and Singapore maintained almost the same position with respect to the estimated EKC line. These results indicate that technological development and technology transfer have been successfully implemented over the most recent 40 years, which has lowered the emissions growth rate compared to the population growth rate. For example, the energy sources for electricity in Japan have been diversified since the 1973 oil crisis. Petroleum accounted for 69.9 percent of the primary energy supply in 1970, but that share was reduced to 40 percent in 2010 because other power sources, including nuclear sources, have been adopted (Agency for Natural Resources and Energy, Japan, 2013). Most countries in Southeast Asia also are moving toward lower carbon economies.

China and India – the two largest emitters of CO_2 in Asia – increased their emissions level per capita over the 40-year period under study. Emissions from Central Asian countries also are growing. With massive population growth, these countries will continue to become a global warming threat.

SO_2 emissions per capita shows a U (N)-shaped trend, as with CO_2 (Figure 3.11), but countries have reduced SO_2 emissions more efficiently than CO_2 emissions. The emissions peak for the imputed results is at 25,000 international dollars per capita, which is at a lower GDP per capita level than the results of the listwise deletion. The results with the imputed dataset show more realistic figures compared with those of the listwise results because we could minimize the bias of the estimators with the imputation.

Over these 40 years, developing countries have shifted to the lower right side of the estimated EKC, which indicates that they have effectively reduced SO_2 emissions per capita with GDP growth (Figure 3.11). In 1970, Japan, Singapore, and Korea, which are the leading economies in Asia, were located above or on the estimated EKC line; by 2012, however, these countries had lowered their SO_2 emission levels, and most of the other countries are also under the estimated average line. Technologies – the source of SO_2 emissions – normally decrease as GDP per capita increases. Therefore, in Asia, where most countries remain in the developing stage, SO_2 emissions per capita is increasing at lower economic levels and has begun to decrease at higher GDP levels, which is consistent with recent studies (e.g., Iwami, 2004; Yaguchi et al., 2007; Coleman, 2009). SO_2 is considered to be one of the local pollutants that is easier to control than global emissions. Sulfur, as a byproduct of industrial production in factories, can be reduced by using an end-of-pipe filter, which is a widely applicable technology even in developing countries. These two factors – being a local pollutant and the existence of applicable clean technology – may have helped cause SO_2 emissions to be lower than the average in 2012.

8. Prediction of emissions level

Figures 3.12 and 3.13 show the predicted levels and shares of CO_2 emissions from 1992 to 2018. Predicted emissions levels are calculated by the estimated parameters. Population and growth rate of GDP per capita are taken from the World Economic Outlook Database April 2013 (WEO2013), which is compiled by the International Monetary Fund.[7] Our estimation results show that the annual CO_2 emissions levels in 2018 in Asia will be almost twice the emissions levels in 2007. China has been the largest emitter, and the second largest emitter, India, will take over the shares from Japan and Korea. The trend is almost identical for SO_2 (Figures 3.14 and 3.15), but the share

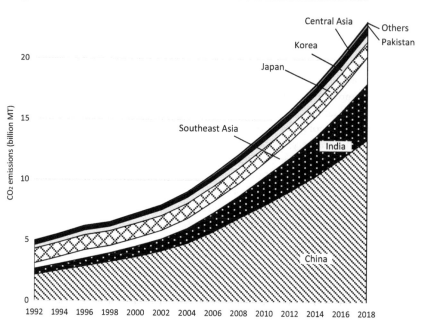

Figure 3.12   Annual trend of predicted CO_2 emissions in Asia

Note: Hong Kong is included in China.

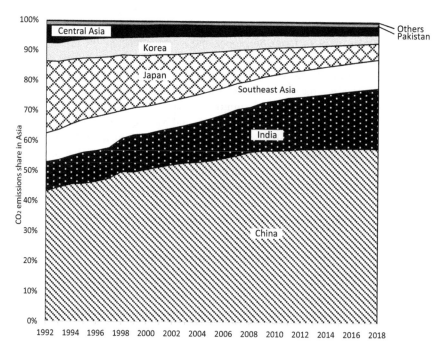

Figure 3.13   Annual trend of predicted CO_2 emissions share in Asia

Note: Hong Kong is included in China.

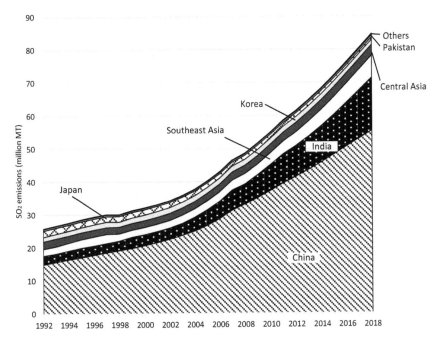

Figure 3.14 Annual trend of predicted SO$_2$ emissions in Asia

Note: Hong Kong is included in China.

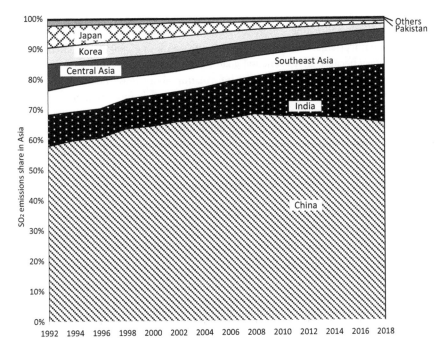

Figure 3.15 Annual trend of predicted SO$_2$ emissions share in Asia

Note: Hong Kong is included in China.

of the developing countries is larger for SO_2. With respect to both CO_2 and SO_2, China, India, and Southeast Asia will be the three largest sources of theses emissions by 2018. Because of increasing population pressures, the decreasing trend in per capita emissions is insufficient to cause a reduction in total CO_2/SO_2 emissions. This result is similar to the conclusion of Coleman (2009) from an EKC estimation of SO_2 emissions in China.

9. Conclusion

Asia is the fastest growing region in the world. Because the EKC indicates the stage that each country fits into, examining the EKC for different emissions in Asia is useful. In this chapter, we demonstrated the application of multiple imputation to estimate the EKC in Asia. First, by carefully choosing the imputation model, we successfully imputed reasonable values into datasets with missing values. Second, we estimated the EKC for Asian countries for four environmental indices – CO_2, SO_2, PM10, and BOD. Finally, we predicted the future emission levels of CO_2 and SO_2 in Asia.

We found that multiple imputation increases the standard errors of the estimated parameters in general and thus evaluates the missing rates from the original datasets properly. Because the relationship between the emissions level and GDP are clearer for CO_2 and SO_2 than for PM10 and BOD, regression parameters for GDP remain significant at a 1 percent significance level after the imputation, such that we can produce an obvious inverted U-shaped curve. The peak of emissions per capita is at a higher level of GDP per capita for the imputed datasets. Comparing the actual emissions level and the estimated EKC reveals that developing countries show improvement in SO_2 emissions levels, but no such trend was observed for CO_2 levels.

We also calculated the projection of future CO_2 and SO_2 emissions levels and each Asian country's share. As a result of rapid population growth, China, India, Southeast Asia, and Central Asia will become the major emitters of CO_2 and SO_2 in Asia. Further studies on environmentally friendly technology and implementation are required to mitigate this trend.

Evaluating the uncertainty of the dataset and future trends in global environmental economic analyses is necessary because environmental goals are set flexibly based on each country's changing situations. Multiple imputation gives us information about how much we can rely on the results of statistical analyses. Furthermore, the results of this study indicate that multiple imputation can serve to expand the datasets for developing countries and environmental indices with missing values. These results will contribute to the construction of inclusive sustainable development indices to confront future international environmental challenges.

Acknowledgement

The authors thank Jue Yang for helpful comments. This research was funded by a Grant-in-Aid for Scientific Research from the Japanese Ministry of Education, Culture, Sports, Science and Technology and Ministry of Environment. The results and conclusions of this chapter do not necessary represent the views of the funding agencies.

Notes

1 Another reason for the use of parametric estimation is that, after multiple imputation, we calculate integrated values of estimated parameters and related standard errors for each of the parameters, which is technically too complicated for nonparametric estimation.
2 Dataset used for the multiple imputation in this chapter is basically the one from the data used in Miyama and Managi (2014).

3 If the country does not exist during the covered period because it is occupied by other countries, the country is excluded from the analysis until its year of independence. Thus, the dataset is unbalanced.

4 This method is a simple example to check the missing mechanisms. More formal tests to determine MCAR are introduced by Little (1988).

5 Western Asia is excluded from the estimation sample in this section because the countries in Western Asia are sometimes considered (at least in part) to be Eastern Europe.

6 Coefficients for year trend and country-fixed effects are averaged to draw the average EKC line.

7 We multiplied 2010 GDP from the Pen World Table (PWT) (in 2005 international dollars) by the growth rate of each country's GDP (in constant national currency) from WEO2013 to derive the projection of GDP per capita from 2011 to 2018.

References

Agency for Natural Resources and Energy, Japan (2013). The White Paper on Energy Usage 2013, Agency for Natural Resources and Energy, Tokyo.

Atici, C. (2012). Carbon emissions, trade liberalization, and the Japan-ASEAN interaction: A group-wise examination. *Journal of the Japanese and International Economies* 26(1): 167–178.

Azomahou, T., Laisney, F., and Nguyen Van, P. (2006). Economic development and CO_2 emissions: A non-parametric panel approach. *Journal of Public Economics* 90(6–7): 1347–1363.

Bertinelli, L., and Strobl, E. (2005). The environmental Kuznets curve semi-parametrically revisited. *Economics Letters* 88(3): 350–357.

Borhan, H., Ahmed, E. M., and Hitam, M. (2012). The impact of CO_2 on economic growth in ASEAN 8. *Procedia-Social and Behavioral Science,* 35: 389–397.

Coleman, A. (2009). A model of spatial arbitrage with transport capacity constraints and endogenous transport prices. *American Journal of Agricultural Economics* 91(1): 42–56.

Coondoo, D., and Dinda, S. (2008). Carbon dioxide emission and income: A temporal analysis of cross-country distributional patterns. *Ecological Economics* 65(2): 375–385.

Dasgupta, S., Laplante, B., Wang, H., and Wheeler, D. (2002). Confronting the environmental Kuznets curve. *The Journal of Economic Perspectives* 16(1): 147–168.

Dempster, A. P., Laird, N. M., and Rubin, D. B. (1977). Maximum likelihood from incomplete data via the EM algorithm. *Journal of the Royal Statistical Society,* Series B (Methodological) 39(1): 1–38.

Fujii, H., and S. Managi. (2013). Which industry is greener? An empirical study of nine industries in OECD countries, *Energy Policy* 57: 381–388.

Galeotti, M., and Lanza, A. (1999). Richer and cleaner? A study on carbon dioxide emissions in developing countries. *Energy Policy* 27(10): 565–573.

Gelman, A., and Hill, J. (2006). *Data Analysis Using Regression and Multilevel/Hierarchical Models.* Cambridge: Cambridge University Press.

Graham, J., Olchowski, A., and Gilreath, T. (2007). How many imputations are really needed? Some practical clarifications of multiple imputation theory. *Prevention Science* 8(3): 206–213.

Grossman, G. M., and Krueger, A. B. (1991). Environmental impacts of a North American Free Trade Agreement. *NBAR Working Paper Series,* Working Paper No. 3914, Cambridge, MA.

Grossman, G. M., and Krueger, A. B. (1995). Economic growth and the environment. *The Quarterly Journal of Economics* 110(2): 353–377.

Heil, M. T., and Selden, T. M. (2001). Carbon emissions and economic development: Future trajectories based on historical experience. *Environment and Development Economics* 6(1): 63–83.

Holtz-Eakin, D., and Selden, T. M. (1995). Stoking the fires? CO_2 emissions and economic growth. *Journal of Public Economics* 57: 85–101.

Honaker, J., and King, G. (2010). What to do about missing values in time series cross-section data. *American Journal of Political Science* 54: 561–581.

Honaker, J., King, G., and Blackwell, M. (2011). Amelia II: A program for missing data. *Journal of Statistical Software* 45(7): 1–47.

Iwami, T. (2004). Economic development and/or environmental quality: Emissions of CO_2 and SO_2 in East Asia. *Discussion Paper F series, March 2004,* Center for International Research on the Japanese Economy, Tokyo.

Jayanthakumaran, K., and Liu, Y. (2012). Openness and the environmental Kuznets curve: Evidence from China. *Economic Modelling* 29(3): 566–576.

Junninen, H., Niska, H., Tuppurainen, K., Ruuskanen, J., and Kolehmainen, M. (2004). Methods for imputation of missing values in air quality data sets. *Atmospheric Environment* 38(18): 2895–2907.

Kabacoff, R. (2011). *R in Action: Data Analysis and Graphics With R*. New York: Manning Publishing Co.

King, G., Honaker, J., Joseph, A., and Scheve, K. (2001). Analyzing incomplete political science data: An alternative algorithm for multiple imputation. *The American Political Science Review* 95(1): 49–69.

Kuznets, S. (1955). Economic growth and income inequality. *The American Economic Review* 45(1): 1–28.

Lee, C.-C., Chiu, Y.-B., and Sun, C.-H. (2010). The environmental Kuznets curve hypothesis for water pollution: Do regions matter? *Energy Policy* 38(1): 12–23.

Little, R.J.A. (1988). A test of missing completely at random for multivariate data with missing values. *Journal of the American Statistical Association* 83(404): 1198–1202.

Managi, S., Hibiki, A., and Tsurumi, T. (2009). Does trade openness improve environmental quality? *Journal of Environmental Economics and Management* 58(3): 346–363.

Marcotullio, P. J. (2006). Faster growth of road transportation CO_2 emissions in Asia Pacific economies: Exploring differences in trends of the rapidly developing and developed worlds. *Bulletin of Science, Technology and Society* 26(2): 121–134.

Mazzanti, M., Montini, A., and Zoboli, R. (2007). Environmental Kuznets curves for GHGs and air pollutants in Italy. Evidence from sector environmental accounts and provincial data. *Economia Politica* 24(3): 369–406.

Millimet, D. L., List, J. A., and Stengos, T. (2003). The environmental Kuznets curve: Real progress or misspecified models? *Review of Economics and Statistics* 85(4): 1038–1047.

Miyama, E., and Managi, S. (2014). Global environmental emissions estimate: Application of multiple imputation, *Environmental Economics and Policy Studies* 16(2): 115–135.

Narayan, P. K., and Narayan, S. (2010). Carbon dioxide emissions and economic growth: Panel data evidence from developing countries. *Energy Policy* 38(1): 661–666.

Orubu, C. O., and Omotor, D. G. (2011). Environmental quality and economic growth: Searching for environmental Kuznets curves for air and water pollutants in Africa. *Energy Policy* 39(7): 4178–4188.

Rubin, D. B. (1976). Inference and missing data. *Biometrika* 63(3): 581–592.

Rubin, D. B. (1977). The design of a general and flexible system for handling non-response in sample surveys. Working document prepared for the U.S. Social Security Administration, Washington, DC.

Rubin, D. B., and Schenker, N. (1986). Multiple imputation for interval estimation from simple random samples with ignorable nonresponse. *Journal of the American Statistical Association* 81(394): 366–374.

Saboori, B., Sulaiman, J., and Mohd, S. (2012). Economic growth and CO_2 emissions in Malaysia: A cointegration analysis of the Environmental Kuznets Curve. *Energy Policy* 51: 184–191.

Shafik, N. (1994). Economic development and environmental quality: An econometric analysis. *Oxford Economic Papers* 46:757–773.

Shu, L., Fantang, Z., Huaiyang, F., and Zhencheng, X. (2012). An empirical test of the environmental Kuznets curve in Guangdong Province, China. *APCBEE Procedia* 1: 204–209.

Song, M.-L., Zhang, W., and Wang, S.-H. (2013). Inflection point of environmental Kuznets curve in Mainland China. *Energy Policy* 57: 14–20.

Stern, D. I. (2004). The rise and fall of the environmental Kuznets curve. *World Development* 32(8): 1419–1439.

Tsurumi, T., and Managi, S. (2010a). Decomposition of the environmental Kuznets curve: Scale, technique, and composition effects. *Environmental Economics and Policy Studies* 11: 19–36.

Tsurumi, T., and Managi, S. (2010b) Does energy substitution affect carbon dioxide emissions–income relationship? *Journal of the Japanese and International Economies* 24: 540–551.

Vincent, J. R. (1997). Testing for environmental Kuznets curves within a developing country. *Environment and Development Economics* 2:417–431.

Yaguchi, Y., Sonobe, T., and Otsuka, K. (2007). Beyond the environmental Kuznets curve: A comparative study of SO_2 and CO_2 emissions between Japan and China. *Environment and Development Economics* 12(3): 445–470.

Yang, J., Managi, S., and Sato, M. (2014). The effect of institutional quality on national wealth: An examination using multiple imputation method. *Environmental Economics and Policy Studies* (June): 1–23.

4

INDEX DECOMPOSITION ANALYSIS FOR TRACKING ENERGY EFFICIENCY TRENDS

Peng Zhou and Beng Wah Ang

1. Introduction

Energy efficiency is now an important public policy consideration in most countries in the face of rising world energy prices, increased volatility in global energy supply, and climate change. It is widely considered to be the most practical and cost-effective way to address the issues of "energy trilemma," i.e. energy security, economic competitiveness, and environmental sustainability. In many countries, including those in Asia, a wide range of measures have been or are being taken to improve energy efficiency across all major energy-consuming sectors in the economy. Naturally, in policy evaluation and performance assessment, the outcomes of these measures preferably should be studied and evaluated in a credible and transparent manner, such as to ascertain whether the intended targets are met. This can be achieved through the design and implementation of a robust accounting system to track and report energy efficiency trends on a regular basis.

One such an energy efficiency accounting system that has been implemented by some national energy agencies and international organizations is built upon the technique of index decomposition analysis (IDA). Originally used to study the impacts of changes in product mix on industrial electricity consumption in the early 1980s, IDA has since the mid-1990s been increasingly used to track sectoral or economy-wide energy efficiency trends. There were new developments and advancements in the technique of IDA over the years, and they have been incorporated by researchers and analysts in studies dealing with drivers of energy use, including the design of energy efficiency accounting systems.

In this chapter, the basic concepts of energy intensity and energy efficiency and how IDA is used to track energy efficiency trends are first reviewed. As there are many decomposition methods that can be adopted within the general IDA framework, we shall then focus on the most popular IDA method, namely the Logarithmic Mean Divisia Index (LMDI) method. The relevant LMDI decomposition analysis formulae are given for various decomposition procedures and how the results obtained can be extended to generate relevant composite indicators for tracking energy efficiency trends are explained. The results of an application study using the data of China finally are presented.

2. Energy intensity versus energy efficiency

2.1 Energy intensity

The term energy intensity (EI) refers to energy use per unit of output or service that is achieved or provided through energy input. In energy demand analysis, where energy consumption is often captured in terms of how it is used in addition to the amount consumed, energy intensity may be defined at different levels of sector or activity disaggregation, e.g. economy-wide, sector, sub-sector, end use, process and device, to serve different needs. Since activity output or service level can be expressed in either monetary or physical terms, there are two common types of EI indicators, namely monetary-based indicators and physical-based indicators.

Both monetary and physical EI indicators are widely used in energy consumption studies. In energy efficiency analysis, physical indicators generally are preferred but monetary indicators often are adopted when appropriate physical indicators cannot be found or the required data are not available. This applies to, for instance, some manufacturing activities such as the production of food, furniture, and electronics products. The choice between the two types of indicators also is dependent on the level of activity or sector disaggregation chosen in an analysis. For example, for economy-wide energy consumption analysis which comprises a spectrum of activities, the activity level is often given by the gross domestic product (GDP). The corresponding EI indicator, the energy-GDP ratio, is a well-known and widely reported monetary EI indicator. Similarly, for the manufacturing industry as a whole, the overall output or activity level is generally given in monetary terms so that all manufacturing activities can be appropriately aggregated, and the most often used EI indicator in this case is the energy use per value added.

In comparison, physical EI indicators more often are adopted at a lower level of sector or activity aggregation, since an appropriate physical indicator that captures the output or service level at such a level is more likely to be available. Examples are energy use in the production of some specific manufacturing products, such as iron and steel, cement, and petrochemicals, where their energy intensities can be given by energy use per ton of the product produced. For some energy-consuming sectors, physical EI indicators can be used at different levels of sector disaggregation. They include, for example, energy use per passenger-kilometre for passenger transport and energy use per unit floor area for buildings. Among the four major sectors of final energy use in an economy, namely transport, residential, industry, and service, physical EI indicators often are adopted for the first two, while monetary EI indicators are more likely to be used for the last two sectors.

2.2 Energy efficiency

Energy efficiency (EE) is a generic term that may be used in many different contexts, including engineering, economic, and environmental. For instance, it is treated by physicists and engineers as a technical efficiency but by economists as an economic efficiency. The definitions used by national energy agencies and international organisations are more general and encompassing, as they must be meaningful, practical, and applicable for all sectors of energy use in an economy. The following are some examples of these encompassing definitions: "How effectively energy is being used for a given purpose" (Canadian Office of Energy Efficiency), "A change to energy use that results in an increase in net benefits per unit of energy" (New Zealand's Energy Efficiency and Conservation Authority), "The ratio of the amount of energy services provided to the amount of energy consumed" (US Energy Information Administration), "A ratio between an output of performance, service, goods or energy, and an input of energy" (European Commission, Directive 2006/32/EC), and "A reduction in the energy used for a given service (heating, lighting, etc.) or level of activity" (World Energy Council).

Conceptually there is little difference among all these definitions. Energy efficiency improvement simply refers to using less energy to provide the same level of energy services or providing more energy services from the same energy input. Energy services are services or benefits arising from the use of energy, which range from specific applications such as lighting, heating, cooling, and moving people and goods to basic human or economic actions that drive energy use. They may be measured by activity indicators such as tonnes or dollars of output of a specific industry activity, tonne-kilometres carried by trucks or railways, and air-conditioning per unit of floor space. The resulting EE indicators, as in the case of the EI indicators, can be physical-based or monetary-based.

It can be seen that the reciprocal of an EI indicator is in fact an EE indicator. Indeed, in energy efficiency analysis, the concept of energy efficiency and that of intensity can be used interchangeably. In tracking energy efficiency trends of an energy-consuming sector or economy-wide, the normal practice is to devise a set of EI indicators, use them to measure, study, and track changes, and the results obtained are aggregated and transformed in an appropriate manner to give changes in energy efficiency trends. These are the steps taken in most accounting systems to track economy-wide energy efficiency trends.

2.3 Composite energy intensity index

The energy-GDP ratio, i.e. energy use per unit of GDP, has long been used by researchers and analysts to track changes in economy-wide energy efficiency. Data on the ratio are widely tabulated in national and international statistical publications. It has some good properties as an EI indicator, including simplicity, readily available data, and ease of understanding. However, changes in the energy-GDP ratio may arise from sources unrelated to energy efficiency, such as activity structure change. As such, an alternative approach is needed to tracking sectoral and economy-wide energy efficiency trends in a more sophisticated and effective way.

An economy or a major energy-consuming sector comprises a spectrum of heterogeneous activities. The alternative approach that has been widely adopted is what is known as the "bottom-up" approach. In this approach, a change in the EI indicator of an activity between two points in time or between two time periods, i.e. the performance change over time, is quantified either in absolute terms or in relative terms by an index. In the latter case, the indexes obtained for various activities can be aggregated level by level in an appropriate and reasonable manner. In this way and depending on the level of sector disaggregation, energy efficiency performance can be evaluated by major sector, such as for transport or industry, or economy-wide. This leads to the creation of composite energy intensity (CEI) indexes which may be used in place of, or to complement, the energy-GDP ratio for tracking energy efficiency trends.

Many Organisation for Economic Development and Co-operation countries have implemented an accounting system that creates CEI indexes or their equivalents to track economy-wide and sectoral energy efficiency trends (Ang et al., 2010). These indexes are derived through aggregating end-use energy intensities to sub-sector intensities, then to sector intensities, and finally to an economy-wide composite index. A commonly used approach to constructing the CEI index is to divide energy consumption in an economy into several major energy-consuming sectors. The index decomposition analysis (IDA) technique is then employed to decompose consumption change in each sector using energy end-use data to single out the energy intensity effect. This effect captures the impact of changes in energy efficiency on energy use in the sector. The aggregation of the estimated intensity effects for all the sectors, with further transformation where appropriate, gives the economy-wide CEI index. At the same time, through applying IDA, other impacts on energy use, such as changes in overall activity level and activity mix, also are revealed.

3. Index decomposition analysis

3.1 Basic identities and formulae

Assume that an economy is divided into m major energy-consuming sectors and for each sector the activity indicators are measured in the same measurement unit. Define the following variables which are normally measured on an annual basis.

E_i: Total energy consumption in sector i

E_{ij}: Energy consumption in sub-sector/end user j of sector i

Q_i: Total activity level of sector i

Q_{ij}: Activity level of sub-sector j in sector i

S_{ij}: Activity share of sub-sector j in sector i ($= Q_{ij}/Q_i$)

I_{ij}: Energy intensity of sub-sector j in sector i ($= E_{ij}/Q_{ij}$)

I_i: Energy intensity of sector i ($= E_i/Q_i$)

The energy consumption in sector i (E_i) as an aggregate indicator can be expressed as the sum of energy consumption in n_i different sub-sectors or end users, which may be further expressed in the form

$$E_i = \sum_{j=1}^{n_i} E_{ij} = \sum_{j=1}^{n_i} Q_i \frac{Q_{ij}}{Q_i} \frac{E_{ij}}{Q_{ij}} = \sum_{j=1}^{n_i} Q_i S_{ij} I_{ij} \tag{4.1}$$

Equation (4.1) is an identity which is the most basic form in IDA applied to energy consumption.

Let $\Delta E_i^{0,T}$ be the change in the energy consumption in sector i from one year to another, say year 0 to year T. According to Eq. (4.1), this change can be explained in terms of three effects, namely the activity effect, structure effect and intensity effect, i.e.

$$\Delta E_i^{0,T} = E_i^T - E_i^0 = \Delta E_{i-act}^{0,T} + \Delta E_{i-str}^{0,T} + \Delta E_{i-int}^{0,T} \tag{4.2}$$

The activity effect refers to the change in the aggregate energy consumption associated with a change in the total activity level of sector i, the structural effect denotes the change associated with changes in the activity shares of sub-sectors, and the intensity effect refers to the change associated with changes in the sub-sector energy intensities.

In Eq. (4.2), the absolute change in the energy consumption is decomposed into three explanatory effects. Similarly, one can decompose the relative change in the energy consumption, i.e. the ratio of energy consumption in year T to that in year 0, into the three effects as follows:

$$D_i^{0,T} = E_i^T / E_i^0 = D_{i-act}^{0,T} \cdot D_{i-str}^{0,T} \cdot D_{i-int}^{0,T} \tag{4.3}$$

In the IDA literature, the form in Eq. (4.2) is referred to as additive decomposition while that in Eq. (4.3) as multiplicative decomposition.

In addition to decomposing changes in energy consumption, researchers also have conducted research on decomposing changes in the aggregate energy intensity. The aggregate energy intensity of sector i, defined as the ratio of energy consumption (E_i) to activity level (Q_i), may be expressed as the following identity

$$I_i = \sum_{j=1}^{n_i} \frac{Q_{ij}}{Q_i} \frac{E_{ij}}{Q_{ij}} = \sum_{j=1}^{n_i} S_{ij} I_{ij} \tag{4.4}$$

Let $\Delta I_i^{0,T}$ denote the change in the aggregate energy intensity of sector i from year 0 to year T. Based on Eq. (4.4), the aggregate energy intensity is composed of two factors, i.e. activity share and sub-sector energy intensity. Therefore, a change in the aggregate energy intensity can be additively decomposed in the following form

$$\Delta I_i^{0,T} = I_i^T - I_i^0 = \Delta I_{i-str}^{0,T} + \Delta I_{i-int}^{0,T} \tag{4.5}$$

where the first and second terms on the right-hand-side of the equation are respectively referred to as the structural effect and the intensity effect. Similarly, one can also decompose the relative change in the energy intensity into the product of structural effect and intensity effect, i.e.

$$R_i^{0,T} = I_i^T / I_i^0 = R_{i-str}^{0,T} \cdot R_{i-int}^{0,T} \tag{4.6}$$

The previous procedure is the basis of IDA and has become a major analytical technique for studying factors driving changes over time in aggregate energy consumption, energy intensity, greenhouse gas emissions, and emission intensity. It also has been used to create CEI for tracking energy efficiency trends. The formulae shown in the foregoing are the most basic form, i.e. only activity, structural, and intensity effects are considered. It is possible to expand and study contributions of other factors if the identities given by Eqs. (4.1) and (4.4) are expressed to include these other factors. The key issue of IDA is then how to derive the contributing effects based on the identity defined in a fair, reasonable, and practical manner.

3.2 Decomposition methods

In IDA a number of decomposition methods have been proposed by researchers to quantify the contributing factors that drive changes in an aggregate of interest. A comprehensive survey of IDA in energy and environmental studies can be found in Ang and Zhang (2000). The strengths and weaknesses of various IDA methods are presented in Ang (2004) and Ang and Liu (2007). Discussions on the properties and linkages of different IDA methods can be found in Ang et al. (2009). The general consensus is that the LMDI method is the preferred method from both the theoretical and application viewpoints. It also has been the most widely used method among researchers and analysts, including for tracking energy efficiency trends. See, for example, Ang et al. (2010), Fernandez Gonzalez et al. (2012), Inglesi-Lotz and Pouris (2012), and Shahiduzzaman and Alam (2013).

In view of its merits and popularity, only LMDI will be introduced in this chapter. An introduction to the method can be found in Ang (2004, 2005). The method has two versions, namely LMDI-I and LMDI-II. Both have very similar functional form. The only difference lies in the weighting scheme, and the scheme for LMDI-II is slightly more complicated than LMDI-I. A comparison between LMDI-I and LMDI-II is provided in Ang et al. (2003).

Table 4.1 shows the LMDI-I and LMDI-II decomposition formulae for quantifying factors contributing to changes in energy consumption and energy intensity as described in Section 3.1. In the table, the logarithmic mean weight function $L(a,b)$, first introduced to IDA by Ang and Choi (1997), is given by

$$L(a,b) = \begin{cases} (a-b)/\ln(a/b) & \text{if } a \neq b \\ 0 & \text{if } a = b \end{cases} \tag{4.7}$$

Table 4.1 LMDI formulae for decomposing changes in energy consumption and energy intensity

		LMDI-I	LMDI-II
Energy consumption	$\Delta E_i^{0,T}$	$\Delta E_{i-act}^{0,T} =$ $$\sum_{j=1}^{n_i} L(E_{ij}^T, E_{ij}^0) \ln \frac{Q_i^T}{Q_i^0}$$	$\Delta E_{i-act}^{0,T} =$ $$\sum_{j=1}^{n_i} \frac{L(E_{ij}^T / E_i^T, E_{ij}^0 / E_i^0) \cdot L(E_i^T, E_i^0)}{\sum_{j=1}^{n_i} L(E_{ij}^T / E_i^T, E_{ij}^0 / E_i^0)} \ln \frac{Q_i^T}{Q_i^0}$$
		$\Delta E_{i-str}^{0,T} =$ $$\sum_{j=1}^{n_i} L(E_{ij}^T, E_{ij}^0) \ln \frac{S_{ij}^T}{S_{ij}^0}$$	$\Delta E_{i-str}^{0,T} =$ $$\sum_{j=1}^{n_i} \frac{L(E_{ij}^T / E_i^T, E_{ij}^0 / E_i^0) \cdot L(E_i^T, E_i^0)}{\sum_{j=1}^{n_i} L(E_{ij}^T / E_i^T, E_{ij}^0 / E_i^0)} \ln \frac{S_{ij}^T}{S_{ij}^0}$$
		$\Delta E_{i-int}^{0,T} =$ $$\sum_{j=1}^{n_i} L(E_{ij}^T, E_{ij}^0) \ln \frac{I_{ij}^T}{I_{ij}^0}$$	$\Delta E_{i-int}^{0,T} =$ $$\sum_{j=1}^{n_i} \frac{L(E_{ij}^T / E_i^T, E_{ij}^0 / E_i^0) \cdot L(E_i^T, E_i^0)}{\sum_{j=1}^{n_i} L(E_{ij}^T / E_i^T, E_{ij}^0 / E_i^0)} \ln \frac{I_{ij}^T}{I_{ij}^0}$$
	$D_i^{0,T}$	$D_{i-act}^{0,T} =$ $$\exp\left(\sum_{j=1}^{n_i} \frac{L(E_{ij}^T, E_{ij}^0)}{L(E_i^T, E_i^0)} \ln \frac{Q_i^T}{Q_i^0}\right)$$	$D_{i-act}^{0,T} =$ $$\exp\left(\sum_{j=1}^{n_i} \frac{L(E_{ij}^T / E_i^T, E_{ij}^0 / E_i^0)}{\sum_{j=1}^{n_i} L(E_{ij}^T / E_i^T, E_{ij}^0 / E_i^0)} \ln \frac{Q_i^T}{Q_i^0}\right)$$
		$D_{i-str}^{0,T} =$ $$\exp\left(\sum_{j=1}^{n_i} \frac{L(E_{ij}^T, E_{ij}^0)}{L(E_i^T, E_i^0)} \ln \frac{S_{ij}^T}{S_{ij}^0}\right)$$	$D_{i-str}^{0,T} =$ $$\exp\left(\sum_{j=1}^{n_i} \frac{L(E_{ij}^T / E_i^T, E_{ij}^0 / E_i^0)}{\sum_{j=1}^{n_i} L(E_{ij}^T / E_i^T, E_{ij}^0 / E_i^0)} \ln \frac{S_{ij}^T}{S_{ij}^0}\right)$$
		$D_{i-int}^{0,T} =$ $$\exp\left(\sum_{j=1}^{n_i} \frac{L(E_{ij}^T, E_{ij}^0)}{L(E_i^T, E_i^0)} \ln \frac{I_{ij}^T}{I_{ij}^0}\right)$$	$D_{i-int}^{0,T} =$ $$\exp\left(\sum_{j=1}^{n_i} \frac{L(E_{ij}^T / E_i^T, E_{ij}^0 / E_i^0)}{\sum_{j=1}^{n_i} L(E_{ij}^T / E_i^T, E_{ij}^0 / E_i^0)} \ln \frac{I_{ij}^T}{I_{ij}^0}\right)$$
Energy intensity	$\Delta I_i^{0,T}$	$\Delta I_{i-str}^{0,T} =$ $$\sum_{j=1}^{n_i} L(V_{ij}^T, V_{ij}^0) \ln \frac{S_{ij}^T}{S_{ij}^0}$$	$\Delta I_{i-str}^{0,T} =$ $$\sum_{j=1}^{n_i} \frac{L(E_{ij}^T / E_i^T, E_{ij}^0 / E_i^0) \cdot L(I_i^T, I_i^0)}{\sum_{j=1}^{n_i} L(E_{ij}^T / E_i^T, E_{ij}^0 / E_i^0)} \ln \frac{S_{ij}^T}{S_{ij}^0}$$
		$\Delta I_{i-int}^{0,T} =$ $$\sum_{j=1}^{n_i} L(V_{ij}^T, V_{ij}^0) \ln \frac{I_{ij}^T}{I_{ij}^0}$$	$\Delta I_{i-int}^{0,T} =$ $$\sum_{j=1}^{n_i} \frac{L(E_{ij}^T / E_i^T, E_{ij}^0 / E_i^0) \cdot L(I_i^T, I_i^0)}{\sum_{j=1}^{n_i} L(E_{ij}^T / E_i^T, E_{ij}^0 / E_i^0)} \ln \frac{I_{ij}^T}{I_{ij}^0}$$
	$R_i^{0,T}$	$R_{i-str}^{0,T} =$ $$\exp\left(\sum_{j=1}^{n_i} \frac{L(V_{ij}^T, V_{ij}^0)}{L(I_i^T, I_i^0)} \ln \frac{S_{ij}^T}{S_{ij}^0}\right)$$	$R_{i-str}^{0,T} =$ $$\exp\left(\sum_{j=1}^{n_i} \frac{L(E_{ij}^T / E_i^T, E_{ij}^0 / E_i^0)}{\sum_{j=1}^{n_i} L(E_{ij}^T / E_i^T, E_{ij}^0 / E_i^0)} \ln \frac{S_{ij}^T}{S_{ij}^0}\right)$$
		$R_{i-int}^{0,T} =$ $$\exp\left(\sum_{j=1}^{n_i} \frac{L(V_{ij}^T, V_{ij}^0)}{L(I_i^T, I_i^0)} \ln \frac{I_{ij}^T}{I_{ij}^0}\right)$$	$R_{i-int}^{0,T} =$ $$\exp\left(\sum_{j=1}^{n_i} \frac{L(E_{ij}^T / E_i^T, E_{ij}^0 / E_i^0)}{\sum_{j=1}^{n_i} L(E_{ij}^T / E_i^T, E_{ij}^0 / E_i^0)} \ln \frac{I_{ij}^T}{I_{ij}^0}\right)$$

Note: $V_{ij}^T = E_{ij}^T / Q_i^T$, $V_{ij}^0 = E_{ij}^0 / Q_i^0$.

4. Composite energy intensity index

We take the energy intensity effect derived from IDA as a proxy for energy efficiency change and use it to create a CEI index. The underlying concept is the same as that described in Section 2.3 except that through the application of IDA information on other drivers of energy consumption, such as the activity and structure effects also are revealed. This procedure has been adopted in the energy efficiency accounting framework developed by many national energy agencies and international organizations. The study by Ang et al. (2010) assesses a number of such accounting frameworks and highlights the strengths of the LMDI-based accounting framework. In the sections that follow, we describe how a CEI index within the LMDI accounting framework can be developed when changes in energy consumption and in energy intensity are respectively decomposed.

4.1 Energy consumption approach

As shown in Table 4.1, the additive decomposition scheme for energy consumption allows the activity, structural, and intensity effects to be quantified. It can be proven that their sum is equal to the absolute change in aggregate energy consumption, which is referred to as zero residual property in IDA. The intensity effect can be conveniently taken as energy savings due to efficiency improvement in period T, i.e.

$$ES_i^T = -\Delta E_{i-int}^{0,T} \tag{4.8}$$

From Eq. (4.8), we can further define an indicator called the hypothetical energy consumption (EH) for sector i. Defined as the energy consumption that would have been had there been no improvement in energy efficiency from period 0 to T, EH is given by

$$EH_i^T = E_i^T - \Delta E_{i-int}^{0,T} \tag{4.9}$$

We can then define a CEI index as the ratio of the actual energy intensity to the hypothetical energy intensity, i.e.

$$CEI_i^{\Delta E} = \frac{E_i^T / Q_i^T}{EH_i^T / Q_i^T} = \frac{E_i^T}{E_i^T - \Delta E_{i-int}^{0,T}} \tag{4.10}$$

As pointed out by Ang et al. (2010), Eq. (4.10) is the energy efficiency improvement indicator used by the Energy Efficiency and Conservation Authority (EECA) of New Zealand. While both LMDI-I and LMDI-II are equally applicable here, the EECA accounting framework is based on the latter.

When the multiplicative LMDI is used, the energy intensity effect obtained can be directly taken as a CEI index (Ang, 2006). Mathematically, the CEI index can be transformed into a weighted product of the energy intensity indexes for all the sub-sectors, i.e.

$$CEI_i^D = D_{i-int}^{0,T} = \prod_{j=1}^{n_i} \left(\frac{I_{ij}^T}{I_{ij}^0} \right)^{w_{ij}^D} \tag{4.11}$$

The weights in Eq. (4.11) are dependent on the choice between LMDI-I and LMDI-II. For LMDI-I we have $w_{ij}^D = L(E_{ij}^T, E_{ij}^0) / L(E_i^T, E_i^0)$, while in the case of LMDI-II we have $w_{ij}^D = L(E_{ij}^T / E_i^T, E_{ij}^0 / E_i^0) / \sum_{i=1}^{n} L(E_{ij}^T / E_i^T, E_{ij}^0 / E_i^0)$.

The weighted product method as an aggregation tool in constructing composite indicators has been recommended in many previous studies. For example, the studies by Zhou et al. (2006) and Zhou and Ang (2009) show that in using this method less information is lost as compared to other aggregation methods. However, it requires that the weights for sub-indicators be first determined. These weights can be generated from appropriate optimization models in an objective way as in Zhou et al. (2010), but this requires additional input from experts which is often difficult to obtain. In contrast, the CEI index derived from the LMDI method uses a set of pre-defined weights with some desirable features, including the zero residual property.

An issue about Eq. (4.11) is the choice between LMDI-I and LMDI-II. Their application will lead to some minor difference in the decomposition results. The studies by Ang (2006) and Ang et al. (2010) recommend LMDI-I due to its simplicity and ease of use. However, for LMDI-II, the sum of the weights is equal to one, which makes Eq. (4.11) a genuine weighted geometric mean. Recently, Fernandez Gonzalez et al. (2012) extend Choi and Ang (2012) and employ LMDI-II to define CEI indexes for 20 European countries. For both LMDI-I and LMDI-II, a simple analytical relationship exists between additive and multiplicative decomposition results. By virtue of the relationship, the CEI index can be directly computed from the intensity effect given by the additive decomposition scheme (i.e. energy savings) and vice versa (Ang, et al., 2010).

4.2 Energy intensity approach

While the intensity effect obtained by decomposing energy consumption change can be used to construct a CEI index, it is also possible to first decompose aggregate energy intensity change and then use the resulting intensity effect to derive a CEI index. Using the intensity effect from the additive LMDI method, we again define an indicator called hypothetical energy intensity (*IH*) for sector *i* with the assumption that there had been no energy efficiency improvement from period 0 to period *T*:

$$IH_i^T = I_i^T - \Delta I_{i-int}^{0,T} \tag{4.12}$$

Similar to Eq. (4.10), a CEI index can be defined as the ratio of the actual energy intensity to the hypothetical energy intensity in period *T*, i.e.

$$CEI_i^{\Delta I} = \frac{I_i^T}{IH_i^T} = \frac{I_i^T}{I_i^T - \Delta I_{i-int}^{0,T}} \tag{4.13}$$

When the multiplicative LMDI is used to decompose aggregate energy intensity change, the intensity effect may be directly taken as a CEI index, which is essentially a weighted product of the energy intensity indexes for all the sub-sectors. Mathematically, the CEI index can be formulated as

$$CEI_i^R = R_{i-int}^{0,T} = \prod_{j=1}^{n_i} \left(\frac{I_{ij}^T}{I_{ij}^0} \right)^{w_{ij}^R} \tag{4.14}$$

It can be seen that the only difference between Eq. (4.11) and Eq. (4.14) lies in the weights used. In Eq. (4.14), w_{ij}^R is equal to $L(E_{ij}^T / Q_i^T, E_{ij}^0 / Q_i^0) / L(I_i^T, I_i^0)$ in LMDI-I while it is equal to $L(E_{ij}^T / E_i^T, E_{ij}^0 / E_i^0) / \sum_{j=1}^{n} L(E_{ij}^T / E_i^T, E_{ij}^0 / E_i^0)$ in LMDI-II. Interestingly, for LMDI-II, decomposing aggregate energy intensity and decomposing aggregate energy consumption produce the same intensity effect.

In summary, a CEI index can be developed through decomposing the change in aggregate energy consumption or energy intensity. Within an LMDI energy efficiency accounting framework proposed by Ang et al. (2010), both LMDI-I and LMDI-II, in additive or multiplicative form, may be used to create a CEI index for tracking sectoral or economy-wide energy efficiency trends. While the additive LMDI method can provide additional information like energy savings, the multiplicative LMDI method is essentially a weighted geometric mean model in which the weights are determined by several logarithm mean weight functions. As in the choice of a decomposition method in IDA studies, different methods or models used will produce different CEI indexes.

4.3 Simple example

Assume that industry is divided only into two sectors. One of the sectors is energy intensive while the other is not. The relevant data are shown in Table 4.2. From year 0 to year T, the aggregate energy intensity increases by 22.5 percent. However, the energy intensities of both sectors drop, which indicates that energy efficiency improvement takes place from year 0 to year T.

Table 4.3 shows the CEI estimates using the methods presented in the foregoing sections. It is found that the CEI indexes are less than unity, which indicates improvement in energy efficiency from year 0 to year T. This is consistent with the observed decreases in the sectoral energy intensities of both sectors. In this example, the CEI indexes based on the additive decomposition scheme are always closer to unity compared to those based on the multiplicative decomposition scheme. Also, the estimates given by the energy consumption approach are generally closer to unity as compared to those based on the energy intensity approach when the same formula is used. In the previous cases, a CEI index closer to unity implies a smaller improvement in energy efficiency. It also can be seen that the results for LMDI-I and LMDI-II are very close to each other.

4.4 Some methodological issues

The formulae in the earlier sections are based on the data for two years and the CEI index for year 0 is implicitly assumed to be unity. This kind of analysis is called non-chaining analysis in IDA. When data are available only for two non-consecutive years, non-chaining analysis is the only option available to the analyst. When yearly time-series data are available, decomposition

Table 4.2 Data for a simple example (arbitrary units)

	Year 0				Year T			
	E_0	Q_0	S_0	I_0	E_T	Q_T	S_T	I_T
Sector 1	60	20	0.2	3.0	120	48	0.4	2.5
Sector 2	40	80	0.8	0.5	27	72	0.6	0.375
Total	100	100	1.0	1.0	147	120	1.0	1.225

Table 4.3 Estimates of CEI index for year T for different procedures (CEI is equal to 1 for year 0)

	Energy consumption approach		Energy intensity approach	
	Additive	*Multiplicative*	*Additive*	*Multiplicative*
LMDI-I	0.853	0.813	0.842	0.812
LMDI-II	0.850	0.809	0.839	0.809

can be conducted for each two consecutive years and the resulting estimates can then be "chained" cumulatively, and this is referred to as chaining analysis. For instance, to compute the CEI index for year T one may use the data for all the $T+1$ years from 0 to T and conduct the decomposition for every two consecutive years. In this way, we can compute a series of CEI indexes with the earlier year treated as the base year. If year 0 is taken as the reference year, the CEI index for year T can be derived by computing the cumulative product of the CEI indexes for all the years. As non-chaining and chaining analyses produce different results, the choice between them becomes necessary in constructing a CEI index series. As pointed out in Ang et al. (2010), chaining analysis generally is preferred as it provides a more representative measure of changes in energy efficiency over time.

Method selection in decomposition analysis is another issue in the creation of CEI. It is known that the LMDI accounting framework has several desirable properties compared to other accounting frameworks for tracking energy efficiency trends. However, within the LMDI accounting framework, as shown in Section 4, there is still a need to choose an appropriate decomposition method. The choice may depend on the characteristics of the data used and study objective. When time-series data are available and the creation of CEI indexes is the main objective, the multiplicative LMDI is more appropriate. In particular, LMDI-II is recommended in view of the consistency results given by the energy consumption approach and the energy intensity approach. If results in absolute terms, including energy savings, are sought, the energy consumption approach using additive LMDI-I is recommended. As shown in Ang et al. (2009), LMDI-I in the additive form is perfect in decomposition not only at the aggregate level but also at the sub-category level, a desirable property which LMDI-II does not possess.

5. Case study

We present a case study on China's manufacturing sector to illustrate the derivation of CEI indexes. The sector consists of 30 sub-sectors, of which two sub-sectors, 'manufacturing of artwork and other manufacturing' and 'recycling and disposal of waste,' are excluded due to changes in sector coverage over time. The energy consumption data were collected from National Bureau of Statistics of China (see http://data.stats.gov.cn/workspace/index?m=hgnd). The activity indicator is given by value added (in 1990 constant prices) and the data from 2000 to 2008 are based on Chen (2011), while those in 2009–2011 were calculated from monthly growth rates by sub-sector. The monthly growth rates of industrial value added for each sub-sector in 2009–2011 were collected from the same website. From 2000 to 2011, the energy consumption increased from 794 to 1,987 million tons of standard coal equivalent (Mtce). Over the same period, the total value added increased from 1,604 to 10,406 billion Yuan. The aggregate energy intensity for the sector, defined as the ratio of energy consumption to total value added, decreased by 61 percent from 2000 to 2011.

The eight decomposition procedures described in Section 4 are employed to compute the CEI indexes in 2001–2011. Figure 4.1 shows the average values of the CEI indexes derived from the eight procedures, respectively for non-chaining and chaining analysis. The aggregate energy intensity index with 2000 as the reference year is also shown in the figure. As revealed by the results, there is a wide gap between the aggregate energy intensity index and the CEI indexes. In fact, progress in energy efficiency would be overestimated using the aggregate energy intensity. Based on the CEI indexes, improvement in manufacturing energy efficiency from 2000 to 2011 was about 50 percent. It also can be seen from Figure 4.1 that the CEI index series derived from

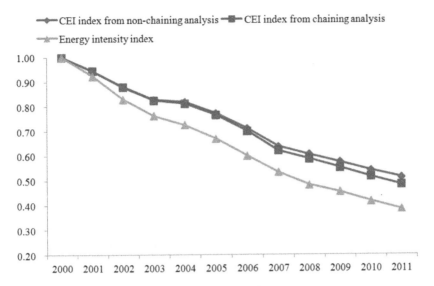

Figure 4.1 CEI indexes from non-chaining and chaining analysis

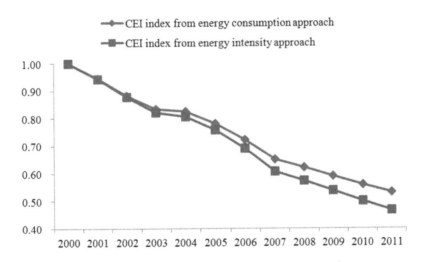

Figure 4.2 CEI indexes from energy consumption and energy intensity approaches

non-chaining analysis is above that of chaining analysis, which means a slower progress in energy efficiency improvement using non-chaining results.

Figure 4.2 compares the average CEI index series derived using the energy consumption approach and that derived using the energy intensity approach. In this particular case, the results show that the energy consumption approach gives higher CEI index estimates and hence slower progress in energy efficiency improvement. The 2011 CEI index is 0.53 for the energy consumption approach, while 0.47 for the energy intensity approach. Figure 4.3 shows the average CEI index series derived by applying LMDI-I and LMDI-II. The differences are so small that the

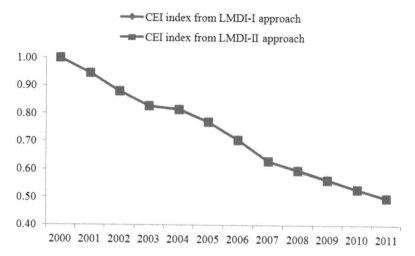

Figure 4.3 CEI indexes from LMDI-I and LMDI-II approaches

two series actually overlap. For instance, the 2011 CEI index for LMDI-I is 0.499, while that for LMDI-II is 0.497. The results show that the choice between LMDI-I and LMDI-II are inconsequential in practice.

6. Conclusion

Tracking economy-wide energy efficiency trends for performance assessment and policy evaluation will grow in importance as countries increasingly put more emphasis on energy efficiency to tackle issues related to energy security, economic competitiveness, and environmental sustainability. It is particular relevant to Asian economies, as growth in their energy demand and energy-related carbon dioxide emissions generally have been high and are expected to remain high in the foreseeable future unless strong measures are taken. There is, therefore, a need for the Asian economies to deploy appropriate accounting systems to serve energy efficiency tracking purposes.

In this chapter, based on the well-established LMDI decomposition technique in IDA, we describe such an accounting system. The energy consumption and energy intensity approaches are introduced that can be used to create CEI indexes for tracking energy efficiency trends. Both LMDI-I and LMDI-II in the additive and multiplicative forms are considered, which leads to a total of eight alternative procedures. While the procedures are described with reference to a sector, they also can be used to create an economy-wide CEI index which involves the aggregation of sectoral results as reported in Ang et al. (2010).

The case study using the data for China's manufacturing sector from 2000 to 2011 shows how the accounting system can be fruitfully applied. In terms of the progress made in energy efficiency, the case study also shows large differences between the results given by the computed CEI indexes and those revealed by the commonly used aggregate energy intensity, i.e. the energy-GDP ratio. This shows the need for creating a CEI index to either replace or supplement the latter in tracking energy efficiency trends and for performance assessment.

References

Ang, B.W., 2004. Decomposition analysis for policymaking in energy: which is the preferred method? *Energy Policy* 32, 1131–1139.

Ang, B.W., 2005. The LMDI approach to decomposition analysis: a practical guide. *Energy Policy* 33, 867–871.

Ang, B.W., 2006. Monitoring changes in economy-wide energy efficiency: from energy-GDP ratio to composite efficiency index. *Energy Policy* 34, 574–582.

Ang, B.W., and K.H. Choi, 1997. Decomposition of aggregate energy and gas emission intensity for industry: a refined Divisia index method. *The Energy Journal* 18(3), 59–73.

Ang, B.W., Huang, H.C., and Mu, A.R., 2009. Properties and linkages of some index decomposition analysis methods. *Energy Policy* 37, 4624–4632.

Ang, B.W., Liu, F.L., and Chew, E.P., 2003. Perfect decomposition techniques in energy and environmental analysis. *Energy Policy* 31, 1561–1566.

Ang, B.W., and Liu, N., 2007. Energy decomposition analysis: IEA model versus other methods. *Energy Policy* 35, 1426–1432.

Ang, B.W., Mu, A.R., and Zhou, P., 2010. Accounting frameworks for tracking energy efficiency trends. *Energy Economics* 32, 1209–1219.

Ang, B.W., and Xu, X.Y., 2013. Tracking industrial energy efficiency trends using index decomposition analysis. *Energy Economics* 40, 1014–1021.

Ang, B.W., and Zhang, F.Q., 2000. A survey of index decomposition analysis in energy and environmental studies. *Energy* 25, 1149–1176.

Chen, S.Y., 2011. Reconstruction of sub2-industrial statistical data in China: 1980–2008. *China Economic Quarterly* 10, 735–776.

Choi, K.H., and Ang, B.W., 2012. Attribution of changes in Divisia real energy intensity index – an extension to index decomposition analysis. *Energy Economics* 34, 171–176.

EERE, 2008. Indicators of Energy Intensity in the United States. Office of Energy Efficiency and Renewable Energy, US Department of Energy. Available at: http://www1.eere.energy.gov/ba/pba/intensityindicators/.

Fernandez Gonzalez, P., Landajo, M., and Presno, M.J., 2012. The Divisia real energy intensity indices: evolution and attribution of percent changes in 20 European countries from 1995 to 2010. *Energy* 58, 340–349.

Inglesi-Lotz, R., and Pouris, A., 2012. Energy efficiency in South Africa: a decomposition exercise. *Energy* 42, 113–120.

Shahiduzzaman, M., and Alam, K., 2013. Changes in energy efficiency in Australia: a decomposition of aggregate energy intensity using logarithmic mean Divisia approach. *Energy Policy* 56, 341–351.

Zhou, P., Ang, B.W., 2009. Comparing MCDA aggregation methods in constructing composite indicators using the Shannon-Spearman measure. *Social Indicators Research* 94, 83–96.

Zhou, P., Ang, B.W., and Poh, K.L., 2006. Comparing aggregating methods for constructing the composite environmental index: an objective measure. *Ecological Economics* 59, 305–311.

Zhou, P., Ang, B.W., Zhou, D.Q., 2010. Weighting and aggregation in composite indicator construction: a multiplicative optimization approach. *Social Indicators Research* 96, 169–181.

5

A CROSS-COUNTRY DECOMPOSITION ANALYSIS OF GREENHOUSE GAS EMISSIONS IN ASIAN COUNTRIES

Hainan Shi, Shunsuke Okamoto, Shigemi Kagawa
and Keisuke Nansai

1. Introduction

Greenhouse gases (GHG) are atmospheric gasses that absorb and reflect radiation within the thermal infrared range. In combination, these processes are considered to be the principle causes of the greenhouse effect, as well as being responsible for the gradual increase in global temperatures (see e.g., Hansen et al., 2001). The emission of greenhouse gasses, such as carbon dioxide, etc., results in part from the combustion of petroleum, coal, and natural gas for goods production, transportation, and electricity (see Raupach, 2007). In order to reduce emissions of GHG, many countries ratified the Kyoto Protocol,[1] the primary objective of which was stated as, "During the period from 2008 to 2012, six types of GHG emissions across countries will be reduced by 5 percent of the total compared to 1990." However, this commitment applies only to Annex I countries,[2] and we need to concentrate on the roles that both Annex I countries and Non-Annex I countries[3] play in global ecology.

The rapid increase observed in non-Annex I emissions primarily is due to their relatively high rates of economic growth. Among the non-Annex I nations, South Korea and China both benefit from increased production competitiveness. The gross domestic product (GDP) of China in 2010 was US$5.88 trillion, which exceeded that of Japan at US$5.46 trillion and was second only to the GDP of the U.S. at US$14.66 trillion (see the World Economic Outlook Database of the International Monetary Fund (IMF)).[4] While economic growth is considered to benefit the world, it also can harm the environment. The emission of carbon dioxide – the main GHG – is increasing sharply. In 2010, CO_2 emissions by China amounted to 3.47 billion tons, ranking second of 178 countries and for of the Non-Annex I parties.[5]

Annex I regions are classified as industrialized countries with high levels of development according to certain criteria. The CO_2 emissions for Germany, Japan, and Australia are several times higher than those of other Annex I regions (see International Energy Agency, 2010). In the case of Japan, whose CO_2 emissions in 2010 were ranked fifth in the world,[6] considerable expenses have been incurred as the country has attempted to improve energy efficiency and reduce fossil fuel consumption (see International Energy Agency, 2010). In order to cut emissions, Annex I countries typically have shifted production of emissions-intensive industries to

Non-Annex I countries. For example, Japan imports a large number of electrical appliances, toys, and household goods from China every year, and China emits large quantities of CO_2 domestically to produce these products; approximately 10 percent of China's CO_2 emissions can be attributed to exports to Japan (see Chapter 14 of Murray and Wood (2010)).

The first such difference is the types of emissions associated with production and consumption, which can be further subdivided into differences in emission intensity, material composition, and final demand. Emission intensity refers to emissions per unit of output. The higher emission intensity is, the more emissions not treated is emitted into the atmosphere; in other words, treatment technology for waste gas is not advanced. Material composition refers to the composition of the materials inputted into industry. The higher material composition is, to the more extent production relies on material inputs; in other words, industry technology is material-intensive.[7] Final demand depends on the consumption or lifestyle of a country; the more final demand is, the more need for consumer goods.

This chapter first estimates CO_2 emissions amounts as not just those generated directly by production but also those generated directly and indirectly by consumption. Then it examines the extent to which each country should take responsibility for the climate change issue. Finally it quantitatively assesses the main sources of cross-country differences in emissions.

Following the Introduction, this chapter is organized as follows: Section 2 presents a short overview of research on GHG emissions embodied in production, consumption, and international trade. Sections 3 and 4 describe the methodology and data used. Section 5 discusses the empirical results and finally Section 6 concludes the chapter.

2. Literature review

Numerous studies have been conducted on the emissions embodied in production and consumption. Lenzen and Murray (2001) analyzed the impact of consumer activities on GHG emissions in Australia. They found that significant emissions in Australia are embodied in the private final consumption of meat products, electricity, retail goods, dining out, and dwellings.[8] In addition, they found that considerable amounts of emissions are attributed to exports of, mostly, primary commodities and concluded that Australia is a net emissions exporter (see page 245 of Lenzen and Murray (2001)).

Bin and Dowlatabadi (2005) used the Consumer Lifestyle Approach to explore the relationship between consumer activities and environmental impacts in the US. In their research, 80 percent of the energy used and the CO_2 emitted in the US results from consumer demands and the economic activities required to support those demands. They also found that direct influences associated with consumer activities (home energy use and personal travel), which account for 4 percent of the US GDP, account for 28 percent and 41 percent of US energy use and CO_2 emissions, respectively. Wei et al. (2007) studied the impact of lifestyle on energy use and CO_2 emissions by China's households from 1999 to 2002. Their study showed that approximately 26 percent of the total energy consumption and 30 percent of CO_2 emissions every year are related to the lifestyles of those households, i.e., energy use by households, food, education, and cultural recreation services are the most energy-intensive and carbon emission-intensive activities.

Numerous studies also have been conducted regarding the role that international trade plays in emissions. Copeland and Taylor (1994) used a North–South trade model to examine links between income, pollution and international trade. The model forecast that free trade increases world pollution and that unilateral transfers from North to South reduce global pollution. Ahmad and Wyckoff (2003) explored the role of trade in goods by examining CO_2 emissions and their relationship with the domestic demand of 24 countries. Their findings showed that the CO_2 emissions generated to satisfy domestic demand in Organisation for Economic Co-operation and Development nations in 1995 were approximately 5 percent higher than emissions related to production. Davis and Caldeira (2010) presented a global, consumption-based CO_2 emissions inventory and calculations of associated energy and carbon intensities. Their findings revealed that 23 percent of global CO_2 emissions were traded internationally, primarily as exports from China and other emerging markets to consumers in developed countries. Peters et al. (2011) developed a trade-linked global database for CO_2 emissions covering 113 countries and 57 economic sectors for the period from 1990 to 2008. They found that the net emissions transfers via international trade from developing to developed countries increased from 0.4 Gt-CO_2 to 1.6 Gt-CO_2. Taken together, these studies show that international trade is a significant factor in explaining the changes in emissions in many countries from a consumption perspective.

Previous research has pointed out the importance of reducing GHG emissions by changing our lifestyle. When we consider the global environmental issue, all these studies have reached the same consensus: consumption in many developed countries has increased in concert with a large proportion of the emissions originating in developing countries (see UNFCCC, 1992). However, they didn't build a systematic model to compare the international differences of roles that industrial sectors play in GHG emission. A cross-country decomposition analysis is needed to solve this question.

3. Methodology

3.1 Basic formulation

The economy-wide supply-demand balance equation can be expressed as:

$$\mathbf{Ax} + \mathbf{f} + \mathbf{e} - \mathbf{m} = \mathbf{x} \tag{1}$$

Where $\mathbf{x}$ is the $k \times 1$ output vector representing gross outputs of k sectors, $\mathbf{A}$ is the $k \times k$ matrix of technical coefficients (input coefficients), $\mathbf{f}$ is the $k \times 1$ final demand vector representing final consumptions of k sectors, $\mathbf{e}$ is the $k \times 1$ export vector representing exports of k sectors, and $\mathbf{m}$ is the $k \times 1$ import vector representing imports of k sectors. It should be noted that the input coefficients $\mathbf{A} = (a_{ij})$ are obtained as $a_{ij} = Z_{ij}/x_j$, where Z_{ij} denotes the domestic intermediate deliveries of sector i to sector j, and x_j represents the total output of commodity j. Solving Eq. (1) yields the following input-output model:

$$\mathbf{x} = (\mathbf{I} - \mathbf{A})^{-1}(\mathbf{f} + \mathbf{e} - \mathbf{m}) = \mathbf{L}(\mathbf{f} + \mathbf{e} - \mathbf{m}) \tag{2}$$

where $\mathbf{I}$ denotes the identity matrix and $\mathbf{L} = (\mathbf{I} - \mathbf{A})^{-1}$ is the Leontief inverse matrix[9] (i.e., direct and indirect requirement matrix). The matrix element l_{ij} of the Leontief inverse matrix represents the output of sector i *directly and indirectly* required to meet per dollar of final demand of sector j.

In order to estimate how much GHGs are emitted to produce goods and services in each country, we defined emission coefficient vectors. As CO_2 accounts for approximately 95 percent of all GHG emissions (see Center for Global Environmental Research, 2011), this chapter only focuses on CO_2 emissions. If $\boldsymbol{\lambda} = (\lambda_j)$ is the $1 \times k$ CO_2 emission coefficient row vector for the amount of CO_2 generated by one dollar of output of sector j, then the jth element of $\boldsymbol{\lambda}\mathbf{L}$ indicates the amount of CO_2 directly and indirectly generated to produce one dollar of final demand (i.e., consumption) of sector j.

Accordingly, we can represent the consumption-based emission formula as follows:

$$Q^c = \boldsymbol{\lambda}(\mathbf{I} - \mathbf{A})^{-1}(\mathbf{F} + \mathbf{E} - \mathbf{M}) \tag{3}$$

where Q^c is the total CO_2 emissions that are directly and indirectly generated to produce final goods and services. Q^c is the consumption-based emissions of a country, and the production-based emission can be simply estimated as follows:

$$Q^p = \boldsymbol{\lambda}\mathbf{X} \tag{4}$$

Here it should be noted that if we focus on the total amount of CO_2 emissions, both the consumption-based emissions (Eq. (3)) and the production-based emission (Eq. (4)) should be concerned.

3.2 Cross-country decomposition analysis of CO_2 emissions

3.2.1 Cross-country decomposition analysis of production-based emissions

Differences exist in the size of the carbon footprints of different countries, and we would like to understand the underlying factors that produce those differences. In this section, cross-country differences in carbon footprints are examined using Structural Decomposition Analysis (SDA) (see Dietzenbacher and Los, 1998, 2000).

In the production-based emissions formula (see Eq. (4)), two major factors underlying differences in cross-country emissions are considered. The first factor arises from the difference in CO_2 emissions per unit of production (intensity effect), while the other arises from differences in the production amount (output effect). By taking these points into consideration, the carbon footprint of two countries (e.g., China and Japan) can be expressed as

$$Q^p(C) = \boldsymbol{\lambda}(C)\mathbf{X}(C) \tag{5}$$

and

$$Q^p(J) = \boldsymbol{\lambda}(J)\mathbf{X}(J) . \tag{6}$$

where C and J represent China and Japan, respectively. The cross-country difference in carbon footprint between these countries can be expressed as

$$\Delta Q = Q^p(C) - Q^p(J) \tag{7}$$

We also can define the cross-country differences in emission intensity vector and output vector as follows:

$$\Delta\boldsymbol{\lambda} = \boldsymbol{\lambda}(C) - \boldsymbol{\lambda}(J) \tag{8}$$

and

$$\Delta\mathbf{X} = \mathbf{X}(C) - \mathbf{X}(J) \tag{9}$$

Eq. (8) and (9) can be transformed as

$$\lambda(C) = \lambda(J) + \Delta\lambda \tag{10}$$

and

$$\mathbf{X}(C) = \mathbf{X}(J) + \Delta\mathbf{X} \tag{11}$$

Substituting Eq. (10) and (11) into Eq. (5), Eq. (7) can be written as follows:

$$
\begin{aligned}
\Delta Q^{p} &= Q^{p}(C) - Q^{p}(J) = \lambda(C)\mathbf{X}(C) - \lambda(J)\mathbf{X}(J) \\
&= \{\lambda(J) + \Delta\lambda\}\{\mathbf{X}(J) + \Delta\mathbf{X}\} - \lambda(J)\mathbf{X}(J) \\
&= \Delta\lambda\mathbf{X}(J) + \lambda(J)\Delta\mathbf{X} + \Delta\lambda\Delta\mathbf{X}
\end{aligned} \tag{12}
$$

Eq. (8) and Eq. (9) can also be transformed as

$$\lambda(J) = \lambda(C) - \Delta\lambda \tag{13}$$

and

$$\mathbf{X}(J) = \mathbf{X}(C) - \Delta\mathbf{X} . \tag{14}$$

Substituting Eq. (13) and (14) into Eq. (5), Eq. (7) can be written as follows:

$$
\begin{aligned}
\Delta Q^{p} &= Q^{p}(C) - Q^{p}(J) = \lambda(C)\mathbf{X}(C) - \lambda(J)\mathbf{X}(J) \\
&= \lambda(C)\mathbf{X}(C) - \{\lambda(C) - \Delta\lambda\}\{\mathbf{X}(C) - \Delta\mathbf{X}\} \\
&= \Delta\lambda\mathbf{X}(C) + \lambda(C)\Delta\mathbf{X} - \Delta\lambda\Delta\mathbf{X}
\end{aligned} \tag{15}
$$

Since the cross-country decomposition equations shown in Eq. (12) and (15) are equivalent, we propose the following cross-country decomposition formula by taking average of Eq. (12) and (15):

$$\Delta Q^{p} = \underbrace{\Delta\lambda \frac{\mathbf{X}(C) + \mathbf{X}(J)}{2}}_{\substack{Cross-country\ intensity \\ effect}} + \underbrace{\frac{\lambda(C) + \lambda(J)}{2} \Delta\mathbf{X}}_{\substack{Cross-country\ output \\ effect}} \tag{16}$$

where the first term on the right-hand side of Eq. (16) is the intensity effect caused by the cross-country difference in emissions per unit output of production and the second term is the output effect caused by the cross-country difference in output levels in both China and Japan.

3.2.2 Cross-country decomposition analysis of consumption-based emissions

Using Eq. (3), the respective carbon footprints of China and Japan can be expressed as follows:

$$Q^{c}(C) = \lambda(C)\mathbf{L}(C)(\mathbf{F}(C) + \mathbf{E}(C) - \mathbf{M}(C)) \tag{17}$$

and

$$Q^{c}(J) = \lambda(J)\mathbf{L}(J)(\mathbf{F}(J) + \mathbf{E}(J) - \mathbf{M}(J)) \tag{18}$$

The difference in the carbon footprint between both countries can simply be formulated by the relation:

$$\Delta Q^c = Q^c(C) - Q^c(J) \tag{19}$$

Since the differences in the emission coefficient vector, Leontief inverse matrix, final demand vector, export vector, and import vector also can be defined as

$$\Delta \boldsymbol{\lambda} = \boldsymbol{\lambda}(C) - \boldsymbol{\lambda}(J), \tag{20}$$

$$\Delta \mathbf{L} = \mathbf{L}(C) - \mathbf{L}(J), \tag{21}$$

$$\Delta \mathbf{F} = \mathbf{F}(C) - \mathbf{F}(J), \tag{22}$$

$$\Delta \mathbf{E} = \mathbf{E}(C) - \mathbf{E}(J), \tag{23}$$

and

$$\Delta \mathbf{M} = \mathbf{M}(C) - \mathbf{M}(J), \tag{24}$$

respectively, substituting Eq. (20)–(24) into Eq. (17) or (18) yields the following two equivalent, cross-country, decomposition formulae:

$$
\begin{aligned}
\Delta Q^c &= Q^c(C) - Q^c(J) \\
&= \boldsymbol{\lambda}(C)\mathbf{L}(C)(\mathbf{F}(C) + \mathbf{E}(C) - \mathbf{M}(C)) - \boldsymbol{\lambda}(J)\mathbf{L}(J)(\mathbf{F}(J) + \mathbf{E}(J) - \mathbf{M}(J)) \\
&= (\boldsymbol{\lambda}(J) + \Delta\boldsymbol{\lambda})(\mathbf{L}(J) + \Delta\mathbf{L})(\mathbf{F}(J) + \Delta\mathbf{F} + \mathbf{E}(J) + \Delta\mathbf{E} - \mathbf{M}(J) - \Delta\mathbf{M}) \\
&\quad - \boldsymbol{\lambda}(J)\mathbf{L}(J)(\mathbf{F}(J) + \mathbf{E}(J) - \mathbf{M}(J)) \\
&= \Delta\boldsymbol{\lambda}\mathbf{L}(J)(\mathbf{F}(J) + \mathbf{E}(J) - \mathbf{M}(J)) + \boldsymbol{\lambda}(J)\Delta\mathbf{L}(\mathbf{F}(J) + \mathbf{E}(J) - \mathbf{M}(J)) \\
&\quad + \boldsymbol{\lambda}(J)\mathbf{L}(J)(\Delta\mathbf{F} + \Delta\mathbf{E} - \Delta\mathbf{M}) + \Delta\boldsymbol{\lambda}\Delta\mathbf{L}(\mathbf{F}(J) + \mathbf{E}(J) - \mathbf{M}(J)) \\
&\quad + \Delta\boldsymbol{\lambda}\mathbf{L}(J)(\Delta\mathbf{F} + \Delta\mathbf{E} - \Delta\mathbf{M}) + \boldsymbol{\lambda}(J)\Delta\mathbf{L}(\Delta\mathbf{F} + \Delta\mathbf{E} - \Delta\mathbf{M}) \\
&\quad + \Delta\boldsymbol{\lambda}\Delta\mathbf{L}(\Delta\mathbf{F} + \Delta\mathbf{E} - \Delta\mathbf{M})
\end{aligned}
\tag{25}
$$

or

$$
\begin{aligned}
\Delta Q^c &= Q^c(C) - Q^c(J) \\
&= \boldsymbol{\lambda}(C)\mathbf{L}(C)(\mathbf{F}(C) + \mathbf{E}(C) - \mathbf{M}(C)) - \boldsymbol{\lambda}(J)\mathbf{L}(J)(\mathbf{F}(J) + \mathbf{E}(J) - \mathbf{M}(J)) \\
&= (\boldsymbol{\lambda}(C)\mathbf{L}(C)(\mathbf{F}(C) + \mathbf{E}(C) - \mathbf{M}(C)) \\
&\quad - (\boldsymbol{\lambda}(C) - \Delta\boldsymbol{\lambda})(\mathbf{L}(C) - \Delta\mathbf{L})(\mathbf{F}(C) - \Delta\mathbf{F} + \mathbf{E}(C) - \Delta\mathbf{E} - \mathbf{M}(C) + \Delta\mathbf{M}) \\
&= \Delta\boldsymbol{\lambda}\mathbf{L}(C)(\mathbf{F}(C) + \mathbf{E}(C) - \mathbf{M}(C)) + \boldsymbol{\lambda}(C)\Delta\mathbf{L}(\mathbf{F}(C) + \mathbf{E}(C) - \mathbf{M}(C)) \\
&\quad + \boldsymbol{\lambda}(C)\mathbf{L}(C)(\Delta\mathbf{F} + \Delta\mathbf{E} - \Delta\mathbf{M}) - \Delta\boldsymbol{\lambda}\Delta\mathbf{L}(\mathbf{F}(C) + \mathbf{E}(C) - \mathbf{M}(C)) \\
&\quad - \Delta\boldsymbol{\lambda}\mathbf{L}(C)(\Delta\mathbf{F} + \Delta\mathbf{E} - \Delta\mathbf{M}) - \boldsymbol{\lambda}(C)\Delta\mathbf{L}(\Delta\mathbf{F} + \Delta\mathbf{E} - \Delta\mathbf{M}) \\
&\quad + \Delta\boldsymbol{\lambda}\Delta\mathbf{L}(\Delta\mathbf{F} + \Delta\mathbf{E} - \Delta\mathbf{M})
\end{aligned}
\tag{26}
$$

By taking the average of Eq. (25) and (26), we finally propose the following cross-country decomposition formula for consumption-based emissions as

$$\Delta Q^c \approx \frac{1}{6}\Delta\lambda \underbrace{\begin{cases} 2\mathbf{L}(C)(\mathbf{F}(C) + \mathbf{E}(C) - \mathbf{M}(C)) + 2\mathbf{L}(J)(\mathbf{F}(J) + \mathbf{E}(J) \\ -\mathbf{M}(J)) + \mathbf{L}(C)(\mathbf{F}(J) + \mathbf{E}(J) - \mathbf{M}(J)) + \mathbf{L}(J)(\mathbf{F}(C) + \mathbf{E}(C) - \mathbf{M}(C)) \end{cases}}_{Cross-country\ intensity\ effect}$$

$$+ \frac{1}{6}\underbrace{\begin{bmatrix} 2\lambda(C)\Delta\mathbf{L}(\mathbf{F}(C) + \mathbf{E}(C) - \mathbf{M}(C)) + 2\lambda(J)\Delta\mathbf{L}(\mathbf{F}(J) + \mathbf{E}(J) - \mathbf{M}(J)) \\ +\lambda(C)\Delta\mathbf{L}(\mathbf{F}(J) + \mathbf{E}(J) - \mathbf{M}(J)) + \lambda(J)\Delta\mathbf{L}(\mathbf{F}(C) + \mathbf{E}(C) - \mathbf{M}(C)) \end{bmatrix}}_{Cross-country\ material\ composition\ effect}$$

$$+ \frac{1}{6}\underbrace{\left\{ 2\lambda(C)\mathbf{L}(C) + 2\lambda(J)\mathbf{L}(J) + \lambda(C)\mathbf{L}(J) + \lambda(J)\mathbf{L}(C) \right\}\Delta\mathbf{F}}_{Cross-country\ final\ demand\ effect} \qquad (27)$$

$$+ \frac{1}{6}\underbrace{\left\{ 2\lambda(C)\mathbf{L}(C) + 2\lambda(J)\mathbf{L}(J) + \lambda(C)\mathbf{L}(J) + \lambda(J)\mathbf{L}(C) \right\}\Delta\mathbf{E}}_{Cross-country\ export\ effect}$$

$$- \frac{1}{6}\underbrace{\left\{ 2\lambda(C)\mathbf{L}(C) + 2\lambda(J)\mathbf{L}(J) + \lambda(C)\mathbf{L}(J) + \lambda(J)\mathbf{L}(C) \right\}\Delta\mathbf{M}}_{Cross-country\ import\ effect}$$

where the first term on the right-hand side of Eq. (27) is the intensity effect caused by cross-country differences in emissions per unit output of production, the second term is the material composition effect caused by cross-country differences in industry technology in both China and Japan, and the third, fourth, and fifth terms are the final demand effect, export effect, and import effect, respectively.

4. Data

The primary data source used in this chapter is the Asian International Input-Output Table 2000 (hereafter referred to as the Asian IO table) compiled by the Institute of Developing Economies, Japan External Trade Organization (see Institute of Developing Economies, 2006). The Asian IO table contains an international IO table, but it does not contain any environmental emissions data. Consequently, GHG emissions data were extracted from the GHG emissions database (hereafter referred to as the environmental Asian IO table) complied by Nansai et al. (2011), which has GHG emissions data for the same sectors specified in the Asian IO table. The emissions for each sector were estimated using International Energy Agency data (IEA, 2007) for fuel origin CO_2 and the United Nations Framework Convention on Climate Change report for non-fuel CO_2, CH_4, N_2O, HFCs, PFCs and SF_6 (UNFCCC, 2011), and the environmental Asian IO table with the GHG emissions was compiled. The Asian IO table and the environmental Asian IO table covers ten countries, 76 sectors, and their associated GHG emissions. In addition to the ten countries – China, Indonesia, Japan, South Korea, Malaysia, Taiwan, Philippines, Singapore, Thailand and the USA, data for the rest of the world also were included. The 76 sectors were aggregated into seven groups (i.e., industries) according to the sector classification codes used in the Asian IO table, which is published by the Institute of Developing Economies, Japan External Trade Organization (see Appendix 5.1) for the sector classification. The Asian IO table contains intermediate input, demand, and national output, as well as international exports and imports. The unit is US$1,000. The environmental Asian IO table lists emissions data for each sector in different countries and the unit is gross ton.

76 industrial sectors and 7 sector classifications

	Sector		Classification
1	Paddy	1	Agriculture, livestock, forestry and fishery
2	Other grain		
3	Food crops		
4	Non-food crops		
5	Livestock and poultry		
6	Forestry		
7	Fishery		
8	Crude petroleum and natural gas	2	Mining and quarrying
9	Iron ore		
10	Other metallic ore		
11	Non-metallic ore and quarrying		
12	Milled grain and flour	3	Manufacturing
13	Fish products		
14	Slaughtering, meat products and dairy products		
15	Other food products		
16	Beverage		
17	Tobacco		
18	Spinning		
19	Weaving and dyeing		
20	Knitting		
21	Wearing apparel		
22	Other made-up textile products		
23	Leather and leather products		
24	Timber		
25	Wooden furniture		
26	Other wooden products		
27	Pulp and paper		
28	Printing and publishing		
29	Synthetic resins and fiber		
30	Basic industrial chemicals		
31	Chemical fertilizers and pesticides		
32	Drugs and medicine		
33	Other chemical products		
34	Refined petroleum and its products		
35	Plastic products		
36	Tires and tubes		
37	Other rubber products		
38	Cement and cement products		
39	Glass and glass products		
40	Other non-metallic mineral products		

(Continued)

	Sector		Classification
41	Iron and steel		
42	Non-ferrous metal		
43	Metal products		
44	Boilers, Engines and turbines		
45	General machinery		
46	Metal working machinery		
47	Specialized machinery		
48	Heavy Electrical equipment		
49	Television sets, radios, audios and communication equipment		
50	Electronic computing equipment		
51	Semiconductors and integrated circuits		
52	Other electronics and electronic products		
53	Household electrical equipment		
54	Lighting fixtures, batteries, wiring and others		
55	Motor vehicles		
56	Motor cycles		
57	Shipbuilding		
58	Other transport equipment		
59	Precision machines		
60	Other manufacturing products		
61	Electricity and gas	4	Electricity, gas, and water supply
62	Water supply		
63	Building construction	5	Construction
64	Other construction		
65	Wholesale and retail trade	6	Trade and transport
66	Transportation		
67	Telephone and telecommunication	7	Services
68	Finance and insurance		
69	Real estate		
70	Education and research		
71	Medical and health service		
72	Restaurants		
73	Hotel		
74	Other services		
75	Public administration		
76	Unclassified		

5. Empirical results

5.1 Production-based emissions in Asian countries and US

Figure 5.1 shows the CO_2 emissions generated *directly* by production in each country. Of the ten countries shown in the figure, the US, China and Japan are the top three emitters and are responsible for 88.7 percent of the CO_2 emissions by the countries listed. For the US, total CO_2 emissions amounted to 5.55 billion tons (almost twice that of China), with "Electricity, gas, and water supply" and "Trade and transport" responsible for 47.2 percent and 30.8 percent of emissions, respectively. In China, total CO_2 emissions amounted to 2.83 billion tons, with "Electricity, gas, and water supply" and "Manufacturing" responsible for 51.6 percent and 32.3 percent of emissions, respectively. Similarly, for the other countries, "Electricity, gas, and water supply" contributes half of the total emissions and is the most CO_2-intensive industry in production activities. In this industry, the "Electricity and gas" sector contributes approximately the entire emissions, primarily because power plants generate electricity by burning fossil fuels and emit large quantities of gas. These findings indicate that it is necessary to promote ways of generating electricity in Asian countries and the US that cause less damage to the environment. Production-based emissions resulting from "Services" amount to less than 8 percent of total emissions. In Singapore and Thailand, "Services" only contributes 0.02 percent toward total emissions.

5.2 Consumption-based emissions in Asian countries and the US

Figure 5.2 shows CO_2 emissions *directly and indirectly* induced by final demand (i.e., consumption activities) in each country. Although emissions from the US (5.84 billion tons), China (2.76 billion tons) and Japan (1.17 billion tons) are the highest of the countries examined, the contributions from each industry are considerably different. Except for "Manufacturing" and "Electricity, gas and water supply," the final demand for "Services" leads indirectly to considerable CO_2 emissions, and this industry accounts for 30 percent of the total emissions in the US. Although the role of "Services" could not be extracted from the data for production-based

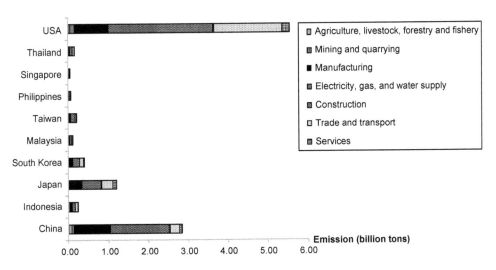

Figure 5.1   Production-based CO_2 emissions in each country

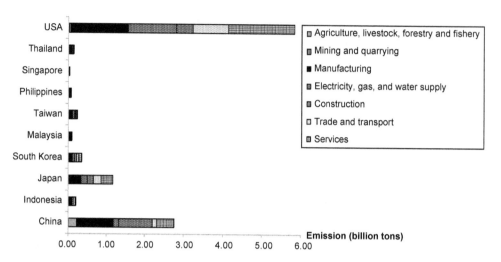

Figure 5.2   Consumption-based CO_2 emissions in each country

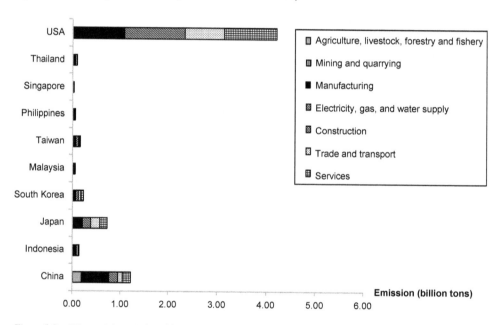

Figure 5.3 CO_2 emissions induced by private consumption in each country

emissions, in consumption-based emissions, we demonstrated that the "Services" industry in developed countries contributes to global warming through the emission of CO_2 to some extent

In order to better understand the relationship between CO_2 emissions and final consumption structure, we classified domestic final demand into four categories: private consumption, government consumption, gross domestic fixed capital formation, and increase in stock. The first three categories constitute more than 90 percent of the total final consumption in every country. Interestingly, private consumption in the US is three times larger than that of China and "Manufacturing," "Electricity, gas, and water supply," "Trade and transport," and "Services" are the main industries of supply. Figure 5.3 shows the CO_2 emissions induced by private consumption in each country. The figure shows that the sectoral contributions of CO_2 emissions induced by private consumption are very similar between the US and Japan and that the manufacturing sector in China plays a more important role in CO_2 emissions than it does in other developed counties.

Government consumption consists almost entirely of "Services," which has relatively low associated CO_2 emissions (see Figure 5.4). In emissions due to gross domestic fixed capital formation, China is the largest carbon emitter (1.31 billion tons), most of which is attributed to the considerable private and public investment (i.e., large final demand in the construction industry).

As shown in Figure 5.7, China's emissions due to exports was 0.85 billion tons, which is higher than 0.83 billion tons of the US, with exports from Taiwan, Japan and South Korea also flourishing. In addition, the large contribution of "Manufacturing" to export emissions (86.8 percent) demonstrates that China really is the world's biggest factory. This is primarily because the main exporting industries in China's manufacturing sectors –"Metal products," "Television sets, radios, audios and communication equipment," "Basic industrial chemicals" and "Wearing apparel" – are all relatively CO_2-intensive.

In the US, "Pulp and paper," "Drugs and medicine," "Industrial chemicals," "Refined petroleum" and "Motor vehicles" are the main export-oriented and CO_2-intensive industries. As a consequence, the magnitude of emissions associated with export (i.e., export emissions) of the manufacturing industry in the US is very large (see Figure 5.7). Taiwan is also a large exporter of manufactured goods, such as "Semiconductors," "Integrated circuits" and "Electronic products," and consequently is also a relatively large emitter of CO_2.

As shown in Figure 5.8, CO_2 emissions induced by imports in the US (i.e., import emissions) account for 1.14 billion tons, which is more than half of the export emissions of the US. "Manufacturing" and "Mining and quarrying" activities (e.g., refining coal and crude petroleum) are

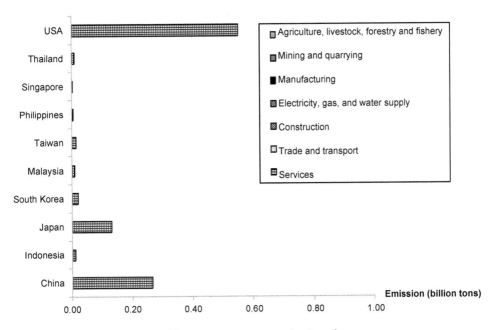

Figure 5.4 CO_2 emissions induced by government consumption in each country

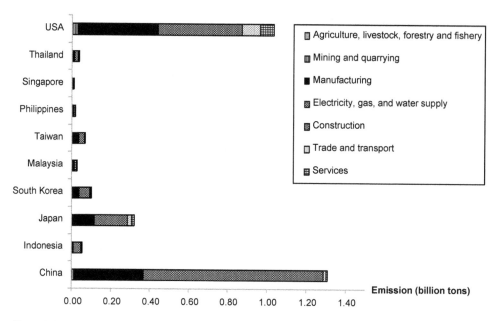

Figure 5.5   CO$_2$ emissions induced by gross domestic fixed capital formation in each country

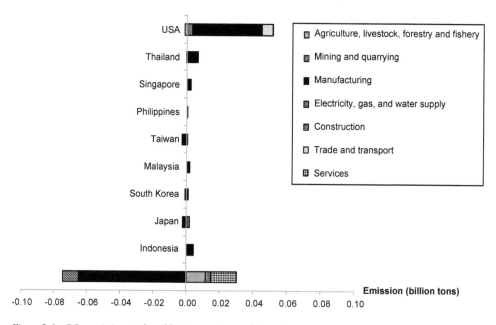

Figure 5.6   CO$_2$ emissions induced by increase in stock in each country

the primary contributors to import emissions. In other words, the US needs to import manufactured goods, coal and crude petroleum in order to satisfy domestic demand. The CO$_2$ induced by producing import goods in other countries is relatively larger than the CO$_2$ induced by producing export goods in the US.

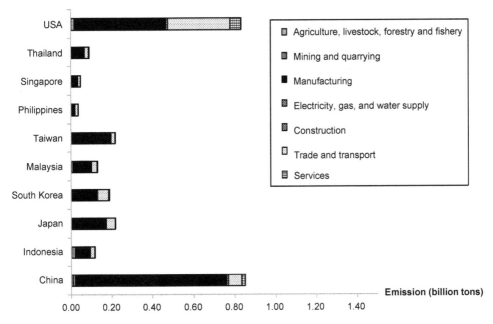

Figure 5.7 CO$_2$ emissions induced by export in each country

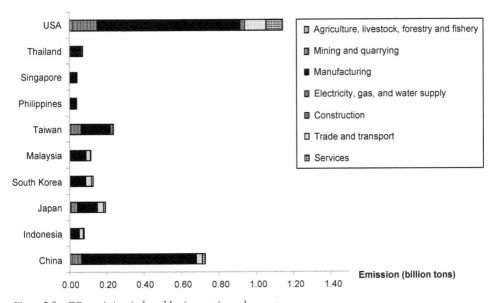

Figure 5.8 CO$_2$ emission induced by import in each country

A comparison between Figure 5.7 and 5.8 shows that in all of the nations surveyed, there are gaps between export and import emissions. We refer to this gap as the "net export emissions" and define these as export emissions minus import emissions. As a measure, the net export emissions of each country are useful for understanding which nations benefit environmentally from international trade.

Table 5.1 CO_2 emissions induced by net export of each country (Unit: billion tons-CO_2)

Country	Net export emissions
China	0.126
Indonesia	0.039
Japan	0.027
South Korea	0.063
Malaysia	0.016
Taiwan	−0.017
Philippines	−0.003
Singapore	0.007
Thailand	0.019
USA	−0.313

Table 5.1 shows the net export emissions of each country. From Table 5.1, the net export emissions of the US and Taiwan are −0.313 billion tons and −0.017 billion tons, respectively, which implies that in the US and Taiwan, the CO_2 emissions induced by imports exceed those induced by exports. This means that both countries benefit environmentally from international trade, because CO_2 is transferred to other countries that produce import goods, especially developing countries. For the US, the negative net export emissions primarily are due to "Manufacturing," which contributes −0.319 billion tons to net export emissions. For Taiwan, the negative net export emissions primarily are due to "Mining and quarrying," which contributes −0.062 billion tons to the net export emissions.

Of the ten countries surveyed, China (0.126 billion tons) ranks as the top net exporter of emissions, which are twice those of South Korea (Table 5.1). Exports related to production transfer emissions from developed countries to China. The low value obtained for the Philippines does not mean that the country has no import emissions or export emissions but rather that this low value is due to offset between them.

5.3 Cross-country decomposition analysis of production- and consumption-based emissions

Table 5.2 shows the result of a cross-country decomposition analysis of consumption-based CO_2 emissions between China and the other countries examined in the study. The difference in consumption-based CO_2 mainly can be explained by three factors: cross-country intensity effect, cross-country material composition effect, and cross-country final demand effect (see Eq. (27)). The table shows that CO_2 gaps (i.e., differences of CO_2) induced by the intensity effect in most countries are positive, except for Indonesia. In addition, compared with other countries, China has low pollution prevention or air quality standards. CO_2 gaps resulting from cross-country differences in material composition are all positive, which indicates that China employs relatively material-intensive industry technology (see footnote 7 for the definition of industry technology). Conversely, the US and Japan have cleaner production and higher material efficiencies compared with China, contributing total reductions of 10.022 billion tons and 5.683 billion tons in emissions compared to China, respectively.

Table 5.2 Difference in consumption-based CO_2 emissions between China and other countries (Unit: billion tons-CO_2)

Country	Intensity Effect	Material Composition Effect	Final Demand Effect	Total
Indonesia	−0.386	1.037	1.914	2.564
Japan	4.096	1.587	−4.095	1.588
South Korea	0.901	0.619	0.897	2.417
Malaysia	0.529	0.378	1.767	2.673
Taiwan	0.177	0.755	1.596	2.529
Philippines	0.621	0.402	1.670	2.692
Singapore	0.720	0.550	1.459	2.728
Thailand	0.676	0.262	1.687	2.625
USA	6.030	3.991	−13.097	−3.075

Table 5.3 Difference in production-based CO_2 emissions between China and other countries (Unit: billion tons-CO_2)

Country	Intensity Effect	Output Effect	Total
Indonesia	−0.742	3.338	2.596
Japan	3.748	−2.116	1.633
South Korea	0.953	1.475	2.428
Malaysia	0.528	2.192	2.720
Taiwan	0.049	2.573	2.621
Philippines	0.694	2.072	2.766
Singapore	0.797	1.996	2.793
Thailand	0.706	1.970	2.676
USA	4.263	−6.977	−2.714

However, the negative CO_2 gaps induced by final demand effect show that the amounts of final demand in the US and Japan are relatively larger. Table 5.2 shows that final demand has a marked effect on increasing the CO_2 emissions levels of the US and Japan, contributing more than 13.097 billion tons and 3.075 billion tons to emissions compared to China, respectively.

Table 5.3 shows the results of a cross-country decomposition analysis comparing the production-based CO_2 emissions of China with those of other countries. The difference in CO_2 emissions can be mainly explained by two factors: cross-country intensity effect and cross-country output effect (see Eq. (16)). The positive output effect shown in Table 5.3 shows that except for Japan and the US, China has a larger economy scale than the other Asian countries in the analysis. In addition, it also produces 2–3 billion tons more emissions than the other countries listed in the table.

5.4 Cross-country decomposition analysis of material composition effects

In order to explore the situation of each sector, knowing the total material composition effect is not sufficient. Consequently, it is necessary to decompose the material composition effects. Because industrial improvements and innovation are at the center of modern society, it is important to determine which industry is most in need of increasing productivity and reducing inputs. Indeed, a more detailed decomposition result would be valuable for Chinese authorities and institutions to formulate effective environmental policy.

To calculate detailed sector-wise material composition effects, we use the following cross-country decomposition formula (see e.g., Casler and Hadlock, 1997).

$$\Delta \mathbf{L} = \mathbf{L}(C) - \mathbf{L}(J)$$
$$= \mathbf{L}(C)(\mathbf{A}(C) - \mathbf{A}(J))\mathbf{L}(J) \tag{28}$$
$$= \mathbf{L}(C)\Delta \mathbf{A}\mathbf{L}(J)$$

If material composition differences in sector j between China and Japan can be expressed as:

$$\Delta \mathbf{A}_j = \mathbf{A}_j(C) - \mathbf{A}_j(J)$$

$$= \begin{bmatrix} 0 & \cdots & 0 & a_{1j}(C) & 0 & \cdots & 0 \\ 0 & \cdots & 0 & a_{2j}(C) & 0 & \cdots & 0 \\ \vdots & \ddots & \vdots & \vdots & & \ddots & \vdots \\ 0 & \cdots & 0 & a_{k,j}(C) & 0 & \cdots & 0 \\ \vdots & \ddots & \vdots & \vdots & \cdots & \ddots & \vdots \\ 0 & \cdots & 0 & a_{m-1,j}(C) & 0 & \cdots & 0 \\ 0 & \cdots & 0 & a_{m,j}(C) & 0 & \cdots & 0 \end{bmatrix} - \begin{bmatrix} 0 & \cdots & 0 & a_{1j}(J) & 0 & \cdots & 0 \\ 0 & \cdots & 0 & a_{2j}(J) & 0 & \cdots & 0 \\ \vdots & \ddots & \vdots & \vdots & & \ddots & \vdots \\ 0 & \cdots & 0 & a_{K,j}(J) & 0 & \cdots & 0 \\ \vdots & \ddots & \vdots & \vdots & & \ddots & \vdots \\ 0 & \cdots & 0 & a_{m-1,j}(J) & 0 & \cdots & 0 \\ 0 & \cdots & 0 & a_{m,j}(J) & 0 & \cdots & 0 \end{bmatrix} \tag{29}$$

$$= \begin{bmatrix} 0 & \cdots & 0 & \Delta a_{1j} & 0 & \cdots & 0 \\ 0 & \cdots & 0 & \Delta a_{2j} & 0 & \cdots & 0 \\ \vdots & \ddots & \vdots & \vdots & & \ddots & \vdots \\ 0 & \cdots & 0 & \Delta a_{k,j} & 0 & \cdots & 0 \\ \vdots & \ddots & \vdots & \vdots & & \ddots & \vdots \\ 0 & \cdots & 0 & a_{m-1,j}(C) & 0 & \cdots & 0 \\ 0 & \cdots & 0 & a_{m,j}(C) & 0 & \cdots & 0 \end{bmatrix}$$

where m is the number of sectors, then Eq. (28) can be rewritten as follows:

$$\Delta \mathbf{L} = \mathbf{L}(C) \sum_{j=1}^{m} \Delta \mathbf{A}_j \mathbf{L}(J) \tag{30}$$

Finally, substituting Eq. (30) into the second term of Eq. (27) yields the following decomposition formula:

Cross - country material composition effect

$$= \frac{1}{6} \left\{ \begin{array}{l} 2\lambda(C)\mathbf{L}(C)\sum_{j=1}^{m}\Delta \mathbf{A}_j\mathbf{L}(J)(\mathbf{F}(C) + \mathbf{E}(C) - \mathbf{M}(C)) + 2\lambda(J)\mathbf{L}(C)\sum_{j=1}^{m}\Delta \mathbf{A}_j\mathbf{L}(J)(\mathbf{F}(J) + \mathbf{E}(J) - \mathbf{M}(J)) \\ + \lambda(C)\mathbf{L}(C)\sum_{j=1}^{m}\Delta \mathbf{A}_j\mathbf{L}(J)(\mathbf{F}(J) + \mathbf{E}(J) - \mathbf{M}(J)) + \lambda(J)\mathbf{L}(C)\sum_{j=1}^{m}\Delta \mathbf{A}_j\mathbf{L}(J)(\mathbf{F}(C) + \mathbf{E}(C) - \mathbf{M}(C)) \end{array} \right\} \tag{31}$$

Table 5.4 shows the results of the sector-wise decomposition analysis estimated by applying Eq. (31) to the Asian IO table with 76 sectors; as stated previously, the 76 sectors were aggregated into seven groups (see Appendix 5.1). The larger value obtained for China implies that China's production is more material-intensive than that of other countries (Table 5.4). Generally, China's largest industrial inefficiencies are most apparent in "Manufacturing," "Construction" and "Services, which contribute to 26.2 percent, 28.1 percent, and 35.8 percent of the total of material composition effects, respectively.

The CO_2 gap between China and other countries can be mainly explained by the differences in material composition in the "Building construction," "Medical and health services," "Other services," "Public administration," "Wholesale and retail trade," "Education and research," "Real estate," "Motor vehicles," "Other construction" and "Specialized machinery;" in the US and Japan, these sectors are responsible for 82.5 percent and 79.2 percent of the total CO_2 gaps, respectively. In "Manufacturing," China still relies on inputting a large quantity of cheap resources, which this leads to low material efficiency and increases emissions. In "Construction," the US and Japan are ranked as the top two most efficient countries, reflecting sound management practices and strong environmental awareness. In "Services," the CO_2 gap is most apparent in "Real estate," "Education and research," "Medical and health services," "Restaurants" and "Public administration."

Interestingly, the minus value indicates that the US, which employs advanced technologies in most industries, is not as efficient as China in "Agriculture, livestock, forestry and fisheries." This is mainly because the US relies on mechanized production, which consumes a lot of materials.

6. Conclusions and policy implications

This chapter presents a new cross-county decomposition method to analyze the sources of GHG emissions of a variety of countries using the Asian IO table. The major findings of this study can be summarized as follows:

The US, China and Japan are the top three CO_2 emitters. When issues related to trade are considered, CO_2 emissions induced by net exports amounted to 0.126 billion tons in China, more than those of other Asian countries. The results showed that emissions were transferred from developed countries (the US and Japan,) to developing countries (China, South Korea, Indonesia, etc.), primarily due to activities in the manufacturing industry. Since global commerce is becoming increasingly pervasive, all countries should be aware of their obligations in international trade, and developed countries should assume more responsibility for emissions than developing countries. In order to cut emissions, standards to limit the export of emission-intensive goods, trade liberalization encouraging trade in low-emission products, and implementation of border adjustment measures (taxes or tariffs) are required when importing goods.

This chapter also discussed GHG emissions gaps among countries using a cross-country decomposition analysis technique. Using China as a benchmark, the differences of consumption-based emissions ranged from −3.075 billion tons (compared to the US) to 2.728 billion tons (compared to Singapore). Excluding Japan and the US, whose final demands are larger than that of China's, the final demand effect contributed to a 60.3 percent difference in the average gap, while the intensity and material composition effects contributed 17.8 percent and 22.0 percent, respectively. China's relative lack of material input efficiency is most apparent in manufacturing, construction, and service industries, such as "Building construction," "Medical and health services," "Wholesale and retail trade," "Education and research," "Motor vehicles," "Specialized machinery" and "Television set, radio, audio and communication equipment." Some of these sectors overlap, and some of these sectors rely on material input to the relative exclusion of science and technology. These ten sectors

Table 5.4 Cross-country decomposition of the sector-wise material composition effect (Unit: million tons-CO_2)

Sector	Country								
	Indonesia	Japan	South Korea	Malaysia	Taiwan	Philippines	Singapore	Thailand	USA
1 Rice paddy	14.25	4.67	9.52	6.27	11.57	9.02	11.90	6.98	11.88
2 Other cereals	17.24	2.88	7.44	14.56	13.29	10.66	13.93	9.73	1.23
3 Food crops	16.79	7.26	8.35	7.14	10.87	6.09	10.24	4.58	4.08
4 Non-food crops	0.84	0.19	0.53	0.22	0.98	0.42	-0.09	0.42	-0.50
5 Livestock and poultry	22.20	-13.35	-3.01	-12.48	-2.34	2.81	1.96	-0.52	-21.43
6 Forestry	1.71	1.07	0.65	1.00	1.03	0.60	1.51	0.93	0.81
7 Fisheries	9.38	1.63	0.12	3.02	4.55	3.69	-2.45	0.19	0.87
8 Crude petroleum and natural gas	5.99	-0.30	4.13	3.71	4.04	2.65	4.32	2.71	6.94
9 Iron ore	0.75	0.20	0.45	0.44	0.45	0.62	0.67	0.63	-0.06
10 Other metallic ores	1.62	0.26	0.56	0.72	0.60	0.80	1.04	0.74	3.95
11 Non-metallic ores and quarrying	0.47	0.16	0.25	0.32	0.43	0.24	0.19	0.23	0.37
12 Milled grain and flour	10.02	1.58	4.23	1.14	4.20	1.32	0.99	1.70	-0.77
13 Fish products	2.79	2.49	0.26	0.25	0.75	0.36	-0.62	-0.49	-3.67
14 Slaughtering, meat and dairy products	6.37	-1.94	0.15	-2.65	0.82	1.85	-0.70	-0.31	-15.33
15 Other food products	38.25	8.54	11.66	-2.71	11.89	10.38	6.75	2.35	14.62
16 Beverages	17.43	15.00	9.08	4.08	10.82	3.63	5.36	5.45	16.26
17 Tobacco	2.63	2.50	2.93	0.47	2.51	3.15	-2.05	3.12	8.04
18 Textiles	0.81	-0.63	-0.16	-1.39	0.75	2.22	-0.32	-1.96	-0.55
19 Weaving and dyeing	3.37	-0.95	0.62	-5.07	-0.19	-0.47	-0.88	-5.02	-2.05
20 Knitting	0.90	0.79	0.67	0.86	0.57	-0.12	-0.15	-0.58	0.34

21 Clothing	8.05	1.20	3.00	−4.77	3.64	3.18	2.19	−7.34	16.79
22 Other textile products	−0.78	0.00	0.03	0.11	−0.04	−0.72	−0.18	0.50	1.63
23 Leather and leather products	7.14	0.01	1.82	−0.69	1.45	2.78	1.37	1.92	3.81
24 Timber	0.04	−0.01	0.00	0.04	−0.02	0.14	0.16	−0.08	−0.07
25 Wooden furniture	3.46	3.45	2.68	1.33	2.83	1.75	1.74	2.28	21.69
26 Other wooden products	−0.31	−0.21	−0.21	−0.25	−0.21	−0.22	−0.31	−0.30	4.53
27 Pulp and paper	4.54	1.87	1.74	2.56	−1.31	3.01	3.27	2.94	7.62
28 Printing and publishing	0.01	3.32	0.54	0.01	0.52	−0.11	0.16	0.02	20.03
29 Synthetic resins and fibers	−0.10	−0.01	−0.10	−0.05	−0.05	0.02	−0.05	−0.02	0.36
30 Basic industrial chemicals	10.23	1.63	4.04	4.63	5.84	2.74	5.04	3.16	7.43
31 Chemical fertilizers and pesticides	−7.78	−2.61	−3.71	−3.99	−4.52	−3.61	−7.18	−3.43	−1.86
32 Drugs and medicines	9.26	3.89	3.27	2.36	6.80	3.36	6.77	3.10	21.97
33 Other chemical products	16.84	9.47	7.75	4.94	9.99	5.39	8.06	5.56	31.84
34 Refined petroleum and its products	−0.50	8.20	3.69	−1.35	−1.67	−1.83	0.48	−1.24	9.77
35 Plastic products	3.23	1.22	0.51	0.45	0.92	0.18	0.71	−0.02	5.50
36 Tires and tubes	1.49	0.07	0.63	0.73	0.61	0.26	0.82	0.71	1.32
37 Other rubber products	2.62	0.68	1.09	1.07	1.00	0.58	2.35	0.73	1.45
38 Cement and cement products	3.70	1.83	1.42	1.55	3.53	1.96	2.43	1.70	2.53
39 Glass and glass products	1.53	0.54	0.48	0.61	0.92	0.12	0.68	0.20	1.72
40 Other non-metallic mineral products	5.27	2.59	2.66	1.72	3.93	−0.01	1.90	1.01	3.15
41 Iron and steel	−4.09	0.25	0.80	−1.77	−3.12	1.25	−4.29	−1.52	1.05

(Continued)

Table 5.4 (Continued)

Sector	Country								
	Indonesia	Japan	South Korea	Malaysia	Taiwan	Philippines	Singapore	Thailand	USA
42 Non-ferrous metal	5.74	1.78	2.64	3.18	1.66	1.79	3.37	3.36	1.22
43 Metal products	4.59	6.03	2.70	2.22	2.72	0.23	4.11	2.72	51.03
44 Boilers, engines and turbines	8.13	4.66	2.84	4.36	5.09	-0.62	7.09	1.73	8.42
45 General machinery	8.54	13.61	5.06	5.49	8.75	-0.58	4.63	3.27	39.22
46 Metal working machinery	7.59	12.25	4.11	4.15	9.44	0.49	4.73	2.36	17.53
47 Specialized machinery	50.36	47.97	22.20	30.62	33.07	-4.81	33.05	21.59	92.28
48 Heavy electrical equipment	3.40	12.74	3.37	1.96	5.02	0.08	2.49	1.72	9.42
49 Television sets, radios, audio and communication equipment	23.72	22.43	21.31	11.37	16.88	17.57	17.55	9.04	62.58
50 Electronic computing equipment	2.38	9.02	4.43	1.98	5.21	1.54	2.87	1.40	31.96
51 Semiconductors and integrated circuits	5.94	2.99	4.70	4.23	5.05	4.32	5.19	3.25	5.97
52 Other electronics and electronic products	2.31	16.72	0.98	1.61	0.83	1.12	1.96	1.21	45.91
53 Household appliances	27.53	16.79	12.46	10.64	7.23	-1.80	12.82	5.48	19.19
54 Lighting fixtures, batteries, wiring and other	12.66	7.14	4.79	6.20	6.58	2.31	6.80	4.84	18.15
55 Motor vehicles	25.71	38.20	12.76	14.52	21.83	1.15	12.87	9.16	222.29
56 Motor cycles	21.79	5.19	4.71	5.61	8.86	3.73	8.08	1.37	1.60
57 Shipbuilding	4.75	1.17	2.28	2.70	4.44	0.50	4.07	1.83	13.97
58 Other transport equipment	11.99	11.05	6.99	6.60	14.51	7.79	10.59	7.37	49.66
59 Precision machinery	2.24	9.07	3.15	1.88	2.82	1.70	2.36	1.51	35.04

60 Other manufacturing products	-0.12	5.37	0.17	-0.01	0.18	-0.05	-0.01	0.46	38.01
61 Electricity and gas	5.28	22.28	3.11	6.53	17.35	-2.86	-2.18	-4.23	1.06
62 Water supply	4.80	12.38	3.35	3.07	7.42	0.88	3.79	2.88	-79.66
63 Building construction	260.88	322.51	176.39	90.43	151.59	160.93	200.72	52.12	681.58
64 Other construction	68.48	163.37	43.58	23.15	45.88	31.18	28.71	18.46	170.34
65 Wholesale and retail trade	19.69	113.32	18.61	13.93	43.52	3.56	3.49	11.00	353.05
66 Transportation	11.53	23.09	2.88	-3.99	12.83	3.82	-1.51	0.51	-0.76
67 Telephone and telecommunication	8.51	23.85	1.29	4.87	10.81	4.11	4.56	2.20	55.61
68 Finance and insurance	5.19	1.16	2.63	1.73	8.51	-4.15	1.47	-1.87	-3.98
69 Real estate	17.34	131.22	19.84	11.22	14.14	10.16	4.80	8.39	271.90
70 Education and research	32.54	93.34	33.92	23.38	41.94	18.34	19.84	17.89	274.94
71 Medical and health service	22.98	93.87	16.46	10.79	29.01	4.93	15.00	6.14	485.11
72 Restaurants	13.91	16.32	6.81	1.63	8.56	1.77	1.02	0.82	48.21
73 Hotels	2.98	4.27	0.47	-0.33	2.04	-0.43	0.45	-2.72	8.73
74 Other services	45.21	139.05	36.33	25.31	74.04	16.70	17.41	4.12	404.16
75 Public administration	50.74	114.23	41.09	17.22	17.78	35.99	29.24	20.07	338.60
76 Unclassified	0.06	-1.02	0.11	0.32	0.94	0.28	0.32	1.57	31.53
Total	1037.04	1586.84	619.12	377.72	755.15	401.55	549.51	261.77	3991.14

mentioned in Section 5.4 account for approximately 75 percent of emissions gaps between China and other countries; in particular, "Building construction," which is the most material-intensive sector in China, accounts for 21.9 percent.

A low-carbon economy is considered to be a necessity to prevent global warming. Over the past 20 years, the combustion of fossil fuels has caused an approximately 75 percent increase in GHG.[10] It, therefore, is important that humans begin searching for alternative energy sources, such as solar power, wind power and nuclear energy. In addition, governments should either reduce or abolish subsidies for fossil fuels. After the global financial crisis, governments have played an increasingly important role in industrial innovations. Japan is well positioned for China to learn from, as the Japanese government has attached great importance to research and development and the protection of property, which have in turn brought about cleaner industry technologies with less material and energy inputs. Further advances in industrial structure also will have the effect of decreasing GHG emissions, but the initial restructuring is likely to be expensive. It, therefore, is imperative that we develop the analytical tools that can be used by nations to monitor the implementation and effectiveness of industrial structure advances for reducing GHGs.

Notes

1 Convened by the United Nations Framework Convention on Climate Change, Third Session of the participating countries in Kyoto, Dec. 1997.
2 Parties include the industrialized countries that were members of the Organization for Economic Co-operation and Development in 1992 and countries with economies in transition, including the Russian Federation, the Baltic States, and several Central and Eastern European States (see the UNFCCC website, http://unfccc.int/parties_and_observers/items/2704.php)
3 Parties are mostly developing countries. Certain groups of developing countries are recognized by the convention as being especially vulnerable to the adverse impacts of climate change (see the UNFCCC website, http://unfccc.int/parties_and_observers/items/2704.php).
4 See the International Monetary Fund website: http://www.imf.org/external/pubs/ft/weo/2011/01/weodata/index.aspx.
5 See the NationMaster website: http://www.nationmaster.com/graph/env_co2_emi-environment-co2-emissions.
6 See the NationMaster website: http://www.nationmaster.com/graph/env_co2_emi-environment-co2-emissions.
7 Following the System of National Accounts (United Nations, 1993), the definition of commodity production technology (or production activity) is different from the definition of industry technology. The industry technology is defined by considering a variety of commodity production technologies. More concretely, the industry technology is defined following the commodity technology assumption which implies that even if the commodity in question is produced by various industries, the commodity has its own technology, regardless of primary and secondary products.
8 Household maintenance.
9 Leontief inverse matrix implies direct and indirect material input structure of the whole economy.
10 IPCC (2001), "Summary for Policymakers." Climate Change 2001: The Scientific Basis. Contribution of Working Group I to the Third Assessment Report of the Intergovernmental Panel on Climate Change. IPCC. http://www.grida.no/climate/ipcc_tar/wg1/pdf/WG1_TAR-FRONT.pdf.

References

Ahmad, N. and Wyckoff, A. (2003) Carbon dioxide emissions embodied in international trade of goods, OECD Science, Technology and Industry Working Papers. Paris: OECD Publishing.
Bin, S. and Dowlatabadi, H. (2005) Consumer lifestyle approach to US energy use and the related CO₂ emissions, *Energy Policy*, 33, 197–208.
Bowen, H.P., Hollander, A., and Viaene, J. (1998) Applied International Trade Analysis. Ann Arbor: University of Michigan Press.

Casler, S.D. and Hadlock, D. (1997) Contributions to change in the input-output model: the search for inverse important coefficients, *Journal of Regional Science*, 37, 175–193.

Center for Global Environmental Research, National Institute for Environmental Studies (2011) National Greenhouse Gas Inventory Report of Japan 2011. National Institute for Environmental Studies, Tsukuba.

Copeland, B.R. and Taylor, M.S. (1994) North-South trade and the environment, *The Quarterly Journal of Economics*, 109, 755–787.

Davis, S.J. and Caldeira, K. (2010) Consumption-based accounting of CO_2 emissions, *Proceedings of the National Academy of Sciences*, 107, 5687–5692.

Dietzenbacher, E. and Los, B. (1998) Structural decomposition techniques: sense and sensitivity, *Economic Systems Research*, 10, 307–323.

Dietzenbacher, E. and Los, B. (2000) Structural decomposition analysis with dependent determinants, *Economic Systems Research*, 12, 497–514.

Hansen, J.E., Ruedy, R., Sato, M., Imhoff, M., Lawrence, W., Easterling, D., Peterson, T., and Karl, T. (2001) A closer look at United States and global surface temperature change, *Journal of Geophysical Research*, 106, 23947–23963.

Institute of Developing Economies (2006) Asian international input-output table 2000, Institute of Developing Economies, Japan External Trade Organization, Japan.

International Energy Agency (IEA) (2007) CO_2 emissions from fuel combustion 1971–2005. Paris: IEA.

International Energy Agency (IEA) (2010) CO_2 emissions from fuel combustion highlights, 2010 edition. Paris: IEA.

Lenzen, M. and Murray, S.A. (2001) A modified ecological footprint method and its application to Australia, *Ecological Economics*, 37, 229–255.

Nansai, K. (2011) Environmental Asian input-output database. Tsukuba: National Institute for Environmental Studies.

Peters, G., Minx, J., Weber, C.L., and Edenhofer, O. (2011) Growth in emission transfers via international trade from 1990 to 2008, *Proceedings of the National Academy of Sciences*, 108, 8903–8908.

Raupach, M. R., Marland, G., Ciais, P., Le Quéré, C., Canadell, J. G., Klepper, G., and Field, C. B. (2007). Global and regional drivers of accelerating CO_2 emissions. Proceedings *of the National Academy of Sciences*, 104, 10288–10293.

Rothman, D.S. (1998) Environmental Kuznets curves – real progress or passing the buck? A case for consumption-based approaches, *Ecological Economics*, 25, 177–194.

UNFCCC (United Nations Framework Convention on Climate Change) (2011) GHG Data. United Nations Framework Convention on Climate Change. http://unfccc.int/2860.php.

UNFCCC (1992) Available at http://unfccc.int/resource/ docs/convkp/conveng.pdf.

United Nations (1993) Revised System of National Accounts, Studies in Methods, Series F, No. 2, Rev.4. Brussels: United Nations.

Wei, Y., Liu, L., Fan, Y., and Wu, G. (2007) The impact of lifestyle on energy use and CO_2 emission: An empirical analysis of China's residents, *Energy Policy*, 35, 247–257.

6

ENVIRONMENTAL TAXES
Practice

Jing Cao

1. Introduction

Due to rapid economic development and population growth, many Asian countries are experiencing deteriorating environmental pollution and natural resource depletion. Environmental taxes, applied more extensively in the European Union, are still relatively new in many Asian countries. Although economists often prefer market-based instruments like environmental taxes to correct externalities or distorted prices to achieve cost-effective goals, in practice command-and-control measures are still dominantly adopted, especially in Asian countries. In recent years, however, environmental taxation policies are playing increasing roles in environmental policy-making in Asian countries.

Environmental taxes have been a popular tool to curb pollution, especially in many European countries, which not only meet governments' aspirations to raise additional revenue, reallocate resources from the private to the public more importantly, correct negative externalities by internalizing the externality costs and reallocating resources for their best uses. In general, the "polluter pays principle" is adopted as a policy guide in environmental tax reform. The goal of environmental taxes (including government levies and other charges) is to send correct price signals to avoid excessive use of natural resources or releasing too much waste, resulting in more efficient use of resources and a reduction in pollution. A pure environmental tax in the textbook definition is referred to as a Pigouvian tax; however, such an idealized tax is rarely used in practice.

Examples of environmental taxes include taxes paid by factories or firms on effluent discharges, such as a sulfur tax or carbon tax, charges on solid wastes or upon the purchase of energy products, such as a gasoline tax in many Asian countries, or a resource tax, for example a tax on coal and oil in China. Feed-in tariffs and tax credits can be viewed as a negative environmental tax. Another special case of environmental tax is a deposit-refund system, where consumers pay a surcharge when they purchase the commodity and receive a refund when they return the product for recycling or disposal (Bohm, 1981; Menell, 1990).

In this chapter we first review various examples of environmental taxes in Asian countries, such as China' pollution levy system, fuel taxes, resource taxes, carbon taxes, feed-in-tariffs and tax credits, and the deposit-refund policy in Asia. We then draw from the academic literature and practices to highlight some lessons and critical issues for the future environmental tax reform.

2. Effluent charges

In economic textbooks, the existence of negative externalities can lead to market failures, so firms may produce too much output at lower than the socially optimal price, thereby deviating from the efficient allocation of resources. To correct this, Pigou came up with the notion of using taxes to correct negative externalities (Pigou, 1932). In theory, the environmental tax should be charged at the Pigouvian tax level (equal to the marginal damage at the optimal pollution level) – that is, the incremental amount that firms spend to reduce pollution; therefore, such a Pigouvian tax can internalize externalities and market failures can be remedied.

Effluent charges are the instruments that are closest to the textbook concept of a Pigouvian tax. In theory, the charge rate should be set equal to marginal damages, but damages are difficult to estimate in practice, especially for economies with rapid growth, such as in many fast-growing developing countries (Sterner and Coria, 2012). Setting the right tax rate is one of the main difficulties; in real-world cases, most effluent charges rely on trial and error. In addition to the purely technical difficulties of estimating the slope of marginal damage and abatement cost curves and other information issues, factors such as political considerations, interest group barriers and capacity building of local environmental protection agencies also are important factors for the success or failure of these taxes in practice. China's pollution levy system and Singapore's water conservation tax are two interesting examples of effluent charges in Asia.

2.1 *China's pollution levy system*

China's pollution levy system is one of the most extensive levy systems in the world. In the late 1970s, the Chinese government launched the wastewater effluent charge system based on the polluters pay principle by drawing on experiences of environmental taxes from the Organisation for Economic Co-operation and Development. The more extensive pollutant discharge levy system started in 1982, covering atmospheric pollution, water pollution, solid waste discharges and noise (Yang and Wang, 1998).

The Chinese levy system is quite unique. Central government determines the charge rate and levy structure, while in the implementation stage, the local (municipal) environmental authorities are responsible for collecting the levies from polluting facilities. According to the levy rules in China, the required levy is only charged on pollution discharges that exceed the standards that are set by the government according to the quantities and concentrations of the pollutants emitted. So it resembles a form of noncompliance fine and incorporates some element of a command-and-control program as well (Sterner and Coria, 2012). More recently this feature has been revised, so the latest water fees and sulfur dioxide charges more resembles Pigouvian charges.

Under the pollution levy system, all enterprises are required to self-report their pollution to the local Environmental Protection Bureau (EPB). The local EPBs inspect the firms from time to time and if the firms were found to have submitted a false report, they need to pay a certain penalty. Since the implementation is solely depending on the enforcement of local authorities and firms' self-reporting system, the effective levy rate varies remarkably among firms across the country: some are paying 100 percent of pollution charges that they are responsible for, while others only may pay a small portion of the real charges. Dasgupta et al. (1997) and Wang and Wheeler (2000) have shown that variations in the actual collection of pollution levies were to a large extent explained by local economic development and environmental quality. The local governments' priority has been local GDP growth and economic development, so the enforcement of the levy system depends more on governments' subjective judgment about whether enforcement will be in conflict with the growth objective. Given the similar economic background, air and water pollution levies are higher in more polluted area; thereby, the more severe the pollution is, the less the bargaining power of the firms with local environmental authorities. Wang et al. (2003) also shows that state-owned enterprises have more bargaining power than private firms; firms facing adverse financial situations have more bargaining power and pay less pollution levies than the required amount (less enforcement).

Due to the fact that the effective levy rate usually is lower than the marginal abatement cost, rational firms pay the levy instead of reducing pollutions(Wang and Wheeler, 1996, 1998; Florig et al., 1995; CRAES, 1997). About 70 to 80 percent of levy funds were returned to enterprises as refunded emissions payments for environmentally beneficial activities, such as purchasing abatement equipment or improve environmental management, and the rest were used for local EBP's own administration costs (Sterner and Coria, 2012). Considering the firms would have some leverage in terms of using levy payments to finance their own abatement projects, firms may be less averse to paying the levy charges compared to the case of environmental taxes, in which most of the revenue goes to the general budget. However, this feature of the levy system also brought substantial efficiency costs and corruption within local EPB, so it was removed and the levy charges were put in the general budget. Nevertheless, the fees are still relatively low and the funds collected are very limited in terms of curbing pollution, although some studies show that the levy system had some positive effects (Wang and Wheeler, 2000). Lin (2013) shows that even with more government inspection, the levy system only works for better verifying plants' self-reported emissions but not for reducing their emissions.

Recently, concerning the ineffectiveness of the current levy system, China's Ministry of Finance has submitted an environmental tax reform plan to the State Council Legislative Affairs Office and currently is in the phase of soliciting opinions from all sides.[1] The goal of the current tax reform is to shift from a pollution levy on sewage, waste gas, solid waste, noise, and etc. to taxes. For instance, as a key pollutant in China, sulfur dioxide (SO_2) is regulated in the 11th Five Year Period. According to the new environmental tax proposal, the current levy charges on SO_2 will be transformed into a sulfur dioxide tax, which will be collected according to the actual monitoring of SO_2 emissions from the major polluting sources, such as power plants, steel plants, etc., while for small firms or for those with emissions data not readily available, the sulfur tax will be charged according to estimates based on the sulfur content in the fuels and related emissions abatement measures. The revenue will be put into the general fiscal budget.[2]

2.2 Singapore's water conservation charges

Singapore does not have a direct green tax on air pollution or waste water, since the air and water have been kept within a safe range that below the U.S. Environmental Protection Agency standards.[3] With an increasing water shortage and cleanup costs on waste water, Singapore first introduced a water conservation tax in 1991 to reflect the scarcity value of water usage. The block tariff is charged at 30 percent of water tariffs for the first 40 cubic meters and 45 percent above 40 cubic meters (Liu and Janjua, 2009).

In 1997, Singapore launched a water pricing reform based on economic efficiency by restructuring a three-tier water and conservation tax into a uniform flat rate; the price incorporates the full cost of recovery as well as increasing water scarcity and the high incremental costs of additional water supplies. As much as possible, the price was flat irrespective of the user (household, industry or construction site) and regardless of the water usage. The new pricing regime comprised two tiers with a threshold of 40 cubic meters per month and the bottom and upper levels pay the water conservation tax, while before the policy the bottom tier is exempted from the water conservation tax. With the reform, Singapore became a pioneering country in introducing marginal cost pricing on water. After the reform, the price of water rose by 120 percent, from S$13 in 1996 to S$30 in 2000. However, the levy on residential water use was still much lower than that in some European countries.

A separate tax rebate on utilities and subsidies targeting low-income households was also introduced to mitigate the distributional impacts of the rising water price. Given the flat rate structure, the reform favored small-size households rather than low-income households. A separate scheme of subsidies and rebates were given on utility bills (including water, electricity and gas); for instance, a U-Save rebate scheme was introduced in 1996 to offset the electricity price rise and Singapore's public housing made the compensation enforcement relatively easy and effective (Tortajada, 2006).

By integrating ecological costs, water scarcity rents, and compensation regimes, Singapore's successful water management program shows that necessity utilities like water do not have to be underpriced for better access. Rather, tackling both water shortage and quality more effectively through marginal cost pricing achieved better performance and made its water industry more competitive.

3. Energy tax

Many environmental pollution problems in Asia occurs due to the inefficient use of energy and resources, and the main reason is due to the market failure of setting wrong price signals on energy use. The energy prices have been kept very low in many developing Asian countries, and a government subsidy on energy is quite common; although in the recent years the distortions have been gradually lessened. The energy tax in Vietnam and the resource tax in China are two examples of taxes imposed on fossil fuel energy. The common problem is that low tax rates work ineffectively in removing the distortions of using energy resources.

3.1 Energy tax in Vietnam

Currently in Vietnam, although there is a tax on coal and gasoline, the level of tax is very low ($0.52 per ton of coal and $0.20 per gallon on gasoline), whereas natural gas is not taxed at all. Given the minuscule size of the taxes, the impacts on energy use are quite limited and more exacerbated by the fuel subsidies on consumers, although arising from equity consideration, most of the subsidies are scaled to protect the poor (IEA, 2011).

3.2 Resource tax in China

The Chinese government started to collect a resource tax on coal, crude oil and natural gas on October 1, 1984, although the original goal of the resource tax was not to protect the environment but to conserve resources. One of the pitfalls of the resources tax is its rate has been unchanged for many years. Given the more than two-digit GDP growth rate and increasing inflation, the constant tax rate is way too low compared to the rising energy prices. Starting from June 1, 2010, the Chinese government launched the first resource tax reform in Xin Jiang province, shifting the unit tax to an ad-valorem tax of 5 percent to 10 percent. The comparison of tax revenue before and after in Xin Jiang province is quite significant; during January to June 2010, the resource tax revenue was only 0.371 billion yuan, while it increased by about six times for the rest of 2010 after the reform, reaching 2.164 billion yuan.[4] Since November 1, 2011, the reform has been extending to the whole nation for crude oil and natural gas. However, the coal sector still remains under a unit tax that is 8 to 20 yuan per ton of coking coal and only 0.3 to

5 yuan for other types of coal.[5] According to the Statistical Review of World Energy 2013, China's total coal consumption has surpassed half of the world's consumption (50.22 percent); therefore, increasing the effective tax on coal by shifting from a unit tax to an ad-valorem tax has very important policy implications in terms of both energy conservation and environmental protection.

4. Environmental taxation in the transport sector

Environmental taxation in the transport sector refers to gasoline tax, congestion fees and certain tax credits or subsidies to promote more environmentally friendly vehicles or use of public transport. Sometimes, non-tax measures also are used, such as managing vehicle ownership and use. Here we summarize various environmental taxes examples in the transport sector in Singapore, China, Japan and Hong Kong.

4.1 Automobile tax and license fees

The Singapore government adopted various pricing measures to manage car ownership and usage, based on the "polluter pays principle." The ownership control measures are complemented by road pricing scheme, so charges are based on both the ownership and usage. Car owners need to pay a registration fee of S$140 and an additional registration fee calculated at the open market value (OMV), an excise duty at 20 percent of the OMV and a goods and services tax of 7 percent; the OMV is assessed by the Singapore customs department, based on the actual vehicle prices. The Singapore strategy is best described as eclectic and pragmatic. Taxes based on the user-based charges and combined with ownership regulation are quite effective in reducing usages.

In China, the vehicle purchase tax is an important tax that impacts the whole economy and may affect air quality and pollution as well. In response to the global financial crisis, the Chinese government formulated a plan to stimulate the sales and market share of smaller vehicles. The Chinese government temporarily reduced the vehicle purchase tax from 10 percent to 5 percent for passenger vehicles less than 1.6 liter in 2009; after December 2009, the rate rose to 7.5 percent. Besides, China also implements vehicle and vessel usage license plate taxes, and the tax base for vehicles is the quantity or the net tonnage of taxable vehicles or vessels. The current tax rate is 15–80 yuan per passenger vehicle per quarter; 4–15 yuan per net tonnage per quarter for cargo vehicles; 5–20 yuan per motorcycle per quarter, and 0.3–8 yuan per non-motored vehicle per quarter.[6]

In Japan, a prefectural automobile tax is paid annually by vehicle owners. An automobile acquisition tax is paid by consumers at the point when they acquire a car, and each year a national motor vehicle tonnage tax is paid by vehicle owners at the time of mandatory inspection. The tax on gasoline and diesel is very high in Japan, currently 152.7 yen/L, about 1.84 US dollars per liter.[7]

In Hong Kong, vehicle owners are required to pay the first registration tax based on the taxable value of vehicle and a vehicle license fee charged according to the type of the vehicle and on a sliding scale with the engine size.

4.2 Gasoline tax

The fuel prices in different countries vary a lot. In some European countries, a liter of gasoline usually cost more than two dollars, while the price in most Asian countries are relatively low.

Table 6.1 reports the spot price of unleaded gasoline and diesel prices for most Asian and Western countries. Most Southeast Asian countries have very low gasoline prices, around 0.85–1.3 US dollars per liter; rich countries such as Japan, Singapore and Hong Kong have higher gasoline prices, roughly around 1.6–2.2 US dollars per liter. Japan has the highest gasoline tax compared to other Asian countries. China's fuel tax rate is similar to the level of the United States', but much lower than Japan and other Northern European countries. It is interesting to see that for a long time the US consumed much higher per capita gasoline than the UK or other European countries (four times higher than the UK), which may be associated with the fact that the gasoline tax in the US is much lower than the European countries. It also suggests that the gasoline tax does work in the long term. In Asian countries, only Hong Kong's gasoline price is slightly lower than the European level, while many other Asian countries are only half-way between the price of the US and European countries, some Asian developing countries even have the lowest fuel prices.

Fuel demand is determined not only by income and fuel prices but also by other factors, such as access to public transport, demand for vehicles and others. There are hundreds of studies on fuel demand elasticities using aggregate time-series national analysis or cross-sectional analysis for different countries. The consensus for Western countries on the long-run fuel demand price elasticity

Table 6.1 Gasoline and diesel tax in selected Asian and Western Countries (Data collected in September 2013)

Country	Unleaded Gasoline Price (US Dollar/L)	Diesel Price (US Dollar/L)	Fuel Tax (Dollar/L)
Malaysia	0.85	0.71	
Indonesia	0.93	1.07	
US	0.93	1.04	0.13 (gasoline) 0.14 (diesel)
Taiwan	1.2	1.11	Fixed annual fuel tax, not tax on fuel usage
Philippines	1.2	1.01	
Thailand	1.23	0.93	
India	1.27	0.88	44–51% of fuel price, varies by states
Japan	1.58	1.35	1.84
Singapore	1.66	1.24	
China	1.67	1.67	0.16 (gasoline) 013 (Diesel)
South Korea	1.78	1.59	
Hong Kong	2.15	1.62	0.88 (gasoline) 0.78 (diesel)
Sweden	2.2	2.24	
UK	2.22	2.28	
France	2.28	2	
Italy	2.43	2.26	
Norway	2.82	2.59	0.92 (gasoline tax and carbon tax)

Source: http://www.mytravelcost.com/petrol-prices/

is around −0.7 or −0.8, while the income is around unity (Sterner, 2012). Cao (2012) applied a cross-sectional data set of Asian countries and found that, the long-run price elasticity is −0.80 and income elasticity is 1.14 in Asian countries. In addition, if dividing the Asian countries into developing and developed countries, the former have higher elasticities then developed countries. The long-run price elasticity in Asian developing countries (China, India, Indonesia, Philippines, and Thailand) is −0.83 and income elasticity is 1.28, while the price elasticity in Asian developed countries (Japan and South Korea) is −0.59 and income elasticity is 0.75. Price elasticities and income elasticities have important policy implications in designing gasoline tax policies to curb vehicle emissions.

5. Carbon tax

Compared to a cap-and-trade system, a carbon tax possesses many advantages: it is simple, straight-forward, and easier to raise government revenue and reconcile with the rest of the fiscal system. The carbon tax often is imposed on the carbon content of various energy types, leading to energy efficiency improvement and pollution reduction along the full production and consumption chain.

With the revenue collected through the carbon tax, the cost on the economy can be alleviated through cutting other more distorted taxes in the preexisting tax system or used to lower tax burdens on energy-intensive and trade-exposed sectors. Tax revenue can also be used to compensate the losers due to the carbon tax, so that to ensure a less regressive impact on the poor, who consume a relatively larger share of energy. However, a carbon tax is more politically difficult compared to cap-and-trade, because in general, especially at the beginning, permits are often allocated in a grandfathered manner.

A carbon tax has been levied in some Northern European countries. For instance, it was first introduced in Finland in 1990, then extended to Sweden, Norway, the Netherlands and Denmark. History shows that the carbon tax has achieved significant reductions in carbon emissions and the use of fossil fuels. The impact on the economy is small; it only slightly affected the growth rate but the employment rate has been increased (Anderson and Ekins, 2009).

The progress on a carbon tax is very slow in some Asian countries, such as China, Japan and the Republic of Korea. Although the Ministry of Finance announced that China will plan to levy a tax on carbon emissions in February 2013,[8] concerns about the impact on economic growth resulted in the nation deferring the carbon tax without a timetable.[9]

The Japanese government introduced a carbon tax (also called the "Tax for Climate Change Mitigation") in October 2012. The tax rates are based on the carbon content of all fossil fuels (JPY 289/tCO2), so it is essentially positioned as an increase in the existing fossil fuel tax (for instance, petroleum and coal tax). To avoid a rapid increase in tax burden, the tax rates are set to gradually increase over a three-and-a-half-year period. The carbon tax revenue is expected to reach 260 billion Japanese yen after 2016. The revenue can be used to fund green initiatives, such as promoting energy efficiency, renewable energy, distributed generation, etc. However, large consumers, such as the iron, steel and cement industries, still are exempted from existing fossil fuel taxes and also are exempted from the carbon tax. The electricity sector is not exempted from the carbon tax, but it can pass on extra costs to end-users. It is estimated that the carbon tax can reduce carbon emissions by 0.5 percent to 2.2 percent in 2020 compared to 1990 benchmark levels.[10]

6. Feed-in tariffs and tax credits on renewable energy

Renewable energy has grown very rapidly in recent years, notably in Asia, due to government support and various tax credits or subsidy policies. The United Nations recently launched its sustainable energy target calling for a global target of doubling the share of renewables by 2030.

Among Asian countries, Japan, China and India have made significant efforts to stimulate the growth of renewable energy.

Japan's renewable energy policy was reviewed and extended through legislation passed in 2009 and a revised Basic Energy Plan was announced in 2010 (IEA, 2012). The new Innovative Strategy for Energy and the Environment was announced in September 2012, which dampens the role of nuclear energy. To compensate for the gap in electricity demand, the strategy calls for renewables to be tripled by 2030 compared to 2010 and reach about 30 percent of total electricity generation. The new feed-in tariff policy was adopted in July 2012 to support wind, solar power and other renewables and other complementary subsidy policies such as investment grants, loans and tax reductions also are being implemented.

China also has made remarkable progress in promoting renewable energy. China passed the Renewable Energy Law and its amendments in 2005. One of the distinctive features was the setting of ambitious targets on renewable energy capacity. Upon approaching the fulfillment of the required targets, new targets have been reset to higher levels before the deadline. For instance, the initial target for renewable's energy share was 10 percent by 2010 and 15 percent by 2020 when the policy goal was made in 2007; however, the 2010 target has been achieved ahead of schedule and the 12th Five Year Plan (2011–2015) raised the 2020 target to 20 percent (Yuan and Zuo, 2011). China also introduced a renewable portfolio standard policy in 2007 through the National Development and Reform Commission (NDRC) Mid- and Long-Term Plan for Renewable Energy. The plan calls for 70 GW of incremental wind capacity, 120 GW of incremental hydropower and 5 GW of additional solar capacity by 2015. Later, a new plan was released in July 2012 that calls for wind capacity to reach 200 GW and solar capacity to reach 50 GW by 2020. To support this aggressive renewable expansion, production-tax incentives, feed-in tariffs and preferable corporate income taxes were implemented (IEA, 2012).

To accompany these ambitious targets, China has introduced favorable renewable energy policies. China has been relying on imported foreign technology for renewable energy by granting low taxes or import tariff exemptions for three decades to boost the development of the high-tech renewable power industry as well as its R&D. With improving technology development, China also endeavored to provide various mechanisms to enhance the commercialization and diffusion of renewable energy; for instance, sharing the extra cost of renewable energy generation among end-users of electricity nationwide, introducing a feed-in-tariff for all renewable energy generation connected to the grid (effective in 2006) and a mandatory grid connection system requiring the grid companies to purchase renewable energy.

Similar to China, India launched the Jawaharlal Nehru National Solar Mission in 2010, targeting to reach 20 GW of grid-connected solar power by 2020. Feed-in tariffs are also applied on solar and wind generation; both in-grid and off-grid solar powers are covered, the latter focused more on rural electrification, solar lighting and heat (IEA, 2012).

The feed-in tariff and relevant supporting policies are crucial to motivate the rapid growth of renewables. The supporting mechanism usually is only for a fixed duration, expecting the generation cost from renewables to eventually drop so that it will be competitive with conventional electricity generation technologies. Subsidies generally are paid to electricity producers directly by giving tax credits on production and investment or providing price premiums and feed-in tariffs. Indirect subsidies include giving preferable bank loans or other mandates to transfer higher costs on end-users. Given the experiences of production tax credits for wind power in the US, to keep the promise support of deployment of renewables to sustain the investor's confidence, is crucial to stimulate renewables development. Inconsistent or myopic policies for the short term cannot stabilize and minimize the risk, since renewables like wind are exposed to greater variations, with boom-and-bust cycles.

7. Deposit-refund systems

Unlike the environmental taxes described previously, deposit-refund-systems are a very special type of Pigouvian tax in which a tax on product consumption is combined with a rebate when the product or its packaging is returned for recycling. Deposit-refund systems have been widely implemented for beverage containers, batteries, electronics and more (Walls, 2011).

The most frequently used is the consumption-based deposit-refund system. Consumers pay a certain amount of fee up-front and then are given a refund for recycling. For instance, in Taiwan consumers who return polyethylene terephthalate (PET) bottles to any of the more than 10,000 established collection locations are paid a refund of NT $2 (about USD 0.06). The deposit-refund system is mandatory, although the refund rate is further reduced. By 1992, Taiwan's PET recycling rate was 80 percent. Similarly, a deposit-refund system on lead-acid batteries was established with retailers and consumers in Delhi, India, where about 90 percent of people returned their used batteries back to a retailer. The consumers obtained a net benefit of 44 to 49 India rupees per kilogram of lead recycled (about 0.7–0.8 USD); retailers were able to retrieve 70 percent of used batteries on average (Gupt, 2012).

8. Environmental tax: critical issues

In theory, economists often view environmental taxes as the most efficient instrument to address environmental and natural resource problems. However, in the real world, a pure environmental tax – a Pigouvian tax – is hard to implement. Although there are many environmental tax instruments being used as described previously, we focus on some key lessons, challenges and other critical issues of environmental taxes so as to shed some light on future policy reforms and academic research.

8.1 Environmental tax rate

The environmental tax rate is one of the most important factors to consider. Ideally it should be set at the Pigouvian tax level. If it is overestimated, in the long run it will hurt competitiveness, causing unnecessary firm closures, unemployment and economic loss. Sterner and Coria (2012) explain that in many eastern European countries with high historic levels of pollution, the marginal damage cost falls when the worst excesses of pollution are cleaned up; however, the tax rate did not reflect the changes in damage costs, causing unnecessary economic disruptions and loss of competitiveness. For this reason, Sterner and Coria (2012) proposed a two-tiered tax on polluters: a zero- or low-level tax up to a certain "permissible" level, then a higher tax rate for the "excess pollution." This regime will alleviate burdens of some firms with less pollution and punish firms with excess pollution. In fact, such a two-tiered tax regime has been implemented in the levy system of China; however, such a regime did not obtain satisfactory results. On one hand, small and inefficient firms (such as small-scale paper plants) are more costly in the production cycle but they still avoid certain pollution charges if their pollution level is within the pollution surcharge threshold. Therefore, there is a conflict between competitiveness and economic efficiency. In the Chinese case, the low rate was set at zero, which encourages firms to operate on a small scale to avoid the charges and the total absolute emissions eventually got out of control. This led the authorities rethink the issue and shift to an alternative command-and-control – total emissions volume – control policy.

Setting the tax rate using the Pigouvian rule is not simple. In the real world the levy rate is often adjusted by trial-and-error according to a given policy target. Only when the target is set as optimal can the trial-and-error practice produce efficient tax policy; otherwise the tax policy would be only cost-effective. In addition, "path dependency" will affect firms' technology options; for instance, if the tax rate is set too low, firms may adopt cheap end-of-pipe abatement technologies that later prove to be insufficient and inferior compared to adopting fundamental technology changes due to the higher environmental tax (Sterner and Coria, 2012). Therefore, even though from the consideration of political feasibility a low tax rate is often charged to meet less resistance from polluters, it is important to set not only a static tax rate but also a dynamic tax rate regime so that firms will have consistent expectations when choosing appropriate abatements.

8.2 Earmarking and revenue recycling

In theory, charges and taxes sometimes mean the same thing. But in the real world, such as in China's case, taxes are reserved for politically determined payments that typically go to the Ministry of Finance, while charges (or fees) are usually administrated by the local or by sectoral agencies and earmarked as specific environmental funds. Charges/fees usually can avoid the complicated political process of passing and modifying tax laws. Especially for local government, the tax revenue that is put in the general budget usually means "lost" revenue, so the local authorizes have less incentives to collect certain environmental taxes.

Economists often view earmarking as inferior than all tax revenues going to the fiscal system, so that public goods (including abatement) can compete equally for public funds (Sterner and Coria, 2012) to achieve economic efficiency. Therefore, earmarking is often a "second-best" strategy that is sometimes useful to help the public or polluters accept the policies more readily or used as a channel to redistribute proceeds to balance the winners and losers. Both the Chinese pollution charge system and Japan's carbon tax use earmarking to promote abatement activities and energy efficiency technologies.

Ideally, after the environmental taxes are collected, the revenue are put into the general budget system under a tax neutral assumption that the total tax revenue is kept the same before and after the tax reform. Therefore, substituting a more distorted tax would sometimes bring "double dividend" – a tax on polluting activities will produce two kinds of benefits: improvement in the environment and improvement in economic efficiency. Fullerton and Metcalf (1998) point out the key to the success of the double dividend is not on revenue per se. Policies that raise product prices through some restrictions on behavior may create scarcity rents; environmental tax policies would be less efficient unless such rents are captured by the government.

Many economists have difficulties with the "free lunch" implied in the "double dividend" debate; theoretical and simulation models suggest that sometimes such a "free lunch" does exist, while others suggest not. Bovenberg and de Mooij (1994) and Goulder (1995) explain the likelihood of "double dividend" from the public finance perspective. They argued that a possible "tax interaction effect" may interfere with the "revenue recycling effects" and in most cases the former exceeds the latter, except under special cases with very high distortional preexisting taxes. Although in theory the "double dividend" may be achievable, it is hard to conduct empirical studies on it in the real world. Nevertheless, focusing on the uncontroversial standpoint – the weak version of the double dividend proposed by Goulder (1995) – revenue recycling to reduce other more distortionary taxes is preferable to a lump-sum return of revenue. Therefore, it should be carefully considered in tax design, especially the question of what other taxes can be swapped with. In Western countries, Sweden and Finland recycled revenue by lowing income taxes; Denmark and the UK swap the tax with lowering employers' social security contributions; the Netherlands reduces the income taxation in the initial phase, then shift toward employers' social security wage component and corporate taxes; and Germany pursued a "mixed" approach, splitting the revenue recycling between the employers' and employees' social security contributions (Andersen and Ekins, 2009).

8.3 *Tax incidence and political feasibility*

After the implementation of an energy tax or environmental tax reform, the poor usually suffer a disproportionately large burden since their energy shares are relatively higher than the rich. In the real world, the tax incidence is more complicated and should be analyzed on a case-by-case basis. In most countries, when imposing a carbon tax the increases prices on coal and oil may affect the poor disproportionately, so the tax incidence is more likely to be regressive (Cao, 2011). However, in some special circumstances this may not hold true. For instance, many rural farmers in south China do not commute frequently and use methane as major energy source instead of coal; thus the impacts of the carbon tax may be less on the poor than on the rich living in the north China, who rely mainly on coal. Therefore, the issues typically are very complex; they combine income distribution and factors associated with geography and rural/urban locations.

In many countries, lobbying campaigns and interest groups often argue that a fuel tax is regressive and would hurt the poor more than the rich. However, empirical studies have shown that the fuel tax in many developing countries is likely to be progressive. Even in the developed countries, by adjusting the lifetime income and other methods, people found the regressivity is somewhat less than what was originally thought (Sterner, 2012). Cao (2012) find the Suits index for the fuel tax in China is positive, ranging from 0.09 in 2002 to 0.24 in 2007. Datta (2012) also finds that in India the direct effects of a fuel tax are progressive, except for kerosene and coal. Yusuf and Resosudarmo (2012) use a computable general equilibrium model to analyze the incidence of reducing vehicle fuel subsidies in Indonesia and also find similar strong evidence on progressivity.

To understand the political economy of the environmental tax, one needs to realize that governance and passing tax law is a complex process. Even though in theory a Pigouvian tax is the optimal policy option, in reality opposition to the tax policy is a real barrier for implementation. In most democratic countries, the choice of policy instruments also is affected by lobbying. In China and other communist countries, monopoly firms or major energy- intensive sectors often have political power that affects not only the targets on abatement but also the choice of instruments. Thus, tax policy might be inferior to grandfathered emissions trading for these interest groups. Cap-and-trade is more politically feasible and the cost burden on existing firms is relatively small. Consumers without bargaining power often bear more tax burdens.

In sum, how to reconcile political feasibility, economic efficiency and fairness are important considerations in any environmental tax reform.

9. Conclusion

In this chapter, we summarized various kinds of environmental tax policies (in broad terms) practiced in Asian countries: pollution levy systems, water conservation taxes, fuel taxes and congestion fees, carbon taxes, feed-in-tariffs and renewable subsidies, and deposit-refund systems. The development of environmental taxation policy in Asian countries is still lagging behind that of developed Western countries, especially European countries. However, with the rapid catch-up on economic development and environmental awareness in Asian developing countries, the gap is gradually shrinking.

The empirical studies on environmental taxation in Asian are still very scarce compared to western countries; learning-by-doing is quite common in many Asian countries. The urgent environmental and resource problems accompanying rapid economic growth pose difficult but not insurmountable challenges ahead, requiring policymakers to adapt and develop their own environmental tax policy regimes for a more sustainable economy. We highlighted some key environmental tax policy designing factors, which are informed by theory as well as by experience.

Although the Pigouvian tax is ideal in terms of economic efficiency, it is difficult to implement in practice especially with pre-existing tax system and trial-and-error is adopted to examine if the taxation tool is cost effective for a given exogenous target. A low tax rate may be more political feasible in the first place but may bring further distortions due to "path dependency" on technology abatement investment choices.

The "double dividend" hypothesis is a quite debated topic; its success or not would attribute to the characteristics of the preexisting taxation distortions, requiring a case-by-case analysis. Earmarking often is used to mitigate the negative impacts on enterprises for competitiveness considerations. However, from the public's economic perspective, this may bring further distortions on public goods competition and resource allocation.

Distributional effects and tax incidences are important factors to consider in order to pass tax laws more easily. Different taxes or the same tax in different countries may bring quite divergent distributional effects or even opposite outcomes. The results also depend on income distribution, rural/urban allocation and other geographical factors. The poor often facing more severe resource depletion and environmental damages and bear disproportionately heavier burdens. Compensation regimes are important factors to consider in environmental tax policy design.

Finally, environmental tax is an exciting academic subject to explore not only in theory but also in practice. Environmental economics and public finance need to extend the boundary with other subjects such as atmospheric science, political science, law, public health and other disciplines. Currently, numerous models are created to strive for optimal solutions or at least cost-effective approaches. However, sometimes reality requires a great deal of sophistication to combine the theoretical foundation with real-world practice to design economically efficient, environmentally effective and more equitable policy solutions. The currently implemented environmental taxation policies already have shaped some useful experience from the Western countries. It is an important challenge to learn how to take lessons from previous environmental tax reforms in the European countries and to adapt and develop strategies and taxation policies that fit each country's own conditions. A careful evaluation of other countries' experience or ex ante policy simulations vs. ex post empirical studies is important and should be integral to the design process. Thus it also requires collaboration not only between countries but also across disciplines and sectors in the policymaking process. Researchers can play an important role to communicate successful experiences and must learn how to convey the policy results to policymakers in a clear and practical way.

Notes

1 http://finance.ifeng.com/a/20131129/11187793_0.shtml
2 http://www.caep.org.cn/english/paper/The-Separate-Environmental-Tax-for-China.pdf
3 The only exception on the PM_{10} exceeding the standard is a result of transboundary haze from Indonesia in 1997 and 2006.
4 http://energy.people.com.cn/GB/15854925.html
5 http://www.gov.cn/zwgk/2011-10/10/content_1965540.htm
6 http://en.wikipedia.org/wiki/Taxation_in_China#Vehicle_and_Vessel_Usage_License_Plate_Tax
7 http://en.wikipedia.org/wiki/Gasoline_and_diesel_usage_and_pricing
8 http://qz.com/55276/china-worlds-largest-emitter-of-greenhouse-gasses-will-tax-carbon/
9 http://www.bloomberg.com/news/2013-03-06/china-backing-away-from-carbon-tax-start-in-2013-official-says.html
10 http://www.env.go.jp/en/policy/tax/env-tax/20121001a_dct.pdf

References

Anderson, M. and P. Ekins (eds.) (2009) *Carbon Taxation: Lessons from Europe.* Oxford and New York: Oxford University Press.

Bovenberg, A. L. and R. A. de Mooij (1994). "Environmental Levies and Distortionary Taxation," *American Economic Review*, 84(4), 1085–9.

Cao, J. (2011). "The Incidence of Carbon Tax in China," presented at the 18th EAERE Annual Conference, June 29–July 2, Rome.

Cao, J. (2012). "Is Fuel Taxation Progressive or Regressive in China." In T. Sterner (ed.), *Fuel Taxes and the Poor,* pp. 128–140. New York: RFF Press and Routledge.

CRAES (Chinese Research Academy of Environmental Sciences). (1997). "A Report on the Study of Design and Implementation of China's Pollution Levy System," CRAES, Beijing.

Dasgupta, S., M. Huq and D. Wheeler (1997). "Bending the Rules: Discretionary Pollution Control in China," Policy Research Working Paper 1761. Development Research Group, the World Bank, Washington, DC.

Datta, A. (2012). "Are Fuel Taxes in India Regressive?" In T. Sterner (ed.), *Fuel Taxes and the Poor,* pp. 141–170. New York: RFF Press and Routledge.

Florig, H., W. Spofford Jr., X. Ma and Z. Ma (1995). "China Strives to Make the Polluter Pay," *Environmental Science and Technology*, 29(6), 268A–273A.

Fullerton, D. and G. Metcalf (1998). "Environmental Taxes and the Double-Dividend Hypothesis: Did you Really Expect Something for Nothing?" *Chicago-Kent Law Review*, 73(1), 221–256.

Goulder, L. (1995). "Environmental Taxation and the "Double Dividend": A Reader's Guide," *International Tax and Public Finance*, 2(2), 157–83.

Gupta, Y. (2012). "Is the Deposit Refund System for Lead-acid Batteries in Delhi and the National Capital Region Effective?" SANDEE Policy Brief, Number 62–12, South Asian Network for Development and Environmental Economics (SANDEE), Kathmandu, Nepal.

Lin, L. (2013). "Enforcement of Pollution Levies in China," *Journal of Public Economics*, 98, 32–43.

Liu, H. K. and S. S. Janjua (2009). "Environmental Taxation and Its Role in Singapore's Approach toward Environmental Sustainable Development." In L. H. Lye et al. (eds.), *Critical Issues in Environmental Taxation – International and Comparative Perspectives,* Volume VII, pp. 3–20. New York: Oxford University Press.

Lu, Y. (2011). "Enhancing Green Tax Measures Concerning Energy Use in Hong Kong." In L. A. Kreiser et al. (eds.), *Environmental Taxation in China and Asia-Pacific,* pp. 150–163. Northampton, MA: Edward Elgar.

Pigou, A. C. (1932) *The Economics of Welfare,* 4th ed. London: Macmillan.

Sterner, T. (2012), "Introduction: Fuel Taxes, Climate, and Tax Incidence." In T. Sterner (ed.), *Fuel Taxes and the Poor,* pp. 1–20. New York: RFF Press and Routledge.

Sterner T. and J. Coria (2012). *Policy Instruments for Environmental and Natural Resource Management,* 2nd ed. New York: RFF Press, Routledge.

Tortajada, C. (2006). "Water Management in Singapore," *Water Resources Development*, 22(2), 227–240.

Walls, M. (2011). "Deposit-Refund Systems in Practice and Theory," RFF Working Paper DP 11–47. Resources for the Future, Washington, DC.

Wang, H., N. Mamingi, B. Laplante, and S. Dasgupta (2003). "Incomplete Enforcement of Pollution Regulation: Bargaining Power of Chinese Factories," *Environmental and Resource Economics,* 24, 245–262.

Wang, H. and D. Wheeler (1996). "Pricing Industrial Pollution in China: An Econometric Analysis of the Levy System," World Bank Policy Research Department Working Paper, No. 1644. World Bank, Washington, DC.

Wang, H. and D. Wheeler (1998). "Endogenous Enforcement and Effectiveness of China's Pollution Levy System," World Bank Development Research Group.: World Bank, Washington, DC.

Wang, H. and D. Wheeler (2000). "Endogenous Enforcement and Effectiveness of China's Pollution Levy System," Policy Research Working Paper 2336, World Bank, Washington, DC.

Yuan, X. and J. Zuo (2011), "Transition to Low Carbon Energy Policies in China – From the Five-Year Plan Perspective," *Energy Policy*, 39, 3855–3859.

Yusuf, A. A. and B. P. Resosudarmo (2012). "Is Reducing Subsidies on Vehicle Fuel Equitable? A Lesson from Indonesian Reform Experience." In T. Sterner (ed.), *Fuel Taxes and the Poor,* pp. 171–180. New York: RFF Press and Routledge.

7

ENERGY AND CLIMATE CHANGE

Takayuki Takeshita

1. Introduction

Climate change is one of the most challenging issues facing the world today. Global awareness of the phenomenon of climate change is growing rapidly, and an increasing number of policy actions are underway to tackle climate change. However, it is indicated that current legislative plans in the aggregate are not sufficient to avoid dangerous climate change (e.g., Riahi et al., 2012). This emphasizes the need for examining quantitative strategies for climate change mitigation that can help achieve global climate stabilization at a safe level.

The energy sector is currently by far the largest source of greenhouse gas (GHG) emissions, accounting for more than two-thirds of the global total (around 90 percent of energy-related GHG emissions being CO_2 and around 9 percent being CH_4) (IEA, 2013). Without policy interventions to achieve global climate stabilization, the energy sector would account for an ever-increasing share of global total GHG emissions (IIASA, 2012). Accordingly, the energy sector has a crucial role to play in tackling climate change.

Thus, the aim of this chapter is to shed light on the question of how future energy systems can meet a global climate stabilization target of 2 °C above pre-industrial levels. For this purpose, this chapter introduces a sustainable energy pathway meeting multiple sustainability goals, such as climate change mitigation over the period 2010–2100 for the whole world and for three developing Asian regions (i.e., Centrally Planned Asia, South Asia, and Other Pacific Asia),[1] which is presented by Riahi et al. (2012) and called the illustrative GEA-Mix pathway.[2] For comparison purposes, a corresponding counterfactual no-policy baseline energy pathway, which is also taken from Riahi et al. (2012) and called the GEA counterfactual pathway, is shown for the whole world and for the three developing Asian regions. These two energy pathways were developed using an integrated assessment modeling framework called MESSAGE[3] (Messner and Strubegger, 1995; Messner et al., 1996; Riahi et al., 2007).

The rest of this chapter is organized as follows. Section 2 describes the methodology for the development of the two energy pathways shown in this chapter. In Section 3, the two energy pathways are shown over the period 2010–2100 for the whole world and for the three developing Asian regions. By comparing the sustainable energy pathway (i.e., the illustrative GEA-Mix pathway) with the no-policy energy pathway (i.e., the GEA counterfactual pathway), the question of what types and levels of demand- and supply-side energy system transformations are required to meet the stringent climate stabilization target is explored. Section 4 concludes the chapter.

2. Methodology for the development of the GEA pathways

2.1 GEA pathways

In addition to the GEA counterfactual pathway, Riahi et al. (2012) present three GEA pathway groups meeting multiple ambitious sustainability goals to represent different emphases in terms of the demand- and supply-side transformations of the energy systems, which were labeled as the GEA-Efficiency, GEA-Mix, and GEA-Supply pathway groups. Although the same socioeconomic and demographic assumptions, such as those on gross domestic product (GDP) and population, are used for all the GEA pathways (including the GEA counterfactual pathway), each pathway group varies substantially with respect to levels of energy demand, leading to pathway groups of low energy demand (GEA-Efficiency), intermediate energy demand (GEA-Mix), and high energy demand (GEA-Supply).

Such different levels of energy demand represent a difference in the assumption about the degree to which efficiency improvements can limit energy demand growth. Low levels of energy demand increase flexibility on the supply side of the energy systems, and vice versa, a more rapid and radical transformation of the supply side increases flexibility on the demand side. Within each pathway group, the alternative choices of transportation system transformation (conventional or advanced) and the portfolio of supply-side options (full or restricted) generate a wide range of alternative GEA pathways with different supply-side characteristics.[4]

For each of the three GEA pathway groups, one illustrative case was chosen that most clearly reflects the main characteristics of the respective group. Of the three illustrative GEA pathways, the illustrative GEA-Mix pathway is regarded as intermediate with respect to many scenario characteristics, such as the emphasis on efficiency improvements and the pace of supply-side transformations. For these reasons, the illustrative GEA-Mix pathway[5] was selected as the sustainable energy pathway in this chapter.

2.2 Sustainability goals of the three GEA pathway groups

All the three GEA pathway groups are designed to describe transformative changes in energy systems required for simultaneously meeting the following four energy-related sustainability goals: (1) to improve energy access, (2) to reduce air pollution and to improve human health, (3) to avoid dangerous climate change, and (4) to improve energy security. These four sustainability goals are defined in terms of specific targets and timelines, which are regarded as ambitious, and are the fundamental drivers of the demand- and supply-side transformations of the energy systems described in the three GEA pathway groups.

For the first and second goals, it is assumed that almost universal access to electricity and clean cooking fuels should be achieved by 2030 and that compliance with the World Health Organization (WHO) air quality guidelines should be achieved for the majority of the world population by 2030 with the remaining populations staying well within the WHO Tier I–III levels by 2030. For the goal of avoiding dangerous climate change, it is assumed that the global mean temperature increase should be limited to 2 °C above pre-industrial levels with a likelihood of more than 50 percent.[6]

On the other hand, energy security concerns typically relate to energy systems' robustness, sovereignty (often quantified as net import dependency in a region), and resilience (often quantified as the diversity of types of primary energy sources in a region) (Cherp and Jewell, 2011). In the three GEA pathway groups, the sovereignty and resilience concerns are addressed, while the robustness concerns are not. The three GEA pathway groups incorporate the sovereignty dimension by limiting energy trade as a fraction of total primary energy supply at a regional scale, but the resilience dimension is not a direct limitation in them.

2.3 Overview of the integrated assessment modeling framework MESSAGE

MESSAGE is a systems engineering optimization model, which represents the whole energy system from resource extraction, imports and exports, conversion, distribution, and the provision of energy end-use services. For the development of the GEA pathways, important inputs to the MESSAGE model are a harmonized set of technical, economic, and environmental parameters, which include reference energy demand (calculated as the product of reference GDP and reference energy intensity), the availability and extraction costs of energy resources, the efficiency of technology options, their capital and operating and maintenance costs, and their pollutant emission factors.

Given these inputs, the MESSAGE model obtains optimal results by minimizing the sum of the discounted costs under various constraints, including those imposed on the multiple sustainability goals (described in Section 2.2). Examples of model results include: price-induced changes in energy demand, deployment of demand- and supply-side measures, primary energy supply by energy source, final energy consumption by fuel, emissions of air pollutants and GHGs, energy system investments, and costs of meeting the sustainability goals. In the model results, GHG emissions reduction is achieved when and where it is most cost-effective.

Table 7.1 shows the regional definition of the three developing Asian regions. In addition, eight world regions are defined in the MESSAGE model. They are: North America, Western Europe, Pacific OECD, Central and Eastern Europe, the Former Soviet Union, Latin America, the Middle East and North Africa, and Sub-Saharan Africa. Detailed scenario data for the individual GEA pathways for these 11 world regions are publicly available in the GEA database (IIASA, 2012).

Table 7.1 Regional definition of the three developing Asian regions

Names of the regions	Countries included
Centrally Planned Asia	Cambodia, China (incl. Hong Kong), Democratic People's Republic of Korea, Laos, Mongolia, Vietnam
South Asia	Afghanistan, Bangladesh, Bhutan, India, Maldives, Nepal, Pakistan, Sri Lanka
Other Pacific Asia	American Samoa, Brunei Darussalam, Fiji, French Polynesia, Gilbert-Kiribati, Indonesia, Malaysia, Myanmar, New Caledonia, Papua New Guinea, Philippines, Republic of Korea, Singapore, Solomon Islands, Taiwan, Thailand, Tonga, Vanuatu, Western Samoa

3. Interpretation of the results of the sustainable energy pathway

3.1 Demand-side energy system transformations

The following three approaches are explored in the three GEA pathway groups as a means of reducing final energy demand: (1) improving technological efficiency, (2) changing the structure of energy services demand (e.g., modal shift), and (3) reducing the level of energy services demand (e.g., mobility demand reduction). The three GEA pathway groups assume that the rapid and pervasive introduction of highly energy efficient end-use technologies will play a central role in reducing final energy demand throughout the time horizon to 2100, which is enabled by effective policies such as improved energy efficiency standards for buildings, appliances, vehicles, and machines; product labeling; and taxes and subsidies. However, to achieve final energy demand reductions represented in the three GEA pathway groups, technological measures to improve efficiency need to be complemented by political, regulatory, and institutional measures to shift and limit energy services demand.

The final energy intensity of the global economy (measured in terms of megajoules of final energy consumed per 2005 US dollars of GDP at market exchange rates) is projected to decline over the course of the century regardless of the two pathways shown in this chapter. Specifically, it declines at an average annual rate of 1.5 percent and 0.8 percent between 2010 and 2100 in the illustrative GEA-Mix pathway and the GEA counterfactual pathway, respectively (compared with 1.2 percent in the period between the early 1970s and now). Such large-scale improvements in the final energy intensity of the global economy require a portfolio of measures that stimulate the adoption of highly energy efficient end-use technologies, changes in the structure of the economy, and changes in energy services demand through lifestyle and behavioral shifts. Energy intensity improvements vary significantly at the regional level: developing regions are projected to experience more rapid energy intensity improvements than today's industrialized regions.

Figures 7.1a–d show the development of final energy demand by sector for the world and for each of the three developing Asian regions in the GEA counterfactual pathway and the illustrative GEA-Mix pathway, respectively. Figure 7.1a shows that expected continuous economic growth in the world more than offsets improvements in the final energy intensity of the global economy in the two pathways, leading to an overall continuous increase in global final energy demand over the course of the century. It should, however, be noted that the growth rate of final energy demand can be suppressed in the illustrative GEA-Mix pathway; for example, levels of final energy demand are stabilized in Centrally Planned Asia (see Figure 7.1b). Globally, final energy demand increases by a factor of 3.4 and 1.8 between 2010 and 2100 in the GEA counterfactual pathway and the illustrative GEA-Mix pathway, respectively.

In the two pathways, the industrial sector remains the largest consumer of final energy in the world and in the three developing Asian regions until 2100 (except for 2010 in South Asia), consuming approximately half of total final energy consumption from 2030 at the latest in the world and in the three developing Asian regions. This implies that energy efficiency improvements in the industrial sector have significant importance for reducing total final energy demand. In the illustrative GEA-Mix pathway, a number of different measures are taken to reduce final energy demand in the industrial sector. These include: (1) the adoption of best available technologies for industrial processes, (2) the retrofit of existing plants, (3) the optimization of industrial systems designs, and (4) further electrification.

Globally, the final energy demand reduction rate in the illustrative GEA-Mix pathway compared with the GEA counterfactual pathway is highest in the transport sector over the period 2010–2100, which is estimated at 48.4 percent in 2050 and 53.5 percent in 2100. This trend

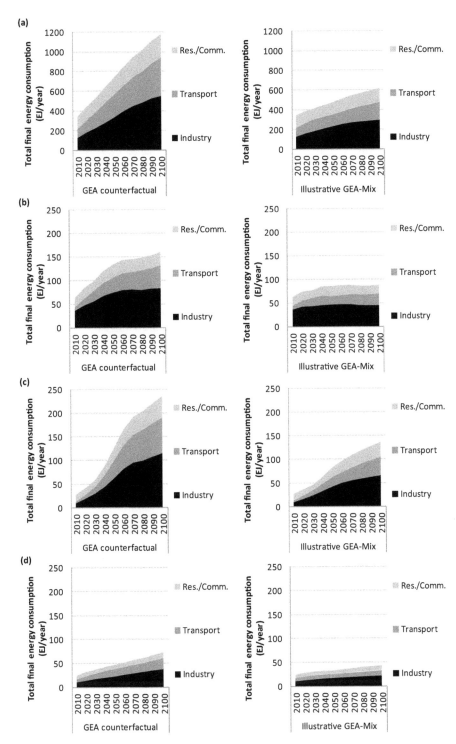

Figures 7.1 (a–d) Final energy demand by sector in the world (a) Centrally Planned Asia (b) South Asia (c) and Other Pacific Asia (d) in the GEA counterfactual and illustrative GEA-Mix pathways

mostly holds for each of the three developing Asian regions, despite increasing reliance on individual mobility provided by cars in these regions. Such a large reduction in final energy demand in the transport sector in the illustrative GEA-Mix pathway results not only from efficiency improvements in the vehicle fleet but also from reduction in transport activity demand (expressed in passenger-kilometers (pkm) per year or tonne-kilometers (tkm) per year) and modal shift towards rail and bus with low energy intensity (expressed in megajoules of final energy consumed per pkm or tkm).

By contrast, in most regions and time points, the final energy demand reduction rate in the illustrative GEA-Mix pathway compared with the GEA counterfactual pathway is lowest in the residential and commercial sector over the period 2010–2100, although the potential efficiency improvements from buildings in terms of energy use avoided are estimated to be among the highest across all energy end-use sectors. In the illustrative GEA-Mix pathway, the potential for energy efficiency improvements for space heating and cooling is tapped, for example, by promoting thermal insulation as well as the retrofit of existing buildings. Also, the increasing penetration of air- or ground-source heat pumps driven by electricity contributes to efficiency improvements in the use of energy for this purpose.

Figures 7.2a–d show the development of final energy consumption by fuel for the world and for each of the three developing Asian regions in the GEA counterfactual pathway and the illustrative GEA-Mix pathway, respectively. In Figures 7.2a–d and 7.3a–c, gases include natural gas, biogas, and synthetic natural gas, while heat includes district heating/cooling and solar thermal heat.

Similar patterns are observed for the global and regional evolution of the final energy mix in the illustrative GEA-Mix pathway. That is, the final energy mix in this pathway changes considerably over the course of the century, as the trend toward more flexible, more convenient, and cleaner energy carriers, such as electricity and gaseous fuels, grows significantly. By contrast, the structure of the final energy mix in the GEA counterfactual pathway would remain almost unchanged in the world and in the three developing Asian regions until 2100, except for the increasing share of electricity and fossil synfuels (which would compensate for the scarcity of the oil resource base). In this pathway, fossil-based energy carriers would continue to account for a significant share of final energy consumption in the world and in the three developing Asian regions.

There are three major characteristics of the structure of the final energy mix in the world and in the three developing Asian regions in the illustrative GEA-Mix pathway. First, oil products, today's prevailing fuels, as well as solid energy carriers (i.e., coal and biomass) are gradually phased out of the final energy market. The use of traditional biomass in the residential and commercial sector is phased out much earlier by 2030 due to improved energy access in developing regions. The share of solid energy carriers shown in Figures 7.2a–d after 2050 is predominantly modern biomass used as a substitute for coal in industrial processes. Second, electricity increases its share dramatically, accounting for 54.2 percent of global final energy consumption in 2100. Third, other grid-delivered or on-site-generated energy carriers (such as natural gas and hydrogen) and biofuels increase their contribution in absolute energy terms. Hydrogen plays a marginal role and is used only for industrial applications.

Figures 7.3a–c show the development of global final energy consumption by fuel for each energy end-use sector in the GEA counterfactual pathway and the illustrative GEA-Mix pathway, respectively. Globally, electricity, natural gas, modern biomass, and hydrogen are the fuels of choice in the industrial sector in the illustrative GEA-Mix pathway, resulting in a reduction in direct CO_2 emissions in this sector. In particular, electricity and natural gas combined account for an increasing and ultimately dominant share of final energy consumption in the industrial

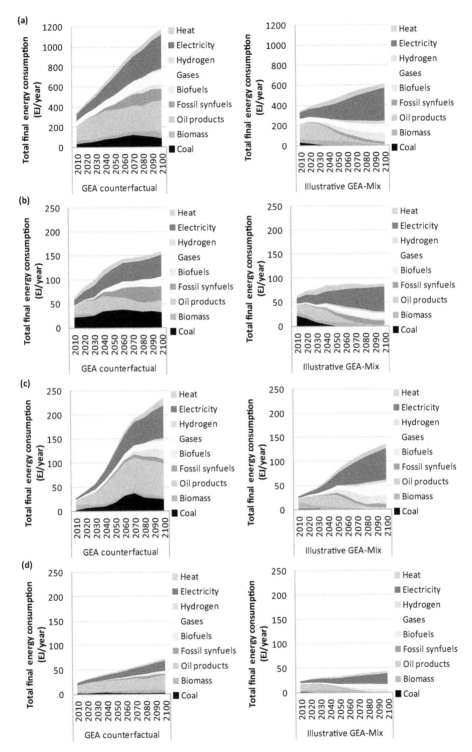

Figures 7.2 (a–d) Final energy consumption by fuel in the world (a) Centrally Planned Asia (b) South Asia (c) and Other Pacific Asia (d) in the GEA counterfactual and illustrative GEA-Mix pathways

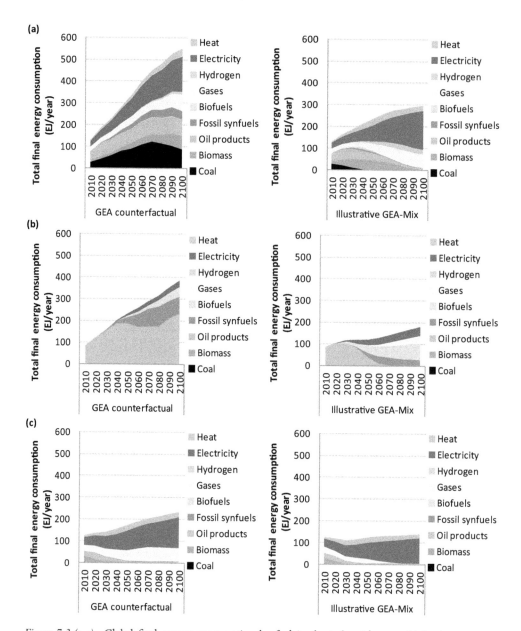

Figures 7.3 (a–c)   Global final energy consumption by fuel in the industrial sector (a) in the transport
sector (b) and in the residential and commercial sector (c) in the GEA counterfactual and
illustrative GEA-Mix pathways

sector in this pathway. Hydrogen is used in direct reduction processes as a substitute for coal.
Although not shown here, these trends also hold for each of the three developing Asian regions.

The transport sector would be dominated by oil products with a smaller contribution from
other liquid fuels and electricity until 2100 in the GEA counterfactual pathway. However, the
dominance of oil products in the transport sector lasts only for the short term in the illustrative
GEA–Mix pathway. In this pathway, biofuels, electricity, and gases (mainly natural gas) replace oil
use in the transport sector and contribute to decarbonizing the transport sector and diversifying

its final energy mix over the medium-to-long term. Hydrogen is not introduced at all in the transport sector mainly because of technical hurdles for hydrogen fuel cell vehicles, their high costs, and extensive requirements for costly hydrogen supply infrastructure. These trends also hold for each of the three developing Asian regions.

Although the limited potential of sustainable bioenergy places an upper limit on the use of biofuels in the transport sector, biofuels account for an increasing share of total final energy consumption in the transport sector and ultimately become the largest source of the fuel supply for the transport sector in the world and in the developing Asian regions except Centrally Planned Asia in the illustrative GEA-Mix pathway. In Centrally Planned Asia in this pathway, fossil synfuels have an increasing share of the final energy mix and play the same role as biofuels do in the world and in the above two developing Asian regions (i.e., South Asia and Other Pacific Asia). Fossil synfuels production is combined with CO_2 capture and storage (CCS) to reduce CO_2 emissions caused by their production.

As regards oil consumption, the transport sector continues to be the largest oil consumer of all energy end-use sectors in the world and in the three developing Asian regions until around the middle of the century in the two pathways. However, in the illustrative GEA-Mix pathway, the industrial sector overtakes the transport sector as the largest oil consumer thereafter. At the global level, the share of the transport sector in global oil consumption in this pathway decreases from 58.5 percent in 2010 to 48.3 percent in 2050 and then to zero from 2080 onwards. It is worth noting that the transport sector ultimately becomes the smallest oil consumer of all energy end-use sectors in the world and in the three developing Asian regions in the illustrative GEA-Mix pathway.

As Figure 7.3c illustrates, the final energy mix in the residential and commercial sector is very similar in the two pathways: electricity, gases, and heat dominate final energy consumption in this sector. This means that even in the GEA counterfactual pathway, the trend toward the decarbonization of the residential and commercial sector would progress over time. The only clear difference between the two pathways is that electricity increases its share at the expense of gases in the illustrative GEA-Mix pathway, whereas gases would continue to be one of the central sources of the fuel supply for this sector until 2100 in the GEA counterfactual pathway. As a result, direct CO_2 emissions in the residential and commercial sector are further reduced in the former pathway. It is also important to note that the electrification rate is highest in the residential and commercial sector of all energy end-use sectors. Although not shown here, solar thermal heat accounts for a larger share of the final energy mix in the residential and commercial sector in Centrally Planned Asia and Other Pacific Asia than in the world.

3.2 Supply-side energy system transformations

Figures 7.4a–d show the development of primary energy supply by energy source for the world and for each of the three developing Asian regions in the GEA counterfactual pathway and the illustrative GEA-Mix pathway, respectively. Here, similar to Riahi et al. (2012), the substitution method is used to calculate primary energy by assuming a 35 percent efficiency for electricity generation from non-combustible sources and an 85 percent efficiency for heat production.[7] Note that secondary energy import is not taken into account in Figures 7.4a–d.

In the GEA counterfactual pathway without any transformational policies to meet the sustainability goals, the global energy system would continue its heavy reliance on fossil fuels: the contribution of fossil fuels to the global primary energy supply would more than double by 2050 (reaching about 900 EJ) and more than triple by 2100 (reaching about 1,300 EJ). By contrast, the primary energy supply mix in the illustrative GEA-Mix pathway is considerably different

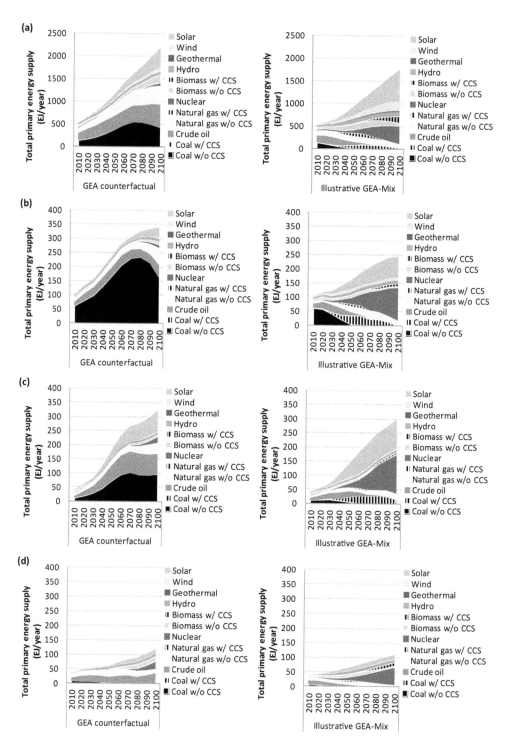

Figures 7.4 (a–d) Primary energy supply by energy source in the world (a) Centrally Planned Asia (b) South Asia (c) and Other Pacific Asia (d) in the GEA counterfactual and illustrative GEA-Mix pathways

from that of today and that in the GEA counterfactual pathway both globally and regionally. In this pathway, renewables (mainly solar, wind, and biomass) and nuclear gain share at the expense of fossil fuels, particularly coal and crude oil, and play an important role in the world and in the three developing Asian regions. Such a phase-out of coal and crude oil is not because of the scarcity of their resource bases but because of the limited carbon emissions budgets under the stringent climate stabilization target. It is interesting to note that even in the GEA counterfactual pathway, the share of renewables in the total primary energy supply in the world and in the three developing Asian regions would increase over time and become pronounced by the end of the century at the latest.

The primary energy structure in the two pathways is characterized by high levels of regional diversity, although this characteristic is less pronounced in the illustrative GEA-Mix pathway. For example, the options for decarbonizing primary energy supply vary by region depending mainly on regional differences in resource supply curves for each primary energy source and in the availability of low-carbon supply-side technological solutions such as nuclear and CCS. Specifically, nuclear, solar, coal with CCS, wind, and biomass with and without CCS are selected in Centrally Planned Asia; nuclear, solar, and coal with CCS are selected in South Asia; and nuclear and biomass with CCS are selected in Other Pacific Asia.

In the two pathways, the share of renewables in total primary energy supply is generally smaller in the three developing Asian regions than in the world. In particular, the global preference for wind and biomass is weak in the three developing Asian regions. This is primarily due to those regions' high population density and to potential land use and other conflicts that limit, for example, their potential for wind energy and/or sustainable bioenergy. Solar becomes by far the largest primary renewable energy source in Centrally Planned Asia and South Asia, whereas biomass, solar, and hydro are the main sources of primary renewable energy supply in Other Pacific Asia. In the illustrative GEA-Mix pathway, the exploitation rate (defined as the ratio of actual production to maximum potential production) is higher for modern biomass than for other renewables partly due to the higher tradability of liquid biofuels compared with electricity and heat. Such large-scale modern biomass production requires large amounts of land and water and thus has a possibility of leading to land scarcity, crop price increases, and biodiversity loss. This implies the need for additional policies to avoid these negative impacts and strict monitoring of biomass production and land use for this purpose.

In the two pathways, especially the illustrative GEA-Mix pathway, the deployment of coal and nuclear occurs intensively in the three developing Asian regions. In the illustrative GEA-Mix pathway, these regions account for 76.3 percent in 2050 and 77.3 percent in 2100 of global primary production of coal and account for 65.3 percent in 2050 and 80.9 percent in 2100 of global primary production of nuclear energy. For nuclear energy to account for such a large share of total primary energy supply in the developing Asian regions, important barriers to nuclear energy implementation, namely safety risks, proliferation risks, and waste management problems, must be addressed.

In the illustrative GEA-Mix pathway, the large-scale commercial deployment of CCS begins in 2030 (see also Figure 7.10). In this pathway, Centrally Planned Asia and South Asia are the regions with the largest and the second-largest cumulative CO_2 storage needs over the century of all the 11 world regions because of their large coal resource base and correspondingly high utilization of coal with CCS. The contribution of coal to the global primary energy supply in this pathway decreases until 2040, but then increases until 2060 and does not completely disappear until 2100 on the condition that CCS can be successfully deployed on a large scale. Furthermore, in this pathway, whereas the vast majority of CO_2 captured by 2050 comes from fossil fuels (i.e., coal and natural gas), biomass in combination with CCS, which enables negative CO_2

emissions, contributes visibly to the primary energy supply mix in the world and in the developing Asian regions except South Asia in the second half of the century and makes a large contribution to achieving the stringent climate stabilization target. For CCS to play such an important role in the developing Asian regions, the challenges associated with financing and technology transfer must be overcome.

Figures 7.5a–d show the development of the import share of primary energy supply for the world and for each of the three developing Asian regions in the GEA counterfactual pathway and the illustrative GEA-Mix pathway, respectively. Also, to examine the diversity of primary

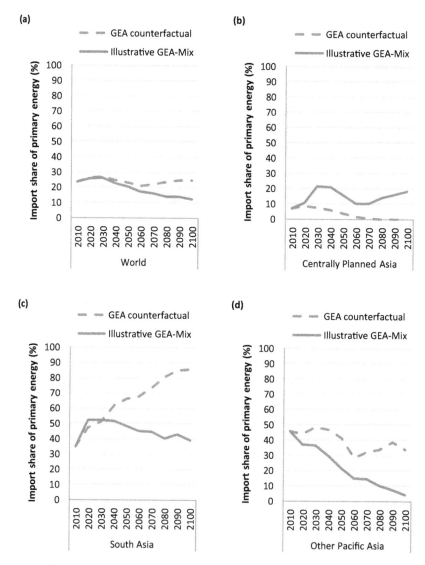

Figures 7.5 (a–d)   The import share of primary energy supply in the world (a) Centrally Planned Asia (b) South Asia (c) and Other Pacific Asia (d) in the GEA counterfactual and illustrative GEA-Mix pathways

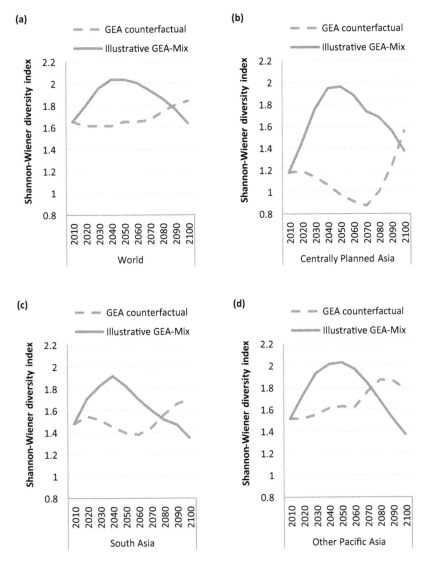

Figures 7.6 (a–d) The Shannon-Wiener diversity index in the world (a) Centrally Planned Asia (b) South Asia (c) and Other Pacific Asia (d) in the GEA counterfactual and illustrative GEA-Mix pathways

energy supply, Figures 7.6a–d show the development of the Shannon-Wiener diversity index (SWDI)[8] for the world and for each of the three developing Asian regions in the GEA counter-factual pathway and the illustrative GEA-Mix pathway, respectively. The SWDI is calculated as follows:

$$SWDI = -\sum_i \left(p_i * \ln\left(p_i \right) \right) \qquad (1)$$

where p_i is the share of primary energy i in total primary energy supply. An increase in the SWDI means an increase in the diversity of primary energy supply.

Figures 7.5a–d and 7.6a–d show that an improvement in energy supply security is, for the most part, achieved as a co-benefit of the decarbonization of the global energy system, taking into account that explicit constraints are not imposed on the diversity of primary energy supply (see Section 2.2). Except for Centrally Planned Asia, the import share of primary energy supply in the illustrative GEA-Mix pathway is generally lower than in the GEA counterfactual pathway. Furthermore, the SWDI (i.e., the diversity of primary energy supply) in the illustrative GEA-Mix pathway becomes much higher than in the GEA counterfactual pathway around the middle of the century in the world and in the three developing Asian regions. However, the results show that there is a trend reversal in which the SWDI in the illustrative GEA-Mix pathway becomes lower than in the GEA counterfactual pathway toward the end of the century in all the 11 world regions except the Middle East and North Africa. This suggests that not only climate change mitigation policies, but also dedicated policies aimed at improving energy supply security are needed to completely meet the four sustainability goals adopted for the GEA analysis.

As shown in Figures 7.2a–d, electricity becomes the most important final energy carrier in the world and in the three developing Asian regions in the illustrative GEA-Mix pathway. Hence, the focus is now placed on examining the optimal mix of electricity generation technologies. Figures 7.7a–d show the development of electricity generation by technology for the world and for each of the three developing Asian regions in the GEA counterfactual pathway and the illustrative GEA-Mix pathway, respectively (PV is an abbreviation for photovoltaics and CSP is an abbreviation for concentrated solar power). It can be seen that electricity generation in the illustrative GEA-Mix pathway becomes higher than in the GEA counterfactual pathway from 2060 onwards in the world, Centrally Planned Asia, and South Asia and from 2030 onwards in Other Pacific Asia. This is mainly because of additional electricity use for CCS and the further electrification of the transport sector in the illustrative GEA-Mix pathway.

Except for the negligible contribution of oil and biomass to the electricity generation mix, the temporal and spatial trends of electricity generation are similar to those of the primary energy supply in the two pathways. In the GEA counterfactual pathway, the electricity generation sector would be dominated by fossil fuels without CCS (excluding oil), with a small but increasing contribution of renewables (mainly solar) and nuclear until 2100 in the world and in the three developing Asian regions. By contrast, in the illustrative GEA-Mix pathway, renewable electricity generation technologies (mainly solar, wind, and hydro), nuclear electricity generation technologies, and fossil-based electricity generation technologies with CCS play an important role, whereas conventional fossil-based electricity generation technologies without CCS are phased out of the electricity generation portfolio. As a result, almost full decarbonization of the electricity generation sector is achieved by the middle of the century in the world and in the three developing Asian regions.

In the illustrative GEA-Mix pathway, fossil fuels with CCS provide a transitional bridge for the electricity generation sector; their contribution increases until around the middle of the century and then declines. This is because electricity supply from fossil fuels with CCS causes non-negligible CO_2 emissions (the rate of CO_2 capture being estimated in the range of 85 percent to 95 percent (IEA and NEA, 2010)). Renewables and nuclear, on the other hand, play an increasing role in this pathway over time and ultimately dominate the electricity generation sector. The temporal trends of electricity generation described previously hold not only for the world as a whole but also for the three developing Asian regions, although the relative importance of each of these low-carbon electricity generation technologies varies by region for the reasons stated in the results for primary energy supply.

Globally and regionally, solar electricity generation technologies (both solar PV and CSP technologies) account for a large share of total electricity generation in the medium to long term

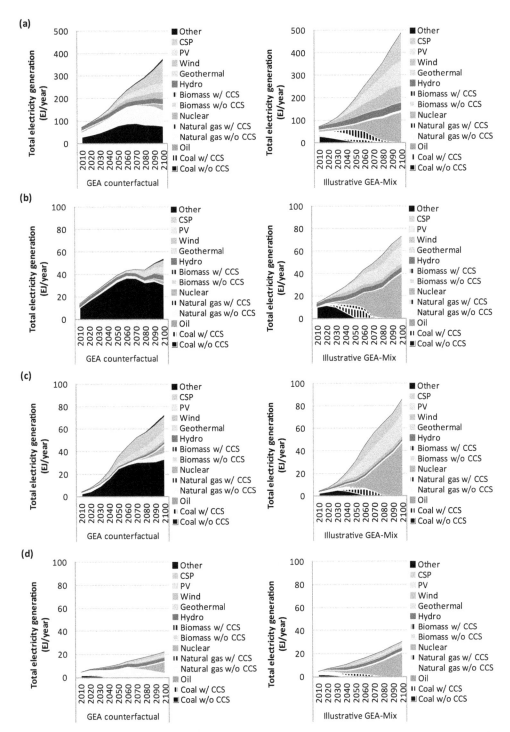

Figures 7.7 (a–d) Electricity generation by technology in the world (a) Centrally Planned Asia (b) South Asia (c) and Other Pacific Asia (d) in the GEA counterfactual and illustrative GEA-Mix pathways

in the illustrative GEA-Mix pathway, whereas flexible electricity generation technologies (such as natural gas combined-cycle power plants and pumped-storage hydropower plants) play a marginal role. This suggests an increasing requirement for technical measures that enable reliable integration of large amounts of electricity from intermittent renewable energy sources into electricity grids. These include, but are not limited to, storage technologies (such as batteries, flywheels, super-capacitors, hydrogen production and storage systems, and super-conducting systems), demand-side management, methods to predict renewable energy supplies many hours ahead, and backup power plants.

As noted in the results for primary energy supply in the illustrative GEA-Mix pathway, the majority of deployment of coal-fired and nuclear electricity generation technologies materializes in the three developing Asian regions. In the illustrative GEA-Mix pathway, the share of these base-load electricity generation technologies in total electricity generation increases from 45.4 percent in 2050 to 56.7 percent in 2100 in Centrally Planned Asia, from 36.5 percent in 2050 to 56.6 percent in 2100 in South Asia, and from 28.9 percent in 2050 to 72.7 percent in 2100 in Other Pacific Asia. In the light of such a large share of base-load electricity generation technologies and a trend toward an increasing difference between maximum and minimum daily electric demand in these regions, solar electricity generation technologies are expected to play a central role in meeting peak load demand.

In the two pathways, the role of biomass in the electricity generation mix is negligible in the world and in the three developing Asian regions. This result and the results of Figures 7.2a–d and 7.4a–d imply that it is cost-effective to preferentially use biomass to supply solid, liquid, and gaseous fuels. This is because conversion of biomass into these fuels is more energy efficient than conversion into electricity and because of the limited supply potential of sustainable bioenergy.

3.3 GHG emissions

Figures 7.8a–d show the development of total GHG emissions for the world and for each of the three developing Asian regions in the GEA counterfactual pathway and the illustrative GEA-Mix pathway, respectively. In the GEA counterfactual pathway, global total GHG emissions would increase monotonically until 2070 to reach 2.5 times larger than 2010 levels. After that time, they would increase only slightly until 2090 and decrease thereafter, reflecting the increasing share of renewables and nuclear in the global primary energy supply (see Figures 7.4a–d). According to Riahi et al. (2012), such a trend for global total GHG emissions might force the global mean temperature increase to reach 5 °C above pre-industrial levels in the long term.

By contrast, global total GHG emissions in the illustrative GEA-Mix pathway exhibit a continuously declining trend from 2010 onwards: they are reduced to 52.2 percent of 2010 levels in 2050 and reach negative levels in 2100 (-2.6 GtCO$_2$-eq), which can be achieved by large-scale deployment of bioenergy combined with CCS and enhancement of the terrestrial sink potential, such as afforestation and reforestation. This suggests the need for very ambitions short-term GHG mitigation policies and their increasing stringency over time under the stringent climate stabilization target. Total GHG emissions in Centrally Planned Asia in this pathway also follow a continuously declining trajectory, whereas those in South Asia and Other Pacific Asia continue to increase until 2040 and 2020, respectively, and decline thereafter. As a result, total GHG emissions in the developing Asian regions except South Asia reach very low to negative levels by 2100 (0.83 GtCO$_2$-eq in Centrally Planned Asia and -0.69 GtCO$_2$-eq in Other Pacific Asia). On the other hand, the level of GHG emissions reduction in this pathway is rather modest in South Asia: total GHG emissions in South Asia in this pathway are reduced to 2.2 GtCO$_2$-eq in 2100, which are 57.2 percent of 2010 levels.

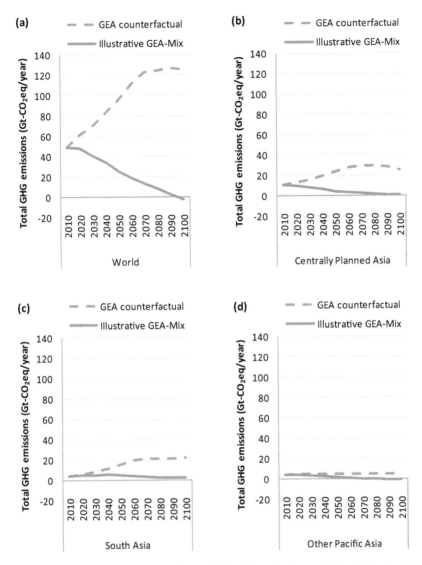

Figures 7.8 (a–d) Total GHG emissions in the world (a) Centrally Planned Asia (b) South Asia (c) and Other Pacific Asia (d) in the GEA counterfactual and illustrative GEA-Mix pathways

To identify the most cost-effective pattern of spatially sharing the burden of a reduction in global total GHG emissions, Figure 7.9 shows the contribution of the 11 world regions to a reduction in cumulative global total GHG emissions over the period 2010–2100 in the illustrative GEA-Mix pathway compared with the GEA counterfactual pathway. The result shows that there is a large difference in regional contribution to a reduction in cumulative global total GHG emissions over this period. It can also be seen that the three developing Asian regions account for a very large share (43.5 percent) of a reduction in cumulative global total GHG emissions over this period, despite a considerable increase in energy services demand and other GHG-emitting activities in these regions. Centrally Planned Asia and South Asia are the largest and the second largest

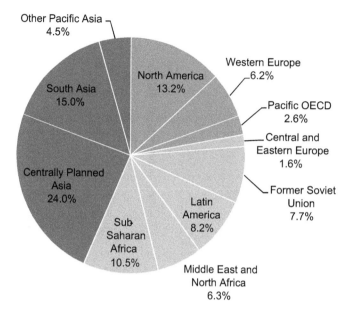

Figure 7.9 Regional breakdown of a reduction in cumulative global total GHG emissions over the period 2010–2100 in the illustrative GEA-Mix pathway compared with the GEA counterfactual pathway

contributors, accounting for 24.0 percent and 15.0 percent of a reduction in cumulative global total GHG emissions, respectively. This means that there is a large low-cost GHG mitigation potential in these regions.

3.4 Contribution of technology options to reducing global energy-related CO_2 emissions under the stringent climate stabilization target

The so-called Kaya identity (Kaya, 1989), which is expressed in equation (2), helps to identify technology options that can contribute to achieving a reduction in global energy-related CO_2 emissions without having a negative impact on economic growth.

$$C_n = \frac{C_n}{C_g} \times \frac{C_g}{PE} \times \frac{PE}{GDP} \times GDP \qquad (2)$$

where C_n is the net global energy-related CO_2 emissions, C_g is the gross global energy-related CO_2 emissions, PE is the global primary energy consumption, and GDP is the global GDP.

The term C_n/C_g represents how widespread the deployment of CCS is, the term C_g/PE represents the carbon intensity of global primary energy consumption, and the term PE/GDP represents the primary energy intensity of the global economy. It can be drawn from equation (2) that the target of reducing net global energy-related CO_2 emissions without compromising economic growth requires a decrease in C_n/C_g, C_g/PE, and/or PE/GDP in equation (2). This means that the deployment of CCS, fuel switching to less carbon-intensive fuels, and energy intensity improvements leading to energy savings are three technology options for meeting this target.

The focus is now placed on examining the contribution of each of the three technology options to reducing net global energy-related CO_2 emissions under the four sustainability goals adopted for the GEA analysis. Net global energy-related CO_2 emissions also can be expressed as follows:

$$C_n = \frac{C_n}{C_g} \times \frac{C_g}{PE_f} \times \frac{PE_f}{PE} \times PE \qquad (3)$$

where PE_f is the global primary fossil energy consumption.

Following the approach proposed by Akimoto et al. (2004), the contribution of each of the three technology options to reducing net global energy-related CO_2 emissions under the constraint that the global mean temperature increase should be limited to 2 °C above pre-industrial levels with a likelihood of more than 50 percent can be derived from equation (4).

$$
\begin{aligned}
C_n^B - C_n^S &= \left(C_g^B - CCS^B\right) - \left(C_g^S - CCS^S\right) \\
&= \left(CCS^S - CCS^B\right) + PE^S\left(\frac{C_g^B}{PE^B} - \frac{C_g^S}{PE^S}\right) + \frac{C_g^B}{PE^B}\left(PE^B - PE^S\right) \\
&= \left(CCS^S - CCS^B\right) + PE^S \frac{PE_f^S}{PE^S}\left(\frac{C_g^B}{PE_f^B} - \frac{C_g^S}{PE_f^S}\right) + PE^S \frac{C_g^B}{PE_f^B}\left(\frac{PE_f^B}{PE^B} - \frac{PE_f^S}{PE^S}\right) \\
&\quad + \frac{C_g^B}{PE^B}\left(PE^B - PE^S\right)
\end{aligned}
\qquad (4)
$$

where CCS is the amount of CO_2 sequestered, and the superscripts B and S denote the GEA counterfactual and illustrative GEA-Mix pathways, respectively.

The first term represents the contribution of CCS, the second term represents the contribution of fuel switching among fossil fuels, the third term represents the contribution of fuel switching to non-fossil fuels, and the fourth term represents the contribution of energy savings on both the demand and supply sides of the energy systems.

Figure 7.10 shows the contribution of each of the three technology options to reducing net global energy-related CO_2 emissions in the illustrative GEA-Mix pathway, which is calculated according to equation (4). It is readily apparent that all the three technology options need to be implemented to meet the stringent climate stabilization target. A large part of the reduction in global energy-related CO_2 emissions results from the decarbonization of energy supply, which is achieved through fuel switching and CCS. Especially fuel switching to non-fossil fuels (such as nuclear, solar, wind, and biomass) makes a significant contribution to reducing global energy-related CO_2 emissions. Energy savings on the demand and supply sides, which are achieved through energy efficiency improvements and price-induced energy demand reductions, also make a sizeable contribution.

Figure 7.10 shows that CCS is the smallest contributor to reducing global energy-related CO_2 emissions in the illustrative GEA-Mix pathway. The global amount of CO_2 captured for storage in this pathway increases until 2060 and then remains almost constant until 2100. It should, however, be noted that the contribution of CCS to reducing global energy-related CO_2 emissions varies significantly depending on levels of energy demand: under high demand levels as is assumed in the GEA-Supply pathways, cumulative global CO_2 storage by 2100 would be approximately 1.5 times larger than that in the illustrative GEA-Mix pathway. Cumulative global CO_2 storage by 2100 amounts to 98.3 $GtCO_2$ and 145.8 $GtCO_2$, respectively, in the illustrative GEA-Mix and illustrative GEA-Supply pathways. These values are much smaller than the best estimate of the global CO_2 storage capacity of approximately 2,000 $GtCO_2$ (Metz et al., 2005), implying that CO_2 storage capacity will not become a problem in the 21st century even under stringent climate stabilization targets.

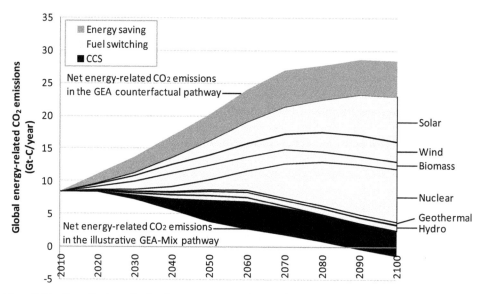

Figure 7.10 Contribution of technology options to reducing global energy-related CO_2 emissions in the illustrative GEA-Mix pathway

4. Conclusions

In this chapter, the illustrative GEA-Mix pathway presented by Riahi et al. (2012) has been shown and discussed in detail as an example of a sustainable energy pathway that can meet not only the ambitious goal of limiting the global mean temperature increase to 2 °C above pre-industrial levels with a likelihood of more than 50 percent but also that of improved energy access, reduced air pollution and improved human health, and energy security. It has been observed from the results of this pathway that early and profound transformations of the demand and supply sides of the energy systems are needed to simultaneously meet these stringent requirements in a cost-effective manner. Such transformations are technologically feasible but pose a formidable challenge for which strong policy interventions, considerable energy investments, and lifestyle and behavioral changes are absolutely essential.

From a short-term perspective, pledges currently in place or in the planning stages, mainly in industrialized countries, need to be tightened to meet the stringent climate stabilization target adopted for the GEA analysis. According to Rogelj et al. (2010) and UNEP (2010), even if all the present pledges made by various countries were to be executed successfully, global GHG emissions would amount to 47.9–53.6 GtCO$_2$-eq in 2020, which are larger than those in the illustrative GEA-Mix pathway. Furthermore, Riahi et al. (2012) estimate globally implemented CO$_2$ price levels that can keep global GHG emissions in 2020 between 2005 and 2010 levels to be in the range of US\$15–45 per tonne of CO$_2$, compared with the current CO$_2$ permit price of just under US\$ 5.2 per tonne of CO$_2$ that prevailed in the EU Emission Trading System[9] as of March 2013 (JPEC, 2013).

There seem to be two important issues not mentioned in this chapter. First, as pointed out by Riahi et al. (2012), special attention should be paid to discussing who must pay for such drastic GHG emissions reduction as those depicted by the illustrative GEA-Mix pathway. To address this equity issue, it is necessary to make a political compromise between industrialized countries (which are responsible for the bulk of the historical increase in atmospheric GHG concentrations) and developing countries (in which a large, low-cost GHG mitigation potential is estimated to exist). Second, in light of the difficulties in drastically cutting GHG emissions, not only mitigation strategies but also adaptation strategies need to be developed to avoid the catastrophic impacts of climate change. It should, however, be kept in mind that mitigation strategies are the first-order task because they are likely to have substantial co-benefits on local and regional environments, human health, and energy security and because there is a possibility that extended and prolonged reliance on adaptation would increase the moral dilemma (Riahi et al., 2012; Smith et al., 2012).

Notes

1 For definitions of regional classification, see Table 1.
2 GEA is an acronym for Global Energy Assessment, a publication by Johansson et al. (2012).
3 These two energy pathways also were developed using an integrated assessment modeling framework IMAGE. The GEA pathways quantified with the IMAGE model are not presented because this model excludes all solar energy technologies other than solar photovoltaics and thus significantly underestimates the potential contribution of solar energy.
4 In total, 41 pathways were developed within the three pathway groups having low, intermediate, and high estimates of energy demand evolution.
5 In Riahi et al. (2012), the GEA-Mix pathway assuming restrictions on the electrification of the transport sector in a conventional transportation world was selected as the illustrative case for the GEA-Mix pathway groups.
6 This likelihood refers to physical uncertainties associated with climate change, such as climate sensitivity, aerosol forcing, and ocean diffusivity, and does not refer to the likelihood of the implementation of political and/or technological measures to meet the goal in the future.
7 There are three main methods for calculating the primary energy equivalent of non-fossil energies (i.e., renewables and nuclear): the substitution method, the direct equivalent method, and the physical energy content method. For details, see, for example, Grubler et al. (2012).
8 For details, see, for example, Stirling (1998) and Jansen et al. (2004).
9 An exchange rate of 1 Euro per US$1.31 was used (MURC, 2013).

References

Akimoto, K., Tomoda, T., Fujii, Y. and Yamaji, K. (2004) "Assessment of global warming mitigation options with integrated assessment model DNE21," *Energy Economics* 26: 635–53.

Cherp, A. and Jewell, J. (2011) "The three perspectives on energy security: intellectual history, disciplinary roots and the potential for integration," *Current Opinion in Environmental Sustainability* 3(4): 202–12.

Grubler, A., Johansson, T.B., Mundaca, L., Nakicenovic, N., Pachauri, S., Riahi, K., Rogner, H.-H., Strupeit, L., Kolp, P., Krey, V., Macknick, J., Nagai, Y., Rogner, M.L., Smith, K.R., Olsen, K.S. and Weinzettel, J. (2012) "Energy Primer," in T.B. Johansson, A. Patwardhan, N. Nakicenovic and L.G. Echeverri (eds.) *Global Energy Assessment – Toward a Sustainable Future*, pp. 99–150. Cambridge: Cambridge University Press.

IEA and Nuclear Energy Agency (NEA) (2010) *Projected Costs of Generating Electricity*. Paris: Organization for Economic Co-Operation and Development.

International Energy Agency (IEA) (2013) *Redrawing the Energy-Climate Map*. Paris: IEA.

International Institute for Applied Systems Analysis (IIASA) (2012) *Publishing on the Internet*. Laxenburg, Austria: IIASA. Online. Available HTTP: <www.iiasa.ac.at/web-apps/ene/geadb> (accessed 1 August 2012).

Jansen, J.C., van Arkel, W.G. and Boots, M.G. (2004) *Designing Indicators of Long-Term Energy Supply Security*, ECN-C-007. Pettern, The Netherlands: Energy Research Center of the Netherlands.

Japan Petroleum Energy Center (JPEC) (2013) *The Latest Trend of the EU-ETS*, JPEC Report No.2. Tokyo: JPEC (in Japanese).

Johansson, T.B., Patwardhan, A., Nakicenovic, N. and Echeverri, L.G. (eds.) (2012) *Global Energy Assessment – Toward a Sustainable Future*. Cambridge: Cambridge University Press.

Kaya, Y. (1989) *Impact of Carbon Dioxide Emission Control on GNP Growth: Interpretation of Proposed Scenarios.* Geneva: Intergovernmental Panel on Climate Change, Response Strategies Working Group.

Messner, S., Golodnikov, A. and Gritsevskii, A. (1996) "A stochastic version of the dynamic linear programming model MESSAGE III," *Energy* 21(9): 775–84.

Messner, S. and Strubegger, M. (1995) *User's Guide for MESSAGE III.* Laxenburg, Austria: IIASA.

Metz, B., Davidson, O.R., de Conlinck, H., Loos, M. and Meyer, L.M. (eds.) (2005) *IPCC Special Report on Carbon Dioxide Capture and Storage.* Cambridge: Cambridge University Press.

Mitsubishi UFJ Research and Consulting (MURC) (2013) *Publishing on the Internet.* Tokyo: MURC. Online. Available HTTP: <www.murc-kawasesouba.jp/fx/past/index.php?id=130301> (accessed 15 September 2013) (in Japanese).

Riahi, K., Dentener, F., Gielen, D., Grubler, A., Jewell, J., Klimont, Z., Krey, V., McCollum, D., Pachauri, S., Rao, S., van Ruijven, B., van Vuuren, D.P., Wilson, C., Isaac, M., Jaccard, M., Kobayashi, S., Kolp, P., Larson, E.D., Nagai, Y., Purohit, P., Schers, J., Vorsatz, D.U., van Dingenen, R. and van Vliet, O. (2012) "Energy Pathways for Sustainable Development," in T.B. Johansson, A. Patwardhan, N. Nakicenovic and L.G. Echeverri (eds.) *Global Energy Assessment – Toward a Sustainable Future*, pp. 1205–305. Cambridge: Cambridge University Press.

Riahi, K., Grubler, A. and Nakicenovic, N. (2007) "Scenarios of long-term socio-economic and environmental development under climate stabilization," *Technological Forecasting and Social Change* 74(7): 887–935.

Rogelj, J., Nabel, J., Chen, C., Hare, W., Markmann, K., Meinshausen, M., Shaeffer, M., MacEy, K. and Hohne, N. (2010) "Copenhagen Accord pledges are paltry," *Nature* 464(7292): 1126–8.

Smith, K.R., Balakrishnan, K., Butler, C., Chafe, Z., Fairlie, I., Kinney, P., Mauzerall, D.L., McKone, T., McMichael, A., Schneider, M. and Wilkinson, P. (2012) "Energy and Health," in T.B. Johansson, A. Patwardhan, N. Nakicenovic and L.G. Echeverri (eds.) *Global Energy Assessment – Toward a Sustainable Future*, pp. 255–324. Cambridge: Cambridge University Press.

Stirling, A. (1998) *On the Economics and Analysis of Diversity*, Paper No. 28. Sussex, UK: University of Sussex.

United Nations Environment Programme (UNEP) (2010) *The Emissions Gap Report Are the Copenhagen Accord Pledges Sufficient to Limit Global Warming to 2 °C or 1.5 °C?* Nairobi, Kenya: UNEP.

8

THEORY OF EMISSIONS TRADING AND TAXATION

Akira Maeda

One of the most significant goals of environmental policy is the reduction of emissions of environmentally affective substances such as air or water pollutants and greenhouse gases (GHG). To attain this goal, policy instruments have been devised in economic theory and are currently being implemented in various ways in many developed countries and regions. Some instruments rely on the behavior of economic agents in economic activities and thus are called market-based instruments (MBIs). These include environmental taxes, subsidies, and tradable permit systems.

This chapter surveys the underlying economic theory for these instruments, describing principles of environmental economic policy, followed by intensive discussion of two selected topics in policy formation for tradable permit systems. The chapter is organized as follows: Section 1 summarizes economic aspects of environmental issues and principles of economic policy instruments. Section 2 focuses on tradable permit systems and discusses the role of initial permit distribution and market power. Section 3 explains the concept of uncertainty regarding tradable permit systems and the theory of the safety valve mechanism.

1. Basics of economic policy instruments

This section summarizes economic aspects of environmental issues and principles of economic policy instruments. A key concept is externality: Externalities are defined as factors whose effects (either positive or negative) are not reflected in the market price of goods. The environment is a common asset of society and thus can be a source of externalities when utilized in individuals' economic activities. To amend externalities, economic theory offers economic measures such as taxation, subsidies, and tradable permit systems.[1]

1.1 The model of externality

Consider an economy in which there are N agents denoted by $i = 1$ to N. Agent i enjoys benefit $B_i(e_i)$ that accrues with the use of the environment, which we call "private benefit." Note that e_i denotes the amount of emission of pollutants or GHGs. Let e_i^{BAU} denote the business-as-usual (BAU) amount of emissions. It represents the state of no control for emissions reduction.

As is usual in economics, we assume that $B_i(e_i)$ is an increasing function of e_i and that marginal benefit is decreasing in e_i:

$$MB_i(e_i) \equiv \frac{dB_i(e_i)}{de_i} \geq 0 \,;\, \frac{dMB_i(e_i)}{de_i} = \frac{d^2B_i(e_i)}{de_i^2} < 0 \,;\, MB_i\left(e_i^{BAU}\right) = 0 \;\; \forall i,$$

$$e_i \in E_i \equiv \left\{ e_i \mid 0 \leq e_i \leq e_i^{BAU} \right\} \;\; \forall i.$$

The total amount of emissions in the economy is defined as follows:

$$e \equiv \sum_{i=1}^{N} e_i \,.$$

The benefit of emitting pollutants for the society, which we call the "social benefit," is defined as a function of e as follows:

$$B(e) \equiv \underset{\{e_i\}}{Max} \sum_{i=1}^{N} B_i(e_i) \;\; \text{s.t.} \;\; e \equiv \sum_{i=1}^{N} e_i \,. \tag{1.1.1}$$

Taking the derivative of B with respect to e, we define marginal social benefit as:

$$MB(e) \equiv \frac{dB(e)}{de} \,.$$

From Equation (1.1.1), we derive that:

$$MB(e) = MB_i(e_i) \;\; \forall i. \tag{1.1.2}$$

The derivation of Equation (1.1.2) is straightforward from the following discussion. From Equation (1.1.1), we have

$$\frac{dB(e)}{de} \equiv \sum_{i=1}^{N} MB_i\left(e_i^{\star}\right) \cdot \frac{de_i^{\star}(e)}{de} \;\; \text{and} \;\; MB_i\left(e_i^{\star}\right) - \lambda = 0 \;\; \forall i,$$

where λ is a Lagrange multiplier, and $\left\{e_i^{\star}\right\}$ represents an optimal distribution of emissions to attain the maximum social benefit.

Because $e = \sum_{i=1}^{N} e_i^{\star}(e)$ holds true, we have $1 = \sum_{i=1}^{N} \frac{de_i^{\star}(e)}{de}$.

Thus, the following equality holds true:

$$\frac{dB(e)}{de} = \lambda \cdot \sum_{i=1}^{N} \frac{de_i^{\star}(e)}{de} = \lambda \,.$$

This outcome proves Equation (1.1.2). (Note that asterisk $\star$ is omitted.) Note that using the envelope theorem[2] would allow us to take a shortcut to obtain the same result.

Similarly, the following properties are obtained:

$$MB(e) \equiv \frac{dB(e)}{de} \geq 0 \,;\, \frac{dMB(e)}{de} = \frac{d^2B(e)}{de^2} < 0 \,;\, MB\left(e^{BAU}\right) = 0 \;\; \text{where} \;\; e^{BAU} \equiv \sum_{i=1}^{N} e_i^{BAU} \,.$$

Apart from benefits, emitting pollutants definitely causes negative effects to the society. Evaluating the effect in monetary terms, we call the effect "social damage," which is a function of e, i.e., $D(e)$. This function has the following properties:

$$MD(e) \equiv \frac{dD(e)}{de} \geq 0 \,; \frac{dMD(e)}{de} = \frac{d^2D(e)}{de^2} > 0 \,.$$

For simplicity of mathematical treatment, we assume that no economic agent suffers "private" damage in addition to the overall social damage as a result of each one's individual emitting activity.

The model presented so far helps explain one of the most important concepts in economics called externality as follows:

Each economic agent behaves so as to maximize her net benefit as follows:

$$\underset{e_i \in E_i}{Max} \quad B_i(e_i) \; \forall i. \tag{1.1.3}$$

The solution to the problem is easily found as follows:

$$e_i^P = e_i^{BAU} \; \forall i.$$

Note that the superscript P indicates that it is an optimal solution to each "private" problem. On the other hand, social optimality is obtained by solving another optimization problem, as follows:

$$\underset{\{e_i\}}{Max} \quad B(e) - D(e) \,. \tag{1.1.4}$$

The optimal solution to the problem e^S, where the superscript S refers to social optimality, satisfies the following condition:

$$MB(e^S) = MD(e^S) \,. \tag{1.1.5}$$

Equations (1.1.2) and (1.1.5) indicate the following:

$$MB_i(e_i^S) = MD(e^S) \; \forall i, \tag{1.1.6}$$

$$e^S \equiv \sum_{i=1}^{N} e_i^S \,. \tag{1.1.7}$$

Note that Equations (1.1.6) and (1.1.7) comprise a set of $(N + 1)$ simultaneous equations containing $(N + 1)$ unknowns. Thus, the solution to the set of simultaneous equations is unique.

We derive the following proposition.

Proposition 1.1.1
With the setting described previously, the following inequalities hold true:

$$0 \leq e_i^S < e_i^{BAU} = e_i^P \; \forall i, \tag{1.1.8}$$

$$e^S < \sum_i e_i^P ,$$
(1.1.9)

$$\left(B\left(e^S\right) - D\left(e^S\right)\right) > \left(B\left(\sum_i e_i^P\right) - D\left(\sum_i e_i^P\right)\right).$$
(1.1.10)

(Proof is easy and thus omitted.)

The inequalities of (1.1.8) state that each level of privately optimized emissions is greater than each socially optimal level of emissions. The inequality of (1.1.9) states that the aggregate of privately optimized emissions is greater than the socially optimal amount of emissions. The inequality of (1.1.10) states that the resulting social net benefit (benefit less damage) for private optimizations is lower than that of socially optimized emissions. These results indicate the negative externality of a market-based economy.

1.2 Taxation and subsidy

To compensate for the negative externality described previously, three economic policy instruments are available. Among these three, taxation is the simplest concept. Suppose that a regulatory authority imposes a per unit tax, t [\$/unit], upon each unit of pollutant emission by an economic agent. This environmental tax forces each emitter to solve the following optimization problem instead of the problem (1.1.3):

$$\underset{e_i \in E_i}{Max} \quad B_i\left(e_i\right) - t\,e_i \;\; \forall i.$$
(1.2.1)

The optimal solution to this problem satisfies the following condition:

$$MB_i\left(e_i^T\right) = t \;\; \forall i.$$
(1.2.2)

Note that the superscript T indicates that it is a solution under the environmental tax scheme. Suppose that the regulator sets t such that the following equality holds:

$$t = MD\left(e^S\right).$$
(1.2.3)

Note that because of Equation (1.1.5), this setting is equivalent to the following:

$$t = MB\left(e^S\right).$$
(1.2.4)

Then, the following proposition holds true:

Proposition 1.2.1
When the regulator sets the environmental tax such that:

$$t = MD\left(e^S\right) \text{ or equivalently } t = MB\left(e^S\right),$$

each agent's amount of emissions under the tax system coincides with that of socially optimized emissions that could have been planned by a social planner for each agent.

$$e_i^T = e_i^S \;\; \forall i.$$

PROOF

From Equations (1.2.2), (1.2.3), and (1.1.6), $MB_i\left(e_i^T\right) = MB_i\left(e_i^S\right)$ $\forall i$ holds true. This proves the proposition. ■

Proposition 1.2.1 suggests that a measure to regulate pollution is to follow the following procedure to introduce a tax system:

Step 1: Estimate socially optimal aggregate emissions (e^s) and the corresponding social marginal damage $MD(e^s)$ (or equivalently social marginal benefit $MB(e^s)$).

Step 2: Set the level of environmental tax such that $t = MD(e^s)$ (or equivalently $t = MB(e^s)$).

Step 3: Implement the system.

The same form of per unit tax discussed previously can be applied to any other public policy plan to compensate for negative externalities other than pollution abatement. In this sense, it has broad applications and is known as a Pigovian tax (also spelled Pigouvian tax), named after the British economist Arthur C. Pigou and his well-known book, *The Economics of Welfare* (1920).

Similar to per unit taxes, subsidies are another economic instrument designed to control pollutant emissions. Consider a regulation scheme with which the regulator provides s [\$] to each economic agent for the agent's per unit emission reduction from the initial level of e_i^{BAU}. The agent's problem of (1.1.3) is modified to the following formulation:

$$\underset{e_i \in E_i}{Max} \quad B_i\left(e_i\right) + s \cdot \left(e_i^{BAU} - e_i\right) \; \forall i. \tag{1.2.5}$$

The solution to this problem must satisfy the following condition:

$$MB_i\left(e_i^Y\right) = s \; \forall i, \tag{1.2.6}$$

where superscript Y represents an optimal solution under the subsidy scheme.

Note that the expression of Equation (1.2.6) has the same form of Equation (1.2.2). In this respect, the subsidy system is based on the same concept as the Pigovian tax and is also called as Pigovian subsidy. The following proposition holds true:

Proposition 1.2.2

Pigovian tax rate t that helps total emissions attain a socially optimal level is identical to that of Pigovian subsidy s, i.e., t = s. Moreover, each agent's emission levels under both systems are identical, i.e., $e_i^T = e_i^Y$ $\forall i$.

PROOF

The proof is evident from Equations (1.2.2) and (1.2.6). ■

1.3 Tradable permits

Another concept of economic instruments that can compensate for negative externality is the use of market mechanisms along with permits for emissions. More specifically, the regulator issues permits, each of which provides the holder the right to emit one unit of a specific pollutant. Then, the regulator makes these permits tradable in the market. This is called *tradable permits*. The word *tradable* can be replaced by *marketable,* while the word *permit* can be replaced by *license* or *allowance.*

The original concept of tradable permit systems appeared in Crocker (1966) and Dales (1968). Based on these studies, Montgomery (1972) developed a rigorous theory of such systems. Tietenberg (1985, 2006) summarizes the history of the development of the theory. The first intensive application of the systems to real-world environmental problems is that for air quality policy in the United States. Klaassen (1996), Joskow et al. (1998), and Ellerman et al. (2000) produced well-known studies on that topic.

Consider a system wherein the regulator sets the total number of permits as l and allocates them to economic agents, allowing permit holders to emit pollutants according to the number of permits they hold. The way of initially allocating permits is an important policy issue, but we do not consider it for a while; it will be discussed in Section 2.

Let $\{l_i\}$ denote the number of tradable permits initially allocated to each agent in the market. By definition, we have the following identity:

$$l = \sum_i l_i .$$

(1.3.1)

Let the market price of these permits be p. Let $\{z_i\}$ denote the number of permits that each agent purchases (or sells) from (to) the market (positive z_i indicates purchasing whereas negative indicates selling). Then, each agent formulates and solves the following problem:

$$\underset{e_i \in E_i}{Max} \quad B_i(e_i) - p \cdot z_i \quad \forall i$$

$$s.t. \quad e_i \leq z_i + l_i$$

(1.3.2)

The solution to the previous problem satisfies the following conditions:

$$MB_i(e_i^M) = p \quad \forall i,$$

(1.3.3)

$$z_i^M = e_i^M - l_i \quad \forall i,$$

(1.3.4)

where superscript M represents an optimal solution under the tradable permit scheme.

Note that z_i can be either positive or negative and that the following equality must hold for the permit market to clear the transactions, which is called the *market clearing condition*:

$$\sum_{i=1}^{N} z_i = 0 .$$

(1.3.5)

Note that Equation (1.3.3) has the same form as Equation (1.2.2). The distinction is that t in Equation (1.2.2) is supposed to be set by the regulator, whereas p in Equation (1.3.3) results from market equilibrium. The following propositions identify the market mechanism to attain the equilibrium:

Proposition 1.3.1

An equilibrium market price of tradable permits satisfies the following conditions:

$$p = MB(l) ,$$

(1.3.6)

$$dp/dl < 0, \tag{1.3.7}$$

$$p > 0 \text{ for } l < e^{BAU} \text{ ; } p = 0 \text{ otherwise.} \tag{1.3.8}$$

PROOF

Recall the definition of social benefit, Equation (1.1.1). With this definition, Equations (1.1.2) and (1.3.3) indicate the following:

$$MB\left(e^{M}\right) = p \tag{1.3.9}$$

$$e^{M} \equiv \sum_{i=1}^{N} e_{i}^{M} . \tag{1.3.10}$$

Equation (1.3.9) solves for total emissions as a function of p as follows:

$$e^{M} = MB^{-1}(p) . \tag{1.3.11}$$

Equations (1.3.4) and (1.3.5), on the other hand, indicate the following:

$$\sum_{i=1}^{N} e_{i}^{M} = \sum_{i=1}^{N} l_{i} .$$

Given Equations (1.3.1) and (1.3.10), this outcome is equivalent to the following:

$$e^{M} = l$$

Thus, Equations (1.3.9) and (1.3.11) are transformed to the following:

$$p = MB(l)$$

$$MB^{-1}(p) = l .$$

Note that the function $MB(e)$ is decreasing in e, i.e., $dMB/de < 0$. Thus, Equations (1.3.7) and (1.3.8) hold true. ∎

Proposition 1.3.2

When the regulator sets the total number of permits such that $l = e^{S}$, the equilibrium market price of permits coincides with a Pigovian tax rate that helps total emissions attain a socially optimal level:

$$p = t. \tag{1.3.12}$$

Moreover, the resulting emission levels of each agent under the scheme attain socially optimal emission levels:

$$e_{i}^{M} = e_{i}^{S} \ \forall i \tag{1.3.13}$$

PROOF

Suppose that l is set to be equal to e^S, i.e., $l = e^S$. Then, Equation (1.3.6) indicates:

$$p = MB\left(e^S\right).$$

From Equation (1.1.5),

$$p = MD\left(e^S\right).$$

Considering Equation (1.2.3), $p = t$ holds true.

Moreover, Equations (1.1.6) and (1.3.3) indicate the following equality:

$$MB_i\left(e_i^M\right) = MB_i\left(e_i^S\right) \ \forall i.$$

This outcome means that:

$$e_i^M = e_i^S \ \forall i. \ \blacksquare$$

The previous proposition demonstrates a concept about the distribution of permits: equilibrium distribution of emissions $\left\{e_i^M\right\}$ is not affected by the initial permit allocation by the regulator $\{l_i\}$ but depends only on the total number of permits l. This result is known as the Coase theorem, named for Coase (1960). The detail is stated in the next section.

Propositions 1.2.1, 1.2.2, and 1.3.2 indicate that there are measures – Pigovian taxes, Pigovian subsidies, and tradable permits – that can be designed to be equivalent to command-and-control regulation to attain socially optimal levels of emissions.

2. Initial permit distribution and market power

The theory of tradable emissions permit markets is closely related to the theory of property rights. It is widely accepted that emissions of atmospheric pollutants can be limited to targeted levels efficiently if the right to emit is defined as a property right and emissions permit trading is instituted in well-conceived markets. According to the well-known Coase theorem (Coase, 1960),[3] the equilibrium of a tradable emissions permit market should be independent of the initial allocation of property rights in that market, assuming that market participants incur no transaction costs and no income effect. In fact, the analysis by Montgomery (1972) shows that the initial distribution of permits has no effect on the cost-efficient attainment of an emissions target. Because of Coase's prevailing conception, the initial allocation of permits has received less attention in economic policy debates in emissions permit markets. This section discusses the role of initial permit distribution in light of the possibility of market distortion in tradable permit markets.[4]

2.1 Market power

One of the presumptions of the Coase theorem is that the market must be perfectly competitive, in the sense that none of the market participants have the ability to control the market. Hence, some previous studies have focused upon the behavior of market participants with market power in emissions permit markets and the economic consequences of that behavior. Hahn (1984) argues that assuming that there is one firm with market power in a permit market, the initial distribution of permits may influence the monopolistic behavior of the firm and thus may affect the degree of efficiency of the market. Hahn shows that unless the firm with market power initially receives an amount of permits equal to the number that it would hold in a competitive environment, the total expenditure on abatement will exceed the cost-minimizing solution. Van Egteren and Weber (1996) extend Hahn's model of firms with market power in permit markets to allow for noncompliance, but their findings regarding the effects of the initial permit distribution on monopolistic behavior essentially agree with those of Hahn. Westskog (1996) extends Hahn's model to consider multiple firms engaging in Cournot behavior, obtaining results that agree with those of Hahn as well. Malik (2002) also extends the works of Hahn and van Egteren and Weber to examine permit markets in which one firm has market power and one or more firms may be noncompliant. In his analysis of the case where all firms are compliant, he shows that the firm with market power may choose to hold more permits than it needs and retire permits from the markets. This result is the one that is not pointed out by Hahn. Misiolek and Elder (1989) examine the behavior of a firm that holds monopolistic power both in its permit market and its product market and argue that the firm can effectively manipulate both markets.

The results of these studies are convincing that: 1) a market participant who initially holds a large proportion of available permits in an emissions permit market would be expected to behave as a monopolist; and 2) a market participant who is the only large permit buyer in the market would be expected to show monopsonistic behavior. On the other hand, an important function of the regulatory authority is to prevent regulated emitters from gaining market power. From the regulatory point of view, it, therefore, might be less important to analyze the behavior and consequences of market power than to understand what proportion of available emissions permits initially allocated to regulated emitters would give those emitters market power. However, no prior studies, including those discussed previously, have explicitly analyzed the conditions on the initial permit distribution for the emergence of emitters with market power.

Tietenberg (1985) spends one chapter on the discussion of market power in various aspects of emissions trading and explores such issues as under what circumstances market power can arise and how serious it is. In his sub-section on "grandfathering" (1985, pp. 133–138), Tietenberg examines the effects of initial distribution of permits on the degree of price manipulation. Illustrating studies including Hahn (1984), Hahn and Noll (1982), and Maloney and Yandle (1984), Tietenberg concludes the following: First, in theory "the larger the number of permits granted to the predatory source above its cost-effective allocation, the more serious the problem" (1985, p. 146). Second, however, numerical analyses by Hahn and others in the context of the U.S. Environmental Protection Agency emissions trading program show that market power "is not normally likely to be a significant problem" (Tietenberg, 1985, p. 147). Although these conclusions may yield some policy implications on a specific permit market, they do not explicitly reveal the necessary and sufficient conditions on the initial permit distribution for the emergence of emitters with market power and thus will be of little help in the more general context of permit markets.

The next sub-section develops an analytical model of an emissions permit market in which a large number of regulated emitters participate and derives the conditions for the emergence of emitters with market power. The emitters represented in this model have similar unconstrained emissions – that is, emissions if no abatement is undertaken – as well as similar abatement cost structures. One might expect that a market comprised of many such participants would be approximated to be competitive. However, it is shown that whether it is competitive or not depends entirely upon the initial distribution of emissions permits; in particular, there is a threshold or border of initial permit holdings that is sufficient for an emitter to have effective market power.

2.2 Model of market makers

Consider an emissions permit market model in which N regulated emitters are engaged in permit trading. There are two types of market participants: "price takers" and "market makers." "Price takers" are market participants who take permit market prices as given, while "market makers" want to control permit market prices by deciding how many permits to buy or sell. Furthermore, let us assume the following.

Assumption 2.2.1 (market participants)

There are two "market makers" in the emissions permit market. They are Emitters 1 and 2, respectively, and can be considered as such without loss of generality. The rest of regulated emitters are "price takers." Furthermore, the number of emitters, N, is infinitely large.

Assumption 2.2.2 (initial permit allocation)

The initial permit holdings of Emitter 1 exceed, or are equal to, its unconstrained emissions (emissions if abatement actions are not undertaken). On the other hand, those of Emitter 2 are less than, or equal to, its unconstrained emissions. (That is to say, Emitter 1 initially holds excess permits while Emitter 2 does not.) The aggregate unconstrained emissions of all other emitters, excluding Emitters 1 and 2, exceeds the aggregate emissions target for all other emitters. (In other words, there is no net excess of permits for all other emitters, excluding Emitters 1 and 2.)

Let us mathematically describe the previous assumptions. The notations are defined as follows.

$i = 1 \cdots N$: Regulated emitters. (N is infinitely large.)

G_i: Unconstrained emissions (emissions if abatement actions are not undertaken) by emitter i.

Y_i: Initial allocation of permits to emitter i. (Emitters are assumed to receive this initial allocation gratis.)

$D_i \equiv G_i - Y_i$: The difference between the unconstrained emissions and the initial permit allocation of emitter i. (When $D_i \geq 0$, the emission rights of emitter i are exhausted. When $D_i \leq 0$, emitter i holds excess emission rights.)

T_i: Permits bought or sold by emitter i. ($T_i > 0$ indicates "buying," while $T_i < 0$ indicates "selling.")

Assumption 2.2.2 reflects the following conditions.

$$D_1 \leq 0, \ D_2 \geq 0, \text{ and } \sum_{i=3}^{N} D_i > 0.$$

All emitters are engaged in permit trading. The total volume of market trade must be equal to zero for the market to be in equilibrium; this is known as the market clearing condition. That is,

$$\sum_{i=1}^{N} T_i^* = 0,$$

where T_i^* is the optimal volume of market trade for emitter i. Given Assumption 2.2.1, the following assumptions provide a further definition of market equilibrium under the economic circumstances it addresses.

Assumption 2.2.3 (the behavior of "price takers")

Each price taker in the market takes permit market prices as given and solves a decision problem that concerns both permit trading and emissions abatement requirements.

Assumption 2.2.4 (Nash game of "market makers")

On the other hand, Emitters 1 and 2 play a Nash game: Each emitter tries to control the total volume of market trades by deciding how many permits of its own to buy or sell. In deciding its own trade volume, each of the two regards the trade volume of the other as given.

Let T_1^* denote Emitter 1's optimal trade volume when Emitter 2 fixes its trade volume at T_2. That is, T_1^* is Emitter 1's best-response function. Similarly, Let T_2^* denote Emitter 2's best-response function when Emitter 1 fixes its trade volume at T_1. Given Assumption 2.2.4, equilibrium is the cross point of their best-response functions. Let $\left(T_1^{**}, T_2^{**} \right)$ denote the cross point. Then, the equilibrium price is calculated, as a function of the cross point, as $S \equiv S_{Nash}\left(T_1^{**}, T_2^{**} \right)$. Given Assumption 2.2.3, emitters 3 to N take this price as given to decide how many permits to buy or sell as well as how much emissions to abate; optimal volumes of market trade for emitters 3 to N are functions of the market price S; that is, $T_i^*(S)$. Thus, Assumptions 3 and 4, combined with the market clearing condition, yield market equilibrium prices.

Let us add an additional assumption on abatement cost structure.

Assumption 2.2.5 (abatement cost functions)

Marginal abatement cost function for each emitter is approximated to be linear in emissions abatement by the emitter; that is, abatement cost function is a quadratic function of abatement. When abatement actions are not undertaken, abatement costs as well as marginal abatement costs are naturally assumed to be zero.

Assumption 2.2.5 is mathematically described as follows.

Let X_i denote emissions abatement by emitter i. Note that these are non-negative. ($X_i \geq 0$) Then, abatement cost function for emitter i is expressed as follows.

$$C_i\left(X_i \right) \equiv c_i X_i^2 / 2.$$

2.3 Market distortion

To compare market prices, let S_{comp} denote possible competitive market prices in a market where all emitters would behave as price takers. If Emitter 1 has effective market power to set a selling price, the permit market price in the previous setting will be higher than the competitive market price level; $S > S_{comp}$. On the other hand, if Emitter 2 in turn has effective market power to set a buying price, the permit market price in the previous setting will be lower than the competitive market price level; $S < S_{comp}$. Hence, estimating how much permit market prices in the previous setting depart from competitive market price levels yields enough information about the market distorted by either Emitters 1 or 2 or both. The following proposition reveals this point.

Proposition 2.3.1 (market distortion when competitive market prices would be positive)

Suppose that the aggregate unconstrained emissions of all emitters is greater than the aggregate emissions target for all emitters; that is, the net shortage of permits in the market is positive:

$$\sum_{i=1}^{N} D_i > 0.$$

(Notice that in this case, competitive market prices would be strictly positive.)

Given Assumptions 2.2.1–5'

1) *if the absolute volume of excess permits of Emitter 1 exceeds the net shortage of permits in the market, then the emitter has effective market power. Moreover, the market price deviates from a competitive price level such that the ratio is equal to 1+{(the absolute volume of excess permits) / (the net shortage of permits) − 1} / 2, and*
2) *if, on the other hand, the absolute volume of excess permits of Emitter 1 does not exceed the net shortage of permits in the market, then no one can have enough market power to control market prices; the market price is approximately equal to a competitive price level.*

These two cases can be expressed as the following formula.

$$S\big/S_{Comp} \cong 1 + Max\left\{\frac{1}{2}\cdot\left(-D_1\Big/\sum_{i=1}^{N}D_i - 1\right), \quad 0\right\} \tag{2.3.1}$$

(Proof is omitted.)

Proposition 2.3.1 has interesting implications. First, whether or not the market prices coincide to competitive price levels depends entirely upon whether or not the absolute volume of initial excess permits of Emitter 1 exceeds the net shortage of permits in the market:

$$S \cong S_{Comp} \text{ if } \sum_{i=1}^{N}D_i \geq -D_1; \; S > S_{Comp} \text{ if } \sum_{i=1}^{N}D_i < -D_1.$$

That is to say, there is a threshold or border for excess permits of Emitter 1 to allow the emitter to have effective market power. Second, notice that the initial permit holding of Emitter 2 has nothing to do with the deviation of market prices from competitive levels. Furthermore, the Nash game structure introduced by Assumption 2.2.4 turned out to have played no significant role in the determination of market equilibrium. This is a consequence of the assumption of large N as in Assumption 2.2.1; the effect of gaming disappears as the presence of players becomes small in a market, in agreement with the well-known conception of "competitive limit."[5] Third, cost parameters do not appear in Equation (2.3.1) and thus have no effect on whether or not the market prices differ from competitive levels. This emphasizes the entire dependence of the price ratio on the initial distribution of permits.

Emitter 1 is a special emitter in the market only because it wishes to become a market maker and happens to initially hold excess permits; there is nothing else special to Emitter 1, including its cost structure. Also notice that Assumption 2.2.2 does not specify whether D_i is positive or negative for emitters 3 to N. Any emitter can become Emitter 1 if it wishes, but in order for its wish to be realized, it must at least have excess permits; in fact, Emitter 2 cannot become an effective market maker because it is a potential buyer. Moreover, there is a threshold for its wish to be realized. In short, if excess permits are initially allocated to an emitter, and if the absolute volume of excess permits of the emitter exceeds the net shortage of permits in the market, then the emitter is entitled to have effective market power.

The entire dependence of the price ratio (S/S_{Comp}) on the permit initial distribution as well as the existence of a threshold for effective market power, as shown in (2.3.1), are important from both theoretical and practical viewpoints. In theory, competitive prices are strictly positive as long as the net shortage of permits in the market is positive and can be calculated as follows.

$$S_{Comp} = \left(\sum_{i=1}^{N}c_i^{-1}\right)^{-1}\cdot\left(\sum_{i=1}^{N}D_i\right) \tag{2.3.2}$$

S_{Comp} does not depend on how permits are initially distributed to emitters but does depend on the sum of D_i only, in agreement with the Coase theorem. Proposition 2.3.1 not only challenges the theorem but goes further to provide us with a criteria; in order to find if a permit market is efficient, we may simply look into whether or not there is an emitter or a group of emitters whose excess permits exceed the net shortage of permits in the market.

The result that the initial distribution of permits affects prices as well as market inefficiency is concluded by Hahn (1984) as well. Proposition 2.3.1 in this chapter, however, contains two important findings that are in contrast to Hahn's. The first important contrast between the result here and Hahn's is the existence of a threshold for market power to be effective. In Hahn, unless the firm with market power initially receives an amount of permits equal to the number that the firm with market power would hold in a competitive market environment, prices set by the firm always depart from competitive levels and thus reduce market efficiency. In Proposition 2.3.1, however, as long as the condition $\sum_{i=1}^{N} D_i \geq -D_1$ is satisfied, the market remains efficient, even though there exist excess initial permits. Since regulated emitters are assumed to be homogeneous with respect to their cost structure, this condition is interpreted as the one that the market does not allow the emergence of emitters with market power. In Hahn, however, such a condition for the emergence of market power cannot be concluded.

Another important contrast is related to the characteristics of market power. While Hahn's analysis shows that with the introduction of market power, permit prices both may increase above and decline below competitive levels, Equation (2.3.1) shows that permit prices never fall below competitive levels. In Hahn, letting Q_i^* denote the number of permits that the firm with market power would hold in a competitive market environment, if the firm initially receives less permits than Q_i^*, then prices set by the firm are lower than competitive levels. On the other hand, if the firm initially receives more permits than Q_i^*, then prices set by the firm are higher than competitive levels. Providing a numerical example, Hahn observes that the former effect of monopsonistic behavior is relatively weak compared to the latter effect of monopolistic behavior. He also predicts "the relative importance of monopolistic and monopsonistic behavior may be quite sensitive to parameter changes" (Hahn, 1984, p. 762). Proposition 2.3.1 – indicating that monopsonistic behavior does not cause a problem – in part supports Hahn's observation on his numerical example and in part denies his prediction on it.

It is also emphasized that an important difference between our analytical settings and Hahn's is the assumption of the large number of market participants, as in Assumption 2.2.1. In general, taking limits to the infinite number of market participants makes the effects of market power disappear in agreement with the conception of "competitive limit." In Proposition 2.3.1, this is the case unless the excess permits granted to Emitter 1 exceed the threshold. In Hahn, however, there is no conception of "limit." It is surmised that if one introduces this conception into Hahn's analytical framework, market prices are always equalized to competitive levels, which coincides with his observation on his numerical example.

Next, let us consider the case where the aggregate unconstrained emissions of all emitters is less than, or equal to, the aggregate emissions target for all emitters. This means that there is a net excess of permits in the market. Since competitive market prices are usually supposed to be zero in this case, Equation (2.3.1) does not make sense. Proposition 2.3.1 should be modified as follows.

Proposition 2.3.2 (market distortion when competitive market prices would be zero)

Suppose that there is a net excess of permits in the market. Given Assumptions 2.2.1–5, Emitter 1 has effective market power to keep the market price being strictly positive. In particular, the market price is approximately equal to (a possible competitive price of the market that excludes Emitter 1) / 2.

(Proof is omitted.)

The implications of Proposition 2.3.2 are basically the same of those of Proposition 2.3.1. A significant feature in addition to Proposition 2.3.1 is that seller's market power keeps market prices from declining to zero.

3. Uncertainty and the safety valve mechanism

As Section 1 in this chapter described, tradable permit systems and environmental taxes are considered to create the same incentive to reduce emissions or pollution. Because of duality, these two policy instruments could, in principle, attain the same emissions reductions at the same cost. However, in practice, this equivalence is conditional upon many practical economic and policy factors, which are addressed in many advanced textbooks. "Uncertainty" is the primary factor that distinguishes tradable permit systems from environmental taxes with respect to the attainment of emissions abatements. In this section, we discuss the effect of uncertainty and an associated policy instrument called the safety valve mechanism.[6]

3.1 The concept of uncertainty

In a classic study of this topic, Weitzman (1974) pointed out that whereas regulated emitters themselves are well aware of their own abatement cost structures, regulators can only learn of such structures with difficulty. Such differences in knowledge produce a state of information asymmetry that creates uncertainty among regulators regarding emissions abatement cost curves. Moreover, at the time of policy design, neither the regulators nor the regulated emitters have complete information regarding the benefit curves of emissions abatement, creating another source of uncertainty. Given the uncertain abatement costs and benefit curves faced by the regulators, Weitzman identified a criterion to judge the comparative advantages between control by price (tax) and by quantity (permits). Weitzman concluded that the difference in comparative advantage provided by price and quantity controls is determined by the relative slope of the social marginal abatement benefit and the marginal abatement cost curve and by uncertainty regarding the identification of the latter curve.[7]

Roberts and Spence (1976) advanced the discussion on the choice of economic instruments to include the consideration of a combination of these instruments in the form of hybrid systems. They explained that by combining the tools of transferable licenses, per-unit penalties, and subsidies, regulators could create a mixed system with which they can implicitly approximate the expected damage function by imposing a piecewise linear penalty function on polluting firms. Therefore, under an uncertain environment – more precisely, information asymmetry between the regulator and firms – regulators can create a better system than that based on the imposition of pure effluent fees or licensing systems.

According to Roberts and Spence (1976), uncertainty is synonymous with information asymmetry between regulated emitters and regulators. The necessity of combining the use of permits and per-unit penalties arises mainly from the premise that a regulator does not have detailed information regarding emissions abatement cost functions. While such information asymmetry may create uncertainty on the side of the regulator, it does not do so on the side of regulated emitters, who know their own cost functions well.

Provided that uncertainty is indeed due to information asymmetry, regulators are assumed to face difficulties in achieving policy goals. This difficulty arises because the implementation of pure permit systems may not lead to the attainment of a socially optimal levels of emissions reduction owing to uncertainty. In contrast, this form of uncertainty does not create difficulties for regulated emitters; given the policy formulated by the regulator, they are always allowed to make their choices and can choose options that will lead to desirable outcomes for their firms. These choices may not lead to socially optimal outcomes; however, this consideration matters only to regulators, not to regulated emitters. Hence, uncertainty as mentioned by Roberts and Spence (1976) does not appear to create problems for regulated emitters. This difference between regulators and regulated emitters raises the question of whether a form of uncertainty exists that creates problems for not only regulators but also regulated emitters. To answer this question, the source of uncertainty must be re-examined.

According to most theories regarding tradable emissions permits, regulated emitters are assumed to not only participate in emissions markets but also to determine and seek to attain their desirable levels of emissions abatement. This premise is based on the assumption that options regarding abatement actions are available at the time of participation in the emissions market. However, this assumption cannot be easily justified in the real world, in which permit trading activities and abatement actions may not be synonymous; unlike engaging in market trading of security-like permits, engaging in instantaneous emissions abatement is practically impossible.

Emissions of GHGs or sulfur dioxide are closely linked to production activities, and thus abatement decisions usually are constrained by long-term production plans. In most cases, investment in abatement technologies at production facilities is required to achieve emissions abatement. Successful implementation of such abatement technologies requires at minimum several months and sometimes years. Moreover, once such an investment decision is made, the plan cannot be easily adjusted until the completion. Thus, physical investments entail not only a time lag between abatement decisions and the achievement of abatement but also inflexibility regarding abatement actions at the time of permit trades. This leads to fundamental changes in the decision frame for emissions abatement and consequently a sequential decision structure within a state of uncertainty.

Permit trading in most existing or planned programs is possible until the end of each compliance period, when actual emissions levels are revealed and reported with certainty. However, abatement decisions, such as those regarding investment in abatement technology, must be made before actual emissions levels, permit market prices, and other factors are known, creating a form of uncertainty that affects abatement decisions.

When emissions abatement decisions must be made within a context characterized by a time lag, abatement inflexibility, and market uncertainty at the time of the abatement decision, regulated emitters may fear that market prices will increase. If they do indeed increase to unaffordable market prices, regulated emitters cannot engage in further emission reduction *ex post facto*. Unaffordable market prices then may force emitters who had planned to purchase permits to declare bankruptcy rather than further reduce emissions. Such a situation highlights the need for a safety valve mechanism.

3.2 Safety valve mechanism

A *safety valve* mechanism is a mechanism for tradable permit systems that allows regulators of a basic cap-and-trade system to set an upper limit on market prices – a so-called "trigger price" – and that guarantees that regulators will sell additional permits if the market price of permits reaches the limit. This mechanism may prevent permit prices from rising to an unsustainable level. Thus, this mechanism may ease price risks for permit market participants.

A primary consideration in using the safety valve mechanism for designing a cap-and-trade system is the means of determining the trigger price. In particular, it is important to identify some rules for setting trigger prices with respect to the total design of tradable permit systems. To address this consideration, this chapter develops an analytical model of a cap-and-trade system equipped with a safety valve mechanism and derives two propositions that provide policymakers with practical guidance in designing a permit market. In developing this model, this analysis focuses on the optimal combination of policy design parameters, namely emissions targets and trigger prices, under uncertainty that arises because of a time lag between an abatement decision and the disclosure of unconstrained actual emissions.

Consider a single-period model in which only the present time (time 0) and one future time period (time 1) are represented. In addition, consider the existence of N regulated emitters who emit pollutants (or GHGs) into the atmosphere at only time 1. The following assumptions are made.

Assumption 3.2.1 (time lag)

Emissions reduction requires prior investment. To reduce emissions at time 1, abatement decisions must be made at time 0. Therefore, decisions regarding the cost and amount of emissions are fixed at time 0.

This assumption asserts that the decision to reduce emissions at time 1 should be taken at time 0, because if the decision is taken at time 1, it would be too late to make the investment necessary for emissions reduction. Given the time lag, regulated emitters are always required to prepare for the economic environment that they will face in the future (that is, time 1). Thus, their decisions must always be made under uncertainty. The following assumption addresses the source of uncertainty.

Assumption 3.2.2 (uncertain business-as-usual emissions)

Business-as-usual (BAU) emissions for time 1 are uncertain for both regulated emitters and regulator at time 0. This uncertainty is only resolved in the future at time 1, when actual emissions can be known without any uncertainty.

To understand that the previous assumption describes the reality to some extent, consider the situation faced by most manufacturers. As manufacturers typically operate on the basis of fiscal years, they usually take investment decisions regarding plant expansion well before the plants are operational or at least at the beginning of the fiscal year. As manufacturers adjust their production activity to meet the demand, the level of total activity may fluctuate on a daily basis. As a result, emissions fluctuate on a daily basis. However, annual emissions are only revealed toward the end of each fiscal year. This situation illustrates that although annual emissions are only revealed *ex post facto*, decisions regarding investments that alter production facilities must be made in advance.

The notations in this model are defined as follows:

$t \in \{0,1\}$: Time indices.

$i = 1 \cdots N$: Indices representing regulated emitters.

X_i: Regulated emitter i's emissions reduction for time 1, fixed at time 0 (a decision variable at time 0) ($X_i \geq 0$).

$X \equiv \sum_{i=1}^{N} X_i$: Sum of X_i, that is, aggregate emissions reduction.

$C_i(X_i)$: Emitter i's abatement cost curve as an increasing convex function of the amount of reduction, as determined at time 0.

$MC_i(X_i) \equiv dC_i / dX_i$: Marginal abatement cost curve, as determined at time 0.

Ω: Set of the states of nature at time 1.

$G_i(\omega)$: Emitter i's quantity of unconstrained BAU emissions when no abatement efforts are made at time 1 in state $\omega \in \Omega$ (random variables).

$G(\omega) \equiv \sum_{i=1}^{N} G_i(\omega)$: Sum of $G_i(\omega)$, that is, the quantity of aggregate BAU emissions at time 1 in state $\omega \in \Omega$ (random variables).

r: Risk-adjusted discount rate between time 0 and time 1.

Note that once the quantity of $\{X_i\}$ is fixed at time 0, the quantity of actual emissions becomes $\{G_i(\omega) - X_i\}$, resulting in aggregate emissions of

$$G(\omega) - X \text{ (equivalently, } \sum_{i=1}^{N} \big(G_i(\omega) - X_i \big) \text{).}$$

This is a random variable depending on state ω at time 1 and is realized at time 1. Given the assumptions stated previously, suppose that the regulator desires to maximize the expected net social benefit as follows:

POLICY GOAL

The regulator desires to control the emissions abatements of regulated emitters to attain the maximum expected net social benefit. The net social benefit is defined as social benefit fixed at time 1 less the sum of regulated emitters' abatement costs fixed at time 0.

To formulate the policy goal, let B denote the social benefit, which is a function of $G(\omega) - X$, that is,

$$B\big(G(\omega) - X\big).$$

By considering the present value of the social benefit comparable to the cost of abatement, the regulator's policy goal can be formulated as the following optimization problem:

$$\underset{\{X_i\}}{\text{Max}} \quad \frac{1}{1+r} E\big[B(G-X)\big] - \sum_{i=1}^{N} C_i(X_i).$$

When a specific functional form for B is assumed, this maximization problem is analytically solved. Let $\{X_i^S\}$ denote the optimal solution set, with the superscript S indicating the social optimum. After formulating the regulator's policy goal, the next consideration is to determine the means of attaining the socially optimal level of emissions abatement, which is addressed in the following section.

When a command-and-control (CAC) policy has been implemented, it is conceptually easy for the regulator to achieve the policy goal: the regulator simply sets emissions abatement standards as $\{X_i^S\}$ and forces regulated emitters to comply with them. When a CAC policy is not available for a particular reason, such as because of societal rejection of compulsory measures, the regulator must use MBIs to regulate emissions. This study hereafter assumes that the regulator uses tradable permits, which are currently one of the most popular MBIs, to attain a socially optimal level of emissions abatement. The outline of the system is as follows:

EMISSION PERMIT SYSTEM

Emission permits are distributed free of charge to each regulated emitter before time 1. These permits represent the right to emit at time 1 and become tradable among emitters at time 1.

Assume that tradable permits are available at time 1. Thus, regulated emitters are able to invest at time 0 to reduce emissions at time 1, enter into forward contracts for permits at time 0, or engage in spot trading at time 1. As discussed previously, the reduction of emissions requires prior investment and is thus subject to time lags. Therefore, if regulated emitters desire to reduce emissions, action must be taken at time 0. In contrast, because regulated emitters know that tradable permits are available at time 1, they can engage in permit trading at both time 0 and time 1.

Forward contracts concern the trading of permits for time 1 at time 0. Parties to a forward contract agree on prices for time 1, which are called "forward prices," at time 0 but make payments and deliveries at time 1. On the other hand, spot trades are made at time 1; thus, price formation, deliveries, and payments are made simultaneously. The nature of the interaction between forward contract formation and spot trading, in particular that concerning relationships between spot and forward prices, has been addressed in the financial economics literature. Most of the research has concluded that forward contracts are "derivatives" of spot prices because forward contract markets are formed on the basis of expectations regarding spot trading markets. In this sense, spot trading markets contribute to forward market formation but the reverse is not true. Because forward contracts are, fundamentally, financial instruments that help market participants to trade risks, they accommodate a wide range of risk preferences in the market. However, they do not reduce the aggregate risk within the market and thus do not affect spot prices that reflect market fluctuations. This chapter focuses on the impact of uncertainty arising from investment inflexibility and the role of spot permit trade markets; forward contracts and the possibility of their formation in the analytical framework are not addressed in the remaining sections of this chapter. Such an omission is based on the understanding that the inclusion of forward markets would not affect any of the findings hereafter presented. For a comprehensive discussion of emissions forward (or futures) markets, see Maeda (2004) and Kijima, Maeda, and Nishide (2010).

The spot prices of tradable permits are determined by the balance between demand and supply at time 1, at which time the prices are realized. At time 0, these prices are treated as random variables dependent upon the realization of emissions at time 1, namely, upon the states of nature. When these prices are realized at time 1, some regulated emitters may feel that they are too high and unaffordable. Despite their concern, the emitters have no choice other than engage in spot permit trading at time 1 because emissions abatements have already been fixed at the time. The only means of addressing their concern would be the implementation of a safety valve mechanism: The regulator sets an upper limit on the spot permit market price, and sells an unlimited number of permits at the trigger price when the market price reaches the trigger price.

According to the framework and assumptions described previously, the actions taken by each regulated emitter can be summarized as follows. First, each emitter chooses a target level of emissions reduction at time 0, based on the forecast of its quantity of BAU emissions for time 1. The decision fixes its emissions reduction cost at time 0. At time 1, when the quantity of actual emissions, which is the quantity of BAU emissions less the quantity of the planned reduction in emissions, is realized, regulated emitters may engage in permit market trading and use the safety valve mechanism when the market price reaches the trigger price. Immediately after time 1, the regulator inspects emitters to determine whether their actual emissions at time 1 are within the authorized permit holding level. Assume that no monitoring or inspection problems exist.[8]

Consider the following notations:

L_i: Emitter i's initial permit holdings or caps, as allocated by the regulator.

$L \equiv \sum_{i=1}^{N} L_i$: Sum of L_is, that is, the aggregate emissions target. The aggregate target is the sum of permits (a policy parameter set by the regulator).

$\phi(\omega)$: Spot market price of permits at time 1 in state $\omega \in \Omega$ (an endogenous variable) ($\phi \geq 0$).

$T_i(\omega)$: Emitter i's trade volume at time 1 in state $\omega \in \Omega$ (a decision variable at time 1).

p: Trigger price, an upper limit on permit market prices (a policy parameter set by the regulator).

$Z_i(\omega)$: Quantity of emitter i's permit holdings purchased from the regulator at the trigger price at time 1 in state $\omega \in \Omega$ (a decision variable at time 1) ($Z_i \geq 0$).

3.3 Trigger price setting

Consider the following assumptions regarding the characteristics of the permit market:

Assumption 3.3.1 (rational expectations)
For all possible states of nature, the regulator and all emitters are able to calculate the market equilibrium price of permits at time 0.

Assumption 3.3.2 (homogeneous beliefs and continuous density functions)
The emitters' probability assignment is homogeneous. The probability measure Q is represented as a continuous distribution density function $F(G_1, G_2, \cdots G_N)$.

Assumption 3.3.3 (competitiveness)
Each emitter produces emissions at such a low level that the impact of its behavior on total emissions, market prices, and other relevant variables is negligible.

Under these assumptions, the abatement decision problem at time 0 for emitter i is given as

$$\underset{X_i \geq 0}{Min} \quad \frac{1}{1+r} E\big[D_i(X_i)\big] + C_i(X_i). \tag{3.3.1}$$

Random variable $D_i(X_i)$ represents the expenditure accrued at time 1 that consists of expenses for purchasing permits from both market and regulator. It is expressed as the result of the following optimization problem:

$$D_i(X_i)[\omega] = \underset{T_i(\omega), Z_i(\omega)}{Min} \phi(\omega) T_i(\omega) + p Z_i(\omega), \tag{3.3.2}$$

$$\text{s.t. } G_i(\omega) - X_i - L_i \leq T_i(\omega) + Z_i(\omega),$$

$$0 \leq Z_i(\omega) \leq G_i(\omega) - X_i.$$

Equations (3.3.1) and (3.3.2) comprise a dynamic optimization problem that is interpreted as follows: At time 0, emitter i decides the level of emissions reduction and awaits to see which state of nature occurs at time 1. Assume that state ω occurs at time 1. In this case, the emitter produces

$G_i(\omega) - X_i$ quantity of emissions. Because the emitter was initially allocated L_i permits, it must obtain an additional quantity of $G_i(\omega) - X_i - L_i$ permits. If the emitter chooses to obtain a quantity of $Z_i \geq 0$ permits from the regulator at the trigger price, the emitter must obtain more than the remaining permits of $G_i(\omega) - X_i - L_i - Z_i$ from the market. Under such constraints, Equation (3.3.2) represents the optimal mix problem of permit trades and use of the safety valve mechanism. By anticipating an optimal balance at time 1, each emitter decides on an optimal level of investment at time 0 for emissions abatement at time 1, as described in Equation (3.3.1).

The permit market at time 1 must be balanced in the sense that total permits purchased must be equal to total permit sold. This condition is described as follows:

Market clearing condition at time 1:

$$\sum_{i=1}^{N} T_i^*(\omega) = 0 , \forall \omega \in \Omega .$$

For simplicity of mathematical expression, the following subsets are defined at time 1:

$$\Omega^1(X) \equiv \left\{ \omega \in \Omega \mid G(\omega) \geq X + L \right\},$$

$$\Omega^2(X) \equiv \left\{ \omega \in \Omega \mid G(\omega) < X + L \right\},$$

where $G(\omega) \equiv \sum_{i=1}^{N} G_i(\omega)$, $X \equiv \sum_{i=1}^{N} X_i$, and $L \equiv \sum_{i=1}^{N} L_i$.

Then, the market clearing condition implies the following:

For $\omega \in \Omega^1(X)$, $\phi(\omega) = p$ and $D_i(X_i)[\omega] = p \cdot \left\{ G_i(\omega) - X_i - L_i \right\}$ $\forall i$.

For $\omega \in \Omega^2(X)$, $\phi(\omega) = 0$ and $D_i(X_i)[\omega] = 0$ $\forall i$.

Thus, the solution to the abatement decision problem described in Equations (3.3.1) and (3.3.2) is given by the following set of equations: (Note that given the convexity of the cost function, the following conditions are sufficient as well as necessary.)

$$\frac{1}{1+r} \frac{d}{dX_i} E\left[D_i(X_i)\right] + MC_i(X_i) = 0 \quad \forall i, \tag{3.3.3}$$

where

$$E\left[D_i(X_i)\right] = p \cdot \int_{\sum_{i=1}^{N}(G_i - X_i - L_i) \geq 0} (G_i - X_i - L_i) f(G_1, G_2 \cdots, G_N) dG_1 dG_2 \cdots dG_N. \tag{3.3.4}$$

Under Assumption 3.3.3, Equations (3.3.3) and (3.3.4) render the following equation, which is satisfied by the level of emissions abatement for emitter i.

$$MC_i(X_i^*) = \frac{1}{1+r} \cdot p \cdot Q\left(\Omega^1(X^*)\right) \quad \forall i. \tag{3.3.5}$$

The fact that (3.3.5) has a solution indicates that if $X_i^* = X_i^S$ $\forall i$ holds, the regulator's policy goal can be achieved. Thus, the next consideration is determining the means of controlling $\left\{ X_i^* \right\}$, the focus of the following section.

For analytical simplicity, we introduce the following two assumptions:

Assumption 3.3.4 (linear marginal cost curves)

Marginal abatement cost functions can be approximated as linear functions, that is,

$$MC_i(X_i) \equiv \frac{1}{1+r} \cdot c_i X_i .$$

Assumption 3.3.5 (normal distribution)

In addition to Assumption 3.3.2, the quantity of aggregate BAU emissions $G \left(\equiv \sum_{i=1}^{N} G_i \right)$ approximately follows a normal distribution with expectation G^e and standard deviation σ. Cumulative normal distribution function $F(x, \sigma)$ is described as follows:

$$F(x; \sigma) \equiv \frac{1}{\sqrt{2\pi}} \int_{-\infty}^{\frac{x-G^e}{\sigma}} e^{\frac{-1}{2}y^2} dy.$$

Given all the assumptions thus far, Equation (3.3.5) implies the following equalities:

$$cX^* = p \cdot \left\{ 1 - F\left(X^* + L; \sigma \right) \right\}, \tag{3.3.6}$$

$$X_i^* = \left(c/c_i \right) X^* \; \forall i, \tag{3.3.7}$$

where $c \equiv \left(\sum_{i=1}^{N} c_i^{-1} \right)^{-1}$.

Note that c, the reciprocal of the sum of the reciprocals of the linear parameters in the emitter's marginal abatement cost functions, represents the linear parameter in the aggregate (or social) marginal abatement cost function. That is,

$$MC(X) \equiv \frac{dC(X)}{dX} = \frac{1}{1+r} \cdot cX,$$

where $C(X) \equiv \min_{\{X_i\}} \sum_{i=1}^{N} C_i(X_i)$ s.t. $X = \sum_{i=1}^{N} X_i$.

Note that Equation (3.3.6) has a definitive solution because the value on the left side is increasing and linear in X^*, while the value on the right side is a decreasing function of X^* within the domain $0 \leq X^* < \infty$. The solution is described as a function of L, p, and σ as follows:

$$X^*(L, p; \sigma),$$

where L represents the aggregate emissions target (cap) set by the regulator and p denotes the trigger price, the two policy parameters that the regulator employs to control aggregate emissions reduction. The following proposition expresses the relationship among these parameters, uncertainty regarding aggregate BAU emissions, and the aggregate reduction level.

Proposition 3.3.1 (sensitivity of aggregate abatement to policy instruments)

Given the assumptions and the framework described previously,

$$\partial X^*/\partial L < 0, \partial X^*/\partial p > 0, \tag{3.3.8}$$

and the following identity holds:

$$-\frac{\partial X^*(L, p; \sigma)}{\partial L} + \frac{p}{X^*} \frac{\partial X^*(L, p; \sigma)}{\partial p} \equiv 1 \; \forall \sigma \in [0, \infty). \tag{3.3.9}$$

(Proof is omitted.)

The implication of Proposition 3.3.1 are the following: The regulator can control the aggregate emissions reduction by changing the aggregate emissions target (L) and the trigger price (p), noting that each emitter's reduction is also subject to control in the same manner, as expressed in Equation (3.3.7). However, these two parameters do not have the same capacity to influence aggregate reduction. As the first term on the left side of Identity (3.3.9) reflects small changes in the aggregate reduction in response to changes in the aggregate emissions target, it can be understood to represent the sensitivity of aggregate emissions reduction to target setting. As indicated in (3.3.8), the sign of the sensitivity is always negative, which implies that an increase in the target level leads to a decline in aggregate reduction. The second term on the left side of Identity (3.3.9) is the percentage change in aggregate emissions reduction in response to the percentage change in the trigger price. This term can be understood to represent the elasticity of aggregate emissions reduction with respect to trigger-price setting. As shown in (3.3.8), its sign of the elasticity is always positive. Thus, Identity (3.3.9) indicates that the sum of the absolute values of the sensitivity to target setting and the elasticity with respect to trigger-price setting is always the unity. If one of these two absolute values is close to the unity, then the other must be close to zero. The balance between them is determined by exogenous uncertainty σ.

Recall that the regulator desires to control emissions reduction to attain a policy goal. Proposition 3.3.1 indicates that uncertainty regarding the quantity of the aggregate BAU emissions strongly impacts the effectiveness of policy parameters in controlling emissions reductions. Thus, examining the impact of uncertainty can lead to identification of policy implications.

For simplicity of mathematical expression, the subsets of policy parameters are defined as follows:

$$A^- \equiv \left\{ (L, p) \mid L + p/(2c) < G^e \right\},$$

$$A^+ \equiv \left\{ (L, p) \mid L + p/(2c) > G^e \right\},$$

$$A \equiv \left\{ (L, p) \mid L + p/(2c) = G^e \right\}.$$

Then, the following proposition is obtained:

Proposition 3.3.2 (impact of uncertainty on emissions reductions)
Given the assumptions and the framework described previously, the following relations hold:

For $(L, p) \in A^-$, $p/(2c) < X^* < G^e - L$ and $\dfrac{dX^*(L, p; \sigma)}{d\sigma} < 0 \ \forall \sigma \in [0, \infty)$.

For $(L, p) \in A^+$, $G^e - L < X^* < p/(2c)$ and $\dfrac{dX^*(L, p; \sigma)}{d\sigma} > 0 \ \forall \sigma \in [0, \infty)$.

For $(L, p) \in A$, $X^* = G^e - L = p/(2c)$. *That is, X^* is independent of σ.*

In particular, if, given L, the trigger price is set at double the marginal abatement cost, that is, $p = 2c(G^e - L)$, then the set of induced emissions reductions $\left\{ X_i^*(L, p; \sigma) \right\}$ is never affected by uncertainty σ.
(Proof is omitted.)

Proposition 3.3.2 demonstrates that as long as the regulator sets policy parameters (L, p) such that $L + p/(2c) = G^e$, the resulting aggregate emissions reduction is $X^* = G^e - L (= p/(2c))$. Thus, the reduction is not affected by uncertainty concerning aggregate BAU emissions. If the regulator does not set parameters in this manner, aggregate reduction is greatly affected by uncertainty, and $X^* = G^e - L$ does not necessarily hold. As the sign of $dX^*/d\sigma$ for $(L,p) \in A^-$ shows, increase in uncertainty decreases aggregate emissions reduction from the level near $G^e - L$ to the level near $p/(2c)$. Similarly, as the sign of $dX^*/d\sigma$ for $(L,p) \in A^+$ shows, increase in uncertainty increases aggregate emissions reduction from the level near $G^e - L$ to the level near $p/(2c)$ as well. Thus, it turns out that increase in uncertainty always shifts the quantity of emissions reductions from the level near $G^e - L$ toward the level near $p/(2c)$. This result is consistent with Proposition 3.3.1.

The regulator can always set its policy goal $(\{ X_i^*(L, p; \sigma) \})$ from Equations (3.3.6) and (3.3.7) as functions of L and p, given uncertainty σ that accrues from the economic conditions and cost structures faced by the regulated emitters. To adjust the goal to the socially optimal levels $(\{ X_i^S \})$, however, it must obtain an exact estimation of this uncertainty σ, which is a difficult task. Proposition 3.3.2 provides a rule for the choice of trigger-price setting as a policy tool despite this difficulty, specifying the condition:

$$p = 2c\left(G^e - L \right).$$

This equality identifies a rule that the trigger price should be set at double the marginal abatement cost.

These findings offer guidance for policymakers regarding the optimal design of a permit market, particularly regarding the combined setting of aggregate emissions targets and trigger prices in a socially optimal manner. Such guidance also is useful in markets characterized by a form of information asymmetry that arises from differences in uncertainty between the regulator and regulated emitters concerning aggregate BAU emissions.

4. Conclusion

This chapter examined principles of MBIs for emissions abatement policies, emphasizing tradable permit systems. As stated in Section 1, the use of tradable permits can substitute for CAC regulation. It relies on market trading that assumes that resources are allocated efficiently according to standard economic theory. In the real world, however, many obstacles hinder efficiency, among which, this chapter highlighted two issues – market power and uncertainty.

Notes

1 There are some advanced textbooks for environmental economics and policy measures, among which the most classic book is written by Baumol and Oates (1988). A survey article of Cropper and Oates (1992) is also a standard classic. The models and formulations presented in this section, however, are original and thus, have no specific reference.

2 Consider a mathematical problem:

$$\text{Max } f(\star) \quad s.t. \ g(x) \le b.$$

We introduce the Lagrangian for the problem as follows:

$$L(x, \lambda) \equiv f(x) - \lambda \cdot (g(x) - b).$$

Then, the optimal solution for the problem $x^*(b)$ must satisfy the following:

$$\partial L(x^*, \lambda^*)/\partial x_i = 0 \ \forall i \ \text{and} \ \partial L(x^*, \lambda^*)/\partial \lambda_j = 0 \ \forall j.$$

This formulation indicates the following equality:

$$df\left(\star\right)\big/db_j = \partial L\left(\star,\boldsymbol{\lambda}\right)\big/\partial b_j = \lambda_j\,.$$

This is called the "envelope theorem."

3 For a representative study on the theory of property rights and the long-standing debate on the Coase theorem, see Parisi (1995). The Coase theorem has been extended in several ways. Boyd and Conley (1997) examined it in the context of first and second welfare theorems, extended the theorem to a general equilibrium frame. Jehiel and Moldovanu (1999) argue for the independence of initial rights distribution from economic efficiency, concluding that even if market participants incur transaction costs, the initial structure of property rights remains irrelevant throughout the reselling of those rights. For other generalizations of the Coase theorem, see, for example, Bernholz (1997; 1999).
4 This section is based on Maeda (2003).
5 See, for example, Mas-Colell, Whinston, and Green (1995, p. 411).
6 This section is based on Maeda (2012).
7 Several studies directly examined and debated Weitzman's conclusions, including Yohe (1976, 1977, 1978), Laffont (1977), Watson and Ridker (1984), Tisato (1994), and Stavins (1996), while several did so indirectly, including Adar and Griffin (1976) and Fishelson (1976). Buchanan and Tullock (1975) and Finkelshtain and Kislev (1997), among others, addressed the political aspects of Weitzman's conclusions.
8 The design of enforcement systems, including that of monitoring and inspection systems, is an important policy issue, but beyond the scope of this chapter, which assumes that neither information asymmetry nor administrative costs are incurred for monitoring and inspection. For studies that focus on enforcement systems, see, for example, Malik (1990), Stranlund and Chavez (2000), Stranlund and Dhanda (1999), and Montero (2002).

References

Adar, Z. and J.M. Griffin (1976). Uncertainty of the choice of pollution control instruments. *Journal of Environmental Economics and Management* 3: 178–188.

Baumol, W.J. and W.E. Oates (1988). *The Theory of Environmental Policy*. Second Edition. Cambridge: Cambridge University Press.

Bernholz, P. (1997). Property rights, contracts, cyclical social preferences and the Coase theorem: A synthesis. *European Journal of Political Economy* 13(3): 419–442.

Bernholz, P. (1999). The generalized Coase theorem and separable individual preferences: An extension. *European Journal of Political Economy* 15(2): 331–335.

Boyd, J.H., III and J.P. Conley. (1997). Fundamental nonconvexities in Arrovian markets and a Coasian solution to the problem of externalities. *Journal of Economic Theory* 72(2): 388–407.

Buchanan, J.M. and G. Tullock (1975). Polluters' profits and political response: Direct controls versus taxes. *American Economic Review* 65(1): 139–147.

Coase, R.H. (1960). The problem of social cost. *Journal of Law and Economics* :1–44.

Crocker, T.D. (1966). The structuring of atmospheric pollution control systems. In *The Economics of Air Pollution*, edited by H. Wolozin, 61–86. New York: W.W. Norton & Co.

Cropper, M.L. and W.E. Oates (1992). Environmental economics: A survey. *Journal of Economic Literature* 30: 675–740.

Dales, J.H. (1968). *Pollution, Property and Prices*. Toronto: University of Toronto Press.

Ellerman, A.D., P.L. Joskow, R. Schmalensee, J-P. Montero, and E. Bailey (2000). *Markets for Clean Air: The U.S. Acid Rain Program*. Cambridge: Cambridge University Press.

Finkelshtain, I. and Y. Kislev (1997). Prices versus quantities: The political perspective. *Journal of Political Economy* 105(1): 83–100.

Fishelson, G. (1976). Emission control policies under uncertainty. *Journal of Environmental Economics and Management* 3: 189–197.

Hahn, R.W. (1984). Market power and transferable property rights. *Quarterly Journal of Economics* 99(4): 753–765.

Hahn, R.W. and R.G. Noll. (1982). Designing a market for tradable emissions permits. In *Reform of Environmental Regulation*, edited by Wesley A. Magat, 119–146. Cambridge, MA: Ballinger.

Jehiel, P. and B. Moldovanu. (1999). Resale markets and the assignment of property rights. *Review of Economic Studies* 66(4): 971–991.

Joskow, P.L., R. Schmalensee, and E.M. Bailey (1998). The market for sulfur dioxide emissions. *The American Economic Review* 88(4): 669–685.

Kijima, M., A. Maeda, and K. Nishide (2010). Equilibrium pricing of contingent claims in tradable permit markets. *Journal of Futures Markets* 30(6): 559–589.

Klaassen, G. (1996). *Acid Rain and Environmental Degradation: The Economics of Emission Trading*. Cheltenham: Edward Elgar.

Laffont, J.-J. (1977). More on price vs. quantities. *Review of Economic Studies* 44(1): 177–182.

Malik, A.S. (1990). Markets for pollution control when firms are noncompliant. *Journal of Environmental Economics and Management* 18: 97–106.

Malik, A.S. (2002). Further results on permit markets with market power and cheating. *Journal of Environmental Economics and Management* 44: 371–390.

Maeda, A. (2003). The emergence of market power in emission rights markets: The role of initial permit distribution. *Journal of Regulatory Economics* 24(3): 293–314.

Maeda, A. (2004). Impact of banking and forward contracts on tradable permit markets. *Environmental Economics and Policy Studies* 6(2): 81–102.

Maeda, A. (2012). Setting trigger price in emissions permit markets equipped with a safety valve mechanism. *Journal of Regulatory Economics* 41(3): 358–379.

Maloney, M.T. and B. Yandle. (1984). Estimation of cost of air pollution control regulation. *Journal of Environmental Economics and Management* 11: 244–263.

Mas-Colell, A., M.D. Whinston, and J.R. Green. (1995). *Microeconomic Theory*. New York: Oxford University Press.

Misiolek, W. S. and H. W. Elder. (1989). Exclusionary manipulation of markets for pollution rights. *Journal of Environmental Economics and Management* 16: 156–166.

Montero, J-P. (2002). Prices versus quantities with incomplete enforcement. *Journal of Public Economics* 85: 435–454.

Montgomery, D.W. (1972). Markets in licenses and efficient pollution control programs. *Journal of Economic Theory* 5: 395–418.

Parisi, F. (1995). Private property and social costs. *European Journal of Law and Economics* 2(2): 149–173.

Pigou, A.C. (1920). *The Economics of Welfare*. London: Macmillan.

Roberts, M.J. and M. Spence (1976). Effluent charges and license under uncertainty. *Journal of Public Economics* 5: 193–208.

Stavins, R.N. (1996). Correlated uncertainty and policy instrument choice. *Journal of Environmental Economics and Management* 30: 218–232.

Stranlund, J.K. and C.A. Chavez (2000). Effective enforcement of a transferable emissions permit system with a self-reporting requirement. *Journal of Regulatory Economics* 18(2): 113–131.

Stranlund, J.K. and K.K. Dhanda (1999). Endogenous monitoring and enforcement of a transferable emissions permit system. *Journal of Environmental Economics and Management* 38: 267–282.

Tietenberg, T.H. (1985). *Emissions Trading: An Exercise in Reforming Pollution Policy*. Washington, DC: Resources for the Future.

Tietenberg, T.H. (2006). *Emissions Trading: Principles and Practice, Second Edition*. Washington, DC: Resources for the Future.

Tisato, P. (1994). Pollution standards vs charges under uncertainty. *Environmental and Resource Economics* 4: 295–304.

Van Egteren, H. and M. Weber. (1996). Marketable permits, market power, and cheating. *Journal of Environmental Economics and Management* 30(2): 161–173.

Watson, W.D. and R.G. Ridker (1984). Losses from effluent taxes and quotas under uncertainty. *Journal of Environmental Economics and Management* 11: 310–326.

Weitzman, M.L. (1974). Prices vs. quantities. *Review of Economic Studies* 41(4): 477–491.

Westskog, H. (1996). Market power in a system of tradable CO_2 quotas. *Energy Journal* 17: 85–103.

Yohe, G.W. (1976). Substitution and the control of pollution: A comparison of effluent charges and quantity standards under uncertainty. *Journal of Environmental Economics and Management* 3: 312–324.

Yohe, G.W. (1977). Comparisons of price and quantity controls: A survey. *Journal of Comparative Economics* 1: 213–233.

Yohe, G.W. (1978). Towards a general comparison of price controls and quantity controls under uncertainty. *Review of Economic Studies* 45(2): 229–238.

9

EMISSIONS TRADING IN PRACTICE

Lessons learnt from the European emissions trading scheme

Regina Betz

Economists have developed a large body of theoretical literature on the advantages of emissions trading schemes (ETSs) over other mechanisms such as regulations.[1] ETSs particularly are lauded as being effective and efficient, as they are theoretically able to achieve a given environmental goal at least cost. However, the real world is more complex than usually assumed in textbooks. How an ETS will actually work in practice, therefore, is difficult to predict.

In 2005, the world's largest ETS was introduced in the European Union (EU) to reduce greenhouse gas (GHG) emissions. After two phases and nine years of operation, it is now a good time to evaluate the actual performance of the EU ETS on empirical, rather than theoretical, grounds. There have been some studies summarising the lessons learned from the EU ETS Phase 1 (Ellerman et al. 2010) and Phase 2 (Wråke et al. 2012 and Laing et al. 2013) or more generally on emissions trading schemes from a global perspective (Newell & Pizer 2013). However, a comprehensive ex-post analysis of the EU ETS two phases is missing and requires a set of different methodologies, such as econometric studies, interviews, and case studies. The main contribution of this chapter will be a framework for evaluating the performance of the EU ETS against the most relevant criteria by drawing on the most recent of such studies, including Phase 1 and 2, and deriving gaps for future research.

Market approaches to tackle environmental externalities have been proposed by Coase (1960) and later by Crocker (1966) and Dales (1968). Such markets are very special, as they would not evolve without intervention and thus must be designed and created by governments. Policymakers establishing those markets must make a choice between many design options and are at the same time influenced by various interest groups. The enormous amount of flexibility poses both opportunities and risks in instrument design. In order to evaluate the performance of the EU ETS, the following criteria are used (Hahn and Stavins 1992): effectiveness; efficiency, including both static and dynamic efficiency; and distributional equity or fairness.

The chapter is structured as follows: after the introduction of the chapter, in Section One the key design features of the EU ETS in Phase 1, 2 and 3 are explained; in Section Two, the evaluation criteria are laid out in more detail; in Section Three, the EU ETS Phase 1 and 2 are evaluated according the criteria; and in Section Four an outlook on the proposed changes to the EU ETS after 2020 is given.

1. Key design features of the EU ETS

In January 2005, the EU launched an EU-wide emissions trading scheme (EU ETS) for CO_2 emissions, covering around 10,800 installations from the energy industry and other carbon-intensive industry sectors across the 25 (now 28) Member States (MS) (EEA 2012).[2] In Phase 2 (2008–2012), the three non-EU members of the European Economic Area – Norway, Iceland and Liechtenstein – joined the scheme and some MS included additional gases from the chemical sector, increasing the number of installations to around 11,800 (2008–2011) and number of countries to 30.[3] From 2012, aviation – including national and international air travel – was added, which increased the number of installations by around 2,000. From Phase 3, some further GHGs and sectors such as petrochemicals, ammonia and aluminium industries were covered. Now the EU ETS accounts for nearly 50 percent of total CO_2 emissions and about 45 percent of all GHGs in the EU.[4]

As it is the cornerstone of European climate policy, the EU expects the ETS to play a major role in helping its MS meet their Kyoto Protocol GHG emissions targets cost efficiently. Under the Kyoto Protocol, the EU has committed to reducing emissions of GHGs by 8 percent by 2008–2012, compared to 1990/1995 base-year levels. This EU-15 target of 8 percent was broken down into differentiated targets for individual MS, while the reduction target for the 12 new MS (which entered the EU after the Kyoto Protocol was agreed to), is 8 percent, with the exceptions of Hungary and Poland (6 percent), Croatia (5 percent) and no targets at all for Cyprus and Malta.

For the post-Kyoto period, the EU has committed itself, without any international agreement, to reducing its overall GHG emissions to at least 20 percent below 1990 levels by 2020 and will reduce them by up to 30 percent should a new global climate change agreement be reached. The EU ETS sector will reduce GHG emissions by 21 percent in 2020 (the annual reduction factor is 1.74 percent), while the non-ETS sector will reduce emissions overall by 14 percent (compared to 2005), varying by MS.

The allocation of permits, which are called European Union Allowances (EUAs), in the EU ETS was specified by each country in its National Allocation Plan (NAP). The allocation thus was left to each MS; however, each NAP was subject to approval by the European Commission. The NAPs specified the total amount of allowances to be allocated in each MS, the allocation rules, and the amount to be allocated for each emitting installation. It also included descriptions of other policies and measures to reduce emissions in the sectors not covered by the EU ETS (non-ETS sector). As shown in Betz et al. (2004), there have been various free allocation approaches and formulas used by MS in Phase 1. Betz et al. (2006) show that there has been resistance to change in most MS, and so NAPs for Phase 2 have remained mainly unchanged from the allocation formulas in Phase 1. However, caps became more stringent from Phase 1 to Phase 2 (see Figure 9.3) . As banking of EUAs was not allowed from Phase 1 into Phase 2, unused EUAs at the end of Phase 1 became worthless and the cap in Phase 2 was not affected by the cap in Phase 1. However, unlimited banking is allowed from Phase 2 onwards, which means that any surplus of allowances in one phase will affect the allowance supply in the next phase.

In Phases 1 and 2, the allocation was almost entirely for free, and auctioning was limited by the European Directive (auction share ≤ 5 percent in Phase 1, ≤ 10 percent in Phase 2). However, those limits have never been reached: auctioning shares have been insignificant in the first two phases, at only 0.13 percent in Phase 1 and 3 percent in Phase 2 (Ellerman et al. 2010) or 4 percent when the left-over of new entrant reserves are taken into account.[5] In Phase 3, the electricity industry has to buy all their allowances (i.e. 100 percent auctioning), though some exemptions exist for electricity industries from Eastern European countries (Bulgaria, Cyprus, Czech Republic, Estonia, Hungary, Lithuania, Poland and Romania) and highly efficient Combined Heat and Power (CHP). The allocation to other sectors starts with a 20 percent auctioning share, reaching 70 percent in 2020 and 100 percent in 2027 (CEC 2009). This will result in around a 40 percent share of auctioning in Phase 3. For installations which belong to a sector which is determined to be at risk of leakage, EUAs will be allocated on the basis of a benchmark (average emissions of the 10 percent highest performing installations of the sector) multiplied by the average production during the period 2005–2008.[6]

The EU ETS also allows a limited number of offsets from the Kyoto Mechanisms Certified Emissions Reductions (CERs) from the Clean Development Mechanism and Emissions Reduction Units (ERUs) from Joint Implementation (JI) to be used for compliance by companies. In Phase 2, the limit for the use of Kyoto Mechanisms had to be specified in the NAP and be approved by the EU Commission (Stephan et al. 2014).[7] The total limit for Kyoto units was 1.4 billion EUAs for Phase 2 (on average around 13.7 percent of the allocation of each installation) and 1.65 billion EUAs over the whole period 2008–2020. The limit varies across MS, as it depended on their position vis-à-vis achieving their Kyoto target internally. In order to record and provide transparency on the issuance, transactions, and surrendering of EUAs, national registries were established which were linked with the Community Independent Transaction Log (CITL). In 2012, the European Union Transaction Log (EUTL) was introduced to accommodate the inclusion of the aviation sector and to enhance security. It replaced the national registries and the CITL. Table 9.1 summarises the key design features over the three phases of the EU ETS.

2. Evaluation criteria

In the following section, the three evaluation criteria of effectiveness, efficiency, and equity are explained, which are later used to assess the EU ETS' performance. ETS are considered superior to other instruments – such as taxes – as they directly set the emissions target, which is argued to be important for an effective policy. Additionally – and in contrast to standards – they are highly flexible in how companies achieve the target, which is argued to be essential for an efficient policy. As will be demonstrated in the following section, the instrument may not meet those expectations, as this is influenced by specific design elements.

2.1 Effectiveness

Assuming mechanisms are in place to ensure compliance, the quantity of allowances issued (emissions budget or cap) determines the amount of GHGs that will be emitted for a particular period. In order to achieve emissions reductions, the number of issued allowances needs to be below the level of emissions that would have occurred without the policy (also called business- as–usual or BAU). However, political pressure may lead to lax emissions targets, or unpredicted economic events may lead to lower BAU emissions than projected, resulting in a target being set that may not reduce emissions below BAU. In such cases, the instrument may still be judged to be effective, as it achieves the given target, but the target is itself ineffective in reducing emissions. The latter is not a fault of the instrument but rather of the target. However, the primary objective of any environmental policy to combat climate change should be to lead to GHG emissions reductions compared to a situation without the policy. Otherwise, significant costs for implementing and operating a policy are incurred with little or no environmental benefit. Therefore, it is important to assess whether the policy achieves any emissions reductions against the BAU scenario. In order to differentiate between those two dimensions – target and instrument – the assessment of effectiveness is divided into two sub-criteria: 1) Is the ETS achieving emissions reductions? (macro dimension); and 2) Is the ETS achieving the given target? (micro dimension).

Table 9.1 Key design features of the EU ETS from Phase 1–Phase 3

Feature	Phase 1	Phase 2	Phase 3
Time frame	2005–2007	2008–2012	2013–2020
Target	Sum of National Targets provided in each National Allocation Plan	Sum of National Kyoto related targets in accordance with the Commission guidance on National Allocation Plans	Harmonised cap determined at European level Linear reduction factor of 1.74% every year (−21% compared to 2005)
Cap	2,082 MtCO$_2$ p.a.	1,998 MtCO$_2$e p.a. + ≈85 MtCO$_2$e for extended scope + ≈200 MtCO$_2$e for aviation from 2012	On average 1,850 MtCO$_2$e over the years 2013–2020 2013: 1,930 MtCO$_2$e p.a. + ≈100 MtCO$_2$e (N$_2$O and PFC) + ≈200 MtCO$_2$e for aviation
Covered Countries	EU 25: 2005/2006 EU 27: from 2007	30 (EU 27 + Norway, Iceland (no installations), Liechtenstein)	31 (EU28 + Norway, Iceland, Liechtenstein)
Covered Sectors	- Power and heat generation - Energy-intensive industry sectors including oil refineries, steelworks and production of iron, aluminium, metals, cement, lime, glass, ceramics, pulp, paper, cardboard, acids and bulk organic chemicals.	As Phase 1 plus: - Civil aviation (from 2012)	As Phase 2 plus: - Nitrous oxide (N$_2$O) from production of nitric, adipic, glyoxal and glyoxylic acids - Perfluorocarbons (PFCs) from aluminium production
Regulated number of installations[1]	2005 10,437 2006 10,678 2007 11,312 Some opt-out of installations	2008 11,303 2009 11,282 2010 11,277 2011 11,195 2012 11,195 + 2,000 (air lines)	≈13,000
Greenhouse Gas	Only Carbon dioxide (CO$_2$) ≈40% of EU GHG	CO$_2$, AU, LT, NL opted-in N$_2$O installations; ≈40% of EU GHG	CO$_2$, N$_2$O and PFCs ≈45% of EU GHG
Accountable units	EU Allowances (EUAs) equals 1 t CO$_2$e Unlimited use of Kyoto Units from Clean Development Mechanism (Certified Emissions Reductions, CERs) excluding CERs generated from sink, nuclear and big hydro projects	EUAs and individual national limits on eligible Kyoto Units (CERs and Emission Reduction Units (ERUs) from Joint Implementation Projects 2008–2012: total limit of 1.4 bn.	EU Allowances (EUAs) and the remaining limits of Kyoto Units resulting in a total limit of 1.6 bn in 2008–2020.

(Continued)

Table 9.1 (Continued)

Feature	Phase 1	Phase 2	Phase 3
Time frame	2005–2007	2008–2012	2013–2020
Threshold	No CO_2e threshold	No CO_2e threshold	25,000 tCO_2 p.a., < 35MW capacity and coverage by other policies
Allocation[2]	Almost 100% free allocation based on approaches specified in National Allocation Plans which vary among member states and were approved by European Commission 0.13% Auctioning	Free allocation (97%) based on approaches specified in National Allocation Plans which vary among member states and were approved by European Commission 4% Auctioning (including left-over from New Entrant Reserves)	Harmonised EU wide rules. Free allocation 1. sectors with a significant risk of carbon leakage based on benchmarks, 2. other manufacturing sectors auctioning starting 2013 at 20% increasing to 70% in 2020 3. 100% Auctioning for power generators from 2013 (excluding generators in 9 Eastern European Countries until 2019) ≈40%
Flexibility	Borrowing between phases not allowed, restricted banking from 1st in 2nd phase	Borrowing between phases not allowed, but unrestricted banking	Borrowing between phases not allowed, but unrestricted banking
Monitoring/reporting /verification	Based on EU monitoring guidelines (tier approach), annually verified reports to national authorities	Based on EU updated monitoring and reporting guidelines.	Based on EU Monitoring and Reporting Regulation (MRR) and Accreditation and Verification Regulation (AVR).
Sanctions	40 €/t CO2e + subsequent surrender + public notification	100 €/t CO2e + subsequent surrender + public notification	100 €/t CO2e + subsequent surrender + public notification
Technical aspects	Annual issuance / surrender, tracking of units by National Registries and European Union Community Independent Transaction Log (CITL)	Annual issuance / surrender, tracking of units by National Registries and EU CITL, 2012 European Union Transaction Log (EUTL)	Annual issuance and surrender, tracking of units by EUTL

Note: Information in the table is retrieved from EEA ETS viewer and from http://ec.europa.eu/clima/policies/ets/index_en.htm.

As shown in the preceding analysis, the micro dimension criteria must be fulfilled as a prerequisite to achieve effectiveness on the macro dimension, but not vice versa.

The major design elements that influence the macro dimension of effectiveness are: 1) the target; 2) potential leakage[8]; and 3) the quality of offsets. The micro dimension is affected by: 1) effectiveness of sanctions; and 2) monitoring, reporting, and verification (M/R/V).

Figure 9.1 illustrates how the *target* should be set to fulfil the micro and macro dimensions of effectiveness. For the macro dimension, the target must at least be set lower (leftward) versus the situation of emissions in BAU in t1. The dotted vertical lines illustrate two different types of ineffective targets. The ineffective target 1 was set below BAU emissions in t0 but above BAU emissions in t1, thus making the target ineffective in t1. The ineffective target 2, in contrast is ineffective in both t0 and t1. Only the dashed vertical line illustrates an effective target (at the macro dimension). Micro dimension effectiveness is achieved if the actual (rather than BAU) emissions are equal to or below the targets set.

With *leakage*, shifts of production and emissions to other countries not covered by an ETS can compromise the effectiveness of the scheme and increases emissions globally, thus again negatively affecting the macro dimension of effectiveness.

The *quality of offsets* also is important, as non-additional offset projects (meaning those that would have occurred in a BAU scenario without the offset scheme) will lead, through the link to the EU ETS, to an actual increase in global emissions as the credits will allow companies in the EU ETS to emit more.

Figure 9.1 also shows the importance of appropriate *sanction* levels. To be effective in the micro dimension, the penalty level for being non-compliant needs to be above the equilibrium permit price. Otherwise, companies will pay the penalty rather than mitigating or buying permits, as it is cheaper.

The importance of M/R/V for the effectiveness of an ETS lies in the fact that a scheme can only lead to real reductions if monitoring is of high quality and cheating is prevented. Shapiro (2007) claims that cap-and-trade schemes provide a higher incentive to cheat than do carbon taxes. This is because neither side in a trade (buyer nor seller) has an incentive to uncover or reveal fraud (e.g. whether the permit sold is the result of real abatement or just understated emissions).

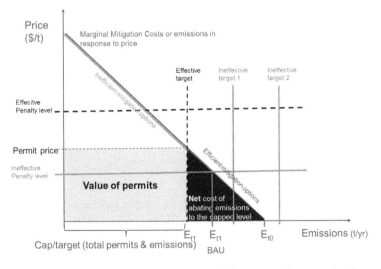

Figure 9.1 Design parameters affecting the efficiency and effectiveness of a cap-and-trade system

Source: Author.

In addition, Brandt and Svendsen (2011) show that there is a risk that even if monitoring occurs by national authorities, they are tempted to give their domestic industries a competitive advantage by allowing them to emit more than they are entitled to or to sell permits without reducing emissions correspondingly.

2.2 Efficiency

The second criterion, *cost efficiency*, refers to achieving an overall emissions target at least cost. Again we distinguish between the macro and micro dimensions, as this gives us the opportunity to assess the following sub-criteria: 1) Is the ETS achieving the emissions reductions at the lowest cost compared to other policies, such as taxes or standards? (macro dimension); and 2) Is the ETS achieving the given target at least cost for an ETS? (micro dimension).

The major design elements that influence the macro dimension of efficiency include: 1) coverage aspects; and 2) the distribution of targets between the covered and non-covered sectors.

From a welfare economic perspective, installations should only be covered by the EU ETS as long as the marginal benefits (e.g. from trading) exceed the marginal costs, including all transactions costs. If for example the transaction costs of including installations in an ETS are high compared to other instruments, it may be cost efficient not to cover all installations with the same policy.

After determining which installations will be included in the ETS and which left outside (non-ETS sector), the respective shares of reduction must be determined, which will lead to the MS achieving its overall reduction target. To achieve an efficient distribution of the reduction burden, the shares should be based on the intersection of aggregated marginal abatement costs of ETS-covered and ETS-non-covered installations, as shown in Figure 9.2.

The micro dimension of efficiency is measured by the performance of the market in achieving an efficient allocation of emissions and abatement over time. From a theoretical perspective, the ETS should potentially be highly cost efficient, since the trading allows flexibility in achieving the emission reductions. The trading between participants with low-cost emissions reduction options and those with only high-cost options maximises the static economic efficiency of the

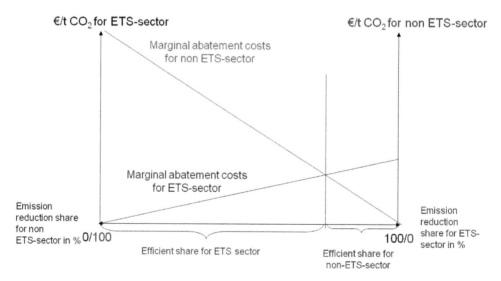

Figure 9.2   Target-sharing of ETS and non-ETS sector

Source: Author.

process. The micro dimension of efficiency also is illustrated in Figure 9.1. To achieve the given target at least cost, those mitigation measures should be implemented that cost less than the permit price, i.e. that are on the marginal mitigation curve to the right of the emissions cap. The total mitigation costs will then be reflected by the shaded triangle. The market would not lead to an efficient allocation if any of the measures with costs above the equilibrium price are implemented, as the total costs would be higher than necessary.

The price for allowances will eventually lead to investments in low-carbon technologies that are cheapest in the long term. This minimisation of costs over time is called *dynamic efficiency*. It includes the increased demand for innovative energy or carbon-saving processes, products, and services that is generated by the price on carbon and which in turn should lead to more research and development (R&D), as well as the invention, adoption, and market diffusion of such innovations.

2.3 Equity

Third, *distributional equity or fairness* relates to the extent to which any group is unfairly disadvantaged or favoured by the scheme and covers intergenerational (between generations) as well as intra-generational (within the same generation) equity. The latter includes international equity aspects of burden-sharing between countries (e.g. developed vs. developing) but also between sectors within one country (e.g. industry vs. households) or within one sector (e.g. low- vs. high-income households). This chapter will focus on the distributional consequences within EU countries. The grey rectangle in Figure 9.1 illustrates the total monetary value of permits. Whoever gets those permits for free will have a monetary benefit (e.g. the government by auctioning them to companies or companies by on-selling the permits or using them to avoid the cost of undertaking abatement). A policy instrument that is regarded as unfair will have difficulty surviving over the long period necessary to reduce GHG emissions to reduce climate change.

Table 9.2 summarises the criteria, dimensions, and design parameters discussed above.

Table 9.2 Summary of evaluation of criteria

Environmental Effectiveness	*Efficiency*	*Equity aspects*
Macro dimension	Macro dimension	Burden sharing between generations
(i) Target: improved	*Coverage*: improved	(inter-generational equity): not assessed
(ii) Leakage: negligible so far	Target setting between ETS	
(iii) Offsets: improved quality	and non-ETS sector: improved	
Micro dimension	Micro dimension	Burden sharing within generations
(iv) Sanctions: improved	Market performance:	(intra-generational equity):
(v) Monitoring/Reporting/	*Static* efficiency negatively	*Country level* (developed vs.
Verification: improved	impacted by free allocation,	developing countries): not assessed
	may improve with auctioning.	
	Dynamic efficiency yet low,	*Sectoral level* (households vs. industry):
	but too early to judge	Allocation method: improved through
		increased share of auctioning but
		mainly depends on how revenue
		is going to be recycled.

Source: Author.

Note: The added judgements to the design elements (e.g. 'improved') is summarising the result of the analysis in Sections 4 and 5. It indicates whether this particular design element of the EU ETS had been modified from Phase 1 to Phase 3 with either a positive or negative effect on the relevant criterion (e.g. effectiveness, efficiency or equity).

3. Evaluation of Phase 1 and Phase 2

3.1 Environmental effectiveness

Design elements that influence the environmental effectiveness of the EU ETS on the macro level include the target, leakage, and use of offsets. Assessment of all those elements is necessary to judge if the introduction of the EU ETS led to any global GHG emissions reductions compared to a situation without the ETS.

To assess the environmental effectiveness of the target, we first compare the number of EUAs distributed to covered installations with the emissions these generated during the first five years of the scheme's operation. Figure 9.3 shows the number of issued EUAs compared to verified emissions in the EU-25 in 2005 to 2012.

As can be seen in Figure 9.4, the cap/target of the Phase 1 (2005–2007) was very weak, as there was an excessive issuance of allowances of about 140 MtCO₂e (allocated EUAs–verified emissions). Verified emissions were higher in 2007 than in 2005 or 2006, as in 2007 the excess allocation was obvious and the spot price of permits collapsed (see Figure 9.5).

Verified and more accurate data, as well as better guidelines on which installations are covered and which are not, was available for Phase 2. However, as is illustrated by Figure 9.6, the proposed budgets in most MS were often significantly larger than what the European Commission approved, and thus the risk of an excess allocation was high in Phase 2. While the announced EU-15[9] emissions trading (ET) budgets for Phase 2 were much stricter than for Phase 1 and required only moderate adjustments from the EU Commission, most proposed EU-12[10] ET budgets appear to be rather generous. However, because of the European Commission's decision to substantially cut several ET-budgets, the EU-wide ET-budget for Phase 2 was significantly

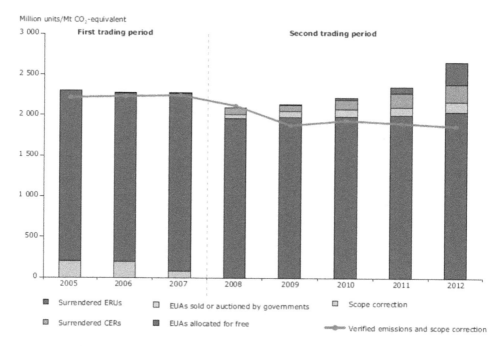

Figure 9.3   Allocated versus verified emissions (million EUAs or MtCO2e), by year

Source: EEA 2013, Figure 2.13

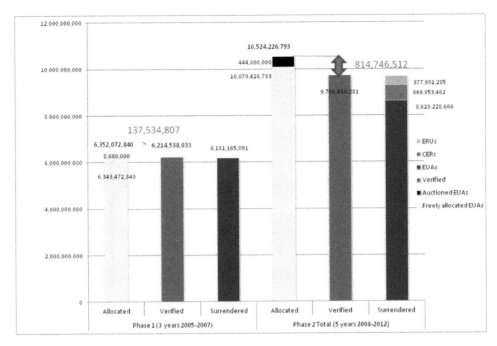

Figure 9.4 Allocated EUAs, verified emissions and surrendered EUAs in Phase 1 and Phase 2

Source: Calculations EEA based on CITL data.

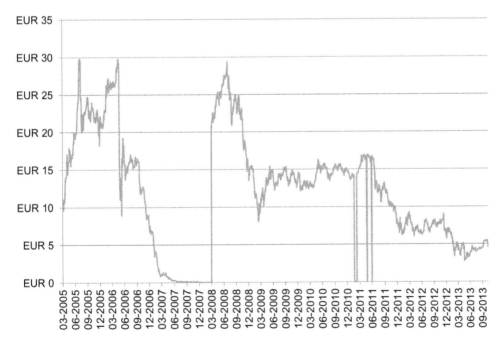

Figure 9.5 EUA spot price development (2005–2013)

Source: Based on data provided by Point Carbon, EEX.

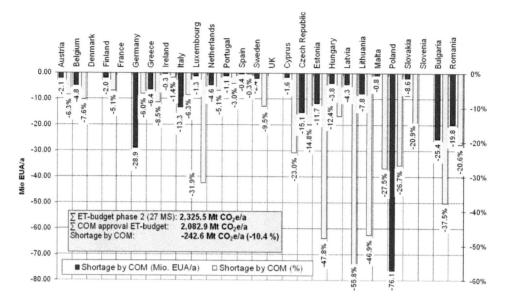

Figure 9.6 Proposed budgets for Phase 2 compared to EU Commission-adjusted budgets (difference in MtCO$_2$e and %)

Source: Divers National Allocation Plans and Commission Decisions, see http://ec.europa.eu/clima/policies/ets/allocation/2008/documentation_en.htm.

Note: The longer the bars, the greater the EU Commission reduced each country's target versus that country's proposal.

more ambitious – about 10.4 percent lower than historical emissions in 2005. This shows how important the role of the EU Commission was to improving the effectiveness of the target but the projections it had in mind when setting the target have again been overly optimistic. Due to the recession, the emissions in Phase 2 were again much lower than expected and EUA prices and emissions have been on a decreasing trend since 2009.

While the announced EU-15 ET budgets for Phase 2 were much stricter than for Phase 1 and required only moderate adjustments from the EU Commission, most proposed EU-1 ET budgets appear to be rather generous (see Figure 9.6).

For 2009 and 2012, the overall position of the EU ETS was again long, indicating that the lower than expected GHG emissions had offset the stricter targets. However, these figures do not reveal if the allocation was actually excessive compared to BAU or whether real abatement occurred. In order to better understand what happened, a counterfactual has to be estimated that tries to quantify the emissions without the EU ETS in each year (BAU emissions levels).

Several econometric studies exist that try to estimate the counterfactual and net abatement effect, but there is only one which includes Phase 1 and 2. This most recent study is undertaken by Gloaguen & Alberola (2013) and concludes that over the first two phases (2005–2011), emissions were reduced by around 1100 MtCO$_2$e compared to the BAU scenario.[11] The study includes 21 countries responsible for around 93 percent of EU ETS emissions. It revealed that more than half of the reduction had been achieved by European climate and energy policies, although the EU ETS did not play a major role. It was estimated that policies which increased renewable production contributed to 500 MtCO$_2$e abatement (40–50 percent) and policies which decreased energy intensity contributed to 10 percent to 20 percent of the reduction. Interestingly, only

300 $MtCO_2e$ (25 percent) of the reduction was attributed to the economic crisis and 20 percent resulted from fuel-switching due to changes in the relation of fuel prices, which lead to substitution effects from coal to gas. The impact of the carbon price was estimated to be negligible, with an effect of 0 to 10 percent.

What are possible reasons for the excess allocation? Apart from poor data quality for base-year emissions[12] and some uncertainty on the coverage of specific installations (e.g. crackers from the chemical industry), the main factor for the excessive allocation was most likely the fact that MS were lobbied extensively by industry for a lax target and determined the cap based on emissions projections instead of historic data (Neuhoff 2011; Betz and Sato 2006). In these cases, uncertainties were combined with overly optimistic economic growth rates. Thus, aiming for only marginal reductions against exaggerated projections is likely to result in an excess allocation of allowances (Grubb & Ferrario 2006).

Another design element that is important with regard to environmental effectiveness is carbon *leakage*. Leakage can occur through different channels, e.g. the production channel (production is transferred outside the EU ETS) or the fossil fuel channel (fuel prices change and led to higher consumption of emissions-intensive fuels outside the EU ETS). Although both of those channels led to higher emissions *ceteris paribus*, there may be some beneficial leakage through spill-overs in the technology channel that actually lower global emissions (Neuhoff 2011). Sectors at risk for carbon leakage are those with high carbon costs (direct and indirect, e.g. through electricity) and high exposure to international trade, as international competition lowers the possibility to pass through carbon costs to consumers. Affected industries include, for example, cement, steel, and paper. Zhang (2012) provides a comprehensive review of carbon leakage and the effectiveness of anti-leakage policies associated with differentiated climate abatement commitments among countries. In addition, the effect of carbon leakage and competitiveness has been estimated by macroeconomic models (Böhringer et al. 2012), as well as empirically (Ellerman et al. 2010; Sartor 2013). The ex-post empirical studies show that there was no statistical evidence of a change in net imports due to the introduction of a carbon price. This means that in Phase 1 and 2 there is little evidence of leakage. However, given that the first and second phase of the EU ETS were dominated by generous free allocations and low carbon prices, the first two phases are a poor indicator of what will happen in the future.

Another factor that may increase or reduce the extent of emissions reductions from the EU ETS from a global perspective is the use of *offsets*. In Phase 1, the use of offsets was negligible, as the excess issuance of EUAs and the banking restrictions on those between Phase 1 and Phase 2 meant companies did not use offsets for compliance but were banking them instead.[13] The cap for offsets was set at 1.4 billion units for Phase 2 and 1.65 billion units for Phase 2 and 3 together. In Phase 2, around 1.05 billion Kyoto units were surrendered for compliance in the EU ETS, 64 percent of which were CERs and 36 percent ERUs (see Figure 9.4, leaving around 600 million for Phase 3. Of those surrendered Kyoto units in Phase 2, around 61 percent were from industrial gas projects.

As mentioned previously, in order to determine the actual contribution to global emission reductions, the quality of the offsets is important – especially their 'additionality'. Schneider (2007) evaluates the additionality of a sample of registered Clean Development Mechanism (CDM) projects and estimates that around 40 percent have not been additional. An econometric study (Zhang and Wang 2011) with a focus on Chinese CDM energy-related projects – excluding CDM projects of industrial gases – also finds problems in proving additionality. It was argued that given the fast changing economy, such as in China, it is difficult to set realistic baselines. Given the fact that CDM projects involving industrial gases like HFC-23 (see Schneider 2011) create perverse incentives to increase their CERs issuance, the real contribution to global emissions reductions from the offset part of the EU ETS =, therefore, is difficult to predict.[14] Those perverse incentives have led to the decision of the European Commission to disallow the use of credits from industrial gases for compliance from Phase 3 onwards.

On ERUs, the situation of additionality is somewhat different. In contrast to CERs, when ERUs are issued they are subtracted from the assigned amount (this is the emissions budget under the Kyoto Protocol) of the host country. This should in theory increase the likelihood of additionality. However, given the high surplus of assigned amount units in most JI host countries, ERUs may have just been used to sell some of their excess assigned amount units into the EU ETS market without verifying the additionality of the JI projects.

From the micro perspective, sanctioning and M/R/V are important design elements that may influence effectiveness. The *penalty* level can have an impact on environmental effectiveness of a scheme, as previously illustrated by Figure 9.1. EU ETS sanctions include a financial penalty (which was increased from 40€/EUA in Phase 1 to 100€/EUA in Phase 2), coupled with a make-good provision (additional surrender of missing permits) and public notification of those installations which are not compliant. The European Environmental Agency (2007) reported that there were only a few operators in Denmark, Portugal, Germany, Spain, and the UK who failed to surrender sufficient allowances.

In total, the shortfall calculated by subtracting the surrendered allowances from the verified emissions was around 33 Million EUAs or around 0.5 percent of the verified emissions in Phase 1 (see Figure 9.4). In Phase 2 the shortfall was even lower with around 500,000 EUAs or 0.01 percent. This decrease over time can be explained by the fact that sanctions are often caused by a mismatch between the reported/verified emissions and the surrendered allowances. This can be illustrated by the experience of the German Emissions Trading Authority. Figure 9.7 from March 2011 shows the number of sanctions (middle grey area) has been decreasing over time from 22 (in 2005) to 4 (in 2007) in Phase 1 and from 11 (in 2008) to 0 (in 2009). In the majority of cases, the charge was dismissed or companies surrendered a

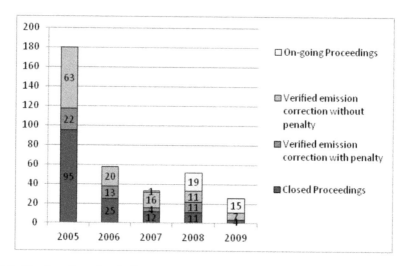

Figure 9.7   Number of sanctions in Germany per year

Source: Graph provided by German Emissions Trading Authority (as of March 30, 2011).

Note: For 2009, additional sanction orders not represented in the figure have been sent but are ongoing proceedings after appeals by the operators.

higher number of allowances than necessary to ensure that they were compliant even in the event that their reported/verified emissions were increased by the authority. Thus, the frequency of sanctions is related to the data quality. The better the quality of verified data, the fewer the sanctions, as there is no need to correct verified emissions and adjust the number of surrendered units. Thus, monitoring and verification experience played a significant role, but overall the design and level of the EU ETS penalty rates seem to be a successful deterrent and kept non-compliance low.

Finally *monitoring, reporting, and verification* may have an impact on the effectiveness of a trading scheme, as they determine the amount of allowances that have to be surrendered. The Monitoring and Reporting Guidelines (MRGs) have been the basis for GHG monitoring in the EU ETS (CEC 2004). They specify different tiers for the calculation of emissions, which depend on the emissions level of the source. In Phase 1, most MS transposed those guidelines into some form of legally binding requirements; however, several exceptions and temporary derogations were made (EEA 2008). In Phase 2, the MRG were replaced to take lessons learnt from Phase 1 into account and to reduce the monitoring costs for small emitters (CEC 2007). The new guidelines include improvements with regard to sampling methods and emissions factors. However, the MRGs only regulate some of the fundamental requirements and aspects of the verification process. Therefore, most MS (except Estonia, France, Portugal, and Slovakia) developed their own verification standards and procedures, as well as accreditation criteria. But even verifiers, who may lose their accreditation if their wrongdoing is detected, have some conflict of interest, as they are paid by the company whose reports they are verifying. Thus, the only instance of proper verification would be the national authorities spot-checking the verified reports. As reported by the European Environmental Agency (EEA 2008) for Phase 1, in 19 MS the national authorities had the authority to check the verified emissions reports and around 44 installations (0.4 percent) from seven MS were reported to have submitted unsatisfactory reports for 2007. However, a much greater problem was missing reports (146 installations, 1.34 percent), especially from installations which had been shut down (EEA 2008).

3.2 Efficiency

To determine the efficiency of the EU ETS from the macro perspective – what is the efficient coverage of sectors, gases, and firm size? – two design elements must be assessed: coverage and the burden sharing between covered and non-covered sectors. Based on CITL data, the EU ETS covers a very large number of small emitters. From a welfare economics perspective, the efficient coverage depends on the ratio between the benefits of coverage and the costs. As theoretically and quantitatively shown by Betz et al. (2010), the efficient coverage depends on the stringency of the target, the distribution of abatement costs, and the transaction costs of regulating companies under different policies.[15] Given the lax targets in Phases 1 and 2, the broad coverage seems inefficient, as the benefits from covering small emitters (e.g. contribution to lower abatement costs) are too low to outweigh the costs of coverage; a phasing-in of smaller emitters when targets become more stringent would be more efficient. Covering small installations with an upstream rather than downstream approach (i.e. higher in the supply chain) may also be more efficient, as it will lower the fixed transaction costs of monitoring, reporting, and verification.

As shown by Schleich et al. (2009), the European Commission again played a crucial role in improving the burden-sharing between ET-covered and ET-non-covered sectors in Phase 2.

Through the ability to use a certain share of offsets for compliance, it is estimated that cost savings in the range of €4–20 billion were achieved (Stephan et al. 2014). The lower estimate is based on the EUA-CER spread and the upper end of the estimate does take demand elasticity into account, meaning it models the EUA price without the use of offsets and compares it to the CER actual price.

From a micro-perspective, efficiency is related to the *market functioning*. In theory, an ETS is an cost-efficient instrument, since it will set a unique price signal for all participants according to scarcity, and the market mechanism will allow those with high mitigation costs to buy and those with low costs to sell. Thus, the scheme eventually will lead to an allocation which is efficient.

This can be derived from the Coase theorem (1960), which states that the bargaining outcome is independent of which party (polluter or sufferer) receives the property rights. The initial allocation will have distributional effects but will not affect the final distribution of permits under certain conditions. Hahn and Stavins (2011) argue that this independence property is of central political importance, as it gives governments the possibility to use permit allocation to gain support for the policy without compromising its effectiveness or efficiency. However, in the real world, it may be difficult to achieve the conditions necessary for an efficient final allocation that is independent of the primary allocation. It would require rational participants (homo economicus) trading in a perfectly competitive market with perfect information and no transaction costs. Translating those requirements into the world of emissions trading, would mean that:

1. participants are well informed about their abatement options and costs, including offset options (perfect information);
2. no transaction costs occur;
3. the demand and supply of permits is well known by all participants and there is no uncertainty about future permit prices (perfect information); and
4. the market is competitive.

To determine the efficiency of the EU ETS market, researchers generally have focussed more on the output side of the market, analysing, inter alia, the development of permit prices and volumes (Lutz et al. 2013 and Aatola et al. 2013) and transaction data (Ellermann and Trotignon 2009). However, these factors only provide a partial answer to the question of whether the market was achieving the given target at least cost. For example, the EUA price development is usually evaluated with a financial market definition of efficiency in mind: markets are judged to be efficient if price development can be explained by changes in the fundamentals (e.g. temperature, fuel prices, economic activity) or if the 'cost of carry model' holds for future markets (Charles et al. 2013). But this is a different interpretation of efficiency and does not answer the question of whether the market achieved a given target at least cost. Recall that market efficiency in the economic sense requires that, for a given target, prices be as low as possible. Given that there was only limited scarcity – if at all – in the EU ETS market in Phase 1 and 2, a price of above zero indicates that the market was not achieving the target at least cost, although price movements may have been explained by fundamentals or other factors such as a lack of information/transparency on overall emissions. In order to understand the 'inefficient' market outcomes, we focus more on the input side: the necessary conditions for markets to work efficiently and how they may be compromised in reality.

The first condition relates to the condition of perfect information. A survey by KfW/ZEW in March 2011 and March 2013 of German companies (compromising 24–30 percent of all regulated installations, responsible for 42–66 percent of emissions) revealed that around 60 percent of the companies did not know their abatement costs (KfW/ZEW 2011 and KfW/ZEW 2013). Not knowing the abatement costs may be rational if the costs associated with attaining that information are higher than the benefits of reducing emissions (Heindl 2011).

The second condition is referring to transaction costs, which means when broadly defined that any gathering of information is costly. Thus, there is a link (overlap) between the conditions of perfect information and transaction costs.[16] However, more common is a narrow definition of transaction costs that limits transaction costs to trading costs – including search and information costs, bargaining, and reaching a decision – but also includes the costs of monitoring and enforcing of contracts (Stavins 1995).

The KfW/ZEW (2011) study reveals that 61 percent of companies mainly met their obligations by shifting long or short allocation positions between their installations without monetary transfers. From an economics point of view, this non-cost-minimising behaviour may be explained by high transaction costs that occur either externally (the benefit of selling on the market would have been low compared to the trading transaction costs) or internally (high organisational barriers and complexities to overcome, e.g. accounting issues or issues of liability).

This is in line with the findings of the study of CITL transfer data from 2005–2007 by Betz and Schmidt (2014) which shows that 98 percent of the accounts were in the passive cluster. According to KfW/ZEW, companies became more active over time. However, 46 percent of the interviewed companies – not installations – did not trade in 2011, and 34 percent did not trade in 2012. From those inactive companies, 55 percent did not trade because of sufficient allocation and 37 percent to prevent speculation. Another survey of about 800 firms across six European countries was undertaken by Anderson et al. (2011) using an innovative interview set-up and combining the interview results with company data from the CITL on emissions and allocations, as well as performance indicators. They find a threshold with regard to company behaviour in the EU ETS market: companies with an excess allocation of about 5,000 permits or more will participate in the market, but those with lesser allocations won't.

In addition to transaction costs, the reluctance to participate in the market may be explained by the fact that not all participants are risk neutral and that there was – and is – uncertainty over future permit prices, the third condition. Baldurson and von der Fehr (2004) have demonstrated theoretically that in a world with uncertainty and risk averse participants, net buyers of permits tend to over-invest in abatement to hedge against possible high future permit prices and net sellers tend to do the opposite.[17] Experiments have shown that this inefficiency may prevail even when companies were able to sell future permits today without transaction costs to hedge future permit price risk. This may be explained by the fact that net sellers did not participate in the futures market and thus net buyers were unable to buy and no futures market evolved (Betz and Gunnthorsdottir 2009).[18] The uncertainty over future permit prices seems to be very high in the EU ETS, given that the supply and demand of permits is affected by outstanding political decisions. For example, at the start of the EU ETS some NAPs had not been approved, and the status of new entrant reserves by countries were not known (i.e. it was not clear if any surplus from the reserves would enter the market). More importantly, appeals against NAP decisions take a long time to settle, and the EU's post-2012 target still depends on the outcome of international climate negotiations and the so called backloading decision. Another caveat is that emissions are reported and publicly released only once a year, which makes it difficult to predict the total demand. As emissions are not evenly distributed, small emitters will have less insight into the overall market position than large emitters (Ellermann et al. 2010).

Finally, relating to the last condition, *market power and market structure* may reduce the efficiency of the ETS. There have been several theoretical papers analysing the effect of market power and initial allocation on the performance of the permit market. They show that due to the market power in the permit market (Hahn 1984) and/or product market (DiSegni Eshel 2005), the initial allocation should be modified to take the strategic behaviour of dominant firms into account.

However, indicators measuring concentration level (Herfindahl-Hirschman Index)[19] have not reflected market power risk in the current EU ETS (Ellermann et al. 2010).[20]

Although in theory, under ideal conditions, the primary allocation approach– auctioning or free allocation – should not have an impact on final allocation of permits and thus efficiency, the EU ETS has shown that there is hardly a NAP that uses a free allocation method that does not distort incentives. This can be illustrated with the following examples (Neuhoff et al. 2006 and Betz et al. 2006):

1. In around ten MS (e.g. Austria, Germany, Netherlands and Poland), allocation in Phase 2 was a function of emissions in 2005, which provided a perverse incentive for less abatement in 2005 in order to receive more permits in Phase 2.
2. The use of free allocations to new entrants, coupled with the withdrawal of allocations to 'ceasing installations' in some MS, has negative effects on efficiency, since it creates perverse incentives to keep inefficient plants in operation.
3. Allocation to new entrants based on benchmarks on installed capacity, as done by several MS, gives perverse incentives to build oversized new installations such as boilers (as in Denmark).[21]

What are the conclusions to be drawn from those findings? First of all, the real world does not fulfil the conditions of the idealised theoretical world that allows the market to achieve an allocation that is independent from the initial allocation of permits. Therefore, we can conclude that the way permits were allocated to companies *did* affect the efficiency of the EU ETS.

What might have been different if full auctioning of permits had been the main allocation method in the EU ETS from 2005 onwards? First, experiments comparing auctioning and grandfathering of permits have shown that auctioning yields better price discovery early on (Restiani 2010). Therefore, one can assume that scarcity or the lack of scarcity in the EU ETS market in Phase 1 would have been discovered earlier. The EU ETS got the first indication that there were likely more permits issued than emissions when verified emissions were published in May 2006 and the permit price collapsed from around 30€/EUA to 10€/EUA (see Figure 9.5). It took until the beginning of 2007 for permit prices to reflect this excess allocation and reach a price of almost 0€/EUA.

Second, under full auctioning, all installations are forced to participate either in investing or buying permits on the market to be compliant. Therefore, a situation in which more than half of the installations do not participate in trading would be unlikely with full auctioning. Compared to a situation with full auctioning, the free allocation in the EU ETS seems to have reduced efficiency, but, on the other hand, it improved environmental effectiveness, as some reduction may have happened due to the (inefficiently) high prices.

Finally, to comprehensively judge whether the market worked in an efficient way in Phase 1 and Phase 2, one would need information on the reference emissions and the abatement costs of each installation.[22] As we do not have this information, it is not possible to judge whether the participating companies behaved in an efficient way. We can only question that a high share of passive regulated companies compared with the substantial trading volume of a small number of companies are characteristics of an efficient market.

With regard to the *dynamic efficiency*, the expected EU Allowance (EUA) price developments are important, as they give companies (emitters and technology companies) an incentive to invest in low-emitting technologies (via R&D and adoption of technologies). EUA prices were extremely volatile at the beginning of the scheme, ranging between €8/EUA and €30/EUA, with a sudden, steep price decline from €30/EUA to around €10/EUA in April 2006 when verified emissions data was released (see Figure 9.5). In Phase 2, a price bubble did occur again; this time the unexpected financial crises triggered the fall of prices. The combination of a lax target, uncertainty about future stringency of the target, and high volatility of permit prices seemed to make long-term investment decisions very risky. The KfW/ZEW survey revealed that around 64 percent of installations have implemented mitigation measures in Phase 2 and 41 percent in Phase 1. However, for most companies the mitigation was a side effect of an investment that would have happened anyway to improve the production process. Those findings are also in line with case studies (Rogge, Schneider, Hoffmann 2011) and interviews (Rogge and Hoffmann 2010) showing that the EU ETS does not yet lead to significantly higher rates of investment and adoption of low-emitting technologies in the electricity generating sector. Only some moderate effects, with an increase in corporate carbon capture and storage research, including pilot projects as well as innovation in the organisational processes, have been measured. The latter effects include the management becoming aware of carbon costs and including these in investment models. However, technology-specific policies and fuel price expectations currently have a much greater effect on companies' investment strategies.

Finally, we can conclude that the EU ETS most likely did not achieve theoretical efficiency, as many of the preconditions have not been fulfilled and allocation methods compromised the incentives.

3.3 Equity

In assessing equity, we will focus on the intra-generational equity aspect in EU countries, as equity with regard to future generations or between developing and developed countries is difficult to judge and beyond the scope of this chapter. To assess the intra-generational equity implications of the EU ETS, the allocation method is the key design element to consider. Recall that the rectangle in Figure 9.1 reflects the monetary value of the permits. The choice of who receives those permits for free has significant distributional effects and raises equity issues that, if mishandled, may reduce the political acceptability of the ETS. Giving those permits to industry for free will generally make high-income households better off compared to low-income households, since the former spend a lower share of their income on emissions-intensive goods and services and tend to benefit more from the higher share values resulting from windfall profits. Furthermore, if all permits are given out for free, the government has no possibility to alleviate undesired regressive effects.

A study by Cludius et al. (2012) assesses the impact of the EU ETS on German households by combining industry data from German environmental and input-output accounts with household-level data based on the German Income and Expenditure Survey. Assuming an average carbon price of €25 per ton of CO_2-e and 100 percent pass-through with no change in consumption patterns, they show that the total impact of the EU ETS on German households in Phase 3 is clearly regressive.[23] This result is driven by the regressive effect of direct electricity consumption, while the indirect effect, which captures the raise in price for consumption of products that use electricity as an input to the production process, is distributed progressively. Overall, the effect seems rather moderate, as the lowest income decile will see a raise in expenditure of 1.09 percent (direct: 0.92 percent/indirect: 0.17 percent) compared to 0.53 percent (0.28 percent/0.25 percent) for the highest income decile.

In addition to the regressive impact, the high share of free allocation led to a high level of windfall profits for electricity producers and other industry sectors that were able to pass on the nominal costs of the permits to customers, even though they received the permits for free. For instance, electricity producers may pass on the opportunity costs (i.e. the profits that could be made by selling the permits on the market) when setting their electricity prices, even though the allowances have been allocated free of charge. This led to significant wealth transfers between consumers and producers, estimated to be around €13 billion per year for Phase 1 (Keppler and Cruciani 2010), which affected low-income households disproportionately, as shown previously. Which companies had the largest surplus of free allocation in Phase 2 has been assessed by Morris (2012) and shows that mainly companies from the steel and cement sector had a surplus of allocation (e.g. ArcelorMittal had a surplus of 123 $MtCO_2e$, around half of their verified emissions). Most of the wealth transfer would be eliminated if companies were obliged to buy the allowances instead of getting them for free, and governments could use the auction revenue to compensate low-income households for the increases in energy and commodity prices associated with the EU ETS. However, the government needs to be cautious to not recycle the revenue in a way that negates the carbon-saving incentives of the carbon price.

4. Outlook and conclusions

Emissions trading schemes are very complex policies that require very careful design processes. The different design elements are highly interrelated (recall coverage and target), and when changing one element, design in other areas may need to be adapted accordingly. Therefore, ETSs may be very vulnerable to a policy design process that tries to accommodate the interests of many stakeholders with conflicting views.

As shown by the experience in the EU, the final design may be compromised, and the original key advantages of an ETS – such as effectiveness, efficiency, and equity – compared to other policies can be diminished or even lost. In addition, policymakers may need to prioritise criteria, as they may require different designs.[24]

Our analysis of the EU ETS has shown that the design has improved over time – though this was very dependent on the institutional setting – but is still far from perfect to deliver efficiency, effectiveness, and equity.

With regard to environmental effectiveness, we can conclude that continued improvements were made, but given the contribution of other policies and the global financial crises, no substantial emissions reductions compared to BAU (macro dimension) were achieved. However, the instrument cannot be blamed for this failure, since it is the target which would need to be adjusted. The European Commission was crucial in ensuring more stringent targets and a more harmonised target setting processes than had the MS acted individually. Starting with the approval process in Phase 1, it then introduced a transparent and objective approval process in Phase 2, and – most importantly – a uniform method for calculating each MS' ET-budget. Finally, in Phase 3, the commission has achieved a harmonised target for all ETS sectors and a more efficient burden-sharing between ETS and non-ETS sectors. However, instead of scarcity, the market has accumulated a high surplus over time, which is estimated to reach 2 billion EUAs by 2015 (see Figure 9.8). After several attempts, the European Commission was able to pass the so called backloading of 900 million EUAs. This will allow the European Commission to reduce the auction volume to later auctions but will not reduce the overall target.

In January 2014, the European Commission proposed a 40 percent reduction target compared to the 1990 emissions level by 2030. This would mean that the linear reduction factor would be increased to 2.2 percent per year from 2021 and that emissions would be reduced by 43 percent compared to 2005 by the EU ETS covered installations. However, the more ambitious reduction factor will not be able to relieve the market imbalance in the short run. Therefore, a proposal for a market stability reserve at the start of Phase 4 has been proposed by the European Commission. The mechanism is supposed to be triggered by surplus volumes: a surplus higher

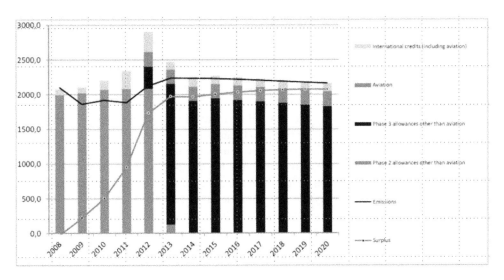

Figure 9.8 Possible surplus development

Source: EC (2012) 234 final

than 833 million allowances will reduce auction volumes and increase the reserve; a surplus below 400 million allowances will release allowances from the reserve and increase auction volumes. These developments show that emissions trading schemes have the potential to start discussions about new mechanisms when policymakers and industry want to keep prices at a certain level. Thus, they may end up in a similar trial-and-error situation as discussed in the context of taxes to achieve a certain price level.

No leakage effect has been measured in Phase 1 or is anticipated for Phase 2, given the almost 100 percent free allocation and low EUA prices. In Phase 3, 164 industrial sectors and sub-sectors were defined to be at risk of carbon leakage and got allocated EUAs based on a BAT benchmark (EC 2011).[25] Again, the free allocation and low prices also reduce the risk of carbon leakage for Phase 3.

The European Commission also has played a role in limiting the use of offsets and setting quality standards, which may improve environmental effectiveness. With regard to sanctions, penalty levels have increased in accordance with the European index of consumer prices in of Phase 3 and will be continually amended. In addition, in Phase 3 the monitoring, reporting, and verification within the EU ETS was based on an EU regulation, which replaced the EU monitoring and reporting guidelines that left MS room for interpretation. This achievement of the commission should make it easier to ensure data quality and, therefore, also should positively affect environmental effectiveness.

The efficiency of the EU ETS from a macro dimension seems also to have increased when taking into account the previously mentioned developments with regard to the burden-sharing between ETS and non-ETS sectors. Similar improvements have been noted with regard to coverage: In Phase 3, the EU directive (EU 2009) also allows the exclusion of installations from the EU ETS if emissions are below 25,000 tCO_2 per year, the capacity is below 35 MW, and they are regulated by other policies (EU 2009). This new opt-out option could increase slightly the efficiency of the EU ETS in Phase 3.[26]

In addition to the harmonisation of the target-setting process, the European Commission increased harmonisation over the allocation process in each phase by publishing NAP guidance documents in Phase 2 and passing a new directive in Phase 3 resulting in harmonised EU-wide benchmarks for free allocation to existing and new entrants in industries defined as being at risk of carbon leakage (EC 2011). What is left to MS is mainly the auction design (if they do not use the central platform) and deciding how the auction revenue will be used. Given the move towards auctioning, the market performance of the scheme may be increased as almost all combustion installations have to become active and buy EUAs.

The higher share of auctioning also may enhance intra-generational equity, as revenue will flow to governments rather than be a windfall to business; recycling the auction revenue to compensate low-income households for the regressive impacts will be possible and should further improve equity.[27] The EU ETS directive (2009) specifies that 50 percent of the auction revenue should be used for specific activities such as demonstration projects for mitigation and adaptation or renewable energy and energy-efficient technologies. However, only a few activities – such as the support of public transportation, energy efficiency measures, financial support for lower and middle income households – will directly lower regressive impacts.

Despite all these positive developments with regard to effectiveness, efficiency on the macro perspective, and potentially equity (summarised in Table 9.2), there is still room for improvement for the EU ETS in the future. Especially static and dynamic efficiency can be improved as they seem negatively affected by high price volatility and the free allocation to sectors with risk of carbon leakage. As Martin et al. (2013) point out, the same reduction in aggregate relocation risk could have been achieved with far less free allowance allocation to industries if compensation is based on the expected marginal impact of relocation. With regard to the high share of companies which have not assessed their abatement potential and the respective costs, it seems that the EU may need some modification, such as additional instruments to complement the ETS, to increase its efficiency. In Sweden, for example, the EU minimum electricity tax can be avoided by energy-intensive industries if they become part of a voluntary agreement called the Programme for Improving Energy Efficiency in Energy-Intensive Industries (PFE), which includes an energy efficiency audit. According to Stenqvist and Nilsson (2011) this programme increased the companies' knowledge of their abatement costs and was successful in reducing emissions. In addition, it needs to be seen if the market stability reserve is sufficient to increase prices, given that it is not reducing the overall quantity of allowances in the system. An ambitious price floor may be a better way to reduce price volatility and support investment (Jotzo and Hatfield-Dodds 2011). Finally, further complementary policies which enhance R&D and technology diffusion are required to achieve the investments in innovation necessary to transform our society into a low-carbon one.

Acknowledgements

The author thanks, without implicating, ZhongXiang Zhang for his valuable comments and suggestions and Martin Jones for his research assistance and proofreading. Support by the Environmental Economics Research Hub financed by the Commonwealth Environmental Research Facilities (CERF) as well as the Swiss Competence Centre for Research in Energy, Society and Transition (CREST) financed by the Swiss Confederation is gratefully acknowledged.

Notes

1 See Tietenberg bibliography http://www.colby.edu/~thtieten/trade.html.
2 In 2007 the EU ETS was extended to 27 MS when Romania and Bulgaria joined the EU. Since 1 January 2014 the EU ETS includes Croatia, due to the country's accession to the EU on 1 July 2013.

3 The total number of installations covered under the EU ETS will change continuously due to new entrants or closures of installations, new gases to be covered, opt-in/opt-out of installations and new countries entering the scheme. In Phase 2, the changes were due to modification of interpretations of the definition of combustion installations, coverage of new gases (countries like France and Belgium [Wallonia] included new gases such as N_2O from adipic acid production) and the entering of Norway, Iceland, and Liechtenstein.

4 See http://ec.europa.eu/clima/policies/ets/index_en.htm.

5 The share of auctioning in 2012 increased by 37 percent compared to 2011 because many EU MS were selling their surpluses in new entrant reserves.

6 The definition is based on the carbon cost in production (CCP) and the exposure to international competition (EIC) and the three criteria used were 1) CCP<5 percent and EIC>10 percent; 2) CCP<30 percent; and 3) EIC<30 percent.

7 There was no quantitative limitation of use of CERs in Phase 1 as it was expected that only a few CERs would be issued. Since ERUs were only able to be produced during the Kyoto Commitment Period from 2008–2012, they were only able to be surrendered in Phase 2. No CERs have been surrendered in Phase 1 (EEA 2008).

8 Leakage is defined as an 'emissions increase abroad caused by unilateral climate policy measures at home' (IPCC 2007).

9 From Austria to UK in Figure 9.6.

10 From Cyprus to Romania in Figure 9.6.

11 Previous studies which estimate the cumulative abatement for Phase 1 (2005–2007) ranged from around 174 $MtCO_2e$ (Anderson and Di Maria 2011) to 210 $MtCO_2e$ (Ellerman et al. 2010). Ellerman et al. (2010) use a simple indicator of CO_2 emissions per Gross Domestic Product (GDP) whereas Anderson and Di Maria (2011) take, like (Gloaguen and Alberola 2013) for instance, temperature changes and fuel price developments into account. For an overview on abatement estimates see Grubb et al. (2013: Table 1).

12 Emissions of covered installations before the ETS, used to set the target.

13 As CERs had no banking limitation from Phase 1 to Phase 2, companies were offering to swap them against non-bankable EUAs.

14 HFC-23 has a very high global warming potential and the costs of reduction are estimated to be very low at US$1 per ton of CO2e. This substantial revenue from the sale of CDM credits may increase the production of industrial gases, leading to non-additional reductions.

15 Betz et al. (2010) compare a 'blanket coverage' with a 'partial coverage' approach, which compares the costs of a broad ETS with the costs of a mix of an ETS and an emissions standard for relatively small emitters.

16 A world without transaction costs will imply perfect information, as gathering of information is costless. However the opposite does not hold, a world with perfect information may still encounter transaction costs.

17 This fact has been supported by the findings of (Abrell et al. 2011), who estimated that firms receiving a tighter allocation than average in the first phase increased reduction efforts of those companies in the second phase and vice versa.

18 The situation may change when more risk-neutral parties, e.g. banks, participate in the spot and future markets, which may increase liquidity.

19 The Herfindahl-Hirschman Index is calculated by summing up the squared market share of each firm competing in the market.

20 In the case of market power, Hintermann (2001) demonstrated that even net permit buyers would have found it profitable to manipulate the permit price upward.

21 The Danish NAP (Danish Government 2007) stated that Denmark reduced the free allocation from 250 EUAs/MW installed capacity in Phase 1 to 100 EUAs/MW in Phase 2 as allowance allocation provided a disproportionately large incentive to built oversized boilers.

22 Remember that, for a market to be efficient, installations with low abatement costs need to reduce emissions and can either be compliant this way or – in case they have over/under-reduced their emissions – they can sell/buy the surplus/shortfall. Those with abatement costs higher than the market price of permits should buy on the market.

23 Although this study assesses the distributional impact in Phase 3, the regressivity of the impact should be similar in Phase 1 and 2. The major difference lies in the size of the effect due to the assumed price level (25€/EUA is much higher than the average price level, which was around 14.46€/EUA in Phase 2 and even lower in Phase 1). A minor difference may be caused by the inclusion of aviation in the

analysis, which was not covered by the EU ETS in Phase 1 and 2 and which leads to a very small, but progressive, impact, thus somewhat lowering the overall regressivity.

24 For example, a recent experimental study has demonstrated that there is a trade-off between compliance incentives (i.e. effectiveness) and efficiency (see Restiani and Betz 2010). This result seems intuitive, as the penalty design that provides higher compliance incentives – e.g. through higher penalty levels – gives companies higher incentives to overinvest in reduction measures to ensure compliance, thus reducing efficiency.

25 The criteria are trade intensity and additional carbon costs as a proportion of gross added value.

26 The study has shown that targets need to be significantly tighter as the one agreed so far for EU ETS in Phase 3 with a reduction of 1.74 percent per year. The study by Betz et al. (2010) has simulated, based on EU ETS data, that for a cost efficient coverage of half of the installations currently under the EU ETS it will require an 8 percent reduction target per year.

27 As the study by Cludius et al. (2012) illustrates, the opportunity for the government to lower the regressivity of the policy depends on the way the revenue is recycled back to households. Comparing two different options, they show that recycling all of the revenue back as lump-sum rebates will make the EU ETS progressive, while a cut in the rate of social security contributions retains the regressivity of the policy, since the unemployed (concentrated in the low income deciles) will not benefit. However, any form of revenue recycling reduces the impact of the policy on consumers.

References

Aatola, P., Ollikainen, M. & Toppinen, A., 2013. Price determination in the EU ETS market: Theory and econometric analysis with market fundamentals. *Energy Economics* 36(October): 380–395.

Abrell, J., Faye, A.N. & Zachmann, G., 2011. Assessing the impact of the EU ETS using firm level data. BETA Working paper no. 2011-15, Strasburg, Germany.

Anderson, B., & Di Maria, C. (2011) abatement and allocation in the pilot phase of the EU ETS. *Environmental & Resource Economics* 48(1): 83–103.

Anderson, B., Leib J., Martin, R., McGuigan, M., Muûls, M., de Preux, L. & Wagner, U.J. (2011) Climate Change Policy and Business in Europe Evidence from Interviewing Managers. Occasional paper, Centre for Economic Performance, http://cep.lse.ac.uk/pubs/download/occasional/op027.pdf.

Baldursson, F.M. & von der Fehr, N.H. (2004) Price volatility and risk exposure: on market-based environmental policy instruments. *Journal of Environmental Economics and Management* 48(1): 682–704.

Betz, R., Eichhammer, W. & Schleich, J. (2004) Designing national allocation plans for EU emissions trading – a first analysis of the outcome. *Energy and Environment*, 15(3): 375–425.

Betz, R. & Gunnthorsdottir, A. (2009) Modelling emissions markets experimentally: The impact of price uncertainty. In: Anderssen R.S., Braddock R.D. & Newham L.T.H. (eds.), 18th World IMAS Congress and MODSIM09 International Congress on Modelling and Simulation. Modelling and Simulation Society of Australia and New Zealand and International Association for Mathematics and Computers in Simulation, July 2009, pp. 1418–1424.

Betz, R., Rogge, K. & Schleich, J. (2006) EU emission trading: an early analysis of national allocation plans for 2008–2012. *Climate Policy* 6(4): 361–394.

Betz, R., Sanderson, T. & Ancev, T. (2010) In or out: efficient inclusion of installations in an emissions trading scheme? *Journal of Regulatory Economics* 37(2): 162–179.

Betz, R. & Sato, M. (2006), Emissions trading: Lessons learnt from the 1st Phase of EU ETS and prospects for the 2nd Phase. *Climate Policy* 6(4): 351–359.

Betz, R. & Schmidt, T. (2014) Transfer patterns in Phase I of the European Union Emissions Trading System: A first reality check based on cluster analysis, Paper presented at the WCRE in Istanbul, http://www.webmeets.com/files/papers/wcere/2014/1042/Cluster%20Analysis%20submitted%20EAERE.pdf.

Böhringer, C., Balistreri, E.J. & Rutherford, T.F. (2012) The role of border carbon adjustment in unilateral climate policy: Overview of an Energy Modeling Forum study (EMF 29). *Energy Economics* 34: S97–S110.

CEC (2004) Commission Decision 2004/156/EC of 29 January 2004 establishing guidelines for the monitoring and reporting of greenhouse gas emissions pursuant to Directive 2003/87/EC of the European Parliament and of the Council, O.J. L 59/1 EN 26.2.2004.

CEC (2007) Commission Decision 2007/589/EC of 18 July 2007 establishing guidelines for the monitoring and reporting of greenhouse gas emissions pursuant to Directive 2003/87/EC of the European Parliament and of the Council, O.J. L 229/1 EN 31.8.2007.

Charles, A., Darné, O. & Fouilloux, J. (2013) Market efficiency in the European carbon markets. *Energy Policy* 60: 785–792.

Chevallier, J. (2011) Carbon Price Drivers: An Updated Literature Review, Working Papers halshs-00586513, HAL, Paris.

Cludius J., Beznoska, M. & Steiner, V. (2012) The European Emissions Trading System: Distributional Issues and the Role of Revenue Recycling, an Empirical Study for German Households. Forthcoming as CEEM working paper.

Coase, R.H. (1960) The problem of social cost. *The Journal of Law and Economics* 3: 1–44.

Crocker, T.D. (1966) The Structuring of Atmospheric Pollution Control Systems. In: Wolozin H (ed.), The Economics of Air Pollution, A Symposium, pp. 61–86.

Dales, J.H. (1968) *Pollution, Property and Prices*. Toronto: University of Toronto Press.

Danish Government (2007) Denmark's National Allocation Plan 2008–12, http://ec.europa.eu/clima/policies/ets/allocation/2008/docs/nap_denmark_en.pdf.

DiSegni Eshel, D.M. (2005) Optimal allocation of tradable pollution rights and market structures. *Journal of Regulatory Economics* 28(2): 205–223.

EC (2011) Commission Decision 2011/278/EU of 27 April 2011 determining transitional Union-wide rules for harmonised free allocation of emission allowances pursuant to Article 10a of Directive 2003/87/EC of the European Parliament and of the Council (notified under document C(2011) 2772), OJ L 130, EN 17.5.2011.

EC (2012) Commission staff working document on information provided on the functioning of the EU Emissions Trading System, the volumes of greenhouse gas emission allowances auctioned and freely allocated and the impact on the surplus of allowances in the period up to 2020 (COM(2012) 416 final), http://ec.europa.eu/clima/policies/ets/cap/auctioning/docs/swd_2012_234_en.pdf.

Ellerman, A.D., Convery, F.J. & de Perthuis, C. (2010) *Pricing Carbon: The European Union Emissions Trading Scheme*. Cambridge: Cambridge University Press.

Ellerman, A.D. & Trotignon, R. (2009) Cross border trading and borrowing in the EU ETS, *The Energy Journal* 30(Special Issue 2): 53–78.

EU (2009) Directive of the European Parliament and of the Council amending Directive 2003/87/EC so as to improve and extend the greenhouse gas emission allowance trading scheme of the Community, 2008/0013 (COD), Brussels.

European Environmental Agency (EEA) (2008) Application of the Emissions Trading Directive by EU Member States – reporting year 2008, EEA Technical report No 13/2008, Copenhagen.

European Environmental Agency (EEA) (2012) EU Emissions Trading System (ETS) data viewer, European Environment Agency, www.eea.europa.eu/data-and-maps/data/data-viewers/ emissions-trading-viewer.

European Environmental Agency (EEA) (2013) Trends and projections in Europe 2013. Tracking progress towards Europe's climate and energy targets until 2020. Brussels: Publications Office of the European Union.

Gloaguen, O. & Alberola, E. (2013) Assessing the factors behind CO_2 emissions changes over the phases 1 and 2 of the EU ETS : an econometric analysis. CDC Climate Research Working Paper No. 2013–15, CDC, Paris.

Grubb, M. & Ferrario, F. (2006) False confidences: forecasting errors and emission caps in CO 2 trading systems. *Climate Policy* 6(4): 495–501.

Hahn, R.W. (1984) Market power and transferable property rights. *Quarterly Journal of Economics* 99(4): 753–765.

Hahn, R.W. & Stavins, R.N. (1992) Economic Incentives for Environmental Protection: Integrating Theory and Practice. *The American Economic Review* 82(2): 464–468.

Hahn, R.W. & Stavins, R.N. (2011) The Effect of Allowance Allocations on Cap-and-Trade System Performance. *Journal of Law and Economics* 54(4): S267–S294.

Heindl, P. (2011) The Impact of Informational Costs in Quantity Regulation of Pollutants: The Case of the European Emissions Trading Scheme. ZEW Discussion Paper No. 11–040, Mannheim.

Hintermann, B. (2001) Market Power, Permit Allocation and Efficiency in Emission Permit Markets. *Environmental and Resource Economics* 49 (3): 327–349.

IPCC (2007) Climate Change 2007 Mitigation of Climate Change, IPCC Fourth Assessment Report, Cambridge University Press, Cambridge.

Jotzo, F. & Hatfield-Dodds, S. (2011) Price floors in emissions trading to reduce policy related investment risks: an Australian view, May 2011, CCEP Working Paper 1105, Canberra.

Keppler, J.H. & Cruciani, M. (2010) Rents in the European power sector due to carbon trading. *Energy Policy* 38(8): 4280–4290.

KfW/ZEW (2011) CO$_2$ Barometer, http://kfw.de/kfw/de/I/II/Download_Center/ Fachthemen/Research/ Grndungsmo33326.jsp.

KfW/ZEW (2013) CO$_2$ Barometer 2013 – Carbon Edition The EU Emissions Trading Scheme: Firm Behaviour During the Crisis. KfW Bankengruppe and Centre for European Economic Research.

Laing, T. Sato, M., Grubb, M. & Comberti, C. 2013. Assessing the effectiveness of the EU Emissions Trading System. Working Paper 126, Centre for Climate Change Economics and Policy, London.

Lutz, B. J., Pigorsch, U. & Rotfuß, W. (2013) Nonlinearity in cap-and-trade systems: The EUA price and its fundamentals. *Energy Economics* 40: 222–232.

Martin, R., Muuls, M., de Preux, L. & Wagner, U. (2013) Industry Compensation Under Relocation Risk: A Firm-Level Analysis of the EU Emissions Trading Scheme, *American Economic Review* 104(8): 2482–2508.

Morris, D. (2012) Losing the lead? Europe's flagging carbon market, The 2012 environmental Outlook for the Eu ETS, http://www.sandbag.org.uk/site_media/pdfs/reports/losing_the_lead.pdf.

Neuhoff, K. (2011) *Climate Policy after Copenhagen, The Role of Carbon Pricing.* Cambridge: Cambridge University Press.

Neuhoff, K., Ahman, M., Betz, R., Cludius, J., Ferrario, F., Holmgren, K., Pal, G., Grubb, M., Matthes, F., Rogge, K., Sato, M., Schleich, J., Tuerk, A., Kettner, C. & Walker, N. (2006) Implications of announced Phase 2 National Allocation Plans for the EU ETS, *Climate Policy* 6(4): 411–422.

Newell, R.G. & Pizer, W.A. (2013) Carbon Markets 15 Years after Kyoto: Lessons Learned, New Challenges. *Journal of Econonomic Perspectives* 27(1): 123–146.

Restiani, P. (2010) Essays in Market Design for Emissions Trading Schemes, Thesis, Sydney.

Restiani, P. & Betz, R. (2010): The Effects of Penalty Design on Market Performance: Experimental Evidence from an Emissions Trading Scheme with Auctioned Permits. EERH Research Report No. 87, Canberra.

Rogge, K. & Hoffmann, V.H. (2010) The impact of the EU emission trading scheme on the sectoral innovation system for power generation technologies – Findings for Germany. *Energy Policy* 38(12): 7639–7652.

Rogge, K., Schneider, M. & Hoffmann, V.H. (2011) The innovation impact of the EU Emission Trading System – Findings of company case studies in the German power sector. *Ecological Economics* 70(3): 513–523.

Sartor, O. (2013) Carbon Leakage in the Primary Aluminium Sector : What evidence after 6 1/2 years of the EU ETS ? CDC Climate Research Working Paper No. 2012–12, CDC, Paris.

Schleich, J., Rogge, K. & Betz, R. (2009) Incentives for energy efficiency in the EU Emission Trading Scheme. *Energy Efficiency* 2(1): 37–67.

Schneider, L. (2007) Is the CDM fulfilling its environmental and sustainable development objectives? An evaluation of the CDM and options for improvement. Berlin: Öko-Institut.

Schneider, L. (2011) Perverse incentives under the CDM: an evaluation of HFC-23 destruction projects. *Climate Policy* 11(2): 851–864.

Shapiro, R. J. (2007) Addressing the Risks of Climate Change: The Environmental Effectiveness and Economic Efficiency of Emissions Caps an Tradable Permits, Compared to Taxes, http://www.consumer institute.org/Report%20on%20Climate%20Change%20-%20Shapiro.pdf.

Stavins, R.N. (1995) Transaction Costs and Tradable Permits. *Journal of Environmental Economics and Management* 29: 133–148.

Steiner Brandt, U. & Tinggaard Svendsen, G. (2011) The Temptation: The Risk of Cheating in the EU ETS. Paper presented at the 2011 Meeting of the European Public Choice Society, University of Rennes, Rennes.

Stenqvist, C., Nilsson, L. J., Ericsson, K., & Modig, G. (2011) *Energy management in Swedish pulp and paper industry – the daily grind that matters.* Paper presented at the 10th ECEEE summer study – energy efficiency first: the foundation of a low carbon society, France, June 6–11, 2011.

Stephan, N., Bellassen, V. & Alberola, E. (2014) Use of Kyoto credits by European installations: from and efficient market to the bubble burst. Climate report No. 43, CDC, Paris.

Wråke, M., Burtraw, D., Löfgren, A. & Zetterberg, L. (2012) What have we learnt from the European Union's emissions trading system? *Ambio* 41(Suppl 1): 12–22.

Zhang, J. & Wang, C. (2011) Co-benefits and additionality of the clean development mechanism: An empirical analysis, *Journal for Environmental Economics and Management* 62(2): 140–146.

Zhang, Z.X. (2012) Competitiveness and leakage concerns and border carbon adjustments. *International Review of Environmental and Resource Economics* 6(3): 225–287.

10

TRADE AND THE ENVIRONMENT

Yasuhiro Takarada,[†] Takeshi Ogawa,[‡] and Weijia Dong[§]

1. Introduction

There is growing concern about the effects of international trade on the environment given increasing globalization. Especially in Asia, the volume of trade has increased considerably in the last two decades. As a result, the trade-and-environment debate has attracted a great deal of interest by researchers and policymakers, with environmental issues discussed not only in trade negotiations through the World Trade Organization (WTO) but also in regional trade agreements (RTAs), whose number in Asia has increased dramatically since the 2000s.[1] The interaction between globalization and environmental quality thus has become an important policy issue given the ongoing integration of the international economy.

The past few decades have seen the publication of a large number of studies concerning the relations between trade and the environment.[2] Both theoretical and empirical analyses in this area already have contributed a deeper understanding of environmental quality and policies. We can explain the basic mechanism regarding the interaction between trade and the environment by focusing on the case where production generates pollution emissions that negatively affect consumer utility (i.e., a negative externality).[3]

To begin, trade liberalization changes the production pattern of an economy through specialization resulting from comparative advantage. This change in production patterns increases pollution emissions when more goods are produced following trade (the scale effect), and the economy has a comparative advantage in "dirty" industries (the composition effect). In a country with comparative advantage in "clean" goods, pollution is likely to decrease through the composition effect. Freer trade then induces income gains in all trading countries (a standard "gains from trade" argument). There also may be spillovers in environmental technologies under freer trade, which enables firms to access and use cleaner technologies more easily (the technique effect).[4] Consequently, as trade has both positive and negative effects, we need to consider carefully the effects of trade on both environmental quality and economic welfare.

Environmental policy is of course required to internalize this negative externality. However, policy may change the comparative advantage structure of the world economy and increase total emissions. Suppose that in the absence of environmental policy, a home country with cleaner technologies has a comparative advantage in pollution-intensive goods because of the prevailing production technology and factor endowments, while a foreign country with dirtier technologies has a comparative advantage in relatively clean goods. If only the home country implements strict environmental regulations, the foreign country could then have a comparative advantage in some pollution-intensive goods, thereby resulting in an increase in total emissions (i.e., carbon leakage). It, therefore, is important to investigate the effects of environmental policy given the presence of trade.

The purpose of this chapter is not to provide a comprehensive overview of this field but rather to explain the features of the available theoretical frameworks and to consider some of the important topics as they relate to Asia, a region where we especially need to increase our understanding.[5] The remainder of the chapter is structured as follows. In Section 2, we review some of the seminal studies and construct the simple general equilibrium model applied in subsequent sections. Section 3 focuses on the differentiated environmental regulations across sectors used to avoid carbon leakage and to support fair trade. The ultimate goal of environmental regulations is to regulate emissions uniformly to minimize the total cost of emissions reduction. However, we readily observe differentiated environmental regulations in countries such as in Asia. To increase our understanding of environmental policy in Asia, we should then consider the effects and implications of differentiated environmental regulations.

In Section 4, we consider the pollution emissions arising from international transport. These emissions relate directly to the volume of trade in goods, and trade itself is concerned with the level of environmental degradation. This topic is especially important for Asian countries because the volume of international transport in Asia has increased rapidly compared with other regions because of the relatively large increase in trade. There is also a close relation between environmental regulations and trade negotiation given that they are included in many RTAs as provisions to support fair trade and foreign direct investment. As the number of RTAs in Asia increases, their role in environmental regulations will become even more important. We discuss recent developments in this area in Section 5. We end the chapter with some concluding remarks in Section 6.

2. Analysis of trade and the environment

2.1 Literature review[6]

The advantage of general equilibrium analysis is that it enables us to consider interactions between industries. Seminal work by Copeland and Taylor (1994) developed a static general equilibrium model of North–South trade to examine the effects of trade on the environment when environmental quality is a local public good. They showed that trade liberalization reduces pollution emissions in the rich North (a human capital abundant country) with strict environmental policy but substantially increases that in the poor South (a human capital scarce country) with weak environmental policy.[7] Thus, the opening up of trade raises the sum of the two countries' local pollution. Intuitively, this is because the production of relatively dirty goods shifts from the North to the South after the opening up of trade. Given that each government optimally implements environmental policy to control local pollution, trade liberalization benefits both countries.

However, when environmental quality is a pure public good (i.e., pollution displays transboundary characteristics), Copeland and Taylor (1995) found that the opening up of trade benefits the South but harms the North. A negative externality is not fully internalized under environmental policy at the national level. Therefore, trade liberalization is likely to increase world pollution. They also demonstrated that international emissions trading (the free international movement of pollution permits) would reduce world pollution relative to that under only goods trade. Intuitively, permit prices internationally equalize with international emissions trading and thus prevent carbon leakage (see also Copeland, 1994).

By using a two-country model, Copeland (1996) investigated the optimal unilateral policy of a home country when the production of goods generates global pollution in both the home and foreign countries. He showed that the home country has an incentive to impose a tax on the pollution content of imports (a pollution content tariff) to control global pollution. This result theoretically supports pollution content tariffs that operate as a kind of the border tax adjustment stipulated in the WTO rules. However, there remains a debate about whether pollution content tariffs are strictly compatible with WTO rules (e.g., WTO, 2009).

A primary feature of these existing studies is the equalization of marginal abatement costs across domestic industries. In other words, the government implements an emissions trading system that involves all emission sources (or equivalently, imposes the same pollution tax across all industries). However, in the real world, countries do not generally uniformly impose environmental regulations on all of their production sectors.

Although this is an important topic, only a few existing studies consider differentiated environmental regulations across sectors. Under differentiated environmental regulations, there is no minimization of the total cost of emissions reduction because there is no equalization of the marginal abatement costs across sectors.[8] However, heterogeneous regulations can be welfare improving when goods are traded and environmental quality is a global public good.

Seminal work by Hoel (1996) showed that a government should impose a lower pollution tax on pollution-intensive tradable sectors to control carbon leakage if it is unable to use (pollution content) tariffs on all traded sectors. Using a trade model, Rauscher (1997) subsequently found that discrimination in emission taxes (so-called ecological dumping) might take place. The government imposes differentiated environmental regulations across sectors to gain from changing the terms of trade in favor of its own economy. The main contribution of both these studies is to provide a rationale for sectorally differentiated environmental regulations.[9]

Recently, there has been some consideration of the welfare effects of emissions trading under these conditions. Marschinski et al. (2012) initially examined the welfare effects of the linking of emissions trading systems (ETSs) between countries with different types of environmental regulations, including partial emission coverage and an economy-wide cap-and-trade system. They found that a country could be worse off with international emissions trading, even if it equalizes marginal abatement costs between countries. The intuition is as follows. Though there are direct gains from emissions trading, a country could be harmed by deterioration in its terms of trade caused by changes in the production of goods through emissions trading. Takarada (2013a) demonstrated that even if an economy is small, emissions trading between domestic industries would harm the economy when there is a reasonable relation between the import tariff rate and the initial disparity of environmental regulations across sectors.

When we consider the effects of trade on the environment in a strategic trade model, we are able to capture how the strategic effects affect environmental regulations. Barrett (1994) developed a two-country model where a firm in each country competes in a third market and showed that governments may then have an incentive to impose weak environmental standards on firms (i.e., the marginal cost of abatement is less than the marginal damage from pollution). Intuitively, this is because of rent seeking through weak environmental regulation, which may create a "race to the bottom" in environmental standards. In Ludema and Wooton (1994), the production of a commodity in the exporting country generates pollution that negatively affects consumer utility in the importing country. They found that the importing country then imposes an import tariff to reduce this negative externality. In contrast, despite national indifference to the externality, the exporting country induces the domestic firm to adopt pollution-abatement technology in order to reduce the tariff imposed by the importing country.[10]

2.2 Basic model

We now explain two useful properties specified in general equilibrium analyses on trade and the environment (e.g., Copeland and Taylor, 2003; Copeland, 2012). We apply the basic model developed in this sub-section to subsequent sections.

Consider a small open economy facing fixed world prices.[11] In this economy, two tradable goods, good 1 and good 2, are produced using (effective) labor as an input. We treat good 2 as the numeraire. We simplify the production function of good i as $X^i = L_i$, where L_i is the amount of labor input in industry i ($i = 1,2$), and one unit of output is produced using each unit of labor. Labor is inelastically supplied and fully employed, $L_1 + L_2 = L$, where L denotes labor endowment.

A firm in industry i can reduce its emissions by employing a fraction θ_i of labor for the purpose of pollution abatement ($0 \leq \theta_i \leq 1$). Given abatement activity, we have

$$x^i = (1 - \theta_i)L_i , \tag{1}$$

$$z_i = \phi^i(\theta_i)L_i , \tag{2}$$

where x^i and z_i are the output of good i and the amount of pollutants in industry i, respectively. For simplicity, we specify the functional forms of $\phi^i(\theta_i)$ as $\phi^1(\theta_1) = (1 - \theta_1)^{1/\alpha}$ and $\phi^2(\theta_2) = (1 - \theta_2)^{1/\beta}$ where $0 < \alpha < 1$ and $0 < \beta < 1$. Given $\alpha \neq \beta$, abatement technologies differ between the two sectors. $\phi^i(\theta_i)$ satisfies $\phi^i(0) = 1$, $\phi^i(1) = 0$, and $d\phi^i/d\theta_i < 0$. $\theta_i = 0$ implies no abatement (i.e., one unit of good i generates one unit of pollution). As a fraction of the input, $\theta_i L_i$, is allocated for abatement activities, the output of goods is necessarily reduced compared with the case of no abatement activity.

From equations (1) and (2), by eliminating θ_i, we obtain $x^1 = z_1^\alpha L_1^{1-\alpha}$ and $x^2 = z_2^\beta L_2^{1-\beta}$. This shows that we can treat pollution as a factor of production, even though it is more properly a joint output. Given abatement activity, the production of goods is with constant returns to scale (CRS) technology using pollution and labor as inputs. Good 1 is pollution (labor) intensive if $z_1/L_1 > (<) z_2/L_2$. This property enables us to use familiar tools in international trade theory.

We next explain the demand side. Consumers have a utility function $u = u\big[q(C_1, C_2), Z\big]$, which we assume is weakly separable, such that $u = q(C_1, C_2) - h(Z)$.[12] Partial utility q is increasing and concave in the consumption of goods 1 and 2 (C_1 and C_2), and h is increasing and convex in total pollution ($Z = z_1 + z_2$). We denote the expenditure of the economy by the expenditure function, $E(p, u, Z)$, where p is the relative price of good 1. $E(p, u, Z)$ has a well-known property, $C_1 = E_p$. Choosing $E_u = 1$, the marginal propensity to consume good 1 is given by pE_{pu}, which is positive when good 1 is normal in consumption.[13]

We obtain the useful property $E_{pZ} = E_{pu}E_Z$, where E_Z (> 0) is the marginal damage caused by an increase in pollution emissions. The sign of E_{pZ} is the same as that of E_{pu}, which implies that E_{pZ} is positive if good 1 is a normal good. We now explain how to derive the property (e.g., Naito, 2003). $E_p(p, u, Z) = C_1(p, I) = C_1(p, E(p, u, Z))$ holds, where $C_1(p, I)$ is the ordinary demand function for good 1, and I is national income. To satisfy the budget constraint, national income I must equal expenditure, $E(p, u, Z)$. The demand for goods is independent of pollution Z because the marginal rate of substitution does not depend on pollution given the utility function $u = q(C_1, C_2) - h(Z)$. Differentiating $E_p(p, u, Z) = C_1(p, E(p, u, Z))$ with respect to Z and u, we obtain $E_{pZ} = (\partial C_1/\partial I)E_Z$ and $E_{pu} = (\partial C_1/\partial I)E_u = \partial C_1/\partial I$, respectively.

Without weak separability of the utility function, we cannot derive the property $E_{pZ} = E_{pu}E_Z$. In general, the demand for goods depends on the amount of pollution emissions, $\tilde{C}_1(p,I,Z)$. E_{pZ} can then be positive (negative), implying that the consumption of good 1 is a complement to (substitute for) pollution.[14]

3. Differentiated environmental regulations across sectors

3.1 The role of differentiated regulations

Sectoral approaches have attracted interest because through these, governments can avoid carbon leakage and support fair trade in world markets (e.g., Baron et al., 2007; Sawa and Fukushima, 2008). Under a sectoral approach, emissions control in an industry employs a sector baseline: the adoption of some reference quantity of greenhouse gases (GHG) per unit of industrial output. As the sectoral approach regulates each industry's emissions differently in considering industry-specific conditions, they are beneficial for trade-exposed and emissions-intensive industries (aluminum, cement, and iron and steel especially).

If adopted globally, firms in a certain industry can then compete in international markets under similar environmental regulations regardless of nationality. Without sectoral approaches, a country may impose environmental regulations strategically to maximize its own welfare (e.g., rent seeking through weak regulations) even if the total emissions of each country are capped through international environmental agreement. Such strategic behavior distorts competition in international markets and reduces economic efficiency.

Sectoral approaches do indeed lead to a higher total cost of GHG reductions, even though they do prevent carbon leakage and support fair trade. This is because there is no equalization of the marginal abatement costs across all emission sources. The feasibility of the sectoral approach also relies on the establishment of a sectoral baseline. This can be problematic given that it can be difficult to collect a suitable record of emissions, especially in developing countries, and we need to determine appropriate baselines to make the regulations effective.

The goal of environmental policy is to regulate pollution emissions uniformly through emissions taxes or an ETS that includes all emission sources, thereby minimizing the total cost of the reduction of emissions. However, the world is currently in an intermediate stage, with different environmental regulations operating across sectors, even in developed countries (e.g., the coverage of an ETS tends to expand but is limited at present).[15] The government has an incentive to regulate trade-exposed and pollution-intensive industries more weakly when there are concerns over carbon leakage and fair trade. In contrast, pollution-intensive industries, such as energy industries (normally, non-tradable sectors), are likely to have more strict regulation because of their large emissions and low monitoring costs. As many Asian countries will regulate GHG emissions more strictly in the near future, they may implement differentiated environmental regulations as a first step and then impose uniform environmental regulations as a second step.[16] For this reason, it is quite important to consider the reasons for, and the effects of, the transition in environmental regulations.

3.2 Theoretical analysis: differentiated regulations under tariffs

We now consider how changes in the enforcement level of sectorally differentiated regulations affect welfare.[17] We develop a small open economy model comprising two goods, good 1 and good 2, and a tariff policy.

The production function of good i is expressed as $X^i = X^i(L_i, Z_i)$, where L_i is the labor input and Z_i are pollution emissions ($i = 1, 2$). $X^i(\cdot)$ is linearly homogeneous and satisfies $X_L^i > 0$,

$X_Z^i > 0$, and $X_{LL}^i < 0$. As the government imposes differentiated environmental regulations across sectors, the amount of pollution permits in each sector, Z_i, is treated as a factor of production specific to sector i (i.e., no emissions trading between the sectors). The government fixes each sector's pollution permits. In contrast, labor is freely mobile between sectors. The utility function is given by $u = u[q(C_1, C_2), Z]$, where $Z (= Z_1 + Z_2)$ are the total emissions of the economy. We assume that the utility function is weakly separable and the goods are normal goods. The economy imports good 1, and the government imposes an ad valorem tariff (a pollution content tariff), t, on good 1. There is full employment of labor, and the goods and labor markets are perfectly competitive.

In equilibrium, the wage rate (the marginal value product of labor) is equal between sectors:

$$pX_L^1(L_1, Z_1) = X_L^2(L - L_1, Z_2). \tag{3}$$

The domestic relative price of good 1 is denoted by $p = (1 + t) p*$, where $p*$ is the world relative price of good 1. The budget constraint of the economy is given by

$$E(p, u, Z) = pX^1 + X^2 + tp^*(C_1 - X^1), \tag{4}$$

where $E(p, u, Z)$ is the expenditure function and $C_1 = E_p$ holds. Designating $E_u = 1$, we can obtain $E_{pZ} = E_{pu}E_Z > 0$ (this property is shown in Section 2.2).

We first investigate the case where the government reduces the pollution permits in sector 2 (the exporting industry), while those in sector 1 (the importing industry) are kept constant. In other words, only environmental regulation in sector 2 becomes stricter. Totally differentiating equations (3) and (4), we obtain

$$\frac{du}{dZ_2} \overset{>}{\underset{<}{=}} 0 \quad \Leftrightarrow \quad X_Z^2 - tp^*X_L^1 \cdot \frac{X_{LZ}^2}{pX_{LL}^1 + X_{LL}^2} \overset{>}{\underset{<}{=}} \left(p^*E_{pu} + 1 - pE_{pu}\right)E_Z. \tag{5}$$

The right-hand-side term and the first left-hand-side term indicate the gain and loss from the reduction in pollution emissions, respectively. These are direct effects. The second term on the left-hand side is the tariff (or indirect) effect.

Importantly, stricter regulation of the exporting sector may harm the economy even if the marginal loss in production of good 2 is less than the marginal benefit in utility, i.e., $X_Z^2 < (p*E_{pu} + 1 - pE_{pu})E_Z$. This is because the second left-hand side term is positive under a positive tariff rate ($t > 0$). The intuition is simple. As a result of the reduction in Z_2, the output of sector 1 increases because of the movement of labor from sector 2 to sector 1 ($dL_1/dZ_2 < 0$). This will decrease the amount of imports because domestic production increases ($dX^1/dZ_2 < 0$). Thus, the economy loses from the reduction in tariff revenue. In particular, under free trade ($t = 0$), the welfare result is standard.

Next, we focus on sector 1 (the importing sector). Similarly, we obtain

$$\frac{du}{dZ_1} \overset{>}{\underset{<}{=}} 0 \quad \Leftrightarrow \quad p*X_Z^1 + tp*X_L^1 \cdot \frac{pX_{LZ}^1}{pX_{LL}^1 + X_{LL}^2} \overset{>}{\underset{<}{=}} \left(p*E_{pu} + 1 - pE_{pu}\right)E_Z. \tag{6}$$

Under a positive tariff rate, the second term on the left-hand side is negative. Therefore, welfare is likely to improve through stricter regulation of the importing sector. This is because the economy benefits not only from reduction of pollution itself but also from an increase in tariff revenue.

Given the presence of tariffs, it is thus important to consider the indirect effect as well as the direct effect of environmental regulations. The policy implication of our results is that when the government protects importing industries using import tariffs and/or imposes pollution-content tariffs to avoid carbon leakage, environmental regulations on importing industries should be relatively strict, while those on exporting industries should be relatively weak.

4. International transport and the environment

4.1 Emissions directly related to trade

There has been growing concern about GHG emissions in international shipping and aviation (considered together as international transport).[18] International transport, especially international shipping, which supports about 90 percent of global trade, is indispensable for the trade in goods, particularly in Asia, where the amount of carbon dioxide emissions from international shipping has increased rapidly since the 1990s. Figure 10.1 depicts the emissions from international shipping with respect to the Association of Southeast Asian Nations (ASEAN) Plus Three (+3), the EU (28 countries), and the North American Free Trade Agreement (NAFTA).[19] The amount of international transport will increase with globalization, which implies that this particular environmental problem will steadily become worse.[20]

The present worldwide environmental framework (the United Nations Framework Convention on Climate Change (UNFCCC)) excludes GHG emissions from international transport. The reason is that it is difficult to identify which countries should be responsible for GHG emissions arising from international transport, with regulations on international transport entrusted to specialized international organizations such as the International Civil Aviation Organization (ICAO) and the International Maritime Organization (IMO).[21]

To date, there has been no effective implementation of environmental regulations concerning international transport. There is also an important difference in the basic principles employed by the UNFCCC, the ICAO and the IMO in that it is common to use the principle of Common but Differentiated Responsibility in multilateral agreements on the environment under the UNFCCC. However, historically both the ICAO and the IMO have adopted the nondiscriminatory principle. This is one reason why it is difficult to take the interests of developing countries into account.

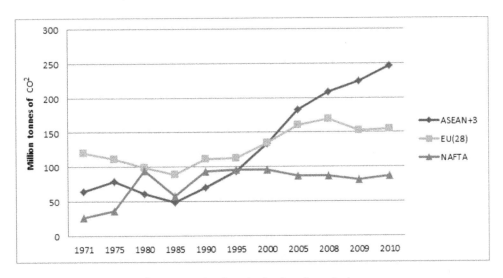

Figure 10.1 CO$_2$ emissions from international marine bunkers (by region).

Data Source: "CO$_2$ Emissions from Fuel Combustion Highlights," IEA (2012: 65–67).

Nonetheless, the IMO and the ICAO have discussed and adopted several environmental regulations. In brief, the IMO considers two types of environmental regulations; namely, direct regulations and market-based measures (MBMs). Of the direct regulations, the Energy Efficiency Design Index (EEDI) is a technical measure and the Ship Energy Efficiency Management Plan (SEEMP) is an operational measure. The EEDI is an index of the amount carbon dioxide emissions per ton and mile made mandatory for new ships, while the SEEMP minimizes the emissions of carbon dioxide by reducing speeds and setting optimal routes, with regulations agreed upon in July 2011 to begin in January 2013.[22] While MBMs are expected to minimize the costs of reducing GHG emissions, the member countries of the IMO have not yet reached an agreement on their use, although various potential measures (e.g., emissions taxes and a global ETS for international shipping) have been proposed by members.[23]

As for international aviation, the ICAO and the International Air Transport Association (IATA) consider types of environmental regulations similar to those for international marine bunkers. In November 2012, the council of the ICAO agreed to form a special high-level group to discuss a global MBM scheme.[24] The IATA has proposed a global sectoral approach to the environment (e.g., a carbon-offset program, improvement of technologies, and MBMs).[25] The EU argued for the necessity of applying the EU ETS to international aviation as a means to strengthen the regulation.[26] In October 2013, the members of the ICAO agreed to develop by 2016 a global MBM for international aviation that can start in 2020, which is an historic milestone for multilateral agreements on the environment.[27]

4.2 *Theoretical analysis: welfare effects*

This sub-section examines the welfare effects of trade liberalization and environmental regulations in a small open economy where both the production of goods and international transportation generate pollution. The main feature of this analysis is that we explicitly consider the international transport sector and its interaction with the final goods sectors through factor markets.

We develop a two-good, three-sector model where international transport is required for importing goods.[28] We assume that the economy imports good 1 and exports good 2. Consumers must use one unit of international transport to import one unit of good 1. We assume a small open economy that uses only domestically produced transport services (no import of transportation services), with the price of international transportation determined endogenously by the market-clearing condition.[29] In contrast, the economy faces fixed world prices of goods.

The two goods, X^1 and X^2, and international transportation, T, are produced employing labor and emissions with CRS technology. We assume the separate allocation of pollution permits between the final goods and international transport sectors to describe the actual situation where a country's emissions cap excludes international transport emissions. Furthermore, while pollution permits for international transportation are specific to that sector, pollution permits for the production of goods can move freely between the sectors. That is, there is emissions trading only for the final goods sectors.

Let $\Omega(L_G, Z)$ be a two-dimensional CRS convex production possibility set, where L_G is the amount of labor available for the production of final goods and Z is a fixed level of pollution emissions from the final goods sectors. Labor is fully employed, $L_G = L - L_T$, where L is the labor endowment and L_T is the labor input in the international transport sector. The production side of the final goods is represented by the gross domestic product (GDP) function, G, which is defined as

$$G(p, L_G, Z) = \max_{X^1, X^2} \left\{ pX^1 + X^2 \middle| (X^1, X^2) \in \Omega(L_G, Z) \right\}. \tag{7}$$

The domestic relative price of good 1 (the imported good) is denoted by $p = p* + t + s$, where $p*$ is the world relative price of good 1, t is trade costs except international transport, and s is the price of international transport services. We can show that the equilibrium denoted by equation (7) is the same as the equilibrium where firms compete competitively and the government implements efficient environmental regulations such as tradable permits or emission taxes (see Copeland and Taylor, 2003).

The value of $G(\cdot)$ denotes the income of the economy earned from final goods production. The GDP function has the following well-known properties (see, e.g., Wong, 1995): $G_p = X^1$, $G_{pZ} = X_Z^1, G_{pL} = X_L^1, G_L = w$, and $G_Z = r$, where w and r are the wage rate and the shadow price of emissions, respectively (r can be treated as an emission tax). Under emissions trading, r becomes the equilibrium permit price. If good 1 is pollution intensive (relatively dirty), G_{pZ} is positive and G_{pL} is negative, which implies that output increases as the amount of pollution permits (Z) rises but decreases as the amount of labor available for final goods production increases (the Rybczynski theorem). In contrast, if good 1 is relatively clean, $G_{pZ} < 0$ and $G_{pL} > 0$ hold.

The CRS production function for international transport services is given by $T = T(L_T, Z_T)$, which satisfies properties such as $T_L > 0, T_Z < 0$, and $T_{LL} < 0$. Z_T denotes pollution emissions from the production of international transport services. While labor is freely mobile between the three sectors, the amount of pollution permits (Z_T) can only be used in the international transport sector.

The budget constraint of the economy is given by

$$E(p, u, Z + Z_T) = G(p, L - L_T, Z) + sT(L_T, Z_T), \tag{8}$$

where $E(p, u, Z + Z_T)$ is the expenditure function. The utility function is assumed to be weakly separable. The market-clearing condition for international transport is as follows:

$$E_p(p, u, Z + Z_T) - G_p(p, L - L_T, Z) = T(L_T, Z_T). \tag{9}$$

The left-hand side is the demand for international transport induced by importing good 1, and the right-hand side is the supply of international transport. Given that labor is mobile between the three sectors, the wage rate must be equal in the three sectors; i.e.,

$$G_L(p, L - L_T, Z) = sT_L(L_T, Z_T). \tag{10}$$

Equations (8), (9), and (10) determine the three endogenous variables, u, s, and L_T.

Now, we examine how trade liberalization (reduction in trade costs t) and a reduction in the amount of pollution permits in the international transport sector affect the price of international transport. Totally differentiating equations (8)–(10), we obtain

$$G_{pL}(G_{pL} - T_L) \geq 0 \quad \Rightarrow \quad \frac{ds}{dt} < 0, \tag{11}$$

$$G_{pL} \leq T_L \quad \Rightarrow \quad \frac{ds}{dZ_T} < 0. \tag{12}$$

From equations (11) and (12), we obtain the following two results. When good 1 is pollution intensive ($G_{PL} < 0$), the price of international transport s is increased by 1) trade liberalization ($dt < 0$) or 2) stricter environmental regulation in the international transport sector ($dZ_T < 0$).

The intuition for result 2) is as follows. The reduction of Z_T decreases the marginal product of labor, which causes labor to move from the international transport sector to the final goods sectors under a given price s. Stricter regulation and subsequent labor movement thus reduce the supply of international transport services. The domestic output of good 1 decreases as a result of the labor movement because $G_{pL} < 0$. Therefore, consumers must import more good 1 from the international market. This will raise the demand for international transport. Thus, stricter regulation increases the price of international transport. Conversely, when good 1 is relatively clean, the domestic output of good 1 increases because of labor movement ($G_{pL} > 0$). In this case, consumer demand for international transport decreases. Therefore, even if stricter regulation reduces the supply of international transport, the price may decrease. We can interpret result 1) by analogy.

We now investigate the welfare effects. From equations (8)–(10), we obtain $du/dt = -T < 0$ and

$$\frac{du}{dZ_T} \begin{array}{c} > \\ < \end{array} 0 \Leftrightarrow E_Z \begin{array}{c} < \\ > \end{array} sT_Z. \tag{13}$$

Here, a decrease in t always benefits the economy because it reduces the trade costs. This result is straightforward. We obtain that welfare may increase (or decrease) with a decrease in the amount of pollution permits (Z_T) depending on the condition. The economy is made better off when the marginal revenue of emissions in the international transport sector (sT_Z) is less than the marginal damage caused by pollution (E_Z). Intuitively, consumers can benefit generally from the reduction of pollution despite their loss from the decrease in imports.

By using a simple trade model, we can depict the interaction between the final goods and international transport sectors, the latter in the past being usually ignored or considered to be an iceberg transportation cost (where the cost of transporting a good uses up only some fraction of the good itself, rather than using any other resources). While a few existing studies have explicitly modeled international transport, none has considered environmental problems (e.g., Samuelson, 1954; Mundell, 1957; Herberg, 1970; Cassing, 1978). Tippichai et al. (2009) analyzed sectoral approaches to transport sectors but did not conduct welfare analysis. Most recently, Abe et al. (2014) analyzed the effects of trade liberalization and environmental regulation in a two-country strategic trade policy model when international transportation generates global pollution. However, they used a one-good partial equilibrium model to shed light on the strategic effects between countries, thereby omitting any interactions between industries through factor movements. In sharp contrast, factor intensity clearly plays an important role in our model.

5. World trading system and the environment

The number of RTAs that contain provisions to protect environmental quality tends to increase, although the issue is traditionally considered within the realm of domestic regulations (see, e.g., Estevadeordal et al., 2009; Jinnah, 2012; Baghdadi et al., 2013; OECD, 2013; WTO, 2013). One way for RTAs to embrace provisions concerning the environment is to include an independent chapter.[30] Another is to include environmental issues in a preface and/or several related chapters in the RTA.[31]

The reason for inclusion of environmental provisions in RTAs is that there are concerns about a race to the bottom. Without environmental provisions, a member country has an incentive to weaken its environmental regulations. Firms in a country with lenient regulations will then have an advantage over other firms in member countries and can use this to increase their exports. Moreover, weak regulations attract inward direct investment that increases employment and technology spillovers. Weak environmental regulations will thus distort free trade and direct investment despite the removal of tariff barriers and investment measures. Therefore, it is necessary to include environmental provisions in RTAs being a commitment by the member countries not to lower environmental regulations. Environmental provisions will not only protect environmental quality but also support fair trade and investment between the parties. If networks of RTAs subsequently expand (i.e., as "building blocks"), this will achieve the worldwide commitment to environmental regulations.

In order to create a win–win–win situation for trade, the environment and development, the elimination of trade barriers on environmental goods and services is important.[32] Freer trade in environmental goods and services will improve market access conditions to more efficient and less expensive clean technologies embodied in such goods and services. This will enhance environmental quality and support sustainable development (see, e.g., Canton, 2007; Dijkstra and Mathew, 2010; Nimubona, 2012).

The WTO negotiations consider several approaches for eliminating trade barriers on environmental goods and services.[33] The first is the "list approach," comprising a list of goods and services proposed for liberalization by all member countries. This does indeed improve environmental quality. However, some of those goods have dual or multiple (nonenvironmental) uses, which do not necessarily improve environmental quality. Thus, it is important to specify an appropriate list. The second approach is the "project approach," where there is the temporary liberalization of a wide variety of goods and services for the duration of a specific environmental project. The range of liberalized goods and services could be larger than the list approach, but the period of trade liberalization is limited. The third approach is the "integrated approach," a mix of the list and project approaches.

As developed countries currently have a comparative advantage in most environmental goods and services, they tend to support the list approach. However, developing countries, which have a comparative disadvantage in environmental goods and seek technology spillovers, are likely to support the project approach or the integrated approach. The members of the WTO have not yet reached an agreement on trade liberalization in environmental goods.

Notably, in September 2012, leaders of the Asia-Pacific Economic Cooperation (APEC) forum agreed on a list of environmental goods on which they will cut tariffs to five percent or less by 2015.[34] This is the first trade negotiation to agree on the trade liberalization of environmental goods. The APEC List of Environmental Goods includes 54 environmental goods on which tariffs in the region are currently as high as 20–35 percent.[35] This agreement could positively affect future trade negotiations on environmental goods.

6. Concluding remarks

The existing literature has examined the interaction between environmental quality and changes in production caused by trade. One outcome is that our knowledge has increased, but some important topics remain outstanding. After constructing a basic model, we consider the effects of differentiated environmental regulations across sectors on welfare to illustrate their implications. Given that we observe differentiated environmental regulations in Asian countries in the intermediate stages of environmental policy, we need to understand more about how each country's environmental regulations relate to its pattern of trade and how the transition of environmental regulations affects welfare. We investigate the emissions from international transport, which we expect to become more severe throughout Asia in the future, to shed light on the effects of environmental regulations on international transport. Such regulations affect trade flows directly and foreign direct investment indirectly. Given that Asia relies proportionately more on trade and direct investment for economic development, we require both theoretical and empirical work to complement the literature on trade and the environment.

We especially need to increase our understanding of the interaction between environmental regulations and RTAs because the latter lead the setting of environmental regulations. Environmental policy is a typical nontariff barrier. Member countries have an incentive to set regional rules to maximize their own welfare, which might be specific to a certain RTA. Therefore, such regional agreements will indeed improve environmental quality through tightening regional environmental regulations but may hinder worldwide agreement on the environment that could minimize total costs for emissions reduction. The number of RTAs will continue to increase in the Asian region. Therefore, more work is necessary to clarify how RTAs affect the level of environmental regulations and emissions.

Acknowledgments

Takarada gratefully acknowledges the financial support of a Grant-in-Aid for Scientific Research (C) #26380335 from the JSPS and the Nanzan University Pache Research Subsidy I-A-2 for the 2014 academic year. Ogawa gratefully acknowledges the Yamada Academic Fellowship.

Notes

[†] Yasuhiro Takarada: Associate Professor, Faculty of Policy Studies, Nanzan University, 27 Seirei-cho, Seto, Aichi 489-0863, Japan. Tel: +81-561-89-2010 (Ext. 3541); Fax: +81-561-89-2012; E-mail: ytakara@ps.nanzan-u.ac.jp. (corresponding author)

[‡] Takeshi Ogawa: Assistant Professor, Faculty of Economic Sciences, Hiroshima Shudo University, 1-1-1 Ozuka-higashi, Asaminami-ku, Hiroshima 731-3195, Japan.

[§] Weijia Dong: Assistant Professor, Graduate School of Economics, Nagoya University, Furo-cho, Chikusa-ku, Nagoya, 464-8601, Japan.

1 See http://www.wto.org/english/tratop_e/region_e/rta_pta_e.htm.

2 Contributions to edited volumes alone include Runge (1995), Rauscher (1999, 2005), Karp and Zhao (2004), UNEP (2005), Gallagher (2008), Copeland (2012), and Jinnah (2012), among others.

3 It is important to examine the effects of trade liberalization under negative production externalities (including environmental capital such as renewable resources). See, for example, Chichilnisky (1994), Brander and Taylor (1997, 1998), Bulte and Damania (2005), Jinji (2006), Rus (2012), and Takarada et al. (2013).

4 See Grossman and Krueger (1993) for discussion of the scale, composition, and technique effects of trade.

5 See, for example, Antweiler et al. (1998), Copeland and Taylor (2003), Frankel and Rose (2005), Managi et al. (2009), Chang (2012), McAusland and Millimet (2013), and Sato (2014) for empirical work.

6 We are unable to provide a comprehensive review of all existing studies because of space limitations. The interested reader is referred to Beghin et al. (1994), Rauscher (1997), Copeland and Taylor (2003, 2004), Takarada (2005), Ishikawa and Kiyono (2006), Managi et al. (2009), and Kiyono and Ishikawa (2013).

7 Copeland and Taylor (1994) assume that the government takes the world prices of goods as given when selecting the pollution taxes on goods. There is support for this assumption given WTO rules that restrict the use of domestic health and environmental policy as trade barriers.

8 For example, Böhringer et al. (2009) used computable general equilibrium models to estimate the economic implications of European Union climate policy, finding that a policy including different carbon prices could make environmental policy more costly.

9 See also Takeda (2005) and Sugiyama and Saito (2009).

10 See also Conrad (1993), Kennedy (1994), and Ulph (1996).

11 The basic settings are from Ch. 2 in Copeland and Taylor (2003).

12 We may alternatively consider a multiplicative form of the utility function $u = q(X_1, X_2)h(Z)$.

13 A subscript in a function represents the partial derivative with respect to the corresponding element (e.g., $E_p = \partial E/\partial p$ and $E_{pu} = \partial^2 E/\partial u \partial p$).

14 For example, a barbecue on the beach is a substitute for pollution because a cleaner environment increases its consumption. An air cleaner is a complement to pollution because consumption increases as the air becomes dirtier.

15 For example, the coverage of the EU ETS in Phase 3 (2013–20) is higher than that of Phase 2 (2008–12) but still less than 50 percent (see, e.g., Parker, 2010). There are several regional ETSs in the US and Canada, including the Regional Greenhouse Gas Initiative and the Western Climate Initiative. Since 2008, Japan has a limited ETS in the form of the Experimental Integrated ETS, as participation is voluntary.

16 In South Korea, sectoral emission restrictions will complement emissions trading from 2013 (see http://p.tl/oZ5o (shortened URL)). In 2011, the Chinese government announced regional ETSs in seven regions (Beijing City, Tianjin City, Shanghai City, Chongqing City, Guangdong, Hubei, and Shenzhen City), though with different levels and types of coverage (e.g., sectors and firms) (see http://www.ndrc. gov.cn/zcfb/zcfbtz/2011tz/t20120113_456506.html). In India, a local ETS applies from 2013 in the textile-producing city of Surat. Duflo et al. (2010) and Sopher and Mansell (2013) provide details of environmental policy in India.

17 We refer to Takarada (2013a) because his model is tractable.

18 See, for example, Olsthoorn (2001), Corbett and Winebrake (2008), DeSombre (2008), and Cristea et al. (2013) for international transport and the environment.

19 ASEAN+3 in Figure 1 consists of the member countries of ASEAN (excluding Laos) plus China, Japan, and South Korea. According to the IEA (2012), the amount of CO_2 emissions from international marine bunkers in ASEAN+3 was 246.86 million tonnes (excluding Laos) in 2010.

20 See also MLIT (2007, pp. 18–19).

21 Article 2.2 of the Kyoto Protocol stipulates that the parties included in Annex I shall pursue the limitation or reduction of emissions of GHG not controlled by the Montreal Protocol from aviation and marine bunker fuels, working through the ICAO and the IMO, respectively. For more information, see http://unfccc.int/methods_and_science/emissions_from_intl_transport/items/1057.php. The GHG emissions from international road transport, such as rail and trucking, are included in the regulation framework of the UNFCCC (the Kyoto Protocol).

22 See, for example, http://www.imo.org/MediaCentre/PressBriefings/Pages/42-mepc-ghg.aspx.

23 See details at http://www.imo.org/OurWork/Environment/PollutionPrevention/AirPollution/Pages/Market-Based-Measures.aspx.

24 See details at http://www.icao.int/Newsroom/Pages/new-ICAO-council-high-level-group-to-focus-on-environmental-policy-challenges.aspx.

25 See, for example, http://www.iata.org/pressroom/facts_figures/fact_sheets/Pages/emissions-approach. aspx, http://www.iata.org/whatwedo/environment/Pages/carbon-offset.aspx, and ICAO (2010: 154–156).

26 The EU was to apply the EU ETS to passenger airlines and cargo carriers from both European and non-European countries in 2012. However, the European Commission postponed implementation for a year following the recommendation of the ICAO council in November 2012. See http://ec.europa. eu/clima/policies/transport/aviation/index_en.htm.

27 See http://www.icao.int/Newsroom/News%20Doc%202013/COM.36.13.A38.Closing.EN.pdf.

28 This model is based on Takarada (2013b).

29 The essence of the following result is valid even with the import of some international transport services, the key point being that domestic import demand mainly affects the price of international transport.

30 For example, Chapter 12 in the China–Swiss Free Trade Agreement (FTA) stipulates environmental issues. The Trans-Pacific Strategic Economic Partnership Agreement, which is an FTA between Brunei Darussalam, Chile, Singapore, and New Zealand, includes an Environment Cooperation Agreement between the parties to complement the FTA.

31 The recognition of environmental issues is sometimes in a preface or chapters in the form of innovations, cooperation, and mutual recognition. For example, the preface of the India–South Korea Comprehensive Economic Partnership Agreement requires the optimal use of natural resources in accordance with the objective of sustainable development. In the Australia–Thailand FTA, the parties affirm obligations relating to international agreements on the environment and conservation to which they are party (Article 703).

32 See http://www.wto.org/english/tratop_e/envir_e/envir_negotiations_e.htm for details.

33 See, for example, UNCTAD (2009) and documents of the Committee on Trade and Environment: http://www.wto.org/english/tratop_e/envir_e/envir_e.htm.

34 See http://www.apec.org/Meeting-Papers/Leaders-Declarations/2012/2012_aelm.aspx.

35 The environmental goods include renewable and clean energy technologies, wastewater treatment technologies, air pollution control technologies, solid and hazardous waste treatment technologies, and environmental monitoring and assessment equipment. See http://www.ustr.gov/about-us/press-office/fact-sheets/2012/september/apec-environmental-goods.

References

Abe K., K. Hattori, and Y. Kawagoshi (2014) "Trade liberalization and environmental regulation on international transportation," *Japanese Economic Review*, vol. 65, pp. 468–482.

Antweiler W., B.R. Copeland, and M.S. Taylor (1998) "Is free trade good for the environment?," *NBER Working Paper* 6707, Cambridge, MA.

Baghdadi, L., I. Martinez-Zarzoso, and H. Zitouna (2013) "Are RTA agreements with environmental provisions reducing emissions?," *Journal of International Economics*, vol. 90, pp. 378–390.

Baron R., J. Reinaud, M. Genasci, and C. Philibert (2007) "Sectoral approaches to greenhouse gas mitigation: Exploring issues for heavy industry," *IEA Information Paper*, OECD/IEA.

Barrett, S. (1994) "Strategic environmental policy and international trade," *Journal of Public Economics*, vol. 54, pp. 325–338.

Beghin J., D. Roland-Holst, and D. van der Mensbrugghe (1994) "A survey of the trade and environment nexus: Global dimensions," *OECD Economic Studies*, vol. 23, pp. 167–192.

Böhringer, C., T.F. Rutherford, and R.S.J. Tol (2009) "The EU 20/20/2020 targets: An overview of the EMF 22 assessment," *Energy Economics*, vol. 31, pp. S268–S273.

Brander, J.A. and M.S. Taylor (1997) "International trade and open access renewable resources: The small open economy case," *Canadian Journal of Economics*, vol. 30, pp. 526–552.

Brander, J.A. and M.S. Taylor (1998) "Open-access renewable resources: Trade and trade policy in a two-country model," *Journal of International Economics*, vol. 44, pp. 181–209.

Bulte, E.H. and R. Damania (2005) "A note on trade liberalization and common pool resources," *Canadian Journal of Economics*, vol. 38, pp. 883–899.

Canton, J. (2007) "Environmental taxation and international eco-industries," *The Fondazione Eni Enrico Mattei (FEEM) Working Papers*, Paper 33. Available at http://services.bepress.com/feem/paper33/.

Cassing, J.H. (1978) "Transport costs in international trade theory: A comparison with the analysis of non-traded goods," *Quarterly Journal of Economics*, vol. 92, pp. 535–550.

Chang, N. (2012) "The empirical relationship between openness and environmental pollution in China," *Journal of Environmental Planning and Management*, vol. 55, pp. 783–796.

Chichilnisky, G. (1994) "North–south trade and the global environment," *American Economic Review*, vol. 84, pp. 851–874.

Conrad, K. (1993) "Taxes and subsidies for pollution-intensive industries as trade policy," *Journal of Environmental Economics and Management*, vol. 25, pp. 121–135.

Copeland, B.R. (1994) "International trade and the environment: Policy reform in a polluted small open economy," *Journal of Environmental Economics and Management*, vol. 26, pp. 44–65.

Copeland, B.R. (1996) "Pollution content tariffs, environmental rent shifting, and the control of cross-border pollution," *Journal of International Economics*, vol. 40, pp. 459–476.

Copeland, B.R. (2012) "Trade and the environment," in *Palgrave Handbook of International Trade*, Bernhofen D., R. Falvey, D. Greenaway, and U. Kreickemeier (ed.), 423–496. New York: Palgrave Macmillan.

Copeland, B.R. and Taylor, M.S. (1994) "North–South trade and the environment," *Quarterly Journal of Economics*, vol. 109, pp. 755–787.

Copeland, B.R. and Taylor, M.S. (1995) "Trade and transboundary pollution," *American Economic Review*, vol. 85, pp. 716–737.

Copeland, B.R. and M.S. Taylor (2003) *Trade and the Environment: Theory and Evidence*. Princeton, NJ: Princeton University Press.

Copeland, B.R. and M.S. Taylor (2004) "Trade, growth and the environment," *Journal of Economic Literature*, vol. 42, pp. 7–71.

Corbett, J.J. and J.J. Winebrake (2008) "International trade and global shipping," in *Handbook on Trade and the Environment*, Gallagher, K. (ed.), 33–48. Cheltenham: Edward Elgar.

Cristea, A., D. Hummels, L. Puzzello, and M. Avetisyan (2013) "Trade and the greenhouse gas emissions from international freight transport," *Journal of Environmental Economics and Management*, vol. 65, pp. 153–173.

DeSombre, E.R. (2008) "Environmental policies and global shipping trade: Club goods as a solution to common-pool resource problems," in *Handbook on Trade and the Environment*, Gallagher, K. (ed.), 204–212. Cheltenham: Edward Elgar.

Dijkstra B.R. and A.J. Mathew (2010) "Liberalizing trade in environmental goods," GEP working paper 10/05, University of Nottingham, Nottingham, UK. Available at http://dx.doi.org/10.2139/ssrn.1577594.

Duflo E., M. Greenstone, R. Pande and N. Ryan (2010) "Towards an emissions trading scheme for air pollutants in India: A concept note." *MoEF Discussion Paper*, Reprint Series Number 229, Prepared for the Ministry of Environment and Forest, Government of India. Available at http://web.mit.edu/ceepr/www/publications/reprints/Reprint_229_WC.pdf.

Estevadeordal, A., K. Suominen and R. Teh (ed.) (2009) *Regional Rules in the Global Trading System*. Cambridge: Cambridge University Press.

Frankel, J.A., and A.K., Rose (2005) "Is trade good or bad for the environment? Sorting out the causality," *Review of Economics and Statistics*, vol. 87, pp. 85–91.

Gallagher, K.P. (ed.) (2008) *Handbook of Trade and the Environment*. Cheltenham: Edward Elgar.

Grossman, G.M. and A.B. Krueger (1993) "Environmental impacts of a North American Free Trade Agreement," in *The Mexico–U.S. Free Trade Agreement*, Garber, P. (ed.), 13–56. Cambridge, MA: MIT Press.

Herberg, H. (1970) "Economic growth and international trade with transport costs," *Zeitschrift für die Gesamte Staatswissenschaft/Journal of Institutional and Theoretical Economics,* Bd. 126, pp. 577–600.

Hoel, M. (1996) "Should a carbon tax be differentiated across sectors?," *Journal of Public Economics*, vol. 59, pp. 17–32.

International Civil Aviation Organization (ICAO) (2010) *Environmental Report: Aviation and Climate Change*. Montréal: ICAO.

International Energy Agency (IEA) (2012) CO_2 *Emissions from Fuel Combustion: Highlights*. Paris: IEA.

Ishikawa, J. and K. Kiyono (2006) "Greenhouse-gas emission controls in an open economy," *International Economic Review*, vol. 47, pp. 431–450.

Jinji, N. (2006) "International trade and terrestrial open-access renewable resources in a small open economy," *Canadian Journal of Economics*, vol. 39, pp. 790–808.

Jinnah, S. (2012) "Trade-environment politics: The emerging role of regional trade agreements," in *Handbook of Global Environmental Politics*, Dauvergne P. (ed.), 386–399. Cheltenham: Edward Elgar.

Kiyono, K. and J. Ishikawa (2013) "Environmental management policy under international carbon leakage," *International Economic Review*, vol. 54, pp. 1057–1083.

Karp, L. and J. Zhao (2004) "The dynamic effects of trade liberalization and environmental policy harmonization," in *Handbook of International Trade, Volume II*, E.K. Choi and Hartigan, J.C. (ed.), 499–525. Malden: Blackwell.

Kennedy, P.W. (1994) "Equilibrium pollution taxes in open economies with imperfect competition," *Journal of Environmental Economics and Management*, vol. 27, pp. 49–63.

Ludema, R.D. and I. Wooton (1994) "Cross-border externalities and trade liberalization: The strategic control of pollution," *Canadian Journal of Economics*, vol. 27, pp. 950–966.

Managi S., A. Hibiki, and T. Tsurumi (2009) "Does trade openness improve environmental quality?" *Journal of Environmental Economics and Management*, vol. 58, pp. 346–363.

Marschinski, R., C. Flachsland and M. Jakob (2012) "Sectoral linking of carbon markets: A trade–theory analysis," *Resource and Energy Economics*, vol. 34, pp. 585–606.

McAusland, C. and D.L. Millimet (2013) "Do national borders matter? Intranational trade, international trade, and the environment," *Journal of Environmental Economics and Management*, vol. 65, pp. 411–437.

Ministry of Land, Infrastructure, Transport and Tourism (MLIT) (2007) *White Paper on Land, Infrastructure, Transport and Tourism in Japan, 2007*, MLIT, Tokyo. Available at http://www.mlit.go.jp/common/000033297.pdf.

Mundell, R.A. (1957) "Transport costs in international trade theory," *Canadian Journal of Economics and Political Science*, vol. 23, pp. 331–348.

Naito, T. (2003) "Pareto-improving untied aid with environmental externalities," *Journal of Economics*, vol. 80, pp. 161–169.

Nimubona, A-D. (2012) "Pollution policy and trade liberalization of environmental goods," *Environmental and Resource Economics*, vol. 53, pp. 323–346.

Organisation for Economic Co-operation and Development (OECD) (2013) "Developments in regional trade agreements and the environment: 2012 update," *OECD Trade and Environment Working Papers 2013/04*, OECD, Paris. Available at http://dx.doi.org/10.1787/5k43m4nxwm25-en.

Olsthoorn, X. (2001) "Carbon dioxide emissions from international aviation: 1950–2050," *Journal of Air Transport Management*, vol. 7, pp. 87–93.

Parker, L. (2010) "Climate change and the EU emissions trading scheme (ETS): Looking to 2020," *CRS Report for Congress*, Congressional Research Service, 7-5700, R41049. Available at http://www.fas.org/sgp/crs/misc/R41049.pdf.

Rauscher, M. (1997) *International Trade, Factor Movements, and the Environment*. Oxford: Clarendon Press.

Rauscher, M. (1999) "Environmental policy in open economies," in *Handbook of Environmental and Resource Economics*, van den Bergh, J.C.J.M. (ed.), 395–403. Cheltenham: Edward Elgar.

Rauscher, M. (2005) "International trade, foreign investment, and the environment," in *Handbook of Environmental Economics vol. 3*, Mäler, K.G. and J.R. Vincent (ed.), 1403–1456. Amsterdam: Elsevier.

Runge, C.F. (1995) "Trade, pollution, and environment protection," in *Handbook of Environmental Economics*, Bromley, D.W. (ed.), 353–375. Cambridge, MA: Blackwell.

Rus, H.A. (2012) "Transboundary marine resources and trading neighbours," *Environmental and Resource Economics*, vol. 53, pp. 159–184.

Samuelson, P.A. (1954) "The transfer problem and transport costs, II: Analysis of effects of trade impediments," *Economic Journal*, vol. 64, pp. 264–289.

Sato, M. (2014) "Embodied carbon in trade: A survey of the empirical literature," *Journal of Economic Surveys*, vol. 28, pp. 831–861.

Sawa, A. and F. Fukushima (2008) "Sectoral approaches as a post-Kyoto framework: A proposal of Japan's Sectoral Approach," the 21st Century Public Policy Institute, Tokyo. Available at http://www.21ppi.org/english/pdf/080321.pdf.

Sopher, P. and A. Mansell (2013) *The World's Carbon Markets: A Case Study Guide to Emissions Trading (India)*: Environmental Defense Fund and International Emissions Trading Associate, Washington, DC. Available at http://www.ieta.org/worldscarbonmarkets.

Sugiyama, Y. and M. Saito (2009) "Ecological dumping under foreign investment quotas," *Journal of Economics*, vol. 98, pp. 137–153.

Takarada, Y. (2005) "Transboundary pollution and the welfare effects of technology transfer," *Journal of Economics*, vol. 85, pp. 251–275.

Takarada, Y. (2013a) "International trade, emissions trading systems, and sectorally differentiated environmental regulations," *RIETI Discussion Paper Series 13-J-042*, the Research Institute of Economy, Trade and Industry, Tokyo.

Takarada, Y. (2013b) "International transport and the environment: Environmental regulations and international emissions trading," *RIETI Discussion Paper Series 13-J-061*, the Research Institute of Economy, Trade and Industry, Tokyo.

Takarada, Y., W. Dong, and T. Ogawa (2013) "Shared renewable resources: Gains from trade and trade policy," *Review of International Economics*, vol. 21, pp. 1032–1047.

Takeda, S. (2005) "The effect of differentiated emission taxes: Does an emission tax favor industry?," *Economics Bulletin*, vol. 17, pp. 1–10.

Tippichai A., A. Fukuda, and H. Morisugi (2009) "Introduction of a sectoral approach to transport sector for post-2012 climate regime: A preliminary analysis using marginal abatement cost curves," *IATTS Research*, vol. 33, pp. 76–87.

Ulph, A. (1996) "Environmental policy and international trade when governments and producers act strategically," *Journal of Environmental Economics and Management*, vol. 30, pp. 265–281.

United Nations Conference on Trade and Development (UNCTAD) (2009) *WTO Negotiations on Environmental Goods and Services: A Potential Contribution to the Millennium Development Goals*. Geneva: UNCTAD.

United Nations Environment Programme (UNEP) (2005) *Environment and Trade, A Handbook, 2nd edition*. Manitoba: UNEP.

Wong, K. (1995) *International Trade in Goods and Factor Mobility*. Cambridge, MA: MIT Press.

World Trade Organization (WTO) (2009) *Trade and Climate Change: A Report by the United Nations Environment Programme and the World Trade Organization*. Geneva: WTO.

World Trade Organization (WTO) (2013) *World Trade Report 2013: Factors Shaping the Future of World Trade*. Geneva: WTO.

11

THE EFFECT OF EXTENDED PRODUCER RESPONSIBILITY ON THE INTERNATIONAL TRADE OF WASTE

Takayoshi Shinkuma and Hajime Sugeta

1. Introduction

Asia is the largest recycling center in the world. End-of-life durable goods such as home appliances and personal computers have been called E-waste. Such goods used in the US, the EU, and Japan have to a large extent been exported into developing countries in Asia. They have also ended up being recycled in the Asian region, especially in China, India, and Pakistan. Although circulation of resources (including the reuse and recycling of material) around the whole world is essential in terms of effective utilization of resources, in these centers of E-waste recycling, serious environmental pollution has been generated by improper recycling methods (Basel Action Network and Silicon Valley Toxics Coalition, 2002).

Our objective in this chapter is to derive an optimal policy to address the problems associated with the international trade of waste. The optimal policy is composed of both a trade restriction represented by a tariff on the importation of E-waste and a domestic recycling system in exporting (developed) countries. While both of these elements are related to each other, they have been introduced independently. Domestic recycling schemes in particular have been established in many developed countries for end-of-life goods on the basis of the concept of Extended Producer Responsibility (EPR), such as product take-back requirements or an Advance Disposal Fee (ADF). The most important feature of these EPR-based policies is that consumers are not required to pay a recycling fee at the time they dispose of end-of-life goods. This characteristic of EPR-based policies successfully removes the incentive for consumers to dispose of end-of-life goods illegally. On the other hand, however, one of the defects of EPR-based policies is that they have not been designed with any consideration of their effect on the international trade of waste.

By using a simple partial equilibrium model in which a developed country exports end-of-life goods as secondhand goods to a developing country, we show that the simple application of EPR-based policies like ADF is not optimal for the developed country exporting end-of-life durable goods. The optimal policy requires that the advance disposal fees paid by consumers at the time they purchase new goods be returned to those consumers who choose to export end-of-life goods as secondhand goods. In other words, it is necessary to subsidize the export of secondhand goods when an EPR policy is introduced.

We also examine the effect of adopting a simple EPR policy in the exporting (developed) country on the production of new goods, on the export of secondhand goods, on the domestic recycling, and on the welfare of both the exporting (developed) country and the importing (developing) country. It will be shown that adoption of a simple EPR policy, compared with the first best, decreases the consumption of new goods, decreases the export of secondhand goods, and increases domestic recycling, while the effect on both the welfare of the exporting (developed) country and that of the importing (developing) country is always negative.

The rest of this chapter is organized as follows. In Section 2, the background of the problem we consider in this chapter is reviewed. In Section 3, we derive the optimal policy that includes a domestic recycling system in a developed country; we also examine the effects of adopting an ADF policy in a developed country on the production of goods, on the export of secondhand goods, and on the domestic recycling in a developed country. In Section 4, we examine the effect of adoption of an ADF policy on the welfare of a developed country and that of a developing country. Our conclusions are drawn in Section 5.

2. Background

2.1 The E-waste problem in Asia

The trade in waste has undergone enormous changes since the Basel Convention came into force in 1992, because the Basel Convention allowed member states to ban the importation of hazardous waste. However, the convention covered neither secondhand goods nor scrap that can be recycled in an environmentally friendly manner. As a result, the export of secondhand goods for reuse and scrap for recycling has been increasing, while there has been a decrease in the export of waste for final disposal from developed to developing countries.

There are reasons for the international trade of E-waste between developed countries and developing countries. First, there is a much larger demand for secondhand goods in developing countries than in developed countries. Second, because recycling operations are labor intensive, domestic recycling in developed countries is discouraged by high wage rates. Thus, while neither reuse nor recycling is profitable in developed countries, end-of-life goods in developed countries can attract positive prices in developing countries because they carry the value of secondhand goods to be reused, as well as the value of resources to be recovered.

The global picture of the E-waste material flow can be split into two closed regions (Shinkuma and Managi, 2011). The first region is comprised of the western half of the US, Japan, Korea, China, Hong Kong, and Southeast Asian countries. While the US, Japan, Korea, and a few Southeast Asian countries like Malaysia and Singapore are exporters of end-of-life goods, China, Vietnam, the Philippines, Indonesia, Cambodia, and Myanmar are importing countries. Southeast Asian countries export scrap to China, the center of recycling in this region, after they have reused secondhand goods originally imported from developed countries.

The second region includes the EU, the eastern half of the US, Africa, the Middle East, and South Asia (including India, Pakistan, Bangladesh, and Nepal). In this region, while the US and the EU are the main exporters of secondhand goods and scrap, the other countries are importers of secondhand goods, with the exception of India and Pakistan, which also import E-waste scrap from other countries. Therefore, in this region India and Pakistan are centers of recycling operations. More recently, the import of secondhand goods by countries in Africa has been increasing, with Nigeria emerging as a new recycling center in this region (Schmidt, 2006).

Behind the international trade of E-waste, in the major centers of E-waste recycling – China, India, and Pakistan – the environment has been severely polluted by recovering gold, copper, and other metals from E-waste (see Basel Action Network and Silicon Valley Toxics Coalition, 2002 and Wong et al., 2007).

As a solution to this problem, several countries have banned the import of secondhand goods that are not covered by the Basel Convention. There is also support for the idea of amending the Basel Convention so that the export from developed to developing countries of scrap that includes any hazardous materials – even for recycling – would be banned. However, Ichinose et al. (2013) estimates the Chinese export demand function of waste and scrap. They show that the substitutability of waste and scraps is weak among the exporting countries, including Japan, the US, the EU, and Hong Kong. The weak substitutability suggests that the contents and also the corresponding level of externality of waste and scrap may differ among the exporting countries. Therefore, their results imply that such a uniform ban on trading hazardous waste as is proposed in the Basel Ban Amendment could be an inefficient environmental policy.

2.2 *Advance disposal fee as an EPR-based policy*

Although the Basel Convention gave an incentive to developed countries to build domestic recycling schemes for end-of-life goods, a stronger driving force was the urgent problem caused by the shortage of disposal sites in several OECD countries, like the EU member countries and Japan. Municipalities traditionally have undertaken treatment of household waste. Even though municipalities have reduced the volume of waste finally disposed of by compressing, incinerating, and recycling it, the amount needing final disposal has been increasing. In several OECD countries, the depletion of final disposal sites has become a serious problem due to resistance to new landfills or incinerators (i.e., the NIMBY problem). As long as municipalities are responsible for managing waste, none of the disposal and recycling costs can be transferred to consumers or producers; to reduce waste generation, it is necessary to transfer the responsibility for waste management from municipalities to consumers or to producers.

EPR is an environmental policy approach in which a producer's responsibility for a product is extended to the post-consumption stage of a product's life cycle. Under the concept of EPR, producers are required to recycle end-of-life goods they produced and dispose of the residuals in an environmentally friendly manner. In addition, an important feature of EPR is that consumers are not required to pay any recycling or disposal-related costs at the time that they dispose of end-of-life goods. This feature encourages consumers to dispose of end-of-life goods in a responsible way.

There are several policies consistent with EPR (OECD, 2001). The most active application of the concept of EPR is a policy that obliges producers to take back their products; this is called a product take-back requirement system. The second type of EPR policy is an ADF. Under an ADF scheme, consumers must pay a recycling fee at the time they purchase new goods. The fees collected by producers are used to subsidize recycling and disposal activities. Although the two policies seem to differ from each other, they produce the same outcome in a competitive market. To see this, note that while in the product take-back requirement system the supply curve for new goods will be shifted upward by the unit recycling cost, in the ADF system the demand curve for new goods will be shifted downward by the unit recycling cost. In spite of the equivalence between the two schemes, in the following sections we consider an ADF system rather than a product take-back requirement system for the sake of simplicity in making comparisons between the first best and the outcome derived under an ADF system.

3. Market equilibrium under an ADF policy compared with the first best

3.1 The optimal policy

In this section we examine the effects of adopting an ADF policy in a developed country assuming an economy in which a developed country exports end-of-life goods as secondhand goods to a developing country. For this purpose, we compare the market equilibrium when the developed country adopts an ADF policy with what happens in the first best. Note that some end-of-life goods can be disposed of illegally in the developed country, and improper recycling also pollutes the environment in the developing country. Therefore, the first best is represented by a competitive market equilibrium if there is no incentive to dispose of end-of-life goods illegally in the developed country and the externality associated with improper recycling in the developing country is internalized.

Because an ADF policy requires a representative consumer in the developed country to pay a recycling fee in advance at the time of purchasing goods, it must distort the consumer's choice between domestically recycling end-of-life goods and exporting them as secondhand goods. Note that under an ADF policy the consumer must pay the advance disposal fee for all end-of-life goods, even though s/he chooses to export some of them as secondhand goods. Therefore, although an ADF policy prevents the consumer from illegally disposing of end-of-life goods, that policy does not generate the first best outcome. This conclusion can be derived in a general setting whenever international trade of waste is taken into consideration.

The first best, however, can be attained by amending an ADF policy. What the government has to do to fix the distortion generated by an ADF policy is to only to return to the consumer the advance disposal fees imposed on the end-of-life goods to be exported as secondhand goods. We shall call such a policy an amended ADF. These statements can be summarized by the following proposition:

Proposition 1[1]

The first best cannot be obtained by a simple ADF policy. To attain the first best, the advance disposal fees that were imposed on the exported secondhand goods should be returned to the consumer.

Under an amended ADF policy, a subsidy is granted for the export of secondhand goods. But transaction costs are not taken into account, and these costs are expected to reach a considerable amount. However, these transaction costs can be avoided by granting a subsidy to exporters, not to the consumer.

3.2 Comparison between the first best and a competitive market equilibrium under an ADF policy

In this section we examine the distortion generated by a simple ADF policy by using a partial equilibrium model. For this purpose, we derive market equilibriums under a simple ADF policy and under an amended ADF policy, respectively. Note that the latter equilibrium represents the first best. We assume that a tax or tariff is set at a sufficient level to internalize the externality generated by improper recycling in the developing country.

We assume that durable goods are produced only in the developed country and new goods also are consumed only in the developed country. It also is assumed that some end-of-life goods are exported to the developing country as secondhand goods and the residuals of end-of-life goods are domestically recycled. These assumptions imply that there is no demand for secondhand goods in the developed country and also there is no demand for new goods in the developing country. In what follows, we consider the market for new goods in the developed country, the market for scrap in the developed country, and the market for secondhand goods in the developing country.

First, we describe how the consumer in the developed country makes a decision about disposing of end-of-life goods under a simple ADF policy. The consumer can export the end-of-life goods as secondhand goods or recycle them domestically. Let q denote the price of the secondhand goods. Assume that exporting of the secondhand goods incurs the cost of handing them to an exporter. The marginal cost of exporting secondhand goods is then denoted by MC. Under a simple ADF policy, the consumer pays the recycling fee denoted by fee_S in advance for the purchase of the new goods, where the subscript S represents a simple ADF policy. In this case, the consumer's net marginal cost of exporting the secondhand goods is $MC - q_S + fee_S$. If, however, the consumer chooses to recycle them, s/he still has to pay the recycling fee denoted by fee_S. This shows that the consumer's marginal cost of recycling is fee_S. It is always optimal for the consumer to choose the option with a smaller marginal cost and thus x_S^u in Figure 11.1 becomes the export of the secondhand goods under a simple ADF policy.

We turn to an amended ADF policy under which the consumer can receive the advance disposal fee when s/he chooses to export end-of-life goods as secondhand goods. Under an amended ADF policy, the consumer's net marginal cost of exporting the secondhand goods is expressed as $MC - q_A$, where the subscript A represents an amended ADF policy. On the other hand, when the consumer chooses to recycle them, the consumer's marginal cost of recycling is represented by fee_A. As in a simple ADF system, it is optimal for the consumer to choose the option with a smaller marginal cost and, therefore, x_A^u in Figure 11.1 becomes the export of the secondhand goods under an amended ADF policy.

We next use the (minimum) marginal cost just derived with regard to the end-of-life goods to derive the demand curve for the new goods in the case where the disposal of the end-of-life goods is taken into account. In Figure 11.2, D^n is depicted as the demand curve for the new goods in the case where the cost of disposing of the end-of-life goods is not taken into account. In the case where such disposal cost is taken into account, we need to subtract the (minimum) marginal cost with regard to the end-of-life goods from D^n to obtain the net WTP for the new goods. Thus after subtraction, the net WTP in each case is derived and denoted by D_S^n and D_A^n in Figure 11.2, respectively. The competitive equilibrium in the market for the new goods, therefore, is given by an intersection of D_S^n or D_A^n with the supply curve S^n.

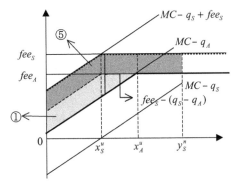

Figure 11.1   The export of the secondhand goods under a simple ADF policy or an amended ADF policy

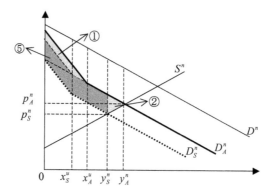

Figure 11.2 The competitive equilibrium in the market for the new goods

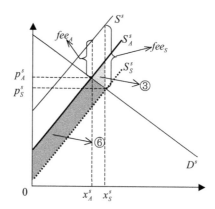

Figure 11.3 The competitive equilibrium in the scrap market

Now the recycling fee paid by the consumer, i.e., *fee*, is utilized as a subsidy granted to recyclers in the developed country. As a result, the supply curve in the scrap market S^s is shifted downward by fee_S under a simple ADF policy and by fee_A under an amended ADF policy, respectively. Hence the competitive equilibrium in the scrap market is given by an intersection of each supply curve with the demand curve for scrap D^s (Figure 11.3).

We turn to the foreign market for secondhand goods. Exporters of secondhand goods buy end-of-life goods from the consumer at the price q. We next examine the effect of improper recycling in the developing country. The secondhand goods brought into the developing country are eventually recycled and then they cause environmental pollution because the recycling processes in that country are generally improper. Let *MEC* denote this marginal external cost. Note that the optimal policy for the developing country is to impose tariffs denoted by *tax* on the imports of secondhand goods and the tax rate should be set at the marginal external cost or *MEC*. As a result, the equilibrium under a simple ADF policy is given by an intersection between S_S^u and D_S^u (Figure 11.4), while that under an amended ADF policy is given by an intersection between S_A^u and D_A^u (Figure 11.5).

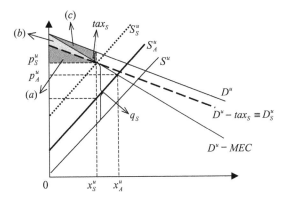

Figure 11.4   The foreign market for secondhand goods under a simple ADF policy

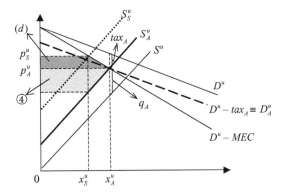

Figure 11.5   The foreign market for secondhand goods under an amended ADF policy

Under a simple ADF policy, a competitive equilibrium can be represented by the following set of equations:

$$p_S^n = S^n(\gamma_S^n)$$

$$p_S^n = D_S^n(\gamma_S^n) \equiv D^n(\gamma_S^n) - \min\{fee_S, MC(\gamma_S^n) - q_S + fee_S\}$$

$$MC(x_S^u) - q_S = 0$$

$$p_S^u = S^u(x_S^u) + q_S \equiv S_S^u(x_S^u)$$

$$p_S^u = D^u(x_S^u) - tax_S \equiv D_S^u(x_S^u)$$

$$tax_S = MEC(x_S^u)$$

$$p_S^s = S^s(x_S^s) - fee_S \equiv S_S^s(x_S^s)$$

$$p_S^s = D^s(x_S^s)$$

$$\gamma_S^n = x_S^u + x_S^s$$

229

where p^n, fee, q, p^u, p^s, tax, y^n, x^u, and x^s are nine unknowns. The last equation shows that the amount of end-of-life goods is equal to the sum of the amount of exports as secondhand goods and the amount of the goods domestically recycled. On the other hand, a competitive equilibrium under an amended ADF policy can be represented by the following set of equations:

$$p^n_A = S^n(y^n_A)$$

$$p^n_A = D^n_A(y^n_A) \equiv D^n(y^n_A) - \min\{fee_A, MC(y^n_A) - q_A\}$$

$$MC(x^u_A) - q_A = fee_A$$

$$p^u_A = S^u(x^u_A) + q_A \equiv S^u_A(x^u_A)$$

$$p^u_A = D^u(x^u_A) - tax_A \equiv D^u_A(x^u_A)$$

$$tax_A = MEC(x^u_A)$$

$$p^s_A = S^s(x^s_A) - fee_A \equiv S^s_A(x^s_A)$$

$$p^s_A = D^s(x^s_A)$$

$$y^n_A = x^u_A + x^s_A$$

By comparing the two competitive market equilibrium solutions, we obtain the following proposition:

Proposition 2

Consumption of new goods and exports of secondhand goods are lesser under a simple ADF policy than under an amended ADF policy, while the recycled amount is greater under a simple ADF policy than under an amended ADF policy.

In what follows, we prove this proposition. Suppose to the contrary that exports of secondhand goods are greater under a simple ADF policy than under an amended ADF policy, i.e., $x^u_S > x^u_A$. Then from Figure 11.1, $q_s > q_A$ must hold. However, this contradicts the situation in Figure 11.4 and Figure 11.5. Therefore, we obtain $x^u_S < x^u_A$. Conversely, we suppose $x^u_S < x^u_A$. Then from Figure 11.4 and Figure 11.5, it follows that $q_s > q_A$.

Suppose next that the amount of goods recycled domestically is lesser under a simple ADF policy than under an amended ADF policy, i.e., $x^s_S < x^s_A$. Then from $x^u_S < x^u_A$, $y^n_S < y^n_A$ must hold. Therefore, from Figure 11.2, it follows that $fee_s > fee_A$. However, as seen from Figure 11.3, this contradicts $x^s_S < x^s_A$. Therefore, we establish $x^s_S > x^s_A$. Conversely, we suppose $x^s_S > x^s_A$. Then we can show that $fee_s > fee_A$ by inspecting Figure 11.3. This completes the proof of Proposition 2.

4. The effect of adoption of a simple ADF policy on welfare

In the case where a developed country that exports end-of-life goods adopts a simple ADF policy, how is the social welfare in both the exporting country and the importing country affected? In what follows, by comparing the two market equilibriums under a simple ADF and an amended ADF policy or the first best, we confirm that social surplus in both a developed country and a developing country decreases when the developed country adopts a simple ADF policy.

To begin with, we examine a change in social surplus in the developed country. Adoption of a simple ADF policy generates the following three effects, which result in a decrease in total surplus in the goods market (a sum of producer surplus and consumer surplus). First, in the case where the consumer chooses to export the end-of-life goods as secondhand goods, s/he can sell them at a higher price under a simple ADF policy than under an amended ADF policy, i.e., $q_s >$ q_A. On the other hand, s/he must pay in advance the recycling fee (*fee*), which is not necessarily paid under an amended ADF policy. As a result, this incurs an additional cost expressed as $\{fee_S - (q_S - q_A)\}x_S^u$. Note that this additional cost imposed on the consumer does not lead to a social loss immediately because some of them or $(fee_S - fee_A)x_S^u$ is just pooled by the producer without being used as a subsidy to the recycling sector. Note that x_S^u denotes exports of end-of-life goods as secondhand goods and the advance disposal fees are not paid back to the consumer under a simple ADF policy. Thus the social loss is represented by the area of the parallelogram inside trapezoid ① in Figures 11.1 and 11.2.

Second, adoption of a simple ADF policy reduces the amount of exports of secondhand goods, i.e., $x_S^u < x_A^u$. The end-of-life goods that were exported as secondhand goods under an amended ADF policy are now recycled domestically under a simple ADF policy. This incurs extra costs for the consumer. These extra marginal costs are given by $fee_A - (MC - q_A)$, which should be integrated from x_S^u to x_A^u to calculate the corresponding additional cost. In Figures 11.1 and 11.2 this cost is represented by the area of the triangle inside trapezoid ①. Third, adoption of a simple ADF policy shrinks the production and consumption of new goods, i.e., $y_S^n < y_A^n$, and thus it reduces social surplus. This reduction is represented by the area of triangle ② in Figure 11.2.

Therefore, adoption of a simple ADF policy results in a reduction of social surplus in the goods market in the developed country represented by the area ① + ② in Figure 11.2. Here an increase in the recycling fee (*fee*) raises the consumer's payment by $(fee_S - fee_A)y_S^n$. This increase in the consumer's payment is represented by ⑤ or the dark shaded area in Figures 11.1 and 11.2. Out of the area ⑤, which is an increment of the recycling fee that the consumer pays, $(fee_S - fee_A)(y_S^n - x_S^u)$ is used as a recycling subsidy received by domestic recyclers. Using $y_S^n = x_S^u + x_S^s$, we note that this recycling subsidy is equal to ③ + ⑥ in Figure 11.3. This recycling subsidy raises social surplus in the scrap market by the area ⑥. That is, ⑥ is gained at the expense of ③ + ⑥ and thus ③ is regarded as social loss in the developed country's scrap market.

On the other hand, in the developing country's market for secondhand goods, an increase in the buying price of end-of-life goods from the developed country ($q_s > q_A$) reduces the amount traded. By noting that a change in the developed country's surplus in this market is a change in the producer surplus, it is represented by the area of trapezoid ④.

Eventually, a decrement in the developed country's social surplus caused by adoption of a simple ADF policy is the area ① + ② + ③ + ④, and thus we confirm that adoption of a simple ADF policy reduces social surplus for the developed country compared with an amended ADF policy or the first best.

We next examine a change in the developing country's social surplus. Suppose that a simple ADF policy is adopted in the developed country and the tariff on imported secondhand goods is set at the optimal level. In this case, the developing country's consumer surplus is expressed as (*a*) and its tariff revenue is given by (*b*) + (*c*) in Figure 11.4. On the other hand, the developing country incurs external costs represented by (*c*), and, therefore, its social surplus amounts to (*a*) + (*b*). If we compare the social surplus of the developing country under a simple ADF policy with that under an amended ADF policy, we can see that adoption of a simple ADF policy leads to a decrease of the social surplus in the developing country by the area of trapezoid (*d*) in Figure 11.5.

We have assumed so far that externality associated with improper recycling was internalized. In the actual economy, however, there are few developing countries that impose the optimal tariff on imports of secondhand goods. In some developing countries, secondhand goods are smuggled in (Shinkuma and Huong, 2009). Therefore, it is worthwhile to examine the effect of adoption of a simple ADF policy on welfare under the assumption that no tariff is imposed on imports of secondhand goods. It can be easily seen that Proposition 2 is still correct in this case. We can also see that adoption of a simple ADF policy always reduces the welfare of the developed country.

However, the effect on the welfare of the developing country becomes ambiguous. When the developed country adopts an amended ADF policy, the developing country earns the social surplus from its secondhand goods market, which is given by its consumer surplus minus its external costs, i.e., $(e) - (f)$ in Figure 11.6. On the other hand, when the developed country adopts a simple ADF policy, the developing country earns the social surplus given by $(g) - (h)$ in Figure 11.7. As illustrated, it is generally ambiguous whether the developing country's social surplus increases or decreases in the case where a simple ADF policy is employed in the developed country. However, it can be stated that adoption of a simple ADF policy increases the social surplus of the developing country if no tariff is imposed on imports of secondhand goods and if the *MEC* associated with improper recycling is sufficiently large.

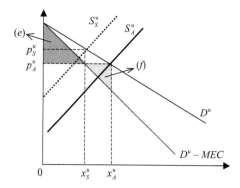

Figure 11.6   The social surplus from the secondhand goods market under an amended ADF policy in a developed country

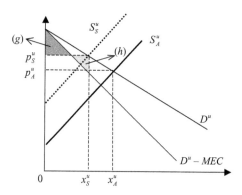

Figure 11.7   The social surplus from the secondhand goods market under a simple ADF policy in a developed country

5. Conclusion

Even though the domestic recycling systems in developed countries comprise, in a broad sense, an international trade policy for waste between developed countries and developing countries, they have been designed without any consideration of the effect on international trade. We show that a simple application of EPR-based policies like an ADF policy cannot be the optimal policy. Optimal policy requires the export of secondhand goods to be subsidized. We also show that adopting a simple ADF policy in an exporting (developed) country, compared with the first best, decreases the consumption of new goods, decreases the export of secondhand goods, and increases domestic recycling.

Because introducing a simple ADF policy decreases the trade volume of secondhand goods, it can be argued that a simple ADF policy can mitigate the environmental pollution associated with recycling E-waste in developing countries. However, a simple ADF policy introduced into a developed country will reduce both the welfare of developed countries and the welfare of developing countries, compared with the first best.

Note

1 See Chapter 8 in Shinkuma and Managi (2011) for a more rigorous proof in a more general setting.

References

Basel Action Network and Silicon Valley Toxics Coalition (2002) "Exporting Harm: The High-Tech Trashing of Asia." Available via DIALOG. http://www.ban.org/E-waste/technotrashfinalcomp.pdf.

Ichinose, D., K. Higashida, T. Shinkuma and M. Kojima (2013) "Should the trade of hazardous waste be uniformly regulated? An empirical analysis of export demand for waste and scrap." *Environment and Development Economics* 18:773–793.

OECD (2001) *Extended Producer Responsibility: A Guidance Manual for Governments.* Paris: OECD.

Schmidt, C.W. (2006) "Unfair trade: E-waste in Africa." *Environmental Health Perspectives* 114:A233–235.

Shinkuma, T. and N.T.M. Huong (2009) "The flow of E-waste material in the Asian region and a reconsideration of international trade policies on E-waste." *Environmental Impact Assessment Review* 29:25–31.

Shinkuma, T. and S. Managi (2011) *Waste and Recycling Theory and Empirics.* New York: Routledge.

Wong, M.H., S.C. Wu, M.J. Deng, X.Z. Yu, Q. Luo, A.O.W. Leung, C.S.C. Wong, W.J. Luksemburg and A.S. Wong (2007) "Export of toxic chemicals – a review of the case of uncontrolled electronic-waste recycling." *Environmental Pollution* 149:131–140.

12

FISHERIES MANAGEMENT IN ASIA

Keisaku Higashida

1. Introduction

Fisheries are renewable resources. If fishers avoid excess harvesting, such resources can be used sustainably. However, when fish stocks are *open access* resources lacking proper management schemes, it is generally difficult to avoid excess investment and a "race to fish." As noted by Hardin (1968), the race to fish results in overexploitation, which may be both biological and economic. In the worst case, a certain fish species may become extinct or at least so depleted that it becomes too costly for fishers to harvest.

According to statistics published by the Food and Agricultural Organization of the United Nations (FAO), both capture and aquaculture production have increased over the last several decades.[1] While the volume of world capture production in 1950 was approximately 16 million tons, the corresponding volume in 2011 was approximately 90 million tons. The increase in aquaculture production is much more dramatic: while the volume in 1950 was less than half a million tons, the corresponding volume in 2011 exceeded 60 million tons.

If the reproductive capacity of the sea had increased dramatically, there would be no cause for concern about the depletion of fish stocks. The reality, however, is quite different, and the depletion of many fish species has become a realistic possibility. According to the FAO (2012), 30 percent of fish species around the world were overexploited as of 2009, and this ratio has increased continuously. By contrast, the ratio of species not fully exploited has continuously decreased and is now roughly 10 percent. A rapid increase in world demand for fish and fisheries products and technological progress have encouraged the increase of production and, accordingly, excess harvesting. Srinivasan et al. (2010) estimated potential catch losses due to unsustainable fishing in all countries' exclusive economic zones (EEZs) and concluded that 36–53 percent of commercial species in more than half of EEZs may have been harvested excessively over the past several decades.

Thus, we must develop fisheries resource management schemes. Many kinds of measures have been considered and implemented and can generally be classified into the following three types: technology control, input control, and output control. It has become clear that each type of measure may have side effects. For example, limits on the size of vessels may give fishers an incentive to increase the power of engines. Total allowable catch (TAC) fosters an intensive race to fish, which results in a very short fishing period and low fish prices. Thus, a combination of more than one measure is needed to mitigate excess investment and overfishing.

Apart from such control measures, one important aspect has drawn attention: rights-based management. As Hannesson (2004, Ch. 1) has shown in his account of the evolution of property rights, human society has experienced many kinds of privatization over hundreds and possibly thousands of years. We can observe that nearly all productive lands are now private property. For example, agricultural land is owned by landlords or farmers, and many industrial sites are owned by firms.

In general, the more scarce a given resource becomes, the more likely it is that the resource is owned privately. On the other hand, if a resource is abundant and not threatened with exhaustion, the resource may be used as common property. Each user of the resource can exploit it to the degree that one desires; in terms of economics, he can choose the amount of extraction or harvesting, so that marginal revenue is equal to marginal cost. In addition, such decision-making is desirable in terms of social welfare because extraction or harvesting behavior gives rise to neither external costs to other users nor the risk of exhaustion.

When a resource becomes scarce, "who uses the resource" and "how it is used" become important questions because efficient use can maximize the benefit from the resource. Establishment of property rights also makes it possible for the society to achieve the sustainable use of resources by avoiding over-exploitation or over-harvesting. This is because owners of resources can plan the sustainable use of resources if they wish to do so.

Fish has long been common property and remains common property in many countries and areas. However, as noted, fish resources have become increasingly scarce over the past several decades. In 1982, the United Nations Convention on the Law of the Sea was adopted in the United Nations Conference on the Law of the Sea after a long discussion that started in the late 1950s. The convention was put into force in 1994, establishing territorial seas, EEZs, and other kinds of legal regimes.[2] The convention clearly advanced a trend toward the establishment of rights to fish resources.

The scarcity of fish resources in Asia is no exception, which implies that there will be a trend toward the establishment of stricter rights to fish resources in this area. Because the demand for fish in Asia has increased rapidly, the natural evolution of rights systems may be too slow to maintain sustainable use. If this is true, we must encourage rights-based fisheries.

In this chapter, we outline two representative types of *rights-based fisheries management – territorial use rights fisheries* (TURF) and *individual transferable quotas* (ITQ) – survey the literature, and review key factors for implementation of these management systems.

Whether rights to fish resources are property rights has become subject to heated debate around the world. In many cases, this type of right is not called a property right but a *use right* or an *access right*. As Dross and Acker (2009) have described in detail, rights to fish resources differ in transferability, exclusivity, durability, and security across countries.[3] Each type of aforementioned rights-based fishery has widely varying characteristics. Systems of TURFs or ITQs differ among countries and areas. In addition, they evolve over time. It is nearly impossible to analyze both types of management systems comprehensively. Therefore, we take examples in Asian countries and examine their effectiveness in economic terms.

In addition, we also consider other key factors that are important to the sustainability of fisheries in Asian countries: aquaculture, agriculture, and environmental issues. On the other hand, we do not address tuna fisheries for the following reason. The purpose of this book is to investigate resource issues in Asia. To solve the problem of overfishing of tuna, we would have to incorporate not only Asian countries but countries outside Asia, such as the US and Mexico. Although the notion of TURF and ITQ can be applied to tuna fisheries management, to consider strongly migratory species comprehensively, we must also investigate international aspects specific to this issue. Thus, we do not focus on tuna fisheries management.

The structure of this chapter is as follows. Section 2 describes the features of Asian fisheries that should be taken into account when introducing rights-based fisheries management. Sections 3 and 4 examine TURF and ITQ, respectively. Section 5 considers key factors in the success of rights-based fisheries management. Section 6 describes other factors: aquaculture, agriculture, and environmental issues. Section 7 provides concluding remarks.

2. Fisheries in Asia

Fisheries in Asian countries face the same problems as fisheries in other parts of the world: over capacity and excess harvesting. In this section, we consider three important features that should be taken into account when authorities in Asian countries develop fisheries management schemes.

First, similar to other parts of the world, both capture and aquaculture production in Asian countries have increased rapidly over the past several decades (see Figures 12.1(a, b) and 12.2(a, b)). Catch amounts have increased continuously, except in Japan and South Korea, where the establishment of 200-mile limits led to decreases in catch amounts after the late 1980s. Parallel with increases in catch amounts, excess investment and overcapacity have reached remarkable levels,

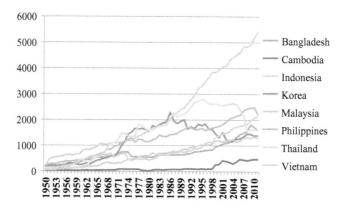

Figure 12.1(a)   Capture Production of Asian Countries (1000 t)

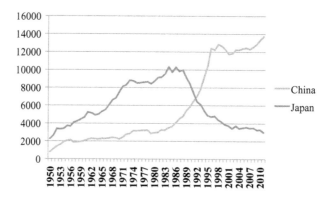

Figure 12.1(b)   Capture Production of Japan and China (1000 t)

Source: FAO Fisheries Statistics. Sea plants, sea animals, and mammals are excluded. http://www.fao.org/fishery/statistics/en

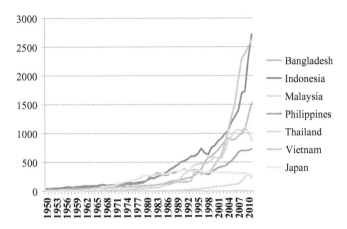

Figure 12.2(a)   Aquaculture Production of Asian Countries (1000 t)

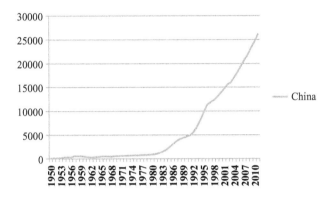

Figure 12.2(b)   Aquaculture Production of China (1000 t)

Source: FAO Fisheries Statistics. Sea plants, sea animals, and mammals are excluded. http://www.fao.org/fishery/statistics/en.

implying that the present harvesting structure is neither efficient nor sustainable. For example, Yagi and Managi (2011) estimated that, according to the data of 2003, the Japanese fisheries industry overall can save 3 billion dollars by decreasing capacity to the optimal level. Other Asian countries have experienced the same problem. For example, see Squires et al. (2003) on Indonesia, Kirkley et al. (2003) and Tai et al. (2000) on Malaysia, and Ahmed et al. (2007) on Thailand.

As a result, each country has seen stock depletion of various species. The Japanese Fisheries Agency publishes reports on the stocks of more than 40 species each year. As of 2005, more than ten species faced serious stock depletion. Moreover, the authority has started to implement stock rebuilding plans for mackerel, snow crab, sailfin sandfish, Japanese anchovy, tiger puffer, and several other species. Lee (2010) describes stock depletion of coastal areas of South Korea over the past several decades. Notably, the South Korean government established the Fish Stock Rebuilding Plan in 2005, a plan that focuses on species that face serious depletion: sailfin sandfish, swimming crab, yellow croaker, and so on.

The second factor is the relationship between the fisheries industry and poverty in developing countries. It is relatively easy for low-income people to enter the small-scale fisheries industry, as initial fixed costs are low. Low-income people are thus able to avoid extreme poverty by engaging in fishing. This implies that stock depletion is likely when fish resources are open access, undermining the interests of fishers generally. Moreover, because fishing communities usually are located in rural areas, fishers tend not to be provided with adequate administrative services. In particular, when they are struck by disaster, they are not given high priority for receipt of aid.

Indeed, fishers often migrate from their original communities to other villages to seek higher or more stable incomes. In addition, farmers enter fisheries when they lose arable land, owing to flood or other kinds of disasters. Islam and Herbeck (2013) surveyed migration in the southern part of Bangladesh, finding that fishers proactively migrate in search of better opportunities. In particular, because Bangladeshi fishers often experience geomorphologic changes of rivers that influence their livelihoods, many fishers migrate. Islam and Herbeck (2013) have clarified the types of fishers that tend to migrate: fishers who also engage in other occupations such as agriculture and trading activities do not tend to migrate.[4]

Moreover, income differentials among fishers are substantial. The simple and intuitive reason for this is that income depends on gear and boats, which fishers own. Fishers with more advanced gear and boats with more horse power earn higher incomes than those with primitive gear and who harvest fish using labor-intensive methods. However, there is one other important cause: in some cases, governments introduce leasing systems for inland water. Under an ordinary leasing system, an inland water area is divided into units, each of which is leased to one fisher or an individual who manages the unit. The owner (lessee) can then determine how many fishers to hire as crew members and the volumes of fish that crew members catch. It is clear that the owner has superior bargaining power relative to crew members and can maximize his own profits. Thus, such a policy generates income differentials. (See Heady (2000) for the case of Bangladesh and Kanchanaroek (2013) for the case of Cambodia.) This system is closely related to the rights-based fisheries management discussed in the following sections. As we will refer to this point later, it is important to elaborate on the whole system of management systems to achieve sustainable use of fish resources and poverty reduction, in particular for developing countries.

The third factor is the traditional formation of fishing communities. Some Asian and Pacific countries have long histories in which fishery communities have functioned as the units in charge of fishery resource management. For example, in Japan, the origin of fisheries communities and its management scheme dates to the feudal era in the 16th century, although it is presumed that fishers at the time had no notion of the sustainability of fish resources. Rather, they had to protect their fish resources from poachers to maintain their livelihoods. Since then, the notion of a commons of the sea has developed among local villagers.

In general, the first factor encourages authorities and fishers to implement rights-based fisheries management, whereas the second may hinder the implementation. At least, authorities must be careful about those last two factors and introduce some additional measures when developing a rights-based fisheries management program.

3. Territorial use rights fisheries (TURFs)

The first rights-based management system we focus on is TURF management, the purpose of which is to allocate rights to use fish resources in specific geographic areas to specific fishers or groups of fishers. This type of management system was formally defined by Christy (1983). In a broad sense, an EEZ is also a type of TURF because use rights of the sea within 200 miles of the shore of a country are allocated to the country. In this sub-section, however, we focus on smaller areas within one country.

It is easy to understand the merits of TURF. Although each fisher may be able to access a smaller area than he could before introduction of the TURF system, smaller numbers of fishers can enter each area. Therefore, even without additional rules and regulations, TURF systems are likely to mitigate overfishing. Usually, entry limitations and other kinds of regulations, such as output and input controls, accompany a basic TURF system. In this respect, a TURF system can be an effective means of achieving sustainable use of fish stocks.

Moreover, according to Wilen et al. (2012), the potential benefits accruing to society by moving from open access to a TURF management system may be greater than usually believed. For example, fishers may decommission redundant vessels, and fishers with low productivity may exit the industry. Hence, this type of system can generate positive incentives for investment in efficient harvesting methods.

Of course, the success of TURF management systems depends on several factors. Wilen et al. (2012) enumerate the following features. First, under open access, too many entrants lead to overexploitation, causing economic benefits to dissipate and fish stocks to become depleted. Thus, TURF management should avoid excess entry. Second, a group of fishers in one territory should be able to monitor and punish poaching. Third, except for TURFs under which only one fisher can use the fish stock in each area, more than one fisher uses the resources. This implies that, without proper rules among groups of fishers, a race to fish may occur among members of groups. Thus, additional rules in each territory are needed. Fourth, territorial use rights must be secure, a basic feature of property rights.

3.1 Legal and economic aspects of Japan's TURF in coastal fisheries

The management method used in Japanese coastal fisheries is a typical TURF management system. Basically, there is one fisheries cooperative association in each village/community. Because many consolidations between adjacent associations have occurred over the past two decades, the number of cooperative associations has decreased. There were, however, 979 associations around the coast of Japan as of March 2013.[5] In some cases, following such consolidations, the customs and culture of fishing activities of affected villages have survived.

Historically, the origin of the TURF system dates to the feudal era in the 16th century.[6] Since then, fishers in villages have come to believe that they (the village) own the sea fronting their villages: the sea has been and will always belong to the villagers in common. This implies that, for community fishers, fish stocks have been common rather than private property. Formally, under the new fisheries act, which was put into operation in 1949, the use rights of fish resources in each area are regulated. Moreover, the Fisheries Cooperative Law, which was also put into operation in 1949, stipulates that each association manages the use rights of fish resources in the sea area that fronts the association.[7] However, the perceptions of fishers have not yet changed very much.

Taking into consideration the rights held in common, there are multiple legal interpretations of use rights of fish resources. Below, we explore the features of use rights in Japanese coastal areas, relating the legal issues to their economic implications.

A use right is called a fishing right. The prefectural government commissions each fisheries cooperative association to manage its fishing rights. Fishers who live in the same local village/community and belong to the association form subgroups for each species, and each subgroup exercises fishing rights over its allotted species. This way of defining fishing rights for individual groups reflects the notion that fish stocks are commonly owned by local inhabitants.

With respect to legal interpretations, there are three types of the ownership of property by more than one person (a group of persons). The important difference is whether there is equity ownership and/or claim rights for partition. The first type of ownership is *joint ownership*. Under this system, each group member has both equity ownership and a claim right for partition. For example, consider joint ownership of a bicycle. Each member has ownership of the bicycle and can transfer his equity to anyone. A buyer of ownership need not belong to the group. The second type of ownership is *joint tenancy*, under which each member has equity ownership but does not have a claim right for partition. In this case, it is impossible for a member of the owner group to transfer his or her equity to a person outside the group. For example, consider assets of cooperative/union. While a member of the cooperative obtains a refund when he withdraws from the cooperative because he has equity ownership, he cannot transfer his equity to a person outside the cooperative. The third type of ownership is *common ownership*, under which each member has neither equity owner-ship nor a claim right for partition. In this case, even if a member gives up ownership, he cannot obtain a refund. Additionally, the group can sell the property/right to another individual or group only when such a transaction is unanimously agreed upon by all members.

As noted above, a fishing right is not a property right but a kind of use right. However, we can use these classifications of property rights to clarify the form of fishing rights in Japanese coastal fisheries. A fishing right is given not to an individual fisher but to a group of fishers. Formally, neither equity ownership nor a claim right for partition is defined by law. Thus, in legal aspect, the form of fishing rights is close to common ownership. On the other hand, in actuality, each fisheries cooperative association determines the number of fishers for each species and regulations such as quotas. Within an association, when one fisher quit fishing a certain species, another member of association is often able to begin the fishing. Therefore, in terms of economics, the form of fishing rights can also be interpreted as that close to joint tenancy.

Now, let us examine the possibility of avoiding excess harvesting under each type of fishing/use right, using a simple model. Consider a sea area in which two fishers, fishers A and B, engage in fishing activities. For simplicity, there is one species of fish in this area, and the fish price, given by p, is constant. The profit for each fisher is

$$\pi_i = pq_i - \alpha_i C_i\left(q_i; q_j\right), \quad i, j = A, B, \; i \neq j,$$

where q_i, α_i, and C_i denote the amount of catch, the technology level, and the total cost, respec-tively.[8] The technology level is fisher-specific, and both fishers are assumed to have the same type of boat. The characteristics of the cost function are as follows:

$$\frac{\partial C_i}{\partial q_i} > 0, \quad \frac{\partial C_i}{\partial q_j} > 0, \quad \frac{\partial^2 C_i}{\partial q_i^2} > 0, \quad \frac{\partial^2 C_i}{\partial q_i \partial q_j} > 0.$$

Moreover, to satisfy the second-order condition and the stability condition, we assume that

$$\frac{\partial^2 C_i}{\partial q_i^2} > \frac{\partial^2 C_i}{\partial q_i \partial q_j}.$$

When each fisher chooses the catch amount to maximize his profit, the first-order condition (FOC) is given by

$$\frac{\partial \pi_i}{\partial q_i} = p - \alpha_i \frac{\partial C_i}{\partial q_i} = 0, \quad i = A, B. \tag{1}$$

However, the FOC for total profit maximization is given by

$$\frac{\partial \hat{\pi}}{\partial q_i} = p - \alpha_i \frac{\partial C_i}{\partial q_i} - \alpha_j \frac{\partial C_j}{\partial q_i} = 0, \; i = A, B, \; i \neq j, \tag{2}$$

where $\hat{\pi}$ denotes the sum of the profits of both fishers. In the former situation, each fisher does not take into consideration the external cost, i.e., that fact that an increase in his catch amount increases the cost to the other fisher. Thus, under open access, excess harvesting occurs because each fisher behaves in accordance with condition (1).

Can each form of fishing right avoid excess harvesting? Fishers have stronger incentives to avoid excess harvesting in cases of joint ownership and joint tenancy than in the case of common ownership. In the former two cases, he will be able to transfer his equity with a higher price if he maintains an abundant fish stock rather than depleting it. This is because the buyer of the equity will then be able to fish at a lower cost. Thus, it is possible in this scenario that fishers A and B take into account total profit, at least in some degree.

However, in the case of joint ownership, additional rules may be needed by fishers for the optimal use of fish stocks with respect to social welfare. For example, consider a situation in which fisher A sells his fishing right to a fisher outside the community, where the new entrant has better technology than that of fisher A. If fishers behave myopically, it is natural to expect the risk of exhaustion to thus increase. Consider a change in the value of α_A, and suppose that, before the transfer, each fisher, including fisher A, chooses his or her catch amount based on condition (1). Because

$$\frac{\partial^2 \pi_A}{\partial \alpha_A \partial q_A} = -\frac{\partial C_A}{\partial q_A}, \quad \frac{\partial^2 \pi_B}{\partial \alpha_A \partial q_B} = 0,$$

it follows that

$$\frac{dq_A}{d\alpha_A} = -\frac{\alpha_B \cdot \partial C_A/\partial q_A \cdot \partial^2 C_B/\partial q_B^2}{\Omega} < 0, \quad \frac{dq_B}{d\alpha_A} = \frac{\alpha_B \cdot \partial C_A/\partial q_A \cdot \partial^2 C_B/\partial q_A \partial q_B}{\Omega} > 0, \quad (3)$$

where

$$\Omega = \alpha_A \alpha_B \cdot \left(\frac{\partial^2 C_A}{\partial q_A^2} \frac{\partial^2 C_B}{\partial q_B^2} - \frac{\partial^2 C_A}{\partial q_A \partial q_B} \frac{\partial^2 C_B}{\partial q_A \partial q_B} \right) > 0.$$

From (3) and the envelope theorem, we obtain that

$$\frac{d\pi_A}{d\alpha_A} = -\alpha_A \frac{\partial C_A}{\partial q_B} \frac{dx_B}{d\alpha_A} - C_A < 0, \quad \frac{d\pi_B}{d\alpha_A} = -\alpha_B \frac{\partial C_B}{\partial q_A} \frac{dx_A}{d\alpha_A} > 0. \quad (4)$$

The inequalities in (4) imply that when a new entrant has better technology than the original fisher, the other fishers lose from this transfer of fishing rights. Moreover, without any output controls, such as TAC, excess harvesting is incentivized, and total profit may decrease.

In the case of Japanese fisheries cooperative associations, each subgroup for each species is subject to various regulations that are voluntarily set by group members: a daily catch limit, a season catch limit, regulations on fishing hours and/or days, regulations on fishing gear, regulations on the size of fish, and so on. In terms of voluntary decision-making with respect to restrictions on fishing, it can be said that this system has been successful thus far. On the other hand, in terms of resource management, fishers have sometimes failed to manage fish stocks effectively, although this failure may be due to climate change or ineffective regulations.

3.2 TURF in other Asian countries

In South Korea, there are many fisheries cooperatives for self-management that are similar to Japanese fisheries associations.[9] However, the history of the formation of associations, the relationship between fishers and authorities, and the present situation differ from those of Japan. At the beginning of the 20th century, under Japanese occupation, fishing rights and fisheries cooperative schemes of the same kind as those established in Japan were introduced. After 1945, the Korean government established three types of cooperative organizations: national, regional, and village fisheries cooperatives. This establishment process was completed by the early 1960s. Subsequently, the central government gradually transferred its power to control fish resources to village cooperatives.

Village cooperatives, like Japanese fisheries cooperatives, have strict regulations and rules. One important difference between Japanese and Korean fishing rights is that any fishing right owned by a village cooperative can be divided and transferred to other village cooperatives. As noted in Section 2, Korea has experienced depletion of fish stocks. At the same time, fishing operations have become individualized, and traditional rules, such as rotation of fishing grounds, have diminished.

Facing serious depletion, in 2001 the Korean Ministry of Maritime Affairs and Fisheries initiated new measures to encourage fishers to establish voluntary self-governance groups. Moreover, for certain species, the authority grants exclusive use rights to group members; thus, this policy is a kind of TURF system. The government provides fishers who establish self-governance groups not only with technical support but financial support. Thus, the Korean TURF system has been established in a top-down way. Uchida et al. (2010) and Uchida et al. (2011) investigated the formation of self-governance groups by Korean fishers, finding that fishers have benefitted from self management of fish resources through TURF systems: revenue increase, cost reduction, stock recovery, and so on.

Other Asian countries also utilize TURF management systems or have adopted such systems in the past.[10] Bangladesh, for example, leased units of inland fishing ground to fishers. In contrast to Japanese and Korean cooperative schemes, each unit was managed by one lessee.[11] The Cambodian government has introduced an interesting scheme for the Tonle Sap wetland, which is the largest floodplain lake in the country and has potentially abundant fish stocks. This wetland is divided into three different zones: conservation zone, open access zone, and private fishing zone. The private zone is divided into units, and each unit is leased to one fisher/manager.[12] Although it differs from a genuine TURF system, Malaysia adopts an area license limitation program, whose purpose is to avoid conflicts between large-scale trawlers and small-scale traditional fishers.[13]

Many TURF systems rely on voluntary management by fishers. Thus, whether TURF management results in success or failure depends on voluntary and cooperative behavior of fishers who engage in fishing activities in the territory. We will discuss the governance problem in Section 5.

4. Individual transferable quotas

The second rights-based fisheries management we focus on is ITQ systems. The requirements for an ITQ system are as follows: a) TAC is determined; b) quotas, which are amounts or shares, are allocated to individual fishers; and c) quotas are transferable among fishers or any entities. Because an ITQ system allocates use rights to individual fishers, this system can be said to be a more advanced measure as compared with TURF schemes in terms of rights-based fisheries management. In an ideal situation, ITQ systems are able to achieve two goals at the same time: they can control the total amount of catch and, accordingly, the resource stock, while achieving economic efficiency. Less efficient fishers sell their quota holdings to more efficient fishers instead of using the quotas for themselves. Thus, the problem of overcapacity is mitigated or avoided, and the total cost of catching a certain amount of fish is minimized. In this section, we first describe the basic function of ITQ systems; then we consider additional measures that may be needed to be combined with a simple ITQ program.[14]

4.1 Basic function of ITQ

In this sub-section, we describe the basic function of an ITQ system using a theoretical model. Consider a fishery with N fishers. Each fisher engages in fishing with one vessel that is large- or small-scale (type L or S, respectively) and harvests fish stock of a single species. The cost structure of each type of vessel is as follows:

$$C_i(q_i) = c_i(q_i) + F_i, \; c_i' > 0, \; c_i'' > 0, \tag{5}$$

where q_i, c_i, and F_i denote the amount of catch, the variable cost, and the fixed cost of type $i(i = L, S)$, respectively.

First, we examine whether an ITQ system achieves the efficiency and, accordingly, the social optimum given the number of each type of vessel: the number of large-scale vessels is n_L and that of small-scale vessels is n_S ($= N - n_L$). At stage 0, the government sets TAC, denoted by $\bar{Q}$, and determines the initial allocation to each fisher. It is assumed that the price of fish is constant, whereas the quota price is determined endogenously. In the first stage, quotas are transacted in a perfectly competitive market. Given the price of quotas (r), each type of fisher determines the amount of catch and, accordingly, the quota amount that s/he buys (or sells) to maximize her/his profit. The profit function for each fisher j is

$$\pi_{i,j} = p(\bar{Q}) q_{i,j} - C_i(q_{i,j}) - r \cdot (q_{i,j} - \bar{q}_j), \; i = L, \tag{6}$$

where $\bar{q}_j$ and p denotes the initial allocation for fisher j and the output/fish price, respectively. From (5) and (6), the FOC is given by

$$p(\bar{Q}) - C_i' - r = 0, \tag{7}$$

and demand for the quota of each fisher is given by $q_i = q_i(r)$. Because we assume that $c'' > 0$, demand curves for quotas are downward sloping. From (6) and the condition that

$$n_L q_L + n_S q_S = \bar{Q}, \tag{8}$$

we obtain the equilibrium outputs and the quota price, which are represented as $q_i^*(n_L, \bar{Q})(i = L, S)$ and $r^*(n_L, \bar{Q})$, respectively. When $C_L' < C_S'$ for any given amount of catch, $q_L^* > q_S^*$ holds. It is noted that the catch amounts are not influenced by the initial allocations ($\bar{q}_j$) as far as the numbers of both types of vessels are fixed.

Then, let us examine whether the equilibrium quota price and outputs achieve the social optimum. Because TAC and, accordingly, the output price is constant, the total profit maximization is equivalent to social welfare maximization. Note that the revenue and expenses generated by quota transactions are cancelled out. Thus, the welfare maximization problem is given by

$$\max_{q_{i,j}} \sum \pi_{i,j}, \qquad s.t. \sum q_{i,j} = \bar{Q} .$$

Then, the FOCs are given by

$$p(\bar{Q}) - C_i' - \lambda = 0, \quad \sum q_j = \bar{Q}, \tag{9}$$

where λ is the Lagrange multiplier. It is obvious that the equilibrium conditions under an ITQ system ((7) and (8)) and the conditions for welfare maximization ((9)) are equivalent.

Next, we consider whether an ITQ system achieves the efficiency given the total number of fishers. To this end, we add the vessel choice stage: in the first stage, given the initial allocation, each fisher chooses the type of vessel s/he uses, and quotas are transacted between fishers in the second stage. We do not consider the case in which a fisher chooses to quit fishing by selling all the quotas he holds.[15] The notion of the equilibrium is a sub-game perfect Nash equilibrium (SPNE) and we solve the determination of the harvesting structure by backward induction.

The second stage is the same as the previous case. Note that if $C'_L < C'_S$ for any given amount of catch, an increase in the number of large-scale fishers necessarily increases the quota price because total demand for quotas increases. In the first stage, each fisher chooses his vessel type so that his profit is maximized. Because we fix the total number of fishers and the TAC level, the profit depends on only the number of large-scale fishers:

$$\Pi_{i,j} = p q^*_{i,j}(n_L) - C_i\left(q^*_{i,j}(n_L)\right) - r^*(n_L) \cdot \left(q^*_{i,j}(n_L) - \bar{q}_j\right), \qquad i = L, S$$

Then, when the following two conditions are satisfied, n^{**}_L and $n^{**}_S (= N - n^{**}_L)$ are vessel numbers in SPNE in that no fisher has an incentive to change her/his own vessel type:

$$\Pi_L(n^{**}_L + 1) < \Pi_S(n^{**}_L), \; \Pi_S(n^{**}_L - 1) < \Pi_L(n^{**}_L).$$

To compare the SPNE with the social optimum, we assume that the numbers of vessels do not need to be integers.

First, we describe the social optimum. The welfare maximization problem can be described as follows:

$$\max_{n_L} n_L \Pi_L + (N - n_L)\Pi_S, \qquad s.t. \; n_L q_L(n_L) + n_S q_S(n_L) = \bar{Q}.$$

The FOC is given by

$$\frac{dSW}{dn_L} = \Pi_L - \Pi_S + \left(p - C'_L\right) \cdot n_L \cdot \frac{dq_L}{dn_L} + \left(p - C'_S\right) \cdot n_S \cdot \frac{dq_S}{dn_L} = 0. \tag{10}$$

When $C'_L < C'_S$ holds and the TAC is fixed, the sum of the third and fourth term is equal to zero. Thus, the condition can be rewritten as $\Pi_L = \Pi_S$.

Let us return to the SPNE. We now consider a more realistic situation: when an ITQ scheme is first introduced, each fisher holds either type of vessel and can determine whether to change the scale of the vessel. To avoid a complicated description of mixed equilibrium strategies, we consider a situation in which each fisher chooses his vessel scale sequentially. Moreover, we assume that, at the outset, there are too many small-scale fishers to optimize social welfare. The fewer large-scale vessels there are, the lower is the equilibrium quota price. Therefore, a large number of small-scale vessels at the outset implies that the quota price in the beginning period is below the social optimum. Small-scale fishers are then incentivized to increase the scales of their vessels. A small-scale fisher compares his present profit, Π_S, with the profit he would receive after changing his vessel scale, which is given by

$$\Pi_L + \frac{d\Pi_L}{dn_L} = \Pi_L + \left(p - C'_L - r\right)\frac{dq_L}{dn_L} - \left(q_L - \bar{q}\right)\frac{dr}{dn_L}. \tag{11}$$

Condition (7) implies that the second term on the right-hand side of (11) is zero. Consider a situation in which large-scale fishers are buyers of quotas in the second stage. Because an increase in the number of large-scale vessels increases the quota price, the final term of (11) is negative. Thus, even if $\Pi_L > \Pi_S$ holds, expectations of a quota price increase may deter a small-scale fisher from changing his vessel scale. In such a case, the condition for social welfare maximization does not hold. When considering vessel scale structure, efficiency may not be achieved by an ITQ system alone. However, if a large number of fishers participate in such a scheme, the effect of a vessel scale change by one fisher on the quota price may be trivial. In such a case, the SPNE is almost equivalent to the social optimum.

4.2 Accompanying regulations

Although economists generally agree that an ITQ system is an effective means of managing fisheries resources and avoiding stock depletion, it is possible that an efficient outcome cannot be achieved with an ITQ system alone. In addition, it is possible that an ITQ system generates side effects. In such cases, some additional measures may be needed.

4.2.1 Quota prices

For an ITQ system to achieve efficiency, quotas must be transacted competitively in the quota market. When fishers transact quotas as price takers, the quota price will be determined such that the harvest structure is efficient. However, like stock prices and foreign exchange rates, quota prices may deviate from a desirable level that achieves efficiency and, moreover, may be unstable. One source of price deviation and instability is speculation.

This possibility of deviation and instability has been examined in experimental studies. For example, Anderson (2004) and Anderson and Sutinen (2005) examine the efficiency of alternative ITQ rules, finding price volatility in several schemes. Anderson and Sutinen (2006) demonstrate large price variations over multiple trading periods, where such variance may be caused by inter-period speculation. They then show that the introduction of initial lease periods mitigates the instability of quota prices under different mechanisms. Moreover, Anderson et al. (2008) study the relationship between cost structures and market share distribution among fishers. Moxnes (2012) investigates a situation in which both capacity and quotas can be traded and compares the effectiveness of ITQs and auctioned seasonal quotas. He also suggests the importance of leasing periods for matching of quotas with capacity.[16]

4.2.2 Overinvestment

As noted in Section 2, over-capitalization is one of major causes of depletion of fish stocks. Therefore, one of the main purposes of introducing an ITQ system is to decrease vessel numbers and/or vessel size. Although an ITQ system generally works for this purpose, as described in the previous sub-section, such a system may not achieve a social optimum. From a theoretical perspective, Vestergaard et al. (2005) consider the non-malleability of capital and, accordingly, sunk costs, demonstrating that exits are delayed.[17] Hannesson (2000, 2007) examines the function of ITQ systems when crew members are paid in shares of catch value. He demonstrates that this payment method leads to overinvestment, a distortion that can be mitigated by a landing tax.

Among additional regulations, one that is commonly observed is an entry ban. Such a measure appears to be reasonable because there are usually too many vessels when an authority decides to introduce an ITQ system. In the long term, it is desirable that the vessel scale structure is the most efficient structure possible. Therefore, whether entry bans can achieve the goal should be examined.

Applying the previous model, we can easily obtain the most efficient vessel structure. Similarly to the previous case, given the total number of fishers, the following conditions must be satisfied: $C'_{L,j} = C'_{S,l}$, $C'_{S,k} = C'_{S,l}$ ($k \neq l$), in so as far as both types of vessels enter the fishery. Because the output price and the TAC are constant, the objective is to minimize total harvesting cost. Thus, the total cost minimization problem can be written as:

$$\underset{n_L, n_S}{Min} \sum_{j=1}^{n_L} \left\{ C_L\left(q_{L,j}\left(n_L, n_S\right)\right) + F_L \right\} + \sum_{k=1}^{n_S} \left\{ C_S\left(q_{S,k}\left(n_L, n_S\right)\right) + F_S \right\}, \ s.t. \ \sum q_{L,j} + \sum q_{S,k} = \bar{Q},$$

where j and k are indices of fishers.

Let us first consider the case in which $AC_L\left(\hat{q}_L \right) < AC_S\left(\hat{q}_S \right)$ holds, where AC denotes the average cost. Moreover, $\hat{q}_i$ ($i = L, S$) represents the unique amount of catch that minimizes the average cost for each type. In this case, the average cost is minimized when a) the number of large-scale vessels is $\bar{Q}/\hat{q}_L$, b) the number of small-scale vessels is zero, and c) the catch of each large-scale vessel is $\hat{q}_L$. The total cost is also minimized.

Next, consider the case in which $AC_L\left(\hat{q}_L \right) > AC_S\left(\hat{q}_S \right)$ holds. Similarly to the previous case, the average cost and, accordingly, the total cost is minimized when a) the number of large-scale vessels is zero, b) the number of small-scale vessels is $\bar{Q}/\hat{q}_S$, and c) the catch of each small-scale vessel is $\hat{q}_S$.

The question is whether this vessel structure can be achieved under an ITQ system. Higashida and Takarada (2011) demonstrate that when large-scale vessels are more efficient than small-scale vessels, long-run efficiency is achieved under an ITQ system alone. However, when small-scale vessels are more efficient than large-scale vessels, long-run efficiency is not achieved; the number of vessels becomes too few relative to a situation in which the total harvesting cost is minimized.

When there are no effective measures for fishery management, either of these two cases can obtain before an ITQ system is introduced.[18] For example, consider a situation in which there are many traditional small-scale fishers, vessel quotas are allocated, and there is no quota transaction scheme. In this situation, it is likely that a large-scale vessel cannot obtain a large amount of quotas and, accordingly, cannot obtain a catch sufficient to earn profits, as a fisher generally must pay large fixed costs to operate a large-scale vessel. Thus, without an ITQ system, small-scale fishers lack incentives to shift their vessels to large-scale ones, and the first case may obtain. However, it is also possible that there is excessive competition between fishers without any effective management measures. In such a case, an excess of investment in vessel size, fishing gear, and so on, may occur. Thus, the second case may obtain. When TAC is implemented without any quota transaction scheme, the second case can arise.

4.2.3 Other factors

In general, when a market is imperfectly competitive, the market cannot achieve efficiency. Anderson (1991) and Armstrong (2008) analyzed, from a theoretical perspective, an imperfectly competitive ITQ market. As expected, in general, the market under imperfect competition cannot realize an efficient situation. It is possible for the number of fishers to decrease after an ITQ system is introduced because more efficient fishers buy quotas from less efficient fishers, and some inefficient fishers exit the fisheries. The market may then become oligopolistic. In this respect, an upper limit on quota holdings by one fisher may be needed.

Production externalities caused by congestion of fishers or stock depletion also appear to inhibit the functioning of ITQ systems. For example, Boyce (1992) demonstrates that the quota price cannot reflect all kinds of externalities. However, as shown by Danielsson (2000), ITQ markets may be able to realize efficient outcomes even if production externalities exist among fishers, if some conditions pertaining to transactions of quotas are combined. Recalling that fisheries resources are exhaustible and that fishers often compete for shoals of fish without considering external costs, clauses pertaining to ITQ systems to discourage the harvesting activities may be needed to achieve efficiency.

Bergland and Pederson (2006) consider a situation in which there is uncertainty regarding harvesting costs, finding that when a portion of the fishers who participate in ITQ transactions are risk averse, the amount of quota transactions is smaller than necessary to achieve an optimum. Moreover, the initial allocation influences the harvesting amounts of fishers. Grafton (1994) examines a case where there is uncertainty regarding output price. Reducing uncertainty faced by fishers can increase total profits achieved, which implies that risk gives rise to inefficiency when fishers are not risk neutral. He suggests that risk-reducing policies, such as a guaranteed minimum output price, may enhance the efficiency of ITQ systems.

Non-compliance can be a serious problem when the number of fishers who participate in and/or the fishing area covered by an ITQ program are very large. Hatcher (2005) demonstrates that penalties for violations of ITQ rules influence quota prices. Chavez and Salgado (2005) also investigate the non-compliance problem and find that illegal fishing may negatively affect fish stocks. Both studies suggest punishment rules that mitigate inefficiencies caused by non-compliant behavior.

Markets in the real world often behave differently than one may expect based on theoretical analysis. In such cases, the causes of malfunctions should be clarified, so that a more comprehensive ITQ system can be developed. For example, taking into consideration informational and behavioral problems, Arnason (1990) and Costello and Deacon (2007) devise more desirable ITQ programs. It is also important to compare ITQ systems with other kinds of resource management measures, for example, taxes.[19]

4.3 The experience of developed countries and the possibility of ITQ in Asian countries

ITQ systems have not been formally introduced into Asian countries. Hence, we mainly describe experiences of countries outside Asia and then briefly consider the possibility of introducing ITQ systems into Asian fisheries.

Hannesson (2004) provides a comprehensive evaluation of the ITQ systems of several countries. According to Hannesson (2004) and other fisheries economists, New Zealand is the most successful country in achieving the goals of ITQ systems. It introduced an ITQ system in 1986. At first, quotas were fixed tonnage quotas, although later they were transformed into share quotas. The fisheries industry has actively participated in this program; for example, it contributes to the assessment of fish stocks. In general, ITQ systems in New Zealand have encouraged the efficiency of fishing activities. Except for the conflict with the Maori, the fisheries of New Zealand that were candidates for ITQ systems are relatively new. Therefore, the government faced fewer objections motivated by sympathy with small-scale traditional fishers. Clark et al. (1988) provide a description of the development and implementation of ITQ systems. Newell et al. (2005) also positively assess ITQ systems of New Zealand, whereas Bisack and Sutinen (2006) recommend modification of ITQ rules for the southern scallop fishery, owing to in-season stock externalities.

Canada, Iceland, and the US also have introduced ITQ systems,[20] with several studies evaluating the effects of ITQ programs in these countries. In general, these programs have encouraged the exit of inefficient fishers and, accordingly, contributed to increased profits and social surplus. This fact also implies the possibility that stock depletion has been avoided compared with what would be the case in the absence of ITQ programs.[21]

Basically, whether an ITQ system works effectively in achieving an efficient harvesting structure depends on how it can be introduced and what kinds of measures can be adopted concurrently. For example, suppose that small-scale traditional fishers are excluded from an ITQ system based on the view that traditional fisheries represent an important culture, so that such fishers are allowed harvest as much as they want. Then, if there are a large number of traditional fishers, the ITQ system may be unable to prevent depletion of fish stocks.

We neither deny the value of culture nor insist that traditional fishers should exit. The point is that ITQ systems may not be appropriate in such situations. In such cases, other types of rights-based management, such as TURF, should be considered. In Asian countries, many fishing areas, particularly in coastal fishing areas, are used by traditional small-scale fishers or a certain area is considered to be commonly owned by fishers of the local community. Thus, we should carefully elaborate a whole picture of an ITQ system when introducing it into such fishing areas.

5. Key factors on rights-based fisheries management

In this section, we identify key factors in rights-based fisheries management, which are important issues for future research.

5.1 Efficiency and distribution

We have thus far investigated both types of rights based fisheries management: TURF and ITQ. A typical TURF system allocates use rights for a certain area to a group of fishers. An ITQ system, by contrast, allocates use rights to individuals. In terms of efficiency, assuming individual rational behavior, an ITQ system is expected to be more effective than a TURF system unless externalities are severe. The reason for this is that the former system stipulates the rights of individuals more clearly than the latter system, and accordingly, each fisher can choose her/his harvesting amount to maximize long-term profits.

However, fishers communicate with each other not only through the quota market but also through other channels. For example, there are often cooperatives in communities that enable fishers to hold meetings routinely and cooperate with each other to establish harvesting rules for the sustainable use of fish stocks. Peer pressure may prevent fishers from engaging in non-compliant activities. In such cases, depending on the characteristics of groups, a TURF system may produce a more efficient outcome than an ITQ system. In particular, if production and stock externalities are severe, a TURF system may function well. Thus, which type of rights-based management is suitable depends on the characteristics of the area, species, and fishers' group.

Distribution is also an important issue. Without any distortions, an ITQ system can produce an efficient outcome that is not influenced by the initial allocation. Income distribution, however, is affected by the initial allocation, which is why some stakeholders object to the introduction of ITQ systems. For example, taking into consideration the difference in harvesting technology, Heaps (2003) examines the effect of introducing an ITQ system on the profit of each fisher. He demonstrates that under a certain rule of initial allocation, a certain fisher may lose from introduction of an ITQ system. Moreover, societies tend to sympathize with traditional fishing and believe that traditions should be maintained for cultural reasons. In such cases, additional measures may be needed. For example, the authority may make a portion of the quotas for small-scale fishers non-transferable. It may also capture a portion of rents from large-scale efficient fishers for redistribution. Additional stakeholders also can be taken into account. For example, Matulich and Sever (1999) consider initial allocations for both the fishing and processing sectors. Thus, in considering distribution, it is also important to examine who has use rights and who should have these rights.

5.2 Governance and behavior of fishers

There is a global trend toward decentralization of fish resource management. One of the important reasons for this trend is that biological, economic, and social situations are different across areas and communities, even in one country. Top-down centralized management schemes seem not to work effectively and will reach a dead end because this type of management is not flexible and enforces common measures on various types of areas/communities. It is costly for the central government to collect information needed to implement a set of measures tailor-made for each community. Thus, it is considered that shifts of authority to local governments or/and communities is desirable in terms of governance efficiency.

As noted in Section 2, inequality and poverty often are serious within areas/communities in Asian developing countries. A rights-based management program implemented by the central government may worsen the problem of income differential. Fishers in local communities usually do not like inequality among members in the same community.[22] In such a case, fishers may be able to introduce additional measures to achieve two goals simultaneously under a rights-based management system: sustainable and efficient use of fish stock and relatively equal distribution of benefit from fishing.

In fact, decentralization has been making a progress in Asian countries for the past few decades. For example, the Korean government has been encouraging self management of fish resources by fishers for the past decade (see Cheong 2004, Lee et al. 2006, Uchida et al. 2010). In Indonesia, decentralization has been growing since 1999. An establishment of a law, the Local Autonomy Law, has given rise to the possibility that coastal areas are managed by provincial, local, and/or district governments, although the situation may be still in transition (see Satria et al. 2006). The Bangladesh government began the decentralization process of inland water fisheries. After twists and turns, it began community-based fisheries management in cooperation with non-governmental organizations (see Kabir et al. 2011, Rahman et al. 2012).

Community-based decentralized management may give rise to interesting rules. For example, a certain number of subgroups in fisheries cooperatives in Japan have introduced an income sharing system, which is called a *pooling system*. A perfect pooling system is defined as follows: a) even if one fisher catches more fish than any other fisher in the group does, and b) even if the average size of catch by one fisher is larger than that by any other fisher in the group, their total revenue is divided by group members equally.

In general, the amount of catch of each fisher is smaller under a pooling system than without any kind of income-sharing system. The reason is that each fisher cannot acquire all of the reward for her/his own effort. Let $N, p, w (0 < w \leq 1), q_i$, and M_i denote the number of fishers, the price of a unit of fish, the ratio of revenue which is equally divided among all fishers, the amount of catch of fisher i, and the income of fisher i, respectively. Then, the income of fisher i is represented as

$$M_i = \frac{1}{N} \cdot p \sum_{i=1}^{N} w q_i + p(1-w) q_i. \tag{12}$$

Differentiation of (12) with respect to q_i yields

$$\frac{\partial M_i}{\partial q_i} = p \cdot \left[\frac{w}{N} + (1-w)\right] < p \ .$$

This inequality suggests that fishers' incentives to harvest as many fish as possible are weaker when there is a pooling system than when there is no income-sharing system. Thus, the possibility of exhaustion of the resource stock decreases.[23]

It may be possible that fishers also lose incentives to catch fish of higher quality. However, if decentralized management continues for a long time, this problem may be solved because of generation of informal relationships between fishers, customs, and peer pressures. As demonstrated by Gaspart and Seki (2003) and Platteau and Seki (2007), preference for social status may make it possible for a fishers' group to achieve an efficient situation with a pooling system. In the community of fishers, social esteem and shame exist and, accordingly, they have incentives to catch high-quality fish to obtain social esteem.

In summary, the point is that fishers are able to develop better management programs for themselves if there are supports and incentives provided by the governing authority. Some communities may choose types of ITQ systems, while others may choose TURF systems.

5.3 Future research

As noted above, biological, economic, and social situations are different across areas and communities, even in one country. Thus, each area/community needs each prescription. In this respect, there is much room for empirical and experimental studies using micro data. The method of field experiments has been making progress and, accordingly, researchers are now able to focus on local areas using experimental approach. So far, some articles have obtained interesting results for fishers' preference and fish resource management in Asian countries (see Nguyen and Leung 2009, Castillo et al. 2011, and Kanchanaroek et al. 2013).[24] Moreover, more advanced theoretical analyses for decentralized management and territorial use rights management of fish stocks will be able to reinforce the persuasiveness of the results of empirical and experimental studies.

6. Other key factors for sustainable fisheries in Asia

6.1 Aquaculture

As shown in Figure 12.2 (a) and (b), aquaculture production also is important for the fisheries industry. At least for some countries, it is as large as capture production. The most important point for aquaculture production is that it can contribute to the alleviation of poverty in rural areas of developing countries.

Whether aquaculture helps low-income people make a profit depends on productivity improvement.

For example, a large part of shrimp seed production is operated by households in Thailand. The hatcheries are called backyard hatcheries because they are located in the backyard of owners. It is important for these small-scale farmers to increase productivity. The farming environment depends on climate, agricultural product, and customs of each area. Therefore, like rights-based management systems for catch production, prescriptions may be different across areas and countries. For example, according to Kongkeo and Davy (2010), the small-scale farmers are more efficient than large-scale ones. Therefore, the expansion of seed production by family-owned enterprises contributes to an increase in aquaculture production.[25] However, Gordon and Bjørndal (2009) find that pond size is important in terms of scale effect in Bangladesh, India, and Indonesia and concluded that many farmers in these countries are too small to realize economic efficiency.

Better risk management is also an important point in terms of alleviation of poverty. In general, small-scale farmers face several kinds of uncertainties, such as diseases, volatile market prices, and institutional changes (see Ha et al. 2013). In fact, farmers perceive that price volatility and diseases are significant risk factors (see Le and Cheong 2010). Therefore, elaboration of risk assessment and management strategies are needed (see also Bunting et al. 2013). Because small-scale farmers are also vulnerable to financial risks, effective microcredit schemes also should be established.[26]

For the management of aquaculture, establishing cooperation and management schemes among farmers are also good strategies. The existence of networks help farmers communicate with each other on ideas, information, and technological progress. This type of network contributes to the improvement of the ability of farmers to adapt themselves to new technologies in Thailand (see Kongkeko and Davy 2010). India also succeeded in introducing best management practices by establishing small groups for a bottom-up management system (see Umesh et al. 2010). The central and local governments are able to support self-management practices by farmers. However, improper policies may deprive farmers of chances to escape from poverty (see, for example, Toan and Schilizzi 2010).

Development of aquaculture may prevent low-income people from engaging in capture production. Thus, aquaculture has high potential for avoiding fish stock depletion and alleviating poverty, if good management strategies are adopted.

6.2 Agriculture and fish farming

Another way of alleviating poverty in rural areas of Asian developing countries is to expand rice-fish farming. Farmers are able to raise commercial fish in their rice fields. There is more than one system for this rice-fish farming. For example, in concurrent rice-farm fishing, fish are raised in the same period in which rice is grown. However, there is another possible method: rice and fish are raised alternately.

The potential of rice-farm fishing is high because the ratio of rice fields in which rice-fish farming is adopted is low in some countries.[27] Rice-fish farming also increases the fish production and income of farmers (Berg 2002, Dey et al. 2005, and Weimin 2010). In some areas, fish farming is more profitable than rice farming (Mekhora et al. 2003). Moreover, rice-fish farming may lead to more efficient and more environmentally friendly use of pesticides, because better use of pesticides makes it possible for farmers to increase the productivity and safety of fish production (Weimin 2010).[28] Thus, the better use of rice fields has high potential for the development of fisheries and the improvement of livelihoods in rural areas of Asian countries.

6.3 Environmental issues

The last key factor is the relationship between the fisheries industry and the environment. The environment in this case does not mean depletion of fish stocks caused by overharvesting. Fishing and farming activities damage the environment other than depleting fish resources. For example, fishing nets and other instruments are sometimes left in the bottom of the sea. Those items may damage the sea environment. People who are conscious of environmental issues may be familiar with the environmental problems relating to aquaculture: salinization, sedimentation, and degradation of mangrove forests.[29] More environmentally friendly methods and technologies have been introduced into shrimp farming. Therefore, the problem of mangrove forests has been mitigated. Nevertheless, the fishing industry certainly generates external costs.

Environmental degradation has adverse effects not only on the productivity of fisheries but also on other kinds of social factors, such as gender issues (Nowak 2008). Thus, in terms of sustainability of fisheries and the livelihood of people, particularly in rural areas, it is important for the authorities and communities to achieve a good balance between economic development and conservation.[30] One possible candidate to help developing countries take environmental aspects of fisheries management into consideration is changes in consumers' consciousness of the environment, in particular in developed countries. There are several kinds of labeling systems in the world that convey information on fishing method and/or fishing stocks. Uchida et al. (2014) find that consumers in Japan willingly pay for proper fisheries management for sustainable use through credible labeling systems. Because developed countries import fish and fish products from developing countries, this type of system may be able to give fishers in developing countries incentives to bear the expenses of avoiding stock depletion and/or environmental degradation.

7. Concluding remarks

In this chapter, we consider the possibility of expanding rights-based fisheries management into fisheries in Asian countries. In some developed countries, such as New Zealand, Australia, and US, ITQ systems have been implemented. They have realized more efficient and sustainable fishing activities. However, some programs also gave rise to side effects. By contrast, few ITQ programs have been introduced in Asian countries. Rather, TURF systems can be observed in these countries. Among rights-based fisheries management, TURF may be consistent with the perception of fishers and the culture of local communities.

Many articles focus on ITQ programs both theoretically and empirically. ITQ markets can be analyzed in a similar way of analyzing ordinary markets in economics. It is easy for economic theory to capture the characteristics of ITQ programs. On the other hand, it is relatively difficult for economics to capture the characteristics of TURF programs, because they include cooperative behavior of fishers and traditional customs.

One important result is that the authorities must develop a rights-based fisheries management system that fits each area/community. Desirable pictures of programs vary from area to area. Fishers also elaborate rules and operation of programs for efficient and sustainable use of fish stocks. To help authorities and fishers implement better fisheries management programs, more research should be conducted, in particular on micro behavior of fishers and the effect of specific measures for each community/area.

Acknowledgements

We gratefully acknowledge financial support from Japan Society for the Promotion of Science under the Grant-in-Aid for Scientific Research on Innovative Areas (25121508).

Notes

1 The data were extracted from the FAO web site: http://www.fao.org/fishery/statistics/en. Note that sea animals and mammals are excluded.
2 See Hoel et al. (2010) and Edeson (2010) for details of international legal regimes for fisheries.
3 More precisely, Dross and Acker (2009) describe the legal aspects of individual transferable quotas (ITQs). See also Arnason (2000).

4 See also Barua et al. (2012) for poverty in fisheries in Bangladesh.

5 The data source is the basic data issued by the Ministry of Agriculture, Forestry, and Fisheries (http://www.maff.go.jp/j/tokei/sihyo/). These data are published only in Japanese.

6 See Cancino et al. (2007), Makino and Matsuda (2005), and Yamamoto (1995) for details.

7 The sea is defined as the property of the nation by the central government of Japan. Thus, this right is a type of use right.

8 Due to space constraints, we do not describe the dynamic aspect explicitly. Moreover, in general, fishers choose their effort levels, and technology is defined as the relationship between effort and catch amounts. In this section, however, technology is attributed to cost differences.

9 For details of the history and recent changes of fisheries management in South Korea, see Cheong (2004) and Lee et al. (2006).

10 TURF schemes, called spatial fishery rights, have been adopted by countries outside Asia. See, for example, Gonzalez (1996), Holland (2000), and Holland (2004), among others.

11 Toufique (1998) investigated the effect of the establishment of use rights in Bangladesh.

12 See Kanchanaroek et al. (2013) for details.

13 See Alam et al. (2002) for details. In contrast to use rights management systems, some countries adopt marine protected area (MPA) schemes for the conservation of biodiversity, such as coral reef habitat. In MPAs, extracting activities are regulated or prohibited. See Gjertsen (2005) and Fernandez and Do (2010) for the cases of the Philippines. Costello and Kaffine (2009) examine the relationship between TURF systems and MPAs and conduct simulations for Southern California to examine the effect of imposing MPA on a fishery managed under TURF systems.

14 Clark (2006) provides basic analysis on the function of ITQ systems.

15 It is considered that both new entry and exit do not occur because of the initial costs for entry and the costs of switching to other industries.

16 On the other hand, Pinkerton and Edwards (2009) refer to the cost of leasing.

17 By employing a laboratory experimental approach, Tanaka et al. (2014) demonstrate that the structure of vessel sizes can converge to the optimum when the total number of fishers is fixed. Schnier and Felthoven (2013) suggest the method of predicting the exit and the degree of consolidation.

18 In the real world, there are various types of vessel scales. The result that an ITQ regime cannot achieve an efficient vessel scale structure when entry is limited holds even if there are more than two types of vessel scales.

19 See Jensen and Vestergaard (2003) and Hansen et al. (2008), among others.

20 Chile has also introduced ITQ systems. In the case of Chile, however, the industry objected to ITQ programs. Accordingly, the programs were partly undermined.

21 On the ITQ programs of Iceland, see Arnason (1993) and Eythórsson (2000), among others. For evaluations of ITQ programs in the Mid-Atlantic Surf Clam and Ocean Quahog fishery, see Adelaja et al. (1998a, 1998b), Weninger (1998), and Brandt (2007). In addition, Squires (1994), Geen and Nayar (1988), Dupont and Grafton (2001), Dupont et al. (2005), and Kompas and Che (2005) also provide evaluations of ITQ systems.

22 This remark is based on the author's interviews with fishers in Japan and Bangladesh.

23 Higashida et al. (2014) examine the factors that encourage the introduction of pooling systems.

24 Other articles focus on other countries outside Asia. For example, see Glecich et al. (2007) and Velez et al. (2010).

25 Setboonsarng and Edwards (1998) examined whether certain fish production strategies are economically viable in northeastern Thailand.

26 For example, see Andersson et al. (2011) for the case of Bangladesh.

27 See Ahmed et al. (2011) for the situation of Bangladesh.

28 In general, improper pesticide use is considered use that damages productivity of fish farming. Klemick and Lichtenberg (2008) find results that support the negative effect of pesticide use for the case of Vietnam, although the damage is very small.

29 The relationship between shrimp farming and degradation of mangrove forest has been a controversial issue. For example, see Janssen and Padilla (1999), Nickerson (1999), Barbier (2000), Primavera (2000), Barbier et al. (2002), Huitric et al. (2002), and Barbier and Cox (2004) among others.

30 For policies and governance problems related to environmental issues, see, for example, Cheung and Sumaila (2008) and Bush et al. (2009). For quantifying method of environmental costs of shrimp farming, Be et al. (1999). Moreover, for the compatibility of environmental, economic, and social purposes under ITQ systems, see Péreau et al. (2012).

References

Adelaja, A., B. Mccay, and J. Menzo (1998a). Market share, capacity utilization, resource conservation, and tradable quotas. *Marine Resource Economics* 13, pp. 115–134.

Adelaja, A., J. Menzo, and B. Mccay (1998b). Market power, industrial organization and tradable quotas. *Review of Industrial Organization* 13, pp. 589–601.

Ahmed, M., P. Boonchuwongse, W. Dechboon, and D. Squires (2007). Overfishing in the Gulf of Thailand: policy challenges and bioeconomic analysis. *Environment and Development Economics* 12, pp. 145–172.

Ahmed, N., K. K. Zander, and S. T. Garnett (2011). Socioeconomic aspects of rice-fish farming in Bangladesh: opportunities, challenges and production efficiency. *Australian Journal of Agricultural and Resource Economics* 55, pp. 199–219.

Alam, M. F., I. H. Omar, and D. Squires (2002). Sustainable fisheries development in the tropics: trawlers and licence limitation in Malaysia. *Applied Economics* 34, pp. 325–337.

Anderson, C. M. (2004). How institutions affect outcomes in laboratory tradable fishing allowance systems. *Agricultural and Resource Economics Review* 33(2), pp. 193–208.

Andersson, C., E. Holmgren, J. MacGregor, and J. Stage (2011). Formal microlending and adverse (or nonexistent) selection: a case study of shrimp farmers in Bangladesh. *Applied Economics* 43, pp. 4203–4213.

Anderson, C. M., M. A. Freeman, and J. G. Sutinen (2008). A laboratory analysis of industry consolidation and diffusion under tradable fishing allowance management, in Todd, C. L., Kroll, S., and Shogren, L, J. eds., *Environmental Economics, Experimental Methods*, pp. 29–46. London & New York: Routledge.

Anderson, C. M., and J. G. Sutinen (2005). A laboratory assessment of tradable fishing allowances. *Marine Resource Economics* 20, pp. 1–23.

Anderson, C. M., and J. G. Sutinen (2006). The effect of initial lease periods on price discovery in laboratory tradable fishing allowance markets. *Journal of Economic Behavior and Organization* 61, pp. 164–180.

Anderson, L. G. (1991). A note on market power in ITQ fisheries. *Journal of Environmental Economics and Management* 21, pp. 291–296.

Armstrong, C. W. (2008). Using history dependence to design a dynamic tradeable quota system under market imperfections. *Environmental and Resource Economics* 39, pp. 447–457.

Arnason, R. (1990). Minimum information management in fisheries. *Canadian Journal of Economics* 23, pp. 630–653.

Arnason, R. (1993). The Icelandic individual transferable quota system: a descriptive account. *Marine Resource Economics* 8, pp. 201–218.

Arnason, R. (2000). Property rights as a means of economic organization, in Shotton, R. ed., *Use of Property Rights in Fisheries Management*, FAO Fisheries Technical Paper 404/1, pp. 14–25.

Barbier, E. B. (2000). Valuing the environment as input: review of applications to mangrove-fishery linkages. *Ecological Economics* 35, pp. 47–61.

Barbier, E. B., and M. Cox (2004). An economic analysis of shrimp farm expansion and mangrove conversion in Thailand. *Land Economics* 80(3), pp. 389–407.

Barbier, E. B., I. Strand, and S. Sathirathai (2002). Do open access conditions affect the valuation of an externality? Estimating the welfare effects of mangrove-fishery linkages in Thailand. *Environmental and Resource Economics* 21, pp. 343–367.

Barua, P., C. Barua, and N. Mallick (2012). *Fisheries of Bangladesh: Dimension in Economic Development*. Saarbrücken: LAP LAMBERT Academic Publishing.

Be, T. T., L. C. Dung, and D. Brennan (1999). Environmental costs of shrimp culture in the rice-growing regions of the Mekong Delta. *Aquaculture Economics and Management* 3, pp. 31–42.

Berg, H. (2002). Rice monoculture and integrated rice-fish farming in the Mekong Delta, Vietnam – economic and ecological considerations. *Ecological Economics* 41, pp. 95–107.

Bergland, H., and Pedersen, P. A. (2006). Risk attitudes and individual transferable quotas. *Marine Resource Economics* 21, pp. 81–100.

Bisack, K. D., and J. G. Sutinen (2006). A New Zealand ITQ fishery with an in-season stock externality. *Marine Resource Economics* 21, pp. 231–249.

Boyce, J. R. (1992). Individual transferable quotas and production externalities in a fishery. *Natural Resource Modeling* 6, pp. 385–408.

Brandt, S. (2007). Evaluating tradable property rights for natural resources: the role of strategic entry and exit. *Journal of Economic Behavior and Organization* 63, pp. 158–176.

Bunting, S. W., R. H. Bosma, P. A. M. van Zwieten, and A. S. Silik (2013). Bioeconomic modeling of shrimp aquaculture strategies for the Mahakam Delta, Indonesia. *Aquaculture Economics and Management* 17, pp. 51–70.

Bush, S. R., N. T. Khiem, and L. X. Sinh (2009). Governing the environmental and social dimensions of pangasius production in Vietnam: a review. *Aquaculture Economics and Management* 13, pp. 271–293.

Cancino, J. P., H. Uchida, and J. E. Wilen (2012). TURFs and ITQs: collective vs. individual decision making. *Marine Resource Economics* 22, pp. 391–406.

Castillo, D., F. Bousquet, M. A. Janssen, K. Worrapimphong, and J. C. Cardenas (2011). Context matters to explain field experiments: results from Colombian and Thai fishing villages. *Ecological Economics* 70, pp. 1609–1620.

Chavez, C., and H. Salgado (2005). Individual transferable quota markets under illegal fishing. *Environmental and Resource Economics* 31, pp. 303–324.

Cheong, S-M. (2004). Managing fishing at the local level: the role of fishing village cooperatives in Korea. *Coastal Management* 32, pp. 191–202.

Cheung, W. W. L., and U. R. Sumaila (2008). Trade-offs between conservation and socio-economic objectives in managing a tropical marine ecosystem. *Ecological Economics* 66, pp. 193–210.

Christy, F. T. (1983). *Territorial use rights in marine fisheries: definitions and conditions*, FAO Fisheries Technical Paper No.227, FAO, Rome.

Clark, C. W. (2006). *The Worldwide Crisis in Fisheries – Economic Models and Human Behavior*. Cambridge: Cambridge University Press.

Clark, I. N., P. J. Major, and N. Mollett (1988). Development and implementation of New Zealand's ITQ management system. *Marine Resource Economics* 5, pp. 325–349.

Costello, C., and R. Deacon (2007). The efficiency gains from *fully* delineating rights in an ITQ fishery. *Marine Resource Economics* 22, pp. 347–361.

Costello, C., and D. T. Kaffine (2009). Marine protected areas in spatial property-rights fisheries. *Australian Journal of Agricultural and Resource Economics* 54, pp. 321–341.

Danielsson, A. (2000). Efficiency of ITQs in the presence of production externalities. *Marine Resource Economics* 15, pp. 37–43.

Dey, M. M., M. Prein, A. B. M. M. Haque, P. Sultana, N. C. Dan, and N. V. Hao (2005). Economic feasibility of community-based fish culture in seasonally flooded rice fields in Bangladesh and Vietnam. *Aquaculture Economics and Management* 9, pp. 65–88.

Dross, M., and H. Acker (2009). Legal aspects of individual transferable quotas. In Hauge, K. H. and D. C. Wilson, eds., *Comparative Evaluations of Innovative Fisheries Management: Global Experiences and European Prospects*, pp. 211–232. Dordrecht and New York: Springer.

Dupont, D. P., and R. Q. Grafton (2001). Multi-species individual transferable quotas: the Scotia-Fundy mobile gear groundfishery. *Marine Resource Economics* 15, pp. 205–220.

Dupont, D. P., K. J. Fox, D. V. Gordon, and R. Q. Grafton (2005). Profit and price effects of multi-species individual transferable quotas. *Journal of Agricultural Economics* 56(1), pp. 31–57.

Eddeson, W. R. (2010). A brief introduction to the principal provisions of the international legal regime governing fisheries in the EEZ. In Ebbin, Syma A., Alf Håkon Hoel, and Are K. Sydnes, eds., *A Sea Change: The Exclusive Economic Zone and Governance Institutions for Living Marine Resources*, pp. 17–30. Dordrecht and Norwell: Springer.

Eythórsson, E. (2000). A decade of ITQ-management in Icelandic fisheries: consolidation without consensus. *Marine Policy* 24, pp. 483–492.

FAO (2012). *The State of World Fisheries and Aquaculture 2012*. Rome: FAO.

Fernandez, C. J., and K. H. P. Do (2010). Logit and principal component analysis of the management of marine protected areas in north-eastern Iloilo, Philippines. *Asia Pacific Development Journal* 17(1), pp. 97–122.

Gaspart, F., and E. Seki (2003). Cooperation, status seeking and competitive behavior: theory and evidence. *Journal of Economic Behavior and Organization* 51, pp. 51–77.

Geen, G., and M. Nayer (1988). Individual transferable quotas in the Southern Bluefin Tuna fishery. *Marine Resource Economics* 5, pp. 365–387.

Gelcich, S., G. Edwards-Jones, and M. J. Kaiser (2007). Heterogeneity in fishers' harvesting decisions under a marine territorial user rights policy. *Ecological Economics* 61, pp. 246–254.

Gjersten, H. (2005). Can habitat protection lead to improvements in human well-being? Evidence from marine protected areas in the Philippines. *World Development* 33(2), pp. 199–217.

González, E. (1996). Territorial use rights in Chilean fisheries. *Marine Resource Economics* 11, pp. 211–218.

Gordon, D. V., and T. Bjørndal (2009). A comparative study of production factors and productivity for shrimp farms in three Asian countries: Bangladesh, India, and Indonesia. *Aquaculture Economics and Management* 13, pp. 176–190.

Grafton, R. Q. (1994). A note on uncertainty and rent capture in an ITQ fishery. *Journal of Environmental Economics and Management* 27, pp. 286–294.

Ha, T. T. P., H. Van Dijk, R. Bosma, and L. X. Sinh (2013). Livelihood capabilities and pathways of shrimp farmers in the Mekong Delta, Vietnam. *Aquaculture Economics and Management* 17, pp. 1–30.

Hannesson, R. (2000). A note on ITQs and optimal investment. *Journal of Environmental Economics and Management* 40, pp. 181–188.

Hannesson, R. (2004). *The Privatization of the Oceans.* Cambridge, MA: MIT Press.

Hannesson, R. (2007). Taxes, ITQs, investments, and revenue sharing. *Marine Resource Economics* 22, pp. 363–371.

Hansen, L. G., F. Jensen, and C. Russell (2008). The choice of regulatory instrument when there is uncertainty about compliance with fisheries regulations. *American Journal of Agricultural Economics* 90(4), pp. 1130–1142.

Hardin, G. (1968). The tragedy of the commons. *Science* 162(3859), pp. 1243–1248.

Hatcher, A. (2005). Non-compliance and the quota price in an ITQ fishery. *Journal of Environmental Economics and Management* 49, pp. 427–436.

Heaps, T. (2003). The effects on welfare of the imposition of individual transferable quotas on a heterogeneous fishing fleet. *Journal of Environmental Economics and Management* 46, pp. 557–576.

Higashida, K., and Y. Takarada (2011). On Efficiency of Individual Transferable Quotas (ITQs) through Reduction of Vessels, Discussion Paper Series #68, Kwansei Gakuin University, Nishinomiya.

Higashida, K., K. Inoue, and T. Abe (2014). What Factors Affect the Establishment of Voluntary Fisheries Management? The Case of Pooling Systems in the Management of Sakhalin Surf Clams by Japanese Fishery Cooperatives, mimeo.

Hoel, A. H., A. K. Sydnes, and S. A. Ebbin (2010). Ocean governance and institutional change. In Ebbin, Syma A., Alf Håkon Hoel, and Are K. Sydnes, eds., *A Sea Change: The Exclusive Economic Zone and Governance Institutions for Living Marine Resources,* pp. 3–16. Dordrecht and Norwell: Springer.

Holland, D. S. (2000). Fencing the fisheries commons: regulatory barbed wire in the Alaskan groundfish fisheries. *Marine Resource Economics* 15, pp. 141–149.

Holland, D. S. (2004). Spatial fishery rights and marine zoning: a discussion with reference to management of marine resources in New England. *Marine Resource Economics* 19, pp. 21–40.

Huitric, M., Carl F., and N. Kautsky (2002). Development and government policies of the shrimp farming industry in Thailand in relation to mangrove ecosystems. *Ecological Economics* 40, pp. 441–455.

Islam, M. M., and J. Herbeck (2013). Migration and translocal livelihoods of coastal small-scale fishers in Bangladesh. *Journal of Development Studies* 49(6), pp. 832–845.

Janssen, R., and J. E. Padilla (1999). Preservation or conversion? Valuation and evaluation of a mangrove forest in the Philippines. *Environmental and Resource Economics* 14, pp. 297–331.

Jensen, F., and N. Vestergaard (2003). Prices versus quantities in fisheries models. *Land Economics* 79(3), pp. 415–425.

Johannes, R. (1997). Traditional law of the sea in Micronesia. *Micronesia* 13(2), pp. 121–127.

Kabir, G. M. S., T. S. Yew, K. M. Noh, and L. S. Hook (2011). Assessing fishers' empowerment in inland openwater fisheries in Bangladesh. *Ecological Economics* 70, pp. 214–2123.

Kanchanaroek, Y., M. Termansen, and C. Quinn (2013). Property rights regimes in complex fishery management systems: A choice experiment application. *Ecological Economics* 93, pp. 363–373.

Kirkley, J. E., D. Squires, M. F. Alam, and H. O. Ishak (2003). Excess capacity and asymmetric information in developing country fisheries: the MalaysianPurse Seine Fishery. *American Journal of Agricultural Economics* 85(3), pp. 647–662.

Klemick, H., and E. Lichtenberg (2008). Pesticide use and fish harvests in Vietnamese rice agroecosystems. *American Journal of Agricultural Economics* 90(1), pp. 1–14.

Kompas, T., and T. N. Che (2005). Efficiency gains and cost reductions from individual transferable quotas: a stochastic cost frontier for the Australian South East fishery. *Journal of Productivity Analysis* 23, pp. 285–307.

Kongkeo, H., and F. B. Davy (2010). Backyard hatcheries and small scale shrimp and prawn farming in Thailand. In De Silva, Sena S., and f. Brian Davy, eds., *Success Stories in Asian Aquaculture,* pp. 67–83. London & New York: Springer.

Le, T. C., and F. Cheong (2010). Perceptions of risk and risk management in Vietnamese catfish farming: an empirical study. *Aquaculture Economics and Management* 14, pp. 282–314.

Lee, K. N., J. M. Gates, and J. Lee (2006). Recent developments in Korean fisheries management. *Ocean and Coastal Management* 49, pp. 355–366.

Lee, S. (2010). *Economics of Rebuilding Fisheries in Korea.* Saarbrücken: LAP LAMBERT Academic Publishing.

Makino, M., and H. Matsuda (2005). Co-management in Japanese coastal fisheries: institutional features and transaction costs. *Marine Policy* 29(5), pp. 441–450.

Matulich, S. C., and M. Sever (1999). Reconsidering the initial allocation of ITQs: the search for a Pareto-safe allocation between fishing and processing sectors. *Land Economics* 75, pp. 203–219.

Mekhora, T., and L. M. J. McCann (2003). Rice versus shrimp production in Thailand: is there really a conflict? *Journal of Agricultural and Applied Economics* 35, pp. 143–157.

Moxnes, E. (2012). Individual transferable quotas versus auctioned seasonal quotas: An experimental investigation. *Marine Policy* 36, pp. 339–349.

Newell, Richard G., J. N. Sanchirico, and S. Kerr (2005). Fishing quota markets. *Journal of Environmental Economics and Management* 49, pp. 437–462.

Nguyen, Q., and P. Leung (2009). Do fisherman have different attitudes toward risk? An application of prospect theory to the study of Vietnamese fisherman. *Journal of Agricultural and Resource Economics* 34(3), pp. 518–538.

Nickerson, D. J. (1999). Trade-offs of mangrove area development in the Philippines. *Ecological Economics* 28, pp. 279–298.

Nowak, B. S. (2008). Environmental degradation and its gendered impact on coastal livelihoods options among Btsisi' households of Peninsular Malaysia. *Development* 51, pp. 186–192.

Péreau, J. C., L. Doyen, L. R. Little, and O. Thébaud (2012). The triple bottom line: meeting ecological, economics, and social goals with individual transferable quotas. *Journal of Environmental Economics and Management* 63, pp. 419–434.

Pinkerton, E., and D. N. Edwards (2009). The elephant in the room: the hidden costs of leasing individual transferable fishing quotas. *Marine Policy* 33, pp. 707–713.

Platteau, J., and E. Seki (2007). Heterogeneity, social esteem and feasibility of collective action. *Journal of Development Economics* 83, pp. 302–325.

Premavera, J. H. (2000). Development and conservation of Philippine mangroves: institutional issues. *Ecological Economics* 35, pp. 91–106.

Rahman H.M. T., G. M. Hickey, and S. K. Sarker (2012). A framework for evaluating collective action and informal institutional dynamics under a resource management policy of decentralization. *Ecological Economics* 83, pp. 32–41.

Ruddles, K., E. Hviding, and R. E. Johannes (1992). Marine resources management in the context of customary tenure. *Marine Resource Economics* 7, pp. 249–273.

Satria, A., M. Sano, and H. Shima (2006). Politics of marine conservation area in Indonesia: from a centralized to a decentralized system. *International Journal of Environment and Sustainable Development* 5(3), pp. 240–261.

Schnier, K. E., and R. G. Felthoven (2013). Production efficiency and exit in rights-based fisheries. *Land Economics* 89(3), pp. 538–557.

Setboonsarng, S., and P. Edwards (1998). An assessment of alternative strategies for the integration of pond aquaculture into the small-scale farming system of Northeast Thailand. *Aquaculture Economics and Management* 2, pp. 151–162.

Squires, D., M. Alauddin, and J. Kirkley (1994). Individual transferable quota markets and investment decisions in the fixed gear Sablefish industry. *Journal of Environmental Economics and Management* 27, pp. 185–204.

Squires, D., I. Omar, Y. Jeon, J. Kirkley, K. Kuperam, and I. Susilowati (2003). Excess capacity and sustainable development in Java Sea fisheries. *Environment and Development Economics* 8, pp. 105–127.

Srinivasan, T. U., W. W. L. Cheung, R. Watson, and U. R. Sumaila (2010). Food security implications of global marine catch losses due to overfishing. *Journal of Bioeconomics* 12, pp. 183–200.

Tai, S. Y., K. M. Noh, and N. M. R. Abdullah (2000). Valuing Fisheries Depreciation in Natural Resource Accounting. *Environmental and Resource Economics* 15, pp. 227–241.

Tanaka, K., H. Keisaku, and M. Shunsuke (2014). A Laboratory Assessment of the Choice of Vessel Size under Individual Transferable Quota Regimes. *Australian Journal of Agricultural and Resource Economics*, forthcoming.

Toan, T. D., and S. G. M. Schilizzi (2010). Modeling the impact of government regulations on the performance of reservoir aquaculture in Vietnam. *Aquaculture Economics and Management* 14, pp. 120–144.

Toufique, K. A. (1998). Institutions and externalities in the inland fisheries of Bangladesh. *Land Economics* 74(3), pp. 409–421.

Uchida, H., Y. Onozaka, T. Morita, and S. Managi. (2014). Demand for ecolabeled seafood in Japanese market: a conjoint analysis of the impact of information and interactions with other labels. *Food Policy* 44, pp. 68–76.

Uchida, E., H. Uchida, J. Lee, J. Ryu, and D. Kim (2011). TURFs and clubs: empirical evidence of the effect of self-governance on profitability in South Korea's inshore (maul) fisheries. *Environment and Development Economics* 17, pp. 41–65.

Uchida, H., E. Uchida, J. Lee, J. Ryu, and D. Kim (2010). Does self management in fisheries enhance profitability? Examination of Korea's coastal fisheries. *Marine Resource Economics* 25, pp. 37–59.

Umesh, N. R., A. B. Chandra Mohan, G. Ravibabu, P. A. Padiyar, M. J. Phillips, C. V. Mohan, and B. Vishnu Bhat (2010). Shrimp farmers in India: empowering small-scale farmers through a cluster-based approach. In De Silva, Sena S., and F. Brian Davy, eds., *Success Stories in Asian Aquaculture*, pp. 41–66. London & New York: Springer.

Velez, M. A., J. J. Murphy, and J. K. Stranlund (2010). Centralized and decentralized management of local common pool resources in the developing world: experimental evidence from fishing communities in Colombia. *Economic Inquiry* 48(2), pp. 254–265.

Vestergaard, N., F. Jensen, and H. P. Jorgensen (2005). Sunk cost and entry-exit decisions under individual transferable quotas: why industry restructuring is delayed. *Land Economics* 81(3), pp. 363–378.

Weimin, M. (2010). Recent developments in rice-fish culture in China: a holistic approach for livelihood improvement in rural areas. In De Silva, Sena S., and F. Brian Davy, eds., *Success Stories in Asian Aquaculture*, pp. 15–40. London & New York: Springer.

Weninger, Q. (1998). Assessing efficiency gains from individual transferable quotas: an application to the Mid-Atlantic surf clam and ocean quahog fishery. *American Journal of Agricultural Economics* 80(4), pp. 750–764.

Wilen, J. E., J. P. Cancino, and H. Uchida (2012). The economics of territorial use rights fisheries, or TURFs. *Review of Environmental Economics and Policy* 6(2), pp. 237–257.

Yagi, M., and S. Managi (2011). Catch limits, capacity utilization, and cost reduction in Japanese fishery management. *Agricultural Economics* 42, pp. 577–592.

Yamamoto, T. (1995). Development of a community-based fishery management system in Japan. *Marine Resource Economics* 10(1), pp. 21–34.

13

NON-RENEWABLE RESOURCES IN ASIAN ECONOMIES

Perspectives of availability, applicability, acceptability and affordability

Youngho Chang and Yanfei Li

1. Introduction

Asian economies have very different natures in their economic structure and level of economic development. Therefore, these economies rely on natural resources to very different extents. Figure 13.1 presents the natural resource rents as a share of GDP for various Asian countries, and there are huge variations among the countries.

Figure 13.1 hints that the dependence of an economy on natural resources seems to have an inverted U-shape relationship with the level of economic development. Less developed economies such as the Philippines and more developed economies such as Japan and South Korea seem to be least reliant on natural resources to contribute to GDP, while fast developing economies such as China, India, and Vietnam and resource-intensive economies such as Indonesia and Malaysia seem to be highly reliant on the extraction of domestic natural resources to contribute to GDP. Figure 13.2 summarizes the average of income groups of economies in the world and reinforces this proposition.

Table 13.1 further decomposes the natural resource rents into five categories of sources, out of which the first four are considered non-renewable resources. More importantly, non-renewable energy resources, including oil, natural gas and coal, constitute the majority of the natural resource rents from non-renewable resources. It also is noted that coal plays a greater role in Asian economies such as China, India, Indonesia, and Vietnam than in the case of world average. Overall, crude oil and coal are the major sources of natural resource rents in Asian economies, followed by minerals and natural gas. Developed Asian economies, such as Japan and South Korea, have almost zero domestic natural resource or non-renewable resource production. These two economies almost entirely rely on imported non-renewable resources, especially non-renewable energy.

Figures 13.3 and 13.4 show specifically the oil production and consumption of Asian economies.

As shown in Figure 13.3 and 13.4, Asian economies as a whole consume far more crude oil than they produce. However, the production and consumption of coal are roughly in balance for these Asian economies combined as shown in Figures 13.5 and 13.6.

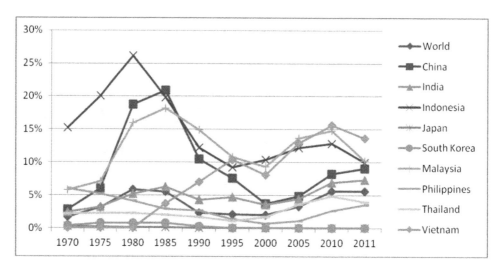

Figure 13.1   Five-year average natural resource rents★ as a share of GDP

Source: World Bank database.

★ Natural resource rents of Asian economies (resource extracted ★ unit rents => resource extracted ★ (unit price − unit cost))

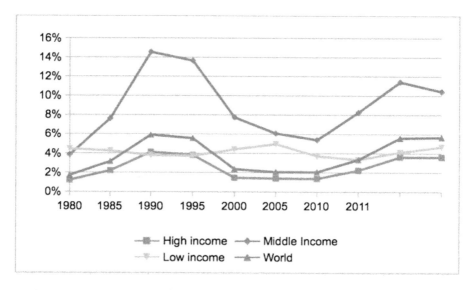

Figure 13.2   Five-year average natural resource rents★ as a share of GDP for different income groups

Source: World Bank database.

Figures 13.4 and 13.6 also show how fast the Asian demand for oil and coal has been growing, mainly due to fast economic growth of the major economies in the region such as China and India. The surge in demand has also in the past decade completely changed world markets for energy, especially those of oil and coal, causing prices to surge. Figure 13.7 shows that spot crude oil prices in the 2010s generally have increased by three-fold from the levels in the 1980s.

Table 13.1 Composition of natural resource rents in Asian economies in 2011

	Total natural resources rents (% of GDP)	Oil rents (% of GDP)	Natural gas rents (% of GDP)	Coal rents (% of GDP)	Mineral rents (% of GDP)	Forest rents (% of GDP)
China	9.1	1.6	0.1	4.4	2.8	0.2
India	7.4	1.3	0.3	3.1	2	0.6
Indonesia	10	3	0.8	4	1.6	0.6
Japan	0	0	0	0	0	0
South Korea	0.1	0	0	0	0	0
Malaysia	10.3	6.4	3.1	0.1	0.2	0.6
Philippines	3.6	0.1	0.3	0.4	2.6	0.2
Thailand	4	2.2	1.3	0.2	0.1	0.3
Vietnam	13.6	7.8	1.1	3.4	0.6	0.7
World	5.7	3.1	0.5	1	1	0.2

Source: World Bank database.

Note: Total share may not be exactly equal to summation of the share of sub-categories due to rounding.

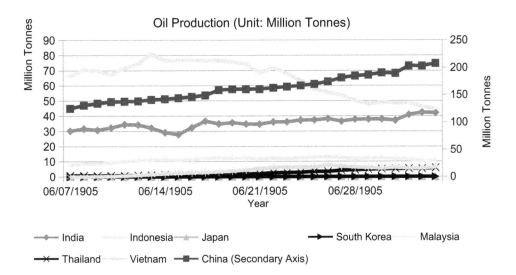

Figure 13.3   Oil production of Asian economies

Source: BP World Energy Statistical Review 2013

Figure 13.8 shows that Asian coal prices have increased by roughly two-fold compared to the levels in the 1980s and slower than the increases in the markets of Japan, Europe and the US, mainly due to relatively abundant reserves and production capacity of coal in the major Asian economies.

The imbalance of production and consumption in non-renewable resources and high and volatile energy prices raise a few critical questions regarding the sustainability of energy supply. First, will ever increasing amounts of non-renewable energy be available to Asian economies in

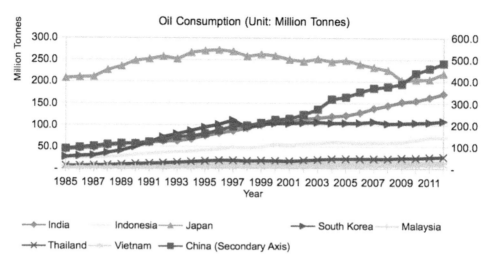

Figure 13.4 Oil consumption of Asian economies

Source: BP World Energy Statistical Review 2013.

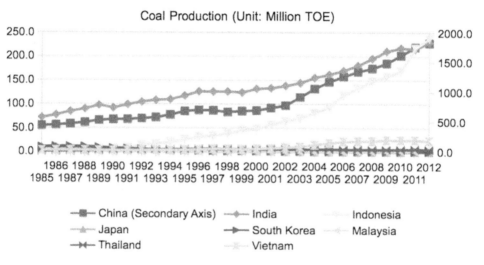

Figure 13.5 Coal production of Asian economies

Source: BP World Energy Statistical Review 2013.

the coming decades, and if not, what other sources of energy should be introduced in a mass scale to replace non-renewable energy? Second, what energy technologies are likely to be applicable in a mass scale to bring sustainable energy supply to Asian economies? Third, will the future trend of energy mix of Asian economies as well as the technologies that bring such an energy mix be acceptable in the consideration of environmental vulnerability, safety, and energy security? Fourth, will such an energy mix and the corresponding technologies be affordable to Asian economies?

This chapter focuses on non-renewable energy resources and reviews the aforementioned issues by applying a 4As framework to sort and analyze information and data from the literature.

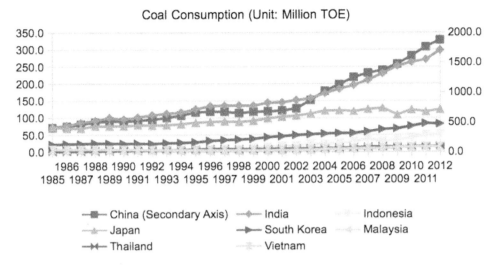

Figure 13.6 Coal consumption of Asian economies

Source: BP World Energy Statistical Review 2013.

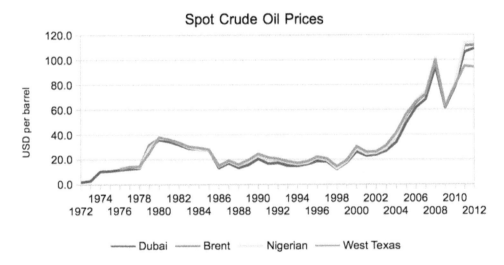

Figure 13.7 Spot crude oil prices 1972–2012

Source: BP World Energy Statistical Review 2013.

The 4As are availability, applicability, acceptability, and affordability, respectively, corresponding to the four key questions raised previously.[1]

The rest of the chapter is organized as follows. Section 2 introduces the 4As framework, based on a brief discussion of the classical Hotelling non-renewable resource economics models. Section 3 reviews the literature regarding issues under each of the four dimensions. Section 4 derives policy implications for Asian economies. Section 5 concludes.

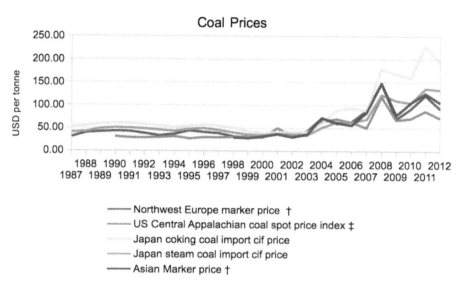

Figure 13.8 Coal prices 1987–2012

Source: BP World Energy Statistical Review 2013.

2. Hotelling rules and the 4A framework: an overview

2.1 Theoretical framework: the Hotelling models

The Hotelling models are a series of developments based on the seminal work of Harold Hotelling (1931). The basic Hotelling model assumes the finite availability of non-renewable resources (fixed amount of reserves). Based on such an assumption, it establishes a supply side equilibrium condition about the resource price and optimal extraction path. The marginal value of extraction from the resource reserve – the resource price less the marginal extraction cost – should equal the value of not extracting from the resource stock – the marginal opportunity cost of depletion. This opportunity cost of depletion is known as user cost, the *in situ* value, and resource rent. Market equilibrium requires that in the long run the *in situ* value to increase at the rate of interest[2] which is externally decided (assuming that extraction cost is independent of the remaining stock). Correspondingly, as an optimal time path of extraction, with a stationary demand curve, extraction decreases as the resource price increases over time.

However, there has not been a persistent increase in non-renewable resource prices over the last 125 years but rather fluctuations around time trends whose direction can depend upon the time period selected as a vantage point. Further development of the basic Hotelling model relaxes a few assumptions, as discussed below, to derive more realistic inferences about the paths for resource prices and extraction (Krautkraemer, 1998).

First, technological changes in resource extraction have been proven empirically to drive the cost of extraction downwards (Barnett and Morse, 1963). This extension derives a resource price path that is U-shaped, namely first decreasing and then increasing.

Second, non-renewable resource stocks should not be assumed as known with certainty, and exploration for new deposits, as well as further development of existing deposits, is an important feature of minerals and non-renewable energy industries.

Third, since the outcome of exploration and development activities cannot be fully antici-pated, expectations about the future value of the resource stock can be revised in response to specific exploration outcomes. Revised expectations about the future value can alter the equilibrium resource price and extraction paths.

Fourth, minerals and non-renewable energy industries are capital-intensive, and the timing and size of investments in extractive capital are functions of the anticipated price path and the cost of capital. Once in place, it may be very costly to adjust the extractive capacity in order to change the extraction rate in response to a change in the resource price path. As a result, the short-run supply of a non-renewable resource may be quite inelastic, and changes in market demand will be resolved with price changes rather than quantity changes. Since the cost of extractive capital assets increases with an increase in the rate of interest, it is no longer necessary that an increase in the rate of interest implies more rapid depletion.

Fifth, non-renewable resources generally occur in deposits of various grades. In an extended Hotelling model, the optimal extraction pattern requires exploiting the deposits in strict sequence from high-quality ore to low-quality ore. Then the optimal response to a price increase can be a decrease of extraction at a higher quality (lower cost) deposit and an increase of extraction at a lower quality (higher cost) deposit so that the average quality of extraction can decline in response to a price increase (Slade, 1988).

Last but not least, the availability of backstop technologies, for example renewable energy technologies in the case of non-renewable energy, deserve a special emphasis in today's circumstances. A backstop technology that provides a substitute for a non-renewable resource at a higher cost can be viewed as a higher cost deposit whose cumulative use is not limited although there may be a finite limit to the availability of the substitute at any particular time. The substitution of solar energy for fossil fuels is the most commonly cited example of a backstop technology. In the absence of stock effects, the *in situ* value of the non-renewable resource increases at the rate of interest until the non-renewable deposit is exhausted just as the resource price reaches the marginal cost at which the backstop technology is available. With a stock effect, the *in situ* value for the non-renewable resource can decline over time (Heal, 1976) and may even be non-monotonic (Farzin, 1992), although the time path for user cost cannot be decreasing if the net benefit function is strictly concave in the resource stock. The arrival of new information about the cost or timing of availability of a backstop technology can revise expectations about the future resource price path, and this can cause the observed time path for user cost to differ from the once-anticipated price path (Swierzbinski and Mendelsohn, 1989).

Other considerations include uncertainty about future resource price, backstop technology availability and the expectation of them, market imperfection, durable non-renewable resources, environmental externalities of non-renewable resource extraction and consumption, and the changing elasticity of demand with respect to resource price (Kraukraemer, 1998; Gaudet, 2007).

The Hotelling model, as mentioned above, is a supply side equilibrium model which assumes constant demand or simplified function of demand. Such is probably mainly due to the fact that the economics of non-renewable resources in history have mostly been driven by developments in the supply side and demand usually grows at a steady rate over time. Since industrialization in Asia, especially China and India, has to a large extent changed the landscape of resource demand, it is probably now equally important to model the demand side in detail as well so as to see how dynamics from both the supply and demand side determine resource prices, extraction paths, exploration activities, and capital investment in exploration and extraction. In addition, there are factors like institutional constraints, social preferences, and geopolitics which also are critical in determining the sustainability of non-renewable energy production and consumption but are not incorporated in the formal Hotelling models. By putting all these factors into consideration under four dimensions, as will be discussed in detail below, the 4As frameworks of economics of non-renewable resources could be more comprehensive and practical as an assessment of the sustainability issue.

2.2 Analytical framework: 4As sustainability assessment for economies

While it is difficult to directly apply the Hotelling models in quantitatively assessing non-renewable resource sustainability for a specific economy, a 4As (availability, applicability, acceptability, and affordability) framework that includes the following four dimensions is applicable to quantitatively assess sustainability for a certain economy. Each of the four dimensions covers certain key factors in determining resource sustainability that are identified in the formal Hotelling models. Some of these factors would be common to all economies while others would be economy-specific.

The availability of resources refers to the geological existence of the energy resources and energy resources that are inexhaustible in duration but limited in the amount available per unit of time. Availability could be specifically reflected in the following issues:

- proven hydrocarbon reserves: conventional (oil, natural gas and coal) and non-conventional (oil sands, shale gas);
- exploration and production expenditure;
- percentage of domestic crude oil production to total petroleum demand; and
- percentage of renewable energy in total energy production.

The applicability of technology refers to technology breakthroughs that can help further exploit proved resources and ensure the conservation and efficient use of the remaining hydrocarbon reserves, as well as renewable energy sources. Applicability could be specifically reflected in the following issues:

- current energy production and consumption technologies, energy conservation and energy efficiency technologies;
- energy intensity level;
- development of renewable energy technologies (including backstop technologies);
- development of non-renewable energy technologies (including backstop technologies);
- production capacity of renewable energies; and
- expenditure on R&D in energy-related technologies: energy production, energy consumption, energy saving, etc.

The acceptability of society considers the perception and safety of the general public when any of the energy resources are used. When energy is one of the inputs in production processes or utilization, energy produces both good and bad effects. Acceptability looks at the tolerance level of the society for the bad in order to enjoy the good produced and the environmental impacts that are associated with the good. Acceptability could be specifically reflected in the following issues:

- energy related carbon dioxide emissions;
- number of operating nuclear generating units;
- key pollutant emissions (Air Quality Index) and the environmental concern about coal; and
- environmental impacts due to non-renewable energy extraction and production.

The affordability can be addressed at a threefold approach – personal, commercial, and national. At the personal level, it evaluates the ability of consumers paying for the energy services provided. At the commercial level, it refers to the viability of the uptake of renewable technologies. Acceptability could be specifically reflected in the following issues:

- per capita energy consumption;
- trade balance of non-renewable energy;
- non-renewable energy market structure and market power;
- average retail prices of electricity (real prices);
- average retail prices of motor gasoline (real prices); and
- residential retail prices of natural gas (real prices).

In the next section, the literature addressing the sustainability of non-renewable energy production and consumption in Asian economies will be reviewed and categorized under the 4A framework to give readers of this chapter an in-depth and comprehensive overview of the development in this issue.

3. Sustainability in non-renewable energy for Asian economies

Availability is conventionally the most critical concern for Asian economies. It used to be equivalent to energy security, which basically means uninterrupted supply to meet increasing domestic demand. In the long run, the consideration of the availability of energy supply has to be extended to climate change and other environmental concerns, alternative (complementary or backstop) energy technologies, regional cooperation, and the cost of acquiring appropriate supply (Hippel et al., 2011b). Therefore, the rest of the discussion of this chapter under the 4As framework also covers technological (institutional) *applicability*, environmental and social *acceptability*, and economic *affordability*. This subsection reviews findings from the literature that fall into each of the four categories.

3.1 Availability

Asian economies face two main challenges regarding availability. First, despite abundant nonrenewable energy reserves that used to enable economies in the region to export non-renewable energy, fast growth in energy demand has in recent decades gradually turned them into net importers of non-renewable energy. As a result, the dependence on imported oil and gas has increased gradually and is expected to further increase. Second, the region traditionally lacks collaboration to make the best use of unevenly distributed non-renewable and renewable energy reserves in the region. Institutional frameworks in terms of energy market integration and infrastructure basis, such as connectivity in power grid and natural gas pipeline networks, are not in place. Each economy in the region has been seeking its own energy security in costly ways. These observations are supported by the evidence summarized as follows.

3.2 Demand and supply situation

Hippel et al. (2011a) study the energy security issues of Northeast Asia economies in detail, including Japan, South Korea, North Korea, Mongolia, China, Hong Kong SAR, Taiwan, and the Far East of Russia. The region's energy consumption share in the world has increased from 18.6 percent in 1999 to 25.2 percent in 2007. The study projects that the region's energy consumption will double in the period of 2005–2030 and 90 percent of the increase will come from China. Oil will see the largest growth – more than double – particularly driven by transport energy demand from China. Coal closely follows the level of growth of oil. Figure 13.9 shows

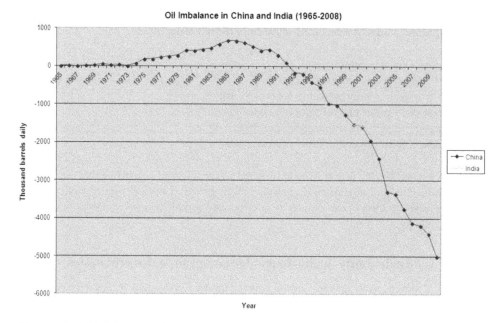

Figure 13.9 Oil imbalance (production less consumption) in China and India

Source: Authors' estimation based on BP World Energy Statistical Review 2013.

how such growth of demand has gradually changed the position of China and India in the global oil market from a net exporter to a net importer, with the gap between demand and supply widening at an unprecedented speed.

About 90 percent of the Association of Southeast Asian Nations' (ASEAN) primary energy supply has been fulfilled by fossil fuels (coal, oil, and natural gas), of which nearly 60 percent is imported from the Middle East (Thavasi and Ramakrishna, 2009).

Cao and Bluth (2013) show that China sources slightly less than 50 percent of its imported oil from the Middle East, 30 percent from Africa, 17 percent from Europe and the Western Hemisphere, and less that 5 percent from Asia-Pacific. Asia-Pacific used to be the most critical source of China's oil imports, but its share gradually shrank from more than 58 percent to 4.7 percent. None used to come to China from Africa, Europe or the Western Hemisphere.

Figure 13.10 summarizes the position of Asia-Pacific economies together in the global oil market. It is evident that the region has the largest gap between oil demand and supply and, therefore, high dependence on imported oil from other parts of the world.

The East Asian and ASEAN regions by themselves have abundant energy resources, both in terms of non-renewables and renewables; however, the reserves are usually far from economic and population centers. This situation requires both massive infrastructure investment and regional collaboration for trans-national transportation/transmission of energy. For example, infrastructure will be needed to develop and transport energy resources (oil and natural gas) from the Russian Far East to South Korea, China, and Japan. Cooperation also is needed on electricity transmission interconnections, energy efficiency, renewable energy, nuclear fuel cycle, and the emergency sharing of energy storage across borders (Hippel et al., 2011a, 2011c).

Japan has established the Energy Silk Road project with China and Turkmenistan and a trans-Asian gas pipeline network, and ASEAN has been pushing for a trans-ASEAN gas pipeline and the ASEAN power grid. Thailand and Myanmar have been cooperating in natural gas exports. The

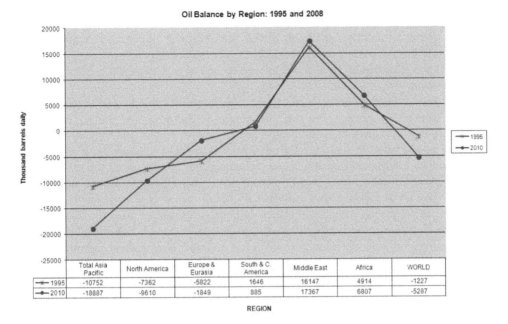

Oil Balance by Region: 1995 and 2008

	Total Asia Pacific	North America	Europe & Eurasia	South & C. America	Middle East	Africa	WORLD
1995	-10752	-7362	-5822	1646	16147	4914	-1227
2010	-18887	-9610	-1849	885	17367	6807	-5287

REGION

Figure 13.10 Oil imbalance (production less consumption) of different regions

Source: Authors' estimation based on BP World Energy Statistical Review 2013.

Philippines and Thailand have agreed on bilateral cooperation in maximizing the use of existing oil storage. The BIMST-EC countries (Bangladesh, India, Myanmar, Sri Lanka, Thailand Economic Cooperation) have proposed to explore, develop and distribute the vast and untapped energy resources in these countries through collaborations and trade (Thavasi and Ramakrishna, 2009).

The Economic Research Institute for ASEAN and East Asia has long been studying energy market integration in the ASEAN region. Chang and Li (2013a) present the results of simulation of an integrated electricity market in ASEAN with an ASEAN Power Grid (APG) that connects member countries to enable trade in electricity. Results indicate that the integrated and open electricity market encourages the development of renewable energy in the region, especially hydropower and wind energy. Chang and Li (2013b) study further policies in addition to EMI to incentivize the development of renewable energy in the power sector. The policies examined are feed-in-tariff (FIT), renewable energy portfolio standards (RPS) and carbon pricing. It is found that FIT is more cost-effective in ASEAN if the APG is in place and member countries can freely trade electricity. These policies not only save the cost of energy for countries but also diversify the energy mix and improve energy securities of countries in the region.

Electricity consumption has been growing strongly in ASEAN countries due to the increasing scale of industry activities, the structural change of industries and shift from low-energy-intensive industries to high-energy-intensive industries, and the shift toward more electricity consumption to substitute for other primary energy consumption. If the current trends continue, electricity demand will grow substantially to 1,955 billion kWh in the region by 2030. However, taking Japan as a benchmark for energy efficiency levels achievable, if a comprehensive set of measures that includes both administrative means and market-oriented ones (especially removing subsidies to electricity tariffs) is used to make sure that energy efficient technologies are adopted and appropriate patterns of energy consuming behavior are developed, levels of future electricity demand in ASEAN economies could be reduced by up to 40 percent (Chang and Li, 2013c).

3.3 Energy conservation and energy efficiency

Energy conservation could be considered another source of energy supply to an economy. In the case of South Korea, according to Park et al. (2013), per capita electricity consumption in 2008 was even higher than that of Japan and developed economies in Europe. There is clearly room for conservation.

Electricity consumption has been growing strongly in ASEAN countries due to the increasing scale of industry activities, the structural change of industries and shifting from low-energy-intensive industries to high-energy-intensive industries, and the shift toward more electricity consumption to substitute for other primary energy consumption. If the current trends continue, electricity demand will grow substantially to 1,955 billion kWh in the region by 2030. However, taking Japan as a benchmark for energy efficiency levels achievable if a comprehensive set of measures that includes both administrative means and market-oriented ones (especially removing subsidies to electricity tariffs) are taken to make sure that energy-efficient technologies are adopted and appropriate patterns of energy consuming behavior are developed, levels of future electricity demand in ASEAN economies could be reduced by up to 40 percent (Chang and Li, 2013c).

Since it is inevitable that Asian economies will turn to external sources for supply of non-renewable energy, it is necessary to look at how Japan as a country extremely lacking in natural resources, including non-renewable energy, has set its energy policies to improve energy security and sustainability. Japan so far is also the most energy efficient economy in the world, yet its energy policies are driving for even higher level of energy efficiency, together with higher energy independence and significantly lower carbon emissions and other GHG emissions.

In 2007, Japan's primary energy mix consisted of 41 percent of petroleum, 22 percent of coal, 18 percent of natural gas, 10 percent of nuclear power, 6 percent of renewable energy, and 3 percent of LPG. In 2010, the Japanese government announced a new Basic Energy Plan (BEP). The new plan focuses on raising Japan's "energy independence ratio" from 38 percent to 70 percent by 2030. The ratio is consisted of two parts: "energy self-sufficiency ratio" (from current 18 percent to 40 percent) and "self-developed fossil fuel supply ratio" (from current 26 percent to future 50 percent). To achieve these goals, Japan plans to bring about a substantial change in its energy mix by 2030, namely to double the share of renewable energy and nuclear power together and reduce the share of non-renewable fossil fuel correspondingly.[3] Moreover, the plan targets reducing absolute primary energy consumption of Japan by 13 percent. However, it is noted that after the Fukushima accident, Japan seems not to be keen in utilizing nuclear power in the country.

Since Japan's hydroelectric potential has been largely exploited, the Japanese government will focus on promoting further development of wind, solar, and biomass energy. Therefore, the government plans to extend the current FIT system, which currently applies only to small-scale electricity generation by photovoltaic (PV) cells, to include wind, geothermal, biomass, and small- to medium-scale hydroelectric plants. The government would increase its support for the introduction of new renewable technologies through such means as tax reductions, subsidies, and support for research and development. It would take steps to deregulate the domestic energy market and prepare the power grid for intermittent sources of supply. Other measures that were considered by the government include introducing sustainability standards for biofuels and expanding the introduction of renewable thermal energy.

The new BEP recognizes that Japan will still have to rely to a substantial extent on coal (17 percent by 2030), which produces the most CO_2 per unit of energy. However, the government would take several steps to reduce CO_2 emissions from coal. It would promote the commercialization of new and more efficient coal-burning technologies, such as integrated gasification combined cycle (IGCC), and require that all new coal plants achieve emissions levels comparable to IGCC. It would also accelerate the development and commercialization of technology for carbon capture and storage (CCS) technologies and require that new coal plants be CCS-ready and then be equipped with CCS technology as soon as it became available.

To reduce CO_2 emissions in the transportation sector, the government would mobilize all possible policy measures to increase the share of new vehicles sales held by next-generation low-emission vehicles, such as hybrids, electric vehicles, and vehicles that run on fuel cells, from the current 10 percent to up to 50 percent by 2020 and up to 70 percent by 2030. It would seek to expand the use of biofuels to around 3 percent of gasoline consumption by 2020 and higher thereafter. It would seek to increase the share of mid- and long-distance transportation held by rail and coastal shipping from the current 55 percent to 80 percent by 2030.

Japan's residential and commercial sectors are perceived to have the greatest potential for reduction in carbon emissions, as between 1990 and 2007 the two sectors' carbon emissions increased by 42 percent and 48 percent, respectively. Measures include promoting the development of net-zero-energy houses and buildings by 2020 and making them the norm for new erections by 2030. It would also promote the adoption of highly efficient water heaters and lighting.

Even further beyond 2030, the new BEP concerns building next-generation energy and social systems, expanding the use of innovative energy technologies, promoting international energy and environmental cooperation, reforming the structure of the energy industry, and promoting public understanding and human resource training. This includes achieving the smart grid and smart communities, promoting the development and installation of smart meters and other energy management systems, diffusing fuel cells and developing a hydrogen supply infrastructure, and accelerating the development and dissemination of innovative energy technologies.

However, two facts are noticeable in reviewing the feasibility of the ambitious plan. First, the possibility of increasing the share of nuclear power by either increasing nuclear power capacity or increase the operation rate of nuclear power plants became lame after the Fukushima nuclear power plant accident. The cost of building and operating nuclear power plants in Japan is also getting higher as the public attitude toward these developments has become more negative.

Second, the industry sector remains the largest energy consumer in Japan, at 46 percent in 2008. However, it also has been the principal target of government efforts to increase energy efficiency since the 1970s – approximately 90 percent of the energy consumption in the sector has long been covered by the Energy Conservation Law, and, partly as a result, the share of energy consumption attributable to the industrial sector has steadily declined from the 1973 level, which was nearly two-thirds. Thus, most of the easy savings in industry already have been exploited.

Given the intermittent nature of renewable energy such as PV solar energy, in the case of Japan, 100 GW of installed PV capacity is only as effective as 40 GW of conventional base- load generation capacities. In addition, concerns remain about the ability of the electricity grid to handle more than a certain amount of electricity from intermittent sources, such as solar and wind. For example, in the case of Japan, the existing power system could accommodate enough PV generating capacity to provide only about 6 percent to 8 percent of the electricity supply, according to opinions of industrial experts. Thus greater penetration by renewables may depend on the development of cost-effective, large-scale electric storage capacity (Duffield and Woodall, 2011).

3.4 Applicability

Applicability mainly concerns energy technologies. Three types of technologies would matter most for the sustainability of energy for Asian economies, namely technologies for the exploration and the extraction of non-renewable energy, renewable energy technologies as the back-stop technologies, and technologies to improve energy efficiency in energy processing, transformation, and final consumption. As Asian economies are not leading in the development or adoption of these technologies, except in some cases for developed economies in the region such as Japan and South Korea, technology transfer/diffusion and adoption in Asian economies is critical in ensuring energy sustainability.

Figures 13.11, 13.12, 13.13 and 13.14 show specifically how energy intensity and particular the intensity of non-renewable energy in Asian economies have changed. These figures show the

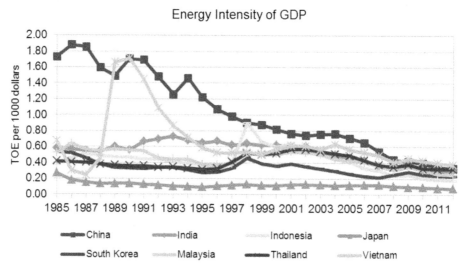

Figure 13.11   Energy intensity of GDP of Asian economies

Source: BP World Energy Statistical Review 2013 and PWT database.

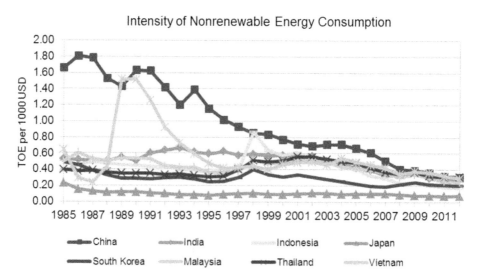

Figure 13.12   Non-renewable energy intensity of GDP of Asian economies

Source: BP World Energy Statistical Review 2013 and PWT database.

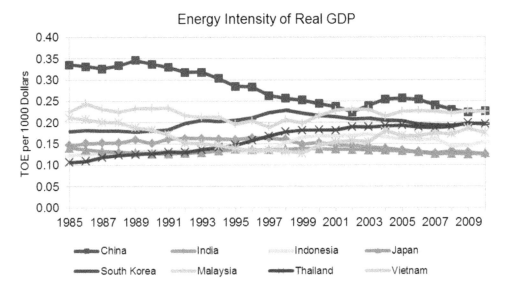

Figure 13.13   Energy intensity of real GDP of Asian economies
Source: BP World Energy Statistical Review 2013 and PWT database.

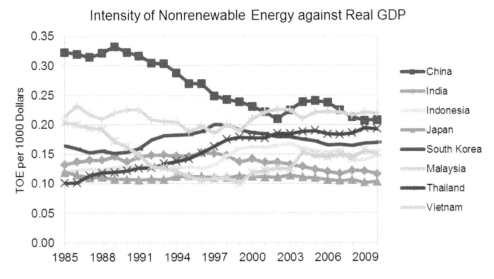

Figure 13.14   Non-renewable energy intensity of real GDP of Asian economies
Source: BP World Energy Statistical Review 2013 and PWT database.

intensity of energy consumption and non-renewable energy consumption respectively of nominal GDP. It is observed that while the intensity of most Asian economies has declined overtime, the energy efficiency gap between those countries and the leading economy in the region, namely Japan, is still significant.

3.4.1 Technological applicability: efficiency, exploration and extraction technologies for non-renewable energy

Behrens et al. (2007)[4] show that while Asian economies experience a spectacular increase in the absolute amount of natural resource use, their overall intensity of natural resource use declines over time, although slower than other parts of the world. On the global level, material intensity, i.e., resource extraction per unit of GDP, decreased by about 25 percent, indicating the relative decoupling of resource extraction from economic growth.

Specifically, the energy intensity of economies in the region has improved over time, due to the replacement of old industrial equipment with more energy efficient newer equipment, phasing out a smaller, older infrastructure (e.g., power plants), and a gradual shift in the structure of the economy toward less energy-intensive industries. This is achieved despite the fact that in the meantime growing personal wealth incurs more household consumption that requires significantly more complementary energy consumption, e.g., more road vehicles and per capita transportation use, homes with greater floor space per person, and the construction of more commercial and residential building space per person (Hippel et al., 2011a).

For example, Andrews-Speed (2009) noticed that China has managed to achieve a sustained decline of energy intensity from 1980 to 2001 but the trend was reversed in 2002. He attributed this to both a shift in the structure of the economy to more energy-intensive industries and to a decline in the rate of technical innovation.

3.4.2 Shale oil

There is an increasing certainty that conventional oil production has peaked or will peak before 2025. It is thus important to examine unconventional oil resources (shale oil, oil sand, tar sand, and extra heavy oil) and possible production. Mohr and Evans (2010) model the production of unconventional oil and conclude that its projected production will not be sufficient to mitigate the peaking of conventional oil. The production of unconventional oil itself will peak around 2076 to 2084.

3.4.3 Shale gas

Shale gas was first commercially produced in 1998 in the US by applying a process known as "hydraulic fracturing" or "fracking" that involves pumping a huge amount of water mixed with chemicals and sand to fracture rock formations so that trapped oil and gas can be extracted. Since then, the two processes (horizontal drilling and hydraulic fracturing) have become the main drivers for extracting shale resources. And the world is full of shale rocks, not limited to the US. In recent years, shale gas has reshaped the US natural gas industry fundamentally. In April 2012, gas prices dipped below US$2/Mbtu for the first time in a decade. This is a quarter of the price of European gas sold at US$9/Mbtu. The world's reserves of gas are almost doubled even by the conservative estimation of proven shale gas reserves around the world. It is noted that estimated shale gas reserves in Asia and Australia are three times as high as conventional natural gas reserves in the region. However, the success of shale gas production has so far been limited to the US (Sultan, 2013; World Energy Council, 2012b).

3.4.4 Energy efficiency and clean energy technologies

China is the major coal consumer in the region as well as in the world. Coal in China is mainly used for power generation and the rest for the production of iron and steel. Improving the efficiency of energy conversion processes and lowering emissions from coal in the power generation sector are critical under the current circumstances. China thus has been investing heavily in the R&D and the application of the relevant technologies.

There are a few clean coal technologies currently being developed in China. First, high-efficiency combustion and advanced-power generation technologies (fluidised bed combustion and supercritical boilers) and integrated gasification combined cycle (IGCC) are already in wide application. Second, coal-transformation technologies such as gasification and liquefaction technologies are being prototyped and are in the demonstration phase. Third, CCS technologies still are being researched and prototyped. The latter two types of technologies are currently expensive technologies to apply, even in developed economies, and this is particularly true about CCS (Chen and Xu, 2010; NEA and IEA, 2010).

Nuclear power development after the Fukushima accident will expect more stringent regulations as well as escalation in costs to improve safety. Reducing the costs while improving safety is the key for the nuclear power industry to survive and grow. Small modular reactors (SMR) that are much cheaper and safer with reduced complexity in design look more preferable. SMR also is more attractive and applicable to developing countries mainly due to lower investment requirement and ease to grid connection (Kessides, 2012).

3.4.5 Renewable energy technologies

International institutions such as the World Bank, the International Finance Corporation, the UN Industrial Development Organization, and the Asian Development Bank have been supporting Asian countries in developing clean/renewable energy and a necessary infrastructure. An Asia-pacific partnership on clean development and climate (AP6), which includes India, China, Japan, South Korea, Australia and the US, was launched in 2006 to promote technology transfer, demonstration, and investment in clean energy and more efficient industrial technologies. Japan so far is the dominant supporter of renewable energy in Asia (Thavasi and Ramakrishna, 2009).

The renewable energy capacity of China, including hydropower, wind, solar PV, and biomass, more than doubled by 2010 compared to the 2005 levels, reaching a total of more than 200 GW (190 GW of this is from hydropower) (Cao and Bluth, 2013).

McLellan et al. (2013) review and analyze Japan's post-Fukushima energy strategy, in which three different scenarios of future energy mix for Japan are proposed, especially regarding the role of nuclear power and renewable energy. Currently nuclear power is about 27 percent of Japan's total primary energy supply. In the extreme scenario, nuclear power will be completely phased out by 2030, while renewable energy will see its share increase from the current 10 percent to 35 percent. Technically, Japan has enough renewable energy resources in terms of solar power and wind power to meet the target share for each of them in the no-nuclear power scenario. If solar PV panels could cover 20 percent of Japan's urban and industrial areas, even at a low efficiency of 10 percent energy conversion rate, the power generated would be enough to meet the target in the extreme scenario.

3.4.6 Institutional applicability: regional cooperation

Hippel et al. (2011c) summarize general factors that determine the success or failure of regional energy cooperation projects, especially focusing on Northeast Asia. There are seven factors, and they are availability and stability of financing; transparency between nations in project planning and operations; transparent and stable system of product pricing; agreement on the regulations relating to the project; limited negative environmental and local social/economic impacts; and demonstrated positive environmental impacts and mutual net benefits in terms of energy security, economic efficiency, and economy development terms. In addition to these generic factors, there are also a few factors specific to the East Asia region. They are the sophisticated nexus of cultural, historical, economical, territorial, political and geopolitical issues that form the environment where the Northeast Asia economies develop and interact with each other, Russia's Eastern energy policy, the influence of the partially-built light water reactors in the Democratic People's Republic of Korea and the geopolitics of the US' involvement in the region.

3.5 Acceptability

Acceptability mainly concerns the environmental impacts of the chosen or dominant energy technologies. Besides GHGs, there is also the concern about the safety of nuclear power. Asian economies are slowing down their progress with nuclear power after the Fukushima accident in 2011 and more interested in developing clean coal with further diversification to natural gas at the same time.

3.5.1 Impacts of non-renewable energy production and consumption

Hippel et al. (2011a) point out that fast growth in energy consumption for Asian economies could negatively affect a number of areas, including impacts on global and regional energy markets in terms of surging prices, marine transport bottlenecks and marine pollution, local land use and environmental impacts for energy infrastructure, local and regional air pollution, and GHG emissions.

According to Cao and Bluth (2013), China's total carbon emissions more than tripled from 1980 to 2005 and carbon emissions per capita also more than doubled. However, the country's carbon intensity of GDP declined drastically, from 2.2 kg/dollar in 1980 to 0.74 kg/dollar in 2000, but slightly increased to 0.76 kg/dollar in 2005.

Specifically in China, coal consumption is responsible for 90 percent of the SO_2 emissions, 70 percent of the dust emissions, 67 percent of the NO_x emissions, and 70 percent of the CO_2 emissions. But as the most abundant energy resource, it will continue to be the dominant energy supply of China for a long time. Therefore, the development and deployment of clean coal technologies are crucial to promote sustainable development in China (Chen and Xu, 2010).

ERIA (2013) tracked the latest energy efficiency and conservation policy proposals by each of the East Asia Summit countries.[5] It is estimated that by 2035, these policies could reduce the future carbon emissions level by 28 percent. Such also applies to the case of China. It is noted that this is merely the number derived from the saving potential from the proposed policies. Technical potential and economic potential of energy savings and, therefore, carbon emissions reductions, are much higher.

3.5.2 Acceptability of nuclear power

According to Hong et al. (2013a), nuclear power is statistically safer than any other fossil fuel or hydropower electricity generation in terms of number of direct fatalities or injuries. Even considering the externalities of the fatalities, injuries, and evacuates that follow a power plant failure (externalities include resource costs, opportunity costs, mental trauma, food and land contamination, and other possible economic losses), considering both the accident probability and the median damage and externalities, nuclear power implies an implicit cost of electricity at US\$1.38 GWh^{-1}, while photovoltaic, hydroelectric power, oil power, and coal power imply US\$0.06 GWh^{-1}, US\$5.87GWh^{-1}, US\$57.7 GWh^{-1}, and US\$40.4GWh^{-1}, respectively.

While radioactive wastes are another concern for nuclear power, coal power generation generates uncontrolled low-level radioactive wastes as well, due to the trace natural uranium and thorium content of coal ashes. The emissions rate is 1.46 g/MWh (Hong et al., 2013b). This is compared to the controlled high-level radioactive wastes from nuclear power generation, which is estimated as 0.713 g/MWh. In addition, Japan's existing spent-fuel storage capacity is enough to treat nuclear power wastes until mid-2020s. An additional 30,000 tons of storage capacity could enable Japan to sustain until 2050, by when the technology to recycle and enrich plutonium from the wastes should be readily matured (Kastuta and Suzuki, 2011).

Hong et al. (2013b) propose a quantitative model to assess the sustainability of a country's energy mix for the power sector. The sustainability criteria that are quantified in the model include the levelized cost of electricity, energy security, GHG emissions, fresh water consumption, heated water discharge, land transformation, air pollutants, radioactive waste disposal, solid waste disposal, and safety issues. The model is applied to assess the sustainability of South Korea's future energy mix in the power sector. By considering all the above mentioned sustainability factors together in the algorithm, it is found that the scenario that maximizes the use of nuclear power yields the fewest overall negative impacts, and the scenario that maximizes renewable energy with fuel cells would have the highest negative impacts. Such negative impacts from maximizing renewable energy are mainly due to the fact that a higher share of renewable energy requires more conventional thermal power generation as a backup capacity and a low load factor means fuel savings would be limited. It is also due to the fact that the higher costs of renewable energy have negative impacts on the competitiveness of the economy. Kim et al. (2011), however, has pointed out the maximum nuclear scenario will not be able to stabilize the GHG emissions path of South Korea. In addition, the feasibility of maximum nuclear share in South Korea, as in other parts of the world as well, will be increasingly uncertain with the evolving influence of civil society debates over the future of nuclear power and the nuclear fuel cycle and waste treatment.

3.5.3 Institutional and market structure issues

Moe (2012) discusses how the vested interests of stakeholders in the energy market could shape the paths of developments in renewable energy and energy efficiency. In the Japanese case, the solar industry has been far more preferred by insiders of the market than wind. This has made it far harder for the wind industry to rise than for solar in Japan. As energy efficiency technologies are not in the way of the interests of insiders and not challenging any vested interest structure, they are a favored approach for over three decades in the economy.

3.6 Affordability

3.6.1 Costs of non-renewable energy

The patterns of costs of non-renewable energy to Asian economies have been fragmented, so do markets for non-renewable energy in this part of the world. The costs of importing non-renewable energy to a certain Asian economy are usually higher than other parts of the world as shown in Figures 13.15 and 13.16. However, these prices seem to apply only to the portion that is acquired from the spot market. To ensure energy security, major Asian economies have been building up overseas non-renewable energy production capacities or shares in foreign supply capacities for decades, with prices secured at different levels in the long-term supply contracts of different natures. Such is especially true for coal and natural gas imported to the region. Fragmented

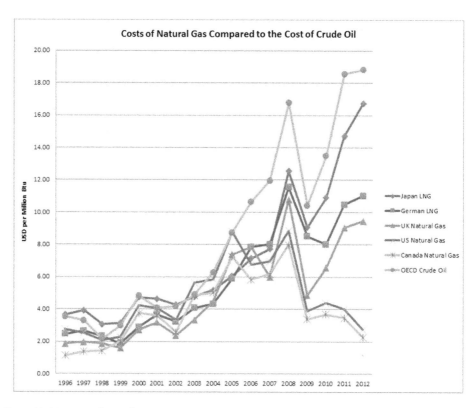

Figure 13.15 Cost of natural gas in various markets of the world compared to the cost of crude oil

Source: BP World Energy Statistical Review 2013.

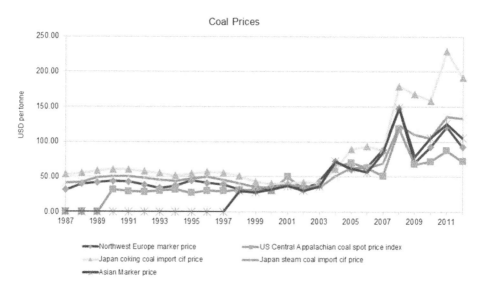

Figure 13.16 Cost of coal in various markets of the world

Source: BP World Energy Statistical Review 2013.

markets for non-renewable energy in the region may benefit individual economies in the short run but in the long run it means low energy security and unstable costs of energy. In the natural gas market of the region, the so-called Asian premium is one of the negative results of the fragmented markets (Chang and Li, 2014; Davoust, 2008).

At the same time, when it comes to final consumption of non-renewable energy, especially in the form of refined products, most Asian economies provide subsidies out of concern for social equity (such as India, Malaysia, Thailand and Indonesia) or the purpose of promoting competitiveness of domestic industries (such as China). As a side effect, these subsidies encourage the use of energy in inefficient ways.

3.6.2 The cost of renewable energy

Park et al. (2013) estimated that for South Korea to achieve 80 percent lower emissions than the 2008 level by 2050 in the power generation sector, the economy has to invest heavily in renewable energy and assume up to 20 percent higher costs of electricity. This result assumes that the economy will gradually phase out nuclear power against the current government's plan to have nuclear contributing some 22 percent of power supply by 2035.[6]

After the Fukushima accident in March 2011, the Japanese government has been considering four possible future energy mixes, including a nuclear-free pathway, and three others with 10 percent to 35 percent nuclear supply coupled with a larger proportion of renewable energy and fossil fuels to replace nuclear energy. According to Hong et al. (2011a) that applies a multi-criteria decision-making analysis, the nuclear-free pathway is estimated to be the most costly choice to Japan in terms of economic costs, environmental costs, and social costs.

Renewable energy also has the potential to help developing Asian economies to relieve their future energy sustainability. Nguyen and Ha-Duong (2009) show that in the case of Vietnam, the economy, which currently relies mainly on natural gas (39 percent), hydropower (37 percent), and coal (16 percent), will turn into mainly relying on coal (44 percent) followed by natural gas by 2030 in the power generation sector as demand for electricity will increase significantly. However, if renewable energy technologies such as small hydro, geothermal, and thermal biomass are adopted, Vietnam can reduce the share of coal in the future by 5 percent, reduce the total discounted cost of electricity by 2.6 percent (which is a surprising result), reduce total CO_2 emissions by 8 percent, and reduce the future imports of coal and natural gas. However, wind energy will have a very limited application in the economy despite its more than 125GW of technical potential, and grid-connected solar will never be adopted, even by 2030.

Hippel et al. (2011a) and Thavasi and Ramakrishna (2009) emphasize the importance of market structure liberalization in the energy sector of Asian economies. It will not only improve efficiency and minimize the costs of energy but also attract enough financial investment into the sector to expand the energy infrastructure.

4. Policy implications

4.1 The future of energy supply and demand

Zhang et al. (2011) provide a comprehensive review on the demand and supply of energy in China, as well as of the country's sustainable development strategy and policies. The energy situation of the country currently can be summarized in five points. First, per capita consumption level is low compared to developed economies. Second, energy consumption grows rapidly but is expected to stabilize around 2050 with low energy efficiency. Third, coal dominates in primary energy mix as the Chinese government constantly emphasizes reliance on domestic energy resources. Fourth, despite the government's self-reliance energy policy, dependence on imported energy, especially oil and natural gas, has been increasing over time. Fifth, energy consumption leads to severe environmental pollution and causes multiple types of economic losses. It is estimated that air pollution by fossil fuels alone causes losses for about 2 to 3 percent of GDP in the short-run. No long-run damages estimation is available yet. Toward sustainability, the Chinese government has taken measures such as legislation for energy conservation and renewable energy development; shutting down low-efficiency small plants in the energy-intensive industries; further raising vehicle fuel efficiency standards; building efficiency public transportation systems and railway transport systems; improving fleet management; giving incentives to alternative fuel and hybrid vehicles; imposing energy consumption taxes; augmenting energy savings regulations and standards; improving public energy saving awareness; providing energy conservation information; and tax recessions for energy saving products, technologies, and equipment. For the promotion of renewable energy, especially solar and wind, the high cost, intermittency of generation, grid connection, and lagging behind in relevant technologies are the main barriers. The government also in recent years prioritized the development of nuclear power, although there were interruptions and delay due to the Fukushima accident in 2011. The challenges to it mainly include public awareness and acceptance, lagging behind in relevant technologies, and lack of nuclear waste treatment and processing capacities.

Fan and Xia (2012) find that energy input mix, industry structure, and technological improvements are the main factors in China that drive its energy consumption. Based on such results, it is forecasted that the country's energy consumption by 2020 could be reduced by as much as 15 percent by optimizing the aforementioned three major factors.

China's policymakers are putting a new emphasis on energy efficiency, conservation, renewable energy, and the shift toward natural gas as the principle primary energy source in the place of coal and oil (Cao and Bluth, 2013).

Specifically regarding China's energy efficiency policies, Andrews-Speed (2009) noted that the economy needs to address a number of existing constraints, which include the reluctance to use economic and financial instruments but instead rely on industrial and social policies, the nature of political decision-making and of public administration, a shortage of technical skills to improve energy efficiency, and social attitudes toward energy.

In less developed economies such as Vietnam, the government is also suggested to shift to market-based energy pricing and remove energy subsidies. In devising energy efficiency policies, the government is reminded to look into both demand side and supply side energy efficiency, while keeping in mind the importance of cross-sectoral opportunities of energy savings (Do and Sharma, 2011).

4.2 Technology and economic structure

On the demand side, Asian economies should put emphasis on the development and adoption of energy efficiency technologies in the process of energy consumption. Although eventually thermal dynamics sets limit to how far energy efficiency can go (the minimum energy requirement for processes of production and services activities) and the marginal return to further R&D to improve energy efficiency of a certain energy use process could decline, the opportunities existing in the numerous processes in various sectors of an economy seem endless.

On the supply side, Asian economies have to look into clean coal technologies, unconventional oil and gas technologies, renewable energy technologies, and nuclear technologies simultaneously, as each of these tracks have embedded uncertainty in terms of how soon the technologies will break through and how much potential these technologies will have. Policies should weigh the relative costs of these technologies, including economic costs, environmental costs, and social costs.

India is a typical low-income developing economy. Its per capita energy consumption is among the lowest in the world, only about one-third of China's and one-fifteenth of the US's. During 2004–2005, India had about 70 million people who do not have access to electricity. Economies like India usually provide substantial subsidies to energy, especially fossil fuels, and the removal of them is politically difficult. In the case of India, diesel, coal, and electricity are all subsidized and the prices of them are lower than the cost of production (Parikh, 2012). Such subsidies encourage inefficient use of energy. Ideally, the fund for subsidies should have been used to financially support the development and diffusion of energy conservation technologies and products and renewable energy supply.

5. Conclusions

In this chapter, the demand and supply trends of non-renewable resources, especially non-renewable energy in major Asian economies, have been reviewed. The discussion focuses on the sustainability of Asian economies' production and consumption of nonrenewable energy by deriving a four dimensional analytical framework – the 4As – based on the implications of theoretical Hotelling models. The framework aims at practically and comprehensively reviewing factors that determine sustainability of non-renewable energy production and consumption in Asian economies.

Asian economies face many challenges in the future sustainability of the production and consumption of energy, especially non-renewable energy. First, most Asian economies are developing economies and, therefore, expect high growth in energy demand as industrialization, urbanization, wealth and income levels, and standard of living all improves while population keeps expanding. Second, more economies will change from net non-renewable energy exporters into net importers and, therefore, dependence on imported non-renewable energy is expected to increase steadily. Third, additional exploitable energy resources are unevenly distributed, especially in the areas remote from the centers of energy consumption. International cooperation is increasing demanded so as to provide proper financial and technological means for the host country to exploit the resource and subsequently move it to consumption centers in neighboring countries. Fourth, as shale oil and shale gas are still to be proven in this part of the world and with abundant coal reserves, Asian economies inevitably will increase the consumption of coal in absolute terms, although the share of coal may decrease; therefore, clean coal technologies should be given priority. Fifth, renewable energy resources gradually will be developed in the region, but they will play a limited role. Sixth, economies with existing nuclear power capacities still have strong willingness to increase the amount and share of nuclear power in their energy mix, while others are actively preparing for the adoption of nuclear power, despite the setback due to the Fukushima accident. Nuclear safety networks and international cooperation/mechanisms in nuclear information exchange, experience sharing, and technology diffusion should be established. Seventh, domestic energy market reforms and other measures to manage energy demand and energy efficiency also should be emphasized, as there is substantial room for energy conservation in most Asian economies. Last but not least, concerns about the environmental impacts of non-renewable energy production and consumption have been rising but no internationally binding mechanisms are at work in the region to contain GHG emissions and other environmental problems. In other words, the production and consumption of non-renewable energy are not properly priced without including negative externality on the environment. International cooperation also is needed in this regard.

In sum, while progress in energy production and consumption technologies, including backstop energy technologies, is expected to relieve energy sustainability and security concerns in the long term, in the short term policies still have a lot do to improve energy efficiency, reform the energy sector, ensure adequate investment into energy infrastructure, and drive for regional cooperation in energy market integration, infrastructure investment, and infrastructure connectivity.

Notes

1 Yao and Chang (2014) have applied the 4As framework to examine energy security in China.
2 If the marginal cost of extraction is independent of the rate of extraction and invariant over time, then resource price will grow at a rate that tends toward the rate of interest as the share of cost in resource price gets smaller and smaller over time.
3 At the Fukushima nuclear power plant, 10 GW of nuclear generating capacity or more than 20 percent of present nuclear generating capacity (about 49 GW) is offline. In addition, with 42 of Japan's 54 reactors offline for maintenance, disaster repairs or safety problems, another 60 percent of nuclear generating capacity is currently down (Moe, 2012).
4 The study applies a material flow accounting method, using domestic extraction data only.
5 Membership of the EAS comprises the ten ASEAN countries (Brunei, Cambodia, Indonesia, Laos, Malaysia, Myanmar, the Philippines, Singapore, Thailand, Vietnam), Australia, China, India, Japan, New Zealand, the Republic of Korea, the United States, and Russia.
6 According to the *Wall Street Journal*, Oct. 15, 2013.

References

Andrews-Speed, P. 2009. China's ongoing energy efficiency drive: Origins, progress and prospects. *Energy Policy*, 37, pp. 1331–1344.

Barnett, H. J. and C. Morse. 1963. *Scarcity and Growth: The Economics of Natural Resource Availability.* Baltimore, MD: Johns Hopkins University Press for Resources for the Future.

Behrens, A., S. Giljum, J. Kovanda, and S. Niza. 2007. The material basis of the global economy – Worldwide patterns of natural resource extraction and their implications for sustainable resource use policies. *Ecological Economics*, 64, pp. 444–453.

Cao, W., and C. Bluth. 2013. Challenges and countermeasures of China's energy security. *Energy Policy*, 53, pp. 381–388.

Chang, Y. and Y. Li. 2013a. Power generation and cross-border grid planning for the integrated ASEAN electricity market: A dynamic linear programming model. *Energy Strategy Reviews*, 2(2), pp. 153–160.

Chang, Y. and Y. Li. 2013b. Renewable Energy and Policy Options in an Integrated ASEAN Electricity Market: Quantitative Assessments and Policy Implications. In F. Kimura, H. Phoumin, and B. Jacobs (Eds.), *Energy Market Integration in East Asia: Renewable Energy and Its Deployment into the Power System*, ERIA Research Project Report 2012, No. 26., Jakarta.

Chang, Y.H. and Y. Li. 2013c. Rapid Growth at What Cost? Impact of Energy Efficiency Policies in Developing Economies. In F. P. Sioshansi (Eds.), *Energy Efficiency: Towards the End of Demand Growth*, 227–250. Oxford and Waltham: Elsevier.

Chang, Y.H. and Y. Li. 2014. Towards An Integrated Asia-Pacific Natural Gas Market. In Y. Wu, F. Kimura, and X. Shi (Eds.), *Energy Market Integration in East Asia: Deepening Understanding and Moving Forward*, 163–187. Jakarta: Routledge-ERIA Studies in Development Economics.

Chang, Y.H. and J.Y. Yong 2007. Differing perspectives of major oil firms on future energy developments: An illustrative framework. *Energy Policy,* 35(11), pp. 5466–5480.

Chen, W. and R. Xu. 2010. Clean coal technology development in China. *Energy Policy*, 38, pp. 2123–2130.

Davoust, R. 2008. Gas price formation, structure and dynamics. Institut Francais des Relations Internationales, Working Paper, IFRI, Paris.

Do, T. M. and D. Sharma. 2011. Vietnam's energy sector: A review of current energy policies and strategies. *Energy Policy*, 39, pp. 5770–5777.

Duffield, J. S. and B. Woodall. 2011. Japan's new basic energy plan. *Energy Policy*, 39, pp. 3741–3749.

Economic Research Institute for ASEAN and East Asia (ERIA). 2013. Analysis on Energy Saving Potential in East Asia. Edited by S. Kimura. ERIA Research Project Report 2012, No. 19, ERIA, Jakarta Pusat, Indonesia.

Fan, Y. and Y. Xia. 2012. Exploring Energy Consumption and Demand in China. *Energy*, 40(1), pp. 23–30.

Farzin, Y. H. 1992. The Effect of the Discount Rate on Depletion of Exhaustible Resources. *Journal of Political Economy*, 92(5), pp. 841–851.

Gaudet, G. 2007. Natural resource economics under the rule of Hotelling. *Canadian Journal of Economics*, 40(4), pp. 1033–1059.

Heal, Geoffrey M. 1976. The relationship be-tween price and extraction cost for a resource with a backstop technology. *Bell Journal of Economics*, 7(2), pp. 371–378.

Hippel, D. Von, T. Savage, and P. Hayes. 2011a. Overview of the Northeast Asia energy situation. *Energy Policy*, 39, pp. 6703–6711.

Hippel, D. Von, T. Suzuki, J. H. Williams, T. Savage, and P. Hayes. 2011b. Energy security and sustainability in Northeast Asia. *Energy Policy*, 39, pp. 6719–6730.

Hippel, D. Von, R. Gulidov, V. Kalashnikov, and P. Hayes. 2011c. Northeast Asia regional energy infrastructure proposals. *Energy Policy*, 39, pp. 6855–6866.

Hong, S., C. J. A. Bradshaw, and B. W. Brook. 2013a. Evaluating options for the future energy mix of Japan after the Fukushima nuclear crisis. *Energy Policy*, 56, pp. 418–424.

Hong, S., C. J. A. Bradshaw, and B. W. Brook. 2013b. Evaluating options for sustainable energy mixes in South Korea using scenario analysis. *Energy*, 52, pp. 237–244.

Hotelling H. 1931. The economics of exhaustible resources. *Journal of Political Economy*, 39, pp. 137–175.

Katsuta, T., and T. Suzuki. 2011. Japan's spent fuel and plutonium management challenge. *Energy Policy*, 39, pp. 6827–6841.

Kessides, I. N. 2012. The future of the nuclear industry reconsidered: Risks, uncertainties and continued promise. *Energy Policy*, 48, pp. 185–208.

Kim, H., E. Shin, and W. Chung. 2011. Energy demand and supply, energy policies, and energy security in the Republic of Korea. *Energy Policy*, 39, pp. 6882–6897.

Klare, M.T. 2008. The new geopolitics of energy. *The Nation*, May 19, 2008.

Krautkraemer, J. A. 1998. Nonrenewable resource scarcity. *Journal of Economic Literature*, 36(4), pp. 2065–2107.

Kruyt, B., D.P.V. Vuuren, H.M. J De Vries, and H. Groenenberg. 2009. Indicators for energy security. *Energy Policy*, 37(6), pp. 2166–2181.

Lewis, T.R. 1976. Monopoly exploitation of an exhaustible resource. *Journal of Environment Economics Management*, 3(3), pp. 198–204.

Lund, H. 2007. Renewable energy strategies for sustainable development. *Energy*, 32(6), pp. 912–919

McLellan, B. C., Q. Zhang, N. A.. Utama, H. Farzaneh, and K. N. Ishihara. 2013. Analysis of Japan's post-Fukushima energy strategy. *Energy Strategy Reviews*, 2, pp. 190–198.

Moe, E. 2012. Vested interests, energy efficiency and renewables in Japan. *Energy Policy*, 40, pp. 260–273.

Mohr, S. H. and G. M. Evans. 2010. Long term prediction of unconventional oil production. *Energy Policy*, 38, pp. 265–276.

Nguyen, N. T. and M. Ha-Doung. 2009. Economic potential of renewable energy in Vietnam's power sector. *Energy Policy*, 37, pp. 1601–1613.

Nordhaus, W.D., H. Houthakker and R. Solow. 1973. The allocation of energy resources. *Brookings Paper on Economic Activity,* (3), pp. 529–576.

Nordhaus, W.D. 1979. *The Efficient Use of Energy Resources*. New Haven: Yale University Press.

Park, N., S. Yun, and E. Jeon. 2013. An analysis of long-term scenarios for the transition to renewable energy in the Korean electricity sector. *Energy Policy*, 52, pp. 288–296.

Parikh, K. 2012. Sustainable development and low carbon growth strategy for India. *Energy*, 40, pp. 31–38.

Pindyck, R.S. 1978a. Gains to Producers from the Cartelization of Exhaustible Resources. *Review of Economics Statistics,* 60(2), pp. 238–251.

Pindyck, R.S. 1978b. Optimal Exploration and Production of Nonrenewable Resources. *Journal of Political Economics*, 86(5), pp. 841–861.

Schmalensee, R. 1976. Resource exploitation theory and the behavior of the oil cartel. *European Economics Review*, 7(3), pp. 257–279.

Slade, M. E. 1988. Grade selection under uncertainty: least cost last and other anomalies, *Journal of Environmental Economics and Management*, 15(2), pp. 189–205.

Sultan, N. 2013. The challenge of shale to the post-oil dreams of the Arab Gulf. *Energy Policy*, 60, pp. 13–20.

Swierzbinski, J. E. and R. Mendelsohn. 1989. Information and exhaustible re-sources: A Bayesian analysis. *Journal of Environmental Economics and Management*, 16(3), pp. 193–208.

Thavasi, V., and S. Ramakrishna. 2009. Asia energy mixes from socio-economic and environmental perspectives. *Energy Policy*, 37, pp. 4240–4250.

World Energy Council. 2012a. *World energy perspective: Nuclear energy one year after Fukushima.* London: World Energy Council.

World Energy Council. 2012b. *Survey of energy resources: shale gas – What's new.* London: World Energy Council.

Yao, L. and Y. Chang. 2014. Energy security in China: A quantitative analysis and policy implications. *Energy Policy*, 67, pp. 595–604.

Zhang, N., N. Lior, and H. Jin. 2011. The energy situation and its sustainable development strategy in China. *Energy*, 36, pp. 3639–3649.

14

MEASURING SUSTAINABLE DEVELOPMENT IN ASIA

Masayuki Sato

1. Introduction

Sustainable development is one of the most important concepts in discussing society's future. In the economic literature, this concept was introduced in the 1970s, then gradually became a key concept following the publication of the Rome Club's seminal report "Limits to Growth" (Meadows et al. 1972) and the double oil shocks in 1973 and 1979. The seminal definition of sustainable development was provided by the Brundtland report (World Commission on Environment and Development, 1987). This report defines sustainable development as "development that meets the needs of the present without compromising the ability of future generations to meet their own needs." Subsequently, many researchers have examined whether or not modern society is sustainable from economic, social, and environmental perspectives.

The data presented in existing research confirms the risk of failure to realize both global and local sustainable development due to resource depreciation and environmental destruction. This is also true in Asian countries. By International Monetary Fund statistics (IMF, 2013), Asian countries experienced quite rapid economic growth after World War II and now produce more than 28 percent of the world's GDP.

In realizing this rapid growth, Asian countries have consumed incredible amounts of resources and emitted a substantial amount of pollutants, including greenhouse gases (GHGs), NO_x, and SO_x. For example, Japan experienced environmental public hazard in the 1960–1970s and China now suffers from serious air pollution. These problems stem from both counties' pursuit of heavy economic activities without considering their effects on either human health or the environment. Furthermore, the demographic situation currently is changing to that of a mature society, i.e., from a population growth period to a period of stabilization or decrease. Although Asia's population is expected to continue to grow until 2050, the productive population rate is expected to show an earlier decline and Japan's already has started to slow (Figure 14.2).

This combination of environmental destruction, resource depreciation, and population structural change (aging society) leaves many people doubting whether or not past economic growth can be sustained. In this sense, many Asian societies confront barriers to achieving economic growth in the traditional way. Instead, a new growth path needs to be forged that can sustain the quality of life per capita for the future by managing our limited productive base.

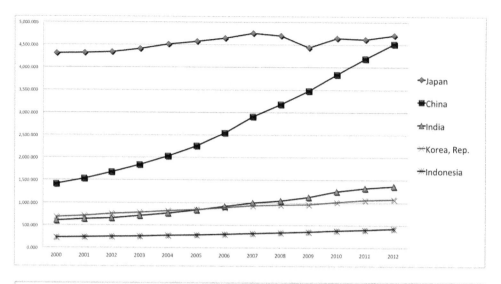

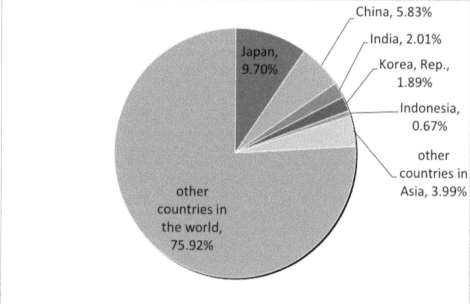

Figure 14.1 GDP in Asia

Source: World Development Indicators.

To monitor the level of each country's sustainability, many indicators have been developed (see Bell and Morse 2008, Stiglitz et al. 2010). Among others, the capital approach introduced by Pearce and Atkinson (1993) for assessing sustainability is attractive due to its well-defined economic theoretical foundations (Arrow et al. 2003). So far, genuine savings (GS) indicators and the Inclusive Wealth Index (IWI) are noted for having both theoretical and empirical proof. In addition, both focus on the change of existing sources (capital stocks) for producing well-being. If the change is non-negative (non-decreasing), the development path can be judged to be

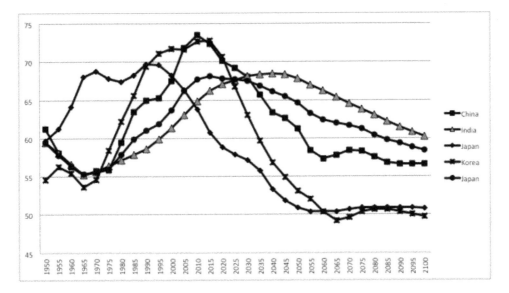

Figure 14.2 Forecasted productive population rate

Source: World Population Prospects.

sustainable. In this chapter, we review the essence of the economic way to assess sustainability mainly with the capital approach.

2. Theoretical framework for assessing sustainability

Arrow et al. (2003) describe this concept of sustainability as a situation leading to non-declining well-being in the future. In this meaning, inclusive wealth (*W*), which is the source of welfare, must be maintained at all points of time. Formally, sustainable development requires

$$V_t = \int_t^\infty U(C_t)e^{-\delta(\tau-t)}d\tau$$

$$\text{and } \frac{dV}{dt} \geq 0 \quad \text{for all } t$$

(1)

where *V*, *U*, *C*, and δ are the well-being function, instantaneous well-being, consumption, and the discount rate, respectively.

As Arrow et al. (2003) suggest, the LHS of Eq. (1) is equal to inclusive wealth under some assumptions, so we can re-write Eq. (1) using vector of capitals as follows:

$$V_t = V(K_t, M, t)$$

(2)

where *K* represents the vector of capital including man-made, human, natural, and other possible capital contributing to production of well-being, and *M* represents institution or other political variables relating to the existing resource allocation mechanism.

Then, as summarized in United Nations University International Human Dimensions Programme on Global Environmental Change and United Nations Environmental Programme

(UNU-IHDP and UNEP 2012), the shadow price of each capital (p_i) can be defined by the marginal contribution of each capital to social well-being:

$$P_K = \frac{\partial V_t}{\partial K} \tag{3}$$

From the total differentiation of (2) and (3), we obtain

$$\frac{dV_t}{dt} = pdK_t + \frac{\partial V}{\partial t} \tag{4}$$

This is the theoretical background of the indicator that focuses on changes of inclusive wealth. It is noteworthy that the term "well-being" is used here for interpreting the definition offered by the Brundtland report. This broader concept includes elements that cannot be incorporated into concepts of "utility" or "welfare" used traditionally in economics, i.e., non-welfare elements such as freedom, fairness, rights, personal conditions, etc. So the formulation presented in this paper includes not only consumption of goods but also other goods/services, e.g., environmental functions, ecosystem services, amenities, or other political and civil matters. Assuming that sustainability should focus more on well-being than welfare, it is clear that utilitarian optimization or market-oriented valuation cannot satisfy sustainability's requirements. Hence for the purposes of economic analysis, considering valuation of non-market goods/services becomes necessary. Basically, the indicator requires measuring the amount of existing capital stock, estimating accounting prices, and calculating total factor productivity (TFP) as a proxy of time capital.

In summary, the capital approach focuses on changes in inclusive wealth, which is calculated as sum of all capitals. If we simply exclude time capital, inclusive wealth is then composed of man-made capital (*KM*), human capital (*KH*), and natural capital (*KN*) evaluated by each's shadow price.

$$W_t = KM_t + KH_t + KN_t \tag{5}$$

Then, the indicator is provided by the time differentiation of Eq. (5) as

$$\frac{dW_t}{dt} = \frac{dKM_t}{dt} + \frac{dKH_t}{dt} + \frac{dKN_t}{dt} \tag{6}$$

Only if the sign of Eq. (6) is non-negative can the development path be considered sustainable. Based on this economic theoretical model, some indicators for assessing sustainability are provided. In the next section, we review a typical sustainability indicator based on capital approach.

3. Database for conducting empirical research

One of the richest current databases is offered by the World Bank under the title "World Development Indicators." A total of 208 countries and regions are included in the database, as well as useful data corresponding to changes in man-made, human, and natural capital.

In this database, adjusted net savings (ANS) is provided as an alias name of genuine savings. Some interesting cases of the ANS path in Asia and other countries are shown in Figure 14.3.

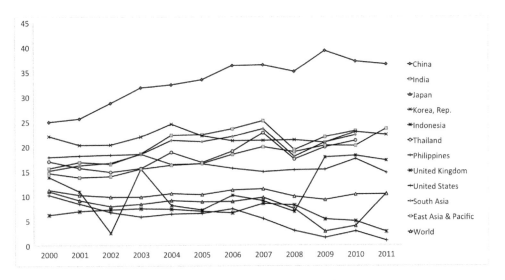

Figure 14.3 Paths of the sustainability indicators (ANS) in Asia and other countries

Source: World Development Indicators

The GS paths show historical transition toward positive numbers, i.e., the sustainable development path. However, they display high volatility, and some countries have a negative trend. Beginning with the case of China, most paths are led by economic factors (man-made capital accumulation). So the revealed pattern doesn't change if we consider human or natural capital perspectives. In addition, this instability can be thought as resulting from a failure to manage the balance between economic development and environmental conservation. Therefore, a policy that stabilizes the GS path is important for countries' future sustainability. We will discuss this trend and the instability of GS paths in Section 4.

First, however, we discuss the limits and the data. This database measures man-made capital change by net national savings and measures human capital by education expenditure. Excluding man-made capital, as Dasgupta (2004) points out, this measures still underestimates human capital because other important factors of human capital formulation, such as health, are omitted. Hence, the IWI approach tries to incorporate health capital by considering the statistical value of life. However, it is considered that more research and data are needed to accurately measure human capital in order to make a better indicator for assessing sustainability.

More serious problems arise when discussing natural capital. First, this indicator includes only changes of forest areas, mineral resource depletion, energy depletion, and damage caused by CO_2 emissions. Furthermore, their shadow prices are approximated by market rents or other exogenous values (such as 1t = $20 as a shadow price of CO_2 emissions). So the database needs to be expanded to reflect both estimations of the amounts of capital and valuations of their shadow prices.

To summarize, three approaches exist to improve the utility and accuracy of research on sustainability assessment. The first approach involves trying to refine the measurement of each capital with exact shadow prices. This includes the following points:

1. Expanding the definition of human capital by including health and that of natural capital by including ecosystems, fisheries resources, land resources, air and water quality, etc. The

project of UNU-IHDP and UNEP is attempting to consider the health component as incorporating human capital and to expand natural capital to include fishery resources and land use. The biggest hurdle likely lies in data availability. Accordingly, the numerical methodology called multiple imputation should be helpful in building a broader dataset for sustainability assessment (Yang et al. 2013).

2. Improving aggregation methods. The main problems involved in this factor include methods of handling global public goods/bads such as CO_2 emissions and how to escape from double-counting. The UNU-IHDP and UNEP follow good practice in that global public bads are aggregated once globally then distributed proportionally to each country.

3. Estimating more precisely the shadow price of each capital input. This relates to the discussion on environmental valuation and benefit transfer.[1] Some elaborate techniques for environmental valuation have been developed (Willis and Garrod 2012). We need to collect the valid shadow price from the valuation research, then apply it to the sustainability indicator. In such an undertaking, valuation databases such as ENVALUE or EVRI and the benefit transfer methodology should be helpful. By using more appropriately estimated shadow price, the sustainability indicator obtains more reliability.

The second approach involves further enhancing existing empirical analysis using available data. Such an undertaking could mean including temporal and spatial aspects. Temporal aspects concern the shape of the indicator's path. Spatial aspects concern relationships among countries. The third approach involves bringing forward discussions of sustainability with reference to the related issues of subjective well-being, social institutions, and policy making.

In the next section, we review the discussions on the second and third approach with some empirical studies. Temporal aspects, spatial aspects and institutional/political aspects are discussed in Sections 4.1, 4.2, 4.3, respectively.

4. Empirical analyses

4.1 Sustainable development path in each country

As shown in Figure 14.1, indicator paths have varied shapes. To confirm this, Table 14.1 summarizes the average, deviation, and trend of paths during the period 1981–2005.

Table 14.1 Indicator paths' characteristics in Asia

Country	Average	Deviation	Trend
China	18.12948568	11.21464544	1.683514563
India	11.32800602	2.328848929	0.566153731
Japan	17.34013266	2.575427649	–0.258759392
Korea Rep.	23.99937988	2.390863117	0.234857874
Pakistan	10.33226292	4.289243534	–0.32951054
Indonesia	13.07099096	19.94180276	–1.008322257
Thailand	20.83410224	3.428544385	0.103868911
United Kingdom	7.333790215	1.27110724	0.044849184
United States	7.421785933	1.275008975	–0.147388046

Source: Sato and Samreth (2008)

Sato et al. (2012) focus on the risk of violating sustainability conditions, meaning their analyses include the effect of volatility. They calculate the following AR(1) process:

$$GS_{t,i} = const_i + \beta GS_{t-1,i} + \varepsilon_i, \tag{7}$$

where $\varepsilon \sim (0, \sigma^2)$ is a normally distributed random term and i is the country index. Then, by projecting the future path for 50 years using this estimated volatility, the probability of the indicator having a negative sign can be calculated. The main results are presented in Table 14.2.

In East and Southeast Asia, the GS of all three countries selected for our study is sustainable. Our findings are consistent with Hamilton and Clemens (1999). However, it is worth noting that even though our estimated result for China shows a moderately high probability of a future negative GS rate, the average time before its initial onset exceeds 200 years. From this result, we can argue that China's GS is likely to satisfy sustainable criteria for the foreseeable future. However, China may need policies that make its GS path less volatile. In South Asia, Hamilton and Clemens (1999) judged Bangladesh and Nepal to be unsustainable, while Arrow et al. (2004) judged them to be sustainable. Our analysis concurs with Hamilton and Clemens (1999), with the results indicating that Bangladesh has a high probability of facing a negative GS rate; however, we differ from Hamilton and Clemens (1999), as well as from Arrow et al. (2004), with regard to the case of Nepal. For India, our result is consistent with both previous studies. However, for the case of Pakistan, our result once again differed from that of previous studies; although they judged Pakistan's GS to be sustainable, our analysis indicates that this may not be the case. From this comparison, the importance of taking into account the shape of temporal path is confirmed. In using a sustainability indicator, the consideration of the shape of historical path is required.

4.2 Relationships between countries: a case of Japan

Unlike the countries whose results we presented above, we cannot confirm the results of a positive sign for Japan at an acceptable degree of certainty. Several reasons contribute to this lack of certainty. Sato et al. (2010) point out that 1) many resource-rich countries show very poor performance and Asian countries depend particularly highly on such natural resources; and 2) previous economic performance was supported by rapid manmade capital accumulation; however, it is unclear whether or not the same growth rate can be maintained.

The first point suggests that under the globalization, we cannot focus on only one country or region when considering sustainability. We need to analyze sustainability across the entire globe as a whole. Many researchers, including Asheim (1996), Hartwick (1995), and Proops and Atkinson (1998), pay attention to the presence of an open economy and international trade. Many high-GS-performance countries depend upon the importation of natural resources, many of which are judged as being "unsustainable" by the same indicator. Such unsustainability stems from serious natural capital depreciation. Atkinson and Hamilton (2002) use an input-output framework to analyze natural resource depletion and the developed countries importing these resources and insist that resource importers should offer assist to resource exporters. This claim should most certainly apply to the case of Japan. Almost all its oil, natural gas, and mineral resource are imported, meaning Japan depends a great deal on foreign forest resources even though Japan itself is heavily forested.

The second point suggests that when the economic growth slows down, maintaining a positive indicator becomes difficult. This raises the question of the appropriate shadow price for man-made, human, and natural capital. Previous studies and data may over-emphasize the

Table 14.2 Some comparisons of previous studies considering path shape

Country	(1) Hamilton and Clemens (1999) GS as percent of GNP	(2) Arrow et al. (2004) GS as percent of GDP	(3) This study						
			Estimated results of AR(1) process			Steady state GS rate	Simulation results		
			constant	β	St. dev. of ε		Initial condition	% of experiencing negative GS in 50 years	Average years before having negative GS
East Asia and the Pacific									
China	21.5	22.72	0.86(1.19)	0.97(0.06)	4.18	26.38	33.20	0.16	218.81
Japan	26.2		1.10(0.97)	0.92(0.05)	1.50	14.46	15.11	0.00	N.A.
Korea Rep.	29.6		3.27(1.64)	0.86(0.07)	2.49	23.72	22.12	0.00	N.A.
Malaysia	18.6		1.22(1.21)	0.90(0.08)	3.46	11.86	9.18	0.57	62.85
Philippines	8.0		2.89(1.53)	0.83(0.10)	3.33	16.80	21.29	0.05	747.32
Thailand	28.1		2.98(1.75)	0.85(0.09)	2.20	20.07	18.56	0.00	N.A.
South Asia									
Bangladesh	2.4	7.14	1.25(0.80)	0.91(0.08)	3.66	13.56	17.51	0.43	83.72
India	7.2	9.47	0.82(0.93)	0.95(0.09)	1.90	17.23	19.35	0.02	1530.84
Nepal	−12.3	13.31	1.43(0.96)	0.94(0.07)	2.79	24.14	23.03	0.02	2087.60
Pakistan	4.7	8.75	2.12(1.06)	0.76(0.11)	2.90	8.88	2.39	0.56	71.43
Sri Lanka	12.4		5.97(2.10)	0.59(0.14)	3.04	14.70	12.47	0.00	N.A.
Other Countries									
United Kingdom	6.6	7.38	1.62(0.70)	0.78(0.08)	1.29	7.38	1.14	0.01	7253.18
United States	9.6	8.94	1.03(0.92)	0.85(0.10)	1.64	7.06	3.31	0.29	180.39

Source: Sato et al. (2012).

economic aspects. In this regard, we need to re-think how to value both human and natural capital based on the earlier discussion of environmental economic valuations. So far, measurement indicators only have used approximate values such as rent or market price. However, the previous discussion on environmental value suggests that it is larger than its market price due to externalities and its multi-dimensional functions. Therefore, it is possible that countries previously judged as sustainable are in fact not sustainable because their depletion of natural capital is larger than their accumulated man-made capital. Despite this, use of the wrong shadow price means that such a country's inclusive wealth is perceived as having increased.

Based on this idea, Sato et al. (2010) try to find international relationships between Japan and resource-rich countries by identifying co-integration. The long-run relationship between variables can be written as

$$GS_{Japan,t} = 470.79^{**} + 2.67^{*}G_{Japan,t} - 0.50I^{M}_{Low,t} + 90.14^{**}I^{H}_{Low,t} + 1.81^{**}I^{N}_{Low,t}$$

where $\star$ and $\star\star$ represents significance at the 10 percent and 5 percent level, respectively.

The results indicate that the resource-rich, low-GS group have positive coefficients of man-made capital investment (*IMlow*) and natural capital depletion (*INlow*), whereas their human capital investment (*IHlow*) coefficient is negative.

The existence of a co-integration relationship among the variables under consideration also implies the existence of a causal relation between these variables. By using a pairwise Granger causality test, we can confirm the existence of a uni-directional (Granger causality) link running from Japan's GS to the natural capital depletion of the defined resource-rich, low-GS group, and *INlow*. This indicates that Japan's GS has an effect on natural capital depletion in resource-rich countries; for the resource-rich country, this relationship and not the influence of other forms of capital causes its GS to decline. On the other hand, Japan's economy clearly depends on imported natural resources. When global natural resources become scarce and prices increase, Japan's GS also will possibly start to decline. Based on this relationship and its impact on potential future sustainability, judging Japan's sustainability by GS only would yield an incomplete and possibly inaccurate conclusion.

As shown in Table 14.2, most high-income countries are determined to be sustainable based on single value or their average GS value without considering natural capital dependencies among counties. As can be seen from our analysis, the GS of the defined high-GS group does relate to the natural capital of the defined resource-rich, low-GS group.

4.3 Other issues

4.3.1 Time capital

As we confirmed, sustainability is judged by the sign of Eq. (4). Previous studies have focused on the first term of RHS in Eq. (4), i.e., the social value of capital change. However, another term remains, i.e., time capital.

Most studies considering time capital assume TFP as a proxy of the second term of RHS in Eq. (4) (Arrow et al. (2004) and Arrow et al. (2012)). By calculating TFP with inputs (labor and capital) and output (GDP), the TFP growth rate is added to the inclusive wealth change. Sato et al. (2013) improved the calculation of TFP for assessing sustainability by considering inclusive inputs and output by using the Malmquist Index (Table 14.3).

Table 14.3 TFP and sustainability assessment

	GS per GNI (1)	Growth rate of unadjusted genuine wealth (2)	Population Growth Rate (3)	Growth rate of Per capita Genuine wealth (before adjusted TFP) (4)	IW-based TFP Growth rate (5)	Inclusive wealth growth adjusted by IW-based TFP (6)	GDP-based TFP Growth rate (7)	Inclusive wealth growth adjusted by GDP-based TFP (8)
China	15.7264	1.2460	1.3200	-0.0740	9.1296	9.0556	-0.0905	-0.1645
India	10.2321	0.5854	2.0083	-1.4229	1.0627	-0.3602	-0.3871	-1.8100
Japan	19.1053	23.6921	0.5771	23.1150	2.1735	25.2884	0.7033	23.8182
Korea Rep.	22.2910	2.8993	1.1859	1.7134	1.2038	2.9173	0.2017	1.9151
Philippines	15.0021	0.8702	2.3767	-1.5065	0.4109	-1.0956	0.0121	-1.4944
Thailand	19.7857	1.0142	1.6390	-0.6248	7.1610	6.5362	0.1741	-0.4508
United Kingdom	8.3496	1.9964	0.2053	1.7911	2.1913	3.9824	0.1727	1.9637
United States	8.7533	2.3784	1.0556	1.3227	8.3258	9.6485	0.1105	1.4333

Source: Sato et al. (2013)

From this table, we can see the difference between traditional GDP-based TFP and inclusive wealth based-TFP. These differences, in turn, affect judgments of sustainability. Overall, TFP is found to be significantly different among the investigated countries, reflecting their varied levels of technological development and efficiency of resource use. Especially in Asian countries, the selection of a TFP measurement is crucial to sustainability assessment outcomes. We can see that the sign of many countries' indicator changes after considering TFP. We should pay attention to the methodology and usage of TFP estimation when considering sustainability.

4.3.2 Institutions

Returning to the discussion of the shape of indicator's path, the issue of what factor stabilizes each country's volatility is interesting. Acemogulu et al. (2003) demonstrated that weak institutions will lead to a high volatility of growth, and Yang (2008) found that by considering ethnic diversity, democracy can be seen to lower growth volatility in ethnically heterogeneous countries. These factors also can be considered important in the context of sustainable development, as institutional variables also may contribute to inclusive wealth changes. Accordingly, we need to consider the possibility that sustainability indicator volatility may be affected by institutions and, therefore, examine both the effect of institutions on GS volatility and the impact of volatility on GS performance by the autoregressive conditional heteroskedasticity in mean:

$$\log(GS_{it}) = c_1 k3 + \beta_1 \sigma_{it}^2 + M_{it}\beta + X_{it}\varphi + \varepsilon_{it}, \tag{8}$$

$$\varepsilon_{it} \sim N(0, \sigma_{it}^2), \tag{9}$$

$$\sigma_{it}^2 = \exp(c_2 + X_{it}K + Z_{it}\gamma) + \phi_1 \sigma_{t-1}^2 + \phi_2 \sigma_{t-2}^2 + \eta_{it}, \tag{10}$$

where GS_{it} represents the transformed genuine savings in country i, σ^2 is the variance of genuine savings reflecting volatility, and t is the time index. M is the vector of the control variables, which appear only in the mean equation. X is the vector of the variables, which are expected to have impacts on both GS and its volatility. For these variables, we mainly focus on institutions (*institution*). The estimation results are given in Table 14.4.

As the result shows, the variable of *institution* contributes both directly and indirectly to the sustainability indicator. This indicates that particular attention should be paid to the indirect contribution of the indicator path's stabilization because Asian countries have relatively large deviations for the indicator (Table 14.1).

5. Conclusion

This chapter reviewed the theoretical framework for assessing sustainability as well as the problems and challenges in conducting empirical analyses. Asian countries are now confronting a new situation; namely, slowing economic development combined with a decreasing productive population. In this situation, the question of how to monitor the sustainability of development is quite important for future economic and environmental policies.

To establish an accurate and reliable indicator for sustainability from an economic perspective, we need to improve theoretical, empirical, and data-gathering research. First, the increasingly strong relationships between Asian countries as a result of active transactions of material and human resources indicate the need to develop an indicator able to capture the interdependency

Table 14.4 Institutions and sustainability indicators

Dependent variable: log(GS)
Sample period: 1984-2008

Independent variables

GS volatility (σ^2)	−0.7988★★★	−0.8140★★★	−0.8486★★★	−0.6972★★★
	(0.2354)	(0.2419)	(0.2384)	(0.2441)
Per capita GDP growth rate (ggdp)	0.1582★★★	0.1864★★★	0.1593★★★	0.1595★★★
	(0.0212)	(0.0221)	(0.0215)	(0.0202)
Age dependency (age_dep)	−0.0540★★★	−0.0703★★★	−0.0475★★★	−0.0569★★★
	(0.0072)	(0.0087)	(0.0076)	(0.0071)
Urban population rate (urban)	−0.1131★★★	−0.1123★★★	−0.1134★★★	−0.1127★★★
	(0.0037)	(0.0050)	(0.0037)	(0.0036)
Institutional factors (institution)	0.0072★★★	0.0071★★★	0.0096★★★	0.0040★★★
	(0.0008)	(0.0008)	(0.0014)	(0.0015)
Inflation rate (inflation)	−0.0001	−0.0001	−0.0001	−0.0001
	(0.0003)	(0.0003)	(0.0003)	(0.0003)
Trade openness (trade)	0.0465★★★	0.0447★★★	0.0673★★★	0.0463★★★
	(0.0020)	(0.0019)	(0.0111)	(0.0020)
Government expenditure (gov_size)	0.0803★★★	0.1191★★★	0.0884★★★	−0.0687
	(0.0175)	(0.0188)	(0.0180)	(0.0540)
(Per capita GDP)★ (institutional factors)		−0.0001★★★		
		(0.0000)		
(Trade openness)★ (institutional factors)			−0.0039★	
			(0.0020)	
(Government expenditure)★ (institutional factors)				0.0268★★★
				(0.0102)
Middle East/North Africa dummy	0.0131★★★	0.0144★★★	0.0117★★★	0.0163★★★
	(0.0038)	(0.0038)	(0.0041)	(0.0041)
Sub-Saharan Africa dummy	−0.0635★★★	−0.0613★★★	−0.0624★★★	−0.0642★★★
	(0.0036)	(0.0038)	(0.0036)	(0.0037)
Constant	0.1326★★★	0.1407★★★	0.1158★★★	0.1514★★★
	(0.0066)	(0.0080)	(0.0104)	(0.0098)

Variance equation

Per capita GDP growth rate (ggdp)	−11.2246★★★	−10.4754★★★	−11.5865★★★	−12.2896★★★
	(1.5099)	(1.4924)	(1.5941)	(1.4802)
Square of per capita GDP growth rate (ggdp^2)	54.2254★★★	51.3985★★★	52.9146★★★	31.1090★★
	(9.4590)	(9.9130)	(9.5697)	(12.6309)
Institutional factors (institution)	−0.3585★★★	−0.2610★★★	−0.3853★★★	−0.3290★★
	(0.0641)	(0.0650)	(0.1195)	(0.1382)

Inflation rate (inflation)	−0.0000	0.0008	−0.0001	0.0007
	(0.0432)	(0.0401)	(0.0460)	(0.0364)
Trade openness (trade)	1.3582***	1.3200***	0.9465	1.4252***
	(0.1903)	(0.1975)	(0.7488)	(0.1972)
Government expend-iture (gov_size)	−1.1285	1.4230	−1.8955	−2.5742
	(1.5732)	(1.6549)	(1.6212)	(4.4807)
(Per capita GDP)*(institutional factors)		−0.0052***		
		(0.0012)		
(Trade openness)*(institutional factors)			0.0793	
			(0.1454)	
(Government expenditure)*(institutional factors)				0.0634
				(0.8687)
Middle East/North Africa dummy	0.1954	−0.0997	0.2832	0.2849
	(0.2634)	(0.2756)	(0.2939)	(0.2931)
Sub-Saharan Africa dummy	0.7247***	0.6311**	0.6959***	0.6881**
	(0.2554)	(0.2493)	(0.2650)	(0.2734)
Constant	−7.0228***	−7.4025***	−6.7813***	−7.0071***
	(0.2562)	(0.2721)	(0.5148)	(0.5963)
σ_{t-1}^2	0.9794***	0.9701***	0.9696***	0.9907***
	(0.0685)	(0.0709)	(0.0704)	(0.0697)
σ_{t-2}^2	0.0290	0.0288	0.0472**	0.0384*
	(0.0213)	(0.0230)	(0.0230)	(0.0214)
Log likelihood	2568.169	2571.747	2569.431	2567.721
Turning point of growth	10.35%	10.19%	10.95%	19.75%
Number of observations	1575.0000	1575.0000	1575.0000	1575.0000

Notes:

1. The numbers in parentheses are standard errors.
2. The asterisks ***, **, and * are 1%, 5%, and 10% of significance levels, respectively.

Source: Sato et al. (2013).

of sustainability in Asia. Second, we need to capture the impact of difficult-to-monitor components such as TFP and institutions. Given the rapid change of technology and systematic institutions in Asia, these components will become increasingly important to realize sustainability. Finally, available databases need to be made richer and capture not just more data but more categories of data. Because sustainability is quite a broad concept, we need not only traditional economic variables but also the other important social and environmental variables collected with a high precision of both measurement and estimation.

Note

1 See also the chapter written by Lindhjem and Tuan in this book.

References

Acemoglu, D., S. Johnson, J. Robinson and Y. Thaicharoen (2003) "Institutional causes, macroeconomic symptoms: volatility, crises and growth," *Journal of Monetary Economics*, 50, pp. 49–123.

Arrow, K., P. Dasgupta, L. Goulder, G. Daily, P. Ehrlich, G. Heal, S. Levin, K.-G. Mäler, S. Schneider, D. Starrett, and B. Walker (2004) "Are we consuming too much?" Journal of Economic Perspectives, 18, pp. 147–172.

Arrow, K., P. Dasgupta, and K.-G. Mäler (2003) "Evaluating Projects and Assessing Sustainable Development in Imperfect Economies," Environmental and Resource Economics, 26, pp. 647–685.

Arrow, K., P. Dasgupta, L. Goulder, K. Munford, and K. Oleson (2012) "Sustainability and the measurement of wealth," *Environment and Development Economics* 17, pp. 317–353.

Atkinson, G. and K. Hamilton (2002) "International trade and the 'ecological balance of payment,'" *Resources Policy*, 28, pp. 27–37.

Asheim, G. B. (1996) "Capital Gains and Net National Product in Open Economies," *Journal of Public Economics*, 59, pp. 419–434.

Bell, S. and S. Morse (2008) *Sustainability Indicators*. London: Earthscan.

Dasgupta, P. (2004) *Human Well-Being and the Natural Environment*. New York: Oxford University Press.

Hamilton, K. and Clemens, M. (1999) "Genuine saving rates in developing countries," *World Bank Economic Review* 13, pp. 333–356.

Hartwick, J. M. (1995) "Constant Consumption Paths in Open Economies with Exhaustible Resources," *Review of International Economics*, 3(3), pp. 275–283.

International Monetary Fund (2013). "World Economic Outlook: a survey by the staff of the International Monetary Fund," IMF, Washington, DC.

Meadows D., J. Randers and D Meadows (1972). *Limits to Growth*. New York: Universe Books.

Pearce, D. W. and G. D. Atkinson (1993) "Capital Theory and the Measurement of Sustainable Development: An Indicator of 'Weak' Sustainability," *Ecological Economics*, 8(2), pp. 103–108.

Proops, J. L. R. and G. Atkinson (1998) "A practical sustainability criterion when there is international trade." In S. Faucheux, M. O'Connor, J. van den Straaten (eds.), *Sustainable Development: Concepts, Rationalities and Strategies,* 169–194. Netherlands: Springer.

Sato, M. and S. Samreth (2008) "Assessing Sustainable Development by Genuine Saving Indicator from Multidimensional Perspectives," MPRA papers, No. 9996, pp. 1–14, Munich University, Germany.

Sato, M., S. Samreth, and K. Sasaki (2013) "The Stability of Sustainable Development Path and Institutions: Evidence from Genuine Savings Indicators", MPRA papers, No. 48983, Munich University, Germany.

Sato, M., S. Samreth and K. Yamada (2012) "A Numerical Study on Assessing Sustainable Development with Future Genuine Savings Simulation," *International Journal of Sustainable Development*, 15(4), pp. 293–312.

Sato, M., S. Samreth and R. Yamaguchi (2010) "Sustainability Dependency under International Relationships: Evidence from Genuine Savings Indicator of Japan," KSI Communications, 006, Kyoto University, Japan.

Stiglitz, J. E., A. Sen and J-P. Fittousi (2010) *Mis-Measuring Our Lives: Why GDP doesn't add up*. New York: The New Press.

UNU-IHDP and UNEP (2012) *Inclusive Wealth Report 2012*. Cambridge: Oxford University Press.

Willis, K. G. and G. Garrod (2012) *Valuing environment and natural resources*. Cheltenham: Edward Elgar.

World Commission on Environment and Development (1987) *Our Common Future*. Oxford: Oxford University Press.

Yang, B. (2008) "Does democracy lower growth volatility? A dynamic panel analysis," *Journal of Macroeconomics*, 30, pp. 562–574.

Yang, J., M. Sato and S. Managi (2013) "National Sustainability Assessment: Measurement of Sustainable Index by Multiple Imputations" mimeo.

15

VALUATION OF ENVIRONMENTAL BENEFITS IN ASIAN COUNTRIES

Suresh Jain, Surender Kumar and Paramjit

1. Introduction

All human activities are dependent on natural resources like forest, land, oceans, rivers, clean air and water and the ecosystem overall. These resources are not utilized sustainably by human beings. The environmental processes provide inputs to the production of goods and services in terms of raw material and also act as sinks for waste and emissions. Environmental resources also have values beyond direct use for various purposes. For example, some resources have value due to cultural or scientific reasons and, sometimes, religious values. Thus, we have to manage all the natural resources and the environment for long-term sustainability for its survival and best use over time.

It is widely accepted that unregulated production and consumption can damage the quality of environmental resources and makes the sustenance of economic development questionable. For these reasons, we must manage the natural environment in ways to safeguard its survival. All the qualitative and quantitative aspects of sustainable development cannot be optimized concurrently in all states. Therefore, any development effort must overcome a continuous and dynamic configuration of the trade-offs. Assessing the appropriate choice in the face of these trade-offs will require knowledge of the benefits and costs involved in alternative decisions. This is important to decide who should use ecological resources how, where and when. Assessments must consider the values of the resources and the compatibility of their possible usages. Generally, many ecological resources are not traded in the markets and hence don't have clear prices. As a result, increasing anthropogenic activities are causing damage to environmental resources. This is important in government decision-making, which is directly concerned with the community interest. Progress has been made in defining environmental values and effects, the methodologies for assessing their economic values, and in defining the role of valuation in policymaking. Improving the use of inadequate resources is one of the major tasks facing any decision-maker. Hence, economic valuation is a very important tool for assessing the accurate cost of environmental damage. It is possible to estimate the potential costs and value of the expected benefits from a proposed program, policy or project and reflect trade-offs inherent in another course of action. The values estimated using different valuation processes have been instrumental in the decision-making process and have led to a number of significant and viable outcomes.

Valuation of environmental benefits or damages from various factors such as air pollution or water pollution is important to determine the optimal levels of environmental quality that society should maintain. However, there are no markets for environmental goods, so it is not possible to get price and quantity data and directly estimate the non-market benefits of preserving environmental quality. Although impacts on ecological resources do not have a direct price, that does not mean they do not have value. This makes a difference between two approaches, i.e. financial analysis deals with goods and services traded in markets; whereas, economic analysis contemplates society's welfare. Therefore, one has to assess environmental damage or degradation while considering the concerned peoples' welfare or health damage due to any project activity or intervention.

The rest of the chapter is organized as follows: Section 2 summaries the basic concepts used in the valuation literature. Economic theory of environmental valuation is summarized in Section 3. Section 4 provides a sketch of various valuation methods. The chapter closes in Section 5 with some concluding remarks.

2. Basic concepts

The benefits provided by an environmental good can be classified into two broad categories: use values and non-use values. Use values are those that accumulate from the physical use of environmental resources, such as recreational amenities, observing wildlife or visiting biodiversity parks. The benefits from productive activities such as agriculture, forestry or fisheries also are included in this category. Non-use benefits refer to the benefits individuals may obtain from environmental resources without directly using or visiting them. In a way, the concept of economic value includes use values and non-use values; wherein, a non-use value considers existence, vicarious, option, quasi-option and bequest value as summarized in Table 15.1. Together they constitute the total value of the environmental good.

Use values refer to the value that individuals derive from the physical use of a resource, including commercial use, recreational use and aesthetic use. It is the economic value associated with the *in situ* use of a resource – e.g. through visiting a recreation site or observing wildlife. There are two subcategories of use values: consumptive use benefits (that contribute to resource depletion), e.g. farming, forestry, fishing, grazing and hunting, which deplete the benefits of these environmental benefits available to others; and non-consumptive use benefits, e.g. boating, hiking, viewing of scenic forests etc.

Non-use value (introduced by John Krutilla, 1967) arises because an environmental good has an existence value or preservation value that arises from situations where individuals derive utility

Table 15.1 Environmental resource valuation using economic classification

Total Economic Value				
Use Values			*Non-use Values*	
Direct Use	*Indirect Use*	*Option Value*	*Bequest Value*	*Existence Value*
Outputs directly consumable	Functional benefits	Future direct andindirect values	Use and non-usevalue of environmental legacy	Value from knowledge of continued existence
Food, biomass, recreation, health and Increased living comfort	Flood control, storm protection, nutrient cycles, carbon sequestration	Biodiversity and conserved habitats	Habitats and prevention of irreversible change	Habitats, species, genetic and ecosystem

Source: EFTEC/RIVM 2000.

from environmental resources without physically interacting with those resources. There are several types of non-use benefits:

Quasi-option value benefits: Benefits are derived by maintaining options by avoiding or delaying irreversible actions. This kind of value may be obtained when future technologies or knowledge enhance the value of a natural resource. Another value stems from the combination of the individual's uncertainty about upcoming demand for the resource and uncertainty about its forthcoming availability.

Bequest benefits: The benefit that the present generation gets from conserving the environment for future generations even if individuals are certain they will never demand *in situ* the services provided by the environmental resource.

Existence values: The benefits obtained from the information that an environmental resource exists. In this case, utility would be derived from the mere presence of ecological resources. The conception also may take account of the benefits achieved from knowing that traditionally important resources are protected.

Vicarious value: The benefits obtained from the indirect consumption of an environmental resource through records and other mass media.

Application of an integrated approach to carry out economic analysis for such impacts can capture the hidden costs and benefits of policy options, as well as the concerted effort and institutional economies of scale that may be achieved through complementary policies that support sustainable development. The primary purpose of environmental regulation and pollution control is to increase net benefits to society. That is, the costs of pollution control should, in principle, be weighed against measures of the marginal benefits of pollution control. These benefits may be in the form of reduced morbidity and mortality and hence increased productivity of labour (USEPA, 2010). In general, decisions related to impacts on the environment include benefits and costs, some with monetary values and some without. In an ideal world, judgments are made where the benefits compensate the costs. Wherever environmental resources are affected by the decision, monetary values need to be weighed against non-monetary values.

3. Theory of environmental valuation

Environmental economics generally deals with goods and services that are not traded in the markets whereas the available literature related to valuation is concerned with marketed goods and services. Therefore, the valuation of environmental resources is done on the basis of these methods. A lot of research has taken place in the last half century in this direction.

If the services of the environment could be purchased in a perfectly functioning market then estimating the marginal willingness to pay would be a straightforward problem. This may be the case for some types of consumptive use benefits. But non-consumptive use benefits and non-use benefits are not reflected in market prices. This is because environmental goods have public good characteristics such as non-excludability and non-rivalry in consumption, and markets for these goods would not function well. The public good character of environmental services leads to market failures. And without a market, there are no price and quantity data from which demand relationships can be estimated.

Environmental valuations assume that an individual is the best judge of his own welfare. The changes in environmental quality certainly has an impact on the level of utility an individual is having given his income level and the set of prices. The changes in environmental quality are reflected through his/her preferences, which can be stated in terms of his/her willingness to pay (WTP), i.e. compensation variation (CV) or willingness to accept (WTA), i.e. equivalent variation (EV) or Marshallian measure of consumer surplus. Therefore, the purpose of this section is to provide explanations of these three measures and the difference between them and how they take into account environmental quality changes.

The very concept of externality implies constraints on the behaviour of consumers in addition to budget. The same is true of detrimental externalities, e.g. in the case of pollution the recipient may prefer and, therefore, would be prepared to pay a price in order to consume zero or less quantity but constraint in this particular case is a 'bad'. Differentiating the expenditure function with respect to Q (Q is a quantity constraint which in this case can be assumed is the level of pollution), the compensated inverse demand function or WTP for changes in Q can be obtained:

$$-\partial E/\partial Q = W\star = W\star(P, Q, U_m) \tag{1}$$

where
E = Expenditure function
U_m = Equilibrium level of utility
P = Price vector of marketed commodities
U'_m = Initial level of utility in equilibrium
U''_m = New level of utility in equilibrium
$W\star$ = Compensated inverse demand function

$$EV = \int^{Q''}_{Q'} W\star (P, Q, U''_m) \, dQ \tag{2}$$

$$CV = \int^{Q''}_{Q'} W\star (P, Q, U'_m) \, dQ \tag{3}$$

$$S_Q = \int^{Q''}_{Q'} W\star (P, Q, M) \, dQ \tag{4}$$

S_Q is the Marshallian consumer's surplus and W(.) is the ordinary demand curve for Q. Apparently, the CV and EV could be computed if the expenditure function or utility function is known. Maler (1974) has shown that due to unknown terms which are function of Q and constants of integration, it is not, in general, possible to solve for the expenditure function by integration. Freeman (1985) reports the circumstances in which the ordinary inverse demand function for Q can be estimated. Accordingly, if W(.) is known, there are two alternatives paths to calculate benefit measures.

a. Hausman (1981) method of calculating exact welfare measures for price changes;
b. Willig (1976) method of errors approximation to the difference between CV, EV and S_Q. Willig has shown that CV and EV are likely to be fairly close in value with the difference depending on the size of income elasticity of the commodity whose price changes.

Randall and Stoll (1980) have established measures of these errors where quantity change rather than price change is involved, and these results are manipulated in environmental economics for the estimation of benefits for the change in environmental quality. Then if there is zero income effect with respect to the commodity, in that situation the three measures approximate to each other.

That is, economic theory explains that maximum WTP is equal to minimum WTA. However, primary surveys show that there are large differences between people's responses to WTP and WTA for traded goods and service. This is due to the reason that persons express their individuality in terms of their rights and belongings; so that the prospect of losing to some degree after it has been consumed for some time signifies a loss of a person's identity.

In Figure 15.1, WTA = AD is the quantity of income required to compensate the individual for forgoing a change in the environmental good from q_o to q_1. This puts the individual on the higher indifference curve at the old quantity q_o. WTP = BC is the amount the individual would be willing to pay after the change to q1 that would leave him as well off as before. WTP implies that the individual has no property rights to the increase in environmental good. It measures the change from the original level of utility with the new level of environmental good. WTA implies that the individual has the property rights to the higher level of environmental services being considered. It is measuring the change from the new level of utility and the original level of environmental good. Here AD>BC implying that WTA>WTP.

Hanemann (1991) shows that the difference between WTP and WTA not only depends on the income effect but also on the substitution effect. If the good in question has fairly close substitutes, the difference will be smaller. Alternatively said, the lesser the substitution effect, the larger the difference between WTP and WTA. When a market good and a non-market good are perfect substitutes, the utility curves are linear – representing frictionless exchange between the two goods (Figure 15.2). The WTA measure is the quantity of the market good necessary to

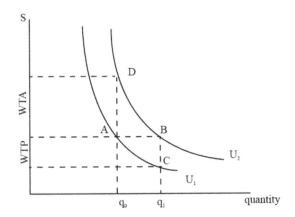

Figure 15.1   WTP and WTA for an environmental benefit or degradation

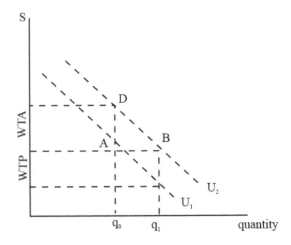

Figure 15.2   WTP and WTA for a marketed good

compensate the individual to forgo a change in q from q_o to q_1. This is the amount AD that puts the individual on the higher indifference curve but maintains the original q_o consumption level. The WTP is the quantity of the market good that one can take from an individual after the change to q_1 while still leaving him as well off as before. This amount is BC. With perfect substitution AD = BC and both equal the average market price of the good.

On the other hand, in Figure 15.1, as the degree of substitutability decreases, the trade-off becomes less desirable, implying that the indifference curves become more curved, thereby creating a greater divergence between WTA and WTP. Thus the WTP-WTA divergence is not some form of cognitive mistake by irrational consumers but is related to the degree of substitutability between the environmental good and the good it is being traded for.

But things are not as simple as they have shown. In all these measure of welfare change, it was assumed that the change has taken place. But Diewert (1976, 1989) has demonstrated that the properties of these measures change even when considering a proposed change in prices, like policy analysis, the end point is not known, so prediction is necessary. This requires additional assumptions so that estimation and predictions can be developed. In the case of environmental commodities, according to Smith, 'For the value of non-market resources, the required assumptions are more detailed because we also must specify the technical indicators of quality that are hypothesized to influence observed behavior' (1993, p. 2).

These three measures are used for the change in welfare for practical purposes. This raises the question of which one should be preferred to others. McKenzie (1983) has dealt with this question. He has shown that EV is an ordinal money metric measure of consumer welfare. The CV also turns out to be an ordinary measure, but it requires the strong assumption of homothetic preferences (Chipman and Moore 1980). With respect to the Marshallian measure of consumer surplus, they have shown that it requires the assumption of homothetic and parallel preferences. This gives an edge to EV over CV and consumer surplus. Thus, the choice between which of the two – WTP or WTA – is the correct measure of an environmental good is not resolved. Since in many cases individuals do not have property rights to the environmental resource and since we want to find the value of an increase in the provision of that good, WTP is the measure that is generally used.

There are two categories of techniques in the literature to the valuation of environmental benefits: indirect methods (dose-response method and revealed preference methods) and stated preference methods. Though the dose-response method does not use consumer's preferences, the revealed preference methods and stated preference methods are based on consumer's preferences, and these methods assume that the consumer is rational; the change in environmental quality is reflected by changes in the consumer's level of welfare change that can be stated in terms of his/her willingness to pay. In both the techniques, the purpose is to elicit individual values for an environmental improvement. Estimation of environmental benefits in monetary values allows the assessment of different benefits in the same entities, which helps in measuring net benefits, which is the sum of all the monetized benefits minus the sum of all monetized costs. This will further help policymakers to make decisions by comparing different benefits with the baseline scenario. It is important to consider each effect individually while valuing impacts of any policy measures and then aggregate the individual values to analyse the complete effects using an integrated approach. However, it also is important to assess the potential trade-offs while considering a number of effects so that each effect will be considered once in the overall analysis while integrating or aggregating their respective values. At times valuation methodology will not be able to capture the accurate environmental benefits due to difficulty in conducting original valuation because of non-availability of funds, time and manpower. Hence in such cases, *benefit transfer* methods generally are used.

4. Methods of environmental valuation

Economic valuation is based on the economic theory of human behaviour and consumer preferences, which revolve around the concept of *utility* that societies know from goods and services, both market and non-market. Different levels and combinations of goods and services afford different levels of utility for any one person. It has been observed that different people have different preferences; different sets of goods and services will appeal more or less to different people. Utility is inherently subjective and cannot be measured directly. Environmental benefits valuation assumes that an individual is the best judge of his or her own welfare. The changes in environmental quality has an impact on the level of utility an individual is having given his income level and the set of prices. Therefore, in order to give 'value', it must be expressed in a quantifiable metric. The changes is environmental quality can be reflected by changes in his/her level of welfare changes. He can state it in terms of his/her WTP, i.e. CV, or WTA, i.e. equivalent EV or Marshallian measure of consumer surplus. The important difference between WTP and WTA is their individual reference utility levels. In the case of WTP, it uses level of utility without enhancement as the reference point; whereas WTA uses the level of utility with the progress as the reference point. Therefore, the purpose of this section is to understand how using different valuation methods people estimate WTA or WTP for an environmental change. There are three approaches, direct method, indirect method and dose-response method, for measuring the value of non-marketed goods and services.

The types of benefits that may arise from environmental policies can be classified in multiple ways (Freeman 2003) (see Table 15.2).

Table 15.2 Different benefits due to an environmental change

Benefit Category	Examples	Commonly Used Valuation Methods
Human Health Improvements		
Mortality risk reductions	Reduced risk of: cancer fatality and acute fatality	Averting behaviours; Hedonics and Stated preference
Morbidity risk reductions	Reduced risk of: cancer, asthma and nausea	Averting behaviours; Cost of illness; Hedonics and Stated preference
Ecological Improvements		
Market products	Harvests or extraction of: food, fuel, fibre, timber, fur and leather	Production function
Recreation activities and aesthetics	Wildlife viewing, fishing, boating, swimming, hiking and scenic views	Production function; Averting behaviours; Hedonics; Recreation demand and Stated preference
Valued ecosystem functions	Climate moderation, flood moderation, groundwater recharge, sediment trapping, soil retention, nutrient cycling, pollination by wild species, biodiversity, genetic library, water filtration, soil fertilization and pest control	Production function; Averting behaviours and Stated preference
Non-use values	Relevant species populations, communities, or ecosystems	Stated preference
Other Benefits		
Aesthetic improvements	Visibility, taste and odour	Averting behaviours; Hedonics and Stated preference
Reduced materials damages	Reduced soiling and reduced corrosion	Averting behaviours and Production/cost functions

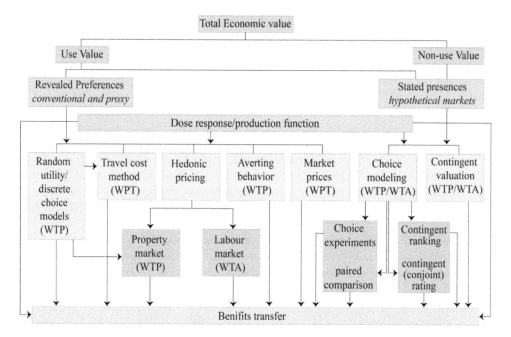

Figure 15.3 Valuation of environmental benefits

Generally, environmental valuation methods can be broadly classified into two categories: revealed preference approaches and stated preference approaches as presented in Figure 15.3. Revealed preference approaches make use of individuals' behaviour in actual or simulated markets to infer the value of an environmental good or service. For example, the value of a wilderness area may be inferred by expenditures that recreationists incur to travel to the area. In the absence of clearly defined markets, the value of environmental resources can be derived from information acquired through surrogate markets. The most common markets used as surrogates when monetizing environmental resources are those for property and labour. Examples of revealed preference methods include the hedonic pricing method (HPM), the travel cost method (TCM), the averting behaviour method (ABM), and the benefit-transfer (BT) method. Stated preference methods attempt to elicit environmental values directly from respondents using survey techniques. The examples of stated preference methods are the contingent valuation method (CVM) and choice modelling (CM).

In the literature various researchers have used the previously mentioned economic valuation methods for assessment of air quality degradation as summarized in Table 15.3.

4.1 *Dose-response method*

Sometimes, benefit estimation methods do not seek to measure the revealed preferences for the environmental good in question. Instead, they calculate a 'dose-response' relationship between pollution and some effect and only then is some measure of the economic value of that effect applied. Examples of dose-response relationships include the effect of pollution on health; the effect of pollution on the physical depreciation of material assets, such as metals and buildings; the effect of pollution on aquatic ecosystems; and the effect of soil erosion on agricultural yields. It requires large datasets, establishment of the dose-response function (for mortality, health, loss

Table 15.3 Valuation studies

Authors	Study Area	Valuation Technique	Environmental Impact/Good to be Valued	Results
O'Garra (2012)	Suva, Fiji	Contingent Valuation	Economic value of goods and services provided by the coastal ecosystems	The study estimated the total economic value of coastal ecosystems within the Navakavu traditional fishing grounds (which cover an area of 18.5 km2) of US$1,795,000 per year.
Jeuland et al. (2010)	Beira, Mozambique	Travel cost approach	Estimation of private benefits of vaccination against cholera	They reported that quantity of vaccines obtained by households and the likelihood of involvement declined as travel cost – in time and transport expenses – increased.
Panduro and Veie (2013)	Aalborg, Denmark	Hedonic price	Classification and valuation of urban green spaces	They reported that access to green space in cities can be linked with both considerably higher and lower housing prices contingent on the type of green space.
Sidique et al. (2013)	Michigan	Travel cost approach	Estimating the demand for drop-off recycling sites	They reported that increased travel costs considerably reduced the frequency of visits to drop-off sites which implied that the usage pattern of a site is influenced by its location relative to where people live.
Chang and Kim (2013)	Seoul, South Korea	Hedonic price	Estimates of rail noise in Seoul	They reported that increase in noise pollution by one unit (dB(A)) resulted in decrease in property value by 0.53%.
Kansal et al. (2009)	Delhi, India	averting behaviour approach	Estimation of marginal health benefits due to air pollution control from thermal power plants	They have estimated total health benefits for entire Delhi city was ~$ 235.2 million; whereas, the capital cost required for controlling air pollution at thermal power plants was ~$217 million at coal-based thermal power plants.
Carlson & Johansson – Stenman, (2000)	Sweden	Contingent Valuation	Benefits from improved air quality	WTP for a 50% reduction of harmful substances where the respondents live and work estimated at about 2000 SEK/year
Navrud, (2001)	Norway	Contingent Valuation	Air pollution and human morbidity: seven lights health symptoms and asthma.	Authors produced mean WTP estimates for the avoidance of 1 and 14 additional days 'light' health symptoms per year.

(Continued)

Table 15.3 (Continued)

Authors	Study Area	Valuation Technique	Environmental Impact/Good to be Valued	Results
Dziegielewska & Mendelsohn, (2005)	Poland	Contingent Valuation	Adverse impact of air pollution on Health: mortality, incidence of bronchitis, asthma, minor health symptoms; Visibility loss, Material damages to historical buildings and Ecosystems damages	Authors produced WTP estimates for a 50% reduction and a 25% reduction in air pollution. Also estimated damage of air pollution as a fraction of the GDP. Historical heritage and ecosystem damage appeared to be significant components of total damage
Desaigues et al. (2004)	France	Contingent Valuation	Air Pollution and Human	Annual WTP for the next 10 years for a medical treatment that would reduce the risk of dying by 1 in 1000 is 412€ and by 5 in 1000 is 563€.
Banfi et al., (2007)	Zurich and Lugano	Choice experiment	Impact of air pollution externalities on human welfare.	Mean WTP for air quality improvements from bad to good is 198 in Zurich and 151 in Lugano (in CHF per month)
			Noise pollution and electro smog were also included into the analysis	Mean WTP for air quality improvements from bad to medium is 198 in Zurich and 94 in Lugano (in CHF per month)
				Mean WTP air quality improvements from medium to good is 70 in Zurich and 57 in Lugano (in CHF per month)
Yoo et al. (2008)	Seoul	Choice Experiment	Environmental costs of air pollution impacts (mortality, morbidity, soiling damages and poor visibility)	Households' monthly WTP for a 10% reduction in the concentrations of major pollutants was approximately 5494 Korean won. Total annual WTP for the entire population was about 203.4 billion Korean won
Wang & Mullahy (2006)	China	Contingent Valuation	Reduced fatal risk by improving air quality	Value of statistical life estimated to be $34,468
Wang & Zhang, (2009)	China	Contingent Valuation	Effects of air pollution on human health	Mean WTP was estimated at 100 Chinese yan per person per year

Study	Location	Method	Topic	Results
Hammit & Zhou (2006)	Three diverse locations in China	Contingent Valuation	Benefits from improved air quality	Median WTP to prevent an episode of cold ranges between US$3 and US$6, WTP to prevent a statistical case of chronic bronchitis ranges between US$500 and US$1000 and the value of statistical life ranged between US$4000 and US$17000.
Belhaz (2003)	Morocco	Contingent Valuation and Hedonic Pricing	Air pollution road traffic Benefits from clean air	Authors produce WTP estimates for a 50% reduction of air pollution
Alberini & Krupnick (2000)	Taiwan	Contingent Valuation	Air Pollution Human Health	Authors produced WTP estimates to avoid minor respiratory illnesses associated with air pollution.
Li et al. (2004)	Shnaghai	Cost Benefit Analysis	Health benefits from pollution reduction	Benefit cost ratio revealed considerable net benefits to be derived
Gupta (2006)	India	Cost of illness	Monetary benefits to individuals from avoided health damages due to reductions in air pollution	Results indicated that the mean worker from Kanpur would gain Rs 165 per year if air pollution were reduced to a safe level
Vrhovcak et al. (2005)	Croatia	Damage cost	External costs of electricity generation in terms of human health	Authors estimated external cost for a bundle of health endpoints
Cesar et al. (2002)	Mexico	Dose – response functions/ Cost of Illness	Health benefits from a number of pollution reduction scenarios	Results suggest that a 10% reduction in ozone was about $760 million (in 1999 U.S. dollars) annually and the benefit for a 20% reduction in ozone and PM was about 1.49 billion annually.
Murty et al. (2003)	Delhi and Kolkata	Health production functions and demand functions for averting and mitigating activities	Air pollution	Annual marginal benefits to a typical household ranged from Rs 2086 in Delhi to Rs 950 in Kolkata if the level of SPM is reduced from current average level to the prescribed safe level.
Komavora (2009)	Moscow	Hedonic pricing	Relationship between air pollution and housing prices	Ecological variable had a negative sign while increasing the level of air contamination from carbon monoxide, nitrogen dioxide, sulphur dioxide and particles.

(*Source*: adapted from Kougea and Koundouri, 2011).

of crops and real estate). Moreover, it requires valuation of mortality, putting a monetary value on life, which is not undisputed.

In general, the dose-response approach is applicable to environmental problems. That is, if there is some damage and it is linked to a cause, the relationship between the cause-and-effect is a dose-response linkage. Once the dose-response relationship is established, these approaches then utilize valuations that are applied to the 'responses'. For example, consider the linkage between air pollution and health. Once the health effects are established, a value of life and/or of illness is applied Markandya (1992) has summarized the procedure as follows:

(i) Estimate a physical damage function of the firm
   R = R(p, other variables)

where R is the physical damage (the response), P is the pollution;

(ii) Calculate the co-efficient of R on P through (typically) statistical regression analysis, i.e. calculate $\partial R/\partial P$ (where ∂ means change in);
(iii) Calculate the change in pollution due to environmental policy, i.e. calculate ΔP;
(iv) Calculate $V.\Delta P(\partial R/\partial P) = V.\Delta R = \Delta D$, where ΔD is the 'damage avoided'.

The essential point here is that the step from the dose-response estimation to the valuation is not as simplistic as is often assumed. In fact, what often is needed is to link the dose-response estimates of the damage to a behavioural model of the demand for the products that are affected. Often, the data simply do not permit the estimation of the more refined model, in which case even the simpler models can be very useful providing their limitations are realized and the kind of biases they are likely to generate are allowed for.

The dose-response tends to be used particularly for two reasons:

1. It is thought that people are unaware of the effects that pollution causes.
2. When eliciting preferences by any one of the direct methods, is not possible for reasons of data, or lack of 'market sophistication' in the population or both to reveal true preferences.

The second reason applies especially in developing countries, where price and expenditure data generally are poor and where the use of CVM has been limited because it is believed that the answers would suffer from strategic, hypothetical and operational biases.

4.2 Revealed preference methods

Use of natural recourses relates to functional benefits, the outputs provide a social benefit from ecosystem functioning; for example, water purification, erosion protection or carbon sequestration. Indirect approaches for measuring the value of non-marketed commodities rely on consumers' choice and revealed preference theory of consumer behaviour is considered superior. Revealed preference theory for describing consumer behaviour relies on the idea that an individual's choice of a consumption bundle that a consumer with given income and prices must be preferred (because of its selection) to all others at that particular set of prices. It is equally true in deriving welfare measures for environmental quality change. As Diewert (1976) demonstrates, Harberger-type (1974) welfare indicators can be interpreted as displaying the effects of revealed preferences through indices that yield correctly signed measures of welfare changes for a wide class of true underlying preference functions (Smith, 1993). For the values of non-marketed resources, the required assumptions are made detailed because the need is to specify the technical indicators of quality that are hypothesized to influence observed behaviour (Smith, 1993).

With respect to these methods, it is worthwhile to quote Smith:

> To appreciate the features of indirect approaches we need do little more than focus on the marginal rate of substitution (MRS) between the non-marketed environmental services and some numeraire as an economic measure of an individual's real value for the last unit here he consumed of a commodity. Consider the exchange of goods on markets. Under these conditions we know that each commodity's relative price reveal the consumers' real (marginal) values. In developing measures of people's value for goods and services, the focus shifts to the typical (representative) individual and the fact that rest values are known once we have the relative price associated with the consumption bundles selected. If the amounts purchased are known, then with sufficient variation in these pairs (i.e. prices and quantities), we can develop conventional valuation measures.
>
> (1993, pp. 2–3)

A variety of revealed preference methods for valuing environmental changes have been developed and are widely used by economists. The following common types of revealed preference methods are discussed in this section:

4.2.1 *Travel cost method*

The travel cost recreation demand model is the straightest forward of the indirect methods. It was initially proposed by Harold Hotelling (1947). According to this model, the visitors to a recreation site pay an implicit price including the opportunity costs of their time. Thus, this approach attempts to evaluate an environmental asset (e.g. national wildlife park) from the perspective of how much time and money people are willing to spend to visit those sites. In this case, people are travelling from different locations only to see the site (e.g. national park), so it means they are spending money and time on travel to see the national park, implying that the site is evaluated highly. The monetary evaluation is attempted by estimating total cost of travel to the site (transportation, entrance fee, etc.) and time factors (one way of calculation is to take proportion of the visitors' incomes).

The travel cost method has been extensively used in the area of environmental and resource economics for estimating demand for leisure amenities (Freeman, 2003). The travel cost approach is useful for valuing the recreational benefits of a site, but it is restrictive as it measures site-specific recreational value. This method has been used by various researchers to study the environmental benefits. For instance, Jeuland et al. (2010) have used the travel cost approach for estimating the private benefits of vaccination against cholera in Beira, Mozambique. They reported that quantity of vaccines obtained by households and the likelihood of involvement declined as travel cost – in time and transport expenses – increased. Further, Sidique et al. (2013) used the travel cost approach for estimating the demand for drop-off recycling sites in Michigan City. They reported that increased travel costs considerably reduced the frequency of visits to drop-off sites, which implied that the usage pattern of a site is influenced by its location relative to where people live. Thus, the travel cost approach is useful and applicable for such areas.

4.2.2 Hedonic pricing method

The theoretical framework for hedonic pricing was established by Rosen (1974). He applied this method in the area of property price. He derives price equations from property sales data by regression and thereby allows valuation of different exogenous attributes of the property itself and its vicinity. The prices of two houses may differ considerably, even with the same facilities like size, structure etc. The prices may reflect the difference of access to the workplace, commercial amenities, environmental facilities such as parks and the environmental qualities of the neighbourhoods. Such differences may imply that people are, to some extent, making a judgement on how much (more) they will spend for the quality of environment. For example, if a person were to choose between two identical houses, a) one situated in clean environment, or b) the other in a polluted area, which one would he/she buy or rent? What if the price of a) is 5 percent higher than b) or 50 percent higher? Similar results have been reported in the literature. For example, Chang and Kim (2013) have applied hedonic price methodology for estimation of rail noise in Seoul, South Korea. They have estimated trade-offs in the context of housing prices, locality, and environment intrusion. They reported that an increase in noise pollution by one unit (dB(A)) resulted in a decrease in property value by 0.53 percent. Further, Panduro and Veie (2013) have used the hedonic price approach for classification and valuation of urban green spaces in the city of Aalborg, Denmark. They have used the generalized additive model for assessing hedonic price. They reported that access to green space in cities can be linked with both considerably higher and lower housing prices contingent on the type of green space. Therefore, hedonic price technique uses property prices to assess how much of the property value differential reflects the difference in environmental values or how much people are willing to pay for an improvement of environmental quality and what the social value of the improvement is.

4.2.3 Averting behaviour method

The averting behaviour method generally assesses values for natural assets from observations of activities people take to avoid or mitigate the augmented health risks or other adverse consequences of decreases in ambient environmental quality (USEPA, 2010). This method depends on the hypothesis that people recognize the undesirable effects of environmental degradation on their health and that they are able to adapt their behaviour to avert or reduce these effects. For example, people experienced negative impacts of poor air quality in a region and hence they have to purchase masks/air filters or health insurance to protect their health from poor air quality. The WTP for a health environment is deducted from people's purchases of goods and amenities to prevent the undesirable effects of air pollution. By estimating the expenditures associated with these averting behaviours, economists can attempt to estimate the value individuals place on small changes in risk (Shogren and Crocker, 1991 and Quiggin, 1992). Since the market prices of products are used to value the environment, this method cannot capture the true value of environmental change. Thus, the validity of this method is debateable because of the theory that people are really buying these goods to safeguard themselves against environmental degradation.

4.2.3.1 CASE STUDY – HEALTH BENEFITS VALUATION USING THE AVERTING BEHAVIOUR APPROACH IN DELHI, INDIA

This study estimated the minimum marginal health benefits using the averting behaviour approach due to air pollution control from thermal power plants in Delhi by adopting the World Bank Emission Guidelines (WBEG) as a regulatory measure. In this study, the authors studied the health benefits by considering three coal-based thermal power plants (Rajghat, Indraprastha and Badarpur) and two natural gas-based thermal power plants (Indraprastha Gas Turbine and Pragati Power). The authors estimated urban air pollution concentration due to thermal power plants using an air quality modelling approach. They used a deterministic air quality model (i.e. ISCST3) for estimating air quality in the study region. They considered two scenarios: one business as usual (BAU) where thermal power plants follow the existing guidelines recommended by the India Ministry of Environment and Forest and an alternative (ALT) scenario where adoption of WBEG is considered. The averting behaviour approach was used to estimate the health benefits due to air pollution control. The minimum marginal household WTP was estimated by considering various factors such as loss of earnings, medical expenses and averting expenditure. A health survey was conducted in 14 zones of Delhi, where 50 households were interviewed from each zone (total 700 households) using random sampling. The authors reported annual marginal benefits of Rs. 66.5 for a household (or Rs. 15.9 per person) in Delhi due to reduction in air pollution by 1 $\mu g/m^3$ through adoption of WBEG. They estimated total health benefits for Delhi city at ~$ 235.2 million; whereas the capital cost required for controlling air pollution at thermal power plants was ~$217 million at coal-based thermal power plants. This study showed that annual costs required for controlling the air pollution at thermal power plants were less compared to annual health benefits estimated by adopting WBEG (Kansal et al., 2009).

4.2.4 Benefit-transfer method

As valuation exercises are costly, researchers need some means of estimating non-market benefits without having to undertake an individual study. Benefits transfer is looked at as a way to make environmental valuation a standardized component of environmental cost–benefit analysis for policymaking and environmental management. Benefits transfer mainly works by taking estimates from one or more original studies and transferring the results to a new context by adjusting for two factors: a) differing socioeconomic characteristics of beneficiaries; and b) differing environmental characteristics of the two different contexts. There are two main approaches to benefit transfers: transfer of adjusted mean WTP values (e.g. fishing – average mean WTP per fishing day); and transfer of benefit functions (e.g. transfer bid curves estimated from other studies). Usually a meta-analysis (a statistical analysis of past valuation studies) is carried out. The transfer error is usually between 20 percent and 40 percent for the first method (absolute transfer error) and can go up to 228 percent for the second method (benefit function transfer error).

4.3 Stated preference approaches – direct methods

Direct use is the most familiar value group, as the economic benefits can be calculated by making use of market information. For instance, a forest may yield annually a certain amount of wood that can be sold or used for heating and construction purposes. With respect to environmental goods, there is one essential attribute which is known as 'publicness' and the problem becomes more complicated, i.e. the environmental resources have along with use values some non-use values which are popularly known as option and existence values (Krutilla, 1967). Therefore, the economists recommend the direct methods of valuation for these types of resources that have non-use values and when no averting or mitigation behaviour exist, i.e. CVM. (In the context of this method, there exists enormous literature both on theoretical and empirical aspects.) Since there is no market for the goods and services in question, a hypothetical market is created. Then the individuals' responses are collected, i.e. their WTP or WTA. Any CVM study must incorporate a full description of the commodity to be valued, method by which payment is to be made and method of eliciting values.

Stated preference valuation approaches make use of questionnaires where candidates either directly ask respondents for their WTP/WTA or ask them choices between packages of attributes and from which options the analysts can infer WTP (WTA). Stated preference methods more generally offer a direct survey approach to estimate individual or household preferences and more specifically WTP amounts for changes in provision of (non-market) goods that are related to respondents' underlying preferences in a reliable mode. Therefore, this approach specifically is useful when measuring impacts on non-market goods, the value of which cannot be exposed using revealed preference methods. Stated preference valuation approaches mainly use two methods: CVM and the choice modelling method for valuation of environmental benefits.

The validity and usefulness of stated preference methods have been questioned almost as long as the methods have been in use. Generally, empirical evaluation of these methods revolves around two issues: hypothetical bias and its scope. The general methodology used under a stated preference study is explained in Figure 15.4. Afroz et al. (2013) have explained the methodology to collect data for valuation of WTP for improving management of waste generated from electrical

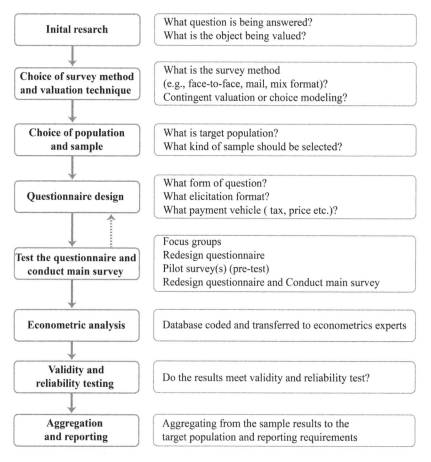

Figure 15.4 Steps involved in a stated preference valuation study

and electronic equipment (WEEE) at household level in the Kuala Lumpur, Malaysia. The objective of this case study was to see the application of valuation of environmental benefits. In this study, the authors have evaluated the awareness among local people about impacts of WEEE and also their WTP for improving overall WEEE waste management and to increase its lifetime. The authors used a questionnaire for conducting the survey in the study area. They selected five residential areas in the city of Kuala Lumpur and questionnaire was distributed in the same localities. They conducted around 350 interviews at the household level. They reported that ~53 percent of the people were WTP for improving overall waste management in the city (for more details, please see Afroz et al., 2013).

4.3.1 Contingent valuation method

This method comes under a direct approach as explained earlier. The CVM was first used by Davis (1963) in a study of deer hunters in Maine. It directly asks people what they are willing to pay for a benefit and/or what they are willing to receive by way of compensation to tolerate a cost in a hypothetical market for environmental goods/services. For example, the method will ask what people are WTP for preservation of native forests, what they are willing to pay for access to clean water or what compensation they are WTA if they are to lose the access to clean water. Major characteristics of the CVM approach is that this is a relatively straightforward way to elicit individuals' valuations of environmental assets (goods), measure non-use values of the environment (e.g. existence value); however, validity and reliability of estimates are questionable due to inherent measurement biases. Generally, people use a payment card method for estimating WTP from affected populations. Payment card is one of the two standard approaches to bring about willingness to pay using closed-ended questions; the second is dichotomous choice. A detailed discussion has been provided in the literature comparing payment card and dichotomous choice elicitation methods and their use by Krupnick et al. (2010). Whereas Champ and Bishop (2006) have reviewed the relative merits of each approach and concluded that both are independent of the study context and neither method is evidently superior to the other. The WTP is a widely used method for valuation of environmental benefits globally. For instance, Heo and Yoo (2013) have used CVM to study the introduction of hydrogen (H_2) fuel cell (FC) buses in South Korea. The study was carried out in the seven metropolitan areas (Seoul, Pusan, Taegu, Kwangju, Ulsan, Daejeon and Incheon). The Korean government involved local people in decision-making before introduction of H_2 FC buses in Korea to understand consumers' attitudes. They reported that the annual mean WTP estimate was US$4.55 per household as of 2007. The result shows that the estimated annual benefits to the affected residents were US$34.7 million. This shows that CVM was expected to be very helpful in policy decisions related to the introduction of H_2 FC buses and investment in H_2 technology development in Korea. However, the various issues that arise with the CVM method are as follows:

- Hypothetical Bias: Difference in actual willingness to pay and willingness to pay revealed in a survey arising from the fact that in actual markets purchasers suffer real costs, while in surveys they do not.
- Information Bias: Distorted evaluation of information.
- Strategic Bias: Causes survey results to differ from actual willingness to pay because individuals have an incentive to not reveal the truth because they can secure a benefit in excess of the costs they have to pay. This arises from the free rider problem.

- Discrepancy between WTP and WTA.
- Choice of response mode: Open ended or closed questions, protest answers, ignoring income constraints etc.
- Voluntary versus forced payments: Compensation issues.

4.3.1.1 CASE STUDY – WILLINGNESS TO PAY FOR MORTALITY RISK REDUCTIONS IN MONGOLIA

This study used stated preference method to estimate the WTP for reductions of mortality risk in Ulaanbaatar, Mongolia. The authors applied CVM for valuation of environmental benefits. They considered a purchasing power parity exchange rate while assessing environmental benefits by improving air quality of the study region. The authors first collected the baseline information related to mortality in the region and also explained the same to the respondents. The authors used a payment card approach for estimating the WTP for reducing mortality risk in Ulaanbaatar city, Mongolia. In the sample design, they considered two scenarios in context to WTP from the respondents. They asked for a reduction of mortality risk by five people in a population of 10,000 for the next ten years and ten people in the same size population. Results showed that income had very positive and significant impacts on WTP. The authors mentioned that the robust variance estimator method has not influenced the regression results and showed that results were not changed by heteroskedasticity. The authors estimated a statistical value of life of approximately $500,000 for annual risk reductions of five people in a population of 10,000, which is almost 3.3 percent of their annual household income (Hoffmann et al., 2012).

4.3.1.2 CASE STUDY – ECONOMIC VALUATION OF A TRADITIONAL FISHING GROUND ON THE CORAL COAST IN FIJI

O'Garra (2012) has estimated economic value of goods and services provided by the coastal ecosystems in a traditional Fijian fishing ground near the capital of Suva using CVM. These resources are taken by residents of four villages, namely Muaivuso, Nabaka, Waiqanake and Namakala, having approximately 600 inhabitants in the year 2007. The aim of the study was to assess the total cost of resources if they were entirely degraded by use of local inhabitants. The author made an assumption that in the absence of new interventions or threats to the resource, the benefits currently received from reefs and mangroves will not change. The questionnaire was used in which a hypothetical market for the good being valued was presented to the respondents who were then asked for their WTP or WTA for the conservation of the Navakavu fishing grounds for future generations, independent of their own use of the resource. The economic values estimated in this study were presented as annual net values. In this study, a 10 percent discount rate was considered based on previous studies carried out by the same author in 2007 (O'Garra, 2007). The study estimated the total economic value of coastal ecosystems within the Navakavu traditional fishing grounds (which cover an area of 18.5 km^2) of US$1,795,000 per year. The present value of the coastal ecosystems over a 99-year time horizon comes to just under US$20 million. It was found that the coral reefs and mangroves make up the largest component of the total economic value (55 percent), followed by fisheries (44 percent). The study highlighted that the mangroves and coral reefs in the Navakavu area provide a valuable coastal protection function. This study did not consider benefits from other recreational activities which might give higher total economic values to the same goods and services provided by the coastal ecosystems (O'Garra 2012).

Table 15.4 Main choice modelling alternatives

Approach	Tasks	Estimates consistent with welfare economies
Choice Experiments	Choose between (usually) two alternatives, versus the status quo	Yes
Contingent Ranking	Rank a series of alternatives	Depends★
Contingent Rating	Score alternative scenarios on ascale of 1–10	Doubtful
Paired Comparisons	Score pairs of scenarios on similar scale	Doubtful

★ In order to interpret the results in standard welfare economic terms, one of the options must always be currently feasible.

Source: Pearce et al., 2002.

4.3.2 Choice modelling method

The CM includes a range of methods, including choice experiments, contingent rating, contingent ranking and paired comparisons. The types of choice modelling are shown in Table 15.4. These are based on the idea that any goods can be thought of as a set of characteristics and if the focus of interest is on the economic value of different characteristics of the goods in question, then choice modelling techniques are more likely to be relevant. CM originated from conjoint analysis and is also a variation on contingent valuation. In comparison to CVM, conjoint analysis describes options by decomposing them into a number of attributes and presents respondents with a choice between j available options (j = 1, 2,.......n). This situation can be made quite realistic by mirroring actual market choice that may depend upon a number of attributes. For example, a forest can be described in terms of its species diversity, age structure and recreational amenities. Changing attribute levels will essentially result in a different goods being produced, and it is on the value of such changes in attributes that CM focuses. There has been a number of applications to estimate the value of recreational and environmental goods in recent years (for example, Opaluch et al., 1993; Adamowicz et al., 1998; Hanley et al., 1998; Morrison and Bennett, 2000). In the literature, CM application has used with a series of choice sets, each containing usually three or more alternative goods. An alternative is a combination of several attributes, with each attribute taking on a value, usually called a level. For instance, an alternative could be described as h hectares of additional forest with p percentage of tree species' that would cost c monetary units. One of the alternatives in each choice set describes the current or future BAU situation and remains constant across the choice sets. From each choice set, respondents are asked to choose their preferred alternative. The attributes used are common across all alternatives. Their levels vary from one alternative to another according to an experimental design (for details, see Bennett and Blamey, 2001)

4.3.2.1 CASE STUDY – NONMARKET VALUES OF MAJOR RESOURCES IN THE KOREAN DMZ AREAS: A TEST OF DISTANCE DECAY IN KOREA

Choi (2013) has estimated the conservation values of the Korean Demilitarised Zone (DMZ), which not only serves as a geopolitical buffer zone between North and South Korea but also as a refuge for various rare animals and plants. The DMZ spans about 238 km from the Imjin River estuary in the west to Myongho-ri in Goseong County in the east, both of which are ecological and geopolitical hotspots. The author has used both CVM and CM methods for estimating economic values. These methods share the same theoretical basis of the random utility maximization theory. The study considered various attributes such as the symbolic space of the DMZ, the number of endangered species, mountains and forests, 43 historical and cultural heritage sites, rivers and their catchments. The questionnaire was used to collect the data from the study area. The estimated conservation values of resources based on the welfare measure of equivalent loss that protects 75 percent of the DMZ area for conservation, 50 percent of the endangered species in Panmunjom, ten special villages, and 50 percent of the cultural heritage sites. The study concluded that the aggregated WTP estimates per person as a one-off payment are US$9.06 and US$34.97, respectively, from the CVM and CM datasets. It is important to note that both values are significantly different at 0.01 levels. The author explained that this may be attributed to strategic behaviour of free-riders, who easily pass the burden of payments to others (Wiser, 2007), which might be easier in the contingent context compare to choice situations (Choi, 2013).

5. Summary and conclusions

The economic analysis is carried out to provide policy and decision-makers' with information on a wide variety of consequences of environmental policies. These estimates are a very important part of analyses which conventionally provide to the policymaking process in appraising of social/environmental benefits and costs – the economic efficiency of a policy. For this reason, this chapter provides rationalized information related with procedures for computing benefits and costs, monetizing benefits estimates and selecting particular inputs and assumptions.

References

Adamowicz, W., Boxall, P., Williams, M. and Louviere, J., 1998. Stated preference approaches for measuring passive use values: choice experiments and contingent valuation. *American Journal of Agricultural Economics* 80: 65–75.

Afroz, R., Masud, M.M., Akhtar, R., Duasa, J.B., 2013. Survey and analysis of public knowledge, awareness and willingness to pay in Kuala Lumpur, Malaysia – a case study on household WEEE management. *Journal of Cleaner Production* 52: 185–193.

Bateman, I.J., Carson, R. T., Day, B., Hanemann, W.M., Hanleys, N., Hett, T., Jones-Lee, M., Loomes, G., Mourato, S., Ozdemiroglu, E., Pearce, D.W., Sugden, R., Swanson, J. 2002. *Economic Valuation with Stated Preference Techniques: A Manual.* Cheltenham: Edward Elgar.

Bennett, J. and Blamey, R. 2001. *The Choice Modelling Approach to Environmental Valuation.* Cheltenham: Edward Elgar.

Champ, P., and Bishop, R., 2006. Is willingness to pay for a public good sensitive to the elicitation format? *Land Economics* 82(2): 162–173.

Chang, J.S., and Kim, D. 2013. Hedonic estimates of rail noise in Seoul. *Transportation Research* Part D 19: 1–4.

Chipman, J.S. and Moore, J.C. 1980. Compensating variation, consumer's surplus and welfare. *American Economic Review* 70: 933–949.

Choi, A.S. 2013. Nonmarket values of major resources in the Korean DMZ areas: a test of distance decay. *Ecological Economics* 88: 97–107.

Davis, R.K. 1963. The Value of Outdoor Recreation: An Economic Study of the Maine Woods. Unpublished Ph.D. dissertation, Harvard University.

Diewert, W.E. 1976. Harberger's welfare indicators and revealed preference theory. *American Economic Review* 66: 143–152.

Diewert, W.E. 1989. Exact and Superlative Welfare Change Indicators. Discussion Paper No. 89–27. Department of Economics, University of British Columbia, Vancouver.

EFTEC/RIVM. 2000. *Valuing the Benefits of Environmental Policy: The Netherlands*, RIVM, London.

Freeman III, A.M. 1985. Methods for assessing the benefits of environmental programs. In *Handbook of Natural Resource and Energy Economics*, A.V. Kneese and J.L. Sweeney (eds.), Chapter 6. Amsterdam: North-Holland.

Freeman III, A.M. 2003. *The Measurement of Environmental and Resource Values: Theory and Methods*. Washington, DC: Resources for the Future.

Hanemann, W.M. 1991. Willingness to pay and willingness to accept: how much they can differ? *American Economic Review* 81: 635–647.

Hanley, N., MacMillan, D., Wright, R., Bullock, C., Simpson, I., Parsisson, D. and Crabtree, B. 1998. Contingent valuation versus choice experiments: estimating the benefits of environmentally sensitive areas in Scotland. *Journal of Agricultural Economics* 49: 1–15.

Harberger, A.C. 1971. Three basic postulates for applied welfare economics: an interpretive essay. *Journal of Economic Literature* 9: 785–797.

Hausman, J.A. 1981. Exact consumer surplus and deadweight loss. *American Economic Review* 71: 662–676.

Heo, J.Y. and Yoo, S.H. 2013. The public's value of hydrogen fuel cell buses: a contingent valuation study. *International Journal of Hydrogen Energy* 38: 4232–4240.

Hoffmann, S., Qin, P., Krupnick, A., et al. 2012. The willingness to pay for mortality risk reductions in Mongolia. *Resource and Energy Economics* 34: 493–513.

Jeuland, M., Lucas, M., Clemens, J., and Whittington, D. 2010. Estimating the private benefits of vaccination against cholera in Beira, Mozambique: a travel cost approach. *Journal of Development Economics* 91: 310–322.

Kansal, A., Khare, M., Sharma C.S., 2009. Health benefits valuation of the World Bank emission guidelines for thermal power plants in Delhi, *India Journal of Environment Planning and Management* 52(7): 881–899.

Kougea, E., and Koundouri, P. 2011. Air quality degradation: can economics help in measuring its welfare effects? In *A Review of Economic Valuation Studies, Indoor and Outdoor Air Pollution*, José Orosa (ed.), 105–126. Available from: http://www.intechopen.com/books/indoor-and-outdoor-air-pollution/air-quality-degradation-can-economics-help-in-measuring-its-welfare-effects-a-review-of-economic-val.

Krupnick, A., Hoffmann, S., and Qin, P. 2010. Willingness to pay for mortality risk reductions. Draft working paper.

Krutilla, J.V. 1967. Conservation reconsidered. *American Economic Review* 57: 777–786.

Kumar, S., and D.N. Rao. 2001. Measuring benefits of pollution abatement using health production function: a case study of Panipat thermal power station. *Environmental and Resource Economics* 20: 91–102.

Kumar, S., and S. Managi. 2009. Valuing the benefits of air pollution abatement. In S. Kumar and S. Managi, (eds.), *The Economics of Sustainable Development: The Case of India,* 107–126. New York: Springer.

Maler, K.-G., 1974. *Environmental Economics – A Theoretical Inquiry*. Baltimore: John Hopkins University Press.

Markandya, A., 1992. The value of the environment: a state of the art survey. In A. Markandya and J., Richardson (eds.), *The Earthscan Reader in Environmental Economics*, 142–166. London: Earthscan.

McKenzie, G. 1983. *Measuring Economic Welfare: New Methods*. Cambridge: Cambridge University Press.

Morrison, M. and Bennett, J., 2000. Choice modelling, non-use values and benefit transfer. *Economics Analysis and Policy* 30: 13–32.

O'Garra, T., May 2007. Estimating the Total Value of the Navakavu Locally Managed Marine Area., Final Report, Coral Reef Initiative for the South Pacific (CRISP) Programme, University of the South Pacific, Vitu Levu Island, Fiji.

O'Garra, T. 2012. Economic valuation of a traditional fishing ground on the coral coast in Fiji. *Ocean & Coastal Management* 56: 44–55.

Ojeda, M.I., Mayer, A.S., and Solomon, B.D. 2008. Economic valuation of environmental services sustained by water flows in the Yaqui River Delta. *Ecological Economics* 65: 155–166.

Opaluch, J., Swallow, S., Weaver, T., Wessells, W. and Wichelns, D. 1993. Evaluating impacts from noxious facilities: including public preferences in current siting mechanisms. *Journal of Environmental Economics and Management* 24: 41–59.

Panduro, T. E., and Veie, K.L. 2013. Classification and valuation of urban green spaces – a hedonic house price valuation. *Landscape and Urban Planning* 120: 119–128.

Pearce D., Zdemiroglu, E. et al. 2002. Economic Valuation with Stated Preference Techniques Summary Guide. Department for Transport, Local Government and the Regions, Eland House, London.

Quiggin, J. 1992. Risk, self-protection and ex ante economic value – some positive results. *Journal of Environmental Economics and Management* 23(1): 40–53.

Randall, A. and Stall, J.R. 1980. Consumer's surplus in commodity space. *American Economic Review* 70: 449–457.

319

Rosen, S. 1974. Hedonic prices and implicit markets – product differentiation in pure competition. *Journal of Political Economy* 82(1): 34–55.

Shogren, J.F., and Crocker, T.D. 1991. Risk, self-protection, and ex ante economic value. *Journal of Environmental Economics and Management* 20(1): 1–15.

Sidique, S. F., Lupi, F. and Joshi, S.V. 2013. Estimating the demand for drop-off recycling sites: a random utility travel cost approach. *Journal of Environmental Management* 127: 339–346.

Smith, V. K. 1993. Non-market valuation of environmental resources: an interpretive appraisal. *Land Economics* 69(1): 1–26.

USEPA (U.S. Environmental Protection Agency). 2010. *Guidelines for Preparing Economic Analyses*, National Center for Environmental Economics. Washington, DC: USEPA.

Willig R.D. 1976. Consumer's surplus without apology. *American Economic Review* 66: 589–597.

Wiser, R.H. 2007. Using contingent valuation to explore willingness to pay for renewable energy: a comparison of collective and voluntary payment vehicles. *Ecological Economics* 62: 419–432.

16

IMPACT OF AGRICULTURAL CHEMICALS ON THE ENVIRONMENT AND HUMAN HEALTH IN ASIA

Are there solutions?

Wasantha Athukorala, Vincent Hoang and Clevo Wilson

1. Introduction

'Some problems are so complex that you have to be highly intelligent and well informed just
to be undecided about them.'

—Laurence J. Peter

Modern commercial agricultural practices in Asia during the last three to four decades involving chemicals (fertilisers and pesticides) have been associated with large increases in food production never witnessed before, especially under the Green Revolution technology in South Asia. This also involves large-scale increases in commercial vegetable crops. However, the high reliance on chemical inputs to bring about these increases in food production is not without problems. A visible, parallel correlation between higher productivity, high artificial input use and environmental degradation and human ill-health is evident in many countries where commercial agriculture is widespread. In this chapter, we focus on the impact of chemical inputs, in particular the impact of pesticides on the environment and on human health in South Asia with special reference to Sri Lanka.

There are numerous negative externalities and private costs arising from agricultural production. It is clear that some of the negative externalities and private costs resulting from agriculture are generated by the very inputs that are used to boost agricultural production. The externalities are in the form of affecting agricultural production and other production processes, wildlife and the environment in general. Therefore, a study of negative externalities and private costs is important, not only to show the impact of agricultural production on the agricultural system itself, other production processes, the environment, wildlife and the health of the producer and third parties but also because such a study can shed light on the private and external costs on the users (e.g. farmers) and those around them, thus showing the need to curb such activities. This brings us to the question of potential solutions that can be adopted. It is clear that in order to bring about a reduction in chemical use (e.g. pesticides), it is important for the market price to reflect the true costs of production. If full costs of production (including private health costs and externalities) are not taken into account in the market price, then resource allocation is inefficient. In the absence of full cost pricing, farmers will use chemicals (e.g. pesticides) if the discounted net present value of stream of returns from doing so is positive (Wilson and Tisdell, 2001). Hence, a transition to a low-chemical production system becomes difficult (or even impossible). Therefore, all other current solutions become only partial or are successful only at the margins. As long as market failure exists, any solution(s) remains suboptimal. We discuss these issues in detail in the chapter with secondary and primary field evidence provided of the environmental impacts and the private health costs to farmers due to direct exposure to pesticides. For this purpose, results of two field studies conducted in Sri Lanka within the last two decades are used. The chapter also asks the question as to whether the true costs of agricultural production will be taken into account. It is argued that the political commitment and the economic costs for both producers and consumers will be large and hence such pricing will not eventuate. This is because the objective of many countries is to produce 'cheap' food, and this is even more pertinent for least developed countries (LDCs), although this approach is diametrically opposed to sustainable food production both from a human health and an environmental point of view. When it comes to market failures of this nature, governments rarely intervene to internalise them and do so only at the margins.

This chapter consists of six sections. The second section discusses agricultural production with special reference to South Asia and discusses the various negative externalities and private costs (involving farmers' health) that are generated. A theoretical discussion is undertaken to show the generation of pollution and the wider consequences resulting from negative externalities and private costs apart from the production that is involved and shows how the internalisation of these problems can be potentially achieved through the price mechanism. We show the necessary conditions for efficient allocation of resources. The third section discusses the problems associated with farmers' exposure to pesticides during handling and spraying on farms and the resulting costs. After a background introduction to agriculture in Sri Lanka and a literature review, we use the results of two major field studies conducted in Sri Lanka during the last 15 years to showcase the magnitude of the problem. Section four attempts to understand why farmers continue to use pesticides despite these high costs, We provide economic justifications for this, especially by drawing attention to the private costs to farmers and negative externalities not reflected in current market prices. Ignoring such costs clearly makes agricultural production inefficient. However, the question that is asked then is: are governments, especially in LDCs, willing or in a position to correct this market failure? This issue is addressed in section five and section six concludes.

2. Agricultural production generates negative externalities

As mentioned in the introduction, there have been large increases in production and productivity, especially in rice and wheat production using Green Revolution technology in South Asia. However, there are numerous negative externalities and private costs due to agricultural production. Some of the negative externalities and private costs resulting from agriculture are generated by the very inputs that are used to boost agricultural production. The externalities are in the form of impacts on agricultural production and other production processes, wildlife and the environment in general. The private costs are the health-related costs suffered by the producer (user of these inputs) and declining agricultural land productivity on the producer's land. Almost all negative externalities and private costs arise from the use of inorganic or chemical inputs.[1] The negative externalities and private costs that are considered in this chapter arise from two of the most harmful agricultural pollutants, namely pesticides and fertilisers. Most of these pollutants break down very slowly in the environment and hence have the potential to accumulate over time. Hence, they have been called 'stock' or conservative pollutants. A good example that is cited in the literature is DDT. Because of the very nature of the pollution that is generated, these pollutants can also give rise to a domino effect, setting off a series of chain reactions. This domino effect will be highlighted in this section, which Zilberman and Marra (1993, p. 247) have described as dynamic in nature. An off-shoot of externalities and private costs arising due to pollution is that if these costs are not taken into account (as it often happens), resource allocation becomes inefficient and market failure occurs.

A simple production function can be employed for agriculture to show the generation of pollution and the wider consequences resulting from it (e.g. externalities and private costs) apart from the production that is involved. The production function shows that output is a function of inputs which can be written as:

$$Y = f(X) \tag{1}$$

X is a vector consisting of many inputs. In the case of agricultural production, in addition to capital (fixed inputs), several variable inputs are used. They include labour, water, pesticides and fertilisers. Some of these inputs, namely agrochemicals, can have a profound effect on production and productivity. This is especially so with hybrid high-yielding varieties (HYVs) which are dependent on these two factors for increased output and productivity. A good example is the HYVs introduced to Asia. The HYVs first introduced to the Asian agricultural fields in the 1960s (the so called Green Revolution[2]) have been associated with increases in cereal production never witnessed before, and in the case of wheat, spectacular growth (see, for example, Farmer, 1986, p. 177; Conway and Barbier, 1990, p. 20; Lipton and Longhurst, 1989, p. 1; Wilson, 1999). As statistics show, both production and productivity[3] have increased. For a detailed discussion on the spectacular increases in output, see Wilson (1999). However, the HYVs (the seeds) are only one component of the Green Revolution package. If the full benefits of this 'miracle technology' are to be harnessed, it is essential to apply large quantities of chemical substances, such as chemical fertilisers and pesticides. Hence, the spectacular increases in cereal production have been accompanied, amongst other inputs, by large increases in the use of fertiliser and pesticides. This is evident in every country/area that has adopted the Green Revolution technology (for a full discussion see, Wilson, 1994, pp. 7–10).

The experience during the last 30-plus years shows that the use of inorganic chemical inputs have been harmful to human health, the agricultural land, other production processes, wildlife and the environment in general (Wilson, 1999). The chemical inputs often have caused serious soil and environmental problems and other side effects. The environmental and health consequences arising from the Green Revolution inputs are many and varied. A visible, parallel correlation between high yields, high artificial input use and environmental degradation and pollution is evident in many countries/areas where the Green Revolution has been successful and where commercial agriculture is widespread. The pollution and the over- exploitation of groundwater is not only affecting the environment and the health of humans but also impacting production and productivity, leading to falling or stagnating yields (IAD, 1994, p. 7; Conway and Barbier, 1990, p. 22; Wilson, 1994, 1999; Athukorala and Wilson, 2012).

The fertilisers (mainly nitrogenous) used have polluted the surface water and groundwater in many areas, with disruptive effects on the environment, wildlife and the health of humans. Pesticides, too, have affected the environment, wildlife, human beings and caused many occupational[4] morbidity and mortality effects due to direct exposure to pesticides. These are some of the private and external costs that have arisen due to agricultural pollution, resulting from the large-scale use of inorganic chemical inputs. We show in the following how this pollution is generated by agricultural production and accumulates in the environment over a period of time.

In order to do this, the production function (1) can be expanded to show all inputs used in the production process:

$$Y = f\left(\overline{X}_1, X_2, X_3, X_4\right) \tag{2}$$

$\overline{X}_1$ = Fixed inputs such as arable land (both in the short term and long term)
X_2 = All variable inputs excluding chemical inputs
X_3 = Chemical inputs (pesticides and fertilisers)
X_4 = Human effort

Although many of the inputs used in the production process can cause pollution- related private costs and negative externalities, in this chapter, as mentioned in the introduction, only the private costs and negative externalities arising from pollution resulting from the use of agro-chemical inputs such as fertilisers and pesticides, (X_3), are considered.

An off-shoot of the agricultural production function is a pollution-generation function (g). We assume that only X_3 causes pollution and affects agricultural productivity, other production processes, human health, the environment and wildlife. There are an N number of farmers in the area, N is large and all of them use the inputs, X_3. This is due to the Green Revolution technology and commercially grown vegetables and other cash crops, where large-scale use of chemical inputs such fertilisers and pesticides are not an uncommon practice. Also, it is assumed that the farmers produce for a market. We can write the pollution-generation function from a single producer at time t as:

$$Z_{it} = g\left(X_{3it}\right) \text{ where } i = 1, \ldots, N \tag{3}$$

Z_t is the quantity of pollution from farm i at time t.
where:

$$\frac{\partial Z_{it}}{\partial X_{3it}} > 0 \tag{4}$$

The second derivative is also positive. This is because pollution increases at an increasing rate as more and more of X_3 are used and also because of the existing level of stock pollution. In other words pollution is exponential.

The use of the inputs, X_3 cause negative externalities and private costs due to the nature of the inputs (which are agro-chemicals), where most of the pollution that is generated from these inputs tend to accumulate over time. As stated earlier, they break down very slowly and can stay in the environment for long periods of time. This we call 'stock' or 'conservative' pollutants (in the case of the Green Revolution, for example, some of the agricultural pollution have been accumulating over the last 30-plus years). Hence, the private costs and the negative externalities (pollution-related) stock accumulation function from X_3, from the N number of farmers at time t can be written as:

$$S_{Nt} = S_{Nt-1} + \sum_{i=1}^{N} Z_{it} \tag{5}$$

S_{Nt} is a stock of pollution,[5] at time t, from the N number of farmers. It is assumed that input use, X_3, by the farmers is the source of the stock pollution.

The stock pollution (i.e. both current and past pollution) causes the negative externalities and private costs. Externalities impose costs outside the farm, while the private costs are picked up by the respective producers. We know that when private costs arising from ill health to the producer from pollution are not taken into account, and in the presence of externalities, resource allocation becomes inefficient. This is because some of the costs arising from production are not taken into account in the market price. Private health costs arising from pollution are not taken into account by farmers due to many reasons. One main reason is that such costs are difficult to quantify and are regarded as indirect costs. Interestingly Sivayoganathan et al. (1995) point out that intangible costs such as discomfort, pain and suffering are considered as a 'normal part of their work' by farmers. Athukorala et al. (2012), too, have come to similar conclusions. In order for the market to internalise the problems, the costs of negative externalities and private costs should be reflected in the market price. When this occurs, we can say that resources have been allocated efficiently. In such a situation, in order to show the necessary condition for efficient resource allocation, let P_t, Q_t and R_t denote output and input prices and the price of pollution[6] in the form of health effects to the producer, generated by his own production activities, respectively, at a particular time t and V denotes a hypothetical shadow price of the externality at time t. Input use of the ith farmer, at time t, when resources are allocated efficiently is done according to:

$$P_t \, \partial Y / \partial X_{3it} = Q_t + R_t + V_t \, \partial Z / \partial X_{3it} \tag{6}$$

where $\dfrac{\partial Y}{\partial X_{3it}} > 0$ and $\dfrac{\partial Z}{\partial X_{3it}} > 0$

When resources are allocated efficiently, the value of marginal product of input use is equal to the sum of the input price, Q_t, plus the price paid for the private cost of pollution, R_t and the cost of marginal externality, by the input, X_3 ($V_t \, \partial Z / \partial X_{3it}$). In the case of externalities, it is important not to ignore the external costs, even though the costs may be picked up by future generations or non-producers. The extent of externalities also gives an indication of the extent of private costs arising from production-related pollution.

As Zilberman and Marra (1993, p. 248–249) have pointed out, ignoring the costs of externalities leads not only to an overuse of the inputs[7] but also to an accelerated build-up of the stock of pollution. Thus, the growth of S_t can impact the environment and wildlife; affect the production processes on the farm, other farms and other production activities; lead to a drop in agricultural output/productivity on the land; affect farmers health and also cause health problems to those living on the farms and outside. Zilberman and Marra (1993), too, confirm that the excessive accumulation of externality in the early periods tends to result in a substantial reduction in productivity in agricultural land in the long run, with output levels declining much below what is required by the efficient solution. The model presented previously shows that pollution generated could build up as a stock, resulting in many private and external costs. When such costs exist, we call such production inefficient. Furthermore, it must be pointed out that it is imperative to take into account the private costs of pollution arising to the producer. This is usually not considered by the producers, as will be shown in Section 3, and these costs are substantial. We show the private costs arising from exposure to pesticides in Section 3. When these pollution-related private costs are not considered, the market price does not reflect the true costs of production and hence resource allocation is inefficient.

There are many examples of declining agricultural productivity as mentioned previously. Studies conducted from the 1960s show that the growth rates for high-yielding varieties developed in Asia in the Green Revolution era have begun to slow down or stagnate (Conway and Barbier, 1990, p. 21; Dhanapala, personal communication, 1994; IAD, 1994, p. 7) and in the case of trial plots, a decline in yields has been observed (IAD, 1994, p. 7). On test plots at the International Rice Research Institute (IRRI) at Los Banos in the Philippines, where the HYVs were developed, varieties which yielded ten tons a hectare in 1966 are now yielding less than seven tons per ha (ibid.). The stagnation in yields experienced in Sri Lanka is attributed to soil fertility decline caused by prolonged intensive monocultures of high yielding cultivars, aided by high chemical inputs on the land (Dhanapala, 1994, personal communication). Declining yields discussed here are not related to the concept of diminishing returns but rather are an end result of pollution. Such pollution which is generated by farmers' activities cause private costs to the farmers themselves, as well as externalities to neighbours. When pollution exists, then the process of diminishing returns is accelerated. For a detailed discussion on the environmental costs of commercial agricultural production in South Asia, see Wilson (2000).

Furthermore, commercial agriculture has also been extracting underground water unsustainably where re-charge is less than water extraction. Athukorala and Wilson (2012) show that extraction of groundwater for onions and other cash crop production has been increasing rapidly during the last two decades in the dry zone areas of Sri Lanka. As a result of overuse, the availability of groundwater gradually has declined, while water quality has deteriorated. The deteriorating water quality has had a negative impact on agricultural production, especially for crops such as onions that are sensitive to increases in salinity levels. Using a stochastic frontier production function, they show farmers' over-use of groundwater in onion cultivation has resulted in decreasing yields.

Another impact that has been widely observed in LDCs, especially Asia, has been the impact of pesticides on human health. Pesticides have affected the users of pesticides (during handling and spraying) and those around them. In some LDC countries in Asia where the use of pesticides is high, the incidence of ill health arising from the use of pesticides also is high. Since exposure to pesticides by farmers is one of the biggest problems arising from commercial agriculture, we devote Section 3 to demonstrating the magnitude of the problem on human health, with special reference to farmers' health in Sri Lanka.

3. Evidence of farmers' pesticide use and its impact on their health and resulting costs

Sri Lanka is one of the success stories in relation to adopting Green Revolution technology in rice varieties in Asia. Furthermore, the country's farmers have moved from growing traditional vegetables to vegetables requiring the frequent use of pesticides and fertilisers. This change in agricultural practices has seen a rapid increase in the use of fertilisers and pesticides. Since the topic of impact of fertilisers and pesticides on health is large, this section concentrates only on some aspects of health related to impacts arising from direct use of pesticides by farmers on their farms and resulting costs to them.

Sri Lanka has been using pesticides since the introduction of Green Revolution technology in the 1960s. Since then, the use of pesticides has grown phenomenally (see, for example, Wilson, 1999). Pesticides (consisting of insecticides, herbicides and fungicides) are used commonly in rice and vegetable cultivation. As much as the farmers have been successful in protecting their crops from pests and diseases, the morbidity and mortality rates also have increased. Table 16.1 shows the extent of hospital admissions and deaths due to pesticide poisoning from 1975 to the mid-2000s. These are country-wide figures reported by government hospitals.

Table 16.1 Hospital admissions and deaths due to pesticide poisoning in Sri Lanka, 1975–1996

Year	Total Pesticide Deaths	Total Pesticide Admissions	Deaths Per100,000 Population	Rank Order*
1975	938	14,653	–	–
1976	964	13,778	–	–
1977	938	15,591	–	–
1978	1029	15,504	–	–
1979	1045	11,372	–	–
1980	1112	11,811	–	–
1981	1205	12,308	–	–
1982	1376	15,480	–	–
1983	1521	16,649	–	–
1984	1459	16,085	–	7th
1985	1439	14,423	–	4th
1986	1452	14,413	–	6th
1987	1435	12,841	8.8	6th
1988	1524	12,997	9.2	6th
1989	1296	12,763	7.7	6th
1990	1275	10,783	8.8	6th
1991	1667	13,837	11.3	4th
1992	1698	15,636	–	4th
1993	1682	16,692	9.5	5th
1994	1421	14,979	8.1	5th
1995	1581	15,740	9.5	6th
1996	1850	21,129	–	6th
1997	2121		11.8	5th
1998				6th
1999	1847		9.7	7th
2000				7th
2001				7th
2002				7th
2003	1310	19505	6.8	6th
2004				10th
2005	1270	16910		7th
2006	1242	17518		11th
2007	1148	17723		12th

Source: Annual health bulletin, Sri Lanka (various issues, 1975–2007).

* Rank order shows the leading causes of deaths in the country. As the rank order shows, pesticide poisoning is a major cause of death in Sri Lanka.

As shown in Table 16.1, the recorded deaths and hospital admissions is high, which reached a peak in the mid-1990s and then shows a marginal decrease. These are aggregated figures and pesticide poisoning recorded is mainly due to intentional (suicides) and accidental ingestion and farmers' exposure to pesticides while handling and spraying. In the case of deaths, the largest number of deaths is due to suicides, while in the case of hospital admissions, the largest number of admissions can be attributed to farmers' exposure to pesticides while spraying on their farms.

The high number of hospital admissions due to farmers exposure to pesticides is not accidental since field surveys repeatedly show that Sri Lankan farmers use pesticides more frequently, more than the recommended levels (Chandrasekera, et al. 1985; Sivayoganathan et al., 1995) and a wide variety of them. In other words, farmers use pesticides more than is privately efficient. They do it in the mistaken belief that increased frequency and increased toxicity will result in higher output. Jayathilake and Bandara (1989) showed from their study that 'absolutely clean crop' attitude and 'quick kill' belief among the farmers have resulted in nearly 77 percent of farmers using stronger concentrations of pesticides than recommended in vegetable cultivation. They also are known to mix several pesticides together (Chandrasekera et al., 1985). These practices not only increase the health hazards to farmers but are also costly.

It must be noted that figures shown in Table 16.1 for hospital admissions is an underestimate since most of the morbidity effects go unnoticed and unrecorded in hospitals.[8] Hoek et al. (1998) stated that 'many cases of intoxication due to occupational exposure may not require admission to a hospital are, therefore, not included in routine health statistics (1997, p. 8). They go on to state that many minor poisoning cases due to occupational exposure are not seen at government hospitals.

Given the high incidence of hospital admissions resulting from exposure to pesticides by farmers, we focus attention on costs resulting from exposure to pesticides by farmers and background information related to farmers' pesticide use in this section. We base our discussion based on two field surveys conducted in 1996 and 2007 to 2008 after a brief review of the relevant literature relating to farmers exposure to pesticides and ill-health.

Perhaps the first detailed study making specific reference to the effect of pesticides on farmers in Sri Lanka showing their harmful effects is by Jeyaratnam et al. (1982) in an article entitled 'Occupational Pesticide Poisoning'. This was a study carried out based on hospital data. The study refers to 23 patients admitted to a government hospital in Sri Lanka with acute pesticide poisoning during the paddy cultivation season of May to July.[9] These patients were diagnosed as having clinical features of acute pesticide poisoning. The chemical class of pesticides used were organochlorines, organophosphates or carbamates, and this was ascertained by examination of the empty bottles of the pesticides provided by the patients or their relatives. Of the 23 patients who were treated in hospital, one patient died. The study found that more than half of the patients developed symptoms either during spraying or within one hour of stopping work. All of the patients were aware of symptoms within four hours after cessation of spraying. When these patients were examined a year after they were hospitalised, many were found to be still suffering from symptoms associated with direct exposure to pesticides during handling and spraying on the farms. This shows that many long-term illnesses can arise due to direct exposure to pesticides, which is an area that remains largely unexplored in Sri Lanka.

More specific studies followed, such as by Chandrasekera et al. (1985).[10] This was a field study (where as the Jeyaratnam et al. 1982 study was based on hospital data) carried out among 288 farmers from vegetable growing areas from four districts. It was found that in the four districts, namely Kandy, Matale, Nuwara Eliya and Badulla, 44 percent, 51 percent, 57 percent and 62 percent of farmers, respectively, complained that they suffered from some illnesses such as faintness, dizziness, headache or vomiting after the application of pesticides to their crops. The study also gives figures not only of farmers hospitalised due to pesticide spraying but statistics of the number of farmers who died due to exposure to pesticides while spraying them on the farms. Dissanayake (1986), too, carried out a similar survey on pesticide use among vegetable growers in Sri Lanka.

Jeyaratnam (1985) in the editorial in the *British Journal of Industrial Medicine* highlighted the health problems faced by farmers using pesticides in Sri Lanka. Jeyaratnam et al. (1987) carried out a rather detailed study to investigate the extent of acute pesticide poisoning in selected agricultural communities in Sri Lanka, Indonesia, Malaysia and Thailand, by which time direct exposure to pesticides had been recognised as a major problem in LDCs.[11] The study confirmed the existence of 'pesticide ill effects' among farmers due to direct exposure to pesticides during handling and spraying in all these countries.

More studies were undertaken since then to show the health hazards arising from pesticide use during handling and spraying by farmers and also to investigate the protective measures taken to avoid symptoms among agro-pesticide applicators in Sri Lanka. They are: Gnanachandran and Siyayoganathan (1989), Jayathilake and Bandara (1989), Dharmawardena (1994), Siyayoganathan et al. (1995) and Van der Hoek et al. (1998). These are detailed studies that show the health hazards arising from direct exposure to pesticides by farmers during handling and spraying on farms and show the inadequacy of precautions taken by farmers using pesticides. The studies showed that direct exposure to pesticides during handling and spraying (often due to inadequate precautions taken) on farms is a major health hazard faced by farmers.

Despite the lack of studies done in the 1960s and 1970s on the dangers of pesticide use (mainly by farmers), legislation was passed in parliament in September 1980 (see Control of Pesticides Parliament Act, No. 33 of 1980) to provide for the safe use of pesticides; to license pesticides used in Sri Lanka; to regulate the import, packing, labelling, storage, formulation, transport, sale of pesticides; and for the appointment of a licensing authority for pesticides and for the establishment of a pesticide formulary committee and for matters connected with it. As a consequence to the Pesticides Act of 1980, a registrar of pesticides was appointed in 1983 with authority to set regulations and standards for pesticides in Sri Lanka. The Malathion Control Act was enacted in 1985. De Alwis (1988) discussed the regulation, formulation, sale and use of pesticides in the country. The statistics discussed in this chapter cover the sale and use of pesticides. It is legally mandatory that the labels of the pesticides give, amongst other items, sufficient information on how to use them (that is, when and how much to use), the period of effectiveness of the pesticide, the pre-harvest interval during which time pesticides should not be used and precautions to be taken in spray preparations and during application. As regards to the sale, the standards are enforced by the pesticide registrar. Furthermore, agricultural extension workers, too, are given regular advice on the handling and use of pesticides, protective measures to be undertaken, the correct dosage and other information related to pesticide use.

However, the problem faced by agricultural extension workers is the non-compliance of farmers in the correct use of pesticides. It is not mandatory for farmers to carry out instructions issued by agricultural extension workers of the Department of Agriculture. Furthermore, policing hundreds of thousands of farmers is not an option that can be easily implemented without incurring large costs. Jeyaratnam et al. (1987) in a brief paper discussed pesticide legislation in LDCs, including Sri Lanka. Apart from legislation to minimise the harmful effects of pesticides, the medical profession have also felt the need for the establishment of a poisons information centre from as early as the 1970s, when pesticides usage was still at a very low level (Fernando, 1988). As a consequence, a National Poisons Information Center was set up in 1988 to disseminate information on all aspects of poisonings, especially pesticides. The problem of pesticide poisoning (affecting farmers and health workers using them, deliberate ingestion for suicides, accidents and homicides) in Sri Lanka has become so acute that the Presidential Task Force on

Formulating a National Health Policy has taken note of the dangers posed by pesticides and has recommended various measures to combat this problem (Sessional Paper, 1993). Fernando (1995) also discussed pesticide poisoning in the Asia-Pacific region and the role of a regional information network to combat the problem of pesticide poisoning in the region. De Alwis (1988) analysed the nature of the market for agro-chemicals in Sri Lanka. We now discuss the results of two field studies conducted within the last two years which show the magnitude of the private costs to farmers exposed to pesticides during handling and spraying.

3.1 Results of two field surveys conducted on farmers' ill-health due exposure to pesticides during handling and spraying

Whilst the literature review covered most of the studies involving farmers exposure to pesticides, not many studies have been conducted which estimate the costs of ill health to farmers as a result of exposure to pesticides while handling and spraying. Figure 16.1 shows a typical farmer in Sri Lanka. Wilson (1999) conducted a comprehensive study that estimated the costs of ill health due to farmers' exposure to pesticides while handling and spraying pesticides on their farms. The survey was conducted from July to September 1996. Another detailed filed survey was conducted by Athukorala (2011) during 2007 to 2008.

Figure 16.1 A typical farmer who handles and sprays pesticides on his farm

Note: Photographed on the 30th of December, 2012 near Wasgamuwa National Park, North Central, Sri Lanka – not far from where the two field studies were undertaken.

In the Wilson (1999) study and as discussed in Wilson (2005), five areas were sampled from the intermediate and dry zones of Sri Lanka where intensive agriculture is widespread to collect a representative cross section of farmers to examine the extent of pesticide use and the health effects arising from such use. The areas covered were Yatawatte, Kandalama, Beligamuwa, Ambana and Polononaruwa in the central and north central provinces of Sri Lanka, within a 75 to 100 mile radius. Only farmers who are regular pesticide users and cultivate land not less than half and not more than three acres were selected. Large-scale cultivators of land were not considered. Farmers cultivating more than half an acre and less than three acres were selected because according to a census carried out in 1982 by the Department of Census and Statistics, the average size of land cultivated in the country was 1.94 acres. Therefore, as the census statistics show, a large number of farmers cultivate a land area which is less than three acres and more than half an acre. The five regions also specialise in growing certain vegetable crops. As a result, the level and intensity of pesticides used and the level of direct exposure to pesticides vary from region to region. Furthermore, the frequency of pesticide use varies from season to season. In the mostly rice growing season (known as Maha), the frequency of pesticide use is less than in the more drier vegetable growing season (known as Yala). Farmers who use pesticides once or twice a week (usually vegetable growers) were more vulnerable to suffer from acute pesticide poisoning than those farmers who used pesticides once a month or 3 to 5 times for the entire cropping season (usually rice growers) and get admitted to hospital or take treatment from a hospital. This is evident in the data collected. Judgment sampling (which is a non-probability sampling technique) was employed to collect the data necessary for the study. This was owing to the impossibility of carrying out a simple random sampling study for the entire country due to financial and time constraints.

The survey unearthed some interesting facts. The survey recorded 103 different brands of pesticides (of which 48 were insecticides, 28 were fungicides and 27 were herbicides – also known as weedicides) being used in the study areas. Of the 103 pesticides being used by farmers in the study area, nine pesticides had been de-registered in Sri Lanka from use since July 1995. The most frequently used pesticides were insecticides. This is shown in Table 16.2. They are used for the control of insects and are the most toxic of all pesticides used. Most of the insecticides used in the study area were organophosphates and carbamates and to a lesser extent organochlorines.

Table 16.2 also shows the quantity of pesticides used by an average farmer in the study area. It is around 356 ounces per farmer per year. In other words, a farmer used more than 22,

Table 16.2 Type and quantity of pesticides used in the study area

Pesticides	Number of Brands	Average use of Pesticide Brands
1. Herbicides	27	1.11
2. Insecticides	48	2.82
3. Fungicides	28	0.99
	Total Use	*Average Use*
Ounces	72,330	356.30

Source: Wilson (1999, 2005).

Survey Period: July to September 1996.

Table 16.3 Handling and spraying exposure to pesticides on a typical pesticide-spraying day

Direct Exposure Time	Average Hours of a Typical Pesticide Spraying Day
Spraying hours per day	5.71
Handling and mixing hours per day	0.19
Total	**5.91**

Source: Wilson (1999, 2005).

Survey Period: July to September 1996.

16-ounce bottles of pesticides a year, most of which are insecticides. In spraying these pesticides, farmers are often directly exposed to these chemicals and some for as long as six hours. Due to the nature of farming (mainly small scale agriculture), pesticide spraying is carried out manually using hand sprayers. Hence the level of direct exposure is very high, which results in high levels of morbidity and even mortality among farmers. A breakdown of the average handling and spraying hours is shown in Table 16.3.

As can be seen from Table 16.3, an average farmer handled and sprayed pesticides for more than half a working day on his farm. The frequency of use varies from one spraying day a month to as much as two spraying days a week during the peak of the cultivating season. The frequency of use can vary greatly from crop to crop and season to season. On average, a farmer handled and sprayed pesticides for around 197 hours a year.

Farmers handling and spraying pesticides are affected due to exposure. A farmer can suffer from many illnesses and the health effects ranging from faintish feelings to blurring vision and tremors. These are the usual acute symptoms which appear on spraying days which have also been documented by other field studies (see, for example, Jeyaratnam, 1985; Siyayoganathan et al., 1995). This is shown in Table 16.4. Similar symptoms appear on non-spraying days as well. Chronic, long-term health effects range from chest pains, blindness, and loss of memory to ulcers, depression, and other illnesses.[12] Due to these morbidity effects, some farmers need hospitalization while some farmers take treatment from a hospital or a physician (but are not admitted to hospital) while others take homemade self-treatment. Thus farmers incur pesticide-related medical expenditures and other costs such as loss of efficiency and loss of leisure time. Furthermore, many working days and hours also are lost due to various illnesses. Discomfort, pain and suffering also are common.

The private short-run costs to the users are expected to be large and the long-term costs are even larger, although difficult to measure. The private costs to the consumers of food crops produced by using pesticides are unknown, although it is also expected to be large. The public costs (hospital costs) also are large. The damage done to the environment should also be high. No study has been conducted to assess the extent of the damage done to fauna, especially birds, fish and insects, but it is quite evident that these fauna, that were once numerous, have decreased in numbers in areas where pesticides are widely used. The various costs incurred by the respondents (farmers) are shown in Table 16.5. A breakdown of the costs incurred due to direct exposure to pesticides for the five regions is also shown in Table 16.5. Apart from the costs arising from direct exposure to pesticides, farmers also incur costs on defensive or precautionary behaviour. A breakdown of the number of respondents (farmers) incurring such costs are shown in Table 16.5.

In the present study, 96 percent of the respondents had suffered some form of after-effect on a typical pesticide spraying day (excludes effects on non-spraying days or long-term effects)

Table 16.4 Frequency of illnesses affecting farmers on a typical pesticide-spraying day

Illnesses recorded on a spraying day	1		2		3		4		5		6	
	No	%	No	%	No	%	No	%	No	%	No	%
Faintish feeling	39	19	11	05	7	03	12	05	77	38	58	36
Headache	61	20	19	09	08	04	24	12	47	24	40	19
Dizziness	32	16	15	07	14	06	16	08	51	23	76	37
Nausea	26	13	14	07	06	03	09	04	47	23	104	51
Excessive salivation	89	44	20	10	02	01	12	06	28	14	52	26
Eye irritation	18	09	14	07	04	02	09	04	21	10	136	66
Eye tearing	14	07	03	01	03	01	13	06	29	14	158	77
Vomiting	04	02	01	0.4	05	02	13	06	51	25	142	69
Weakness of muscles	24	12	07	03	04	02	07	03	23	11	138	67
Difficulty in breathing	13	06	10	04	04	02	07	03	26	13	143	70
Twitching of eye lids	11	05	07	03	00	00	08	04	12	06	165	91
Cramps	14	06	06	03	04	02	06	03	15	07	175	86
Diarrhea	00	00	01	0.4	00	00	03	01	03	01	25	12
Twitching of muscles in the face	17	08	11	05	03	01	08	04	10	04	154	75
Twitching of muscles in the body	41	20	12	05	05	02	07	03	26	12	112	55
Blurring vision	16	08	08	04	05	02	06	03	15	07	152	74
Tremor	04	18	04	02	02	01	09	04	36	18	146	71

Source: Wilson (1999, 2005).

Survey Period: July to September 1996.

Note:
1 Every Day,   2 Almost Every Day,   3 About Half of the Time,   4 Now and then, but less than half of the time,   5 Rarely,   6 None of the time.

during the year before the survey, not necessarily leading to hospitalization or taking treatment from a physician, but, however, incurring costs due to self-treatment, loss of working days, efficiency at work and loss of leisure time. On a typical spraying day or soon afterwards (usually within four hours), 20 percent of the farmers interviewed had been admitted to hospital and incurred costs, 30 percent had taken treatment from a doctor and incurred costs and another 64 percent, although not hospitalized or did not require treatment from a physician, nevertheless took homemade self-treatment and incurred other private costs. Furthermore, 42 percent of the respondents incurred costs on non-spraying days and 35 percent incurred costs due to long-term illnesses resulting from direct exposure to pollution. Table 16.5 shows the extent of the costs arising from direct exposure to pesticides and precautionary measures taken.

As Table 16.5 shows. there is considerable variation in the number of respondents incurring costs across regions. Furthermore, there is considerable variation in precautionary costs as well.

Table 16.5 Number of respondents incurring costs due to pesticide pollution in the study area

Respondents	Beligamuwa		Ambana		Kandalama		Yatawatte		Polonnaruwa		Total	
	42		31		46		53		31		203	
	No.	%	No.	%	No.	%	No.	%	No.	%	No.	%
Medical and other costs												
A	13	30%	06	19%	08	17%	08	15%	06	19%	41	20%
B	09	21%	04	13%	23	50%	22	41%	04	13%	62	30%
C	33	78%	30	97%	20	43%	25	47%	28	90%	136	64%
NSD	21	50%	14	45%	34	73%	14	26%	04	13%	87	42%
LTC	09	21%	07	22%	23	50%	25	47%	07	23%	71	35%
Defensive costs												
PC	20	48%	31	97%	32	69%	25	47%	16	51%	123	61%
OC	04	10%	09	29%	21	46%	26	49%	03	10%	66	32%
All	22	52%	31	100%	32	69%	40	75%	17	55%	142	70%
EP	42	100%	31	100%	46	100%	49	92%	27	87%	195	96%

Source: Wilson (1999, 2005).

Survey Period: July to September 1996.

A: Respondents admitted to hospital and incurring private costs (includes all costs associated with pesticide pollution).

B: Respondents consulting a doctor and incurring private costs (includes all costs associated with pesticide pollution).

C: Respondents not admitted to hospital or consulting a doctor, but seeking some form of treatment and incurring private costs (includes all costs associated with pesticide pollution).

NSD: All private costs incurred on non-spraying days due to exposure to pesticides (includes costs on medicine, consultation and other costs).

LTC: All long-term private costs incurred due to direct exposure to pesticides (includes costs on medicine, consultation and other costs).

PC: Number of respondents incurring costs on some form of protective gear.

OC: Number of respondents incurring costs apart from costs on protective gear (for example, costs incurred on special storage and hiring labour).

ALL: Includes all respondents incurring costs on protective clothing and other defensive behaviour.

EP: Number of respondents suffering from acute illnesses described in the interview on a typical pesticide spraying day (excludes non-spaying days and long-term illnesses) and incurring costs. There were eight respondents in the sample (n = 203) who did not incur any costs.

From the table we can see that in areas where precautionary costs are high, then, in general, the number of those admitted to hospitals (serious illnesses) and taking treatment from physicians (moderate illnesses) is low. There are, however, exceptions to this rule. In the case of Polonnaruwa, the amount of precautions taken is low and also the number of respondents needing hospitalization and treatment from a physician also is low. This is because Polonnaruwa is mainly a paddy growing area and the frequency of pesticide use is low (on average, one pesticide spray a month). Table 16.5 suggests that when protective measures are undertaken, they could to some extent minimize the extent of serious and moderate illnesses; however, many pesticide users could yet suffer from mild symptoms. This is because the precautions taken are inadequate to prevent mild symptoms. For example, take Ambana, where the precautionary costs are high and, therefore, serious and moderate illnesses are low while the mild symptoms are high. On the other hand, when the precautionary costs are low, as for, example, in Beligamuwa and Yatawatte, then the serious and moderate illnesses tend to increase. These figures, however, should be treated with caution since only a small sample of farmers has been surveyed.

The survey also estimated the average cost of illnesses due to direct exposure to pesticides arising on pesticide spraying days, non-spraying days and long-term illnesses. The survey estimated losses in the following categories under direct and indirect costs. The estimated direct private costs were: any privately purchased drugs, laboratory and other investigation costs done privately, costs of transport to the patient and costs involved with special diets, hired labour due to inability to work on sick days and other losses due to direct exposure to pesticides (such as crop damage due to inability to look after crops such as from theft and damage from wild animals). A major portion of the losses resulting from direct exposure to pesticides were from imputed value of lost time rather than from out-of-pocket expenses. Thus, the valuation of time is critical. The indirect private costs are: loss of working days, loss of efficiency and the time a patient spends visiting hospitals or a doctor. We tried to estimate the loss of efficiency for the farmers on their farm resulting from direct exposure to pesticide-related illnesses because most farmers during the pilot survey complained that their efficiency decreased following a direct exposure to pesticide-related illness, which was substantial. While this procedure is subjective, it addresses a real economic consequence of illnesses of this sort. The inclusion of leisure hours is also no doubt subjective, but it also shows the economic consequences of the illnesses. The inclusion of leisure hours is all the more important when we consider that loss of leisure hours affects productivity. It must be mentioned that estimating the number of leisure hours lost as well as lost productivity is a difficult task. Leisure hours were taken to be any time spent at home after work such as: reading a newspaper, watching television, listening to the radio, pursuing a game or a hobby or time spent with the family. Sleeping hours are not included nor was the time spent attending to domestic chores. Loss of efficiency was defined as the lessening of one's productivity while working. The estimation of work hours lost and time spent travelling to hospital and seeking treatment is less troublesome to calculate. Once the lost time has been calculated, the conversion to monetary terms was straightforward. This is because, as noted by Harrington et al. (1989, p.128) the losses in many of these categories depend to a considerable extent on the value of time. Following Becker (1965), lost work time, efficiency, leisure hours, time spent travelling to hospital was calculated at the prevailing hourly average wage rate in the areas for the interviewed farmers. The hourly wage rate was derived by dividing an average days' labour wage by the number of hours worked. The average cost of labour for a day in the study area in 1996 was taken as Rs 150 (approximately US$1.15 based on October 2013 exchange rates) and the number of hours worked for this sum was eight hours. The average cost of labour was arrived by dividing the wage rates prevalent in the study areas to spray pesticides by the number of hours worked per day. Sections four and five of the questionnaire obtained data on the hours worked and also the wage rates paid. Hence, we arrived at a wage rate of Rs 18.75 per hour (approximately US$0.15 based on October 2013 exchange rates). This figure was then used to arrive at the estimates shown in Table 16.6.

Table 16.6 provides estimates of the total and average cost to farmers arising from direct exposure to pesticides. As can be seen, the direct average total cost due to direct exposure to pesticides for a year is more than an average month's salary (the average monthly salary is Rs 4,748.17 – approximately US$36.53 based on October 2013 exchange rates). The direct private out-of-pocket costs for medical care are a small portion of the total cost. Time costs (indirect

Table 16.6 Private out-of-pocket and time costs due to direct exposure to pesticides

Item	Direct		Indirect	
	Total Costs	*Average Costs*	*Total Costs*	*Average Costs*
Time spent on travelling/ seeking treatment			70,856.25	349.04
Hired labour due to inability to work	82,072	404.28		
Other costs: Private medical expenditure Special diets, travel costs	212,584	1047.21		
Loss of work days/ hours on farm			312,121.85	1,537.54
Loss of efficiency on farm			164,709.35	811.37
Leisure time losses			176,414.08	869.03
Long-term	90,750	447.04		
Total (RS)	385,404	1898.53	724,101.53	3,566.98
Total (US)	2964.7	14.61	5570	27.5

Survey Period: July to September 1996.

Note:

(1) The costs considered are for one year. The costs incurred by farmers for the period June 1995–June 1996 were considered for this study.

(2) Long-term costs are those costs arising from a permanent nature as opposed to the short-term illnesses described in the questionnaire (please see section three of questionnaire). The long-term illnesses considered were those diagnosed by a physician as arising from direct exposure to pesticides. Suffers have to incur costs on treatment, etc. every year due to long-term illnesses. For this study only the costs incurred from long-term illnesses for one year (June 1995–June 1996) were considered.

costs) make up the rest, with loss of productivity and leisure time accounting for more than half the loss. Once these costs are added, the private costs of direct exposure to pesticides is more than an average farmer's monthly income. In other words, a farmer on average suffered costs which amounted to more than a month's income per year in 1997. It must be noted here that a very large portion of the medical direct costs have not been included for this estimation for lack of hospital data. The medical costs are no doubt very large.

One-and-a-half decades later, another major survey (Athukorala, 2011) was undertaken. One of the main objectives of this survey was to determine the costs of ill-health arising from farmers. The survey selected six villages in the Galnawa divisional secretariat area in the Anuradhapura district[13] for the study. Face-to-face interviews were conducted among randomly selected farmers. Survey techniques used in this survey were similar to the one employed by Wilson (1999). Of the 257 interviews conducted, the data from 246 interviews are used in the analysis due to erroneous or irrational reporting.

Furthermore, 217 hospitalised farmers due to exposure to pesticides while spraying were also interviewed in their villages. As discussed in Athukorala et al. (2012), the farmers studied in this part of the survey were those who have been treated by physicians for symptoms arising from exposure to pesticides while spraying on farm crops. These farmers, like the general farmers, cultivate their own land and they include both men and women. This study surveyed farmers in the Anuradhapura, Kurunagala and Ampara districts. For this part of the survey, 36 hospitals were visited (this includes some dispensaries) to obtain the medical records of the affected (hospitalised) farmers. In general, doctors maintain records under three headings. They are accidental poisoning, spray poisoning and observations when doctors suspect a patient needs treatment due to pesticide-related illnesses. The survey was conducted during the period September 2007 to February 2008. The survey was conducted as follows: Once the interviewers visited a hospital in the selected area, they requested doctors to provide addresses of those patients who have been diagnosed as suffering from ill-health due to exposure to pesticides. Permission was then sought from patients (farmers) to conduct the interviews. Only farmers who provided their consent to take part in the survey were interviewed. Data from 221 farmers were collected using direct interviews. Due to some incomplete responses, the study uses responses of 217 farmers.

The average number of self-reported illnesses on a typical pesticide spraying day is three and two for the hospitalized and general farmers, respectively. The average level of education is higher for the general farmers. As expected, the quantity of pesticides used per month (in litres), number of pesticides types used, frequency of use (pesticides used per month) and direct exposure to pesticides (per day/hours) were higher for hospitalized farmers than for the general farmers. The health symptoms most commonly reported by all respondents (both samples) included headaches (68 percent), eye irritation and tearing (49 percent), pain in muscles, joints, or bones (31 percent), a rash or cramps (30 percent) and difficulty in breathing (16 percent).

Using this data, the medical costs under different scenarios were investigated. This analysis considered the variation of costs to farmers who have different experiences of illnesses due to direct exposure to pesticides. The average cost was calculated for farmers classified as serious (A – hospitalisation), moderate (B – a doctor is consulted, but no hospitalization is required) and mild cases (C – no visits to the doctor, yet medication is taken). A farmer may have experienced one, two or all three of the above. Table 16.7 shows medical costs incurred by the two groups of farmers. As can be seen, there is considerable variation in the costs incurred for the three categories. It is interesting to note that the reported average costs of hospitalized farmers are higher than that of the general farmers for most of the three categories and on non-spraying days.

Table 16.7 shows that on a typical pesticide spraying day or soon afterwards, approximately 4.8 percent of the general farmers interviewed had been admitted to hospital and incurred costs while 8 percent had taken treatment from a doctor. This figure is consistent with other studies conducted (see, for example, Murray et al. 2002; Garming and Waibel, 2009). Approximately 56 percent of the general farmers took homemade self-treatment and incurred other private costs. Approximately 71 percent of this group said that they have suffered from some form of acute ill-health and incurred costs from pesticide spraying days during the last three years. However, 34 percent of the interviewed farmers in this group said that they did not suffer any form of ill-health and did not incur any form of expenditure due to exposure to pesticides during the previous cultivation season.

Of the hospitalised farmers, the majority (45 percent) incurred all forms of costs (i.e. A, B and C) and 84 percent said that they had been hospitalized plus taken treatment at home without consulting a doctor. The monthly average medical costs due to direct exposure to pesticides to farmers who suffered from all three categories of costs were approximately Rs. 325 and Rs. 287 (approximately US$2.5 and 2.2 based on October 2013 exchange rates) for the hospitalised and general farmers, respectively. The average monthly medical costs to farmers suffering from ill-health due to exposure to pesticides are approximately Rs. 229 and Rs. 169 (approximately US$1.76 and 1.3) for the hospitalised and general farmers, respectively. The estimated average monthly costs for pesticide exposure on non-spraying days are Rs. 51 and Rs. 29 (approximately

Table 16.7 Medical costs incurred under different scenarios[1] (Rs./per month) (See note for exchange rate calculation in US$)

Scenarios	Hospitalised farmers	Percentage	General farmers	Percentage
A, B and C	324.74 (0.72)	45.62	287.28 (0.64)	1.63
A and B	250.50 (0.56)	13.82	262.50 (0.58)	1.22
A and C	180.19 (0.40)	23.96	165.00 (0.37)	1.22
A	157.77 (0.35)	16.58	138.33 (0.31)	0.81
B and C	–	–	154.16 (0.34)	1.63
B	–	–	120.71 (0.27)	1.22
C	–	–	53.20 (0.11)	56.50
Average	228.30 (0.51)	100.00	168.74 (0.37)	64.23
NSDs	50.94 (0.11)	–	29.28 (0.06)	–
Zero Cost	0.00	0.00	0.00	35.77
N	217	–	246	–

Source: Athukorala et al. (2012).

Note:

i. Monthly medical costs for a typical cultivation season for farmers who have different experiences due to exposure to pesticides are reported in the table. The medical costs for hospitalised farmers or those who take treatment for being sick soon after spraying (within 12 hours) or while spraying/mixing pesticides were calculated. For the general farmer's sample, only 158 farmers reported any form of costs. NSD denotes average medical costs incurred due to exposure to pesticides on non-spraying or mixing days. Zero costs refer to farmers who did not fall into any of the above mentioned categories during the specified cultivation seasons.

ii. Costs as a ratio of daily wages are shown in parentheses.

iii. The 2013 (October) exchange was 1US$ = Rs 130

1. These costs were calculated using average monthly health costs as well as by taking into account the number of times a farmer has suffered from ill-health. For example, medical costs of general farmers who have experienced B and C (Rs.154.16) heath costs is greater than the cost of the farmers who have only been hospitalised (Rs. 138.33). The reason for this is that the frequency of hospital visits is lower than B and C.

US$0.40 and 0.3) for the two respective groups. The cost for the general farmers who are in category C (mild cases) is low (Rs. 53, US$41). This is because most of the farmers in this group resort to homemade treatment, which does not incur significant costs.

In addition to incurring medical expenditures, loss in earnings from being unable to work is a large cost to farmers (see, for example, Wilson, 1999; Huang et al. 2000; Garming and Waibel, 2009). Therefore, the lost earnings of farmers who have had different experiences of ill-health were estimated. The opportunity cost of lost labour hours due ill-health from direct exposure to pesticides is used for this purpose. The estimated lost earnings and mitigating expenditures is shown in Table 16.8.

Table 16.8 shows the opportunity costs of lost labour hours due to pesticide-related illnesses for the hospitalized as well as the general farmer's sample. The monthly labour costs of farmers who fall into all three categories are approximately 13 and 10 hours for hospitalised and general farmers, respectively. However, the average monthly costs to farmers from loss of labour hours are Rs. 475 (approximately US$3.7) for the hospitalized sample, which is equal to the value of a day's wage. For the general farmer group, it is approximately Rs.340 (approximately US$2.6),

Table 16.8 Lost earnings due to exposure to pesticides and mitigating expenditures (Rs./per month) (See note for exchange rate calculation in US$)

Scenario	Lost earnings*		Averting expenditures**	
	Hospitalised farmers	*General farmers*	*Hospitalised farmers*	*General farmers*
A, B and C	731.25 (1.62)	590.62 (1.31)	23.51 (0.05)	34.56 (0.07)
A and B	519.37 (1.15)	379.68 (0.84)	44.30 (0.09)	54.58 (0.12)
A and C	316.94 (0.71)	412.50 (0.91)	43.65 (0.09)	41.83 (0.09)
A	332.81 (0.73)	346.87 (0.77)	65.23 (0.14)	56.91 (0.12)
B and C	–	253.12 (0.56)	–	50.77 (0.11)
B	–	241.07 (0.53)	–	53.92 (0.12)
C	–	177.15 (0.39)	–	68.39 (0.15)
Average***	475.09(1.05)	343.01 (0.76)	44.17 (0.09)	51.57 (0.11)
N	217	246	217	246

Source: Athukorala et al. (2012).

Note:

i. * The daily wage rate in Sri Lanka varies between Rs. 400 and Rs. 500 for different areas. However, Rs. 450 was used as the average daily wage rate. Accordingly, the hourly wage rate is assumed as Rs.56.25 when calculating the loss in earnings. ** Mitigating expenditure mainly includes costs incurred on wearing protective clothing, marks, gloves and shoes. *** Average for general farmers is calculated using only 158 farmers who have at least one experience of the above scenarios.

ii. Costs as a ratio of daily wages are shown in parentheses.

iii. The 2013 (October) exchange was 1US$ = Rs 130

which is equal to the value of two-thirds of their daily labour rate. This means that during a typical cultivation season, farmers are losing between half to one day value of labour each month due to ill-health from exposure to pesticides. However, most of the farmers are not aware of the value of health-related loss of labour hours lost due to pesticide exposure. This indicates that the opportunity cost of lost labour hours is low – a problem common to markets not fully monetised.

The averting expenditure undertaken by farmers to reduce exposure to pesticides is shown in Table 16.8. In the study areas, pesticide spraying is undertaken every two to six days. However, the extent of the precautions taken is low for both farmer groups. A similar conclusion is drawn by Wilson (2005) in a study analysing the averting behaviour of pesticides of farmers in Sri Lanka. One of the interesting observations of the data here is that the average monthly averting expenditure of farmers who said that they had incurred no costs from spraying pesticides is more than double (Rs.108.50 – US$0.84) the average of farmers who reported expenditures due to pesticide related ill-health (See Table 16.9).

According to Table 16.9, the average estimated total costs incurred by the hospitalized sample is approximately Rs. 800 (US$6.16). This is equal to approximately 3 percent of an average farmer's monthly income during a typical cultivation season. This figure is Rs. 590 (US$4.54) for the general farmer's sample, equivalent to a loss of approximately 2 percent of their monthly farm income. In this study, we have not estimated the magnitude of the benefits of using pesticides. However, the majority of farmers (87 percent) surveyed were of the view that their crop loss will be more than 75 percent if they do not use pesticides on their crops. The costs to farmers who have incurred all three types of medical expenditures are relatively higher for both samples. It is

Table 16.9 Estimated total costs to farmers due to exposure to pesticides (Rs./per month) (See note for exchange rate calculation in US$)

Scenario	Hospitalised farmers	As a percentage of farm income	General farmers	As a percentage of farm income
A, B and C	1136.17 (2.52)	4.37	970.21 (2.15)	3.45
A and B	864.40 (1.92)	3.32	725.52 (1.61)	2.58
A and C	591.33 (1.31)	2.27	668.33 (1.48)	2.00
A	602.18 (1.34)	2.31	561.29 (1.25)	1.99
B and C	–	–	482.06 (1.07)	1.71
B	–	–	432.85 (0.96)	1.54
C	–	–	307.89 (0.68)	1.10
Average	798.52 (1.77)	3.07231	592.25 (1.32)	2.10

Source: Athukorala et al. (2012).

Note:

i. Total costs include mainly medical, labour and averting costs. Medical costs include both costs incurred on spraying days and non-spraying days. The sample average income is used to show the total costs as a percentage of farmers' average income. Average farm incomes of hospitalised and general farmers were Rs.25,991 and Rs. 28,113 respectively.

ii. Costs as a ratio of daily wages are shown in parentheses.

iii. The 2013 (October) exchange was 1US$ = Rs 130

Rs. 1,136 and Rs. 970 (US$8.74 and 7.47) for hospitalised and general farmers, respectively. As a percentage of farm income it is approximately 4 percent and 3 percent for the two groups, respectively.

It is important to note that more than 60 percent of total costs incurred were due to lost earnings representing a hidden cost to farmers. Labour is a scare resource during the peak cultivating and harvesting periods in Sri Lanka but less so during other periods. Farmers are, therefore, less likely to put a high valuation on their lost labour or opportunity cost of lost hours in non-peak cultivating and harvesting periods when spraying usually takes place. This is one of the reasons why most farmers do not take into account this large cost when deciding to use pesticides.

4. Understanding the reasons as to why farmers continue to use chemicals such as pesticides despite the high costs

As was shown in the previous section, farmers' exposure to pesticides is high and the resulting economic costs also are high. However, despite these costs, farmers continue to use pesticides. In order to implement policies for farmers to reduce the current use of pesticides and their high exposure, it is important to understand why farmers continue to use pesticides despite the high costs. There are many reasons for this paradox, and they differ widely across regions and countries and may not follow a similar pattern where the use of pesticides is common place. Wilson and Tisdell (2001) have discussed this issue in detail. They point out that farmers will use pesticides if the discounted net present value of stream of returns from doing so is positive. Such a situation can support the use of unsustainable pest control strategies and is more likely to do so the higher the real discount rate. This is usually considered to be higher in LDCs than in more developed countries (MDCs). As Managi (2006) shows, pollution levels (in this case exposure to pesticides) will begin to show a decrease after reaching some threshold income. This is typically the inverted U shaped environmental Kuznets curve where it is hypothesised that as income increases, pollution decreases after reaching some threshold income. For farmers in LDCs, this is a long way off or may never reach the 'threshold income' required for pollution to show a decrease because farmers in these countries are caught in a 'pesticide trap' and, as Section 3 indicated, the large health costs are reducing the real incomes of farmers.

Hence, to use less sustainable techniques is more likely in LDCs. It is also possible that farmers in LDCs are less informed about pesticides than those in MDCs.

Furthermore, Wilson and Tisdell (2001) pointed out that market systems encourage the adoption of biophysically unsustainable techniques such as the use of pesticides in agriculture. Such techniques lower current costs and boost yields in the short-run but eventually lower yields and raise costs of production in the longer term. They point out that initially the use of pesticides is likely to increase the supply and reduce market prices, thereby forcing non-adopters to adopt despite their reservations. In short, farmers not using pesticides could be forced to use pesticides to avoid economic losses. Defensive use of pesticides becomes necessary by non-users so as to ensure their economic survival. Once the new technique is used, it may be difficult to revert to the previous process, except at a high cost, even when the cost of production of employing the new technique eventually rises above that of the old. Hysteresis is present.

They also show that farmers may use pesticides for reasons other than the above. There may be ignorant about the sustainability of pesticide use. Pesticides use may be believed to be more sustainable than is in fact the case. Pesticides are an integral part of commercially grown HYVs (for example, Green Revolution varieties). Without the use of pesticides, high yields of some crop varieties may not be sustained. Furthermore, the pesticide industry has an incentive to push their use by advertising and promotion, and this could create a bias in favour of their use (see, for example, Tisdell et al., 1984). Hence, the use of chemicals in agriculture may be encouraged in preference to the use of natural ingredients available to farmers (Tisdell, 1999). Agricultural research also could become biased towards pesticides. The market failure results in the use and development of agricultural techniques which lack sustainability and which reduce long-term economic welfare (Tisdell, 1999). This is especially so if there is no countervailing argument from consumers or activists against their use. Loans obtained by farmers for the purchase of inputs (for example, pesticides and fertilisers) may also be a barrier to switching to other strategies. Damage to agricultural land from the use of pesticides occurs over a period of time. Hence, costs arising may not initially look serious. Furthermore, farmers do not compensate for the numerous externalities except in the case of production externalities. As shown by Wilson (1999), although farmers in Sri Lanka were willing to pay a higher price to use safer pesticides or adopt Integrated Pest Management (IPM) strategies and biological control of pests and diseases, such services are not easily available to farmers in these countries. IPM is practiced in many countries but has been on a small-scale for many reasons. IPM in developing countries is more the exception than the rule. Farmer knowledge and management of crop disease also is an important factor in the use of pesticides.

It is also likely that in the majority of cases, the short-term health effects arising from pesticide use and the disutility from that ill health are underestimated by farmers. This is because costs resulting from exposure to pesticides accrue over a period of time (for example, one year) and include time costs as well. Lack of medical facilities in developing countries makes the problem more complicated. As a result, lack of diagnosis attributed to pesticide exposure often ignores the dangers of pesticide use. Ill health then is attributed to another cause. The long-term relationship between dose and effect is complicated and because of the time involved is less easy to prove (Pimentel and Greiner, 1997). Another reason is that farmers in developing countries have no easy alternatives to subsistence farming. Subsistence farming on the other hand requires very little capital and skill. Furthermore, subsistence farmers use some of their produce for home consumption, thus covering a large part of the family expenditure. Hired labourers using pesticides may not know the true health impacts of pesticide use until severely affected. Hence, for one or more reasons mentioned above, farmers become locked into 'unsustainable' agricultural systems.

5. Unaccounted private costs of pollution and externalities in the market price and solutions at the margins

Decision-makers around the world are now aware of the impact of exposure to pesticide on human health and on the environment. However, the reasons as to why farmers continue to use pesticides despite the obvious costs as discussed above are not easy to overcome. In short, the solutions available are expensive and hence, especially in developing countries, the choice is between cheap food production at the expense of farmers' health or alternatively expensive food with better health outcomes for farmers and the environment. For example, as pointed out in the previous section, the short-term health effects arising from pesticide use and the disutility from that ill health are underestimated by farmers. It appears that the most pressing issue is the production of cheap food where for farmers the discounted net present value of returns from using pesticides is positive. As discussed in detail in Section 2, it is important to take into account the costs of private costs of pollution (e.g. farmers' health costs) and externalities in the market price of the goods produced. However, this is not an option that governments in LDCs (and also in developed countries) have taken on board. Furthermore, some countries such as Sri Lanka still provide subsidies for chemical inputs such as fertilisers which inevitably lead to their over-use. Gallagher et al. (2009) referring to pesticides state: 'Although, undocumented it is important to realise the subsidies also mean kickbacks to decision-makers granting large contracts to supplies of pesticides and thus there is a strong reluctance to remove subsidies once started, no matter how much science and field evidence' (p. x). The problems created by agricultural subsidies are so large that it has been called 'wicked' (see, for example, Conklin, 2006). For an excellent discussion on subsidies in relation to Africa, see Ricker-Gilbert et al., (2013). As an alternative, regulation (sometimes involving bans), promoting IPM and direct action have been preferred even in the presence of poor institutional capacity and weak budgets to effectively implement such policies.

IPM has been promoted in many Asian as well as in other countries to reduce the dependence on pesticides and their benefits have been widely discussed (see, for example, Gallagher, n.d.; Gershon et al., 2004; Gallagher, et al. 2009). Pimentel (1997) points out that Indonesia in the late 1980s invested as much as US$1 million a year in ecological/biological research, followed by extension programmes (usually supported by large donor organisations such as the World Bank and the UN Food and Agriculture Organisation) to train farmers to conserve natural predators of pests. He mentions that the investments in biological pest controls in the 1980s in Indonesia have shown remarkable success, with biological pest control and low pesticide use where yields have increased by 12 percent by the mid-1990s.

Another approach used by decision-makers in countries in Asia (and elsewhere) to reduce the toxicity of pesticides is to ban certain pesticides such as organophosphates and organochlorines and also ban pesticide advertisements. Sri Lanka is one country that has banned certain pesticides and that is considering legislation on banning pesticide advertisements. Roberts et al. (2003) state that in relation to pesticide-induced deaths in Sri Lanka, the ban of certain pesticides in the mid-1990s was beneficial. However, they go on to state that 'switching to other highly toxic pesticides, as one was banned and replaced in agricultural practice by another' (p. x). Field evidence in Sri Lanka (see, for example, Athukorala and Wilson, 2012) show that farmers are still being affected in a large way while handling and spraying pesticides. Than (2013) states that some of the banned pesticides (organophosphates) in some countries are still being used in other countries such as India. So, too, is the use of organochlorine pesticides (see, for example, Okoya et al., 2013).

Another approach used to reduce farmers' exposure to pesticides is farmer education on the harmful impact of exposure to pesticides and to provide guidelines on the safe use of pesticides and the importance of taking safety precautions when spraying. This approach has been going on for decades, but studies (see, for example, Wilson, 1999; Athukorala, 2011) show such policies are extremely difficult to implement successfully. Furthermore, subsistence farmers are unable to afford protective gear and limit pesticide spraying (see, for example, Wilson, 1999). A similar situation exists in other countries of Asia and developing countries in other continents.

Furthermore, in the case of rice varieties, increased number of pest-resistant rice varieties has been developed (and are in the process of being developed) and are introduced to farmers. These schemes are carried out by (or with the help of) IRRI and research units of some agricultural departments in Asian countries. As a result, the need for the use of insecticides is minimised. However, the amount of money available for research and development is small (and limited) and is not common among vegetable crops.

What is clear from the previous discussion is that although several approaches have been tried to reduce pesticide use with varying degrees of success, such measures have not been sufficient to transition to low pesticide use. In fact, what has been tried has provided solutions only 'at the margins' rather than confronting the main issue – that is the need for the market price to reflect the full cost of pesticide use by taking into account the private health costs resulting from direct exposure to pesticides and the costs of negative externalities. Only then is it possible for alternative solutions such as IPM strategies to endure. This is because in the absence of full-cost pricing farmers will use pesticides if the discounted net present value of stream of returns from doing so is positive (Wilson and Tisdell, 2001). Thus, such a situation can support the use of unsustainable pest control strategies and is more likely to do so, the higher the real discount rate (ibid).

Having advocated a full pricing system to create an environment to potentially transition to a low-pesticide use system, it is pertinent to ask the question whether such a transition is possible in reality? Unfortunately, the answer to this is 'unlikely'. This is not because the magnitude of the damage incurred to farmers and the environment is not known to policy decision-makers, but because it involves a large political commitment and an economic cost to both farmers (users of agricultural chemicals) and consumers. This is politically unsustainable. If such a policy is to be implemented then the price of food production will inevitable increase but the objective is to produce 'cheap' food, although this approach is diametrically opposed to sustainable food production, both from a human health and an environmental point of view. Furthermore, there is the problem of having to disentangle from the current 'locked-in' path dependent systems (Cowan and Gunby, 1996) the agricultural systems in Asia and most other countries operate in (Wilson and Tisdell, 2001). Some countries (e.g. Sweden) have tried to reduce the dependence on pesticides and Pimentel (1997) states that this is due to socio-political reasons. In low-medium income Asian countries (e.g. Sri Lanka, India, Pakistan, Indonesia) pesticide poisoning and damage to the environment from pesticides is not a major socioeconomic issue but cheap food production is. In such a situation the latter prevails.

6. Conclusions

The chapter examined the impact of agricultural chemicals on the environment and human health in mostly South Asian countries with a special focus on Sri Lanka. It was acknowledged that agricultural productivity and production have shown a remarkable increase, especially after the introduction of Green Revolution varieties in wheat and rice and commercially grown vegetable crops. The Green Revolution varieties were first introduced in the 1960s and commercially grown crops were cultivated on a large scale a few decades later. However, this success has not come without a cost. The increase in food production has been reliant of the heavy use of agrochemicals, namely fertilisers and pesticides. As a result, a visible parallel correlation between higher productivity, high artificial input use and environmental degradation and impaired human health is evident in many countries where commercial agriculture is widespread. This chapter discussed in detail the various negative externalities that arise from chemicals and pesticides and furthermore the private costs that farmers incur while handling and spraying pesticides on farms. The chapter discussed in detail the private health costs incurred by farmers from two field surveys conducted in Sri Lanka during the last two decades. It was show that the costs are very large.

Attention was then focussed on the need to take into account these costs (i.e. negative externalities and private health costs) in the market price in order to internalise the problems. At present, none of these costs are reflected in market prices of agricultural produce and hence market failure exists. A theoretical discussion was undertaken to how the internalisation of these problems can be remedied through the price mechanism. We show the necessary conditions for efficient allocation of resources.

The chapter examined the important question as to why farmers continue to use chemicals such as pesticides despite the high costs discussed, especially given the private health costs. It was shown that there are many reasons for this paradox, and they differ widely across regions and countries and may not follow a similar pattern where the use of pesticides is commonplace. It was argued that farmers will use pesticides if the discounted net present value of stream of returns from doing so is positive. This shows the importance of taking into account all the costs of negative externalities and private costs in the market price. Ignoring such costs it was argued can increase the use of chemical inputs such as pesticides and is more likely to do so, the higher the real discount rate. This is usually considered to be higher in LDCs than in more developed countries.

Given this situation, are there solutions available and if so are they likely to be implemented? Section Five discussed the various issues involved. It was argued it is important to take into account all costs arising from production to create an environment to potentially transition to a low-pesticide use system. However, this is 'unlikely'. It is not because the magnitude of the damage incurred to farmers and the environment is not known to policy decision-makers, but because it involves a large political commitment and an economic cost to both farmers (users of agricultural chemicals) and consumers. This is politically unsustainable. This is because the price of food production will inevitably increase but the objective of most governments, especially in LDCS is to produce 'cheap, affordable' food. In many countries, including those discussed in the chapter, pesticide poisoning of farmers and the damage caused to the environment from pesticides is not a major socioeconomic issue but cheap food production is. In such a situation, cheap food production takes precedence. The inability to consider all the associated costs of agricultural production in the market price thus makes attempted solutions by governments suboptimal and partial. This is because the trigger required to transition agricultural production to a low-chemical production system is missing. Hence, the issues remain intractable.

Notes

1 However, there are exceptions to this rule. For example, water logging and salination also cause many externalities.
2 According to John Harris (1987, p. 229), this expression was deliberately coined with the phrase 'Red Revolution' and the notion that LDCs were to undergo far-reaching changes as a result of an agricultural revolution rather than because of radical political transformation.

3 The impact of the Green Revolution on wheat and rice production is a function of both the area sown with the new wheat and rice varieties and the increase in yields per unit of land.

4 Occupational refers to farmers engaged in farming activities who handle and spray pesticides.

5 There is natural degradation of the stock of pollution. However, it is assumed that the rate of pollution accumulation is greater than the natural rate of degradation. Hence, a build up of stock of pollution. The factors that influence the breakdown of chemical pollution such as fertilisers and pesticides were discussed earlier in this chapter.

6 The prices can be both hypothetical shadow prices and/or existing market prices.

7 Here the inputs are overused or increased, in order to increase the total product or output, which is increasing at a decreasing rate. In other words, average product and marginal product are decreasing.

8 It is interesting to note that farmers treated for pesticide poisoning (possibly for other illnesses too) as out-patients are not recorded in hospitals. Furthermore, occupational- related cases are not properly recorded in the registers and simply categorized as organophosphates (OP's), agro chemical poisoning or pesticide poisoning. Hence, it is difficult to attribute the poisoning due to an occupation, suicides or accidents. Only in certain cases is there specific identification of the cause which attributes it to an occupational nature. This applies to fatal cases as well. On the other hand, suicide- related cases are properly identified. Hence, there is a considerable amount of under- reporting of both morbidity and mortality cases resulting from the use of pesticides by farmers in Sri Lanka. Furthermore, since there is a considerable level of 'private practice' by doctors in rural areas, patients treated for exposure to pesticides during use on farms are never reported and hence go unnoticed. Hence, the statistics available, are an under-representation of the real dangers arising from direct exposure to pesticide pollution by farmers.

9 Pesticide spraying by paddy farmers is at its highest during the 'Yala' season because of increased attacks by pests during this period of the year. This phenomenon is thought to be due to the longer day length, resulting in increased photoperiodism and increased vegetative growth of the plants making them more susceptible to pest attack. During the season when these workers were poisoned, there was a major outbreak of 'Brown-Hopper' pest infestation resulting in the excessive use of pesticides (Jeyaratnam et al., 1982).

10 Perhaps this is the first field study undertaken to study the use of pesticides by farmers and the health effects.

11 Studies that highlight the health problems of direct exposure to pesticides by farmers in the Asian region include: Loevinsohn (1987); Lum et al. (1993); Rola and Pingali (1993); Kishi et al. (1995); Antle and Pingali (1994); Other work outside Asia includes: Forget (1991); Mwanthi and Kimani (1993); Sharma et al. (2012).

12 These observations were made by farmers based on their perceptions of ill health using pesticides which were confirmed by physicians. In the US many studies have established these links. For example, see Hoar et al. (1986), Nielson and Lee (1987), Blair and Zahm (1993), Blair et al. (1993), Boyle and Zardize (1993), Brown et al. (1993) and Collins et al. (1993).

13 Anuradhapura district was selected because it is an agricultural district with high rates of poisonings in Sri Lanka. A secretariat division and six villages were selected randomly. The selection of villages for the sample was conducted using the list of active farmers in the area provided by the village agricultural extension officer. Every third name on the list was selected for the interview.

References

Antle, J. M. and Pingali, P. 1994. 'Health and productivity effects of pesticide use in Philippine rice production,' *Resources*, vol. 144, 16–19.

Athukorala, W. 2011. Essays on irrigation development, farm production and unaccounted costs: Theory and empirical evidence. PhD Thesis, Queensland University of Technology, Brisbane, Australia.

Athukorala, W. and Wilson C. (2012). 'Groundwater overuse and farm-level technical inefficiency: evidence from Sri Lanka,' *Hydrogeology Journal*, vol. 20, 893–905.

Athukorala, W., Wilson C. and Robinson T. 2012. 'Determinants of health costs due to farmers' exposure to pesticides: an empirical analysis,' *Journal of Agricultural Economics*, vol. 63, no. 1, 158–174.

Becker, G. S. 1965. A theory of the allocation of time, *Economic Journal*, vol. 75, 493–517.

Blair, A., Dosemeci, M. and Heineman, E. F. 1993. 'Cancer and other causes of death among male and female farmers from twenty three states,' *American Journal of Industrial Medicine*, vol. 23, no. 5, 729–742.

Blair, A. and Zahm, S. H. 1993. 'Patterns of pesticide use among farmers: implications for epidemiologic research,' *Epidemiology,* vol. 4, no. 1, 55–62.

Boyle, P. and Zardize, G. 1993. 'Risk factors for prostate and testicular cancer,' *European Journal of Cancer,* vol. 29A, no.7, 1048–1055.

Brown, L. M., Burmeister, L. F., Everett, G. D. and Blair, A. 1993. 'Pesticide exposure and multiple myeloma in Iowa men', *Cancer Causes Control,* vol. 4, no. 2, 153–156.

Chandrasekara, A. I. Wettasinghe, A. and Amarasiri, S. L. 1985. Pesticide usage by vegetable farmers, paper presented at Annual Research Conference ISTI, Gannoruwa, Sri Lanka.

Collins, J. J., Strauss, M. E., Levinskas G. J. and Conner, P. R. 1993. 'The mortality experience of workers exposed to 2,3,7,8 tetrachlorodibenzopdioxin in a trichlorophenol process accident,' *Epidemiology,* vol. 4, no.1, 713.

Conklin, J. 2006. 'Wicked problems and social complexity.' In: *Dialogue Mapping: Building Shared Understanding of Wicked Problems,* (chapter 1). Chichester, UK: Wiley.

Conway, G. R. and Barbier, E. B. 1990. *After the Green Revolution.* London: Earthscan Publications.

De Alwis, L. B. C. and Salgado, M. S. C. 1988. 'Agrochemical poisoning in Sri Lanka,' *Forensic Science International,* vol. 36, 81–89.

De Alwis, N. 1988. 'Regulation of import, formulation, sale and use of pesticides in Sri Lanka.' In: *Use of Pesticides and Health Hazards in the Plantation Sector,* Friedrich Ebert Stiftung (ed.), pp. 69–88. Colombo: Friedrich Ebert Stiftung.

Dhanapala, M. P. 1994. Personal communication, July.

Dharmawardena, L. I. M. 1994. 'Pesticide poisoning among farmers in a health area in Sri Lanka,' *Ceylon Medical Journal,* vol. 39, 101–103.

Dissanayake, D. 1986. Pesticide use in intensive vegetable cultivations in Sri Lanka – insights from a farm level study. Unpublished B.Sc. Thesis, University of Ruhuna, Sri Lanka.

Farmer, B. H. 1986. 'Perspectives on the Green Revolution in South Asia,' *Modern Asian Studies,* vol. 20, 175–199.

Fernando, P. R. 1988. *Management of Pesticide Poisoning,* Pesticide Association of Sri Lanka, Colombo, Sri Lanka.

Fernando, P. R. 1995. 'Pesticide poisoning in the Asia-Pacific region and the role of a regional information network,' *Clinical Toxicology,* vol. 33, pp. 677–682.

Forget, G. 1991. 'Pesticides and the third world.' *Journal of Toxicology and Environmental Health,* vol. 32, 11–31.

Gallagher, K. D., Ooi, P. A. and Kenmore, P. E. 2009. 'Impact of IPM Programs in Asian Agriculture." In: Integrated Pest Management: Dissemination and Impact (Vol. 2), E Peshini, R., and Dhawan, A. (eds.), pp. 347–358. India: Springer.

Gallagher, K. D. n.d. 'Stopping subsidies for pesticides in Indonesian rice production.' *Sustainable Development International.* Food and Agriculture, Organization, Rome, Italy, 71–74.

Garming, H. and Waibel, H. 2009. 'Pesticides and farmer health in Nicaragua: a willingness-to-pay approach to evaluation,' *The European Journal of Health Economics,* vol. 10, 125–133.

Gershon, F., Murgai, R. and Quizon, J. B. 2004. 'Sending farmers back to school: the impact of farmer field schools in Indonesia,' *Applied Economic Perspectives and Policy,* vol. 26, 45–62.

Gnanachandran, S. and Sivayoganathan, C. 1989. 'Hazards associated with the spraying of pesticides to chilli and brinjal in the Jaffna district,' *Tropical Agricultural Research,* vol. 1, 132–141.

Harrington, W., Krupnick, A. J. and Spofford, Walter, O. Jr. 1989. 'The benefits of preventing an outbreak of giardiosis,' *Journal of Urban Economics,* vol. 25, 116–137.

Harris, J. 1987. 'Capitalism and peasant production: The Green Revolution in India.' In: *Peasants and Peasant Societies,* Shanin, T. (ed.), pp. 101–112. Oxford: Blackwell.

Hoar, S. K., Blair, A., Holmes, F. F., Boysen, C. D., Robel, R, J., Hoover, R. and Fraumeni, J. F. 1986. 'Agricultural herbicide use and risk of lymphoma and soft tissue sarcoma,' *Journal of American Medical Association,* vol. 256, 1141–1147.

Huang, J., Qiao, F., Zhang, L. and Rozelle, S. 2000. 'Farm Pesticide, Rice Production, and Human Health,' EEPSEA Research Reports, International Development Research Centre, Ottawa.

International Agricultural Development 1994, 'Green Revolution blues,' vol. 14, no. 6, 7–9.

Jayathilake, J. and Bandara, J. M. R. S. 1989. 'Pesticide use by vegetable farmers: case study in a multiple cropping system in Sri Lanka', *FAO Quarterly Newsletter, Asia and Pacific Plant Protection Commission,* vol. 32, no. 2, 28–38.

Jeyaratnam, J. 1985. 'Health problems of pesticide usage in the Third World,' *British Journal of Industrial Medicine,* vol. 42, 505–506.

Jeyaratnam, J., Alwis Seneviratne, R. S. De and Copplestone, J. F. 1982. 'Survey of pesticide poisoning in Sri Lanka,' *Bulletin of the World Health Organization*, vol. 60, no. 4, 615–619.

Jeyaratnam, J., Luw, K. C. and Phoon, W. O. 1987. 'Survey of acute pesticide poisoning among agricultural workers in four Asian countries,' *Bulletin of the World Health Organization*, vol. 65, no. 4, 521–527.

Kishi, M., Hirschhorn, N., Djajadisastra, M., Satterlee, L. N., Strowman, S. and Dilts, R. 1995. 'Relationship of pesticide spraying to signs and symptoms in Indonesian farmers,' *Scandinavian Journal of Work Environmental Health*, vol. 21, 124–133.

Lipton, M. and Longhurst, R. 1989. *New Seeds and Poor People*. Baltimore: John Hopkins University Press.

Loevinsohn, M. E. 1987. 'Insecticide use and increased mortality in rural central Luzon, Philippines,' *Lancet*, vol. 13, June, 1359–62.

Lum, K.Y., Jusoh Mamat, M. D., Cheah, U. B., Castaneda, C. P., Rola, A. C. and Sinhaseni, P. 1993. 'Pesticide research for public health and safety in Malaysia, the Philippines and Thailand.' In: *Impact of Pesticide Use on Health in Developing Countries*, G. Forget, T. Goodman, and A. de. Villiers (eds.), 31–48. Ottawa: International Development Research Centre.

Managi, S. 2006. 'Are there increasing returns to pollution abatement? Empirical analytics of the environmental Kuznets curve in pesticides,' *Ecological Economics* vol. 58, no. 3, 617–636.

Mwanthi, M. A. and Kimani, V. N. 1993. 'Agrochemicals: a potential health hazard among Kenya's small-scale farmers.' In: *Impact of pesticide use on health in developing countries*, Forget, G, Goodman T., and Villers, De A. (eds.), pp. 106–114. Ottawa: International Development Research Centre.

Nielson, E. G. and Lee, L. K. 1987. *The Magnitude and Costs of Groundwater Contamination from Agricultural Chemicals: A National Perspective*, Agricultural Economic Report No. 576. Washington DC: U.S. Department of Agriculture.

Okoya, A.A., Ogunfowokan, O.A, Asubiojo, O. I. and Torto, N. 2013. 'Organochlorine pesticide residues in sediments and waters from cocoa producing areas of Ondo State, Southwestern Nigeria,' *ISRN Soil Science* (Open Access Journal), Article ID 131647, 12 pages, http://dx.doi.org/10.1155/2013/131647.

Pimentel, D. and Greiner, A. 1997. 'Environmental and socioeconomic costs of pesticide use.' In: *Techniques for Reducing Pesticide Use: Economic and Environmental Benefits*, Pimentel, D. (ed.), pp. 51–78. Chichester, UK: John Wiley and Sons.

Ricker-Gilbert, J., Jayne, T. and Shively, G. 2013. 'Addressing the "wicked problem" of input subsidy programs in Africa,' *Applied Economic Perspectives and Policy*, vol. 35, no. 2, 322–340.

Roberts, D.H., Karunarathna,A., Buckley, N. A., Manuweera, G., Sheriff, R. and Eddleston, M. 2003. 'Influence of pesticide regulation on acute poisoning deaths in Sri Lanka,' *Bulletin of the World Health Organization* vol. 81, 789–798.

Rola, A. C. and Pingali, P. L. 1993. *Pesticides, Rice Productivity, and Farmers Health*. Manila: International Rice Research Institute/Word Resources Institute.

Sharma, R.D., Thapa, B. P., Manandhar, H. K., S. M. Shrestha, S.M. and Pradhan, S. B. 2012. 'Use of pesticides in Nepal and impacts on human health and environment,' *The Journal of Agriculture and Environment*, vol. 13, June: 67–72.

Sessional Paper. 1993. Report of the presidential task force on formulation of a national health policy for Sri Lanka, No. 2, pp. 27.

Sivayoganathan, C., Gnanachandran, J., Lewis, J. and Fernando, M. 1995. 'Protective measure use and symptoms among agropesticide applicators in Sri Lanka', *Social Science and Medicine*, vol. 40, no. 4, 431–436.

Szmedra, P.I. 1991. Pesticide use in agriculture. In: *Handbook of Pest Management in Agriculture*, vol. I, Pimentel, D. (ed.), pp. 649–678. Boston: CRC Press.

Than, K. 2013. 'Organophosphates: a common but deadly pesticide,' *National Geographic*, Published July 18, http://news.nationalgeographic.com/news/2013/07/130718-organophosphates-pesticides-indian-food-poisoning/.

Tisdell, C.A. 1999. 'Economics, aspects of ecology and sustainable agricultural production.' In: *Sustainable Agriculture and Environment*, Dragun, A.K., and Tisdell, C. (eds.), pp. 37–55. Cheltenham: Edward Elgar.

Tisdell, C.A., Auld, B. and Menz, K.M. 1984. 'On assessing the biological control of weeds,' *Protection Ecology* vol. 6, 169–179.

Van Der Hoek, W., Konradsen, F., Athukorala, K. and Wanigadewa, T. 1998. 'Pesticide poisoning: a major health problem in Sri Lanka,' *Social Science and Medicine*, vol. 46, 495–504.

Wilson, C. 1994. How sustainable has the Green Revolution proved to be? South Asia with special reference to Sri Lanka, M.Phil Dissertation, University of Cambridge, Cambridge, UK.

Wilson, C. 1999. Cost and Policy Implications of Agricultural Pollution with Special Reference to Pesticides, PhD thesis, Department of Economics, University of St Andrews, St. Andrews, UK.

Wilson, C. 2000. 'Environmental and human costs of commercial agricultural production in South Asia,' *International Journal of Social Economics*, vol. 27, 816–846.

Wilson, C. 2005. 'Exposure to pesticides. Ill-health and averting behaviour: costs and determining the relationships,' *International Journal of Social Economics,* vol. 32, 1020–1034.

Wilson, C. and Tisdell, C. 2001. 'Why farmers continue to use pesticides despite environmental, health and sustainability costs,' *Ecological Economics,* vol. 39, 449–462.

Zilberman, D. and Marra, M. 1993. 'Agricultural externalities.' In: *Agricultural and Environmental Resource Economics*, Carlson, G, A, Zilberman, D. and Miranowski, A. (eds.), 221–267. New York: Oxford University Press.

17

BENEFIT TRANSFER OF NATURE CONSERVATION VALUES IN ASIA AND OCEANIA BASED ON META-ANALYSIS

Data heterogeneity and reliability issues

Henrik Lindhjem and Tran Huu Tuan

1. Introduction

According to the Millennium Ecosystem Assessment (MEA), more than 60 percent of the world's ecosystems are being degraded or used unsustainably (MEA 2005). And Asia fares no better than other parts of the world. Following on from MEA, economists and other professions have worked to document and value the loss of ecosystem services, for example through initiatives such as the Economics of Biodiversity and Ecosystem Services (TEEB) (Kumar 2010). The aim is to "recognize and demonstrate" for policymakers, bureaucrats, businesses and the general public the magnitude of the welfare loss in order to "capture" such un-internalized ecosystem service values in decisions. An important part of this effort has been to utilize the existing and relatively large non-market valuation literature in environmental economics in order to estimate values of ecosystem services in new local policy contexts or scaled up (e.g., for regional or national level uses) (see e.g., de Groot et al. 2012 for a recent example of the latter). This practice is termed "benefit or value transfer," as economic values of (an) ecosystem service(s) derived from a study or compiled based on the literature are transferred, often in adjusted form, to a new policy site or context.

An increasingly common way to conduct benefit transfer is to use meta analytic techniques to statistically synthesize the valuation literature and to estimate one or more transfer functions. Inserting values for relevant policy context variables describing the ecosystem service, the affected population etc., may then be a more reliable way of transferring values than more simplistic unit value transfers (see e.g., Lindhjem and Navrud 2008, Lindhjem and Navrud forthcoming, Brander and Florax 2006, Brander et al. 2012). However, there are also many challenges involved in conducting meta-analytic benefit transfer (MA-BT) (see e.g., Nelson and Kennedy 2009 and Boyle et al. 2013 for overviews and discussions). In this chapter, we first demonstrate the use of meta analysis (MA) to review and take stock of the literature on non-market valuation of (changes in) ecosystem services from conservation of different types habitat, biodiversity and endangered species in Asia and Oceania.[1] We then attempt to answer the following research questions of particular relevance to practical use of MA for benefit transfer. How sensitive are the meta-regression results and particularly the value forecasts (benefit transfers) for unstudied (policy) sites to: 1) the "scope of the MA," i.e., the level of heterogeneity of the good valued and the valuation methods used; and 2) the choice of meta-regression models?

The analysis contributes to our understanding and refinement of MA methodology in environmental economics, where the meta-analyst typically is left to make a number of practical choices, potentially introducing different subjective biases (Hoehn 2006; Rosenberger and Johnston 2009). An important analyst choice both for the robustness of MA models and their suitability for use in benefit transfer applications relates to the scope of the MA, i.e., the trade-off between the number of observations and the acceptable level of heterogeneity in the data, as pointed out by e.g., Engel (2002) and Nelson and Kennedy (2009). Another related choice and of particular interest in this chapter is which model to choose for MA-BT; for example, which covariates to include and how to treat insignificant variables (Stapler and Johnson 2009). There are different practices and little is known of resulting empirical effects, though, for example, Lindhjem and Navrud (2008, forthcoming) and Johnston and Thomassin (2010) have shown that the precision of MA-BT applications depends on such choices, sometimes in unexpected ways.

Previous MA studies primarily have analyzed the values of more homogenous types of environmental goods (e.g., water and air quality, recreation days) often within the same country (Rosenberger and Loomis 2000; Van Houtven et al. 2007). However, there is a trend toward using MA and BT for more complex goods in international settings (e.g., wetlands, coral reefs, forests, biodiversity, agricultural land preservation) (see e.g., Brander et al. 2006, 2007; Jacobsen and Hanley 2009; Lindhjem 2007; Richardson and Loomis 2009; Barrio and Loureiro 2010).

To explore the research questions, we divide our dataset into two levels of heterogeneity: endangered species (more similar good and methods used) and nature conservation more generally (more heterogeneity in good and methods used). We then estimate a number of random effects meta-regression models for these two main datasets using different procedures and subsets of the data investigating explanatory power and the robustness of results. These meta-regression models and estimated meta-equations are then the basis for estimating the level of forecast (or transfer) errors for unstudied sites broken down by type of models, nature conservation habitat, geographic region and valuation method used, based on a jackknife resampling technique used in MA by e.g., Brander et al. (2006) and Lindhjem and Navrud (2008).

The outline of the chapter is a follows. The next section explains the underlying theory of MA-BT and one common and general way to go about testing reliability and validity of MA-BT based on different types of data, regression models and contexts. In Section 3 we explain the meta-database we assembled containing studies valuing nature conservation in Asia and Oceania. From these studies we extracted information that was coded as the most relevant explanatory variables to estimate the MA functions used as basis for benefit transfer. Section 4 briefly presents the meta-regression results, with emphasis on the differences between models and data partitions and the resulting explanatory power of the models. Section 5 presents results of the reliability tests of these models for BT, while Section 6 concludes.

2. Validity and reliability of meta-analytic benefit transfer

2.1 Underlying theory of MA-BT

We define "nature conservation" broadly as the conservation or active management of a natural terrestrial or aquatic ecosystem, resource or amenity, Q. The economic value of an increase in the level of nature conservation (Q) is the change in the quantity and/or quality (QUAL) of Q, or some set of ecosystem services provided by Q, and is referred to as consumers' surplus or willingness to pay (WTP). From the standard indirect utility function, the bid function for a representative individual j for this change can be given by (Bergstrom and Taylor 2006):

$$WTP = f(P_j, M_j, Q_j^T - Q_j^R, QUAL_j^T - QUAL_j^R, SUB_j^T - SUB_j^R, H_j) \qquad (1)$$

Where P = a price index of market goods (assumed constant), M = (individual or household) income (assumed constant), $Q^T - Q^R$ and $QUAL^T - QUAL^R$ are the changes in quantity and quality from a reference situation ("status quo") (R) to a target state-of-the-world (T), SUB = substitutes for Q available to individual j, H = non-income household or individual characteristics. Further to make (1) elastic enough for use in MA, we assume, following Bergstrom and Taylor (2006), a "weak structural utility theoretic approach" where the underlying variables in the bid function are assumed to be derivable from some unknown utility function. At the same time, flexibility is maintained to introduce explanatory variables into the model, such as study design and different valuation methods that do not necessarily follow from (1), as is typically done in practical MA. This is the most common approach in MA. In this process the empirical specification chosen for (1) needs to trade off the availability of information reported in valuation studies with the range of potentially relevant explanatory variables. For example, information about substitute sites to a national park will mostly not be reported, even if important for WTP. In addition, if information *is* reported, for example about the exact change in the valued nature conservation, this change may not be easily comparable across sites and studies. No MA studies are free of this problem. Some try to map changes to a common unit of measurement in terms of hectares or to a water quality ladder or similar, though such simplified common units may mask differences in other dimensions of the good important to individuals (see e.g., Lindhjem 2007). There are no easy solutions, and in our rather general case, we interpret mean WTP from different studies as welfare estimates for a (small, though not marginal) change in Q and/or in one or more elements in an attribute vector of QUAL describing the quality of the nature site. We then use dummy variables to detect differences in WTP depending on the type of habitat or change valued.

2.2 Validity and reliability of MA-BT

Before explaining the underlying data to estimate an empirical meta-regression specification of (1), we discuss a common procedure used here to test validity and reliability of using MA for benefit transfer. MA-BT involves transferring one or more estimated meta-regression equations to an unstudied policy site and inserting values from this site for the geographic, socioeconomic, good characteristics variables and relevant year, and predicted or forecast annual WTP per household. The values of methodological variables would typically be set at some best practice level at the average sample value (Stapler and Johnston 2009) or drawn from the MA sample distribution (Johnston et al. 2006) since there is no such information for an unstudied policy site. In our case, we avoid this problem by using the meta-models to predict (see the following).

To the extent observable characteristics of the habitats/good valued and the population explain a significant portion of the variation in WTP and not only the methodological differences between studies, it gives us confidence that MA-BT may be a credible alternative to a new valuation study as input for example in cost-benefit analysis. The performance of MA-BT could only be accurately assessed if we knew the "true value," or an estimate of this, for a range of sites and then used the MA models to predict the value at those sites and calculate so-called transfer errors (TE) (equation 2)[2]:

$$TE = \frac{\mid WTP_T - WTP_B \mid}{WTP_B}, \qquad (2)$$

where T = Transferred (predicted) value from study site(s), B = Estimated true value ("benchmark") at policy site. Validity[3] has traditionally required "that the values, or the value functions generated from the study site, be statistically identical to those estimated at the policy site" (Navrud and Ready, 2007, pp. 7), i.e., that TE is statistically indistinguishable from zero. More recently BT validity assessment has shifted focus somewhat to the concept of reliability for policy use, which requires that TE is relatively small (but not necessarily zero). This shift comes from the realization that BT can be considered valid even if the standard hypothesis of TE = 0 is rejected – in fact the most appropriate null hypothesis is that TE>0 since environmental benefits from theory should be assumed to vary between contexts (see Kristofersson and Navrud 2005). However, there is no agreement on maximum TE levels for BT to be reliable for different policy applications, though 20 and 40 percent have been suggested (Kristofersson and Navrud 2007).

Lindhjem and Navrud (2008), Johnston and Thomassin (2010) and a few other studies use different "benchmark" values from within their sample or from new studies to "simulate" the true value to assess TE performance. Based on this, we carry out an assessment of how our MA models based on different subsets of the data forecast nature conservation values in Asia and Oceania. We will use a jackknife data splitting technique, used e.g., by Brander et al. (2006) and Lindhjem and Navrud (2008), where we estimate n-1 separate meta-regression equations to predict (or forecast) the value of the omitted observation in each case, which mimics the value of a "policy site." We then calculate the percentage difference between observed and predicted values, the TE in our exercise, and the overall median and mean TE for all observations.[4] This measure gives a good indication of how far off our MA models would be in a real BT exercise, depending on different methodological choices and level of heterogeneity of the meta-regression analysis. We also break down the results and assess specifically the precision of the main regression models used for BT for different species and habitat types, valuation methods and geographical regions.

3. Meta-data sources and variable coding

To provide the reader with sufficient background information for understanding the MA-BT reliability assessments that will be conducted and the process of carrying out a MA, we explain the meta-data sources and the coding of the data in this section, and the meta-regression models and results in Section 4. Details can be found in Lindhjem and Tuan (2012).

The meta-database includes studies available in English up to 2009 valuing nature conservation in Asia and Oceania. A final meta-dataset of 550 mean WTP estimates (i.e., observations) from 95 studies was compiled (see supplementary appendix in Lindhjem and Tuan 2012 for a complete list).[5] The database covers a range of habitats (terrestrial and marine), geographical sub-regions, ecosystem services and valuation methods. The most frequently used method is contingent valuation (CV), with 77 studies, while the travel cost method (TCM) comes second with only 14 studies. A small number of studies (five) use other methods, such as the hedonic pricing method (HPM) or calculate the value of wetlands and forests using the market price approach.

Information extracted from the studies was coded for the most important variables, drawn from theory and previous empirical studies, in a spreadsheet with between one and 36 observations drawn from each study (average 5.8). The same study typically has several sub-samples varying the methods used, scope and other aspects of the good valued giving rise to multiple WTP estimates. Table 17.1 below gives the variable names, definitions, mean and standard

Table 17.1 Definition of meta-analysis variables and descriptive statistics

Variables	Description	Mean (SD)*
Dependent variable:		
WTP 2006	WTP in 2006 prices (US$)	133 (461)
Methodological variables:		
SP	Binary: 1 if stated preference, 0 if otherwise	.84 (.35)
DC	Binary: 1 if SP using dichotomous choice, 0 if otherwise	.51 (.50)
TCM	Binary: 1 if travel cost method, 0 if otherwise	.07 (.25)
Hholdpay	Binary: 1 if household's WTP, 0 if individual	.67 (.46)
Month	Binary: 1 if payment is a monthly payment, 0 if otherwise	.35 (.47)
Nonpara	Binary: 1 if estimate is non-parametric (Turnbull), 0 otherwise	.07 (.25)
Interview	Binary: 1 if it is an in-person interview, 0 otherwise	.60 (.48)
Mandatory	Binary: 1 if it is a mandatory payment vehicle, 0 if voluntary	.69 (.88)
Good characteristics variables:		
Mammal	Binary: 1 if it is a mammal, 0 otherwise	.04 (.20)
Turtle	Binary: 1 for sea turtle, 0 otherwise	.06 (.24)
Species	Binary: 1 for primarily species, 0 if other habitats/services	.23 (.42)
Terrestrial	Binary: 1 for terrestrial habitats, 0 if other habitats/services	.32 (.47)
Marine	Binary: 1 if marine habitat (beach, sea, watercourse, lake, river), 0 other habitats/services	.29 (.45)
Wetland	Binary: 1 for wetlands, 0 if other habitats/services	.07 (.26)
Nonuse	Binary: 1 for primarily non-use, 0 otherwise	.77 (.41)
Socioeconomic variables:		
Income	Continuous: Mean household income from sample (PPP adjustment, 2006)	14,318 (17,258)
GDP	Continuous: GDP 2006 from country for survey.	14,524 (12,191)
Geographic characteristics (countries and regions):		
Australia	Binary: 1 if the study in Australia, 0 otherwise	.19 (.39)
Philippin	Binary: 1 if a study in the Philippines, 0 otherwise	.22 (.42)
Oceania	Binary: 1 if a study in Oceania, 0 other region	.21 (.40)
East	Binary: 1 if a study in East Asia, 0 other region	.18 (.38)
Southeast	Binary: 1 if a study in Southeast Asia, 0 otherwise	.44 (.48)
Southwest	Binary: 1 if a study in Southwest Asia, 0 otherwise	.04 (.19)
South	Binary: 1 if a study in South Asia, 0 otherwise	.13 (.33)
Other variables:		
EEPSEA**	1 if the study is funded by EEPSEA, 0 otherwise	.39 (.48)
Journal	1 if it is a published paper, 0 otherwise	.47 (.49)
Year	Continuous: from 0 (2006) to 26 (1979)	6.36 (4.07)

Notes: *The Mean (SD) is for overview purposes given for the whole dataset. The scope of the dataset is limited in the model runs in the next section. Further not all variables are used in all models.
**EEPSEA = Environment and Economy Program for Southeast Asia.

Source: Reproduced from Lindhjem and Tuan (2012).

deviation for all variables that were included in final meta-regressions. The variables are divided into five categories: 1) Methodological, 2) Good characteristics, 3) Socioeconomic, 4) Geographic characteristics, and 5) Other. Since there is no standardized way of reporting welfare estimates in the literature, a wide variety of units are typically used, e.g., WTP per individual or household, per unit of area,[6] per visitor, for different time periods (e.g., per month, per visit, per year, one-time amount etc.) and in different currencies and reporting years. To deal with this problem, we standardized the values to a common metric following standard MA practice, i.e., WTP (US$ in 2006 prices) per household per year as a default, and coded WTP per individual, WTP per month etc. using dummies.[7] Values from different years were converted to 2006 prices using GDP deflators from the World Bank World Development Indicators. Purchase Power Parity (PPP)-corrected exchange rates were used to correct for differences in price levels between countries (Ready and Navrud 2006).

4. Meta-regression models and results

4.1 Dividing the data into two levels of heterogeneity

For the meta-regressions, the dataset was divided into two primary levels of scope, according to level of homogeneity of the good and methods used: Level 1: Species; and Level 2: Biodiversity and nature conservation more generally. The species data include WTP estimates from 16 studies using CV to value the preservation of single or multiple species providing 124 estimates that will be used in the meta-regression analysis. Although the species are different, we consider the preservation of them as a good with many similar attributes in valuation, as compared to nature and biodiversity conservation more generally. In addition, methodological heterogeneity is reduced since all the studies in this level use CV.

The second level of the data include the studies from Level 1 and all the rest of the studies that value nature conservation more generally, with different types of methods (though the majority also use CV here). This dataset includes welfare estimates for a relatively more heterogeneous good. All in all, the Level 2 dataset contains between 67 to 95 studies and 390 to 550 estimates, depending on the cleaning procedures and the subsets of the data used in the meta-regressions. The details of the Level 1 and 2 datasets are given in Tables A1 and A2, respectively, in the supplementary appendix to Lindhjem and Tuan (2012). We run several meta-regression models based on these two levels of data to explain variations in welfare estimates and to investigate effects of different dimensions of heterogeneity on transfer errors.

4.2 Meta-regression model

As most studies provide more than one WTP estimate, one sensible approach is to treat the data as a panel to account for the correlation between the errors of estimates from the same study (Nelson and Kennedy 2009).[8] Our empirical specification of equation (1) above can then be written as:

$$WTP_{ij} = \alpha + \sum_{k=1}^{n} \beta_k x_{kij} + \mu_{ij} + \varepsilon_i \tag{3}$$

where WTP is the i'th observation from the j'th stratum (here study), α is a constant. The variation in WTP_{ij} is to be explained by a vector of covariates k = 1,.., n, denoted by x_{kij} (as defined in Table 17.1), with a panel effect μ_{ij} and an error $\varepsilon_i \sim N(0, \sigma^2)$. We also assume that μ_{ij}, ε_i and x_{kij} are uncorrelated within and across studies. A Breusch-Pagan Lagrange multiplier (LM) statistic

Table 17.2 Test of random vs. fixed effects panel structure (N = 550, j = 95)

	b Fixed effects model	B Random effects model	b-B	S.E.
Income variable	.0305127	−.0494427	.0799554	.2193994
p> χ^2: 0.7155				

test of whether panel effects are significant was conducted. The null hypothesis is that an equal effects model is correct ($H_0 : \mu_{ij} = 0$), and the alternative that a panel effects model is correct ($H_1 : \mu_{ij} \neq 0$). If the hypothesis of fixed effects in the Breusch-Pagan LM test is rejected, the random effects model assuming heterogeneous effect sizes across studies and within models should be more efficient in estimation. We chose a double-log specification of (3), common in the MA literature, which fitted our data better than linear or other specifications. For a model with income as the only explanatory variable,[9] the Breusch-Pagan LM test showed that a model with equal effects was rejected, confirming the appropriateness of a panel estimation model (χ^2 = 274.90, p = 0.000 with N = 550 and j = 95).

In order to test whether a random effects specification (which has a panel specific error component) is outperformed by a fixed effects model (which keeps the panel specific error component constant), a Hausman χ^2 test was performed for the whole dataset. The null hypothesis is that the random effect specification is correct, i.e., the panel effects are uncorrelated with other regressors, and the alternative that the fixed effect specification is correct (Zandersen and Tol 2009). The results in Table 17.2 show that the random effects model (B) cannot be rejected, and thus, is the one we use.

We also performed the Hausman test for all the models used in this study, i.e., for different subsets of the data and different explanatory variables included, and find that a random effects model is the best estimation approach for Level 1 and 2 of our data.

4.3 Meta-regression results for level 1: species

Results of six regression models are reported in Table 17.3 for the Level 1 (species) data. Starting with Model 1.5, this is a model that includes all explanatory variables in Table 17.1 of relevance to the Level 1 data. Only one regional dummy and two species type dummies are used, as estimates are thinly spread across categories. Models 1.1 to 1.4 (and 1.6) are versions of Model 1.5 where adding different subcategories of variables illustrates changes in the explanatory power of the models. Model 1.1 contains methodological characteristics of the CV method only, Model 1.2 adds good characteristics, Model 1.3 adds country variables (instead of region dummy in Model 1.5), Model 1.4 includes income and the survey year variables, and Model 1.6, finally, excludes all methodological variables. In this latter model, we test whether the variation can be explained only by the kind of variables that are relevant for BT.

Going from Model 1.1 to 1.4, the models gradually explain more of the variation in WTP for species preservation, as judged by the R^2. Adding country specifics and income and year in Models 1.3 and 1.4, for example, help explain another 25 to 31 percentage points of the variation compared to Models 1.1 and 1.2. Model 1.4, the best fitting of the models, obtains an overall R^2 of 0.81, which is very high compared to other MA studies (R^2 for Model 1.5 is almost as high).

It is comforting for our belief in the validity of the data and for the potential use of such value estimates for BT that around half of the explained variation in the best model is due to non-study specific, observable characteristics related to the good, geographical area, year of study and income level of the population surveyed. Model 1.6 drives home the same point, with a R^2 of 61 percent. This model may be of particular interest for testing in MA-BT how ignoring methodological differences translates into BT errors predicting values for new sites.[10] Individual parameter estimates in the best Model 1.4 conform fairly well with expectations where such priors exist (including estimates of income elasticity of WTP in the plausible range of 0–1)[11] (see Lindhjem and Tuan 2012 for a discussion). Note for example, that mammals are valued significantly higher than other species types in four out of five models, likely due to a "charisma" effect. Some conformity with expectations for explanatory variables gives us some confidence that the data reflect reliably elicited, contingent preferences.

4.4 Meta-regression results for level 2: biodiversity and nature conservation

In Table 17.4 we present results of five regression models using the more heterogeneous Level 2 data (nature and biodiversity conservation values). In this case, we include the fuller range of explanatory variables (e.g., covering different valuation methods) using different subsets of the data. We keep the same methodological variables (except including the dummy for stated preference estimates) for the sake of comparing the robustness of the results with Level 1. Further, we include the habitat/good characteristics variables that are significant across at least one of our four models. Finally, geographic region dummies were included if significant or if data from these regions dominate our dataset.

Similar to the models in Table 17.3, we first run a fully specified Model 2.4 using all variables in Table 17.1 and then we exclude in Model 2.5 method variables. Model 2.1 investigates the full dataset of 550 observations, inserting GDP as proxy for unreported income information, while Model 2.2 excludes studies that did not report income information (both of these practices are common in the MA literature). Since many studies do not report sample income, 119 observations are lost in Model 2.2. Model 2.3 contains the Model 2.2 observations, excluding values estimated using other methods than CV, CM and TCM.[12] Model 2.2 and 2.3 (and the resulting TE results below) are chosen to investigate the trade-off between including fewer observations and a more accurate measure of income and increasing the dataset at the cost of a more imprecise income measure. Model 2.3 reduces methodological heterogeneity, which may also affect BT performance.

Given the heterogeneity of the good included in the Level 2 data, our fully specified Model 2.4 does not do very well in controlling for this heterogeneity. The model explains only 13.5 percent of the variation. This is only slightly increased for Model 2.1, to a R^2 of 16 percent, which offers the best combination of covariates for the full dataset. However, it is nevertheless comparable to the 25–26 percent obtained in two national-level MA studies of the recreation activity days in the US (a more homogenous good, see Rosenberger and Loomis 2000 and Shresta and Loomis 2003).[13] The R^2 for the full dataset here is higher than the random effects MA models of international biodiversity studies in Jacobsen and Hanley (2009).

Enhancing methodological homogeneity in Model 2.3 increases the explained variation further to 46 percent, the same level as for example found in the MA of Brander et al. (2006) of international wetland valuation studies. Removing the methodological variables from the fully specified Model 2.4 reduces the explanatory power to a low 9.5 percent in Model 2.5 – an aspect that may invalidate that model for BT purposes. There are no guidelines in the literature on what the minimum level of explanatory power should be for MA-BT.

Table 17.3 Meta-regression models for Level I: Species studies (standard error of coefficients in parentheses)

Variable#	Model 1.1	Model 1.2	Model 1.3	Model 1.4	Model 1.5	Model 1.6
	Method variables	+ Species types	+ Country variables	+ Income and year	All variables	No method variables
Constant	1.149	2.262 ★★★	1.010	−9.949★★★	13.939★★	−.455
	(.757)	(.834)	(1.155)	(3.043)	(5.510)	(3.861)
DC	1.462★	.646	1.191	1.542★★★	1.300★★	
	(.792)	(.819)	(.782)	(.537)	(.583)	
Hholdpay	.095	.103	.709	1.818★★★	2.162★★	
	(.789)	(.813)	(.785)	(.638)	(.944)	
Month	.176	.668	1.274★	.320	1.032★★	
	(.676)	(.629)	(.718)	(.569)	(.430)	
Nonpara.	−.257★★	−.277★★	−.271★★	−.278★★★	−.275★★★	
	(.120)	(.119)	(.111)	(.107)	(.107)	
Interview	1.577★★★	.145	.970	−.701	.148	
	(.506)	(.738)	(.889)	(.820)	(.587)	
Mandatory	.196	.203★	.241★★	.208★	.220★★	
	(.121)	(.120)	(.113)	(.109)	(.108)	
Turtle		−.417	−.710	−1.013★★★	−.867★★	.004
		(.530)	(.509)	(.326)	(.386)	(.469)
Mammal		1.748★★	.788	1.498★★	1.620★★★	2.574★★★
		(.862)	(.844)	(.595)	(.595)	(.470)
Australia			1.034	−1.723★		
			(.937)	(.963)		
Philippin			−.987★★★	−.141		
			(.228)	(.332)		
Southeast					−.270	−.587★★
					(.280)	(.288)
EEPSEA					−2.768	−.441
					(2.001)	(1.720)
LnIncome				.876★★★	.803★★★	.505★★
				(.266)	(.225)	(.228)
LnYear				2.145★★★	3.848★	−.669
				(.611)	(2.074)	(1.445)
Summary statistics:						
R^2: within	.077	.077	.190	.253	.255	.168
R^2: betw.	.573	.764	.881	.961	.953	.727
R^2: overa.	**.354**	**.500**	**.755**	**.816**	**.813**	**.611**
Sigma_u	.801	.712	.674	.386	.442	.630
Sigma_e	.464	.464	.437	.421	.420	.435
Rho	.748	.701	.704	.457	.525	.677
N	124	124	124	124	124	124
# studies	16	16	16	16	16	16

Note: ★p < 0.10, ★★p < 0.05, ★★★p < 0.01. STATA 9.2 used. # Blank space means variable not included in regression.

Source: Reproduced in slightly adapted form from Lindhjem and Tuan (2012).

Table 17.4 Meta-regression models for Level 2: Biodiversity and nature conservation (standard error of coefficients in parentheses)

Variable#	Model 2.1	Model 2.2	Model 2.3	Model 2.4	Model 2.5
	GDP inserted for income	Income reported	Only SP and TCM	All variables	No method variables
Constant	3.455★★	4.058★★★	3.448★★★	6.554★★★	5.522★★★
	(1.513)	(1.221)	(1.104)	(1.800)	(1.664)
SP	−.450	−1.713★★★	−1.769★★★	−2.593★★★	
	(.321)	(.279)	(.225)	(.628)	
DC	.580★★★	.011(.181)	−.065	.760★★★	
	(.213)		(.140)	(.221)	
TCM				−2.657 ★★★	
				(.676)	
Hhldpay	.335	.025(.260)	.008	−.085	
	(.290)		(.273)	(.332)	
Month	.606	1.377★★★	1.448★★★	1.021★★	
	(.376)	(.309)	(.310)	(.404)	
Nonpara	−.252	−.209	−.220★	−.267	
	(.243)	(.174)	(.125)	(.237)	
Interview	.080	−.009	.176	.153	
	(.298)	(.249)	(.220)	(.309)	
Turtle	−.026	−.117	−.275		
	(.665)	(.490)	(.495)		
Mammal	1.666★★★	1.885★★★	1.715★★★		
	(.614)	(.494)	(.495)		
Marine	.888★★★	.562★★	.554★★	.046	.134
	(.308)	(.266)	(.272)	(.447)	(.437)
Wetland	−.991★★	1.258★★★	1.218★★★	−1.967★★★	−1.718★★★
	(.429)	(.421)	(.414)	(.538)	(.528)
Species				−.942★★	−.372
				(.439)	(.423)
Terrestrial				−1.143★★★	−.893★
				(.446)	(.442)
Nonuse	.057	−.240	−.084	.175	.093
	(.237)	(.217)	(.179)	(.237)	(.210)
Oceania	.755★	.677 ★	.588	.994	.513
	(.458)	(.405)	(.405)	(.647)	(.630)
East	−.204	.180	−.105	−.421.638	−.646
	(.413)	(.356)	(.370)		(.632)
Southeast	−.766★	−.323	−.841★★	−.879	−.975
	(.412)	(.356)	(.382)	(.670)	(.665)
South				.131	.433
				(.751)	(.731)
EEPSEA	−.449★★	−.561★	.188	−.357	−.266
	(.389)	(.310)	(.368)	(.403)	(.406)

Journal	−.318	−.263	−.017	−.096	−.354
	(.341)	(.304)	(.318)	(.371)	(.366)
LnIncome	−.022	.062	.103	−.027	−.068
	(.133)	(.107)	(.091)	(.140)	(.136)
LnYear	.281	.213	.180	.168	.020
	(.236)	(.193)	(.189)	(.262)	(.256)
Summary statistics:					
R^2 within	.124	.124	.212	.179	.103
R^2:betwen	.172	.550	.572	.155	.074
R2: overall	**.159**	**.337**	**.459**	**.135**	**.095**
Sigma_u	.955	.708	.764	1.032	1.037
Sigma_e	1.083	.809	.582	1.066	1.108
Rho	.437	.434	.632	.484	.466
N	550	431	390	550	550
# studies	95	70	67	95	95

Note: *p < 0.10, **p < 0.05, ***p < 0.01. STATA 9.2 used. # Blank space means variable not included in regression.

Source: Reproduced in slightly adapted form from Lindhjem and Tuan (2012).

Despite a higher degree of heterogeneity than for the Level 1 dataset, the data show some degree of regularity, and many of the parameters have the expected signs, as further discussed in Lindhjem and Tuan (2012). However, the results are not as clear and there is more "noise" than for the more homogenous Level 1 data. The next step is to test the effects of the different meta-regression models and the two data levels on BT reliability, i.e., estimated transfer errors.

5. Assessment of transferability of nature conservation values

This section reports the results of conducting the assessment of transfer errors using the different meta-regression models and the two levels of data, as described in Section 2.2. We then break down the TE results into transfers conducted for species and habitat types, valuation methods and geographical regions and provide a brief sensitivity analysis.

5.1 Estimated overall mean and median transfer errors

We start by reporting the results for the six models using the Level 1 and Level 2 data. We have used the models to predict each of the observations in the dataset that have been left out in turn. Based on this, we obtain n individual TE estimates from which we derive overall mean and median TE (results for the Level 1 data reported in Table 17.5).[14]

First, using fully specified models such as Models 1.4 and 1.5 for the Level 1 data yields fairly high precision at around median TE of 23 percent to 24 percent (mean 45–46 percent) (Table 17.4). Mean TE is low compared to other studies performing this check, e.g., Lindhjem and Navrud (2008) (62–266 percent), Brander et al. (2006, 2007) (74–186 percent), Stapler and Johnston (2009) (152 percent), Richardson and Loomis (2009) (34–45 percent for a within-sample test), indicating a level of precision that could be acceptable for policy use.

Table 17.5 Median and mean transfer error (percent) for models Level 1: Endangered species

	Model 1.1	Model 1.2	Model 1.3	Model 1.4	Model 1.5	Model 1.6
	Method variables	+ Species types	+ Country variables	+ Income and year	All variables	No method variables
Median	61	59	33	24	23	36
Mean	108	85	58	46	45	67
N	124	124	124	123	123	123

Table 17.6 Median and mean transfer error (percent) for models Level 2: Biodiversity and nature conservation

	Model 2.1	Model 2.2	Model 2.3	Model 2.4	Model 2.5
	GDP inserted for income	Income reported	Only SP and TCM	All variables	No method variables
Median	71	52	46	77	64
Mean	7344	377	89	5277	8363
N	547	428	387	547	547

Precision increases with the more fully specified models, as expected. Interestingly, introducing species dummies to Model 1.1 reduces median TE by only 2 percentage points in Model 1.2 compared to an almost halving of median TE from introducing country variables in Model 1.3. Model 1.6, which uses only observable values at the "policy site" (i.e., no methodological controls included), still manages to predict values with a median precision of 36 percent. Stapler and Johnston (2009) find that using the hypothetical "ideal" values for the methodological variables instead of the means in the sample in a fully specified MA-BT model, gives a TE gain overall of only 26 percentage points (from 151.9 to 125.6 percent). In an earlier study Johnston et al. (2006) find that the choice of values for methodological variables may have a large impact on forecasts. Although ignoring methodological differences between studies altogether may not generally be a sensible approach in MA-BT, our case illustrates at least that loss in precision is relatively low as long as the good and methods used are relatively similar. In the sensitivity analysis that follows, we also ran the BT tests using reduced versions of Models 1.1 to 1.4, excluding variables not significant at the 20 percent level, which is a common procedure in the literature to simplify the MA-BT process (Lindhjem and Navrud 2008).

For the Level 2 data, the median TE of Models 2.1 to 2.3 are, somewhat surprisingly, a bit higher but very much comparable to the Model 1.1 to 1.4 Level 1 results, despite lower explanatory power (Table 17.6). However, the Level 2 data produce more high TE values (i.e., the mean is much higher than the median). Only for Model 2.3 is the mean TE anywhere near acceptable levels.

Keeping to the median TE, Models 2.4 and 2.5 do a poorer job at controlling heterogeneity as judged by the TEs of 77 and 64 percent, respectively, compared to Models 1.5 and 1.6 for Level 1. However, although the mean TEs are in the thousands, it is somewhat surprising that medians are not influenced more by the low explanatory power of Models 2.4 and 2.5 for Level 2. Confer the sensitivity analysis below for a version of Model 2.5, based on the including only SP and TCM estimates, as in Model 2.3.

Reducing methodological heterogeneity for the Level 2 data from Model 2.2 to 2.3 reduces median TE from around 52 to 46 percent, while mean TE comes down from an unacceptably high level of 377 percent to a more reasonable 89 percent. For both Level 1 and 2 models, there is generally an inverse relationship between the level of explained variation and TE, as expected. Hence, increasing degree of homogeneity of the data in terms of good characteristics (biodiversity and nature conservation in general to endangered species) increases the precision, as does the enhanced homogeneity of valuation methods used within Level 2. However, in median terms, the gain in precision is perhaps not as highly related to explanatory power or homogeneity, as expected. Even with a heterogeneous dataset, median TE may approach acceptable levels for policy use.

5.2 Illustration of predicted (transferred) and observed values

For mean TE the results can be clearly seen from a plot. The plot of observed log WTP values (estimates sorted in ascending order) vs. predicted (zigzag line,) for Model 1.4 (Level 1 data) is first illustrated in Figure 17.1. The forecasts follow the observed values well except at the extremities of the data, a characteristic of forecasting models and an effect of using a relative measure of TE. Lindhjem and Navrud (forthcoming), as noted previously, use both an absolute and relative measure of TE to get a more balanced picture.

For comparison, Model 2.1 (the whole dataset, 550 observations) for Level 2 is plotted in Figure 17.2. This plot shows a lower level of precision than for Level 1 in Figure 17.1 (however, note that the scale is different). It is even clearer from this plot that the predictions are reasonably well aligned in the center of the data but miss substantially for small and large WTP values.

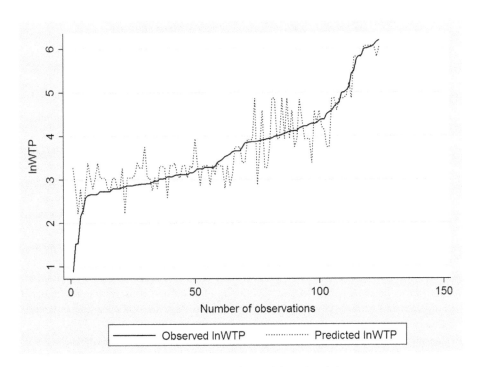

Figure 17.1 Plot of predicted vs. observed lnWTP for Model 1.4 (Level 1)

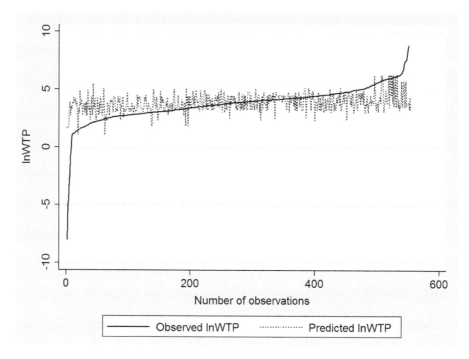

Figure 17.2   Plot of predicted vs. observed lnWTP for Model 2.1 (Level 2)

5.3 Transfer errors for species and habitat types, valuation methods and geographical regions

We also break down estimated median and mean TE from Tables 17.5 and 17.6 for Models 1.1 to 1.4 and 2.1 to 2.3, for different subsets of the Level 1 and 2 data, i.e., by different characteristics of the good (Levels 1 and 2), valuation methods and geographical region (Level 2). In other words, are the models more or less precise if used for specific BT purposes and contexts?

First, TE for the four Level 1 models predicting values for preservation of turtles, mammals and other species are given in Table 17.7. Precision increases from Model 1.1 through to 1.4 for all species types. WTP for mammal preservation is predicted with a median (mean) precision of 16 (17), percent, while for other species median TE doubles. These are generally relatively low TE estimates.

In Table 17.8, we split the estimated TE for species and different types of habitats for the Level 2 data. The precision is generally higher for the endangered species (for example, median TE of 36 percent for Model 2.3). Model 2.3 predicts WTP for terrestrial and marine habitats with the same median error of 40 percent to 46 percent (means at around 100 percent), while wetlands and other habitats have higher median errors. The similarity (homogeneity) in the change of environmental quality (ensure conservation) among the endangered species studies may be the reason that their values are predicted at a higher level of precision. Santos (1998) argues that the prediction errors he obtains in a MA of CV studies of landscape conservation are higher than those estimated in Loomis' (1992) study of rivers within the same US state due to landscapes being a more heterogeneous good.

Enhancing methodological homogeneity from Model 2.2 to 2.3 (i.e., removing estimates using market price or hedonic methods) reduces TE especially for terrestrial habitats. This is an indication that other valuation methods introduce substantial noise for terrestrial habitat valuation

Table 17.7 Median (mean) transfer error in percent for different species, Models 1.1–1.4, Level 1 data

	Turtle	*Mammal*	*Other species*
Model 1.1	45 (169)	50 (120)	67 (75)
Model 1.2	52 (114)	43 (86)	65 (71)
Model 1.3	32 (97)	36 (61)	33 (39)
Model 1.4	24 (69)	16 (17)	32 (43)
# of obs.	**34**	**19/20**	**70**

Table 17.8 Median (mean) transfer error in percent for different habitat types, Models 2.1–2.3, Level 2 data

	Terrestrial habitats	*Marine habitats*	*Endangered species*	*Wetlands*	*Other habitats*
Model 2.1	86 (545)	63 (605)	47 (85)	71 (92838)	77 (184)
Model 2.2	62 (1134)	44 (105)	36 (60)	77 (116)	78 (79)
Model 2.3	46 (104)	40 (106)	36 (57)	71 (119)	81 (75)
# obs.	81–173	129–162	121–129	31–41	17–37

Table 17.9 Median (mean) transfer error in percent for different valuation methods, Models 2.1–2.3, Level 2 data

	CV	*CM*	*TCM*	*Others*
Model 2.1	64 (157)	70 (159)	73 (104785)	93 (1776)
Model 2.2	41 (81)	78 (167)	101 (141)	84 (3882)
Model 2.3	41 (71)	26 (149)	105 (145)	–
# of obs.	121–423	50	17–37	37

Table 17.10 Median (mean) transfer error in percent for different regions, Models 2.1–2.3, Level 2 data

	Southeast Asia	*Oceania*	*East Asia*	*South Asia*	*Southwest Asia*
Model 2.1	59 (16000)	80 (209)	66 (163)	80 (1605)	45 (76)
Model 2.2	42 (102)	61 (81)	68 (304)	67 (3184)	44 (43)
Model 2.3	37 (90)	59 (76)	68 (110)	21 (27)	36 (36)
# of obs.	69–244	16–116	26–99	10–41	12–21

in the MA. In Table 17.9, we break down TE by valuation methods used (Level 2 data, as all data in Level 1 is CV). WTP estimates derived by CV has a median (mean) TE of 41 (71) percent in the most homogenous Model 2.3. Estimates derived by TCM or other valuation methods generally have higher TE than stated preference methods. This result is also confirmed (for CV) in a recent study by Kaul et al. (2013).

Finally, breaking the TE estimates down by region in Table 17.10 shows that using the model to predict values in Southeast Asia produces the lowest TE, which is partly due to the larger number of estimates from this region. Except for some very high TE estimates pulling up the mean, median TE for transfers to all regions are below 80 percent and approaching acceptable levels for policy use.

5.4 Sensitivity analysis of overall transfer error results

In the sensitivity analysis we first display the results of reduced Models 1.1 to 1.4 and Models 2.1 to 2.3 for the Level 1 and Level 2 data,[15] where variables not significant at the 20 percent level have been excluded. This is, as noted, a common procedure to simplify the MA-BT process. These models are then used to calculate transfer errors (Tables 17.11 and 17.12), which can be compared to results in Tables 17.5 and 17.6 in Section 5.1. Results show that TE levels are very similar to estimates in Tables 17.4 and 17.5 and there is no clear relationship between TE and reduced vs. full versions of the models.[16] This may mean that this simplification of the MA-BT procedure may be worth doing, as little is gained in precision.

We also ran a version of Model 2.5 for Level 2 based on the more methodologically homogenous dataset used for Model 2.3. The purpose of this is to check how much of the TE for Model 2.5 is due to methodological heterogeneity not accounted for. This produced median TE of 49 percent (mean 108 percent) (see Table 17.13), down from 64 percent in Table 17.6, caused by only excluding hedonic and market price method observations (having no methodological covariates).[17] It seems that keeping methodological heterogeneity in source valuation studies low may give a MA dataset that can produce close to reliable transfers just by the controlling for policy-relevant variables in the transfers and ignoring methodological variation.

Table 17.11 Median and mean transfer error (percent) for reduced Models 1.1–1.4, Level 1 data

	Model 1.1a	Model 1.2a	Model 1.3a	Model 1.4a
Median	69	44	68	25
Mean	108	77	103	44
N	124	124	124	123

Table 17.12 Median and mean transfer error (percent) for reduced Models 2.1–2.3, Level 2 data

	Model 2.1a	Model 2.2a	Model 2.3a
Median	67	58	46
Mean	10449	279	86
N	547	428	387

Table 17.13 Median and mean transfer error for alternative version of Model 2.5

	Model 2.5b
Median	49
Mean	108
N	387

6. Concluding remarks

This chapter has first reviewed and taken stock of the growing literature on non-market valuation of (changes in) ecosystem services from conservation of different types habitat, biodiversity and endangered species in Asia and Oceania. We have then primarily attempted to investigate the following two research questions of particular relevance to practical use of MA for benefit transfer. How sensitive are the meta-regression results and particularly the value forecasts (benefit transfers) for unstudied (policy) sites to; 1) the "scope of the MA," i.e., the level of heterogeneity of the good valued and the valuation methods used; and 2) the choice of meta-regression models?

Dividing our dataset into two levels of heterogeneity in terms of good characteristics and valuation methods (Level 1: endangered species and CV data, and Level 2: Biodiversity and nature conservation more generally), we show that the degree of regularity and conformity with theory and empirical expectations as well as the explanatory power of our MA models is higher for the more homogenous dataset of endangered species values, as expected. The analysis of the more homogenous endangered species data show that around half of the variation in the best model is due to non-study specific observable characteristics of the good and population surveyed, boding well for use of such data in BT applications.

Subjecting both our dataset levels to assessment of benefit transfer error TE using the MA models to predict observations one-by-one when excluded from the datasets, show for the best models median (mean) TE of 24 (46) percent for the endangered species data and 46 (89) percent for the more heterogeneous nature and biodiversity data. This is in the low range compared to other MA studies. At face value these results suggest that such levels of forecasting errors may in general approach acceptable levels for policy use. Both median and mean TE results also are robust and relatively low for all the meta regression models tested on the Level 1 data.

However, there is substantial variation in our estimated TE for the Level 2 data. Even if lower explanatory power of the meta-regression models does not substantially decrease the BT precision as measured with median TE within and between the two data levels, mean TE "explodes" for four out of five models for the more heterogeneous Level 2 data. Due caution, therefore, needs to be exercised when blindly using very heterogeneous valuation data (both in terms of methods and types of ecosystem services or habitats valued) for MA-BT. More testing and exploration of these issues clearly are needed but there also are encouraging signs from our analysis of the Level 2 data. By reducing some of the methodological variation (and not other heterogeneity per se), i.e., excluding WTP estimates derived from hedonic and market price methods), the mean TE was reduced substantially.

We also broke down the TE results for different species and habitat types, valuation methods and geographical regions for both levels of the data. In the best model for the Level 1 data, values for mammal conservation are predicted with a median error of only 16 percent, while this doubles for other species types (turtles, other). Note that caution should be exercised in using values for single species for BT, as such estimates may include values of biodiversity or habitats more generally (see e.g., Veisten et al. 2004). For the Level 2 data, precision is generally higher using BT for the endangered species part of the data (median TE of 36 percent), while WTP for terrestrial and marine habitats are predicted with the same median error of 40 percent to 46 percent. Wetlands and other habitats have higher median errors. Further, breaking down the results by valuation methods shows that the CV estimates are predicted with the lowest error (median TE of 41 percent). This was also found in another study by Kaul et al. (2013). Finally, predicting values for Southeast Asia yields the highest precision compared to other regions.

This chapter has only started to investigate issues that may be important in determining the reliability of using meta-analysis as basis for benefit transfer. As international and national processes following up on MEA and TEEB demand valuation of ecosystem services in Asia and elsewhere, environmental economists increasingly will be called upon to utilize existing value information in new contexts. This requires continued methodological development and testing of BT methods to ensure that such efforts are able to contribute reliable and decision-relevant information about people's preferences for ecosystem services in the future.

Acknowledgements

We would like to thank Vic Adamowicz, Ståle Navrud and Randall Rosenberger for constructive comments. Funding from the Environment and Economy Programme for Southeast Asia (EEPSEA) is greatly appreciated.

Notes

1 This part of the analysis draws heavily on Lindhjem and Tuan (2012) and more details and discussions of results can be found there and in the accompanying supplementary appendix to that paper.
2 Lindhjem and Navrud (forthcoming) in addition also use an absolute measure of TE (in monetary terms), since this matter more in practical use of results: $TE = |VSL_T - VSL_B|$
3 In the BT literature the term "convergent validity" is sometimes used.
4 The mean prediction error is often termed Mean Absolute Percentage Error (MAPE).
5 27 very high or low (2 standard deviations of the mean) were excluded in the final dataset that counted 550 observations.
6 Studies that reported results with per unit of an area were excluded, as the total size typically was not given.
7 For WTP per visit from CV or TCM studies, we calculated WTP per visit per year (if the study had information about how many trips a person would make per year, we converted to WTP per year).
8 There are also many alternative and simpler statistical approaches that are used in the literature. See e.g., Lindhjem et al. (2011) for an alternative.
9 A comprehensive test would have included other explanatory variables with different model specifications, but for sake of simplicity and brevity, we only present the model with the income variable here.
10 Note that the models are directly comparable since they all include the same observations
11 Due to the double log specification, coefficients on GDP/income can be interpreted as elasticities.
12 The TCM variable is the "hidden" category in Model 2.3, now that other non-SP methods are excluded. In Models 2.1 to 2.2 the TCM variable is excluded as it is not significant across models.
13 Since R^2 obtained from random effects models is not directly comparable to standard R^2 for OLS, the comparison should be interpreted with caution.
14 To account for econometric error in transforming ln(WTP) to WTP using antilog, we add standard deviation ($s^2/2$), which estimate varies when the sample changes, prior to transformation of ln(WTP) (see e.g., Johnston et al. 2006)
15 The regression results are left out here for the sake of brevity, only the corresponding transfer error results are included. For the regression results, see Tuan and Lindhjem (2009).
16 We also ran the same TE simulations using a rule-of-thumb of p > 0.1 instead of p > 0.2 for the reduced models, detecting no clear(er) relationship with TE.
17 We acknowledge that reducing methodological heterogeneity may also implicitly reduce good heterogeneity, as some types of nature conservation values may be more likely to be estimated using particular methods.

References

Barrio, M., and Loureiro, M. (2010) "A meta-analysis of contingent valuation forest studies," *Ecological Economics* 69:1023–1030.
Bergstrom, J.C., and Taylor, L.O. (2006) "Using meta-analysis for benefits transfer: Theory and practice," *Ecological Economics* 60:351–360.

Brander, L.M., Braeuer I., Gerdes, H. et al. (2012) "Using meta-analysis and GIS for value transfer and scaling up: Valuing climate change induced losses of European Wetlands," *Environmental and Resource Economics*, 52(3):395–413.

Brander, L.M. and Florax, R.J.G.M. (2006) "The Valuation of Wetlands: Primary Versus Meta-Analysis Based Value Transfer." In Carruthers, J.I. and Mundy, B. (eds.), *Environmental Valuation: Interregional and Intraregional* Perspectives, 193–210. Aldershot: Ashgate.

Brander, L.M., Florax, R.J.G.M., and Verrmaat, J.E. (2006) "The Empirics of wetland valuation: A comprehensive summary and a meta-analysis of the literature," *Environmental and Resource economics* 33:223–250.

Brander, L.M., van Beukering, P., and Cesar, H. (2007) "The recreational value of coral reefs: a meta-analysis," *Ecological Economics* 63(1):209–218.

Boyle, K.J., Parmeter, C.F., Boehlert, B.B., Paterson, R.W. (2013) "Due diligence in meta-analyses to support benefit transfers," *Environmental and Resource Economics* 55(3):357–386.

de Groot, R., Brander. L., van der Ploeg, S., Costanza, R., Bernard, F., Braat, L., Christie, M., Crossman, N., Ghermandi, A., Hein, L., Hussain, S., Kumar, P., McVittie, A., Portela, R., Rodriguez, L. C., ten Brink, P., van Beukering, P. (2012) "Global estimates of the value of ecosystems and their services in monetary units," *Ecosystem Services* 1(1):50–61.

Engel, S. (2002) "Benefit Function Transfer versus Meta-analysis as Policy-Making Tools: A Comparison." In: Florax, R.J.G.M., Nijkamp, P. and Willis, K.G. (eds.), *Comparative environmental economic assessment*, 133–153. Cheltenham, Edward Elgar.

Hoehn, J.P. (2006) "Methods to address selection effects in the meta regression and transfer of ecosystem values," *Ecological Economics* 60(2):389–398.

Jacobsen, J.B., and Hanley, N. (2009) "Are there income effects on global willingness to pay for biodiversity conservation," *Environmental and Resource Economics* 43:137–160.

Johnston, R.J., Besedin, E.Y., Iovanna, R., Miller, C.J., Wardwell, R.F. and Ranson, M.H. (2005) "Systematic variation in willingness to pay for aquatic resource improvements and implications for benefit transfer: a meta-analysis," *Canadian Journal of Agricultural Economics* 53(2–3):221–248.

Johnston, R. J., Besedin, E. Y., and Ranson, M. H. (2006) "Characterizing the effects of valuation methodology in function-based benefits transfer," *Ecological Economics* 60(2):407–419.

Johnston, R.J., Kukielka, J.B. and Duke, J.M. (2008) "Systematic Variation in Willingness to Pay for Agricultural Land Preservation." Paper presented at the 2008 Workshop on Meta-Analysis in Economics and Business, Nancy, France, October 17–18, 2008.

Johnston, R.J., Thomassin, P.J. (2010) "Willingness to pay for water quality improvements in the United States and Canada: Considering possibilities for international meta-analysis and benefit transfer," *Agricultural and Resource Economics Review* 39(1):114–131.

Kaul, S., Boyle, K. J., Kuminoff, N.V., Parmeter, C.F., Pope, J.C. (2013) "What can we learn from benefit transfer errors? Evidence from 20 years of research on convergent validity," *Journal of Environmental Economics and Management* 66(1):90–104.

Kristofersson, D. and Navrud, S. (2005) "Validity tests of benefit transfer – Are we performing the wrong tests?" *Environmental and Resource Economics* 30:279–286.

Kristofersson, D. and Navrud, S. (2007) "Can Use and Non-Use Values be Transferred Across Countries?" In: Navrud, S. and Ready, R. (eds.), *Environmental Value Transfer: Issues and Methods*, 207–225. Dordrecht, The Netherlands: Springer.

Kumar, P. (2010) *The Economics of Ecosystems and Biodiversity: Ecological and Economic Foundations*. London: Earthscan.

Lindhjem, H. (2007) "20 Years of stated preference valuation of non-timber benefits from Fennoscandian forests: A meta-analysis," *Journal of Forest Economics* 12(4):251–277.

Lindhjem, H. and Navrud, S. (2008) "How reliable are meta-analyses for international benefit transfers?" *Ecological Economics* 66(2–3):425–435.

Lindhjem, H. and Navrud, S. (forthcoming)"Reliability of meta-analytic benefit transfers of international value of statistical life estimates: Tests and illustrations." In: Johnston, R., Rolfe, J., Rosenberger, R. and Brouwer, R. (eds.), *Benefit Transfer of Environmental and Resource Values: A Handbook for Researchers and Practitioners*. The Netherlands: Springer.

Lindhjem, H. and Tuan, T.H. (2012) "Valuation of species and nature conservation in Asia and Oceania: A meta-analysis," *Environmental Economics and Policy Studies* 14(1):1–22.

Lindhjem, H., Navrud, S., Braathen, N.A. and Biausque, V. (2011) "Valuing mortality risk reductions from environmental, transport and health policies: A global meta-analysis of stated preference studies," *Risk Analysis* 31(9):1381–1407.

Loomis, J. B. (1992) "The evolution of a more rigorous approach to benefit transfer – Benefit function transfer," *Water Resources Research* 28(3):701–705.

Millennium Ecosystem Assessment (MEC) (2005) *Synthesis Report.* Washington, DC: Island Press.

Navrud, S. and Ready, R. (2007) "Lessons learned for environmental value transfer." In: Navrud, S. and Ready, R. (eds.), *Environmental Value Transfer: Issues and Methods,* 238–290. The Netherlands: Springer.

Nelson, J.P. and Kennedy, P.E. (2009) "The use (and abuse) of meta-analysis in environmental and natural resource economics: An assessment," *Environmental and Resource Economics* 42:345–377.

Ready, R. and Navrud, S. (2006) "International benefit transfer: Methods and validity tests," *Ecological Economics* 60:429–434.

Richardson, L. and Loomis, J. (2009) The total economic value of threatened, endangered and rare species: An updated meta-analysis,: *Ecological Economics* 68(5):1535–1548.

Rosenberger, R. and Johnston, R. J. (2009) "Selection effects in meta-valuation function transfers: Avoiding unintended consequences," *Land Economics* 85(3):410–428.

Rosenberger, R.S. and Loomis, J.B. (2000) "Using meta-analysis for benefit transfer: In-sample convergent validity tests of an outdoor recreation database," *Water Resources Research* 36(4):1097–1107.

Rosenberger, R. and Stanley, T.D. (2007) "Publication Effects in the Recreation Use Values Literature," Annual Meeting of the American Agricultural Research Association, July 29-August 1, 2007, Portland, Oregon.

Santos, J.M.L. (1998) *The Economic Valuation of Landscape Change. Theory and Policies for Land Use and Conservation.* Cheltenham: Edward Elgar.

Shrestha, R.K. and Loomis, J.B. (2003) "Meta-analytic benefit transfer of outdoor recreation economic values: Testing out-of-sample convergent validity," *Environmental and Resource Economics* 25:79–100.

Stapler, R.W. and Johnston, R.J. (2009) "Meta-analysis, benefit transfer, and methodological covariates: Implications for transfer error," *Environmental and Resource Economics* 42:227–246.

Tuan, T.H. and Lindhjem, H. (2009) "Meta-analysis of nature conservation values in Asia & Oceania: Data heterogeneity and benefit transfer issues." In: Lindhjem, H. (ed.), *Methodological issues in meta-analysis, benefit transfer and environmental valuation.* PhD Thesis. Department of Economics and Resource Management, Norwegian University of Life Sciences, As, Norway.

Van Houtven, G., Powers, J. and Pattanayak, S.K. (2007) "Valuing water quality improvements using meta-analysis: Is the glass half-full or half-empty for national policy analysis?" *Resource and Energy Economics* 29(3):206–228.

Veisten, K., Hoen, H.F., Navrud, S. and Strand, J. (2004) "Scope insensitivity in contingent valuation of complex environmental amenities," *Journal of Environmental Management* 73(4):317–331.

Zandersen, M. and Tol, R.S.J., 2009. A Meta-Analysis of Forest Recreation Values in Europe. *Journal of Forest Economics* 15, 109–130.

18

EFFECT OF THE ANNOUNCEMENT OF CONSERVATION AREA AND FINANCIAL TARGETS ON CHARITABLE GIVING FOR FOREST CONSERVATION

A natural field experiment study in East Asia

Yohei Mitani, Koichi Kuriyama and Takahiro Kubo

1. Introduction

Charitable giving can contribute to the environment. More than $300 billion was donated to charity in the United States in 2012, which was responsible for 2 percent of the country's GDP (Giving USA, 2013). Environmental or animal-related organizations received 3 percent of the total giving in the same year. Compared to donation activities in the Western countries, much less fundraising efforts have been made in East Asia. Eastern Asian countries except Hong Kong were ranked relatively low in the World Giving Index ranking, in which Japan was ranked 105th out of 153 countries (Charities Aid Foundation, 2011). In 2007, total donations in Japan amounted to just only 0.11 percent of the country's GDP. Also, the percentage of individual donors in Japan was only 19 percent in the same year, compared with 88 percent in the United States (Giving USA, 2008).

We study the economics of charitable giving for private forest conservation surrounding a potential United Nations Educational, Scientific and Cultural Organization (UNESCO) world natural heritage site in Japan. In the Western world and Japan, non-industrial private forest (NIPF) occupies the majority of forestland and provides important habitat for wildlife (Shogren and Tschirhart, 2001). The direct regulation approach has not been successful in providing the right incentives for forest conservation on private land since serious conflicts erupted between NIPF landowners and the government in many countries (Hanley et al., 2012). Instead, voluntary incentive schemes have been increasingly used in recent years for forest conservation on NIPF land (Mitani and Lindhjem, 2015). In the United States and most of Europe, conservation initiatives increasingly emphasize more direct payment approaches, such as land purchases, easements, and financial incentives, in which direct payments are targeted specifically to ecosystem services of interest (Ferraro and Kiss, 2002). We examine the use of charitable giving as a means of collecting payment for ecosystem services from the ecosystem services buyers.

A growing literature utilizes field experiments to identify the causal effect of some policy or institutions in the applied economics fields (Levitt and List, 2009). Regarding the economics of charity, a large body of experimental economics research has employed laboratory experiments to develop voluntary contribution mechanisms that lessen the free-rider problem (Ledyard, 1995). However, an external validity concern has been expressed in the applied fields, such as the economics of charity and environmental economics, as to whether the behavior of experimental participants in a laboratory reflects the behavior of people in the real field. To this end, economists have extended randomized experiments from the laboratory to fields (Harrison and List, 2004). In the economics of charity, a series of natural field experiments (NFE) have shown some devices that increase charitable donations (Landry et al., 2006). NFE are those randomized experiments conducted in environments where subjects naturally make a targeted decision and do not know that they are participating in an experiment (Harrison and List, 2004). Thus, subjects neither know that they are being manipulated and randomized into an experimental treatment nor that their behavior is subsequently inspected. While an increasing number of papers employ NFE in the fields of energy, development, labor, and charitable giving, a very limited number of applications exist in the field of environmental and resource economics (List and Price, 2013). We use a NFE to test the effect of announcing fundraising targets and seed donations. This is the first study that uses a NFE to investigate donation behaviors in East Asia and the first to our knowledge that explores the economics of charitable giving for private forest conservation around a potential UNESCO world natural heritage site.

We experimentally manipulate a solicitation of nearly 700 individuals for a National Trust campaign to test the effect of announcing fundraising targets and seed donations. In particular, we employed two non-mechanism treatments in addition to a control group: one with additional information regarding a conservation area goal and another with additional information regarding a financial goal. We find no effect of announcing a financial goal on both participation and donation size. We find statistical evidence that announcing a conservation area goal slightly increases the probability of participation but has no effect on the amount donated. In addition, we investigated the effects of individual's membership status and past donations. Our regression analyses show that individuals who are currently members and/or past time donors are more likely to participate and donate higher and also individuals who donated earlier to the current campaign tend to participate more but do not necessarily donate higher.

The remainder of this chapter proceeds as follows. The next section summarizes important findings in the economics of charitable giving and provides a theoretical framework for this chapter. Section 3 describes our field experimental design. Section 4 demonstrates the findings and Section 5 concludes.

2. Theoretical framework

Fundraising efforts are characterized as an individual's voluntary contributions to a public good, which typically rely on a voluntary contribution mechanism (VCM). A VCM payoff function for individual i (π_i) can be defined as follows:

$$\pi_i = w - c_i + m \sum_{j \in N} c_j, \tag{1}$$

where w is an endowment, c_i is individual i's contribution to a public good, and m represents a marginal per capita return (MPCR) from the public good. This VCM has a unique Nash equilibrium with zero contribution as long as the MPCR is less than one. Since this primitive fundraising effort mechanism suffers from a free-rider problem, a central question in the economics of charitable giving is how fundraisers can increase donations by refining the mechanism. To answer the question, researchers investigate both the number of donors (participation) and total money raised (donation size) as target variables.

A large literature in experimental economics has shown that provision point mechanisms (PPM) can lessen the free-rider problem (Ledyard, 1995). The PPM goes back to a conjecture by Brubaker (1975) that less free-riding would occur if contributions needed to exceed a specified threshold (i.e., provision point) before a public good is provided than in the simple setting of voluntary contribution. Let T be a pre-announced, common-knowledge provision point. In a PPM with money-back guarantee, if $\sum_{j \in N} c_j < T$, individual i's payoff is w for all i. If $\sum_{j \in N} c_j \geq T$, individual i's payoff function is given by Equation 1. Only if total contributions reach the threshold, the public good is provided. Failure to reach the threshold results in a refund of all contributions. This PPM has multiple Nash equilibria, which consist of two sets of efficient and inefficient Nash equilibria. The inefficient equilibrium is a free-riding zero-contribution Nash equilibrium. Efficient Nash equilibria in which the threshold is exactly met and the public good is provided are characterized by two constraints, efficiency and individual rationality, as follows: $\sum_{j \in N} c_j = T$ and $c_i \leq m \sum_{j \in N} c_j$, for all i (Bagnoli and Lipman, 1989). Thus, economic theory suggests that PPM increases total contribution (or average contribution) compared with VCM. The theoretical prediction has been supported by experimental evidence. Cadsby and Maynes (1999) employ a threshold public goods experiment with continuous contribution, money- back guarantee, no rebate and homogeneous induced-values to show that PPM increases average contributions compared with VCM. Rondeau et al. (2005) compare results from public goods experiments using VCM and PPM and find that PPM results in significantly higher contribution levels.

The lessons learned from theory and laboratory experiments have been brought and extended to the economics of charitable giving (List and Lucking-Reiley, 2002). Fundraising campaigns tend to use a threshold good, where charitable organizations provide a public good only if the charitable donation reaches some minimum threshold of contributions. In the economics of charity, a series of NFE have shown that publicly announced seed money increases charitable donations, which is consistent with a theory of fundraising for threshold public goods (Landry et al., 2006). Announcement of seed money holds two possible positive effects as an elimination device and credibility device. First, seed money eliminates the zero-contribution Nash equilibrium in PPM (Andreoni, 1998). Second, announcement of seed money can show potential donors credibility and the value of the public good (Landry et al., 2006). A possible negative effect is that seed money reduces the necessary money amount to make the threshold, which can lower individual contributions. List and Lucking-Reiley (2002) conducted a NFE, dividing 3,000 direct-mail solicitations for a university capital campaign into six treatments, comparing total contributions across a different level of seed money. They find that increasing seed money clearly increases both the participation rate of donors and the average contribution from participants. The NFE evidence suggests that the announcement of seed money works well (Rondeau and List, 2008). However, there have been very few NFE applications specifically to payments for ecosystem services (Alpizar et al., 2008) and none to donations to private forest conservation.

We extend a NFE study of charitable giving beyond analyzing economic mechanism effects to ecological, non-mechanism dimensions. Though very little attention has been paid to the non-mechanism treatment effects (Landry et al., 2006), an ecological point of view also can matter when designing charitable donations for biodiversity conservation on private forestland (Hanley et al., 2012). Connected habitats are ecologically more valuable than fragmented habitats for many species (Heilman et al., 2002). This leads us to examine the effect of announcing conservation area targets and seed donations with respect to conservation parcels, in comparison with financial targets. Our solicitee (i.e., potential contributor) i is assumed to have the following ex post utility with Andreoni (1990)'s impure altruistic motivation:

$$U_i = u(w - c_i) + g(\textstyle\sum_{j \in N} c_j) + \gamma f(c_i),\qquad\qquad(2)$$

where $u(\cdot), g(\cdot)$, and $f(\cdot)$ are increasing and concave. Positive γ implies the warm-glow effect from giving itself. We compare between two non-mechanism treatments in addition to a control group: one with additional information regarding a conservation area goal and another with additional information regarding a financial goal. These different non-mechanism information sets might differently affect either potential donors' perception of a public good, through of $g(\cdot)$, or their impure satisfaction from giving, through $\gamma f(\cdot)$. We examine whether introducing an ecological point of view prompts contributors to increase their participation and donation amount.

3. Experimental design

We designed a NFE to better understand how different information sets, conservation area versus financial, regarding fundraising targets and seed donations affect the participation rate and the unconditional donation amount.

3.1 National trusts fundraising campaign in Amami, Japan

The Association of National Trusts in Japan conducted a fundraising campaign from March 4 until June 30, 2013, to acquire approximately 100 ha of private forestland in Setouchi Town on Amami islands, Japan (National Trust Japan, n.d.). Amami islands are located far south of the Japanese home islands (28°16'N, 129°21'E), approximately 250 km north of Okinawa (Figure 18.1). Some 15 million years of repeated cataclysm and climate changes since 2 million years ago have created a unique subtropical forest ecosystem on the islands, where a large number of endangered and epidemic species exist (Kagoshima Prefecture, 2007). The government of Japan applied for the inclusion of the islands on UNESCO's provisional list of candidates for world natural heritage sites in 2013. The government aims to secure UNESCO world natural heritage status for the islands in 2016. The fundraising campaign site is located near the world natural heritage candidate site. The financial target of the campaign was 20 million JPY, which covers the conservation area target of 100 ha forestland, divided into 28 land plots.

3.2 Experimental treatments

To test the effect of announcing fundraising targets and seed donations, we employed three treatment groups: a control group (C); area target treatment group with additional information regarding a conservation area goal (T1A); and financial target treatment group with additional information regarding a financial goal (T2F). The text of the solicitation letter was identical across treatments, except for the following:

Control group (C)

"We have conducted a fundraising campaign *Amami-no-kurousagi Trust Campaign* since March 2013. Thanks for your support we have already received 18.67 million JPY as of June 14. We would like you to consider making a contribution *by June 30, the end of the campaign.*"

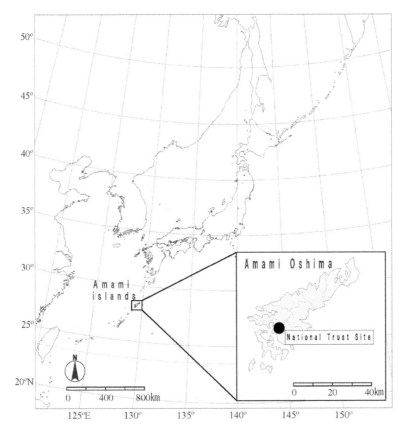

Figure 18.1 Study area

Conservation area target (T1A)

"We have conducted a fundraising campaign *Amami-no-kurousagi Trust Campaign* since March 2013. Thanks for your support we have already received donations to cover 27 of 28 land plots as of June 14. We are soliciting donations to cover *the remaining one more land plot* to reach our goal of 100ha forest conservation. To reach the campaign's goal of 28 land plots, we would like you to consider making a contribution *by June 30, the end of the campaign.*"

Financial target (T2F)

"We have conducted a fundraising campaign *Amami-no-kurousagi Trust Campaign* since March 2013. Thanks for your support we have already received 18.67 million JPY (93 percent of our goal) as of June 14. We are soliciting donations to cover *the remaining 1.33 million JPY.* To reach the campaign's goal of 20 million JPY, we would like you to consider making a contribution *by June 30, the end of the campaign.*"

Table 18.1 summarizes all information available for potential solicitees (donors) by treatments at the time when our NFE was conducted. Some information was available on the website of the organization, which was out of our experimental control (see Table 18.1).

Table 18.1 Information by treatments

Information Types	C	T1A	T2F	Web★
Information regarding Targets				
Financial goal of 20M JPY	No	No	Yes	Yes
Area goal of 28 plots with the total area of 100ha	No	Yes	No	Yes
Information regarding Seed Donations				
1.3M more to reach the goal	No	No	Yes	No
One more land plot to reach the goal	No	Yes	No	No

★ Web: Information available on the webpage of National Trusts, which is out of our experimental control.

Table 18.2 Comparison of control and treatment groups

	Control	*T1: Area*	*T2: Finance*	*Total*
All (N)	228	228	228	684
Male (%)	50.9%	50.0%	49.6%	50.1%
Members (%)	33.3%	33.3%	33.3%	33.3%
Previous Members (%)	37.3%	36.8%	36.8%	37.0%
Previous Time Donors (%)	14.9%	15.4%	15.4%	15.2%
Previous Money Donors (%)	14.5%	14.5%	14.5%	14.5%
Early Current-Campaign Donors (%)	3.9%	4.4%	4.8%	4.4%

3.3 Stratified randomization and implementation

The experiment was conducted by mail with 684 individuals. We collaborated with the National Trust Japan for the actual addressing, mailing of the 684 solicitation letters, and collecting donations. All letters were mailed on June 18, 2013, by the organization, and we requested that solicitees respond by June 30. Our experimental pool consisted of about 700 individuals who are either members of the organization, previous members, or previous money or time donors who have donated to the organization.

We employed a between-subjects design, where potential donors were randomly assigned to either a control group (C), area target treatment (T1A), or financial target treatment (T2F). Since our warm list was relatively short as a mail fundraising NFE (List and Lucking-Reiley, 2002), we employed a stratified randomization to eliminate particular sources of differences between groups (Bruhn and McKenzie, 2009). To implement a stratified randomization, the organization provided us the following information: potential donors' membership status, previous time and money donations, and gender. We stratified on these characteristics: current members, past members, non-member previous money donors, non-member previous time donors, early current campaign donors (who have already made a donation to the current campaign), and male. Table 18.2 shows that characteristics are balanced across groups.

4. Experimental results

Table 18.3 presents summary statistics of the experimental results for all three treatments. In total, we received 47 donation checks during the experimental period from 47 different individuals. The average participation rate was 6.87 percent, and the total money raised was 346,000 JPY. The conservation area target treatment (T1A) produces the highest participation rate (7.46 percent) and total money raised (123,000 JPY), while the average donation conditional on contributing of the T1A is not the highest. Wilcoxon-Mann-Whitney tests of the differences in the number of donors and the average unconditional money raised show that there is no statistically significant difference across all three treatments as the last two rows of Table 18.3 report. Table 18.4 reports the distribution of raw donation amounts across all three treatments. These descriptive statistics suggest that there is no clear indication that our treatments affect the participation rate and donation amounts.

To control for observable and unobservable differences in donors and allow us to focus on our treatment effects, we conduct regression analyses of the participation decision and unconditional

Table 18.3 Summary of results

	Control	T1: Area	T2: Finance	Total
The Number of Donors	15	17	15	47
Participation Rate (%)	6.58%	7.46%	6.58%	6.87%
Total JPY Raised	118000	123000	105000	346000
Average JPY Unconditional	517.5	539.5	460.5	505.8
Average JPY Conditional	7866.7	7235.3	7000.0	7361.7
Total Number Solicited	228	228	228	684
WMW-Test (vs. Control)★				
The Number of Donors	–	0.37 (0.71)	0.00(1.00)	–
Average JPY Unconditional	–	0.39 (0.69)	−0.03(0.97)	–

★ z-value from Wilcoxon-Mann-Whitney test and p-value in parentheses.

Table 18.4 Distribution of donation amounts

Amount	Control	T1: Area	T2: Finance	Total
0	213	211	213	637
1000	3	1	7	11
2000	1	3	0	4
3000	3	2	1	6
4000	1	0	0	1
5000	2	4	3	9
10000	4	6	3	13
30000	0	1	0	1
50000	1	0	1	2
Total	228	228	228	684

Table 18.5 Estimation results

	Model 1 (Probit) Donation (Binary)		Model 2 (OLS) Amount (Unconditional)	
	Coef.	Std. Err.	Coef.	Std. Err.
T1: Area	0.091	0.031 ★★★	19.127	66.551
T2: Finance	−0.034	0.041	−61.221	46.743
Male	0.059	0.073	−178.542	138.700
Members	5.007	0.268 ★★★	1443.544	12.232 ★★★
Time Donors	4.254	0.271 ★★★	141.321	7.010 ★★★
Early Donors	0.757	0.344 ★★	140.686	126.269
Const.	−6.034	0.288 ★★★	100.572	66.549
N	684		684	
Pseudo/Adj R2	0.267		0.043	
Log Likelihood	−125.6		–	

★★★ $p < 0.01$; ★★ $p < 0.05$

donation amount. First, we estimate a probit regression of the participation decision on dummy variables for our experimental treatments and other individual characteristics. Our subjects can be categorized into the following donor types: members, previous members, non-member previous time donors, and non-member previous money donors. To account for unobservable heterogeneities at the donor-type level, we cluster the robust standard errors by donor type. Model 1 in Table 18.5 shows the estimation result. Regarding our treatment effects in comparison with the control group, the result shows that announcing a conservation area goal slightly increases the probability of participation at the 1 percent risk level while announcing a financial goal does not have statistically significant effect on the probability of participation. Also, the result suggests that individuals who are currently members, past time donors, or donated earlier to the current campaign are statistically more likely to participate.

Second, we estimate a linear regression model of the (unconditional) amount donated on dummy variables for our experimental treatments and other characteristics. We again cluster the standard errors by donor type. Model 2 in Table 18.5 shows the estimation result. The result suggests no statistical significant treatment effect on the unconditional amount donated, compared with the control group. Also, the result suggests that individuals who are currently members or past time donors are statistically more likely to donate higher.

5. Concluding remarks

In this study, we explore the use of charitable giving as a means of collecting payment for private forest conservation from the ecosystem services buyers. Since an ecological point of view can be important when designing fundraising campaigns for biodiversity conservation, we extend a NFE study of charitable giving beyond analyzing economic mechanism effects to ecological, non-mechanism dimensions. We use a NFE to examine the effect of announcing conservation area targets and seed donations regarding conservation parcels, in comparison with financial targets and monetary seed donations. We solicited contributions for a National Trust campaign using direct mail from nearly 700 individuals, randomly divided into three experimental treatments: a control group, a conservation area target treatment, and a financial target treatment.

We raised 346,000 JPY in total with a participation rate of 6.87 percent. We investigated the effects of individual's membership status and past donations. Our regression analyses show that individuals who are currently members and/or past time donors are more likely to participate and donate higher and that individuals who donated earlier to the current campaign tend to participate more but do not necessarily donate higher. The result is consistent with the previous findings (Lange and Stocking, 2009).

Regarding our treatment effects, we find statistical evidence that announcing a conservation area goal slightly increases the probability of participation but has no effect on the amount donated, while we find no effect of announcing a financial goal on both participation and donation size. The result provides insight into the design of charitable campaigns for private forest conservation, suggesting that introducing an ecological point of view in combination with financial information might prompt contributors to increase their participation. Further investigation with bigger sample size is needed to establish the ecological, non-mechanism effects on donation behavior for biodiversity conservation.

This is the first study that uses a NFE to investigate donation behaviors in East Asia and the first that explores the economics of charitable giving for private forest conservation surrounding a potential world natural heritage site. The advantage of using NFE over laboratory, artificial field, and framed field experiments is that NFE are conducted in environments where subjects naturally make a targeted decision and do not know that they are participating in an experiment (Harrison and List, 2004). Thus, NFE are more likely to have higher external validity, implying that the results produced from NFE are relatively easy for practitioners and policymakers to understand (List and Price, 2013). A shortcoming of NFE compared with laboratory experiments is the relative difficulty of implementation and replication since conducting NFE is often opportunistic and requires cooperation of outside organizations. Especially in Japan compared with the Western countries, it seems more difficult to find organizations or sites willing to collaborate with researchers to implement large-scale field experiments.

References

Alpizar, F., Carlsson, F. and Johansson-Stenman, O. (2008) "Anonymity, reciprocity, and conformity: evidence from voluntary contributions to a national park in Costa Rica," *Journal of Public Economics*, 92(5), 1047–1060.

Andreoni, J. (1990) "Impure altruism and donations to public goods: a theory of warm-glow giving," *Economic Journal*, 100(401), 464–477.

Andreoni, J. (1998) "Toward a theory of charitable fund-raising," *Journal of Political Economy*, 106(6), 1186–1213.

Bagnoli, M. and Lipman, B. L. (1989) "Provision of public goods: fully implementing the core through private contributions," *Review of Economic Studies*, 56, 583–601.

Brubaker, E. R. (1975) "Free Ride, Free Revelation, or Golden Rule," *Journal of Law and Economics*, 18, 147–161.

Bruhn, M. and McKenzie, D. (2009) "In pursuit of balance: randomization in practice in development field experiments," *American Economic Journal: Applied Economics*, 1(4), 200–232.

Cadsby, C. B. and Maynes, E. (1999) "Voluntary provision of threshold public goods with continuous contributions: experimental evidence," *Journal of Public Economics*, 71(1), 53–73.

Charities Aid Foundation. (2011) World Giving Index. https://www.cafonline.org/pdf/world_giving_index_2011_191211.pdf.

Ferraro, P. J. and Kiss, A. (2002) "Direct payments to conserve biodiversity," *Science* 298, 1718–1719.

Giving USA. (2008) http://nonprofit.about.com/od/trendsissuesstatistics/a/giving2008.htm.

Giving USA. (2013) http://nonprofit.about.com/od/trendsissuesstatistics/a/giving2013.htm.

Hanley, N., Banerjee, S., Lennox, G. D., Armsworth, P. R. (2012) "How should we incentivize private land-owners to 'produce' more biodiversity?" *Oxford Review of Economic Policy*, 28(1), 93–113.

Harrison, G. W. and List, J. A. (2004) "Field experiments," *Journal of Economic Literature*, 42, 1009–1055.

Heilman, G. E., Strittholt, J. R., Slosser, N. C., and Dellasala, D. A. (2002) "Forest Fragmentation of the conterminous united states: assessing forest intactness through road density and spatial characteristics," *BioScience*, 52(5), 411.

Kagoshima Prefecture. (2007), "Relics of Evolution Japan: Heritage of the Amami Islands Japan," Department of Environment and Residential Life, Kagoshima Prefecture, Japan.

Landry, C., Lange, A. List, J.A., Price, M., and Rupp, N. (2006) "Toward an understanding of the economics of charity: evidence from a field experiment," *Quarterly Journal of Economics*, 121, 747–782.

Lange, A. and Stocking, A. (2009) "Charitable Memberships, Volunteering, and Discounts: Evidence from a Large-Scale Online Field Experiment," *NBER Working Paper* No. 14941, Cambridge, MA.

Ledyard, J. (1995) "Public goods: A survey of experimental research." In *Handbook of Experimental Economics*, Kagel, J. H. and Roth, A. E. (eds.), 111–194. Princeton, NJ: Princeton University.

Levitt, S. D. and List, J. A. (2009) "Field Experiments in economics: the past, the present, and the future," *European Economic Review*, 53, 1–18.

List, J. A. and Lucking-Reiley, D. (2002) "The effects of seed money and refunds on charitable giving: experimental evidence from a university capital campaign," *Journal of Political Economy*, 110(1), 215–233.

List, J. A. and Price, M. K. (2013) "Using Field Experiments in Environmental and Resource Economics," *NBER Working Paper* No. 19289, Cambridge, MA.

Mitani, Y. and Lindhjem, H. (2015) "Forest Owners' Participation in Voluntary Biodiversity Conservation: What does it take to forego forestry forever?" *Land Economics*, forthcoming.

National Trust Japan (n.d.) http://www.ntrust.or.jp/trust_project/amakuro/newpage2.html.

Rondeau, D. and List, J. A. (2008) "Matching and challenge gifts to charity: evidence from laboratory and natural field experiments," *Experimental Economics*, 11(3), 253–267.

Rondeau, D., Poe, G. L., and Schulze, W. D. (2005) "VCM or PPM? A comparison of the performance of two voluntary public goods mechanisms," *Journal of Public Economics*, 89(8), 1581–1592.

Shogren, J. F. and Tschirhart, J. (2001) *Protecting Endangered Species in the United States: Biological needs, Political Realities, Economic Choices.* Cambridge, New York and Melbourne: Cambridge University Press.

19

COASTAL DEVELOPMENT, CORAL REEFS AND MARINE LIFE IN ASIA

Tourism's double-edged sword

Clevo Wilson and Clem Tisdell

1. Introduction

A large proportion of the world's population, including those of Asian countries, live in close proximity to the coastline. Coastlines are being developed at a faster rate than ever before and there is now a growing body of literature to show that such activities are affecting the quality of coastal ecosystems and its wildlife (see, for example, Jennings, 2004; Siler et al., 2014; Duke et al., 2007). This in turn is impacting negatively on the fishing and the tourism industries, amongst others. Millions of people depend on these sectors for their livelihoods and, unsustainable development can only make the plight of those who rely on these resources worse. The tourism industry in the coastal regions is particularly at risk since the industry relies heavily on coastal ecosystems to attract visitors. This chapter discusses the strong links that exist between coastal development, tourism, marine ecosystems and its wildlife, drawing attention to two well-known species widely used in tourism, namely whales and sea turtles, and discussing their conservation in relation to tourism. The chapter is divided into six sections. The second section examines why it is important to strike a balance between coastal development and protecting ecosystems. In this section, we discuss the major identified causes of coastal ecosystem degradation from the published literature, and the third section focuses attention on tourism development in the Asian region, which is one of the major reasons for coastal degradation. A diagrammatic approach is used to illustrate that planning of coastal tourism development which takes into account environmental impacts could result in economic benefits to the areas and regions concerned. The negative impacts on tourism when coastal ecosystems are damaged are discussed in section four. Section five shows the economic benefits resulting from sea turtle and whale watching-based tourism in Australia, and section six examines tourism as a conservation tool. In this section, the differing experiences of sea turtle tourism in Sri Lanka and Australia are discussed based on our published work. The final section concludes.

2. Why it is important to strike a balance between coastal development and protecting ecosystems?

It is estimated that millions of the world's population are living in close proximity to the sea (see Figure 19.1), and as Goudarzi (2006) noted, there has been more than a 35 per cent increase in populations living on the coasts since 1995, and this figure is increasing. In fact, coastlines are fast

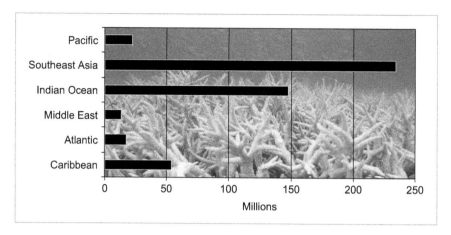

Figure 19.1 Number of people living within 100 km from the coast (coral reefs)

Source: Burke et al. (1998).

becoming overpopulated, and in some countries, the majority of the population lives on the coast. A good example is Australia. In some of the populated countries, including countries in Asia and Australasia, the coastal population density can be more than 100 people per square km and is predicted to increase (Subramanian, 2012). There are several countries in Asia (e.g. Sri Lanka, Bangladesh, India) that fall into this category. This is not only restricted to urban areas, but population growth also is fast spreading into rural areas. As a consequence, during the past few decades increasing portions of coastlines have become urbanized in many countries, with some of the biggest changes being witnessed by Asian counties with rapid economic growth.

What is more important and why we should be more concerned about protecting coastal eco-systems is that most of these populations depend on coastal ecosystems for their livelihoods. Despite rapid urbanisation, a large part of coastal populations is involved in fishing and this often involves traditional fishing. For example, coral reefs contribute about one-quarter of the total fish catch, providing food for millions of people in Asia alone (Birkeland, 1997; Subramanian, 2012). Local inhabitants also depend on other resources from coastal ecosystems, such as from sand and coral mining and the use of mangroves (UNEP, 2006). As is now well recognised, coral reefs are one of the most biologically rich ecosystems on earth (see, for example, Charles et al., 2009). It is estimated that about 4,000 species of fish and 800 species of reef-building corals are now known to science (see, for example, Paulay, 1997; Charles et al., 2009). Coastal ecosystems, especially coral reefs, have the potential to provide the necessary raw materials for new drugs (see, for example, Fenical, 1996). They provide a wide range of environmental services which are difficult to quantify but are extremely valuable to coastal communities and visitors. Some of them include recreational services, especially for the tourism industry. Coral reefs are a major drawcard for recreational fishers, snor-kelers, and scuba divers who spend millions of dollars each year on these and associated activities. Apart from these economic benefits, some of the marine life, such as sea turtles, whales and dol-phins, create economic opportunities to coastal communities through nature-based tourism. Reefs, mangroves and beaches also provide protection to coastal inhabitants (see, for example, Das and Vincent, 2009). These are some of the benefits to communities that coastal ecosystems provide.

In addition, coastal communities have been benefiting from tourism, both local and foreign, during the last few decades. Tourism is one of the fastest growing sectors in the world (Burke et al., 2001; United Nations World Tourism Organisation, 2012) and coastlines are a prime attraction to tourists (Subramanian, 2012). In addition, revenue generated from tourism to coastal communities is often larger in per capita dollar terms compared to traditional activities such as fishing (see, for example, UNEP, 2011). The amount of employment generated from tourism also is large, and there are many countries in Asia and Australasia that rely heavily on revenue generated from tourism. Countries in these regions (and elsewhere) are rapidly expanding their infrastructure development activities to take advantage of tourism revenue (see, for example, IOSEA Marine Turtle Memorandum of Understanding, 2014, database).

The question that is being asked, however is, can the expansion of human activities, whether it is tourism or fishing that depend on coastal ecosystems for their activities, continue without negative consequences? The evidence that is emerging shows that overutilisation of coastal resources is affecting the quality of coastal ecosystems, including fisheries and wildlife such as sea turtles. They in turn have negative impacts on the tourism industry.

We know that coastal ecosystems are extremely rich in biodiversity and are highly productive (see, for example, Souter and Linden, 2005; IOSEA Marine Turtle Memorandum of Understanding, 2014, database). Coastal ecosystems support the marine food chain, which in turn provides food for the human population. As is well documented, coral reefs, sea grass beds and mangroves are some of the most productive ecosystems (UNEP, 2006). Souter and Linden (2005), for example, point out that the yearly production of fish is in the range of 20 tons per square kilometre among coral reefs (for other detailed studies on this topic see UNEP, 2011). However, fish production can only be high if coastal ecosystems are healthy. If the marine environment is damaged, fish production and productivity are likely to drop, as is already happening in some countries (UNEP, 2011).

Souter and Linden (2005) in their study state that 'decreasing productivity of coastal waters is now the norm throughout much of the Indian Ocean. The catch per effort is steadily going down affecting the livelihoods of coastal communities.' There are many reasons for the decreasing and loss of productivity of coastal ecosystems. Some of them are local, while a few can be attributed to regional/global phenomena such as global warming.

The existing literature (e.g. Burke et al.,1998; Souter and Linden, 2005; Subramanian, 2012) show that the degradation of coastal ecosystems can be roughly categorized into: overexploitation of the marine environment, coastal development (for example tourism), pollution resulting from inland human activity and marine-based pollution. Interestingly, as Figure 19.2 shows, following

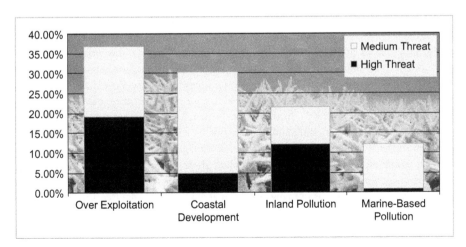

Figure 19.2 Main threats to coral reefs

Source: Burke et al. (1998).

Burke et al. (1998), that human overexploitation of coastal resources and over-development pose the biggest threats to reef ecosystems, followed by pollution resulting from human land-based (e.g. agricultural and industrial pollution) and marine activities. Interestingly, action taken to reduce these market failures often remains weak, and in many countries, especially in low-mid income countries, such action is yet to materialize.

As is clear from Figure 19.2, human overexploitation of coral reefs is one of the major causes for the destruction of coral reefs. Overfishing affects fish size, their abundance, and the composition of species within reef communities (see, for example, UNEP, 2011). Destructive fishing practices include blast fishing, fishing with cyanide and other poisonous chemicals, and trawling (FAO, 2002). These methods directly damage reef ecosystems. Because these methods are generally nonselective, large numbers of other species, along with undersized target species, may be destroyed. For more details see Burke et al. (1998).

When the impacts shown in Figure 19.2 occur, symbiotic relationships that normally exist are severely disrupted. For example, when fishing exceeds natural recruitment and fishermen use more effective and destructive techniques, they destroy the ecosystems even more. These practices increase the vulnerability of coastal ecosystems (for example, the effects of the Tsunami in December 2004 – see, Das and Vincent, 2009). The problems are compounded further due to climate change. Temperature increases lead to coral bleaching, which now occurs periodically in almost the entire Asian and Australasian regions (see, for example, CRC Reef Research Centre, 2005).

The second major threat that is identified by Burke et al. (1998) is coastal development. It is evident from available data that the growth of coastal cities and towns has resulted in a range of threats to costal ecosystems. It is not uncommon for coral reefs and mangroves to be reclaimed for the construction of airports, hotels and for other infrastructure such as expansion of ports. A good example of large-scale port expansion taking place is in Australia. For example, in February 2014, the Abbot Point coal terminal expansion, which will be one of the largest ports in the world, was approved. The dredged spoil will be dumped in the Great Barrier Reef Marine Park (World Heritage listed) area, which is likely to damage the marine ecosystem, including corals (Peterson, 2014). This also is likely to impact fisheries and tourism activity in the area. Development of new ports and expansion of ports is not uncommon in Asia and Australasia and is increasing to keep pace with economic activity. Furthermore, in many low-income countries of Asia (as is the case in East Africa and the Pacific), coastal/coral ecosystems are mined for sand and limestone. In some countries such as Sri Lanka it is a lucrative cottage industry.

The activities of hotels and resorts directly affect sea turtle nesting sites. Very often the best nesting grounds are taken over for tourist development. Hatchlings are disoriented by lights. Vehicles and tourists on beaches affect sea turtle nests and jet skis are a major hazard as well. Garbage and fishing tackle also are an issue. For a discussion on these issues, see Wilson and Tisdell (2001).

Furthermore, unregulated tourism poses a threat to coral reefs and other coastal ecosystems (see, for example, Hawkins et al., 2005). In unregulated situations it is not uncommon to see tourists destroying corals through trampling and boat anchoring also causes further damage (Souter and Linden, 2005; UNEP, 2006). In mostly low-income countries, the tourist demand for curios results in over-harvesting of marine resources. They include shells, corals and sea turtle products.

Another major threat is run off from agriculture, industries, tourist hotels and resorts, which impact on adjoining ecosystems in many countries, including Australia (see, for example. Tisdell et al., 1992). As is well known, effluents and other forms of pollution (e.g. nitrate pollution) promote algal blooms. Algal blooms have been recorded in several countries of Asia, including Indonesia and Thailand (see, for example, Tisdell et al.,1992). They also affect marine wildlife such as sea turtles, dolphins, and string rays – marine resources that are natural assets for nature-based tourism activities.

Burke et al. (1998) also identified marine-based pollution as a threat to coral reefs. However, in comparison to the other three stresses, marine-based pollution is less significant, but is a major cause for coral reef degradation. Oil spills and discharge of oil and other chemical material by passing ships and accidents pose an unknown threat to coral reefs (see, for example, UNEP, 2006). However, some studies suggest that the effects are mostly short term in nature. As Burke et al. (1998) point out, in the long term, oil spills could leave reef communities more vulnerable to other types of disturbances.

The previous discussion was mainly based on the impacts on coral reefs. However, it must be mentioned that all the above activities are likely to affect nearby mangroves, sea grass beds and other associated habitats. As is now well known, these ecosystems serve as nurseries for many marine species. In many parts of the world, mangroves are being overexploited for fuel wood, to make room for aquaculture ponds and for other coastal development activities such as tourism (see, for example, Tisdell et al.,1992; Souter and Linden, 2005; Duke et al. 2007).

Figure 19.3 shows the threats to coral reefs globally based on the four risk factors discussed previously. They are overexploitation by human activities, coastal development, inland pollution, erosion and marine-based pollution.

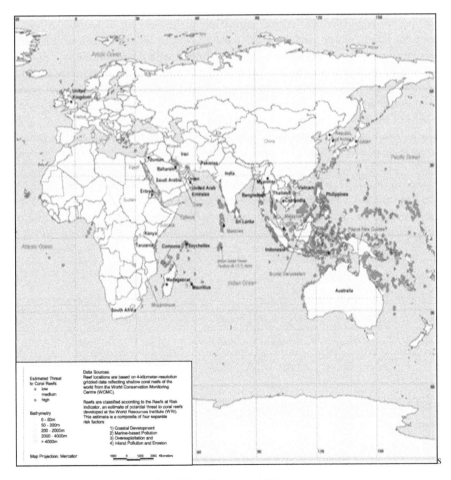

Figure 19.3   Potential threats to coral reefs from human activities

Source: Adapted from Bryant et al. (1998).

To identify the potential threats to coral reefs on a global scale, 13 factors were considered in Figure 19.3. They are cities, settlements, airports and military bases, population density, mines, tourist resorts, ports, oil tanks and wells, shipping routes, and areas where blast fishing or fishing using poisons is known to occur. Additionally, a watershed-based model was used to estimate potential erosion within the watershed to produce an estimate of areas potentially threatened by inland pollution and sedimentation. The 13 threat surfaces were integrated with data on coral reef locations, resulting in a global classification of potential threats to coral reefs. It must be mentioned here that only data pertaining to coral reefs have been used to create Figure 19.3. The figure does not show threats to other coastal ecosystems from overexploitation of resources and coastal development.

The next section focuses attention on tourism development in the Asian and Australasian region, which is a major reason for coastal development.

3. Tourism development in the Asian region

As mentioned in the introduction, tourism is one of the world's largest and fastest growing industries, and the situation in Asian and Australasian countries is no different. Worldwide, international tourism grew at an average annual rate of 4.3 per cent between 2000 and 2012, exceeding the billion visitor mark in 2012. Table 19.1 shows international tourist arrivals and revenues for the Asian and Australasian regions compared with the rest of the world.

As can be seen, international tourism numbers have shown a rapid increase between 2000 and 2012. The trends are similar for most of the Asian tourist destinations apart from a few exceptions (UN Statistical database, various years). Countries like Sri Lanka have seen a rapid increase in tourist arrivals after the end of the civil war in 2009.

There are several reasons for the global increase in tourist numbers. They include rising levels of disposable income, especially in China and India, improvements in transportation and the introduction of low-cost airline services, easier access to destinations and the growing number of new market niches, such as nature-based tourism. For more details, see Tisdell and Wilson (2012). Revenue from tourism is a major foreign exchange earner for some countries, especially for those small countries in the Asian and Australasian region. The socio-economic impact of tourism is very large, contributing to millions of jobs and incomes in the region (World Travel and Tourism Council, 2013). The creation of employment is direct and indirect and many sectors of the

Table 19.1 International tourist arrivals and receipts in Asia and Australasia, 2000–2012

Destination	Arrivals (in millions)			Receipts (in US $ millions)		
	2000	2005	2012	2000	2005	2011
World	678	805	1,035	475B★	679B★	1042B★
Asia Pacific	110.1	153.6	232.9	85,332	135,826	299,740
North-East Asia	58.3	85.9	122.8	39,427	64,964	149,487
South East Asia	36.1	48.5	84.0	26,838	33,981	84,311
South Asia	6.1	8.1	14.0	4,794	9,947	24,230
Oceania	9.6	11.1	12.1	14,269	25,934	41,713

Source: United Nations World Tourism Organisation (2000–2012).

★*Note*: B = billion

economy benefit. In 2012, for example, the direct contribution from travel and tourism to GDP in Southeast Asia alone was more than US $100 billion and was approximately 4.5 per cent of the whole economy's GDP (World Travel and Tourism Council, 2013). In other regions too, the contribution from the tourism sector is high. Clearly, tourism is an important sector for most of the Asian and Australasian countries. However, it must be noted that much tourism is highly reliant on coastal resources and ecosystems to provide the quality of services to tourists and also to maintain the current revenues generated, level of employment and other benefits.

The threats to coastal ecosystems from overexploitation of resources, unplanned coastal development, and pollution have a direct impact on tourism activities and its revenue and employment. This is because tourism relies heavily on high-quality beaches, coral reefs, wildlife, recreational fishing and associated attractions for its long-term survival and also to add value to tourist destinations. If these invaluable resources are damaged or destroyed, the quality of tourism will suffer together with adverse socio-economic consequences. In such situations, not only will the quality of tourism suffer but also the number of tourists and the number of days spent in an area will be reduced. Needless to say, the amount of money that tourists spend also will be reduced. It also is likely that in such situations, 'budget' tourists could replace high-spending tourists in some areas. There also is evidence to show that low-spending tourists could contribute and even accelerate socio-economic problems prevailing in some tourist destinations (Huybers, 2007). Low-spending tourists also are likely to spend less for conservation of wildlife and entry fees to nature reserves and national parks in countries visited.

On the other hand, better planning of coastal development with a view to attract tourists can pay economic dividends. If this tourism development is poorly planned, the demand of tourists to visit the area may decline as discussed and could be illustrated as shown by curve ABCDE in Figure 19.4.

The cost of catering for the tourist visits when development is poorly planned might be as shown by HDJ. This could be 'budget tourists' as opposed to high-spending tourists who keep away from such areas. However, with planning of development that takes account of environmental factors and preservation of natural attractions, the demand to visit the area might be as shown by curve ABCFG. Note here the extra number of tourists visiting the area which is shown by X_2. This also includes extra days spent in an area by tourists. But an extra cost is involved for

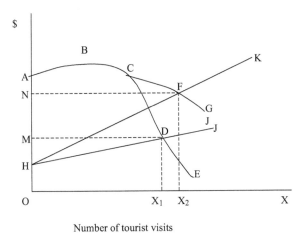

Number of tourist visits

Figure 19.4 The planning of coastal tourism development which takes account of environmental impacts can have economic benefits

this planned development, which also entails protecting the natural resources which the tourism industry depends on for sustaining the tourism industry. The cost of catering for tourist visits is now assumed to be as indicated by HFK, which of course, is higher than development that is poorly planned. It can be seen visually that the area of HFN exceeds that of HDM. It also can be proven to be the case mathematically. Consequently, the producers' surplus (their net revenue) in the tourist area increases as a result of planning which takes greater account of environmental factors that complement the tourism industry.

In the next section, we provide examples from secondary studies to showcase how tourism can be negatively affected when environmental factors such as coastal ecosystems are damaged either from unplanned development or from adverse weather events such as El Niño which leads to coral bleaching amongst other impacts.

4. Negative impacts on tourism when coastal ecosystems are damaged

As mentioned in the earlier section, coastal tourism relies heavily on healthy coastal ecosystems. If coastal ecosystems are affected, the quality and quantity of tourists visiting a coastal region is likely to suffer and the income from tourism is likely to decrease. When the tourism sector suffers, it gives rise to many socio-economic problems. These will be discussed referring to some selected research conducted in the early part of the 2000s.

First, we provide an example of a coastal ecosystem which the tourism industry relies on heavily, namely coral reefs. For instance, 85 per cent of tourists (WWF, 2014) who visit Australia travel to see the Great Barrier Reef. However, if coral reefs are damaged due to excessive tourism activities, the number of tourists visiting coral reefs is likely to decline. Furthermore, the quality of tourists also is likely to decline. There is clear evidence to demonstrate the impact on tourism when coral reefs are damaged (see, for example, UNEP, 2006).

The example selected for this chapter is taken from a study conducted by Cesar (2000) in the Philippines in 2000. In the summer of 1998 there was widespread bleaching of coral reefs in the Indian-Pacific Ocean (CRC Reef Research Centre, 2005). Many coral reefs in the Asian or Australasian region suffered as well (ibid.). For instance, it is estimated that 30 per cent to 50 per cent of the coral reefs around El Nido in the Philippines suffered from coral bleaching (Cesar, 2000). He showed that two years since the bleaching occurred, there was clear evidence to show that the quality of tourists visiting El Nido had been affected.

El Nido is located on the island of Palawan and the local economy relies heavily on tourism. As stated in Cesar (2000), the two resorts in the area attracted approximately 17,000 visitors in 2000. The tourists who visit El Nido are of two main groups, namely backpackers and resort tourists, roughly 50 per cent from each category. As a can be seen from Table 19.2, most of the tourists are from Europe. The rest are from Asia and the US.

Table 19.2 Number of tourists by country of origin and type of accommodation in El Nido – 1999 data

	Europe	*Japan*	*Korea*	*Philippines*	*US*	*Others*	*Total*
Cottages	4728	193	193	1598	675	620	8005
Resorts	1363	2331	1368	2413	804	328	8607
Total	6091	2524	1561	4011	1479	948	16612
% of total	37%	15%	9%	24%	9%	6%	100%

Source: Cesar (2000).

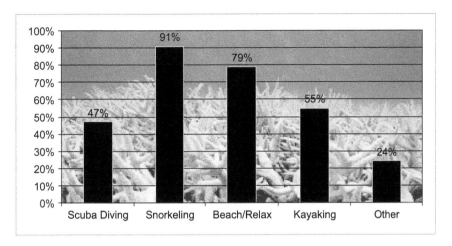

Figure 19.5   Activities undertaken by tourists in El Nido – multiple activities possible

Source: Cesar (2000).

As Cesar (2000) notes, the resort tourists are high-spending tourists while backpackers spend less. They are 'budget' tourists. He categorised the tourists who visit El Nido into three groups based on purpose of visit namely: a) divers, b) honeymooners, and c) general ecotourists/ relaxers. As would be expected, most of the daily activities of the tourists are related to the sea and the beaches. The types of sea-related activities undertaken by the tourists are shown in Figure 19.5.

Apart from the types of sea activities undertaken by the tourists, most of the visitors to the area had a clear interest in the marine environment. The survey conducted by Cesar (2000) showed that only five per cent of those interviewed said that the 'marine life' was not important. El Nido was a popular tourist destination prior to the 1998 coral bleaching and as pointed out by Cesar, resort tourism since the mid-1980s had roughly doubled and budget tourism had increased five-fold at the same time.

Interviews conducted by Cesar (2000) among key informants (e.g. dive instructors, resort managers and cottage owners) showed that resort tourists were affected most because the resorts have specialized in catering to the exclusive high-end of the dive market, and Bacuit Bay was advertised as a pristine diving area. Over the two years after the bleaching, the area had lost this image due to reef degradation. Interestingly, according to information provided by the key informants, coral bleaching had not impacted budget tourist arrivals. This is because fewer budget tourists dive during their stay and make fewer dives. According to the key informants, the degradation of the reef was not only due to coral bleaching but due to other factors such as the 1998 typhoon (also linked to El Niño), destructive fishing (which is common) and tourism damage arising from boat anchoring and trampling on reefs by divers.

According to key informants, approximately 80 per cent of resort guests were divers, and after the coral bleaching this figure at dropped to roughly ten per cent. In order to deal with the drop in dive tourists (low room occupancy) the resorts had shifted their marketing to attract other groups of tourists. Most often such groups spend less in resorts. The drop in occupancy rates suggests that the loss in tourists specialized in diving is a loss to the resorts.

Cesar (2000) estimated the loss of tourism revenue for El Nido from coral bleaching-related effects, which is shown in Table 19.3.

Table 19.3 Loss in net revenue to the Philippine economy due to coral bleaching in El Nido (In net present value (NPV) in '000 US$ over the period 2000–2025)

	Annual loss to Local Economy	NPV Permanent	NPV Permanent	NPV Temporary	NPV Temporary
		3% discount rate	9% discount rate	3% discount rate	9% discount rate
Budget tourists	10	179	99	49	40
Resort tourists	1500	26,815	14.893	7,349	5971
Total losses	1510	26,992	14.992	7398	6010

Source: Cesar (2000).

Cesar (2000) presents the results of two scenarios in Table 19.3. One scenario assumes a situation where the tourism revenue losses are only temporary and that the damage disappears (gradually) over a ten-year period due to the recovery of corals. In the second scenario, he estimates the losses in tourism revenue if the damage is permanent or there is no significant recovery of the coral ecosystem. Discount rates of three per cent and nine per cent per year are used to estimate the net present value of the losses. As can be seen, total losses are estimated to be between US$15.0 and 27.0 million depending on the discount rate used. On the other hand, if the damage to corals is temporary, the cost would be between US$6.0 to 7.4 million.

Furthermore, in addition to loss in revenue for hotels and resorts, the degradation of coastal ecosystems such as coral reefs also can affect tourists' holiday satisfaction and thereby create a loss in their welfare. Furthermore, 'future' tourism prospects for the areas also can be affected because we know that 'word of mouth' promotion is an important aspect of attracting visitors to destinations. Dissatisfied tourists are likely to give negative feedback when they return from holiday. Hence, tourist numbers drop, as shown in Figure 19.4.

Cesar (2000) assessed the satisfaction of tourists based on photos shown. Tourists were asked to express their willingness to pay for 'better reef quality'. The specific question was how much tourists were willing to pay extra to go to a hypothetical remote area on Palawan where reefs were not affected by coral bleaching and which were, in all other respects, identical. The results showed that divers were prepared to pay considerably more than snorkelers. He estimated that an average diver was willing to pay as much as US$202 for the experience than an average snorkeler, who was willing to pay only a sum of US$26.

Not only is occupancy and spending within the hotels affected when the quality of coastal ecosystems decline, but it also affects other sectors that depend on tourism for their business. They include transport, restaurants, those who provide leisure services and a host of other sectors. In other words, when tourists visit an area they incur expenditures in the local area in addition to what they pay for their accommodations and food. National parks and nature reserves also loose out, and in some countries, tourism revenue is used to pay for rangers and provide other facilities (Tisdell and Wilson, 2012).

The next example shows the impacts on tourism revenue and employment when a marine conservation park is affected due to bleaching, destructive tourism activities (coral mining) and to some extent marine pollution.

The example is from Sri Lanka and the conservation park is Hikkaduwa Nature Reserve, located in the south-western part of the island. After the bleaching in the late 1990s, the effects of which were exacerbated due to destruction of coral reefs and pollution, only half of the 80 registered glass-bottom boats were in operation during 2000 and 2001 (Amaralal et al. 2002, cited and discussed in Souter and Linden, 2005). They further point out that the number of daily trips per boat dropped five to ten times compared to before the bleaching event in 1998. Surveys conducted in 2000 and 2001 have showed that the snorkelling and glass-bottom boat industries were the most affected due to the degraded coral reefs along the south coast of Sri Lanka (Amaralal et al., 2002, cited and discussed in Souter and Linden, 2005).

The Sri Lankan case study is not an isolated one. There are many such examples that can be cited from other countries where degradation has taken place either due to coral bleaching or degradation caused by human activities (see, for example, Subramanian, 2012; IOSEA Marine Turtle Memorandum of Understanding, 2014, database). Those countries that have high levels of damage as shown in Figure 19.3 are more vulnerable and are more likely to suffer from loss in tourism revenues. What should be kept in mind is that only threats to coral reefs from human activities were shown in Figure 19.3. Other ecosystems apart from coral reefs should be considered as well. It was not possible to show the threats to the entire coastal ecosystem due to human activities because of the large data requirements. However, this does not mean that no threats exist. We know by judging from the current rates of coastal development in some of the Asian and Australasian countries that threat levels are likely to be high.

The example from Cesar (2000) from the Philippines demonstrated that the number of high-spending tourists could decline when coastal ecosystems suffer from degradation. This was illustrated in Figure 19.4. These numbers are likely to be replaced by budget tourists (e.g. backpackers), who spend less money. Hence, even if overall numbers increase (this is another possibility, but not shown in Figure 19.4), the total tourist revenue is still less because the quality of tourists has changed. What is important to note here is that when tourist numbers drop, the hotel room rates also will have to be reduced. Hence, a drop in tourism revenue. There is evidence to show that high-quality tourism can be replaced with cheaper forms of tourism which are linked to drugs and prostitution. It is claimed that crime is also an outcome of such tourism (see, for example, Uriely and Belhassen, 2006; Haralambopoulos, 1996).

The example from Sri Lanka showed that the numbers of tourists visiting a particular nature-based tourism site (for example, a marine reserve or a national park) also would decline when there is environmental degradation. As a result, revenue from fees to such sites will decline. Furthermore, those who provide services also are affected. In the case of Hikkaduwa Nature Reserve, boat operators were severely affected (Amaralal et al., 2002, cited and discussed in Souter and Linden, 2005). The revenues they were earning were reduced by more than half. Hence, there is loss of income. Therefore, a whole chain of service providers who rely on the tourism industry are affected as a result. Some examples include restaurants, gift shops, transport and a host of other services. Hence, there is loss of income and unemployment in the local area.

There is another aspect to the deterioration of coastal ecosystems and loss of marine wildlife. When there is deterioration of coral reefs or any other coastal ecosystem and wildlife, our studies (see, for example, Tisdell and Wilson, 2002; Wilson and Tisdell, 2003) clearly show that tourists are likely to spend fewer days in an area. Hence, there is loss in income and unemployment because of the loss in expenditures to the area. Our studies show that because of the presence of marine wildlife such as sea turtles, whales, and penguins, tourists spend more extra days in areas where wildlife viewing takes place. They incur extra expenditures. We also know from our studies that such tourists are more educated and most often belong to high-income groups (see, for example, Tisdell and Wilson (2002) and Wilson and Tisdell (2003)). The economic benefits to the regions resulting from two forms of marine-based wildlife tourism, namely sea turtle and whale watching, respectively, are discussed in the next section as illustrative examples.

5. Economic benefits resulting from sea turtle and whale watching-based tourism in Australia

Sea turtle and whale watching-based tourism in Bundaberg (Mon Repos) and Hervey Bay in Queensland, Australia, is seasonal in nature, yet these two nature-based tourism activities make a significant contribution to the respective regions. Tisdell and Wilson (2002) and Wilson and Tisdell (2003) have estimated the economic impact of visitor spending to the Bundaberg (Mon Repos) and Hervey Bay regions and whether or not visitors would have visited these two regions if not for the presence of sea turtles and whales, respectively. In these two studies we found that approximately 40 per cent of the respondents would not have visited Bundaberg (Mon Repos) if sea turtle viewing was absent. Similarly, approximately 42 per cent would not have visited if whale watching did not occur in Hervey Bay. The proportion of tourists who would not have visited these two areas if not for the presence of sea turtles and whales is shown in Table 19.4.

Furthermore, of the surveyed visitors to Mon Repos, 19 per cent of those who said that they would have come to Mon Repos even in the absence of sea turtles were of the view that they would have reduced their stay within a 60 km radius if there had been no sea turtles in the area. The number of reduced days in the Bundaberg area was 1.34 days on average for this group. Of those visitors who said they would have visited Hervey Bay even if whales did not occur, 22 per cent said that they would have reduced their stay if whales did not occur in the bay. The number of reduced days was 1.58 days per average person.

Given the numbers of visitors coming to watch sea turtles and whales, the economic benefits are quite significant. During the 1999 to 2000 sea turtle season for instance (the year in which this study was undertaken), 23,500 visitors came to Mon Repos (the visitor numbers have remained more or less the same in the late 2000s since visitor numbers are capped). The number of visitors to Hervey Bay to watch whales was 62,670[1] in 2000. Since this study was undertaken in 2000, visitor numbers have increased, except during the global financial crisis, although it is difficult to provide accurate figures. It also should be noted that whale watching has spread along the eastern coast of Australia (e.g. Gold Coast and Brisbane) with the increasing number of whales. In order to determine the economic benefits to the two areas (region(s)) from these two

Table 19.4 Surveyed visitors who came to the Bundaberg and Hervey Bay due to the presence of sea turtles and whales

Category	Number of Respondents		Percentage	
	Sea Turtles	Whales	Sea Turtles	Whales
Number of respondents whose visit did not depend on the presence of sea turtles & whales in the Bundaberg and & Hervey Bay region(s)	280	380	54	54
Number of respondents whose visit depended on the presence of sea turtles & whales in the Bundaberg & Hervey Bay region(s)	208	296	40	42
Locals	25	26	05	04
No Response	06	–	01	–
Total	519	702	100	100

Source: Wilson and Tisdell (2003)and Tisdell and Wilson (2012).

Note: Surveys were conducted during the period December,1999 to February 2000 for sea turtles and for whales during the period July 2000 to September 2000.

Table 19.5 Average daily expenditures of surveyed sea turtle and whale watchers

Region(s)	Aus $
Bundaberg	24.88
Mon Repos	10.57
Bundaberg and Mon Repos	35.45
Hervey Bay	125.97

Source: Wilson and Tisdell (2003) and Tisdell and Wilson (2012).

Note: The expenditures incurred by sea turtle viewers in Bundarberg and Mon Repos were estimated separately. This was because visitors incur expenditures (e.g. entrance fees and purchasing souvenirs) inside the Mon Repos Conservation Park as well. The expenditure at Hervey Bay is higher because the whale watching fee on average during the study was Aus $70 per adult.

species, a question was devised in each of the questionnaires which was aimed at determining the expenditures for these two nature-based tourism activities, respectively, within a 60 km radius. Table 19.5 shows the average daily expenditures of surveyed visitors.

The average expenditure per respondent on accommodation, food, travel, souvenirs purchased, recreational activities in the region (Bundaberg and Mon Repos) within a 60 km radius was Aus $35.45 during the 1999 to 2000 season. Assuming that this is the average expenditure of the approximately 23,500 sea turtle viewers at the time, the total direct expenditure in the region from sea turtle viewing is approximately Aus $833,075. Since the average number of days spent by these visitors is 3.21 days, the amount of expenditure in the region for the sea turtle season was approximately Aus $2.68 million for the season. When only the expenditures at Bundaberg were taken into account, the total tourist expenditure in the region associated with those who watched sea turtles at Mon Repos was approximately Aus $1.9 million. In the case of whales, assuming that the average expenditure of 62,670 whale watchers in the Hervey Bay region for 2000 was Aus $125.97, then the total direct expenditure was approximately Aus $7.89 million. Since the average number of days spent by whale watchers was 3.76 days, the expenditure in the region during the season was approximately Aus $30 million. These estimates, if anything, are on the conservative side. When the multiplier effects are considered, the benefits to the region(s) are likely to be even larger. The importance of sea turtle and whale watching could be even greater to the region(s) considering the fact that a large number of visitors would not have come or reduced the number of days spent in the region(s) if these two species did not occur. This was confirmed by the two studies. The loss of income to the regions in such an event is large. Therefore, considering the short seasons and the scarcity of the wildlife that is being viewed, the income generated from these nature-based tourism activities is significant. In fact, these two nature-based activities (excluding other tourism activities) are among some of main tourist attractions in this predominantly agricultural region.

6. Tourism can potentially be used as a conservation tool

It is estimated that between 20 per cent to 40 per cent of all international tourists have an interest in some form of wildlife watching (see, for example, Agrawal and Baranwal, 2012, citing previous studies) and many more tourists visit coral reefs and beaches. For example, as mentioned before, some studies suggest that as many as 95 per cent of international tourists who visit Australia visit the Great Barrier Reef. Therefore, it is potentially possible to use tourism revenue and tourist payments for the conservation of coastal ecosystems and marine wildlife. This is from tourism revenue generated from entrance fees to nature reserves and national parks and from visitors' willingness to pay for conservation. In the Asian and the Australasian region, the existence of entry fees is mixed, with many Australian national parks charging no fee (Wilson and Tisdell, 2004; Tisdell and Wilson, 2012, chapter 3).

In the former case, some or all of the entrance fees may be re-invested for conservation purposes. A study by Wilson and Tisdell (2004) showed that visitors were willing to pay an entrance fee to enter a national park if the money were re-invested for conservation and provision of visitor facilities in the park in question. Furthermore, our studies (see, for example, Tisdell and Wilson, 2001) show that visitors are willing to pay extra for the conservation of wildlife such as sea turtles.

6.1 Tourism and sea turtle viewing in hatcheries in Sri Lanka

A number of private operators maintain sea turtle hatcheries mainly for tourist viewing in Sri Lanka. These operators purchase turtle eggs from collectors, bury them in a fenced sandy area near a beach to hatch and hold them for a few days before releasing them to the ocean. The operators claim that their activities involve ecotourism and contribute to sea turtle conservation (Gampell, 1999). Such programmes for sea turtles are quite common (Wyneken, 2001; Tisdell and Wilson, 2012, chapter 10), and it is widely accepted that well-managed sea turtle hatcheries can play a positive role in turtle conservation when in *situ* conservation is not possible or practical (IUCN/SSC Marine Turtle Specialist Group, 1999). In Sri Lanka, the collection and consumption of sea turtle eggs is widespread and tourism dollars enable hatchery owners to purchase collected eggs at a price above market selling price. These operators claim that they ensure more eggs hatch than otherwise and that they increase the chances of hatchlings entering the sea.

Hatcheries are not new. For example, they have been in existence in Sri Lanka since the 1970s (Fernando, 1977). They initially involved purchasing eggs from collectors who otherwise would have sold these in the local village market or elsewhere for human consumption. Although at that time conservation was the prime reason for the establishment of the first hatchery, they soon attracted visitors, both local and foreign. Subsequently, a visitor charge was levied and most of the money was used to purchase more eggs from illegal collectors. Because of the high demand from tourists to view turtle hatchlings and the income generated, many hatcheries currently operate and all receive fee-paying visitors. This form of viewing is promoted as a form of 'nature-based tourism' activity, and the hatchery operators claim that the main objective is the conservation of sea turtles. However, Amarasooriya (2001) claimed that only two hatcheries out of the nine in operation at that time had conservation in mind as their main objective and the rest are primarily operated for tourism revenue.

In the early 2000s, it was estimated that over one million eggs have been used in hatcheries during the 1980s and 1990s, and in the 2000s the use of eggs in hatcheries has accelerated rapidly. For example, the three hatcheries in existence in 1981 to 1982 used 48,934 eggs at the time (Wickramasinghe, 1982), and in 2000, the nine existing hatcheries used around 300,000 eggs (Amarasooriya, 2001), a 513 per cent increase (for more details, see, Tisdell and Wilson, 2012, chapter 10).

Sea turtle hatcheries in Sri Lanka attract many tourists, both domestic and foreign, and are part of the itinerary of many tour operators in Sri Lanka (see, for example, Responsible Travel, 2003). Travel guides and tourist brochures showcase these hatcheries as part of the natural attractions of Sri Lanka (see, for example, Bradnock and Bradnock, 1998). A study conducted among foreign tourists holidaying in south-western Sri Lanka by Wilson, Amarasooriya and Mackensen (2002) in early 2002 found that approximately 80 per cent of the surveyed foreign tourists were aware of sea turtle hatcheries in Sri Lanka. Only 19 per cent did not know about their existence and one per cent did not answer this question. Of those who said 'yes', 40 per cent said they knew about the presence of turtle hatcheries before their arrival in Sri Lanka. The study found that

66 per cent of those tourists who were aware of the hatcheries had either visited or intended to visit them during their stay in Sri Lanka.

Even among those tourists who were not aware of the presence of sea turtle hatcheries, 50 per cent said that they would consider visiting a hatchery. Almost one-third (31 per cent) of those tourists who said that they had already visited or intended visiting a hatchery said that this was or would be an important part of the stay on the south-western coast of Sri Lanka. However, 22 per cent of the respondents did not answer this question.

Almost all sea turtle hatcheries in Sri Lanka are dependent on tourist dollars (entrance fees, donations and sale of souvenirs) for their operations, and interestingly, some of them operate only during the main tourist season (Hewavisenthi, 1993). Although these actions show that some hatchery operators may be driven by tourism revenue rather than conservation, the situation in Sri Lanka demonstrates that there is the potential to channel tourism dollars towards sea conservation and even other wildlife. Figure 19.6 shows a map of Sri Lanka where sea turtle hatcheries operate (marked in grey), which also are areas which are visited most by tourists.

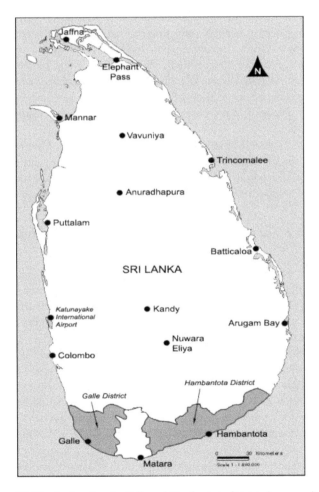

Figure 19.6   Map of Sri Lanka showing the Galle and Hambantota districts (grey areas), the only two locations for turtle hatcheries in Sri Lanka

Source: Tisdell and Wilson (2012, chapter 6).

The Wilson, Amarasooriya and Mackensen (2002) survey found that the majority of responding foreign tourists were supportive of sea turtle-based tourism in hatcheries and thought they involved a better form of turtle use than consumptive use. Of those who answered this question, 77 per cent said it is a better form of turtle use than their consumptive use, while only 18 per cent said they did not think that hatchery-based tourism is a better form of turtle use.

What the findings of the sea turtle research show is that in some circumstances, sea turtles hatcheries are the only practical solution to protecting sea turtles, as is the case on the south-western coast of Sri Lanka, where population density is high and sea turtle egg consumption is widespread. In such situations, tourism based on hatcheries can potentially make a valuable contribution to the conservation of sea turtles provided they are well managed. This is not an uncommon practice is some parts of Asia (for example, Indonesia and Malaysia) and is now being proposed in Australia at Mon Repos to make sea turtle viewing-based tourism viable throughout the year (Queensland Government, 2013).

It is interesting to note that despite sea turtle hatcheries being on the itinerary of many tour operators and being promoted as an in-situ conservation solution, such hatcheries are strictly speaking illegal in Sri Lanka and some Asian countries. However, because the operators of hatcheries have convinced the public and tourists that they make a positive contribution towards sea turtle conservation, their presence is 'unofficially' sanctioned and the collection of eggs for hatcheries is 'justified'. Surprisingly, there are few, if any, prosecutions for illegally collecting turtle eggs. Australia's interest in a limited sea turtle hatchery is very interesting and will no doubt be monitored scientifically. Interestingly, the move to establish a hatchery has been influenced by tourism and the potential to generate revenue to justify sea turtle-related conservation efforts.

The next section discusses the nature-based tourism experience at Mon Repos Conservation Park in Bundaberg discussed previously. While the interference in sea turtle life-cycle is more marked in Sri Lanka, which deals with only eggs and hatchlings, the sea turtle tourism that takes place at Mon Repos beach interferes very little with the natural life-cycle of sea turtles.

6.2 Sea turtle-based tourism and its contribution to conservation at Mon Repos

The creation of the Mon Repos Conservation Park and nature-based tourism activities is an interesting one. In the late 1960s, a group of citizens and organisations tried to have a national park established at Mon Repos beach for the purpose of protecting nesting turtles. This was because the site was an important loggerhead rookery, and under proper management the rookery could have been an important tourist attraction, such as the fairy penguins on Phillip Island in the Bass Strait (Australia). Penguin viewing on Phillip Island is another successful nature tourism-based activity that has been successful in terms of economic benefits to the region and conservation benefits to the penguins. If not for the presence of penguins and the economic opportunities they have created, it is likely that the site would have been developed for housing or even for a tourist resort (for more details on this study, see, Tisdell and Wilson, 2012, Chapter 12). A similar success story is also reported for New Zealand (Tisdell and Wilson, 2012, Chapter 13).

However, one local council (Woongarra Shire Council) was not convinced that the local area would gain from extra tourists coming to watch sea turtles and thought that most of the gains would go to Bundaberg (commercially, a different council) in a town much larger than the two villages in close proximity to Mon Repos beach. The councillors preferred the extra rates (taxes) from potential commercial development (e.g. housing) at Mon Repos beach. Although the

Queensland Cabinet agreed in 1968 to create Mon Repos National Park, more than a decade passed before steps were taken to establish a suitable protected area at Mon Repos Beach in 1981 (for further details see, Tisdell and Wilson, 2005b).

With growing crowds of turtle-watching visitors, research staff at Mon Repos commenced a formal turtle-watching programme in 1985. It was felt that this would be the most efficient way of catering for the growing number of visitors to the site and would help with crowd control. In mid-1990s, facilities were created to cater to turtle-watching tourists at Mon Repos with the construction of the building for an information centre and amphitheatre. These were intended to educate visitors about sea turtles, especially their biology and ecology and threats to their survival. During the 1994 to 1995 sea turtle season, a service fee was charged for the first time. This marked the commencement of commercialised ecotourism at this site. The charging of a fee for entry to the park in the evening or night during the turtle season continues. Its main purpose seems to be to raise funds to help cover costs associated with visitors at the site. Visitor numbers are now limited to approximately 300 per evening (since the 2004–2005 season) and are coordinated through a booking system. This has been done to manage the site to ensure low impacts on sea turtle nesting and hatchlings.

The number of tourists visiting Mon Repos has been growing since the 1990s. This is shown in Table 19.6. As can be seen from Table 19.6, the number of visitors has increased rapidly and if not for the daily limits placed on the number of tourists, the visitor numbers could be even higher.

Currently the type of tourism that occurs at Mon Repos Beach in connection with turtle-watching satisfies most of the basic conditions required for ecotourism. It is: 1) nature-based; 2) educational; and 3) careful of the environment and conservation-oriented. Furthermore, it: 4) involves local people; and 5) benefits the local community economically.

The type of tourism practiced is careful of the environment and informative (Tisdell and Wilson, 2002). During the turtle-nesting season, tourists are only allowed on the beach at night under the supervision of officers of the Queensland Parks and Wildlife Service and trained volunteers, mostly from the local community. The maximum size of each group is 70. Appropriate logistics and behaviour are adopted so as not to interfere with the natural behaviour of the sea turtles.

The ecotouristic venture relies heavily for its viability on help from volunteers from the local community and elsewhere. This helps build local political support for the turtle conservation project and assists with crowd control and management. In addition, the direct economic injection to the local community is significant, as shown in the last section. Furthermore, there is scientific spin-off. At the same time as tourists are viewing turtles, scientists and volunteers gather scientific data about the nesting of turtles or the nesters themselves and about hatchlings. This is of assistance for determining whether or not population recovery of turtles is underway. The presence of this tourism at Mon Repos has incidental conservation benefits. Predators, such as introduced foxes, are not likely to predate on turtles when they are accompanied by people.

Table 19.6 Visitors to Mon Repos to view sea turtles – selected years

Turtle season	2007/08	2005/06	2004/05	2000/01	1999/00	1998/99	1994/95
Visitor Numbers	24 731	24 745	28 281	24 270	23 284	18 421	14 858

Source: Queensland Environmental Protection Agency, Australia, unpublished data.

Note: It must be mentioned here that tourism numbers have grown since the 2007/08 seasons (see, Queensland Government, 2013) except in years where southeast Queensland has been affected by natural disasters, such as floods during the last few years.

Programmes to control the presence of such predators in the park have been instituted and these have been partly financed by visitor fees.

In 1991, a further flow-on conservation benefit was the declaration of the adjoining Woongarra Marine Park for the prime purpose of protecting sea turtles offshore, particularly in the breeding season. It is interesting to note that the Burnett Shire Council, the local government successor to the Woongarra Shire Council, keenly supports sea turtle conservation and the form of ecotourism associated with it. This is a complete turn around in attitude to that of 1968 when the Woongarra Shire Council opposed the creation of a park of the present type at Mon Repos. In fact, as mentioned earlier, plans are afoot to encourage turtle viewing throughout the year at Mon Repos, with the establishment of a sea turtle hatchery that can hold 50 sea turtles (Queensland Government, 2013).

Our survey (Tisdell and Wilson, 2002) of visitors to Mon Repos rookery in the 1999 to 2000 season showed that visitors experiences had several positive consequences for sea turtle conservation:

- Most believed after their experience that more should be done to conserve sea turtles;
- A large proportion said that after the event they were prepared to donate more for programmes to conserve sea turtles than if they had not visited Mon Repos; and
- Many respondents said that they would alter their behaviour so as to be more considerate of sea turtles. For example, 62 per cent of respondents said they would be more careful in disposing of plastics, 68 per cent said they would switch off lights near beaches, 47 per cent would take greater care with fishing gear, and 73 per cent said they would refrain from consuming turtle eggs, meat or soup while overseas. Changed behaviours in relation to several other factors affecting turtle conservation also were mentioned.

Therefore, the evidence is quite strong that the development of sea turtle tourism at Mon Repos Beach has contributed positively to the conservation of sea turtles. Tourism numbers have increased and are likely to increase further with the proposed year-round sea turtle viewing at Mon Repos. Investments in the environment and its surroundings, although time-consuming and expensive, has had many conservation benefits as well as increased tourist numbers. This is akin to what was shown by ABCFG in Figure 19.4.

Interestingly, other conservation measures undertaken in the area are also paying off. Prawn trawling was banned during the sea turtle breeding season; and it was made mandatory for trawlers to install turtle excluder devices. A few years after these measures were undertaken, sea turtle nesting at Mon Repos was shown to increase. This is shown in Figure 19.7.

The recovery data until 2005 is shown in Figure 19.6, and this trend is continuing to increase. This goes on to demonstrate that appropriate action can restore the damage caused by overexploitation of coastal ecosystems, although expensive. This (and other costs associated with Mon Repos investments) is similar to HFK in Figure 19.4. There are potential benefits from the increase in sea turtles at Mon Repos. The increase in the number of sea turtles means that the waiting time for tourists to view turtles is less and also it is possible to increase the number of tourists given access to view turtles per night. This increases visitor satisfaction, which is vital, especially when it comes to seeking visitor donations/payments for conservation work. The nature-based tourism experiences discussed in this section are a reminder for other countries with development pressures that planning of coastal development which takes account of the environment (including wildlife), results in economic benefits to the areas or regions.

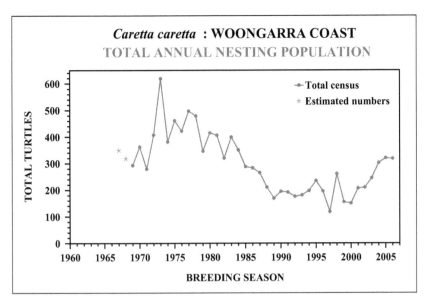

Figure 19.7 Number of loggerhead sea turtles nesting at Mon Repos is increasing

Source: Queensland Environmental Protection Agency, Australia, unpublished data.

Note: The data reported in until 2005. However, the recovery is likely to continue given that the protection measures introduced in the 1990s are in place.

7. Conclusion

This chapter showed that the damage to coral reefs in some regions of Asia and Australasia is high. From Figure 19.3 (and data used to compile), it also can be assumed that the damage to other coastal ecosystems is high. Many studies conducted (see, for example, Souter and Linden, 2005; UNEP, 2006) also show that in such situations, fisheries output and productivity is likely to fall. For a region where the majority of the population in the region depends on coastal and marine resources for their livelihoods, the drop in returns from these resources can have serious consequences. Loss in income and unemployment are likely to increase, exacerbating prevailing poverty. In short, the current use of coastal resources in many countries of the region is unsustainable and recovery efforts are warranted. Needless to say, it involves costs, but the welfare benefits to the inhabitants of these regions also are likely to be high by reducing the negative externalities of overdevelopment.

As was shown, if coastal ecosystems and marine wildlife are depleted, the quality and quantity of tourism numbers will be affected. This is likely to lead to many socio-economic problems, both direct and indirect. Hence, it is imperative that urgent action is taken to remedy the situation. Remedial actions that can be taken are many. However, it is important to do the following as a starting point.

It is important to set aside coastal ecosystems for conservation purposes. Australia is a good example of this. It is equally important to reduce the current destructive practices in the exploitation of marine resources for human needs. Human activity and commercial development of conservation sites should be reduced or altogether eliminated as showcased from the example provided from Mon Repos. Certain marine wildlife species such as sea turtles can be used as flagship species around which conservation actions can be undertaken. When adequate land (beaches) and marine reserves (including coral reefs) are set aside for sea turtles, other marine species will benefit. The marine reserves will provide an opportunity for ecosystems (including corals) to recover and fish and other marine populations to increase (see, for example, UNEP, 2011; Edgar, 2014). Such recovery will ultimately help local people through increased fish availability. Tourism (both quality and quantity) will benefit, too, for reasons explained in this chapter. Tourism revenue will increase and so will tourism dollars for conservation. The Mon Repos example is a good case in point where a healthy ecosystem with sea turtles can co-exist with sustainable tourism activities.

Currently, many of the Asian and Australasian countries do not have a tourism policy where it is mandatory for hotels and resorts to integrate coastal ecosystem and wildlife protection in their operations. In other words, there is no policy to address or pay to for action to reduce the impact of negative externalities. It is imperative to design policies to address these issues. After all, the tourism industry depends heavily on coastal resources for its survival and revenue. The fishing industry in some countries has improved their fishing practices by using sea turtle excluder devices in their fishing vessels, which have reduced sea turtle mortality. The example from Mon Repos is one such example. In a similar way, hotels in coastal areas can play a proactive role in coastal ecosystem conservation and wildlife and minimise the threats created by the leisure industry. Some of the actions that can be undertaken would result in tourists paying more for their visits (such as HFK shown in Figure 19.4) but could have the support of tourists. In fact, our studies show that tourists are often supportive of conservation practices adopted by institutions. For example, some of the action that can be taken in the case of sea turtle conservation include setting aside some parts of beaches for sea turtles, adjusting lighting that does not affect nesting turtles or disorient hatchlings, reducing or removing heavy vehicles from beaches, reducing access to tourists to certain beaches and even funding sea turtle and other marine conservation projects. Our studies show that the majority of tourists are willing to pay for conservation activities if sufficient benefits can be seen. Of course different situations require different solutions. The actions mentioned above are only a guide. In fact any conservation measures adopted to protect coastal ecosystems from overdevelopment also will benefit tourists. In such cases, visitor satisfaction is likely to be high, which in turn will benefit the tourism industry. Given the importance of coastal resources to the long-term survival and viability of the tourism industry, it is important to guide the hotel industry, for example, in this direction.

However, taking initial action is fraught with many difficulties. It is not always easy to convince decision-makers, the hotel industry and the local population to take appropriate action. Nevertheless, it is imperative that the exploitation of coastal ecosystems and development is made sustainable. Otherwise, the majority of the current and future generations are bound to suffer through welfare losses.

Note

1 The number of whale watching visitors to Hervey Bay in 1998 and 1999 were 82,511 and 77,859, respectively (QNPWS, 2001).

References

Agrawal, K. & Baranwal, H. 2012. 'Environmental sustainability of tourism,' *Research Journal of Economics and Business Studies*, vol. 1, number 9, pp. 1–7, http://www.theinternationaljournal.org/ojs/full/vol01no09_rjebs.pdf.

Amaralal, K.H., Vidanage, S.P. & Wimalasena, H.D. 2002. 'Impacts of coral bleaching on tourism in Sri Lanka,' Socio-economic and Market Research Division, NARA, Colombo, Sri Lanka.

Amarasooriya, K. 2001. 'The role of sea turtle hatcheries in the conservation of sea turtle fauna of Sri Lanka,' paper presented at the 21st World Sea Turtle Symposium, Feb. 24–28, 2001, Philadelphia, PA.

Bryant, D., Burke, L., McManus, J. & Spalding, M. 1998. *Reefs at risk – a map based indicator of threats to the world's coral reefs.* Washington, DC: World Resources Institute.

Burke, L., Bryant, D., McManus, J. & Spalding, M. 1998. *Reefs at risk – analysis of threats to coral reefs*, Washington, DC: World Resources Institute.

Burke, L., Kura Y., Kassem, K., Revenga, C., Spalding, M. & McAllister, D. 2001, *Pilot analysis of global ecosystems: coastal ecosystems.* Washington, DC: World Resources Institute.

Birkeland, C. (ed.) 1997. *Life and death of coral reefs.* New York: Chapman and Hall.

Cesar, H. 2000. *Impacts of the 1998 coral bleaching event on tourism in El Nido, Philippines*, Coastal Resources Center Coral Bleaching Initiative, http://www.crc.uri.edu/download/tourism_elnido.pdf.

Charles R., Sheppard, C., Davy, S.K. & Pilling, G.M. 2009. *The biology of coral reefs.* Oxford: Oxford University Press.

CRC Reef Research Centre 2005. *Coral bleaching and global climate change,* http://www.reef.crc.org.au/publications/brochures/1998event.htm.

Das, S. & Vincent, J.R. 2009. 'Mangroves protected villages and reduced death toll during Indian super cyclone,' *Proceedings of the National Academy of Sciences*, vol. 106, pp. 7357–7360.

Duke, N.C., Meynecke J.-O., Dittmann S., Ellison, A.M., Anger, K., Berger, U., Cannicci, S., Diele, K., Ewel, K.C., Field, C.D., Koedam, N., Lee, S.Y., Marchand, C., Nordhaus, I. & Dahdouh-Guebas, F. 2007, 'A world without mangroves?' *Science*, vol. 317, no. 41, pp. 41–42.

Edgar, G. J., Stuart-Smith, D., Willis, J., Kininmonth, S., Baker, C., Banks, S., Barrett, S., Becerro, A, Bernard, A., Berkhout, J., Buxton, C., Campbell, J., Cooper, A., Davey, M., Edgar, S. Försterra, G., Galván, D., Irigoyen, A., Kushner, D., Moura, R., Parnell, P., Shears, N., Soler, G., Strain, E., and Thomson, R. 2014. 'Global conservation outcomes depend on marine protected areas with five key features,' *Nature (0028-0836)*, vol. 506, no. 7487, pp. 216–220.

Fenical, W. 1996. 'Marine biodiversity and the medicine cabinet: the status of new drugs from marine organisms,' *Oceanography*, vol. 9, no. 1, pp. 23–27.

Fernando, R. 1977. 'Turtle hatcheries in Sri Lanka,' *Marine Turtle Newsletter*, no. 3, p. 8.

Food and Agriculture Organisation. 2002. *The ecosystem approach to fisheries – issues, terminology, principles, institutional foundations, implementation and outlook,* ftp://ftp.fao.org/docrep/fao/006/y4773e/y4773e00.pdf.

Gampell, J. 1999. 'To save the turtles,' *Reader's Digest,* May (Asian Version).

Goudarzi, S. 2006. *Flocking to the coast: World's population migrating into danger*, Live Science, http://www.livescience.com/4167-flocking-coast-world-population-migrating-danger.html.

Haralambopoulos, N. 1996 'Perceived impacts of tourism – the case of Samos,' *Annals of Tourism Research,* vol. 23, pp. 503–526.

Hawkins, J.P., Roberts, C.M., Kooistra, D., Buchan, K. & White, S. 2005. 'Sustainability of scuba diving tourism on coral reefs of Saba, *Coastal Management*, vol. 33, pp. 373–387.

Hewavisenthi, S. 1993. 'Turtle hatcheries in Sri Lanka: boon or bane?' *Marine Turtle Newsletter* vol. 60, pp. 19–21.

Huybers, T. 2007. *Tourism in developing countries.* Cheltenham: Edward Elgar.

Indian Ocean South-East Asian Marine Turtle Memorandum of Understanding (IOSEA). 2014. *Welcome to the IOSEA marine turtle MoU website*, http://www.ioseaturtles.org/index.php.

International Ecotourism Society. 1998. Ecotourism Statistical Fact Sheet, IOSEA database – archives. International Ecotourism Society, Washington, DC.

International Union for the Conservation of Nature/SSC Marine Turtle Specialist Group. 1999. *A Global Strategy for the Conservation of Marine Turtles,* http://www.tortugas.unam.mx/mtsg/english/mtsg_publications-english.htm.

Jennings, S. 2004. 'Coastal tourism and shoreline management,' *Annals of Tourism Research*, vol. 31, pp. 899–922.

Paulay, G. 1997. 'Diversity and distribution of reef organisms.' In Charles Birkeland (ed.), *Life and death of coral reefs*, pp. 298–353. New York: Chapman and Hall.

Peterson, F. 2014. 'Great Barrier Reef Marine Park Authority approves plan to dump Abbot Point spoil,' http://www.abc.net.au/news/2014-01-31/abbot-point-spoil-dredging-approved/5227774.

Queensland Government. 2013. 'Gateway Visitor Centre, Draft Master Plan for Consultation, Mon Repos,' Discussion Paper, http://www.nprsr.qld.gov.au/managing/plans-strategies/pdf/mon-repos-master-plan-dp.pdf.

Responsible Travel. 2003. *Holidays in Sri Lanka: Virgin forests and coastal greenway*, http://www.responsible-travel.com/Trip/Trip100616.htm.

Souter, D. & Linden, O. (eds.) 2005. *Coral reef degradation in the Indian Ocean, status report*, published by CORDIO, Department of Botany and Environmental Science, University of Kalmar, Sweden.

Subramanian, V. 2012. 'Coastal environments of Asia.' In V. Subramanian (ed.), *Coastal environments: Focus on Asian coastal regions*, pp. 1–18. The Netherlands: Springer.

Tisdell, C., Khan, H., Viryasiri, S., Prichard, S., Doeleman, J.A., Watson, M., Wirakartakusumah, M.D. & Marsh, J.B. 1992. 'Marine pollution and tourism.' In J.B. Marsh (ed.), *Resources and environment in Asia's marine sector*, pp. 381–396. London: Taylor and Francis.

Tisdell, C. & Wilson, C. 2001. 'Wildlife-based tourism and increased support for nature conservation financially and otherwise: evidence from sea turtle ecotourism at Mon Repos,' *Tourism Economics*, vol. 7, no. 3, pp. 233–249.

Tisdell, C. & Wilson, C. 2002. *Economic, educational and conservation benefits of Sea turtle-based ecotourism: a study focused on Mon Repos*, Cooperative Research Centre for Sustainable Tourism, Gold Coast, Queensland, Australia.

Tisdell, C. & Wilson, C. 2005a. 'Do open-cycle hatcheries relying on tourism conserve sea turtles? Sri Lankan developments and economic-ecological considerations,' *Environmental Management*, vol. 35, pp. 1–12.

Tisdell, C. & Wilson, C. 2005b. 'Does ecotourism contribute to sea turtle conservation? Is the flagship status of turtles advantageous?' *Maritime Studies*, vol. 3 & 4, pp. 145–167.

Tisdell, C. & Wilson, C. 2012. *Nature-based tourism and conservation: new economic insights and case studies*. Cheltenham: Edward Elgar.

United Nations Environmental Programme. 2006. *Marine and coastal ecosystems and human well-being*, http://www.unep.org/pdf/Completev6_LR.pdf.

United Nations Environmental Programme. 2011. *Fisheries – investing in natural capital*, http://www.unep.org/greeneconomy/Portals/88/documents/ger/GER_3_Fisheries.pdf.

Uriely, N. & Belhassen, Y. 2006. 'Drugs and risk-taking in tourism,' *Annals of Tourism Research*, vol. 33, no. 2, pp. 339–359.

Wickramsinghe, S. 1982. 'Turtle hatcheries in Sri Lanka,' *Marine Turtle Newsletter*, vol. 22, pp. 3–4.

Wight, P.A. 1993. 'Sustainable ecotourism: balancing economic, environmental and social goals within an ethical framework,' *Journal of Tourism Studies*, vol. 4, no. 2, pp. 54–56.

Wilson, C. & Tisdell, C. 2001. 'Sea turtles as a non-consumptive tourism resource especially in Australia,' *Tourism Management*, vol. 22, pp. 279–288.

Wilson, C. & Tisdell, C. 2003. 'Conservation and economic benefits of wildlife-based marine tourism: sea turtles and whales as case studies,' *Human Dimensions of Wildlife*, vol. 8, pp. 49–63.

Wilson, C. & Tisdell, C. 2004. 'Attitudes to entry fees to national parks: results and policy implications from a Queensland case study,' *Economic Analysis and Policy*, vol. 34, pp. 79–102.

World Travel and Tourism Council 2013, *Travel and Tourism – Economic Impact, South-East Asia*, http://www.wttc.org/site_media/uploads/downloads/south_east_asia2013_1.pdf.

World Wide Fund for Nature 2014, *Coastal development problems: tourism*, http://wwf.panda.org/about_our_earth/blue_planet/problems/tourism/tourism_pressure/.

Wyneken, J. 2001. 'The migratory behaviour of hatchling sea turtles beyond the beach,' 2nd ASEAN Symposium and Workshop on Sea Turtle Biology and Conservation, http://www.arbec.com.my/sea-turtles/art13julysept01.htm.

20

AN ASSESSMENT OF BIODIVERSITY OFFSETS AND MITIGATION ACTIONS

Case studies on mining, energy and paper and pulp sectors in India

Tania Bhattacharya and Shunsuke Managi

1. Background

Biodiversity loss could be considered as one of the greatest economic problems of this century. First, it is economic growth and industrial development which causes large biodiversity loss and damages to the ecosystem. The rapid growth of the population from around two billion in 1900 to more than seven billion by 2010, along with a massive increase in income and corresponding resource consumption, already has affected earth's natural ecosystems severely (Helm and Hepburn, 2012). Second, loss of biodiversity and ecosystems may significantly reduce future productivity of the economy as well. In other words, businesses are intimately linked with biodiversity and ecosystem services in two basic ways. First, they impact ecosystems and services though their activities. Second, the survival of all businesses, irrespective of sectors, depends on biodiversity and ecosystem services as inputs to their production(Hansonet, 2012).

With the current rate of extinction, by end of this century we may have endangered half of the species on the earth (Wilson, 1994; Thomas et al., 2004). We might be living through one of the great extinction episodes in geological history (Barnosky, 2011). Such adverse impacts on ecosystem will dramatically affect the overall production and consumption pattern for human beings in the years to come (Helm and Hepburn, 2012). Nevertheless, actions for biodiversity protection and conservation still are inadequate compared to its requirement. The last few years, however, have witnessed growing interest in the use of biodiversity offset mechanisms by governments, banks and companies (Bhattacharya and Managi, 2013) to mitigate the negative impacts of loss of biodiversity and ecosystem. The targets set by the Convention of Biological Diversity (CBD) for the year 2010 are yet to be achieved in all respects, including required policy interventions, gathering required amounts of international funding, relevant mechanisms and processes for technology transfer and patent issues, among others (Butchart et al., 2010). It has been further envisaged that unless the business and commercial activities mainstream biodiversity protection and conservation, it is difficult to achieve the targeted level of mitigation actions mainly due to lack of finance and technological innovation (Bhattacharya and Managi, 2013).

The definition of biodiversity offsets provided by the Business and Biodiversity Offset Program mainly discusses the measurability of the conservation outcomes which are performed to compensate the significant adverse effects on biodiversity and ecosystem due to certain business activities (BBOP, 2012). The goal of biodiversity offsets, therefore, is to ensure at least a zero sum impact or a net gain impact of biodiversity on the ground with respect to species composition, habitat structure, ecosystem function and people's use and cultural values associated with biodiversity. The principles of biodiversity offset mechanisms, especially in the case of business activities that cause biodiversity losses, are so far identified under ten different categories such as: no net loss, additional conservation benefits, adherence to the mitigation hierarchy, limits to offset activities, stakeholder engagement, and adherence to the equity principle and following the principle of transparency are the major issues in the process of developing offset mechanisms (BBOP, 2012).

As the 'no net loss' or a 'net gain' of biodiversity is increasingly getting acknowledged as a core part of society's expectation, more legislation and investment conditions requiring biodiversity offsets are expected in the coming years, along with various voluntary activities. The coming years are a vital period for any company, government, financial institution or civil society organisation wishing to influence global policy and practice on biodiversity offsets. As a matter of fact, the companies should now start considering how their long-term business opportunities and licence to operate might benefit from being a leader in utilising biodiversity offset techniques and policies. The public sector developers also need to consider biodiversity offsets to help governments to meet their biodiversity conservation commitments and simultaneously enable the governments to meet the expectations of local stakeholders.

With a background of assessment on international activities on biodiversity conservation by the multinational companies that are prone to affect biodiversity by their operational processes, this study focuses particularly on India due to India's increasing presence in the global business arena. Many favourable factors, including increasing domestic demand, presence of ancillary and supportive labour skills of international calibre, and pervasive confidence for looking beyond domestic markets, offer a unique business environment for Indian companies to go global and thus increasing their ecological footprints as well. Biodiversity and ecosystems are thus an important factors for Indian business and their sustainability in the longer term at a global scale. It has been observed that the multinational companies who have direct supply chain links to ecosystems are keener to adopt business policies like offset mechanisms and conservation and protection of biodiversity. It is thus a priority of the global Indian companies to adopt and develop such practices following their counterparts in the international business arena.

India is one of the 17 "mega diverse" countries in the world and enriched with different ecosystems like forests, grasslands, wetlands, coastal, marine and deserts. India also is rich in traditional knowledge associated with biological resources (Bhattacharya and Managi, 2013). For India, the conservation of its biodiversity is crucial because it provides several goods and services necessary for human survival and is directly linked with providing livelihoods and improving socio-economic conditions of more than 300 million people.[1] India's National Policy and Macro-level Action Strategy on Biodiversity (1999) includes regeneration and rehabilitation of threatened species; participation of state governments, communities, people, non-governmental organisations (NGOs), industry and other stakeholders; and research and development to understand the values of biodiversity among others. India has enacted the Biological Diversity Act 2002, which primarily aims at regulating access to biological resources and associated traditional knowledge to ensure equitable sharing of benefits from this usage, which is in accordance with the provision of Article 15 of the CBD. India also has announced a grant of $50 million for strengthening the institutional mechanism of biodiversity conservation in India and other developing countries by the name of the Hyderabad Pledge.

2. National biodiversity policies of India and their primary focus

India has a long history of conservation and sustainable use of natural resources. Perhaps India is the first developing country in the world to enact a formal forest conservation act at a national level. Over the years, India has developed a stable organizational structure and a strong legal and policy framework for protection of environment in the country. India is also one among the parties of CBD, which requires all parties to prepare national biodiversity strategies and action plans for conservation and sustainable use of biological diversity. Accordingly, India developed a National Policy and Macrolevel Action Strategy on Biodiversity in 1999. Thereafter, an externally aided project on a National Biodiversity Strategy and Action Plan (NBSAP) also was implemented in the country during 2000 to 2004, adopting a highly participatory process involving various stakeholders. Meanwhile, India also enacted the Biological Diversity Act in 2002, Section 36 which empowers the central government to develop a national biodiversity action plan. After approval of the National Environment Policy (NEP) in 2006, preparation of the National Biodiversity Action Plan (NBAP) was taken up by revising and updating the document prepared in 1999 and by using the final technical report of the NBSAP project. The NBAP draws upon the main principle in the NEP that human beings are at the centre of concerns of sustainable development, and they are entitled to a healthy and productive life in harmony with nature. Business being part of the social existence of the mankind, therefore, is responsible to follow a sustainable mechanism which can ensure peaceful coexistence of nature and humans.

2.1 Biodiversity conservation policies and business in India

Business is linked to the ecosystem and biodiversity in two different ways: first, through impacts of the environment on business activities, and second, through factor inputs to the production process. For example, the cosmetics and pharmaceutical sector benefits from access to wild genetic resources but in turn impacts these resources through overexploitation (Sukhdev, 2012). The NEP (2006) thus emphasizes the importance of public–private partnerships in environmental management to conserve and protect the local ecosystem and biodiversity. Recently, the Ministry of Environment and Forests (MOEF) has also developed the guidelines for 'Institutionalizing Corporate Environmental Responsibility,' with an objective to further streamline and strengthen environmental actions, going beyond legal compliance, by business organisations. The largest Indian business community, the Confederation of Indian Industry, has been actively engaged in promoting the 3Ps approach of 'People, Profit and Planet' to spread the message of sustainable business following conservation of natural resources, habitats and ecosystems around us. Besides, the national government also is working together with various international organizations like the United Nations Development Programme and Global Environment Facility to promote sustainable business in 15 major production sectors, including fisheries, aquaculture, forestry and agribusiness etc. The effect of businesses on ecosystem services, however, has been largely neglected so far, mainly due to ambiguous property rights, lack of market prices, insufficient information and high transaction costs. The major drivers of biodiversity loss, e.g., demand for food and water, pollution, and global warming impacts, are on the rise in countries like India and many developing countries. As a matter of fact, business in India is slowly creating negative externalities on society in general and local communities in particular, due to lack of understanding of the long-term effects.

3. Methodology and data

It has been identified that the primary impact of ecosystems on business activities and vice versa are seen mainly in the sectors like mining, paper and pulp and electricity generation (Bhattacharya and Managi, 2013). For the paper and pulp sector, the main source of vulnerability comes from procurement of wood for pulp production. Thus ecosystem affects the raw material supply for this sector. On the other hand, the mining and electricity sector affects the ecosystem due to their unsustainable operation on the ground. Thus in this study we have selected two different sets of industries to demonstrate the up and downstream impacts of business and biodiversity. The main objective of this study is to assess the activities to achieve sustainable business in the context of ecosystem and biodiversity conservation in India in three major industrial sectors and to identify the gaps and way forward to improve the activities in the future. In the process of conducting this study, we looked into the current status and issues of biodiversity in the Indian paper and pulp and mining and electricity generating companies in the context of their operational impact on local ecosystems and biodiversity and vice versa. Nevertheless, at the beginning we also conducted an assessment of activities of the global leaders in the respective sector to set the background for comparison of the activities of the corresponding Indian companies, which further leads to the assessment of necessary offset policies required in the country. Section 3 thus deals with the international scenario of ecosystem and biodiversity conservation in the selected sectors. Section 4 describes the Indian situation of three different industrial sectors regarding their policies and plans to conserve ecosystem and biodiversity. Finally, Section 5 summarises the findings of the assessment, which further leads towards policy recommendations.

In India, the major concern for a biodiversity-related study is to obtain reliable and useful information. Though the business sector is working on biodiversity and ecosystem conservation and management, maintaining a database for their activities is still a distant future. However, the main source of information regarding companies' environmental activities is still in their websites, where they publish relatively easy to understand and activity-wise information related to environment conservation activities including biodiversity and ecosystems. Besides, for any detailed analysis on business activities related to biodiversity conservation, it is essential to conduct primary data collection and surveys. In India there are very few attempts so far to conduct such primary research on business sectors' activities towards biodiversity conservation. Therefore, in this study a hybrid methodology has been developed.

For monitoring, measuring, and assessing a company's progress towards sustainability and corporate responsibility Szekely and Knirsch (2005) identified 11 main approaches : (1) surveys, (2) award schemes, (3) investor's criteria, (4) benchmarking, (5) sustainability indexes, (6) external communication tools, (7) accreditation processes, (8) standards and codes, (9) sustainability indicators, (10) metrics for sustainability performance, and (11) non-quantifiable sustainability initiatives. Among these, in this chapter we applied option 1, i.e. survey method; option 4, i.e. benchmarking; option 5, i.e. metrics for sustainability performance; and option 11, i.e. non-quantifiable sustainability initiatives in our methodology.

For the first part of this study, the data have been collected from the respective companies' websites. We thoroughly analysed the contents of these companies' corporate social responsibility reports, sustainability reports and/or annual papers (depending on the availability from each company's website) to study their operational impacts and related offset policies and initiatives. Then for the next part of the study, i.e. in the case of India, the data have been collected through questionnaire survey, interview and field survey to demonstrate what are the impacts that these three sectors create on biodiversity and ecosystems and what are the different offset techniques they follow to reduce these impacts on the ecology.

Based on the information collected, we have created four major indicators for assessment of the companies' initiatives and activities towards biodiversity conservation and protection. The four indicators are: (1) sustainability, (2) biodiversity awareness, (3) biodiversity conservation activity, and (4) biodiversity conservation policy. Under each indicator, selected companies are assessed based on their level of achievement which is levelled as nascent, developing or matured. Selection of level is determined based on certain predetermined conditions. For the sustainability parameter, the companies that have their sustainability papers published and also completed any clean development mechanism (CDM) project are identified as matured. The companies that have not yet published any sustainability papers but completed any CDM project are identified as developing. The companies that have no sustainability paper or never did any CDM project are identified as in their nascent stage. This content analysis-based assessment is to categorise the companies taking initiatives to conserve biodiversity and ecosystems in the entire process of their business activities.

4. International scenario

In the process of conducting a comparative assessment of the selected business sectors in India, in terms of their activities related to biodiversity and ecosystem conservation, we first conducted a thorough investigation of various activities related to ecosystem and biodiversity conservation by the globally ranked international companies from the same sectors. The following section further describes how each selected sector is performing under different categories of actions to conserve and protect ecosystems and biodiversity.

4.1 Paper and pulp sector

From the Global Forest Resources Assessment (2006) we get that 30 percent of the world's land area is covered by forest. In the global context, the paper and pulp industry, which depends on the forest for their raw material procurement, has a significant role in the global sustainable development because of their unique raw material basis and increasing internationalization (Mikkila and Toppinen, 2008).

From the review of the biodiversity offset and mitigation policies of the paper and pulp sector leaders worldwide (for example: Fibria Celulose S.A. (Brazil), International Paper (US), Hudson Pulp and Paper (US), Stora Enso Oyj (Finland), etc.) we observe that they have different mitigation and offset initiatives along with biodiversity conservation and rehabilitation programs. Key components of biodiversity strategy taken up by the paper and pulp companies involve concurrent and post-closure rehabilitation and the utilization of biodiversity offsets as a tool for conservation. By implementing impact assessment techniques and environment management tools like environment impact assessment (EIA), environmental units (UMAS), and environmental management systems (EMS) etc., these companies try to control their impacts on biodiversity and ecosystems along with the impacts on the overall environment. Biodiversity conservation policies of the major paper and pulp companies worldwide are mainly divided into four major different categories of activities:

1. **Operational policy-driven activities**: This category of action includes various financial, operational and planning-related mitigation actions. For example, forest conservation certification i.e. Forest Stewardship Council (FSC) certification is one of the most popular initiatives. Similarly, investment policy in forest conservation and regeneration of forestland also is part of the overall initiatives to conserve biodiversity.

2. **Long-term business planning**: This category of action includes mid- to long-term planning of business which takes care of the issues like ecological landscape planning and not converting natural forests, protected areas or areas in an official conservation process into plantations unless it is clearly in line with the conservation regulations.

3. **Direct mitigation actions**: This category of activities includes actions which are directly related to conservation, protection and restoration of the biological diversity and ecosystem in the areas of company operation. For example, paper and pulp companies are heavily involved in rehabilitation of degraded forest and land areas for ecological restoration (promoting silviculture is part of such activities). It has been observed that these companies are spending more than 10 percent of their CSR budget in such activities, which are often considered as long-term business investment too. As a matter of fact, companies also are involved in community engagement in such restoration and rehabilitation activities via education, capacity building and even sometimes employing community members to restore the local degraded areas.

4. **Research and development activities:** Companies also are taking measures to protect the environment, ecology and biodiversity by promoting research in these areas. Often companies are building research laboratories for conducting research on plant species which can work at a faster rate to restore the degraded forest and can maintain the soil quality as well. Database development also is a big contribution that the companies are making which can help future research in this area.

4.2 *Mining sector*

Mining operation also affects local ecology. The Global Biodiversity Outlook of the CBD lists habitat conversion driven by industrial expansion as one of the major causes of biodiversity loss. This is especially true for industries such as mining, oil and gas and power that need access to biodiversity-rich areas either for extraction or for building infrastructure (Secretariat of the Convention on Biological Diversity, 2010). From the review of the biodiversity offset and mitigation policies of the mining sector leaders worldwide (for example: Newmont Mining Corp. (US), Barrick Gold Corp. (Canada), Xstrata plc (UK), Rio Tinto Group (Australia) etc.), we observe that they have different mitigation and offset initiatives along with biodiversity conservation and rehabilitation programs. Key components of biodiversity strategies taken by the mining companies involve concurrent and post-closure rehabilitation and the utilization of biodiversity offsets as a tool for conservation. Implementing impact assessment techniques and environment management tools like EIA, net positive impact (NPI) accounting and offset design methodology, UMAS and EMS etc., these companies try to control their impacts on biodiversity levels along with other environmental impacts. Biodiversity policies of the major mining companies worldwide mainly consist of the following:

1. **Minimizing impacts during mining**: This category of action includes minimizing impacts of mining by stockpiling topsoil, establishing nurseries to grow local plant species, preventing animals from entering the active part of a mining operation, undertaking erosion control, treating water prior to returning it to the environment and practicing concurrent reclamation.

2. **Mitigating long-term impacts:** This category of action leads towards mitigating long-term impacts of loss of ecosystems and biodiversity and leaving behind (upon closure) restored lands that will support productive post-mining land uses. This also includes not exploring mining within World Heritage Sites and geographically defined protected areas.

3. **Biodiversity management actions in different phases:** This set of activities includes actions during pre- and post-mining to conserve, protect and restore local ecosystems and biodiversity due to mining activities. Pre-construction phase includes installation of shaft site perimeter fencing, installation of shaft site sediment and erosion control measures and commencement of noxious weed management throughout entire site. Construction phase action includes plant, machinery and people to be contained by shaft site perimeter fencing and ecologist being present during tree removal and clearance (to minimise the disturbance to hollow-dependent native fauna.) Finally the post-construction phase includes screening trees, rehabilitation of temporarily disturbed areas, maintenance weed management in rehabilitated areas and management of grazing and agriculture.

4. **Research and development activities:** This category of action includes creating facilities for research on ecosystem conservation and facilities for preservation, education and sensitization of the stakeholders and promoting in-house biodiversity training of people.

4.3 Power sector

From the review of the biodiversity offset and mitigation policies of the leading energy companies worldwide, for example: Duke Energy Corp. (US), Energias de Portugal S.A. (Portugal), Enagas S.A. (Spain), Spectra Energy Corp. (US), etc., we observe that they have different mitigation and offset initiatives, along with biodiversity conservation and rehabilitation programs compared to the companies in developing countries. Throughout the life cycle of power generation, transmission and distribution, the activities create negative impacts on global biodiversity. Collision with power lines are threats for bird lives (Ferrer and Janss, 1999). Power lines also are barriers to wildlife movement (Treweek, 1999). The combined effects of several power lines which pass through different forest areas could affect many forest species and habitats significantly (Soderman, 2006). In power/electric transmission line EIAs, it is important to address biodiversity issues as early as possible to offset and mitigate impacts effectively, to compare different alternatives and to choose the best alternative with least negative impacts (Soderman, 2006).

By implementing impact assessment techniques and environment management tools like EIA, UMAS and EMS, etc., these companies try to control their impacts on biodiversity along with other environmental factors. On the basis of the reviews of Finnish electricity power transmission lines (Soderman, 2006) and other studies in Finland (Soderman, 2005), and also as studied in other countries, e.g. in the UK (Cooper and Sheate, 2002), in the US (Cooper and Canter, 1997) and Canada (Ross, 1998), it could be further recognised that the mitigation actions against cumulative impacts of developments on biodiversity are not adequately taken up in project EIAs as of now. However, biodiversity policy of the major energy companies worldwide mainly consists of the following:

1. **Preventive measures**: The majority of the global power utility companies are following certain preventative measures to offset the negative impacts of biodiversity and ecosystem loss due to their business activities. However, such mitigating measures and policies are dependent on the location of operation, mainly due to the local ecological characteristics and regulatory requirements. Since the impact of loss of biodiversity and ecosystems has relatively less direct affect on day-to-day business operations of the energy/power utility companies, therefore, globally we observed rather passive action on biodiversity conservation by them. In several cases, we also observed that these companies are including ecology and biodiversity conservation under the regular environmental impact assessment reports. Integrating biodiversity into the EMS, setting goals and indicators, as well as standards, for

the control, monitoring and audits are also observed as popular mechanism among those companies.

2. **Long-term planning**: We also observed that the power companies are keen to integrate biodiversity conservation into their company strategies and in their infrastructure development projects. Implementing preventive approaches to minimize the negative impacts of new infrastructure on biodiversity throughout the entire life cycle is also a popular preventive approach in this sector.

3. **Research and development activities**: This category of action includes creating facilities for research on ecosystem conservation, facilities for preservation, education and sensitization of the stakeholders and promoting in-house biodiversity training of people.

5. Case study on Indian companies

In this section we discuss the Indian situation of biodiversity and ecosystem conservation in the selected business sector. As the Indian economy is growing at a faster rate and it is suspected that its ecological footprint also will be relatively high compared to other developing countries, it is thus important to evaluate progress and activities of the Indian business sector in the context of ecological footprint and its mitigation for sustainable development. It is also important to understand how the national policy on biodiversity is affecting the business sector's response to biodiversity. India being one of the hot spots of biological diversity in the world, it, therefore, is important to understand the relationship between businesses, government policy and biodiversity conservation and mitigation activities in the county as a whole.

In this section, we first discuss the national and state policies on biodiversity related to the selected business sectors for this study and then we discuss the findings we obtained from the questionnaire survey and interviews of the experts from the respective sectors and companies. We also discuss the national policies related to the sectors for comparison of policy guideline and actual implementation in the country.

5.1 Overview of national biodiversity policies

India is one of the 17 mega-diverse countries in the world. Its total land area covers only 2.4 percent of the earth's total land area but consist of 8 percent of total plant and animal species existing currently on the earth. Within India's ten biogeographic and agroclimatic zones, certain extremely important ecological habitats exist like alpine forest, desert ecosystem, coastal and marine ecosystem and wetland. India is the home of four biodiversity hotspots in the world, indicating high endemism among species within the country, which covers agricultural crops and domestic animals too. As a matter of fact, India has 16 major types of forest and 251 subtype of forests within its territory. Thus, India has a long history of conservation and sustainable use of natural resources. Perhaps India is the first developing country in the world to enact a formal forest conservation act at a national level. Over the years, India has developed a stable organizational structure and a strong legal and policy framework for protection of environment in the country. India is also a party to the CBD, which requires all parties to prepare national biodiversity strategies and action plans for conservation and sustainable use of biological diversity. Accordingly, India developed a National Policy and Macrolevel Action Strategy on Biodiversity in 1999. Thereafter, an externally aided project on the NBSAP also was implemented in the country during 2000 to 2004, adopting a highly participatory process involving various stakeholders. Meanwhile, India also enacted the Biological Diversity Act in 2002, Section 36 of which empowers the central government to develop a national biodiversity action plan. After approval of the

NEP in 2006, preparation of the NBAP was taken up by revising and updating the document prepared in 1999 and by using the final technical report of NBSAP project. The NBAP draws upon the main principals in the NEP that human beings are at the centre of concerns of sustainable development, and they are entitled to a healthy and productive life in harmony with nature. Business being the part of the social existence of the mankind, therefore, is responsible to follow a sustainable mechanism which can ensure peaceful coexistence of nature and humans.

5.2 Importance of Biodiversity Act of 2002 for business in India

Traditionally Indian laws are protective towards the country's natural resources, environment and wildlife. Besides biodiversity-specific laws and regulations, there are several federal acts which are complementary to the National Biodiversity Act of 2002, like the Environment Protection Act 1986, the Forest Conservation Act 1980, the Wildlife Protection Act 1972 etc., and can act to strengthen the legal teeth of the Biodiversity Act of 2002 further. Apart from natural resource protection, there are couple of other acts related to protection of traditional habitats (Tribal Area Protection Act), conservation of lakes etc. which also are adding legal teeth to the biodiversity protection act. In India, acts and regulations related to national parks and sanctuaries are some of the toughest in the world. According to the MOEF), India has 668 protected areas in the country as of 2010. However, together they constitute just 4.90 percent of the total area of the country. Among these, 102 are national parks, 515 are wildlife sanctuaries, 47 are conservation reserves and four are community reserves. Continuous amendments of environmental acts (forest, air, water etc.) are creating huge challenges too to the companies in India to operate. As a matter of fact, in India, the clear message of the national government towards the business community is conducting sustainable business without any alternatives. Environment and especially biodiversity protection is constitutionally a concurrent matter of federal and state governments. Therefore, in addition to several federal laws, there are several state-specific laws and regulations as well which vary from state to state. Finally, the presence of more than ten different federal Acts related to biodiversity protection with more than 50 different state policies and regulations have created perhaps the most protected legal environment in India in the context of ecosystem and biodiversity conservation. Therefore, the business sector needs to be aware and careful in India while doing business to avoid future conflict and legal actions by the state or any stakeholders legally present in the country.

5.2.1 Paper and pulp industry in India

India is the 15th largest paper producer in the world. The Indian paper and pulp industry produces more than six million tonnes annually from more than 600 mills. This sector provides employment to more than 1.5 million people and fetches revenue to the national government of India of around Rs.25 billion. In the last 50 years, the number of paper mills increased from 17 mills to 660. So far, India is self-sufficient in terms of its paper production and consumption. Currently per capita paper consumption in India is around 7 kg, which is far below than the world average and even below the Asian average of 28kg per capita. By 2020, it is expected to go up the level of 20 kg. The domestic paper market mainly is dominated by the big companies with their captive plantations. However, the types of raw material used for paper production in India are divided into three main categories: wood based, agriculture residue based and recycled paper based. Currently, 32 percent of wood-based paper production is gradually getting replaced by non-timber and non-wood-based paper production, mainly due to environmental reasons and its related regulation.

5.2.2 National policies on biodiversity and forestry conservation for the paper and pulp sector

In the Indian context, the MOEF's broad objectives regarding biodiversity policies, i.e. conservation and survey of flora, fauna, forests and wildlife, prevention and control of pollution, forestations and regeneration of degraded areas, protection of the environment and ensuring the welfare of animals, go along with the environment and biodiversity protection policies of the paper and pulp industries. As per MOEF, the tools to achieve these objectives are mainly: EIA; eco-regeneration; assistance to organizations implementing environmental and forestry programmes; assistance to organizations including animal welfare programmes; promotion of environmental and forestry research, extension, education and training; dissemination of environmental information; international cooperation; and creation of environmental awareness among all sectors of the country's population.

These objectives are supported by a set of legislative and regulatory measures aimed at the preservation, conservation and protection of the environment and biodiversity. Some of them are the Water Prevention and Control of Pollution Act of 1974, the Air Prevention and Control of Pollution Act of 1981, the Environment Protection Act of 1986, the Wildlife Protection Act of 1972 and the Forests Conservation Act of 1980. Besides the legislative measures, a National Conservation Strategy and Policy Statement on Environment and Development (1992) and a National Forest Policy (1988) also have been evolved. Further to the reference of additional progress in the terms of bilateral activities, especially in the paper and pulp business sector, the second meeting of the India-Finland Joint Working Group on Environment (September 2003 in Helsinki, Finland) focused on areas of mutual cooperation in the field of climate change, sustainable development and environmental technology in hazardous waste treatment for the paper and pulp industry.

5.2.3 Biodiversity offset policies in the Indian paper and pulp sector

To obtain information regarding the current status of the Indian paper and pulp companies in the context of their activities related to conservation of biodiversity and ecosystem, we conducted a nationwide survey. We prepared a questionnaire consisting of 20 different questions covering all aspects of business activities and their corresponding responses to ecosystem and biodiversity conservation. Survey questions are divided into three main categories: volume of business, potential impacts of business activities on biodiversity and company polices to mitigate impacts of loss of biodiversity and ecosystems. We got responses from all the major Indian paper and pulp companies. In the highest ranked paper company of India, the virgin fibre is obtained through farm forestry and social forestry plantations promoted by the company on 130,000 ha. Apart from the previous, recycled paper is used in the manufacturing of paper and paperboard. In this company, no industrial enzymes are used in paper and paperboard manufacture and thus its operational impact on environment and ecosystem is less. To assess their impact on the environment, including ecosystems and biodiversity, these major paper companies use EIA techniques.

Regarding biodiversity protection policies, the major-most paper company of India has mainly taken up forest conservation actions and Forest Stewardship Council (FSC) certification. For example, it has got FSC chain of custody certification for its four units. It also got FSC certification for 8,000 ha under forest management. Also all its paper units are International Organization for Certification (ISO) 9000, 14000 and Occupational Safety and Health Administration (OSHA) certified. This company promotes farm forestry wherein the pulpwood tree plantations are grown by the farmers on their own land. With tree plantations, agricultural crops are encouraged as intercrop. Apart from the previous, it has shown agro-biodiversity to the FSC. Moreover, bio-diversity conservation plots are opened up with the help of farmers wherein the natural growth of trees, shrubs and herbs is protected; water bodies are created for fish culture; apiary promoted; paddy cultivation taken up; medicinal plants are grown and also eucalyptus plantations. In this company, the internal mechanism exists under corporate Environment Health and Safety on biodiversity.

Another major paper company of India also has forest conservation certification and follows National Forest Policy 1988 by government of India, while they don't have any other biodiver-sity protection policies as of now. But they have planned to follow related policies in the near future while setting up new plants. Other related activities include: CDM project for improving rural livelihoods through carbon sequestration by adopting environment friendly technology-based agro-forestry practices. Also it has tie-ups with many NGOs who work for climate change and forestry protection. This company uses amylase for starch conversion in their operation process which reduces the environmental impact to an extent. Also it takes up conversion of native starch to reduce viscosity. However, as forestry protection and biodiversity protection policy, they mainly take up afforestation and pulp wood plantation. Also they have taken up FSC certification.

One Indian paper company who has large market share in the state of West Bengal uses alpha amylase enzyme for reduction of raw starch viscosity (3 kg/month only) in their paper produc-tion. They claim to create no environmental impact because of the usage of very low quantity for surface sizing along with the starch. It carries out an EIA study to know the environmental impacts (including impacts on biodiversity) before any project start up. After project commis-sioning, all environment conditions and regulations are complied. Full-fledged environmental management system exist to monitor the impact on the environment on a day-to-day basis. This company has achieved the certification of ISO 9001, 14001 and OSHAS 18001 and Total Pro-ductivity Maintenance excellence certificate from the Japan Institute of Plant Management.

5.3 Coal mining industry in India

Mining has now become an integral part of the sustained economic development of a mineral-rich country like India.[2] The world's largest coal reserves are held by the US, Russia, China, Australia and India put together. According to the 2012 BP Statistical Energy Survey, India has coal reserves of 60,600 million tonnes, equivalent to 102 years of current production and 7.03 percent of the world's total. India's lignite reserves are estimated at 6.5 billion tonnes. Most of India's coal is characterised by high ash content, low sulphur content (generally 0.5 percent), low iron content in ash, low refractory nature of ash, low chlorine content and low trace element concentration. Most of the coal production in India comes from open-pit mines, which contribute more than 81 percent of the total production. A number of large open-pit mines of over 10 million tonnes per annum capacity are in operation. Underground mining currently accounts for around 19 percent of national output. Most of the production is achieved by conventional board and pillar mining methods.

About 88 percent of the total coal production in the country is produced by various subsid-iaries (a total of 390 mines) of Coal India Ltd., which is the largest supplier of coal (and one of the largest taxpayers) in the country. Although Coal India is currently state controlled, efforts are being made to open the industry to Indian private investors. At present all private mines are allowed to operate only if they are producing coal to supply a specific industry (e.g. power station industry).

5.3.1 National policies on biodiversity and forestry conservation for coal mining

The MOEF) of India has taken several important policy steps for biodiversity protection in the context of mining operation in the country. MOEF of India is now very strict about the mining industry for issuing licenses and continuing permission for their operation based on different environment clearing issues, including forestry clearance and biodiversity loss. For example, the government of India said it has stopped operations in 23 iron ore mines in Joda as they could not submit proof of the necessary clearances including documents like forest clearance, mining lease, and surface rights.[3]

The Indian Constitution itself mentioned the regulation of mining activities in the county in the entry of Section 54. The national policy also mentions the introduction of improved mining technology, especially for the coal mines in the county, including increased collaboration with international companies having advanced technologies. Besides, there are certain areas of research and development that have been prioritised by the MOEF in the coal/other mining sector e.g., improved mining techniques; promoting the use of new technologies such as fluidized bed combustion; land reclamation systems for areas degraded by opencast mining; environmental protection through improvement in ventilation and environmental conditions in underground mines; new methods for coal beneficiation; clean coal technologies; alternative modes for coal transportation, extraction and use of environmental friendly sources of energy such as coal bed methane. The National Conservation Strategy and Policy Statement on Environment and Development in 1992, along with the National Forest Policy, state a major policy instrument of the government for integrating conservation considerations in the policies and programmes of mining owned and operated by the government.

5.3.2 Biodiversity offset policies in the Indian mining (coal) sector

In this study, the major coal mining companies of India were surveyed about their operational issues and related impacts on biological diversity, awareness and policies to protect biodiversity and ecosystem. Primary data has been collected during site visits and experts' interviews in different coal mines of West Bengal State of India to see what initiatives they are taking to mitigate their impacts on local ecology. Also, while it was not possible to visit the mines, the questionnaire survey and interviews were conducted to collect data and information from the mining companies. All the major Indian coal mining companies, like-Tata Steel, Eastern Coal Field Limited, Bharat Coking Coal limited, Jindal Steel, Hindalco Industries and National Aluminium Company were surveyed. The total production of the companies surveyed in this study covers more than 70 percent of the national coal production and has the biggest open-mine production share in the country. Figure 20.1 shows the national distribution and location of coal fields in India. This indicates that the eastern part of India is the main source of coal production in the country.

From our visit to different coal mines, we see that mainly open-cast mines create more negative impacts on local ecology and biodiversity than the underground mines. Impact areas include: land degradation, deterioration of air quality, groundwater contamination, siltation in river basin (impact on surface water), displacement of local habitats and displacement of local flora and fauna from the biosphere.

The major coal mines were visited for this study, which includes both open-cast coal mines and underground coal mines (colliery) as well. The impact on the environment due to extraction of coal is being monitored constantly by the companies and adequate measures are undertaken for control of air, water and noise pollution, land degradation, deforestation etc. According to one

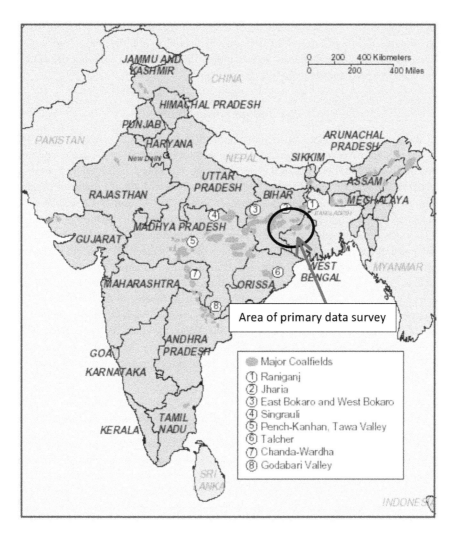

Figure 20.1   Indicative map of Indian coal fields

of the major coal mine companies in the state of West Bengal, they planted around 19,5000 trees during the years 2011 to 2012 covering an area of 78 ha. The main activity related to biodiversity protection taken up by the major coal mining companies is called flora restoration action (FRA). FRA includes pre-construction phase, construction phase, and post-construction phase. Pre-construction phase further includes installation of perimeter fencing, installation of sediment and erosion-control measures, noxious weed management throughout the restoration site, etc. Construction phase includes plant, machinery and people to be contained by shaft site perimeter fencing. Post-construction phase includes screening trees, rehabilitation of temporarily disturbed areas, maintenance weed management in rehabilitated areas and management of grazing and agricultural activities in the restored areas.

The mining sites we visited are yet to reach the level of fully developed stage regarding biodiversity offset initiatives, as most of the restorations are only 10 to 15 years old. The mining companies also are working on biodiversity and ecosystem conservation action plans on a regular basis.

They also are involved in capacity building of their own staff members in terms of developing understanding about ecosystems and the importance to conserve it in the mining process. Mining companies are also engaging the local communities in the context of developing the mining reclamation plan, especially for the open cast mining.

5.4 Indian power sector

India is the world's sixth largest energy market. India's total primary energy consumption is around 400 million ton of oil equivalent (MMtoe). However, in terms of per capita consumption (2.4 boe), India is still far below than the world average (11.3 boe). India's energy consumption is expected to grow at an annual pace of 3.2 percent along with GDP growth of 7 percent to 9 percent per annum. Though during the recent years (FY2011 and 2012) India's economic growth slowed down significantly, it is expected to bounce back to the previous level in the near future. Along with other energy demand, electricity demand is growing at the fastest rate of around 5 percent to 6 percent per annum in India as the rate of electrification and modernization is happening in the energy sector of the economy. Due to economic growth, affordability of household electronic items has increased by more than 15 percent in the last decade and it increases the electricity demand in the domestic sector by more than 8 percent. As a matter of fact, electricity supply has become a pre-condition for sustained economic growth of the country.

Ironically, Indian energy supply is expected to be skewed towards coal until the next couple of decades as India has plenty of low-cost domestic coal reserve. As a result, India's continued economic growth also will continue to pressurise the country's environmental condition, as coal is the dirtiest fossil fuel in the world.

5.4.1 Biodiversity and forestry policies for power sector in India

The MOEF also has taken several important policy steps for biodiversity protection which can be applicable to the electricity sector in the country as well and could be outlined for the sector as described in the following. Agenda 21 at the national scale focuses on the role of efficiency in energy production, transmission, distribution and consumption and on the use of environmentally sound energy systems, such as advanced fossil fuel technologies and new and renewable sources of energy for controlling environmental damage. It integrates biodiversity concerns into measures for energy conservation and adoption of renewable energy technologies with a focus on local biomass resources and dissemination of improved fuel wood stoves and solar cookers. It also intends to promote the usage of non-conventional/environmentally friendly sources of energy (such as coal bed methane), clean coal technologies and alternative modes for coal transportation which would help to reduce the impact on biodiversity.

According to the theme in Agenda 21, activities in the energy sector may cause severe impacts on the environment right from the mining stage through the processing stage to the final use of fuels in power generation or for transport. One of the mechanisms is to develop and implement integrated enforceable and effective laws and regulations that are based on sound social and ecological principles. Another mechanism is the use of economic and market-based instruments that incorporate environmental costs in the decisions of producers and consumers.

An important dimension of sustainable energy systems is the direct social impact of energy development, such as resettlement and rehabilitation of people displaced by clearing of land for mining or setting up large hydropower plants. One example, also presented by the World Business Council for Sustainable Development (2012) in their recently published report, is of the Reliance Industries' Jamnagar oil refinery in Gujarat where they are working with local communities to enhance the biodiversity potential of the land.[4] Addressing the social impacts of energy projects is an important component of sustainable energy development. In India, such policy measures are adopted under the national priority and vision of long-term energy supply and sustainable development planning. Inclusive growth and integrated energy planning of India are the basic guidelines in the country in terms of developing sustainable energy and electricity development planning.

However, in the oil sector the major themes are compliance with sulphur emissions norms and improvements in fuel quality. All Indian refineries comply with the applicable minimum national standards prescribed for SO_2. Measures adopted by the oil companies operating within the county to comply with the national target include usage of low-sulphur fuel oil, desulphurization of refinery fuel gas in sulphur recovery unit, taller stacks for better dispersion etc.

5.4.2 Biodiversity offset policies in the Indian power sector

In this study, the major power and energy companies of India were contacted to know about their operational impacts, awareness and policies to protect biodiversity and ecosystem. We followed the questionnaire survey and interview method to collect data and information. We got responses from all the major power and energy companies like Damodar Valley Corporation Of India , West Bengal Power Development Corporation Limited, Oil and Natural Gas Corporation of India, Indian Oil Corporation Limited, Reliance Energy Limited, Calcutta Electric Supply Corporation etc.

For most of the power companies in India, there are no specific policies or actions related to biodiversity protection. But technological renovation has been done to mitigate the pollution. Technology also is used to protect natural resources. Related to biodiversity and forestry, forest conservation is done as a main activity. Though they don't have any specific policies, they follow all the related acts and regulations of the government of India while setting up new plants. It is seen in the case of old power stations that there were no biodiversity policies followed while they were set up. But for any new plant set up, biodiversity conservation and protection policies are adopted and implemented.

Climate change and carbon sequestration awareness exists in some of the power companies but on a limited scale. The conventional government power companies just follow environmental rules and regulation for compliance purpose and hence no new initiatives are taken apart from them. Global environmental effects are not taken into consideration for most of the government organisations in India. Forest conservation and plantation always was there in the common social activities. The companies are largely concerned about their operational impacts on biodiversity, especially on the marine life/river fishes and species while they intake water for thermal power generation.

One of the major power generating company in West Bengal is producing power mainly from coal and hydro resources. The company has no specific biodiversity-related policy but environmental conservation is streamlined in their policymaking processes. Conservation of forest during construction of transmission and distribution lines and also setting up new power plants is very much in line with the National Forest Conservation Act of India. It also conducts EIA for all new projects as required by law, which ensures the conservation and protection of environment, ecology and biodiversity in general. This power company also invests money in terms of developing and using new and advanced technologies which can reduce impact on the environment. They have introduced new transmission technology which requires less land area. As a matter of fact, this new technology is conducive for forest conservation. In the context of research and development in the area of ecology and biodiversity, this company has a research institute near Hazaribagh which is working on soil conservation, forest conservation and plantation techniques. Under the corporate social responsibility activity, it also conducts various rural education and training program in the operation areas. In general, this major power company is concerned about the environmental impacts of their operation and do work towards mitigation of impacts though biodiversity specific activities are yet to come.

6. Result and analysis

The result presented in this study are mainly obtained from the field survey and questionnaire survey with the selected companies in the respective business sectors. For the paper and pulp sector, data and information were collected mainly by questionnaire survey method. Only 44 percent responded to this survey. For the mining sector, we used a field survey as well as questionnaire survey. Among six major mining companies in India, we obtained primary data from two and secondary data from four companies. The responses factor in this sector is around 33 percent. For the power sector, all selected companies responded to our survey and questionnaire either by mail or by direct interviews. Here our response factor is around 100 percent.

In Table 20.1 and Table 20.2 a summary of the findings has been represented. Here it was intended to find out the state of the companies (nascent stage/developing stage/matured stage)

Table 20.1 Status of the three sectors with respect to sustainability and biodiversity awareness

Unit: percentage of total responses obtained from companies

Type of business	Sustainability			Biodiversity awareness		
	Nascent	*Developing*	*Matured*	*Nascent*	*Developing*	*Matured*
Paper & Pulp★	0	50	25	0	50	50
Mining	0	66	34	0	0	100
Power sector (Elec. Gen/Dist)	0	100	0	0	100	0

Note:★ 25% of the paper and pulp companies surveyed didn't respond on sustainability indicator.

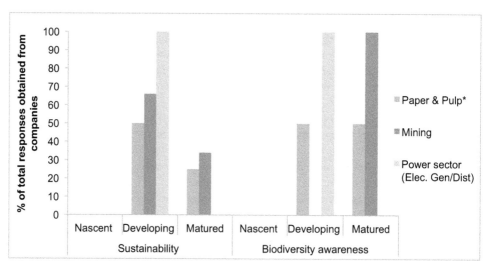

Table 20.1a Schematic representation of Table 20.1

Table 20.2 Status of the companies with respect to biodiversity planning and actions

Type of business	Biodiversity planning			Biodiversity protection action		
	Nascent	Developing	Matured	Nascent	Developing	Matured
Paper & Pulp★		75		50	50	0
Mining ★		66			66	
Power sector (Elec. Gen/Dist)	75	25	0	75	25	0

Note: ★ 25% and 34% of total companies surveyed under the paper and pulp and mining sector respectively didn't respond on biodiversity planning indicator.

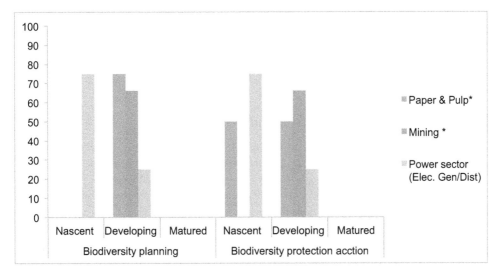

Table 20.2a Schematic representation of Table 20.2

with respect to sustainability, biodiversity awareness, biodiversity planning and the actions taken for biodiversity protection. For the sustainability parameter, the companies who have their sustainability reports published and also completed any CDM projects have been identified as in the matured stage of sustainability. The companies who have not yet published any sustainability reports but done any CDM projects have been identified as in their developing stage of sustainability. The companies who do not have any sustainability report or never did any CDM project could be identified as in their nascent stage of sustainability.

Table 20.1 shows the status of the companies with respect to biodiversity awareness. Here, the companies who have clear ideas about why biodiversity protection is important and also are aware about the CBD and convention of the parties (CBD member countries) are identified as in their matured stage of biodiversity awareness. The companies who are aware about biodiversity and the importance of its protection but not aware about international activities have been identified as in their developing stage of biodiversity awareness.

Table 20.2 shows the status of the companies with respect to biodiversity planning and actions taken for biodiversity protection. The companies that don't have any policy yet related to biodiversity protection or have plans to take up any related policies (unless there are any mandatory acts from the government to be implemented) in the near future have been identified in their nascent stage of biodiversity planning. The companies who may not have taken up any biodiversity protection policy yet but are enthusiastic about the same while mainly setting up new operational units have been identified as in their developing stage of biodiversity planning. While the companies that already have many policies and actions in the area of biodiversity protection and also have taken up projects for the same along with utilizing new and innovative technologies to reduce net biodiversity loss have been identified as in their matured stage of biodiversity planning.

Regarding the actions taken for biodiversity protection, the companies that have not yet taken any policy implementation related to biodiversity protection rather than just doing the forest conservation in the operational area have been identified as companies in their nascent stage of actions for biodiversity protection. The companies that have taken up specific projects related to reducing the net biodiversity loss, already have number of biodiversity offset policies along with the forest conservation and plantation actions have been identified as the companies in their developing stage of actions taken up for biodiversity protection. The matured stage of biodiversity protection actions was granted for the companies who have many offset and mitigation actions and policies at par with the sustainable world leaders in the international field related to biodiversity protections.

7. Conclusion and recommendations

This study reveals the overall picture of the Indian paper and pulp, mining and power sectors regarding their awareness of biodiversity protection and related planning and mitigation actions in the processes of their daily business activities. In the first part of this study, we have also done a review of the status of the world's market leaders in the context of their biodiversity offset policies and mitigation measures. From the analysis of the study of the Indian companies in the selected business sectors, we observe that the mining sector is more conscious compared to the paper and pulp and power sector regarding the impacts they create on the local ecology and the related mitigation and offset policies. One of the major reasons for this is the impact they create on biodiversity, including the local flora and fauna species, mainly through their open-cast mining operations is quite visible and significant. Among the other two sectors, we find that the paper and pulp sector is doing better regarding awareness and actions related to biodiversity protection than the power sector. Public-owned power companies (state electricity authorities) are in the nascent stage in this regard while the semi-government and private organizations still could be considered as in the developing stage of building sustainable development practices within their businesses. For example: BirdLife International on 16 October 2012 launched an e-Atlas of Marine-Important Bird Areas during COP11. The e-Atlas will act as an inventory and carry data of around 3,000 important bird areas from across the world and can play a major role in conserving the CBD target for protection of 10 percent of coastal and marine areas by 2020.[5] So the power companies should try different biodiversity offset policies related to their transmission lines which may protect birds' lives. Finally, based on the conclusions and findings, we propose the overall recommendations for the Indian companies in the respective business sectors in the context of their future activities towards biodiversity conservation as follows:

• Promoting national and state government activities regarding creation of awareness and generating importance of biodiversity protection among the stakeholders. Increasing staff training and internal meetings on capacity building related to conservation and ecosystem and biological diversity in the context of their respective business activities.

- More specific acts should be taken up by the government which follows the CBD's rules and regulations.
- Mainstreaming the biodiversity policy along with other environmental and sustainability policies taken up by the private companies.
- Engaging NGOs and non-profit organizations in partnership to implement more biodiversity offset initiatives. Effective utilization of corporate social responsibility activities is essential in this context.
- More R&D should be done in this field to find innovative technologies to reduce the impacts on biodiversity and other innovative techniques to reduce the net loss of global biodiversity.

Notes

1 For further information see: http://www.cbd.int/doc/newsletters/news-biz-2012-11-en.pdf.
2 Source: http://www.teriin.org/events/docs/fimi.pdf.
3 Source: http://articles.timesofindia.indiatimes.com/2011-01-22/bhubaneswar/28362376_1_mining-lease-iron-ore-mines-mining-plan
4 http://www.cbd.int/doc/newsletters/news-biz-2012-11-en.pdf
5 http://www.jagranjosh.com/current-affairs/cop-11-held-in-hyderabad-emphasised-on-the-well-being-of-biodiversities-1350904072-1

References

Anuradha R.V., Taneja B. and Kothari A. 2001. Policy Making and Community Registers in India. International Institute for Environment and Development, London.
Barnosky, A. D., Nicholas, M., Susumu, T., Guin W., Brian S., Tiago Q., Charles M., McGuire, J., Lindsey, E., Maguire, K., Mersey, B. and Ferrer, E. 2011. Has the Earth's sixth mass extinction already arrived? *Nature* 471:51–57.
Bekessy, S., Wintle, B. A., Lindenmayer, D. B., Mccarthy, M. A., Colyvan, M. and Burgman, M. A. 2010. The Biodiversity bank cannot be a lending bank. *Ecological Economics* 53(4):439–616.
Bhattacharya, T.R. and S. Managi. 2013. Contributions of the private sector to global biodiversity protection: case study of the fortune 500 companies. *International Journal of Biodiversity Science, Ecosystem Services & Management* 9(1):65–86.
Biodiversity banking in India. India Environmental Portal. http://www.indiaenvironmentportal.org.in/topic-tree.
Biodiversity hotspot in India. http://www.biodiversityofindia.org/index.php?title=Biodiversity_hotspots_in_India.
Business and Biodiversity Offsets program. http://bbop.forest-trends.org/.
Cooper L.M. and Sheate W.R. 2002. Integrating cumulative effects assessment into UK. *Impact Assessment Review* 22:403–425.
Cooper, T. and Canter, L. 1997. Documentation of cumulative impacts in environmental impact statements. *Environmental Impact Assessment Review* 17(6):385–411.
Department for Environment, Food and Rural Affairs. http://www.defra.gov.uk/environment/natural/biodiversity/uk/offsetting/.
Department of Environment & Conservation. 2006. Biobanking: An investigation of market-based instruments to secure long-term biodiversity objectives. Department of Environment & Conservation, NSW, Sydney.
Energy and Biodiversity Initiative (EBI). 2005. Paper on Progress. Washington, DC: The Center for Environmental Leadership in Business, Conservation International.
Global Forest Resources Assessment. 2005. Progress Towards Sustainable Forest Management, FAO Forestry paper 147, UN Food and Agriculture Organization, Rome.
Hanson, C, Ranganathan, J., Iceland, C. and Finisdore, J. 2012. *The corporate ecosystem services review.* Meridian Institute and World Resources Institute, Washington, DC.

Helm, D. and Hepburn, C. 2012. The economic analysis of biodiversity: an assessment. *Oxford Review of Economic Policy* 28(1):1–21.

Indian Ministry of Environment and Forestry. 2008. National Biodiversity Action Plan, Government of India, New Delhi.

Janss, G.F.E. and Ferrer, M. 1999. Avian electrocution of power lines: European experiences. In M. Ferrer and G.F.E. Janss (eds.), *Birds and power lines: Collision, electrocution, and breeding*, pp. 145–164. Madrid: Quercus.

Leibig, K., Alker, D., Chih, K., Horn, D., Illi, H. and Wolf, J. 2002. Governing biodiversity. Access to Genetic Resources and Approaches to Obtaining benefits from their use: the case of Philippines, Reports and Working Papers 5/2002, Bonn German Development Institute.

Maiti, S.K. 1997. Economic valuation of environmental impacts of open-cast coal mining project: An appraisal in Indian context. In V.P. Upadhaya (ed.), *Issues of Environment and Sustainability*, pp. 112–125. Bhubaneswer: Nandighosh.

Maiti, S.K. 2002. Ecological environment. In N.C. Saxena et al. (eds.), *Environmental Management in Mining Areas*, pp. 110–14. Jodhpur: Scientific Publishers.

Maiti, S.K. 2006a. Ecorestoration of coalmine OB dumps – with special emphasis on tree species and improvements of dump physico-chemical, nutritional and biological characteristics. *MGMI Transactions* 102(1&2):21–36.

Maiti, S.K. 2006b. Properties of minesoil and its affects on bioaccumulation of metals in tree species: a case study from a large opencast coalmining project. *International Journal of Mining, Reclamation and Environment* 20(2):96–110.

Maiti, S.K. 2007a. Bioreclamation of coalmine overburden dumps – with special emphasis on micronutrients and heavy metals accumulation in tree species. *Environmental Monitoring and Assessment* 125:111–122.

Maiti, S.K. 2007b. Ecological impact assessment of surface mining project. In K.K. Singh et al. (eds.), *Environmental degradation and protection*, Vol. 2, pp. 1–31. New Delhi: MD, Publication Pvt. Ltd.

Maiti, S.K., Nandhini, S. and Das, M. 2005. Accumulation of metals by naturally growing herbaceous and tree species in iron ore tailings. *International Journal of Environmental Studies* 62(5):503–563.

Maiti, S.K., Shee, C. and Ghose, M.K. 2007. Selection of plant species for the reclamation of mine degraded land in the Indian context. *Land Contamination & Reclamation* 15(1):55–66.

National Biotechnology Development Strategy. 2007. Department of Biotechnology, Ministry of Science and Technology, India.

Richerzhagen, H.M. 2004. The effectiveness of access and benefit sharing in Costa Rica: implications for national and international regimes. *Ecological Economics* 53:445–460.

Roe, D., Sukhdev, P., Thomas, D. and Munroe, R. Banking on Biodiversity: a natural way out of poverty. http://www.indiaenvironmentportal.org.in/papers-documents/banking-biodiversity-natural-way-out-poverty.

Ross, W. 1998. Cumulative effects assessment: learning from Canadian Case studies. *Impact Assessment and Project Appraisal* 16(4):267–276.

Siebenhuner, B., Dedeurwaerdere, T. and Brousseau, E. 2005. Biodiversity conservation, access and benefit sharing and traditional knowledge. *Ecological Economics* 53:439–444.

Soderman, T. 2006. Treatment of biodiversity issues in impact assessment of electricity power transmission lines: A Finnish case review. Environmental Impact Assessment Review 26(4):319–338.

The Economics of Ecosystems And Biodiversity (TEEB). 2010. Paper for Business. Geneva: UNEP.

Thomas, C.D., Cameron, A., Green, R.E., Bakkenes, M., Beaumont, L.J., Collingham, Y.C., Erasmus, B.F., De Siqueira, M.F., Grainger, A., Hannah, L., Hughes, L., Huntley, B., Van Jaarsveld, A.S., Midgley, G.F., Miles, L., Ortega-Huerta, M.A., Peterson, A.T., Phillips, O.L. and Williams, S.E. 2004. Extinction risk from climate change. *Nature* 427(6970):145–8.

Treweek, J. 1999. Ecological Impact Assessment. Malden, MA: Blackwell Science.

United Nations. 1992. Convention on Biological Diversity (Article 2). Rio de Janeiro: UNEP.

Walpole, M., Almond, R.E.A., Besancon C. and Butchart, S. 2009. Tracking progress toward the 2010 biodiversity target and beyond. *Science* 325:1503–1504.

Walter, V.R. 2005. *Millennium Ecosystem Assessment: Ecosystem and Human Well-being*. Washington, DC: Island Press.

Wilson, E.O. 1994. Biodiversity: challenge, science, opportunity. *American Zoologist* 34:5–11.

21

TECHNOLOGICAL CHANGE AND THE ENVIRONMENT

Surender Kumar*

1. Introduction

Technological advancements play a crucial ameliorating role in managing the long-standing problems of environment and climate change. Long-term sustainability of economic growth requires understanding about the environmental impacts of technological changes as the environmental impacts of economic activities are profoundly associated with the rate and direction of technological changes. Environmental technologies include not only the end-of-pipe technologies such as scrubbers for use on industrial smokestacks or catalytic converters for automobiles. They also include the technologies that change the production processes, such as improved energy efficiency. Moreover, note that environmental problems and associated policy responses evolve over long time horizons, and the cumulative impacts of technological changes are likely to be large. Most of the models of technological measurement are concerned with exogenous technological change, but economists cite use of economic instruments such as pollution taxes and emissions trading permits for the advancement of environmental technologies.

Environmental technological development is prone to various market failures that arise due to environmental externalities, public good externalities or knowledge externalities, network externalities, asymmetric information, and uncertainty problem and the problems of general purpose technologies; therefore, policies should be targeted to correction of these various kinds of market failures. At a minimum, environmental-friendly technological development requires correction for environmental externality and/or knowledge market failures.

The emphasis of on-going climate change mitigation negotiations should be on developing ways for reducing greenhouse gas emissions through adoption of clean technologies. A natural way to approach this question is the identification of the extent to which the pace of technological advance, the direction of technological advance, and changes in the substitutability of inputs due to changes in relative energy prices and exogenous forces such as developments in general science and technology. Energy economists often cite market-based instruments such as energy taxes for encouraging energy-saving technological progress. Energy policy interventions may change the constraints and incentives that affect technological change (TC). For instance, changes in current relative energy prices may induce substitution of energy by other factors of production and changes in its long-run prices may induce development of new energy-saving technologies.

421

Although this chapter reviews the literature on the economics of technological change and environment, it is more concentrated on a few applications that measure the technological changes that involve not only the extent of advancement but also its direction, input and output bias and factor substitutions and relate these changes to environmental/climate policy options. For a recent detailed review on energy, environment and technological changes, see Pope et al. (2010). Therefore, we mainly confine ourselves to the review of the literature on the measurement of technological progress, especially using the frontier approaches. Measuring technological advancements using frontier approaches not only helps in measuring of the extent of the pace of technological advance but also in identifying the direction of technological advance and changes in the substitutability of inputs due to changes in relative energy prices and exogenous forces such as developments in general science and technology. Using frontier approaches, we also can measure the extent of technological diffusion.

The chapter is organized as follows: Section 2 not only reviews the measurement of environmental technological changes using the production frontier approach, it also provides a detailed conceptual framework. The framework is not confined to the exogenous and neutral technological changes but also shows how the technological advancements are decomposed into exogenous and induced innovations and how they are decomposed into neutral and biased technological changes. Section 3 reviews the theoretical and empirical studies of environmental policy and technological progress. The studies related to climate change and technological changes are reviewed in Section 4. The chapter closes in Section 5 with some concluding remarks.

2. Measurement of technological change

Technological advancements happen in three stages: inventions, innovations and diffusions of technologies. Invention means finding a new product or a new production process and innovations imply commercial availability of those products or processes. Note that it is not necessary that all the inventions are converted into the innovations, and it is also not necessary that inventor and innovator are the same firms or individuals. A firm or an individual can innovate without ever inventing by finding an existing technical idea that was never commercialized and bringing a new product or process based on that idea to the market. Inventions and innovations are the product of a process which is generally known as research and development (R&D). A widespread and successful adoption of an innovation in relevant applications by individuals and firms is known as the diffusion of technology, and a combination of these three stages is known as technological change.

Technological changes are measured in two different ways: counting of patents and using production function/frontier. Whenever a new invention takes place, it gets patented, and the number of patents in a particular area is considered an indicator of the technological developments in that area. Patents may not be able to capture all the technological developments in an area since all the inventions are not converted into innovations; that is, inventions might not be widely deployed (Basberg, 1987). For example, if a firm produces a lot of useless patents that are never deployed, the firm should not be rated as innovative relative to another firm with the same or fewer number of patents that are more useful.

Though the modern theory of technological advancements has its roots in the work of Josef Schumpeter, the measurement of technological change and its contribution in economic growth for the first time saw its day in the work of Robert Solow in 1957. The long-term economic growth rate in Solow's model actually is independent of the rate of saving and capital accumulation and the sustained rate of growth he assumes as the result of improvement in labour productivity, presumably the result of technological advancement.

2.1 Measurement of technological change using production function/frontiers

The measurement of the rate and direction of TC rests fundamentally on the concept of a production possibility frontier, a set of combinations of inputs and outputs that are technically feasible at a point in time,

$$T\ (Y, I, t) \leq 0, \tag{1}$$

where Y represents a vector of outputs, I represents a vector of inputs, and t is time. Technological change is represented by movement of this frontier that makes it possible over time to use given input vectors to produce output vectors that were not previously feasible. An outward shift in the frontier implies technological improvements, as the firms can produce more outputs with the given level of inputs.

In most of the empirical applications, by making separability and aggregation assumptions, and taking the output as a scalar measure, the production technology is represented by the production function,

$$Y = f\ (K, L, E; t), \tag{2}$$

where Y is now a scalar measure of aggregate output (for example, gross domestic product), and a single composite of capital goods, K, a single composite of labour inputs, L, and a single composite of environmental inputs, E (for example, waste assimilation). Again, technological change means that the relationship between these inputs and possible output levels changes over time.

Logarithmic differentiation of Equation (2) with respect to time yields

$$y_t = A_t + \beta_{Lt}\ l_t + \beta_{Kt}\ k_t + \beta_{Et}\ e_t, \tag{3}$$

where lowercase letters represent the percentage growth rates of the corresponding uppercase variable, the β's represent the corresponding logarithmic partial derivatives from Equation (2) and the t indicates that all quantities and parameters may change over time. The term A_t corresponds to "neutral" technological change, in the sense that it represents the rate of growth of output if the growth rates of all inputs were zero. But the possibility that the β's can change over time allows for biased technological change; that is, changes over time in relative productivity of the various inputs. Equations (2) and (3) are most easily used to measure either process innovations or product innovations. In Equation (3), if all the inputs and outputs are measured properly and inputs yield only normal returns, then all endogenous contributions to output should be captured by returns to inputs, and there should be no residual difference between the weighted growth rates of inputs and the growth rate of output. Even if there is any positive residual, then it is interpreted as evidence of some source of exogenous technological change.

In the literature to measure innovations, two approaches are widely used: the growth accounting approach and econometric approach. The growth accounting approach relies on neoclassical production theory. Under constant returns to scale β's in Equation (3) are taken as factor shares, and thereby A_t is calculated as the arithmetic residual after share-weighted input growth rates are subtracted from the growth rate of output (Denison, 1979). The econometric approach estimates the parameters of Equation (3) from time series data and infers the magnitude of A_t as an econometric residual after the estimated effects of all measurable inputs on output have been allowed for (Jorgenson and Griliches, 1967; Jorgenson and Stiroh, 2000).

Measurement of TC using Equations (2) and (3) does not distinguish between the effects of innovation and diffusion; that is, representation of technological change as A_t shows improvement in productivity but does not provide the underlying information necessary to separate such improvements into movements of production frontier and the movement of existing firms towards the frontier. Note also that innovations can be undertaken either by the manufacturers or the users of industrial equipment, and this point has special significance for environment-related technological changes. When the innovations are undertaken by the manufacturers of industrial equipment, then the innovations are embodied in new capital goods and diffuse through the users via the purchase of these goods. Innovations may occur through the changes in practices that are implemented with existing equipment via the users of industrial equipment. Moreover, firms may develop new equipment for their own use, which they then may or may not undertake to sell to other firms. The fact that the locus of activity generating environment-related technological change can be supplying firms, using firms or both has important consequences for modelling the interaction of technological change and environmental policy.

The embodiment of new technology in new capital goods creates an ambiguity regarding the role played by technology diffusion with respect to Equations (2) and (3). One interpretation is that these equations represent 'best practice'; that is, what the economy would produce if all innovations made to date had fully diffused. In this interpretation, innovation would drive technological change captured in Equation (3); the issue of diffusion would then arise in the form of the presence of firms producing at points inside the production possibility frontier. Frontier estimation techniques (Aigner and Schmidt, 1980) or data envelopment methods (Fare, Grosskopf and Lovell, 1994) would be needed to measure the extent to which such sub-frontier behaviour is occurring. Alternatively, one can assume that the users of older equipment make optimal, informed decisions regarding when to scrap old machines and purchase newer ones that embody better technology. In this formulation, observed movements of the frontier – measured technological change – comprise the combined impacts of the invention, innovation and diffusion processes.

In the earlier literature on energy and environmental policy models, TC is incorporated as an exogenous variable, i.e. technological developments are autonomous and do not depend upon on policy or economic variables and there is very little empirical evidence on induced technological developments. However, recently some attempts have been made to model policy-induced technological changes in the climate-economy models.[1] Energy policy interventions may change the constraints and incentives that affect technological change. For instance, changes in current relative input prices induces factor substitution given the production technology and serve as scarcity signals, and changes in the long-run prices induce the development of new technologies and serve as innovation signals. The importance of relative prices as a stimulator of technological advancement is traceable to Hicks (1932). Hicks argues that 'a change in relative prices of factors of production is itself a spur to invention, and to invention of a particular kind – directed to economizing the use of a factor which has become relatively expensive' (1932, pp. 124–125). If for example relative energy prices rise, technological change will be energy saving, i.e. the theory of induced innovation addresses the impact of relative prices on the direction of technological change (Hayami and Ruttan, 1971).

The frontier approach used to measure total factor productivity (TFP) differs from that used conventionally where the contribution of TFP to output growth is measured residually after accounting for growth in all inputs. The conventional measurement of TFP assumes there is an aggregate production function that represents the production technology of all firms and that firms are operating on their production frontiers, producing the maximum possible output given their inputs and realizing the full potential of their technology (see survey of Nadiri, 1970; Murillo-Zamorano, 2004; Murty and Kumar, 2004; Kumar and Khanna 2009). These studies treat TFP as analogous to technical change. They either disregard pollution or model it as an additional input (which is not consistent with the material balance approach as discussed in Murty and Russell, 2002). The frontier approach used to measure TFP is based on the premise that firms do not operate on their production frontier due to organizational and other reasons and are technically inefficient; thus technical progress is not the only source of growth in TFP. Instead, TFP growth can be decomposed into that due to technical progress and changes in technical efficiency. This approach towards TFP measurement can be used to obtain a measure of the environmental productivity (EP). EP is the ratio of two estimates of TFP, one obtained under the assumption that emissions are weakly disposable and the other obtained by ignoring the generation of these emissions. The EP can be interpreted as the efficiency with which environment-friendly technologies are utilized and the costs of these technologies (e.g. Jaffe et al., 2003).

2.2 Measurement of technological change using multiple outputs framework

Kumar and Managi (2009a) develop a framework for the measurement of technological progress in the presence of multiple outputs in which some of them are undesirable. Technological change can be decomposed into two components – innovation and diffusion – and the transformation function[2] is best suited to measure technological change (Jaffe et al., 2003). The transformation function represents 'best practice', i.e. what the economy would produce if all innovations made to date had fully diffused; therefore, the shift in transformation function captures innovations. The role of diffusion would then arise if some firms are not adopting 'best practice' and operating at points inside the transformation frontier. The movement of these firms towards the frontier can be termed as 'catch-up' effect or technological diffusion (TD).[3] The present study tends to extend the literature on induced technological progress by measuring both innovations and diffusion.

There is considerable theoretical and empirical literature on induced innovation hypothesis.[4] That literature typically analyses the inducement effect in a framework of conventional representation of production technology, such as cost, production or profit functions. Distinguishing between factor substitution and shift of transformation frontiers is problematic with the conventional representations. That is, in conventional representations the first order comparative static optimization conditions cannot be followed since the direct derivatives of the demand and supply functions with respect to prices cannot be unambiguously signed, given the presence of the cross derivatives (Celikkol and Stefanou, 1999; Paris and Caputo, 2001).

Directional distance function can be used as a representation of production technology. This function simultaneously seeks to expand output and contract inputs. It is particularly well suited to the task of providing a measure of technical efficiency in the full input-output space and satisfies all those properties that are satisfied by the conventional representations. Using the dual Hotelling lemma, one can derive the inverse of input demand and supply functions from the directional distance function and also can estimate Morishima elasticities of substitution (MES) which signals factor scarcity without explicitly including the current prices in the representation of production technology. The inclusion of long-run prices can play the role of shifter of production technology, i.e. innovation signals.

2.2.1 Directional distance function

Directional distance function seeks to expand the desired output, e.g. GDP, and contract inputs such as labour, capital and energy and inherits its properties from the production technology, T.[5] More formally the function is defined as:

$$D(x, y; g) = \max_{\beta} \left\{ \beta : \left(y + \beta \cdot g_y, x - \beta \cdot g_x \right) \in T \right\} \tag{4}$$

Where $T = \{(x,y): x \text{ can produce } y\}$, and $y = (y_1,...,y_M) \in \Re_+^M$ and $x = (x_1,...,x_N) \in \Re_+^N$ are output and input vectors, respectively. The solution, β^* gives the maximum expansion and contraction of outputs and inputs, respectively. The vector $g = (g_y, -g_x)$ specifies in which direction an output–input vector, $(y, x) \in T$ is scaled so as to reach the boundary of the technology frontier at $(y + \beta^* \cdot gy, x - \beta^* \cdot gx) \in T$, where $\beta^* = D(x, y; g)$. This means that the producer becomes more technically efficient when simultaneously increasing outputs and decreasing inputs. The function takes the value of zero for technically efficient output–input vectors on the boundary of T whereas positive values apply to inefficient output vector below the boundary. The higher the value the more inefficient is the input–output vector, i.e. the directional distance function is a measure of technical inefficiency.[6]

Directional distance function and profit function are dual to each other (Färe and Grosskopf, 2000) and the dual Hotelling lemma, i.e. the derivatives of directional distance with respect to output and input quantities provide inverse supply and demand functions (Hudgins and Primont, 2004). The profit function is defined as:

$$\pi(p,r) = \max_{x,y} \{py - rx : (x, y) \in T\}$$

$$= \max_{x,y} \{py - rx : D(x, y; g) \geq 0\}$$

since $(x,y) \in T \Leftrightarrow (x - D(x,y; g)g_x, y + D(x,y; g)g_y) \in T$ by the free disposability assumption. Thus profit may be defined by the unconstrained maximization problem:

$$\pi(p,r) = \max_{x,y} \{p(y + D(x, y; g)g_y - r(x - D(x, y; g)g_x)\}$$

$$= \max_{x,y} \{py - rx + D(x, y; g)(pg_y + rg_x)\}$$

The first order conditions are:

$$-r + \nabla_x D(x, y; g)(pg_y + rg_x) = 0$$

$$p + \nabla_y D(x, y; g)(pg_y + rg_x) = 0$$

or

$$\frac{r}{pg_y + rg_x} = \nabla_x D(x, y; g)$$

$$-\frac{p}{pg_y + rg_x} = \nabla_y D(x, y; g) \tag{5}$$

These are inverse demand and supply functions for input demand and output supply respectively. Prices are normalized by the number, $pg_y + rg_x$.

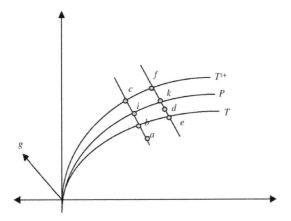

Figure 21.1 Luenberger productivity indicators

Finally, the directional distance function satisfies the translation property

$$D\left(x, y + \alpha \cdot g_y, x - \alpha \cdot g_x; g\right) = D\left(x, y; g\right) - \alpha \qquad (6)$$

where α is a positive scalar. The translation property states that if output is expanded by αg_y and inputs are contracted by αg_x, then the value of the distance function will be more efficient with the amount α.

2.2.2 *Luenberger index of technological change*

Kumar and Managi (2009b) extend the Luenberger measure of productivity change or TC,[7] introduced by Chambers et al. (1996) and Chambers (2002), to a measure that also accounts for energy price-induced innovations. The Luenberger productivity indicator is decomposed into two component measures: innovation and diffusion. We decompose innovation further into exogenous innovations (ETC) and energy price-induced innovations (ITC). This can be illustrated through Figure 21.1.

Suppose a firm in the year t with input-output (x^t, y^t) vector is operating at point a, and in the year $(t + 1)$ with the input-output vector (x^{t+1}, y^{t+1}) is at d. The technologies at these two points of time are specified as T and T^{t+1}. The shift in technology from T to T^{t+1} is the combination of energy price induced and exogenous innovations, i.e. shift in the production technology from T to P is induced by the factors such as change in relative long-term energy prices and the shift from P to T^{t+1} is due to some external factors such as advancement in science and technology. Therefore we get:

Diffusion $= (b - a) - (f - d)$
Innovation $= 0.5((f - e) + (c - b)) = 0.5(((f - k) + (k - e)) + ((c - j) + (j - b)))$

or

Innovation $= 0.5((f - k) + (c - j)) + 0.5((k - e) + (j - b)) = ETC + ITC$

Thus technological diffusion is measured by the distance of points *a* and *d* from the transformation functions T^t and T^{t+1}, respectively.[8]

Following Chambers (2002), the directional output distance function is parameterized using a (additive) quadratic flexible functional form. In our case, with one output, three inputs, time trend and long-run relative energy prices, the particular form is

$$D^{kt}(x^{kt}, y^{kt}, b^{kt}; g, t, \bar{r}) = \alpha_0 + \sum_{n=1}^{3} \alpha_n x_n^{kt} + \beta_1 y^{kt} + \gamma_1 t + \gamma_2 \bar{r}^{kt}$$

$$+ \frac{1}{2} \sum_{n=1}^{3} \sum_{n'=1}^{3} \alpha_{nn'} x_n^{kt} x_{n'}^{kt} + \sum_{n=1}^{3} \delta_{n1} x_n^{kt} y^{kt} + \sum_{n=1}^{3} \eta_{n1} x_n^{kt} t + \sum_{n=1}^{3} \eta_{n2} x_n^{kt} \bar{r}^{kt} \qquad (7)$$

$$+ \frac{1}{2} \beta_2 y^{kt} y^{kt} + \mu_1 y^{kt} t + \mu_2 y^{kt} \bar{r}^{kt} + \frac{1}{2} \gamma_{11} t.t + \varphi t \bar{r}^{kt} + \frac{1}{2} \gamma_{22} \bar{r}^{kt} . \bar{r}^{kt}$$

with

$$\alpha_{nn'} = \alpha_{n'n}; \beta_1 - \sum_{n=1}^{3} \alpha_n = -1; \delta_{n1} - \sum_{n=1}^{3} \alpha_{nn'} = 0; \beta_2 - \sum_{n=1}^{3} \delta_{n1} = 0; n = 1, 2, 3.$$

where $g = (1, -1)$, 1 refers to g_y and -1 refers to $-g_b$; and t is a time-trend, $\bar{r}$ is the long-run energy prices.

The specification of (7) allows for neutral and biased technological changes. The effect of neutral exogenous technological change is captured by the coefficients γ_1 and γ_{11} and the effect of neutral induced technological change is captured by the coefficients γ_2 and γ_{22}. The extent of input biased exogenous and induced technological change are captured by the coefficients η_{n1} and η_{n2} respectively; the effect of changes in output due to exogenous and induced factors (i.e. scale augmenting technological change) is captured by the coefficients μ_1 and μ_2, respectively. In addition, the interaction between exogenous and induced factors is captured by the coefficient φ. The directional distance function is parameterized in quadratic form; hence it is possible to apply Diewert's (1976) quadratic identity lemma.[9] Using this identity, changes in the directional distance function from one period to the next can be written as:

$$(D^t - D^{t+1}) = 0.5 \left[\frac{\partial D^t}{\partial y} + \frac{\partial D^{t+1}}{\partial y} \right].(y^{t+1} - y^t) + 0.5 \sum_{n=1}^{3} \left[\frac{\partial D^t}{\partial x_n} + \frac{\partial D^{t+1}}{\partial x_n} \right].(x_n^{t+1} - x_n^t)$$

$$+ 0.5 \left[\frac{\partial D^{t+1}}{\partial t} + \frac{\partial D^t}{\partial t} \right] + 0.5 \left[\frac{\partial D^{t+1}}{\partial \bar{r}} + \frac{\partial D^t}{\partial \bar{r}} \right].(\bar{r}^t - \bar{r}^{t+1}) \qquad (8)$$

where D^t is short for $D(x^t, y^t; g, t, \bar{r})$. Technological change (*TC*) can be defined as:

$$TC = -0.5 \left[\frac{-\partial D^{t+1}}{\partial y} + \frac{-\partial D^t}{\partial y} \right].(y^{t+1} - y^t) + 0.5 \sum_{n=1}^{3} \left[\frac{\partial D^{t+1}}{\partial x_n} + \frac{\partial D^t}{\partial x_n} \right].(x_n^{t+1} - x_n^t) \qquad (9)$$

Technological change can be broadly defined as the difference of the weighted average rates of change in outputs and inputs, where the weights are derivatives of directional distance function

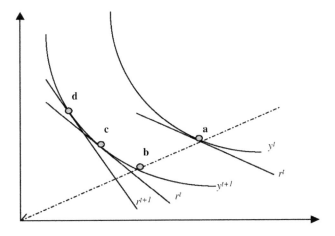

Figure 21.2　Decomposition of energy price-induced innovation

with respect to (negative) output and (positive) inputs respectively. Rearranging equation (8), TC can be decomposed as:

$$TC = \underbrace{(D^{t+1} - D^t)}_{Diffusion} - 0.5\underbrace{\left[\frac{\partial D^{t+1}}{\partial t} + \frac{\partial D^t}{\partial t}\right]}_{ETC} - 0.5\underbrace{\left[\frac{\partial D^{t+1}}{\partial \bar{r}} + \frac{\partial D^t}{\partial \bar{r}}\right].(\bar{r}^{t+1} - \bar{r}^t)}_{ITC} \qquad (10)$$

　　Equation (9) provides a meaningful decomposition of TC into diffusion, exogenous innovations, ETC, and energy-price induced innovations, ITC, respectively. Negative values of the derivatives of directional distance function with respect to time-trend and long-run energy prices imply positive ETC and ITC, respectively. Therefore, the negative value of each components of productivity index implies positive change in TC.[10]

　　The TC, either exogenous or induced, can be further decomposed into two categories: changes due to shifts in the production technology and change in usage decisions regarding use of a particular input due to change in its relative prices along the new production technology frontier. The changes of production technology can be sub-divided into two categories: neutral technological changes and biased technological changes. Neutral technological change implies a shift in the technological frontier, i.e. isoquant towards the origin making it possible to produce the same level of output with lesser quantities of inputs, and biased technological change implies a change in the slope of frontier and the decision point of the firm is not on the ray to the origin even without change in relative prices. Newell et al. (1999) take the term 'innovation' to encompass the combined effect of all these change in a microeconomic product-level phenomenon. The decomposition of technological change or innovation can be illustrated through Figure 21.2.

　　Suppose to produce GDP at point t an economy is employing two factors of production, namely, capital and energy. Further assume that this economy takes decision at point **a**, given technical possibilities represented by y^t and the slope of price line r^t which represent the relative price of energy relevant for the choice of optimal choice of energy efficiency. Assume also that, at some time $t + 1$, technical possibilities have improved as represented by the shift of the isoquant from y^t to $y^{t + 1}$, and that energy prices also have changed so that the price line now has the slope of r^{t+1} instead of r^t. Accordingly, the optimal production decision is now taken at point **d**.

The improvement can be decomposed between points **a** and **d** into the movements from **a** to **b**, from **b** to **c**, and from **c** to **d**. Point **b** is the point on the new isoquant that lies on a ray to the origin from the initial point **a**. Hence, the movement from **a** to **b** represents equi-proportionate lesser usage of capital and energy, measuring neutral technological change. Point **c** lies at the tangency between the new isoquant and the old price line, thus the movement from **b** to **c** measures the effect on energy use of the tilt in the isoquant between time t and $t + 1$, which we call bias in the usage of inputs or biased technological change. Finally, the point **d** is the new optimum and the movement from **c** to **d** is the 'substitution effect' brought about by the change in price from r^t to r^{t+1} along the new production isoquant y^{t+1}. Sections 2.3 and 2.4 deal with the measurement of factor usage bias and the elasticity of substitution in directional distance function context.

2.2.3 Factor using bias

Generally there are two approaches for measuring the factor using bias of technological change. Hicks suggested a pairwise comparison approach based on the marginal rate of technical substitution. However, this approach becomes cumbersome to interpret the results for three or more inputs case.

Binswanger (1974) introduced multifactor input bias measures using the changes in factor cost share attributed to technical change. Antle (1984) develops a profit-based multifactor measure of biased technical change, which is similar to the cost-share approach. Antle (1984) defines the impact of technical progress on input decisions for factor i as the proportionate change in the cost-share of elasticity of factor I, $\frac{\varepsilon_i}{\varepsilon}$ due to proportionate change in ETC, measured by $B_{it}^E = \frac{\partial \ln(\varepsilon_i/\varepsilon)}{\partial \ln t}$, and due to proportionate change in ITC, measured as $B_{it}^I = \frac{\partial \ln(\varepsilon_i/\varepsilon)}{\partial \ln \bar{r}}$, where

$$\frac{\varepsilon_i}{\varepsilon} = -\frac{\partial \ln G}{\partial \ln r_i} \bigg/ -\sum_{i=1}^{n} \frac{\partial \ln G}{\partial \ln r_i} \text{, G is the convex profit function of normalized input prices and}$$

exogenous variables such as long-term relative energy prices, time trend etc.; t is the measure of exogenous technical change and $\bar{r}$ is the measure of relative price change in factor prices with which we are interested in measuring the bias of ITC. In the present study, it is the relative change in the prices of energy.

As noted earlier, the profit function and directional distance function are dual to each other. Using Hotelling lemma, one can derive the input demand functions as the derivative of profit function with respect to input prices. Similarly, using the dual Hotelling lemma, we can derive the inverse of the input demand functions as the derivative of directional distance function with respect to input quantities. The measures of factor using bias for exogenous and induced technical change can be expressed as follow:

$$\frac{\varepsilon_i}{\varepsilon} = -\frac{\partial \ln D}{\partial \ln x_i} \bigg/ -\sum_{i=1}^{n} \frac{\partial \ln D}{\partial \ln x_i}$$

$$B_{it}^E = \frac{\partial \ln(\varepsilon_i / \varepsilon)}{\partial \ln t} \tag{11}$$

$$B_{it}^I = \frac{\partial \ln(\varepsilon_i / \varepsilon)}{\partial \ln \bar{r}}$$

The factor using bias associated with technological progress is:

$$
i^{th} \text{ factor } \begin{cases} Saving \\ Neutral \\ Augmenting \end{cases} \text{ when } B_{it}^{k} \begin{cases} > \\ = \\ < \end{cases} 0
$$

for $k = E, I$ and i = labour, capital and energy.

2.2.4 Elasticity of substitution

Sue Wing (2006) develops a theory in the context of climate change policy by adding external-ities and environmental taxation to Acemoglu's (2002) model. Sue Wing shows that an environ-mental tax always biases production away from the dirty good towards the clean good. However, this does not necessarily mean that the environmental tax also biases innovation towards research on the clean good. Rather, this depends on the substitutability between clean and dirty inputs. If the clean input is not readily substitutable for the more expensive dirty input, the absolute quan-tity of dirty R&D exhibits a hump-shaped profile so that it increases under small environmental taxes but declines under higher environmental taxes. That is, a low environmental tax encourages research to make the dirty input more productive, so as to get more output from each unit of the dirty input.

Using the same framework of directional distance function, one can estimate the curvature of the boundary of the production technology. The curvature measures how the input price ratio changes as the relative input intensity (ratio of inputs) changes. Following Blackorby and Russell (1989) and Grosskopf et al. (1995), the indirect MES between different inputs are defined as:

$$
\sigma_{ij} = \frac{\partial \ln(r_i / r_j)}{\partial \ln(x_j / x_i)}
$$

and in terms of directional distance function the MES, following Färe et al. (2005) can be specified as:

$$
\sigma_{ij} = x_j \star \left(\frac{D_{ij}(x, y; g)}{D_i(x, y; g)} \right) - x_j \star \left(\frac{D_{jj}(x, y; g)}{D_j(x, y; g)} \right) \tag{12}
$$

Where $x_j^{\star} = x_j - D(x, y; g)$ and r is the vector of factor prices and the subscripts on the dis-tance functions refer to partial derivatives with respect to inputs: e.g. $D_{ij}(x, y; g)$ is the second order partial derivative of the distance function with respect to x_j. The first derivatives of the distance function with respect to inputs yield the normalized shadow price of that input; therefore, the first line of the definition may be thought of as the ratio of percentage change in shadow prices brought about by a one-percentage change in the ratio of inputs. Higher and positive values of σ_{ij} (higher in absolute terms) indicate limited substitution possibilities between inputs.

Here it should be noted that the Morishima and Allen elasticities yield the same result in the two-input case; when the number of inputs exceeds two, however, they no longer coincide.

Moreover, the MES may not be symmetric, i.e. $\sigma_{ij} \neq \sigma_{ji}$. This is as it should be and allows for the asymmetry in the substitutability of different inputs.

3. Environmental policy and technological change

The most widespread method of treating technological change in environmental policy modelling is to consider it an exogenous variable – simply an autonomous function of time. The fundamental distinction between exogenous technological change and endogenous technological change is that with exogenous technological change, production possibilities depend only on time, whereas with endogenous technological change, these possibilities can depend in a variety of ways on past, present, and/or future expected prices and policy. Thus, with endogenous technological change, current technological possibilities for producing output with various combinations of capital, labor and emissions limits depend on past activities. In turn, there is a dependence of future technological possibilities on current actions.

In the short run, optimal level of pollution in a society is determined at the point where the marginal cost (MC) of pollution abatement is equal to the marginal benefits of a cleaner environment. The trade-off between the marginal cost of abatement and the benefits of cleaner environment is altered through the introduction of technology in the equation. Environmental technological innovations are supposed to reduce the marginal cost of achieving a given unit of pollution reduction. These innovations also may change the shape and slope of these marginal costs.

The innovation of a technology that reduces the marginal costs of abatement shifts the innovating firm's marginal costs of abatement downwards and this shifts the industry's marginal costs of abatement from MC to MC' as depicted in Figure 21.3. This will lead to cost savings of e_mAB for achieving a given level of abatement e'. Adoption of the technology by all firms in the industry will reduce each firm's marginal costs of abatement and shift the industry marginal costs of abatement even further, to MC", and leads to further social gains. Optimal agency response occurs when the policymaker adjusts the optimal level of abatement taking into account the new marginal costs of abatement. The optimal level of abatement is now set at e" and social welfare increases by the amount CAD. Different environmental policy instruments vary in the incentives they provide to a firm to undertake innovation in a marginal cost of abatement reducing technology.

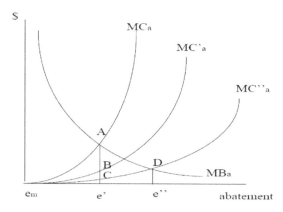

Fig. 21.3 Innovations and marginal costs of abatement

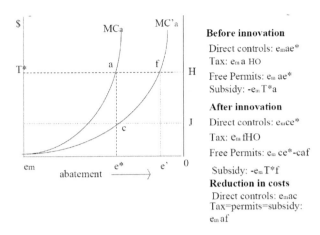

Before innovation

Direct controls: e$_m$ae*

Tax: e$_m$ a HO

Free Permits: e$_m$ ae*

Subsidy: -e$_m$ T*a

After innovation

Direct controls: e$_m$ce*

Tax: e$_m$ fHO

Free Permits: e$_m$ ce*-caf

Subsidy: -e$_m$ T*f

Reduction in costs

Direct controls: e$_m$ac

Tax=permits=subsidy:

e$_m$ af

Figure 21.4 Impact of innovation on costs of abatement under alternative policies

Environmental policy helps in shaping the direction of technological change. In the absence of environmental policy, firms have no incentive to use clear equipment or to find new ways of emissions reduction. This can lead early, pre-policy predictions of the net benefits of environmental regulation to be lower than evaluations after the fact, as newly developed technologies lower the costs of complying with regulation (Harrington et al., 2000). More recently, environmental economists have paid increasing attention to estimating the rate at which technology improves, as well as the role of technology policy itself to supplement the effects of environmental policy.

The basic model consists of three stages. First, an innovating firm decides how much to invest in R&D by setting its marginal cost of innovation equal to the expected marginal benefits. Second, polluting firms decide whether or not to adopt the new technology, use an (inferior) imitation of it or do nothing. Finally, firms minimize pollution control expenditures by setting their marginal costs equal to the price of pollution. Policy instruments affect the innovation incentives primarily through three effects: 1) an abatement cost affect, reflecting the extent to which innovation reduces the costs of pollution control; 2) an imitation effect, which weakens innovation incentives due to imperfect appropriability; and 3) an emissions payment effect, which can weaken incentives if innovation reduces firms' payments for residual emissions. The relative strength of these effects will vary across policy instruments and particular applications, with no instrument clearly dominating in all applications.

Milliman and Prince (1989) examine the incentives provided by alternative environmental policies for a firm to innovate and adopt a technology, which reduces the marginal costs of abatement. There are three steps in the process of technological change: a) innovation by a firm; b) diffusion to other firms in the industry; and c) optimal agency response by adjusting environmental policy parameters in response to innovations.

Five policies are examined here: direct controls, emissions subsidies, emissions taxes, marketable permits distributed free and auctioned marketable permits.

In Figure 21.4, direct controls on emissions limit emissions to e★, the tax on emissions and the price of permits needed to achieve an equivalent level of pollution is T★ and the subsidy for reducing emissions below e$_m$ is T★.

3.1 Impact of alternative policies on incentives to innovate

Incentives to adopt end-of-pipe technologies that only serve to reduce emissions must come from environmental regulation. Therefore, it is not surprising that studies addressing adoption of environmental technologies find that regulations dominate all other firm-specific factors. In contrast, energy efficiency and fuel-saving technologies may be adopted more slowly, as it is cost savings, rather than a direct regulatory requirement, that often matters. This can be influenced by policies that raise energy prices. However, to the extent that fuel prices do not capture the external costs of energy use, such as carbon emissions, energy prices alone will not encourage a socially optimal level of adoption for energy efficiency technologies. With direct controls on emissions, the costs of abatement prior to innovation at $e^\star$ are $e_m ae^\star$. After innovation these costs decrease to $e_m ce^\star$. The gain due to innovation is $e_m ac$.

Under an emissions tax policy, costs of abatement prior to the innovation are the costs of abatement plus the tax payments on remaining emissions $= e_m ae^\star + e^\star aHO = e_m aHO$.

Under the tax policy, after the innovation, the costs of abatement decrease to $e_m fe'$ and the tax payments are now $e'fHO$, with total costs of abatement equal to $e_m fHO$. The reduction in total costs of abatement to the firm are: $e_m af$.

Under a free permit policy with $e^\star$ permits, initial costs of abatement are $e_m ae^\star$. After innovation, the innovating firm's marginal costs of abatement decreases while that of the others stays at MC_a as before. At price $T^\star$ the innovating firm will increase abatement to e' and sell $e^\star - e'$ permits, earning a revenue of $e^\star afe'$. However, the additional abatement it has to undertake implies costs of $e^\star fe'$. Hence the net gain in revenue is caf. The reduction in costs of abatement for $e^\star$ emissions is $e_m ac$. Total gains are $e_m ac + caf = e_m af$.

Under a subsidy policy that subsidizes at rate $T^\star$ for reducing emissions below e_m, the costs of abatement prior to innovation net of subsidy payments received are: $- e_m ae^\star + T^\star ae^\star e_m = e_m T^\star a$. After the innovation, at the same subsidy rate $T^\star$, the firm increases abatement to e' and now its costs of abatement are: $e_m fe'$ and the subsidy payments it receives are $e_m T^\star fe'$. As compared to the pre-innovation costs, its costs are now $e_m T^\star f$ and the gain to the firm is $e_m T^\star f - e_m T^\star a = e_m af$.

Under auctioned permits, costs of abatement plus cost of permits auctioned at price $T^\star$ prior to innovation are the same as under an emissions tax because it now has to pay for the permit to pollute each unit, like under an emissions tax policy: $e_m aHO$. After innovation, with the price of the permits at $T^\star$, the gains from innovation are again identical to an emissions tax. Hence direct controls provide the least reduction in costs of abatement due to innovation (see Figure 21.5).

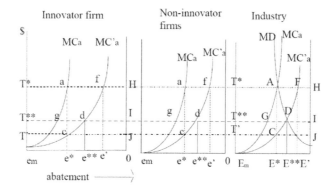

Figure 21.5 Innovation and its impact on different firms and industry under different policies

Gains to the innovating firm from promoting diffusion

Under a direct control policy: $e_m ce^\star - e_m ce^\star = 0$
Under an emissions tax: $e_m fH0 - e_m fH0 = 0$
Under an abatement subsidy: $e_m T^\star f - e_m T^\star f = 0$
Under an auctioned permit policy: $e_m cJ0 - e_m fHO = cfHJ$
Under a free permits policy: $(e_m ce^\star - caf) - e_m ce^\star = -caf$

Gains to the non- innovating firm adopting the new technology

Reduction in abatement costs:
Under a direct control policy: $e_m ac$
Under an emissions tax: $e_m af$
Under an abatement subsidy: $e_m af$
Under an auctioned permit policy: $e_m aHO - e_m cJO = e_m aHJc$
Under a free permits policy: $e_m ae^\star - e_m ce^\star = e_m ac$

3.2 Impact of alternative policies on incentives to innovate due to diffusion of technology to other firms in the industry

Studies of the diffusion of environmental technologies within firms focus on two main questions. First, what is the theoretical and empirical potential for induced diffusion of lower-emissions technologies? Specifically, how do environmental policy instruments that implicitly or explicitly increase the economic incentive to reduce emissions affect the diffusion rate of these technologies? Second, to what extent have market failures in energy and equipment markets limited historical diffusion rates of energy efficient technologies?

For the innovator firm, with an unchanged emissions tax rate, subsidy rate or standard on emissions, diffusion of the technology to the other firms in the industry lead to no change in abatement costs. Under a free permit policy, prior to diffusion, the innovating firm becomes a seller of permits and earns revenue of $e^\star afe'$ after it adopted the new technology. After the diffusion of the technology to all firms, the demand for permits will fall and the price of permits will fall to T'. Net loss in revenues is area caf. Hence diffusion has a negative impact on incentives to innovate when a marketable permit is used.

Under auctioned permits, the diffusion of the technology to all firms in the industry will reduce each firm's marginal costs of abatement and increase abatement to $e^{\star\star}$. The price of permits will fall to T' and this will lead to post diffusion costs of abatement of $e_m cJO$. Compared to costs $e_m fHO$ for the innovator without diffusion, the gain due to diffusion is cfHJ. Unlike an emissions tax, which if kept constant at $T^\star$ does not affect the incentives for innovation due to diffusion, auctioned permits create positive incentives for innovation due to the gains in revenue caused by diffusion.

3.3 Industry incentives to promote optimal agency response

Change in industry costs of abatement with optimal agency response under:

Direct controls: $E_m CE^\star - E_m DE^{\star\star} < 0$
Emissions Subsidy: $- E_m T^\star F - E_m T^{\star\star}D < 0$
Emissions Tax: $E_m FHO - E_m DIO > 0$

Auctioned Permits: $E_mCJO - E_mDIO < 0$

Free Permits: $E_mCE\star - E_mDE\star\star < 0$

3.4 Incentives to innovate under alternative policies with optimal agency response

After the environmental agency responds to the reduction in abatement costs and changes the tax rate to equate the new marginal costs of abatement to the marginal benefits of adoption, the tax rate will fall to $T\star\star$. The costs of abatement under the tax are now: $e_mde\star\star + e\star\star dIO = e_mdIO$. The gain due to innovation is $e_maHO - e_mdIO = e_maHId$.

Under direct controls, the increase in optimal abatement standard to $e\star\star$ implies that costs of abatement are: $e_mde\star\star$. As compared to pre-innovation costs of $e_mae\star$ the gains from innovation are uncertain.

3.5 Gains to the innovator from the entire process of technological change

Direct Control: $e_mae\star - e_mde\star$ uncertain

Emissions Subsidy: $e_mT\star a - e_mT\star\star d$ uncertain

Emission Tax: $e_maHO - e_mdIO > 0$

Auctioned Permits: $e_maHO - e_mdIO > 0$

Free Permits: $e_mae\star - e_mde\star$ uncertain

The gains from the entire process of innovation are uncertain under a subsidy and a marketable permits policy. Auctioned permits and emissions tax are the only two policies that provide positive gains from the process of innovation. Both policies are identical in their incentives for innovation.

This approach is focusing on end-of-pipe abatement of pollution and ignores potential for abatement by adopting technologies that change the production process and reduce pollution at source. It also assumes that all firms in the industry are identical and respond identically to the introduction of an abatement technology. Pollution is considered to be easily monitored and all the policies considered are pollution-based policies. This may not be possible in the case of non-point pollution, where it is difficult to identify the polluters and to measure the pollution generated by them. It also does not consider the impact of abatement on industry output and input-use.

Recently, Fischer and Newell (2008) use a micro approach to study a broader set of policy options that provide incentives to the firms in the adoption of new technologies reducing carbon emissions and encourage the firm in innovating and adoption of renewable energy technologies. They evaluate the relative performance of policies according to incentives provided for emissions reduction and economic efficiency and also assess how the nature of technological progress and the degree of knowledge spill overs affects the desirability of different policies. Although the relative cost of individual policies in achieving emissions reductions depends on parameter values and the emissions target. Based on their empirical analysis they rank the different policies as follows: 1) emissions price, 2) emissions performance standard, 3) fossil power tax, 4) renewables share requirement, 5) renewables subsidy, and 6) R&D subsidy. Nonetheless, an optimal portfolio of policies – including emissions pricing and R&D – achieves emission reductions at significantly lower cost than any single policy.

Most empirical studies of environmental technology adoption focus on one of the two questions. First are the studies examining the relationship between environmental policy and adoption. The focus on adoption of pollution-control techniques. A common finding in this literature is that environmental regulation is necessary to encourage adoption of pollution-control techniques. Second are the studies asking whether adoption eventually reaches socially efficient levels or if market failures hinder the adoption of environmentally friendly technologies. These studies primarily focus on the adoption of energy efficiency technologies.

Although difficult to categorize neatly, the most commonly used approaches model endogenous technological change in one of three ways: direct price-induced, R&D-induced and learning-induced. Direct price-induced technological change implies that changes in relative prices can spur innovation to reduce the use of the more expensive input (e.g. energy) in accordance with the Hicks-induced innovation hypothesis. R&D-induced technological change allows for R&D investment to influence the rate and direction of technological change. It often involves an explicit knowledge capital stock. Finally, learning-induced technological change allows for the unit cost of a particular technology to be a decreasing function of the experience with that technology. Learning-by-doing is the most commonly employed method used in this approach, where the unit cost of a technology is typically modelled as a decreasing function of its cumulative output.

Title IV of the 1990 Clean Air Act Amendments (1990 CAAA) introduces an emissions permit trading system to regulate SO_2 emissions from US thermal power plants. The policy was implemented to reduce damage from acidification while achieving the lowest compliance costs.[11] The often-cited measure of the success of the program is that the market allowance prices were substantially lower than the marginal compliance costs initially predicted. The decline in compliance costs can be attributed to three factors: i) a decline in fuel prices coupled with a reduction in rail transportation costs for low sulphur western coal; ii) exogenous technological progress that would have occurred in the absence of the program; and iii) the technological progress that has been ignited by the allowance trading program (Burtraw et al., 2005). Using a production frontier approach, this study disentangles these effects by estimating exogenous (i.e. the aggregate of (i) and (ii)) and technological progress induced by the allowance system (i.e. (iii)) that occurred from 1995 to 2007.

Environmental policy is designed to enhance incentives for the development and utilization of environmentally friendly technologies beyond static efficiency (Kneese and Schulze, 1975).[12] Firms change their technology in various directions depending upon prices and costs, which may be influenced by environmental regulations. Several theoretical studies show the advantages of market-based instruments over command-and-control regulations for inducing technological progress.[13] Some recent studies have empirically examined the dynamic effects of environmental policy in the US electricity sector (Keohane, 2002; Popp, 2003). Keohane (2002) has found an increase in the adoption of new scrubber technology after the 1990 CAAA. Popp (2003) used patent data to measure the level of innovation. He found that while successful patent applications for flue gas desulfurization units were higher before the introduction of the 1990 CAAA, the post-1990 CAAA had more positive environmental effects. However, Lange and Bella (2005) find that while scrubbers installed under the 1990 CAAA are less expensive to purchase and operate than older scrubbers, these cost reductions appear as a one-time drop rather than a continual decline.

We now turn to empirical applications measuring the role of market-based instruments in technological developments. The US's SO_2 trading program is considered as one of the successful applications of the market-based instruments in the area of environment. Innovations under SO_2 allowance trading are not limited to scrubbing; rather, other abatement options, such as organizational changes at the firm, market, and regulatory level, as well as process changes, are also allowed (Burtraw, 2000). Kolstad and Turnovsky (1998) and Considine and Larson (2006) showed that technological change has conserved sulphur, thereby supporting the notion that technological progress has been responsible, at least in part, for the drop in the abatement costs of SO_2 emissions. Similarly, Carlson et al. (2000) found the approximate 20 percent declines in marginal abatement costs from 1985 to 1995 can be attributed to exogenous technological changes. However, these studies do not distinguish the technological progress that is exogenous (that is, technological progress that happened even in the absence of allowance trading) and the technological changes that were ignited by allowance trading. This study fills this void by decomposing the technological progress into exogenous and induced components so that the contribution of the allowance trading system can be explicitly recognized.

Kumar and Managi (2010b) measure TC for US thermal power plants from 1995 to 2007. TC is similar in nature to any investment process, as it requires time and adjustment that is not instantaneous, and the choice of technology is influenced by long-term prices. A time trend variable is used to measure exogenous innovation.[14] Similarly, the inclusion of long-term allowance prices, as a factor accounting for shifts in the transformation function, is used to measure the induced innovation effect.

The U.S. Environmental Protection Agency holds auctions of allowances each year and electric utilities and brokers also can sell their allowances at these auctions. The auctions are held in two categories: 1) a spot allowance auction, and 2) an advance allowance auction. The first category consists of allowances that are sold and can be used in the same year for compliance purposes, while the latter category includes allowances that become usable for compliance seven years after the transaction date, although they can be traded earlier. Thus, the spot allowance auction prices can be considered current prices, and the advance auction prices may be used as long-term emission prices.[15]

The notion that long-run prices may serve as a stimulating factor for innovation is a critical component of the price-induced innovation model. Changes in current prices induce factor substitution, whereas changes in long-run prices induce the development of new technologies and may lead to shifts in the technology frontier. The movements in allowance prices may help in understanding the evolution of the allowance trading market. At the opening of Phase I of the program in 1995, the average spot prices were about US$130 per ton at current prices and fell to about US$66 per ton in 1996. Thereafter, allowance prices experienced an upward trend, and in 1999, they reached US$200 per ton.[16] Kumar and Managi (2010b) find that allowance prices continuously increased to US$860 but then in 2007 declined to US$433. The seven-year advance auction price increased during 2002 to 2005 and reached its highest value at US$260 in 2005 but then declined. Some studies (Carlson et al., 2000) have shown that the rate of increase in allowance prices corresponds roughly to the opportunity cost of holding emissions allowances in the bank.

Kumar and Managi (2010b) decompose TC into two components: ETC and ITC. Overall, they observe a positive ETC effect of the magnitude of about eight percent per year from 1995 to 2007. During the initial years, they observe an increasing trend in ETC, but then it starts to decline and reaches its lowest growth rate of about five percent in 2001 to 2002. Afterward, it starts to increase at a rate of about 11.5 percent in 2005 to 2006. Similarly, during Phase I, they observe significant growth in ETC for both, plants required to participate in Phase I and plants not required to do so; the ETC growth rate is higher for the group required to participate in Phase I.

That is, the growth rate of ETC was about nine percent per year for the plants that participated in Phase I, while other plants observed an ETC growth rate of about eight percent per year. The positive and substantial contribution of ETC to TFP indicates that the progress of general science and technological made a significant contribution during these time periods. This finding is contrary to the findings of Gollop and Roberts (1983), Yaisawarng and Klein (1994), and Kolstad and Turnovsky (1998), all of which show both positive and negative productivity growth at different times over their sample periods.

Measurement of technological progress induced by the allowance trading system is their main concern. Kumar and Managi (2010b) observe that electricity-generating plants experience positive ITC effects during the period under study, i.e. electricity-generating plants are able to increase electricity and reduce the emissions of SO_2 and NO_x from 1995 to 2007 due to introduction of an allowance trading system. Yearly results indicate that the growth rate of ITC is about 0.14 percent per year. Moreover, it is also evident that the growth rate of ITC is higher during Phase II of the program relative to Phase I. Here it should be noted that the contribution of ITC to TC increases over the period under study. At the beginning of the allowance trading system, the contribution of ITC to TC was about one percent; this rate has increased to about two percent by 2006.

Both Phase I and non-Phase I groups witnessed positive ITC effects during Phase I of the allowance trading program. The ITC growth rate is higher for plants required to participate in allowance trading during Phase I in comparison to their non-Phase I counterparts. The ITC growth rates are about 0.13 and 0.10 percent per year for these Phase I and non-Phase I groups, respectively. Moreover, they observe that the contribution of ITC to TC is higher in the former group relative to the latter group. For the plants that participated during Phase I, the contribution of ITC to TC is about 1.5 percent per year, whereas for the other group, it is about 1.2 percent per year on average.

The pattern of technological change in these two groups of plants is consistent with the pattern of SO_2 emissions reductions during Phase I. Ellerman et al. (2000) found that the SO_2 emissions not only substantially fall to previous levels, but they also fall relative to levels that would have seemingly been achieved in the absence of allowance trading during Phase I of the program. Recall that Phase II of the trading program started in January 2000, and since then, all electricity-generating plants were required to participate in the trading. That is, they are now restricted to emitting 1.2 pounds of SO_2 per million BTUs of heat input. From 2000 to 2001, electricity-generating plants experienced increased ITC effects of about 0.14 percent. In addition, the performance of Phase I plants is slightly higher in comparison to other plants from 1998 to 1999. This finding is in accordance with the estimates of the patterns of emissions reductions between these two groups. Ellerman (2003) found that about 83 percent of the reductions in SO_2 emissions in 2001 from the projected baseline occurred at large, dirty plants, that is, Phase I plants.

Moreover, Kumar and Managi (2010b) observe that the timing of ITC effects is in line with economic theory. ITC effects are larger in years that have seen higher long-term allowance prices, e.g. the seven-year allowance auction price is higher. For example, the long-term prices are higher in Phase II relative to Phase I, and the ITC effect is 0.15 percent per year during Phase II relative to 0.10 percent per year during Phase I. The ITC effect is higher during years when long-term allowance prices are higher than in the preceding years.

Exogenous TC output bias results indicate that from 1995 to 2007, ETC effects increased electricity and reduced emissions except for the initial two years. In 1995 and 1996, ETC effects reduced both electricity and emissions. ETC output bias results also show that over the period under study, technological progress increased electricity less but reduced emissions more so, as the magnitude of bias reduces electricity and increases emissions over time in absolute terms. Similar results are obtained regarding induced technological progress. In general, the magnitude of bias arising from exogenous forces is higher than the bias arising from allowance prices, thus suggesting that exogenous innovations effects dominate price-induced technological progress.

Exogenous output bias results indicate that the Phase I plants experienced technological progress that increased electricity and NO_x emissions and reduced SO_2 emissions during Phase I. However, in this group, exogenous technological progress reduced electricity and increased emissions in 1995. ETC continued to increase NO_x emissions only up to 1997, after which it reduces NO_x emissions. Similar trends are observed with respect to induced technological progress. Among non-Phase I plants, exogenous technological change increases electricity and reduces emissions, except in 1996. In 1996, ETC reduces both electricity and emissions. These findings are in line with the observed behaviour of SO_2 and NO_x emissions. Between 1985 and 1998, Färe et al. (2007) observed substitutability between the emissions of SO_2 and NO_x. Output bias resulting from induced innovation indicates that allowance price changes lead to technological progress, which in turn results in an increase in electricity and a reduction in emissions.

4. Technological change and climate policy

Most of the empirical studies on induced innovations are conducted using firm-level industrial data and measure technological progress either in terms of inputs (e.g. investments or R&D spending in energy saving innovations (ESI)) or outputs (e.g. the number of patents filed, granted or cited in the area of ESI). But at macro level, though data on energy R&D spending is collected in some countries, to get the comparable data across countries is a daunting task. Moreover, the data collected by International Energy Agency on energy R&D do not encompass deployment activities, which are essential components in technological progress (Gallagher et al., 2006).

Popp (2002), using output measure of ESI, analyses the induced innovation hypothesis on a macroeconomic level. He uses U.S. patent data from 1970 to 1994 to estimate the effect of energy prices on innovations and finds positive association between energy prices and energy saving innovations. Patent data cannot be an appropriate measure of technological change because inventions might not be widely deployed (Basberg, 1987). For example, if a country produces a lot of useless patents that are never deployed, the country should not be rated as innovative relative to another country with the same or less number of patents that are more useful.

Newell et al. (1999) also provide evidence of energy price-induced innovations using a product-characteristics framework. Using most tangible output metric of ESI, they find that the energy prices have positively affected the energy efficiency of electrical appliances. Gallagher et al. (2006) point out that this output metric is again loaded with problems since technologies are discrete and not often well defined, and ESIs relate to more energy-efficient system integration, which relies heavily on the accumulated knowledge of those doing the integration.

In contrast to pollution-control technologies, energy efficiency technologies will diffuse even without environmental policy in place, as they offer users the opportunity of cost savings.

Fisher-Vanden et al. (2006) use a panel of 22,000 Chinese large and medium enterprises to study improvements in energy efficiency. Between 1997 and 1999, total energy use fell by 17 percent. 54 percent of this decline can be explained by price changes. Technological change, measured by firm-level R&D, accounts for 17 percent of this change, and changes in ownership account for another 12 percent. Looking more closely at the role of technological change, they find that imported technology saves labor and energy, whereas internal R&D from Chinese firms saves capital and energy. They explain this difference by noting that technological change responds to the resource scarcities in the country supplying the technology. They also find that a firm's in-house technological activities are important for creating absorptive capacity needed for successful diffusion of imported technology.

Nordhaus (2002) compares this endogenous technological change specification with the specification in DICE (Dynamic Integrated Model of Climate and the Economy) (where carbon intensity only is affected by mitigation efforts substituting abatement for consumption). His primary conclusion is that induced innovation is likely to be less powerful of a factor in reducing emissions than substitution.

One important feature underlying these results is a crowding-out effect where expansion of knowledge generation in one sector comes at a cost to other sectors due to the limited pool of knowledge-generating resources (i.e. there is a positive and increasing opportunity cost to R&D in one sector). A carbon-tax policy serves to spur R&D in the alternative energy sector but discourages R&D in non-energy and conventional energy sectors due both to slower growth of output in those industries and the limited pool of knowledge-generating resources. On the other hand, the knowledge spill over effects, whereby policy-induced R&D has social returns above private returns, provide additional benefits from a climate policy above the environmental benefits. However, the presence of endogenous technological change with spill overs does not imply the possibility of zero-cost carbon abatement, unless the spill overs overwhelm the crowding out effect, a largely empirical question.

Changes in production factors are expected to change the constraints and incentives that affect technological change (TC). The importance of relative prices as a stimulator of TC is traceable to Hicks, who argues that 'a change in relative prices of factors of production is itself a spur to invention, and to invention of a particular kind – directed to economizing the use of a factor which has become relatively expensive' (1932, pp. 124–125). In general, the theory of induced innovation addresses the effects of relative prices on the direction of TC (Hayami and Ruttan, 1971).

It is expected that the increase in long-term oil prices will economies the use of oil and substitute it with other relatively cheap energy inputs such as coal. The change in the composition of energy inputs has implications for emissions. For example, the decrease in oil use as a result of higher oil prices may lead to increase in the use of coal, and as a result, the emissions of carbon, in the absence of any regulation, will be higher.

Most empirical studies are conducted using firm-level industrial data and measure TC either in terms of inputs (e.g. investments and R&D expenditures in energy-saving innovations) or in terms of outputs (e.g. the number of patents filed, granted or cited in the area of ESIs). For example, Popp (2002) tests the induced innovation hypothesis using US patent data from 1970 to 1994 to estimate the effect of energy prices on innovations. However, patent statistics can be misleading since many patents never see commercial application, many innovations are not patented, and some are subdivided into multiple patents, each covering one or more aspects of the innovation (e.g. Basberg, 1987). In addition, changes in patent policies over time may again make patent counts a misleading indicator of innovation, particularly over longer time periods (Managi, et al., 2005).

The TECH needs to be estimated in terms of measures of market penetration, the economic benefits of technologies, technological learning, energy efficiency and changes in the energy mix (Gallagher et al., 2006), and the transformation function is the best instrument for measuring the rate and direction of TECH (Jaffe et al., 2003).

There is a considerable theoretical and empirical literature on the measurement of induced innovation effects.[17] This literature typically analyses the inducement effect in the framework of a conventional representation of production technology, including cost, production and profit functions. Distinguishing between factor/output substitution and shifts in the production technology frontier is problematic with such conventional representations. This is because current and long-run prices appear along with the input–output vectors. As a result, the comparative static relations of the stated price-induced innovation model do not follow basic economic conditions. That is, the direct derivatives of the demand and supply functions with respect to prices cannot be signed given the presence of the cross-derivatives (Celikkol and Stefanou, 1999; Caputo and Paris, 2005).

Moreover, traditional measures of productivity do not account for the production of harmful by-products, such as CO_2 and SO_2 emissions, which may lead to environmental damage. Some recent studies include environmental externalities and conclude that measures including environmental indicators differ from traditional measures.[18]

Technological change is similar in nature to any investment process, as it requires time and adjustment that is not instantaneous, and the choice of technology is influenced by long-term prices. A time trend variable is also included in the country-specific frontier to account for ETC.[19] They also address the dual measures of input bias arising from ITC and ETC as well MES between different pairs of inputs. Thus they generate each of these measures for each country and at each time period.[20] The results show that developed countries experienced higher exogenous technological progress in comparison with developing countries and the gap between the two groups has increased over the sample period.

On average and across the world, they observe an absence of energy price-induced technological progress; most of the technological progress is attributed to exogenous technological progress. However, Kumar and Managi (2009b) find that both groups of countries observed substantial energy price-induced technological progress when long-term oil prices were rising, although the growth rate is more volatile in developed countries than in developing countries.

On the one hand, Kumar and Managi (2009b) find that the direction of technological progress was GDP-increasing and emissions-reducing in the 1970s in the developed countries when oil prices were rising. However, the direction was both GDP- and emissions-increasing during the 1980s and the 1990s. The result that only increasing energy prices encourages energy-saving technological progress is consistent with the theoretical arguments of price-induced technological progress. The results on the output bias provide important implications for the environmental (or carbon) taxation debate; for example, energy prices induce technological progress that internalizes the externalities. The output bias leads to technological change biased in favour of emissions and against GDP. On the other hand, technological change is GDP-reducing and emissions-increasing in developing countries. These results imply that developing countries are insensitive to increasing energy prices. Therefore, we need to be careful about the interpretation of energy price increases or energy taxation with regard to developing countries. Moreover, the heterogeneity of results recalls that future research could be directed towards more in-depth analyses of individual countries on this issue.

Kumar and Managi (2010a) are interested in whether there are any relationships between income and intertemporal environmental performance in the spirit of the environmental Kuznets curve. The objective of this paper is as follows. First, they measure productivity change for environmental (non-market) outputs such as carbon dioxide (CO_2) and sulphur dioxide (SO_2) emissions using country-level data for 51 developed and developing countries over the period of 1971 to 2000. They measure EP extending the TFP literature (see Färe et al., 2005; Managi et al., 2005). During the study period, when public policies and public concern for global warming were minimal, Kumar and Managi (2010a) examine business-as-usual trends in costs of abatement and EP in CO_2. In the case of local pollution of SO_2, environmental policies have been implemented and, therefore, higher EP is expected if regulations are implemented effectively. Then, the changes in EP in different countries are linked with their respective per capita income to examine an EKC-type relationship. They then discuss the implications for developed and developing countries.

Kumar and Managi (2009a) studied CO_2 and SO_2 emissions using country-level data over the period of 1971 to 2000 for 51 developed and developing countries. Intertemporal environmental performance, called EP, is proposed and is found to be increasing on average over the years when both emissions are considered. When the performance of each emission is measured separately, they have a similar trend, but with a slight difference. That is, the score in EP in SO_2 is larger than that of CO_2. This might be because local pollution of SO_2 has been regulated and there are incentives to improve its performance, especially in developed countries.

Developing countries were catching up to the developed countries in their pollution abatement management in the 1970s and early 1980s. However, Kumar and Managi (2009a) are not able to find any catch up effect after 1985 in the static sense. They identify this problem by using nonparametric estimation of generalized additive models. This lack of a catch-up effect may be explained by technological progress being faster in developed countries. Once they consider dynamic changes in efficiency as EP, they find a catch up of the low income group to the high income group. Our results are not pessimistic because they observe the catch-up of low income countries. However, it is not optimistic either because overall EP of both SO_2 and CO_2 show developed countries improve much more than developing countries. If these relationships continue in the future, it is hard to expect convergence in performances. Although our study is different from traditional convergence studies and instead they examine the transformation of production processes by quantifying the opportunity cost of adopting alternative environmentally superior technologies, their results for CO_2 appear to be consistent with the study by Aldy (2007), which did not find CO_2 emissions convergence. Kumar and Managi (2009a) results suggest they must be careful to suggest any developed countries' technological and management assistances to developing countries and may need further efforts to increase their environmental efficiency level apart from those associated with economic development.

A change in trade openness may stimulate technological change that reverses the pollution haven effect (Maria and Smulders, 2004). This study contributes to the literature by considering a simultaneous reduction of pollution emissions with the expansion of good outputs. Kumar and Managi (2009a) investigate how the changes in trade openness are related to induced innovations that are not only GDP increasing but also emissions saving.

Kumar and Managi (2009a) measure technological change in terms of the economic benefits of technologies by using a production possibility frontier. In particular, a directional distance function is applied to measure technological change for 76 countries over the period of 1963 to 2000. The technological change effect is decomposed into its exogenous and endogenous effects by trade. They find significant trade-induced technological change, and that the size of the trade-induced technological change is about one-third of the overall technological change. Finally, they analyse the biased technological change that provides important implications for the policy debate about the effect of trade openness on the environment. They find trade-induced technological changes are GDP saving and emissions augmenting. Therefore, there might be international technology spill overs in market output. However, pollution-saving technological diffusion is not induced by trade. Instead, they find increases in the relative supply of pollution from trade openness. Therefore, trade-induced technological progress does not internalize negative externalities. This paper uses macroeconomic data to measure the trade induced environmental and economic outcomes. Future study on industry level, using the variety of economic indicators, and covering different time periods, would be a step further for forthcoming research to test whether trade and technological performance have been able to significantly or systematically affect the environment.

5. Conclusions

Technological advancements help in lowering the environmental impacts of economic activities. New and better technologies make production processes environmentally friendly and production becomes more efficient and produces environmentally benign products. Due to market failures arising due to twin externalities of environment and knowledge markets failing to provide incentives for environmentally benign technological progress, firms under-invest in R&D activities that lead to technological advancements. Therefore, the role of environmental policy is imperative. Properly crafted environmental policy increases incentives for environmental R&D.

Environmental technological advancements are measured either by counting the patents or using production function/frontier approach. Patents may not be the best measure of technological advancement, as many patents are not deployed in practice. Conventional measures of productivity, such as growth accounting approaches or production function-based approaches, measure innovations but are not able to properly measure the diffusion on technological progress. Frontier- based approaches measure not only the innovations as the shift in the frontier, but also the movement of observations towards the frontier is considered as the diffusion of technological progress. Note that the advantage of the frontier approach is that it captures the effect of the knowledge that has been available but could not find a place in practice along with the new developments which are measured using the patent approach.

In the present chapter, we have not thoroughly reviewed the literature in the areas of environment and technological progress. This chapter provided the methodological framework in the presence of environmentally harmful products such as emissions of carbon and sulphur for measuring the complete technological progress; either it is autonomous or policy induced or it is neutral or embodied in some outputs or inputs. It also measures the effect of policy options on the substitution possibilities. To illustrate the framework, it reviews some of the studies conducted in the area. The chapter also reviews the theoretical and empirical issues concerning the various environmental and climate policy options that affect the technological innovating and adopting behaviour of the firms.

Note that, most of the available literature is concerned either with the autonomous tech-nological progress or policy-induced technological change. Environmental technological advancements are not just constrained by the market failures arising due to environmental and knowledge externalities but also due to network externalities, asymmetric information and the uncertainty problem. The existing literature on the measurement of technological progress is not able to capture the later effects and the future research should concentrate on these concerns also.

Notes

* Professor, Department of Business Economics, University of Delhi, South Campus, Benito Juarez Road, New Delhi 110021, e-mail: surender672@gmail.com

1 See special issues of the *Energy Journal* (2006), *Energy Economics* (2006) and *Ecological Economics* (2005) as evidence of recent attempts on modeling endogenous technological progress in the area. There are few studies that empirically measure the induced technological progress due to changes in environmental policy parameters, for example, Lichtenberg (1986, 1987), Lanjouw and Mody (1996), Jaffe et al. (1997), Newell et al. (1999), Nordhaus (1999) and Popp (2002).

2 Transformation function describes a production possibility frontier, that is, a set of combinations of inputs and outputs that are technically feasible at a point in time.

3 Directional distance function constitutes the transformation function using the data of the countries under study; thus, it is a relative measure of technical inefficiency across countries. It can identify if the practices adopted by the most efficient country are diffused to other countries. This is not equivalent to saying that most efficient country uses only the latest innovations, i.e. directional distance function cannot say anything about the diffusion within a country.

4 See *Hayami and Ruttan (1971), Binswanger (1974, 1978)* and Thirtle and Ruttan (1987) for a summary of this literature.

5 For properties of directional distance function see, Fare et al. (2005).

6 Directional distance function can be used for the case of multiple outputs and multiple inputs. In our study the output is a scalar rather than a vector.

7 Productivity change is generally decomposed into technical change and efficiency change components. We use the term technological change in place of productivity change; technical change is termed as innovations and efficiency change is termed as technological diffusion or catch-up effect.

8 The reference (benchmark) technology may be of t or t + 1 period. In order to avoid choosing an arbitrary benchmark, we specify the technological change index or innovations index as the arithmetic mean of the two indexes.

9 Orea (2002) used the quadratic identity lemma for parametric decomposition of Malmquist productivity index using output distance function.

10 In the discussion of results, for the sake of convention we have multiplied each of the component by minus one.

11 The allowance trading program was divided in two phases. Phase I affected 110 of the dirtiest plants and remained operative from 1995 to 1999. Units in phase I could emit at a rate of 2.5 pounds of SO_2 emissions per million British Thermal Units (mBTUs) of heat input. All other units of fossil-fueled power plants could annually emit at the rate of 1.2 pounds of SO_2 emissions per mBTUs of heat input. Phase II has been in operation since January 2000. In this phase, all major plants can emit at a rate of 1.2 pounds of SO_2 emissions per mBTUs of heat input. Under the emissions trading system, the firms have an incentive to find the lowest-cost means of achieving compliance and to reap financial rewards for developing these means. Some recent studies (Carlson et al., 2000; Swinton, 2004) empirically examine the cost effectiveness of allowance trading systems.

12 'over the long haul, perhaps the most important single criterion on which to judge environmental poli-cies is the extent they spur new technology towards the efficient conservation of environmental quality' (van Soest, 2005, pp. 236).

13 See Requate (2005) for a survey of theoretical literature on dynamic incentives provided by various environmental policy instruments. Jaffe et al. (2003) has reviewed the literature on environmental policy and technological change.

14 Technological progress occurs due to both inducements and advancements in general science and technology. Therefore, a time trend is included to account for the impact of scientific innovation on production technology (Lansink et al., 2000, pp. 500, footnote 1).

15 Allowance auction price information was obtained from the U.S. Environmental Protection Agency website (http://www.epa.gov/airmarkets/auctions/factsheet.html) on December 23, 2008.

16 The temporarily jump in allowance prices in 1999 can be attributed in part to the planning for Phase II of the program, as well as to the tightening of particulate matter ambient health standards (Burtraw et al., 2005).

17 See Hayami and Ruttan (1971), Binswanger (1974, 1978), Thirtle and Ruttan (1987) for recent literature reviews.

18 See, for example, Hailu and Veeman (2000), Färe et al. (2005) and Kumar (2006).

19 Technological progress occurs both due to inducements and advancements in general science and technology. Therefore, a time trend is included as an argument in the transformation frontier to account for the impact of scientific innovation on the production technology (Lansink et al., 2000, p. 500, footnote 1).

20 In the energy consumption, oil accounts for most of the consumption of hydrocarbons, although the use of natural gas has risen in the past decades or so and there is high positive correlation between oil and natural gas prices. Moreover, oil accounts for about 35 percent of global annual use of primary energy, with much of that oil coming from politically unstable regions (Gallagher et al., 2006); therefore, it is assumed that it is oil price volatility which induces technological progress which is energy saving.

References

Acemoglu, D. (2002). 'Directed technical change,' *The Review of Economic Studies* 69, 781–809.

Aigner D. J., and Schmidt, P. (1980). 'Specification and estimation of frontier production, profit and cost functions,' *Journal of Econometrics* 13, 1–138.

Aldy, J.E. 2007. 'Divergence in state-level per capita carbon dioxide emissions.' *Land Economics* 83(3), 353–369.

Antle, J.M. (1984). 'The structure of U.S. agricultural technology, 1910–78,' *American Journal of Agricultural Economics* 66, 414–421.

Basberg, B. (1987). 'Patents and the measurement of technological change: a survey of the literature,' *Research Policy* 16, 131–41.

Binswanger, H.P. (1974). 'The measurement of technical change biases with many factors of production,' *American Economic Review* 64, 964–976.

Binswanger, H.P. (1978). 'Measured biases of technical change: the United States.' In H.P. Binswanger and V.W. Ruttan, eds., *Induced Innovation: Technology, Institutions, and Development*, pp. 215–242. Baltimore, MD: John Hopkins University Press.

Blackorby, C., and Russell, R.R. (1989). 'Will the real elasticity please stand up?' *American Economic Review* 79, 882–888.

Burtraw, D. (2000). 'Innovation under the tradable sulfur dioxide emissions permits program in the US electricity sector,' Discussion Paper No. 00–38, Resource for Future, Washington, DC.

Burtraw, D., Evans, D.A., Krupnick, A., Palmer, K. and Toth, R. (2005). 'Economics of pollution trading for SO_2 and NOx,' *Annual Review of Environment and Resource* 30, 253–289.

Caputo, M.R. and Paris, Q. (2005). 'An atemporal microeconomic theory and an empirical test of price-induced technical progress,' *Journal of Productivity Analysis* 24, 259–281.

Carlson, C., Burtraw, D., Cropper, M. and Palmer, K.L. (2000). 'Sulfur dioxide control by electric utilities: what are the gains from trade?' *Journal of Political Economy* 108(6), 1292–1326.

Celikkol, P. and Stefanou, S. (1999). 'Measuring the impact of price induced innovation on technological progress: application to the U.S. food processing and distribution sector,' *Journal of Productivity Analysis* 12, 135–151.

Chambers, R.G. (2002). 'Exact nonradial input, output and productivity measurement,' *Economic Theory* 20, 751–765.

Chambers, R.G., Chung, Y. and Färe, R. (1996). 'Benefit and distance functions,' *Journal of Economic Theory* 70, 407–419.

Considine, T.J. and Larson, D.F. (2006). 'The environment as a factor of production,' *Journal of Environmental Economics and Management* 52(3), 645–662.

Diewert, W.E. (1976). 'Exact and superlative index numbers,' *Journal of Econometrics* 4, 115–145.

Ellerman, D. (2003). 'Ex-post evaluation of tradable permits: the US SO_2 cap-and-trade program,' Working Paper MIT/CEEPR 03–003, MIT Center for Energy and Environmental Policy Research, Cambridge, MA.

Ellerman, D., Joskow, P.L., Schmalensee, R., Montero, J.P. and Bailey, E.M. (2000). *Markets for Clean Air: The US Acid Rain Program.* New York: Cambridge University Press.

Färe, R., and Grosskopf, S. (2000) 'Theory and applications of directional distance functions,' *Journal of Productivity Analysis* 13, 93–103.

Färe, R., Grosskopf, S. and Lovell, C.A. (1994). *Production Frontiers.* Cambridge: Cambridge University Press.

Färe, R., Grosskopf, S., Noh, D., and Weber, W. (2005). 'Characteristics of a polluting technology: theory and practice,' *Journal of Econometrics* 126, 469–492.

Färe, R., Grosskopf, S., Norris, M. and Zhang, Z. (1994). 'Productivity growth, technical progress, and efficiency change in industrialized countries,' *American Economic Review* 84, 66–83.

Färe, R., Grosskopf, S., Pasurka, C., and Weber, W. (2007). 'Substitutability among undesirable outputs,' Working Paper, Oregon State University, Corvallis, OR.

Färe, R., Grosskopf, S. and Weber, W. (2005) 'Shadow prices of Missouri public conservation land,' *Public Finance Review* 26(6), 444–460.

Fischer, C. and Newell, R. (2008). 'Environmental and technology policies for climate mitigation,' *Journal of Environmental Economics and Management* 55(2), 142–162.

Fisher-Vanden, K., Jefferson, G., Ma and Xu, J. (2006). 'Technology development and energy productivity in China,' *Energy Economics* 28(5/6), 690–705.

Gallagher, K.S., Holdren, J.P. and Sagar, A.D. (2006). 'Energy-technology innovation,' *Annual Review of Environment and Resource* 31, 193–237.

Gollop, F.M. and Roberts, M.J. (1983). 'Environmental regulations and productivity growth: the case of fossil-fueled electric power generation,' *Journal of Political Economy* 91, 654–674.

Grosskopf, S., Margaritis, D. and Valdmanis, V. (1995). 'Estimating output substitutability of hospital services: a distance function approach,' *European Journal of Operational Research* 80, 575–587.

Hailu, A. and Veeman, T.S. (2001). 'Non-parametric productivity analysis with undesirable outputs: an application to the Canadian pulp and paper industry,' *American Journal of Agricultural Economics* 83, 605–616.

Harrington, W., Morgenstern, R.D. and Nelson, P. (2000). 'On the accuracy of regulatory cost estimates,' *Journal of Policy Analysis and Management* 19(2), 297–322.

Hayami, Y., and Ruttan, V.W. (1971). *Agricultural Development: An International Perspective*, Baltimore. MD: John Hopkins University Press.

Hicks, J.R. (1932). *The Theory of Wages.* New York: St. Martin's Press.

Hudgins, B.L. and Primont, D. (2004) 'Directional technology distance functions: theory and applications,' Working Paper #10, Department of Economics, Southern Illinois University, Carbondale, IL.

Jaffe, A. B., Newell, R. G. and Stavins, R. N. (2003). 'Technological change and the environment.' In K.G. Mäler and J. Vincent, ed., *Handbook of Environmental Economics*, vol. 1, pp. 461–516. Amsterdam: North-Holland.

Jaffe, A. B. and Palmer, K. (1997). 'Environmental regulation and innovation: a panel data study,' *Review of Economics and Statistics* 79, 610–619.

Jorgenson, D. and Griliches, Z. (1967). 'The explanation of productivity change,' *Review of Economic Studies* 34, 249–283.

Jorgenson, D.W. and Stiroh, K.J. (2000). 'Raising the speed limit: U.S. economic growth in the information age,' *Brookings Papers on Economic Activity* 1, 125–211.

Keohane, N.O. (2002). 'Environmental Policy and the Choice of Abatement Technique: Evidence from Coal-Fired Power Plants,' Presented at the 2nd World Congress of Environmental and Resource Economists, June 24–27, 2002, Monterey, CA.

Kneese, A.V. and Schulze, C L (1975). *Pollution, Prices and Public Policy.* Washington, DC: Brookings.

Kolstad, C.D., and Turnovsky, M.H.L. (1998). 'Cost functions and non-linear prices: estimating a technology with quality differentiated inputs,' *Review of Economics and Statistics* 80, 444–453.

Kumar, S. (2006). 'Environmentally sensitive productivity growth: a global analysis using Malmquist-Luenberger Index,' *Ecological Economics* 56, 280–293.

Kumar, S. (2010). *Energy Prices and Induced Innovations: A Directional Distance Function Approach.* Saarbrücken: VDM Publishing House.

Kumar, S. and Khanna, M. (2009). 'Measurement of environmental efficiency and productivity: a cross country analysis,' *Environment and Development Economics* 14, 473–495.

Kumar, S. and Managi, S. (2009a). 'Trade-Induced technological change: analyzing economic and environmental outcomes,' *Economic Modelling* 26(3), 721–732.

Kumar, S. and Managi, S. (2009b). 'Energy price-induced and exogenous technological change: assessing the economic and environmental outcomes,' *Resource and Energy Economics* 31(4), 334–353.

Kumar, S. and Managi, S. (2010a). 'Environment and productivities in developed and developing countries: the case of carbon dioxide and sulfur dioxide,' *Journal of Environmental Management* 91(7), 1580–1592.

Kumar, S. and Managi, S. (2010b). 'Sulfur dioxide allowances: trading and technological progress,' *Ecological Economics* 69(10), 623–631.

Lanjouw, J.O. and Mody, A. (1996). 'Innovation and the international diffusion of environmentally responsive technology,' *Research Policy* 25, 549–71.

Lansink, A. O., Silva, E. and Stefanou, S. (2000). 'Decomposing productivity growth allowing efficiency gains and price-induced technical progress,' *European Review of Agricultural Economics* 27(4), 497–518.

Litchtenberg, F.R. (1986). 'Energy prices and induced innovation,' *Research Policy* 15, 67–75.

Litchtenberg, F.R. (1987). 'Changing market opportunities and the structure of R&D investment: the case of energy,' *Energy Economics* 9, 154–158.

Managi, S., Opaluch, J.J., Jin, D. and Grigalunas, T.A. (2005). 'Environmental regulations and technological change in the offshore oil and gas industry,' *Land Economics* 81(2), 303–319.

Maria, C.D. and Smulders, S.A. (2004). 'Trade pessimists vs technology optimists: induced technical change and pollution havens,' *Advances in Economic Analysis and Policy* 4(2), Article 7.

Milliman, S.R. and Prince, R. (1989). 'Firm incentives to promote technological change in pollution control,' *Journal of Environmental Economics and Management* 17, 247–265.

Murillo-Zamorano, L. R. (2004). 'Economic efficiency and frontier techniques,' *Journal of Economic Survey* 18(1), 33–77.

Murty, M.N. and Kumar, S. (2004). *Environmental and Economic Accounting for Industry.* New Delhi: Oxford University Press.

Murty, S. and Russell, R. (2002). *On Modelling Pollution Generating Technologies.* Riverside, CA: University of California.

Nadiri, M.I. (1970). 'Some approaches to the theory and measurement of total factor productivity: a survey,' *Journal of Economic Literature* 8(4), 1137–1177.

Newell, R.G., Jaffe, A.B. and Stavins, R.N. (1999). 'The induced innovation hypothesis and energy-saving technological change,' *Quarterly Journal of Economics* 109, 941–975.

Nordhaus, W.D. (1994). *Managing the Global Commons: The Economics of Climate Change.* Cambridge, MA: MIT Press.

Nordhaus, W.D. (2002). 'Modeling induced innovation in climate-change policy.' In A. Grübler, N. Nakićenović and W.D. Nordhaus, eds., *Modeling Induced Innovation in Climate Change Policy,* pp. 259–290. Washington, DC: Resources for the Future.

Orea, L. (2002). 'Parametric decomposition of a generalized Malmquist productivity index,' *Journal of Productivity Analysis* 18, 5–22.

Paris, Q., and Caputo, M.R. (2001). 'Price-induced technical progress and comparative statics,' *Economics Bulletin* 15(8), 1–8.

Popp, D. (2002). 'Induced innovation and energy prices,' *American Economic Review* 92, 160–180.

Popp, D. (2003). 'Pollution control innovations and the Clean Air Act of 1990,' *Journal of Policy Analysis and Management* 22(4), 641–60.

Popp, D., Newell, R.G. and Jaffe, A.B. (2010). 'Energy, the environment, and technological change.' In B.H. Halland and N. Rosenberg, eds., *Handbook of the Economics of Innovation,* vol. 2, pp. 873–938. Burlington, VT: Academic Press.

Requate, T. (2005). 'Dynamic incentives for environmental policy instruments: a survey,' *Ecological Economics* 54, 175–195.

Sue Wing, I. (2006). 'Representing induced technological change in models for climate policy,' *Energy Economics* 28, 539–562.

Swinton, J.R. (2004). 'Phase I completed: an empirical assessment of the 1990 CAAA,' *Environmental and Resource Economics* 27(3), 227–246.

Thirtle, C.G. and Ruttan, V.W. (1987). 'The role of demand and supply in the generation and diffusion of technical change.' In F.M. Scherer, ed., *Fundamentals of Pure and Applied Economics,* vol. 21 in the *Economics and Technological Change Section*, pp. 1–184. New York: Harwood Academic Publishers.

van Soest, D.P. (2005). 'The impact of environmental policy instruments on the timing of adoption of energy-saving technologies,' *Resource and Energy Economics* 27, 235–247.

Yaisawarng, S. and Klein, J.D. (1994). 'The effects of sulfur dioxide controls on productivity change in the U.S. electric power industry,' *Review of Economics and Statistics* 76, 447–460.

22

PRODUCTIVITY, INSTITUTIONS AND CLIMATE CHANGE

Lessons for Asian countries

Surender Kumar and Shunsuke Managi

1. Introduction

Climate change is unequivocal and its vagaries in terms of economic impacts and costs of mitigating carbon emissions have made it an issue of central concern. The impacts of climate change and carbon emissions mitigation policy can be observed in terms of the productivity of factors of production. Though the link between temperature and productivity is talked about in the classic writings of Montesquieu (1750). Marshall (1890) and Huntington (1915), it is less discussed in the literature on the impacts of climate change (Dell et al., 2008). The objective of the present study is to measure a relationship between cumulative total factor productivity (TFP) and average temperature over the last three decades for 88 countries over a span of 15 years (1994–2008) and the role of institutions in lowering the climate change impacts on TFP.

Institutions are defined in terms of property and contracting rights. The incentive structure shapes the direction of economic growth in an economy, which is determined by the institutions in which it is operating (North, 1991). Acemoglu et al. (2001, 2005) find that the economies where property rights are secure and contracting rights are enforced are doing better in economic terms relative to those economies where these institutions are weak. Therefore, it is hypothesized that the better institutions help in lowering the vagaries of climate change and provide incentives for technological adoption and innovations so that the carbon emissions are mitigated at lower cost.

Note that in the Asian region, most of the population is poor and institutions are weak, as a result the Asian population is more vulnerable to climatic changes. A large body of cross-country empirical work has identified the importance of institutional quality for either growth or income levels; this chapter aims to identify the role of institutions in addressing climate change concerns. In the developed countries, there are better property right and contracting institutions relative to developing countries. For example, Banerjee and Iyer (2005) show that Indian districts in which property rights were historically given to landlords had lower levels of investment and productivity than districts where property rights were assigned to cultivators, arguing that this reflects the greater security of tenure in non-landlord districts.

Climate change mitigation policy requires transformations in production technology by adopting low-carbon technologies and diverting some productive resources towards abatement. Since the different countries are operating at different levels of resource availability and policy environments, the mitigation policy is supposed to create differing levels of impacts in terms of productivity. We intend to quantify these costs of abatement and impacts on productivity through measuring productivity under different scenarios: carbon emissions are not regulated (i.e., strong disposability of carbon emissions) and these emissions are regulated (i.e., weak disposability of carbon emissions). Measuring productivity under different scenarios will provide insights on the extent to which technological adoptions and innovations can be relied upon to mitigate carbon emissions and on the validity of concerns about the economic impact of carbon abatement (Kumar and Khanna, 2009).

The directional output distance function is used as an analytical tool for measuring TFP under both the scenarios: strong and weak disposability of carbon emissions. The distance function can take care of a multiplicity of outputs where some of the outputs, such as CO_2 emissions, are bad, which need to be reduced. For measuring productivity and its components, the distance function requires only quantitative information on various inputs and outputs. We compute the value of directional output distance function using a non-parametric data envelopment analysis (DEA) approach. The computed values of TFP and its components are regressed on various geographic variables such as precipitation and average temperature and the variables measuring institutions to get an idea of the impact of climate change and its mitigation policies using truncated regression with robust standard errors.

We observe that though during the study period the productivity growth is happening across both the groups, developed and developing countries, the differing levels of productivity growth help in explaining the increasing economic divergence between these groups. As expected, it is found that carbon emissions can be mitigated at lower cost in developing countries but the carbon emissions mitigation lowers their growth potential, which requires that these countries be adequately compensated. Moreover, it is found that better property rights help in lowering the impacts of climate change under the business-as-usual scenario (in the absence of carbon emissions regulations), implying that secure and enforceable property and contracting rights increase the opportunities of technological adoption and increase resource productivity in these countries, thus lowering the impact of climate vagaries.

The chapter is organized as follows: Section 2 provides a brief review of the related literature. Section 3 describes the methodology followed in the chapter and data. Section 4 presents the empirical results. Concluding remarks and policy recommendations are provided in Section 5.

2. Related literature

To understand the differing levels of development among countries, the TFP measurement is very close to the heart of economists, and productivity changes are measures in terms of Solow's residues. These conventional approaches use gross domestic product (GDP) as output and labor and capital as inputs but ignore the production of emissions that take place as a result of economic activities performed by these countries. In the last two decades, there are developments in the productivity literature that take into consideration the production of both desirable outputs such as GDP and bad outputs such as carbon emissions. Some of these studies have treated the emissions as inputs,[1] while others treated them as a synthetic output such as pollution abatement (e.g., Gollop and Robert, 1983). Murty and Russell (2002) noted that the treatment of emissions as inputs is inconsistent with the material balance approach. The approach adopted by Gollop and Robert to treat the reduction in emissions as desirable output creates a different nonlinear transformation of the original variable in the absence of base constrained emissions rates (Atkinson and Dorfman, 2005). To overcome this problem, Pittman (1983) proposed that GDP and emissions should be treated non-symmetrically. Following Chung et al. (1997), we use the directional output distance function to calculate the production relationships involving GDP and emissions while treating them asymmetrically.[2]

Studies on the economic impacts of climate change can be put in to three categories: sectoral studies, studies using integrated assessment models (IAM), and econometric studies trying to directly establish a link between income and climate change variables. Sectoral studies examine climate's role in specific sectors, primarily agriculture (Deschênes and Greenstone, 2007; Madison et al., 2007; Mendelsohn, 1994; Schlenker et al., 2006) and health (Bosello et al., 2006) and then construct an overall prediction of climate change impacts by aggregating these sectors. Faced with these different sectoral channels, the IAM approach takes some of these channels, specifies their effects and then adds them up (e.g., Mendelsohn et al., 2000; Nordhaus and Boyer, 2000; Tol, 2002; Nordhaus, 2010). The IAM approach is based on many assumptions about which effects to include, how each of these effects operates, and how to add them up. Dell et al. (2008) and Horowitz (2009) take a direct approach, measuring the impact of temperature and precip-itation on the national income. They econometrically estimate a reduced form equation meas-uring a relationship between income and temperature. In these two studies, the difference lies in the measurement of the temperature variable. Dell et al. (2008) take annual variation in the temperature in the second half of 21st century, whereas Horowitz (2009) takes monthly average temperature data over 1960–2005 to measure the impact of climate change on income.

The main objective of the study is to investigate the impact of climate change on productiv-ity growth and then how better institutions help in alleviating the impacts. Modern theories of economic growth recognize the fact that difference across nations in per capita income is due to productivity differences, but they assume that per capita income or the growth rate of per capita income is the function of conventional factor (such as capital per worker) accumulation along with technologies. In the last decade, studies starting with Hall and Jones (1999) have started to consider institutions and governance along with geographic factors as the determinants of differences in per capita income or productivity across nations. In the recent studies, Nordhaus (2006) recognizes that climatic factors matter most in determining the growth of a nation's per capita income.

Institutions are the "rules of the game" that shape political, economic and social interaction in a society and establish the incentive structure in an economy (North, 1991). Property right regimes, in particular, are important factors in institutional analysis (North, 1991). It takes, how-ever, resources to define and protect property rights and to enforce agreements. North (1990, p. 54) asserts that "the inability of societies to develop effective, low-cost enforcement of contracts is the most important source of both historical stagnation and contemporary underdevelopment in the Third World," because the absence of secure property and contractual rights discourages investment and specialization. Property rights determine who can participate in decision-making and ultimately use resources. For example, a subsidy or tax cannot be defined independently of property rights. Thus, well-defined property rights could lead to efficient resource use (Bromley, 1995). Acemoglu et al. (2001), Easterly and Levine (2003), and Rodrik et al. (2004) conclude that the institutions determine the growth trajectory in a country rather than its geography, while Sachs (2003) and Nordhaus (2006) argue that geography is the main determinant of the growth rate in a country. Our empirical strategy is to use regression analyses to measure the impact of institutions on productivity and its components under strong and weak disposability in the pres-ence of climatic factors. These regressions provide an understanding about the role of institutions in mitigating the impacts of climate change and emissions mitigation strategies.

3. Methodology and data

The analysis is undertaken for a set of 88 countries including 26 developed countries and 62 developing countries for the period 1994–2008. In the absence of direct data on the costs of carbon abatement, we rely on a distance function approach that incorporates both the desirable output (GDP) and the undesirable output (CO_2) to provide a measure of "how far" each country's output vector is from the best practice input frontier, given an input vector. This approach recognizes pollution as an undesirable output that is not freely disposable; rather it is weakly disposable; that is, some productive resources have to be given up in order to reduce the level of pollutants. The extent to which a country would need to sacrifice its desirable output to reduce pollution represents its opportunity cost of pollution reduction, referred to here as environmental efficiency (EE). Countries that are less constrained are considered to be more environmentally efficient because they have chosen a more appropriate mix of desirable outputs, undesirable output, and inputs. In less constrained economies, it is possible to reduce emissions of carbon at lower cost but it might affect their growth potential in terms of lower productivity growth when the emissions of carbon are weakly disposable.

Suppose that a country employs a vector of inputs $x \in \Re_+^N$ to produce a vector of good outputs $y \in \Re_+^M$, and bad outputs $b \in \Re_+^I$. Let $P(x)$ be the feasible output set for the given input vector x and $L(y, b)$ is the input requirement set for a given output vector (y, b). Now the technology set is defined as:

$$P(x) = \{(y,b) : x \text{ can produce}(y,b)\}, x \in \Re_+^N \tag{1}$$

We assume that the good and bad outputs are null-joint; a country cannot produce good outputs in the absence of bad outputs, i.e., if $(y,b) \in P(x)$ and $b = 0$ then $y = 0$. The output is strongly or freely disposable if

$$(y,b) \in P(x) \text{ and } \hat{y} \leq y \text{ imply } (\hat{y},b) \in P(x) \tag{2}$$

Strong disposability of the bad outputs excludes production processes that generate undesirable outputs that are costlier to dispose. In such cases, bad outputs are considered as being weakly disposable and

$$(y,b) \in P(x) \text{ and } 0 \leq \theta \leq 1 \text{ imply } (\theta y, \theta b) \in P(x) \tag{3}$$

Moreover, it is assumed that the good and bad outputs are null-joint in the production process. It states that every bad output is produced by some country, k, and that every country, k, produces at least one bad output (in multiple bad output situations).

The directional distance function seeks to increase the good outputs whilst simultaneously reducing the bad outputs. Formally it is defined as:

$$\vec{D}_o(x, y, b; g) = \sup\{\beta : (y,b) + \beta g \in P(x)\} \tag{4}$$

where g is the vector of directions in which outputs can be scaled. Following Chung et al. (1997), the direction taken is $g = (y, -b)$, such that as the good outputs are increased and the bad outputs are decreased.[3]

3.1 Malmquist-Luenberger productivity index

Using directional distance functions, we define the Malmquist-Luenberger (ML) productivity index. The ML index is very much based on the traditional Malmquist indexes – the main difference being that they are constructed from directional distance functions rather than

Shepherd distance functions. Chung et al. (1997) define the ML index of productivity between period t and t+1 as:

$$ML_t^{t+1} = \left[\frac{\left(1 + \vec{D}_o^{t+1}\left(x^t, y^t, b^t; y^t, -b^t\right)\right)}{\left(1 + \vec{D}_o^{t+1}\left(x^{t+1}, y^{t+1}, b^{t+1}; y^{t+1}, -b^{t+1}\right)\right)} \frac{\left(1 + \vec{D}_o^t\left(x^t, y^t, b^t; y^t, -b^t\right)\right)}{\left(1 + \vec{D}_o^t\left(x^{t+1}, y^{t+1}, b^{t+1}; y^{t+1}, -b^{t+1}\right)\right)} \right]^{\frac{1}{2}} \quad (5)$$

The index can be decomposed into two component measures of productivity change:

$$ML_t^{t+1} =$$

$$\underbrace{\left[\frac{1 + \vec{D}_o^t\left(x^t, y^t, b^t; y^t, -b^t\right)}{1 + \vec{D}_o^{t+1}\left(x^{t+1}, y^{t+1}, b^{t+1}; y^{t+1}, -b^{t+1}\right)} \right]}_{MITECH_t^{t+1}} \times$$

$$\quad (6)$$

$$\underbrace{\left[\frac{\left(1 + \vec{D}_o^{t+1}\left(x^t, y^t, b^t; y^t, -b^t\right)\right)\left(1 + \vec{D}_o^{t+1}\left(x^{t+1}, y^{t+1}, b^{t+1}; y^{t+1}, -b^{t+1}\right)\right)}{\left(1 + \vec{D}_o^t\left(x^t, y^t, b^t; y^t, -b^t\right)\right)\left(1 + \vec{D}_o^t\left(x^{t+1}, y^{t+1}, b^{t+1}; y^{t+1}, -b^{t+1}\right)\right)} \right]^{\frac{1}{2}}}_{MITECH_t^{t+1}}$$

The first term, MLEFFCH represents the efficiency change component, a movement towards the best practice frontier while the second, MLTECH, the technical change, i.e., a shift. If there have been no changes in inputs and outputs over two time periods, then $ML_t^{t+1} = 1$. If there has been an increase in productivity, then $ML_t^{t+1} > 1$, and finally, a decrease when $ML_t^{t+1} < 1$. Changes in efficiency are captured by $MLEFFCH_t^{t+1}$, which gives a ratio of the distances the countries are to their respective frontiers, in time periods t, and t + 1. If $MLEFFCH_t^{t+1} > 1$, then there has been a movement towards the frontier in period t + 1. If $MLEFFCH_t^{t+1} < 1$, then it indicates that the country is further away from the frontier in t + 1 and hence has become less efficient. If $MLTECH_t^{t+1} > 1$ implies technical change enables more production of good and less production of bad outputs and if $MLTECH_t^{t+1} < 1$, there has been a shift of the frontier in the direction of fewer good outputs and more bad outputs (Kumar, 2006).

Note that the previous procedure measures adjunct year productivity growth. To construct cumulative productivity growth, we create a chain approach by having a chain multiplication of indices for computing cumulative productivity growth and its components for the terminal year 2008.

We use DEA to compute the directional distance functions. To measure the ML index, four DEA programs need to be solved for each observation. Two of them use observations and technology for time period *t*, or *t + 1*, and the other two use mixed periods; for example, technology calculated from period *t* with the observation *t + 1*. Mixed period problems can cause difficulties in calculation, whereby the observed data in period *t + 1* is not feasible in period *t*. For example, the observation $(\mathbf{y}^{t+1,k}, \mathbf{b}^{t+1,k})$ may not belong to the output set $P^t(\mathbf{x}^{t+1})$. To minimize this problem, we follow Kumar (2006), whereby multiple year "windows" of data are the reference technology. All frontiers are constructed from three years of data.

In the second stage, we econometrically estimate a reduced form equation measuring the relationship between temperature measured as an average of data from 1980 through 2008 and various measures of productivity and its components under different scenarios. We run a separate regression of each of the group, as well as a regression for all the observations for cumulative productivity growth and its components under both the scenarios. Generally, the regressions are run using Tobit model that recognizes the censored nature of productivity and its determinants which, by definition, is constrained to zero toward the left. Simar and Wilson (1999) show that productivity and its component scores are correlated with the explanatory variables, and the estimates obtained using Tobit model will be inconsistent and biased. We use the approach proposed in Simar and Wilson (2007) with a truncated regression. We assume that the distribution of error term is truncated normal with zero mean (before truncation), unknown variance, and (left) truncation point determined by the condition $ui \geq 1 - \alpha(determinants) - qi\alpha - vi$. We compute the robust standard errors for the estimates of parameters.

We obtain the data on five variables, namely GDP, CO_2, labor, capital stock, and commercial energy consumption for 88 countries,[4] a mix of developed and developing countries for the period of 1994 to 2008 to measure efficiency and productivity growth. The choice of period and countries is based on the availability of complete balanced panel data. Out of these five variables, the first two, GDP and CO_2 are considered as proxies of good and bad outputs, respectively, and the remaining three are used as inputs. Data on the GDP, CO_2, labor force, and capital stock is collected from Extended Penn Tables (Version 4) and energy consumption is from the World Development Indicators (WDI, World Bank). GDP and capital stock are measured in 2005 US dollars, whereas CO_2 and energy consumption is measured in thousand metric tons. The labor force data is in millions of workers.

4. Empirical results

The cumulative growth rates of all the variables used in the study for both of the groups, i.e., developed and developing countries, are presented in Table 22.1. Note that the growth rate of CO_2 emissions is substantially lower than that of energy consumption in the developed countries, but it is opposite in developing countries. It implies that in the developed countries, energy consumption has decoupled from CO_2 emissions or these countries are following less carbon-intensive growth relative to their counterparts in developing countries. Alternatively, this implies that most of the carbon mitigating technological progress is concentrated in the developed world. This corroborates the fact that about 80 percent of all clean energy innovations are concentrated in just six developed countries, namely, the US, Japan, Germany, Korea, France, and the UK (Jishnu, 2011).

Table 22.2 sums up the main results of total factor productivity growth, which describe the cumulative performance of each group.[5] Recall that index values greater (less) than one denote improvements (deterioration) in the relevant performance. Here we calculate the ML index and its components for both cases: weak and strong disposability of CO_2 emissions.

We calculate ML productivity indices as well as the efficiency-change and technical-change components for each country in our sample. Instead of presenting the disaggregated results for each country and year, we discuss the summary of the cumulative performance of each country over the entire 1994 to 2008 time period. The cumulative ML index value of 1.16 indicates that the cumulative productivity growth for the sample countries was 16 percent. On average,

Table 22.1 Growth rates of key variables in 2008 over 1994

	GDP	CO_2	Energy	labor	Capital
Overall	66.79	38.44	36.73	24.27	82.76
Developed Countries	40.86	4.01	11.81	13.41	54.51
Developing Countries	125.37	90.16	75.38	26.81	143.35

Table 22.2 Descriptive statistics of various measures of productivity in 2008 over 1994

Variable	Developed Countries				Developing Countries			
	Mean	Std. Dev.	Min	Max	Mean	Std. Dev.	Min	Max
EFFCH$_S$	0.98	0.15	0.74	1.43	0.92	0.21	0.39	1.40
TC$_S$	1.22	0.17	1.00	1.73	1.26	0.18	1.04	1.89
PC$_S$	1.20	0.28	0.75	1.97	1.15	0.25	0.54	1.80
EFFCH$_W$	1.00	0.13	0.75	1.43	1.05	0.11	0.75	1.42
TC$_W$	1.22	0.15	1.02	1.69	1.06	0.17	0.90	1.83
PC$_W$	1.22	0.24	0.76	1.91	1.11	0.20	0.80	1.76
ENVEFF	0.80	0.20	0.19	1.00	0.75	0.24	0.13	1.00

this growth was due to technical change; the world witnessed an average technical progress of 25 percent over the study period (Table 22.2). This cumulative progress in TFP is 20 percent for developed countries, whereas in developing countries it increased by 15 percent. From these overall average figures of progress in TFP changes in countries, it may be argued that effectively all GDP growth in the post-1994 period was due to input accumulation and technological changes. The figures on the standard deviation of the indices show that there is much diversity among the developed countries relative to developing countries with respect to changes in TFP and its components.

Figure 22.1 shows a relationship between the per capita income in 1995 and cumulative productivity growth. We observe a positive relationship between productivity growth and per capital income implying, per se, that productivity growth is one of the key reasons for growth in per capita income. But the desegregation of productivity change in catch-up effect and technological progress shows that the catch-up effect observed an inverted "U-shaped" relationship and technological progress a "U-shaped" relationship with respect to per capita income. This implies that in the middle-income countries, much of the productivity growth can be attributed to technological diffusion, but in low- and high-income countries the productivity growth observed is due to technological progress.

Figure 22.2 shows the relationship between carbon sensitive productivity growth and its components with per capita income. Similar to the strong disposability case, we find a positive association between carbon sensitive productivity growth and per capita income. But note that the case under weak disposability is just the opposite of the strong disposability case when we decompose the productivity growth between efficiency change and technical change. We find technological diffusion is negatively associated with the per capita income but most of the carbon-sensitive technological progress happens to be in the higher income countries.

The estimates of carbon efficiency as EE, represented as the ratio of production inefficiency under weak disposability to strong disposability of CO_2 emissions show that most countries observe value less than one, i.e., there are carbon inefficiencies in all the study years. The results imply that, on average, most of these countries have carbon-binding production technologies. For example in 2008, the average scores are 0.75 and 0.80 for the developing and developed countries, respectively. In this case, inefficiency in the developing countries is higher in comparison with developed countries. In the case of major economies, the US observes non-binding production technology whereas China has the most binding production technology, followed by India. This implies that the major economies such as China and India can reduce CO_2 emissions

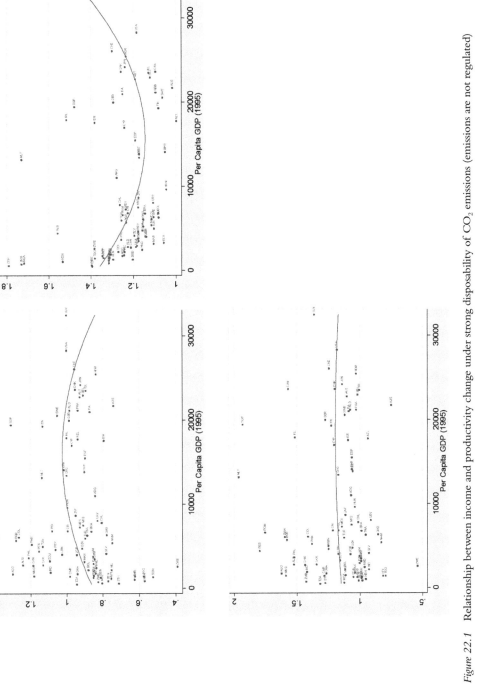

Figure 22.1 Relationship between income and productivity change under strong disposability of CO_2 emissions (emissions are not regulated)

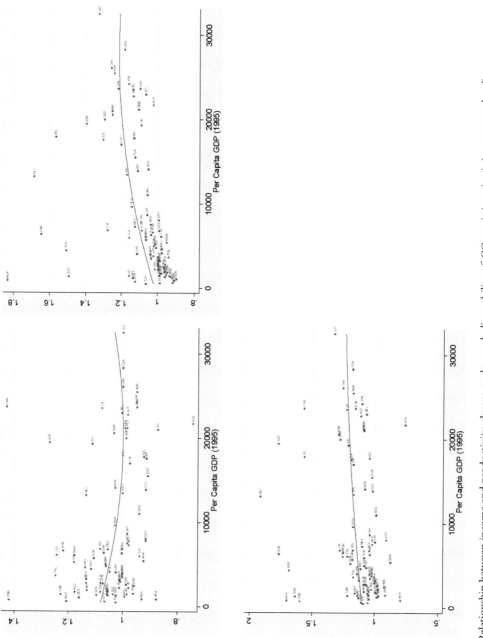

Figure 22.2 Relationship between income and productivity change under weak disposability of CO_2 emissions (emissions are regulated)

at lower cost in comparison to the US, Japan or the Organisation for Economic Co-operation and Development group, but if the emissions regulation conditions are imposed without any compensation, these developing economies also lose the most in term of lost GDP.

When countries' efficiency scores differ under the assumption of weak disposability and strong disposability of CO_2, they suffer congestion from the emissions. That is, if these countries were to reduce emissions, they have to sacrifice their GDP. Once this inefficiency is translated into loss of desirable output, the results indicate that developing countries would have to lose more of their GDP because of congestion of production technologies. As a whole, countries in our sample would lose 23 percent of GDP in 2008 on average because of carbon-binding production technology. The relative output loss because of the imposition of costly abatements for developing countries is higher than the overall average of the entire sample.

Again we observe that all counties have lower growth in TFP when CO_2 is considered as an undesirable output in comparison to the conventional TFP growth. This finding corroborates with Kumar and Khanna (2009); they find similar results for the period 1971 to 1992 when there was no binding on the carbon emissions of any country. Nevertheless, it was both technological and efficiency changes that governed the change in overall productivity indices in all countries. The ratio of TFP measures under weak and strong disposability condition can be interpreted as the intertemporal efficiency showing how well environmentally friendly technologies and managements are utilized (e.g., Jaffe et al., 2003; Kumar and Managi, 2010).

The cumulative change in the productivity index when CO_2 was weakly disposable was 14 percent. This cumulative TFP measure was the sum of a positive change in innovation of 10 percent and a positive efficiency change of 4 percent. In developed counties, it was technological changes that governed the change in the overall productivity index in most of the countries, whereas in the developing countries, carbon-sensitive productivity growth is governed by the diffusion in technologies, i.e., catch-up effective was dominating.

4.1 Impact of climate change and institutions on productivity growth

As our interest is in measuring the impact of climate on productivity, a measure of long-run average temperature will be the most useful single climate variable. Nordhaus (2006) uses the geographic average of temperature, but his unit of observation was a one-degree latitude/longitude cell, rather than countries and cells without economic data were excluded. If one is interested in using the country-level data, then a country's temperature averaged over the entire country will include economically irrelevant areas. We use the temperature data from the Nordhaus' g-econ project.[6] Nordhaus' g-econ project provides temperature data at one-degree latitude/longitude cells averaged over the period of 1980 to 2008. To have country-level data, we exclude the cells without economic data.

Figure 22.3 and 22.4 provide a tentative idea about the relationship between productivity under different scenarios and average temperature. Both the figures show a strong and negative relationship between productivity growth and temperature level, i.e., the hotter countries observe lower levels of productivity growth relative to colder countries. This relationship, though known since the 18th century (Montesquieu, 1750), has been further established using national data by Dell et al. (2008) and Horowitz (2009) and sub-national data by Nordhaus (2006) in the context of income-temperature relationship. There are, of course, many possible reasons why hotter countries have lower productivity growth, such as climate's effects on disease, agriculture, capital depreciation, worker productivity, or human behavior in the form of culture or institutions. Nordhaus (1994) discusses wide-ranging pathways of how temperature has been viewed as a factor in economic activity, particularly at the individual level, as when worker or student performance is affected by ambient temperature.

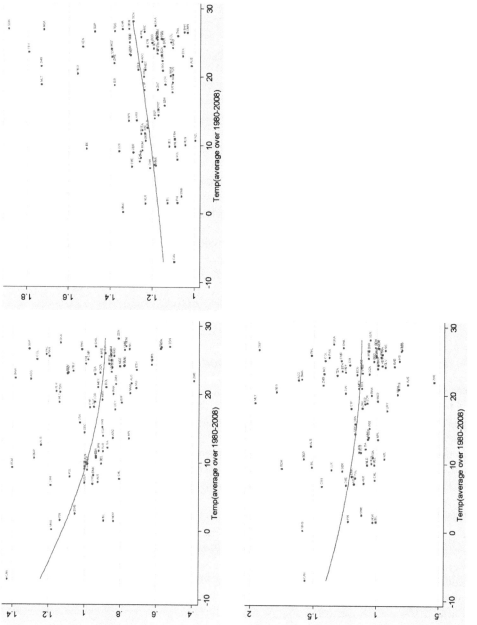

Figure 22.3 Relationship between temperature and productivity change under strong disposability of CO_2 emissions

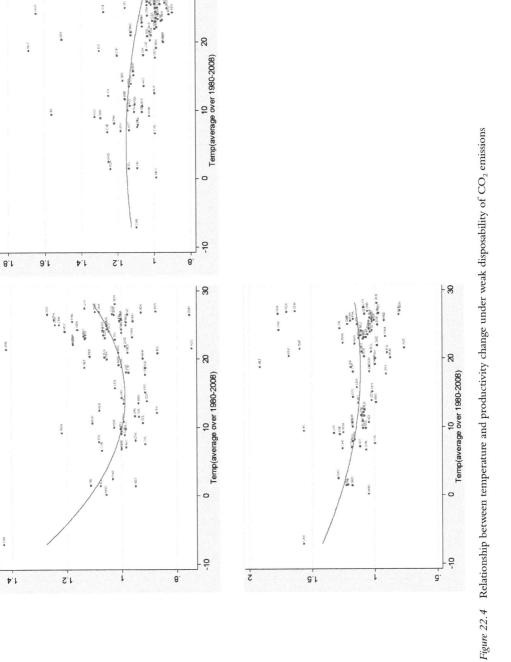

Figure 22.4 Relationship between temperature and productivity change under weak disposability of CO_2 emissions

Note that the negative relationship between productivity growth and temperature levels is governed by the catch-up effect when the productivity growth is measured conventionally. However, a negative relationship between temperature-carbon sensitive productivity is the function of both the negative relationships between temperature and technological diffusion as well temperature and technological progress (Figure 22.4), though a positive relationship between temperature and technological diffusion is observed when the average temperature is more than 20°C.

To examine the relationship between productivity and its determinants, the study considers variables such as level of productivity in the initial year, average temperature in a country over the period of 1980 to 2008, soil quality in a country, average protection against appropriation of property rights (AVEXPRO), and Simeon extended index of formalism (SDFORMALISM). The source of data on soil quality is Nordhaus' g-econ project. A low value of the index of soil quality implies high water level.

The convergence theory could be restated in the relationship between productivity and lagged technical inefficiency. This relationship would state that those countries that were near the production frontier would see a lower level of productivity growth than those that were farther away. Therefore, the positive relationship between productivity level and lagged productivity level would indicate the presence of convergence hypothesis (Kumar, 2006). A positive relation between cumulative productivity (CP) and initial productivity shows divergence across countries, and a negative relation between CP components and initial inefficiency indicates divergence across countries.

Table 22.2a provides the descriptive statistics of the determinants of productivity and its components for both developed and developing countries. In the developed countries, the average temperature is about 10°C, whereas in the developing countries group the temperature is about 21°C and more than their counterpart group. Similarly, in the developed countries the index value of soil quality is 48.5, though in the developing countries group the average value of soil quality index is about 80. Note that in respect to both the climatic factors, there is higher variability in the developed country group relative to the developing countries group. The situation is opposite with respect to institutional variables in developed and developing countries. In the developing countries the value of AVEXPRO is substantially lower and SDFORMALISM is higher relative to the developed countries group, and there is high variability with respect to these variables in the developing countries in comparison to developed countries. The regression results are presented from Table 22.3 to 22.5.

Tables 22.3a and 22.3b provide the parameters estimates of productivity determinants under strong and weak scenarios, respectively. We find a positive association between cumulative productivity and its initial level, which helps in explaining the growing inequality between countries. Divergence is happening even within the developing countries under both the scenarios. Soil quality levels impact productivity growth positively in developed countries, whereas the temperature levels affect growth in developing countries negatively. A negative association between temperature level and cumulative productivity level for the

Table 22.2a Descriptive statistics of variables used in regressions

Variable	Developed Countries					Developing Countries				
	Obs	Mean	Std. Dev.	Min	Max	Obs	Mean	Std. Dev.	Min	Max
Soil Quality	26	48.50	34.07	0	139.67	62	79.37	40.88	12.88	182.68
Temperature	26	10.36	7.20	−7.08	26.60	62	21.10	6.23	0.24	28.16
AVEXPR	25	9.48	0.67	7.23	10.00	57	6.55	1.28	1.64	9.00
SDFORMALISM	26	3.09	0.80	1.58	5.25	53	4.08	1.01	1.68	5.91

sample of developing countries under strong disposability indicates that climate change impacts are more pronounced in the developing countries. Moreover, better property rights and less complex systems help in increasing the productivity level in developed countries under both of the scenarios.

Table 22.3a Determinants of productivity change under strong disposability of CO_2 emissions

Variable	All Countries			Developed Countries			Developing Countries		
	Variant1	Variant2	Variant3	Variant1	Variant2	Variant3	Variant1	Variant2	Variant3
Productivity96	1.044	0.748	0.666	2.326	3.939	2.754	1.012	0.641	0.684
	1.99	1.77	1.74	1.41	3.15	1.75	1.95	1.51	1.84
Temperature	−0.003	−0.008	−0.005	0.002	−0.002	0.004	−0.009	−0.014	−0.014
	−0.71	−1.4	−1.68	0.23	−0.12	0.33	−1.58	−2.65	−3.09
Soil Quality	−0.002	−0.002	−0.001	−0.004	−0.003	−0.003	−0.001	−0.001	−0.001
	−2.14	−1.85	−1.83	−2.34	−3.21	−2.53	−1.59	−1.23	−1.45
Sdformalism	0.014			−0.119			0.043		
	0.46			−1.37			1.47		
AVEXPR		0.021			0.181			0.002	
		0.71			1.67			0.08	
Constant	0.215	0.815	0.675	−0.619	−0.909	−1.481	0.229	0.857	0.827
	0.38	1.85	1.64	−0.3	−0.49	−0.86	0.41	2.07	2.04
sigma	0.229	0.245	0.243	0.221	0.216	0.238	0.209	0.229	0.228
	9.37	10.24	11	5.96	5.11	5.28	9.61	10.58	11.17
Observations	79	82	88	26	25	26	53	57	62
Log pseudolikelihood	4.189	−1.137	−0.425	2.37	2.79	0.479	7.636	3.04	3.79

Note: values in second row represent t-statistics

Table 22.3b Determinants of productivity change under weak disposability of CO_2 emissions

Variable	All Countries			Developed Countries			Developing Countries		
	Variant1	Variant2	Variant3	Variant1	Variant2	Variant3	Variant1	Variant2	Variant3
Productivity96	1.794	2.04	1.894	2.511	4.22	2.894	1.703	2.066	1.871
	3.2	4.19	3.86	1.64	4	1.86	2.69	4.17	3.76
Temperature	−0.004	−0.006	−0.004	−0.002	−0.007	−0.001	−0.005	−0.003	−0.002
	−1.39	−1.27	−1.53	−0.22	−0.57	−0.05	−1.8	−1.2	−0.92
Soil Quality	−0.0014	−0.001	−0.001	−0.003	−0.003	−0.003	−0.001	−0.0003	−0.001
	−2.25	−1.86	−1.86	−2.02	−2.8	−2.03	−1.46	−0.6	−0.83
Sdformalism	−0.021			−0.11			0.005		
	−0.77			−1.53			0.17		
AVEXPR		−0.015			0.198			−0.022	
		−0.7			1.97			−1.26	

(Continued)

Table 22.3b (Continued)

Variable	All Countries			Developed Countries			Developing Countries		
	Variant1	Variant2	Variant3	Variant1	Variant2	Variant3	Variant1	Variant2	Variant3
Constant	−0.438	−0.641	−0.637	−0.803	−0.994	−1.589	−0.508	−0.754	−0.717
	−0.71	−1.3	−1.25	−0.43	−0.62	−0.94	−0.74	−1.62	−1.41
sigma	0.173	0.184	0.183	0.198	0.185	0.214	0.142	0.155	0.159
	7.04	7.05	7.48	6.21	4.94	5.11	5	5.99	6.63
Observations	79	82	88	26	25	26	53	57	62
Log pseudolikelihood	26.479	22.53	24.48	5.259	6.749	3.236	28.30	25.46	25.758

Note: values in second row represent t-statistics

Table 22.4 Determinants of efficiency change under weak disposability of CO_2 emissions

Variable	All Countries			Developed Countries			Developing Countries		
	Variant1	Variant2	Variant3	Variant1	Variant2	Variant3	Variant1	Variant2	Variant3
Efficiency96	0.144	0.133	0.144	0.392	0.513	0.379	0.107	0.098	0.108
	2.93	3.01	3.13	2	1.83	1.74	1.78	1.62	2.1
Temperature	−0.001	−0.002	−0.001	−0.008	−0.010	−0.008	0.002	0.002	0.001
	−0.32	−0.46	−0.23	−1.52	−1.42	−1.3	1	0.94	0.72
Soil Quality	−0.0003	−0.001	−0.0004	−0.001	−0.001	−0.001	−0.0003	−0.0004	−0.001
	−0.77	−1.29	−1.26	−1.56	−1.44	−1.35	−0.74	−0.94	−1.43
Sdformalism	0.006			−0.05			0.0118		
	0.38			−1.39			0.6		
AVEXPR		−0.009			0.070			0.005	
		−0.77			1.99			0.35	
Constant	1.006	1.13	1.032	1.263	1.772	1.088	0.941	0.974	1.022
	14.98	7.79	25.03	7.97	4.52	15.79	8.48	8.36	21.94
sigma	0.109	0.111	0.109	0.103	0.102	0.109	0.100	0.104	0.103
	8.09	8.88	9.04	5.45	4.42	4.73	6.96	8.25	8.72
Observations	79	82	88	26	25	26	53	57	62
Log pseudolikelihood	62.88	64.109	69.68	22.316	21.52	20.74	46.67	48.22	53.03

Note: values in second row represent t-statistics

Table 22.4a Determinants of efficiency change under strong disposability of CO_2 emissions

Variable	All Countries			Developed Countries			Developing Countries		
	Variant1	Variant2	Variant3	Variant1	Variant2	Variant3	Variant1	Variant2	Variant3
Efficiency96	−0.029	−0.002	−0.008	0.211	0.256	0.194	−0.037	−0.027	−0.029
	−0.87	−0.06	−0.26	0.96	0.92	0.84	−1.08	−0.84	−0.92

Temperature	−0.006	−0.006	−0.007	−0.007	−0.008	−0.006	−0.009	−0.01	−0.013
	−1.55	−1.46	−2.72	−1.05	−0.9	−0.82	−1.71	−2.23	−3.42
Soil Quality	−0.001	−0.001	−0.001	−0.002	−0.001	−0.001	−0.001	−0.001	−0.001
	−1.04	−1.21	−1.54	−2.03	−1.55	−1.72	−1	−1.26	−1.6
Sdformalism	−0.027			−0.071			−0.039		
	−1.46			−1.75			−2.15		
AVEXPR		0.011			0.061			0.046	
		0.57			1.41			2.29	
Constant	1.007	1.02	1.134	1.317	1.662	1.068	1.056	0.924	1.314
	13.56	4.6	20.61	7.42	3.42	12.08	8.07	4.17	11.51
sigma	0.167	0.181	0.180	0.122	0.131	0.133	0.174	0.183	0.189
	10.95	11.54	12.01	5.72	4.6	4.86	9.85	10.36	10.77
Observations	79	82	88	26	25	26	53	57	62
Log pseudolikelihood	29.367	23.686	25.85	17.85	15.438	15.628	17.437	15.829	15.12

Note: values in second row represent t-statistics

Table 22.5a Determinants of technical change under strong disposability of CO_2 emissions

Variable	All Countries			Developed Countries			Developing Countries		
	Variant1	Variant2	Variant3	Variant1	Variant2	Variant3	Variant1	Variant2	Variant3
Efficiency96	0.056	0.041	0.049	−0.492	−0.441	−0.499	0.069	0.062	0.063
	2.29	1.59	2.08	−2.1	−1.98	−2.19	2.56	2.53	2.55
Temperature	0.004	0.001	−0.003	0.005	0.002	0.005	0.004	0.0017	−0.005
	1.54	0.21	−1.72	1.36	0.48	1.43	1.33	0.62	−1.8
Soil Quality	−0.001	−0.0004	−0.0002	−0.002	−0.002	−0.002	0.0003	0.0004	0.001
	−1.02	−0.62	−0.41	−2.19	−2.96	−2.46	0.57	0.67	0.8
Sdformalism	−0.024			−0.029			−0.013		
	−1.14			−0.68			−0.53		
AVEXPR		0.023			−0.071			0.045	
		1.43			−1.08			1.78	
Constant	1.26	1.407	1.164	1.432	2.024	1.33	1.122	1.42	1.045
	15.87	8.58	21.82	7.71	3.06	18.53	10.24	7.1	12.02
sigma	0.149	0.165	0.163	0.121	0.118	0.123	0.144	0.158	0.161
	8.71	8.35	7.76	7	7.54	7.07	6.49	6.83	6.35
Observations	79	82	88	26	25	26	53	57	62
Log pseudolikelihood	38.34	31.22	35.018	18.048	17.867	17.64	27.615	24.348	25.238

Note: values in second row represent t-statistics

Table 22.5b Determinants of technical change under weak disposability of CO_2 emissions

Variable	All Countries			Developed Countries			Developing Countries		
	Variant1	Variant2	Variant3	Variant1	Variant2	Variant3	Variant1	Variant2	Variant3
Efficiency96	−0.304	−0.335	−0.332	−0.547	−0.487	−0.561	−0.276	−0.327	−0.302
	−3.46	−4.27	−4.52	−2.12	−1.86	−2.13	−2	−3.21	−3.22
Temperature	−0.0003	1.59E−06	−0.0004	0.002	−0.001	0.003	−0.002	−0.001	−0.001
	−0.12	0	−0.2	0.74	−0.16	0.89	−1.01	−0.45	−0.56
Soil Quality	−0.001	−0.0003	−0.0004	−0.002	−0.002	−0.002	0.0001	0.0003	0.0002
	−1.09	−0.54	−0.85	−2.31	−3.07	−2.4	0.28	0.73	0.46
Sdformalism	−0.029			−0.050			−0.022		
	−1.64			−1.47			−0.9		
AVEXPR		0.003			−0.076			0.008	
		0.23			−1.23			0.53	
Constant	1.349	1.215	1.247	1.501	2.062	1.323	1.301	1.153	1.199
	21.25	8.34	32.09	9.16	3.32	20.15	14.78	8.93	19.67
sigma	0.129	0.146	0.142	0.115	0.115	0.121	0.124	0.146	0.142
	5.34	6.41	6.44	7	6.06	6.18	3.41	4.72	4.69
Observations	79	82	88	26	25	26	53	57	62
Log pseudolikelihood	49.286	41.52	46.74	19.437	18.539	18.11	35.25	28.928	33.06

Note: values in second row represent t-statistics

Table 22.4 presents the regression results for the determinants of efficiency change (catch-up effect). Under strong disposability, neither divergence nor convergence is observed in either of the groups. However, if the disposal of emissions is restricted, then there is convergence in technological adoption across countries and within the groups of developed and developing countries. When the disposal of CO_2 emissions is free, the temperature increases lower the technological diffusion in developing countries but better property rights help in lowering the impact of climate change and spread the diffusion. Soil quality is not related to technological diffusion. Less complex systems improve the diffusion in developed countries. The process of the diffusion is negatively affected in developed countries due to climate change under weak disposability of emissions. However, better property rights in developed countries help in improving the process of technological diffusion.

Tables 22.5a and 22.5b provide the regression results for the determinants of technological change. Under strong disposability, there is divergence in innovation in developed countries but convergence in developing countries. But if the disposal is made costly, divergence in innovation is common in both of the groups. Better property rights help in improving the innovations in developed countries under weak disposability and in developing countries under strong disposability. However, innovations are not related to temperature changes under either of the scenarios.

5. Conclusions and policy recommendations

Temperature and institutions determine choices and provide incentives; therefore, they are important in lowering the vagaries of climate change measured in terms of climate change impacts in terms of productivity. Their relationships to productivity is analyzed in the literature

(Montesquieu, 1750; Acemoglu and Johnson, 2005). However, it is less discussed in the literature on the impacts of climate change (Dell et al., 2008). This chapter intends to measure the relationships with productivity measures adjusted for the regulation of carbon emissions and institutions along with climate change variables and draw policy lessons for Asian countries.

This study involves two stages: in the first stage it estimates TFP, and in the second stage, the impacts of climate change and institutions on TFP are estimated using truncated regressions. We measure TFP for a group of 88 countries over the period of 1994 to 2008 using directional output distance function. It estimates TFP under two scenarios: carbon emissions are not regulated and these emissions are regulated. The comparison between the two scenarios provides an idea about the costs of regulation of carbon emissions, i.e., the cost of mitigating carbon emissions.

In this study, productivity growth has been found both in developed and developing countries and their divergence in productivity growth has been increasing. Note the divergence in growth in productivity is happening not only between the groups of countries but also within the group of developing countries. When CO_2 is considered, there is higher potential for reduction of CO_2 emissions in developing countries at lower cost. However, the costly disposable of emissions lowers their growth potential in terms of loss in productivity growth.

Under scenarios when carbon emissions are not regulated, the developing countries are found to be more vulnerable to climate change problems and better property rights help in lowering the impacts of climate change through improving the process of technological adoption in developing countries. Climate change reduces the productivity growth in developing counties by lowering the process of technological adoption and better property and contracting rights result in higher productivity. The results of the study also show that better institutions encourage technological adaptation and innovations under the weak disposability of carbon emissions scenario. This implies that rights that secure individual property from any kind of expropriation and enforceable contracting rights could be the tools of good climate policy, i.e., better institutions help in adapting to changing climate and mitigate carbon emissions at lower cost by finding new technologies.

In addition, we find a potential win-win opportunity to reduce CO_2 while increasing GDP given that a country's distance from the best-practice frontier is higher for developing countries than for developed countries. The countries in our sample would lose 23 percent of GDP in 2008 on average. This is because of carbon-binding production technology. The relative output loss by the imposition of costly abatements for developing countries is higher than the overall average of the entire sample. This finding implies that it is cheaper to reduce carbon emissions in developing countries, but if they are not adequately compensated and required to reduce the emissions, their growth potentially will be hindered and will further accentuate the growing divergence between developed and developing countries. Therefore, international climate policy should not only rely solely on emissions trading to mitigate carbon emissions in a cost effective manner but also try to institute technology and funds transfers from developed countries to developing countries so that carbons emission can be abated cost effectively and in a just way.

Notes

1 See Pittman (1981), Cropper and Oates (1992), Kopp (1998), Reinhard et al. (1999), and Murty and Kumar (2004).

2 Recently the same approach was followed by many studies, including Kumar (2006), Kumar and Khanna (2009), and Kumar and Managi (2009, 2010), which use macro level data sets.

3 For details on directional distance function and estimation of productivity and efficiency using Malmquist-Luenberger Index and its computation through DEA, see Kumar (2006).

4 Developed countries: Australia, Austria, Belgium, Canada, Cyprus, Denmark, Finland, France, Greece, Iceland, Ireland, Israel, Italy, Japan, Luxembourg, Malta, Netherlands, New Zealand, Norway, Portugal, Singapore, Spain, Sweden, Switzerland, United Kingdom, United States.

Developing countries: Albania, Algeria, Angola, Argentina, Bahrain, Bangladesh, Benin, Bolivia, Botswana, Brazil, Bulgaria, Cameroon, Chile, China, Colombia, Costa Rica, Ecuador, El Salvador, Ethiopia, Gabon, Ghana, Guatemala, Haiti, Honduras, Hungary, India, Indonesia, Iraq, Jamaica, Jordan, Kenya, Lebanon, Malaysia, Mexico, Mongolia, Morocco, Mozambique, Namibia, Nepal, Nicaragua, Nigeria, Oman, Pakistan, Panama, Paraguay, Peru, Philippines, Poland, Romania, Senegal, South Africa, Sri Lanka, Sudan, Tanzania, Thailand, Togo, Tunisia, Turkey, Uruguay, Vietnam, Zambia, Zimbabwe.

5 Disaggregated results for each country are available from the authors on request.

6 See http://gecon.yale.edu/ for dataset and detailed description.

References

Acemoglu, D., S. Johnson and J. Robinson. (2001) Reversal of Fortune: Geography and Institutions in the Making of the Modern World Income Distribution, *Quarterly Journal of Economics*, 117:1231–1294.

Acemoglu, D. and J. Simon. (2005) Unbundling Institutions, *Journal of Political Economy*, 113:949–995.

Atkinson, S. E. and R.H. Dorfman. (2005) Crediting Electric Utilities for Reducing Air Pollution: Bayesian Measurement of Productivity and Efficiency, *Journal of Econometrics* 126:445–468.

Banerjee, A. and L. Iyer. (2005) History, Institutions and Economic Performance: The Legacy of Colonial Land Tenure Systems in India, *American Economic Review* 95(4):1190–213.

Bosello F., R. Roson and R.S.J. Tol. (2006) Economy-Wide Estimates of the Implications of Climate Change: Human Health, *Ecological Economics* 58:579–591.

Bromley, D.W. (Ed.) (1995) *Handbook of Environmental Economics.* London: Blackwell Publications Ltd.

Chung, Y., R. Färe and S. Grosskopf. (1997) Productivity and Undesirable Outputs: A Directional Distance Function Approach, *Journal of Environmental Management* 51:229–240.

Cropper, M.L. and W.E. Oates. (1992) Environmental Economics: A Survey, *Journal of Economic Literature* 30(2):675–740.

Dell, M., B.F. Jones and B.A. Olken. (2008) Climate change and economic growth: Evidence from the last half century, NBER Working Paper #14132, Cambridge, MA.

Deschênes, O. and M. Greenstone. (2007) The Economic Impacts of Climate Change: Evidence from Agricultural Output and Random Fluctuations in Weather, *The American Economic Review* 97(1):354–385.

Easterly, W. and R. Levine. (2003) Tropics, Germs, and Crops: How Endowments Influence Economic Development, *Journal of Monetary Economics* 50:3–39.

Gollop, F.M. and M.J. Roberts. (1983) Environmental Regulations and Productivity Growth: the Case of Fossil-Fuelled Electric Power Generation, *Journal of Political Economy* 9(4):654–74.

Hall, R.E. and C. Jones. (1999) Why Do Some Countries Produce So Much More Output Per Worker Than Others? *Quarterly Journal of Economics* (February):83–116.

Horowitz, J.K. (2009) The Income-Temperature Relationship in a Cross-Section of Countries and its Implications for Predicting the Effects of Global Warming, *Environmental and Resource Economics* 44:475–493.

Huntington, E. (1915) *Civilization and Climate.* New Haven, CT: Yale University Press.

Jaffe, A.B., R.G. Newell and R.N. Stavins. (2003) Technological Change and the Environment. In *Handbook of Environmental Economics*, K.-G. Mäler and J. Vincent, (Eds.) pp. 461–516. Amsterdam: North-Holland, Elsevier Science.

Jinshu, L. (2011) No Climate for Cleantech, *Down to Earth*, November 1–15, p. 50.

Kopp, G. (1998) Carbon Dioxide Emissions and Economic Growth: A Structural Approach, *Journal of Applied Statistics* 25(4):489–515.

Kumar, S. (2006) Environmentally Sensitive Productivity Growth: A Global Analysis Using Malmquist–Luenberger Index.," *Ecological Economics* 56 (2): 280–293.

Maddison, D., M. Manley and P. Kurukulasuriya. (2007) The Impact of Climate Change on African Agriculture, Policy Research Working Paper #4306, The World Bank, Development Research Group. Washington, DC: The World Bank.

Marshall, A. (1920) *Principles of Economics.* London: Macmillan and Co.

Mendelsohn, R., W. Morrison, M. Schlesinger and N. Andronova. (2000) Country-Specific Market Impacts of Climate Change, *Climatic Change* 45(3–4):553–569.

Mendelsohn, R., W. Nordhaus, and D. Shaw. (1994) The Impact of Global Warming on Agriculture: A Ricardian Analysis, *American Economic Review* 84(4):753–71.

Montesquieu, C.d. (1750) *The Spirit of Laws.* London: J. Nourse & P. Vaillant.

Murty, M.N. and S. Kumar. (2004) *Environmental and Economic Accounting for Industry.* New Delhi: Oxford University Press.

Murty, S. and R. Russell. (2002) On Modelling Pollution Generating Technologies. Working Paper Series, No. 02–14, Department of Economics, University of California, Riverside, CA.

Nordhaus, W.D. (2006) Geography and Macroeconomics: New Data and New Findings, *PNAS* 103(10):3510–3517.

Nordhaus, W.D. (2010) Economic Aspects of Global Warming in a Post Copenhagen Environment, *PNAS* 107(26):11721–11726.

Nordhaus, W. D. and J. Boyer. (2000) *Warming the World: The Economics of the Greenhouse Effect.* Cambridge, MA: MIT Press.

North, D.C. (1990) *Institutions, Institutional Change and Economic Performance.* Cambridge: Cambridge University Press.

North, D.C. (1991) Institutions, *Journal of Economic Perspective* 5(1):97–112.

Pittman, R.W. (1981) Issues in Pollution Control: Interplant Cost Differences and Economies of Scale, *Land Economics* 57(1):1–17.

Pittman, R.W. (1983) Multilateral Productivity Comparisons with Undesirable Outputs, *The Economic Journal* 93:883–891.

Reinhard, S., C.A.K. Lovell and G. Thijssen. (1999) Econometric Estimation of Technical and Environmental Efficiency: An Application to Dutch Dairy Farms, *American Journal of Agricultural Economics* 81(1):44–60.

Rodric, D., A. Subramanian and F. Trebbi. (2004) Institutions Rules: The primacy of Institutions Over Geography and Integration in Economic Development, *Journal of Economic Growth* 9:131–165.

Sachs, J. (2003) Institutions Don't Rule: Direct Effect of Geography on Per capita income, NBER Working Paper No. 9490, Cambridge, MA.

Schlenker, W., W.M. Hanemann and A.C. Fisher. (2006) The Impact of Global Warming on U.S. Agriculture: An Econometric Analysis of Optimal Growing Conditions, *The Review of Economics and Statistics* 88(1):113–125.

Simar, L. and P. Wilson. (1999) Of course we can bootstrap DEA scores! But does it mean anything? Logic trumps wishful thinking, *Journal of Productivity Analysis* 11:93–97.

Simar, L. and P. Wilson. (2007) Estimation and Inference in Two Stage, Semi-Parametric Models of Productive Efficiency, *Journal of Econometrics* 136:31–64.

Tol, R.S.J. (2002) Estimates of the Damage Costs of Climate Change, *Environmental and Resource Economics* 21:47–73.

23

DETERMINING FUTURE ENVIRONMENTAL VALUE

Empirical analysis of discounting over time and distance

Tetsuya Tsurumi, Kei Kuramashi, Shunsuke Managi, and Ken-Ichi Akao

1. Introduction

Economists have argued about various discount rates. Strotz (1955–56) first suggested that there is no reason to consider a time-consistent discount rate such as an exponential function. Over the past five decades, various functional theoretical forms have been proposed, including exponential, hyperbolic, and quasi-hyperbolic. Simultaneously, empirical studies have found there is a possibility that observed discount rates are not constant over time. The data tend to not fit exponential functional forms but rather hyperbolic ones; this implies declining discount rates. Furthermore, empirical studies have found that discount rates vary across objects. Fredrick et al. (2002) summarized the annual discount rates found in previous empirical studies. Table 23.1 summarizes annual discount rates estimated in previous literature. The literature suggests various annual discount rates, and the results depend on the type of goods, the time range, and/or the estimation methods. In this chapter, we consider the discount rates on environmental values, and especially on long-term problems, as these are not empirically addressed in previous literature.

It is crucial to adopt appropriate discount rates. In the literature on climate change, Nordhaus (1992) employed a utility discount rate of 3 percent, while Cline (1992) adopted a utility discount rate of 0 percent to place as much weight on future generations as on the present. The latter is referred to as a utilitarian ethical perspective; it implies that we need rapid action to prevent global warming. Similar to Cline (1992), Stern (2007) adopts a utilitarian ethical perspective and thus employs a utility discount rate of only 0.1 percent per annum.[1] Nordhaus (2007) and Dasgupta (2006, 2007) argue that Stern's utility discount rate is quite low and recommend that historic market interest rates be applied. These researchers apply discount rates based on market interest rates, which reflect the sum of many actual individual choices. Historic market interest rates have averaged around 6 percent, and most previous research applied consumption discount rates at roughly this level (Hepburn et al., 2010). The differences among discount rates produce critical differences among long-term environmental values such as climate change.

Furthermore, when we consider long-term discount rates, we need to consider the effect of "uncertainty." Weitzman (1998, 2001) suggests that if we take uncertainty into consideration, the discount rate declines over time. Behavioral economists and psychologists have found evidence

Table 23.1 Annual discount rates in the literature

Study	Good(s)	Time Range	Annual Discount Rate(s)
Maital & Maital (1978)	Money & coupons	1 year	70%
Thaler (1981)	Money	3 mos. to 10 yrs.	7% to 345%
Houston (1983)	Money	1 yr. to 20 yrs.	0.23
Benzion et al. (1989)	Money	6 mos. to 4 yrs.	9% to 60%
Shelley (1993)	Money	6 mos. to 4 yrs.	8% to 27%
Chapman & Elstein (1995)	Money & Health	6 mos. to 12yrs.	11% to 263%
Wahlund & Gunnarsson (1996)	Money	1 mos. to 1 yrs.	18% to 158%
Cairns & van der Pol (1997)	Money	2 yrs. to 19 yrs.	13% to 31%
Green et al. (1997)	Money	3 mos. to 20 yrs.	6% to 111%
Johannesson & Johansson (1997)	Life years	6 yrs. to 57 yrs.	0% to 3%
Cairns & van der Pol (1999)	Health	4 yrs. to 16 yrs.	0.06
Ganiats et al. (2000)	Health	6 mos. to 20 yrs.	negative to 116%
Hesketh (2000)	Money	6 mos. to 4 yrs.	4% to 36%
van der Pol & Cairns (2001)	Health	2 yrs. to 15 yrs.	6% to 9%

Source: Fredrick et al. (2002).

of preference reversals. One theory consistent with preference reversals is that people have diminishing impatience and tend to discount the future with a declining discount rate. A large number of empirical studies argue that impatience in the present is higher than impatience with respect to future tradeoffs (Ainslie, 1992; Frederick et al., 2002; Della Vigna, 2009; Hepburn et al., 2010).

In this study, we consider various objects' discount rates in the long run. Previous literature does not consider long-term discount rates, such as those that discount over a 100-year period (See Table 23.1). We also consider not only time discount rates but also "distance discount rates." There is a possibility that willingness to pay (WTP) for environmental conservation differs according to the location where conservation is provided. For example, we may donate more money for local environmental problems than for those in foreign countries. This argument is unique to this research area.

The remainder of the chapter is organized as follows: In Section 2, we present an overview of our surveys and show descriptive statistics. In Section 3, we explore how our estimated discount factors fit previously proposed functional forms. In Section 4, we conclude.

2. The surveys

We conducted three surveys in Japan. They occurred from February 17 to 20, 2010; from February 17 to 20, 2011; and from January 20 to 23, 2012, respectively. The results of these surveys are summarized in Table 23.2. To consider both time and distance discount rates, we investigate WTP for various environmental conservation initiatives. We assume that environmental conservation is conducted at various times and in various places, as discussed later. To obtain the WTP for environmental conservation, we apply a contingent valuation method (CVM). We apply three CVMs to confirm robustness. They include a single-bounded dichotomous choice method, a double-bounded dichotomous choice method, and a card verification method. We then show the results of the three surveys.

Table 23.2 Overview of the three surveys

	Survey 1	*Survey 2*	*Survey 3*
Period	Feb. 17–20, 2010	Feb. 17–22, 2011	Jan. 20–23, 2012
Sample	7,231	4,002	1,113
Area	All prefectures in Japan	All prefectures in Japan	All prefectures in Japan
Environmental evaluation method	Contingent valuation method (CVM): single-bounded dichotomous choice	Contingent valuation method (CVM): double-bounded dichotomous choice	Contingent valuation method (CVM): card verification methods
Place where the environmental problems occur	Local (Japan), Southeastern Asia, South America	Various place in Japan, foreign country	Local (Japan) and foreign country
Time when the environmental problems occur (years later)	5, 20, 100	0, 5, 10, 20, 50, 100, 200	0, 5, 10, 20, 50, 100, 200

Table 23.3 All scenarios: 2010 survey

Environment	*Where the destruction occurs*	*When the destruction occurs*
Dam development	Local (Japan), Southeast Asia, South America	5, 20, 100
Water source forest	Local (Japan), Southeast Asia, South America	5, 20, 100
Water pollution (river)	Local (Japan), Southeast Asia, South America	5, 20, 100
Agricultural damage by global warming	Local (Japan), Southeast Asia, South America	5, 20, 100

Note: We use single-bounded dichotomous choice to obtain the WTP.

2.1 The 2010 survey

The 2010 survey applied four scenarios to obtain the WTP. The four scenarios are as follows: a) biodiversity destruction due to a dam development project; b) destruction of a water-source forest; c) water pollution (river); and d) agricultural damage due to global warming. To consider the effects of time, we assume the following three times when the destruction occurs: 1) five years later, 2) 20 years later, and 3) 100 years later. Additionally, to consider the effects of place, we divide the survey sample into the following three groups where the destruction occurs: 1) a local area, 2) a certain country in Southeast Asia, and 3) a certain country in South America. The scenarios are summarized in Table 23.3.

We apply a single-bounded dichotomous choice to obtain the WTP. Figure 23.1 shows the relationship between the estimated WTP and time. The results indicate that the discount rates tend to decrease over time. There is a possibility that the functional form of the discount rates is hyperbolic or quasi-hyperbolic and not exponential. On the other hand, Figure 23.2 shows the relationship between the estimated WTP and distance. The results indicate that there is a clear

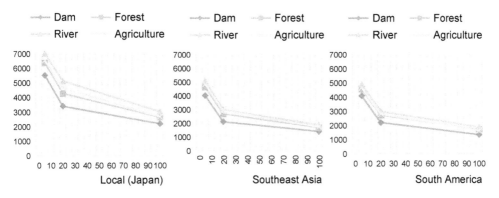

Figure 23.1   Relationship between time on WTPs (2010 survey)

Notes: The vertical line indicates the WTP (yen) for environmental conservation. The holizontal line indicates the time (year) the environmental degradation occurs. We use a single-bounded dichotomous choice to obtain the WTP.1.

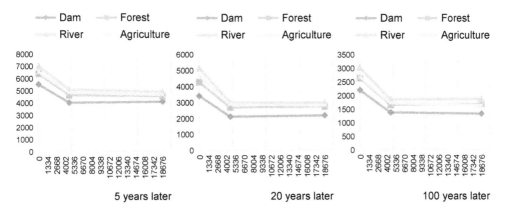

Figure 23.2   The relationship between distance and the WTP (2010 survey)

Notes: The vertical line indicates the WTP (yen) for environmental conservation. The holizontal line indicates the distance (km) from Japan to the place where the environmental degradation occurs. We use a single-bounded dichotomous choice to obtain the WTP.

difference between the WTP in Japan and that in foreign countries. In addition, we cannot find a difference between the WTP in Southeast Asia and South America. This may imply that we tend to differentiate between domestic and foreign environmental problems and that there are few differences in the WTP among foreign countries.

2.2 The 2011 survey

The 2010 survey indicates that with regard to environmental conservation of four objects, the time discount rates decrease over time. In the 2011 survey, we consider "ultra-long-term" discount rates. Previous studies tend to consider relatively short-term discount rates, as seen in Table 23.1. In the 2010 survey, we consider discount rates for 100 years into the future, while in the 2011 survey we consider those for 200 years hence. It is important to consider ultra-long-term

Table 23.4 The 2011 survey outline

	Where the destruction occurs	*When the destruction occurs*
PLACE 1	Somewhere in the municipality where a respondent lives	0, 5, 10, 20, 50, 100, 200
PLACE 2	Somewhere in the municipality next to PLACE 1	0, 5, 10, 20, 50, 100, 200
PLACE 3	Somewhere in the prefecture where a respondent lives (except for the area covering PLACES 1 and 2)	0, 5, 10, 20, 50, 100, 200
PLACE 4	Somewhere in the prefecture next to PLACE 3	0, 5, 10, 20, 50, 100, 200
PLACE 5	Somewhere in the region where a respondent lives (except for the area covering PLACES 1, 2, 3, and 4)(Hokkaido, Tohoku, Kanto, Chubu, Kinki, Chugoku, Shikoku, and Kyushu regions)	0, 5, 10, 20, 50, 100, 200
PLACE 6	Somewhere in the region next to PLACE 5	0, 5, 10, 20, 50, 100, 200
PLACE 7	Somewhere in the foreign countries	0, 5, 10, 20, 50, 100, 200

Note: We use a double-bounded dichotomous choice to obtain the WTP. We suppose water pollution as environmental degradation.

discount rates because an environmental problem such as global warming strikes a note of warning against future damage.

We also consider distance discount rates in the 2011 survey. In the 2010 survey, we consider the difference in discount rates among foreign countries. In the 2011 survey, we consider the difference in the domestic country's discount rates. The 2011 survey assumes seven places where environmental degradation occurs.[2] The first (PLACE 1) is somewhere in the municipality where a respondent lives. The second (PLACE 2) is somewhere in the municipality next to PLACE 1. The third (PLACE 3) is somewhere in the prefecture where a respondent lives (except for in PLACES 1 and 2). The fourth (PLACE 4) is somewhere in the prefecture next to PLACE 3. The fifth (PLACE 5) is somewhere in the region where a respondent lives (except for the areas of PLACES 1, 2, and 3, and 4). Here regions refer to Hokkaido, Tohoku, Kanto, Chubu, Kinki, Chugoku, Shikoku, and Kyushu. The sixth location (PLACE 6) is somewhere in the region next to PLACE 5. The seventh (PLACE 7) is somewhere in the foreign countries. Concerning the environmental objects, the 2011 survey concentrates on one type of object, i.e., water pollution, because in this survey we focus attention on the ultra-long-term discount rates and on the difference in discount rates among domestic countries. We summarize the survey outline in Table 23.4.

Figures 23.3 and 23.4 show the estimated WTP for environmental conservation against future water pollution. Figure 23.3 refers to the relationship between the WTP and time, while Figure 23.4 refers to the relationship between the WTP and distance.

Figure 23.3 implies that, as in the 2010 survey, the time discount rates decrease over time. We find that the annual discount rates around 200 years are slightly smaller than those around 100 years. We also find that a respondent tends to place an emphasis on his or her own municipality. The WTP in PLACE 2 (the neighborhood municipality) is apparently smaller than that in PLACE 1 (the municipality where a respondent lives). And it is notable that there are few differences in the WTP among PLACES 2, 3, 4, 5, and 6. This may suggest that we tend to place an emphasis on the location where we live, while we tend to place an equal but lesser emphasis on locations within the domestic country. We also note that the WTP in foreign countries (PLACE 7) are smaller than those in PLACE 2 to PLACE 6. We, therefore, can divide the WTP

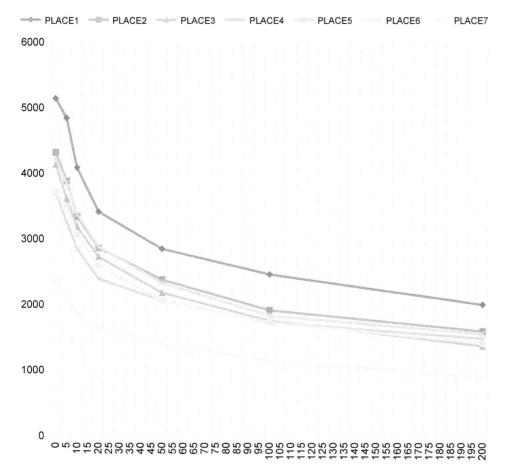

Figure 23.3 WTP for environmental conservation against water pollution and time (2011 survey)

Note: The vertical line indicates the WTP (yen). The horizontal indicates the time (year). The estimation method is a double-bounded dichotomous choice.

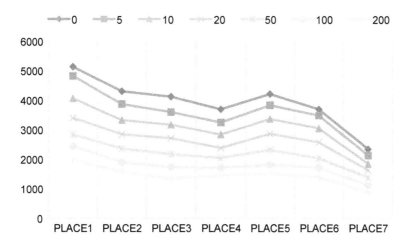

Figure 23.4 The WTP for environmental conservation against water pollution and for distance (2011 survey)

Note: The vertical line indicates the WTP (yen). The horizontal line indicates the place where water pollution occurs. The estimation method is a double-bounded dichotomous choice.

into three groups. The first group includes PLACE 1, which has the highest WTP; the second group includes PLACES 2, 3, 4, 5, and 6, which have mid-range WTPs, and the third group includes PLACE 7, which has the lowest WTP. Figure 23.4 also suggests the same findings for these three groups.

To sum up, we find that the time discount rates tend to decrease for the ultra-long-term time period and that there are roughly the following two distance discount rates in the domestic country: one is the WTP for the local place where a respondent lives and the other is the WTP for other locations within the domestic country.

2.3 The 2012 survey

In the 2010 and 2011 surveys, we find there are various time and distance discount rates. It also is important to note individual WTPs. In the 2012 survey, therefore, we apply card verification methods to obtain individual WTPs. Table 23.5 shows our survey outline. Similar to the 2011 survey, in the 2012 survey we concentrate on water pollution (river). Figure 23.5 shows the average individual WTPs for environmental conservation against water pollution. We find that time discount rates decrease over time and that the WTPs in the local area are larger than those of foreign countries, as is the same in the 2010 and 2011 surveys.

Table 23.5 The 2012 survey outline

Where the destruction occurs	*When the destruction occurs*
Local area where a respondent lives	0, 5, 10, 20, 50, 100, 200
Somewhere in foreign countries	0, 5, 10, 20, 50, 100, 200

Note: We use card verification methods to obtain the WTP. We suppose water pollution as environmental degradation.

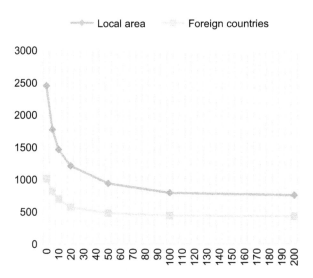

Figure 23.5 WTPs (yen) for environmental conservation against water pollution and time (2012 survey)

476

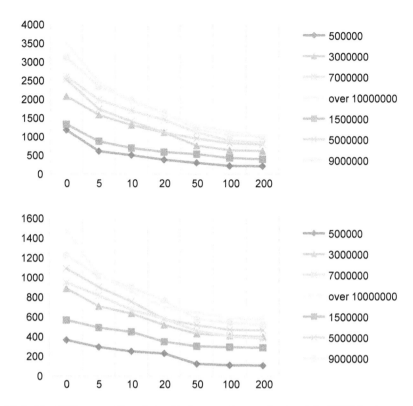

Figure 23.6 The 2012 survey: The relationship between income (yen) and the WTP (yen)

Hereafter, we show the relationship between some indices and the WTP in terms of descriptive statistics. Figure 23.6 shows the average WTP by income group. As expected, we find that income is positively correlated with the WTP. On the other hand, Figure 23.7 implies that age also is positively correlated with the WTP. Because the positive correlation of age and income is not applicable for people older than 60 years of age (see Figure 23.8), there is a possibility that older people tend to place more value on environmental conservation than younger people.

Next, Figure 23.9 shows the relationship between gender and the WTP. We do not find an apparent relation between them. On the other hand, Figure 23.10 implies that there is a possibility that people who have children tend to place more value on environmental conservation than people who do not, especially in the time period from 0 to 20.

To consider the relationship between the above indices with the WTP, we apply the ordinary least squares (OLS) regression. Tables 23.6 and 23.7 show the estimation results for the WTP for local areas and for foreign countries, respectively. Here, we do not find a statistically significant relation between families with children and the WTP, while we find a statistically significant relationship between income and the WTP and between age and the WTP.

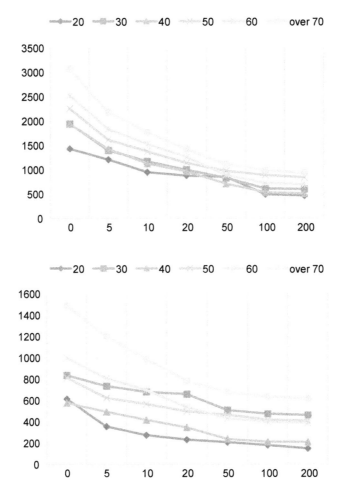

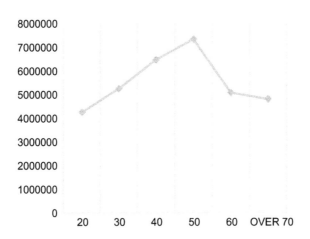

Figure 23.7 The 2012 survey: The relationship between age and the WTP (yen)

Figure 23.8 The 2012 survey: The relationship between age and income (yen)

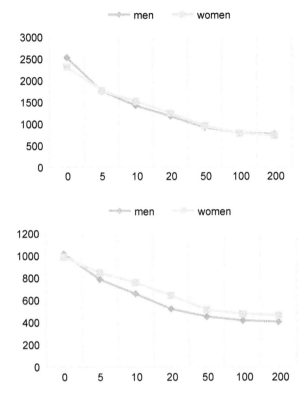

Figure 23.9 The 2012 survey: The relationship between gender and the WTP (yen)

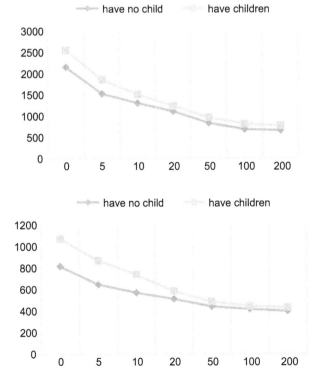

Figure 23.10 The 2012 survey: The relationship between families with and without children and the WTP (yen)

Table 23.6 Determinants of the WTP for environmental conservation against water pollution in the local area

	0	5	10	20	50	100	200
Income	1.652★★★	1.218★★★	0.998★★★	0.811★★★	0.680★★★	0.641★★★	0.594★★★
	(6.35)	(5.75)	(5.10)	(4.38)	(3.98)	(4.00)	(3.75)
Age	39.733★★★	25.233★★★	21.325★★★	15.876★★★	9.657★★★	11.895★★★	10.655★★★
	(5.17)	(4.03)	(3.69)	(2.90)	(1.92)	(2.51)	(2.28)
Sex	142.633	−65.313	−143.589	−111.160	−61.755	−16.067	16.875
	(0.74)	(−0.42)	(−0.99)	(−0.81)	(−0.49)	(−0.14)	(0.14)
Children	249.473	114.047	170.561	163.476	67.243	84.766	80.050
	(1.06)	(0.60)	(0.97)	(0.98)	(0.44)	(0.59)	(0.56)
Const.	−720.327	−276.605	−142.316	5.114	69.584	−201.024	−163.006
	(−1.51)	(−0.71)	(−0.40)	(0.02)	(0.22)	(−0.69)	(−0.56)

Note: Values in parentheses are t-values. ★, ★★ and ★★★ indicate "significant" at the 10% level, the 5% level and the 1% level, respectively. Dependent variable is WTPs (yen). Estimation method is Ordinary Least Squares (OLS).

Table 23.7 Determinants of the WTP for environmental conservation against water pollution in foreign countries

	0	5	10	20	50	100	200
Income	0.799★★★	0.556★★★	0.432★★★	0.393★★★	0.384★★★	0.357★★★	0.352★★★
	(5.17)	(4.12)	(3.42)	(3.37)	(3.55)	(3.36)	(3.35)
Age	22.700★★★	17.171★★★	13.094★★★	9.377★★★	9.639★★★	9.384★★★	9.129★★★
	(4.97)	(4.31)	(3.51)	(2.72)	(3.01)	(2.99)	(2.94)
Sex	−4.431	−78.718	−117.081	−139.741	−79.983	−76.992	−77.195
	(−0.04)	(−0.79)	(−1.25)	(−1.62)	(−1.00)	(−0.98)	(−0.99)
Children	102.444	49.564	41.519	89.006	117.289	128.823	117.803
	(0.74)	(0.41)	(0.36)	(0.85)	(1.20)	(1.34)	(1.24)
Const.	−700.524★★	−426.893★	−214.621	−54.500	−171.797	−172.056	−174.151
	(−2.48)	(−1.73)	(−0.93)	(−0.26)	(−0.87)	(−0.88)	(−0.90)

Note: Values in parentheses are t-values. ★, ★★ and ★★★ indicate "significant" at the 10% level, the 5% level and the 1% level, respectively. Dependent variable is WTPs (yen). Estimation method is Ordinary Least Squares (OLS).

3. Exponential, hyperbolic, or quasi-hyperbolic?

As already mentioned in Section 1, the functional forms of discount rates are under discussion. In this section, we use our survey data to test the fitness of the functional forms. We test the following three functional forms: exponential, hyperbolic, and quasi-hyperbolic. We apply nonlinear least-squares estimation to find the functional form that best fits our estimated discount factors. The functional forms to be tested are as follows:

$$f_E(D) = e^{-kD} \tag{1}$$

$$f_H(D) = 1/(1+kD) \tag{2}$$

$$f_{QH}(0) = 1, \ f_{QH}(D) = \beta \times \delta^D \tag{3}$$

where equation (1), equation (2), and equation (3) correspond to the exponential, hyperbolic, and quasi-hyperbolic functions, respectively.[3] *f(D)* is a discount factor. *D* is time or distance. *k* refers to the parameter that governs the degree of discounting. β and δ are constants between 0 and 1. We show data on discount factors obtained from our survey in Appendix B. Hereafter, we show the estimation results.

3.1 Functional forms of time discount factors

First, Tables 23.8 to 23.10 show the estimation results of the nonlinear least-squares concerning the time discount factors obtained from the 2010 survey (Hence, *D* refers to 0, 20, and 100). The results indicate that the hyperbolic functions show the best fit to our data in all cases because their residuals are the least among the three functions. The results are robust regardless of where the environmental degradation occurs and what the environmental problem is.

Second, Tables 23.11 to 23.13 show the estimation results of the 2011 survey (Hence, *D* refers to 0, 5, 10, 20, 50, 100, and 200). Similar to Tables 23.8 to 23.10, the estimation results indicate that the time discount factors best fit the hyperbolic functions regardless of where the environmental degradation occurs. It is also notable that even if we take the ultra-long-term time discount rates (i.e., 200) into consideration, the discount factors fit the hyperbolic functions.

Table 23.8 Non-linear least squares estimation in survey in 2010 (local) (*D*: time)

Function	parameter	Local (dam)	Residual	Local (forest)	Residual	Local (water)	Residual	Local (agri.)	Residual
Exponential	κ	0.012*	0.019	0.011*	0.012	0.0094**	0.0055	0.010**	0.0066
Hyperbolic	κ	0.021*	0.0066	0.018**	0.0037	0.015**	0.0012	0.016**	0.0013
Quasi-hyperbolic	β	0.91	0.028	0.93*	0.018	0.95*	0.008	0.95*	0.0096
	δ	0.99***		0.99***		0.99***		0.99***	

Note: *D* = 0, 20, 100 (N = 3). Local corresponds to Local (Japan). *, ** and *** indicate "significant" at the 10% level, the 5% level and the 1% level, respectively.

Table 23.9 Non-linear least squares estimation in survey in 2010 (Southeastern Asia) (*D*: time)

Function	parameter	SA (dam)	Residual	SA (forest)	Residual	SA (water)	Residual	SA (agri.)	Residual
Exponential	κ	0.016	0.030	0.014	0.022	0.013	0.021	0.014*	0.019
Hyperbolic	κ	0.033*	0.0092	0.027*	0.0063	0.026*	0.0062	0.025*	0.0049
Quasi-hyperbolic	β	0.90	0.049	0.91	0.034	0.91	0.032	0.92	0.029
	δ	0.99***		0.99***		0.99***		0.99***	

Note: *D* = 0, 20, 100 (N = 3). SA corresponds to Southeastern Asia. *, ** and *** indicate "significant" at the 10% level, the 5% level and the 1% level, respectively.

Table 23.10 Non-linear least squares estimation in survey in 2010 (South America) (*D*: time)

Function	parameter	SAM (dam)	Residual	SAM (forest)	Residual	SAM (water)	Residual	SAM (agri.)	Residual
Exponential	κ	0.017	0.026	0.013★	0.019	0.012★	0.019	0.014★	0.017
Hyperbolic	κ	0.033★	0.0066	0.024★	0.0057	0.023★	0.0060	0.025★★	0.004
Quasi-hyperbolic	β	0.90	0.041	0.91	0.029	0.91	0.029	0.92★	0.026
	δ	0.99★★★		0.99★★★		0.99★★★		0.99★★★	

Note: *D* = 0, 20, 100 (N = 3). SAM corresponds to South America. ★, ★★ and ★★★ indicate "significant" at the 10% level, the 5% level and the 1% level, respectively.

Table 23.11 Non-linear least squares estimation in survey in 2011 (*D*: time)

Function	parameter	PLACE1	Residual	PLACE2	Residual	PLACE3	Residual
Exponential	κ	0.0079★★★	0.017	0.0087★★★	0.017	0.0097★★★	0.016
Hyperbolic	κ	0.014★★★	0.0068	0.015★★★	0.0063	0.017★★★	0.005
Quasi-hyperbolic	β	0.88★★★	0.012	0.87★★★	0.011	0.87★★★	0.0099
	δ	0.99★★★		0.99★★★		0.99★★★	

Note: *D* = 0, 5, 10, 20, 50, 100, 200 (N = 7). ★, ★★ and ★★★ indicate "significant" at the 10% level, the 5% level and the 1% level, respectively.

Table 23.12 Non-linear least squares estimation in survey in 2011 (*D*: time)

Function	parameter	PLACE4	Residual	PLACE 5	Residual	PLACE6	Residual	PLACE7	Residual
Exponential	κ	0.0081★★★	0.021	0.0087★★★	0.015	0.0079★★★	0.013	0.0076★★★	0.014
Hyperbolic	κ	0.015★★★	0.0092	0.015★★★	0.0047	0.013★★★	0.0044	0.013★★★	0.0053
Quasi-hyperbolic	β	0.85★★★	0.012	0.89★★★	0.010	0.90★★★	0.01	0.88★★★	0.0082
	δ	0.99★★★		0.99★★★		0.99★★★		0.99★★★	

Note: *D* = 0, 5, 10, 20, 50, 100, 200 (N = 7). ★, ★★ and ★★★ indicate "significant" at the 10% level, the 5% level and the 1% level, respectively.

Table 23.13 Non-linear least squares estimation in survey in 2012 (*D*: time)

Function	parameter	Local (Japan)	Residual	Foreign country	Residual
Exponential	κ	0.024★★	0.038	0.010★★	0.040
Hyperbolic	κ	0.042★★★	0.014	0.021★★	0.019
Quasi-hyperbolic	β	0.76★★★	0.026	0.78★★★	0.022
	δ	0.99★★★		0.99★★★	

Note: *D* = 0, 5, 10, 20, 50, 100, 200 (N = 7). ★, ★★ and ★★★ indicate "significant" at the 10% level, the 5% level and the 1% level, respectively.

Finally, Table 23.14 refers to the estimation results of the 2012 survey (Hence, *D* refers to 0, 5, 10, 20, 50, 100, and 200). The results also suggest that the data best fits the case of the hyperbolic functions.

Overall, the three surveys yield similar results. It is, again, notable that we use three kinds of CVMs to obtain the WTP. In other words, our results are not changed by a difference in the CVM techniques. Furthermore, we find that, regardless of what environmental objects we conserve and/or where the conservation occurs, the time discount factor tends to fit the hyperbolic functions. Our results, thus, imply that the time discount rates for environmental conservation tend to decline over time.

3.2 Functional forms of distance discount factors

Tables 23.15 to 23.17 refer to the estimation results of the distance discount factors obtained from the 2010 survey (Hence, *D* refers to 0, 4616, and 18702). The residuals imply that the quasi-hyperbolic functions best fit our data. This suggests that distance discount factors rapidly decrease in the near future and then gradually decline at a constant rate. What should be noted here is that we obtain a different functional form from the time discount factors. The goodness of fit to the quasi-hyperbolic functions may imply that Japanese people tend to place great value on local environmental problems compared with the value they place on those of the foreign countries'. As is shown in Figure 23.2, the estimated WTP for Southeast Asia and those for South America are almost similar. Our results may imply that Japanese people tend to assign environmental problems to the following two separate categories: domestic and foreign.

Table 23.14 Non-linear least squares estimation in survey in 2010 (Dam) (*D*: distance)

Function	Parameter	Dam_5	Residual	Dam_20	Residual	Dam_100	Residual
Exponential	κ	0.000021	0.018	0.000032	0.034	0.000035	0.029
Hyperbolic	κ	0.000026	0.016	0.000049	0.027	0.000055	0.021
Quasi-hyperbolic	β	0.96★	0.012	0.95★	0.022	0.96★	0.015
	δ	0.97★★		0.95★★		0.94★★	

Note: D = 0, 4616, 18702 (N = 3). ★, ★★ and ★★★ indicate "significant" at the 10% level, the 5% level and the 1% level, respectively.

Table 23.15 Non-linear least squares estimation in survey in 2010 (Forest) (*D*: distance)

Function	parameter	Forest_5	Residual	Forest_20	Residual	Forest_100	Residual
Exponential	κ	0.000023	0.017	0.000032	0.032	0.000032	0.019
Hyperbolic	κ	0.00003	0.014	0.000048	0.025	0.000049	0.025
Quasi-hyperbolic	β	0.97★	0.0091	0.96★	0.019	0.96★	0.019
	δ	0.96★★		0.95★★★		0.95★★	

Note: D = 0, 4616, 18702 (N = 3). ★, ★★ and ★★★ indicate "significant" at the 10% level, the 5% level and the 1% level, respectively.

Table 23.16 Non-linear least squares estimation in survey in 2010 (Water) (*D*: distance)

Function	parameter	Water_5	Residual	Water_20	Residual	Water_100	Residual
Exponential	κ	0.000024	0.016	0.000040	0.037	0.000035	0.033
Hyperbolic	κ	0.000032	0.013	0.000066	0.026	0.000054	0.025
Quasi-hyperbolic	β	0.97★	0.0079	0.96★	0.020	0.96★	0.019
	δ	0.96★★		0.94★★		0.94★★	

Note: *D* = 0, 4616, 18702 (N = 3). ★, ★★ and ★★★ indicate "significant" at the 10% level, the 5% level and the 1% level, respectively.

Table 23.17 Non-linear least squares estimation in survey in 2010 (Agri.) (*D*: distance)

Function	parameter	Agri._5	Residual	Agri._20	Residual	Agri._100	Residual
Exponential	κ	0.000022	0.014	0.000036	0.030	0.000035	0.026
Hyperbolic	κ	0.000029	0.012	0.000055	0.022	0.000052	0.018
Quasi-hyperbolic	β	0.97★	0.0070	0.96★	0.016	0.97★	0.012
	δ	0.96★★★		0.94★★		0.95★★	

Note: *D* = 0, 4616, 18702 (N = 3). ★, ★★ and ★★★ indicate "significant" at the 10% level, the 5% level and the 1% level, respectively.

4. Summary and conclusions

In this study, we consider the functional forms of discount rates concerning not only time but also distance. To consider environmental value, we estimate the WTP for environmental conservation, focusing on Asia. We assume conservation is done for various objects such as dam development, water-source forest conservation, water pollution (river), and agricultural damage caused by climate change. We also assume conservation is done in various years and places. Furthermore, to obtain the WTP, we apply the following three kinds of CVMs: single-bounded dichotomous choice, double-bounded dichotomous choice, and card verification methods. Applying non-linear least squares, we find that discount factors for time tend to fit the hyperbolic functions and those for distance tend to fit the quasi-hyperbolic functions. The results for time are robust for changes in CVMs, environmental objects, and places. Even if we consider the ultra-long term, the hyperbolic functional forms tend to fit the discount factors. On the one hand, the results for distance are robust for changes in CVM, environmental objects, and time.

What suggestions can we offer? The hyperbolic functions imply that people tend to discount more in the near future and less in the distant future. On the other hand, the quasi-hyperbolic function implies that people tend to place great value on environmental problems in the domestic country rather than in foreign countries. These results are believed to offer material for discussions on long-term environmental degradation.

Notes

1 This percentage refers to the exogenous risk of humanity becoming extinct because of some disaster.
2 We show a map of Japan in Appendix A. The boundary of Appendix A refers to that of the prefectures. There are 47 prefectures in Japan and there are eight regions (Hokkaido, Tohoku, Kanto, Chubu, Kinki, Chugoku, Shikoku, and Kyushu region). In addition, Japan has 1,742 municipalities (January 1, 2013).

3 There are various forms concerning hyperbolic functions in the literature, For example, Ainslie (1975) proposes $f(D) = 1/D$, Hernstein (1981) proposes $f(D) = 1/(1 + kD)$, and Lowenstein and Prelec (1992) propose $f(D) = 1/(\alpha + kD)^{\gamma/\lambda}$. Although we adopt $f(D) = 1/(1 + kD)$, the estimation results from Tables 8 to 17 were almost the same as the estimation results using $f(D) = 1/D$ or $f(D) = 1/(\alpha + kD)^{\gamma/\lambda}$.

References

Ainslie, G., 1975. "Specious Reward: A Behavioral Theory of Impulsiveness and Impulse Control," *Psychological Bulletin* 82(4), 463–96.

Ainslie, G., 1992. *Picoeconomics*. Cambridge: Cambridge University Press.

Benzion, U., A. Rapport and J. Yagil, 1989. "Discount Rates Inferred From Decisions: An Experimental Study," *Management Science* 35, 270–84.

Cairns, J. and M. van der Pol, 1997. "Constant and Decreasing Timing Aversion for Saving Lives," *Social Science & Medicine* 45(11), 1653–59.

Cairns, J. and M. van der Pol, 1999. "Do People Value Their Own Future Health Differently from Others' Future Health?" *Medical Decision Making*, 19(4), 466–72.

Chapman, G.B. and A.S. Elstein, 1995. "Valuing the Future: Temporal Discounting of Health and Money," *Medical Decision Making* 15(4), 373–86.

Cline, W., 1992. *The Economics of Global Warming*. Washington, DC: Institute for International Economics.

Dasgupta, P., 2006. *Comments on the Stern Review's Economics of Climate Change*, Foundation for Science and Technology at the Royal Society, London, November 8.

Dasgupta, P., 2007. "Commentary: The Stern Review's economics of climate change," *National Institute Economic Review*, 99, 4–7.

DellaVigna, S., 2009. "Psychology and Economics: Evidence from the Field," *Journal of Economic Literature* 47(2), 315–72.

Frederick, S., G. Loewenstein and T. O'Donoghue, 2002. "Time Discounting and Time Preference: A Critical Review," *Journal of Economic Literature*, 40(2), 351–401.

Ganiats, T.G., R.T. Carson, R.M. Hamm, S.B. Cantor, W. Sumner, S.J. Spann, M.D. Hagen and C. Miller, 2000. "Health Status and Preferences: Population-Based Time Preferences for Future Health Outcome," *Medical Decision Making*, 20(3), 263–70.

Green, D., K. Jacowitz, D. Kahneman and D. McFadden, 1997. "Referendum Contingent Valuation, Anchoring, and Willingness to Pay for Public Goods," *Resource and Energy Economics*, 20(2), 85–116.

Hepburn, C., S. Duncan and A. Papachristodoulou, 2010. "Behavioural Economics, Hyperbolic Discounting and Environmental Policy," *Environmental Resource Economics* 46, 189–206.

Herrnstein, R., 1981. "Self-Control as Response Strength." In C.M. Bradshaw, E. Szabadi and C.F. Lowe (eds.), *Quantification of Steady-State Operant Behavior*, pp. 3–20. Amsterdam: Elsevier/North-Holland.

Hesketh, B., 2000. "Time Perspective in Career-Related Choices: Applications of Time- Discounting Principles," *Journal of Vocational Behavior*, 57, 62–84.

Houston, D.A., 1983. "Implicit Discount Rates and the Purchase of Untried, Energy-Saving Durable Goods," *Journal of Consumer Research*, 10, 1236–46.

Johannesson, M. and P-O. Johansson, 1997. "Quality of Life and the WTP for an Increased Life Expectancy at an Advanced Age," *Journal of Public Economics*, 65, 219–28.

Loewenstein, G. and D. Prelec, 1992. "Anomalies in Intertemporal Choice: Evidence and an Interpretation," *Quarterly Journal of Economics*, 107(2), 1573–97.

Maital, S. and S. Maital, 1978. "Time Preference, Delay of Gratification, and Intergenerational Transmission of Economic Inequality: A Behavioral Theory of Income Distribution." In O. Ashenfelter and W. Oates (eds.), *Essays in Labor Market Analysis*, pp. 179–99. New York: Wiley.

Mazur, J.E., 1987. "An Adjustment Procedure for Studying Delayed Reinforcement." In M.L. Commons, J.E. Mazur, J.A. Nevin and H. Rachlin (eds.), *The Effect of Delay and Intervening Events on Reinforcement Value*, pp. 55–73. Hillsdale, NJ: Erlbaum.

Nordhaus, W.D., 1992. "An optimal transition path for controlling greenhouse gasses," *Science*, 258, 1315–19.

Nordhaus, W.D., 2007. "A review of the Stern Review on the economics of climate change," *Journal of Economic Literature*, 45(3), 686–702.

Shelley, M.K., 1993. "Outcome Signs, Question Frames and Discount Rates," *Management Science*, 39, 806–15.

Stern, N., 2007. *The Economics of Climate Change: The Stern Review*. Cambridge: Cambridge University Press.

Strotz, R.H., 1955–6. "Myopia and Inconsistency in Dynamic Utility Maximization," *Review of Economic Studies*, 23(3), 165–80.

Thaler, R., 1981. "Some Empirical Evidence on Dynamic Inconsistency," *Economic Letters*, 8, 201–7.

van der Pol, M., M. Marjon and J. Cairns, 2001. "Estimating Time Preferences for Health Using Discrete Choice Experiments," *Social Science & Medicine*, 52, 1459–70.

Wahlund R. and J. Gunnarsson, 1996. "Mental Discounting and Financial Strategies," *Journal of Economic Psychology*, 17(6), 709–30.

Weitzman, M.L., 1998. "Why the Far Distant Future Should Be Discounted at Its Lowest Possible Rate," *Journal of Environmental Economics and Management,* 36, 201–8.

Weitzman, M.L., 2001. "Gamma Discounting," *American Economic Review*, 91(1), 261–71.

APPENDIX A

Appendix A   A map of Japan

Note: There are 47 prefectures in Japan

APPENDIX B

Appendix B1 Time discount factors in Survey in 2010 (time 0 = 1)

time	local (dam)	local (forest)	local (water)	local (agri.)	SA (dam)	SA (forest)	SA (water)	SA (agri.)	SAM (dam)	SAM (forest)	SAM (water)	SAM (agri.)
0	1	1	1	1	1	1	1	1	1	1	1	1
20	0.617021	0.670131	0.731819	0.7122	0.522739	0.577706	0.586798	0.596684	0.533595	0.6	0.607655	0.60396
100	0.397527	0.414108	0.431062	0.410879	0.342079	0.356494	0.363941	0.356062	0.324914	0.368943	0.38068	0.349548

Note: Concerning time, we consider 5 years as the most recent year (i.e., 0) to define discount factors. Here, local corresponds to Local (Japan), SA corresponds to Southeast Asia, and SAM corresponds to South America.

Appendix B2 Distance discount factors in Survey in 2010 (Distance 0 = 1).

Distance	Dam_5	Dam_20	Dam_100	Forest_5	Forest_20	Forest_100	Water_5	Water_20	Water_100	Agri._5	Agri._20	Agri._100
0	1	1	1	1	1	1	1	1	1	1	1	1
4616	0.727769	0.616564	0.626258	0.727445	0.627115	0.626236	0.725104	0.581414	0.612198	0.741395	0.621144	0.642483
18702	0.741589	0.64132	0.60613	0.714848	0.640038	0.636882	0.6981	0.579656	0.616507	0.713891	0.605394	0.60733

Note: Unit of distance is km (0 corresponds to Local (Japan), 4616 corresponds to Southeast Asia, and 18702 corresponds to South America). 5, 20, 100 correspond to the time when environmental deterioration occurs.

Appendix B3 Time discount factors in Survey in 2011 (time 0 = 1)

time	PLACE1	PLACE2	PLACE3	PLACE4	PLACE5	PLACE6	PLACE7
0	1	1	1	1	1	1	1
5	0.941451	0.898403	0.873911	0.878575	0.909414	0.942349	0.907973
10	0.793814	0.773432	0.770329	0.767674	0.798486	0.824892	0.788804
20	0.664268	0.662115	0.659729	0.64517	0.679991	0.698276	0.697201
50	0.553978	0.550798	0.527348	0.555855	0.551798	0.553879	0.592875
100	0.477728	0.441796	0.422798	0.464922	0.431646	0.465248	0.479644
200	0.387473	0.367739	0.329622	0.399083	0.365894	0.379041	0.377863

Appendix B4 Time discount factors in Survey in 2012 (time 0 = 1)

time	Local (Japan)	Foreign country
0	1	1
5	0.722062	0.805618
10	0.595786	0.691751
20	0.492661	0.563792
50	0.381217	0.472755
100	0.321584	0.435926
200	0.306137	0.424277

24

INEQUALITY AND THE ENVIRONMENT

Makiko Nakano and Shunsuke Managi

1. Introduction

Traditionally, researchers have been interested in the relationship between environmental quality and economic activities. Separating economic growth from environmental deterioration has attracted great attention. Therefore, the environmental Kuznets curve (EKC) hypothesis has been discussed in many studies.[1]

Recent studies reviewed in the following sections have focused on the effect of inequality on environmental quality. Some researchers are concerned that achieving economic growth might not be enough to construct a sustainable society, not only from the viewpoint of distribution, but also from that of environmental issues. However, the number of studies investigating the relationship between inequality and the environment is much smaller than those investigating the relationship between economic growth and the environment. Therefore, this chapter focuses on the relationship between inequality and the environment. We conduct a review of the available literature and present the results of our empirical estimation.

Many studies have used the Gini coefficient as a proxy of income inequality. However, this approach often suffers from missing values and limited observations. Therefore, we use data pertaining to the "loss" of the Human Development Index (HDI) due to inequality, which are calculated by the United Nations Development Programme (UNDP). To our knowledge, this study is the first to use this index as the variable of inequality. Using this index, we are able to consider several kinds of inequality in addition to income inequality. Our empirical results show that in the member countries of the Organisation for Economic Co-operation and Development (OECD), more inequality results in increased CO_2 emissions. Moreover, in non-OECD countries, the opposite results are obtained.

This chapter is structured as follows. In Section 2, we overview inequality in Asian countries. Section 3 reviews the literature investigating inequality and the environment. In Section 4, we present the estimation models and data used in our study. Section 5 discusses the results. Finally, Section 6 provides concluding remarks.

2. Overview of inequality in Asia

The Asian region has experienced high economic growth. However, the region faces growing inequality. The Asian Development Bank (2012) noted that "of the 28 countries that have

491

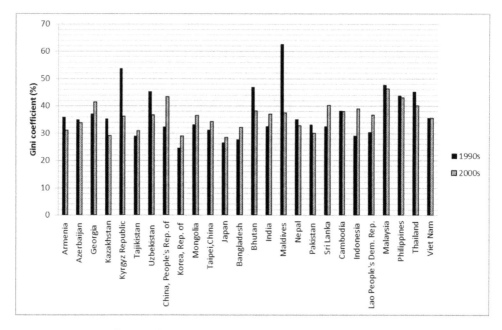

Figure 24.1   Gini coefficients of Asian countries (1990s and 2000s)

Note: With the exception of Japan, the data are obtained from the Asian Development Bank (2012).
The data for Japan are obtained from Nishizaki et al. (1998) and the website of the Ministry of Internal
Affairs and Communications, Statistics Bureau.

comparative data between the 1990s and 2000s, 11 – accounting for about 82 percent of developing Asia's population in 2010 – experienced rising inequality of per capita expenditure or income, as measured by the Gini coefficient,"[2] and warned that "rising inequality can damp the poverty impact of economic growth, and even undermine the basis of growth itself."

Figure 24.1 shows the Gini coefficient for Asian countries, comparing the inequality between the 1990s and the 2000s. Georgia, China, the Republic of Korea, Mongolia, Taipei, Japan, Bangladesh, India, Sri Lanka, Indonesia, and the Lao People's Democratic Republic have experienced expanding inequality.

The Gini coefficient is calculated based on income or expenditure, depending on the availability of statistics. Therefore, this index focuses on economic aspects. In order to enable further investigation into inequality, UNDP (2010) developed the Inequality-adjusted Human Development Index (IHDI) and calculated loss of HDI caused by inequality. In the index, UNDP (2010) classified inequality into three categories: first, a long and healthy life (life expectancy); second, access to knowledge (education); and third, a decent standard of living (income). These indices are further explained in Section 4. Figure 24.2 shows the loss due to inequality.

Therefore, many researchers tend to focus on inequality itself, and a vast amount of literature is devoted to this aspect. We introduce a small portion of these studies here.

According to the Asian Development Bank (2012), the Gini coefficient for China increased from 32.4 in the 1990s to 43.4 in the 2000s. Many studies have addressed the inequality issue in China. For example, Liu (2013) used a new approach called the sequential panel selection method to conclude that 20 regions in China have not experienced a decrease in income inequality. Zheng and Kuroda (2013) examined the effect of knowledge infrastructure and transportation infrastructure on regional inequality and growth in China using simultaneous equations

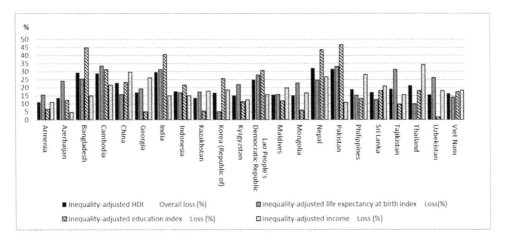

Figure 24.2 Loss in the Human Development Index caused by inequality in 2010

Note: The data are obtained from UNDP (2010).

methods. Li and Luo (2008) argued that the government should shift to a more labor-intensive development strategy, support small and medium enterprises, and unify the labor market.

For India, the Gini coefficient increased from 32.5 in the 1990s to 37.0 in the 2000s (Asian Development Bank, 2012). Barua and Chakraborty (2010) showed that regional inequality in India has been increasing and examined the effect of economic liberalization on interregional inequality. Asadullah and Yalonetzky (2012) addressed the inequality issue from the viewpoint of educational opportunity.

For the Republic of Korea, the Gini coefficient increased from 24.5 in the 1990s to 28.9 in the 2000s (Asian Development Bank, 2012). Sato and Fukushige (2009) examined the determinants of the Gini coefficient for income and expenditure. They investigated the effect of opening the goods and capital markets on income inequality. Sung and Park (2011) focused on the redistribution effects of tax and benefits in order to reduce inequality.

Therefore, various studies have dealt with inequality issues. However, the number of studies focusing on the relationship between inequality and environmental issues is considerably less. Therefore, in the next section, we introduce such studies, which are not limited to Asia.

3. Literature on inequality and the environment

The various ways in which inequality affects the environment have been investigated in the following literature.

Boyce (1994) proposed the political economy argument. He theoretically proposed the power-weighted social decision rule (PWSDR),[3] according to which the degree of environmental degradation is determined by the balance of power between the winner, who derives the net benefit from the environmental degrading activity, and the loser, who bears the net cost. When the winners are more powerful than the losers, the environmental issue will worsen. Torras and Boyce (1998), Boyce et al. (1999), and Boyce (2007) also examined the effect of inequality on the environment from the viewpoint of the political economy. These studies suggest that greater inequality of power results in greater environmental degradation, especially for environmental issues, such as air and water pollution, whose damage emerges in the short term.[4]

Among the many kinds of power inequalities, most of the empirical analyses in such literature have focused on income. The impact of income inequality on the environment was reviewed by Boyce (2007). Torras and Boyce (1998) used the Gini coefficient as a measure of income inequality to examine the impacts on air and water pollution, access to safe water, and sanitation facilities. The results differ across environmental impacts. For example, for sulfur dioxide (SO_2) and smoke, higher inequality is associated with greater environmental damage in low-income countries, while this does not hold for high-income countries. For heavy particles, higher inequality is associated with a better environment in low-income countries. Boyce et al. (1999) also considered other power inequalities besides income inequality. They investigated the relationship among power distribution, the environment, and public health using cross-sectional data of 50 US states. A measure of power distribution was derived from voter participation, tax fairness, Medicaid access, and educational attainment. They constructed a composite index as a measure of environmental policy. They found that more equal distribution of power is associated with stronger environmental policies and lower environmental stress and that both environmental stress and power inequality are associated with adverse public health outcomes.

Scruggs (1998) believed that two implicit assumptions were made in Boyce (1994), who argued that equality results in a better environment. The assumptions are that the rich prefer environmental degradation and that democratic social choice generally results in the best outcome. Scruggs (1998) argued that these assumptions are too restrictive. Scruggs (1998) employed the Gini coefficient in the empirical analysis and argued that the results suggesting a systematic positive relationship between inequality and the environment, such as water and air pollution, are not robust enough.

Magnani (2000) showed that individual heterogeneity, relative income effect, and political framework are important to decrease the environmental burden. Magnani (2000) empirically examined the effect on public R&D expenditure for environmental protection using data from OECD countries and found that the Gini coefficients did not show a significant impact. On the other hand, when the ratio of income shares of the first and fourth quintile of the income distribution is used as the index of inequality, the estimated impacts were negatively significant in some models.

Heerink et al. (2001) focused on the relationship between income and environmental damage. When the relationship is concave, redistributing income from rich households to poor households increases the total level of environmental damage. Therefore, decreasing inequality increases the environmental burden. This contradicts the PWSDR. However, when the relationship between income and environmental damage is convex, decreasing inequality reduces the environmental damage. This is in agreement with the PWSDR. In the empirical analysis, Heerink et al. (2001) used the Gini coefficient as the index of inequality and showed that income equalization improves access to safe water and urban sanitation. They showed that deforestation also could be prevented by income equalization. However, their results indicated that income inequality reduces the problems associated with CO_2 emissions and soil nutrient depletion.

Coondoo and Dinda (2008) used the Lorenz curve and the specific concentration curve to show that the distributional inequality of income as well as the mean income is associated with environmental damage. They showed that environmental damage changes its characteristics from a luxury good to a necessary good, and further to an inferior good, as income grows. They tried to theoretically link intra-country income distribution and intra-country demand for environmental damage. For their empirical analysis, they used the cointegration approach and focused on inter-country income distribution. Their results showed that inter-country income inequality has a significant effect on mean CO_2 emissions levels and inter-country inequality of CO_2 emissions levels.

Vona and Patriarca (2011) used the dynamic model and theoretically showed that in rich countries, environmental innovations are promoted by equal income distribution. In their empirical analysis, they examined the effects of income inequality (Gini coefficient) on the development of environmental technologies (public environmental R&D, turnover of eco-industries, and the quota of priority patent applications in selected environmental domains) using OECD data, since innovations tend to be conducted by rich countries. The results showed that inequality negatively affects environmental innovations and per capita income tends to be the paramount factor in poorer ones.

Farzin and Bond (2006) conducted an empirical analysis and found that the effects of democracy and freedom on the environment differ among pollutants. The effect of income inequality measured by the Gini coefficient also varied depending on the pollutants. The interaction term between income inequality and the degree of democracy was positively estimated for CO_2 and ambient SO_2 concentrations. Therefore, more inequality increased CO_2 and ambient SO_2 concentrations, and this effect was found to be stronger for democratic countries. However, the interaction terms were negative for non-methane volatile organic compounds (VOCs) and SO_2 emissions. For CO_2, VOCs, and SO_2 emissions, the signs of the interaction terms among income inequality, degree of democracy, and gross domestic product (GDP) are the opposite of the signs of the interaction terms between inequality and democracy.

Kempf and Rossignol (2007) adopted the political-economy perspective and used the endogenous growth model to examine the relationship between inequality and the environment in a growth economy. Based on the majority decision-making rule in politics, they theoretically showed that the poorer the median voters, the more they value material wellbeing over environmental protection. Therefore, public expenditure is used to support material growth instead of environmental protection. This means that the more unequal the society, the more damage to the environment.

UNDP (2011) discuss the issues of sustainability and equity from a broad perspective, including how environmental damage affects inequality.

4. Model and data

In Section 3, we reviewed the previous literature. In Sections 4 and 5, we introduce our empirical study. In the previous studies, the Gini coefficient was the most popular index of inequality. Our study is unique in that we use the loss in the HDI due to inequality, which was calculated by UNDP (2010), as the index of inequality. Using this index, we can consider several kinds of inequalities in addition to income inequality. We do not restrict our sample to Asian countries, since such a restriction would reduce our sample size.

In this section, we present the econometric models and the data used to examine the relationship between inequality and the environment. Notably, we focus on CO_2 emissions. CO_2 has global, indirect, and long-term impacts. Therefore, it is quite difficult to identify the income level at which CO_2 emissions start to decrease, compared to other substances that have short-term and local impacts.[5] Therefore, we have to further investigate the possible factors influencing CO_2 emissions. Accordingly, we estimate expression (1).

$$\ln (CO_2 \text{ per capita}_i) = \alpha + \beta_1 \ln (GDP \text{ per capita}_i) + \beta_2 \{\ln (GDP \text{ per capita}_i)\}^2 + \beta_3 Popdensity_i + \beta_4 Urbanpop_i + \beta_5 Democracy_i + \beta_6 Inequality_i + u_i \tag{1}$$

The dependent variable is the log of CO_2 per capita in each country. The data of CO_2 emissions were calculated using the sectoral approach by the International Energy Agency (2012).

The dependent variables include the log of GDP per capita and its square. These terms are included to observe the impact of economic wealth on CO_2 emissions. GDP is measured by purchasing power parity (current international \$). The data are sourced from World Development Indicators (WDI) published by the World Bank.

Popdensity indicates population density, measured by people per square km of land area. The data are obtained from WDI. For areas with low population density, the transport sector may tend to emit large amounts of CO_2 given the poorer availability of public transportation. For details about the link between population density and CO_2 emissions, see Grazi et al. (2008).

Urbanpop indicates the share of the urban population in the total population. The data are obtained from WDI. Rivera-Batiz (2002) discussed that urbanization might be associated with agglomeration economies, leading to new industries, goods, and services. This means that innovation is stimulated. According to Dinda (2004), technological progress entails mixed effects. One aspect is that technological progress allows higher efficiency in the use of energy. Another aspect is that new technologies might produce potential dangers in the environment. Torras and Boyce (1998) noted that while urbanization is related to heavier pollution, it may reduce the environmental burden through economies of scale.

Democracy indicates the degree of democracy. Democracy is likely to be associated with the environment. For example, Farzin and Bond (2006) argued that democracy contributes to the environment in that people can state their preference for the environment more effectively compared to autocracy. In our analysis, the data for democracy are obtained from the Polity IV Project. We use the polity2 score as the independent variable. This score ranges from +10 (strongly democratic) to –10 (strongly autocratic).

Inequality indicates the index of inequality. The previous studies reviewed in Section 3 focused on income inequality. In our analysis, in addition to income inequality, we analyze inequality in a broader sense. The *Human Development Report* published by UNDP provides calculations of the HDI. According to the UNDP (2010), the HDI measures the average achievements in three basic dimensions of human development: a long and healthy life (life expectancy index), access to knowledge (education index), and a decent standard of living (income index) (for details about the HDI, see UNDP (2010)). The UNDP (2010) has developed IHDI. According to its technical note, "The IHDI accounts for inequalities in HDI dimensions by 'discounting' each dimension's average value according to its level of inequality. The IHDI equals the HDI when there is no inequality across people but is less than the HDI as inequality rises." UNDP (2010) reports not only the IHDI and the HDI but also the "loss" due to inequality in each dimension, which is explained as follows: "The 'loss' in potential human development due to inequality is given by the difference between the HDI and the IHDI and can be expressed as a percentage." Therefore, we use the "loss" due to inequality as the measure of inequality. In particular, we use two indices. The first index is the overall loss index, which includes inequalities in all the three dimensions (we name the variable *Overall_loss*). The second index is the income loss index, which shows the inequalities related to income (we name the variable *Income_loss*).

Due to data availability, our sample period is restricted to the year 2010, which is the only year for which both the IHDI and CO_2 emissions values are available at the date when we collected the data. The sample countries are those for which IHDI data are available. However, when data of other variables are missing for a country, we exclude it from the sample. We separate the sample countries into OECD and non-OECD countries, since these two groups tend to have different characteristics.[6]

Table 24.1 Descriptive statistics

OECD	Mean	Std. Dev.	Min	Max
ln (CO_2 per capita)	−11.62	0.42	−12.30	−10.78
ln (GDP per capita)	10.55	0.27	10.15	11.35
Popdensity	164.19	151.19	2.87	508.86
Urbanpop	78.87	10.004	60.51	97.46
Democracy	9.77	0.61	8	10
Overall_loss	9.3	2.42	6.5	16.7
Income_loss	17.17	3.63	11.3	23.9
non-OECD	Mean	Std. Dev.	Min	Max
ln (CO_2 per capita)	−13.37	1.36	−16.81	−10.34
ln (GDP per capita)	8.68	0.97	5.92	10.19
Popdensity	107.10	145.40	1.75	1160.99
Urbanpop	54.20	19.05	13.44	93.31
Democracy	4.24	5.76	−9	10
Overall_loss	22.88	9.92	6.1	45.3
Income_loss	24.55	12.04	4.4	68.3

Inequality might be an endogenous variable. Therefore, we conduct the test of endogeneity. When inequality is found to be an endogenous variable, we use the instrumental variable method. In doing this, the additional instrumental variable is *Younpop*, which indicates the share of the young population (under age 14 years) in the total population. We obtain this data from WDI. We use robust standard errors in the estimation.

The descriptive statistics are shown in Table 24.1.

5. Results

The results for OECD and non-OECD countries are summarized in Table 24.2 and Table 24.3, respectively.

In the analysis of OECD countries, the robust Durbin–Wu–Hausman test could not reject the hypothesis that the inequalities are exogenous. The values of test statistic are 0.09 and 0.25 in each model. Therefore, we use the ordinary least squares with robust standard errors. In the analysis of non-OECD countries, the robust Durbin–Wu–Hausman test rejected the null hypotheses that *Overall_loss* is exogenous at 5 percent and that *Income_loss* is exogenous at 1 percent. Therefore, we use the instrumental variable method with robust standard errors for non-OECD countries.

ln (GDP per capita) is positively significant for non-OECD countries and not significant for OECD countries. This might be partly because the variance for OECD countries is small. The quadratic term is not significant for non-OECD countries. Therefore, for non-OECD countries, CO_2 levels increase as the GDP increases.

Urbanpop is positively significant only for OECD countries. Therefore, living in urban areas in OECD countries emits much CO_2.

Democracy is negatively significant for non-OECD countries. The degree of democracy differs widely among non-OECD countries, ranging from −9 to 10 for non-OECD countries, and

Table 24.2 Results for OECD countries

Dependent variable	Log of CO_2 per capita	
ln (*GDP per capita*)	14.6776 (1.19)	6.4497 (0.53)
{ln (*GDP per capita*)}^{2}	−0.6384 (−1.12)	−0.2562 (−0.46)
Popdensity	−0.0003 (−0.48)	−0.0001 (−0.18)
Urbanpop	0.0183* (2.09)	0.0167* (1.94)
Democracy	0.1483 (1.26)	−0.0484 (−0.34)
Overall_loss	0.1124*** (3.48)	
Income_loss		0.0543** (2.62)
Constant	−99.2539 (−1.47)	−52.8905 (−0.80)
Sample size	22	22
R^2	0.49	0.46

Note: Values in parentheses are *t*-values. *, **, and *** denotes significance at the 10%, 5%, and 1% level, respectively.

Table 24.3 Results for non-OECD countries

Dependent variable	Log of CO_2 per capita	
ln (*GDP per capita*)	2.4252** (2.42)	3.3218** (2.43)
{ln (*GDP per capita*)}^{2}	−0.0828 (−1.32)	−0.1251 (−1.52)
Popdensity	−0.00004 (−0.14)	−0.0005 (−1.13)
Urbanpop	−0.0035 (−0.53)	−0.0004 (−0.05)
Democracy	−0.0295** (−2.21)	−0.0109 (−0.56)
Overall_loss	−0.0447*** (−3.62)	
Income_loss		−0.0485*** (−2.76)
Constant	−26.7677*** (−6.70)	−31.3531*** (−5.61)
Sample size	81	82
Wald's χ^2	483.78	308.17
Test of endogeneity	4.75	11.03

Note: Values in parentheses are *z*-values. *, **, and *** denotes significance at the 10%, 5%, and 1% level, respectively.

from 8 to 10 for OECD countries. In non-OECD countries, democracy might be associated with CO_2 reduction. However, the relationship is not robust, since it is not significant when we use *Income_loss* as the index of inequality.

The effect of inequality differs between OECD and non-OECD countries. For OECD countries, inequality is positively significant. This result is consistent with those of Vona and Patriarca (2011) and Kempf and Rossignol (2007), namely that environmental degradation worsens as inequality grows in rich countries and democratic countries, respectively.

The situation described in Kempf and Rossignol (2007) might be partly similar to the situation in some OECD countries. It seems that the existence of inequality makes the introduction of positive environmental policies difficult.

Although Japan is not included in our sample (due to missing data), we present an example from Japan. Japan could not have introduced effective climate change policies. Although the country introduced an emissions trading scheme in 2005, it was implemented on a voluntary basis only.[7] In 2012, the tax policy for climate change mitigation was introduced. However, the tax rate is not high.[8] The Ministry of Health, Labor and Welfare (2013) noted that the Gini coefficient for Japan increased in the 2000s. Before the redistribution of income, the Gini coefficient was 0.4720 in 2000, 0.5263 in 2006, and 0.5536 in 2011.[9] GDP per capita growth rates were 2.1 percent in 2000, 1.7 percent in 2006, 4.7 percent in 2010, and −0.9 percent in 2011 (World Bank, 2013). Therefore, in the 2000s, Japan's condition pertaining to inequality and economic growth rate was not good. It is possible that the growing inequality is one of the reasons for the failure in introducing effective environmental policies in Japan. However, it is difficult to separate the effect of inequality from that of low economic growth in order to attribute one or the other to the failure in introducing specific policies.

Korea is included in our sample as an OECD member country. Among the 22 OECD countries in the sample, Korea ranked 1st in *Overall_loss* and 9th in *Income_loss* in 2010. GDP per capita growth rates were 7.6 percent in 2000, 4.7 percent in 2006, 5.8 percent in 2010, and 2.9 percent in 2011 (World Bank, 2013). Although per capita growth rates are higher than those in Japan, it is not easy to introduce climate change policies in this country either. For example, around 2010, Korea postponed the introduction of an emissions trading scheme, the future of which remains unclear.[10] Both countries assigned higher priorities to industrial competitiveness and business conditions.

In non-OECD countries, inequality is negatively significant. This result is consistent with the situation described in Heerink et al. (2001), that decreasing inequality increases environmental burden when the relationship between income and environmental damage is concave. Like our study, their empirical result shows that inequality has a negatively significant effect on CO_2 emissions per capita.

6. Conclusion

This chapter examined the relationship between inequality and the environment. In many cases, large inequality itself is of great concern. In addition, some researchers are interested in the effects of inequality on the environment. Previous studies have shown both positive and negative relationships depending on the characteristics of the countries and their environmental problems.

We conducted an empirical analysis focusing on CO_2 emissions. The effects of inequality differ among OECD and non-OECD countries. In OECD countries, the environmental situation worsens as inequality increases. In non-OECD countries, the opposite results are obtained.

We need detailed data for each country in order to investigate specific characteristics for individual countries.

Notes

1 For example, see Dinda (2004).

2 According to the Asian Development Bank (2012), the term "developing Asia" indicates "the 44 developing member countries of the Asian Development Bank and Brunei Darussalam, an unclassified regional member."

3 Boyce (2007) summarized five types of power (purchasing power, decision power, agenda power, value power, and event power) influencing decisions on environmental protection. Boyce (2007) noted that depending on the society in question, these powers are correlated to wealth, income, race, ethnicity, gender, age, and so on.

4 Another contribution of these studies is their examination of the possibility that less powerful people bear a disproportionate cost of environmental degradation. For example, the location of hazardous waste sites tends to be correlated to power. For a review on this issue, see Boyce (2007).

In this article, however, we focus on how inequality in a society affects the overall environment burden.

5 For a related literature review and discussion on this issue, see Dinda (2004).

6 Our sample includes the following countries. OECD countries: Australia, Austria, Belgium, Canada, Denmark, Finland, France, Germany, Greece, Ireland, Israel, Italy, Korea (Republic of), Luxembourg, Netherlands, Norway, Portugal, Spain, Sweden, Switzerland, United Kingdom, United States.

Non-OECD countries: Albania, Angola, Armenia, Azerbaijan, Bangladesh, Belarus, Benin, Bolivia (Plurinational State of), Brazil, Bulgaria, Cambodia, Cameroon, Chile, China, Colombia, Congo, Congo (Democratic Republic of the), Costa Rica, Croatia, Cyprus, Czech Republic, Dominican Republic, Ecuador, Egypt, El Salvador, Estonia, Ethiopia, Gabon, Georgia, Ghana, Guatemala, Haiti, Honduras, Hungary, India, Indonesia, Jordan, Kazakhstan, Kenya, Kyrgyzstan, Latvia, Lithuania, Mexico, Moldova (Republic of), Mongolia, Morocco, Mozambique, Namibia, Nepal, Nicaragua, Nigeria, Pakistan, Panama, Paraguay, Peru, Philippines, Poland, Romania, Russian Federation, Senegal, Serbia, Slovakia, Slovenia, South Africa, Sri Lanka, Syrian Arab Republic, Tajikistan, Tanzania (United Republic of), Thailand, Togo, Trinidad and Tobago, Tunisia, Turkey, Turkmenistan, Ukraine, Uruguay, Uzbekistan, Venezuela (Bolivarian Republic of), Viet Nam, Yemen, Zambia. In the analysis for *Income_loss*, we also included Malaysia.

7 Tokyo city introduced a mandatory emissions trading scheme. However, it is limited to facilities in Tokyo city.

8 Details for this tax can be found at the website of the Ministry of the Environment http://www.env. go.jp/en/policy/tax/env-tax.html.

9 According to the Ministry of Health, Labor and Welfare (2013), after redistribution of income, the values of the Gini coefficients become 0.3814, 0.3873, and 0.3791 for 2000, 2006, and 2011, respectively.

10 According to Lee (2013), one of the major reasons for this is Japan's failure in introducing a mandatory emissions trading scheme. In this case, the introduction of mandatory emissions trading in Korea alone would have reduced its competitiveness, since these two countries are market competitors.

References

Asadullah, M.N. and Yalonetzky, G. (2012) "Inequality of Educational Opportunity in India: Changes Over Time and Across States," *World Development*, Vol. 40, pp. 1151–1163.

Asian Development Bank. (2012) *Asian Development Outlook 2012: Confronting Rising Inequality in Asia.* Mandaluyong City, Philippines: ADB.

Barua, A. and Chakraborty, P. (2010) "Does Openness Affect Regional Inequality? A Case Study for India," *Review of Development Economics,* Vol. 14, pp. 447–465.

Boyce, J.K. (1994) "Inequality as a Cause of Environmental Degradation," *Ecological Economics*, Vol. 11, pp. 169–178.

Boyce, J.K. (2007) "Inequality and Environmental Protection." In Baland, J.M., Bardhan, P., Bowles, S. (eds.) *Inequality, Cooperation, and Environmental Sustainability*, pp. 314–348. Princeton, NJ: Princeton University Press.

Boyce, J.K., Klemer, A.R., Templet, P.H. and Willis, C.E. (1999) "Power Distribution, the Environment, and Public Health: A State-level Analysis," *Ecological Economics*, Vol. 29, pp. 127–140.

Coondoo, D. and Dinda, S. (2008) "Carbon Dioxide Emission and Income: A Temporal Analysis of Cross-country Distributional Patterns," *Ecological Economics*, Vol. 65, pp. 375–385.

Dinda, S. (2004) "Environmental Kuznets Curve Hypothesis: A Survey," *Ecological Economics*, Vol. 49, pp. 431–455.

Farzin, Y.H., and Bond, C.A. (2006) "Democracy and Environmental Quality," *Journal of Development Economics*, Vol. 81, pp. 213– 235.

Grazi, F., van den Bergh, J.C.J.M. and van Ommeren, J.N. (2008) "An Empirical Analysis of Urban Form, Transport, and Global Warming," *The Energy Journal*, Vol. 29, pp. 97–122.

Heerink, N., Mulatu, A. and Bulte, E. (2001) "Income Inequality and the Environment: Aggregation Bias in Environmental Kuznets Curves," *Ecological Economics*, Vol. 38, pp. 359–367.

International Energy Agency (2012) *CO₂ Emissions from Fuel Combustion.* Paris: IEA.

Kempf, H. and Rossignol, S. (2007) "Is Inequality Harmful for the Environment in a Growing Economy?" *Economics and Politics*, Vol. 19, pp. 53–71.

Lee, S.C. (2013) "Policy Design and Process of Low Carbon Policy in Japan and Korea: Case Study on Emission Treading Scheme," *The Meijo Review*, Vol. 13, pp. 159–172 (in Japanese).

Li, S. and Luo, C. (2008) "Growth Pattern, Employment, and Income Inequality: What the Experience of Republic of Korea and Taipei, China Reveals to the People's Republic of China," *Asian Development Review*, Vol. 25, pp. 100–118.

Liu, W.C. (2013) "Reexamining the Income Inequality in China: Evidence from Sequential Panel Selection Method," *Economic Modeling*, Vol. 31, pp. 37–42.

Magnani, E. (2000) "The Environmental Kuznets Curve, Environmental Protection Policy and Income Distribution," *Ecological Economics*, Vol. 32, pp. 431–443.

Marshall, M.G. and Gurr, T.R. (accessed in July 2013) "Polity IV Project: Political Regime Characteristics and Transitions, 1800–2012," http://www.systemicpeace.org/polity/polity4.htm.

Ministry of Health, Labor and Welfare (2013) *Income Redistribution Survey Report* (in Japanese). Tokyo: Ministry of Health, Labor and Welfare.

Ministry of Internal Affairs and Communications, Statistics Bureau. (accessed in October 2013) http://www.stat.go.jp/data/zensho/2009/keisu/yoyaku.htm.

Ministry of the Environment. (accessed in October 2013) http://www.env.go.jp/en/policy/tax/env-tax.html.

Nishizaki, F., Yamada, Y. and Ando, E. (1998) "Income Disparity in Japan – from the Viewpoint of International Comparison," *Economic Analysis – Series of Policy Research Viewpoint*, Vol. 11. (in Japanese), pp. 1–51.

Rivera-Batiz, F.L. (2002) "Democracy, Governance, and Economic Growth: Theory and Evidence," *Review of Development Economics*, Vol. 6, pp. 225–247.

Sato, S. and Fukushige, M. (2009) "Globalization and Economic Inequality in the Short and Long Run: The Case of South Korea 1975–1995," *Journal of Asian Economics*, Vol. 20, pp. 62–68.

Scruggs, L.A. (1998) "Political and Economic Inequality and the Environment," *Ecological Economics*, Vol. 26, pp. 259–275.

Sung, M.J. and Park, K.B. (2011) "Effects of Taxes and Benefits on Income Distribution in Korea," *Review of Income and Wealth*, Vol. 57, pp. 345–363.

Torras, M. and Boyce, J.K. (1998) "Income, Inequality, and Pollution: A Reassessment of the Environmental Kuznets Curve," *Ecological Economics*, Vol. 25, pp. 147–160.

United Nations Development Programme (2010) *Human Development Report 2010 – 20th Anniversary Edition. The Real Wealth of Nations: Pathways to Human Development.* New York: UNDP.

United Nations Development Programme (2011) "Human Development Report 2011 – Sustainability and Equity: A Better Future for All." New York: UNDP.

Vona, F., Patriarca, F. (2011) "Income Inequality and the Development of Environmental Technologies," *Ecological Economics*, Vol. 70, pp. 2201–2213.

World Bank (2013) "World Development Indicators," (July 2, 2013 version), http://data.worldbank.org/data-catalog/world-development-indicators (accessed in July 2013).

Zheng, D. and Kuroda, T. (2013) "The Role of Public Infrastructure in China's Regional Inequality and Growth: A Simultaneous Equations Approach," *The Developing Economies*, Vol. 51, pp. 79–109.

25

VOLUNTARY STANDARDS AND DETERMINANTS

Analysis of ISO 14001 certification

Yutaka Ito, Shunsuke Managi and Toshi H. Arimura

1. Introduction

Pursuing sustainability is becoming a key business imperative, and an increasing number of companies have recognized the importance of considering the future of both people and the planet for the long-term success of their businesses (Hay et al., 2005; Kleindorfer et al., 2005; Fujii et al., 2013). Because of the impact of business activities on the three "pillars of sustainability" (i.e., profit, people, and planet) (Elkington, 1994), public concerns for the management of emissions by facility oversight, corporate social responsibility, environmentally friendly products, and the adoption of voluntary standards have been increasing over the past several decades.

Voluntary standards were developed to overcome weaknesses in traditional regulatory instruments such as command-and-control approaches (Fujii et al., 2011). The United States, for example, has experienced a great deal of success with its 33/50 program, which is a voluntary emissions reduction program introduced in 1991 to complement existing environmental regulations (Innes and Sam, 2008; Khanna and Damon, 1999; Fujii and Managi 2013). Such programs are recognized as being more flexible, effective, and less costly than traditional approaches (Arimura et al., 2008; Miyamoto and Managi, 2014), and they also are expected to play an important role in supplementing direct regulation through a command-and-control approach and indirect regulation, such as deposit-refund systems, charges and taxes, emissions trading, and financial assistance (Dawson and Segerson, 2008; Iwata et al., 2010; Murase, 2003).

An environmental management system (EMS) is a systematic process designed to manage the environmental impacts of a business and reduce the environmental risk associated with business activities (Bansal and Bogner, 2002; Bansal and Hunter, 2003; Cary and Roberts, 2011; Seymour and Ridley, 2005). In 1996, the International Organization for Standardization (ISO) adopted the new international standard ISO 14001,[1] and it provides the criteria for environmental management systems. To adopt ISO 14001, a firm must meet the requirements of the following five main elements based on the principles of continuous improvement (Plan, Do, Check, and Act [PDCA]): environmental policy, planning, implementation and operation, checking and corrective action, and management review.

Despite being a voluntary standard, its adoption may lead enterprises to improve the control and management of their process, products, and services. ISO 14001 also helps to reduce costs and increase profits over the medium and long term (Epstain and Roy, 1997). Hence, adoption of EMS ISO 14001 has constituted one of the most important elements of global corporate sustainability, especially in higher pollution emissions industries, such as mining, paper production, chemical production, construction, automotive services, and industrial coating (Barla, 2007; Comoglio and Botta, 2012; Gavronski et al., 2008; Newbold, 2006; Rodríguez et al., 2011; Zhang et al., 2014).

As shown in Figure 25.1, the number of ISO 14001 adoptions around the world has steadily increased to 285,844 at the end of 2012 since ISO 14001 was released in 1996 (ISO, 2012). ISO 14001 certificates have been issued across 167 countries, and the region with the highest number of certifications is East Asia and the Pacific, followed by Europe, North America, Central and South America, and Central and South Asia. However, the total number of certificates in 2012 was 9.1 percent higher than the 2011 figures, whereas the growth rate was half that of the 2009 figures (which saw numbers rise by 18.2 percent) and the second lowest rate following 4.1 percent in 2011. This trend indicates that the rate at which organizations are renewing or gaining certifications is now slowing down.

As indicated in Table 25.1, the top three countries with the total number of certificates issued were China, Japan, and Italy, whereas the top three for growth in the number of certificates in 2012 were China, Spain, and Italy. The number of organizations in Japan certified with ISO 14001 exceeds 27,774; however, it has been decreasing from 39,556 in 2009. In addition, these data highlight huge regional and international disparities in the uptake of the standard, with the vast majority of the 285,844 certified systems located in Europe (40 percent) and East Asia and the Pacific (51 percent).

Accordingly, organizations may have low expectations of effectiveness of the standard and its audits. To fill the gaps between these countries and regions and to be renewed, understanding the factors that promote or prevent organizations from becoming involved in a voluntary standard system is a primary issue, especially for countries that still have a lower number of certifications but have high economic potential, such as Indonesia, India, etc. Therefore, in the following sections, we introduce previous work in this field according to three groups. In Sections 3 to 5, we suggest the importance of considering features in each county for promoting ISO 14001 certifications by conducting an empirical analysis using Organisation for Economic Co-operation and Development (OECD) survey data. Considering the importance of voluntary action in emerging Asian countries, it is imperative to study global data using country-specific data.

2. Background of ISO 14001 adoption

Previous literature regarding ISO 14001 adoption is mainly classified into three groups. The main purpose of the first group is to analyze whether implementing environmental management is related to improved economic performance (Cormier and Magnan, 1999, 2003; Cormier et al., 2004; Darnall et al., 2007; Hackston and Milne, 1996; Hart and Ahuja, 1996; Hibiki et al., 2003; King and Lenox, 2002; Nakamura et al., 2001; Nakao et al., 2007; Nishitani, 2009, 2011; Nishitani et al., 2011, 2012; Patten, 1991; Roberts, 1992; Ruf et al., 2001; Zeng et al., 2010). For example, Nishitani (2009) found that there is a positive relationship between economic performance and initial ISO 14001 adoption; he also indicated that the determinants of the initial ISO 14001 adoption differed among the years of adoption and suggested that the adoption of ISO 14001 positively influenced a firm's added value by increasing demand and improving productivity (Nishitani, 2011). Hence, it is expected that the implementation of an EMS will improve economic performance while reducing environmental impact.

The objective of the second group is to examine the effectiveness of environmental policy instruments such as the U.S. Toxic Release Inventory (TRI) or pollutant release and transfer

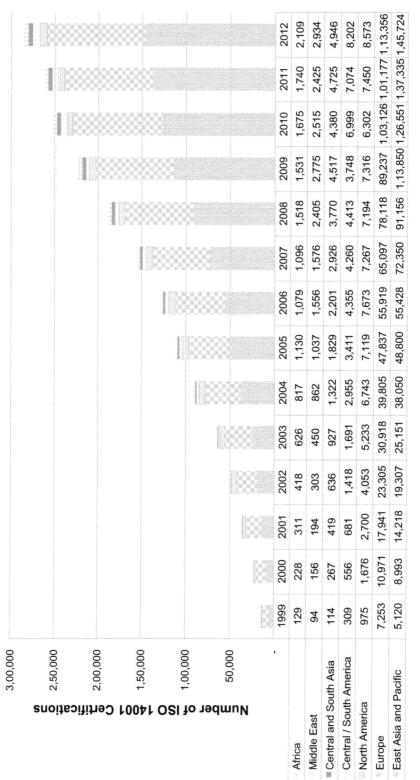

	1999	2000	2001	2002	2003	2004	2005	2006	2007	2008	2009	2010	2011	2012
Africa	129	228	311	418	626	817	1,130	1,079	1,096	1,518	1,531	1,675	1,740	2,109
Middle East	94	156	194	303	450	862	1,037	1,556	1,576	2,405	2,775	2,515	2,425	2,934
Central and South Asia	114	267	419	636	927	1,322	1,829	2,201	2,926	3,770	4,517	4,380	4,725	4,946
Central / South America	309	556	681	1,418	1,691	2,955	3,411	4,355	4,260	4,413	3,748	6,999	7,074	8,202
North America	975	1,676	2,700	4,053	5,233	6,743	7,119	7,673	7,267	7,194	7,316	6,302	7,450	8,573
Europe	7,253	10,971	17,941	23,305	30,918	39,805	47,837	55,919	65,097	78,118	89,237	1,03,126	1,01,177	1,13,356
East Asia and Pacific	5,120	8,993	14,218	19,307	25,151	38,050	48,800	55,428	72,350	91,156	1,13,850	1,26,551	1,37,335	1,45,724

Number of ISO 14001 Certifications

Figure 25.1 The total number of ISO 14001 certifications in each region from 1999 to 2012 (ISO, 2012).

Table 25.1 Top Ten countries for ISO 14001 certificates in 2012

Ranking	Country Name	Number of ISO certified facilities	Proportion in the world
1	China	91590	32.0%
2	Japan	27774	9.7%
3	Italy	19705	6.9%
4	Spain	19470	6.8%
5	United Kingdom	15884	5.6%
6	Korea, Republic of	11479	4.0%
7	Romania	8633	3.0%
8	France	7975	2.8%
9	Germany	7034	2.5%
10	United States of America	5699	2.0%

registers (PRTRs) (see Cohen and Santhakumar, 2007; Hibiki and Managi, 2010, 2011).[2] There are many types of empirical research on such policy instruments, especially in the US. For example, Melnyk et al. (2003) found that the adoption of ISO 14001 significantly reduced waste within the production process for US manufacturing firms. King et al. (2005) used sample data derived from the TRI for 7,899 US manufacturing facilities from 1995 to 2001 and found that ISO 14001 was associated with the existence of a functioning EMS and that these systems were associated with improved environmental performance. Potoski and Prakash (2005) examined data for 3,709 facilities that were regulated as major pollution sources under the US Clean Air Act from 1995 to 1996 and 2000 to 2001. They found that ISO 14001-certified facilities achieved a greater reduction in TRI pollution emissions than did non-certified facilities. Using a sample of 169 US electronics plants in 1999, Russo and Harrison (2005) found that ISO 14001 certification was associated with greater emissions based on data from the TRI. Based on a TRI data for 242 US facilities in the electronics industry, Russo (2009) found that the early adoption of ISO 14001 was associated with lower emissions, whereas late adoption was not. In Japan, Arimura et al. (2008) examined a sample of 792 Japanese manufacturing facilities operating in 2002 and found that ISO 14001 adoption helped reduce natural resource use, solid waste generation, and wastewater effluent. These studies generally suggest that there is a positive relationship between the implementation of ISO 14001 adoption and environmental performance, which implies that the voluntary approach is appropriate for reducing environmental impacts.[3]

The last group analyzes the determinants of ISO 14001 adoption, such as the customer's behavior (Arimura et al., 2008; Nakamura et al., 2001; Neumayer and Perkins, 2004; Nishitani, 2009, 2010, 2011), stockholder's influence (Arimura et al., 2008; Cormier and Magnan, 1999, 2003; Hibiki et al., 2003), and firm size (Arimura et al., 2008, 2011; Cormier and Magnan 1999, 2003; Hibiki et al., 2003; Nakamura et al., 2001; Nishitani, 2009; Patten and Crampton, 2004; Welch et al., 2000, 2002;). For example, Nakamura et al. (2001) analyzed the characteristics of ISO 14001-certified firms using a survey of 193 Japanese manufacturing firms listed on the first section of the Tokyo Stock Exchange. They found a positive effect of firm size, export orientation, pressure from civil society, and the firm's environmental responsibility on ISO 14001 adoption and a negative effect of the debt ratio and size of knowledge capital on ISO 14001 adoption.

Additional studies and research have evaluated the adoption of environmental management systems in diverse countries, such as in the US (Babakri et al., 2003), Slovenia (Selih, 2007), Spain (Rodríguez et al., 2007, 2011), Hong Kong (Hui et al., 2001), Germany (Morrow and Rondinelli, 2002), Australia (Zutshi and Sohal, 2004), Turkey (Turk, 2009), and Brazil (Gavronski et al., 2008), among others. The common finding is that the environmental preferences and pressures of stakeholders and firm characteristics influence firms to adopt ISO 14001 (see Nishitani, 2009).

3. Model and data description

To perform an econometric analysis of the survey data, we utilize binary probit models. If ISO_i^* is the facility i's net benefits from adopting ISO 14001, then ISO_i^* is determined by

$$ISO_i^* = \delta'_{ISO} X_i + \varepsilon_{iISO}, \tag{1}$$

Where X_i is a set of exogenous variables and ε_{iISO} is an idiosyncratic error. We assume that the facility will adopt ISO 14001 if its net benefit is greater than or equal to zero and ISO_i^* equals one if $ISO_i^* \geq 0$ and is equal to zero otherwise. The exogenous variables used in this model are explained in the next section.

In this study, we used the data collected from a 12-page survey developed by the OECD Environment Directorate and academic researchers from Canada, France, Germany, Hungary, Japan, Norway, and the United States. One of the authors of this chapter, Arimura, was involved in the development of the survey and data collection. The purpose of the survey was to collect information regarding environmental practices and performance from manufacturing facilities with 50 employees or more in these countries. The survey asked questions on: 1) management systems and tools in the facility; 2) environmental measures, innovation, and performance; 3) influence of stakeholders and motivations for environmental practices; 4) public environmental policy; 5) facility characteristics; and 6) firm characteristics.

To reduce reporting bias, the survey respondents were guaranteed anonymity. Additionally, the OECD examined nonresponse bias by evaluating the general distribution of its survey respondents and assessed the industry representation and facility size of the survey sample relative to the distribution of facilities in the broader population; statistically significant differences were not found (Johnstone, 2007). The summary statistics of variables used for estimation are presented in Table 25.2. Our final sample contained 2,318 facilities after removing incomplete responses, and it showed that 30.4 percent of the facilities had adopted ISO 14001.

Using information from the survey, we constructed a set of exogenous variables. The implementation of quality control was likely to affect the adoption of ISO 14001, whereas it did not directly affect environmental performance because it was not designed to improve environment management. Quality control and ISO 14001 involve similar PDCA cycles, and introducing a PDCA cycle incurs an adjustment cost because employees must be trained and familiarized with the system. With a similar cycle already in place under quality control, the adjustment cost is lower and the facility finds it easier to adopt ISO 14001. Therefore, we included a dummy variable, *OMPQMS*, which was set to one if the facility implemented quality control. As shown in Table 25.1, 77.4 percent of the facilities in our sample had implemented quality control.

Because many organizations continue to outsource manufacturing to low-cost countries in Asia, the Caribbean, Eastern Europe, and Latin America, the frequency and severity of supply-chain disruptions significantly increase. To avoid and/or reduce these types of risks, facilities may be more likely to attempt to green their supply chain by requiring that their suppliers undertake particular environmental measures, and it also is possible that these facilities may offer assurances

Table 25.2 Summary statistics of dependent and explanatory variables ($N = 2318$)

Variable	Mean	S.D.	Description
ISO 14001	0.3037	0.4600	Dummy for ISO 14001
OMPQMS	0.7735	0.4186	Dummy for quality management
REQSUPL	0.3934	0.4886	Dummy for requiring suppliers to undertake environmental measures
VOLAGR	1.7826	0.6797	Applicability of voluntary agreement
SUBSIDY	1.8546	0.7444	Applicability of subsidy or tax preferences
FRMQUOT	0.1993	0.3996	Dummy for listed firm
FACAGE	42.4713	30.3626	Facility age
FACEMPL	321.594	414.1997	The number of employees
AMTIMG	2.4478	0.6068	Importance of image
AMTSAV	2.3805	0.6282	Importance of cost savings
NATIONAL	0.3930	0.4885	Dummy for national market
REGIONAL	0.1247	0.3304	Dummy for regional market
GLOBAL	0.4055	0.4911	Dummy for global market
CANADA	0.0720	0.2586	Dummy for facilities in Canada
FRANCE	0.0591	0.2359	Dummy for facilities in France
GERMANY	0.2317	0.4220	Dummy for facilities in Germany
HUNGARY	0.1225	0.3280	Dummy for facilities in Hungary
JAPAN	0.3167	0.4653	Dummy for facilities in Japan
NORWAY	0.0824	0.2750	Dummy for facilities in Norway
USA	0.1156	0.3198	Dummy for facilities in the USA

to suppliers that they provide safe goods by adopting ISO 14001. Hence, we included a dummy variable, *REQSUPL*, which was set to one if the facility requires suppliers to undertake environmental measures; otherwise, it is zero. In our sample, 39 percent of the facilities required suppliers to undertake environmental measures.

Because environmental policy can be a determining factor for the adoption of ISO 14001, we controlled for two types of policy instruments, each of which was set to one if the facilities reported voluntary participation in environmental programs (*VOLAGR*) and subsidies/tax preferences (*SUBSIDY*) that are applicable to their facility's production activities. Facility managers indicated if these policy instruments were "not important," "moderately important," or "very important," which were set to one, two, or three, respectively.

To capture the heterogeneity of environmental managers, the survey asked managers to evaluate the importance of corporate profile/image (*AMTIMG*) and cost savings (*AMTSAV*) with respect to their facility's environmental practices. For each of these motivations, these variables were set to one, two, or three if the motivation was "not important," "moderately important," or "very important," respectively.

Our model includes basic facility and firm characteristics, such as the number of employees in the facility (*FACEMPL*) and age of the facility (*FACAGE*). Firm size may be an important determinant of the adoption of ISO 14001 for two significant reasons. First, larger firms experience more pressure from their various stakeholders regarding their environmental performance, and they are more likely to be the primary targets of environmental regulatory agencies because they have increased public visibility and sometimes are regarded as the largest polluters. Thus, larger firms are more susceptible to negative publicity regarding their environmental performance (Gonzalez-Benito and Gonzalez-Benito, 2006; Neumayer and Perkins, 2004; Welch et al., 2000, 2002). Second, ISO 14001 adoption requires comparatively high initial and long-term maintenance costs because firms must change their production processes and organizational structure (Arimura et al., 2008; Chin and Pun, 1999; Melnyk et al., 2003; Nakamura et al., 2001; Neumayer and Perkins, 2004). Such an enormous cost for adoption is less significant for larger firms than for smaller ones. Therefore, larger firms have a greater incentive to adopt ISO 14001.

We also include a dummy variable that indicates whether a facility is listed on a stock exchange (*FRMQUOT*), and it is used as a proxy for shareholder pressure. Stockholders also influence a firm's ISO 14001 adoption because they have a voice in its decisions. A reduction in pollution contamination by the firm could increase the confidence of its stockholders (Khanna and Damon, 1999; Welch et al., 2000). If a firm believes that its stockholders expect a reduction of current and future pollution, which would reduce the risk of environmental liabilities and provide higher profitability, the firm is more likely to adopt ISO 14001 to signal its commitment to environmental management (Hibiki et al., 2003; Welch et al., 2000). Because the expectation of lower risk and higher profitability in the future influences stock and dividend prices in the long term, long-term stockholders are more responsive to environmental management than other stockholders. Therefore, long-term stockholders are more eager for ISO 14001 adoption, and firms with more long-term stockholders are more strongly motivated to adopt it.

We also control for market scope by using four dummy variables that are set to a value of one if the facility's market scope is "*LOCAL*," "*NATIONAL*," "*REGIONAL*" (neighboring countries), or "*GLOBAL*." Firms face demand-side incentives to adopt ISO 14001 (Neumayer and Perkins, 2004). Foreign customers may demand more visible signs of commitment to environmental protection because they have less opportunity to monitor the performance of a firm. ISO 14001 is regarded as the international benchmark for assessing a firm's environmental performance (Nakamura et al., 2001; Rondinelli and Vastag, 2000). Thus, firms that have more foreign customers are more likely to adopt ISO 14001. Here, the omitted reference case is the local market. In our model, the industry dummy and country dummy are also included. The country dummy of Canada is used as the omitted reference case in each specification. In addition, we also include the interaction term between the country dummy and explanatory variables to capture the feature of each country regarding ISO 14001 adoption. In this chapter, six types of specifications are implemented, of which five types of specifications include the interaction term.

4. Results and discussion

The estimated coefficients of the ISO 14001 adoption equations are presented in Table 25.3. This table presents the results from the probit regression estimations. The dependent variable for the entire column is a dichotomized ISO adoption variable in which the adoption value is one and non-adoption is zero. Specification 1 shows the determining factors for the adoption of ISO 14001 by a facility without interaction term variables. Interaction terms between each country dummy are listed to the left of the specifications from 2 to 6, and the independent variable is listed below the title of the specification. For example, the interaction term between *REQSUPL* and the country dummy for each country are included in specification 2.

For specification 1, the coefficients for quality control (*OMPQMS*), requirement to undertake environmental measures (*REQSUPL*), facility size (*FACEMPL*), voluntary agreement (*VOLGAR*), initial public offering (*FRMQUOT*), and motivation or image related to an environmental

Table 25.3 Estimation results of each specification

Variable	Non-interaction term	Interaction Term				
	Specification 1 (BASIC)	Specification 2 (REQSUPL)	Specification 3 (FACEMPL)	Specification 4 (FRMQUOT)	Specification 5 (SUBSIDY)	Specification 6 (AMTSAV)
CONSTANT	−3.619(0.295)***	−3.748(0.319)***	−3.446(0.324)***	−3.414(0.312)***	−3.612(0.44)***	−3.951(0.55)***
OMPQMS	0.845(0.102)***	0.856(0.103)***	0.833(0.102)***	0.836(0.102)***	0.851(0.102)***	0.842(0.102)***
REQSUPL	0.659(0.064)***	0.399(0.183)**	0.665(0.065)***	0.678(0.065)***	0.657(0.065)***	0.662(0.065)***
FACEMPL	0.001(0.00)***	0.001(0.00)***	0.001(0.00)***	0.001(0.00)***	0.001(0)***	0.001(0)***
FACEMPL2	0.00(0.00)***	0.00(0.00)***	0.00(0.00)***	0.00(0.00)***	0.00(0.00)***	0.00(0.00)***
VOLAGR	0.117(0.053)**	0.127(0.054)**	0.115(0.054)**	0.104(0.054)*	0.12(0.054)**	0.113(0.054)**
FRMQUOT	0.289(0.083)***	0.3(0.084)***	0.271(0.084)***	0.017(0.184)	0.285(0.084)***	0.296(0.084)***
FACAGE	0.00(0.001)	0.00(0.001)	0.00(0.001)	0.00(0.001)	0.00(0.001)	0.00(0.001)
SUBSIDY	−0.121(0.051)**	−0.121(0.051)**	−0.125(0.051)**	−0.118(0.051)**	0.115(0.136)	−0.118(0.051)**
AMTIMG	0.237(0.06)***	0.24(0.061)***	0.233(0.06)***	0.236(0.06)***	0.23(0.06)***	0.229(0.061)***
AMTSAV	−0.095(0.055)*	−0.096(0.055)*	−0.091(0.055)*	−0.094(0.055)*	−0.088(0.055)	−0.408(0.162)**
NATIONAL	0.06(0.141)	0.036(0.143)	0.063(0.141)	0.03(0.142)	0.057(0.141)	0.056(0.142)
REGIONAL	0.522(0.164)***	0.488(0.165)***	0.507(0.164)***	0.512(0.164)***	0.528(0.164)***	0.527(0.165)***
GLOBAL	0.375(0.148)**	0.342(0.149)**	0.375(0.148)**	0.375(0.148)**	0.38(0.148)***	0.369(0.148)**
Country dummy						
FRANCE	0.577(0.188)***	0.705(0.244)***	0.347(0.264)	0.565(0.227)**	1.158(0.508)**	1.04(0.658)
GERMANY	0.488(0.157)***	0.681(0.205)***	0.39(0.209)*	0.312(0.190)*	0.396(0.408)	1.244(0.559)**
HUNGARY	0.345(0.167)**	0.629(0.229)***	0.255(0.233)	0.155(0.200)	0.423(0.479)	1.055(0.665)
JAPAN	1.105(0.156)***	1.068(0.202)***	0.864(0.209)***	0.88(0.187)***	1.11(0.392)***	0.888(0.551)
NORWAY	0.948(0.175)***	1.143(0.221)***	0.658(0.244)***	0.866(0.208)***	1.099(0.458)**	1.165(0.637)*
USA	0.241(0.163)	0.459(0.215)**	0.292(0.228)	0.255(0.223)	−0.215(0.451)	1.398(0.655)**

(Continued)

Table 25.3 (Continued)

Variable	Non-interaction term	Interaction Term				
	Specification 1 (BASIC)	Specification 2 (REQSUPL)	Specification 3 (FACEMPL)	Specification 4 (FRMQUOI)	Specification 5 (SUBSIDY)	Specification 6 (AMTSAV)
Interaction term						
CANADA		0.536(0.33)	0(0.00)	−0.111(0.326)	−0.246(0.229)	0.456(0.254)★
FRANCE		0.228(0.323)	0.001(0.00)	−0.277(0.348)	−0.547(0.219)★★	0.259(0.248)
GERMANY		0.094(0.226)	0(0.00)	0.371(0.257)	−0.198(0.162)	0.13(0.193)
HUNGARY		−0.019(0.257)	0(0.00)	0.551(0.328)★	−0.277(0.183)	0.177(0.231)
JAPAN		0.565(0.213)★★★	0.001(0.00)★★★	0.785(0.25)★★★	−0.248(0.158)	0.552(0.185)★★★
NORWAY		0.002(0.297)	0.001(0.001)★	−0.305(0.358)	−0.33(0.2)★	0.373(0.237)
Log likelihood	−1074.3	−1066.3	−1068.4	−1062.9	−1070.7	−1066.8
Pseud R2	0.245	0.251	0.249	0.253	0.248	0.25
N	2318	2318	2318	2318	2318	2318

Note: The table shows the maximum simulated likelihood estimates of ISO 14001 adoption. In addition to the variables listed here, the regressions include industry dummies. Standard errors are in parentheses. ★, ★★, and ★★★ indicate the significance at the 10%, 5%, and 1% levels, respectively. Industry dummies are included in the model, although their coefficients are not reported here. The results of the interaction term of the US are not reported because all of the results were omitted. However, all of the variables that were statistically significant in Table 25.3 had the same signs and statistical significance in the cases without the US facilities.

approach (*AMTIMG*) are positive and statistically significant. Therefore, facilities that implement quality control and require suppliers to undertake environmental measures are more likely to attempt adopting ISO 14001. The larger sized and listed facilities also tend to adopt ISO 14001.

With regard to market scope, the *REGIONAL* and *GLOBAL* dummy variables are positive and statistically significant, whereas the *NATIONAL* dummy is not statistically significant. Therefore, facilities with more foreign customers are more likely adopt ISO 14001. These results are consistent with previous literature (Arimura et al., 2008; Arimura et al., 2011; Bansal and Hunter, 2003; Hibiki et al., 2003; Nakamura et al., 2001; Nishitani, 2009; Welch et al. 2002; Wu et al., 2007; Yiridoe et al., 2003). However, subsidy/tax preferences (*SUBSIDY*) and cost savings (*AMTSAV*) are negative and have a statistically significant correlation with the adoption of ISO 14001. The age of the facility (FACAGE) is not statistically significant.

In other specifications, the coefficient signs of these independent variables are consistent with specification 1; however, certain results are not significant, such as *FRMQUOT* in specification 4, *SUBSIDY* in specification 5, and *AMTSAV* in specification 5.

With respect to the country dummy, numerous countries are statistically positive or not significant for all of the specifications. These results indicate that facilities located in France, Germany, Hungary, Japan, Norway, and the US are more likely to have a higher number of ISO 14001 certifications relative to facilities in Canada. The following section explains the results of the interaction term.

4.1 Discussion of the interaction term

In specification 2, the interaction term between the country dummy and *REQSUPL* are not significantly correlated with ISO 1400 adoption except for in Japan, which indicates that the Japanese facilities that require suppliers to undertake specific environmental performance measures are more likely to adopt ISO 14001 relative to the facilities without such a requirement. This result might be complemented by previous research (Arimura et al., 2011) that indicates that Japanese facilities with an EMS certified to ISO 14001 are 40 percent more likely to assess their suppliers' environmental performance and 50 percent more likely to require that their suppliers undertake specific environmental practices.

From the results of specification 3, we found that the probability of ISO 14001 adoption has a statistically positive correlation with the interaction dummy between *FACEMPL* and the Japanese or Norwegian facilities. Therefore, there is an increased tendency for relatively larger facilities in these countries to adopt ISO 14001 compared to small facilities, and this tendency is higher than in other countries.

Similar to specification 3, the interaction dummy of Japan with *FRMQUOT* also is statistically significant and positive in specification 4, which is also true for Hungary. These results imply that the environmental preferences and pressures of stakeholders and/or the financial flexibility that results from joining the market might influence the adoption of ISO 14001 in these two countries compared to other countries.

The estimation result of specification 5 shows that the interaction dummies for France and Norway with *SUBSIDY* are negatively and positively correlated with ISO 14001 adoption, respectively. Therefore, in the case of France, facilities that considered the impacts of environmental policy, such as a subsidy or tax on their facilities and activities, to be important were less likely to adopt ISO 14001. This result may indicate that environmental policies that promote voluntary approaches by facilities are not influential. Lastly, specification 6 indicates that Japanese and Canadian facilities that consider environmental practices to be a relatively important motivation for cost savings are more likely to adopt ISO 14001. As expected, differences can be found regarding the factors that affect ISO 14001 adoption in different countries according to the interaction term.

5. Conclusion

ISO 14001 has proven to be both popular and effective at providing a global framework through which organizations across the world manage their impacts on the environment. By focusing on ISO 14001 adoptions, we found that the determinants of ISO 14001 adoptions were similar to those shown in previous work. In addition, by including the interaction terms between country dummies and determinant variables, we showed that the effects of certain determinants are different in each country. Our results and the results of previous studies imply strong causal connections between ISO adoption and country effect. Of course, country effect includes several factors (culture, regulations, support of government, etc.). Considering the future importance of Asian countries, additional analyses focusing on Asia are required. In future work, we must show in more detail the causality between each factor, including country effect and ISO adoption.

Notes

1 There are many international standards of environmental management, such as the Global Reporting Initiative guidelines for corporate sustainability reports. See Veleva and Ellenbecker (2000) for details
2 Several studies were also conducted to evaluate the effect of ISO 14001 adoption on environmental performance instead of using pollution emissions data. For instance, Arimura et al. (2011) analyzed the effects of ISO 14001 on green supply chain management and found significant but previously unnoticed spillover effects of ISO 14001 and government promotion of voluntary action. Inoue et al. (2013) also empirically showed that as the ISO 14001 improves facilities, those facilities are likely to spend more on environmental R&D. The facility age and market concentration also positively affects environmental R&D.
3 Past studies are not necessarily in agreement on the effectiveness of certified EMS, especially European countries. For example, Ziegler and Rennings (2004) found that EMS certification does not significantly affect environmental innovation and abatement behavior at German manufacturing facilities. Using UK data, Dahlström et al. (2003) showed that neither ISO 14001 nor EMS has a positive effect on compliance with environmental regulations.

References

Arimura, T., Darnall, N., and Katayama, H., 2011. Is ISO 14001 a gateway to more advanced voluntary action? The case of green supply chain management. *Journal of Environmental Economics and Management* 61, 170–182.

Arimura, T., Hibiki, A., and Katayama, H., 2008. Is a voluntary approach an effective environmental policy instrument? A case of environmental management systems. *Journal of Environmental Economics and Management* 55, 281–295.

Babakri, K.A., Bennet, R.A., and Franchetti, M., 2003. Critical factors for implementing ISO 14001 standard in United States industrial companies. *Journal of Cleaner Production* 11, 749–752.

Bansal, P. and Bogner, W.C., 2002. Deciding on ISO 14001: economics, institutions, and context. *Long Range Planning* 35, 269–290.

Bansal, P. and Hunter, T., 2003. Strategic explanations for the early adoption of ISO 14001. *Journal of Business Ethics* 46, 289–299.

Barla, P., 2007. ISO 14001 certification and environmental performance in Quebec's pulp and paper industry. *Journal of Environmental Economics and Management* 53, 291–306.

Cary, J. and Roberts, A., 2011. The limitations of environmental management systems in Australian agriculture. *Journal of Environmental Management* 92, 878–885.

Chin, K. and Pun, K., 1999. Factors influencing ISO 14000 implementation in printed circuit board manufacturing industry in Hong Kong. *Journal of Environmental Planning and Management* 42, 123–134.

Cohen, A.M. and Santhakumar, V., 2007. Information disclosure as environmental regulation: a theoretical analysis. *Journal of Environmental Planning and Management* 37, 599–620.

Comoglio, C. and Botta, S., 2012. The use of indicators and the role of environmental management systems for environmental performances improvement: a survey on ISO 14001 certified companies in the automotive sector. *Journal of Cleaner Production* 20, 92–102.

Cormier, D. and Magnan, M., 1999. Corporate environmental disclosure strategies: determinants, costs and benefits. *Journal of Accounting*, Auditing and Finance 14, 429–451.

Cormier, D. and Magnan, M., 2003. Environmental reporting management: a continental European perspective. *Journal of Accounting and Public Policy* 22, 43–62.

Cormier, D., Gordon, I.M. and Magnan, M., 2004. Corporate environmental disclosure: contrasting management's perception with reality. *Journal of Business Ethics* 49(2), 143–165.

Dahlstrom, K., Howes, C., Leinster, P. and Skea, J., 2003. Environmental management systems and company performance: assessing the case for extending risk-based regulation. *European Environment* 13, 187–203.

Darnall, N., G.J. Jolley and B. Ytterhus. 2007. Understanding the relationship between a facility's environmental and financial performance. In: Johnstone, N. ed., *Environmental Policy and Corporate Behavior*, pp. 213–259. Cheltenham, UK: Edward Elgar Publishing, in association with OECD.

Dawson, N.L. and Segerson, K., 2008. Voluntary agreements with industries: participation incentives with industry-wide targets. *Land Economics* 84, 97–114.

Elkington, J., 1994. Towards the sustainable corporation: win-win-win business strategies for sustainable development. California Management Review 36, 90–100.

Epstain, M.J. and Roy, M.J., 1997. Using ISO 14001 for improved organizations learning and environmental management. *Environmental Quality Management* 7, 21e30.

Fujii, H., Iwata, K., Kaneko, S. and Managi, S., 2013. Corporate environmental and economic performances of Japanese manufacturing firms: empirical study for sustainable development, *Business Strategy and Environment* 22(3), 187–201.

Fujii, H. and Managi, S., 2013. Decomposition of toxic chemical substance management in three U.S. manufacturing sectors from 1991 to 2008, *Journal of Industrial Ecology* 17(3), 461–471.

Fujii, H., Managi, S. and Kawahara, S. 2011. The pollution release and transfer register system in the U.S. and Japan: an analysis of productivity, *Journal of Cleaner Production* 19(12), 1330–1338.

Gavronski, I., Ferrer, G. and Paiva, E.L., 2008. ISO 14001 certification in Brazil: motivations and benefits. *Journal of Cleaner Production* 16, 87–94.

Gonzalez-Benito, J. and Gonzalez-Benito, O., 2006. A review of determinant factors of environmental proactivity. Business Strategy and the Environment 15, 87–102.

Hackston, D. and Milne, M.J., 1996. Some determinants of social and environmental disclosures in New Zealand companies. *Journal of Accounting Auditing and Accountability* 9, 77–108.

Hart, S.L. and Ahuja, G., 1996. Does it pay to be green? An empirical examination of the relationship between emission reduction and firm performance. Business Strategy and the Environment 5, 30–37.

Hay, R.L., Stavins, R.N. and Vietor, R.H.K., 2005. *Environmental Protection and the Social Responsibility of Firms: Perspectives from Law, Economics and Business.* Washington, DC: RFF Press.

Hibiki, A., Higashi, M. and Matsuda, A., 2003. Determinants of the Firm to Acquire ISO14001 Certificate and Market Valuation of the Certified Firm, Tokyo Institute of Technology Discussion Paper, No. 03-06. Tokyo Institute of Technology, Tokyo.

Hibiki, A. and Managi, S., 2010. Environmental information provision, market valuation, and firm incentives: an empirical study of the Japanese PRTR system. *Land Economics* 86, 382–393.

Hibiki, A. and Managi, S., 2011. Does the housing market respond to information disclosure? Effects of toxicity indices in Japan. *Journal of Environmental Management* 92, 165–171.

Hui, I.K., Chan, A. and Pun, K.F., 2001. A study of the environmental management system practices. *Journal of Cleaner Production* 9, 241–256.

Innes, R. and Sam, A., 2008. Voluntary pollution reductions and the enforcement of environmental law: an empirical study of the 33/50 program. *The Journal of Law and Economics* 51, 271–296.

Inoue, E., Arimura, T. and Nakano, M., 2013. A new insight into environmental innovation: does the maturity of environmental management systems matter? *Ecological Economics* 94, 156–163.

International Organization for Standardization, 2012. ISO survey, Survey Data. http://www.iso.org/iso/home/standards/certification/iso-survey.htm?certificate=ISO%209001&countrycode=AF.

Iwata, K., Arimura, T. and Hibiki, S., 2010. An empirical analysis of determinants of ISO 14001 adoption and its influence on toluene emission reduction (in Japanese). *Nihon Keizai Kenkyuu* 62, 16–38.

Johnstone, N., 2007. *Environmental Policy and Corporate Behaviour.* Cheltenham: Edward Elgar Publishing.

Khanna, M. and Damon, L.A., 1999. EPA's voluntary 33/50 program: impact on toxic releases and economic performance of firms. *Journal of Environmental Economics and Management* 37, 1–25.

King, A. and Lenox, M., 2002. Exploring the locus of profitable pollution reduction. *Management Science* 48, 289–299.

King, A., Lenox M. and Terlaak, A. 2005. The strategic use of decentralized institutions: exploring certification with the ISO 14001 Management Standard. *Academy of Management Journal* 48(6), 1091–106.

Kleindorfer, P.R., Singhal, K. and VanWassenhove, L.N., 2005. Sustainable operations management. Production and Operations Management 14, 482–492.

Melnyk, S.A., Sroufe, R.P. and Calantone, R., 2003. Assessing the impact of environmental management systems on corporate and environmental performance. *Journal of Operations Management* 21, 329–351.

Miyamoto, T. and S. Managi, S. 2014. Intra-industry spillover effects of ISO 14001 adoption in Japan, *International Journal of Ecological Economics & Statistics* 34(3), 20–36.

Morrow, D. and Rondinelli, D., 2002. Adopting corporate environmental management systems: motivations and results of ISO 14001 and EMAS certification. *European Management Journal* 20, 159–171.

Murase, S., 2003. WTO/GATT and MEAs: Kyoto protocol and beyond. http://www.gets.org/gets/harmony/projectpapers.html.

Nakamura, M., Takahashi, T. and Vertinsky, I., 2001. Why Japanese firms choose to certify: a study of managerial responses to environmental issues. *Journal of Environmental Economics and Management* 42, 23–52.

Nakao, Y., Amano, A., Matsumura, K., Gemba, K. and Nakano, M., 2007. Relationship between environmental performance and financial performance: an empirical analysis of Japanese corporations. Business Strategy and the Environment 16, 106–118.

Neumayer, E. and Perkins, R., 2004. What explains the uneven take-up of ISO14001 at the global level? A panel-data analysis. *Environment and Planning A*. 36, 823–839.

Newbold, J., 2006. Chile's environmental momentum: ISO 14001 and the large-scale mining industry e Case studies from the state and private sector. *Journal of Cleaner Production* 14, 248–261.

Nishitani, K., 2009. An empirical study of the initial adoption of ISO 14001 in Japanese manufacturing firms. *Ecological Economics* 68, 669–679.

Nishitani, K., 2010. Demand for ISO 14001 adoption in the global supply chain: an empirical analysis focusing on environmentally conscious markets. Resource and Energy Economics 32, 395–407.

Nishitani, K., 2011. An empirical analysis of the effects on firms' economic performance of implementing environmental management systems. Environmental and Resource Economics 48, 569–586.

Nishitani, K., Kaneko, K., Fujii, H. and Komatsu, S. 2011. Effects of the reduction of pollution emissions on the economic performance of firms: an empirical analysis focusing on demand and productivity. *Journal of Cleaner Production* 19, 1956–1964.

Nishitani, K., Kaneko, K., Fujii, H. and Komatsu, S. 2012. Are firms' voluntary environmental management activities beneficial for the environment and business? An empirical study focusing on Japanese manufacturing firms. Journal of Environmental Management 105, 121–130.

Patten, D., 1991. Exposure, legitimacy, and social disclosure. Journal of Accounting and Public Policy 10, 297–308.

Patten, D. M. and Crampton, W., 2004. Legitimacy and the internet: an examination of corporate web page environmental disclosures. Advances in Environmental Accounting and Management 2, 31–57.

Potoski, M. and Prakash, A., 2005. Covenants with weak swords: ISO14001 and facilities' environmental performance. *Journal of Policy Analysis and Management* 24, 745–769.

Roberts, R.W., 1992. Determinants of corporate social responsibility disclosure: an application of stakeholder theory. Accounting, Organizations and Society 17, 595–612.

Rodríguez, G., Alegre, F.J. and Martínez, G., 2007. The contribution of environmental management systems to the management of construction and demolition waste: the case of the autonomous community of Madrid (Spain). Resources, Conservation and Recycling 50, 334–349.

Rodríguez, G., Alegre, F.J. and Martínez, G., 2011. Evaluation of environmental management resources (ISO 14001) at civil engineering construction worksites: a case study of the community of Madrid. Journal of Environmental Management 92, 1858–1866.

Rondinelli, D. and Vastag, G., 2000. Panacea, common sense, or just a label? The value of ISO 14001 environmental management systems. European Management Journal 18, 499–510.

Ruf, B.M., Muralidhar, K., Brown, R.M., Janney, J.J. and Paul, K., 2001. An empirical investigation of the relationship between change in corporate social performance and financial performance: a stakeholder theory perspective. *Journal of Business Ethics* 32, 143–156.

Russo, M.V., 2009. Explaining the impact of ISO 14001 on emission performance: a dynamic capabilities perspective on process and learning. *Business Strategy and the Environment* 18, 307–19.

Russo, M.V. and Harrison, N.S., 2005. Organizational design and environmental performance: clues from the electronics industry. *Academy of Management Journal* 48: 582–593.

Selih, J., 2007. Environmental management systems and construction SMEs: a case study for Slovenia. *Journal of Civil Engineering and Management* 13, 217–226.

Seymour, E.J. and Ridley, A.M., 2005. Towards environmental management systems in Australian agriculture to achieve better environmental outcomes at the catchment scale: a review. Environmental Management 33, 311–329.

Turk, A.M., 2009. The benefits associated with ISO 14001 certification for construction firms: Turkish case. *Journal of Cleaner Production* 17, 559–569.

Veleva, V. and Ellenbecker, M., 2000. A proposal for measuring business sustainability – addressing shortcomings in existing frameworks. *Greener Management International* 31, 101–120.

Welch, E.W., Mazur, A. and Bretschneider, S., 2000. Voluntary behavior by electric utilities: levels of adoption and contribution of the climate challenge program to the reduction of carbon dioxide. *Journal of Policy Analysis and Management* 19, 407–425.

Welch, E.W., Mori, Y. and Aoyagi-Usui, M., 2002. Voluntary adoption of ISO 14001 in Japan: mechanisms, stages and effects. Business Strategy and the Environment 11, 43–62.

Wu, S.Y., Chu, P.Y. and Liu, T.Y., 2007. Determinants of a firm's ISO 14001 certification: an empirical study of Taiwan. *Pacific Economic Review* 12, 467–487.

Yiridoe, E.K., Clark, J.S., Marett, G.E., Gordon, R. and Duinker, P., 2003. ISO 14001 EMS standard registration decisions among Canadian organizations. *Agribusiness* 19, 439–457.

Zeng, S.X., Meng, X.H., Yin, H.T., Tam, C.M. and Sun, L., 2010. Impact of cleaner production on business performance. *Journal of Cleaner Production* 18, 975–983.

Zhang, W., Wang, W. and Wang, S., 2014. Environmental performance evaluation of implementing EMS (ISO14001) in the coating industry: case study of a Shanghai coating firm. *Journal of Cleaner Production* 64, 205–217.

Ziegler, A. and Rennings, K. 2004. Determinants of environmental innovations in Germany: do organizational measures matter? A discrete choice analysis at the firm level. ZEW Discussion Paper no. 04–30, Centre for European Economic Research, Mannheim.

Zutshi, A. and Sohal, A., 2004. Adoption and maintenance of environmental management systems: critical success factors. *Management of Environmental Quality: An International Journal* 15, 399–419.

26

JAPANESE DOMESTIC ENVIRONMENTAL POLICY

With a focus on climate change and air pollution policy

*Toshi H. Arimura**

1. Introduction

The Japanese government has implemented a range of environmental policies. Economists often promote the use of economic instruments such as tax or emissions trading schemes aiming for economic efficiency. The introduction of economic instruments, however, faces opposition from various stakeholders in many countries. Japan is no exception; a regulatory approach is often used to control environmental impacts.

Japanese environmental policy may be characterized by command-and-control types of regulation. This chapter outlines some of the major environmental regulations enacted over the past 15 years and introduces an economic analysis of these regulations.

We will focus on air pollution policy and climate policy.[1] Specifically, we will emphasize policies that are evaluated from the viewpoint of economics or quantitative analysis. The next section outlines air pollution policy. Section 3 explains the energy conservation act and its major provisions. Section 4 presents emissions trading schemes in Japan. Voluntary actions by the private sector are explained in Section 5. Section 6 discusses the international offsets for carbon mitigation. The carbon tax is explained in Section 7. Renewable energy policy is explained in section 8. Section 9 concludes this chapter.

2. Air pollution policy

The ambient air quality in Japanese metropolitan areas improved during the 1980s through the reduction of SO_2 emissions. Nitrogen oxide (NO_x) and particulate matter (PM)[2] emissions then became the major concern in the 1990s. By the 1990s, a great share of the NO_x and PM emissions in urban areas were from automobiles.

2.1 Automobile NO_x Act and NO_x PM Act

In addition to the emissions gas standard, which is a typical regulation of exhaust gas, a unique regulation was introduced in 1992 to address the NO_x issue: the Automobile NO_x Act (hereafter called "the NO_x Act"). The NO_x Act is a type of command-and-control regulation in which owners are forced to replace their old vehicles with new, cleaner ones (Oka et al., 2007).

Despite these efforts, the concentration of NO_x in metropolitan areas did not improve in the 1990s. Among roadside air pollution monitoring stations in the nonattainment areas, only 43 percent met the national ambient air quality standard for NO_x in 1998. The environmental standard for PM was even worse; only 36 percent of roadside air pollution monitoring stations met the standard in 1998.

The heavy usage of diesel trucks was responsible for this situation. Consequently, the Automobile NO_x-PM Act (NO_x-PM Act), a revised version of the NO_x Act, was enacted in 2001 to decrease the concentration of PM and NO_x in nonattainment metropolitan areas.

The NO_x-PM Act has a provision called the "vehicle type regulation." The vehicle type regulation prohibits the use and registration of automobiles in the nonattainment areas after certain grace periods unless the automobiles satisfy the 2005 emissions standard. This is a unique regulation since it regulates vehicles in use.

Iwata and Arimura(2009) conducted a cost-benefit analysis of this provision and found that the net benefit of the regulation was approximately 681 billion yen and thus that the NO_x-PM Act yielded great benefit for the society. The researchers also posited the importance of economic instruments by demonstrating that the net benefit would have doubled had economic instruments been used.

The target of the NO_x PM Act was PM_{10}. In 2009, for the first time in Japan, the ambient air quality standard for $PM_{2.5}$ was set. It remains to be seen how Japan will achieve this standard. An appropriate cost-benefit analysis of control measures is desirable.

3. Energy Conservation Act

After the NO_x PM Act was adopted, carbon mitigation became a major environmental policy issue. The government has implemented various climate policies for different sectors of the Japanese economy. Several regulations have their basis in the Act on the Rational Use of Energy (Energy Conservation Act).

3.1 *Energy management under the act on the rational use of energy*

Established in 1979, the Energy Conservation Act aimed to promote energy savings, mainly in the manufacturing sector. Manufacturing facilities were the regulation unit of this act, with each facility being required to meet the energy intensity target of a 1 percent annual reduction. The facilities subject to the regulation must appoint an energy manager, obey the standards of judgment prescribed in the act, and submit an annual report and medium- and long-term plans for achieving targets related to the rational use of energy.

Subsequently, the scope of the regulation was expanded to cover the service sector.[3] For example, the hotel industry became subject to the regulation. Arimura and Iwata (2015) examined the effectiveness of the 1 percent annual reduction for the hotel industry, finding that from 2002 to 2004, the hotel industry achieved the target for fossil fuel but slightly missed the target for electricity.

3.2 *Top runner program*

The top runner program is one of the most famous mitigation policy measures under the Energy Conservation Act. This program was introduced in 1999 to reduce energy consumption from transportation and household/commercial sectors.[4] The program assumes the form of "a maximum standard value system" (METI, 2010). The program sets the energy efficiency targets for various products, such as electric appliances or vehicles. Producers are required to achieve an efficiency level based on the weighting average of their products by the sales volume.

One unique future of the program is that it incorporates "potential technological improvements" in setting the standard. Consequently, the program requirement may be stringent. For example, Geller et al. (2006) noted that: "In some cases, the required efficiency improvement is over 50 percent."

The scope of the top runner program has been expanding. When the program was introduced in 1999, 11 products, including passenger cars and air conditioners, were subject to this regulation. More products have since been included in this regulation. Most recently, printers and two other products were added to this program in 2013 for a total of 26 types of products subject to the top runner program.

Several studies have quantitatively investigated the impacts of the program. Kainou (2006, 2007) conducted a cost-benefit analysis of the top runner program. The study concluded that the benefits exceed the costs and that the overall program generates benefits of approximately 180 billion yen with CO_2 reductions of 25 Mt per year on average. The analysis, however, indicates the importance of ex ante cost-benefit analysis in designing the program because the cost exceeds the benefit for certain appliances.

Kimura (2010) examined the top runner program and reported an improvement in efficiency. According to the information from the Energy Conservation Center, Japan (ECCJ) (2008), the requirement of energy efficiency improvement from 1997 to 2003 or 2004 for major products ranged from 16 percent to 80 percent. The study found that all products achieved the target. At the same time, the investigation indicated that the unique feature of the Japanese market structure potentially played an important role in successfully implementing the program.

The success of the program appears to be still valid based on the recent data. According to a report issued by the Minister of Economy, Trade and Industry (METI),[5] dramatic improvement was achieved for many products. For instance, fuel efficiency for passenger vehicles improved by 48.8 percent by 2010. The efficiency of refrigerators and DVD recorders also improved by more than 40 percent. Caution may be required in interpreting the results. Manufacturers are facing pressures from various stakeholders to improve the energy efficiency of their products. Therefore, it may be too simplistic to attribute all the improvement to the top runner program.

Hamamoto (2011) examined the impact of the program on firms' R&D efforts. The study found that, together with the labeling systems, the program increased R&D expenditures of appliance producers by 9.5 percent. By contrast, the study found a negative result for motor vehicle production, possibly due to the exhaust gas regulation for diesel vehicles.

The top runner program is now combined with the labeling program. Depending on the achievement of efficiency, each product may use different types of labels to display the energy efficiency level (METI, 2010).

4. Emissions trading schemes in Japan

In September 2009, after winning the majority in the lower house election, the Democratic Party of Japan proposed the 25 percent reduction of greenhouse gas (GHG) emissions relative to the 1990 level. To achieve this target, three major policy instruments were proposed. One instrument was a domestic emissions-trading scheme (ETS). The potential for a domestic ETS has been intensively discussed among policymakers and tested via several voluntary or experimental ETSs. Due to their voluntary nature, some Japanese firms have participated, while others have not.

4.1 Discussion of the cap-and-trade scheme in Japan

The discussion of the domestic cap-and-trade scheme was intense in 2010. Arimura et al. (2012) conducted a corporate survey to determine which issues regarding the cap-and-trade scheme would be important were it to be introduced. The group listed 15 issues based on the discussion within the central environmental council under the Ministry of the Environment. These issues include "allocation methods" (auctioning or grandfathering and total emissions or emissions per unit) or the "aggregate cap." Among these issues, an important economic factor is competitiveness and carbon leakage. A total of 76 percent of the responding firms consider these issues to be extremely or moderately important.

Under the ETS, energy-intensive industries competing with firms facing no regulation could lose their competitive edge, which may lead to a reduction in their production. This factor is called the competitiveness issue. In many countries, energy-intensive industries are opposed to the ETS. Political support from the industry, including energy-intensive industries, is indispensable to the introduction of an ETS.

Carbon leakage is another important issue. An ETS may lead such industries in nations with regulations to reduce production. Consequently, production from energy-intensive industries can move to countries with lower energy efficiency and less stringent regulations, such as China and India. This phenomenon could cause carbon leakage by increasing emissions in developing countries. To avoid potential leakage, governments must be cautious in introducing stringent regulation on energy-intensive industries.

Several studies have tackled these competitiveness/leakage issues in the Japanese economy. Sugino et al. (2013) estimated which industrial sector would face the competitiveness issue under the cap-and-trade scheme. They found that, if criteria in the Waxman–Markey proposal (H.R. 2454) in the US Congress were applied, then 23 out of 401 industries would be considered as energy-intensive trade-exposed (EITE).

As a countermeasure against the competitiveness/leakage issues, several methods are discussed. In the US Congress, cap-and-trade proposals such as the Waxman-Markey proposal included the border carbon adjustment (BCA). In Japan, the BCA also was studied under the Ministry of Finance. Applying the Fischer-Fox type of static multiregional computable general equilibrium (CGE) model (Fisher and Fox, 2007) to the Japanese economy, Takeda et al. (2014) analyzed the application of the BCA to the Japanese economy. The researchers demonstrated that the carbon tariff is not sufficient for addressing the competitiveness/leakage issue in the Japanese economy; an export rebate is crucial for mitigating the competitiveness issue in the Japanese economy. It also was found that the BCA in Japan significantly affects carbon leakage to China. Finally, the study also found that the BCA is effective in protecting the competitiveness of the iron and steel sector among all sectors.

Representing another means of managing competitiveness/leakage issues are output-based allocations (OBAs). Under OBAs, tradable permits are distributed freely to firms involved in international competition, based on their output. This unique idea was proposed in the Lieberman-Warner and Waxman-Markey bills in the US to address the international competitiveness and carbon leakage issues.

Following Fischer and Fox (2007), Takeda et al. (2014) empirically investigated the effects of OBAs on the Japanese economy. They found that an OBA mitigates leakage and damage to energy-intensive sectors in the Japanese economy. The macroeconomic impact, however, is less desirable. Considering leakage, competitiveness, and macroeconomics, the study revealed that combinations of auctions and OBAs in energy-intensive and trade-exposed sectors are desirable.

Another approach toward the competitiveness issue is to use international credits or offsets. Takeda et al. (2012b) examined the economic impacts of international offsets on the Japanese economy.

They constructed a multi-regional recursive dynamic CGE model to evaluate the economic situation in 2020, assuming that US, Japan, EU27, Australia, and New Zealand achieve the Copenhagen Pledge. Using the model, the researchers considered a scenario in which Annex B regions purchase certified emissions reductions (CERs) from non-Annex B regions. The researchers conducted simulations by changing the amount of CER supply and examined two cases: one with the restriction on CER usage and one without the restriction.

The results were illustrated in Figure 26.1. The vertical axis exhibits the reduction of GDP from the business-as-usual scenario where no carbon regulation is imposed. Each pair of bars corresponds to the amount of CER supply shown above. The following results were found. First, without the restriction of CER usage, the benefit for the Japanese economy in both income and GDP increases as the supply of CER increases. The use of CERs dramatically reduces the negative impacts on the EITE sector. With the restriction of CER usage, however, the purchase of CERs by the Japanese economy reaches the limit when the supply is 400 MtCO$_2$. Therefore, even if the supply increases further, the amount of the domestic reduction in the Japanese economy does not decrease. Even after the CER purchase reaches the limit, however, the Japanese economy gains income because the declining CER price decreases payments to foreign countries. However, the GDP decreases slightly as the CER supply increases after CER purchasing reaches the limit. This decrease in GDP may occur because other Annex B regions are able to increase their production through the purchase of CERs with the lower prices, which in turn decreases Japanese exports.

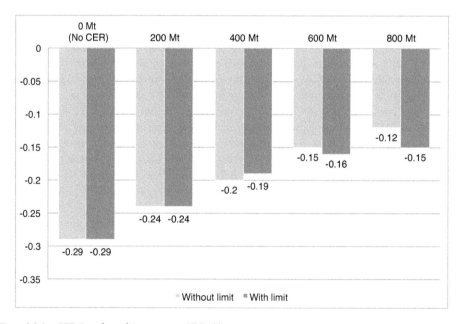

Figure 26.1 CER Supply and impacts on GDP (%)

4.2 Voluntary emissions trading schemes

After the discussions under the Ministry of the Environment (MOE) and METI, the government decided not to introduce a mandatory ETS in 2010. Although there are no mandatory ETSs in effect at the national level in Japan, the national government had introduced several voluntary or experimental ETSs.

MOE launched Japan's Voluntary Emissions Trading Scheme (J-VETS) in 2005 to disseminate knowledge and experience regarding a domestic cap-and-trade ETS, which is a voluntary ETS scheme. By 2008,[6] 84 organizations participated in J-VETS. The greatest number of transactions was 51, which was recorded in 2007. The largest emissions reduction was 382,625 t-CO_2 during the period from 2007 to 2009. Overall, by the final period of 2012, the reduction in CO_2 was reportedly 220 million tons.

In addition to this experimental ETS, in 2008, METI launched the Domestic Credit Scheme, also known as the Domestic CDM, to mitigate GHG emissions from industries. If small and medium enterprises undertake a GHG emissions-reduction project using finance or technologies provided by a larger firm, then credits for the emissions reductions resulting from the project would be issued to the large firm. These credits may be used to comply with other emissions-reduction targets, such as those set under the Voluntary Action Plan (VAP) by Keidanren (Japanese Business Federation). Allowed projects under the Domestic CDM include biofuel or renewable energy projects. By the end of September 2013, approximately 1,500 projects were registered under the Domestic CDM. By then, 1,266 projects were verified, and the total amount of credits issued was 1,181,989 t-CO_2.

In 2008, the Ministry of the Environment introduced another offset scheme, called the Japan Verified Emission Reduction Scheme (J-VER). Five types of domestic projects are eligible for this verification scheme: forest management, agriculture and improvement of fertilizer, biofuel, renewable energy, and emissions reductions in small and medium enterprises (SMEs). Local governments as well as private firms may implement J-VER projects. The credits may be freely traded. By the end of September 2013, approximately 253 projects were registered under the J-VER. Of the registered projects, 231 projects were verified. In total, 552,235 t-CO_2 credits were issued from these projects.

During the early stage of the first Kyoto commitment period, policymakers discussed whether to create a domestic ETS for Japan to achieve a potential mid-term target for the second Kyoto commitment period. In response to the heated discussion regarding the ETS, the Japanese government introduced in 2008 the Experimental Emissions Trading Scheme (EETS), which is an experimental integrated domestic market for emissions trading. The aim of the EETS was to determine an appropriate ETS for Japan. Specifically, the aim was to test and evaluate options, such as the choice of absolute- or intensity-based emissions caps. Participants could trade emissions permits and credits generated through domestic CDM projects, thereby achieving their voluntary emissions-reduction target (absolute- or intensity-based). If a participant is in a sector with the target under the VAP, then the participant's targets must be consistent with the VAP.

Despite these efforts, a cap-and-trade scheme was not introduced at a national level. Moreover, in 2013, the J-VER and the Domestic CDM were integrated into one system, called the J-Credit Scheme. Credits from this scheme may be used to achieve the emissions target set in Keidanren's Commitment to a Low Carbon Society.

4.3 Tokyo ETS

Although the national government has not been able to introduce a mandatory ETS, the Tokyo prefectural government successfully introduced an ETS, namely, the Tokyo Emissions Trading Scheme (Tokyo–ETS), in 2010 (Morotomi, 2014). This ETS is the first cap-and-trade ETS in Japan.[7]

The target of this scheme is large facilities and buildings. If these facilities consume 1,500 kilo-liters of oil equivalents per year in Tokyo Prefecture, they must reduce their emissions. To mitigate the burden, the Tokyo ETS offers three types of domestic offset credits: 1) small- and medium-sized installation credits within the Tokyo area; 2) outside Tokyo Prefecture credits; and 3) renewable energy certificates. International credits, however, cannot be used to offset GHG emissions in this scheme.[8]

In 2013, 1,392 facilities are subject to the Tokyo ETS. By August of 2013, a reduction of 63,000 CO_2-tons was reported. The amount of small- and medium-sized installation credits issued that year was approximately 3,000 t-CO_2, The amount of renewable energy credits was approximately 120,000 tons of CO_2.

5. Voluntary environmental actions by private sectors

Despite the absence of the cap on emissions or the carbon tax, Japanese manufacturing sectors successfully controlled the growth of GHG emissions during the first commitment period of the Kyoto Protocol, at least until the Great East Japan Earthquake caused problems in the nuclear power plants in Fukushima. This success may be attributed to voluntary environmental actions by private sectors and to the Energy Conservation Act.

5.1 Voluntary action plan by the Japanese business federation

A part of this success can be attributed to the VAP by Keidanren The VAP was announced in 1997 along with the signing of the Kyoto Protocol. Most major Japanese firms have been involved with the VAP through their associated industrial associations. Under the VAP, industrial associations set targets for GHG emissions. Some industrial associations set absolute targets for GHG emissions or energy consumption. Others set intensity targets for GHG emissions (e.g., CO_2 tons per kwh) or for energy consumption.

The VAP consists of four phases. The first phase is to set targets.[9] Second, the firms are engaged in reducing their emissions or energy consumption. Third, the performance of each industrial association is assessed at the end of each year. Finally, the performances are publicized and reviewed. This four-phase process is repeated annually.

Although the VAP is voluntary, the Japanese government depended on the VAP to achieve the Kyoto target. The government had essentially incorporated the VAP into the Kyoto Protocol Target Achievement Plan[10] (KPTAP) and implicitly uses the voluntary targets as the targets in the KPTAP. There is no guarantee, however, that private firms will achieve their emissions intensity targets in the VAP because the penalty for non-achievement is not explicit, due to the nature of the "voluntary" scheme. In addition, the VAP's targets may be too lenient, enabling firms to achieve them easily.

How well has the VAP performed? The results for the manufacturing sectors and the power sectors may be summarized as follows: In FY2011, 34 sectors[11] participated in the follow-up of the VAP. The total emissions of CO_2 from these participating firms in 1990 was 584 million tons, representing 44 percent of total emissions in 1990. In 2010, the reported emissions level was 443, representing a 12.3 percent reduction from the 1990 emissions levels. Among the 34 participating sectors, CO_2 emissions were reduced from the 1990 level in 24 sectors. These 34 sectors face different types of targets.[12] Of these sectors, 14 face absolute CO_2 emissions targets, of which 13 sectors successfully reduced their CO_2 emissions. Five sectors have absolute targets of energy consumption, all of which successfully reduced their energy consumption relative to the 1990 level. All 10 sectors with CO_2 intensity targets have improved their intensities compared to the

1990 level. Among 12 sectors with energy intensity targets, 10 sectors have improved the intensity relative to the 1990 level.

Several studies have examined the effectiveness of the VAP. Wakabayashi and Sugiyama (2007) examined VAP performance. Based on a qualitative analysis of the annual reports of participating associations, the authors concluded that the iron and steel industries and the power sector reduced their GHG emissions.

Using a unique firm-level panel data set, Sugino and Arimura (2011) empirically investigated the effects of the VAP on investments in energy conservation and efficiency. The authors examined whether the type of target plays a role in VAP performance and concluded that firms with absolute targets are more likely to invest in energy-saving processes compared to those with intensity targets.

Wakabayashi (2013) conducted a study on the VAP. Specifically, the study examined the VAP as a case study together with two other cases of corporate voluntary environmental activities. The study found that the VAP plays a role in sharing information among member firms and in assisting the small- and medium-size firms.

Japanese industry also is preparing for the post-Kyoto period. Keidanren announced Nippon Keidanren's Commitment to a Low Carbon Society (CLCS). Notably, Keidanren uses the word "commitment" rather than "voluntary action." This fact demonstrates Keidanren's strong desire to contribute to a low-carbon society. The major structure of the CLCS consists of the following four goals:[13] 1) establishment of reduction targets for domestic business operations up to the year 2020; 2) strengthen cooperation with other interested groups; 3) contributions at the international level; and 4) development of innovative technologies. The effectiveness of this commitment should be monitored and carefully examined.

Despite its success, the strategic implications of the VAP should not be forgotten Kolstad (2010, p. 359) claims that voluntary actions by private firms may be partly motivated by their desire to preempt regulatory actions. By taking a voluntary environmental action, private firms may be able to avoid stringent emissions targets, carbon taxes or ETSs. This may be an interesting topic for researchers to examine.

5.2 Voluntary environmental actions by individual firms

Voluntary environmental actions by individual firms also are an important component of mitigation strategies. One of the most popular voluntary environmental actions taken by individual firms is ISO14001, the certificate of environmental management systems by the International Organization for Standardization (ISO).

In the early stage of ISO14001 adoption, Japanese firms dominated in terms of the number of certificates earned. Using data on Japanese manufacturing firms, Nakamura et al. (2001) found that larger and/or export-oriented firms are more likely to adopt ISO14001. Furthermore, the researchers found that pressure from civil society and expectations related to environmental responsibility promote adoption. Nisthiani (2010) found that the environmental preferences and pressures of customers in environmentally conscious markets is an important factor in ISO14001 adoption.

The other studies investigated the effectiveness of ISO14001 in Japan. Arimura et al. (2008) examined the effectiveness of ISO14001 on natural resource usage, including fossil fuels and electricity. The authors found that ISO14001 is indeed effective in reducing the usage of these resources. Other studies examined the effectiveness of ISO14001 on other type of environmental impacts. For example, Iwata et al. (2010) demonstrated that ISO14001 is effective in controlling chemical substances.

Furthermore, Arimura et al. (2011) examined the effectiveness of ISO14001 from another perspective. The authors found that ISO14001 certification promotes green supply chain management, which is a collection of pro-environmental practices in companies' supply chains. Therefore, the promotion of ISO14001 by local governments (Arimura et al. 2008) is even more meaningful because it helps not only firms receiving assistance from the local government but also firms in the supply chain through the adoption of ISO14001.

6. International offset schemes: CDM and JCM

As discussed in Section 5, the reduction of GHG outside Japan, e.g., international offsets, has been an important issue in policy discussions. This section discusses the past and future of international offsets relevant for Japan.

6.1 Clean Development Mechanism

To achieve the target under VAPs, the Clean Development Mechanism (CDM) has played an important role for certain industrial associations. Specifically, the CDM has been indispensable for energy-intensive industries such as power companies and the iron and steel industries. For other industries, however, the CDM may not have been relevant (Arimura et al. 2012).

How has the CDM been perceived by Japanese firms? The corporate survey on the national ETS by Arimura et al. (2012) asked firms what would be desirable as a complement to the cap-and-trade scheme. The respondents were requested to choose from three schemes: 1) a domestic CDM; 2) an international offset such as the CDM; or 3) an offset credit scheme such as the J-VETS. These results revealed that more firms prefer domestic schemes to international ones, implying that CDM under the United Nations Framework Convention on Climate Change (UNFCCC) is the least popular option as an offset.

The researchers identified factors that may lessen firms' incentives to participate in CDM projects. The potential candidates for problems were as follows: 1) additionality requirements that are too strict (additionality); 2) too much time to audit, register and issue credits (lengthy process); 3) geographic imbalances; 4) smaller volumes of CERs than expected (CER volumes); and 5) other problems (others). The firms were asked to assess the importance and to choose their answers from among "very important," "moderately important," and "not important" for each potential problem.

Figure 26.2 displays responses from the CDM-participating firms. The figure reveals that the lengthy process is the most important problem. The second-most important problem is "additionality." "CER volume" is the third-most important problem. This result implies that firms are likely to take opportunity costs seriously when deciding to participate in projects.

6.2 Joint Crediting Mechanism

Given these situations, the Joint Crediting Mechanism[14] (JCM) is proposed to address these issues associated with CDM. The Japanese government has been working to devise new schemes that are acceptable to Japanese industry and to the international community and that are accompanied by environmental integrity. The JCM is similar to the CDM in essence: it uses advanced technology of the developed countries (host countries) to reduce GHG in developing countries (called partner countries).

The JCM and CDM, however, differ in several respects. First, in terms of governance, the JCM is expected to have a decentralized structure, in contrast to the centralized structure of

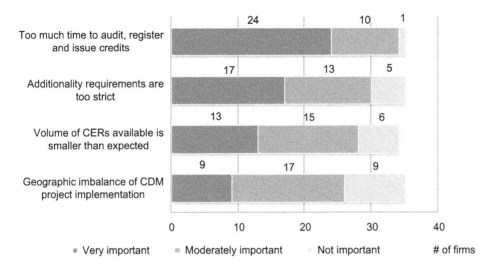

Figure 26.2 Importance of the problems in the CDM scheme (36 CDM Participating Firms)

CDMs, for which the CDM-Executive Board (EB) or United Nations have strong stakes in the approval process. Specifically, an investing government (such as Japan) and a partner country (a host country) are expected to form a joint committee that measures and verifies GHG-reduction projects. In this way, the joint committee may reduce the transaction costs that investors would have incurred under CDM schemes.

Second, the types of eligible projects differ between the JCM and the CDM. For example, in CDM schemes, the export of an energy-efficient appliance to developing countries is not allowed. By contrast, such projects are expected to be eligible for the JCM. In fact, several feasible studies are being implemented for these types of projects. The additionality requirement is one reason why these activities are not eligible for the CDM. To address this issue of the proof of additionality, it is expected that the JCM will take a different approach, which remains under discussion.

How is the JCM managed under the UNFCCC? A new market mechanism proposed by the EU, such as the sector-crediting system (Bolscher et al., 2012), is under consideration as a new mechanism. By contrast, the JCM is treated as one program of various approaches in the Conference of the Parties.

How many developments have been achieved for the JCM? Starting in 2010, METI and MOE financed several feasibility studies. These programs financed 30 feasibility study projects in 13 countries in the 2010 fiscal year (FY). In FY2011, 79 FS projects were financed. In FY2012, 79 projects were financed. By August 2013, the Japanese government had successfully signed official documents for the JCM with seven countries, including Mongolia, Bangladesh, Ethiopia, Kenya, Maldives, Vietnam, and Laos.

How do Japanese firms perceive the new mechanism of JCM? In 2012, a research team at the Research Institute of Trade and the Environment at Waseda University led by the author conducted a corporate survey on the JCM. The result is summarized in Table 26.1.

The table categorizes firms into four types: 1) firms participating in FS (11 firms); 2) firms that considered FS but not did participate (22 firms); 3) firms with JCM knowledge that did not consider FS (171 firms); and 4) firms that did not know about the JCM (191 firms). The survey listed ten issues associated with the JCM and asked which issue would be important. One point

Table 26.1 Potential issues in the JCM

	FS participants (11 Firms)	Considered participation (22 Firms)	Have not considered but knows JCM (171 Firms)	Does not know JCM (191 Firms)
Investment from counterparts	81.8	86.4	51.5	38.7
Subsidy from the host country	100.0	86.4	62.0	43.5
Gain offsets/credits beforehand	81.8	50.0	51.5	36.6
Direct financing from the Japanese Government	100.0	95.5	59.6	50.3
Establishment/Investment support from pensions funds/institutional investors	72.7	68.2	47.4	35.1
Insurance system that deal with political risks	90.9	72.7	50.3	40.3
Funds run by government institutions and public firms	90.9	72.7	48.5	40.3
Information on technology in the host country	100.0	86.4	58.5	46.6
Coordination with the international framework	100.0	90.9	66.1	48.2

noted from this result is that both firms with FS experience (column A) and with FS consideration only (column B) consider coordination with the international framework to be an important
issue. Therefore, to achieve greater participation from Japanese firms, the government must
coordinate with the UNFCCC. Therefore, it is important to determine the system of measurement, reporting and verification (MRV) that is considered to be reliable under UNFCCC. However, this may be a challenging task because one motivation of the JCM proposal by the Japanese
government was to simplify the MRV process, which, if it is too simple, may be not permitted
under the UNFCCC or may not be acceptable among the international community. Therefore,
the Japanese government must devise a balance between simplicity and reliability.

7. Carbon tax

For the last two decades, the Ministry of the Environment has tried and failed several times to
introduce a carbon tax. Finally, in October 2012, the "Carbon Dioxide Tax of Global Warming
Countermeasure" was introduced. The tax rate is conservative at 289 yen per CO_2 ton for all
fossil fuels.

7.1 Burden of carbon tax

The carbon tax is known to be an efficient policy instrument. Several papers have examined the
effectiveness of the carbon tax in the Japanese economy. The introduction of the carbon tax has,
however, become controversial because it may be burdensome on households or industries. Several economic impact analyses of carbon tax proposals have been performed.

Input-output models often have been used to analyze the short-term burden of such policies (Sugino et al., 2011; Shimoda and Watanabe, 2004; Fujikawa, 2000). These studies examined the burden of the carbon tax on households (by income class) or on specific industries and often proposed a specific proposal to mitigate the burden on specific groups.

7.2 Potential of the double dividend in the Japanese economy

The carbon tax is expected to increase in three stages, up to 289 yen per CO_2 ton. After the full introduction, the tax revenue is expected to be 262 billion yen.[15] Because the tax rate is low, the direct effects of reducing GHG emissions may be limited. It is expected, however, that the tax revenue will contribute to emissions reduction in the long term. The revenue of the carbon tax goes to a special account for energy policy. Therefore, the usage of the carbon tax is restricted to the GHG mitigation policy or to the promotion and development of new energy, including renewable energy.

From an economic viewpoint, the use of the tax revenue is an important issue. Economists often promote using carbon tax revenue to reduce other distorting taxes such as the labor tax or corporate tax, which is known as a double dividend (Kolstad, 2010). Several studies have examined the size of the double dividend in the Japanese economy.

For instance, using a CGE model, Takeda (2007) examined the size of the double dividend when the revenue from carbon taxes was used to cut corporate taxes. The study found that the GDP would increase in the short and medium terms, with a GDP increase of 0.9 percent expected 25 years after the introduction of the carbon tax.

Other studies quantitatively examined the impacts of the double dividend when the carbon tax revenue was allocated to reducing taxes on labor in the form of a social security premium on wages. Takeda et al. (2014) found that this tax recycling would increase GDP. Furthermore, according to Kawase et al. (2003), GDP would increase if the carbon tax revenue were used to cut the consumption tax. These studies suggest that the superior revenue recycling of the carbon tax may improve macroeconomic performance, such as GDP.

8. Renewable energy policy

The Great East Japan Earthquake of March 2011 has shifted the focus of the policy discussion from climate policy to the energy supply issue. Even before the earthquake, however, several polices were adopted to promote renewable energy.

8.1 Renewable portfolio standard

In 2003, the renewable portfolio standard (RPS) was introduced to increase power generation from renewable energy. Basically, the RPS mandates electric utilities to generate a certain amount of electricity from renewable energies. Under the RPS, renewable energy includes wind, solar, geothermal, hydro and biomass (including solid waste). The share of the renewable energy in power generation was 0.6 percent in 2003. Although the share increased due to the RPS, the effect was limited. Even in 2008, the share was only 1.0 percent; therefore, renewable energy's penetration into the power market was limited.

8.2 Feed-in tariff

Given the limitation of the RPS, the government decided to adopt a feed-in tariff (FIT) to address climate and energy issues by promoting renewable energies in Japan. The FIT was introduced in

Table 26.2 Values of feed-in tariff

Energy Sources		April, 2013 - March, 2014		
	Capacity		*Price (yen/kWh)*	*Duration (Years)*
Solar	More than 10kW		37.8	20
	Less than 10kW		38	10
Wind	More than 20kW		23.1	20
	Less than 20kW		57.75	20
Geothermal	More than 1.5MW		27.3	15
	Less than 1.5MW		42	15
Medium & Small Hydropower	1,000kW - 3MW		25.2	20
	200kW - 1,000kW		30.45	20
	Less than 200kW		35.7	20
Biomass	Gasification		40.95	20
	Wood fired power plant	Timber from forestthinning	33.6	20
		Other woody materials	25.2	20
		Recycled wood	13.65	20
	Wastes(Excluding woody wastes)		17.85	20

November 2009. The FIT is the system in which utilities must purchase the electricity power generated from solar energy with a fixed price. Concurrently, the utilities may pass costs on to the electricity customers. The purchase rates are 48 yen/kwh for residential use and 24 yen/kwh for non-residential use.

Facing the nuclear accident in Fukushima I March 2011, Prime Minister Kan from the Democratic Party of Japan decided to take even more aggressive measures toward renewable energy. The Act on Special Measures concerning the Procurement of Renewable Electric Energy by Operators of Electric Utilities was passed in August 2011. Under this new act, the FIT target was expanded to include wind, geothermal, biomass and micro-hydro resources. Table 26.2 shows the values of the expanded FIT for different various sources.

One important feature of this new act is that all the electrical power generated by renewable energy – not just the surplus – is purchased by power companies.[16] The power generation by renewable energy increased sharply due to the revised FIT. In 2009, when the FIT was first introduced, the share of renewable energy was 1.1 percent. This share grew to 1.6 percent in 2012 following the FIT expansion.

9. Concluding remarks

This chapter outlined recent Japanese environmental policy with a focus on air pollution and GHG mitigation. We mainly discussed policies reviewed by an economic approach with an emphasis on empirical methods. By reviewing the literature on the evaluation of Japanese environmental policies, we find that ex ante quantitative analysis of environmental policy may contribute to the improvement of policy or to policy design. Quantitative economic analyses should be incorporated more thoroughly in designing Japanese environmental policy.

Notes

* I appreciate the financial support from Japanese Ministry of the Environment.
1 Solid waste generation has been another important environmental issue for the Japanese economy. Readers who are interested in the issues of solid waste generation should refer to Shinkuma and Managi (2011).
2 In this study, PM represents PM_{10}, which has a particulate diameter of less than 10 μm.
3 The act was amended several times. Due to the 2008 amendment, the regulation is now implemented at the firm (or a business operator) level rather than at the facility level. The scope of the regulation was dramatically expanded by this amendment. For instance, logistics companies in the transportation sector or convenience store chains in the commercial sector are now subject to the regulation.
4 The most updated information, as of 2010, regarding the top runner program in English is available at http://www.enecho.meti.go.jp/policy/saveenergy/toprunner2010.03en.pdf.
5 http://www.meti.go.jp/committee/summary/0004310/017_s02_00.pdf.
6 J-VETS was integrated into the EETS in 2008. Therefore, no more new participants joined the J-VETS.
7 The Tokyo ETS created a successor of the similar system. Saitama Prefecture, a neighborhood prefecture of Tokyo, started its own local ETS.
8 Tokyo Prefecture is a member of the International Carbon Action Partnership. Therefore, it is worth noting how Tokyo's scheme links with international markets in the future.
9 The targets become more aggressive if the results from the previous year satisfy the prior targets. However, if the targets are not reached, then those from the previous year remain the same.
10 The details of the Kyoto Protocol Target Achievement Plan are available at http://www.kantei.go.jp/foreign/policy/ondanka/index_e.html.
11 In principle, one industrial association corresponds to one sector in the VAP.
12 Sugino and Arimura (2011) found that the different types of targets have different impacts on the energy-saving investment. Specifically, firms with absolute targets are more likely to invest in energy-saving technologies compared to firms with intensity targets.
13 See http://www.keidanren.or.jp/en/policy/2013/003_commitment.pdf.
14 JCM was initially proposed as the "Bilateral Offset Crediting Mechanism." Later, it was renamed the Joint Crediting Mechanism.
15 http://www.env.go.jp/policy/tax/about.html.
16 This change does not apply to solar power generation by households.

References

Arimura, T. H., Darnall, N. and Katayama, H. (2011) "Is ISO 14001 a gateway to more advanced voluntary action? A case for green supply chain management," *Journal of Environmental Economics and Management* 61:170–182.

Arimura, T. H., Hibiki, A. and Katayama, H. (2008) "Is a voluntary approach an effective environmental policy instrument? A Case for environmental management systems," *Journal of Environmental Economics and Management* 55(3):281–295.

Arimura, T. H. and Iwata, K. (2015) *An Evaluation of Japanese Environmental Regulations: Quantitative Approaches from Environmental Economics.* The Netherlands: Springer, forthcoming.

Arimura, T. H., Miyamoto, T., Katayama, H. and Iguchi, H. (2012) "Japanese firms' practices for climate change: Emission mission trading schemes and other initiatives," *Sophia Economic Review* 57:31–54 (in Japanese).

Bolscher, H., Van der Laan, J., Slingerland, S., Sijm, J. Bakker, S., Mikunda, T., Wehnert, T., Sterk, W., Hoogzaad, J., Wemaere, M. and Conway, D. (2012) *Design options for sectoral carbon market mechanisms.* The Netherlands: Ecorys.

Fischer, C., and Fox, A. K. (2007) "Output-based allocation of emission permits for mitigating tax and trade interactions," *Land Economics* 83(4):575–599.

Fujikawa, K. (2000) "Load of Carbon Tax by Region and Income Group Input- Output Analysis," Innovation & I-O Technique 10(4):35–41 (in Japanese).

Geller, H., Harrington, P., Rosenfeld, A. H., Tanishima, A. and Unander, F. (2006) "Policies for increasing energy efficiency: Thirty years of experience in OECD countries," *Energy Policy* 34:556–573.

Hamamoto, M. (2011) "Energy efficiency regulation and R&D activity: A study of the top runner program in Japan," *Low Carbon Economy* 2:91–98.

Iwata, K. and Arimura, T. H. (2009) "Economic analysis of a Japanese air pollution regulation: An optimal retirement problem under vehicle type regulation in the NO_x–Particulate Matter Law," *Transportation Research Part D* 14(3):157–167.

Iwata, K., Arimura, T. H. and Hibiki, A. (2010) "An empirical study on determinants of ISO14001 and its effect on reduction in toluene emission in Japan," *JCER Economic Journal* 62:16–38 (in Japanese).

Kainou, K. (2006) "Quantitative policy evaluation of the Top Runner method household appliance efficiency standards regulations in Japan by cost-benefit analysis," Research Institute of Economy, Trade and Industry Discussion Paper Series, 06025, RIETI, Tokyo, Japan (in Japanese).

Kainou, K. (2007) "Quantitative policy evaluation of the Top Runner method regulations for fuel consumption standards for passenger cars in Japan by cost-benefit analysis," Research Institute of Economy, Trade and Industry Discussion Paper Series, 07006, RIETI, Tokyo, Japan (in Japanese).

Kawase, A., Kitaura, Y. and Hashimoto, K. (2003) "Environmental tax and the double dividend: A computational general equilibrium analysis," *Public Choice Studies* 41:5–23 (in Japanese).

Kimura, O. (2010) "Japanese top runner approach for energy efficiency standards," SERC Discussion Paper, 09305, SERC, The Central Research Institute of Electric Power Industry, Tokyo, Japan (in Japanese).

Kolstad, C. D. (2010) *Environmental Economics*, 2nd ed. New York: Oxford University Press.

Ministry of Economy, Trade and Industry (METI) and Agency of Natural Resources and Energy (2010) "Top Runner Program: Developing the world's best energy-efficiency appliance," Tokyo, Japan (in Japanese).

Mori, Y. and Welch, E. W. (2008) "The ISO 14001 environmental management standard in Japan: Results from a national survey of facilities in four industries," *Journal of Environmental Planning and Management* 51(3):421–445.

Morotomi, T. (2014) "Climate change policy from the bottom up: Tokyo's cap-and-trade scheme and multi-level governance." In Niizawa, H. and Morotomi, T., (Eds.), *Governing Low Carbon Development and the Economy – Based on the Experiences of Japan and East Asia*. Tokyo: UN Press, forthcoming.

Nakamura, M., Takahashi, T. and Vertinsky, I. (2001) "Why Japanese firms choose to certify: A study of managerial responses to environmental issues," *Journal of Environmental Economics and Management* 42:23–52.

Nishitani, K. (2010) "Demand for ISO 14001 adoption in the global supply chain: An empirical analysis focusing on environmentally conscious markets," *Resource and Energy Economics* 32:395–407.

Nordqvist, J. (2007) "The Top Runner policy concept: Pass it down?" *ECEEE Summer Study* 1209–1214.

Oka, T., Fujii, Y., Ishikawa, M., Matsuo, Y. and Susami, S. (2007) "Maximum abatement costs for calculating cost-effectiveness of green activities with multiple environmental effects." In Huppes, G., and Ishikawa, M. (eds.), *Quantified Eco-Efficiency (Eco-Efficiency in Industry and Science)*, 41–47. Dordrecht, Netherlands: Springer.

Shimoda, M. and Watanabe, T. (2006) "Re-examination of the Scheduled Carbon Tax on the Basis of IO Analysis: A Quantitative Analysis on Household Burden by Income Class and by Region," *The Business Review of Aichi Gakuin University* 46(3):47–62 (in Japanese).

Shinkuma, T. and Managi, S. (2011) "Waste and recycling: theory and empirics," *Routledge Studies in Ecological Economics* 13:1–168.

Sugino, M. and Arimura, T. H. (2011) "The effects of voluntary action plans on energy-saving investment: an empirical study of the Japanese manufacturing sector," *Environmental Economics and Policy Studies* 13(3):237–257.

Sugino, M., Arimura, T. H. and Morgenstern, R. (2013) "The effects of alternative carbon mitigation policies on Japanese industries," *Energy Policy* 62:1254–1267.

Sugino, M., Arimura, T. H. and Morita, M. (2012) "The impact of carbon tax on the industry and household: an input output analysis," *Environmental Science* 25(2):126–133 (in Japanese).

Takeda, S. (2007) "The double dividend from carbon regulations in Japan," *Journal of the Japanese and International Economies* 21(3):336–364.

Takeda, S., Horie, T. and Arimura, T. H. (2012a) "A Computable General Equilibrium Analysis of Border Adjustments under the Cap-and-Trade System: A Case Study of the Japanese Economy," *Climate Change Economics* 3(1): pp.(1250003)1–30.

Takeda, S., Arimura, T. H., Tamechika, H., Fischer, C. and Fox, A. (2014) "Output-Based allocation of emissions permits for mitigating the leakage and competitiveness issues for the Japanese Economy," *Environmental Economics and Policy Studies* 16(1):89–110.

Takeda, S., Kawasaki, H., Ochiai, K. and Ban, K. (2010) "An analysis of the Medium-term target for CO_2 reduction by the JCER-CGE Model," *Review of Environmental Economics and Policy Studies* 3(1):31–42 (in Japanese).

Takeda, S., Sugino M., Arimura, T. H. and Yamazaki, M. (2012b) "Economic analysis of clean development mechanism and international linking emission trading scheme." In Arimura, T. H. and Takeda, S. (Eds.), *Economics of Emission Trading Schemes and Energy Efficiency,* 41–61. Tokyo: Nippon Hyoron Sha Co. Ltd. (in Japanese).

Wakabayashi, M. (2013) "Voluntary Business Activities to Mitigate Climate Change: Case Studies in Japan," *Energy Policy Communication* 63:1086–1090.

Wakabayashi, M. and Sugiyama, T. (2007) "Japan's Keidanren voluntary action plan on the environment." In Morgenstern, R. D. and Pizer, W. A. (Eds.), *Reality Check: The nature and Performance of Voluntary Environmental Programs in the United States, Europe, and Japan,* 43–63. Washington, DC: RFF Press.

27

PROGRAMS, PRICES AND POLICIES TOWARD ENERGY CONSERVATION AND ENVIRONMENTAL QUALITY IN CHINA

ZhongXiang Zhang

1. Introduction

Since launching its open-door policy and economic reforms in late 1978, China has experienced spectacular economic growth and hundreds of millions of the Chinese people have been raised out of poverty. In this course, China has been heavily dependent on dirty-burning coal to fuel its rapidly growing economy. Moreover, until recently, China had valued economic growth above environmental protection. A combination of these factors has given rise to unprecedented environmental pollution and health risks across the country (Ho and Nielsen, 2007; The World Bank, 2007; CAEP, 2013).

While being confronted with rampant conventional environmental pollution problems, China became the world's largest carbon emitter in 2007 (IEA, 2007). The number one position put China in the spotlight just at the time when the world's community started negotiating a post-Kyoto climate regime under the Bali roadmap. There was renewed interest and debate on China's role in combating global climate change. Given the fact that China has since 2007 been the world's largest carbon emitter and its emissions have continued to rise rapidly in line with its industrialization and urbanization on the one hand, and the fact that China overtook Japan as the world's second largest economy on the other hand, China is seen to have greater capacity, capability and responsibility for taking on climate commitments. The country is facing great pressure both inside and outside international climate negotiations to be more ambitious in combating global climate change.

Clearly, China's rampant environmental pollution problems and rising greenhouse gas emissions and the resulting climate change are undermining its long-term economic growth. China, from its own perspective, cannot afford to and, from an international perspective, is not meant to, continue on the conventional path of encouraging economic growth at the expense of the environment. Instead, concerns about a range of environmental stresses and energy security as a result of steeply rising oil imports have sparked China's determination to improve energy efficiency and cut pollutants and to increase the use of clean energy in order to help its transition to a low-carbon economy.

To that end, China has incorporated for the first time in its five-year economic plan an input indicator as a constraint requiring that energy use per unit of GDP be cut by 20 percent during the 11th five-year period running from 2006 to 2010. This five-year plan also incorporated the goal of reducing SO_2 emissions and chemical oxygen demand (COD) discharge by 10 percent by 2010, relative to their 2005 levels. This is widely considered an important step toward building a "harmonious society" through "scientific development." Just prior to the Copenhagen Climate Change Summit, China further pledged to cut its carbon intensity by 40 to 45 percent by 2020 relative to its 2005 levels in order to help reach an international climate change agreement at Copenhagen or beyond and reaffirmed its plan to have alternative energy sources to meet 15 percent of the nation's energy requirements by 2020.

This chapter focuses on China's efforts toward energy conservation and environmental quality. The article discusses a variety of programs, prices, and other economic and industrial policies and measures targeted for energy saving and pollution cutting and the associated implementation and reliability issues. The chapter ends with some concluding remarks and recommendations.

2. Major programs and initiatives

Given the inevitable trend that China's energy demand will continue to rise over the next two decades and beyond, the key issue is how China can drive its future energy use and carbon emissions below the projected baseline levels to the extent possible. In this regard, improving energy efficiency is considered the cheapest, fastest and most effective way to keep energy growth under control and address environmental concerns. This section highlights a few major programs and initiatives to exemplify China's efforts toward energy conservation and emissions abatement.

2.1 The Top 1,000 Enterprises Energy Conservation Action Program

Given that industry accounts for about 70 percent of the country's total energy consumption (Zhang, 2003), this sector is crucial for China to meet its goal. So the Chinese government has taken great efforts toward changing the current energy inefficient and environmentally unfriendly pattern of industrial growth. To that end, China is exploring industrial policies to encourage technical progress, strengthen pollution control and to promote industrial upgrading and energy conservation. On the specific energy-saving front, China established the Top 1,000 Enterprises Energy Conservation Action Program in April 2006. This program covered 1,008 enterprises in nine key energy supply and consuming industrial subsectors. These enterprises each consumed at least 0.18 million tons of coal equivalent (tce) in 2004 and all together consumed 33 percent of the national total and 47 percent of industrial energy consumption in 2004. The program aimed to save 100 million tce cumulatively during the period 2006 to 2010, thus making a significant contribution to China's overall goal of 20 percent energy intensity improvement (NDRC, 2006a).

In May 2006, the National Development and Reform Commission (NDRC), China's top economic planning agency, signed energy-saving responsibility agreements with governments of 31 provinces or their equivalent to allocate the overall energy-saving target of those top 1,000 enterprises to each province or equivalent. These governments in turn signed with those top 1,000 enterprises located in their regions. To ensure that the goal is met, achieving energy efficiency improvements has become a criterion for job performance evaluations of the heads of these enterprises. This will help them realize that they should take their jobs seriously because they have an important part to play in meeting energy-saving goals.

While there are areas that need further improvements (Price et al., 2010), this program has gone very much as planned as far as the energy-saving goal is concerned. The first year's results show that more than 95 percent of these enterprises appointed energy managers, and the program achieved energy savings of 20 million tce in 2006 (NDRC and NBS, 2007). In 2007, energy savings of 38.17 million tce were achieved, almost doubling the amount of energy savings in 2006 (NDRC, 2008c). In November 2009, NDRC (2009) reported that the Top 1,000 Program had realized energy savings of 106.2 million tce by the end of 2008, two years ahead of schedule to achieve its cumulative goal for the program over the whole five-year period. In September 2011, NDRC reported that the Top 1,000 Program had been estimated to achieve total energy savings of 150 million tce during the 11th five-year plan period (NDRC, 2011b).

2.2 The 10,000 Enterprises Energy Conservation Low Carbon Action Program

To help to meet the goals of energy saving and carbon intensity reduction for the 12th five-year plan, NDRC and 11 other central government organizations (NDRC and Eleven Other Central Government Organization, 2011) in December 2011 announced the expansion of the Top 1,000 Program to the 10,000 Enterprises Energy Conservation Low Carbon Action Program. This enlarged program covered 16,078 enterprises. These enterprises include those industrial and transportation enterprises consuming energy of 10,000 million tce or more and other entities consuming energy of 5,000 tce in 2010. Together these enterprises consumed at least 60 percent of the national total in 2010. Shandong province is set to have the highest energy-saving targets of 25.3 million tce, while Jiangsu province comes in second with an energy-saving target of 22 million tce and has the maximum number of enterprises (1,221) under the program. The program aims to save 250 million tce cumulatively during the period 2011 to 2015 (NDRC, 2012).

In December 2013, NDRC reported the performance results for 2012 of the 10,000 Program. Of 14,542 enterprises examined, 3,760 enterprises exceeded their energy-saving targets, accounting for 25.9 percent; 7,327 enterprises fulfilled their energy-saving goals, accounting for 50.4 percent; and 2,078 enterprises basically fulfilled their energy-saving goals, accounting for 14.34 percent. While 1,377 enterprises, or 9.5 percent of the program's enterprises, failed to meet their targets, the program had achieved total energy savings of 170 million tce over 2011 to 2012, meeting 69 percent of the total energy-saving goal during the 12th five-year plan period (NDRC, 2013e).

2.3 Low-carbon city development pilot program

The past three decades of economic reforms have witnessed a shift in the control over resources and decision-making to local governments. This devolution of decision-making to local governments has placed environmental stewardship in the hands of local officials and polluting enterprises that are more concerned with economic growth and profits than the environment. The ability of, and incentives for, lower-level governments to effectively implement energy-saving and pollution-cutting policies, therefore, are critical (Zhang, 2011a, 2012). With increasingly stringent energy-saving and carbon-intensity goals, China started experimenting with low-carbon city development in a batch of five provinces and eight cities on in July 2010. This experiment was further expanded to a second batch of 29 provinces and cities in December 2012 (Wang et al., 2013).

Globally as well as in China, cities have contributed the most to economic output and have accordingly given rise to most of CO_2 emissions. In China, cities are responsible for more than 60 percent of total energy consumption (CAS, 2009), and their contribution continues to increase given the expected urbanization rate of 65 percent in 2030 (Li, 2014). Clearly, given unprecedented urbanization, cities will play an even greater role in shaping energy demand and CO_2

emissions. Therefore, cities are the key to meeting China's proposed carbon-intensity target in 2020 and whatever climate commitments beyond 2020 that China may take. The low-carbon city development experiment in these ten provinces and 32 cities in the context of government decentralization will serve as the test ground to see whether they can stand up to the challenges.

Wang et al. (2013) identifies several problems and challenges for China's low-carbon city development, including the absence of a sound carbon accounting systems, lack of low-carbon specific evaluation systems, insufficient government-enterprise interactions and excessive budget dependence on land concession. While these are areas that need further improvements, there are encouraging signs that this low-carbon pilot program is moving in the right direction. The NDRC evaluation reveals that the ten pilot provinces cut their carbon intensity by 9.2 percent in 2012 relative to their 2010 level, much higher than the national average carbon-intensity reduction of 6.6 percent (NDRC, 2014). In addition, while it is not mandated by the central government, all these pilot provinces and cities set CO_2 emissions to peak in 2030 or earlier; 15 pilot provinces and cities even aim for CO_2 emissions to peak in 2020 or earlier, with Shanghai publicly announcing its peak year in 2020, Suzhou in 2020 and Ningbo in 2015, respectively (E. Wang, 2014). Zhang (2011a, 2001b) argues from six angles that China could cap its greenhouse gas emissions between 2025 and 2032 or around 2030. The practice and ambition of these piloted regions set the good example of keeping their emissions under control and made positive contribution to overall low-carbon development in China and thus could make China's carbon emissions peak occur even earlier than the aforementioned timeline.

2.4 *Mandatory closures of small power plants while building larger, more efficient units*

For power generation, coal-fired power plants dominate total electricity generation in China, accounting for about 75 percent of total capacity and more than 80 percent of total power generation. China's total installed capacity of coal-fired power plants is more than the current total of the US, the UK and India combined. As the largest coal consumer, power and heat generation is consuming more than half of total coal use. This share is expected to rise to well above 60 percent in 2020, given the rapid development of coal-fired power generation. Thus, efficient coal combustion and power generation is of paramount importance to China's endeavor of energy saving and pollution cutting. To that end, China has adopted the policy of accelerating the closure of thousands of small, inefficient coal- and oil-fired power plants. The total combined capacity that needs to be decommissioned is set at 50 gigawatts (GW) during the period of 2006 to 2010.

In addition to mandatory closures at many small power plants, NDRC instituted a series of incentives for small, less-efficient power plants to shut down. Feed-in tariffs for small plants were lowered, power companies were given the option to build new capacity to replace retired capacity, and plants designated for closure were given electricity generation quotas which could be used to continue operation for a limited time or sold to larger plants (Williams and Kahrl, 2008; Schreifels et al., 2012). These incentive-based policies helped the government surpass the goal of closing 50 GW of small thermal power plants. By the end of 2008, China had closed small plants with a total capacity of 34.21 GW, relative to a total capacity of 8.3 GW decommissioned during the period of 2001 to 2005 (NDRC, 2008b). By the end of the first half year of 2009, the total capacity of decommissioned smaller and older units had increased to 54 GW, having met the 2010 target of decommissioned 50 GW one and half years ahead of schedule (*Sina Net*, 2009; Wang and Ye, 2009). By the end of 2010, the total capacity of decommissioned smaller and older unites had increased to 76.8 GW (*China News Net*, 2011), more than the entire current power capacity of Great Britain and almost ten times the total capacity decommissioned during the period of 2001 to 2005.

The Chinese government's policy concurrently has focused on encouraging the construction of larger, more efficient and cleaner units. By the end of 2012, 75.6 percent of fossil fuel-fired units comprised units with capacities of 300 MW and more, relative to 42.7 percent in 2000 (Zhu, 2010; NDRC, 2013c). The combined effect of shutting down smaller, less-efficient power plants and building larger, more-efficient plants led the average coal consumed per kWh of electricity generated to decline to 326 gce/kWh by 2012 or a 12.8 percent reduction relative to its 2005 levels of 374 gce/kWh (CEC, 2011; CEC and EDF, 2012).

Due to higher thermal efficiency and relatively low unit investment costs, China's power industry has listed supercritical (SC) power generation technology as a key development focus. To date, this generation technology is the only advanced, well established and commercialized clean power generation technology in the world. As a result, an increasing number of newly built plants are more efficient supercritical or ultra-supercritical (USC) plants. China now leads the world, having 54 USC plants of unit capacity of 1GW in operation by 2012 (NDRC, 2013c). With cost comparative advantages over other cleaner coal technologies, such as integrated gasification combined cycle and polygeneration technologies, SC and USC technologies will be developed and deployed in China.

3. Energy prices

Before the post-1978 economic reform, China's economic management structure was modeled principally on that of the former Soviet Union, an essential feature of which was the adoption of a united state pricing system. Under this pricing system, the state-set prices of goods, including those of energy, did not reflect either the production costs nor the influence of market forces. The structure of state-set prices also was irrational: the same type of goods were set at the same prices regardless of their qualities, thus resulting in the underpricing and undersupply of goods of high quality. Over a very long period, this pricing system remained unchanged so that its inflexible and restrictive nature became increasingly apparent. Thus, the outdated pricing system had to be changed.

In 1984, the government required state-owned enterprises (SOEs) to sell up to a predetermined quota of goods at state-set prices but allowed SOEs to sell above the quota or surplus at prices within a 20 percent range above the state-set prices. In February 1985, the 20 percent limit was removed and prices for surplus could be negotiated freely between buyers and sellers (Wu and Zhao, 1987). At that point, the dual pricing system was formally instituted. Such a pricing system introduced, among others things, economic efficiency in the use of resources and generally was considered a positive, cautious step toward a full market price.[1]

Under this dual pricing system, SOEs still received allocations for part of their energy inputs at the state plan prices, which were kept much lower than the market prices. As a result, these enterprises have weak incentive for investment in energy conservation. Confronted with energy shortages and insufficient energy conservation investment, China reformed its energy prices as part of sweeping price reforms initiated in 1993. While the overall trend of such energy-pricing reform has been to move away from pricing completely set by the central government in the centrally planned economy toward a more market-oriented pricing mechanism, the pace and scale of the reform differs across energy types.[2]

Coal pricing reform has been most extensive in terms of both pace and scope. The dual pricing system was introduced in 1984 where enterprises were required to sell up to a predetermined quota at state-set prices but were allowed to sell above the quota at market prices. As part of sweeping price reforms initiated in 1993, coal price has since been set differently, depending on its use. Under a two-track system for coal prices, the price of coal for non-utility use, the so-called market coal, has been determined by the market. But the price of coal for utility use, the so-called power coal, is based on a "guiding price" that has been set by the NDRC substantially below market prices. In 2004, NDRC abolished its guiding price for power coal and set price bands for negotiations between coal producers and electricity generators. NDRC widened those bands in 2005 and scrapped them altogether in 2006 (Williams and Kahrl, 2008). NDRC proposed in May 2005 a coal-electricity price "co-movement" mechanism that would raise electricity tariffs if coal prices rose by 5 percent or more in no less than six months and allowed electricity generators to pass up to 70 percent of increased fuel costs on to grid companies. In December 2012, the State Council abolished the two-track system for coal prices, allowing the price of coal for utility use to be determined by the market just as the price of coal for non-utility use is. Moreover, it revised the coal-electricity price co-movement mechanism, allowing an adjustment in electricity tariffs if fluctuations in coal prices go beyond 5 percent or more in 12 months and allowing electricity generators to pass up to 90 percent of increased fuel costs on to grid companies instead of the existing 70 percent threshold (The State Council, 2012).

Similar to coal, a dual-pricing system for crude oil was introduced in 1984 and was virtually eliminated in 1993. Since 1998, domestic crude oil prices have tracked international prices but refined oil product prices have not. To address this disconnect, the government has implemented since May 2009 a pricing mechanism whereby domestic petroleum product prices would be adjusted upward if the moving average of international crude oil prices based on the composited crude oil price rose by more than 4 percent within 22 consecutive working days. To better reflect refiners' costs and adapt to fluctuations in global crude oil prices, NDRC launched in March 2013 an automatic petroleum product pricing mechanism, shortening the current 22-working-day adjustment period to ten working days and removed the 4 percent threshold. The composition of the basket of crude oils to which oil prices are linked also will be adjusted (Liu, 2012; Zhu, 2013).

Natural gas prices also have undergone reforms (Xinhua Net, 2013). A breakthrough in the reform area was changing the existing cost-plus pricing to the "netback market value pricing" in Guangdong province and the Guangxi Zhuang Autonomous region. Under this new pricing mechanism, pricing benchmarks are selected and pegged to prices of alternative fuels that are formed through market forces to establish a price linkage mechanism between natural gas and its alternative fuels. Gas prices at various stages will then be adjusted accordingly on this basis (NDRC, 2011c). This new mechanism, which has been widely adopted in Europe, will better trace and reflect market demand and resource supplies, as well as guiding reasonable allocations. Until the Guangdong and Guangxi pilot reform program is implemented in the entire country, NDRC plans to lunch three-tier-tariffs for household use of natural gas across the whole country before the end of 2015 (China Economic Net, 2014). These price reforms and the pilot scheme in Guangdong and Guangxi will help to establish a market-oriented natural gas pricing mechanism that fully reflects demand and supply conditions.

The government still retains control over electricity tariffs. But in order to encourage coal-fired power plants to install and operate flue gas desulfurization (FGD) and denitrification facilities, the government has offered since 2004 a price premium to electricity generated by coal-fired power plants with FGD capacity (NDRC and SEPA, 2007) and since November 2011 a price premium for electricity generated by power plants with flue gas denitrification capacity. The level and scope of the price premium were amended since their initial implementation in order to achieve the mandated emissions reductions (NDRC, 2013a, b). China also charged differentiated power tariffs for companies classified as "eliminated types" or "restrained types" in eight energy-guzzling industries from October 2006 onwards (NDRC, 2006b). NDRC has implemented since July 2012 three-tier-tariffs for household electricity use and since January 2014 expanded the three-tiered electricity pricing approach to the aluminum sector to phase out outdated production capacity and promote industrial restructuring more quickly (NDRC and MIIT, 2013; Gao, 2013). Similar tiered power pricing policy is expected to be implemented in other industries, such as cement, to force upgrades in the drive for sustained and healthy development.

4. Supportive economic policies

The central government also is providing supportive economic policies to encourage technical progress and strengthen pollution control to meet the energy-saving and environmental-control goals. To support the ten energy-saving projects, China's Ministry of Finance and the NDRC (Ministry of Finance and NCRC, 2007) award enterprises in east China 200 yuan and enterprises in the central and western part of the country 250 yuan for every tce saved per year since August 2007. Such payments are made to enterprises that have energy metering and measuring systems in place that can document proved energy savings of at least 10,000 tce from energy-saving technical transformation projects. Since July 2011, such awards are increased to RMB 240 for enterprises in East China, and RMB 300 for enterprises in the Central and Western part of the country for every tce saved per year and at the same time, the minimum requirements for total energy savings from energy-saving technical transformation projects are lowered to 5000 tce from the previously required amount of 10000 tce (Ministry of Finance and NDRC, 2011). China also introduces market mechanism, developing energy management companies (EMCs) to promote energy saving. China had only three EMCs in 1998 (China News Net, 2008). This number increased to more than 80 by 2005 and further increased to more than 800 in 2010 (NDRC, 2011a). The NDRC and the Ministry of Finance of China award EMCs 240 yuan for every tce saved, with another compensation round of no less than 60 yuan for every tce saved from local governments (The State Council, 2010). As a result of an increasing number of EMCs and the award policy, the total annual energy saving by EMCs increased to 13 million tce in 2010 from 0.6 million tce in 2005 (NDRC, 2011a). Moreover, with one-third of China's territory widely reported to be affected by acid rain, which is formed by SO_2 along with NO_2, reducing SO_2 emissions has been a key environmental target in China. In its economic blueprint for 2006 to 2010, China incorporated for the first time the goal of reducing SO_2 emissions by 10 percent by 2010. With burning coal contributing 90 percent of the national total SO_2 emissions and coal-fired power generation accounting for half of the national total, the Chinese central government has mandated that new coal-fired units must be synchronously equipped with FGD capacity and that plants built after 1997 must have begun to be retrofitted with FGD before 2010. And policies favorable to FGD-equipped power plants are being implemented, e.g., the on-grid tariff incorporating desulphurization cost, priority given to being connected to grids, and being allowed to operate longer than those plants that do not install desulphurization capacity. Some provincial governments provide even more favorable policies, leading to priority dispatching of power from units with FGD in Shandong and Shanxi provinces. Moreover, the capital cost of FGD has fallen from 800 yuan/kW in the 1990s to about 200 yuan/kW (Yu, 2006), thus making it less costly to install FGD capacity. As a result, newly installed desulphurization capacity in 2006 was greater than the combined total over the past 10 years, accounting for 30 percent of the total installed thermal (mostly coal-fired) capacity. By 2011, the coal-fired units installed with FGD increased to 630 GW from 53 GW in 2005. Accordingly, the portion of coal-fired units with FGD rose to 90 percent in 2011 of the total installed thermal capacity from 13.5 percent in 2005 (Sina Net, 2009; CEC and EDF, 2012). As a result, by the end of 2009, China had cut its SO_2 emissions by 13.14 percent relative to its 2005 levels (Xinhua Net, 2010), having met the 2010 target of a 10 percent cut one year ahead of schedule.

5. Industrial policies

In addition to supportive economic policies and market-based environmental instruments, governments are exploring industrial policies to promote industrial upgrading and energy conservation. With the surge in energy use in heavy industry, China's Ministry of Finance and the State Administration of Taxation started levying export taxes from November 2006 on a variety of energy- and resource-intensive products to discourage exports of those products that rely heavily on energy and resources and to save scarce energy and resources. This includes a 5 percent export tax on oil, coal and coke; a 10 percent tax on non-ferrous metals, some minerals and 27 other iron and steel products and a 15 percent tax on copper, nickel, aluminum and other metallurgical products. Simultaneously, imports tariffs on a range of items, including 26 energy- and resource-intensive products such as oil, coal and aluminum, were cut from their current levels of 3 to 6 percent to 0 to 3 percent. From July 1, 2007, China's Ministry of Finance and the State Administration of Taxation (2007) eliminated or cut export tax rebates for 2,831 exported items. This is considered as the boldest move to rein in exports since China joined the World Trade Organization in December 2001. Among the affected items, which account for 37 percent of all traded products, are 553 "highly energy-consuming, highly-polluting and resource-intensive products," such as cement, fertilizer and non-ferrous metals, whose export tax rebates were completely eliminated. This policy will help to enhance energy efficiency and rationalize energy- and resource-intensive sectors, as well as to control soaring exports and deflate the ballooning trade surplus. From the point of view of leveling the carbon-cost playing field, such export taxes increase the price at which energy-intensive products made in China, such as steel and aluminum, are traded in world markets. For the EU and US producers, such export taxes imposed by their major trading partner on these products take out at least part, if not all, of the competitive pressure that is at the heart of the carbon leakage debate. Being converted into the implicit carbon cost, the estimated levels of CO_2 prices embedded in the Chinese export taxes on steel and aluminium are very much in the same range as the average price of the EU allowances over the same period. Zhang (2009 and 2010b) have argued that there is a clear need within a climate regime to define comparable efforts toward climate mitigation and adaptation to discipline the use of unilateral trade measures at the international level. As exemplified by export tariffs that China applied on its own during 2006 to 2008, defining the comparability of climate efforts can be to China's advantage (Zhang, 2010b).

China's Ministry of Commerce and the State Environmental Protection Agency (Ministry of Commerce and SEPA, 2007) in October 2007 were in an unusual collaboration to jointly issue the anti-pollution circular. Targeted at its booming export industry, this new regulation would suspend the rights of those enterprises that do not meet their environmental obligations to engage in foreign trade for a period of more than one year and less than three years. A significant portion of China's air pollution can be traced directly to the production of goods that are exported. In the Pearl River delta, a major manufacturing region in southern China, Streets et al. (2006) found that 37 percent of the total SO_2 emissions in the region, 28 percent of NO_x, 24 percent of particulate matter (PM), and 8 percent of volatile organic compounds (VOCs) were caused by export-related activities. In the city of Shenzhen alone, the regional leader in industrial development and trade, 75 percent of VOCs, 71 percent of PM, 91 percent of NO_x, and 89 percent of SO_2 emissions from the industrial sector were released through the manufacture of exported goods. Effectively implemented, this policy will help polluting enterprises that export their products to pay attention to the environmental effects of their products and produce more environmentally friendly products.

In the transport sector, the excise tax for vehicles has been adjusted over time to incentivize the purchases of energy-efficient cars. The excise tax levied at the time of purchase was first introduced in 1994 when China reformed its taxing system, and the rate increases with the size of engines, set at 3 percent for cars with engines of 1.0 liter or less, 8 percent for cars with engines of more than 4 liters, and 5 percent for cars with engines in between. To further rein in the production and use of gas-guzzling cars and promote the production and use of energy-efficient small cars, from September 1, 2008, the rate for small cars with engines of 1.0 liter or less further decreased to 1 percent, whereas the rate for cars with engines of no less than 3 liters but no larger than 4 liters is set at 25 percent. Cars with engines of larger than 4 liters are now taxed at the highest rate of 40 percent (Sina Net, 2006; *People Net*, 2008; Zhang, 2010a).

6. Market-based instruments

Market-based instruments, such as pollution charges, green taxes, tradeable permits and penalties for the infringement of environmental regulations, are common ways to internalize externality costs into market prices. Many Asian countries have traditionally relied on rigid command-and-control (CAC) approaches. With the poor environmental performance of such approaches and the cost and complexity associated with their implementation, more and more countries in this region are transforming from current reliance on CAC regulations to market-based policy instruments. The added abatement costs will be imposed on polluting companies as part of production cost that can be reduced by cutting pollution. This is seen to increase not only cost-effectiveness but also flexibility in complying with the set environmental regulations.

With one-third of China's territory widely reported to be affected by acid rain, the formation of which SO_2 is crucial to, reducing SO_2 emissions has been the key environmental target in China. China has since 1996 levied charges for SO_2 emissions in the so-called Two Control Zones based on the total quantity of emissions and at the rate of 0.20 yuan per kilo of pollution equivalent (Yu, 2006). Since July 1, 2003, this charge was applied nationwide and the level of this charge was raised step-by-step. From July 1, 2005, onwards, the charge was applied at the level of 0.60 yuan per kilo of pollution equivalent. The pollutants that are subject to pollution charges are broadened to include NO_x as well, which is charged at the rate of 0.60 yuan per kilo of pollution equivalent since July 1, 2004 (SDPC et al., 2003). To help to meet the energy saving and environmental control goals set for the 11th five-year economic plan, the Chinese government planned three steps to double the charges for SO_2 emissions from the existing level to 1.2 yuan per kilo of pollutant equivalent within the next three years (The State Council, 2007). Local governments are allowed to raise pollution charges above the national levels. Since 1999, Beijing levied charges of 1.2 yuan per kilo of pollution equivalent for SO_2 emissions from coal of high sulfur content (SDPC et al., 2003). Jiangsu province raised charges for SO_2 emissions from the existing level of 0.6 to 1.2 yuan per kilo of pollution equivalent from July 1, 2007, onwards, three years ahead of the national schedule (People Net, 2007; Sina Net, 2007). China's Ministry of Finance, the State Administration of Taxation and the Ministry of Environmental Protection (MEP) have proposed levying environmental taxes to replace current charges for SO_2 emissions and chemical oxygen demand, a water pollution index. This proposal is subject to the approval of the State Council. While their exact implementation date has not yet been set, it is generally expected to be introduced during the 12th five-year plan period running from 2011 to 2015. As experienced with environmental taxes in other countries (Zhang and Baranzini, 2004), such taxes initially will be levied with low rates and limited scope, but their levels will increase over time. Once implemented, the long-awaited environmental taxes will have far-reaching effects on technology upgrading, industrial restructuring and sustainable development in China.

To shut down plants that are inefficient and highly polluting and to keep the frenzied expansion of offending industries under control, the NDRC ordered provincial governments to implement differentiated tariffs that charge more for companies classified as "eliminated types" or "restrained types" in eight energy-guzzling industries, including cement, aluminum, iron and steel, and ferroalloy from October 1, 2006, onwards. While provinces like Shanxi charged even higher differentiated tariffs than the levels required by the central government (Zhang et al., 2011), some provinces and regions have been offering preferential power tariffs to struggling, local energy-intensive industries. The reason for this repeated violation is the lack of incentive for local governments to implement this policy, because all the revenue collected from these additional charges goes to the central government. To provide incentives for local governments, this revenue should be assigned to local governments in the first place, but the central government requires local governments to use the revenue specifically for industrial upgrading, energy saving and emissions cutting (Zhang, 2007a, 2007b, 2010). In the recognition of this flaw, the policy was adjusted in 2007 to allow local provincial authorities to retain revenue collected through the differentiated tariffs, providing stronger incentives for provincial authorities to enforce the policy (Zhou et al., 2010). Partly for strengthening China's longstanding efforts to restructure its inefficient heavy industries, and partly because it was faced with the prospect of failing to meet the ambitious energy-intensity target set for 2010, the NDRC and other five ministries and agencies jointly ordered utilities to stop offering preferential power tariffs to energy-intensive industries by June 10, 2010. Such industries will be charged with the punitive, differentiated tariffs. Those utilities that fail to implement the differentiated tariffs will have to pay a fine that is five times that of the differentiated tariffs multiplied by the volume of sold electricity (J. Zhu, 2010).

To avoid wasteful extraction and use of resources while alleviating the financial burden of local governments, China needs to reform its current coverage of resource taxation and to significantly increase the levied level. Since the tax-sharing system was adopted in China in 1994, taxes are grouped into taxes collected by the central government, taxes collected by local governments and taxes shared between the central and local governments. All those taxes that have steady sources and broad bases and are easily collected, such as the consumption tax, tariffs and the vehicle purchase tax, are assigned to the central government. The value-added tax (VAT) and the income tax are split between the central and local governments, with 75 percent of VAT and 60 percent of the income tax going to the central government. This led the central government's share of total government revenue to go up to 55.7 percent in 1994 from 22 percent the previous year. In the meantime, the share of the central government's total government expenditures rose by just 2 percent. By 2009, local governments accounted for only 47.6 percent of the total government revenue but their expenditures accounted for 80 percent of total government expenditures in China. To be able to pay their expenditures for culture and education, supporting agricultural production, the social security subsidiary and so on, local governments have little choice but to focus on local development and GDP. That in turn enables them to enlarge their tax revenue by collecting urban maintenance and development taxes, contract taxes, arable land occupation taxes, urban land use taxes and so on.

Alleviating the financial burden of local governments is one avenue to incentivize them not to focus on economic growth alone. Enlarging their tax revenue is the key to helping them cover a disproportional portion of the aforementioned government expenditures. In the tax-sharing system adopted in 1994, onshore resource taxes are assigned to local governments, while the central government is collecting revenues from resource taxes offshore. In 1984, resource taxes were levied at 2 to 5 yuan per ton of raw coal and 8 yuan per ton of coking coal, with the weighted average of 3.5 yuan per ton of coal. For crude oil, the corresponding tax is levied at 8 to 30 yuan per ton. While the prices of coal and oil have significantly increased since 1984, the levels of their resource taxes have remained unchanged over the past 25 years (Zhang, 2011b). As a result, the resource taxes raised amounted to only 33.8 billion yuan, accounting for about 0.57 percent of China's total tax revenues and about 17.5 percent of the national government expenditures for environmental protection, which amounted to 193.4 billion yuan in 2009 (NBS, 2010). Therefore, to avoid wasteful extraction and use of resources while alleviating the financial burden of local governments, the method of levying taxes on resources in China should be changed. Such taxation should be levied based on revenues. In addition, current resource taxes are only levied on seven types of resources, including coal, oil and natural gas. This coverage is too narrow, falling far short of the purposes of both preserving resources and protecting the environment. Thus, overhauling resource taxes also includes broadening their coverage so that more resources will be subject to resource taxation.

Clearly, broadening the current coverage of resource taxation and significantly increasing the levied level also help to increase local government's revenues while conserving resources and preserving the environment. The Chinese central government started a pilot reform on resource taxation in Xinjiang, China's northwestern border area of abundant resources and numerous opportunities for growth and expansion. Since June 1, 2010, crude oil and natural gas are taxed by revenues rather than volume in Xinjiang. While it was enacted as part of a massive support package to help Xinjiang achieve leapfrog-like development, which is considered a strategic choice to deepen the country's western development strategy and tap new sources of economic growth for China, this new resource tax will help to significantly increase revenues for Xinjiang. It is estimated that the new resource tax levied at a rate of 5 percent will generate additional annual revenues of Yuan 4 to 5 billion yuan for Xinjiang (Dai, 2010). This is a significant increase, in comparison with the total resource tax revenues of 1.23 billion yuan in 2009, inclusive of those from other resources other than crude oil and natural gas (NBS, 2010). This will contribute to 17 to 21 percent of the total tax revenues for Xinjiang, in comparison with the contribution level of about 4.1 percent in 2009.

There have been intensified discussions on levying a resource tax on coal by revenues. China is most likely to overhaul the current practice and levy a tax on coal by revenues in 2014. Coal-rich provinces, like Shanxi and Inner Mongolia, have studied options to levy a tax on coal by revenues. The tax rates are proposed to be 2 to 10 percent, depending on the extent to which current fees and charges are cut or abolished. Specifically, assuming a coal price of 465 yuan per ton, Shanxi proposes to levy a tax at 2.2 percent if the charge for the coal sustainable development fund (which charges 8–23 yuan per ton, depending on the type of coal) remains; 7.4 percent if that charge is abolished. If coal price is assumed at 440 yuan per ton, then Shanxi proposes to levy a tax at 2.4 percent if the charge for the coal sustainable development fund remains; 7.6 percent if that charge is abolished (Xing, 2013; Wang et al., 2014).

China has been experimenting with SO_2 emissions trading in Hubei, Hunan, Jiangsu, and Zhejiang provinces and Tianjin metropolitan city. Zhejiang province has implemented provincial-wide trial SO_2 emissions quotas that can be purchased and traded since 2009. It, as well as Jiangsu, is experimenting with trading COD permits in Taihu Basin. In Jinxing city, 890 enterprises were reported to participate in the paid use and trade of pollution quotas by mid-November 2009, representing rising trends of both volume and prices of quotas transacted (CAEP, 2009). Even in Shanxi province, China's coal and power base, power-generating plants sold SO_2 emissions quotas to the State Grid. The tradeable permits scheme thus entered the essentially operational stage in the province after years of preparation.

Moreover, China had relied mostly on administrative means to achieve its 20 percent energy-saving goal for 2010. Qi (2011) shows that during the 11th five-year plan period, the total amount of CO_2 reduction reached 1.25 billion tCO_2e through mandatory regulations and auxiliary financial stimuli, while only 0.035 billion tCO_2e were reduced as a result of market-based instruments. In the end, the country has had limited success in meeting that goal. Learning from this lesson in the 11th five-year period and confronted with increasing difficulty in further cutting energy and carbon intensities in the future, China has realized that administrative measures are effective but not efficient. It is becoming increasingly crucial for China to harness market forces to reduce its energy consumption and cut carbon and other conventional pollutants and genuinely transition to a low-carbon economy. In the meantime, evidence suggests that environmental tax reforms and greenhouse gas emissions trading schemes in the Organisation for Economic Co-operation and Development work (Andersen et al., 2007; Andersen and Ekins, 2009; Ellerman et al., 2000, 2010).

To that end, China is experimenting with low-carbon provinces and low-carbon cities in six provinces and 36 cities. Aligned with such an experiment, NDRC has approved seven pilot carbon trading schemes in the capital of Beijing; the business hub of Shanghai; the sprawling industrial municipalities of Tianjin and Chongqing; the manufacturing center of Guangdong province on the southeast coast; Hubei province, home of Wuhan Iron and Steel; and in Shenzhen, the Chinese special economic zone and across the border from Hong Kong. There are features in common in these pilot trading schemes. All the pilot schemes run from 2013 to 2015. During the pilot phase, banking is allowed, but allowances cannot be carried forward beyond 2015. Borrowing is not authorized to improve the liquidity of the carbon market. All regimes allow to a different degree the use of the Chinese Certified Emission Reductions (CCERs) that meet the requirements of China's national verification regulation. Of the seven pilot emissions trading cities, Shenzhen's emissions trading scheme (ETS) includes the largest number of enterprises. Trading started in June 2013 at about 28 yuan per ton of CO_2. Allowances are currently traded at about 84 yuan per ton, with prices peaking at 140 yuan per ton. As the country's first carbon trading scheme in operation, Shenzhen's ETS is just a baby step when you look at the total amount of the regulated emissions compared to the country's total emissions of more than 8 billion tons in 2012, but it is hailed as a landmark step for China in building a nationwide carbon ETS planned for later this decade. With 388 million tons of allowances set for 2013, Guangdong positions itself as the world's second largest carbon market behind the EU ETS. Trading started in December 2013 with 0.12 million tons of allowances traded at 60 to 61 yuan per ton. Based on these piloted schemes, China aims to establish a national carbon trading scheme, hopefully by 2016.

7. Implementation and reliability issues

It should be emphasized that enacting the aforementioned policies and measures targeted for energy saving and pollution cutting just signals the goodwill and determination of China's leaders. To actually achieve the desired outcomes, however, requires strict implementation and coordination of these policies and measures. It has been stipulated that leaders of local governments and heads of key state-owned enterprises are held accountable for energy savings and pollution cutting in their regions and that achieving the goals of energy efficiency improvements and pollution reductions has become a key component of their job performance evaluations. But no senior officials have been reported to take responsibility for failing to meet the energy-saving and pollution-cutting targets to date, not to mention having been asked to step down from their positions on these grounds, except for the mayor of Beijing municipality and the governor of Shanxi province, who stepped down for the mismanagement of the severe acute respiratory syndrome epidemic and large coal-mining accidents.

Another example is the enforcement of FGD operation to ensure that those units equipped with FGD capacities always use it. The government offered a 0.015 RMB/kWh premium for electricity generated by power plants with FGD capacity installed to encourage the installation and operation of FGD at large coal-fired power plants. The premium was equivalent to the average estimated cost of operating the technology. However, this price premium was provided for FGD-equipped power plants regardless of FGD performance. This created an incentive for power plants to install low-cost, poor-quality FGDs in order to obtain the price premium but not to operate the FGD (Schreifels et al., 2012). When NDRC conducted field inspections in July 2006, it found that "up to 40 percent of those generation units with FGD facility did not use it" (Liu, 2006). Given that FGD costs are estimated to account for about 10 percent of the power generation cost (Peng, 2005), combined with lack of trained staff in operating and maintaining the installed FGD facility and lack of government enforcement, this should not come as a surprise unless there is adequate enforcement. Even if the installed FGD facilities were running, they do not run continuously and reliably. MEP field inspections in early 2007 found that less than 40 percent of the installed FGD were running continuously and reliably (Xu et al., 2009).

This does not apply to power generation alone. MEP field inspections in early 2013 found 70 percent of the desulphurization facilities installed in iron and steel plants in Herbei province, in which seven of the ten most polluted cities in China are located, were not running continuously and reliably. Some plants stopped running the desulphurization facility at 8 o'clock in the evening and then started its operation at 8 o'clock in the morning, illegally discharging SO emissions in the evening (Wang and Wei, 2013). Even more alarming is that coal-fired plants were supposed to emit 1.44 million tons of SO_2 emissions in 2012 if they complied with the new emissions standards that took into effect in the beginning of 2012, but they actually emitted 8.83 million tons of SO_2 emissions, based on the data released by the MEP (X. Zhang, 2014). With more than 90 percent of coal-fired generation capacity already equipped with FGD, the government desulphurization policy should thus switch from mandating the installation of FGD to focusing on enforcing units with FGD to operate through online monitoring and control.

Clearly, implementation holds the key. This will be a decisive factor in determining the prospects for whether China will cleanup its development act. There are encouraging signs that the Chinese government is taking steps in this direction. For example, given that the aforementioned price premium for FGD-equipped power plants was based on the installation of FGD facility, not its operation or performance, when requiring continuous emission monitoring systems (CEMS) at coal-fired power plants in May 2007, NDRC and MEP modified the price premium to address FGD performance, basing the electricity price premium on FGD operation and performance. The revised policy continued to provide a price premium of 0.015 RMB/kWh for power plants operating FGDs, but a penalty of 0.015 RMB/kWh is imposed for plants operating FGDs between 80 percent and 90 percent of total generation and a penalty of 0.075 RMB/kWh for plants operating FGDs less than 80 percent of the time. Regardless of the duration of FGD operation, all plants were ordered to return the compensation for their desulphurization costs in proportion to the time when their FGD facilities were not in operation (NDRC and MEP, 2007; Xu, 2011). In its 2008 assessment of the total volume reduction of major pollutants, MEP found that FGD facilities of five coal-fired power plants were either in improper operation or their online monitoring and control data were false. These plants were ordered to return the compensation for their desulphurization costs in proportion to the time when their FGD facilities were not in operation and to make necessary adjustments in the specified period (K. Zhang, 2009). Based on its 2012 assessment of the total volume reduction of major pollutants in all provinces or equivalent and eight central state-owned enterprises, MEP issued a penalty on 15 enterprises involved in improper operation of their desulfurization facilities or desulfurization data falsification. These enterprises were ordered not only to return the compensation for their desulphurization costs in proportion to the time when their desulfurization facilities were not in operation but also had to pay a fine up to five times the compensation amount they received (Qin and Qi, 2013).

The efficacy of basing policies on performance, not process, suggests that the accuracy of SO_2 data is critical. Nowadays emission reports are verified by the central government. Prior to that, it was undertaken by the local environmental protection bureaus (EPBs), as MEP and NDRC mandated the installation of CEMS and the transfer of real-time data to EPBs in May 2007. This had led to nationwide underreporting of emission levels. While in the 11th five-year plan, MEP and EPBs collected SO_2 data from CEMS at most power plants, data quality concerns limited the use of the data (Zhang et al., 2011 and Zhang and Schreifels, 2011). To ensure the reliability of emissions data, MEP instituted an inspection program for provinces, fuel suppliers, and major emitters. Based on the analyses of MEP inspectors, MEP rejected 30 percent to 50 percent of SO_2 reductions claimed by some provinces. This inspection system raised the level of accountability for plant owners and operators, but MEP's investment in the inspections in terms of both staff and financial resources was large. Staff at regional supervision centers spent up to 60 percent of their time conducting these inspections (Schreifels et al., 2012).

Implementation also raises concern about the reliability of energy data. This will be even a bigger issue at local levels because of the lack of reliable local energy statistics. The limited capacity and rampant data manipulation have turned the compilation of local energy statistics into a numbers game. NDRC reported that from 2011 to 2012, national energy intensity declined by 5.5 percent according to data from the National Bureau of Statistics. By contrast, national energy intensity declined by 7.7 percent based on aggregated local statistics during the same period (NDRC, 2013d). This differential in national energy intensity reductions suggests that local governments have overstated their achievement in energy conservation by 40 percent. Because of the mismatch between local and national statistics, even if each region claims to have met its energy-saving goal, China would still fail to meet the national target. Local government reporting based on unreliable local energy statistics are perceived to have a better perspective on the attainment of their energy-saving goals. Therefore, they do not feel the same level of urgency and pressure as the central government. This is seriously undermining the attainment of the national energy-saving target.

8. Concluding remarks

China has gradually recognized that the conventional path of encouraging economic growth at the expense of the environment cannot be sustained. It has to be changed. To that end, China has implemented and strengthened a variety of programs, prices, and other economic and industrial policies and measures targeted to energy saving and pollution cutting. While these policies and measures are helpful in keeping China's energy demand and pollution under control, they fall short of the purposes of both preserving energy and resources and protecting the environment. It is fair to say that lack of strict implementation and coordination of these policies and measures, and lack of appropriated incentives to get local governments' cooperation, contributed to the undesired outcomes. But this is mainly because China relied most on costly administrative measures to meet its energy saving target in 2010. In the end, China missed that target.

Having learned from the lessons of the 11th five-year period and confronted with increasing difficulty in further cutting energy and carbon intensities in the future, China has realized that administrative measures are effective but not efficient. It is becoming increasingly crucial for China to harness market forces to reduce its energy consumption and cut carbon and other conventional pollutants and genuinely transition to a low-carbon economy. The Chinese leadership is well aware of this necessity. This is clearly reflected by the key decision of the third plenum of the 18th Central Committee of the Communist Party of China in November 2013 to assign the market a decisive role in allocating resources. However, to have the market to play that role, getting energy prices right is crucial because it sends clear signals to both producers and consumers of energy. While the overall trend of China's energy pricing reform since 1984 has been moving away from the pricing completely set by the central government in the centrally planned economy toward a more market-oriented pricing mechanism, the pace and scale of the reform differs across energy types.

To date, the reform on electricity tariffs has lagged far behind, and accordingly the government still retains control over electricity tariffs. While China has been reforming the electricity industry structure since 2002, transmission, distribution and sale of electricity are operated in integration by two main grid companies, State Grid and China Southern Power Grid, and several local grid companies, such as Inner Mongolia Grid and Shaanxi Grid. As the designated sole buyers of electricity from generators and distributors and sellers of electricity, they monopolize their respective areas. Their monopoly power and thereby the lack of competition in the electricity market has been heavily criticized. However, separation of transmission and distribution is not an option. The most feasible approach would be to start reforming the electricity sale side by setting up an electricity power trading market. In this regard, direct purchase for major electricity users, as piloted in Yunnan province, should be actively promoted. That will help to infer the cost of electricity transmission and distribution and help the government to set the appropriate level of the grid's transmission and distribution charges in future electricity power structure reform. While splitting the grid is not an option to achieve this goal, separating electricity sale from the grid's transmission and distribution is a must to establish a competitive electricity power market. Then the electricity sale side can be opened and electricity-selling companies independent of grids can be set up in each region. As such, marketing trade will be performed on both the electricity generation side and the sale side and an open, nationwide electricity power market will be established to create a market-based system for electricity pricing. This is considered as the more realistic option to move electricity power reforms forward. In the meantime, given that meeting the goal of cutting NOx emissions has been lagged far behind the government's set schedule as a result of high costs involved and thereby coal-fired power plants' reluctance to install and operate denitrification facilities, the government could consider raising the current level of price premium for denitrification in order to encourage such plants to install and run denitrification facilities continuously and reliably.

Even if the aforementioned energy price reform is undertaken, however, from a perspective of the whole value chain of resource extraction, production, use and disposal, energy prices still do not fully reflect the cost of production. Thus, combined with the pressing need to avoid wasteful extraction and use of resources, getting energy prices right calls for China to reform its current narrow coverage of resource taxation and to significantly increase the levied level. The resource tax levied on crude oil and natural gas by revenues rather than by existing extracted volume, which started in Xinjiang in June 2010 and then was applied nationwide in November 2011, is the first step in the right direction. China should broaden that reform to coal, overhauling the current practice and levying a tax on coal by revenues. This also will help to increase local government's revenues and alleviate their financial burden to incentivize them not to focus on economic growth alone.

Correct energy prices from a perspective of the whole energy value chain also needs to include negative externalities. Clearly, the imposition of environmental taxes or carbon pricing can internalize externality costs into the market prices. Currently, China is experimenting with low-carbon provinces and low-carbon cities in six provinces and 36 cities. Aligned with such an experiment, the central government has approved seven pilot carbon-trading schemes. The seven regions are given considerable leeway to design their own schemes and these trading schemes, which share some common features but also have differing features, have been put into operation since June 2013. Based on these piloted schemes, China aims to establish a national carbon trading scheme, hopefully by 2020. However, in terms of timing, given that China has not yet levied environmental taxes, it is better to introduce environmental taxes first, not least because such a distinction will enable China to disentangle its additional efforts toward carbon abatement from broad energy-saving and pollution-cutting efforts.

Finally, it should be emphasized that implementation holds the key. This will be a decisive factor in determining the prospects for whether China will cleanup its development act. There are encouraging signs that the Chinese government is taking steps in this direction.

Notes

1 See Wu and Zhao (1987) and Singh (1992) for general discussion on pros and cons of the dual pricing system and Albouy (1991) for its impact on coal.
2 See Zhang (2014) for detailed discussion on the evolution of price reforms for coal, petroleum products, natural gas and electricity in China and some analysis of these energy price reforms.

References

Albouy, Y. (1991) Coal Pricing in China: Issues and Reform Strategy, World Bank Discussion Papers No. 138, The World Bank, Washington, DC.

Andersen, M. S., T. Barker, E. Christie, P. Ekins, J. Fitz Gerald, J. Jilkova, J. Junankar, M. Landesmann, H. Pollitt, R. Salmons, S. Scott, and S. Speck. (2007) "Competitiveness Effects of Environmental Tax Reforms (COMETR)." Final Report to the European Commission, DG Research and DG TAXUD, National Environmental Research Institute, University of Aarhus, Denmark.

Andersen, M. S. and P. Ekins, (eds.) (2009) *Carbon-energy Taxation: Lessons from Europe*. New York: Oxford University Press.

China Economic Net (2014) Focus on the reform of natural gas prices. http://www.ce.cn/cysc/ztpd/12/ws/.

China Electricity Council (CEC) (2011) Annual Development Report of China's Power Industry 2011, CEC, Beijing.

China Electricity Council (CEC) and Environmental Defense Fund (EDF) (2012) Studies on Pollution Cutting in China's Power Industry, CEC and EDF, Beijing.

China News Net (2008) "The World Bank: a significant energy saving with the rapid development of China's energy management industry over the past decade," January http://news.sohu.com/20080116/n254683016.shtml.

China News Net (2011) "China decommissioned 76.825 GW of smaller and older coal-fired unites during the 11th five-year period," September 28, http://www.chinanews.com/ny/2011/09-28/3358876.shtml.

Chinese Academy for Environmental Planning (CAEP) (2009) "National research and pilot project on environmental economics and policy: 2009 report," CAEP, Beijing.

Chinese Academy for Environmental Planning (CAEP) (2013) "China Green National Accounting Study Report 2010," CAEP, Beijing.

Chinese Academy of Sciences (CAS) (2009) *China Sustainable Development Strategy Report: China's Approach Towards A Low Carbon Future*. Beijing: Science Press.

Dai, L. (2010) "Oil and gas-producing areas in Xinjiang call for the adjustment for the distribution of resource tax revenues," *People Net*, November 29, http://finance.sina.com.cn/china/dfjj/20101129/07149023055.shtml.

Ellerman, A. D., F. J. Convery, C. de Perthuis, E. Alberola, B. K. Buchner, A. Delbosc, C. Hight, J. H. Keppler, and F. C. Matthes (2010) *Pricing Carbon: The European Union Emissions Trading Scheme*. Cambridge: Cambridge University Press.

Ellerman, A. D., P. L. Joskow, J. P. Montero, R. Schmalensee, and E. M. Bailey (2000) *Markets for Clean Air: The US Acid Rain Program*. Cambridge: Cambridge University Press.

Gao, S. Y. (2013) "NDRC to implement tiered power prices for aluminum smelters, the production costs expected to increase," *Caixin Net*, December 23, http://industry.caijing.com.cn/2013-12-23/113726942. html.

Ho, M. and C. Nielsen (2007) *Clearing the Air: The Health and Economic Damages of Air Pollution in China*, Cambridge, MA: MIT Press.

International Energy Agency (IEA) (2007) *World Energy Outlook 2007*. Paris: International Energy Agency.

Li, W. (2014) "Study on China's Future Energy Development Strategies," *People's Daily*, February 12, p. 12, http://www.drc.gov.cn/zxxw/20140212/1-223-2878725.htm.

Liu, C. (2012) "Lack of transparency over parameters to set domestic prices of gasoline and diesel triggered suspension," *Time Weekly*, March 29, http://news.sina.com.cn/c/sd/2012-03-29/151024195106. shtml.

Liu, S. X. (2006) "Why did 40% of generation units with FGD facility not use it?" *China Youth Daily*, August 8, http://zqb.cyol.com/content/2006-08/08/content_1471561.htm.

Ministry of Commerce of China and the State Environmental Protection Agency (SEPA) (2007) "A circular on strengthening the environmental supervision of export-engaged enterprises," http://www.gov.cn/ zwgk/2007-10/12/content_775030.htm.

Ministry of Finance of China and National Development and Reform Commission (NDRC) (2007) "A circular on interim measures for fund management of financial incentives for energy-saving technical transformation," available at: http://www.mof.gov.cn/zhengwuxinxi/caizhengwengao/caizhengbu-wengao2007/caizhengbuwengao200711/200805/t20080519_27902.html.

Ministry of Finance and National Development and Reform Commission (NDRC) (2011), "A circular on measures for fund management of financial incentives for energy-saving technical transformation," Beijing, June 21, available at: http://www.gov.cn/zwgk/2011-06/24/content_1891712.htm.

National Bureau of Statistics of China (NBS) (2010) *China Statistical Yearbook 2010*. China Statistics Press, Beijing.

National Development and Reform Commission (NDRC) (2006a) The top 1,000 enterprises energy conservation action program. NDRC Environment & Resources No. 571, NDRC, Beijing.

National Development and Reform Commission (NDRC) (2006b) Suggestions for improving the policy on differentiated tariffs, NDRC, Beijing.

National Development and Reform Commission (NDRC) (2008a) A circular on the evaluation of energy saving in 2007 of the top 1,000 enterprises, NDRC, Beijing.

National Development and Reform Commission (NDRC) (2008b) China had decommissioned fossil fuel-fired small plants with a total capacity of 25.87 GW since 1 January 2006, NDRC, Beijing.

National Development and Reform Commission (NDRC) (2009) Performance of the Thousand Enterprises in 2008. NDRC Proclamation No. 18, NDRC, Beijing.

National Development and Reform Commission (NDRC) (2011a) A rapid development of energy service industry: energy saving and pollution cutting during the 11th five-year period in retrospect, NDRC, Beijing.

National Development and Reform Commission (NDRC) (2011b) The thousand enterprises exceeded the energy-saving target during the 11th five year plan period, NDRC, Beijing.

National Development and Reform Commission (NDRC) (2011c) A circular on pilot reform on natural gas pricing mechanism in Guangdong Province and Guangxi Zhuang autonomous region, NDRC Price No. 3033, NDRC, Beijing.

National Development and Reform Commission (NDRC) (2012) List and energy-saving targets of the ten thousand enterprises committed to energy-saving and low- carbon activities, NDRC Proclamation No. 10, NDRC, Beijing.

National Development and Reform Commission (NDRC) (2013a) NDRC expanded the pilot scope of the price premium for coal-fired power plants equipped with denitrification facility, NDRC, Beijing.

National Development and Reform Commission (NDRC) (2013b) Further improvement of the policy on renewable energy and environmental-related electricity pricing, NDRC, Beijing.

National Development and Reform Commission (NDRC) (2013c) China's policies and actions for addressing climate change, NDRC, Beijing.

National Development and Reform Commission (NDRC) (2013d) The grim situation of energy conservation and emissions reduction, significant potential of industry development: analysis of energy conservation and emissions reduction in the first half of 2013, NDRC, Beijing.

National Development and Reform Commission (NDRC) (2013e) Energy conservation performance of the 10,000 enterprises, Circular No. 44, NDRC, Beijing.

National Development and Reform Commission (NDRC) (2014) Promoting low-carbon development pilot to press forward a change in the model of economic development, NDRC, Beijing.

National Development and Reform Commission (NDRC) and Eleven Other Central Government Organizations (2011) A circular on the ten thousand enterprises energy conservation low carbon action program, NDRC Environment & Resources No. 2873, NDRC, Beijing.

National Development and Reform Commission (NDRC) and Ministry of Environmental Protection (MEP) (2007) A circular on the interim administrative measures for price premium for coal-fired power plants equipped with FGD facility and FGD operation, NDRC Price No. 1176, NDRC, Beijing.

National Development and Reform Commission (NDRC) and Ministry of Industry and Information Technology (MIIT) (2013) A circular on levering aluminum smelters with tiered power prices, NDRC Price No. 2530, NDRC, Beijing.

National Development and Reform Commission (NDRC) and National Bureau of Statistics (NBS) (2007) Bulletin on energy use of the top 1000 enterprises, NDRC, Beijing.

National Development and Reform Commission (NDRC) and State Environmental Protection Agency of China (SEPA) (2007) Administrative measures for power price premium for FGD by coal-fired power plants and the operation of FGD facility, NDRC, Beijing.

Peng, J. G. (2005) "Five top risks facing thermal power companies," *China Power Enterprise Management*, October, http://www.cnki.com.cn/Article/CJFDTotal-ZGDQ200510012.htm.

People Net (2007) "Jiangsu will raise the levels of pollution charges from 1 July 2007," June 11, http://politics.people.com.cn/GB/14562/5848072.html.

People Net (2008) "Adjustments for vehicle excise taxes will take place since 1 September, up for cars with large engines and down for small cars to 1 percent," August 14, http://auto.people.com.cn/GB/1049/7663221.html.

Price, L., X. Wang and J. Yun (2010) "The challenge of reducing energy consumption of the top-1000 largest industrial enterprises in China," *Energy Policy*, Vol. 38, No. 11, pp. 6485–6498.

Qi, Y. (ed.) (2011) *Annual Review of Low-Carbon Development in China 2011–2012*. Beijing: Social Science Academic Press (in Chinese).

Qin, F. and D. Qi (2013) "MEP severely punishes enterprises involving desulfurization data falsification, several enterprises with China in their names receive the penalty tickets," *Shanghai Securities News,* May 16, http://news.xinhuanet.com/energy/2013-05/15/c_124711794.htm.

Schreifels, J., Y. Fu and E. J. Wilson (2012) "Sulfur dioxide control in China: policy evolution during the 10th and 11th five-year plans and lessons for the future," *Energy Policy*, Vol. 48, pp. 779–789.

Sina Net (2006) "Special topic on paying close attention to adjustments in consumption tax policy," available at: http://finance.sina.com.cn/focus/gzxfstz/index.shtml.

Sina Net (2007) "Jiangsu will double the charges for atmospheric pollutants from 1 July," June 11, http://news.sina.com.cn/c/2007-06-11/012711994856s.shtml.

Sina Net (2009) "SO_2 cutting goal expected to come ahead of schedule," July 7, http://finance.sina.com.cn/roll/20090707/04346447872.shtml.

Singh, I. (1992) "China: industrial policies for an economy in transition," World Bank Discussion Papers No. 143, The World Bank, Washington, DC.

State Development and Planning Commission (SDPC), Ministry of Finance, State Environmental Protection Agency and State Economic and Trade Commission (2003) Administrative measures on the levying levels of pollution charges, http://www.sepa.gov.cn/epi-sepa/zcfg/w3/ling2003-31.htm.

Streets, D. G., C. Yu, M. H. Bergin, X. Wang and G. R. Carmichael (2006) "Modeling study of air pollution due to the manufacture of export goods in China's Pearl River Delta," *Environmental Science and Technology*, Vol. 40, No. 7, pp. 2099–2107.

The State Council (2007) Comprehensive work plan for energy saving and pollution cutting, http://news.xinhuanet.com/politics/2007-06/03/content_6191519.htm.

The State Council (2010) A circular of the National Development and Reform Commission and other departments to speed up the implementation of energy management contract to promote the energy service industry, http://www.gov.cn/zwgk/2010-04/06/content_1573706.htm.

The State Council (2012) The guiding suggestion for deepening the reform of utility coal market, The General Office, No. 57, http://www.gov.cn/zwgk/2012-12/25/content_2298187.htm.

The World Bank (2007) *Cost of Pollution in China: Economic Estimates of Physical Damages*. Washington, DC: World Bank.

Wang, C., J. Lin, W. Cai and Z. X. Zhang (2013) "Policies and practices of low carbon city development in china," *Energy & Environment*, Vol. 24, Nos. 7–8, pp. 1347–1372.

Wang, E. (2014) "15 piloted regions expected to reach co₂ emissions peak before 2020," *21st Century Business Herald*, January 21, http://biz.21cbh.com/2014/1-21/zNMDA0MTdfMTA0OTYzNA.html.

Wang, L. (2014) "China's coal consumption peaks at 4100 MT in 2020," *Economic Information Daily*, March 5, http://finance.chinanews.com/ny/2014/03-05/5910245.shtml.

Wang, L., Q. Zhao, Y. Liu and B. Wei (2014) "Approaching the time to levy coal resource taxes, *Economic Information Daily*," January 9, http://www.gmw.cn/ny/2014-01/09/content_10070821.htm#blz-insite.

Wang, Y. and W. Wei (2013) "Ministry of environmental protection: Over 70% of the steel companies failed to meet the emissions standards," *China Securities Journal,* October 23, http://finance.china.com.cn/stock/20131023/1895794.shtml.

Wang, P. and Q. Ye (2009) "China about to release new energy development plan by the end of 2009," *Xinhua Net*, August 9, available at: http://news.sina.com.cn/c/2009-08-09/140918397192.shtml.

Williams, J. H. and F. Kahrl (2008) "Electricity reform and sustainable development in China," *Environmental Research Letters*, Vol. 3, No. 4, pp. 1–14.

Wu, J. and R. Zhao (1987) "The dual pricing system in China's industry," *Journal of Comparative Economics,* Vol. 11, No. 3, pp. 309–318.

Xing, Y. (2013) Coal resource taxes about to be up and running, *Caixin Net*, September 13, http://economy.caixin.com/2013-09-13/100582573.html.

Xinhua Net (2010), "NDRC: the 11th five-year pollution-cutting goals met ahead of the schedule," March 10, http://news.sina.com.cn/c/2010-03-10/152019834186.shtml.

Xinhua Net (2013) "Special topic on the adjustments of natural gas prices for non-residential users," http://www.xinhuanet.com/energy/zt/rht/10.htm.

Xu, Y. (2011) "Improvements in the operation of SO₂ scrubbers in China's coal power plants," *Environmental Science & Technology*, Vol. 45, No. 2, pp. 380–385.

Xu, Y., R. H. Williams and R. H. Socolow (2009) "China's rapid deployment of SO₂ scrubbers," *Energy & Environmental Science*, Vol. 2, No. 5, pp. 459–465.

Yu, Z. F. (2006) "Development and application of clean coal technology in Mainland China." In: Zhang, Z. X., and Bor, Y. (Eds.), *Energy Economics and Policy in Mainland China and Taiwan*, pp. 67–88. Beijing: China Environmental Science Press.

Zhang, D., K. Aunan, H. M. Seip and H. Vennemo (2011) "The energy intensity target in China's 11th five-year plan period – local implementation and achievements in Shanxi Province," *Energy Policy*, Vol. 39, No. 7, pp. 4115–4124.

Zhang, K. (2009) "Ministry of environmental protection penalizes 8 cities and 5 power plants based on the assessment of pollutant-cutting," *China Business News*, July http://finance.sina.com.cn/roll/20090724/04006522664.shtml.

Zhang, X. (2014) "Solving the negative consequences of burning coal," *Caixin Century*, No. 2, http://magazine.caixin.com/2014-01-10/100627227.html.

Zhang, X. and J. Schreifels (2011) "Continuous emission monitoring systems at power plants in China: Improving SO₂ emission measurement," *Energy Policy*, Vol. 39, No. 11, pp. 7432–7438.

Zhang, Z. X. (2003) "Why did the energy intensity fall in China's industrial sector in the 1990s?: the relative importance of structural change and intensity change," *Energy Economics*, Vol. 25, No. 6, pp. 625–638.

Zhang, Z. X. (2007a) "China's reds embrace green," *Far Eastern Economic Review*, Vol. 170, No. 5, pp. 33–37.

Zhang, Z. X. (2007b) "Greening China: Can Hu and Wen turn a test of their leadership into a legacy?" Presented at the Plenary Session on Sustainable Development at the Harvard College China-India Development and Relations Symposium, March 30–April 2, New York, NY.

Zhang, Z. X. (2009) "Multilateral trade measures in a post-2012 climate change regime? What can be taken from the Montreal Protocol and the WTO?" *Energy Policy* Vol. 37, pp. 5105–5112.

Zhang, Z. X. (2010a) "China in the transition to a low-carbon economy," *Energy Policy*, Vol. 38, pp. 6638–6653.

Zhang, Z. X. (2010b) "The U.S. proposed carbon tariffs, WTO scrutiny and China's responses," *International Economics and Economic Policy*, Vol. 7, Nos. 2–3, pp. 203–225.

Zhang, Z. X. (2011a) *Energy and Environmental Policy in China: Towards a Low-carbon Economy*. Cheltenham: Edward Elgar.

Zhang, Z. X. (2011b) "In what format and under what timeframe would china take on climate commitments? A roadmap to 2050," *International Environmental Agreements: Politics, Law and Economics*, Vol. 11, No. 3, pp. 245–259.

Zhang, Z. X. (2012) "Effective environmental protection in the context of government decentralization," *International Economics and Economic Policy*, Vol. 9, No. 1, pp. 53–82.

Zhang, Z. X. (2014) "Energy prices, subsidies and resource tax reform in China," *Asia and the Pacific Policy Studies*, Vol. 1, No. 3, pp. 439–454.

Zhang, Z. X. and A. Baranzini (2004) "What do we know about carbon taxes? An inquiry into their impacts on competitiveness and distribution of income," *Energy Policy*, Vol. 32, No. 4, pp. 507–518.

Zhou, N., M. D., Levine and L. Price (2010) "Overview of current energy-efficiency policies in China," *Energy Policy*, Vol. 38, pp. 6439–6452.

Zhu, J. H. (2010) "Six ministries and agencies claim those utilities that fail to implement the differentiated tariffs will face a penalty equaling to five times that of supposed revenues," *People Net*, May 22, http://finance.sina.com.cn/chanjing/cyxw/20100522/07037984663.shtml.

Zhu, J. H. (2013) "The adjustment period of oil prices shortened to 10 working days, with the 4 percent threshold scrapped," *People Net-People's Daily*, March 27, http://energy.people.com.cn/n/2013/0327/c71661-20928257.html.

Zhu, X. R. (2010) "China Electricity Council released data on fossil fuel-fired power plants in 2009," *China Energy News*, July 19, http://paper.people.com.cn/zgnyb/html/2010-07/19/content_572802.htm.

28

MEASURING EMBODIED EMISSIONS FLOWS FOR THE INTERDEPENDENT ECONOMIES WITHIN CHINA

Sören Lindner, Dabo Guan and Klaus Hubacek

1. Introduction

In the past decades, China has undergone dramatic economic and social changes. Following a 'catch-up' strategy to the leading economies in the world for nearly 30 years, the country achieved an average annual growth rate of 9.8 percent. China has overtaken Japan to become the second strongest economy after the US. Despite the remarkable performance of its economic engine and the resulting pace of growth, the distribution of reform benefits have been uneven across Chinese regions (Feng et al., 2009, Guan et al., 2010). China can be perceived as a group of co-evolving, disparate economies rather than a homogenous entity. On the one hand, China has fast-developing urban growth centers in the coastal areas, but on the other hand, there are vast rural areas in internal regions associated with distinct income, lifestyle and expenditure patterns (Hubacek et al., 2001). Citizens living in the coastal mega-cities increasingly gain in wealth and adopt energy-intense Western lifestyles, whereas regions in western China still lag behind in economic development and living low-carbon lifestyles (Chen, 2010; Guan et al., 2008).

One result of rising economic growth is the steady increase in energy demand and related emissions of greenhouse gases (GHG), in particular CO_2 emissions. The need to decrease CO_2 emissions in China, however, is urgent; in 2007 the country overtook the US as the top emitter of annual CO_2 emissions (Guan et al., 2009). Today, 70 percent of energy consumption relies on the most emission-intensive source – coal. In the context of international climate agreements, China is facing more and more pressure to set in place proper policies to reduce emissions. Currently, regional authorities across Chinese provinces continue to focus on sustainable economic growth, with large-scale investment efforts in balancing socioeconomic disparities between regions without much consideration of associated emissions of such policies. Traditionally, interregional trade within China was low, but the government, realizing the economic benefit from international trading with other countries, applied this same concept to stimulate and encourage interregional trade for stimulating growth of less developed regions (Okamoto et al., 2010). The challenge is how to foster economic development of those poor regions while at the same avoiding further growth in emissions for China as a whole.

There are clear signs that climate policy will play a stronger role for China in the near future. Prior to the Copenhagen Climate Summit in 2010, China had committed to a voluntary emissions reduction target and pledged to reduce its carbon emissions intensity by 40 percent to 45 percent in 2020 compared to 2005 levels (Li and He, 2011). The 12th five-year plan contains an outline for establishing step-by-step a carbon emissions trading market as one policy option for meeting the carbon reduction targets. In addition, several policies have been set in place in the recent past aiming at reducing energy intensity in the electricity sector and heavy industry (Carraro and Masseti, 2010; de Coninck, 2007). Several scholars have suggested implementation of a regional approach in China to emissions reduction (Zhang, 2010; Chen et al., 2005; Wang, 2009; Guan and Hubacek, 2010) or a focus on individual sectors, in particular the electricity sector (He et al., 2007; Hao and Nakata, 2008).

This recent shift in attitude gives reason to think that domestic climate policy has moved up the political priority list in China, and it is worth investigating opportunities for effective design and implementation of such policies. In this context, an important question arises: how can commitment to a national target be implemented most effectively taking into consideration the diversity between regions? One possibility for China is to focus on production-related emissions reduction efforts in individual regions rather than pursuing a unified national effort. CO_2 reduction commitments could be established for well-developed regional economies first, while leaving less developed regions initially out of an emissions reduction scheme (Guan and Hubacek, 2010). Another approach would be to allocate emissions obligations to each region according to the triggered emission by consumption activities. There are two different emissions inventory accounting methods associated with above approaches: 1) production-based accounts for emissions from domestic production including exports (Peters, 2008); and 2) consumption-based accounting complements the production-based accounting approach by including CO_2 emissions along the whole supply chain associated with final consumption (Wiedmann, 2009). Researchers have revealed that a consumption-based accounting method provides a better understanding of the common but differentiated responsibility between countries in different economic development stages (Peter and Hertwich, 2008; Wiedmann, 2009). Great research efforts have been made in estimating global and country level CO_2 emissions from both production and consumption perspectives (see Wiedmann, 2009; Davis and Caldeira, 2010; Peters et al., 2011), but few studies have conducted analyses at the subnational level, which are especially important for large developing countries like China. This is largely due the difficulties in tracing interregional trade flows where very little data are available from official statistical offices.

This chapter presents an environmental, extended multi-region input-output (MRIO) model based on the latest publicly available provincial level data in 2002 that captures interregional trade flows to final demand of eight economic regions within China. The model is used to estimate and compare production and consumption emissions for each region, which will provide a better understanding of regional responsibilities for emissions in China. Our work is one of the few early attempts to estimate regional consumption-based carbon footprints and embodied emissions in interregional trade within China.

2. Selective literature review, method and data

2.1 *Environmental input-output analysis and its applications to China*

Input-output analysis (IOA), which can analyze the interdependence of industries in an economy, is one of the most widely applied methods in economics and was developed by Wassily Leontief in the late 1930s (Miller and Blair, 2009). Walter (1973) firstly applied IOA to estimate the pollution content of trade between countries.

Within the context of input-output modeling, the MRIO is known as a simplified form of the interregional IO model (IRIO), requiring less computation and statistical data (Miller and Blair, 2009). MRIO has its origin in regional economics, but after Leontief created a world MRIO model (1977), the concept has been increasingly used for international trade analysis (e.g., Polenske, 1980). One of the advantages seen with MRIO modeling is that it takes into account differences in domestic and foreign production technology (Peters, 2008).

In recent years, many MRIO models have been developed to quantify emissions embodied in trade. The comprehensive overview has been done by Wiedmann (2009). More recent studies, for example, conducted by Davis and Caldeira (2010) and Peters et al. (2011) traced the embodied emissions in global supply chains over years. Those analyses have provided quantitative evidence in the debate of allocations of emissions responsibilities between producers and consumers.

Input-output analysis has been used previously for China to show imbalances in consumption of resources between regions. For example, Hubacek et al. (2001) applied IOA to land use change in China by assessing how socioeconomic changes affect land use at the regional level. With regards to carbon embodied in trade, studies primarily focus on international trade of China with other countries: Zhang et al. (2009) used IOA coupled with a structural decomposition analysis (SDA) to investigate energy related CO_2 emissions in China between 1991 and 2006. They showed that increasing levels of economic activity leads to the largest increase of CO_2 emissions in all major economic sectors. Analyzing reasons for China's rise in emissions, Guan et al. (2008) assessed the emissions drivers of China from 1980 to 2030. They found that mainly household consumption, but to some extent also growth in exports and capital investments, have been responsible for the increase in CO_2 emissions.

Studies attempting to capture environmental impacts based on interregional trade within China are scarce. Liang et al. (2007) applied an MRIO to measure differences in energy use efficiency and to capture embodied emissions in China, but they only used a highly aggregated version with four sectors in each region to forecast future economic scenarios between 2010 and 2020. Several authors discussed potential errors and uncertainties associated with MRIO models (Munksgaard et al., 2005; Peters and Hertwich, 2007; Wiedmann et al., 2007). For example, errors can occur throughout compilation of input-output tables or the estimation method of trade flows. Su et al. (2010) used an eight-region model for China to test the effect of different levels of sector aggregation on emissions embodied in exports. They found that an aggregation level of 40 to 45 sectors is sufficient for obtaining the overall share of embodied in a region's export. In another study, Su et al. (2010b) looked into the effect of spatial aggregation on embodied emissions using an eight-region model of China. They found that levels of aggregation affects the total CO_2 embodied in exports and generally recommend models with high spatial disaggregation. The validity of such models with high spatial disaggregation, however, greatly relies on availability of data.

2.2 Methodology

The basic structure of an input-output system consists of a set of n linear equations with n unknowns, which we can present in a matrix formulation. In general, the total output, X, of an economy is given by the sum of intermediate output, z, of industries $(i,j ..n,)$ and final demand, f:

$$X_i = z_{i1} + \dots + z_{ij} + \dots Z_{in} + f_i = \sum_{j=1}^{n} z_{ij} + f_j \qquad (1)$$

By defining a technical coefficient, A_j, as

$$A_j = \frac{z_{ij}}{x_j} \tag{2}$$

the fixed dependency of inter-sectoral flow between i and j (z) to total output of sector j (xj) is shown. The basic Leontief inverse tells us that for each unit change in demand output changes as well:

$$x = (I - A)^{-1}f = Lf \tag{3}$$

where A represents the technical coefficient matrix, I the Inverse matrix and x is total output of a region. The total output of a regional economy with m sectors, (m indexes the region of interest) can be expressed as

$$x_m = A_m x_m + f_m \tag{4}$$

2.2.1 Interregional trade flows

Interregional trade flows in the MRIO model are estimated by sector and are in monetary units (RMB). We can denote the total flow, T, of goods i in an economy with m regions irrespective of the sector of destination, as

$$\begin{pmatrix} T_i^1 \\ T_i^2 \\ \vdots \\ T_i^m \end{pmatrix} \begin{pmatrix} z_i^{11} & z_i^{12} & \cdots & z_i^{1m} \\ z_i^{21} & z_i^{22} & \cdots & z_i^{2m} \\ \cdots & \cdots & \ddots & \cdots \\ z_i^{m1} & z_i^{m2} & \cdots & z_i^{mm} \end{pmatrix} \tag{5}$$

Dividing each element by its total gives the coefficient denoting the proportion of all goods i used in a region, m, that comes from each other region s ($s = 1,...,m - 1$). We call this proportion

$$c_i^{ms} = \frac{z_i^{ms}}{T_i^s} \text{ or in matrix form } C^{ms} = \begin{bmatrix} c_1^{ms} & 0 & \cdots & 0 \\ 0 & c_2^{ms} & \cdots & 0 \\ \vdots & \vdots & \ddots & \vdots \\ 0 & 0 & \cdots & c_m^{ms} \end{bmatrix} \tag{6,7}$$

In a MRIO we also define an interregional matrix, stemming from the definition of an interregional coefficient which indicates the proportion of a good i used in region m that came from within that region:

$$c_i^{mm} = \frac{z_i^{mm}}{T_i^s} \text{ or in matrix form } C^{mm} = \begin{bmatrix} c_1^{mm} & 0 & \cdots & 0 \\ 0 & c_2^{mm} & \cdots & 0 \\ \vdots & \vdots & \ddots & \vdots \\ 0 & 0 & \cdots & c_m^{mm} \end{bmatrix} \tag{8,9}$$

A general form that fits multi-region cases can be expressed as:

$$(I - CA)x = Cf \qquad (10)$$

and solve for x to obtain the Leontief form for multi-regional analysis:

$$x = (I - CA)^{-1} Cf \qquad (11)$$

2.2.2 Calculating emissions embodied in trade and emissions embodied in consumption

The methodology is described in detail by Peters (2006). This section briefly summarizes. Environmental impacts are calculated by introducing a pollution vector, y:

$$y_m = Y_m x_m = Y_m (I - A_m)^{-1} f_m \qquad (12)$$

The final demand vector, f_m, is composed of final domestic demand for consumption goods of rural and urban household (*rh, uh*), capital investment (*ci*), and government expenditure (*ge*). The total consumption can be expressed as the sum of all subcategories. For an economy with m regions, we define a vector of final demand as

$$f_m = \sum f_{rh} + f_{uh} + f_{ci} + f_{ge} \qquad (13)$$

Final demand can be further decomposed into products produced domestically, and imports from other regions, s, where s = (1…m − 1). $f_m = f_{mm} + \sum_s e_{sm}$. Each region has exports, $e_m = \sum_m e_{ms}$ and imports $i_m = \sum_s i_{sm}$ which can be constructed from trade data (discussed in Section 2.4). Furthermore the inter-industry requirement is split in a MRIO into inputs within a region and industry input of products from a region *s* into *m*: $A_m = A_{mm} + \sum_s A_{sm}$.

We can re-write (5) as

$$Y_m = Y_m x_m = Y_m \left(I - A_{mm} \right)^{-1} \left(f_{mm} + \sum_s e_{ms} \right) \qquad (14)$$

In order to be able to capture emissions from domestic demand and domestic production we decompose equation (7) into

$$Y_{mm} = Y_m \left(I - A_{mm} \right)^{-1} f_{mm} \qquad (15)$$

Which gives the domestic demand, and in order to obtain the emissions embodied in trade (EET) from region *m* to *s* we define

$$Y_{ms} = Y_m \left(I - A_{mm} \right)^{-1} e_{ms} \qquad (16)$$

Total emissions embodied in imports (EEI) as

$$y_m^i = \sum_s f_{m} \qquad (17)$$

Total emissions embodied in exports (EEE) as

$$y_m^e = \sum_s y_{ms} \tag{18}$$

Production emissions (y_{pm}) of a region are the sum of domestic emissions (excluding imports) and exports:

$$y_{pm} = y_{rr} + y_{ms} \tag{19}$$

In a similar fashion, we calculate the emissions embodied in consumption (indirect emissions). Following this approach allows considering the full life cycle of emissions of imported goods. This is achieved by splitting imports into the receiving region between domestic inter-industry demand and final demand. The two approaches give the same total amount of emissions embodied in consumption for a region. Considering exports to final demand of a region s to m we write:

$$e_{sm} = e_{sm}^{ii} + f_{sm} \tag{20}$$

Exports to industry of region m are expressed as:

$$e_{sm}^{ii} = A_{sm} x_s \tag{21}$$

The standard MRIO then becomes:

$$x_m = A_{mm} x_m + f_{mm} + \sum_{m \neq s} A_{ms} x_s + \sum_{m \neq s} f_{ms} \tag{22}$$

2.3 Data for constructing Chinese multiregional input-output table 2002

The foundation of the constructed Chinese multiregional input-output table are datasets published by China's National Bureau of Statistics (NBS, 2006) which consist of 30 single region input-output tables (IOTs) at provincial level for mainland China in 2002 (except Tibet). Those tables are the latest publicly available for China's regions with 42 × 42 commodity by commodity input-output tables that are also identical with the format of the national input-output table. The final demand category in each IOT consists of rural and urban households' consumption, government expenditure, capital formation and trade column(s). However, the availability of trade activities of IOTs varies. The detailed description and related treatments is provided in Section 2.4.2 below. We grouped the 30 provinces into eight regions following two criteria: 1) geographic proximity of provinces, and 2) similar socioeconomic conditions. This is shown in Figure 28.1. The eight regions are as follows: North East, including Heilongjiang, Jilin and Liaoning; Beijing Tianjin, including Beijing and Tianjin; North Coast, including Hebei and Shandong; East Coast, including Jiangshu, Zhejiang and Shanghai; South Coast, including Fujian, Guangdong and Hainan; Central Region, including Anhui, Henan, Hubei, Hunan, Jiangxi and Shanxi; North West, including Neimenggu, Shannxi, Gansu, Ningxia and Xinjiang; and South West, including Sichuan, Chongqing, Yunnan, Guizhou, Qinghai and Tibet.[1] League table of Figure 28.1 shows the respective average regional GDP per capita for each region.

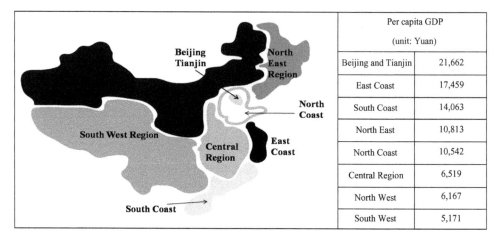

	Per capita GDP (unit: Yuan)
Beijing and Tianjin	21,662
East Coast	17,459
South Coast	14,063
North East	10,813
North Coast	10,542
Central Region	6,519
North West	6,167
South West	5,171

Figure 28.1   Map of eight economic regions used for this study (not drawn to scale)

2.4 Building the Chinese multiregion input-output model

2.4.1 Data estimation for interregional commodity flow

One of the critical challenges to build the Chinese MRIO is to estimate the trade flow of the commodities of the 42 sectors, Zi, between provinces and regions. First, we collected the total freight transportation data by transport modes (i.e., rail, road, air, and ship) for each region in the 2002 Chinese Transportation and Communication Yearbook (NBS, 2003). Second, we obtained the rail freight transportation data in 29 commodities details and interregional rail freight trade flow matrix (total physical volume between 30 provinces) from the Chinese Railway Statistics Yearbook. Third, we assume all freights transported by other modes (e.g., road, air and ship) will follow the same pattern as rail freight transportation to be delivered between Chinese provinces. Fourth, we apply the "gravity coefficient method" (GCM) (Leontief and Strout, 1963) to estimate interregional commodity flows. Following Leontief and Strout, we assume that trade flow from region m to s is proportional to the total amount produced in region r and consumed in region s and inversely proportional to the cost of moving commodities between them. This ratio is then weighted by a gravity-trade coefficient, called Q, which is an empirical constant that is negatively related to per-unit transportation costs (Lin and Polenske, 1995). Trade flow of commodities, zi, can thus be defined as:

$$z_i^{rs} = \frac{x_i^{r} x_i^{s}}{\sum_{r} x_i^{r}} Q_i^{rs} \tag{23}$$

where x_i^{r} is the total output of i in region r, and x_i^{s} the total purchases of i in s, $x_i^{\cdot\cdot}$ the total production of commodity i in the system and Q_i^{rs} is the trade coefficient, which can be estimated at step 3 described above.

In addition, all data are in provincial level, and we need to aggregate them into regions, and then estimate the trade flow as described above. We proceeded the following way: 1) we balanced individual regions by cancelling out domestic imports and exports between provinces that represent one region; and 2) we applied the gravity coefficient method GCM to all trade flow activities between regions by summing the trade flow of all provinces presenting one region to provinces of all other regions.

2.4.2 Separating the trade columns for each province

Some of the 2002 province IO tables provide information on domestic and international trade in four columns (domestic import, domestic export, international import and international export), whereas other provinces reflect trade in only two total columns (total export and total import). Those provinces with only two columns are Jilin, Fujian, Shanxi, Henan, Jiangxi, Hunan, Hubei, Inner Mongolia, Shaanxi, Yunnan, Ningxia, Gansu and Qinghai. Few provinces only provide one column to account for trade, which represents the difference between the export (domestic and international outflow) and import (domestic and intl. inflow). Heilongjiang, Shandong, Sichuan, Chongqing and Guizhou are provinces with only one trade column. For constructing the MRIO we needed to transform all tables into one four-column format, which means splitting the two-column and one-column tables into four-columns. The Chinese custom statistics provides some valuable information regarding to the total amount of international exports and imports for every province in China.

For those one-column tables, we first obtained the total of domestic imports/exports from regional statistics yearbook published by National Bureau of Statistics on yearly basis. Second, we gain the total of international trade from Chinese custom statistics. Third, we used the average structural information of the provinces in the same regions (e.g., assuming Heilongjiang has the same trade pattern as Northeast – average of Jilin and Liaoning provinces) and adapted their ratio of (domestic) inflow and outflow to total use in order to split the total import and export into four columns.

2.5 Energy and emission inventory for 30 Chinese provinces

We constructed CO_2 emissions embodied in trade from energy consumption by industry sector. The energy data was extracted and converted to emission data for the 30 provinces individually and stems mainly from two official Chinese statistics sources: 1) the Chinese Energy Statistics Yearbook that provides energy balance sheets for every province, and 2) the Regional Statistics Yearbook that provides final energy consumption in sectoral details. The complete dataset for every province consists of 18 types of fuel, heat, and electricity consumption in physical units. Fuel types can be broken down into primary energy forms such as crude oil, coal and gas, and secondary products (e.g., coke, coke oven gas, refined petroleum products) into which the primary energy is transformed. In order to avoid double counting, we needed to carefully consider how to allocate primary energy when constructing total energy consumption. Typically in energy studies, primary energy that goes into transformation sectors (secondary sectors) is removed from those sectors, and the secondary energy is then allocated to industry users (Peters et al., 2006). In energy input-output analysis (EIOA), however, this method is not appropriate because energy should be allocated to the industry that combusts the fossil fuel. Therefore, as an example, we do not include inputs into refining, coking and coal cleaning into the total energy consumption. An adjustment is made for electricity: here we add all thermal power and heating supply inputs to the sector "Electric Power, Steam and Hot Water Production and Supply" and then remove the electricity and heat sectors from the total energy consumption to avoid double counting. The details of conversion and data manipulation steps are described in Peters et al. (2006).

CO_2 emissions from combustion of fuels and industrial processes were calculated using the Intergovernmental Panel on Climate Change reference approach (IPCC, 2006). Each fuel type has a specific potential carbon emissions factor (kg carbon/10^6KJ) as well as a fraction of oxidized carbon. Each sector in each province is multiplied by these two factors to give CO_2 emissions in mega tons (Mt). The energy and emissions data for both years comprise 38 production sectors and two households sectors (urban and rural). In a final step, we disaggregate the 38 sector from the energy data to fit 42 input-output economic sectors.

Several authors have pointed toward underreporting; for example, in the case of coal consumption published in Chinese official energy statistics for the period of 1996 to 2004 (Sinton, 2001; Streets et al., 2001). Despite this issue, we have to rely on the most updated data from the Chinese statistical agencies, as it is the most consistent dataset and published on a regional scale.

In fact, energy data availability in some Chinese provinces is poor. Almost one-third of the provinces either only publish regional energy balance sheets without details of sectoral final energy consumption patterns or publish the final energy consumption data in a format different from the national classification. Therefore, we have made great effort to normalize every energy dataset at provincial level to the same standard as the national classification. For provinces like Hubei or Yunnan which only provides four to five energy categories (i.e., coal, oil, gas, electricity and heat), we disaggregate categories into the national standard of 18 energy types based on either regional or national averages. Other provinces such as Shanghai and Guangxi have never published energy consumption data in sectoral details; we use energy consumption pattern from an economically similar province as a proxy. For instance, we assume that Shanghai has the same industrial energy consumption pattern as Zhejiang, which is also one of the economically developed regions in East Coast China.

3. Results

3.1 Domestic emissions per sector

We investigate the main economic sectors contributing to regional production emissions and the major causes of triggered emissions in sectoral details. In all regions, electricity production contributes the highest amount of production emissions – for example, 68 percent of total generated emissions in the North West, 54 percent in the Central and 60 percent in the East Coast. As a comparison, the non-metal mineral production sector, ranked number two for total production emissions, causes only 9 percent, 19 percent and 15 percent of emissions in the above three regions, respectively. Other sectors mainly responsible for production emissions are coal mining and petroleum processing and coking (Central Region), as well as metals smelting and pressing, chemicals, and transport and warehousing. Our results show four sectors have triggered the most emissions: construction, electricity, agriculture and, in case of East Coast, machinery and equipment. In comparison to the other sectors contributing to consumption emissions, construction is leading with 14 percent of the total emissions in the North West, 12 percent in the Central region and 10 percent on the East coast. Electricity production is actually the second main contributor of consumption emissions in the Central and North West region.

We also calculated the relative carbon intensity of the ten main polluters in each region with the highest amount of production emissions, expressed in $kgCO_2$/sectoral GDP (billion yuan), indexed to the national average of each sector, as shown in Figure 28.2. For example, carbon intensity of coal mining and coking in the North West exceeds the national average intensity of that sector by a factor of close to 5 (492 percent). In the East Coast and Central Region, carbon intensity of electricity production lies just slightly above the national average. Metal ore mining in the East Coast and petroleum processing in the Central Region are sectors with very high carbon intensity when compared to the national average. The carbon intensity analysis gives us an indication of levels of efficiency per sector and region. For example, carbon intensity of electricity production (dark blue bar) is as high as the national average in the East Coast and higher in North

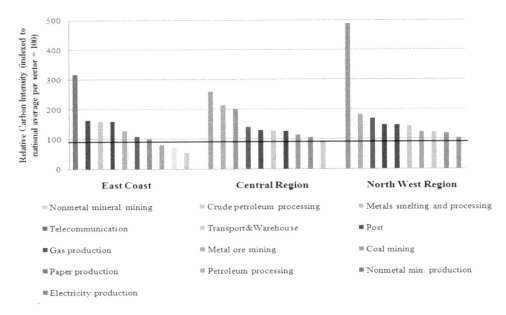

Figure 28.2 Relative carbon intensity indexed to the national average of each sector

West and Central region – showing that electricity production in the East Coast is more efficient than in the other regions. Overall, primary industry, like crude petroleum processing, metals smelting and processing, and coal mining in Central and North West is much more carbon intense than the national average. Central region, and to a lesser extent North West region, are export regions into East Coast of the products from the primary industry that are processed further in other regions. Our results, therefore, detect that downstream of a product chain, carbon intensities are high and these intense production processes are driven largely by demand from well-off regions.

3.2 Embodied emissions in interregional trade

China's interregional trade is very active. For example, 47 percent of North East production emissions are embodied in exports, and for East Coast the figure is 74 percent, Central Region 77 percent, Beijing-Tianjin and South West both 87 percent, North West 77 percent, North Coast 76 percent, and South Coast 67 percent. This indicates that, except for North East, in all other regions more than two-third of domestically occurred emissions are actually for producing goods and services for exports which are consumed by other Chinese regions or countries, and only one-third or less are to fulfill domestic final demand.

Consumption-based emission accounting allows one to trace the origin of emissions through the entire production supply chain. Here we take into account that some imports are destined to intermediate demand of a region, from where they are re-allocated as exports to final demand of another region (reflected in Equation 21). Figure 28.3 compares the embodied emissions in imports (EEI) with emissions from domestic consumption in order to understand what fraction of the total embodied emission in consumption (EEC) are imported. Two regions stick out: South West, with the lowest per capita GDP, is importing 94 percent of their total consumption based emissions. Beijing-Tianjin, with the highest per capita GDP, is importing 54 percent of total EEC. It also shows the highest amount of EEC per capita. Central Region, the North Coast, North

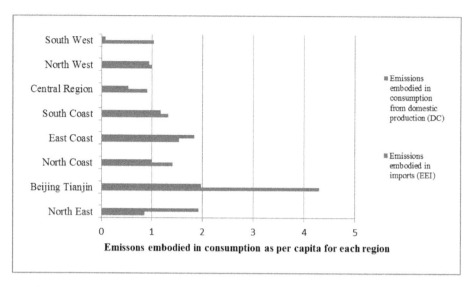

Figure 28.3 Emissions embodied in consumption split between EEI and domestic consumption

West and South Coast all embody more emissions in imports than they produce domestically for consumption, and domestic consumption in the North East makes up 56 percent of total EEC. Only two regions (North East and East Coast) actually produce more emissions domestically than they import. We find that the emissions embodied in imports vary between Chinese regions: in some regions it exceeds 50 percent of total EEC. In general, results from the EEC accounting method show that many regions can be responsible for emissions occurring outside their borders. However, not only the economically well-off regions have a high amount of emissions embodied in trade but also regions with low developed production structure like the South West. Similar to our findings from comparing export emissions with emissions for domestic final demand, we see a high fraction of emissions embodied in imports relative to domestic consumption. In other words, significant amount of production for a region's final demand occurs outside the region's own border.

Table 28.1 shows the origin of EEI for each region. Central Region and East Coast are the main manufacturing bases for most of Chinese regions. Overall, EEI for the two regions are 618 Mt CO_2 and 601 Mt CO_2, which accounts for 24 percent and 23 percent of total EEI between Chinese regions, respectively. But they have similarities and differences in terms of their exports to other Chinese regions. Both regions exports commodities to fulfill other regions' capital formation activities, which accounts for 36 percent and 32 percent of EEE in Central Region and East Coast, respectively. In terms of other exports, Central Region usually provides consumption in other regions with large-scale machinery, processed food and non-metal mineral products, while East Coast provides with small industrial equipment, wearing apparel and chemicals etc. Between the two regions, they exchange overall 223 Mt CO_2 (i.e. 88 Mt CO_2 + 145 Mt CO_2) via bilateral trade, which accounts for more than 40 percent of each region's total EEI. Furthermore, both regions contribute to more than 60 percent of total EEI to every other region, except North East and Beijing-Tianjin, which chooses more adjacent regions as main importing origins. For example, more than 80 percent of EEI of Beijing-Tianjin is mainly from the North Coast, Central Region and North West.

Table 28.1 Origin of EEI for each region (results are given in Mt CO2)

North East

Total	298.6
EEI	**91.7**
origin:	
North West	22.8
East Coast	20.8
North Coast	17.9
Central Region	12.2
Beijing Tianjin	9.9
South Coast	5.4
South West	2.8

Beijing and Tianjin

Total	152.4
EEI	**104.3**
origin:	
North Coast	44.3
Central Region	30.3
North West	12.4
North East	6.9
East Coast	6.8
South West	1.8
South Coast	1.8

East Coast

Total	461.3
EEI	**210.4**
Central Region	88.0
North Coast	53.1
South Coast	20.5
North West	19.1
South West	15.7
North East	7.8
Beijing Tianjin	6.3

South Coast

Total	302.5
EEI	**160.7**
Central Region	57.4
East Coast	42.1
South West	34.2
North Coast	11.8
North West	5.7
Beijing Tianjin	2.9
North East	2.8

North Coast

Total	378.2
EEI	**221.6**
origin:	
East Coast	130.7
South Coast	30.2
North West	17.7
South West	16.8
North West	15.9
Beijing Tianjin	7.0
North East	3.4

North West

Total	502.5
EEI	**317.5**
origin:	
South Coast	145.0
East Coast	54.2
Beijing Tianjin	51.4
North Coast	31.4
North East	22.6
South West	12.8
Central Region	9.2

South West

Total	217.6
EEI	**112.5**
Central Region	91.2
East Coast	36.8
North Coast	17.9
South Coast	13.8
North West	12.2
Beijing Tianjin	11.6
North East	11.1

Central Region

Total	284.3
EEI	**266.2**
origin:	
Central Region	103.7
East Coast	82.2
North Coast	28.5
South Coast	26.1
North West	12.9
Beijing Tianjin	7.5
North East	5.2

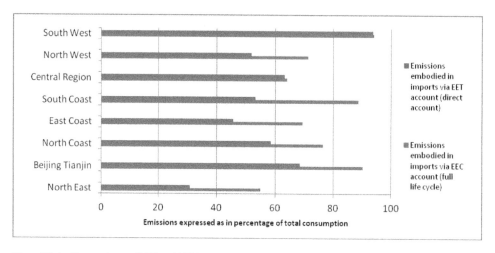

Figure 28.4   Comparison of EEI and EEC

Furthermore, the above analysis cannot illustrate the full picture of embodied emissions in interregional trade between Chinese regions. We compare the results calculated from the EEI and EEC to tackle the "passing through" emissions embodied in "re-export products" (Peters, 2006). Both approaches are from consumption-based accounting perspective. The EEI accounting method allocates all imports of the receiving region to its final consumption, whereas the EEC method allocates those imports to intermediate demand (from where they could be exported again to final consumption of another region) and final consumption of the importing region. We see from Figure 28.4 that these two accounting methods indeed give different results, although the difference in South West and Central Region is very small. The emissions embodied in imports obtained by the EEC are higher in all regions than through the EEI method, suggesting that considering re-export of imports into a region increases the overall emissions embodied in imports of regions. The difference between EEI and EEC is greatest in the wealthiest regions, South Coast and East Coast and Beijing-Tianjin, suggesting that in these regions there are significant amount of commodities that have been exported to other regions for further processing and being imported to fulfill their own consumption.

3.3 Emissions embodied in final consumption

Figure 28.5 provides an interregional comparison between the production-based and consumption-based emissions accounting methods. If we measure per capita carbon footprint by using the consumption-based emissions accounting approach (as shown in Figure 28.5), our result largely complies with the findings from previous studies that per capita consumption in rich regions is having a larger footprint than the ones in poor regions. In contrast, emissions accounting using a production-based approach shows that many less-developed regions (e.g., Central Region and North West) would have larger per capita carbon footprints than the more developed regions (e.g., South Coast). This is mostly due to the difference in production structures between regions. Central Region and North West are largely engaged in carbon-intensive productions such as cements, steel and coking, whereas South Coast has relatively more electronic products in its production mix.

564

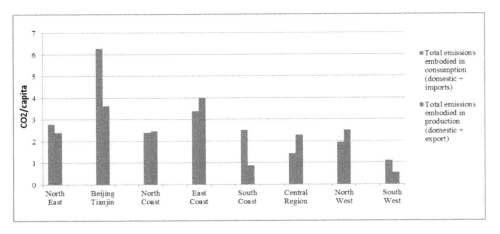

Figure 28.5 Comparison of emissions embodied in production and emissions embodied in consumption (total)

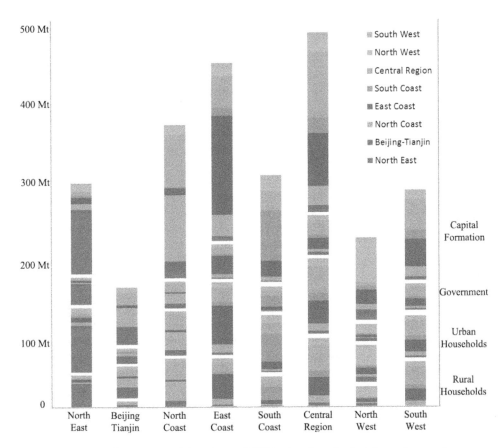

Figure 28.6 Regional comparion of the origins of EEC broken down by final demand categories

The biggest variance can be seen in Beijing-Tianjin in terms of the difference between consumption and production carbon footprints. The region has higher emissions embodied in consumption then production. A similar phenomena can be observed in the other rich region – South Coast. The main driver of consumption-triggered emissions is capital formation, which accounts for about half of total embodied emissions for regional consumption for both regions. However, the commodities consumed by capital formation (e.g., cements and steels) are largely relying on imports. For instance, Beijing-Tianjin production can only satisfy 28 percent of its consumption of capital-related products, and the figure for South Coast is 47 percent. The gaps are mainly fulfilled by imports from Central Region and East Coast. In a poor region like South West, consumption-triggered emissions also are larger than the production-related emissions. This is largely due to the fact that many areas in South West are still in the initial stage of industrialization, where many final products are imported to fulfill its consumption.

Figure 28.6 illustrates the amount and the origins of embodied emissions triggered by different final demand categories for every region. The hight of each column represents the total emissions caused by overall final demand in each region. Further, each column is broken down into four subcategories: the bottom bar is emissions triggered by rural household consumption; the lower middle bar is urban household consumption; the upper middle bar is govermental consumption; and the top bar is by capital formation or investments. Every bar is color-coded to illustrate the origins (within China) of the embodied emissions.

Capital formation (top section) is the largest driver in emission generation for all regions. North East and East Coast dominately produced goods and services to fulfill their capital-related activities domestically, while both rich regions like Beijing-Tianjin and poor regions like South West largely rely on imports from other regions to satisfy their capital formation.

4. Conclusion

Given the spatial economic disparity in China, this chapter constructs an environmental, extended multiregional input-output model to assess the amount of emissions embodied in interregional trade between Chinese regions on a sector level. Our results indicate several immediate opportunities for China's climate policy.

First, sectoral carbon intensities have great regional disparities. The belief that environmentally sound technologies are the key to climate change mitigation and that intellectual property rights protection is one of the biggest obstacles that should be waived for developing countries is enshrined in the UN Framework Convention on Climate Change. However, great technological inequalities have remained and even grown, not just between North and South or even amongst developing countries, but even within a country such as China. Nevertheless, over the past decade, China has acquired (and has begun to manufacture) many state-of-the-art low-carbon technologies. For example, 38 percent of the world's newly constructed or operated super-critical (SC) and ultra-super-critical (USC) power plants exist in China, and the main technologically intensive elements such as boilers, turbines and generators are produced domestically by Harbin Boiler Works and Shanghai Dongfang (Ueno, 2009). However, these advanced technologies usually are retained in a small number of large enterprises in those well-off regions. While there are limited offers on new low-carbon technologies that can be given from international channels, much effort can be invested in leveling the technological inequalities between Chinese regions. Almost all heavy industries with carbon-intensive production in China are state-owned enterprises. In other words, the authorities can greatly influence the firms' decisions on technology transfer or even with direct accessibility to the low-carbon technologies. In principle, the national council can coordinate design and implement effective mechanisms and channels to encourage technology transfers between the more and lesser developed regions of China. Some efforts have been achieved. For example, the authorities have placed SC and USC on the list of technologies given R&D support for deployment while mandating that small-scale power plants (< 1MW) should be replaced with large (>800 MW) SC and UC plants.

Secondly, China trades actively between regions, resulting in embodied emissions flows associated with trade. Except North East, the other regions generate about two-third of their domestic emissions to produce goods and services for export. In other words, all regions receive significant amount of embodied emissions from other regions to satisfy their consumption. Further, a large fraction of embodied emissions to rich regions are via "re-export" products. This implies that regions like South Coast and Beijing-Tianjin receive a significant amount of goods and products for final consumption, whereas Central Region re-exports some of their imports. Therefore, rich regions act as strong sink regions of embodied emissions. Guan and Hubacek (2010) argued that the rich Chinese regions with similar carbon footprints to many developed countries would be better able to afford a CO_2 reduction target. Our analysis indicates that it will be appropriate to set target from a consumption- rather than a production- based emissions accounting approach. The potential benefits can be: 1) more emissions reduction by setting a same ratio of reduction target given the fact of consumption emissions (152 Mt CO_2) in Beijing-Tianjin is about double its production emissions (88 Mt CO_2); 2) driving de-carbonization of the supply chain for rich regions where much primary processing occurs in relatively poor regions.

Note

1 There is no input-output table available for Tibet, however the economic contribution (e.g., GDP) from Tibet to overall China is small (0.1 percent of national GDP in 2002). Further the geographic conditions and economic production and consumption pattern in Tibet are relatively similar with Qinghai province, which is also a plateau region. Hence, we assume Tibet has the same input-output configuration as Qinghai but with Tibet economic outputs that can be found in Chinese Statistics Yearbook (National Bureau of Statistics, 2003).

References

Ahmad, N. (2003). A framework for estimating carbon dioxide emissions embodied in international trade of goods. STI Working Paper STI/SD/WAF, vol. 20. Organisation for Economic Co-operation and Development, Paris, France.

Anderson, J. (1979). A theoretical foundation for the gravity equation. *The American Economic Review, 69*(1), 106–116.

Atkinson, G., Hamilton, K., Ruta, G., & Van Der Mensbrugghe, D. (2011). Trade in "virtual carbon": Empirical results and implications for policy. *Global Environnemental Change, 21*(2), 563–574.

Bertini, S., & Paniccia, R. (2008). Polluting my neighbours: linking environmental accounts to a multi-regional input–output model for Italy, methodology and first results, International Input–Output Meeting on Managing the Environment, July 9–11, 2008, Seville, Spain.

Bodansky, D. (2010). The Copenhagen Climate Change Conference. *The American Journal of International Law, 104*(2), 230–240.

Bradley, R., Baumert, K. A., Childs, B., Herzog, T., & Pershing, J. (2007). *Slicing the Pie: Sector-Based Approaches to International Climate Agreements*. Washington, DC: World Resources Institute.

Cai, W., Wang, C., Chen, J., Zhang, Y., & Lu., X. (2007). Comparison of CO_2 emission scenarios and mitigation opportunities in China's five sectors in 2020. *Energy Policy, 36*, 1181–1194.

Carraro, C., & Masseti, E. (2010). Energy and Climate Change in China. Working Paper. Fondazione Eni Enrico Mattei.

Chiang, Y., & Wang. N. (2009). Environmental regulations and emissions trading in China. *Energy Policy, 38*(7), 3356–3364.

Chen, A. (2010). Reducing China's regional disparities: Is there a growth cost? *China Economic Review, 21*(1), 2–13.

Chen, R., Guerrero, D. China's New Climate Diplomacy in the COP16. Focus on Trade Working paper No. 155, Manila.

Chen, W., Wu., Z. Gao., P. & Xu., S. (2005). Carbon emission control strategies for China: A comparative study with partial and general equilibrium versions of the China MARKAL model. *Energy, 32*, 59–72.

de Coninck, H. (2007). Trojan horse or horn of plenty? Reflections on allowing CCS in the CDM. *Energy Policy, 36*(3), 926–936.

Démurger, S. (2001). Infrastructure Development and Economic Growth: An Explanation for Regional Disparities in China? *Journal of Comparative Economics, 29*(1), 95–117.

Feng, K., Hubacek, K, & Guan, D. (2009). Lifestyles, technology and CO_2 emissions in China: A regional comparative analysis. *Ecological Economics, 69*(1), 145–154.

Giljum, S., Lutz, C., & Jungnitz, A. (2008). The Global Resource Accounting Model (GRAM). A methodological concept paper. *SERI Studies 8*, Elsevier, Amsterdam.

Gordon, I. (1976). Gravity demand functions, accessibility and regional trade. *Regional Studies, 10*(1), 25.

Guan, D., & Hubacek, K. (2010). China can offer domestic emission cap-and-trade in post 2012. *Environmental Science & Technology, 44*(14), 5327.

Guan, D., Hubacek, K., Weber, C. L., Peters, G. P., & Reiner, D. M. (2008). The drivers of Chinese CO_2 emissions from 1980 to 2030. *Global Environmental Change, 18*(4), 626–634.

Guan, D., Peters, G. P., Weber, C. L., & Hubacek, K. (2009). Journey to world top emitter: an analysis of the driving forces of China's recent CO_2 emissions surge. *Geophysical Research Letters, 36*(4), 1–5.

Hi, S., & He, J. (2011). Impact of China's domestic Carbon Emissions Trading Scheme. Conference Paper for the 19th IIOA Conference, July 2011, Alexandria, VA.

Hubacek, K., & Sun, L. (2001). A scenario analysis of China's land use and land cover change: incorporating biophysical information into input–output modeling. *Structural Change and Economic Dynamics, 12*(4), 367–397.

Hubacek, K., & Sun, L. (2005). Economic and societal changes in China and their effects on water use. A scenario analysis. *Journal of Industrial Ecology, 9*(1–2), 187–200.

Intergovernmental Panel on Climate Change (IPCC) 2006. *2006 IPCC Guidelines for National Greenhouse Gas Inventories,* edited by S. Eggleston et al., Institute for Global Environmental Strategies, Hayama, Japan.

Leontief, W., & Strout, S. (1963). Multiregional input–output analysis. *Structural interdependence and economic development.* In Input–Output Economics, Wassily Leontief (Ed.), 223–257. Oxford: Oxford University Press.

Liang, Q., Fan, Y., & Wei, Y. (2007). Multi-regional input–output model for regional energy requirements and CO2 emissions in China. *Energy Policy, 35*(3), 1685–1700.

Lin, J., Zhou, N., Levine, M., & Fridley, D. (2008). Taking out 1 billion tons of CO2: The magic of China's 11th Five-Year Plan? *Energy Policy, 36*(3), 954–970.

Lin, X., & Polenske, K. (1995). Input–Output Anatomy of China's Energy Use Changes in the 1980s. *Economic Systems Research, 7*(1), 67.

Lindall, S., Olsen, D., & Alward, G. (2006). Deriving multi-regional models using the IMPLAN national trade flows model. *Journal of Regional Analysis and Policy, 36*(1), 76–83.

Ma, H., Oxley, L., & Gibson. J. (2009). Gradual reforms and the emergence of energy market in China: Evidence from tests for convergence of energy prices. *Energy Policy 37,* 4834–4850.

Miller, R., & Blair, P. D. (2009). *Input-output analysis: foundations and extensions* (2nd ed.). Cambridge; New York: Cambridge University Press.

Minx, J., Peters, G., Wiedmann, T., & Barrett, J. (2008). GHG emissions in the global supply chain of food products. International Input–Output Meeting on Managing the Environment, July 9–11, 2008, Seville, Spain.

Munksgaard, J., & Pedersen, K. (2001). CO2 accounts for open economies: producer or consumer responsibility? *Energy Policy, 29*(4), 327–334.

Munksgaard, J., Wier, M., Lenzen, M., Dey, C. (2005). Using Input-Output Analysis to Measure the Environmental Pressure of Consumption at Different Spatial Levels. *Journal of Industrial Ecology 9*(1–2), 169–185.

National Bureau of Statistics (NBS). (2003). Yearbook House of China Transportation and Communication 2003. Chinese Transportation and Communication Yearbook. NBS, Beijing.

National Bureau of Statistics (NBS). (2006). National Bureau of Statistics, 2002 Input–Output Table of China, China Statistics Press, Beijing.

National Development and Reform Commission (NDRC). (2007). National Development and Reform Commission. China's National Climate Change Programme. NDRC, Beijing.

Norman, J., Charpentier, A., & MacLean, H. (2007). Economic Input-Output Life-Cycle Assessment of Trade Between Canada and the United States. *Environmental Science & Technology*, *41*(5), 1523–1532.

Peters, G. P. (2006): Opportunities and challenges for environmental MRIO modelling: Illustrations with the GTAP database. 11th International Input Output Conference, Istanbul, Turkey.

Peters, G. P. (2008). From production-based to consumption-based national emission inventories. *Ecological Economics*, *65*(1), 13–23.

Peters, G., & Hertwich, H. (2007). CO_2 Embodied in International Trade with Implications for Global Climate Policy. *Environmental Science and Technology*, *42*(5), 1401–1407.

Peters, G. P., Weber, C., & Liu, J. (2006). Construction of Chinese energy and emissions inventory. Norwegian University of Science and Technology Industrial Ecology Programme Reports and Working Papers, Norwegian University of Science and Trondheim University, Trondheim.

Polenske, K. R. (1980). *US multiregional input-output accounts and model* (Vol. 6). Lexington, KY: D.C. Health & Co.

Schulz, N. 2009. Delving into the carbon footprints of Singapore – comparing direct and indirect greenhouse gas emissions of a small and open economic system. *Energy Policy 38*, 4848–4855.

Sinton, J. E. (2001). Accuracy and reliability of China's energy statistics. *China Economic Review*, *12*(4), 373–383.

Streets, D., Gupta, S., Waldhoff, S., Wang, M., Bond, T., & Yiyun, B. (2001). Black carbon emissions in China. *Atmospheric Environment*, *35*(25), 4281–4296.

Su, B., Huang, H. C., Ang, B. W., & Zhou, P. (2010). Input-output analysis of CO_2 emissions embodied in trade: The effects of sector aggregation. *Energy Economics*, *32*(1), 166–175.

Teather, D. (2010). China overtakes Japan as world's second-largest economy, *The Guardian*, http://www.guardian.co.uk/business/2010/aug/16/china-overtakes-japan-second-largest-economy.

Ueno, T. (2009) *Technology Transfer to China to Address Climate Change Mitigation*. The Climate Policy Program, Resources for the Future, Washington, DC.

Walter, I. (1973). The pollution content of American trade. *Economic Inquiry*, *11*(1), 61–70.

Wang, H., & Nakata, T., (2009). Analysis of the market penetration of clean coal technologies and its impacts in China's electricity sector 2009. *Energy Policy, 37*, 338–351.

Weber, C. L, & Matthews, H. S. (2007). Embodied Environmental Emissions in US International Trade, 1997–2004. *Environmental Science & Technology*, *41*(14), 4875–4881.

Wiedmann, T. (2009). A review of recent multi-region input-output models used for consumption-based emission and resource accounting. *Ecological Economics*, *69*(2), 211–222.

Wiedmann, T., Lenzen, M., Turner, K., & Barrett, J. (2007). Examining the global environmental impact of regional consumption activities – Part 2: Review of input–output models for the assessment of environmental impacts embodied in trade. *Ecological Economics, 61*, 15–26.

Wilson, A. G. (1971). A family of spatial interaction models, and associated developments. *Environment and Planning A*, *3*(1), 1–32.

Zhang, M., Mu, H., & Ning, Y. (2009). Accounting for energy-related CO_2 emission in China, 1991–2006. *Energy Policy*, *37*(3), 767–773.

Zhou, X., & Kojima, S. (2010). How does trade adjustment influence national emissions inventory of open economies? Accounting embodied carbon based on multi-region input–output model, Institute for Global Environmental Strategies, Hayama, Japan.

29

MATERIAL FLOW ACCOUNTING OF THE UK

Linking UK consumption to global impacts with an example of imports from China

Dabo Guan, Ashok Chapagain, Jan Minx, Martin Bruckner and Klaus Hubacek

1. Introduction

The speed of economic globalization and integration has accelerated over the last two decades to an extent where the supply chains of most products have been fragmented all over the world. However, the big picture remains that while Organisation for Economic Co-operation and Development (OECD) countries are the main consumers of world produce, a range of developing countries are becoming the main providers of the resource-intensive products at the cost of a wide range of impacts on their environment. Based on the criteria of the ecological footprint, it is estimated that the total consumption in the UK is more than three times larger than the present regenerating capacity of the planet Earth, meaning that the UK consumption is far beyond environmental limits of the globe (WWF, 2006). A significant portion of resource-intensive products are mainly produced and imported from developing countries. Significant pollution and environmental impacts have been left in the mining site during the materials mining processes. For example, from extraction to combustion, every step in the process of using coal damages the environment; coal extraction produces water, air and noise pollution as well as impacts on aquifers, water systems and land. The spread of coal dust, as well as other environmental problems, occurs with coal transportation. Damages from coal combustion include air pollution resulting from dust, NO_X, sulfur oxides (SO_X), CO_2 and mercury. These pollutants would cause respiratory disease and seriously impact public health. A recent report, "The true cost of coal," released by Greenpeace states that the environmental and social costs associated with China's use of coal came to RMB1.7 trillion – that's about 7.1 percent of the nation's GDP in 2005. Further, more than 31,000 coal miners in China died from accidents down the mines between 2000 and 2006.

The EU's import from China has increased six-fold between 1995 and 2007 from € 34 billion to € 242 billion; 17 percent of total EU-27 imports now originate from China, making China the largest exporter to the EU. Measured by value, three countries, Germany (21 percent), the Netherlands (16 percent) and the UK (14 percent) were the main EU importers from China that together account for more than half of all EU imports from China. If we break down the imports in terms of commodity categories, China's exports to EU/UK are carbon- and resource- (material and water) intensive. For example, carbon/material-intensive products such as metallic products; information, communication and technological products; machinery and transport equipment; and miscellaneous manufactured goods account for 65 percent of EU imports from China. Relatively water-intensive products such as clothing and footwear, food, animal/vegetable oils and fats, and chemical products account for the rest.

It is necessary to understand these material flow linkages between the developed countries and developing countries before addressing global sustainability challenges. In an increasingly interconnected world, no nation or region acting alone can meet this challenge. The aim of this chapter is to investigate international material flows driven by the UK's consumption. We use 20 indicators of material flows to illustrate the natural materials imported either directly or indirectly to fulfil the UK's production and consumption activities in 2004 via a multilateral trade model between the UK, EU, non-EU OECD countries, China, and the rest of the world.

In this chapter, we employ ten materials flow indicators and greenhouse gas (GHG) emissions to assess the embedded material/emission flows to an "earlier" ascendant – the UK and its environmental implications to the rest of world and in particular a newly ascending country – China – through a multiregional trade model. Section 2 provides a selective overview of the application of world system theory in environmental studies; Section 3 describes the model constructions and data compilation; Section 4 presents material flows to fulfil UK's economy; Section 5 illustrates the magnitude, origins, and the environmental implications of material flows triggered by the UK's consumption; and finally Section 6 concludes.

2. World system theory and the environment

One of the dominant theories and frames to understand the interdependencies in the globalizing world system is the world system theory (Mol, 2011), which was firstly articulated by Wallerstein (1974). He aimed at achieving "a clear conceptual break with theories of 'modernization' and thus provide a new theoretical paradigm to guide our investigations of the emergence and development of capitalism, industrialism, and national states" (Skocpol, 1977, p. 1075). In particular, Wallerstein (1974; 1979) studied how ascending economies and states (such as the Dutch Republic, the British empire, the US, and Japan) managed to become hegemonic powers through a global division of labor as well as exploitation and unequal exchange of surplus goods and services with peripheral regions and states. Here we provide a summary of world system theories' development and application to environmental studies. A comprehensive review is provided by Burns et al. (2003).

The world system theory has been applied to studying the social, political, and economic inequalities via these unequal exchanges between the hegemonic and peripheral countries with particular focus on income inequalities (e.g., Chase-Dunn, 1975, 1998; Chase-Dunn & Hall, 1997; Kentor, 2001; Kick, Byron, Davis, Burns, & Gubin, 1995) and urbanization (e.g., Kentor, 1981; London & Smith, 1988; Smith, 1996; Timberlake & Kentor, 1983).

But since the mid-1990s, environmental issues have become more central topics in world system studies. Theorist have paid increasing attention to how natural resources extracted and traded and the associated environmental degradation in peripheral countries (e.g., developing countries) in order to satisfy the further expansion and growth of core countries (e.g., developed countries) and classes. In particular, a number of cross-national studies have been done from the world-system perspective that shed light on problems such as GHG emissions (Burns, Byron & Kick, 1997; Roberts & Grimes, 1997); international patterns of accumulation and transfer of hazardous waste (Frey, 1995); the ecological footprint (York, Rosa & Dietz, 2002); as well as studies of deforestation (Burns, Kick, Murray & Murray, 1994).

In recent years, researchers have investigated whether China is a new ascending economy that extracts resources and pollutes peripheral countries (i.e., oil extraction in Africa and deforestation in South Asia) (Mol, 2011). A central theorem of environmental scholars in the world systems theory tradition is "environmentally unequal exchange" between ascending global powers and peripheral nations and communities, leading to the destruction of natural environments in these latter places. It seems that the existing world system studies have mainly focused on the direct trade of natural materials; for example, Ciccantell (2009) investigates China's efforts in acquirement of raw materials by "stealing" the earlier ascendant's (e.g., Japan's) raw materials peripherals. But they have largely ignored one of the main triggers of such "unequal exchange" – that is, materials and emissions embedded in manufactured products that are produced in some ascending countries and delivered to those hegemonic countries for consumption.

3. Method

3.1 Multiregional input-output table

We employ multiregional input-output analysis (MRIO) as the main engine to drive the study. Input-output analysis is one of the most effective tools to model interactions between economic activities and the natural environment. This tool was developed by Wassily Leontief in the late 1930s with a subsequent recognition with a Nobel Prize in Economics in 1973.

The constructed UK MRIO model in this chapter is based on the existing model developed by Stockholm Environmental Institute (SEI). The existing model is represented with its full input-output data in supply and use format whereas the four world regions (UK, EU, non-EU OECD, and rest of world) are represented by their domestic and import transaction matrices. Imports to the UK are distinguished by region and by destination to intermediate and final demand. SEI's model is in the detail of 178 economic commodity sectors. Wiedmann et al. (2010) gives detailed explanations to the method and data used to build the model. The framework used for the UK-China MRIO is presented in Table 29.1.

China is the world largest manufacturer and the UK is one of the main destinations of Chinese exports. Hence, it is worthwhile to give some attention to the material flows between the UK and China. We pulled out China from the "rest of world" in the SEI model and use multilateral trade data to link between the UK and other regions. However, the Chinese input-output data are available in most disaggregated sectoral details (2002) with 122×122 sectors. The most recent table is for the year 2005 with the format of 42×42. In order to perform the research in the best way, we update the 2002 table to the year 2005 with the sectoral detail of 122×122 sectors by using the 2005 42×42 table as a benchmark. Furthermore, we disaggregated Chinese input-output tables into 178×178 sectors with RAS balancing techniques. RAS is a widely used method for updating an input-output table over a certain time period; the basic method is described in Miller and Blair (1985).

3.2 Material flow analysis

The principle concept underlying material flow analysis (MFA) is a simple model interrelating the economy and the environment where the economy is an embedded subsystem of the environment. Material flow accounting and analysis is an approach to determine the flow of materials through the economy. The inputs to the system are raw materials, water and air extracted from the natural system, which are then transformed into products and finally reemitted to the natural system as outputs in the form of waste and emissions. The total input equals the total output plus

Table 29.1 Multi-regional input-output (MRIO) system used for the present study

	Intermediate demand					Final demand					Total output
	UKu	Region e	Region o	Region c	Region w	UKu	Region e	Region o	Region c	Region w	
UKu											
Region e											
Region o											
Region c											
Region w											
Primary inputs											
Total inputs											
Factor inputs (environmental loads)											

Legend: UK$_u$ (United Kingdom), Region e (OECD Europe countries, Austria, Belgium, Czech Republic, Denmark, Finland, France, Germany, Greece, Hungary, Iceland, Ireland, Italy, Luxembourg, Norway, Poland, Portugal, Slovak Republic, Spain, Sweden, Switzerland, Turkey, United Kingdom), Region 0 (OECD non-Europe countries (superscript o) (Canada, Mexico, United States, Australia, Japan, Korea, New Zealand), China$_c$ (China), Region w (non-OECD countries except China = rest of the world).

net accumulation of materials in the system. Thus, the increasing global environmental problems such as climate change, the loss of biodiversity, or desertification that are associated with waste generation and emissions are directly related to the scale of material input. As the level of current global resource use is already unsustainable, any increase in material consumption in developing countries for ensuring an equitable quality of life must be compensated by a subsequent decrease in resource use by industrialized countries.

MFA provides a direct quantitative measure of the actual material flows through an economy. It quantifies the linkage of human activities and environmental problems and serves as a system-wide diagnostic procedure related to environmental problems, supports the planning of adequate management measures, and provides for monitoring the efficacy of those measures. MFA allows early warning and supports precautionary measures. It detects problem shifting between regions and sectors. MFA provides aggregated information to support decision- making. It can be applied at different levels of economic activity.

The main shortcomings of MFA are the aggregation of different qualities of material flows to derive aggregated indicators and the weak links between MFA indicators and environmental impacts. Big material flows dominate all indicators and bias interpretations of aggregated results. Aggregated MFA indicators can, to a large extent, be dominated by only one material category, which can lead to misinterpretations of results, as detailed information on developments of other material groups or economic sectors is diluted or obscured. The collection and interpretation of MFA data, therefore, should always be carried out on a level that disaggregates economic sectors and/or material groups.

Using input-output methodologies, the material flow accounts capture the mass balances in an economy, where inputs (the weight of domestically extracted raw materials, water, air, and imports) equal outputs (the weight of domestic consumption, exports, waste, and emissions). All materials used in production and consumption are taken into account – called "used materials." In addition to used material extraction, this also includes estimates on unused extraction, i.e., overburden from mining activities and unused residuals of biomass extraction, which refers to "unused materials." The total amount (used + unused materials) is referred to as "total materials" in this chapter.

3.3 Data on material flow accounting

Since the beginning of the 1990s, when the first material flow accounts on the national level were presented, MFA has been a rapidly growing field of scientific interest, and major efforts have been undertaken to harmonize methodological approaches developed by different research teams. In international working groups on MFA, standardization for accounting and analysing material flows on the national level was achieved and published in methodological guidebooks by EUROSTAT (2007) and the OECD (2007b). In many EU and OECD countries, MFA is already part of the official environmental statistics reporting system. MFA data also are available for an increasing number of emerging and developing countries (see OECD, 2007a).

A large and increasing number of material flow studies are available from national and international statistical offices, environmental agencies, and research institutions (see OECD, 2007b). The first global dataset (covering 188 countries) in a time series of 1980 to 2002 was compiled by Sustainable Europe Research Institute in EU-funded projects (see www.materialflows.net, and Behrens, Giljum, Kovanda & Niza, 2007) following the nomenclature and categorization of materials listed in the handbook for economy-wide material flow accounting published by the Statistical Office of the European Union (EUROSTAT, 2001). This international database (currently available up to 2006) on natural resource extraction is mainly based on international statistics from the International Energy Agency, the Food and Agricultural Organisation of the United Nations, the British Geological Survey, the United States Geological Survey, and the German Federal Institute for Geosciences and Natural Resources (see Giljum et al., 2004 for details). In total, the database comprises 267 different material commodities from five material groups (fossil fuels, metal ores, industrial minerals, construction minerals, and biomass).

The MRIO table constructed for this chapter contains 178 economic sectors, which is one of the most disaggregated sectoral breakdowns in the world. Especially, the economic sectors such as the organic food production sector, FSC (Forest Stewardship Council) forestry sector and energy generation by different supply sources are separately disaggregated so that one can assess the impacts on biodiversity driven by the changes of consumption behaviors via material flow analysis.

3.3.1 Allocation of raw material extraction to industries in the IO table

For the MRIO-based calculation of material flows, the allocation of the material extraction data to economic sectors is a key decision, as detailed data of sectoral primary resource extraction and use is missing. However, if material extraction would strictly be allocated to the primary extracting sectors, based on OECD input-output data, only three aggregated material categories could be separated, in particular biomass, fossil fuels, and minerals. It is obvious that such an allocation would produce significant errors with regard to the composition of materials used in different sectors. Another approach, which allocates specific raw material inputs to those industries that serve as the main recipient of raw material inputs at the first stage of further processing also was identified as source of errors, as some countries export significant shares of their raw material extraction without previous processing. Table 29.2 summarizes the allocation scheme between the material flow data and the MRIO model.

Table 29.2 Allocation of MFA categories to economic sectors in UK–China MRIO model

Code	Sector	Material category	UK	EU27 (excl. UK)	OECD (non-EU)	China	RoW
1	Conventional growing of cereals, vegetables, fruits and other crops	Cereals, crops, fruits, vegetables, etc.	85.2%	85.2%	85.2%	90%	90%
2	Organic growing of cereals, vegetables, fruits and other crops		1.7%	1.7%	1.7%	1%	1%
3	Growing of horticulture specialties and nursery products		13.2%	13.2%	13.2%	9%	9%
4	Conventional farming of livestock (except poultry)	Grazing	99%	99%	99%	98.2%	98.2%
5	Organic farming of livestock (except poultry)		1%	1%	1%	1.8%	1.8%
8	Forestry, logging and related service activities (conventional)	Wood	99.4%	90%	99%	90%	99%
9	Forestry and logging and related service activities ('sustainable'/FSC)		0.6%	10%	1%	10%	1%
10	Fishing	Fish	100%	100%	100%	100%	100%
13	Mining of coal and lignite; extraction of peat	Coal, peat	100%	100%	100%	100%	100%

(Continued)

Table 29.2 (Continued)

Code	Sector	Material category	UK	EU27 (excl. UK)	OECD (non-EU)	China	RoW
14	Extraction of crude petroleum and natural gas and service activities incidental to oil and gas extraction, excluding surveying	Oil, gas	100%	100%	100%	100%	100%
15	Mining of uranium and thorium ores	Uranium	100%	100%	100%	100%	100%
16	Mining of iron ores	Iron ore	100%	100%	100%	100%	100%
17	Mining of non-ferrous metal ores, except uranium and thorium ores	Non-ferrous	100%	100%	100%	100%	100%
18	Mining and quarrying of stone, gravel, clays, salt, etc.	Other minerals	100%	100%	100%	100%	100%

Note: RoW stands for "rest of the world."

3.3.2 Indicators of material flows

In this chapter, we employ ten different materials: Food, Grazing, Wood, Fish, Coal and peat, Oil and gas, Uranium, Iron ore, Non-ferrous ores, and Construction and industrial minerals, as the indicators to assess the material flows between the UK and the world with special investigation between UK and China. Furthermore, we also classify the ten materials into two categories: "used extractions" and "total extractions." The category of used materials is defined as the amount of extracted resources that enters the economic system for further processing or direct consumption. All used materials are transformed within the economic system. Unused extraction refers to materials that never enter the economic system and, thus, can be described as physical market externalities. This category comprises overburden and parting materials from mining, by-catch from fishing, wood and agricultural harvesting losses, as well as soil excavation and dredged materials from construction activities. The total extractions include both used and unused extractions, which can be a more appropriate term to serve this chapter to evaluate the biodiversity impacts driven by consumption.

4. Results

In order to fulfill its production and final consumption needs, the UK in 2004 consumed 52,292 million tons of "used materials" in total. As shown in column of used materials in Table 29.3, the consumption of non-ferrous ore takes the dominating portion, 44,534 million tons, which accounts for 86 percent of the total materials consumption in the UK. Iron ores ranks the second largest raw material consumption, at 5,864 million tons, which accounts for 11 percent of the total. The rest, 3 percent, is shared among construction materials (1.56 percent), oil & gas (0.82 percent), coal & peat (0.4 percent), food (0.37 percent), grazing (0.31 percent), uranium (0.11 percent), wood (0.05 percent) and fish (less than 0.01 percent).

If we take the "unused materials" into consideration, UK's consumption of materials in 2004 will be more than doubled to 106,805 million tons, which indicates that the overburden from mining activities and unused residuals of biomass extraction is even higher than the actual consumption. The major contribution to the increase is from non-ferrous ore and iron ore consumption, which accounts for 86 percent and 10 percent of the total increase, respectively. The amount of unused materials of non-ferrous ore and iron ore consumption is 46,625 and 5,318 million

Table 29.3 Material consumption in the UK

	Used Materials		Unused Materials		Total Materials	
	MT	%	MT	%	MT	%
Food	192	0.37%	44	0.08%	236	0.22%
Grazing	164	0.31%	0	0.00%	164	0.15%
Wood	25	0.05%	4	0.01%	29	0.03%
Fish	1	0.00%	0	0.00%	1	0.00%
Coal & peat	212	0.40%	1366	2.51%	1578	1.48%
Oil & gas	427	0.82%	62	0.11%	490	0.46%
Uranium	60	0.11%	948	1.74%	1007	0.94%
Iron ore	5864	11.21%	5318	9.75%	11182	10.47%
Non-ferrous ores	44534	85.16%	46625	85.53%	91159	85.35%
Construction materials	814	1.56%	144	0.27%	959	0.90%
Total	**52292**	**100%**	**54513**	**100%**	**106805**	**100%**

tons, respectively (as shown in column "unused material" in Table 29.3). If we compare the figures with the amount of used materials, we can identify that for every ton of non-ferrous ore and iron ore consumed in the UK, 1.1 and 0.9 tons of ores would be waste/lost in the original mining sites, respectively, which would result in significant impacts on local environment and biodiversity. Furthermore, although the material consumption of uranium and coal and peat cannot drive significant increase of total material consumption due to their small portion of used consumption, their environmental/biodiversity impacts would be vast. As shown in Table 29.3, in order to deliver 60 million tons of uranium and 212 million tons of coal and peat to satisfy UK's production and consumption, 948 million tons of uranium and 1,366 million tons of coal and peat were left in the mining sites in the form of waste or residual. In the other words, every ton of uranium or coal and peat consumed in the UK would result in 15.9 or 6.5 tons of uranium or coal and peat waste or residual, respectively, where the mining activities occurred.

If we investigate the origins of the "used materials" consumed in the UK's production and consumption processes in 2004, it is almost entirely are imported (98.8 percent). Of the total amount of used materials consumed in the UK, 53 percent (27,713 million tons) is from non-EU OECD countries (e.g., US, Japan and Australia), 28.8 percent (15,055 million tons) is from the rest of world (e.g., developing countries without China), 16.2 percent (8,453 million tons) is from EU27, and is 0.8 percent from China (425 million tons).

If we take the "unused materials" into consideration, the total materials from other countries "flow" into the UK are 105,896 million tons, accounting for 99.2 percent of the UK's overall materials consumption. The imports from non-EU OECD countries are 60,037 million tons, which accounts for more than half of UK's total material use (56 percent). The rest of world ranks as the second largest total materials exporter to the UK, with 30,537 million tons (29 percent of total UK material consumption). EU-27 provides 14,515 million tons of materials to the UK (13 percent of material consumption) and China exports 806 million tons of total materials to the UK, which is about 1 percent of total UK material consumption.

As there are wide variations in the quantity and origin of these imports for different products, it is important to analyse them by individual material categories. Furthermore, these imports are driven by different actors in the UK. Hence, a breakdown of this analysis is presented for ten different material categories in the following sections.

4.1 Food

4.1.1 Used food materials consumption

In the year 2004, the UK economy consumed 192 million tons of materials in "Food," of which 35 percent – 68 million tons – is from its domestic production. Out of which, there are 56 million tons (29 percent) from EU27 countries; 48 million tons (25 percent) from the rest of world; 16 million tons (8 percent) from non-EU OECD countries and 4 million tons (2 percent) from China.

Of the 192 million tons of food materials consumed in the UK, the conventional growing of cereals, vegetables, fruits and other crops accounts for 91 percent; the organic growing of cereals, vegetables, fruits and other crops only accounts for 2 percent; and the growing of horticulture specialities and nursery products takes the rest, at a 7 percent share.

In 2004, the UK economy consumed 3,414 thousand tons of organic cereals, vegetables and fruits, of which one-third was grown in the UK, 37 percent was imported from other EU-27 countries, 18 percent from the rest of world, 10 percent from non-EU OECD countries, and 2 percent from China.

Figure 29.1 – "Food" – illustrates the major production sectors that are the major drivers to food materials consumption in the UK when accounting for both direct and indirect material consumptions. For example, crop production is responsible for 27 percent of food materials; food processing, including meat processing, fruit, oil and dairy products, are responsible for 26 percent; hotel and restaurant are responsible for 9 percent; livestock farming and wholesales and retails are responsible for 6 percent each; production of drinks and tobacco are responsible for 4 percent; and the rest, 22 percent, is consumed by all other sectors.

The left graph illustrates the origins of the ten materials consumed by the UK economy. The right graph illustrates the ten material consumption patterns by the top 20 material-intensive sectors in the UK's economy. Due to the scale of non-ferrous ores and iron ores consumption in the UK are significantly larger than other material indicators, a separated scale is used that is placed at the top of the figure.

4.1.2 Total food materials consumption

If we take the "unused materials" into consideration, the UK's food materials use will be 236 million tons, 23 percent more than it actually entered the economy (used materials). That is about 44 million tons of food materials being wasted during the planting and extraction process. In terms of material efficiency (used materials/total materials) of food materials, UK's material production is the lowest – 78 percent – which means that for every ton of food materials generated in the UK, only 78 percent can be used in economic purposes. The efficiency of the material imported from China and the rest of world figures are 81 percent, showing a large scale of biomass waste, mainly in developing countries.

4.2 Grazing

The UK economy consumed 164 million tons of materials in the "Grazing" category in 2004. Out of this, conventional livestock accounts for 99 percent and the rest (1 percent) is for organic livestock. Out of the total 164 million tons, 88 million tons is from its domestic production,

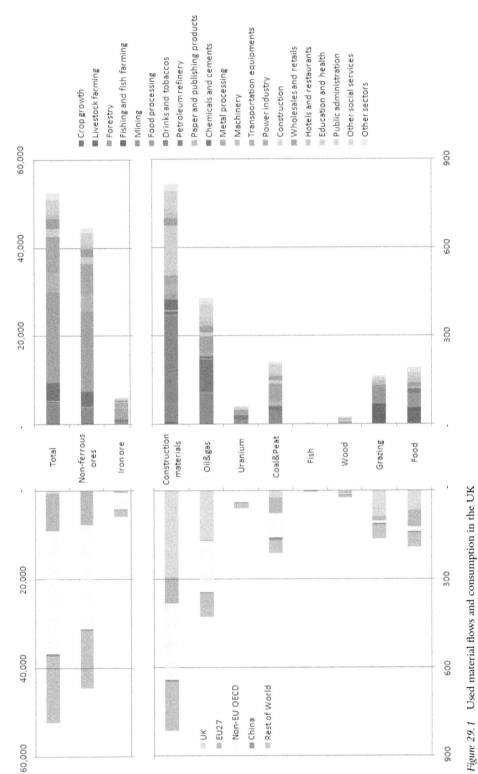

Figure 29.1 Used material flows and consumption in the UK

49 million tons (30 percent) from the rest of world, 15 million (9 percent) from EU-27 countries, 9 million tons (5 percent) from non-EU OECD countries, and 4 million tons (2 percent) from China.

Figure 29.1 – "Grazing" – illustrates the major production sectors that are the major drivers to grazing materials consumption in the UK when accounting for both direct and indirect material consumptions. The largest sector is livestock farming (39 percent), followed by food processing (28 percent, mainly for meat processing and dairy products), hotel and restaurant (9 percent), wholesales and retails (4 percent), and the rest, 20 percent, by all other sectors.

4.3 Wood

4.3.1 Used "wood" materials consumption

The UK economy consumed 25 million tons of materials in the "wood" category in 2004, of which 20 percent – 4.8 million tons – is from domestic resources. There are 9.6 million tons (39 percent) from the rest of world, 7.5 million tons (31 percent) from the EU-27 countries, 2.3 million tons (9 percent) from non-EU OECD countries, and 0.3 million tons (<1 percent) from China. Conventional forestry products account for 96 percent; sustainable forestry (e.g., FSC wood) only accounts for 4 percent of the total "used wood: material consumed in the UK.

In 2004, the UK economy consumed 996 thousand tons of FSC wood, of which 3 percent was grown in the UK, 81 percent was imported from other EU-27 countries, 10 percent from the rest of world, 3 percent from China, and 2 percent from non-EU OECD countries.

Figure 29.1 The largest sector is construction (17 percent), followed by paper and publishing products production (10 percent), forestry (17 percent), wholesales and retails' (5 percent), hotel and restaurant, education and health and public administration (4 percent each), production of drinks and tobacco'(4 percent), and the rest, 43 percent, by all other sectors.

4.3.2 Total "wood" materials consumption

If we take the "unused materials" into consideration, the UK's wood materials use will be 28.5 million tons, 21 percent more than actually entered the economy (used materials), which means that there are about 4 million tons of wood materials were wasted during the logging process. In terms of material efficiency (used materials/total materials) of wood materials, EU-27 material production is the lowest – 84 percent – which means every ton of wood materials generated in the UK, only 84 percent can be used in economic purposes. The efficiency of the wood logging in the UK as well as imported from China and the rest of world is 87 percent.

The wood materials consumed in the UK are mainly non-FSC produced, which would result in large-scale deforestation and biodiversity loss at the original sources. We've selected wood as an example to examine the biodiversity impacts in Chinese forestry sites driven by the consumption of wood material in the UK.

4.4 Fish

The UK economy consumed 1.1 million tons of materials in the "fish" category in 2004, of which more than two-third – 666 thousand tons – is from its internal sources. There are 254 thousand tons (23 percent) from the rest of world, 120 million tons (11 percent) from non-EU OECD countries, 57 thousand tons (5 percent) from the EU-27 countries, and 5 thousand tons (0.4 percent) from China.

If we account for both direct and indirect material consumptions via the whole production supply chain to investigate which production sectors are the major drivers to fish materials consumption in the UK, fishing and fish farming are the largest, with 28 percent of fish materials consumption, followed by food processing (28 percent), hotel and restaurant (20 percent), wholesales and retails (4 percent), and the rest, 20 percent, by all other sectors, as shown in Figure 29.1 – "Fish."

4.5 Coal and peat

4.5.1 Used coal and peat materials consumption

The UK economy consumed 211 million tons of materials in the "coal and peat" category in 2004, of which 12 percent (25 million tons) is extracted from its own sources, 81 million tons (38 percent) from non-EU OECD countries, 54 million tons (26 percent) from the EU-27 countries, 42 million tons (20 percent) from the rest of world, and 10 million tons (5 percent) from China.

If we account for both direct and indirect material consumptions via the whole production supply chain to investigate which production sectors are the major drivers to coal and peat materials consumption in the UK, the power industries are the largest, with 25 percent of coal and peat material consumption, followed by coal mining and other mining industries (19 percent), construction and wholesales and retails (6 percent each), hotel and restaurant, education and health and public administration (4 percent each), other social services (7 percent), and the rest, 21 percent, for all other sectors, as show in Figure 29.1 – "Coal and Peat."

4.5.2 Total coal and peat materials consumption

If we take the "unused materials" into consideration, the UK's coal and peat material use will be 1,578 million tons, about seven and half times more than actually entered the economy (used materials). This is about 1,366 million tons of coal and peat being wasted during the mining and extraction processes. In terms of material efficiency (used materials/total materials) of coal and peat materials, it is lowest in the non-EU OECD countries, with merely 11 percent, meaning that of every ton of coal and peat extracted in these countries for export to the UK, only 110 kg is being used for economic purposes. The efficiencies of the coal and peat extraction in the UK, EU-27 and the rest of world are 15 percent, 14 percent and 15 percent, respectively. Surprisingly, the efficiency in China for extraction of the coal and peat extraction is 57 percent, much higher compared with other countries.

4.6 Oil and gas

The UK economy consumed 427 million tons of materials in the "oil and gas" category in 2004, of which 39 percent (168 million tons) is extracted from its territory. There are 173 million tons (41 percent) from non-EU OECD countries, 83 million tons (19 percent) from the rest of world, 3.6 million tons (1 percent) from the EU-27 countries, and 0.2 million tons (less than 0.1 percent) from China.

If we account for both direct and indirect material consumptions via the whole production supply chain to investigate which production sectors are the major drivers to oil and gas materials consumption in the UK, the largest sector is petroleum refinery and nuclear fuel processing industries (26 percent), followed by extraction of crude oil and gas (23 percent), power industries (12 percent), wholesales and retails (5 percent), hotel and restaurant and public administration (4 percent each), construction and education and health sectors (3 percent each), other social services (6 percent), and the rest, 14 percent, by all other sectors, as show in Figure 29.1 – "Oil and gas."

4.7. Uranium

4.7.1 Used uranium consumption

The UK economy consumed 60 million tons of uranium in 2004, of which 65 percent (39 million tons) is from non–EU OECD countries (mainly from Australia), 19 million tons (32 percent) from the rest of world, 1 million ton (2 percent) from the EU-27 countries.

The largest driving sector is petroleum refinery and nuclear fuel processing industries (27 percent), followed by extraction of crude oil and gas (19 percent), power industries (14 percent), wholesales and retails and public administration (5 percent each), hotel and restaurant (4 percent), construction and education and health sectors (3 percent each), other social services' (7 percent), and the rest, 13 percent, by all other sectors.

4.7.2 Total uranium consumption

Taking the "unused materials" into account, UK's uranium use was 1,007 million tons in 2004, which is about 17 times more than it actually entered the economy (used materials). There is about 948 million tons of uranium raw materials being wasted during the mining and extraction processes. In terms of material efficiency (used materials/total materials) of uranium, EU-27 countries have the highest efficiency, which is 10 percent; for all other countries it is only 6 percent. That means for every ton of uranium generated for exporting to the UK in these countries, only 60 to 100 kg actually is being consumed in the UK.

4.8 Iron ores

4.8.1 Used iron ores consumption

The UK economy consumed 5,864 million tons of materials in the "iron ores" category in 2004, of which 100 percent is imported. The largest exporter is non–EU OECD countries with 3,722 million tons (64 percent), followed by the rest of the world (1,544 million tons, 26 percent), the EU-27 with 470 million tons (8 percent), and China with 128 million tons (2 percent).

If we account for both direct and indirect material consumption via the whole production supply chain to investigate the major drivers to iron ores materials consumption in the UK, the largest is metal processing industries (41 percent), followed by transportation equipment production sectors (15 percent), machinery production sectors (9 percent), chemicals and cements production industries (8 percent), mining sectors (7 percent), construction and wholesales and retails (4 percent each), health and education (2 percent), hotel and restaurant (2 percent), public administration (2 percent), other social services sectors (3 percent), and the rest 4 percent by all other sectors, as show in Figure 29.1 – "Iron ores."

4.8.2 Total iron ores consumption

If we take the "unused materials" into consideration, the UK's iron ores consumption will be 11,182 million tons, 90 percent more than actually entered the economy (used materials), which means that there are about 5,317 million tons of iron ores being wasted during the mining and extraction processes. In terms of material efficiency (used materials/total materials) of iron ores, it is lowest in non–EU OECD countries, with 53 percent, meaning that of every ton of iron ores generated for exporting to the UK, only 530 kg is actually exported and used for economic purposes in the UK. The efficiencies of the iron ores extraction in EU-27, China, and the rest of world are 63 percent, 53 percent and 58 percent, respectively.

4.9 Non-iron metal ores

4.9.1 Used non-iron ores consumption

The UK economy consumed 44,534 million tons of materials in the "non-iron ores" category in 2004, of which 100 percent is imported. There are 23,409 million tons (53 percent) from non-EU OECD countries, 13,093 million tons (29 percent) from the rest of world, 7,756 million tons (17 percent) from the EU-27 countries, and 274 million tons (less than 1 percent) from China.

If we account for both direct and indirect material consumption via the whole production supply chain to investigate which production sectors are the major drivers to non-iron ores consumption in the UK, the largest sector is processing industries (41 percent), followed by transportation equipment production sectors (15 percent), machinery production sectors (9 percent), chemicals and cements production industries (8 percent), mining sectors (7 percent), construction and wholesales and retails (4 percent each), health and education, hotel and restaurant and public administration (2 percent each), other social services sectors (3 percent), and the rest, 4 percent, by all other sectors, as seen in Figure 29.1 – "Non ferrous ores."

4.9.2 Total non-iron ores consumption

If we take the "unused materials" into consideration, the UK's non-iron ores consumption was 91,159 million tons in 2004, which is more than twice what actually entered the economy (used materials). This means that there are about 46,625 million tons of non-iron ores being wasted during the mining and extraction processes. In terms of material efficiency (used materials/total materials) of non-iron ores, it is lowest in non-EU OECD countries with only 46 percent, which means every for ton of non-iron ores extracted for exporting to the UK, only 460 kg can be actually used for economic purposes in the UK. The efficiencies of the iron ores extraction in EU-27, China and the rest of world are 63 percent, 53 percent, and 58 percent respectively. The environmental impacts at extraction sites are investigated in Section 3.2 together with iron ores.

4.10 Construction materials

4.10.1 Used construction materials consumption

The UK economy consumed 814 million tons of materials in the "construction materials" category in 2004, of which 292 million tons (36 percent) is from imports. There are 261 million tons (32 percent) from non-EU OECD countries, 167 million tons (21 percent) from the rest of world, 90 million tons (11 percent) from the EU-27 countries, and 4 million tons (less than 1 percent) from China.

If we account for both direct and indirect material consumption via the whole production supply chain to investigate the major drivers to non-iron ores consumption in the UK, the largest sector is quarry mining with 44 percent, followed by construction sectors (21 percent), machinery production and chemicals and cements production sectors (4 percent each), transportation equipment and wholesales and retails (3 percent each), health and education, hotel and restaurant and public administration (2 percent each), other social services sector (5 percent), and the rest, 9 percent, by all other sectors, as show in Figure 29.1 – "Construction materials."

4.10.2 Total construction materials consumption

If we take the "unused materials" into consideration, the UK's construction material consumption will be 959 million tons, 18 percent more than it actually entered the economy (used materials), which means that there are about 144 million tons of non-iron ores being wasted during the mining and extraction processes. In terms of material efficiency (used materials/total materials) of construction materials, UK material production is the lowest (78 percent). This means that every for ton of construction materials generated for exporting to the UK, only 780 kg can be actually exported and used for economic purposes in the UK. The efficiencies of the iron ores extraction in EU=27, non-EU OECD countries, China, and the rest of world are 89 percent, 89 percent, 95 percent, and 90 percent, respectively.

4.11 GHG emissions

In order to fulfill production and final consumption needs, the world produces 974 million tons of GHG emissions measured in CO_2 equivalent (CO_2e) terms. CO_2 emission is the major contributor to GHG emissions, which forms 76.1 percent of the total – 741 million tons. CH4 emission is the second largest among the six GHGs, which forms 14.4 percent of the total – 140 million tons CO_2e. N_2O forms 7.2 percent of the total – 70 million tons CO_2e. HFC forms 1.7 percent of the total – 17 million tons CO_2e. HFC forms 0.2 percent of the total – 2 million tons CO_2e. SF6 forms 0.3 percent of the total – 3 million tons CO_2e.

In terms of producer emissions accounting approach, the UK's production (excluding household emissions) generates 573 million tons CO_2e GHG emissions that account for 59 percent of the total. In order to produce UK's imports, EU-27 countries produce 122 million tons CO_2e GHG emissions that account for 13 percent of the total; non-EU OECD countries produce 123 million tons CO_2e GHG emissions that account for 13 percent of the total; China produces 16 million tons CO_2e GHG emissions that account for 2 percent of the total; and the rest of world produces 140 million tons CO_2e GHG emissions that account for 14 percent of the total.

If we take both direct and indirect effects to investigate which economic sectors are the major contributors to overall emissions – 974 million tons CO_2e – we find that the tertiary industry is responsible for almost half of the emission, while secondary industry is responsible for about 45 percent of the emissions, and primary industry takes the rest, at less than 10 percent responsibility for the emissions. If we look in detail about the specific sectors in tertiary industry, as shown in Figure 20.2, the wholesales and retails sector is responsible for 8 percent of total emissions; construction, hotel and restaurant, education, and health and public administration are responsible for 5 percent of the total emissions each; and other services sector (e.g., banking and finance) is responsible for 11 percent of total emissions. In contrast, among the secondary industry, the power generation sector is responsible for 10 percent; petroleum production and chemicals and cements production sectors are responsible for 5 percent each; metal processing and products and the transportation equipment production sectors are responsible for 4 percent each; the electrical and electronics and machinery production sectors are responsible for 3 percent each, and the other industrial sectors is responsible for 11 percent. In primary industry, the agriculture and mining sectors are responsible for 5 percent and 4 percent, respectively.

Of the 573 million tons of CO_2e GHG emissions generated in the UK, 29 percent or 164 million tons is produced due to other countries' consumption (e.g., embedded in the UK's exports). Of the 122 million tons of CO_2e GHG emissions generated in the EU-27 countries, 21 percent or 26 million tons is discharged in order to produce necessary goods and services to fulfil the UK's exports production. Similarly, of the 123 million tons CO_2e GHG emissions generated in

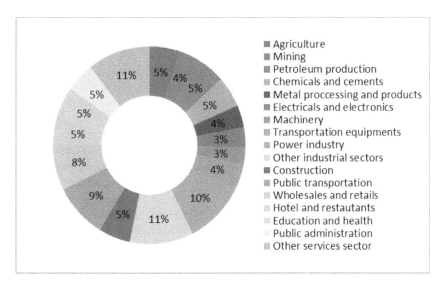

Figure legend:
■ Agriculture
■ Mining
■ Petroleum production
▨ Chemicals and cements
■ Metal proccessing and products
▨ Electricals and electronics
▨ Machinery
▨ Transportation equipments
▨ Power industry
▨ Other industrial sectors
■ Construction
▨ Public transportation
▨ Wholesales and retails
▨ Hotel and restautants
▨ Education and health
Public administration
▨ Other services sector

Figure 29.2. Main economic sectors to contribute GHG emissions

the non-EU OECD countries, 29 percent or 36 million tons is generated in order to produce necessary goods and services to fulfil the UK's exports production. Of the 16 million tons CO_2e GHG emissions generated in China, 15 percent or 3 million tons is generated in order to produce necessary goods and services to fulfil the UK's exports production. Of the 140 million tons CO_2e GHG emissions generated in the rest of world, 21 percent or 30 million tons is generated in order to produce necessary goods and services to fulfil the UK's exports production. Thus, of the total – 974 million tons of CO_2e GHG emissions generated to sustain UK's economic activities – 27 percent or 259 million tons are generated for UK's export production to fulfill other countries' consumption.

Nevertheless, the majority of the emissions is generated to satisfy the UK consumers' needs. If we account for UK's GHG emissions from consumer emissions accounting approach (GHG footprints), the UK is responsible for 716 million tons of CO_2e GHG emissions in 2004. The population in the UK is approximately 59.87 million in 2004. Therefore, the UK's per capita GHG footprint is 16 tons CO_2e in 2004.

5. Environmental impacts of China–UK material trade

5.1 The impact of UK coal consumption to China's environment

Natural resources, having a direct relation to biodiversity, are the primary and key inputs for China's economic production as well as industrialization. A total of 95 percent of China's energy and 80 percent of industrial and agricultural raw materials are provided by natural resources. However, significant pollution and other environmental impacts have been left in the mining sites during the materials mining processes.

In order to sustain rapid economic growth, China produces on average six billion tons of mining ores per year. China is the third largest mining ores production country but the largest country in terms of consuming iron ores, making China a topper in production of pig iron around the globe. China's mining activities have left huge amounts of pollution (e.g., air pollution, land contamination, and water pollution) and caused local ecological crisis (Hu, 2009). The wastewater discharged after coal or other non-metal ores mining usually contains large amounts of heavy metals and other toxic materials, which is directly released to freshwater bodies to contaminate both surface and underground water (Hu, 2009). Furthermore, mining activities have occupied and damaged large amount of cultivated land. The cumulative contaminated land caused by mining activities reached 36 million hectares by 2005, which is about 30 percent of total Chinese cultivated land. The contaminated land due to heavy metal pollution is 25 million hectares, in which 3 percent (0.7 million hectares) are so seriously contaminated that they would not be suitable for cultivation activities (Hu, 2009).

China's economic production and consumption largely rely on coal. From extraction to combustion, every step in the process of using coal damages the environment. For example, coal extraction produces water, air and noise pollution, as well as impacts on aquifers, water systems, and land. The spread of coal dust, as well as other environmental problems, occurs with coal transportation. Damages from coal combustion include air pollution resulting from dust, NO_X, sulfur oxides (SO_X), CO_2, and mercury. These pollutants can cause respiratory disease and seriously impact public health. A recent report – "The true cost of coal" – released by Greenpeace, states that the environmental and social costs associated with China's use of coal came to RMB1.7 trillion – that's about 7.1 percent of the nation's GDP in 2005. Further, more than 31,000 coal miners in China died from accidents down the mines between 2000 and 2006.

Air pollution is caused by extraction process, transportation, and combustion. In the extraction process, large amount of coal bed gas (e.g., methane) are released. According to the National Development and Reform Commission, the emissions of coal bed gases reached 15.33 billion cubic meters in 2005, in GHG terms equivalent to the emission of 220 million tons of CO_2. Solid waste such as coal gangue is an important by-product during extraction and washing coal. The spontaneous combustion of gangue emits large amounts of toxic and harmful gases such as SO_2, CO_2, and carbon monoxide (CO), which negatively affects biodiversity and has human consequences. According to statistics from the State Administration of Coal Mine Safety (2006), there are 1,500 spoil tips of coal gangue, with 389 long-term self-igniting ones, leading to serious pollution of the surrounding area and harm to the health of local residents, even resulting in deaths (Zhang, 2005).

Further, there are about 6,000 coal storage sites in China, most without any anti-dust facilities. This not only leads to a loss of coal resources but also pollution. It is estimated that 10 million tons of coal dust are wasted each year for this reason (Mao, Sheng & Yang, 2008). Coal extraction and washing also are water-intensive processes. The extraction of coal from the ground could result in a drying up of groundwater and a lowering of the water table (Mao et al., 2008), which is a prospective threat to future generations and the regular working of ecosystem services. Of the 96 major state-owned coal mines, 71 percent face water shortages and 40 percent have a serious shortage of water. The damage to water resources is particularly serious in the major coal production areas of Shanxi, Shaanxi, and the western part of Inner Mongolia, leading to irreversible losses (Mao et al., 2008). Washing one ton of coal generally uses four to five cubic meters of water. Some 40 million cubic meters of water are used to wash coal every year (Zhang, 2005). The wastewater from coal washing contains a large amount of slime, mud, sediment, and heavy metals (Liu, 2004), which further contaminates original water bodies, leading to negative impacts on biodiversity and regular human needs.

The extraction and processing of coal produces a large amount of coal gangue, which is one of the largest sources of solid waste in China, occupying a large area of land for a long period of time. It also leads to air and water pollution, destroying large amounts of arable land. The weight of coal gangue produced each year is equivalent to 10 percent of coal extracted. In 2006, 1,600 coal gangue heaps in China, which is equal to a total of 4.2 billion tons of gangue, occupied

173-thousand hectares of land – increasing at the rate of 70 million tons and 200 hectares of land every year (Zhao, 2007).

Weber et al. (2008) argued that at least one-third of Chinese carbon emissions are due to export production, which OECD countries accounted for 60 percent. Although the UK only accounts for 3 percent of total Chinese exports (National Bureau of Statistics, 2009), its production and consumption activities would have certain impacts on the Chinese environment.

6. Conclusion

Mining activities usually leave significant amounts of waste and emissions in the local environment where the materials are produced. In order to satisfy production and consumption activities in the UK, 107 billion tons of natural raw materials was either consumed or wasted at mining sites globally in 2004, while 974 million tons of CO_2e GHG emissions was produced.

The consumed materials by the UK economy were mainly provided not by itself but by other countries, for example, non-EU OECD countries (53 percent) and the rest of the world countries (29 percent). From our results, the consumed materials by the UK economy from China only accounted for 1 percent of the total. However, the real figure might be larger as our model is not a full multiregional model, which can only capture the intermediate material flows between China and UK but not China with the other countries. In other words, the UK imported large amounts of material-intensive products from EU and non-EU OECD countries (e.g., the US and Canada), which may be produced in China and other developing countries. A step forward would be to consider trade between UK, China, and other trade partners from where China imports raw materials, for example Africa.

The overall purpose would be to learn how to work in a triangle that links resource providers, manufacturers, and end consumers in a sustainability context through dialogue and cooperation based on both theoretical and quantitative evidence of social-economic and environmental performance.

References

Behrens, A., Giljum, S., Kovanda, J., & Niza, S. (2007). The material basis of the global economy: world-wide patterns of natural resource extraction and their implications for sustainable resource use policies. *Ecological Economics*, 64(2), 444–453.

Burns, T. J., Byron, L. D., & Kick, E. L. (1997). Position in the world system and national emissions of greenhouse gases. *Journal of World-Systems Research*, 3(3), 432–466.

Burns, T. J., Kick, E. L., & Byron, L. D. (2003). Theorizing and rethinking linkages between the natural environment and the modern world system: deforestation in the late 20th century. *Journal of World-Systems Research*, 14(2), 357–390.

Burns, T. J., Kick, E. L., Murray, D. A., & Murray, D. A. (1994). Demography, development and deforestation in a world-system perspective. *International Journal of Comparative Sociology*, 35(3–4), 211–239.

Chase-Dunn, C. (1975). The effects of international economic dependence on development and inequality: a cross-national study. *American Sociological Review*, 40, 720–738.

Chase-Dunn, C. (1998). *Global Formation: Structures of the World-Economy*. Lanham, MD: Rowman & Littlefield.

Chase-Dunn, C., & Hall, T. D. (1997). Ecological degradation and the evolution of world-systems. *Journal of World-Systems Research*, 3, 403–431.

Chen, Q., Kang, C., Xia, Q., & Guan, D. (2011). "Primary Exploration on Low-Carbon Technology Roadmap of China's Power Sector." *Energy*, 36(3), 1500–1512.

Ciccantell, P. S. (2009). China's economic ascent and Japan's raw-material peripheries. In H.-F. Huang (Ed.), *China and the Transformation of Global Capitalism*, pp. 109–129. Baltimore, MD: John Hopkins University Press.

EUROSTAT. (2001). *Economy-Wide Material Flow Accounts and Derived Indicators. A Methodological Guide.* Luxembourg: Statistical Office of the European Union.

EUROSTAT. (2007). Economy-wide material flow accounting – a compilation guide. Compiled by Weisz, H. et al., *IFF Institute for Social Ecology.* Luxembourg: Statistical Office of the European Union.

Frey, R. S. (1995). The international traffic in pesticides. *Technological Forecasting and Social Change*, 50, 151–169.

Giljum, S., Behrens, A., Jölli, D., Vogt, K., Kovanda, J., Niza, S., et al. (2004). *Material input data for the GIN-FORS model: Technical Report.* Vienna: Sustainable Europe Research Institute.

Hu, Z. (2009). China's 20 years' land reclamation and ecological reconstruction. *Review and Forward Looking Science & Technology Review,* 27(17), xx.

Kentor, J. (1981). Structural determinants of peripheral urbanization: the effects of international dependence. *American Sociological Review*, 46, 201–211.

Kentor, J. (2001). The long term effects of globalization on income inequality, population growth, and economic development. *Social Problems*, 48, 435–455.

Kick, Edward L., Davis, Byron L., Burns, Thomas J., & Gubin, Oleg I. (1995). "International Multiple Networks in World-System Approaches." In M.G. Everett and K. Rennolls (eds.) *International Conference on Social Networks*, Vol. 3, pp. 237–248. London: Greenwich University Press.

Liu, C. (2004). Theory and practice of cost and price of coal for sustainable development. In *Collection Of Theses from 2004 High Level Forum.* World Health Organisation: Geneva.

Liu, Z., Geng, Y., Lindner, S., & Guan, D. (2012). "Uncovering China's greenhouse gas emission from regional and sectoral perspectives." *Energy*, 49(1), 1059–1068.

London, B., & Smith, D. A. (1988). Urban bias, dependence, and economic stagnation in noncore nations. *American Sociological Review*, 55, 454–463.

Mao, Y., Sheng, H., & Yang, F. (2008). *The True Cost of Coal.* Amsterdam: Greenpeace International.

Miller, R. E., & Blair, P. D. (1985). *Input-Output Analysis: Foundations and Extensions.* Englewood Cliffs, NJ: Prentice-Hall.

Mol, A. P. J. (2011). Chinas ascent and Africa's environment global environmental change. *Human and Policy Dimensions*, 21(3), 785–794.

National Bureau of Statistics. (2009). *China Statistical Yearbook 2009.* Beijing: China Statistics Press.

OECD. (2007a). *Measuring Material Flows and Resource Productivity. Inventory of Country Activities.* Paris: Organisation for Economic Co-operation and Development.

OECD. (2007b). *Measuring Material Flows and Resource Productivity. The OECD guide.* Paris: Organisation for Economic Co-operation and Development.

Roberts, J. T., & Grimes, P. (1997). Carbon intensity and economic development 1962–91. *World Development*, 25, 191–198.

Skocpol, T. (1977). Wallerstein's world capitalist system: a theoretical and historical critique. *American Journal of Sociology*, 82(5), 1075–1090.

Smith, D. A. (1996). *Third World Cities in a Global Perspective: The Political Economy of Uneven Urbanization.* Boulder, CO: Westview Press.

State Administration of Coal Mine Safety. (2006). *China Coal Industry Year Book.* Beijing: China Coal Industry Publishing House.

Timberlake, M., & Kentor, J. (1983). Economic dependence, overurbanization and economic growth: a study of less developed countries. *The Sociological Quarterly*, 24, 489–507.

Wallerstein, I. (1974). *The modern World System I: Capitalist Agriculture and the Origins of the European World-Economy in the Sixteenth Century.* New York: Academic Press.

Wallerstein, I. (1979). *The Capitalist World-Economy.* Cambridge: Cambridge University Press.

Weber, C. L., Peters, Glen P. , Guan, D., & Hubacek, K. (2008). The contribution of Chinese exports to climate change. *Energy Policy*, 36(9), 3572–3577.

Wiedmann. T., R. Wood, J. Minx, M. Lenzen, Guan, D., & Harris, R. (2010). A climate footprint time series of the UK – results from a multi-region input-output model. *Economic System Research*, 22(1), 19–42.

WWF. (2006). Living Planet Report 2006. Switzerland: WWF International.

York, R., Rosa, E., & Dietz, T. (2002). Bridging environmental science with environmental policy: plasticity of population, affluence, and technology. *Social Science Quarterly*, 83(1), 18–34.

30

ENERGY AND ENVIRONMENTAL POLICY IN KOREA

Suduk Kim and Yungsan Kim

1. Introduction

On August 15, 2008, the Korean government announced with great fanfare an initiative to reduce 30 percent of greenhouse weighted potential (GWP) greenhouse gas (GHG) emissions by 2020. The initiative, named the Low Carbon Green Growth Initiative, also was publicly declared before international society at the Copenhagen COP 15.[1] Numerous follow-up policy measures have been prepared in short order. The Presidential Committee on Green Growth was established in January 2009 and started to prepare the framework act on this initiative.

Massive R&D support for conventional and renewable energy technology development is to be provided with the announcement of the 3rd Master Plan for New and Renewable Energy Technology Development and Promotion (2008–2030). A legal framework for Low Carbon Green Growth also was provided by the enactment of the Framework Act on Low Carbon, Green Growth on January 13, 2010. Many of the existing energy- and environment-related legislation acts were subordinated under the new framework, including the preexisting framework act on energy. Policy measures such as GHG and Energy Target Management (June 2009), enactment of the Smart Grid Law (November 2011), Green Building Support Law (February 2012), and the legislation on the allocation and trading of GHG emissions (May 2012) followed.

The idea of cleaning up the environment and fighting global warming is universally embraced. It is for the good of the whole human race. Especially those industries that benefit from the generous government support of R&D and subsidies for renewable energy eagerly welcome policy measures to implement the idea. Realization of the goals, however, also requires restriction of business activities in conventional quarters of the economy to varying degrees. It could be in the form of new taxes or new regulations. Such measures are not popular and may even face strong resistance from the stakeholders affected by them. These measures are the real challenges that put the government's will and skill to accomplish the goals to the test. In this period of economic difficulty, does the government have the will to push the environmental agenda before economic stimulation? Does it have the skill and the public support to overcome any social conflicts caused by the restrictive measures?

There are several studies that examine the effects of various policy measures. For example, Kim (2011) discusses the environmental impact of the energy sector and the potential energy tax reform. Oh et al. (2012) applied a computable general equilibrium (CGE) model to assess the economic impact of technological development and the introduction of a revenue-neutral carbon tax for GHG reduction. Lim (2011) tried to find the major issues of climate convention-related negotiations drawn from CGE model simulation results. Lim et al. (2012) provided a simulation result that shows that real GDP can grow without increasing CO_2 emissions when R&D subsidies are combined with a carbon tax. But we also need to ask if those policy measures will be effectively implemented. It is still too early to answer this question, when most of the policy measures have been just introduced or have yet to take effect.

By examining the legal framework, the governance structure and the details of the policy measures adopted so far, however, we may at least be able to get a glimpse of their potential and the government commitment toward the announced goals. Recent trends are not very promising; GHG emissions are fast increasing. The legislation on the allocation and trading of GHG emissions has been under controversy ever since the Korean National Assembly passed a law to start a carbon emissions trading scheme from January 2015. The Presidential Committee on Green Growth has maintained a low profile since the inauguration of the new president. In this chapter, we provide our assessment of the Korean environment and energy policies and discuss the problems and challenges.

The remainder of the chapter is organized as follows. Section 2 provides an overview of the Korean economy, GHG emissions and energy. Section 3 explains the tasks and policy measures to combat climate change from the perspective of mitigation measures. In this section, detailed discussions on three major mitigation policies, namely, GHG emissions reduction, renewable energy promotion and energy efficiency improvement, are discussed. Especially for GHG emissions reduction and renewable energy promotion policies, GHG and energy target management, emissions trading system, the introduction of a carbon tax and feed-in tariff, renewable portfolio standard, and renewable fuel standard are discussed in detail. This section assesses the achievements so far and discusses the problems, including the challenges for the future. Section 4 concludes the chapter.

2. Overview of the Korean economy, GHG emissions and energy

With the per capita GDP increasing from less than 100 USD in 1960 to 20,757 USD in 2011, Korea has transformed itself from one of the poorest countries into the 15th largest economy of the world during the last 50 years. But recently, economic growth has been sluggish, with the annual growth rate dipping below three percent. In the energy sector, the average annual growth rate for primary energy consumption since 1998 is 3.53 percent, with renewable energy growing at 10.61 percent.

Figure 30.1 shows the major economic indicators of Korea since 1990. During that period of time, GDP per capita increased 3.57 times, and primary and final energy consumption increased 2.96, and 2.74 times, respectively. With the increasing consumption of energy, GWP GHG emissions also increased. Figure 30.2 shows how GWP GHG emissions increased during the same period. It is easily seen that the GHG emissions pattern closely matches the economic activity and the energy consumption patterns. Especially during the Asian financial crisis that hit Korea severely in 2008, both energy consumption and GHG emissions decreased drastically. Except for that period of time, both energy consumption and GHG emissions kept increasing continuously. The difference between total and net GWP GHG emissions from the figure is explained by GHG absorption from land use, land-use change and forestry.

Figure 30.3 shows the composition of GHG emissions sources. The energy sector has been more than 80 percent of GHG emissions sources except the two years of 1995 and 1996, with its weight of 85.3 percent in year 2010. The recent trend of continuously increasing weight of the

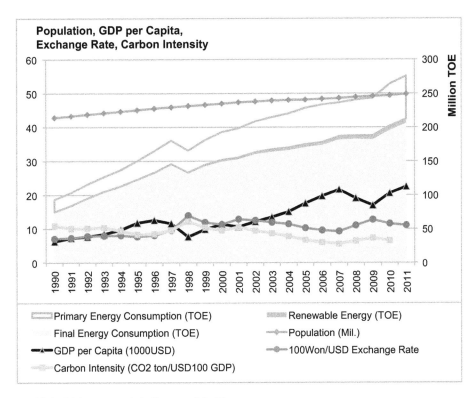

Figure 30.1 Major economic indicators of the Korean economy
Source: KEEI (2012a).

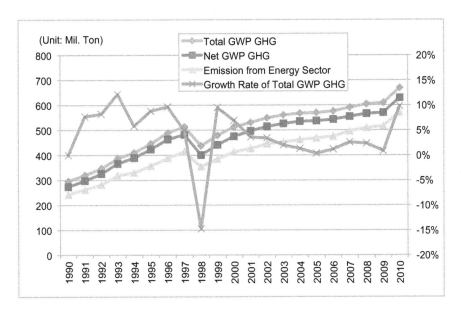

Figure 30.2 Global warming potential GHG emissions trend
Source: GIR (2012).

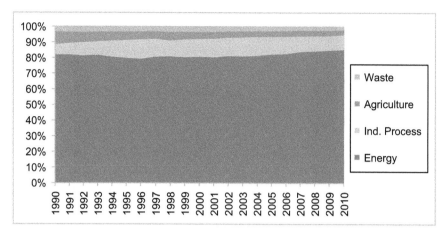

Figure 30.3   GWP GHG emissions by sources

Source: GIR (2012).

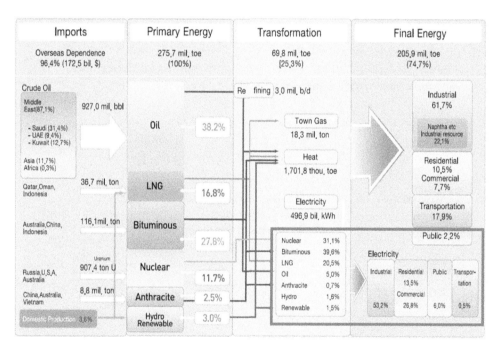

Figure 30.4   2011 energy balance flow

Source: KEEI (2012b).

energy sector in GHG emissions since 1996 is noteworthy. Industrial process, whose weight is gradually declining, also is related to the energy sector in terms of GHG emissions, since it utilizes non-energy petroleum products such as naphtha, asphalt, lubricant, wax residue, etc.

Figure 30.4 summarizes the significance of electricity in Korea's energy sector in the 2011 energy balance flow. The electricity sector is shown in the lower right corner. Korea depends on imports for 96.4 percent of the total primary energy supply. Out of 275.7 MTOE of total primary energy supply, 38.2 percent is comprised of oil. After going through the transformation process, electricity accounts for 19.01 percent of the total final energy of 205.9 MTOE. A further examination reveals, however, that 38.9 percent of primary energy sources are consumed to generate this expensive final energy of electricity. As depicted in the figure, the industrial sector consumes 53.2 percent of the power supply, while commercial and residential sectors consume 26.8 percent and 13.5 percent, respectively.

3. Legal framework and government organizations

3.1 Politics and environmental policy trends

Korea's environmental awareness grew with its political democratization. After decades of dictatorship backed by the military, Korea reached full-fledged democracy in 1998, with the election of the opposition leader Kim Dae-Jung as the president.

Although there has been environment-related legislation before, it can be said that real attention to the environment was first paid during President Kim's government (1998–2002). The main policy objective of his "Government of the People" was to overcome the economic difficulties resulting from the Asian currency crisis, which hit the Korean economy in mid-1997. In addition to economic restructuring to cope with these difficulties, his government also focused on the welfare of the people suffering from severe socioeconomic transition in the crisis. Of his top ten policy priorities, the eighth was "to create a hospitable environment and comfortable culture." That included the promotion of a pleasant natural environment (forestry, pollution-free metropolitan areas, water and coastal ocean) and care of the home land (waste reduction, eco-friendly industry, conservation with development). Within the framework of economic restructuring, his government emphasized energy conservation and increased energy supply capacity.

The next president, Roh Moo-Hyun (2003–2007), mostly focused on issues arising from the unbalanced development of urban and rural areas, cooperation among north-eastern Asian countries and the reunification of the Korean peninsula. His policy of balanced economic development naturally paid attention to sustainable development in both energy and environment issues. Stable energy supply, water management, management of national territory and ecosystem, etc. advanced by the presidential committee on sustainable development could be regarded as the major environmental policy process adopted by his government.

President Lee Myung-Bak (2008–2012) emphasized the market economy to mobilize human capital and promote the "future growth engine for next generations." Under the motto of "Global Korea," his government listed projects such as an eco-friendly economy, energy diplomacy, northeast Asian oil hub, climate change and energy, the development of ecological parks and a grand canal, and active protection of people from various disasters. His environmental policy was highlighted when he announced a national GHG emissions reduction plan of Low Carbon Green Growth on August 15, 2008. This initiative aims to reduce by 30 percent GWP GHG emissions by 2020 based on the business-as-usual energy forecast scenario. This target is the highest of the GHG-reduction recommendations for developing countries by the Intergovernmental Panel on Climate Change. The Presidential Committee on Green Growth was established in January 2009 and started to prepare the framework act on this initiative.

To promote this program, and at the same time to develop a future growth engine, his government opened offices for climate change response policies in most of the government ministries. Massive R&D support for conventional and renewable energy technology development was announced in the 3rd Master Plan for New and Renewable Energy Technology Development and Promotion (2008–2030). A legal framework for Low Carbon Green Growth also was provided by the enactment of the Framework Act on Low Carbon, Green Growth on January 13, 2010. The preexisting framework act on energy was subordinated to this new act. The introduction of GHG and energy-target management was confirmed (June 2009), and the enactment of a smart grid law (November 2011), green building support law (February 2012), and the legislation on the allocation and trading of greenhouse gas emissions (May 2012) followed. The legislation on the allocation and trading of greenhouse gas emissions caused great controversy since the Korean National Assembly passed a law to start a carbon emissions trading scheme from January 2015.

Although President Lee's policies seem to have very clear targets on the environment and energy sectors, the actual policy implementation by his government has been exactly the opposite. The energy sectors of gas and power remained in the public sector without introducing market competition.[2] A smart grid demonstration project was initiated without allowing retail competition. Energy conservation always has been a hollow claim without any proper energy policy attached. Policy adjustment of the adaptation and mitigation actions among the major ministries, especially between the Ministry of Environment and the Ministry of Knowledge Economy (currently, Ministry of Industry, Trade and Energy), was not properly managed. Figure 30.1 clearly shows the result of such policy ambivalences: during his government, total energy consumption has increased faster than during other governments. As a result, the energy sector's proportion of GHG emissions increased.

The current president, Park Geun-Hye, who was inaugurated in February 2013, presented five national policy targets, with major focus on employment and welfare issues arising from the sluggish economy. The new motto is "Creative Economy," and a brand-new Ministry of Science, ICT and Future Planning has been ordained to handle this goal. Her government's environmental policy is well stated in the 4th policy target of "the society with security and harmony." Prevention of disaster from the fields of air, marine, nuclear, energy supply system, and the systematic management of environmental damage are proposed. At the same time, existing environmental policies for mitigation and adaptation continue to be observed since her policy targets clearly include GHG emissions reduction, active response to climate change, stable energy supply and the promotion of renewable energy to achieve a pleasant and sustainable environment.

It is still too early to assess the energy and environmental policy of the current government. Detailed plans for future nuclear power promotion, renewable energy promotion targets, and restructuring of the current energy price system are discussed in the 2nd National Energy Master Plan announced in January 2014. Since the environmental policy pursued by the previous government has backfired in various aspects, it is not clear whether the basic principle of the framework act on low carbon green growth will survive in this government. The fact that the Presidential Committee on Green Growth co-chaired by the prime minister has been demoted to a committee under the prime minister's office does not bode well for such prospects.

Most environmental policy issues can be discussed within the framework of adaptation and mitigation. The following sections attempt to explain Korean environmental policy within this framework in conjunction with the governance structure based on currently identifiable policies.

3.2 Legal framework for environmental policies

As already noted in the discussion on the governmental and environmental policy changes, the environment-related legal framework is not well organized. It is not easy to identify all the laws and acts of Korea regarding the environment, either. Tables 30.10 and 30.11 in the Appendix of

Environment Related Legislation, each with the Ministry of Environment (ME) as the office in charge (total of 52) and with other ministries as the office in charge (total of 66), have been prepared based on the 2012 white paper on the environment by ME. Environment-related laws enacted before 1990 include Water Supply & Waterworks Installation Act (Dec. 31, 1961), Waste Cleaning Act (Dec. 30,1961), Environmental pollution Prevention Act (Nov. 5, 1963), Act on Poison and Deleterious Material (Dec. 13, 1963), Sewerage Act (Aug. 3, 1966), Act on the Protection of Birds, Mammals & Hunting (Mar. 30, 1967), Environmental Conservation Act (Dec. 31, 1977), Compound Waste Treatment Corporation Act (Dec. 30, 1979), Natural Park Act (Jan. 4, 1980), Environmental Pollution Prevention Corporation Act (May 1, 1983), and Waste Management Act (Dec. 31, 1986).[3]

Brief examination of the two tables would reveal that the environment-related legislation acts are extremely complicated with vast areas of overlapping jurisdictions. Also, legal experts point out that they take the form of over-delegation. They take the form of a separate law system, overlapping in its contents with other environmental regulations, sometimes even contradicting them. They usually take a regulator-oriented framework and excessively depend on direct regulation. As such, they are criticized to be inefficient and unrealistic. According to Koh (2012), the introduction of an integrated environmental law is necessary to protect the environment more efficiently. Integration and harmonization of environmental laws are said to generate a simpler process, more transparent potential for deregulation, and stronger environmental protection. From this perspective, the enactment of the Framework Act on Low Carbon, Green Growth on January 13, 2010, is notable. The legislative intent of this framework act is written in article 1 as "to promote the development of the national economy by laying down the foundation necessary for low carbon, green growth and by utilizing green technology and green industries as new engines of growth, so as to pursue harmonized development of the economy and environment and to contribute to improvement of the quality of life of every citizen and to a mature, top-class, advanced country that shall fulfill its responsibility in the international community through the realization of a low-carbon society." It intends to integrate all of the existing legislation on sustainable economic development and the quality of the environment as a framework act and to ordain all future legislation within its framework.

Caution is required in referring to the categorization of environment-related laws in the two tables, since it was prepared by ME, which mostly focuses on adaptation policy. However, this is the only currently available document on the summary of related legislation.

3.3 Current government structure

The Ministry of Strategy and Finance (MOSF) announced the government organization of the new government on March 2, 2013. Table 30.1 summarizes the names of ministries and their major affiliations, with acronyms.

For a better understanding of the organizational structure, an organization chart is prepared in Figure 30.5. MSIP and MOF are newly established ministries while major adjustment of jurisdiction has been made for several ministries such as MOE, MOFA, MOSPA, MAFRA, MOTIE and MOLIT as noted with bold boxes in this figure. MSIP, a newly established ministry ordained to manage science, ICT and future planning, has jurisdiction over vast areas of the government. A lot of science- and technology-related jurisdictions of the previous government have been moved to this ministry from the National Science and Technology Commission, Ministry of Science and Education, Ministry of Knowledge Economy, Ministry of Security and Public Administration and Ministry of Culture, Sports and Tourism. MOF is newly established to

Table 30.1 Acronyms of the ministries and their major affiliations

	Name of the Ministry		Major Affiliations
		PS	Presidential Secretariat
		PMO	Prime Minister's Office
		NHRCK	National Human Rights Commission of Korea
		NIS	National Intelligence Service
		KCC	Korea Communications Commission
MOSF	ministry of strategy and finance	NTS	National Tax Service
		NCS	Korea Customs Service
		PPS	Public Procurement Service
		NSO	National Statistics Office
MSIP	ministry of science, ICT & Future Planning		
MOE	ministry of education		
MOFA	ministry of foreign affairs		
MOU	ministry of unification		
MOJ	ministry of justice	SPO	Supreme Prosecutors' Office
MND	ministry of national defense	MMA	Military Manpower Administration
		DAPA	Defense Acquisition Program Administration
MOSPA	ministry of security and public administration	NPA	National Police Agency
		NEMA	National Emergency Management Agency
MCST	ministry of culture, sports and tourism	CHA	Cultural Heritage Administration
MAFRA	ministry of agriculture, food and rural affairs	RDA	Rural Development Administration
		KFS	Korea Forest Service
MOTIE	ministry of trade, industry and energy	SMBA	Small and Medium Business Administration
		KIPO	Korean Intellectual Property Office
MW	ministry of health and welfare		
ME	ministry of environment	KMA	Korea Meteorological Administration
MOEL	ministry of employment and labor		
MOGEF	ministry of gender equality and family		
MOLIT	ministry of land, infrastructure and transport	MACCA	Multifunctional Administrative City Construction Agency
MOF	ministry and oceans and fisheries	KCG	Korea Coast Guard

Source: English websites of ministries and affiliations.

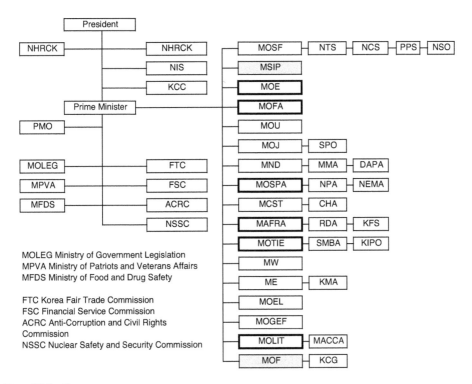

Figure 30.5 Current government structure

Note: Adjustment of jurisdiction has been made for the ministries within bold boxes.

Source: MOSF (March 23, 2013).

combine the marine and fishery jurisdictions that used to be separately managed by Ministry of National Territory and Ministry of Agriculture and Food.

Among the ministries with major jurisdiction adjustment, MOFA is redesigned to focus on foreign affairs by transferring its role on trade policy and administration to MOTIE, while MOTIE has to give up most of its technology-related jurisdictions to MSIP. There has not been much jurisdictional adjustment for ME.

3.4 Environmental policy and government organization

As was noted earlier, the Framework Act on Low Carbon Green Growth puts the prime minister's office at the top of energy and environmental policy coordination. This had been previously managed by the Presidential Committee on Green Growth co-chaired by the prime minister. Figure 30.6 shows the structure of this organization.

As the main government sector for environmental policy, the Ministry of Environment manages the following major environmental policies:

- Green growth,
- Water quality and water ecosystem,
- Water supply, sewerage, soil and groundwater,

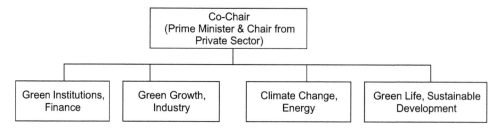

Figure 30.6 Organization of Presidential Committee on Green Growth

Source: Available at https://www.greengrowth.go.kr/.

- Waste and recycling,
- Territorial and natural environment,
- Air pollution and climate change, and
- International cooperation.

Especially for the GHG emissions reduction management, KMA, an affiliate of ME, is to monitor and forecast climate change. The Greenhouse Gas Inventory and Research Center of Korea, established in June 2010 as the premier research institute for climate change, is designated as a think-tank for low-carbon green growth, playing the role of an information hub of comprehensive and efficient greenhouse information management to accelerate green growth. It currently operates the integrated electronic administration of the national greenhouse gas management system.

Environmental policies can be divided into two broad categories: mitigation and adaptation. Mitigation involves reducing the magnitude of climate change itself and can be subdivided into two alternative strategies: emissions reductions (dealing with the problem at its very source), and geo-engineering (attempting to offset the climate changes themselves through other means, for example carbon capture and sequestration, of human intervention in the climate system). Adaptation, by contrast, involves efforts to limit our vulnerability to climate change impacts through various measures, while not necessarily dealing with the underlying cause of those impacts (See Figure 30.7).[4]

For the adaptation to climate change, the Korean government (2010) announced the sectors for adaptation and assigned the ministries in charge as is shown in Figure 30.7. Overall coordination of adaptation measures is to be conducted by the Ministry of Environment. Most of the government ministries and agencies are to cooperate for adaptation measures; for example, ME is to work for adaptation sectors such as health, water management, ecosystem, climate change monitoring, forecast and industry adaptation, energy with MW, MOLIT, MAFRA, MOE, KMA, and MOTIE.

The Ministry of Trade, Industry and Energy[5] is to set policy directions on industry, trade and energy. For energy policy directions, it lists four main policy goals, namely:

- Manage the national energy supply – prevention of accidents
- Promote overseas energy development projects
- Implement environmentally responsible growth policies
- Combat climate change

This is a slight change in policy directions from the previous MOTIE's policy target of "securement of stable energy supply for sustainable economic development." For "combat

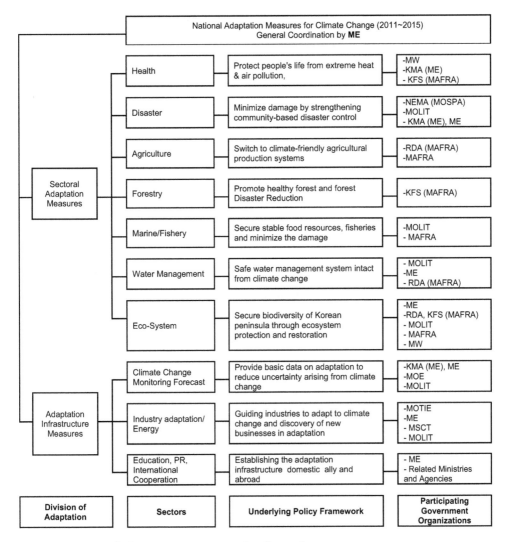

Figure 30.7 National adaptation measures to combat climate change

Source: Recompiled based on the Government of Korea (2010).

Note: Names of ministries are based on the previous government and the organizational chart has not been revised, yet.

climate change," the policies of establishment of a carbon market, promotion of voluntary agreement to reduce greenhouse gas emissions, and support for research and development pertaining to green technologies are newly included in addition to the existing energy policies such as energy conservation, efficiency improvement and renewable energy promotion with the reduction of the reliance on fossil fuels. For "reduction of GHG emissions from the energy sector," energy sources such as renewable energy and nuclear power are promoted. At the same time, rational energy utilization and energy conservation policy is mandated for the industry, building and transportation sectors.

For "promotion of renewable energy," a penetration target of 11 percent by 2030 has been set and a renewable portfolio standard has been adopted since 2012, with additional support for its supply and technology development through R&D. For "energy conservation," an efficiency improvement target of 46 percent by 2030 has been set and follow-up energy demand management policy will be administered.

As discussed, most of MOTIE's policies are geared toward mitigation actions. Adaptation actions, such as the prevention of accidents in the process of managing national energy supply, however, also are explicitly mentioned.

Table 30.2 shows the mitigation policies, measures and instruments with their key constraints or opportunities combined with the current government organizations potentially to participate. The selection of the government organizations is subjectively made based on the explanation in the column "Policies, measures and instruments shown to be environmentally effective" and current jurisdictions of the Korean government organization. For most of the mitigation policies, measures and instruments that require incentive structures based on government budget, MOSF is expected to participate. At the same time, sectors such as energy supply, transport, building and industry are clearly under the jurisdiction of MOTIE. Other sectors such as agriculture, forestry/forests and waste would expect the participation of MAFRA, KFS, PPS (MOSF), MOLIT and ME.

It is interesting to note here that there has been an acute dispute between MOTIE and ME for both defining their roles in the actual implementation of climate change related measures and understanding the importance of mitigation or adaptation policy. ME by its nature puts emphasis on adaptation, while MOTIE focuses on mitigation. While implementing adaptation measures such as the installation of a monitoring system at industrial chimneys for air pollution detection, ME may think that these measures are within its own realm of policy implementation. But MOTIE, which is in charge of the industry and has its own office for climate change, may think differently.

4. Tasks and policy measures to combat climate change

The laws and government organizations explained in the previous section have produced many policy measures and action plans. Discussions in the previous section indicate that environmental policy for adaptation measures covers a wide range of socioeconomic issues and would not be easy to cover here. Instead, it would be better to focus on the environmental policy for mitigation actions. Mitigation actions can be broadly divided into three categories by their strategic goals: GHG emissions reduction, renewable energy promotion and energy efficiency improvement. This section explains the details of these policies and plans.

4.1 GHG emissions reduction

4.1.1 GHG and energy target management

The GHG and energy target management program is a hands-on approach for select large energy users that together account for about 60 percent of the total GHG emissions. It sets specific goals for their emissions reduction, energy savings and energy efficiency enhancement and then monitors their progress. The program was announced in 2009 and a pilot program was launched with 48 energy-intensive companies in 2010. The official program took effect in March 2011, starting with 410 largest companies or plants and gradually expanding the target companies. Table 30.3 shows the schedule and the criteria for selecting the target companies.

ME, MAFRA, MOTIE and MOLIT are in charge of the program's implementation, with the Ministry of Environment playing the leading role. The implementation is both top-down and

Table 30.2 Key sectoral mitigation policies with potential government organizations to participate

Sector	Policies, measures and instruments shown to be environmentally effective	Key constraints or opportunities (Normal font = constraints; Italics = opportunities)	Government organizations to participate
Energy supply	Reduction of fossil fuel subsidies; taxes or carbon charges on fossil fuels	Resistance by vested interests may make them difficult to implement	- MOTIE - MOSF
	Feed-in tariffs for renewable energy technologies; renewable energy obligations; producer subsidies	*May be appropriate to create markets for low-emission technologies*	- MOTIE - MOSF
Transport	Mandatory fuel economy; biofuel blending and CO2 standards for road transport	Partial coverage of vehicle fleet may limit effectiveness	- MOLIT - MOTIE - ME
	Taxes on vehicle purchase, registration, use and motor fuels; road and parking pricing	Effectiveness may drop with higher incomes	- MOSF - MOTIE - ME
	Influence mobility needs through land-use regulations and infrastructure planning; investment in attractive public transport facilities and non-motorized forms of transport	*Particularly appropriate for countries that are building up their transportation systems*	- MOLIT - MOTIE
Agriculture	Financial incentives and regulations for improved land management; maintaining soil carbon content; efficient use of fertilizers and irrigation	*May encourage synergy with sustainable development and with reducing vulnerability to climate change, thereby overcoming barriers to implementation*	- MAFRA - MOSF
Buildings	Appliance standards and labeling	Periodic revision of standards needed	- MAFRA - MSIP - MOE
	Building codes and certification	Attractive for new buildings. Enforcement can be difficult	- MAFRA - MOTIE
	Demand-side management programs	Need for regulations so that utilities may profit	- MOTIE - ME
	Public sector leadership programs, including procurement	*Government purchasing can expand demand for energy-efficient products*	- PPS (MOSF)
	Incentives for energy service companies (ESCOs)	*Success factor: access to third party financing*	- MOTIE - MOSF

(Continued)

Table 30.2 (Continued)

Sector	Policies, measures and instruments shown to be environmentally effective	Key constraints or opportunities (Normal font = constraints; Italics = opportunities)	Government organizations to participate
Industry	Provision of benchmark information; performance standards; subsidies; tax credits	May be appropriate to stimulate technology uptake. Stability of national policy important in view of international competitiveness	- MOTIE - MOSF
	Tradable permits	Predictable allocation mechanisms and stable price signals important for investments	- ME - MOTIE - MOSF
	Voluntary agreements	Success factors include: clear targets, a baseline scenario, third-party involvement in design and review and formal provisions of monitoring, close cooperation between government and industry	- ME - MOTIE - MOLIT
Forestry/forests	Financial incentives (national and international) to increase forest area, to reduce deforestation and to maintain and manage forests; land–use regulation and enforcement	Constraints include lack of investment capital and land tenure issues. *Can help poverty alleviation*	- KFS (MAFRA) - MOSF - MOLIT
Waste	Financial incentives for improved waste and wastewater management	*May stimulate technology diffusion*	- ME, MOSF
	Renewable energy incentives or obligations	Local availability of low-cost fuel	- MOTIE - MOSF
	Waste management regulations	Most effectively applied at national level with enforcement strategies	- ME

Source: Compiled based on IPCC (2007).

Table 30.3 Schedule of energy target management

Criteria	By the end of 2011		From Feb. 2012		From Jan. 2014	
	Company	*Plant*	*Company*	*Plant*	*Company*	*Plant*
By CO_2 (Ton)	125,000	25,000	87,500	20,000	50,000	15,000
By Energy (Tera Joules)	500	100	350	90	200	80
(TOE)	12,000	2,400	8,400	2,100	4,800	1,900
Expected Number of Target Companies or Plants	170	240	220	250	300	280

Sources: BIS, http://www.bsigroup.co.kr/, KEEI, http://www.keei.re.kr/keei/download/seminar/100831/ S2-1.pdf (in Korean).

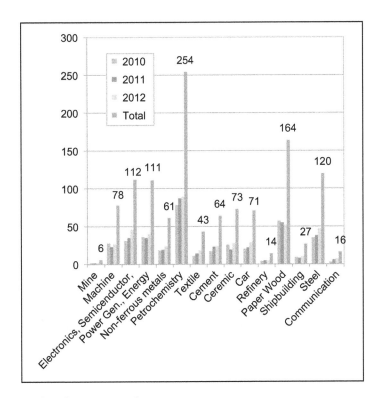

Figure 30.8 Number of companies under energy target management

Source: Green Business Projects, http://www.greencompany.or.kr/eng/main/main.aspx.

bottom-up. The reduction goals are first set at the national level, then at the sector level and finally at the industry level. Individual target companies and the ministry in charge negotiate the annual company-level reduction goals considering the company's investment plans, reduction potential and the upper-level reduction goals. Once the goals are set for the target companies, the ministry reviews their execution plans and monitors their progress. It also provides various financial and technical support. Figure 30.8 shows the number of companies selected for energy target management from 2010 to 2012 out of 15 different industrial sectors.

4.1.2 Emissions trading system

In May 2012, the Korean National Assembly passed a law to start a carbon emissions trading system (ETS) from January 2015, and the government announced its implementing ordinances in November 2012. The master plan was announced in January 2014 and the general rules on rights allocation, trading, certification, etc. was announced in September 2014.

Though enacting legislation for the ETS is all but finished, there are still controversies surrounding it. The business society is expressing concern about the impact on the economy and is requesting the government to consider delaying its introduction. It points to the recent global recession and the crisis in the European emissions trading market for the reasons. It also points out that even some of the advanced countries like the US, Japan, and the biggest emitter, China, do not have a national ETS yet and argues that the early adoption by Korea may jeopardize its competitiveness. It also demands that the free rights allocation period should be extended to beyond 2020.

But, as the seventh biggest emitter of CO_2 (in 2010), Korea recognizes its duty to contribute to the world's effort to reduce GHG, though it is not a signatory of the Kyoto Protocol. The government has already announced its goal of reducing GHG emission by 30 percent from business-as-usual by 2020. The proponents of ETS insist that it is the most cost-effective way of reducing emissions and that Korea should be the leader in the global effort to reduce GHG instead of waiting for others to act first.

The trading scheme will be cap-and-trade. The government first sets the emissions reduction goal at the national level for the planning period of ten years, with adjustment every five years. The goals at the sector level will be set next, followed by those of the industry level. Based on these goals, emissions caps are determined at the sector and industry levels, and finally emissions caps for individual companies are determined considering their past emissions levels and available technologies. ME is to be the primary government authority over this program. However, there are channels through which other ministries can be involved so that the interests of various sectors can be represented. One of such channels is the Emission Rights Allocation Committee in charge of the major issues on emission rights allocation and trading. The committee will be filled with the deputy ministers of the related ministries and chaired by MOSF. There are lower level committees such as the Allocation Review Committee and the Validation Committee, also to be filled with officials from various ministries.

The scheme will include all the sectors and industries covered by the energy target management program. Companies emitting more than 125,000 CO_2t/year and plants emitting 25,000 CO_2t/year are mandatorily included. Voluntary participation is allowed. Those who are included in the energy target management program are to be exempted. In the first stage of the program (2015–2017), 100 percent of the emissions rights will be allocated to individual companies for free. The proportion will go down to 97 percent for the second stage (2018 –2020) and to 90 percent or less afterwards. However, those industries determined to be export-intensive or highly affected by the scheme are to be granted free allocation. Figure 30.9 in the Appendix shows the implementation process of the ETS and Table 30.4 summarizes and compares target management and ETS.

4.1.3 Introduction of carbon tax

Korea does not have a carbon tax but has a transportation, energy and environment tax and a driving tax. These taxes are similar to the carbon tax in that they are added to transportation fuel prices, but they are not applied to other sources of GHG emissions. They are special purpose

Table 30.4 Comparison of energy target management program and emissions trading scheme

	Target Management	*ETS*
Goal Setting	National goal: 30% reduction against BAU by 2020 – goals by sectors and industries set in accordance with the national goal	
Measuring Reporting Verifying	Use the same system	
Operation mode	Command and control	Market mechanism
Planning interval	Single year	Multi-year (5 years)
Outsourcing	Not allowed	Allowed
Methods for attaining goals	Reduction only	Reduction + Rights purchase, borrowing, offsetting
Reward for over attainment	None	Rights sales or carry-over
Penalty level	10 million won max. (fixed)	Fines proportional to over-emission

Source: Prime Minister's Office, Nov. 13, 2012.

taxes, the revenue from which is earmarked for transportation- and environment-related purposes and those taxes on fuel prices are scheduled to expire by the end of 2015 after a series of consecutive extensions in 2009 and 2012. With the termination of these taxes approaching, in addition to the relatively simple tax structure of car-ownership-related taxes for potential tax system restructuring (HRI, 2010), the introduction of a carbon tax is being hotly debated in Korea. Proponents argue that these taxes should be replaced by a carbon tax with broader scope to address the plan for GHG reduction. It also seems to appeal to politicians due to its wider tax base, which can more than make up for the tax revenue reduction due to the termination of the existing taxes. The opponents, mostly from the business sector, argue that a carbon tax would impose too much burden on the Korean economy considering Korea's energy-intensive industrial structure. They argue that a new carbon tax in addition to other existing energy taxes and the new emissions trading system would impose double taxation on Korean industry and so would weaken its competitiveness.[6]

4.2 Renewable energy promotion

4.2.1 Feed-in tariff

Korea introduced a feed-in tariff (FIT) for renewable energy generation in 2002. The program gradually expanded coverage until it was terminated and replaced by the renewable portfolio standard (RPS) in 2012. It applied to such renewable energy generation as photovoltaic, wind, hydro, bioenergy, waste combustion, ocean energy and fuel cell. It supported these renewable energies by purchasing the generated power at very generous prices above the market price to cover the high cost. The purchase prices were guaranteed for 15 years (20 years optional for photovoltaic). However, there were limits for total coverage applied to photovoltaic, wind, and fuel cell at 500MW, 1000MW, and 50MW, respectively. Tables 30.5 and 30.6 show the guaranteed prices. No new support is to start after 2011. For reference, the average wholesale price for electricity in 2011 was KRW 126.63 /kWh.

Table 30.5 FIT support for renewable energy production (2009)

Energy source		Capacity criteria	Category		Guaranteed price (Won/kWh) Fixed	Guaranteed price (Won/kWh) Variable*	Annual adjustment
Wind		≥ 10kW	–		107.29	–	–2%
Hydro		≤ 5MW	usual	≥ 1MW	86.04	SMP+15	
				< 1MW	94.64	SMP+20	
			special	≥ 1MW	66.18	SMP+ 5	
				< 1MW	72.8	SMP+10	
Waste combustion (including RDF)		≤ 20MW	–		–	SMP+ 5	
Bioenergy source	LFG	≤ 50MW	≥ 20MW		68.07	SMP+ 5	
			< 20MW		74.99	SMP+10	
	Biogas	≤ 50MW	≥ 150kW		72.73	SMP+10	
			< 150kW		85.71	SMP+15	
	biomass	≤ 50MW	lignocellulose		68.99	SMP+ 5	
Ocean energy	Tide	≥ 50MW	max gap	w/ dike	62.81	–	
			≥ 8.5m	w/o dike	76.63	–	
			max gap	w/ dike	75.59	–	
			< 8.5m	w/o dike	90.5	–	
Fuel cell		≥ 200kW	biogas fuel		227.49	–	–3%
			other fuel		274.06	–	

Source: MKE (2008).

★ SMP: System marginal price in Korean wholesale power market.

Table 30.6 FIT support scheme changes for photovoltaic power generation (Won/kWh)

Start year	Install place	Support period (yr)	≤ 30kW	> 30kW ≤ 200kW	> 200kW ≤ 1MW	> 1MW ≤ 3MW	> 3MW
2009	–	15	646.96	620.41	590.87	561.33	472.7
		20	589.64	562.84	536.04	509.24	428.83
2010	Land	15	566.95	541.42	510.77	485.23	408.62
		20	514.34	491.17	463.37	440.2	370.7
	Building	15	606.64	579.32	546.52	–	–
		20	550.34	525.55	495.81	–	–
2011	Land	15	484.52	462.69	436.50	414.68	349.20
		20	439.56	419.76	396.00	376.20	316.80
	Building	15	532.97	508.96	480.15	–	–
		20	483.52	461.74	435.60	–	–

Source: MKE (2009).

4.2.2 Renewable portfolio standard

The RPS program started in 2012 to replace the existing FIT program. Power generation companies with over 500MW capacity are to supply a certain amount of electricity generated with renewable energy. Currently 13 companies have this duty. The aggregate renewable proportion is to increase gradually from two percent in 2012 to a maximum of ten percent in 2022. The generation quantity for each company is individually determined considering total generation and the energy source. Special favor is given to photovoltaic generation with a separate target quantity to be distributed to the participating companies. Also different weights are assigned to different renewable energy sources considering their effects on the environment and the economy, generation cost and GHG reduction. The renewable generation supported by FIT is not eligible for RPS.

The participating companies can generate the renewable electricity themselves or purchase renewable energy certificates (REC) from others. Or they can put off up to 20 percent of their annual assignment to the next year.[7] To encourage private sector participation, the six affiliates of KEPCO should outsource at least 50 percent of photovoltaic generation. REC's are traded in the Korea Power Exchange for one day every month.

During the first year of RPS implementation in 2012, 842 MW of renewable generation capacity was newly added, which is impressive compared with the 1024 MW cumulative installed capacity during the ten years prior to RPS. On the other hand, however, only 64.7 percent of the annual generation target was fulfilled. For photovoltaic, it was 95.7 percent but for others it was 63.3 percent. As a result, even after the allowed 30 percent carry-over,[8] many generation companies face fines. The total amount of the penalty is US23 million dollars.[9] The penalty determined is 1.31 times of the original estimation based on the unfulfilled obligation (597,889 REC, 9.03 percent) times average REC price (KRW 32,331 per REC) of non-PV. It is reported that the penalty will be finalized considering the conditions of the participant (see Table 30.7).

Table 30.7 Weights for power generation by renewable energy types

Renewable energy source	Weight	Details on Installation		
		Type	*Place*	*Capacity*
Photovoltaic	0.7	land	5 land types (farm land, forestry, etc.)	
	1		others	> 30kW
	1.2			≤ 30kW
	1.5	Building or other existing structure		
Other renewables	0.25	IGCC, product gas		
	0.5	waste, land fill gas		
	1	Hydro, onshore wind, bioenergy, RDF, waste gasification, tide with dike		
	1.5	Lignocellulosic biomass power generation, offshore wind (within 5 km)		
	2	Offshore wind (over 5km), tide w/o dike, fuel cell		

Source: MOTIE (2010).

4.2.3 Renewable fuel standard

Korea is also to introduce a renewable fuel standard (RFS). In June 2013, the National Assembly passed an amendment to the Renewable Energy Development, Utilization and Promotion Act to introduce RFS for transportation fuels from 2014 to 2020 in three stages. Since 2012, Korea has had a regulation that transportation diesel fuel should include at least two percent bio-diesel. The new law will gradually increase this ratio up to five percent by 2020. Also bio-gas and bio-ethanol will be included in the program from 2017 and 2020, respectively. Domestic oil-refining companies and oil importers bear the responsibility of meeting the RFS. According to a study, this new program is expected to reduce CO_2 emissions by 3 million to 3.8 million tons.[10] However, as of September 2013, the implementation of RFS is expected to be postponed due to the high dependence on imported bio-fuels.[11]

4.3 Energy efficiency improvement and other policy measures

In 2008, the government announced the 4th Master Plan for Rational Energy Use, which lays the groundwork for energy efficiency policies for 2008 to 2012.[12] It aims to improve energy efficiency by 11.3 percent by 2012 and 23.5 percent by 2017. It contains scores of policy initiatives in four areas: energy efficiency R&D, energy demand management, market creation and improvement, and social and regulatory infrastructure. Some of the initiatives are symbolic or look like slogans, such as green government buildings and promoting energy-saving life style, and some seem to be simply government wishes. For example, the government has not acted on the plan to revamp the electricity tariff structure yet although it has 100 percent control of the tariffs. However, other initiatives have substance involving specific actions. For instance, the plan to ban incandescent light bulbs from 2013 has actually been carried out.[13] Energy demand management plans apply to four sectors: industry, transportation, buildings, and the public sector (see Table 30.8).[14]

In 2010, 15 green energy technologies were selected for mid- and long-term energy technology targets. It clearly shows that PV, wind and fuel cell are strategically selected for future technology development targets among eight renewable energies and three new energies defined by law.[15] For the utilization of fossil fuel, it is noted that cleaner use of fossil fuel such as clean coal technology and integrated gasification combined cycle (IGCC) are explicitly mentioned for technology development in addition to carbon capture and storage (CCS) (see Table 30.9).

It is shown from the Table 30.9 that nuclear energy is categorized as clean energy production in Korea since it does not emit CO_2 in its power generation process. Nuclear power has been producing more than 30 percent of electric power since 1986. Korea, with very limited indigenous energy resources, has been heavily dependent upon nuclear power. It produced more than 40 percent of total electric power until as recently as 2006. After the 2011 Fukushima accident, however, with increasing concerns over nuclear safety and the fraud scandal in nuclear power plant construction and maintenance, a team of 58 from South Korea's nuclear safety agency inspected all 23 of the nation's nuclear plants in November 2012. As a result, the proportion of nuclear power generation dropped below 30 percent for the first time since 1986. Min et al. (2012) discusses the potential environmental issues of nuclear power in north-eastern Asian countries examining the seasonal wind directions and China's nuclear plans. With massive promotion plans of over 280GW nuclear power in China, including inland nuclear power plants and in areas potentially overlapping with seismic zones, any nuclear-related environmental issue could be a problem of all countries in this region, they argued.

Table 30.8 Summary of energy efficiency policies in 4th Master Plan for Rational Energy Utilization

Area	Sector	Policies	Office in Charge
Energy efficiency R&D	Core technology	Building energy efficiency system (BEMS) R&D	MOTIE, MOLIT
		Electricity use efficiency R&D	MOTIE
		Energy storage R&D	MOTIE
		Green Car R&D	MOTIE, MOLIT, ME
		LED R&D	MOTIE
	Application	7 top energy-intensive equipment R&D	MOTIE
		6 green home appliances R&D	MOTIE
Demand management	Industry	Expand support for energy clinic	MOTIE
		Customize energy policy for energy-intensive plants by size	MOTIE
		Expand Energy Saving through Partnership(ESP) program	MOTIE
		Tax and financial support for energy saving investments	MOSF, MOTIE
		Strengthen linkages between energy assessment and energy investment	MOSF, MOTIE
		Support energy service company(ESCO)	MOTIE
	Transportation	Improve fuel efficiency labeling	MOTIE
		Keep raising fuel efficiency standards	MOTIE
		Better support hybrid vehicle promotion	MOSF, MOSPA, MOTIE, MOLIT, ME
		Infrastructure for Eco-driving	MOTIE, MOLIT, ME
		Introduce energy-intensive transportation company reporting system	MOTIE, MOLIT, ME
		Promote 'no driving day' program	MOLIT
		Introduce new public transport	MOLIT
		Promote rail traffic	MOLIT
		Promote bicycle riding	MOSPA, MOLIT
		Eco-friendly and efficient airport, port, fishing boats	MAFRA, MOLIT
		Advanced logistics system	MOKIT

(Continued)

Table 30.8 (Continued)

Area	Sector	Policies	Office in Charge
	Buildings	Effective energy planning consulting	MOTIE, MOLIT
		Expand community energy service(CES) program	MOTIE
		Strengthen energy-saving building design standards	MOTIE
		Expanding building energy efficiency rating certification	MOTIE
		Expand green building supply	MOLIT, ME
		Introduce total building energy consumption design	MOLIT
		Expand voluntary agreement with energy-intensive buildings	MOTIE
		Smart meter program	MOTIE
	Public sector	Green government buildings	MOSPA
		Green governmental IT	MOSPA
		Promote regional energy program	MOTIE
		Total energy consumption cap for public buildings	MOTIE
Market creation and improvement	Market creation	Expand energy efficiency product certification	MOTIE
		Support promote high energy efficiency products	MOSF, MOTIE
	Market change	Home appliances energy efficiency 'Top-Runner" program	MOTIE
		Expand energy efficiency rating labeling	MOTIE
		CO_2 level in energy efficiency labels	MOTIE
	Market close	Expand minimum efficiency standard, ban incandescent light bulbs	MOTIE
		Standby power warning label	MOTIE
Social and regulatory infrastructure	Rational energy price structure	Electricity rate by voltage	MOSF, MOTIE
		Introduce dynamic pricing in electricity	MOSF, MOTIE
		Allow gas rate differences by consumption pattern	MOSF, MOTIE
		Optimal transportation fuel portfolio	MOSF, MOTIE
		Heat price cap by area	MOSF, MOTIE
		Incentive to reduce fuel cost for heating	MOSF, MOTIE
	Promote energy-saving life style	Promote energy saving and GHG reduction	MOTIE, MOLIT, ME
		Early education for energy saving	MOE, MOTIE
		Carbon points and carbon rebate program	ME, MOTIE

Source: Prime minister's office and Ministry of Trade, Industry, and Energy, press release, December 15, 2008.

Table 30.9 Green energy technologies

Clean Energy Production	PV, Wind, Hydrogen and Fuel Cell, IGCC, Nuclear
Cleaner Fossil Fuel	Cleaner Fuel, CCS
Energy Efficiency Improvement	Power Sector IT, Energy Storage, Small Co-generation, Heat Pump, Superconducting, Car Battery, Building Energy, LED

Source: MKE(2010).

4.4 Evaluation of tasks and policy measures

With numerous legislative and organizational preparations, Korea now has the institutional infrastructure for active environment and energy policies. However, this does not mean that it is committed to the environmental policy targets it has already announced. As discussed in Section 3.1, the government's stand toward the environment is affected by politics. Actual implementation of future environmental policies currently scheduled and expected, such as ETS and the introduction of a carbon tax, is still controversial and thus faces many uncertainties. A simple change in the governmental ordinance or a delay of scheduled programs can materially affect the effectiveness of these policies.

Closer examination of past policy implementation results provides some insight toward this. During the period of 2000 to 2010, carbon intensity dropped 3.76 percent and renewable energy supply increased by more than 10 percent, both in annual growth rate. However, primary energy and final energy consumption increased by 4.18 percent and 2.66 percent per annum, respectively. As a result, total CO_2 emissions increased by 2.67 percent per year. Especially during the period of 2005 to 2010, CO_2 emissions increased by 4.17 percent per year. This period overlaps with President Lee's government, which declared "Green Growth" as its top priority. The relative success of renewable energy promotion on the one hand and the fast increase of CO_2 emissions on the other imply a possible bias in policy implementation. The continuously high growth rate of renewable energy supply and lowering of carbon intensity suggest that future R&D support for technology development in the energy and environment sector will continue. Supporting new technology is popular and faces little objection. For continuous implementation of other measures, however, a major modification of policy measures is expected. First, the accomplishment rate of a renewable energy obligation target other than PV (Photovoltaics) for the first year of its introduction is only 63.3 percent. The postponement of implementation of RFS due to high dependence on imported bio-fuels is another recent policy change. Second, the accomplishment of a CO_2 emissions reduction target is rather uncertain. The emissions increase from 2011 to 2013, which is not yet officially publicized, in addition to the 17.6 percent emissions increase confirmed during the previous five years poses a serious threat to a successful target accomplishment. The CO_2 reduction policy faces strong resistance from the emitters and places an immediate burden on the whole economy. As a result, it may suffer from "not in my term" syndrome, passing its implementation to the next government and imposing ever-increasing burdens on future generations.

5. Conclusion

In this chapter, a brief survey on Korean environment and energy policy is presented. This overview provides information on the current status of the Korean economy, GHG emissions, and energy supply and demand structure. Review of the changes in the legal framework reveals the characteristics of the current environmental regulation system. It is isolated, overlapping in its contents with other environmental regulations and sometimes even contradictory to other regulations. The prospect of the current energy and environmental policy is still uncertain, although much of the environmental policy had been openly announced by the previous government.

To avoid the complexity of discussion, the chapter focuses on the tasks and policy measures to combat climate change from the perspective of GHG mitigation. So it offers more detailed examination of the three major categories of mitigation measures: GHG emissions reduction, renewable energy promotion and energy efficiency improvement. For GHG emissions reduction, GHG and energy target management, emissions trading system and carbon tax policy have been examined, while the examination of FIT, RPS and RFS are conducted for the renewable energy promotion policy. Again, the successful progress of these policy measures may depend on the new government's initiatives and surrounding economic conditions.

Obviously this review of Korean environment and energy policy is not only incomprehensive but also incomplete. Issues such as a better coordination framework for the adaptation and mitigation policies, which require the participation of most of the government organizations, collection of related information and analysis, could be an interesting topic for further investigation.[16]

Notes

1 15th Conference of Parties was held at Copenhagen on December 2009.
2 See Kim et al (2013) for current state of Korean electricity market liberalization.
3 Dates in parentheses denote those of enactment. For further details, refer to Appendix.
4 John A. Dutton, e-education, Adaptation vs. Mitigation, Department of Meteorology, Pennsylvania State University, https://www.e-education.psu.edu/meteo469/node/175.
5 http://www.motie.go.kr/language/eng/policy/Epolicies.jsp.
6 For further references on the discussions of carbon tax and restructuring of current energy and environment tax system, refer to Kang et al. (2011) and Kim (2011).
7 It is up to 30 percent until 2014.
8 Actual carry-over is 26.3 percent.
9 Based on the press release on Sept. 16. For prior estimation on this penalty, refer to MOTIE (2013). Won/dollar exchange rate of 1,100 applied.
10 These figures were presented by Lim, Eu-Soon at a public hearing organized by Ministry of Knowledge Economy on Feb. 2, 2013.
11 This view was expressed by a government officer who participated in a seminar organized by a National Assembly member on Sep. 11, 2013.
12 5th Master Plan is not out yet.
13 The ban is to take effect from 2014.
14 KEEI (2010) is a preliminary research paper published for the preparation of the 5th Master Plan for Rational Energy Utilization, although it was not officially adopted by government.
15 New and Renewable Energy Development, Utilization and Promotion Act, enacted on 2006 and recently amended on 2013.
16 Almost all independent activities for information gathering and research are being conducted by entities such as NSO under PMO, KEMCO (Korea Energy Management Corporation), KESIS (Korea Energy Statistics Information System, http://www.kesis.net/) of KEEI under MOTIE, KECO (Korea Environment Management Corporation), GIR, NGMS under ME, KMA under ME, KIER (Korea Institute of Energy Research) under MISP, KFS under MAFRA, MOLIT-related statistics (https://stat.molit.go.kr/) under MOLIT, etc.

References

GIR (Greenhouse Gas Inventory and Research Center of Korea) (n.d.), http://www.gir.go.kr.
GIR (Greenhouse Gas Inventory and Research Center of Korea) (2012), National Greenhouse Gas Inventory Report of Korea, Seoul, Korea (in Korean).

Government of the Republic of Korea (2010), Climate change adaptation measures according to the enactment of the framework act on low carbon, green growth 2011–2015.

Government of the Republic of Korea (2014), The 2nd Master Plan for National Energy (in Korean).

Green Business Projects (n.d.), Management of Targets for GHGs and Energy, http://www.greencompany.or.kr/eng/main/main.aspx.

HRI (Hyundai Research Institute) (2010), Recommendations for the Potential Carbon Tax Introduction to Domestic Car Industry, VIP Report, 10–23, Seoul, Korea.

IPCC (2007), IPCC Fourth Assessment Report: Climate Change, http://www.ipcc.ch/publications_and_data/ar4/syr/en/contents.html.

Kang, M.O., Kang, K.K. and J.W. Cho (2011), Introduction of the Carbon Tax and Reforming the Current Energy Tax System: The Case of Korea, Green Growth Research, 2011–07, Korea Environment Institute, Seoul, Korea.

KEEI (2010), Korea Energy Economics Institute, A Research for the 5th Master Plan for Rational Energy Utilization, Seoul, Korea (in Korean).

KEEI (2012a), Korea Energy Economics Institute, 2012 Yearbook of Energy Statistics, Seoul, Korea (in Korean).

KEEI (2012b), Korea Energy Economics Institute, Energy Info., Seoul, Korea.

Kim, S., Y. Kim and J.S. Shin (2013), The Evolution of the Korean Electricity Market. In *Evolution of Global Electricity Markets: New Paradigms, New Challenges, New Approaches*, ed. by Fereidoon Sioshansi, pp. 679–713, London: Academic Press.

Kim, S.-R. (2011), A Study on Policy Directions for Environmentally-friendly Energy Tax Reform in Korea, *Korean Energy Economic Review*, Vol. 10, No. 2, 143–167 (in Korean).

Koh, M-H. (2012), Development of Korean Environmental Law and Its Desirable Amendment Direction, *Korea Public Law Research*, Vol. 9, No. 3, 555–581 (in Korean).

Lim, J. K. (2011), Major Issues of Post-Kyoto Negotiation and Their Implications: An Economic Analysis by Using a CGE Model, *Environmental and Resource Economics Review*, Vol. 18, No. 3, 457–493 (in Korean).

Lim, J-S. and Y.-G. Kim (2012), Combining carbon tax and R&D subsidy for climate change mitigation, *Energy Economics* 34, S496-S502.

ME (Ministry of Environment) (2012a), Environmental Statistics Yearbook, Vol.1 & 2 (in Korean), Seoul, Korea.

ME (Ministry of Environment) (2012b), White Paper on the Environment, Seoul, Korea (in Korean).

Min, E., Y. Zhang, H.-G. Kim, and S. Kim (2012), Can China, Korea and Japan Avoid the Controversy Over Nuclear Energy, *The Journal of Energy and Development*, Vol. 37, No. 2, 143–178.

MKE (Ministry of Knowledge Economy) (2008a), The 3rd Master Plan for New and Renewable Energy Technology Development and Promotion (2008–2030), Seoul, Korea (in Korean).

MKE (Ministry of Knowledge Economy) (2008b), The 4th Master Plan for Rational Energy Utilization (2008–2012) (in Korean), Korea.

MKE (Ministry of Knowledge Economy) (2009), The Revised Guidance of the Operating Regulations on Renewable Energy Feed-in Tariff Support Schemes, Seoul, Korea (in Korean).

MKE (Ministry of Knowledge Economy) (2010), Energy Technology Development Plan, Seoul, Korea (in Korean).

MOSF (Ministry of Strategy and Finance) (2012), Press Release, Seoul, Korea (in Korean).

MOTIE (Ministry of Trade, Industry and Energy) (2010), Detailed Regulations on RPS, press release, Seoul, Korea (in Korean).

MOTIE (Ministry of Trade, Industry and Energy) (2013a), 2012 REC price for RPS, press release, May 17, Seoul, Korea.

MOTIE (Ministry of Trade, Industry and Energy) (2013b), White Paper on Industry and Trade, vol. 1 & 2, http://www.mke.go.kr/motie/in/pl/motiepaper/motiepaper.jsp.

NGMS (National Greenhouse Gas Management System), n.d. http://master.gir.go.kr/.

Oh, J.G. and G.L. Cho (2012), Economic Impact of Technological Development and Revenue Neutral Carbon Tax for GHG Reduction, *Environmental and Resource Economics Review*, Vol. 21, No. 2, 371–416 (in Korean).

Prime Minister's Office and Ministry of Trade, Industry, and Energy (2008), Press release, Dec. 15, Seoul, Korea (in Korean).

APPENDIX

Table 30.10 Enactment of environment-related legislation (ME as Office in Charge)

'60 (Total of 6 Acts)	'70~'80 (Total of 9 Acts)	'90~2012(Total of 52 Acts)	Office in charge
1 Environmental Pollution Prevention Act (Enacted on Nov.5,'63)	Environmental Conservation Act (Enacted on Dec.31,'77)	Framework Act on Environmental Policy	ME
2		Clean Air Conservation Act	ME
3		Framework Act on sustainable development	ME
4		Environmental Education Promotion Act	ME
5		Environmental Health Act	ME
6		Indoor Air Quality Management Act	ME
7		Noise & Vibration Control Act	ME
8		Foul Odor Prevention Act	ME
9		Special Act on Metropolitan Air Quality Improvement	ME
10		Water Quality and Ecosystem Conservation Act	ME
11		Act Relating to Han River Water Quality Improvement & Community Support	ME
12		Act on Nakdong River Watershed Management & Community Support	ME
13		Act on Geum River Watershed Management & Community Support	ME
14		Act on Yeongan & Sumjin River Watershed Management & Community Support	ME
15		Natural Environment Conservation Act	ME
16		Act on Special Measures for the Control of Environmental Offenses	ME

No.	Act	Former Act	Competent ministry
17	Environmental Dispute Adjustment Act		ME
18	Act on Antarctic Activities and Environmental Protection		MOFA, MOF, ME
19	Act to facilitate the purchase of eco-friendly products		ME
20	Act on Environment Related testing and inspection		ME
21	Environmental Improvement Expenses Liability Act		ME
22	Asbestos Damage salvation Act		ME
23	Asbestos Safety Act		ME
24	Act to promote and support the reuse of water		ME
25	Act to facilitate the purchase of green products.		ME
26	Artificial light pollution Prevention Act		ME
27	Natural Park Act	Natural Park Act (Enacted on Jan.4,'80) Act on the Protection of Birds, Mammals & Hunting (Enacted on Mar.30,'67)	ME
28	Special Act on the Ecosystem Conservation of Small Islands such as Dokdo Island		ME
29	Wetland Conservation Act		MOF, ME
30	Environmental Impact Assessment Act		ME
31	Soil Environment Conservation Act		ME
32	Act on the Protection of the Baekdu Daegan Mountain System		KFS
33	Wildlife Protection Act	(the Act on the left)	ME
34	National Trust Act on cultural heritage and natural environment assets		MOF, ME
35	Biodiversity Conservation and Utilization Act		ME

(Continued)

Table 30.10 (Continued)

	'60 (Total of 6 Acts)	'70~'80 (Total of 9 Acts)	'90~2012 (Total of 52 Acts)	Office in charge
36		Environmental Pollution Prevention Corporation Act (Enacted on May 1, '83)	Environmental Management Corporation Act	ME
37			Development of & Support for Environmental Technology Act	ME
38	Act on Poison and Deleterious Material (Enacted on Dec.13,'63)		Toxic Chemicals Control Act	ME
39			Persistent organic pollutant Management Act	ME
40	Waste Cleaning Act (Enacted on Dec.30,'61)	Waste Management Act (Enacted on Dec.31,'86)	Waste Control Act	ME
41			Act on the Disposal of Livestock Wastewater	ME
42			Act on the circulation of electrical, electronic products and automotive resources	ME
43			Act on the Control of Trans-boundary Movement of Hazardous Wastes & Their Disposal	ME
44			Act on the Promotion of Construction Waste Recycling	ME
45			Promotion of Waste Disposal Facilities & Assistance, etc. to Adjacent Areas Act	ME
46			Metropolitan Landfill Site Management Corporation Act	ME
47		Compound Waste Treatment Corporation Act (Enacted on Dec.30,'79)	Act on the Promotion of Saving and Recycling of Resources	ME
48	Sewerage Act (Enacted on Aug.3,'66)		Sewerage Act	ME
49	Water Supply & Waterworks Installation Act (Enacted on Dec.31,'61)	Water Supply & Waterworks Installation Act	Water Supply & Waterworks Installation Act	ME
50			Management of Drinking Water Act	ME
51			Special Act to Support 2012 World Conservation Congress	ME
52			Framework Act on Low Carbon, Green Growth	PMO, ME

Source: ME (2012) and Korea Legislation Research Institute, http://elaw.klri.re.kr/eng_service/main.do.

Table 30.11 Environment-related legislation (other than ME as Office in Charge)

	Name of Legislation	Sector	Office in charge
1	Road Traffic Act,	Air Pollution	SPO
2	Road Traffic Act,	Noise	SPO
3	Assembly and Demonstration Act	Noise	SPO
4	Act on the punishment of misdemeanors,	Other	SPO, KCG
5	Healthy schools Act	Noise	MOE
6	Automobile Management Act,	Air Pollution	MOLIT
7	Construction Machinery Management Act,	Air Pollution	MOLIT
8	Groundwater Act,	Air Pollution	MOLIT
9	River Act,	Air Pollution	MOLIT
10	Act on aggregate collection	Air Pollution	MOLIT
11	dam construction and the surrounding area support Act,	Air Pollution	MOLIT
12	National territories act	In general	MOLIT
13	National Territory Planning and Utilization Act,	In general	MOLIT
14	Building codes, city parks and greenery Act,	In general	MOLIT
15	City parks and green space Act,	In general	MOLIT
16	Acquisition of land for public utilities and Compensation Act,	In general	MOLIT
17	Urban Development Act,	In general	MOLIT
18	Industrial Sites and Development Act,	In general	MOLIT
19	Housing Site Development Promotion Act	In general	MOLIT
20	Metropolitan Area New Airport Construction Promotion Act	In general	MOLIT
21	Seoul Metropolitan Area Readjustment Planning Act,	In general	MOLIT
22	Urban and residential environments improvement Act	In general	MOLIT
23	Special law on the development of inland and east–west south coast	In general	MOLIT
24	Housing Act	In general	MOLIT
25	Jeju Special Self-Governing Province and Free International City installation Promotion Act	In general	MOLIT, MOSPA
26	Pesticide Control Act,	Agriculture	MAFRA
27	Farmland Act	Agriculture	MAFRA
28	Animal Protection Act,	Agriculture	MAFRA
29	Plant Protection Act,	Agriculture	MAFRA
30	Livestock Act,	Livestock	MAFRA
31	Dairy Promotion Act,	Livestock	MAFRA
32	Grassland Law	Livestock	MAFRA
33	Special Act on the Promotion and Development of rural areas and the quality of life of the farmers and fishermen	Agriculture	MAFRA, MOF
34	Rural Maintenance Act,	Agriculture	MAFRA, MOF

35	Agriculture Fisheries disaster prevention Act	Agriculture	MAFRA, MOF
36	Cultural Heritage Act,	Other	CHA
37	International Conference Industry Promotion Act,	In general	MCST
38	Tourism Promotion Act,	Other	MCST
39	Science and Technology Basic Law	Other	MISP
40	Forest Basic Law,	Forest	KFS
41	Erosion control Act,	Forest	KFS
42	Mountain management Act	Forest	KFS
43	Petroleum and alternative fuels, Business Act, Energy Law,	Air Pollution	MOTIE
44	Energy fundamental law	Air Pollution	MOTIE
45	Community Energy Act,	Air Pollution	MOTIE
46	New and renewable energy development, utilization and Promotion act,	Air Pollution	MOTIE
47	Ozone Layer Regulations Act	Air Pollution	MOTIE
48	Industrial Cluster Development and Factory Establishment Act,	In general	MOTIE
49	Mining damage prevention and recovery Act	In general	MOTIE
50	Special Act on the deregulation of measures related to business activities,	Other	MOTIE
51	Environmentally friendly industrial structure promotion Act,	Other	MOTIE
52	Mining Security Act,	Other	MOTIE
53	Mining Act,	Other	MOTIE
54	Foreign Trade law	Other	MOTIE
55	Small Stream management Act	Air Pollution	NEMA
56	Natural Disaster Countermeasures Act,	Other	NEMA
57	Act on hot spring management	Air Pollution	MOSPA
58	Special act on the support of Surrounding areas of US Forces in Korea	In general	MOSPA
59	Nuclear Safety Act,	Air Pollution	NSSC
60	Nuclear Damage Compensation Act,	Air Pollution	NSSC
61	Marine Environmental Management Act,	Air Pollution	MOF
62	Newport Construction Promotion Act	In general	MOF
63	Fisheries Act,	Fishery & harbor	MOF
64	Fishing village and port law,	Fishery & harbor	MOF
65	Port Act	Fishery & harbor	MOF
66	Inland Fisheries Act,	Other	MOF

Source: ME (2012).

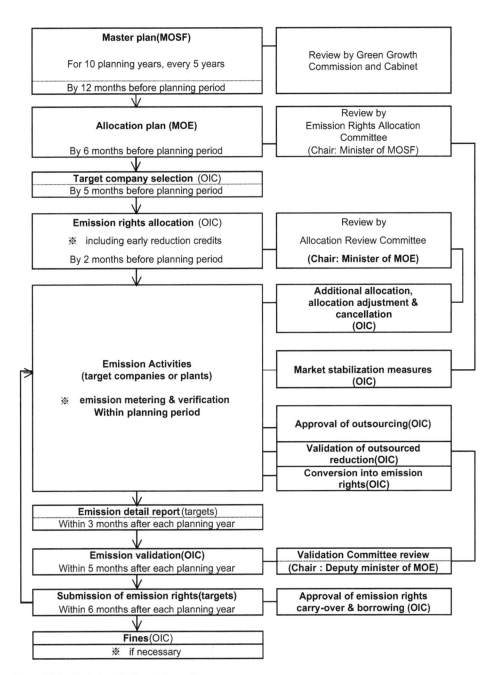

Figure 30.9 Emission Trading Scheme Process

Source: Prime Minister's Office, Nov.13, 2012

31

ENVIRONMENTAL AND RESOURCE POLICY IN INDIA

Priyadarshi Shukla and Diptiranjan Mahapatra

1. Introduction

"The world has enough for everyone's need, but not enough for everyone's greed."
—Mahatma Gandhi

The primacy of development or environment has been on the minds of India's policymakers for a long time. The sentiments were eloquently expressed in a question raised by India's Prime Minister Indira Gandhi at the UN World Environmental Conference in Stockholm in 1972: "Are not poverty and need the greatest polluters?" (CSE, 2013). The two-sidedness of this statement is at the roots of all environmental debates, movements, actions and progress in India. The poverty and the needs relate to different kinds of environmental issues. The poor, who depend on the environment for their livelihoods, are the victims of environmental degradation. They have been the prime movers of the environmental policies. The rising nouveau riche, whose *needs* are delivered though the unregulated markets and their *greed* finding means for fulfillment through the nexus of market and state actors, have caused impediments to wise use of the environment and natural resources. India's environment and natural resource policies are evolving through the struggle of these two divergent forces.

In the early decades since independence, in the absence of environmental laws and implementation machinery, the environmental degradation and exploitation of natural resources went on increasingly unfettered. The environmental laws and policies lagged behind the rapid pace of decline in environmental quality and rise in unsustainable exploitation. The government actions were in the firefighting mode; they responded to the issues that were raised by popular movements or as legal cases in filed the courts in the public interest. The big-ticket items included cleaning of the holy river Ganges, alleviating air pollution affecting the iconic historical monument Taj Mahal and the environment degradation by large damns. Controlling pollution from industry remained sidestepped in the guise of protecting jobs. The ultimate shock to this complacent policy equilibrium came in December 1984 from the Bhopal gas tragedy, considered the world's worst industrial disaster. The Environment (Protection) Act (1986), which followed the Bhopal tragedy, came in as a comprehensive law that instituted and empowered the implementing agencies, the Central and the State Pollution Control Boards, to act effectively and swiftly.

The economic reforms since 1991 have brought the environment and development issues further into focus in the context of globalization. The timing coincided with the emerging global environmental issues, e.g., climate change and biodiversity, which formed the key agenda of the United Nations Conference on Environment and Development (also called The Earth Summit) in Rio de Janeiro in 1992. Prior to that, the government of India had been active in global environmental policy negotiations such as the Montreal Protocol on Substances that Deplete the Ozone Layer. Economic globalization though brought a different perspective on the old development versus environment debate. The competition among the nations to gain competitive advantage gained precedence over the national and sub-national environmental issues. The competitive advantage of the national industries, as an objective of the state policy, superseded the sustainability of the national environment and natural resources. The expectations that economic globalization will have a benign influence on the quality of the national environment thus were belied, at least in the immediate term.

The damage to air, soil, and water quality and the overexploitation of over-ground and underground natural resources continued unabated in the wake of rapid economic growth. The preoccupation with economic globalization caused further policy and legal distortions in allotment and exploitation of natural resources. The combination of economic globalization with distorted domestic institutions having weak implementation capacity and inadequate regulatory and judicial safeguards has resulted in prices of goods and services that do not adequately reflect the social costs, thereby resulting in glaring market failures(Pigou, 1920; Coase, 1960; Baumol and Oates, 1975; Hohmeyer, 1988). This aside, the regulatory capture (Stigler, 1971; Spiller, 1990) by dominant regulated firms, information asymmetry between the regulator and the regulated (Lewis, 1996), and incomplete scientific understanding especially of environmental problems, have rendered India's regulatory process anemic.

Wise use of "environment" and "natural resources" are the cornerstones of sustainable growth that maximizes the common good. The policies for the allocation of scarce resources in India have fallen far short of the wise-use paradigm. Rights to use environmental goods and natural resources are allocated as largesse by state actors to preferred clients. This outcome is politically improper, socially inequitable and economically Pareto inefficient and distortive of all related competitive markets. This reality, wherein the environmental rights and natural resources are usurped by the entrenched classes, contradicts with the vision of India's 12th Five-Year Plan (Planning Commission, 2011a), which aims to achieve "inclusive" growth whereby the endowed environment and natural resources are distributed asymmetrically to favor the disadvantaged section of society. The distortion is stark when viewed vis-à-vis the constitutional values of "right to life," a fundamental right under Article 21 of the Indian Constitution that entails the consumption of natural resources and a clean environment as essential for the wholesome quality of life.

India is at the crossroads of a transition to high economic growth, the point at which many countries have faltered in protecting the environment and natural resources in ways that serve the best interest of the citizens. This chapter is focused on the in situ dynamics of the environment and natural resource policies in India and issues thereof, the future vision of the national policymakers and remarks on future directions whereby India can transit to a green growth path that makes it possible to reconcile environment and development objectives and avert the false sequencing trap of "economic growth now and environment after."

1.1 Vision: sustainable development

The government of India (GoI) has been actively pursuing initiatives that address the issues of sustainable development and environmental change. The most significant commitments are the Millennium Development Goals (MDGs) signed in September 2000, the Five-Year Plan, and the National Action Plan on Climate Change (NAPCC) announced by GoI in June 2008. India's MDG framework recognizes all 53 indicators of the United Nations Development Group's 2003 framework for monitoring of the eight goals of MDGs (GoI 2011a). The relevant goal for the discussion of this chapter is goal seven: ensure environmental sustainability. With regard to the NAPCC, eight missions that focus on solar energy, energy efficiency, sustainable habitat, water, sustaining the Himalayan eco-system, green India, sustainable agriculture, and strategic knowledge for climate care are being implemented by the nodal ministries to address vulnerability to climate change and enhance capacity at central and state levels. Finally, recognizing the growing conflict between development and ecosystem engendering disenchantment and exclusion, the basic theme of the 12th Five Year Plan (2012–2017) – "faster, sustainable and more inclusive growth" – could not have been more timely (Planning Commission, 2011a).

The Ministry of Environment and Forest (MoEF), the nodal ministry in charge of environment, is actively engaged in promoting international cooperation through regional, bilateral and multilateral initiatives in the arena of environment and ecology through bodies like the Economic and Social Council for Asia and Pacific and the South Asian Association for Regional Cooperation and multilateral bodies such as the Commission on Sustainable Development and the Global Environment Facility. The MoEF also serves as the nodal agency for the United Nations Environment Programme, the South Asia Cooperation Environment Programme and the International Centre for Integrated Mountain Development, as well as, for follow up on the United Nations Conference on Environment and Development.

1.2 Constitution of India: ownership of natural resources and environment

The Constitution of India has delineated, with precision, the contours of ownership of minerals and natural resource through various entries such as Union List (List 1), State List (List II), and the Concurrent List (List III) as enumerated in the seventh schedule. Summarily, the proprietary title to onshore minerals is assigned to the constituent states, while the minerals situated in the offshore areas are under the exclusive control of the central government. However, when read in its entirety through the conditionality outlined in clauses (1) to (3) of Article 246 of the Constitution, what emerges is the preponderance of the central government's powers in the area of regulation of mines and mineral development even with regards to the onshore minerals, leaving only a small window called the minor minerals where the states can make their own rules and regulations. Besides, under Entry 53 of List I, parliament has the power to make legislation for regulation and development of oil fields, mineral oil resources, petroleum, petroleum products, other liquids and substances declared by parliament by law to be dangerously inflammable. This basically means that regardless of location of these resources, there has to be equitable distribution of natural gas amongst the states i.e., its benefit has to be shared by the whole country.[1]

But, when it comes to ownership of environment, the clarity between state and central government is not as clear. In fact, environment as such does not find mention in any of the three lists. Under the constitutional scheme of division of powers, the subjects of "forests" and "protection of wild animals and birds" that earlier existed in the State list were later moved to the Concurrent list in 1976 through the 42nd amendment. Land and water are state subjects, excepting the regulation and development of inter-state rivers only to the extent when it is specifically decided by the Parliament to be taken care of in public interest.

1.3 Law making and implementation

The following main legislation and policies are the instruments that support, assist and guide the various ministries to attain the objectives of preservation, conservation and protection of environment and natural resource:

1. Indian Forest Act, 1927
2. The Forest (Conservation) Act, 1980
3. The Air (Prevention and Control of Pollution) Act, 1981
4. The Environment (Protection) Act, 1986
5. The Biodiversity Act, 2002
6. The National Green Tribunal Act, 2010
7. The Water (Prevention & Control of Pollution) Act, 1974
8. The Water (Prevention & Control of Pollution) Cess Act, 1977
9. The Hazardous Waste (Management and Handling) Rules 1989, 2003, 2008
10. The Bio – Medical Waste (Management and Handling) Rules 1988, 2003
11. The Municipal Solid Wastes (Management and Handling) Rules 2000
12. The Plastics Manufacture and Usage Rules, 1999
13. The Noise Pollution (Regulation & Control) Rules, 2000
14. Environmental Impact Assessment Notification, 2006 as amended 2009
15. National Environmental Policy, 2006
16. Fly Ash Management Rule, 2008
17. Easement Act, 1884
18. Land Acquisition Act, 1894
19. Indian Forest Act, 1927
20. The Wildlife (Protection) Act, 1972
21. Forest (Conservation) Act, 1980
22. The Environment (Protection) Act, 1986
23. National Forest Policy, 1988
24. The Panchayati Raj Act, 1994;
25. Several state laws on the pricing and contracting of non-timber forest produce

The institutional setup of the MoEF includes a number of directorates, divisions, regional offices, subordinate offices, boards, autonomous institutions and one public sector undertaking.[2] The Central Pollution Control Board (CPCB), a 100 percent grants-in-aid institution of the MoEF, in coordination with State Pollution Control Boards (SPCB) or Pollution Control Committees implements plans and programs relating to abatement of pollution. One of the mandates of the CPCB is to plan and cause to be executed a nationwide program for prevention, control and abatement of water or air pollution. With regard to the sharing of responsibility, the central government formulates the overarching policy and regulatory framework, while the state government's job is to enforce its implementation. Once industries get operational, the approach adopted to regulate pollution from industrial and domestic sectors is through Industry Specific Minimum National Standards as developed by the CPCB. All the SPCBs must ensure that ambient environmental quality or emissions standards as prescribed by the CPCB or central government are not derogated through command-and control type measures (see Table 31.1 for details on polluting units).

Environment clearances, stipulating various conditions, are granted as per the procedure prescribed under the Environment Impact Assessment Notification 2006 under the Environment

Table 31.1 State–wise polluted industrial units

State	No. of water polluting units	% of units satisfying standards	No. of air polluting units	% of units satisfying standards	No. of highly polluting units HPUs	% of HPUs with facilities to satisfy standards	Estimated number of hazardous waste generating units
Andhra Pradesh	2820	90.85	2520	79.84	220	96.36	744
Assam	95	13.68	86	32.56	15	60	31
Bihar	116	29.31	1386	40.55	40	82.5	146
Goa	32	100	18	100	7	100	28
Gujarat	8098	32.16	5757	54.87	200	95	1362
Haryana	2580	53.72	1513	26.76	2580	40.19	178
Himachal Pradesh	975	28.82	983	74.67	12	50	25
Karnataka	8015	57.83	6902	46.33	113	91.15	333
Kerala	2250	35.6	1528	24.41	24	91.67	229
Madhya Pradesh	526	–	526	68.63	88	98.86	191
Maharashtra	7169	62.29	7008	58.86	318	95.59	1763
Manipur	0	0	26	100	4	–	–
Meghalaya	14	0	81	0	1	100	–
Orissa	–	–	–	–	–	–	–
Punjab	3280	49.72	8299	17.62	51	76.47	174
Rajasthan	692	–	430	–	49	97.95	174
Tamil Nadu	6338	–	6998	–	188	98.4	1465
Uttar Pradesh	454	48.9	281	80.07	627	83.41	591
West Bengal	62	59.68	6188	–	64	81.25	413

Source: Central Pollution Control Board (CPCB).

(Protection) Act of 1986. The stages in environment clearance process comprise of screening, scoping, public consultation and appraisal. The prescribed time period for taking a decision on an environment clearance case is 105 days after the submission of the final environmental impact assessment and environment management plan report by the project proponent to the ministry. Various steps taken by MoEF to fast-track the environment clearance process without compromising the quality of the appraisal or the integrity of the environment include continuous monitoring of the status of pending projects; regular and longer duration meetings of expert appraisal committees for consideration of projects in different sectors; streamlining of process, etc. The compliance of stipulated environment clearances conditions by the industry is monitored by the six regional offices of Ministry of Environment and Forests, CPCB and the concerned SPCB and Union Territory Pollution Control Committees. In order to ensure checks and balances, necessary powers have been delegated to the state governments and SPCB and committees to take appropriate action in case of any violation.

However, the environment impact assessment (EIA) in its current form suffers from flaws, important amongst them is the fact that EIA reports are commissioned by the project proponents themselves and, obviously, there are almost negligible chances that the consultants hired for the preparation of the report would ever go against the sponsor i.e., the project proponent. At times, states and other departments exert pressure on the MoEF for expeditious clearance of projects and also for allowing relaxation. For example, the National Highways Authority of India recently took the MoEF to the Supreme Court seeking to delink MoEF's criterion that takes up the environment clearance only after the forest clearance[3] has been obtained.

The National Green Tribunal (NGT) was established under the National Green Tribunal Act of 2010 for effective and expeditious disposal of cases relating to environmental protection and conservation of forests and other natural resources, including enforcement of any legal right relating to the environment and giving relief and compensation for damages to persons and property and for matters connected therewith or incidental thereto. The NGT is making all endeavors for disposal of the cases by the tribunal within the time limit of six months and most of the cases have been disposed within that time.

Environment and resource law-making in India is still evolving and has been influenced largely by certain major events and developments, a series of judicial interventions and pronouncements, and commitment to various multilateral environmental agreements. Among the notable actors that have contributed to this evolution are the central government, the Supreme Court, state government, industry and the civil society. At times, conflicting interests between various stakeholders morphs into impasses and blame games.

2. Regulatory landscape: status

The government of India's approach toward correcting environmental market failures has been primarily through traditional command-and-control-type regulations, although the economic instrument approach is slowly evolving (for details, see e.g., Weitzman, 1974; Roberts and Spence, 1976; Weitzman, 1978; Stavins, 1996; Montgomery, 1972; and Pizer, 2002). It is in the year 2010, the GoI took a first step toward implementing the polluter-pays principle by imposing a coal tax of Rs. 50 (Rs. stands for Indian Rupee) to create a fund for promoting clean energy called the National Clean Energy Fund. Similarly, there have been ongoing discussions regarding setting up of an environment restoration fund that could act as a deterrent for noncompliance and violations by industries (MoEF, 2013). Further, with its recently introduced pilot emissions trading program,[4] possibly the first in any developing country, and also the green ratings project, India undeniably is making serious attempts to ride on the environment regulation frontier. However,

Table 31.2 Details of water tax collected and grants disbursed (in Rs. Crore)

Year	Water tax collected	Grants to SPCB	Grants to CPCB	Total
2005–2006	56.4	76.52	47.04	123.56
2006–2007	170.3	76.51	47.12	123.63
2007–2008	190.84	130.34	47.96	178.3
2008–2009	228.99	79.8	50.63	130.43
2009–2010	207.01	209.96	54.77	264.73
Total	853.54	573.13	247.52	820.65

Source: Performance Audit of Water Pollution in India, CAG, 2011.

the importance of institutional and political constraints for mainstreaming these innovations as policy instruments cannot be overlooked.

Besides the command-and-control approach, the government also has introduced major economic incentives for pollution abatement in India. For example, the Water Cess Act 1977 empowered the state pollution control boards to levy a water tax on local authorities supplying water to consumers and on industries on consumption of water in certain specified activities. Unfortunately, the low water tax (Rs 0.10–0.40 per cubic meter) incentivizes wastage and is probably an important contributor to water pollution from Indian industry (see Table 31.2 for detail on water tax collection).

3. Environmentalism in India

Indian environmentalism has a long history and has found voice across the country covering varied environmental issues. The people's movement for a better environment, which started as an idea, e.g., the "Chipko movement" in 1973 aiming to save trees, has become pervasive and is still evolving (see for example, Zhang, 2010; Guha, 1988, Guha and Martinez-Alier, 1997; Sinha, Baviskar and Philip, 2006). For most of the populace, environmentalism usually conjures up images of rural Indians confronting state-sponsored development. Unsurprisingly, as India began the experiment with the free-market in 1991, concerns raised by the environmentalists were and are still viewed as anti-development. Over the years, this has given rise to two distinct forms of environmentalism: a green agenda for the *nouveau riche* and the rising middle class and a resource-scarce future that forces the poor to defend their livelihoods (Bauer, 2006). A most recent and vivid example is the case of Bauxite mining project that is discussed later in detail.

The difference between Indian and Western environmentalism centers on the question of "need." Indian environmental movements look at the surroundings as a source of sustenance and, hence, think it should be preserved, while their Western counterparts take action out of a sheer desire to protect the environment that has no strong correlation, albeit in the short run, to their own survival (for discussion, see e.g., Guha, 2013; Narain, 2002).

3.1 Judiciary

An early intervention by the Supreme Court of India in preserving the environment was made in 1980 when the apex court gave direction to the Municipal Council of Ratlam City to facilitate the construction of proper drains and also cautioned that a paucity of funds could not be an alibi by the local authorities to fail to carry out their basic duties.[5] Unfortunately, the Ratlam judgment remained inconsequential with regard to its impact on the functioning of municipalities and, as a result, municipalities, often citing budgetary constraints, have managed to get away with poor public service in provisioning. Subsequently, public interest litigation came into prominence and started altering the landscape of judicial activism and the role of the higher judiciary in India. To this end, M.C. Mehta, a lawyer practicing in the Supreme Court, became the champion of many public causes. Notable amongst his petitions that have resulted into landmark decision by the Supreme Court are: 1) orders assigning strict liability for the leak of oleum gas from a factory in New Delhi;[6] 2) directions to check pollution in and around the Ganges River;[7] 3) the relocation of hazardous industries from the municipal limits of Delhi;[8] 4) directions to state agencies to check pollution in the vicinity of the Taj Mahal;[9] 5) the shift to the use of compressed natural gas (CNG) by government-run buses;[10] and 6) an order that required privately-run auto-rickshaws (three-wheeled public vehicles) to shift to the use of CNG. Another landmark judicial intervention happened in 1996 when Almitra Patel filed a petition before the court for a violation of Article 21, the right to life and a healthy environment, arising because of "faulty and deficient" garbage disposal practices in urban centers. Subsequently, with the submission of the report by the court- constituted committee and deliberations, the MoEF finally propagated the Municipal Solid Waste (Management and Handling) Rules on October 3, 2000, that entails setting up of waste processing and disposal facilities, improvement of existing landfill sites and identification of landfill sites for future.

Notwithstanding the fact that the judicial interventions have, more often than not, improved quality of life, many observers have expressed apprehensions over growing environmental jurisprudence.[11] It is imperative that the courts exercise extreme caution in examining that while remedying a constitutional imbalance, or correcting executive error or removing legislative omission, whether or not they are overstepping their domain and getting into the realm of executive policymaking. It is likely that such frequent judicial interventions might result in reduced incentives for executive agencies to improve their functioning.

3.2 Expert committees

In order to achieve a transparent process, GoI constitutes expert committees to assist the decision-making authorities in arriving at the proper decision. At times, the authority empowered to take a decision may accept the view expressed by one committee in preference to another for plausible reasons. They are not bound to accept the view of any committee. It is also believed that consulting various committees strengthens the decision-making process. With regard to the environment and natural resource sector, with a view to ensure multi-disciplinary input required for appraisal of this critical sector, expert committees have been constituted for environmental and economic issues arising in many sectors, e.g., mining projects; industrial projects; thermal power projects; river valley, multipurpose, irrigation and hydro Projects; infrastructure development and miscellaneous projects; nuclear power projects; pricing of natural resource and more.

Inadvertently, India's strength of a multi-tier system in the decision-making process at times becomes a constraint, with the process itself contributing to procrastination. At times the expert committee's composition and conflicts of interest, design and functioning at a fundamental level defeat the very objective of getting an independent evaluation. In some cases, the selection of experts in the committee contributes to the bias. The procedural fairness, both real and perceived, are important ingredients of public decision-making and in this context, the process of decision-making, as opposed to the actual decisions, is vital (See Table 31.3 for a description of committees on environment).

Table 31.3 Expert committees on the environment

Committee Name	Year	Focus Area
Technical Expert Committee (TEC) on Genetically Modified (GM) crops, constituted by the Supreme Court	2012	To study genetically modified crops
Expert Committee for Lavasa city Project, Pune	2011	To examine the penalty and creation of environmental restoration fund
M.S. Swaminathan Expert Committee	2004	To review the existing CRZ notification
Expert Committee	2008	To evolve environmental standards
Expert Committee on climate change	2007	To look into the impacts of climate change
Technical Committee constituted by the Genetic Engineering Appraisal Committee	2006 and 2009	To study the safety and efficacy aspects of Bt brinjal
CPCB Expert Committee	2009	To develop national emissions standard for petrochemical manufacturing units (basic and intermediate products)
Expert Committee on MSW	2009	To evolve a roadmap for proper management of wastes in the country
Expert Committee on Biodiversity Management Committee	2010	To prepare guidelines on creating structures, running administration and maintaining of accounts and other related matters
Development of Environmental Standards	2010	To evolve environmental standards and consequent upon the adoption of the National Environment Policy–2006
Expert Committee on Bio-Medical Waste Management	2010	To evaluate the new state of the treatment technologies for disposed of bio-medical waste

Source: Ministry of Environment and Forest (MoEF).

3.3 Civil society organizations

The state, as mandated by the constitution, has the duty to provision sovereign functions, including public goods. However, the state may not always be able to reach out to the recipients for a variety of reasons. An often-advocated remedy is to provision public goods through the market via private operators. The markets though create exclusion through price, and in such cases the civil society organizations can play an effective role for socially inclusive redistribution of environmental public goods. The state then becomes an enabler of meaningful and constructive participation of civil society in the existing governance structure in a transparent and verifiable manner.

Environment and natural resources are the primary sources of livelihood of the rural poor. These common property resources are most vulnerable to the disturbances in the ecosystem. India has a dynamic civil society and non-governmental organization community. They play an active role in bringing to notice of the government and the judiciary the abuse of environmental and natural resources and of the unfair exclusion of any section of the citizens from the products and services of the environment and natural resources. Notably, civil society organizations have actively worked in key areas such as fair water distribution and minimizing the health effects of environmental degradation, such as by poor indoor and outdoor air quality and preventing unauthorized mining activities. While playing an active role in influencing environmental policymaking and its implementation for the redistribution of environmental goods, civil society organizations often come into conflict with state agencies and groups having alternate interests. This is universally expected, especially in a functioning democracy; the huge delays in the Indian judicial system often lead to lose–lose outcomes. Judicial and administrative reforms, therefore, are vital to bringing about the social equilibrium that can prevent avoidable conflicts among state and non-state players that may make the society worse-off.

4. Environmental and resource policies

The GoI's environmental policies primarily are motivated by the sovereign responsibility of maintaining a clean and healthy environment, as per the Articles 48A and 51A(g) of the Constitution and the eminent judicial interpretation of Article 21. The National Environment Policy of 2006 is one such effort directed toward mainstreaming environmental concerns in all development activities without derogating the existing and disparate policies, such as the National Forest Policy, 1988; the National Conservation Strategy and Policy Statement on Environment and Development, 1992; the Policy Statement on Abatement of Pollution, 1992; the National Agriculture Policy, 2000; the National Population Policy, 2000; and the National Water Policy, 2002.

The central theme of these polices hinge on the principle that environmental protection is an integral part of the development process. The policies then suggest preventive actions through precautionary principles, economic efficiency, and conservation of resources, as under:

- Precautionary principle through pollution-prevention strategies;
- Polluter pays principle;
- Assessment of production and consumption patterns;
- Cost-benefit analysis;
- Internalization of environmental costs;
- Efficiency in use of resources;
- Cost minimization;
- Waste minimization and cleaner production; and
- Multi-stake holder participation.

With regard to natural resources, sustainable use of resources has been embedded into national decision-making through various policy statements, such as the National Forest Policy, the National Wildlife Action Plan, the National Biodiversity Action Plan, the National Environment Policy; legislative measures, such as the Environment (Protection) Act, the Wildlife (Protection) Act, the Biological Diversity Act; and programs such as Joint Forest Management and afforestation. All these policies, plans and programs, with an embedded appreciation of the needs of the local communities, have emphasized the need to respect the existing resources with an eye on intergenerational equity.

To this end, the Ashok Chawla Committee on Allocation of Natural Resources has examined the allocation of eight natural resources (minerals, coal, petroleum, natural gas, spectrum, land, water and forests) and has recommended several methods of allocation for different sets of natural resources, including the use of market-linked processes, which in some cases include auction as the preferred mode (GoI, 2011c). The thrust of the committee's recommendations, most of which have been accepted by the Group of Ministers, is generally to move toward a transparent system of allocation and pricing of identified natural resources. Further, GoI has introduced the

Mines and Minerals (Development and Regulation) Bill of 2011, wherein there is a provision for sharing of benefits with the local population that would grant monetary benefits to families affected by mining-related activities and the creation, management and maintenance of local infrastructure in areas affected by mining related operations.

As per the Mines and Minerals Development and Regulation Act of 1957, the holder of a mining lease shall pay royalties in respect of any mineral removed or consumed by him or by his agent, manager, employee, contractor or sub-lessee from the leased area at the rate for the time being specified in the second schedule in respect of that mineral. Further, as per section 9A(1) of the Mines and Minerals Development and Regulation Act, the holder of a mining lease shall pay to the state government every year dead rent at such rate as may be specified, for the time being, in the third schedule for all the areas included in the instrument of lease. However, the leaseholder shall pay either the royalty for any mineral removed or consumed or the dead rent, whichever is greater.

The same act also specifies that royalties, revisable upward only once in three years, are levied on ad valorem basis for all major minerals excepting nine minerals for which royalties are charged on tonnage basis. The ad valorem system of computing royalties allows for levy after taking into account various price slabs of minerals and captures increases or decreases in the price of minerals. The major royalty accrued states are Rajasthan, Orissa, Andhra Pradesh, Madhya Pradesh, Karnataka and Chhattisgarh. The royalty collected for major minerals by the states for 2002 to 2003 and 2010 to 2011 as received from respective state governments is given in Table 31.4. GoI is currently examining the recommendations of one study group on revision of royalty rates and dead rent for major minerals (other than coal, lignite, and sand for stowing).

As mentioned earlier, in India, the proprietary title to onshore minerals vests in the federating states. However, this ownership is subject to legisla-tion governing regulation and control of mining enacted by the Parliament. This dichotomy has given rise to instances of conflicts between the central government and the state, giving an impression that despite the state being the owners

Table 31.4 Royalty collections for major minerals (excluding coal and lignite) during 2002–03 to 2009–10 for important mineral-producing states (Rs. in Crore)

States	2002–03	2003–04	2004–05	2005–06	2006–07	2007–08	2008–09	2009–10	2010–11
Chhattisgarh	552.36	637.17	694.61	121.62	144.15	148.8	153.89	474.4	1201.74
Jharkhand	797.65	900.16	916.2	51	86.29	86.88	63.24	319.04	440.42
Karnataka	83.89	143.62	210.94	149.86	172.26	135.53	184.14	427.09	647.35
Tamil Nadu	297.34	324.5	324.82	77.62	85.55	86.82	104.24	130.57	319.71
Rajasthan	399.68	457.96	589.79	350.06	810.28	761.79	659.81	987.31	–
Andhra Pradesh	769.93	766.56	864.53	170.38	202.95	232.37	242.85	370.38	566.23
Orissa	440.57	547.2	663.61	247.17	320.66	336.23	431.35	894.44	–
Maharashtra	400.69	475.92	568.24	68.1	57.69	78.97	107.43	84.61	–
Madhya Pradesh	590.69	646.71	733.72	157.75	186.85	208.88	191.44	351.45	338.09
Goa	14.81	17.87	17.44	18.08	22.46	26.48	27.46	285.91	974.19
Gujarat	172.63	217.9	238.95	–	131.61	168.46	157.86	192.91	

Source: GoI, 2011b, Mineral Royalties, Ministry of Mines; Rajya Sabha unstarred question 1490 answered on December 5, 2011.

of the resources, the mine owners are benefitting beyond reasonable returns. Recently, the state of Odisha sought imposition of a mineral resource rent tax on super-normal profits[12] made by iron ore mining companies operating in the state. In reply, the central government has been citing the provisions of the national and state mineral funds, district mineral foundation payments etc. as proposed in the impending Mines and Minerals (Development and Regulation) Bill, that could possibly be used for the benefit of the mining areas and the local people displaced by the mining activities.

4.1 Energy sector

4.1.1 Fossil energy

India's energy dependency has shown growth both in depth, i.e., quantity imported and also in breadth, i.e., variety imported. As a result, India's import dependence increased from 11 percent (34 Mtoe) in 1990 to 35 percent (236 Mtoe) in 2009 (IEA, 2012). As a percent of total demand, crude topped the list with 81 percent, representing 162 Mtoe in terms of the absolute volume of import, while natural gas in the form of liquefied natural gas (imports of 10 Mtoe were 21 percent of total natural gas demand in 2009 (IEA, 2012). The rising coal import, despite India's huge coal endowments, has added a new twist to energy security concerns. The environmental concerns and other procedural and structural delays in clearing coal mining projects have led to coal imports surging by 650 percent in the last seven years to 82 million tons in 2012 to 2013. The growing import of coal has been a subject of intense public scrutiny and public discourse in recent times.

In order to intensify energy exploration activities and lessen the import dependency, the government of India has been periodically revising the exploration and production policy based on evolving market dynamics. With the aim of attracting private investment and infusing technology from around the world, the New Exploration and Licensing Policy (NELP) and Coal Bed Methane (CBM) Policy in the late 1990s, for example, opened the sector to competition by incorporating innovative production sharing contracts (PSPs). Under NELP, the government's take depends on sharing of "profit oil" based on the pre-tax investment multiple with cost recovery, while contracts under CBM provide for revenue-sharing based on production linked payment without cost recovery. With nine rounds of NELP auctions of oil and gas blocks completed, certain constraints have been observed in the working of the existing contractual and fiscal model as corroborated by the Ashok Chawla Committee on Allocation of Natural Resources (GoI, 2011c) and also observed by the Comptroller and Auditor General in its audit report on PSCs in hydrocarbon exploration (CAG, 2011). Considering the shortcomings, it is expected that the tenth round of NELP is likely to be based on new terms wherein a bidder shall be asked to quote the amount of oil or gas output it is willing to offer to the government from the first day of production, as suggested by the Rangarajan Committee (GoI, 2012).

Similarly, for coal that hitherto was governed through a discretionary allocation policy, the government through its notification Competitive Bidding of the Coal Mines Rules, 2012, approved the coal block auction policy for private companies based on competitive bidding. The methodology (Press Information Bureau, PIB, 2013) calls for production-linked payment on a rupee per ton basis, plus a basic upfront payment of 10 percent of the intrinsic value of the coal block. In order to arrive at the intrinsic value, it is suggested to refer to the net present value of the block calculated through the discounted cash flow method. Finally, to benchmark the selling price of coal at the mine mouth, it is recommended to base it with the international free on board price from the public indices like Argus or Platts after adjusting it by 15 percent to provide for inland transport cost.

Evidently, the Indian policymakers have used heterogeneous policies for fossil energy. Three conclusions that follow are: 1) the policy changes often followed significant international events that affected the global fossil fuel market; 2) the policy perspective has been short-term; 3) a multitude of disconnected policy instruments are used, some of which may be at cross purpose; and 4) there is an increasing trend in the use of market-oriented policy instruments.

4.1.2 Renewable energy

Renewable energy under the nodal agency the Ministry of New and Renewable Energy has emerged as an integral part of the government agenda of "sustainable and more inclusive growth." Besides having a contribution of 12.5 percent of grid-connected power generation capacity, renewable energy-based decentralized and distributed applications have benefited millions of people in rural villages by meeting their cooking, lighting and other energy needs in an environmentally friendly manner.

The rural energy programs have been driven by diverse objectives such as clean energy supply, energy access, alleviating indoor air pollution, jobs in the rural informal sector, rural entrepreneurship and mitigation of greenhouse gases and black carbon emissions. These programs formally came on the policy agenda after the two oil shocks in the 1970s. Their immediate goals were to enhance national energy security and to provide clean energy options to rural populations faced with high energy prices and depleting local energy resources. The programs include supply-side and demand-side policies, and its implementation architecture predominantly targets local biomass resources by measure that enhance penetration of improved cook-stoves, family and community level biogas plants, bio-mass gasifier for local electricity generation, solar street lighting for village community and efficient irrigation pumps.

Notable programs (and year of launch) are: National Programme on Biogas Development (1980), National Programme on Improved Cook-stoves (1986), Integrated Rural Energy Programme (1985), Rural Energy Entrepreneurship and Institutional Development (2000) and Women and Renewable Energy Development (2000). At the national level, the annual targets are decided during the budget exercises and these are allocated to the states, which may add funds from own budget based on their priorities.

With regard to grid-based power, the Electricity Act of 2003 provides for regulatory interventions for promotion of renewable energy sources through 1) determination of tariff; 2) specifying renewable purchase obligation (RPO); 3) facilitating grid connectivity; and 4) promotion of development of market. The National Tariff Policy 2006 requires the State Electricity Regulatory Commissions (SERCs) to fix a minimum percentage of RPOs from such sources taking into account availability of such resources in the region, its impact on retail tariffs, and procurement by distribution companies at preferential tariffs determined by the SERCs. The NAPCC suggests increasing the share of renewable energy in the total energy mix at least up to 15 percent by 2020.

The government also has recently decided oil marketing companies will procure ethanol only from domestic sources to achieve the mandatory requirement of blending 5 percent ethanol with petrol by October 2013 in areas of the country where sufficient quantity of ethanol is available. In other parts of the country, blending of ethanol may be increased progressively, depending upon the availability of ethanol, to reach the mandatory level. Further, certain states, for example the state of Maharashtra, has imposed a tax of Rs. 0.08 per unit from May 1, 2008, on the sale of electricity to commercial and industrial consumers. The tax is to be used for supporting schemes for generation of renewable energy.

4.1.3 Nuclear energy

India has a long history of nuclear legislation, starting with the Atomic Energy Act of 1948, which was replaced by Atomic Energy Act of 1962. India is a member state of the International Atomic Energy Agency (IAEA) and has signed various conventions including the Convention on Nuclear Safety. The central government has set up agencies and organizations such as the Atomic Energy Commission, the Bhabha Atomic Research Centre, the Nuclear Power Corporation of India and the Atomic Energy Regulatory Board. Following the national nuclear policy, these organizations have conducted R&D and have helped to set up 20 operating nuclear power reactors with installed capacity of 4,780 MWe (megawatt electrical) that were commissioned over the past four decades – from the year 1969 to 2011.

Prior to 2008, India faced a fuel supply problem as it did not permit IAEA's full scope safeguards on its nuclear program. As a result, the Nuclear Suppliers Group (NSG) could not sell uranium to India. The major concern then was the short supply of yellow cake uranium (U_3O_8) from indigenous sources, which resulted in the reduced plant load factor to below 50 percent. The fuel supply was even a greater concern as seven more units, with a capacity of 5,300 MWe, were under various stages of construction and commissioning. But the nuclear fuel supply constraint was mitigated in 2008 with the signing of the United States-India Nuclear Cooperation Approval and Non-proliferation Enhancement Act. The NSG then relaxed the restriction on the supply of uranium. This helped India to fully utilize the existing nuclear power plants and also envisage new nuclear power capacity.

India has embarked upon a three-stage nuclear power program based on a closed nuclear fuel cycle. The first stage, which is already in the commercial domain, comprises setting up of pressurized heavy water reactors that use natural uranium as fuel. The second stage, which is in the technology demonstration stage, is geared to set up fast breeder reactors using plutonium produced by reprocessing of spent uranium fuel from the first stage. The third stage, which is in the technology development stage, will be based on the thorium-uranium-233 cycle in specifically designed advanced heavy water reactors for which uranium-233 is obtained by irradiation of thorium (DAE, 2006).

India now is aiming at bigger nuclear power targets, reaching 20,000 MWe in 2020 and 60,000 MW (Grover, 2011) by 2030. As per our analysis, even if we were to stop at 10,000MWe of pressurized heavy-water reactor by 2020, which is half of what the Department of Atomic Energy is planning to install, the shortfall of yellow cake as per our calculation would be closer to 330 tons per annum. Hence, the currently known reserves of indigenous uranium in the country are not sufficient in terms of fuel supply to run atomic power stations in the country. Understandably, to overcome the shortage of fuel India has entered into various collaboration agreements with the US, Canada, and Russia etc. that include the Indo-U.S. Joint Statement 2005, for a renewed global civil nuclear energy cooperation.

After the Fukushima accident, the public perception became more adverse toward nuclear power plants. This is affecting the new proposed plants where local communities are resisting the construction of nuclear power plants.. But India's planning process has continued to regard nuclear power as a key energy to hedge against energy security concerns and low-carbon energy transition. The GoI has been reaching out to stakeholders through various consultative processes by forming a high level committee of specialists to review and recommend safety upgrades as required to handle extreme external events of natural and human origin.

4.1.4 Energy efficiency

India's rapid growth has outpaced its energy needs, resulting into an increasing dependency on oil and coal imports. In the energy efficiency context, India has huge "catching up" to do. Energy efficiency can net "low hanging fruits"; it can deliver energy savings at low or even negative costs. The saved energy can alleviate energy security concerns, reduce investments in back-up electricity generation, and also make the best use of existing supply capacities to improve energy access. In recognition of this, GoI enacted the Energy Conservation Act of 2001 with the purpose to aid, enhance and enforce the efficient use of energy and its conservation. The act instituted a Bureau of Energy Efficiency (BEE) (GoI, 2001) empowered with the legal authority to institute and enforce energy standards, disseminate information and operationalize technical and economic instruments to promote energy savings that are economically and environmentally sustainable. Notable among the achievements of BEE include appliance standards and labeling, building codes and a perform, achieve and trade mechanism (BEE, 2013) to promote efficiency in large, energy-intensive industries.

GoI's push for energy efficiency has targeted two key economic front: 1) rationalizing energy prices by eliminating distortionary energy subsidies, and 2) taking non-price initiatives such as labeling of appliances; the Super-Efficient Equipment Program to accelerate the introduction and deployment of super-efficient appliances; assistance to promote energy efficiency in groundwater pumping by farmers and building codes. The National Mission on Enhanced Energy Efficiency included in NAPCC has mandated near-term energy savings targets that can deliver energy savings and also reduce greenhouse gas emissions.

4.2 Water

With the availability of only 4 percent of global fresh water, India is water short. With increasing demand, the challenges seem menacing but not insurmountable if action focused toward water resources development, conservation and optimum use are instituted. The annual utilizable water resources of the country have been assessed at 1,123 billion cubic meters (BCM), of which 690 BCM is from surface water and 433 BCM from groundwater sources (Planning Commission, 2011b). As per Central Water Commission data, the per capita availability of water, presently around 1,720.29 cum has declined over the years. It is estimated that a major part of the future water demand is going to come from domestic and industrial sectors. Under the Constitution, water, including the rural water supply, is primarily a state subject and the central government comes in only in the case of issues related to inter-state river waters. However, over the years, loosely defined property rights have engendered environmental, ecological, social, and human rights concerns. To address this so as to avoid the pitfalls of the tragedy of the commons (Hardin, 1968) and also to establish good governance and integrated planning of the water resources through a comprehensive overarching legal framework at the national level, it is increasingly felt that shifting of water as a subject under the concurrent list of the Indian Constitution is desirable.

Water pricing in India lacks clarity with regard to the cost recovery principles that results in substantial undervaluation in tariff setting for all segments of users, i.e., urban, rural and industrial. Either uniform volumetric charges for metered charging or a flat rate charge for unmetered charging are the usually employed tariff recovery mechanisms. The distortion in the extant structure has resulted in situations wherein the largest consumers, i.e., the industrial water users, are meeting their demand through groundwater extraction since it is less expensive to extract water compared to paying the service provider's tariffs. Even in cases where a handful of industrial consumers are being provisioned by water utilities, the rates at which these consumers are getting the service are much lower than the true cost of the water provided.

In some places, though, a mix of quantity as well as price instruments, such as, but not limited to, connection fees, water taxes, water charges, meter rent, license fees, water rationing by time-of-day supply, meter maintenance charges, and development and fixed charges for capital renovation of the water system are used for cost recovery. Additionally, some of the utilities levy wastewater charges on households, such as connection charges or drainage or sewerage charges for discharging wastewater to the sewer network. The effective utilization of water resources is still far from what would be economically efficient and environmentally sustainable. India is already a water-stressed nation. This, compounded with added stresses in the future from intensive agriculture, industrialization, population pressures and climate change, can lead to future water crises unless a mix of economic, and in the short run even command-and-control-type measures, are urgently initiated to stem unsustainable water use.

4.3 Land use and forestry

Under the Indian Constitution, land is a state subject, but the state, while bringing in its own laws, could only upgrade but not derogate any relevant central legislation. In India, land as a subject of discourse and land acquisition as a process always has been a contentious issue, both in political and apolitical circle alike. Market imperfections, anaemic property rights and private and public litigation are a few attributes of the exiting land market that have resulted in many battles both in and out of the courtrooms. Market distortions are further exasperated because of the out-dated Land Acquisition Act 1894, the existing law on compulsory acquisition of land and private property. Singur, Nandigram, Kalinganagar, Jaitapur and Bhatta Parsaul are places where enforcement of eminent domain (Munch, 1976) by the sovereign and the subsequent resistance from the peasants have resulted in bitter disputes (Ghatak and Ghosh, 2011). It is too early to comment on the efficacy of the recently passed Right to Fair Compensation and Transparency in Land Acquisition, Resettlement and Rehabilitation Act of 2013, which replaced the antiquated 1894 law. Beyond intentions and expectations, the new bill, if successful, can reduce transaction costs in land acquisition and can bring transparency and fairness in compensation and efficient economic valuation in the acquisition of land for the public purpose. Since 2008, the policies have aimed to transit from the extant "presumptive" property title system to "conclusive" or the Torrens system (Morris and Pandey, 2007; Sinha, 2009) by launching a major program called the National Land Records Modernization Program.

Article 48A of the Constitution of India requires the state to protect and improve the environment and to safeguard the forests and wildlife of the country. The laws that govern the use and protection of forest lands include the Forest (Conservation) Act, 1980; the Scheduled Tribes and Other Traditional Forest Dwellers (Recognition of Forest Rights) Act, 2006; and the Indian Forests Act, 1927.I n the case of tribal communities, there are specific constitutional provisions and laws that govern land relations in tribal areas like the fifth and sixth schedule and the Panchayats Extension to Scheduled Areas Act, and the various state laws or government orders concerning Adivasi land. Besides, several court judgments also guide policymakers, especially in cases where forest and tribal land is set to be diverted for non-forest purposes.

The Supreme Court in *Samatha vs State of AP 1997*[13] instructed that government land, tribal land, and forest land in scheduled areas could not be leased to non-tribal or private companies for mining or industrial operations. It is well documented that despite stringent provisioning, over the years many of these rights have been ignored, weakened or violated and large tracts of such land have been diverted for private purposes (CAG, 2013). Economic growth in an emerging economy like India inevitably requires land to build assets on. What is of paramount importance then is to balance economic development and social equity. Hence, the question of diversion of land is of less consequence than the issue of compensation and rehabilitation in the interest of intra-generational and intergenerational justice. Given the instances of abuse of sovereign power (Gonsalves, 2010; Guha, 2007; Desai, 2011; Morris and Pandey, 2007; Sarkar, 2007; Singh, 2012; CAG, 2013; Ramanathan, 2011; Sarkar, 2011; Sarma, 2011), it is unsurprising that the Supreme Court of India is playing a proactive role to ensure protection of the rights of marginalized sections of society[14] by issuing interim orders and judgments on various issue such as tree felling, operation of saw mills, violations of approvals for forest diversion, de-reservation of forests and many other matters related to compensatory afforestation (see Table 31.5 for an estimate of land degradation across states).

In its orders, the apex court has fixed the responsibility for ensuring the proper carrying out of compensatory afforestation on the MoEF and ordered the setting up of the Central Empowered Committee (CEC) with explicit functions of monitoring the implementation of the court's orders. Following this, the MoEF constituted the Compensatory Afforestation Fund Management and Planning Authority for management of the monies received from the user agencies toward compensatory afforestation, additional compensatory afforestation, penal compensatory afforestation, net present value (NPV) of forest land, catchment area treatment plan funds, etc. For calculating the NPV per hectare of forest in India, the following monetary value of goods and services provided by the forest is usually considered: 1) value of timber and fuel wood; 2) value of non-timber forest products; 3) value of fodder; 4) value of eco-tourism; 5) value of bio-prospecting; 6) value of ecological services of forest; 7) value of flagship species; and 8) carbon sequestration value (see Chopra Committee Report, 2006 for a detail discussion).

However, a challenge for the policymakers is how to value the intangibles and what discount rate to be used. With regard to the methodology, several options such as, but not limited to, opportunity cost, replacement cost, travel cost, contingent value method and social benefit cost analysis are explored. As for discounting, a social discount rate that represents societal time preferences could be used. In practice though, there is no agreement on the value of the social discount rate (IPCC, 1995) because of the embedded public goods character of the products that are not available in the market in discrete form. Chopra Committee (2006) has recommended a 5 percent social discount rate, but the CEC preferred a reduction and accepted a 4 percent social discount rate. It should be noted that the CEC consulted with eminent economists and was of the view that the social discount rate should be around 2 percent in India.[15]

The National Mission for Green India is a new initiative under the NAPCC with an objective to increase forest and tree cover on a five million ha area, to improve quality of forest cover on another five million ha area, to ameliorate forest-based livelihoods of local communities and also to improve ecosystem services such as carbon sequestration, biodiversity and hydrological services. The state-wise details of funds released for carrying out preparatory activities under the mission are given in the Table 31.6.

4.4 Marine resources

With a coastline of 8,118 km and extremely diverse ecosystems, India's marine and coastal ecosystems constitute an important natural resource. Following the provisions contained in the UN Convention on Law of the Sea, signed and ratified by India, GoI has enacted various legislation for protection and regulation of marine resources. The Territorial Waters,

Table 31.5 State-wise extent of various kinds of land degradation in India (area in thousand hectares)

S.N.	Name of the States	Water Erosion	Wind Erosion	Water Logging	Salinity/ Alkalinity	Soil Acidity	Complex Problem	Degraded Area	Geographical Area	Degraded Area (%)
1	Andhra Pradesh	11518	0	1896	517	905	156	14992	27505	54.5
2	Arunachal Pradesh	2372	0	176	0	1955	0	4503	8374	53.8
3	Assam	688	0	37	0	612	876	2213	7844	28.2
4	Bihar + Jharkhand	3024	0	2001	229	1029	0	6283	17387	36.1
5	Goa	60	0	76	0	2	24	162	370	43.9
6	Gujarat	5207	443	523	294	0	1666	8133	19602	41.5
7	Haryana	315	536	146	256	0	214	1467	4421	33.2
8	Himachal Pradesh	2718	0	1303	0	157	0	4178	5567	75
9	Jammu & Kashmir	5460	1360	200	0	0	0	7020	22224	31.6
10	Karnataka	5810	0	941	110	58	712	7631	19179	39.8
11	Kerala	76	0	2098	0	138	296	2608	3886	67.1
12	MP & Chhatisgarh	17883	0	359	46	6796	1126	26210	44345	59.1
13	Maharashtra	11179	0	0	1056	517	303	13055	30771	42.4
14	Manipur	133	0	111	0	481	227	952	2233	42.6
15	Mizoram	137	0	0	0	1050	694	1881	2108	89.2
16	Meghalaya	137	0	7	0	1030	34	1208	2243	53.9
17	Nagaland	390	0	0	0	127	478	995	1658	60
18	Orissa	5028	0	681	75	263	75	6122	15571	39.3
19	Punjab	372	282	338	288	0	0	1280	5036	25.4
20	Rajasthan	3137	6650	53	1418	0	110	11368	34224	33.2
21	Sikkim	158	0	0	0	76	0	234	710	33
22	Tamil Nadu	4926	0	96	96	78	138	5334	13006	41
23	Tripura	121	0	191	0	203	113	628	1049	59.9
24	UP & Uttaranchal	11392	212	2350	1370	0	0	15324	29441	52
25	West Bengal	1197	0	710	170	556	119	2752	8875	31
26	Delhi	55	0	6	10	0	11	82	148	55.4
27	A & N Islands	187	0	0	9	0	9	205	825	24.8
28	Chandigarh	0	0	0	0	0	0	0	0	0
29	D & N Haveli	0	0	0	0	0	0	0	0	0
30	Daman & Diu	0	0	0	0	0	0	0	0	0
31	Lakshadweep	0	0	0	0	0	0	0	0	0
32	Pondicherry	0	0	0	0	0	0	0	0	0
	Grand Total (Million ha)	**93.68**	**9.48**	**14.3**	**5.94**	**16.03**	**7.38**	**146.82**	**328.6**	

Source: Planning Commission, Report of the Working Group on Environment and environmental regulatory mechanisms in environment and forests for the 11th Five-Year Plan (2007-2012).

Table 31.6 State wise details of funds released and utilized under Green India Mission (Rs. in Lakhs)

S.NO.	Name of State	Amount Released	Amount Utilized
1	Maharashtra	405.77	361.55
2	Jharkhand	147.00	75.50
3	Kerala	194.60	122.79
4	Tamil Nadu	72.15	59.73
5	Gujarat	133.80	114.81
6	Rajasthan	275.25	50.00
7	Himachal Pradesh	126.50	105.00
8	Jammu & Kashmir	64.00	22.82
9	Orissa	107.50	8.80
10	Punjab	125.50	122.27
11	Haryana	357.00	201.00
12	Chhattisgarh	972.00	331.89
13	Assam	130.00	125.00
14	Andhra Pradesh	89.53	5.00
15	Manipur	40.50	40.50
16	Nagaland	141.50	141.50
17	Tripura	350.50	84.44
18	Karnataka	267.45	232.86
19	Madhya Pradesh	823.50	66.51
20	Uttar Pradesh	119.50	74.25
21	Uttarakhand	51.00	11.00
	Total	**4994.55**	**2357.22**

Source: Annexure referred in reply to part (c) of Lok Sabha unstarred question no. 5321 due for answer on April 29, 2013, http://164.100.47.132/Annexture/lsq15/13/au5321.htm.

Exclusive Economic Zone and other Maritime Zones Act of 1976 provides for specific designated areas for the protection of marine environment and resources in the exclusive economic zones and the continental shelf. The Offshore Areas Mineral (Development and Regulation) Act of 2002 provides for development and regulations of mineral resources in the territorial waters, continental shelf, exclusive economic zones and other maritime zones of India. Regarding living resources, Maritime Zones of India (Regulation of Fishing by Foreign Vessels) Act of 1981 provides for the regulation of fishing by foreign vessels in certain maritime zones of India. Further, potential fishing zone advisories for the adjoining sea off the east coast, west coast, Lakshadweep Islands and Andaman and Nicobar Islands are not issued during the breeding season with a view to protect juvenile fishes. A few other international agreements having repercussion on marine resources and to which India is a party includes the Agreement related to Part XI of the UN Convention on Law of the Sea, 1995 Fish Stock Agreement and Convention for the Conservation of Antarctic Marine Resources and related agreements.

5. Human settlement and environment policies

According to the 2011 census (GoI, 2011d) India's population was 1.21 billion. The urban population (377.1 million) accounted for 31.63 percent. Over the 20 years from 1991 to 2011, the population increased by 43 percent; the urban population rising by 73 percent and rural by 43 percent. Whereas the overall percent of urban population is still relatively low, e.g., compared to China, the rise in absolute numbers has been significant – a 1.8 percent per annum growth rate from 1991 to 2011. The rapid rise in urban population (2.8 percent per annum growth rate from 1991 to 2011) has added to the stress on urban environment and resources. This is manifest in poor access to clean air, land, safe drinking water and sanitation. The rapid "suburbanization" (Hallegatte and Fay, 2012), i.e., the faster expansion of rural areas adjacent to India's major metropolitan cities, is adding further stress to the urban system.

The rising population in rural areas and intensification of agriculture has led to rural environmental and resource crises such as manifested in scarcity of common property resources like water and gathered biomass fuels and increased use of chemical fertilizer and pesticides. Deforestation, salinization and desertification have added further pressure on lands and land productivity. Rural development, therefore, has been a key policy area where government has instituted various development programs such as Mahatma Gandhi National Rural Employment Guarantee Act, Pradhan Mantri Gram Sadak Yojana, National Rural Livelihood Mission and Indira Awaas Yojana being implemented by the Ministry of Rural Development. These programs directly aim at improvement in the quality of life in rural areas through employment generation, development of rural infrastructure and provision of other basic amenities. In addition, environment and resource-oriented programs are initiated to align environmental and development goals to gain multiple co-benefits like reduced indoor air pollution from clean energy resources and improved water use from sustainable agriculture practices.

5.1 Rural environment policies

Biomass, wood, agricultural residues, animal dung, charcoal, and forest residues constitute the major source of cooking energy in India, and as per the 2011 census, 495 of the households in the country use firewood for cooking (World Bank, 2013a). An extreme negative externality from use of biomass arises from health hazards from indoor air pollution, especially that of women and young children, who spend considerable amount of time indoors. Recent research regarding the impact of indoor air pollution on human health in India has put an estimate of about Rs.865 billion or 1.3 percent of GDP in 2009, of which about 68 percent is associated with chronic obstructive pulmonary disease 32 percent with acute respiratory illness, and the balance, 10 percent, linked to morbidity (World Bank, 2013a).

The over-dependency on agriculture for livelihood by nearly 60 percent of the population has led to a scenario whereby the land-labor ratio is skewed toward excess labor compared to what a profit-maximizing production function would have employed. This has shifted the excess farm labor to look for other means of sustenance such as fishing, grazing, and exploiting other natural resources on common lands for survival. Here, open access property rights have led to overfishing and overgrazing beyond the natural regeneration rate of water bodies and grasslands, leading to the tragedy of the commons (Hardin, 1968). The lack of clarity on land title, absence of a land lease market, absence of reverse mortgages, and restrictions on land trade have added to the woes of land dependents, rooting them to the land. An Achilles' heel of the agriculture policies is the subsidy for electricity, fertilizer and water. The underpricing, at times even the free supply, has resulted in over-exploitation and inefficient use of scarce resources, leading to severe environmental externalities from water logging, water wastage and soil quality deterioration.

5.2 Urban environment policies

Urban environment in India suffers the most because of juxtaposition of human settlements and economic activities that are growing unbridled and rapidly. According to an UN assessment report (UN, 2012), India's urban population is going to reach 50 percent by about 2044 from nearly 30 percent at present. Conflicts with biodiversity hotspots and coastal zones already are visible and if ignored, may have significant adverse implications for the country's environment, ecology and sustainability. The ambient air quality deterioration in cities is manifest in the higher concentration of respirable suspended particulate matter resulting from construction and vehicular exhaust emissions. Lack of scientific assessments that apportion pollutions to sources and their impacts on urban ecosystems has resulted in blind spots and consequent inaction. The CPCB carried out source apportionment studies in six cities in the year 2007. These studies showed that contribution from vehicles to the ambient air quality measures in PM10 ranged from 2 percent to 48 percent (Bangalore: 11–23 percent, Chennai: 35–48 percent, Delhi 9–21 percent, Kanpur: 15–17 percent, Mumbai: 8–26 percent, and Pune: 2–10 percent) but there is little policy follow-up. The water pollution from domestic sewage remains a major concern. But the responses have been are sparse as managing domestic sewage comes within the jurisdiction of urban local bodies. For the total discharge in the country of 38,000 million liters per day (MLD) of sewage, the treatment capacity is limited to 11,000 MLD.

For stemming vehicular pollution, the government has taken several steps through the following:

1. Bharat Stage IV emission standards (equivalent to EURO IV standards) for all categories of new vehicles (except two- and three-wheelers) in 13 mega-cities, namely Delhi, Mumbai, Kolkata, Chennai, Bangalore, Hyderabad, Ahmedabad, Pune, Surat, Kanpur, Agra, Lucknow and Sholapur from the year 2010.
2. Sulfur content in diesel and petrol reduced further to 0.005 percent (50 mg/kg) in the 13 mega-cities by 01.04.2010. The amount of sulfur in diesel and petrol is 0.035 percent (350 mg/kg) and 0.015 percent (150 mg/kg), respectively, in the rest of the country.
3. The Bharat Stage III standards have been implemented for all categories of two- and three-wheelers all over the country.
4. Auto fuels compliant to B.S III (whole country) and B.S IV (for 13 cities) specifications are made available in the respective cities.
5. Pollution under control norms have been implemented for both gasoline and diesel vehicles.
6. Alternate clean fuels like CNG, liquefied petroleum gas (LPG), electric vehicles, bio-diesel etc. have been promoted/encouraged and incentivized.
7. By-passes have been constructed to avoid unnecessary entry into the city of heavy-duty vehicles and other vehicles carrying cargo for other destinations.
8. Mass transport system has been strengthened to discourage use of private vehicles (including diesel cars).
9. Notification of ambient air quality standards with respect to 12 pollutants and preparation of action plans to meet these standards.
10. Emphasis on preparation of master plan/development plan of metro cities and preparation of compatible land use plan, including not permitting industries in non-conforming areas.
11. Environmental clearance has been made mandatory for establishment of certain categories of polluting industries, building construction and infrastructure projects.

In addition, the Sustainable Urban Transport Project was initiated since 2010 and 2011 under Jawaharlal Nehru National Urban Renewal Mission to strengthen the capacity of state governments and cities in planning, financing, implementing, operating and managing sustainable urban transport systems. The intention is to assist states and cities in preparing and implementing demonstration "green transport" projects as pilots toward reduction of greenhouse gases in the urban environment.

6. Economic policies and environment

There are different schools of thoughts about the correlation between the economic growth and environmental quality. The "limits to growth" paradigm presumes resources as constraining factors for economic growth. On the other hand, the proponents of green growth postulate that economic growth and good environment complement each other. Empiricists have demonstrated the environmental Kuznets curve hypothesis, which theorizes the existence, albeit contentious, of an inverted-U relationship between environmental quality and economic growth. Notwithstanding the differences, there is a general agreement that natural resources and the environment play a vital role in the economy either as a direct input, such as mineral resources, or indirectly as an enabler, such as a carbon sink. Still, barring a few, the ecosystem services remain non-monetized positive externalities that are neither internalized in the firm's production function nor in the national accounts.

6.1 Resource and product pricing

The GoI's strategy on natural resource pricing has not followed the conventional economic efficiency rationale. While the government is aware that the "first-best pricing" would provide greater surplus, it is also sensitive to the fact that doing so would mean that economically weaker section of population would be priced off. But by adopting policies that deviate from the "first-best" mean that distortions are visible elsewhere in the economy. For example, despite having a substantial import dependency, India's energy prices have remained misaligned with international benchmarks and are artificially kept lower than the global prices for many products. While targeted subsidies have a place in a developing economy, their use for political reasons distorts the welfare objective. At a microeconomic level, the underpricing has led to: 1) reduced incentives to be energy efficient, 2) leakages across subsidized and unsubsidized segments, 3) fiscal imbalances, and 4) lack of motivation to optimally invest in the sector. Nonetheless, several initiatives for rationalizing the resource prices, in different sectors, are underway. The earlier practice of pricing coal was on gross calorific value and resulted in 30 percent to 50 percent lower price for domestic coal compared to imported coal. This is being corrected now following the international best practice of pricing on the basis of useful heat value.

Similarly, in case of pricing of petroleum products, even though the government dismantled the Administered Pricing Mechanism in 2002, it has since continued to modulate the retail prices by not allowing pass-through of changes in the international crude price. As recommended by the Rangarajan Committee in 2006, the public sector oil marketing companies pay trade parity price for purchase of diesel and import parity price for purchase of Public Distribution System (PDS) kerosene and domestic LPG from the refineries. As per the refinery gate price effective August 2013, the oil marketing companies are incurring under-recovery of Rs. 10.22 per liter on sale of diesel (to retail consumers), Rs. 33.54 per liter on PDS kerosene and Rs. 411.99 per 14.2 kg cylinder on subsidized domestic LPG [16] (see Table 31.7 for an estimate on under-recovery).

In electricity pricing, political expediencies and exigencies have taken precedence over sound economic and financial principles, with a result that the tariffs are very low, especially for agriculture and rural consumers, but also far lower than the economic value for many other categories of consumers. This jeopardizes the financial health of the utilities and distribution companies and forces them to overcharge the urban and industrial consumers, who are then driven to find alternatives like captive power generation that have inferior scale economy. Electricity subsidies are cascading the distortion in the electricity market from the entire chain of inputs to the final outputs. This has prevented the modernization of the power sector and has contributed to the loss of competitiveness of several key manufacturing and service industries. Apart from this, the more evident outcome is the sustained demand-supply gap that has led to frequent power cuts, secondary investment in inefficient small-sized power generation technologies such as diesel generators, and damage to appliances and machines due to frequent power tripping, which have ill-affected the quality of life of consumers. Correction of distortions in electricity pricing is one area where huge economic gains are evident but where political will, followed by implementation of a strategic action plan, can be the prime mover to untie the Gordian knot.

Table 31.7 Under recoveries to oil marketing companies on sale of sensitive petroleum products (in Rs. Crores)

(a) As India imports about 80% of its crude oil requirement, international oil prices play a decisive role in the domestic pricing of sensitive petroleum products. The public sector oil marketing companies (OMCs) viz. Indian Oil Corporation Limited, Bharat Petroleum Corporation Limited and Hindustan Petroleum Corporation Limited pay trade parity price to refineries when they buy diesel, and pay import parity price for PDS kerosene and domestic LPG. Accordingly, OMCs ought to fix retail prices based on this cost. However, the retail prices, which are modulated by the Government, are generally lower. The difference between the required price based on trade parity/import parity and the actual selling price realized (excluding taxes and dealer's commission) represents the under-recoveries of OMCs.

(b) In tandem with the steady increase in international oil prices, the OMCs' under-recoveries have also been rising. The details of the under-recoveries incurred by OMCs on the sale of sensitive petroleum products from the year 2005-06 to 2012-13 are given below:

Products	2005–06	2006–07	2007–08	2008–09	2009–10	2010–11	2011–12	2012–13
Petrol★★	2723	2027	7332	5181	5151	2227★★	–	–
Diesel#	12647	18776	35166	52286	9279	34706	81192	92061
Domestic LPG^	10246	10701	15523	17600	14257	21772	29997	39558
PDS Kerosene	14384	17883	19102	28225	17364	19484	27352	29410
Total	**40000**	**49387**	**77123**	**103292**	**46051**	**78190**	**138541**	**161029**

Note:

★★ Under-recovery on petrol is only up to June 25, 2010.

#Effective 18.01.2013, the government has taken decision to sell diesel to all consumers taking bulk supplies directly from the installations of OMCs at the non-subsidized market determined price.

^Effective 13.09.2012/18.01.2013, the government has taken decision to restrict the supply of subsidized LPG cylinders to each consumer to nine cylinders annually.

Source: Petroleum Planning & Analysis Cell (PPAC), 2013; http://ppac.org.in

6.2 Waste management and waste recovery

Municipal solid waste management in India is a state subject and it is the responsibility of the state government or urban local bodies to plan, design, implement, operate and maintain the solid waste management system in the urban areas. The municipal solid waste generation in urban areas, state-wise, is given in Table 31.8. the Ministry of New and Renewable Energy is promoting energy recovery from urban and industrial wastes, but the initiatives on energy recovery are still in the initial stages. Different types of financial and fiscal incentives for recovery of energy from urban, industrial and agricultural wastes and residues include capital subsidy, concessional customs and excise duty rates and support for R&D of new and more efficient technologies. Instruments like "build, own, operate, and transfer" are supported in the areas of bio-methanation, combustion and gasification technologies for power generation. The feed-in tariff rates of Rs. 2.59 to Rs. 4.25 per kWh makes the electricity from such sources fairly competitive. Gradual adoption of improved waste management practices, including waste segregation, is improving heat recovery. A list of municipal and urban waste based power projects taken up so far can be found in Table 31.9.

The MoEF has instituted e-waste rules, effective since May 1, 2012. The rules are based on extended producers responsibility, which mandates the producers to collect e-waste generated from the end of life of their products by setting up collections centers or take back systems either individually or collectively. Recycling of the collected e-waste is to be done only in facilities authorized and registered with SPCBs or PCCs. Finally, wastes generated are required to be sold to a registered or authorized recycler or re-processor having environmentally sound facilities.

Notwithstanding the measures described above, waste recovery in India, through legal mandates and formal measures exist, is still in the initial stage. An active informal sector has been delivering sizable waste recovery, though the working conditions in the informal sector have been dismal and unsustainable. Waste management and waste recovery practices have the potential to deliver multiple social, economic and environmental co-benefits as India makes the transition to urbanization and industrialization.

6.3 Environmental innovations

Environmental innovations and related R&D thrust in India has been through demand-pull policies. For example, in the energy sector, measures like feed-in tariffs are instituted to bring about technological change. Such measures are good to promote penetration of existing technologies, but they do not spur innovations (Weber and Hemmelskamp, 2005), especially in developing countries, since in the near-term the change in production frontier comes from technology transfer rather than domestic innovations. The demand-side measures for achieving environmental targets, e.g., emissions tax or cap-and-trade, have marginal effect in the near-term on the technological frontier. India's participation in the Clean Development Mechanism, for instance, did induce sizable mitigation activities, but these had little effect on domestic technology innovations. Still, such technology transfers do induce innovations for local adaptations and to that extent have contributed to shifting the technology frontier, albeit marginally.

A key issue with environmental innovations is that there is no reliable, let alone free or vibrant, market in India for the supply of environmental public goods like waste recovery, air pollution or clean water supply. The consumers in these markets are the governments. The

Table 31.8 Estimated state-wise MSW generation during the year 2008 for urban India

S. No.	States/UTs	Municipal solid waste (MSW) Generation (Tons Per Day)
1.	Andaman & Nicobar	146.531
2.	Andhra Pradesh	25353.613
3.	Arunachal Pradesh	265.71
4.	Assam	3794.17
5.	Bihar	9408.294
6.	Chandigarh	1389.159
7.	Chattisgarh	4858.481
8.	Dadra Nagar Haveli	59.704
9.	Daman & Diu	73.98
10.	Delhi	22526.265
11.	Goa	937.521
12.	Gujarat	24588.124
13.	Haryana	7530.141
14.	Himachal Pradesh	642.275
15.	Jammu & Kashmir	3016.141
16.	Jharkhand	7060.148
17.	Karnataka	22845.629
18.	Kerala	9983.801
19.	Lakshadweep	36.559
20.	Madhya Pradesh	19347.071
21.	Maharashtra	55052.207
22.	Manipur	698.443
23.	Meghalaya	525.243
24.	Mizoram	616.104
25.	Nagaland	390.038
26.	Orissa	6178.866
27.	Pudducherry	994.048
28.	Punjab	10504.627
29.	Rajasthan	15687.05
30.	Sikkim	65.173
31.	Tamil Nadu	37167.161
32.	Tripura	620.234
33.	Uttarakhand	2626.57
34.	Uttar Pradesh	40281.443
35.	West Bengal	27445.574

Source: Lok Sabha Annexure unstarred question 465 dated November 26, 2012, http://164.100.47.132/LssNew/psearch/QResult15.aspx?qref=137514.

Table 31.9 List of municipal and urban waste-based power projects

No.	Project promoters	Location	Capacity (MW)	Technology	Project cost (Rs. in crores)	Present status
1	M/s. Timarpur Okhla Waste Management Private Ltd. (TOWMCL), Jindal ITF Centre, 28 ShivajiMarg, New Delhi (Promoted by Jindal Urban Infrastructure Ltd.)	Old NDMC Compost plant, New Okhla tank, New Delhi	16	Combustion	188.28	Commissioned
2	M/s East Delhi Waste processing Company (P) Ltd., New Delhi(Promoted by DIAL, IL&FS Energy Dev. Co. Ltd. (IEDCL) and SELCO International Ltd.)	Gazipur, Delhi	12	Combustion	155.42	Under installation
3	M/s Srinivasa Gayatri Resource Recovery Limited No. 303, Shreshta Bhumi Complex, No. 87, K.R. Road, Next to GayanaSamaja, Bangalore	Village Mandur, Bangalore	8	Combustion	70.33	Under installation
4	M/s RDF Power Projects Ltd.401, Galada Towers, Adjacent Lane to Pantaloons, Begumpet, Hyderabad	Chinnaravulapally Village, BibinagarMadal in Nalgonda District, A. P.	11	Combustion	114.11	Under installation
5	M/s. Delhi MSW Solutions Ltd., Sector–5, Pocket No–1, Bawana Industrial Area, Bawana, New Delhi. (promoted by RamkyEnviro Engineers Ltd., Hyderabad)	Bawana, Delhi	24	Combustion	268.27	Under installation
6	M/s. Rochem Separation Systems (India) Pvt. Ltd., 101, HDIL Towers, Anant Kanekar Marg, Bandra (E), Mumbai.	Pune	10	Gasification	90.00	Under installation
7	M/s. Solapur Bio-Energy Systems Pvt. Ltd., CBD Belapur, Navi Mumbai.	Solapur	3	Bio-methanation	40.89	Under installation

Source: Annexure referred to in reply to Part (c) of the Lok Sabha Unstarred Question No. 4241 for 22nd March 2013, Retrieved from http://164.100.47.132/annexture/lsq15/13/au4241.htm on 10th October 2013.

lax implementation, budget shortages and high transaction cost of dealing with the bureaucracy all add up to pose enormous risk for innovative firms or entrepreneurs. The supply-side push for technology development in India is driven, to an extent, through government laboratories. But the paucity of funds, absence of technology targets and bureaucratic functioning has led to inferior supply of innovations from laboratories as compared to their scientific capabilities.

Environmental R&D is contingent on the rise of environmental industry. India is passing through the early stage of building up environmental services and industry. The government of India, rather than providing subsidies, would get better R&D responses from industry and service sectors if environmental laws are backed with mandated environmental standards and their strict implementation. This will create demand certainty, which is fundamental to investments in innovations. The demand-pull will then create its own supply-push and associated innovations. A credible environment innovation policy regime should also take into account the fact that, in absence of basic innovations and swift implementation, India will get locked-in into an unsustainable high natural resource consumption phase.

6.4 Disaster and insurance

India's vulnerability, in varying degrees, to a large number of natural as well as man-made disasters could be ascribed to expanding population, urbanization and industrialization, development within high-risk zones, environmental degradation and climate change. The severity of this scenario may be gauged from the fact that around 58.6 percent of the landmass is prone to earthquakes of moderate to very high intensity; more than 40 million hectares (12 percent of land) is prone to floods and river erosion; of the 7,516-km-long coastline, close to 5,700 km is prone to cyclones and tsunamis; 68 percent of the cultivable area is vulnerable to drought; and hilly areas are at risk from landslides and avalanches. Besides, vulnerability to emergencies of chemical, biological, radiological and nuclear origin cannot be ruled out. GoI has been systematically trying to look at the problem from a proactive prevention, mitigation and preparedness-driven approach rather than the erstwhile relief-centric response.

As per the Global Climate Change Vulnerability Index that identifies risks to populations, company operations, supply chains and investments, six of India's biggest cities figure in a list of the top 25 cities exposed to risks of environmental disasters. To this end, GoI took a major step by enacting the Disaster Management Act of 2005, which envisaged the creation of the National Disaster Management Authority headed by the prime minister; State Disaster Management Authorities headed by the chief ministers, and District Disaster Management Authorities headed by the collector or district magistrate or deputy commissioner, to spearhead and adopt a holistic and integrated approach to disaster management.

The government funds cannot cover the full damages caused by disasters. The government at best can mobilize services, as public goods, to minimize damages before, during and after the disasters. It would deal with disaster in the aggregate; it cannot be an efficient insurer who would provide individual compensations as the insurers would do based on the individual insurance cover and the premium paid by the insured. Therefore, the financial tools such as catastrophic risk financing, risk insurance, catastrophe bonds, microfinance and insurance etc. have a role and government at best may provide marginal fiscal incentives to such arrangements to the extent that coverage is in the public interest. This role of the government is pivotal to bringing in the private sector to the insurance market and also to overcome the moral hazard and adverse selection problems that are common to the insurance sector.

7. India in the global environmental regime

India is an active proponent and participant in the framing of global environmental conventions, laws and treaties. In turn, the environmental law-making in India is influenced significantly by the transnational environmental laws. In a number of instances, even the Supreme Court has guided the executives to follow the environmental principles agreed in the international conventions and treaties to which India is a signatory.

7.1 India in global environment regime

Starting with the UN Conference on the Human Environment in 1972 in Stockholm, today India is very much part of numerous global environmental regimes such as, but not limited to (Planning Commission, 2006):

1. United Nations Conference on the Human Environment 1972: The treaty calls upon governments and peoples to exert common efforts for the preservation and improvement of the human environment.
2. Convention on International Trade in Endangered Species of Wild Fauna and Flora1975: The agreement aims to ensure that international trade in specimens of wild animals and plants does not threaten their survival.
3. Ramsar Convention, 1971: The Convention on Wetland provides a framework for national action and international cooperation for the conservation and right use of wetlands and their resources.
4. The Basel Convention on the Control of Transboundary Movements of Hazardous Wastes 1989 (signed and ratified in 1992): The convention aims at minimizing hazardous waste production wherever possible.
5. United Nations Conference on Environment and Development 1992: The conference had three sub-declarations: 1) Agenda 21, 2) Rio Declaration, and 3) Millennium Development Goals.
6. Framework Convention on Climate Change 1992: The convention set the overall framework for intergovernmental efforts to tackle the challenge posed by climate change.
7. Vienna Convention 1985: The convention provided the framework under which the Montreal Protocol was negotiated. It aims for protecting human health and the environment against the adverse effects of ozone depletion.
8. Convention on Biological Diversity1992: This convention outlines principles for conservation of biological diversity, the sustainable use of its components and the fair and equitable sharing of the benefits arising out of the utilization of genetic resources.
9. Convention to Combat Desertification 1996: The objective of this convention is to strengthen the capacity of countries experiencing serious drought and/or desertification.
10. Rotterdam Convention on Prior Informed Consent Procedure for certain Hazardous Chemicals in International Trade 2002 (Ratified May, 24, 2005): The convention aims to promote shared responsibility and cooperative efforts among parties in the international trade of certain hazardous chemicals, and also to enable the countries to monitor and control trade in such hazardous chemicals.
11. Stockholm Convention on Persistent Organic Pollutants 2001(signed in May 2002, ratified in September 2005): The convention is a global treaty to protect human health and the environment from persistent organic pollutants.

12. Chemical Weapons Convention: This convention is a universal, nondiscriminatory, multilateral, disarmament treaty that bans the development, production, acquisition, transfer, use and stockpile of all chemical weapons.

13. Strategic Approach to International Chemicals Management 2006: The treaty aims to develop a strategic approach to international chemicals management and the three essential components of the SAICM include: 1) an overarching policy strategy; 2) global plan of action; and 3) a Dubai declaration.

14. World Trade Organization (WTO) agreements: While WTO has no specific agreement dealing with the environment, there are a number of declarations, for example, the Doha Ministerial Conference 2001, that include provisions dealing with trade and environmental concerns.

7.2 Climate change

India has engaged actively in various multilateral negotiations on climate change. India signed the United Nations Framework Convention on Climate Change (UNFCCC) on June 10, 1992 and ratified it on November 1, 1993. Within the climate change negotiations, India has emphasized the principles of "equity" and the "common but differentiated responsibilities." On emissions mitigation, India has kept a consistent position of advocating allocation of "equal per capita emissions rights" to all countries. India has made a voluntary pledge to reduce the emissions intensity of the nation's GDP by 20 percent to 25 percent between years of 2005 to 2020 (GoI, 2010) and has endorsed the global climate stabilization target of limiting the temperature rise to under 2°C.

India signed the Kyoto Protocol (KP) to the UNFCCC on August 26, 2002. As a developing country, though India had no emissions limitations commitment under the KP, it has contributed significantly to the greenhouse gas emissions mitigation by being an active participant in the Clean Development Mechanism (CDM) of the KP. India's private sector responded well to the CDM and registered numerous projects in diverse areas of mitigation and thereby gained sizable certified emissions reductions that were traded in the EU Emissions Trading System.

Toward responding to climate change, India has followed a "development focused" approach to climate change policies (Shukla, 2006) with aims to align climate actions with national development goals (Shukla, 2005). India realized very early that climate change is not solely an environmental issue but the manifestation of style and mode of development (Heller and Shukla, 2003; Sathaye et al., 2006). India's "National Action Plan on Climate Change (NAPCC)" (GoI, 2008) released by the prime minister's office in June 2008, is an eminent example of this approach. NAPCC includes a variety of mitigation and adaptation actions, implemented through eight national missions that are institutionalized in and implemented through relevant ministries.

Recognizing the importance of adapting to the vulnerability in the future climate change, India has been active in shaping the various financial instruments of the UNFCCC such as the Green Climate Fund as an operating entity of the financial mechanism of the UNFCCC that was established at the 16th session of the Conference of Parties to the UNFCCC held in Cancun, Mexico, in December 2010. The government of India is actively pursuing strategies internally to address the issues of mitigation, vulnerability and adaptation to climate change by undertaking various scientific studies (INCAA, 2010; GoI-MoEF, 2004, GoI-MoEf, 2012)

GoI adopted the NAPCC in 2008 with eight missions, namely 1) National Solar Mission, 2) National Mission on Enhanced Energy Efficiency, 3) National Mission on Sustainable Habitat, 4) National Water Mission, 5) National Mission for Sustaining the Himalayan Ecosystem, 6) Green India Mission, 7) National Mission for Sustainable Agriculture, and 8) National Mission for Strategic Knowledge for Climate Change. These missions are implemented by the respective ministries on the basis of detailed plans that are approved by the prime minister's Council on Climate Change. Besides, GoI has been actively pursuing and encouraging the states to prepare State Action Plan on Climate Change at the state level to address climate change.

The national missions, e.g., National Solar Mission and Mission on Enhanced Energy Efficiency, aim to coordinate policies that overcome technological, financial, and market barriers to the penetration of solar and energy efficient technologies, respectively. The legal, institutional and policy initiatives that have followed these missions are targeting the entire value chain of the energy sector as well as integration with related environmental concerns like water stresses and air quality. It then seeks to find the mechanisms through which development policies can exert the leverage effect on the drivers of climate change.

7.3 Biodiversity

With only 2.5 percent of the world's land area, India accounts for 7.8 percent of the recorded species of the world, including 45,500 recorded species of plants and 91,000 recorded species of animals (MoEF, 2009). India has adopted a multipronged approach to preserve its immensely rich biodiversity. As a signatory to the Convention on Biological Diversity, India's policies follow the convention's three goals: 1) conservation of biological diversity; 2) sustainable use of the components of biological diversity; and, 3) fair and equitable sharing of the benefits arising out of the utilization of genetic resources. In accordance, biodiversity is labeled as a critical national priority because of its vital nexus with the local livelihoods of a sizable population.

With an exceptional diverse ecological habitats like forests, grassland, wetlands, coastal and marine ecosystems and desert ecosystems, GoI has taken concrete steps for the conservation of biological diversity through: survey and making inventory of floral and faunal resources; assessment of the forest cover to develop an accurate database for planning and monitoring; establishment of a protected area network of national parks, wildlife sanctuaries, conservation and community Reserves; designating biosphere reserves for conservation of representative ecosystems; and undertaking of species-oriented programs, such as Project Tiger and Project Elephant; complemented with ex situ conservation efforts. In addition, Biological Diversity Act 2002 has also been enacted with the aim to conserve biological resources of the country and regulation of access to these resources to ensure equitable sharing of benefits arising out of their use, under which a National Biodiversity Authority and State Biodiversity Boards have been set up for implementing the provisions of the act.

However, despite these measures, threats to biological resources persist due to unguarded development and illegal poaching, such as of tigers, whose organs have a lucrative market. Besides protective measures to stem the damages, attention is increasingly being paid to the preservation of the genetic pools of species under threat of extinction or protection against epidemics. A recent instance is that of creating a second habitat for the Asiatic lions, who now exist only in a single habitat, to protect them from extinction. The policy of trans-boundary cooperation has been paying dividends in cases such as the cooperation with Bangladesh for preservation of Bengal tigers.

7.4 Trade and environment

The ongoing negotiations on trade and environment under the Doha Round contain elements that are relevant for the environment, even in case of global issues like climate change. In trade negotiations though, India has shown reluctance to accept agreements on IT and environmental goods that are proposed by a group of developed nations "plurilaterally" at the WTO. Instead,

India has advocated the environmental project approach (EPA) that fully responds to the objectives of the Doha Ministerial Declaration, i.e., to eliminate tariff and non-tariff barriers to trade in environmental goods and services.

Unlike the "list" approach that solely focuses on trade in goods and is silent on environmental services, the "project" approach addresses the explicit mandate to include environmental services in addition to issues relating to non-tariff barriers. Because of the lack of support for EPA, India and Argentina jointly floated the "integrated approach" for liberalization of all goods and services for designated projects, such as water and waste water management, environmental monitoring and renewable energy, etc.

On climate change, India has been active in undertaking mitigation and adaptation measures, together with compensation for the full incremental costs and transfer of clean technologies from the developed nations. India has advocated making special and differential treatment element an essential part of any discussion on environment goods and services. While remaining active in the framing of global environmental laws and their implementation, India, like most developing countries, has been vigilant to ensure that the "environment" or issues like "human rights" are not used as a pretext for restricting trade.

8. Environment and corporations: the conflict

The fair distribution of the value of environmental common property resources has confounded most governments, India being no exception. Natural resources are repositories of wealth. Competitive markets can reward its owner with the best value. In India, by law, the national or state governments own these resources inherently. In theory, an ideal government would distribute the resources in a manner that maximizes social welfare. A combination of competitive markets and ideal governments, though, rarely exist anywhere. The combination of political exigencies and motives for super-profits, together with corporate power, in reality skew the distribution in favor of corporations. In its extreme, the conflict of interest even manifest in wars, as often witnessed in resource-rich regions.

A similar conflict of interest arises in distribution of the direct value of ecosystem services and the existence or option values of ecosystems in contingent markets. A significant portion of option value may fairly belong to the future generations. In the absence of rules, the direct market value is appropriated by the in situ nexus of private and state actors, leaving little for the rest of the society or future generations. The misallocations, disguised on efficiency and expediency grounds, result in win–win situation for the small section of beneficiaries, imposing a "lose" option on the rest of the society.

In India, as in most countries, the conflict of public and private interests in allocation of environmental goods and natural resources has been at the center of intense public debates and people's movements seeking reversals of unfair allocations. In India, government policies have reflected the public concerns through various regulations, policies and administrative measures, many of which are already narrated in earlier sections. But India needs even more stringent regulatory and administrative safeguards to ensure that resources are managed in a sustainable and equitable manner. Specific policies such as transparent auction of natural resource assets and corporate declaration of green practices as a part of the corporate social responsibility (CSR) obligations are among the small first steps.

The businesses are increasingly recognizing the need to switch from a "profit only" mindset to a more holistic approach to doing business that addresses the three broad components of sustainability, i.e., "people, planet and profits." However, competition distorted by greed often drives corporations to find short-cuts that circumvent social accountability and legal culpability.

In recent decades, the economic reforms in India with their singular focus on economic growth have enhanced competition and this added to pressures on ecosystems and natural resources. Corporations have been in the middle of several of the environmental controversies, as in the following cases cited, wherein the legal and administrative remedies were sought through public activism. Sometimes, corporate projects get entangled in the struggle for dominance among state actors or political factions. The cases following show that enlightened public oversight, proactive judiciary and clean administration are vital to avert the corporate versus public interest conflicts. In the end, though, the corporations will have to find the right balance for their own sustainability and the governments have to frame clear rules that stop unlawful encroachments on environmental and natural resource assets and which at the same time reduce the transaction costs of undertaking legitimate development activities.

8.1 Lavasa

Lavasa is one of the biggest and poshest residential property development projects in India, located in pristine hills in the state of Maharashtra. The project development started in 2004, with the environment clearances granted by the government of Maharashtra through the Hill Station Development Act of 1996. The MoEF's environment impact assessment notification (1994) and the environment clearance under the Environment Protection Act (1986) were bypassed. Wrapped under the environment, the real conflict was between the powers and jurisdiction of the state and the central governments. The MoEF concluded the state's clearance to be illegal and called it a case of conflict of interest and recommended that the state government withdraw the clearance and not repeat the practice in future. Finally, in order to overcome this impasse, MoEF recommended that Lavasa set up an environmental restoration fund, set aside a profit percentage earmarked for the CSR and submit a revised development plan.

8.2 Vedanta

The case of Bauxite Mining Project, a joint venture between the Odisha Mining Corporation and Sterlite Industries, a subsidiary of the multinational Vedanta Aluminum, is remarkable because it signals the first-ever environmental referendum in India. In the case of *Orissa Mining Corporation Ltd. Versus Ministry of Environment and Forest,*[17] the Supreme Court in April 2013 directed the Gram Sabha (the village council), the smallest unit of local governance, to consider whether scheduled tribes and other traditional forest dwellers, like Dongaria Kondh, Kutia Kandha and others, have any religious rights, i.e., rights of worship, over the Niyamgiri Hills. Further, the apex court also empowered the Gram Sabha to examine whether the proposed mining area Niyama Danger, 10 km away from the peak, would in any way affect the abode of Niyam-Raja (the king of Niyamgiri). On the conclusion of the proceeding before the Gram Sabha determining the claims submitted before it for which the Supreme Court awarded three months, the MoEF was authorized to then take a final decision on the grant of Stage II clearance for the Bauxite Mining Project of M/s. Sterlite (parent company of Vedanta) within two months thereafter. At the time of writing, all the 12 gram sabhas selected by the Odisha government have voted unanimously to reject the mining operations.[18]

8.3 Okhla bird sanctuary

The case of the Okhla bird sanctuary[19] presents a number of anomalies with regard to interpretation of the extant environmental impact assessment (EIA) notification and also showcases the classic conflict between the central government and state in terms of reach and jurisdiction of

MoEF over the state. First, the construction of one memorial project, practically adjoining the Okhla bird sanctuary, despite being a potential threat to the sensitive and fragile ecological balance of the sanctuary, could not be stopped because there is no law to stop it. Second, the project, despite being large in size with the total area of 33.43 hectares and a built-up area with the hard landscaped area and the covered areas put together coming to 1,05,544.49 square meters, did not fall within the ambit of the EIA notification simply because this is how the EIA notification is framed. The Supreme Court while closing the verdict did admit this to be not an ideal or a very happy outcome. The case pointed to the failure of the central and the state governments for so far not having been able to evolve a principle to notify the buffer zones around sanctuaries and national parks to protect the sensitive and delicate ecological balance required for the sanctuaries eventually resulted in an unhappy and anomalous situation.

9. Conclusions: toward inclusive green growth

Evidently, India's policymakers have enacted environmental laws and framed good policies, but these are short on implementation. Over the past two decades, since early the 1990s, India's economic policies have been focused on liberalizing markets and integrating the national economy with the global economy. These new economic orientation has raised contentious debates on the impacts of these policies on the environment: i.e., whether the economic transition path endogenously will lead to a clean economy or will it succumb to "environmental colonialism" and import pollution. While the differences among either side of the arguments remain, the generally agreed middle position is that conscious and proactive environmental policies are needed and their implementation is vital to not only to limit the environmental damage but also to find "greening" opportunities during the economic transition from low to middle income.

The Indian economy experienced high economic growth averaging 8.2 percent during the first four years of the 11th Five-Year Plan (2007–2012). Affected by the global financial crisis, the GDP growth declined to 6.2 percent and 5 percent in the last two financial years – 2011 to 2012 and 2012 to 2013. But the inclusiveness and sustainability of the growth pattern is questioned (Dreze and Sen, 2013). Others also have noted that in the recent period India had high economic growth but witnessed impoverishment and the exclusion of large sections of population from the benefits of development (Hussain, 2012).

The studies on India's environment have noted rising environmental damages accompanying the economic growth. A World Bank estimate for India showed that the exports from polluting industries almost doubled to around 20 percent between 1997 and 2006 (Hindustan Times, 2006). A recent World Bank report (World Bank, 2013a) estimates the total cost of environmental degradation in India, which includes outdoor air pollution, indoor air pollution, croplands degradation, inadequate water supply and sanitation, pastures degradation and forest degradation, at Rs. 3.75 trillion (US$80 billion) annually, i.e., 5.7 percent of GDP in 2009. While the numbers could be debated, what is pivotal is how to ensure long-term sustainable growth that reckons the true social costs of consumption and production through a paradigm shift toward green growth. Fundamentally this underscores the importance of making ecosystems, i.e., human as well as natural elements, integral to the development process rather than external elements.

Referring to a report by the World Bank, The Economist (2008, pp. 33–34) reported that: "By 2020, according to the World Bank, India's water, air, soil and forest resources will be under more human pressure than those of any other country." But this future is not cast in stone. It can be altered for the better if India can institute laws, policies and the governance system that can harness the growth and development benefits while proactively managing its negative effects. This needs a framing that leapfrogs the conventional framing wherein economic growth and development are seen as inherent opposites to be reconciled by policies and measures. The green growth framing (The World Bank, 2012) offers a way to overcome this contradiction by viewing economic growth and environment as reinforcing aspects of development and societal well-being.

A starting agenda of policymaking in India for environment and natural resources is to *first* correct the distortive distribution of environment and natural resources and *second* to institutionalize policies and *third* to institute implementation machinery that can harmonize environment and development policy toward inclusive green growth. Evidently, the green growth rational is vital for an emerging economy like India where altering in the short-run the investments, e.g., in infrastructures, can prevent long-term lock-ins into adverse environmental impacts and unsustainable resource consumption patterns. The paradigm views natural resources and environmental services not as means but as the ends which, if ameliorated through well-use practices and innovations, could enhance productivity, improve livelihoods, create jobs and reduce poverty.

The importance of equitable and environmentally sustainable development is reflected in the central theme, "Inclusive Green Growth" (GoI, 2013, p. 10) of the 12th Five-Year Plan (2012–2017). The stated vision is "of India moving forward in a way that would ensure a broad-based improvement in living standards of all sections of the people through a growth process which is faster than in the past, more inclusive and also more environmentally sustainable." Similarly, the eight missions under India's National Action Plan on Climate Change emphasize development and environment objectives, including protecting ecosystems, agricultural sustainability, biodiversity and quality of life, in addition to climate change mitigation and adaptation measures (GoI, 2008).

The transition to inclusive green growth for India will require a re-framing of development and environmental objectives, laws, implementation architecture and greater awareness on the synergies and tradeoffs. Solutions could be in the form of policies, incentives, infrastructure choices, pricing and other instruments. Monitoring mechanisms will need to be in place to understand the nature and extent of impacts from these policies. A number of indicators exist on measuring growth, human well-being, environment; these include the indicators of the MDGs, the set of Sustainable Development Indicators, the Human Development Index, biophysical capacity, ecological footprints, greenhouse gas emissions measures, ambient air and water pollution indicators, measures of the stocks of natural capital and indicators of natural resource and energy productivity (UNEP, 2012). India's commitments to the UN Sustainable Development Goals post-2015 – an outcome of the Rio+20 Conference – will be another opportunity to commit to the inclusive green growth vision in the global, national and local contexts.

To this end, Indian planning may consider using extended production functions in which output (Y) is not only a function of labor (L) and capital (K), but also of environmental resources (E): $Y = f(L, K, E)$. This would further reinforce the conviction that trade and environment can be mutually reinforcing to deliver "green growth." Evidently, as the growing literature on green growth (World Bank, 2013a, 2013b, 2013c) points out, green growth is necessary; it is affordable, desirable and measurable. To this end, India has initiated studies to assess the feasibility of developing sector-wise uniform methodology for natural resource accounting for developing a framework for green national accounts. The expert group constituted under the Ministry of Statistics and Programme Implementation, the nodal ministry on this subject, has developed a framework of green national accounts for India. The ongoing deliberations aim to identify data requirements for the implementation of the recommended framework and elicit suggestion for bridging the data gaps before the government takes the next step toward adopting the green national accounting system for India.

In recent years, several good practices have emerged in the country in the form of agricultural innovations, waste management plans in cities, new financing models for renewable energy and energy efficiency, forest management practices, etc. However, widespread implementation will require institutional capacities for implementing programs and policies. Elements of good governance include decentralized decision-making, efficiency (transparency, administration, service delivery and infrastructure investments), equity, and security of environmental resources, disaster preparedness and crime control and prevention (UNCHS, 2000). A detailed assessment of best practices is needed to understand the factors for success – implementation mechanisms, financing model, innovation, context variables, and governance architecture.

The Indian economy is at an important threshold where a change in the development pattern has the possibility of providing growth that is cleaner, resource efficient and environmentally compatible. It can transit a sizable population out of poverty. Green growth does not require a radically different paradigm but an alteration in the existing vision. While the potential for green growth exists, it is not automatic that it will be realized. India will need the political will; the processes for assessment of altering societal and environmental dynamics, rapid policy responses that can seize opportunities and avert harm and implementable measures and a governance structure for lawful and effective implementation.

Notes

1 See, Supreme Court of India case *Special Reference No. 1 of 2002 Versus Union Of India Writ* Petition (Civil) No. 852 of 1991.
2 An organizational chart showing an outline of the environmental regulatory set-up in India can be found in Chatterjee (2009).
3 http://www.business-standard.com/article/economy-policy/green-nod-nhai-says-ball-now-in-ministry-s-court-113011700016_1.html, Retrieved on 14th October 2013
4 http://articles.timesofindia.indiatimes.com/2013-06-06/surat/39788147_1_emission-trading-scheme-gujarat-pollution-control-board-pilot-project.
5 See, *Municipal Council, Ratlam versus Vardhichand* AIR 1980 SC 1622.
6 See, *M.C. Mehta versus Union of India*, (1987) 1 SCC 395.
7 See, *M.C Mehta versus Union of India* (1988) 1 SCC 471.
8 See, *M.C. Mehta versus Union of India*, (1996) 4 SCC 750.
9 See, *M.C. Mehta versus Union of India*, (1996) 4 SCC 351.
10 See, *M.C. Mehta versus Union of India*, (1998) 8 SCC 648.
11 D.P. Shrivastava Memorial Lecture, 'The role of the judiciary in environmental protection' by K.G. Balakrishnan, Chief Justice of India Venue, High Court of Chattisgarh, Bilaspur, March 20, 2010.
12 http://pib.nic.in/newsite/PrintRelease.aspx?relid=98685.
13 Supreme Court Case *Samatha Versus State Of Andhra Pradesh with Hyderabad Abrasives and Minerals Private Limited Versus State Of Andhra Pradesh* Civil No. 4601 of 1997; 4602 of 1997 .
14 See for example, *T.N. Godavarman Thirumulpad versus Union of India*, W.P. (Civil) No. 202 of 1995.
15 See for example, *T.N. Godavarman Thirumulpad versus Union of India*, W.P. (Civil) No. 202 of 1995.
16 Lok Sabha unstarred question no 3412, answered on August 30, 2013.
17 See writ petition (civil) no. 180 of 2011.
18 http://www.thehindu.com/news/national/12th-gram-sabha-too-votes-against-vedanta-mining/article5039304.ece.
19 See *In Re Versus Union Of India with Construction Of Park At Noida Near Okhla Bird Sanctuary Anand Arya Versus Union Of India with T.N. Godavarman Thirumulpad Versus Union Of India*.

References

Bauer, J. R. (Ed.). (2006), *Forging Environmentalism: Justice, Livelihood, and Contested Environments*. Armonk, NY: ME Sharpe.
Baumol, W.G. and Oates, W.E. (1975), *The Theory of Environmental Policy: Externalities Public Outlays, and the Quality of Life*. Englewood Cliffs, NJ: Prentice-Hall.
BEE (Bureau of Energy Efficiency) (2013), http://www.bee-india.nic.in/.

Coase, R. (1960), 'The Problem of Social Cost,' *Journal of Law and Economics* 3:1–44.

CAG (Comptroller and Auditor General) (2011), *Performance Audit of Hydrocarbon Production Sharing Contract (PSC)*, Report No. 19, http://saiindia.gov.in/english/home/Our_Products/Audit_report/Government_Wise/union_audit/recent_reports/union_performance/2011_2012/Civil_%20Performance_Audits/Report_19/Report_19.html.

CAG (Comptroller and Auditor General) (2013), *Compensatory Afforestation in India*, Report No. 21 of 2013, http://saiindia.gov.in/english/home/Our_Products/Audit_Report/Government_Wise/union_audit/recent_reports/union_compliance/2013/Civil/Report_21/Report_21.html.

Chatterjee, T.(2009), 'Reorienting Environment Policy in India Towards a Local Area-Based Development and Management Paradigm,' *The Journal of Transdisciplinary Environmental Studies* 8(1):1–16.

Chopra Committee Report (2006), 'Report of the Expert Committee on Net Present Value,' http://www.iegindia.org/npvreport.pdf.

CSE (Centre for Science and Environment) (2013), 'Exploring the Myth – Poverty Is the Biggest Polluter,' http://www.cseindia.org/oslo2007/index.asp.

DAE (Department of Atomic Energy) (2006), 'Shaping the Third Stage of Indian Nuclear Power Programme,' http://dae.nic.in/writereaddata/.pdf_32.

Desai, M. (2011), 'Land Acquisition Law and the Proposed Changes,' *Economic & Political Weekly* 46(26–27):95–100.

Dreze J. and S. Amartya (2013), *An Uncertain Glory: India and Its Contradictions*. Allen Lane, UK: Alliance Publishers.

Economist, The (2008), "India and Pollution: Up to their Necks in It," July 17, http://www.economist.com/node/11751397/print?story_id=11751397.

Ghatak, M. and Ghosh, P. (2011). 'The Land Acquisition Bill: A Critique and a Proposal,' *Economic & Political Weekly* 41:65–72.

GoI (Government of India) (2001), *The Energy Conservation Act, 2001*, http://www.powermin.nic.in/acts_notification/pdf/ecact2001>.pdf .

GoI (Government of India) (2008), National Action Plan on Climate Change, Prime Minister's Council on Climate Change, Government of India, Delhi.

GoI (Government of India) (2010), Ministry of Environment & Forest, Government of India, Communication to United Nations Framework Convention on Climate Change, https://unfccc.int/files/meetings/cop_15/copenhagen_accord/application/pdf/indiacphaccord_app2.pdf.

GoI (Government of India) (2011a), *Millennium Development Goals: India Country Report 2011*, Central Statistical Organisation, Ministry of Statistics and Programme Implementation, Government of India, Delhi.

GoI (Government of India) (2011b), *Mineral Royalties*, Ministry of Mines, Indian Bureau of Mines, Government of India, Delhi.

GoI (Government of India) (2011c), *Ashok Chawla Committee Report on Allocation of Natural Resources (CANR)*, http://www.infraline.com.

GoI (Government of India) (2011d), Census of India: Provisional Population Tables (Paper 1 of 2011, Series 1), http://www.censusindia.gov.in/2011-prov-results/data_files/india/paper_contentsetc.pdf.

GoI (2013), Twelfth Five Year Plan (2012–2017): Faster, More Inclusive and Sustainable Growth, Vol. I. New Delhi: SAGE Publications India Pvt Ltd.

GoI-MoEF (Ministry of Environment and Forests, Government of India) (2004), India's Initial National Communication to the United Nations Framework Convention on Climate Change, Ministry of Environment and Forests, Government of India, Delhi.

GoI-MoEF (Ministry of Environment and Forests, Government of India) (2012), India Second National Communication to the United Nations Framework Convention on Climate Change. Ministry of Environment and Forests, Government of India, Delhi.

Gonsalves, C. (2010), 'Judicial Failure on Land Acquisition for Corporations,' *Economic & Political Weekly* 32:37–42.

Grover R.B. (2011), 'Policy Initiative by the Government of India to Accelerate the Growth of Installed Nuclear Capacity in the Coming Years,' *Energy Procedia* 7:74–78.

Guha, A. (2007), 'Peasant Resistance in West Bengal a Decade before Singur and Nandigram,' *Economic & Political Weekly* 15:3706–3711.

Guha, R.(2013), 'The past and present of Indian environmentalism,' http://www.thehindu.com/opinion/lead/the-past-present-of-indian-environmentalism/article4551665.ece>.

Guha, R. (1988), 'Ideological Trends in Indian Environmentalism,' *Economic and Political Weekly* 23(49):2578–2581.

Guha, R., & Martinez-Alier, J. (1997), *Varieties of Environmentalism: Essays North and South*. London: Earthscan Publications Ltd.

Hallegatte, S. and Fay, M. (2012), *Inclusive Green Growth: The Pathway to Sustainable Development*. Washington, DC: World Bank.

Hardin, G. (1968), 'The Tragedy of the Commons.' *Science* 162(3859):1243-1248.

Heller, T. and Shukla, P.R (2003), 'Development and Climate – Engaging Developing Countries.' In J.E. Aldy and Pew Center on Global Climate Change, et al. (eds.), *Beyond Kyoto: Advancing the International Effort against Climate Change*, pp. 111–140. Washington, DC: The Pew Center on Global Climate Change.

Hindustan Times (2011), 'India Exports from Polluting Firms Rising,' June 20, http://www.hindustantimes.com/India-news/NewDelhi/Indian-exports-from-polluting-firms-rising/Article1-711417.aspx.

Hohmeyer, O. (1988), *Social Costs of Energy Consumption*. Berlin: Springer.

Hussain, M. (2012), 'Twelfth Five Year Plan: Taking "Inclusive Development" from Myth to Reality,' *Economic and Political Weekly*, December 29, http://www.epw.in/web-exclusives/twelfth-five-year-plan.html.

IEA (International Energy Agency) (2012), 'Understanding Energy Challenges in India: Policies, Players and Issues,' https://www.iea.org/publications/freepublications/publication/India_study_FINAL_WEB.pdf.

INCCA (Indian Network for Climate Change Assessment) (2010), Climate Change and INDIA: A 4X4 Assessment – A Sectoral and Regional Analysis for 2030s, Ministry of Environment and Forests, Government of India, Delhi.

IPCC (International Panel of Climate Change) (1995), *IPCC Second Assessment Report: Climate Change 1995*. Geneva: UNEP.

Lewis, T.R. (1996), 'Protecting the Environment When Costs and Benefits Are Privately Known,' *The Rand Journal of Economics* 27(4):819–847.

MoEF (Ministry of Environment and Forests) (2009), 'India's Fourth National Report to the Convention on Biological Diversity,' http://envfor.nic.in/downloads/public-information/in-nr-04.pdf.

MoEF (Ministry of Environment and Forests) (2013), 'Report of the Committee for inspection of Adani PortandSEZ,'http://envfor.nic.in/content/report-committee-inspection-ms-adani-port-sez-ltd-mundra-gujarat.

Montgomery, D. (1972), 'Markets in Licenses and Efficient Pollution Control Programs,' *Journal of Economic Theory* 5:395–418.

Morris, S. and A. Pandey (2007), 'Towards Reform of Land Acquisition Framework in India,' *Economic & Political Weekly*, 22:2083–2090.

Munch, P. (1976), 'An Economic Analysis of Eminent Domain,' *The Journal of Political Economy* 84(3):473–97.

Narain, S. (2002), 'Changing environmentalism,'http://www.india-seminar.com/2002/516/516%20sunita%20narain.htm.

PIB (Press Information Bureau) (2013), Coal Block Auction Methodology approved, Ministry of Coal, Government of India.

Pigou, A.C. (1920), *The Economics of Welfare*. London: Macmillan.

Pizer, William A. (2002), 'Combining Price and Quantity Controls to Mitigate Global Climate Change,' *Journal of Public Economics* 85(3):409–434.

Planning Commission (2006), 'Report of the Working Group on environment and environmental regulatory mechanisms in Environment and Forests for the Eleventh Five Year Plan (2007–2012),' http://planningcommission.nic.in/aboutus/committee/wrkgrp11/wg_envtal.pdf.

Planning Commission (2011a), 'Faster, Sustainable and More Inclusive Growth: An Approach to the Twelfth Five Year Plan (2012–17),' http://planningcommission.gov.in/plans/planrel/12appdrft/approach_12plan.pdf.

Planning Commission (2011b), 'Working Group Report on "Land and Water" for the Twelfth Five Year Plan (2012–2017),' http://planningcommission.gov.in/aboutus/committee/index.php?about=12strindx.htm.

Press Information Bureau (2013), Coal Block Auction Methodology Approved, September 25, Government of India, Ministry of Coal, Delhi.

Ramanathan, U. (2011), 'Land Acquisition, Eminent Domain and the 2011 Bill,' *Economic & Political Weekly* 46(44):10–14.

Roberts, M.J., and M. Spence (1976), 'Effluent Charges and Licenses under Uncertainty,' *Journal of Public Economics* 5(3–4):193–208.

Sarkar, A. (2007), 'Development and Displacement: Land Acquisition in West Bengal,' *Economic & Political Weekly* 42(16):1435–42.

Sarkar, S. (2011), 'The Impossibility of Just Land Acquisition,' *Economic & Political Weekly* 46(41):35–38.

Sarma, E.A.S. (2011), 'Sops for the Poor and a Bonus for Industry,' *Economic & Political Weekly* 46(41):32–34.

Sathaye, J., Shukla, P.R. and Ravindranath, N.H. (2006), 'Climate Change, Sustainable Development and India: Global and national concerns,' *Current Science* 90(3):314–325.

Shukla, P.R. (2005), 'Aligning Justice and Efficiency in the Global Climate Regime: A Developing Country Perspective.' In W.S. Armstrong & R.B. Howarth (eds.), *Advances in the Economics of Environmental Resources, Volume 5: Perspectives on Climate Change: Science, Economics, Politics, Ethics*, pp. 121–144. Oxford: Elsevier.

Shukla, P.R. (2006), 'India's GHG Emission Scenarios: Aligning Development and Stabilization Paths,' *Current Science* 90(3):384–395.

Singh, R. (2012), 'Inefficiency and Abuse of Compulsory Land Acquisition: An Enquiry into the Way Forward,' *Economic & Political Weekly*, May 12, pp. 46–53.

Sinha, R. (2009), *Moving towards Clear Land Titles in India*, http://www.fig.net/pub/fig_wb_2009/papers/country/country_sinha.pdf.

Sinha, S., Baviskar, A. and Philip, K. (2006), 'Rethinking Indian Environmentalism. Industrial Pollution in Delhi and Fisheries in Kerala.' In J. Bauer (ed.), *Forging Environmentalism. Justice, Livelihood, and Contested Environments*, pp. 189–256. Armonk, NY: M.E. Sharpe, PM.

Spiller, P. (1990), 'Politician, Interest Groups, and Regulators: A Multiple-Principals Agency Theory of Regulation, or "Let Them Be Bribed",' *Journal of Law and Economics* 33:65–101

Stavins, R.N. (1996), 'Correlated Uncertainty and Policy Instrument Choice,' *Journal of Environmental Economics and Management* 30:218–232.

Stigler, J.G. (1971), 'The theory of Economic Regulation,' *The Bell journal of Economics and Management Science* 2(1):3–21.

UN (United Nations) (2012), *The Cities and Biodiversity Outlook*, http://www.cbd.int/en/subnational/partners-and-initiatives/cbo.

UNCHS (UN Centre for Human Settlements) (2000), 'United Nations Centre for Human Settlements (Habitat) – The Global Campaign for Good Urban Governance,' *Environment & Urbanization* 12(1):197–202.

UNEP (United Nations Environmental Programme) (2012), Measuring Progress Towards a Green Economy, United Nations Environment Programme, Nairobi.

Weber, K. M. and Hemmelskamp, J. (Eds.). (2005), *Towards Environmental Innovation Systems*. Berlin: Springer.

Weitzman, M.L. (1974), 'Prices vs. Quantities,' *Review of Economic Studies* 41(4):477–491.

Weitzman, M. L. (1978), 'Optimal Rewards for Economic Regulation,' *American Economic Review* 68(4):683–691.

World Bank (2007), 'India: Strengthening Institutions for Sustainable Growth. Country Environmental Analysis,' South Asia Environment and Social Development Unit South Asia Region, Report No. 38292-IN. Washington, DC: World Bank.

World Bank (2012), 'Inclusive Green Growth: The Pathway to Sustainable development,' Washington, DC: World Bank.

World Bank (2013a), 'India: Diagnostic Assessment of Select Environmental Challenges – An Analysis of Physical and Monetary Losses of Environmental Health and Natural Resources,' (Volume 1 of 3), http://www.worldbank.org/en/news/press-release/2013/07/17/india-green-growth-necessary-and-affordable-for-india-says-new-world-bank-report.

World Bank (2013b), 'India – Diagnostic Assessment of Select Environmental Challenges,' Vol. 2 of 3: Economic Growth and Environmental Sustainability: What Are the Tradeoffs?' http://www.worldbank.org/en/news/press-release/2013/07/17/india-green-growth-necessary-and-affordable-for-india-says-new-world-bank-report.

World Bank (2013c), 'India – Diagnostic Assessment of Select Environmental Challenges," Vol. 3 of 3: Valuation of Biodiversity and Ecosystem Services in India,' http://www.worldbank.org/en/news/press-release/2013/07/17/india-green-growth-necessary-and-affordable-for-india-says-new-world-bank-report.

Zhang, S. (2010), 'Conceptualising the Environmentalism in India: Between Social Justice and Deep Ecology.' In Q. Huan (ed.), *Eco-socialism as Politics: Rebuilding the Basis of Our Modern Civilisation*, pp. 181–190. London: Springer.

INDEX